PRINCIPLES
OF
SALES LAW

By

James J. White
Professor of Law, University of Michigan
Member, Michigan Bar

Robert S. Summers
Professor of Law, Cornell University
Member, Oregon and New York Bars

CONCISE HORNBOOK SERIES®

WEST®
A Thomson Reuters business

Mat #16525154

© 2009 Thomson Reuters
    610 Opperman Drive
    St. Paul, MN 55123
    1–800–313–9378
Printed in the United States of America

ISBN: 978–0–314–90802–5

Preface

This work is a modified and much reduced version of the relevant parts of the 5th Edition of J. White and R. Summers, The Uniform Commercial Code, Volume 1 (2006).

*

Acknowledgement

Professor White acknowledges the assistance of Mark R. Christy, '10, University of Michigan Law School, of Christine Lee, '10, Cornell Law School and the patience and thoroughness of his administrative assistant, Janis Weston.

Professor Summers acknowledges the invaluable assistance of Christine Lee, '10, Cornell Law School.

*

Summary of Contents

Table of Contents

*

PRINCIPLES
OF
SALES LAW

*

Chapter 1

2001 REVISION OF ARTICLE 1

Analysis

§ 1–1 Article 1 Revision

In 2001 Article 1 was revised. While that revision made a relatively small number of substantive changes, the old substance now sometimes appears in new Sections, so one must be careful in reading cases decided before the revision and in applying the new law to old cases. At this writing 35 states have adopted the 2001 revision of Article 1.

The substantive changes concern scope of the Article, applicability of supplemental principles of law, the concept of good faith and choice of law. Rules on course of performance have been brought from Article 2 to Article 1. Hence, insofar as adopted, these rules clearly apply to all of the UCC, not just to Article 2. There is a new section (1–108) on the relation to "UETA" (Uniform Electron-

1

ic Transactions Act) and "E–Sign" (Electronic Signatures in Global and National Commerce Act). The mysterious statute of frauds (1–206), whose presence in old Article 1 was probably an historical anomaly, is gone. The changes with respect to choice of law are theoretically the most important, but the failure of most states to adopt the new choice of law rules has diminished that importance.[1]

§ 1–2 UCC Purposes and Policies and the Applicability of Supplemental Principles of Law

Revised 1–103 combines subsections (1) and (2) of pre-revision 1–102 (concerning the underlying purposes and policies of the UCC) with pre-revision 1–103 (concerning the applicability of supplemental principles of law). The provisions have been combined in this section to reflect the relationship between the UCC's purposes and policies and the extent to which other law is available to supplement the UCC.[1]

Textual Comparison

§ 1–103. Construction of [Uniform Commercial Code] to Promote its Purposes and Policies; Applicability of Supplemental Principles of Law.~~1–102. Purposes; Rules of Construction; Variation by Agreement.~~

~~(1) This Act shall~~(a) [The Uniform Commercial Code] must be liberally construed and applied to promote its underlying purposes and policies~~.~~, which are:

~~(2) Underlying purposes and policies of this Act are~~

~~(a)~~(1) to simplify, clarify, and modernize the law governing commercial transactions;

~~(b)~~(2) to permit the continued expansion of commercial practices through custom, usage, and agreement of the parties; and

~~(c)~~(3) to make uniform the law among the various jurisdictions.

... ~~:~~

~~§ 1–103. Supplementary General Principles~~ of Law Applicable

(b) Unless displaced by the particular provisions of ~~this Act~~ [the Uniform Commercial Code], the principles of law and

---

§ 1–1

1. See Revised Article 1, Prefatory Note (Draft for Approval, Aug. 10–17, 2001), available at http://www.law.upenn.edu/bll/ulc/ucc1/ucc161401.htm. See generally, K. Patchel, on the Article

1 Revision Process, 54 SMU L. Rev. 603 (2001).

§ 1–2

1. § 1–103, Changes from former law (2001).

equity, including the law merchant and the law relative to capacity to contract, principal and agent, estoppel, fraud, misrepresentation, duress, coercion, mistake, bankruptcy, ~~or~~and other validating or invalidating cause ~~shall~~supplement its provisions.

Except for minor stylistic changes, the language of subsection (a) of revised 1–103 is the same as subsections (1) and (2) of prerevision 1–102. The Comments with respect to this subsection are also substantially the same as the Comments on subsections (1) and (2) of pre-revision 1–102. The language of subsection (b) of revised 1–103 is nearly identical to pre-revision 1–103.

The Comments to revised 1–103(b) are more elaborate than, and otherwise differ from, the Comments that accompanied the comparable statutory language in the old Code. These new Comments merit study by anyone who must argue that "other law" supplements or does not supplement a Code rule. They are the result of a prolonged attempt by the Drafting Committee to state more exactly what law supplements the UCC and what does not.

The language in Comment 1 to old 1–103 that appeared to allow supplementation by any law that was not "explicitly displaced" by a provision of the Code is gone. It is enough that a rule is displaced; it need not be "explicitly displaced." The advocates of greater protection from outside law also won an extended Comment that explained that a court should bar not only outside law that was displaced by a provision but also outside law that was inconsistent with the purposes and policies of the Code:

> The language of subsection (b) is intended to reflect both the concept of supplementation and the concept of preemption. Some courts, however, had difficulty in applying the identical language of former Section 1–103 to determine when other law appropriately may be applied to supplement the Uniform Commercial Code, and when that law has been displaced by the Code. Some decisions applied other law in situations in which that application, while not inconsistent with the text of any particular provision of the Uniform Commercial Code, clearly was inconsistent with the underlying purposes and policies reflected in the relevant provisions of the Code. *See, e.g., Sheerbonnet, Ltd. v. American Express Bank, Ltd.*, 951 F.Supp. 403 (S.D.N.Y. 1995). In part, this difficulty arose from Comment 1 to former Section 1–103, which stated that "this section indicates the continued applicability to commercial contracts of all supplemental bodies of law except insofar as they are explicitly displaced by this Act." The "explicitly displaced" language of that Comment did not accurately reflect the proper scope of Uniform Commercial Code preemption, which extends to displacement of other law that is inconsistent with the

purposes and policies of the Uniform Commercial Code, as well as with its text.

One might wonder about the authoritative status of a Comment that urged rejection of outside law not in conflict with any "provision" of the Code but only with its "purposes and policies." Does the explicit reference to "displace[ment] by a particular provision" mean that conflict with a policy or purpose is not enough? This is not so clear, and, in our view, the case is not helped by the choice of *Sheerbonnet*[2] as an example of a court gone wrong in its use of the common law; we think the *Sheerbonnet* case was probably rightly decided. *Sheerbonnet* was an Article 4A case; its critics cite to the language of the Comments to 4A–102 on its "careful and delicate balancing" of various rights in Article 4A and on the injury to commerce if that balancing were upset by the intrusion of the common law. Invariably where parties do an electronic transfer of funds, there are other important parts of the transaction that must be governed by law beyond Article 4A and the "delicate balancing" of the drafters in Article 4A does not change that.

Sources of Other Law that May Supplement the UCC

Both pre-revision 1–103 and revised 1–103(b) provide that the principles of law and equity that may supplement the UCC provisions include "the law merchant and the law relative to capacity to contract, principal and agent, estoppel, fraud, misrepresentation, duress, coercion, mistake, bankruptcy, or other validating or invalidating cause." Comment 4 to revised 1–103 follows Comment 3 to pre-revision 1–103 in confirming that the list of sources of supplemental law in 1–103(b) is intended merely to be illustrative and is not exhaustive.

While the primary focus of revised 1–103 is on the relationship between the UCC and principles of common law and equity as developed by the courts, the Drafting Committee recognized that state law is increasingly statutory, and not only are there a growing number of state statutes addressing specific issues that come within the scope of the UCC, but in some states many general principles of common law and equity have also been codified.[3] Thus, Comment 3 to 1–103 makes it clear that the principles of 1–103(b) remain relevant to the analysis of the relationship between a state statute and the UCC when the statute relates to a matter within the scope of the UCC. More specifically, the mere fact that an equitable principle is stated in statutory form rather than in judicial decisions should not change the analysis of whether the principle can be used to supplement the UCC under 1–103(b).

2. Sheerbonnet, Ltd. v. American Express Bank, Ltd., 951 F.Supp. 403 (S.D.N.Y. 1995).

3. See § 1–103, Comment 3 (2001).

Comment 3 to revised 1–103 addresses consumers' concerns to some extent. In most states, laws protecting consumers are statutory. If these consumer protection statutes are specifically intended to provide additional protection to the consumers as a class they will not be preempted even if they do not have a provision that specifically grants them superiority over the UCC.

§ 1–3   Section 1–108, E–Sign, and UETA

Section 1–108 came to Revised Article 1 late. It did not even appear in the Draft for Approval at the NCCUSL 2001 Annual Meeting.[1] It specifies the relationship of Article 1 to the federal Electronic Signatures in Global and National Commerce Act (E–Sign).[2] Section 1–108 states:

> This article modifies, limits, and supersedes the Federal Electronic Signatures in Global and National Commerce Act, 15 U.S.C. § 7001 *et seq.*, except that nothing in this article modifies, limits, or supersedes section 7001(c) of that Act or authorizes electronic delivery of any of the notices described in Section 7003(b) of that Act.

To understand section 1–108 and the same language in 2–108(4), one needs to know something about UETA (state law) and its federal counterpart, E–Sign. The origin of E–Sign can be traced to UETA. In order to resolve some of the issues relating to the widespread use of the Internet for sale of goods, and to provide uniformity, NCCUSL promulgated UETA in 1999. It allows the use of electronic records and electronic signatures in many transactions, including Articles 2 and 2A transactions, but does not apply to transactions under other articles. As of July, 2006, 46 states, the District of Columbia and the U.S. Virgin Islands had adopted UETA. Congress feared that UETA would not create uniformity in electronic contracting law because some states might not adopt it and others threatened to enact forms of UETA with additional provisions, omissions or both. To forestall the nonuniformity that could arise from states' failure to enact UETA and from rogue versions of UETA, Congress enacted E–Sign in 2000. E–Sign covers the same territory as UETA.

Section 103 of E–Sign[3] provides that section 101 of E–Sign (the major section of E–Sign that specifies the general rule of validity of electronic signatures, contracts or other records) does not apply to a contract to the extent it is governed by the UCC other than Articles

§ 1–3

1. Revised Article 1 (Draft for Approval, Aug. 10–17, 2001), available at http://www.law.upenn.edu/ bll/ulc/ uccl/ ucc161401.htm.

2. 15 U.S.C. § 7001 et seq. (2000).

3. 15 U.S.C. § 7003.

2 and 2A and pre-revision 1–107 and 1–206. But this blanket exemption applies only to parts of the UCC "in effect." Apparently the drafters of Revised Article 1 and Amended Article 2 feared that the revision might not get the protection of the 103 exemption because of the "in effect" language. Since arguably none of the revisions or amendments were "in effect" when E–Sign was passed, the drafters were not confident that the 103(a)(3) exemption from E–Sign would apply.

Out of an excess of caution the drafters have inserted section 1–108 to comply with a different exemption provision of E–Sign, section 102. Section 102(a)(2) of E–Sign allows states to exempt certain law from E–Sign's preemption:

> (a) In general
>
> A State statute, regulation, or other rule of law may modify, limit, or supersede the provisions of section 7001 of this title with respect to State law only if such statute, regulation, or rule of law—
>
> . . . .
>
> (2)(A) specifies the alternative procedures or requirements for the use or acceptance (or both) of electronic records or electronic signatures to establish the legal effect, validity, or enforceability of contracts or other records, if—
>
>> (i) such alternative procedures or requirements are consistent with this subchapter and subchapter II of this chapter; and
>>
>> (ii) such alternative procedures or requirements do not require, or accord greater legal status or effect to, the implementation or application of a specific technology or technical specification for performing the functions of creating, storing, generating, receiving, communicating, or authenticating electronic records or electronic signatures; and
>
> (B) if enacted or adopted after June 30, 2000, makes specific reference to this chapter.[4]

Revised 1–108 provides that Article 1 modifies, limits, and supercedes E–Sign.[5] Assuming that Revised Article 1 meets all of the

---

4. 15 U.S.C. § 7002(a).

5. Except that nothing in Revised Article 1 modifies, limits, or supercedes Section 101(c) of E–Sign (imposing additional requirements for consumer disclosures in electronic forms) or authorizes electronic delivery of any of the notices described in Section 103(b) of that Act (such as court orders or notices, notice of cancellation or termination of utility services, notice of cancellation of health insurance, notice of recall of a product, etc.). See UCC § 1–108 (2001); 15 U.S.C. § 7001(c); 15 U.S.C. § 7003(b).

conditions in section 102(a)(2) of E–Sign,[6] what will 1–108 accomplish and what did the drafters fear? We are told that the language of section 1–108 was drafted by the UETA committee for insertion in many NCCUSL statutes to protect them from unforeseen modification by the federal law.

Here the drafters might have feared that application of E–Sign to Article 1 would allow E–Sign to enter Articles 3 and 4 by the back door. Article 3 still requires that a negotiable instrument be "written" and "signed" (see sections 3–103(a)(8) and (10) and section 3–104). If E–Sign were to apply to Article 1, conceivably it would modify the definition of "writing" and "written" in 1–201(b)(43) and the analogous use of "signed" in 1–201(b)(37). If those definitions were effectively modified to permit the writings and signatures to be electronic, the sections that include those words in Article 3 would be so changed and, *mirabile dictu*, one would have electronic negotiable instruments without a single formal change to any word in Article 3.[7]

§ 1–4　General Definitions, Section 1–201

Only a few of the general definitions have been changed by Revised Article 1, and most of those changes are modest.

a.　*Agreement, Section 1–201(b)(3)*

Pre-revision 1–201(3) defined "agreement" as "the bargain of the parties in fact as found in their language or by implication from other circumstances including course of dealing or usage of trade or course of performance as provided in this Act (sections 1–205, 2–208, and 2A–207)."

---

6. Comment 1 to § 1–108 says Revised Article 1 has satisfied all three criteria listed in Section 102(a)(2) of E–Sign. It is noteworthy that E–Sign recognizes electronic contracts and records as well as electronic signatures, see 15 U.S.C. § 7001(a), but Revised Article 1 has not recognized electronic signatures yet, see *supra* § 1–4. However, the first sentence of Section 102(a)(2) of E–Sign only requires the state law to specify "the alternative procedures or requirements for the use or acceptance (or both) of electronic records *or* electronic signatures to establish the legal effect, validity, or enforceability of contracts or other record." 15 U.S.C. § 7002(a)(2) (emphasis added). Thus, Section 1–102(a)(2) of E–Sign arguably does not require a state law to provide for both electronic records and electronic signatures before it may preempt E–Sign.

7. Another effect of revised § 1–108 is that E–Sign will cease to apply to records for the discharge of claims or rights arising out of an alleged breach, which is governed by revised 1–306. Though E–Sign will not be applicable, revised § 1–306 itself has explicitly provided that disclaimers of claims or rights may be memorialized in an "authenticated record." The official comments accompanying revised § 1–306 say that, in this context, a party may "authenticate" a record by attaching to—or logically associating with a record that is not written—an electronic sound, symbol or process with the present intent to adopt or accept the record. See UCC § 1–306 (2001). Thus, revised 1–306 recognizes both electronic records and electronic signatures by itself.

Revised 1–201(b)(3) provides, " 'Agreement', as distinguished from 'contract', means the bargain of the parties in fact, as found in their language or inferred from other circumstances, including course of performance, course of dealing, or usage of trade as provided in Section 1–303."

According to a literal reading of pre-revision 1–201(3) and 1–205, the "agreement" of the parties is composed of three sources: express terms, course of dealing, and usage of trade. Except in Article 2 (where course of performance is defined), course of performance would not have been a source for the meaning of the parties' agreement under pre-revision Article 1.

Commentators and courts were in doubt about the place of course of performance in Articles other than Article 2. For example, one commentator argued that pre-revision 1–205 simply did not attempt to deal with the legal consequences of post-agreement events such as those defined in 2–208 as course of performance.[1] In Westinghouse Credit Corp. v. Shelton,[2] the Tenth Circuit held that a secured party's course of performance in accepting late payments might be used to interpret the meaning of the parties' contract. Despite its conclusion that "course of performance" is not an element of the meaning of agreement in Article 1, the court reached to find a connection between Article 2 and Article 9 so to introduce course of performance into the security agreement.

New section 1–303 brings course of performance to Article 1 (making it directly applicable to contracts in all Articles) and the definition of "agreement" specifically refers to course of performance as a source of the parties' agreement.

The pre-revision definition of "agreement" included a second sentence which provided that "[w]hether an agreement has legal consequences is determined by the provisions of this Act." This sentence has been moved to the Comments in Revised Article 1.

The pre-revision definitions of "agreement" and "contract" included cross-references to each other at the end of the text. These cross-references were removed on the recommendation of the Committee on Style, but the Drafting Committee still wanted a signal to highlight the differences between the two definitions. To do that the Committee inserted the phrase "as distinguished from 'contract-agreement' " at the beginning of the definitions.

After the revision, it is clear that "agreement" means bargain of the parties in fact, and such agreement may be found in four

§ 1–4

1. Memorandum from Dennis Patterson to Article 1 Comm., 2 (Nov. 3, 1992) [hereinafter Patterson Memo] (on file with one of the authors) (citing Dugan, Buyer–Secured Party Conflicts Un-

der Section 9–307(1) of the Uniform Commercial Code, 46 U. Colo. L. Rev. 333, 340 (1975)).

2. 645 F.2d 869 (10th Cir. 1981).

sources: express terms, course of performance, course of dealing, and usage of trade. Not all agreements of the parties have legal consequences. Whether an agreement has legal consequences is determined by applicable provisions of the UCC and, to the extent provided in revised 1–103, by the law of contracts. "Contract" means the total *legal* obligation that results from the parties' agreement as determined by the UCC and supplemented by any other applicable laws. Thus, "contract" includes (i) parties' bargain in fact that has the legal consequences of creating legal obligations, and (ii) legal obligations imposed by the law in the absence of agreement of the parties, such as gap fillers in the UCC.[3] None of this is really different in the revision from what it was before.

b. *Conspicuous, Section 1–201(b)(10)*

The definition of "conspicuous" has been changed to reflect electronic commerce and communication. The Drafting Committee originally hoped to defer consideration of the definition of conspicuous (which appears in several articles[4]) until completion of the Article 2 drafting process, but they could not wait.[5] By far the most important use of the adjective in the UCC is in section 2–316 where the law grants a safe harbor to certain disclaimers of implied warranties if they are "conspicuous." There is later a discussion of the more extensive Amended Article 2 definition of "conspicuous" below.

Textual Comparison

§ 1–201. General Definitions.

(10) "Conspicuous"., with reference to a term, meansA term or clause is conspicuous when it is so written, displayed, or presented that a reasonable person against whichom it is to operate ought to have noticed it. A printed heading in capitals (as: NonNegotiable Bill of Lading) is conspicuous. Language in the body of a form is "conspicuous" if it is in larger or other contrasting type or color. But in a telegram any stated term is "conspicuous".Whether a term or clause is "conspicuous" or not is fora decision byfor the court. Conspicuous terms include the following:

(A) a heading in capitals equal to or greater in size than the surrounding text, or in contrasting type, font, or color to the surrounding text of the same or lesser size; and

---

3. For example, implied warranties of merchantability under § 2–314 are part of the "contract" but not of the "agreement."

4. §§ 2–316, 2A–211, 2A–214, 2A–303, 3–104(d), 3–311, 7–104, 7–203, 7–210, 7–402, 7–403, 8–204, and 8–209 (2003).

5. See, e.g., § 1–201(11) (Discussion Draft, Nov. 2000), available at http://www.law.upenn.edu/bll/ulc/ucc1/ucc 11100.htm.

(B) language in the body of a record or display in larger type than the surrounding text, or in contrasting type, font, or color to the surrounding text of the same size, or set off from surrounding text of the same size by symbols or other marks that call attention to the language.[6]

The definition in Revised Article 1 follows the pre-revision definition in two aspects: (1) it states the general standard that, to be conspicuous, a term ought to be noticed by a reasonable person; (2) it reaffirms that "conspicuousness" is an issue for the court.

The pre-revision definition envisioned only "conspicuous" terms or clauses in writing. The new definition in Revised Article 1 provides for conspicuous terms in writing as well as in electronic forms. The pre-revision 1–201(10) provided, "A term or clause is conspicuous when it is so written that a reasonable person against whom it is to operate ought to have noticed it." In revised 1–201 " 'Conspicuous' means so *written, displayed, or presented* that a reasonable person against which it is to operate ought to have noticed it." So it recognizes that an electronic statement can be conspicuous.

The approved methods for making something conspicuous are slightly different in the new version. The chart below compares the old and new definitions.

	Old definition	**New definition**
For a **heading** to be "conspicuous," it must be	(i) in capitals.	(i) in capitals and equal to or greater in size than the surrounding text; or (ii) in contrasting type, font, or color to the surrounding text and equal to or greater in size than the surrounding text.
For **language** in the **body** of a form to be "conspicuous," it must be	(ii) in other contrasting type or color	(i) in larger type than the surrounding text; (ii) in contrasting type, font, or color to the surrounding text of the same size; or (iii) set off from surrounding text of the same size by symbols or other marks that call attention to the language.

The new definition makes it clear that a heading may be "conspicuous" by being in contrasting type, font, or color even if it

---

6. § 1–201(b)(10) (2001).

is not in capitals. It also recognizes that language set off by "symbols" or "marks" from the surrounding text is conspicuous. Finally, it provides that for either a heading or language in the body to be "conspicuous," it usually needs to be equal to or greater in size than the surrounding text.

Comment 10 appears to deny safe harbor status to the various formulations in the statutory text: "the test is whether attention can reasonably be expected to be called to it," and "[t]he statutory language should not be construed to permit a result that is inconsistent with that test." This Comment is likely a response to the consumer groups' objection to the safe-harbor provisions. In its memo to the Uniform Law Commissioners of July 1997, the Consumers Union expressed its concern that, if read literally, the revised definition would render *per se* conspicuous any text in a contrasting color or font, even if the font were hard to read or the color offered a poor contrast.[7] The Consumers Union gave the example of credit card solicitations, that sometimes print the required disclosure box in very light gray ink on white paper.[8] Another example, if revised 1–201(10) is to be read literally, is a form which uses 12–point font throughout the document except one paragraph which uses 8–point font, and within that paragraph, one sentence uses 9–point font. Because this sentence is in larger type than its "surrounding text," it may qualify as "conspicuous." The Consumers Union suggested that the basic standard should be whether a reasonable person against whom the term is to operate should have noticed it.[9]

One of us (the one who was a member of the Article 1 Drafting Committee) is doubtful that the quoted commentary is supported by the statutory text. (Usually the Comments are prepared by the Committee chair and the reporter and are not necessarily considered or debated by the Committee.) Barring most unusual circumstances, we would find that terms meeting the tests of (10)(A) and (B) are, ipso facto, conspicuous. We note that there is no reference on "calling attention" in (A) and we read the last clause of (B), on calling attention, to modify only "symbols or marks."

Comparison of Definitions in Revised Article 1 and Amended Article 2

The failed Article 2 amendments (not adopted in any state) had a definition of conspicuous that is different from the Revised Article 1 definition. Because the Article 2 proposal contemplated transactions conducted through electronic agents without the need for review by a person, it may be persuasive, even if not law. In section

---

7. See Memorandum from Gail Hillebrand to Uniform Law Commissioners.

8. *Id.*

9. *Id.*

2–103(1)(b), the Amended Article 2 definition of "conspicuous" added: "A term in an electronic record intended to evoke a response by an electronic agent is conspicuous if it is presented in a form that would enable a reasonably configured electronic agent to take it into account or react to it without review of the record by an individual."

The Amended Article 2 definition also indicates a way to make a term attention-calling in transactions concluded through electronic agents. The method is to place or display the term in a way that an electronic agent cannot proceed without taking action with respect to the particular term. This method also applies to transactions done by a human on the buyer or consumer side. When an online shopper is required to check a box associated with a particular term before he or she can proceed with the online purchase, this term is "conspicuous" under Amended Article 2 even if it is of the same type, font, color, and size as the surrounding text and not set off from surrounding text by symbols or other marks. Terms placed or displayed in this way should be "conspicuous" under the Revised Article 1 definition as well because they would meet the general test of whether "a reasonable person against which it is to operate ought to have noticed it." Amended Article 2 is more explicit.[10]

c. Good Faith, Section 1–201(b)(20)

The definition of good faith has undergone a gradual evolution from mere "honesty in fact" to "honesty in fact and the observance of reasonable commercial standards." The most recent tiny step in this evolution is the modification of the definition in Revised Article 1: " 'Good faith,' except as otherwise provided in Article 5, means honesty in fact and the observance of reasonable commercial standards of fair dealing." The change in Article 1 from the former three word "honesty in fact" definition ("narrow definition") to the new ten word definition ("broad definition") is tiny because Articles 3, 4 and 9 already have the longer definition, and because a variation of the longer definition always applied to merchants in Article 2.[11]

---

10. Because current Articles 2 and 2A do not have separate definitions of "conspicuous" and current Sections 2–103 and 2A–103 provide that the general definitions in Article 1 are applicable to these two Articles, those states that adopt Revised Article 1 will have a broader definition of conspicuous applicable to Articles 2 and 2A than before. However, to have a formal definition of "conspicuous" compatible with transactions done by electronic agents without the need for review by a person, states have to adopt the Amended Articles 2 and 2A. But even after that, the Article 1 definition will continue to apply to conspicuous requirements in other Articles of the UCC.

11. " 'Good faith' in the case of a merchant means honesty in fact and the observance of reasonable commercial standards of fair dealing in the trade." § 2–103(1)(b) (1994). Later, Article 2A explicitly incorporated this definition. See § 2A–103(3) (1999). Then, other Articles broadened the applicability of Article 2 standard of "good faith" by adopt-

Despite the insignificance of the proposal to change Article 1, the bankers have opposed it and have successfully blocked the new definition in some states.[12] Why the bankers, who are already subject to the broader definition in their Article 3, 4, and 9 transactions, oppose it in Article 1 is not clear to us. Perhaps they fear its application by analogy to the non-Article 9 parts of loan collections and contracts. Perhaps they think that their actions in closing and setting off bank accounts are not now subject to the broader definition in Article 4. In any case, at this writing it appears that a large number of states will keep the old "honesty in fact" in Article 1.

But how is the law changed by the addition of a requirement that one observe reasonable commercial standards of fair dealing? This is sometimes described as the "objective" part of the definition; it tells one to conform somehow to the others' standards, to

ing it for all parties rather than just for merchants. Thus, Sections 3–103(a)(4) (i.e. 3–103(a)(6) after 2002 amendments to Article 3), Section 4–104(c), 4A–105(a)(6), 8–102(a)(10), and 9–102(a)(43) have adopted the broad definition of "good faith." Only revised Article 5 uses the narrow definition, and only Article 6 and Article 7 are without definitions of "good faith." While revised Article 6 does not define good faith, Comment 2 to revised 6–102 says "this Article adopts the definition of 'good faith' in Revised Article 1 in all cases, even when the buyer is a merchant." It seems to indicate that the broad definition in Ar-

ticles 3, 4, 4A, 8 and 9 may be acceptable for Article 6 too. It should also be noted that revised Article 7 (last revised or amended in 2003) also adopted the broad definition. See § 7–102(a)(6) (2003).

Because of this trend of broadening the definition of "good faith" in all other Articles of the UCC (except Article 5), the Drafting Committee decided to move the broad definition in Articles 3, 4, 4A, 8 and 9 to Article 1, which will apply to all other Articles of the UCC except Article 5. The following table shows the development of the definition of "good faith" in the UCC. (See table below.)

	Pre–2001 revision of Art. 1	2001 revision of Art. 1 to its adoption	Post-adoption of Revised Art. 1
Art. 1	Narrow Definition	Narrow Definition	Broad Definition
Art. 2/2A	Variation of Broad Definition	Variation of Broad Definition	Follow Art. 1
Art. 3	Broad Definition	Broad Definition	
Art. 4/4A			
Art. 5	Narrow Definition	Narrow Definition	Narrow Definition
Art. 6	None.	Follow Art. 1 (Narrow)	Follow Art. 1 (Broad)
Art. 7	None.	Broad Definition after 2003 revision	
Art. 8	Broad Definition	Broad Definition	
Art. 9			

12. See, e.g., Alabama, Idaho, Virginia, and Hawaii. See Act of May 17, 2004, § 7–1–201, 2004 Ala. Acts 524 (to be codified at Ala. Code. § 7–1–201); Act of Mar. 10, 2004, ch. 43, sec. 19, § 28–1–201, 2004 Idaho Sess. Laws (to be codified at Idaho Code § 28–1–201); Va. Code Ann. § 8.1A–201 (2004); H.R. 1259, 22d State Legis. (Haw. 2003).

commercial standards. Both of us have written about defining good faith,[13] and neither of us is sanguine about our ability to define the idea. The commercial standards language will come into play most often where a contract gives one party discretion, and the other argues that the first exercised that discretion in a way not consistent with reasonable commercial standards. We can imagine a franchisee's complaining about a franchisor's behavior or an output buyer's complaining that the seller was giving too much or too little. Most of the cases that we can envision fall under Article 2 where merchants have always been subject to the longer definition. So we repeat, why the fuss over Article 1?[14]

Assuming (contrary to our belief) that insertion into Revised Article 1 will give greater play to the definition than it had formerly, let us consider one threatening possibility that lies buried in the commercial standards language. That is the possibility that courts will misconstrue the reasonable commercial standards language to impose a duty of care, not just an obligation of fairness. The text is clear, and the commentary even clearer, that observa-

---

13. Robert S. Summers, "Good Faith" in General Contract Law and the Sales Provisions of the Uniform Commercial Code, 54 Va. L. Rev. 195 (1968); James J. White, Good Faith and the Cooperative Antagonist, 54 SMU L. Rev. 679 (2001). See also M.L. Moses, The New Definition of Good Faith in Revised Article 1, 35 UCC L.J. 47 (2002).

14. With respect to transactions under Amended Articles 2 and 2A, the requirement of "observance of reasonable commercial standards of fair dealing" will apply not only to merchants but also to non-merchants after Revised Article 1 is adopted. Read literally, this means that even consumers should observe "reasonable *commercial* standards of fair dealing" in addition to showing honesty in fact.

Consumer representatives had objected strongly to inclusion of the word "commercial" in the Revised Article 1 definition and expressed the concern that inclusion of the word would impose "commercial" standards on those not professionally in commerce. See Letter from William B. Davenport and Harry C. Sigman, Jenner & Block, to Professor Geoffrey C. Hazard, Jr., Chairman of Permanent Editorial Board for the Uniform Commercial Code (Oct. 13, 1993) (on file with one of the authors). Professor Farnsworth also wondered "if there are 'commercial' standards for consumers under Article 2." See Memorandum

from E. Allan Farnsworth, Columbia University School of Law, to Donald J. Rapson (Oct. 13, 1992) (on file with one of the authors).

Believing that leaving out the word "commercial" should not make a substantive difference, the ABA Article 1 Review Task Force recommended omission of the word "commercial" and defining "good faith" as "honesty in fact and the observance of reasonable standards of fair dealing in the conduct or transaction concerned." The Task Force believed that omission of this word would provide flexibility in application of the definition in consumer situations and permit consideration of the degree of sophistication of the individual consumer not professionally in commerce. See Final Report of ABA UCC Article 1 Review Task Force Re: Revised Definition of Good Faith (Oct. 13, 1993).

For reasons unclear to us, the word "commercial" is still included in the revised definition. It's unclear what it would mean to require consumers in a sales transaction to observe reasonable commercial standards of fair dealing.

In addition, Revised Article 1 will remove the words "in the trade" from the end of the definition of "good faith" in current Articles 2 and 2A. This change presumably will exclude industry-specific commercial standards.

tion of reasonable commercial standards of *fair dealing* is not equivalent to a requirement of due care. For example, a bank could have thoroughly negligent check collection and processing procedures and yet not be in bad faith. The rule could mean that I will not treat you less fairly than I treat others, not that I will use as much care as others. In Articles 3 and 4 one court has this wrong,[15] but most courts have it right.[16]

The February 1997 Draft of Article 1 said that "the augmented definition of 'good faith'" should not inappropriately encourage courts to "avoid the effects of the UCC provisions perceived as being utilized in a commercially unreasonable way."

Comment 4 to section 3–103 provides, "Although fair dealing is a broad term that must be defined in context, it is clear that it is concerned with the fairness of conduct rather than the care with which an act is performed. Failure to exercise ordinary care in conducting a transaction is an entirely different concept than failure to deal fairly in conducting the transaction. Both fair dealing and ordinary care . . . are to be judged in the light of reasonable

---

15. See Maine Family Fed. Credit Union v. Sun Life Assurance Co., 727 A.2d 335, 343 (Me. 1999) (The Supreme Judicial Court of Maine admitted that the Credit Union could meet the subjective standard of good faith ("honesty in fact" or "pure heart and empty head" standard) because it took the instruments without notice of any possible dishonor, defect, fraud, or illegality. The court, however, upheld a jury verdict that the Credit Union did not meet the objective standard of good faith. According to the court, the objective standard requires the conduct of the holder to comport with industry or "commercial" standards applicable to the transaction and that those standards be reasonable standards intended to result in fair dealing. The court held that the Credit Union's failure to place a hold on the uncollected funds for a reasonable period of time under the circumstances did not comport with commercial standards that were reasonably structured to result in fair dealing.). See also Agriliance, L.L.C. v. Farmpro Servs., 328 F.Supp.2d 958, 970 (S.D. Iowa 2003) ("Whether reasonable commercial standards of fair dealing were observed . . . is ultimately a question of whether a reasonable lender (Farmpro) and reasonable bank (Central Bank) would have had reason to know of the potential competing claim . . . that they should have inquired about how the check was funded before accepting it.")

16. See, e.g., San Tan Irrigation Dist. v. Wells Fargo Bank, 197 Ariz. 193, 3 P.3d 1113, 1116 (App. 2000) (holding it unnecessary to decide whether the bank acted carelessly because the fair dealing prong of the good faith definition is concerned with the fairness of conduct rather than the care with which an act is performed); Wachovia Bank, N.A. v. Federal Reserve Bank of Richmond, 338 F.3d 318, 323 (4th Cir. 2003) ("To determine whether Wachovia acted in conformity with reasonable commercial standards of fair dealing, we consider the fairness of Wachovia's actions, rather than any negligence on its part." "While the FRB does allege that Wachovia's check processing procedures did not conform to reasonable commercial standards, the FRB has not made a showing that Wachovia failed to comply with reasonable commercial standards of fair dealing."); Gerber & Gerber, P.C. v. Regions Bank, 266 Ga.App. 8, 596 S.E.2d 174, 178 (2004) (stating that reasonable commercial standards of fair dealing are different from reasonable commercial standards of due care and holding that it was a question of fact whether the bank violated the reasonable commercial standards of fair dealing when it violated known commercial banking practices).

commercial standards, but those standards in each case are directed to different aspects of commercial conduct."

Comment 10 to section 8–102 provides, "The reference to commercial standards makes clear that assessments of conduct are to be made in light of the commercial setting." None of these exhortations or explanations was restated in the Comments to Article 1, but the drafters probably assumed that reiteration was not necessary.

Moreover, the Permanent Editorial Board (PEB) commentary on pre-revision 1–203 (obligation of good faith) recognized that different standards of "good faith" were adopted in pre-revision Article 1 (subjective standard) and in some other Articles (subjective and objective standards). Even so the PEB commentary reached a conclusion which would apply with equal force to both standards. This was added to the Official Comment to pre-revision 1–203, "[T]he doctrine of good faith merely directs a court towards interpreting contracts within the commercial context in which they are created, performed, and enforced, and does not create a separate duty of fairness and reasonableness which can be independently breached."[17]

Matters Unchanged by the New Definition of Good Faith in Article 1

(1) "Good faith" under Article 5 will continue to have the narrow definition. According to Comment 3 to 5–102,

> The narrower definition of "honesty in fact" reinforces the "independence principle" in the treatment of "fraud," "strict compliance," "preclusion," and other tests affecting the performance of obligations that are unique to letters of credit. This narrower definition—which does not include "fair dealing"—is appropriate to the decision to honor or dishonor a presentation of documents specified in a letter of credit. The narrower definition is also appropriate for other parts of revised Article 5 where greater certainty of obligations is necessary and is consistent with the goals of speed and low cost. It is important that U.S. letters of credit have continuing vitality and competitiveness in international transactions.

(2) The original broad definition of "good faith" in Articles 3, 4, 4A, 8 and 9 will be replaced with the broad definition of "good faith" in Article 1, but no substantive change will be brought to these Articles. (There would be a significant and unintended change in the law if a state used the narrow definition of good faith in Revised Article 1 and then deleted the definitions of good faith from the other articles.)

---

17. See UCC Text PEB Commentary No. 10 (Feb. 10, 1994).

(3) Most importantly, the change in the definition of "good faith" is unlikely to resolve any of the problems courts have faced in dealing with this term under its pre-revision narrow definition. Courts and commentators have had difficulty in determining what is and what is not good faith performance and very little success in agreeing on standards that might give a court guidance. It is unlikely that the revised definition will help to resolve this difficulty in any way.

State Enactments

Thirty-five states and the Virgin Islands have adopted Revised Article 1, but not all of them have adopted the broad definition of "good faith" in Revised Article 1. For example, the definitions of "good faith" adopted by a sample of eight of these jurisdictions are as follows:

Delaware, Minnesota, Texas, Virgin Islands	Adopted the Revised Article 1 definition.
Alabama, Idaho, Virginia	Maintained the Pre–Revision Article 1 definition.
Hawaii	"Good faith" means honesty in fact.

d. Record, Section 1–201(b)(31)

Revised Article 1 has adopted for all of the UCC the definition of "record" that first appeared in 1995 in revised Article 5 (5–102(a)(14)) and was later used in revised Article 9 (9–102(a)(69)): "information that is inscribed on a tangible medium or which is stored in an electronic or other medium and is retrievable in perceivable form."

A discussion of an ABA working group in 1994 affords some insight into this new definition:

Any "writing" is also a "record." A "record" need not be permanent or indestructible but must, at the time of creation, be durable. The term "record" does not include any oral or other communication which is not stored or preserved by any means. A "record" may be created without the knowledge or intent of any party.

Like the terms "written" or "writing", the term "record" does not establish the purposes, permitted uses or legal effects which a "record" may have under particular section of the Code. For example, the fact that a record no longer exists, or may no longer be accurate or reliable, should not affect the determination of whether or not a "record" existed.

While the definition includes writings, its principal utility is to identify non-written compilations of information that have sufficient permanence to be recognized as having the same status as a writing. Examples of records would include e-mails, information on electronic web sites, and similar compilations that are not technically "electronic" but that are retrievable. While it is clear that oral communications cannot be records, the status of an audiotape or a recorded "voice-mail" is not so obvious. We suspect that audiotapes are records and the same is probably true of voice-mails, but some might argue that things so easily erased as a telephone voice-mail should not be regarded as "retrievable."[18]

In sum, the inclusion of "Record" in Revised Article 1 is not revolutionary; the word has been in Article 5 for almost a decade and students of Article 5 and 9 are now familiar with the idea. As we note below, Revised Article 1 does not specify how one would perform the electronic equivalent of a signature on these "Records." The Revised Article 1 definitions make no reference to the usual form of electronic signature, an "authentication," and the definition of "signed" in 1–201(b)(37) is limited to inscriptions on writings.[19] It is not too large a request to ask courts to accept authentications of the kind described in 9–102(a)(7)(B) for records that are used in transactions under other Articles. The Comments to revised 1–306 suggest as much: "a party may 'authenticate' a record by (i) signing a record that is a writing or (ii) attaching to or logically associating with a record that is not a writing an electronic sound, symbol or process with the present intent to adopt or accept the record."[20] Technically this instruction applies only to revised 1–306, but it reflects the Drafting Committee's understanding of the term.

e. Signed, Section 1–201(b)(37)

Revised 1–201(b)(37) defines "signed" as including "using any symbol executed or adopted with present intention to adopt or accept a writing." The new definition limits "signatures" to in-

---

18. E-mails are easily "erasable" but typically linger on in computer memories even after they disappear from the screen.

19. In the drafting process of Revised Article 1, the Drafting Committee considered adding a new definition of "authenticate," whose relation to the term "signed" would be similar to the relation of "record" to "writing." Indeed, Revised Article 9 includes a definition of "authenticate." According to revised § 9–102(7), "Authenticate means: (A) to sign; or (B) to execute or otherwise adopt a symbol, or encrypt or simi-larly process a record in whole or in part, with the present intent of the authenticating person to identify the person and adopt or accept a record." See § 9–102(7) (1999). Thus, "authenticate" may be used with respect to any record as defined in § 9–102(69) including electronic forms, while "signed" will be used with respect to writings in cases where a signed paper is required. Therefore, revised Article 9 has made electronic signatures possible.

20. See § 1–306, Changes from former law (2001).

scriptions on writings[21] and makes only one substantive change: it replaces "intention to authenticate" with "intention to adopt or accept." According to Comment 37 to revised 1–201, this change was made because other articles now use the term "authenticate" (e.g., Article 9). To avoid confusion, the Drafting Committee decided to use the words "adopt or accept", which are used in 9–102(a)(7) in connection with the Article 9 definition of "authenticate."

In 2001 when the revision of Article 1 was adopted, the Drafting Committee's preferred approach appeared to be to use the term "signed" for writings only, and to enlarge the scope of "authenticate" to include both traditional signatures in writing and electronic signatures. By 2003, the drafters of Article 2 took a different approach; they enlarged the scope of "signed" to include both written and electronic signatures. Amended 2–103(1)(p) provides, " 'Sign' means, with present intent to authenticate or adopt a record: (i) to execute or adopt a tangible symbol; or (ii) to attach to or logically associate with the record an electronic sound, symbol, or process."[22] In addition, the 2003 amendments to Article 2A and the revision of Article 7 added a new definition of "sign" that is identical to the Amended Article 2 definition.[23] So in Amended (or revised) Articles 2, 2A and 7 "sign" and "signed" mean one thing, and mean another in all of the other Articles. The drafters of Article 1 could not use the Amended Article 2 definition without appearing to authorize non-written negotiable instruments, something the drafters have been unwilling to do.

Assigning different meanings to the same term in different Articles of the UCC is never a good idea, but careful reading and meticulous sorting of Article 3 and 4 transactions from others will minimize the difficulties. More threatening is the possibility that a contract, which is not clearly subject to a particular Article, will require a "signature" or a "signed document." The parties to the contract may then fall into dispute on the question whether an authenticated e-mail, for example, satisfies the contract as something that is "signed."

§ 1–5 Relocation of Substantive Provisions, Sections 1–202 through 1–206

In four cases the drafters moved material out of the definitions provisions on the ground that the material stated substantive rules of law, not definitions.

---

21. See § 1–201, Comment 37 (2001) ("This provision refers only to writings, because the term 'signed,' as used in some articles, refers only to writings.").

22. § 2–103(p) (2003).

23. See § 2A–103(dd) (2002), § 7–102(11) (2003).

a.   Notice and Knowledge, Section 1–202

The rules on notice and knowledge have been moved to 1–202. The only substantive change in these rules is the deletion of the reference to the "forgotten notice" doctrine. The last sentence of pre-revision 1–201(25) provided: "The time and circumstances under which a notice or notification may cease to be effective are not determined by this Act." This sentence was deleted in revised 1–202. However, the Draft for Approval dated August 10–17, 2001 still included a sentence in its Comments which says, "This subsection leaves open the time and circumstances under which notice or notification may cease to be effective. Therefore such cases as *Graham v. White–Phillips Co.*, 296 U.S. 27, 56 S.Ct. 21, 80 L.Ed. 20 (1935), are not overruled." Eventually even the commentary reference to the "forgotten notice" doctrine disappeared. We are not sure why.

b.   Distinguishing Leases From Security Interests, Section 1–203

In pre-revision Article 1, the definition of "security interest" consisted of a short paragraph that stated the basic principle that resolves most issues, followed by over 50 lines of clarification and qualification whose only purpose was to distinguish "true leases" from documents that are leases in form but security agreements in substance. This extended rule even contains a nested definition of the term "present value," which is used partly to distinguish between true leases and security interests. The portion of the pre-revision definition of "security interest" that distinguishes true leases from security interests has been moved to a separate substantive section. As a result, the remaining portion of the definition is shorter and clearer. The definition of "present value" now enjoys its own subsection 1–201(b)(28).[1]

c.   Value, Reasonable Time and Presumptions, Sections 1–204, 205 and 206

The definitions of "value" and "presumption" in pre-revision 1–201(44) and (31) have been moved to new sections 1–204 and 1–206 respectively, and subsections (2) and (3) of pre-revision 1–204 have been moved to new section 1–205, but their substance is not changed.

§ 1–6   Choice of Law, Section 1–301

Section 1–301 is the most ambitious section in Revised Article 1, and, as this treatise is written in 2009, its prospects are not promising. As indicated in Section 1–1 above, Revised Article 1 has

§ 1–5
1.   § 1–201(b)(28) (2001).

been adopted in 35 states and one territory, but none of the states adopted more than a fragment of 1–301, and most kept old 1–105 verbatim or in substance. Because of this failure to win over the states, we omit consideration of 1–301 here; those interested may refer to Section 1–H of Volume 1 of our treatise on the UCC.

§ 1–7   Variation by Agreement, Section 1–302

Revised 1–302 combines the rules from subsections (3) and (4) of pre-revision 1–102 and subsection (1) of pre-revision 1–204. There is no substantive change in the rules.[1] The old Comments to pre-revision 1–102(3)(4) and 1–204 have been moved to this section with only stylistic changes, and a new Comment 2 has been added.

Textual Comparison

§ 1–302.   Variation by Agreement.

(From pre-revision 1–102(3))

(a) Except as otherwise provided in subsection (b) or elsewhere in [the Uniform Commercial Code], ~~T~~the effect of provisions of ~~this Act~~[the Uniform Commercial Code] may be varied by agreement~~, except as otherwise provided in this Act and except that~~.

(b) ~~T~~the obligations of good faith, diligence, reasonableness, and care prescribed by ~~this Act~~[the Uniform Commercial Code] may not be disclaimed by agreement.~~but t~~ The parties,~~may~~ by agreement, may determine the standards by which the performance of those~~such~~ obligations is to be measured if those~~such~~ standards are not manifestly unreasonable.

(From pre-revision 1–204(1))

Whenever [the Uniform Commercial Code]~~this Act~~ requires any action to be taken within a reasonable time, ~~any~~time ~~which~~that is not manifestly unreasonable may be fixed by agreement.

(From pre-revision 1–102(4))

(c) The presence in certain provisions of ~~this Act~~[the Uniform Commercial Code] of the ~~words~~phrase "unless otherwise agreed", or words of similar import, does not imply that the effect of other provisions may not be varied by agreement under this section~~subsection (3)~~.

This dutiful repetition of the words of the former statute misleads as to the substantial proposals for change that were considered and rejected. There were three main objections to the

§ 1–7

1. See also § 1–302, Changes (2001).

old law: 1) the rule was not sufficiently explicit on the question when contracting parties can bind a third person who is not a party to the contract; 2) the old law did not identify provisions that are non-variable but that do not say so; 3) under the old law, it was unclear whether one could opt out of the UCC by adopting a trade code or another body of law such as the UNCITRAL rules or the CISG.

The drafters in 1997 sought to meet all of these objections. The Draft reads as follows: "[T]he effect of provisions of [the Uniform Commercial Code] [on the rights and obligations of parties with respect to each other] may be varied by agreement [between those parties]. [Such an agreement may include agreement that a trade code or similar record will govern the relationship between the parties.]"[2] Language in the third and fourth brackets was intended to meet the first and second objections, and the fifth bracket to meet the third objection.

Four years after the 1997 proposals, none remained in the statute and only the third earned extensive treatment in the Comments. The right of parties to adopt trade codes or other bodies of law as their "law" is recognized by new Comment 2:

> An agreement that varies the effect of provisions of the Uniform Commercial Code may do so by stating the rules that will govern in lieu of the provisions varied. Alternatively, the parties may vary the effect of such provisions by stating that their relationship will be governed by recognized bodies of rules or principles applicable to commercial transactions. Such bodies of rules or principles may include, for example, those that are promulgated by intergovernmental authorities such as UNCITRAL or Unidroit (*see, e.g.*, Unidroit Principles of International Commercial Contracts), or non-legal codes such as trade codes.

Why did the drafters pull back from the first two tasks and relegate the third to the Comments? We suspect that attempts like the draft of 1997 demonstrated how difficult it would be to deal with these issues in a definitive and comprehensive way without reference to particular cases in specific contexts. It is easy to see that two persons cannot by agreement confer negotiability on an otherwise nonnegotiable instrument or that a debtor and creditor cannot change the rules of priority of secured creditors in a way that would hurt a third party. But what about the agreement of creditor one with a debtor to allow creditor two priority? Isn't creditor two a third party beneficiary of the deal between debtor

---

2. § 1–303(a) (Discussion Draft, Sept. 1997), available at http://www.law. upenn.edu/bll/ulc/ucc1/sept97.htm.

and creditor one? The problem is evident, and, we suspect, the committee saw it.

§ 1–8   Course of Performance etc., Section 1–303

Textual Comparison

§ ~~1–205.~~1–303. Course of Performance, Course of Dealing, and Usage of Trade.

(a) A "course of performance" is a sequence of conduct between the parties to a particular transaction that exists if:

(1) the agreement of the parties with respect to the transaction involves repeated occasions for performance by a party; and

(2) the other party, with knowledge of the nature of the performance and opportunity for objection to it, accepts the performance or acquiesces in it without objection.

~~(1)~~(b) A "course of dealing" is a sequence of ~~previous~~conduct concerning previous transactions between the parties to a particular transaction ~~which~~that is fairly to be regarded as establishing a common basis of understanding for interpreting their expressions and other conduct.

~~(2)~~(c) A "usage of trade" is any practice or method of dealing having such regularity of observance in a place, vocation, or trade as to justify an expectation that it will be observed with respect to the transaction in question. The existence and scope of such a usage ~~are to~~must be proved as facts. If it is established that such a usage is embodied in a~~written~~ trade code or similar ~~writing~~record, the interpretation of the ~~writing is for the court.~~record is a question of law.

~~(3)~~(d) A course of performance or course of dealing between the parties ~~and any~~or usage of trade in the vocation or trade in which they are engaged or of which they are or should be aware is relevant in ascertaining the meaning of the parties' agreement, may give particular meaning to ~~and supplement or qualify~~specific terms of ~~an~~ the agreement, and may supplement or qualify the terms of the agreement. A usage of trade applicable in the place in which part of the performance under the agreement is to occur may be so utilized as to that part of the performance.

~~(4) The~~(e) Except as otherwise provided in subsection (f), the express terms of an agreement and any applicable course of performance, course of dealing, or usage of trade ~~shall~~ must be construed ~~wherever~~whenever reasonable as consistent with each other~~;~~. ~~but when~~If such construction is unreasonable:

(1) express terms prevail over course of performance, course of dealing, and usage of trade; ~~control both~~

(2) course of performance prevails over course of dealing and usage of trade; and

(3) course of dealing ~~controls~~prevails over usage of trade.

~~(5) An applicable usage of trade in the place where any part of performance is to occur shall be used in interpreting the agreement as to that part of the performance.~~

(f) Subject to Section 2–209 and Section 2A–208, a course of performance is relevant to show a waiver or modification of any term inconsistent with the course of performance.

~~(6)~~(g) Evidence of a relevant usage of trade offered by one party is not admissible unless ~~and until he~~ that party has given the other party ~~such~~ notice ~~as~~ that the court finds sufficient to prevent unfair surprise to the ~~latter~~other party.

In a 1992 memo to the ABA Task Force on Article 1,[1] Professor Patterson argued that course of performance should come to Article 1 for two reasons. First, to make it applicable to deals under all of the Articles was consistent with contract law, for the Restatement does not single out contracts for the sale of goods for special treatment. Second, the policy used to justify 2–208's incorporation of course of performance in Article 2—that the parties know best what they mean and that their own performance of the contract best shows that meaning—applied equally in cases not under Article 2.[2]

Convinced by Professor Patterson, the committee brought course of performance to Article 1 in section 1–303 where the committee used language insignificantly different from the deleted language from 2–208. Adding course of performance as a basis to find the meaning of parties' agreement slightly complicated the rules concerning choice between what were now four sources of meaning: express terms, course of performance, course of dealing, and usage of trade. Like pre-revision 1–205, section 1–303 asks the court to try to find agreement among the sources of meaning and, failing that, sets up a hierarchy from express terms to usage of trade.

Putting course of performance into Article 1 raised two additional issues.[3] First, the Drafting Committee believed that a course of performance which might otherwise create a defense to the obligation of a party to a negotiable instrument should not be

---

§ 1–8

1. Patterson Memo, *supra* § 1–4, note 1.

2. *Id.*

3. See § 1–304, Revision Notes (Discussion Draft, Feb. 1997), available at http://www.law.upenn.edu/bll/ulc/ucc1/art1feb.htm.

available as a defense against a holder in due course who took the instrument without notice of that course of performance. The Drafting Committee resolved this issue by adding a sentence in the first paragraph of the Comment: "It should be noted that a course of performance that might otherwise establish a defense to the obligation of a party to a negotiable instrument is not available as a defense against a holder in due course who took the instrument without notice of that course of performance."[4]

Second, the Drafting Committee concluded that Article 1 needed a statement about course of performance and waiver or modification. So we have 1–303(f): "Subject to Section 2–209 and Section 2A–208, a course of performance is relevant to show a waiver or modification of any term inconsistent with the course of performance."

Revised 1–303 made two small additional changes to pre-revision 1–205. The definition of "course of dealing" was changed from "a sequence of previous conduct between the parties...." to "a sequence of conduct concerning previous transactions between the parties...."[5] This change eliminates any implication that negotiations leading up to a contract are themselves course of dealing. And the former reference to "written trade code or similar writing" was replaced with "trade code or similar record" to account for trade codes in electronic form.[6]

§ 1–9 Waiver or Renunciation of Claim or Right After Breach, Section 1–306

Section 1–306 comes from pre-revision 1–107 which provided, "Any claim or right arising out of an alleged breach can be discharged in whole or in part without consideration by a *written* waiver or renunciation *signed* and *delivered* by the aggrieved party." (Emphasis added.)

Revised 1–306 provides, "A claim or right arising out of an alleged breach may be discharged in whole or in part without consideration by *agreement* of the aggrieved party in an *authenticated record*." (Emphasis added.)

This section changes former law in two respects. First, pre-revision 1–107, requiring the "deliver[y]" of a "written waiver or renunciation," merges the separate concepts of the aggrieved party's agreement to forego rights and the manifestation of that agreement. Revised 1–306 separates those concepts, and explicitly requires agreement of the aggrieved party. (Since signing a writing would surely be an agreement, adding the word "agreement" is

---

4. § 1–303, Changes from former law (2001).

5. § 1–303(b) (2001).

6. See § 1–303(c) (2001).

hardly a change.) By providing for memorialization in an authenticated record, the new section does make a change. In this context, a party may "authenticate" a record by (i) signing a record that is a writing or (ii) attaching to or logically associating with a record that is not a writing an electronic sound, symbol or process with the present intent to adopt or accept the record. The Comment references 1–201(b)(37) (definition of "signed") and 9–102(7) (definition of "authenticate"). The combined language of those provisions is similar to the definition of "sign" in amended 2–103(p).[1]

The drafters omitted the following language (that had been in the Comments to 1–107) from the Comments to 1–306:

> There may, of course, also be an oral renunciation or waiver sustained by consideration but subject to Statute of Frauds provisions and to the section of Article 2 on Sales dealing with the modification of signed writings (section 2–209). As is made express in the latter section this Act fully recognizes the effectiveness of waiver and estoppel.

Why the omission? Maybe the reporter was intentionally playing down the statute of frauds.

§ 1–9

1. See *supra* § 1–4(e) (discussion of definition of "signed").

Chapter 2

SCOPE OF ARTICLE 2, AND OFFER, ACCEPTANCE, AND CONSIDERATION THEREUNDER

Analysis

§ 2–1 Introduction—Scope of Article 2 and Its Expanded Concept of Contract

Article 2 includes 104 provisions subsumed under the following seven headings:

Part 1. Short Title, General Construction and Subject Matter

Part 2. Form, Formation and Readjustment of Contract

Part 3. General Obligation and Construction of Contract

Part 4. Title, Creditors and Good Faith Purchasers

Part 5. Performance

27

Part 6.   Breach, Repudiation and Excuse

Part 7.   Remedies

The drafters of "old," that is, the Article 2 currently in force patterned the sequence of sections in the Article after the sequence of events in sales.[1]

The primary scope section is section 2–102 of Article 2 which provides:[2]

> Unless the context otherwise requires, this Article applies to transactions in goods; it does not apply to any transaction which although in the form of an unconditional contract to sell or present sale is intended to operate only as a security transaction nor does this Article impair or repeal any statute regulating sales to consumers, farmers or other specified classes of buyers.

Section 2–105(1) defines "goods" as "all things * * * which are movable at the time of identification to the contract for sale other than the money in which the price is to be paid, investment securities (Article 8) and things in action." Included in this definition of goods are "unborn young of animals and growing crops and other identified things attached to realty." Sections 2–105 through 2–107 define key terms relevant to the scope of Article 2. We will see in Section 2–2 below that the Uniform Electronic Transfers Act (UETA) has bearing here as well.

Article 2, and other articles of the Code also include several sections that resolve specific issues as to the scope of Article 2. Thus section 2–105(1) states that "goods" does not mean investment securities, and the section refers to "Article 8" which includes numerous provisions on investment securities. Where the provisions of Article 8 do not deal with a matter, however, courts have tended to apply Article 2 by analogy.[3]

Under certain Article 2 sections, such as 2–401, 2–505, 2–707, and 2–711(3), specialized Article 2 "security interests" arise which are subject not only to Article 2 on sales but, with the exceptions set forth in 9–110, are subject as well to the provisions of Article 9.

§ 2–1

1. Although the official text of Article 2 went through many proposed revisions over the past fifteen years, as of this writing, Amended Article 2, has not been adopted in any state, and is not likely to be.

2. See generally, Note, The Uniform Commercial Code As a Premise for Judicial Reasoning, 65 Colum. L. Rev. 880 (1965); Note, UCC Application by Analogy, 6 Ind. L. Rev. 108 (1972); Murray,

The Spreading Analogy of Article 2 of the Uniform Commercial Code, 39 Fordham L. Rev. 447 (1971); Rapson, A "Home Run" Application of Established Principles of Statutory Construction: UCC Analogies, 5 Cardozo L. Rev. 441 (1984).

3. See, e.g., Chadwell v. English, 652 P.2d 310, 313, 34 UCC 1644 (Okl. App. 1982). Cf. Kottis v. Cerilli, 612 A.2d 661, 666 18 UCC2d 701 (R.I. 1992).

Of course, most ordinary consensual security interests in goods arise in the first place not under Article 2 but under Article 9. But even as to these, although Article 9 governs the security aspects of the transaction, Article 2 applies to certain other aspects at least where the transaction also involves the sale of goods. Thus, for example, Article 2's warranty provisions govern disputes as to the quality of goods sold subject to a security interest, but the validity, perfection, and foreclosure of that interest are controlled by Article 9. And where a transaction in goods is in the form of a contract to sell or a present sale yet is intended to operate only as a secured transaction, 2–102 provides that Article 2 "does not apply."

Moreover, 2–102 provides that Article 2 does not "impair or repeal any statute regulating sales to consumers, farmers, or other specified classes of buyers." Such other statutes may be state or federal. Frequently, both Article 2 and one or more other regulatory statutes will apply. For example, Article 2 may apply to warranty terms while the Uniform Consumer Credit Code or other state consumer regulatory law governs the "door-to-door" aspects of the sale. Another important category of examples consists of state or federal legislation dealing with farmers and agricultural products. Still another category of statutes controls the transfer of title to automobiles or aircraft. Today there are also local statutes governing aspects of the sale of pets and domestic animals. In all of the above categories, both Article 2 and the other statutes may apply, and when the two conflict, the other statutory law typically controls.

But the specific provisions in Article 2, other Code articles and other regulatory statutes only treat, and in terms resolve, a limited number of the scope issues that have arisen in the cases. Most of the scope issues that have arisen in the now vast case law fall into the following categories: (1) cases posing the issue of whether goods are involved at all, (2) cases in which goods are plainly involved, yet the transaction is not a sale, but say, a financing arrangement, a lease, etc., (3) cases of a hybrid nature involving goods and non-goods such as realty, and (4) cases of a hybrid nature involving goods and services.

In the first category above, a major subset consists of those cases involving contracts for the sale and licensing of computer software. Courts, sometimes hesitantly, have generally held under section 2–102 that computer software are "goods." However, a related question is whether, even though particular software constitutes "goods," it still may fall outside Article 2 because the distribution of the software is not a "transaction" in goods. This somewhat separate issue arises because software dealings often involve attendant circumstances to which the phrase "transaction" in goods does not felicitously apply. Factors bearing on this are whether, for example, the software is created from scratch or customized from existing software, whether the deal more closely resembles a sale or a licensing agreement, or whether the sale of software is accomplished by provision of services. There is a vast body of case law here. As one court put it with regard to software licenses, "in Massachusetts and across most of the nation, software licenses exist in a legislative void" and "Article 2 technically does not govern software licenses, but for the time being, the court will assume that it does".[4] Another court put it thus: "in many states, it is not clear whether 'license' agreements ... are contracts for the sale of 'goods' and therefore within the UCC * * * ".[5]

There are, however some discernible patterns as to criteria that are being used to differentiate between transactions that fall under the UCC and those that do not. In considering whether a particular software transaction qualifies as a transaction in goods some courts have classified an ordinary mass market software sale as such a transaction in goods.[6]

However, where the purchaser is not a mass market consumer, some courts have looked to a second criterion and have held that entirely new software made from scratch (i.e. "concept to realization") does not fall under the purview of Article 2, and distinguished this result from other cases in which the sales were of preexisting software with custom modifications or upgrades.[7] Another court reached the same result by turning to a third criterion of applying the logic used in some "hybrid" cases and finding that the contract called for the software developer's "contribution of knowledge and expertise to the design and development of a product that included a software component."[8] Applying the predomi-

---

4. See, e.g., I. Lan Sys. v. Netscout Serv. Level Corp., 183 F.Supp. 2d 328, 46 UCC2d 287 (D. Mass. 2002).

5. Arbitron, Inc. v. Tralyn Broad., Inc., 400 F.3d 130, 56 UCC2d 883 (2d Cir. 2005).

6. See ProCD, Inc. v. Zeidenberg, 86 F.3d 1447, 1450, 29 UCC2d 1109 (7th Cir. 1996) (treating "licenses as ordinary contracts accompanying the sale of products", and affirming the district court's decision stating that the mass market software transaction at issue was a transaction in goods because purchasers do not make periodic payments, the software company does not retain title for the purpose of a security interest, and no set expiration date for the licensed right exists); Olcott International & Co. v. Micro Data Base Systems, Inc., 793 N.E.2d 1063, 51 UCC2d 352 (Ind. App. 2003) (purchase of pre-existing standardized software modules). See also,

Smart Online, Inc. v. Opensite Technologies, Inc., 2003 NCBC 5, 51 UCC2d 47, 2003 WL 21555316 (N.C. Super. Ct. 2003).

7. Data Processing Servs. v. L.H. Smith Oil Corp., 492 N.E.2d 314, 1 UCC2d 29 (Ind. Ct. App. 1986) (finding the design, development, and implementation of a data processing system to be a service). See also, True N. Composites, L.L.C. v. Trinity Indus., 65 Fed. Appx. 266, 50 UCC2d 683 (Fed. Cir. 2003) (stating "the UCC does not distinguish between specially made goods that are customized from existing products and goods that are entirely specially made"); Pearl Invs., LLC v. Standard I/O, Inc., 257 F.Supp.2d 326, 50 UCC2d 377 (D. Me. 2003).

8. Multi–Tech Sys. v. Floreat, Inc., 47 UCC2d 924, 2002 WL 432016 (D. Minn. 2002).

nant purpose test, the court found that the "software ... provided ... at best was incidental to the predominant purpose of those agreements."[9] Another court also applied the predominant purpose test, but reached the opposite result because "services [we]re only incidental to the sale of goods."[10] A number of courts have recognized certain software transactions to be hybrid transactions.[11]

A fourth criterion is manner of payment. An upfront or single payment is an indication of a sale of a good according to several courts.[12] Payment in installments would indicate a transaction more akin to a licensing agreement or contract for services.

In the process of seeking to amend Article 2, the drafters struggled with the foregoing problems of scope from 1990 to 2003. The formal resolution was that a few words were changed in the definition of goods. Section 2–103(k) of Amended Article 2 included the upshot that goods "do not include information." To deal with the software issue that the committee was struggling with, NCCUSL drafted the Uniform Computer Information Transactions Act (UCITA) without the ALI's involvement. Of course, Amended Article 2 has not been adopted anywhere, and UCITA has only been adopted in Virginia and Maryland. The resistance to adopting UCITA stems from a perception that it weakens consumer protections and is overly favorable to software producers.[13] The history regarding Amended Article 2 and UCITA is dealt with in a related work by your authors.[14]

9. Id at *4.

10. Arlington Electrical Constr. v. Schindler Elevator Corp., 1992 WL 43112, at *7 (Ohio Ct. App. 1992). See also, Advent Sys. v. Unisys. Corp. 925 F.2d 670, 13 UCC2d 669 (3d Cir. 1991).

11. RRX Indus. v. Lab–Con, Inc., 772 F.2d 543, 41 UCC 1561 (9th Cir. 1985); Schroders, Inc. v. Hogan Sys., Inc., 137 Misc. 2d 738, 522 N.Y.S.2d 404, 4 UCC2d 1397 (1987); Systems Design & Management Information, Inc. v. Kansas City Post Office Employees Credit Union, 14 Kan.App.2d 266, 788 P.2d 878, 11 UCC2d 775 (1990); Wharton Management Group v. Sigma Consultants, Inc., 1990 WL 18360, 50 UCC2d 678 (Del. Super. Ct. 1990); Camara v. Hill, 157 Vt. 156, 596 A.2d 349, 15 UCC2d 1216 (1991); Synergistic Technologies, Inc. v. IDB Mobile Communications, Inc., 871 F.Supp. 24, 27 UCC2d 428 (D.D.C. 1994); PC COM v. Proteon, Inc., 946 F.Supp. 1125, 32 UCC2d 663 (S.D.N.Y. 1996); Dahlmann v. Sulcus Hospitality Techs., Corp., 63 F.Supp.2d 772, 39 UCC2d 299 (E.D. Mich. 1999);

Nielsen Media Research, Inc. v. Microsystems Software, Inc., 2002 WL 31175223 (S.D.N.Y. 2002); ePresence, Inc. v. Evolve Software, Inc., 190 F.Supp.2d 159, 47 UCC2d 132 (D. Mass. 2002); Smart Online, Inc. v. Opensite Technologies, Inc., 2003 NCBC 5, 2003 WL 21555316, 51 UCC2d 47 (N.C. Super. Ct. 2003); Mortgage Plus, Inc. v. DocMagic, Inc., 55 UCC2d 58, 2004 WL 2331918 (D. Kan. 2004); KSM Associates, Inc. v. ACS State Healthcare, LLC, 2006 WL 847786 (E.D.Pa. 2006).

12. SoftMan Prods. Co., LLC v. Adobe Sys., 171 F.Supp.2d 1075, 45 UCC2d 945 (C.D. Cal. 2001); Smart Online, Inc. v. Opensite Technologies, Inc., 2003 NCBC 5, 51 UCC2d 47, 2003 WL 21555316 (N.C. Super. Ct. 2003); Dealer Mgmt. Sys. v. Design Auto. Group, Inc., 355 Ill.App.3d 416, 290 Ill.Dec. 971, 822 N.E.2d 556, 55 UCC2d 965 (2005).

13. Neil Gross, *This Law Is User-Unfriendly*, Bus. Wk., April 17, 2000, at 94.

14. James J. White & Robert S. Summers, Revised Article 1 and Amend-

With neither Amended Article 2 nor UCITA likely to be widely adopted, our view on the proper approach to mixed transactions is as follows: Where there are legal issues about both hardware and software, we doubt it makes sense in the usual case to treat one part under one body of law and the other part under another body. In some cases the dispute will involve only the hardware or the software and not both; in other cases it may make sense to apply Article 2 or UCITA by analogy.

What general approach should courts take when deciding whether to apply Article 2 to non-sale transactions? We believe that the best general approach for courts to take is to determine what policy objectives the particular Code section in question implicates, and then, in light of those policies, determine whether the particular facts of the transaction invite the application of the section by analogy. We call this a "policy approach", and it differs significantly from certain other general approaches to be found in the cases. Of course, there may be a competing body of law, too, the policies of which must also be considered. And in a proper case, that body of law should control, not Article 2.

The approach we advocate has been adopted in a number of cases. Thus, the Idaho Supreme Court in Glenn Dick Equipment Co. v. Galey Construction, Inc.[15] articulated this approach in these terms:[16]

> In order to determine which provisions are applicable, we will look to the commercial setting in which the problem arises and contrast the relevant common law with Article 2—we will use Article 2 as "a premise for reasoning only when the case involves the same considerations that gave rise to the Code provisions and an analogy is not rebutted by additional antithetical circumstances."

Another general issue arises in the "hybrid" cases where there is a combination of properties consisting of non-goods as well as goods, or a combination of services with a sale of goods. Suppose, for example, that seller contracts to sell a going business consisting of goods, realty and goodwill. Or suppose a party undertakes to install a plumbing system in a house under construction and is also to provide the copper tubing. In such "hybrid" cases, a minority of courts apply Article 2 to the sale of goods aspects of the transaction only,[17] whereas a majority apply Article 2 if the "predominant

---

ed Article 2—Substance and Process, Supplement to Accompany Uniform Commercial Code Practitioner Treatise Series, Volumes 1–4, 52–55 (2005).

15. 97 Idaho 216, 541 P.2d 1184, 18 UCC 340 (1975). See also Printers II, Inc. v. Professionals Publishing, Inc.,

615 F.Supp. 767, 42 UCC 381 (S.D.N.Y. 1985), aff'd, 784 F.2d 141 (2d Cir. 1986).

16. 97 Idaho at 222, 541 P.2d at 1190, 18 UCC at 348.

17. The leading case is Foster v. Colorado Radio Corp., 381 F.2d 222, 4 UCC 446 (10th Cir. 1967).

purpose" of the whole transaction was a sale of goods, and in that event, the majority usually applies Article 2 to the whole.[18] If a sale of goods is not the "predominant purpose," then Article 2 does not apply at all. It may be added that in the overwhelming majority of cases, Article 2 has been found applicable. Here we offer a caveat about the predominant purpose test. It presupposes that if Article 2 is to apply or not apply, it should apply (or not apply) to the whole of the transaction. In many cases it does make sense only to apply one body of law to the whole transaction. Thus in Hudson v. Town and Country True Value Hardware, Inc.,[19] the Tennessee Supreme Court invoked the test and applied a single non-goods measure of damages to the whole transaction rather than the Article 2 measure to the goods and a non-Article 2 measure to the non-goods. We applaud this result but not on the ground that in this case the non-goods were "predominant." Rather, we applaud it in light of the more specific reason the court gave. It suggested that applying two bodies of law—one to the goods aspect and one to the non-goods aspect would present "insurmountable problems of proof in segregating assets and determining their respective values at the time of the original contract and at the time of resale, in order to apply two different measures of damages."[20]

Many of the hybrid cases deal with franchise or distributorship agreements. The majority approach is to apply the UCC to such agreements. We wonder whether this approach is correct; we would agree that the Code could be applied by analogy.

§ 2–2　Contract Formation Under Article 2 Including Internet and Other Digital Contracts

We now briefly turn to the expanded concept of contract in Article 2. The expansion we address consists of the expansion of contract in existing Article 2 as compared to contract as conceived in pre code statutory law and case law. Some of the enacted Article 2 provisions on the formation of contracts[1] for the sale of goods have not only radically altered sales law but have influenced the Restatement (Second) of Contracts as well.[2] In most fundamental

18. See, e.g., Bonebrake v. Cox, 499 F.2d 951, 14 UCC 1318 (8th Cir. 1974); De Filippo v. Ford Motor Co., 516 F.2d 1313, 16 UCC 1199 (3d Cir. 1975), cert. denied, 423 U.S. 912, 96 S.Ct. 216, 46 L.Ed.2d 141 (1975).

19. 666 S.W.2d 51, 38 UCC 6 (Tenn. 1984).

20. *Id*. at 54, 38 UCC at 9.

§ 2–2

1. Murray, Contracts: A New Design for the Agreement Process, 53 Cornell L.

Rev. 785 (1968); Project, The Uniform Commercial Code and Contract Law: Some Selected Problems, 105 U.Pa. L. Rev. 836 (1957); Note, Contractual Interactions and the Uniform Commercial Code, 89 Yale L.J. 1396 (1980).

2. See Braucher, Freedom of Contract and the Second Restatement, 78 Yale L.J. 598 (1969).

terms, Article 2 expands our conception of contract. It makes contracts easier to form, and it imposes a wider range of obligations than before. Contract formation is easier in several ways. Parties may form a contract through conduct rather than merely through the exchange of communications constituting "offer and acceptance." Section 2–204(1) says, "A contract for sale of goods may be made in any manner sufficient to show agreement, including conduct by both parties which recognizes the existence of such a contract." Sections 2–206(1) and 2–207(3) also expressly allow for the formation of contracts partly or wholly on the basis of such conduct.[3] Further, Article 2 reduces the formalities required for contract formation. The statute of frauds (section 2–201) requires only a writing that "indicate[s]" a contract was made,[4] and 2–206 and 2–207(1) abandon the requirement that an acceptance must coincide precisely with all terms of the offer. Section 2–204(3) also states: "Even though one or more terms are left open a contract for sale does not fail for indefiniteness if the parties have intended to make a contract and there is a reasonably certain basis for giving an appropriate remedy." As we will see, Article 2 itself helps provide this "reasonably certain basis" through numerous provisions which fill gaps in an agreement that might otherwise fail for indefiniteness.[5]

Article 2 contracts are also expansive in content. Thus 1–201(11) defines "contract" as the "total legal obligation which results from the parties' agreement," and 1–201(3) defines "agreement" to mean "the bargain of the parties in fact as found in their language or by implication from other circumstances including course of dealing or usage of trade or course of performance as provided in this Act."[6] Section 1–205 defines course of dealing and usage of trade while section 2–208 defines course of performance. The Code therefore adds to sales agreements much that is not made express by the parties. Section 1–103 on supplemental general principles also feeds much general contract law into Article 2 sales contracts. Further, 1–102(3) and 1–203 of the Code impose obligations of good faith which may be thought of as part of any Article 2 contract.[7] And Article 2 broadens the notion of contract insofar as

---

3. See §§ 2–3 and 2–6 *infra.*

4. See Chapter 3.

5. See Chapter 4.

6. A leading case on the enlarged concept of agreement is Nanakuli Paving and Rock Co. v. Shell Oil Co., Inc., 664 F.2d 772, 32 UCC 1025 (9th Cir. 1981).

7. Summers, "Good Faith" in General Contract Law and the Sales Provisions of the Uniform Commercial Code,

54 Va. L. Rev. 195 (1968). See Restatement, Second, Contracts § 205. Summers, The General Duty of Good Faith—Its Recognition and Conceptualization, 67 Cornell L. Rev. 810 (1982). Numerous cases now apply 1–203. See, e.g., Baker v. Ratzlaff, 1 Kan.App.2d 285, 564 P.2d 153, 21 UCC 1217 (1977); Neumiller Farms, Inc. v. Cornett, 368 So.2d 272, 26 UCC 61 (Ala. 1979); Zapatha v. Dairy Mart, Inc., 381 Mass. 284, 408 N.E.2d 1370, 29 UCC 1121 (1980); T.W.

2–202 on parol evidence permits parties to prove "extrinsic" terms not provable under various pre-Code versions of the parol evidence rule.

a. Contracts Made Electronically

A growing number of contracts are now made, to some extent, by digital interaction between persons or between machines. These electronic contracts are, for example, made between two persons as by e-mail, made between a person and an electronic agent (such as the phone robot at Sears or United Airlines), or made in still other electronic fashion, perhaps between two robots or two other electronic agents!

Electronic contracting is addressed in UETA, the Uniform Electronic Transactions Act, which as of May 2009 had been adopted in the District of Columbia, the U.S. federal jurisdiction, the Virgin Islands, and in every state except Illinois, New York, and Washington. Congress has addressed electronic contracting at the federal level by adopting "E–Sign" in 2000, the Electronic Signatures in Global Commerce Act.

Prefatory note A to UETA stresses that "in the context of Articles 2 and 2A, the UETA provides the vehicle for assuring that such transactions may be accomplished and affected via an electronic medium." However, the prefatory note is also emphatic that UETA is "NOT a general contracting statute—the substantive rules of contracts remain unaffected by UETA. Nor is it a digital signature statute." The prefatory note goes on to stress:

> Finally, recognition that the paradigm for the Act involves two willing parties conducting a transaction electronically, makes it necessary to expressly provide that some form of acquiescence or intent on the part of a person to conduct transactions electronically is necessary before the Act can be invoked.

Accordingly, section 5 of the Act provides that "this Act applies only to transactions between parties each of which has agreed to conduct transactions by electronic means." Evidence of such agreement can take a variety of forms, including: explicit agreement by the parties, course of dealing, substantial negotiations through e-mail, or performance in accord with terms agreed upon electronically.

We can identify at least three types of "electronic contracting." First, electronic contracting occurs when two individuals, acting as agents or on their own behalf, use digital data to make contracts. These interactions might be by email, over the Internet, or by some other form of digital communication. And UETA recognizes e-mail

Oil, Inc. v. Consolidated Edison Co., 57 N.Y.2d 574, 457 N.Y.S.2d 458, 443 N.E.2d 932, 35 UCC 12 (1982) (alternative holding).

communications with e-mail signatures as adequate to satisfy the Statute of Frauds and otherwise to form an enforceable contract. Second, electronic contracting occurs when both parties use electronic agents. Section 14(1) of UETA recognizes contracts "formed by the interactions of electronic agents of the parties, even if no individual was aware of or reviewed the electronic agents' actions or the resulting terms and agreements." An example would be an electronic shopping agent programmed to scour internet websites in search of the lowest price on an item such as a digital camera. Third, electronic contracting occurs under Section 14(2) of UETA when a contract is formed by the interaction of at least one electronic agent and an individual, acting on the individual's own behalf or for another person. An internet purchase by an individual from L.L. Bean (where the purchaser is communicating with Bean's computer by filling in a digital form and sending credit card numbers) is an example of such electronic contracting.

The need to adopt the revision to Article 2 to accommodate electronic contracting was greatly diminished by the widespread adoption of UETA before that revision effort was concluded. UETA solves most of the electronic contracting issues in all of the foregoing types of electronic contracts: (1) where one of the contracting agents is electronic, as in the above L.L. Bean example, meaning either acting as agents or as acting on their own behalf, and (2) where both agents use electronic means either as agents or as acting on their own behalf. (See especially UETA (4)(a) and (b) and Comment 5.)[8]

b. *Internet Contracts*

Internet contracts for the license of software and the sale of goods have earned their own terminology. Most of the cases involve the purchase and sale of licenses for the use of a computer program, but the Internet is also often used to purchase goods, and some of the cases here involve contracts to buy computers or other goods.

In the early license cases, the contracts were called "shrinkwrap" contracts—so because the software to be licensed was on a disk in a box and the box was covered by a transparent plastic "shrinkwrap" cover. The notorious case, ProCD, Inc. v. Zeidenberg,[9] is such a case. Cases like *ProCD* wrestle with the question whether the licensee, who does not see the license before he pays, is nevertheless bound by the license.

---

8. For a discussion of the ways that Amended Article 2 would have imposed rules that differed from UETA, see J. White & R. Summers, Article 2—Substance and Process, Supplement to Ac- company Uniform Commercial Code Practitioner Treatise Series, Volumes 1– 4, at 87–88 (2005).

9. 86 F.3d 1447 (7th Cir. 1996).

The more recent iteration of this license transaction does not involve a disk or any other tangible representation of the product. It is a license to use software that will be downloaded electronically. If the contract is for the purchase of goods, the buyer makes a contract over the Internet exactly as if he were a licensee, but, in the case of goods, the fight will not be about the terms of the license but about warranties, disclaimers or the like. In these cases the licensee or buyer downloads the digital contract terms from the licensor's web site. The licensee or buyer often pays by authorizing an electronic debit.

Even though the terms of the contract in the Internet cases are not enclosed in a plastic wrapper, the vernacular for Internet cases mimics the shrinkwrap terminology; it identifies the two common modes of contracting as "browsewrap" and "clickwrap." In the latter the licensor/seller might present a rectangular box somewhere on the licensor/seller's site that invites the licensee/buyer to form the contract by clicking on a box marked "I Agree" or "I Accept." In the browsewrap cases the licensee/buyer presumably "browses" through the web site and, when he is satisfied, downloads the software or somehow otherwise indicates his agreement to the licensor/seller's terms. The difference between "browse" cases and "click" cases is that the licensee/buyer's acceptance of the licensor/seller's terms is more ambiguous in the former than in the latter.

Notwithstanding claims to the contrary from computer-centrics, the arguments about the efficacy of all three of these modes of contract formation are but a reiteration of well known disputes that have grown out of contracting by use of standard forms in other settings. Here, as in most form contract cases, the question is either whether the licensee/buyer has sufficiently signified his agreement or, alternatively, whether it is fair to hold him to the contract when the harshness of the terms is reviewed in light of the licensee/buyer's possible inability to perceive them from the licensor/seller's form.[10]

---

10. The ALI has recently issued its proposed final draft of the Principles of the Law of Software Contracts. The following section is relevant to the enforcement of standard form contracts:

§ 2.02 Standard–Form Transfers of Generally Available Software; Enforcement of the Standard Form

(a) This section applies to standard-form transfers of generally available software as defined in § 1.01(1).

(b) A transferee adopts a standard form as a contract when a reasonable transferor would believe the transferee intends to be bound to the form.

(c) A transferee will be deemed to have adopted a standard form as a contract if

(1) the standard form is reasonably accessible electronically prior to initiation of the transfer at issue;

(2) upon initiating the transfer, the transferee has reasonable notice of and access to the standard form before payment or, if there is no payment, before completion of the transfer;

1. Clickwrap

With no exceptions that we have found, courts have found clickwrap agreements sufficient to show agreement.[11] Unlike browsewrap agreements, clickwrap agreements require clear action by the user and assent is expressly given, not implied by the circumstances. The Sprecht case[12] involved both a clickwrap agreement and a browsewrap agreement. The clickwrap agreement was required for installation of Netscape's Communicator—a software program that permits Internet browsing. A user attempting to install the program would be shown scrollable text containing the license agreement and could not proceed with installation without clicking a "Yes" button to indicate acceptance of the license terms. By analogy to shrinkwrap cases, the court noted that these contracts are often sufficient to show assent:

> Just as breaking the shrinkwrap seal and using the enclosed computer program after encountering notice of the existence of governing license terms has been deemed by some courts to constitute assent to those terms in the context of tangible software, so clicking on a webpage's clickwrap button after receiving notice of the existence of license terms has been held by some courts to manifest an Internet user's assent to terms governing the use of downloadable intangible software.[13]

(3) in the case of an electronic transfer of software, the transferee signifies agreement at the end of or adjacent to the electronic standard form, or in the case of a standard form printed on or attached to packaged software or separately wrapped from the software, the transferee does not exercise the opportunity to return the software unopened for a full refund within a reasonable time after the transfer; and

(4) the transferee can store and reproduce the standard form if presented electronically.

(d) Subject to § 1.10 (public policy), § 1.11 (unconscionability), and other invalidating defenses supplied by these Principles or outside law, a standard terms is enforceable if reasonably comprehensible.

(e) If a transferee asserts that it did not adopt a standard form as a contract under subsection (b) or asserts a failure of the transferor to comply with subsection (c) or (d), the transferor has the burden of production and persuasion on the issue of compliance with the subsections.

Principles of the Law of Software Contracts § 2.02 (1998) (Proposed Final Draft 2009).

11. *E.g.,* Caspi v. Microsoft Network LLC, 323 N.J.Super. 118, 732 A.2d 528 (App. Div. 1999) (upholding agreement where users required to review license terms in scrollable window and click "I Agree" or "I Don't Agree"); Forrest v. Verizon Commc'ns Inc., 805 A.2d 1007 (2002) (upholding agreement where user required to click an "Accept" button after scrolling through terms).

12. Specht v. Netscape Commc'ns Corp., 306 F.3d 17 (2d Cir. 2002).

13. *Id.* at 22 n. 4.

Courts enforce these agreements[14] unless the court finds the contract objectionable on grounds applicable to general contract law— e.g., that the contract is unconscionable.[15]

2. Browsewrap

Browsewrap agreements attract more scrutiny. Here assent is implied, not expressly indicated; instead of scrolling through the terms of an agreement and clicking on an icon expressing assent, a user can proceed with installation without any unequivocal statement of his agreement. Often there is a hyperlink to the terms located somewhere on the vendor's website; the outcome often depends on the location and conspicuousness of the link.

Only a handful of cases have dealt with these agreements, and their enforceability is still uncertain. An early case that dealt with browsewrap agreements, Pollstar v. Gigmania, Ltd.,[16] left the general question of enforceability open. The court suggested enforcement would be problematic when notice of the terms was in small gray print on a gray background. Moreover, the text stating "use is subject to license agreement" was not underlined (a common practice to show a hyperlink), so the court noted that many users might not be aware that the license agreement was linked to the home page. However, the court did discuss the possibility that the agreement could be enforceable based on reasoning in *ProCD*.[17] In *ProCD*, Judge Easterbrook discussed some of the many commercial transactions in which people pay for products before receiving the terms: insurance, airline tickets, concert tickets, drugs.[18] While declining to rule on the enforceability of the browsewrap agreement in question, the *Pollstar* court noted that, based on the examples and reasoning in *ProCD*, the agreement may be "valid and enforceable."[19]

Another case found that notice was conspicuous when a blue hyperlink entitled "Terms and Conditions of Sale" appeared on numerous web pages that the plaintiffs completed in the ordering process. In Hubbert v. Dell Corp.,[20] the court found that the blue hyperlinks should be treated "the same as a multipage written paper contract" in that they simply take "a person to another page of the contract...."[21] The court concluded that, "the hyperlink's contrasting blue type makes it conspicuous."[22]

14. Principles of the Law of Software Contracts § 2.02 cmt. b (Tentative Draft No. 1 2008) (citing multiple cases that have upheld clickwrap agreements).

15. *See, e.g.,* Comb v. Paypal, Inc., 218 F. Supp. 2d 1165, 1177 (N.D. Cal. 2002) (finding a User Agreement and arbitration clause unconscionable under California law discussing factors like the relative sophistication of the plaintiff, lack of mutuality, and costs of arbitration).

16. 170 F. Supp. 2d 974 (E.D. Cal. 2000).

17. ProCD, Inc. v. Zeidenberg, 86 F.3d 1447 (7th Cir. 1996).

18. *Id.* at 1451.

19. *Pollstar*, 170 F. Supp. 2d at 982.

20. Hubbert v. Dell Corp., 359 Ill. App.3d 976, 296 Ill.Dec. 258, 835 N.E.2d 113 (Ct.App. 2005).

21. *Id.* at 983–84.

22. *Id.*

Sprecht v. Netscape Communications Corp.,[23] one of the leading cases, found that the browsewrap agreement was unenforceable because of the location of the terms. The court found that a reasonably prudent user would not learn of the existence of license terms when the "sole reference to . . . [the] license terms on the . . . webpage was located in text that would have become visible to plaintiffs only if they had scrolled down to the next screen."[24] Plaintiffs "were required neither to express unambiguous assent to the program's license agreement nor even to view the license terms or become aware of their existence before proceeding with the invited download of the free plug-in program."[25] The court rejected the defendant's arguments that the scroll bar location put the plaintiffs on notice that the portion submerged contained a notice of license terms. The court concluded that "where consumers are urged to download free software at the immediate click of a button, a reference to the existence of license terms on a submerged screen is not sufficient to place consumers on inquiry or constructive notice of those terms."[26]

DeFontes v. Dell Computers Corp.[27] follows the logic in Sprecht. There the plaintiffs bought computers from Dell subject to the Terms and Conditions Agreement that could be accessed in at least three places: (1) a hyperlink on Dell's website, (2) a copy of the terms sent with an order confirmation, and (3) a copy sent with the computer when shipped. When discussing the hyperlink on the bottom of the page, the court agreed with the reasoning in Sprecht and noted that it was "not sufficient to put Plaintiffs on notice of the terms and conditions of the sale of the computer."[28]

But entering the interior web pages might show consent when the home page contains a prominent notice. In Ticketmaster Corp. v. Tickets.Com, Inc.,[29] Ticketmaster placed a notice on its home page that told users that by proceeding into interior web pages they were accepting certain conditions. A competitor, Tickets.Com, employed an electronic program called a "spider" which could automatically enter the interior web pages of the Ticketmaster site and extract information for use on the Tickets.Com website. Such use was in violation of one of the conditions of the agreement which prohibited use of information for commercial purposes. The court said that it "would prefer a rule that required an unmistakable

23. Specht v. Netscape Commc'ns Corp., 306 F.3d 17 (2d Cir. 2002).

24. *Id.* at 23.

25. *Id.*

26. *Id.* at 32.

27. DeFontes v. Dell Computers Corp., 2004 WL 253560, 52 UCC2d 795 (2004).

28. *Id.* at *6.

29. Ticketmaster Corp. v. Tickets.Com, Inc., No. CV99–7654–HLH (VBKx), 2003 WL 21406289 (C.D. Cal. Mar. 7, 2003).

assent to the conditions easily provided by requiring clicking on an icon which says 'I agree' or the equivalent. Such a rule would provide certainty in trial and make it clear that the user had called to his attention the conditions he or she accepted when using the web site."[30] However, the court recognized that "the law has not developed this way. Use of a cruise ship ticket with a venue provision printed on the back commits one to the venue provided".[31] The court notes that a person's acts can constitute acceptance and distinguished *Sprecht* by pointing out that the notice in Ticketmaster was visible or known.

In another case involving Ticketmaster, a court held that using a website to purchase tickets manifests assent when notice of the terms is conspicuous. In Druyan v. Jagger,[32] the plaintiff purchased tickets to see a Rolling Stones concert, but the concert was rescheduled when Mick Jagger got a sore throat. The contract did not entitle the plaintiffs to a refund, so they claimed that the defendants did not provide a timely notice of the fact that the concert was being rescheduled. The Terms of Use said that any event was subject to rescheduling and provided no specific time requirement for notice. The users in this case had to click on a "Look for Tickets" button located right above a statement that explicitly stated that "By clicking on the 'Look for Tickets' button or otherwise using this website, you agree to the Terms of Use." The court found the Terms of Use to be "sufficiently conspicuous to be binding on the plaintiff as a matter of law."[33]

In Register.com v. Viero, Inc., notice of terms appeared only after the transaction was complete, but assent arose from the buyer's repeated use of the site.[34] Register.com was one of more than fifty companies appointed a registrar of domain names by the Internet Corporation for Assigned Names and Numbers (ICANN). Part of the agreement with ICANN required Register.com to update information about applicants registering domain names and to allow free public query of its WHOIS information (contact information on registrants who applied for domain names). Register.com also engaged in the business of selling web-related services to entities that maintain web sites. The defendant Verio was a competitor and accessed the free public information in a series of automated queries run by an Internet program. After accessing the information, a legend appeared that prohibited the accessing party from using the data to transmit mass unsolicited, commercial

---

30. *Id.* at *8.

31. *Id.* (citing Carnival Cruise Lines v. Shute, 499 U.S. 585, 111 S.Ct. 1522, 113 L.Ed.2d 622 (1991)).

32. Druyan v. Jagger, 508 F. Supp. 2d 228 (S.D.N.Y. 2007).

33. *Id.* at 237.

34. Register.com, Inc. v. Verio, Inc., 356 F.3d 393 (2d Cir. 2004).

advertising. Verio violated this prohibition by sending out mass solicitations to potential business clients. Verio argued that it never assented to the restriction because the notice did not appear until after it submitted the query and received the data. According to the court this "argument might well be persuasive if its queries addressed to Register.com's computers had been sporadic and infrequent."[35] But in this case "Verio was daily submitting queries, each of which resulted in its receiving notice of the terms Register.com exacted."[36] The court also found "no reason why the enforceability of the offeror's terms should depend on whether the taker states (or clicks) 'I agree.' "[37] Finally, the court noted that while the Internet is a novel setting for contract formation, traditional contract law still applies: "While new commerce on the Internet has exposed courts to many new situations, it has not fundamentally changed the principles of contract."[38] Verio knew of the terms and had the choice of either accepting the offer of the contract subject to the conditions of the offer or declining to use the site and take the benefits.[39]

Given the uncertainty about the enforcement of browsewrap agreements and the fact that courts will likely enforce clickwrap agreements, why do online vendors ever use browse-wrap agreements? Presumably the rational online vendor is balancing the costs of uncertain enforceability with the benefits of a simple transaction. The purpose of these websites is both to advertise and attract customers and to make contracts. Stern clickwrap agreements may be incompatible with the first purpose, attracting customers. Contrary to the fears of consumer advocates, there is evidence that these agreements do not include "the kinds of pro-seller terms that are standard for boilerplate contracts with consumers in other contexts."[40] In fact, the average consumer probably benefits from the simpler design of browsewrap agreements.[41] As Judge Easterbrook noted in Hill v. Gateway 2000, Inc.,[42] customers are better off when vendors do not have to recite entire contracts

---

35. *Id.* at 401.

36. *Id.*

37. *Id.* at 403.

38. *Id.*

39. *Id.*

40. Ronald J. Mann & Travis Siebeneicher, Just One Click: The Reality of Internet Contracting, 108 Colum. L. Rev. 984, 999 (2008) (surveying 500 retailers' websites and finding both that few sites use agreements that ensure enforceability and that a relatively small number contain pro-seller terms like disclaimers, limitation of damages, choice of forum, etc.).

41. See Gary M. Olson & Judith S. Olson, Human–Computer Interaction: Psychological Aspects of the Human Use of Computing, 54 Ann. Rev. Psych. 491, 500 (2003) ("There are design prescriptions gleaned from empirical studies of web-searching behavior that claim that if in three clicks users do not find information that at least suggest they are on the right track, they will leave the site.").

42. Hill v. Gateway 2000, Inc., 105 F.3d 1147, 1149 (7th Cir. 1997).

over the phone before customers can purchase products. Similarly, if customers are forced to scroll through a long list of terms or assent to specific provisions (like agreeing to a forum selection clause), many customers may just scroll to the end without reading or abandon the site for one that is easier to use.

In the end, we wonder at the courts' and commentators' concern over Internet contracts. These judicial and academic brows—so tightly furled over Internet contract terms—belie considerable foolishness and even hypocrisy. Nobody reads form contracts. When was the last time you read a form contract on the Internet or in print? A long time ago, we bet. We believe that most do what we do—click "I Agree" without reading a word of the contract. Most of us do that with the expectation that we will never need the contract and—if, god forbid, we do—in the hope that the market will have forced the licensor/seller to have written a passable contract. So judicial inquiry about the conspicuousness and clarity of form contract terms is a waste and a fraud unless it really is a covert investigation of the fairness of the contract.

§ 2–3   Battle of the Forms and the Like Under Existing Section 2–207

Many sales contracts are not fully bargained, not carefully drafted, and not understandingly signed or otherwise acknowledged by both parties. Often, here is what happens: underlings of seller and buyer each sit in their offices with a telephone and a stack of form contracts. Today the "stack of forms" is more likely on the party's hard drive and it may be transmitted from there digitally to the other party. Seller's lawyer has drafted seller's forms to give seller advantage. Buyer's lawyer has drafted buyer's forms to give buyer advantage. The two sets of forms naturally diverge. They may diverge not only in substantive terms but also in permissible methods of contract formation.

The process of "contracting" begins with an underling telephoning another underling or with the dispatch of a form. When the process ends, there will usually be two forms involved, seller's and buyer's. The documents will usually have the same bargained terms such as price, quality, quantity and delivery terms. But on other terms the forms will diverge in important respects. Frequently this will pose no problem, for the deal will go forward without breakdown. But sometimes the parties will fall into dispute even before the occasion for performance. More often, one or both will perform or start to perform and a dispute will break out. In all these cases the parties will haul out their forms and read them—perhaps for the first time—and they will find that their forms diverge. Is there a contract? If so, what are its terms?

Section 2–207 is the Code's solution to this and related problems. This section reads in full:

(1) A definite and seasonable expression of acceptance or a written confirmation which is sent within a reasonable time operates as an acceptance even though it states terms additional to or different from those offered or agreed upon, unless acceptance is expressly made conditional on assent to the additional or different terms.

(2) The additional terms are to be construed as proposals for addition to the contract. Between merchants such terms become part of the contract unless:

(a) the offer expressly limits acceptance to the terms of the offer;

(b) they materially alter it; or

(c) notification of objection to them has already been given or is given within a reasonable time after notice of them is received.

(3) Conduct by both parties which recognizes the existence of a contract is sufficient to establish a contract for sale although the writings of the parties do not otherwise establish a contract. In such case the terms of the particular contract consist of those terms on which the writings of the parties agree, together with any supplementary terms incorporated under any other provisions of this Act.

Unfortunately the section is like an amphibious tank that was originally designed to fight in the swamps, but was sent to fight in the desert. The original drafter of 2–207 designed it mostly to keep the welsher in the contract. The drafter had cases like Poel v. Brunswick–Balke–Collender Co.[1] in mind. There the buyer's underling sent back its own order form which happened to coincide with the seller's terms except in one minor respect. It added: "The acceptance of this order * * * in any event you must promptly acknowledge." The seller failed to acknowledge, and the buyer for other reasons backed out. When the seller sued the buyer, the court held that the buyer's order form did not constitute an acceptance.[2] At common law an acceptance had to be a mirror image of the offer. The buyer's form therefore could not be an acceptance; it was a counteroffer.[3] The rigidity of the common law rule ignored the

---

§ 2–3

1. 216 N.Y. 310, 110 N.E. 619 (1915).

2. For what may have been a modern welsher case, see Autonumerics, Inc. v. Bayer Indus., Inc., 144 Ariz. 181, 696 P.2d 1330, 39 UCC 802 (App. 1984).

3. Some commentators argue that the mirror image rule was seldom applied so rigidly as to allow parties to welsh. See Baird and Weisberg, Rules Standards, and the Battle of the Forms: A Reassessment of § 2–207, 68 Va. L. Rev. 1217, 1233–36 (1982).

modern realities of commerce. Where preprinted forms are used to structure deals, they rarely mirror each other, yet the parties usually assume they have a binding contract and act accordingly. Section 2–207 rejects the common law mirror image rule and converts many common law counteroffers into acceptances under 2–207(1).

But it is a mistake to think of 2–207 as a law dealing principally with contract formation. Parties to sales much more often call on courts to use 2–207 to decide the terms of their contract after they exchange documents, perform, or start to perform and then fall into dispute. Here the courts are not deciding whether there is a contract. They are answering a different question: what are its terms? This is not only a different but also a more difficult problem for the law than that of keeping the welsher in.

Not only does 2–207 suffer from being designed for the swamps yet called on to fight in the desert, it also suffers because the desert terrain has proved to be so varied. We discuss ten different types of cases with which 2–207 must deal. And these are not all. We believe each type arises often in real life; Section 2–207 deals with several well, with others not so well. (We number these cases with some trepidation, for we realize that those who can analyze, do, and those who cannot, number.) The ten are:

(1) Express Term in Second Form Different from Terms in First

(2) Express Term in First Form but Second Form Silent

(3) Term in Second but not in First Form

(4) Term in Second Form but not in First and Second Form a Counter Offer ("Expressly Conditional")

(5) At Least One Form Insists on All Its Terms and Expressly Prohibits a Contract on Any Other Terms

(6) Prior Oral or Other Agreement

(7) Non–Form Agreements

(8) Second Form not an Acceptance

(9) Contract by Conduct

(10) A Non–Merchant, so 2–207(2) not Applicable

In our discussion of these cases, a central problem will be this: how may 2–207 be interpreted so as not to give an unearned and unfair advantage to the contracting party who by pure happenstance sends the first or in other cases the second form? When the parties send their forms blindly and blindly file the forms they receive, it makes little sense to give one an advantage over the other with respect to unbargained terms *simply* because one mailed the first form. Yet avoiding favoritism because of timing is a difficult task under 2–207.

1. Express Term in Second Form Different From Terms in First

Assume that buyer sends a purchase order which provides that any dispute will be governed by arbitration. Seller responds with an acknowledgement which provides that any dispute will not be resolved by arbitration. At least if the *bargained* terms on the purchase order and acknowledgement agree, we would find that the seller's document is a definite and seasonable expression of acceptance under 2–207 and that a contract has been formed by the exchange of the documents. We would thus bind any party who seeks to get out of the contract before either performs.

Assume that the seller ships the goods, the buyer receives and pays for them, and the parties fall into dispute about their quality. Does the contract call for arbitration or does it not? Buyer will argue that buyer's document was the offer (and it appears to us that buyer's document was the offer since it was sent first)[4] and that seller's document operated as an acceptance of all of the terms on buyer's form. Furthermore, buyer will correctly point out that seller's term (no arbitration) was not an additional term which could come into their contract under 2–207(2) but was a "different" term and therefore could not become part of the contract under 2–207(2). Section 2–207(1) applies to an *acceptance* that "states terms additional to or different from those offered." But the text of 2–207(2) only refers to "additional" terms, and the drafters could easily have inserted "or different" if they had so intended. Yet it would be more than a little difficult to view a different term in an acceptance as a proposal for addition to the contract where the offer already includes a contrary term. It is not possible to have different terms on the same subject as "a part" of the same contract.[5]

First, the seller offeree might respond that his "no arbitration" document differed from the buyer's ("arbitration") so substantially that it did not constitute an "acceptance" under 2–207(1). But in our view, it is clear that a document may be an acceptance under 2–207(1) and yet differ substantially from the offer. The wording of 2–207(2)(b) supports this, too, for it presupposes that a contract can be formed under 2–207(1) even though the acceptance includes an additional term that "materially alters" the offer.

But how much can an acceptance differ? Certainly there is some limit. We think that in the usual purchase order-acknowledge-

---

4. Of course, whoever sends the first form is generally the offeror.

5. Comment 3 to 2–207, which says that 2–207(2) determines whether "ad-

ditional or different terms will become part of the agreement," goes beyond the text except insofar as it applies to confirmations of a prior agreement.

ment context the forms do not approach this limit at least if the forms do not diverge as to price, quality, quantity, or delivery terms, but only as to the usual unbargained terms on the reverse side concerning remedies, arbitration, and the like. Here we would reject the seller offeree's argument. A case that goes to the very edge in finding a document to be an acceptance is Southern Idaho Pipe & Steel Co. v. Cal–Cut Pipe & Supply, Inc.[6] There, the Idaho Supreme Court held that an acceptance occurred even though the buyer's "accepting" form was the same form sent by the seller, the buyer having stricken the seller's delivery date, inserted his own and returned the form. There the parties may still have been bargaining over the delivery date, a fact not present in our hypothetical case.

Second, in our hypothetical case, the seller might contend that its document (seller's acceptance) was "expressly made conditional on assent to the additional or different terms" under 2–207(1). This argument finds some support in the well-known case, Roto–Lith, Ltd. v. F.P. Bartlett & Co., (which has since been repudiated by the First Circuit),[7] where the First Circuit held that any responding document "which states a condition materially altering the obligation solely to the disadvantage of the offeror"—here, a disclaimer—was expressly conditional and thus did not operate as an acceptance. We would reject that argument also, for it is inconsistent with our interpretation of the word "acceptance" in 2–207(1) and contrary to the drafter's policy stated above to whittle down the counteroffer rule. Further, Comment 4 to 2–207 refers to disclaimers as "material" alterations under 2–207(2)(b), a reference that would be redundant if disclaimers always made an offer expressly conditional under 2–207(1).

Third, the seller may argue that seller's acceptance is only an acceptance of the terms on which the two documents agree, and they did not agree on arbitration, nor do Code gap fillers provide for arbitration. This argument finds no explicit support in 2–207, but one of us (White) thinks part of Comment 6 supports it:

> If no answer is received within a reasonable time after additional terms are proposed, it is both fair and commercially sound to assume that their inclusion has been assented to. Where clauses on confirming forms sent by both parties conflict each party must be assumed to object to a clause of the other conflicting with one on the confirmation sent by himself. As a result the requirement that there be notice of objection which is found in subsection (2) is satisfied and the conflicting terms do not become a part of the contract. The contract then consists of the terms originally expressly agreed to, terms on

---

6. 98 Idaho 495, 567 P.2d 1246, 22 UCC 25 (1977).

7. 297 F.2d 497, 500, 1 UCC 73 (1st Cir. 1962).

which the confirmations agree, and terms supplied by this Act, including subsection (2). The written confirmation is also subject to Section 2–201. Under that section a failure to respond permits enforcement of a prior oral agreement; under this section a failure to respond permits additional terms to become part of the agreement.

In the end, how would our hypothetical case come out under the Code? One of us (White) would turn to the foregoing comment and find that the two terms cancel one another. On this view the seller's form was only an acceptance of terms in the offer which did not conflict with any terms in the acceptance. Thus the ultimate deal would not include an arbitration clause. The Code does not expressly authorize this result, but White believes it does not bar it either.[8]

Summers believes that Comment 6 is not applicable. In his view Comment 6 applies only to variant terms on confirming forms, not to variant terms on forms one of which is an offer and the other an acceptance under 2–207(1) (a distinction itself drawn in Comment 1). Thus, in our hypothetical case, the buyer offeror's arbitration clause controls, for the seller's no-arbitration clause, as a different term embodied in the accepting form, simply falls out; 2–207(2) cannot rescue it since that provision applies only to additional terms. White answers that, among other things, this reading gives the sender of the first form (the buyer here) an unearned advantage. Summers does not agree that the "advantage" is entirely unearned. The recipient of the first form at least had an opportunity to object to its contents. Moreover, Summers believes that White's approach is relatively more unfair to the offeror than Summers' approach is to the offeree. According to Summers, offerors have more (even if only a little more) reason to expect that their clauses will control than offerees have to expect that their clauses will. After all, when the offerees send their forms they will have already received a form from the offerors, and offerees know full well that forms of different parties rarely coincide. But even if the offeror's advantage is to some extent unearned, the text of 2–207, according to Summers, appears plainly to authorize it. Section 2–207(1) presupposes an outstanding offer and explicitly applies only to an acceptance (or confirmation). Thus we are to begin the analysis with the offer the terms of which control exclusively except insofar as 2–207 provides otherwise. Section 2–207 does not provide otherwise as to different terms. As to additional terms, the section

---

8. Many cases involve arbitration clauses. See Marlene Indus. Corp. v. Carnac Textiles, Inc., 45 N.Y.2d 327, 408 N.Y.S.2d 410, 380 N.E.2d 239, 24 UCC 257 (1978) (in New York, a clause for arbitration is never "minor" under 2–207(2)!). Southeastern Enameling Corp. v. General Bronze Corp., 434 F.2d 330, 8 UCC 469 (5th Cir. 1970) (clause part of the contract; not merely an exchange of forms); Universal Oil Products Co. v. S.C.M. Corp., 313 F.Supp. 905, 7 UCC 813 (D.C. Conn. 1970) (clause part of contract).

provides otherwise only insofar as these survive 2–207(2). Summers adds that if the drafters intended the White approach, they could have easily drafted the section accordingly.

Most of the decisions agree with White. For example, the Tenth Circuit canvassed the cases on our dispute in Daitom, Inc. v. Pennwalt Corp.[9] The court purported to side with White and remarked that the Summers position "misses the fundamental purpose of the UCC in general and 2–207 in particular, which is to preserve a contract and fill in any gaps if the parties intended to make a contract and there is a reasonable basis for giving an appropriate remedy." With respect, Summers considers this to be a question-begging characterization, and he awaits the court's answer to his specific textual and other arguments.[10]

Consider this further problem. Assume for example that the offer contains an otherwise valid disclaimer of warranties and that the acceptance contains a conflicting express warranty. According to White, neither become part of the contract under 2–207(1) despite the fact that a contract is formed. Likewise neither enters the contract through 2–207(2) because the term in the acceptance is a different, not an additional term. Moreover by its terms 2–207(3) does not apply to this case but applies only to the case where "the writings of the parties do not otherwise establish a contract." Is it possible, nonetheless, that an *implied* warranty enters the contract directly as a gap filler without reference to 2–207(3)? White believes that it does and that indeed most of the gap fillers do not depend upon 2–207 to enter the contract. He says there are many contracts adequately formed by an offer and an acceptance which a gap filler dealing with price or warranty or terms of delivery would enter without any reference to 2–207. On White's view, that seems the proper result. He thinks that the court in Bosway Tube & Steel Corp. v. McKay Machine Co.[11] reached just this result by applying both 2–207(1) and 2–207(3). It seems to him that the court's result is correct (but that it is technically incorrect in finding that 2–207(3) can apply to a case in which the court has already found a 2–207(1) contract). On White's analysis the foregoing outcome favors neither party. The Code may provide a term substantially identical to one of those rejected. So be it. At least a term so supplied has the merit of being a term that the drafters considered fair.

Summers believes White misreads 2–207, both in text and in spirit. Summers would, in the foregoing further hypothetical case,

---

9. 741 F.2d 1569, 39 UCC 1203 (10th Cir. 1984).

10. What happens to an additional term that fails to survive 2–207(2)? Comment 3 says that to become part of the contract, such a term must then be expressly agreed to by the other party.

Such an agreement can be manifested in writing or by conduct.

11. 65 Mich.App. 426, 237 N.W.2d 488, 18 UCC 857 (1975). White also cites the case of Lea Tai Textile Co. v. Manning Fabrics, Inc., 411 F.Supp. 1404, 19 UCC 1080 (S.D.N.Y. 1975).

uphold the offeror's otherwise valid disclaimer as to both express and implied warranties. The offeree's term is a different term and falls out.

We add, finally, that in a large number of cases courts have had to decide whether a contract initially formed under 2–207 was modified under either 2–208 or 2–209. Courts have frequently had difficulty in determining the scope and interrelations of the above sections. Suppose buyer sends a purchase order. Seller sends an acknowledgment that includes a warranty and disclaimer. The disclaimer "materially alters" under 2–207(2). Later, with knowledge of the warranty and disclaimer, the buyer acknowledges the disclaimer. Does it then become part of the contract (as a modification) under 2–209(1)? Some courts have said "yes!"

2. Express Term in First Form but Second Form Silent

Assume that buyer sends a form to seller and that it explicitly provides for arbitration. Seller sends back an acknowledgement that is silent on the question of arbitration. Buyer's argument in this case will be the same as in Case 1: "seller's document was an acceptance of the terms on my document including the one dealing with arbitration." Comment 6 does not operate here since there are no terms on the form that "conflict." Despite the argument that this outcome gives the buyer-offeror an unearned advantage, we think that buyer-offeror is correct and that terms contained in buyer-offeror's document which are not contradicted by the acceptance become part of the contract.

Consider this variation. The offeror's form includes a term contrary to a gap filler and the accepting form is silent. Is the accepting form to be construed as impliedly including the contrary Code gap filler? And if so, is it an "additional" or a "different" term? In Idaho Power Co. v. Westinghouse Electric Corp., the accepting party apparently claimed that its silent acceptance included full consequential damages under the Code gap-filler rule, even though the offer specifically limited liability. Apparently, the accepting party also argued that its forms thus included a "different" term and that the two terms cancelled each other, with the resulting gap being filled by the Code. The court did not agree, and correctly upheld the offeror's clause limiting liability.[12]

3. Term in Second but Not in First Form

This is the problem of the *Roto–Lith* case.[13] In that case the buyer sent an offer—a purchase order—to seller. Though the offer

---

12. 596 F.2d 924, 26 UCC 638 (9th Cir.1979). Neither of us would allow a mere gap filler to knock out an explicit contrary term in the offer.

13. Roto–Lith, Ltd. v. F.P. Bartlett & Co., 297 F.2d 497, 1 UCC 73 (1st Cir. 1962).

was silent as to warranties, Code gap-fillers (e.g., 2–314) might supply them. Subsequently seller returned an acknowledgment that contained a disclaimer. The court ultimately found that the seller's document was "expressly conditional" and therefore not an acceptance but a counteroffer, accepted by the buyer's performance in receiving and using the goods. Under that case the seller got all of his terms, disclaimer included.[14]

On the facts, we would find the second document to be an acceptance and would reject the *Roto–Lith* assumption that it was expressly conditional and therefore a counteroffer. Of course, the offeror could specify in the offer that acceptance must be in the exact terms of the offer, with the result that any additional or different terms would constitute a counteroffer.[15] Similarly under 2–207(1), an acceptor could explicitly make acceptance "expressly conditional" on the offeror's assent to additional or different terms, and thus also a counteroffer. Because neither is true in our hypothetical, we would find that a contract was formed upon the exchange of documents without reference to the subsequent performance. This case differs from Case 2 in that the acceptor (offeree) does not get all of his or her terms in the contract under subsection (1). Rather the additional (not "different") term[16] in the acceptance that did not appear in the offer must pass through subsection (2) of 2–207 to become part of the contract. That subsection reads in full as follows:

> The additional terms are to be construed as proposals for addition to the contract. Between merchants such terms become part of the contract unless:
>
>   (a) the offer expressly limits acceptance to the terms of the offer;
>
>   (b) they materially alter it; or
>
>   (c) notification of objection to them has already been given or is given within a reasonable time after notice of them is received.

---

14. In the First Circuit, *Roto–Lith* no longer lives. See Ionics, Inc. v. Elmwood Sensors, Inc., 110 F.3d 184, 32 UCC2d 1 (1st Cir. 1997) (overruling *Roto–Lith* application of 2–207(1) language after the comma as in conflict with the purpose of 2–207, noting if *Roto–Lith* were to apply then 2–207(3) would be preempted, and instead applying 2–207(3) to create an implied warranty).

15. This is what the offeror did in Salt River Project Agricultural Improvement & Power District v. Westinghouse Electric Corp., 143 Ariz. 437, 694 P.2d 267, 37 UCC 75 (App. 1983), opinion approved and vac'd in part, 143 Ariz. 368, 694 P.2d 198, 40 UCC 418 (1984).

16. Comment 4 to 2–207 supports characterizing these as "additional." See also Album Graphics, Inc. v. Beatrice Foods Co., 87 Ill.App.3d 338, 42 Ill.Dec. 332, 408 N.E.2d 1041, 30 UCC 53 (1980); Wheaton Glass Co. v. Pharmex, Inc., 548 F.Supp. 1242, 35 UCC 65 (D.N.J. 1982).

Doubtless the parties in our case are merchants, but in the absence of a contrary course of dealing or usage of trade, a disclaimer "materially alters" the contract, and the disclaimer would not become part of the contract.

Whether a term contained in an acceptance materially alters the terms of the offer can be a complex question.[17] Comment 4 to 2–207 explains that a material alteration is one that would "result in surprise or hardship if incorporated without express awareness by the other party."[18] Clauses that Code comments consider to be material alterations include: a warranty disclaimer, a clause contradicting usage of the trade in determining permissible quantity leeways, a clause giving the seller the right to cancel the contract if the buyer fails to pay any invoice on a timely basis, and a clause requiring complaints to be made in an unreasonably short period of time.[19] Non-material changes, according to the comments, include: a force majeure clause, requirement that complaints be made in a timely fashion, a reasonable interest charge on overdue accounts, and a limitation of remedies. The cases on materiality generally conform to the comments.

Acceptors rarely win the argument that their additional terms are only immaterial alterations under 2–207(2). A principal reason for their losing record is that their non verbal acts contradict their verbal arguments. Who goes to the appellate court with lawyers hired at hundreds of dollars per hour to dispute a term that is not material?

4.   Term Found in Second Form but Not in First, and Second Form a Counter Offer ("Expressly Conditional")

Section 2–207(1) provides:

A definite and seasonable expression of acceptance or a written confirmation which is sent within a reasonable time operates as an acceptance even though it states terms additional to or different from those offered or agreed upon, unless acceptance is expressly made conditional on assent to the additional or different terms.

The language of subsection (1) contemplates contract formation by two quite different routes. Up to the comma is one route, call it Route A. After the comma is a second route, call it Route B. Subsection (3) provides still a third route, through "conduct of both parties," call it Route C. As we have seen, and will see further, the

---

17. See, e.g., Transamerica Oil Corp. v. Lynes, Inc., 723 F.2d 758, 37 UCC 1076 (10th Cir. 1983); Luedtke Eng'g Co. v. Indiana Limestone Co., 740 F.2d 598, 39 UCC 400 (7th Cir. 1984).

18. UCC § 2–207, Comment 4.

19. Id.

terms of any resulting contracts will vary, depending on which route to contract formation a court adopts.

Here we deal with route B—where the second document is not an acceptance because it is expressly conditional. A return form of an offeree that invokes the language after the comma, i.e. expressly conditions "acceptance", becomes a traditional common law counteroffer. But under the cases so far, this language is *not* easily invoked. The offeree must state a counteroffer very clearly. For example, suppose a buyer sends an offer that is silent about arbitration. The seller offeree sends a return form providing for arbitration and explicitly stating that contract formation between the parties is expressly conditional on the buyer offeror's assent to the terms of the seller offeree's form. Here, of course, there is statutory and case law warrant for the conclusion that the seller offeree has made a counteroffer. But language that is only a little less clear is not likely to be so regarded.[20] Courts routinely characterize even deviant documents as acceptances and not as counteroffers as a way of preventing surprise to the original offeror who may not have read the claimed counterofferor's form—an "anti-last shot" policy. For example, if it were easy for a seller offeree to invoke Route B, then seller offeree could readily become a counterofferor, and the original offeror-buyer's form would be superseded as the offering form. If a court were then to hold (as the *Roto–Lith* court did) that the buyer's receipt and use of the goods constituted an acceptance of the seller's counter-offer, a contract would be formed entirely on seller's terms.

Suppose the seller offeree has sent a return form clearly constituting a counteroffer under subsection 1 (so invoking Route B) and providing for arbitration. He then ships the goods. Here, the buyer might expressly assent to the seller's return form. In that event, the terms on seller's counter-offering form control. This, of course, is standard common law doctrine.[21] But what if the buyer does not assent expressly but merely receives and accepts the goods shipped by the seller? Most courts under the Code hold that such an "acceptance" merely by conduct does not constitute "assent" within the meaning of 2–207(1) after the comma (Route B). Instead, no contract on seller's counteroffer is formed and seller does not have the right to arbitration as provided on his counter-offering form. Instead, the contract is formed (via Route C) under 2–207(3),

---

20. Dorton v. Collins & Aikman Corp., 453 F.2d 1161, 10 UCC 585 (6th Cir. 1972) ("The acceptance of your order is subject to all of the terms & conditions on the face & reverse side hereof, *including arbitration*"; not expressly conditional). See also McCarty v. Verson Allsteel Press Co., 89 Ill.App.3d 498, 44 Ill.Dec. 570, 411 N.E.2d 936, 30 UCC 440 (1980) (acceptance which encloses its conditions of sale not expressly conditional).

21. See Restatement (Second) of Contracts, § 19 (1979).

and terms are supplied by the gap-filler provisions of Article 2.[22] Since these gap-fillers do not provide for arbitration, there is no such term. Professor White finds this overall solution congenial because the "neutral" Code gap fillers control terms. Summers finds this solution contrary to the common law, which does recognize "conduct acceptances." Summers believes that the seller offeree's clear counteroffer and the buyer's knowing receipt and acceptance of the goods should at least in some cases form a contract under 2–207(1), section 1–103, and the common law. Summers especially laments a Ninth Circuit case in which the seller offeree not merely sent a clear counteroffer under the terms of subsection One after the comma, but in response to the buyer's objection, orally insisted on the very terms of the counteroffer. Because the buyer did not explicitly assent thereto and thereafter merely accepted the goods, the court decided that seller's counteroffer did not control. Instead, 2–207(3) (Route C) was held applicable to determine contract terms as well as contract formation.[23] Here Summers notes that no semblance of an "anti-last shot policy" in the name of preventing unfair surprise could possibly be applicable to favor this counterofferee. White notes that seller could have declined to ship in the face of buyer's silence.

It is important to differentiate cases in which contracts are formed under Route B pursuant to "expressly conditional" counter offers from those cases in which the seller offeree sends back a non-acceptance (e.g., "I reject your offer"), yet thereafter ships the goods and the buyer accepts them. Section 2–207(3)—Route C—fits the latter case more comfortably that it fits the former.

5. At Least One Form Insists on All Its Terms and Expressly Prohibits a Contract on Any Other Terms

One or both parties may send a document that contains a conspicuous term stating that any contract formed as a result of an exchange of documents must consist of all the terms in that form and no others. Such a term in an accepting form would also signify that the acceptance is "expressly conditional" and thus would bar the formation of a contract at that point under the language of 2–207(1) after the comma.[24]

The proper subsection One analysis is not as easy if the term appears not in the acceptance but in the offer. On the one hand, if

22. See, e.g., Dorton v. Collins & Aikman Corp., 453 F.2d 1161, 10 UCC 585 (6th Cir. 1972).

23. Diamond Fruit Growers, Inc. v. Krack Corp., 794 F.2d 1440, 1 UCC2d 1073 (9th Cir. 1986).

24. Salt River Project Agr. Improv. and Power Dist. v. Westinghouse Electric Corp., 143 Ariz. 368, 694 P.2d 198, 40 UCC 418 (1984) ("The conditions stated below shall take precedence over any conditions which may appear on your standard form * * *"; held not an acceptance but, in effect, a counteroffer).

the restrictive language in an offer is read to mean "I agree to contract only if your acceptance contains all of my terms and I hereby object to any additional terms," presumably a responding document that contains the same terms plus some additional ones is still an acceptance under 2-207(1). However, the additional terms would be viewed as proposals for addition to the contract and would be excluded from the contract under 2-207(2)(a) and 2-207(2)(c).[25] On the other hand, if the offer is read to mean "This offer can be accepted only by a document that contains neither additional nor different terms," any response that contains either additional or different terms would not constitute an acceptance and the case would fall entirely outside 2-207(1) and 2-207(2).[26]

The courts have had difficulty in dealing with these cases,[27] and the drafters of the Code apparently had similar problems in anticipating them. Under the interpretation that makes a responsive document containing additional terms an acceptance, both 2-207(2)(a) and 2-207(2)(c) preclude those additional terms from becoming part of the contract.[28] It is not clear to us that 2-207(2)(a) could ever alone preclude such an additional term from becoming part of the agreement. We warn the reader to approach restrictive language in an offer with caution.

Once the language is interpreted, the problems are much less worrisome. Where the restrictive term in the offer is construed to make an acceptance possible even though the responding document contains additional terms, we have the case described in category 3 above—except that notice has already been given under 2-207(2)(c). Where the restrictive language in the offer is construed to limit forms of acceptance to documents that neither add nor contradict, no contract exists at the conclusion of the exchange of forms since no 2-207(1) acceptance occurred. Of course, a contract may be formed under 2-207(3).[29]

25. See Lounge-A-Round v. GCM Mills, Inc., 109 Cal.App.3d 190, 166 Cal. Rptr. 920, 29 UCC 778 (1980) (offer that did not permit alteration of its terms held accepted but without additional terms).

26. See Tecumseh Int'l Corp. v. City of Springfield, 70 Ill.App.3d 101, 26 Ill. Dec. 745, 388 N.E.2d 460, 26 UCC 645 (1979) (where an offer expressly limits acceptance to terms of offer and the acceptance proposed different delivery terms, no contract).

27. See, e.g., Tunis Mfg. Corp. v. Mystic Mills, Inc., 40 A.D.2d 664, 337 N.Y.S.2d 150 (1972) (arbitration clause in seller's acceptance excluded); Alan Wood Steel Co. v. Capital Equip. En-

ters., Inc., 39 Ill.App.3d 48, 349 N.E.2d 627, 19 UCC 1310 (1976) (express warranties in buyer's purchase order excluded).

28. See CBS, Inc. v. Auburn Plastics, Inc., 67 A.D.2d 811, 413 N.Y.S.2d 50, 26 UCC 40 (1979) (offer insisting on its own terms also held implicitly to object to additional term in acceptance).

29. See Boise Cascade Corp. v. Etsco, Ltd., 1984 WL 178957, 39 UCC 410 (D. Or. 1984) (where both offer and acceptance limited any resulting contract to their own terms, no contract could be formed on exchange of forms). Cf. Challenge Machinery Co. v. Mattison Machine Works, 138 Mich.App. 15, 359 N.W.2d 232, 39 UCC 1578 (1984) (where

Assume that no contract exists under 2–207(1) yet the parties perform. A court can find a contract in one of two ways. First, a court can take the common law, *Roto–Lith,* approach and find that the second document is a counteroffer and hold that subsequent performance by the party who sent the first document constitutes acceptance. This gives one party (who fortuitously sent the second document) all of its terms.[30] In our view, Code drafters rejected this approach, and the drafters sent us to section 2–207(3), which reads in full as follows:

> Conduct by both parties which recognizes the existence of a contract is sufficient to establish a contract for sale although the writings of the parties do not otherwise establish a contract. In such case the terms of the particular contract consist of those terms on which the writings of the parties agree, together with any supplementary terms incorporated under any other provisions of this Act.

Section 2–207(3) is only applicable when the writings of the parties do not otherwise establish a contract yet their conduct evidences a contract.[31] Additionally, it presumes that there have been "writings of the parties" in which they failed to reach an agreement. Absent such, 2–207(3) is inapplicable and the proper analysis focuses on 2–204.[32] Not every court has grasped the relation between 2–207(3) and 2–204. Note that contract formation under subsection (3) gives neither party the relevant terms in its document, but fills out the contract with the standardized provisions of Article 2.[33] As a practical matter this solution may put a seller at a disadvantage, for seller will often wish to undertake less responsibility for the quality of his goods than the Code imposes or else wish to limit its damages liability more narrowly than would the Code.

both offer and acceptance insist on own terms, contract formed on those terms on which the forms agree).

30. See Gilbert & Bennett Mfg. Co. v. Westinghouse Electric Corp., 445 F.Supp. 537, 22 UCC 920 (D. Mass. 1977).

31. Challenge Machinery Co. v. Mattison Machine Works, 138 Mich.App. 15, 359 N.W.2d 232, 39 UCC 1578 (1984) (2–207(3) only applies if there is no contract under 2–207(1) but conduct of parties indicates a contract exists).

32. See Album Graphics, Inc. v. Beatrice Foods Co., 87 Ill.App.3d 338, 42 Ill.Dec. 332, 408 N.E.2d 1041, 30 UCC 53 (1980) (2–207(3) contemplates the exchange of writings between the parties which do not reach agreement); Lock-

wood Corp. v. Black, 501 F.Supp. 261, 30 UCC 1231 (N.D. Tex. 1980), aff'd, 669 F.2d 324 (5th Cir. 1982); Preston Farm & Ranch Supply, Inc. v. Bio–Zyme Enters., 625 S.W.2d 295, 32 UCC 712 (1981) (using 2–204 to form the contract).

33. C. Itoh & Co. (America) Inc. v. Jordan Int'l Co., 552 F.2d 1228, 21 UCC 353 (7th Cir. 1977); McCarty v. Verson Allsteel Press Co., 89 Ill.App.3d 498, 44 Ill.Dec. 570, 411 N.E.2d 936, 30 UCC 440 (1980) (where contract is formed under 2–207(3), the Code fills all gaps left where writings do not agree); Leonard Pevar Co. v. Evans Products Co., 524 F.Supp. 546, 32 UCC 720 (D. Del. 1981) (under 2–207(3) the Code gap fillers supply terms where writings of parties do not agree).

After this problem flowered in *Roto–Lith*, the Code's Permanent Editorial Board added a new Comment 7 to 2–207, which reads in full as follows:

> In many cases, as where goods are shipped, accepted and paid for before any dispute arises, there is no question whether a contract has been made. In such cases, where the writings of the parties do not establish a contract, it is not necessary to determine which act or document constituted the offer and which the acceptance. See Section 2–204. The only question is what terms are included in the contract, and subsection (3) furnishes the governing rule.

One might argue with some justification that the comment is an *ex post facto* attempt to alter and shore up a demonstrably unsatisfactory statutory scheme. Be that as it may, the comment offers a certain and sensible rule that should alleviate the pains most courts would feel with 2–207 in cases of the type under consideration.

6. *Prior Oral or Other Agreement*

In many cases the parties first reach an oral or other informal agreement covering the essence of the deal. Thereafter, one or both sends a "confirmation" form that includes terms different from or additional to those previously agreed on orally. If the parties file the forms as usual without reading them and perform, and if a dispute then arises, is there a contract? If so, on what terms?

Here it is tempting to say that 2–207(1) does not apply at all because the section contemplates contract formation by offer and acceptance, and the offer and acceptance already occurred orally prior to the exchange of forms. By the same token, 2–207(3) would not apply, for it contemplates contract formation through performance, and here the contract was already formed orally prior to performance. Thus, it might seem that a court should not resort to 2–207 either to form the contract or to determine terms in any case in which the parties actually entered an oral agreement prior to their form-shuffling exercises.

Yet section 2–207(1) uses the word "confirmation." And Comment 1 to 2–207 indicates the drafters did intend at least that sections 2–207(1) and (2) apply "where an agreement has been reached * * * orally * * * and is followed by one or both of the parties sending formal memoranda embodying the terms so far as agreed upon and adding terms not discussed."[34] Section 2–207(1) provides:

> A definite and seasonable expression of acceptance or a written confirmation which is sent within a reasonable time operates

---

34. § 2–207, Comment 1.

as an acceptance even though it states terms additional to or different from those offered or agreed upon, unless acceptance is expressly made conditional on assent to the additional or different terms.

Moreover, 2–207(1) speaks of a confirmation that operates as an acceptance despite the fact that it states terms additional to or different from those agreed upon. Prior oral agreement cases in which one or both of the parties follow up with a confirming form are to be run through 2–207(1) and (2) with whatever results those subsections and the rest of Article 2's provisions on terms dictate.[35] Thus, in American Parts Co. v. American Arbitration Association,[36] the parties had initially reached an oral understanding. The seller had sent a confirming form which purportedly recited the contract terms (including quantity), added an arbitration clause, and provided that the entire form would become controlling if the "buyer accepts delivery of all or any part of the goods herein described." The buyer allegedly refused to accept some of the goods, and the seller then sought arbitration. The buyer sought a stay, and the seller moved for summary judgment. In denying summary judgment the court assumed that under 2–207(1) a confirming form can constitute an "acceptance" even where there has already been an oral offer and acceptance. As a corollary, certain additional terms in the confirmation may become (retroactively, as it were) a part of the original contract by virtue of the operation of 2–207(2).[37] But the court also noted differences between those forms falling in 2–207(1) that are confirmations and those that are not.[38]

What if the parties reach an oral or other informal agreement for the sale of fabric and nothing was said about arbitration, yet the seller later sent a confirmation containing an arbitration clause? This clause would "materially alter" and thus not survive 2–207(2). But the original oral agreement itself, would, of course incorporate any applicable trade usage. Let us assume that there was a trade

35. For cases adopting this approach, see Dorton v. Collins & Aikman Corp., 453 F.2d 1161, 10 UCC 585 (6th Cir. 1972) (also explicitly rejects *Roto–Lith* approach); Windsor Mills, Inc. v. Collins & Aikman Corp., 25 Cal.App.3d 987, 101 Cal.Rptr. 347, 10 UCC 1020 (1972) (arbitration clause in seller's form was material alteration and not part of contract); Frances Hosiery Mills, Inc. v. Burlington Indus., Inc., 285 N.C. 344, 204 S.E.2d 834, 14 UCC 1110 (1974) (arbitration clause in seller's form was material alteration).

36. 8 Mich.App. 156, 154 N.W.2d 5, 6 UCC 119 (1967) (facts taken from affidavits).

37. *Id*. at 172, 154 N.W.2d at 14, 6 UCC at 129.

38. *Id*. at 174, 154 N.W.2d at 15, 6 UCC at 130–31. The court correctly held that 2–207(1) does not permit confirmations to be expressly conditional on assent to additional or different terms. A party should not be able to escape an oral contract through a confirmation. See Luria Bros. & Co. v. Pielet Bros. Scrap Iron & Metal, Inc., 600 F.2d 103, 26 UCC 1081 (7th Cir. 1979) (differing terms in confirmatory memoranda do not negate antecedent oral agreement).

usage to arbitrate. In Schubtex, Inc. v. Allen Snyder, Inc.[39] the court indicated that the trade usage would be part of the oral agreement and thus would be binding upon the buyer notwithstanding cases holding that arbitration clauses are always material alterations.[40] Trade usage and the course of dealing are always relevant to determine the content of an oral agreement in the first place.[41]

When a confirmation states a term different from the original oral or other informal agreement, the different term falls out. The benchmark for determining additionalness or differentness is the prior agreement, not the other confirmation form.[42] Thus if a supplier of metal and a purchaser orally agree to the sale of a set quantity of brass at a firm price of $1.17 per pound, that will be the contract price notwithstanding a different price in one of the two confirming forms.

If the seller responds with a confirmation of a term not in the informal agreement and the buyer's confirmation states a conflicting term, the two knock each other out.[43] Comment 6, however, provides that if Article 2's gap fillers then supply a term, it is binding.

Once there has been an effective confirmation under 2–207(1) and the full terms of the agreement have been established under 2–204 and 2–207(1) & (2) it is erroneous to resort to 2–207(3) to add additional terms to the contract based upon the subsequent conduct

---

39. 49 N.Y.2d 1, 424 N.Y.S.2d 133, 399 N.E.2d 1154, 27 UCC 1166 (1979).

40. *Id.* at 6, 424 N.Y.S.2d at 135, 27 UCC at 1168–69 (dictum).

41. See Jones Apparel Group, Inc. v. Petit, 75 A.D.2d 504, 426 N.Y.S.2d 739, 28 UCC 633 (1980) (dictum) (custom and usage of an industry might support finding an agreement to arbitrate in oral agreement); Ernest J. Michel & Co. v. Anabasis Trade, Inc., 72 A.D.2d 715, 422 N.Y.S.2d 79, 27 UCC 909 (1979), order aff'd, 50 N.Y.2d 951, 431 N.Y.S.2d 459, 409 N.E.2d 933, 29 UCC 55 (1980) (course of dealing relevant to express agreement to arbitrate); BICC Cables Corp. v. Teledyne Industries, Inc., 1994 WL 853628, 27 UCC2d 103 (Ind. Cir. 1994) (factual issue of whether trade usage commonly involves remedy limitation will determine whether term enters contract).

42. See "or agreed upon" in 2–207(1). See Dorton v. Collins & Aikman Corp., 453 F.2d 1161, 10 UCC 585 (6th Cir. 1972) (confirmation must be compared to oral agreement to determine if it states additional or different terms); Blair Int'l, Ltd. v. LaBarge, Inc., 515 F.Supp. 891, 32 UCC 13 (E.D.Mo. 1981), aff'd in part, rev'd in part, 675 F.2d 954, 33 UCC 1242 (8th Cir. 1982) (requirement of irrevocable letter of credit in second confirmation not an additional term even though first confirmation form silent on this issue because term had been part of original oral agreement); Power Press Sales Co. v. MSI Battle Creek Stamping, 238 Mich.App. 173, 604 N.W.2d 772, 39 UCC2d 964 (1999) (confirmation materially altered prior oral agreement).

43. See § 2–207(2)(c) and Comment 6. It has been said that for this purpose, the informal agreement includes terms supplied by Code gapfillers. See Western Indus., Inc. v. Newcor Canada Ltd., 739 F.2d 1198, 38 UCC 1458 (7th Cir. 1984); Ward Transformer Co. v. Distrigas of Massachusetts Corp., 1992 WL 316072, 18 UCC2d 29 (E.D.N.C. 1992).

of the parties. Thus in McKenzie v. Alla–Ohio Coals, Inc.[44] the court erred in finding that a penalty clause in a confirmation, which had been objected to, became part of the contract through the conduct of the parties pursuant to 2–207(3). If it later became part of the contract, this would be because the parties so modified the contract by course of performance[45] or by virtue of an estoppel.[46] Again, 2–207(3) does not apply if a contract is already formed.

7. Non–Form Agreements

In this type of case there is no pattern, or at least no continuous pattern of exchange of printed forms. One party may send a typewritten one. The parties may exchange letters. The parties may send printed forms that differ so substantially that the second cannot be an acceptance; then one party responds further with a letter or a typed form or some such document, yet the parties never write down their agreement in one document. If one of the parties walks away, or worse yet, if both perform and then something goes wrong, is there a contract? If so, what are its terms? Since there is no "definite and seasonable expression of acceptance," no contract can exist under 2–207(1) before the comma, or under 2–204, or 1–103 unless and until the parties begin to perform, further writings are exchanged, or an oral agreement entered. The case of Construction Aggregates Corp. v. Hewitt–Robins, Inc.,[47] is illustrative. This was not a typical battle of the forms situation; the parties appeared to have negotiated most (if not all) of the terms of the contract, to have consulted their lawyers about the terms, and to have corresponded with one another orally and in writing about various terms. Thus the case was not one in which only the parties' documents pass in the mail and are placed in files until a difficulty arises under the contract; there was real bargaining. The court found that one of the seller's later transmissions constituted a counteroffer which the buyer had accepted by seeking to make only one change in it and by failing to raise any other objections to it. The court found that the seller's "acceptance" was expressly conditional under the last clause of 2–207(1) and that the buyer assented to those conditions. Thus we do not have the case where the parties performed in the face of two conflicting documents. Rather it is a case where the parties reached a bargained agreement on all the terms (or so the court found).

We well understand that a clever lawyer can make a colorable claim that every case falls within our seventh classification, is therefore beyond the reach of 2–207, and adrift on the murky sea of

44. 1979 WL 30087, 29 UCC 852 (D.D.C. 1979).

45. See UCC § 2–208. See cases cited *supra* in this section.

46. See UCC § 1–103.

47. 404 F.2d 505, 6 UCC 112 (7th Cir. 1968), cert. denied, 395 U.S. 921, 89 S.Ct. 1774, 23 L.Ed.2d 238 (1969).

common law. We hope that courts will reject these arguments and will only rarely permit buyers and sellers who communicate principally through printed purchase order-acknowledgment forms to escape the grip of 2–207. Absent further legislative action, we believe that judicial use of 2–207 in these cases is still the best avenue for the development of a certain and consistent body of law.

But what are those "rare" cases in which the courts may properly permit the parties to escape the grip of 2–207 altogether? This hard question is for the courts.

8. Second Form Not an Acceptance

Not all return documents are 2–207(1) "acceptances." If the return document diverges significantly as to a dickered term, it cannot be a 2–207(1) acceptance. For example, if the purchase order calls for the sale of 200,000 pounds of lard at ten cents a pound and the acknowledgment responds with 200,000 pounds at fifteen cents a pound, the second document is not an acceptance under 2–207(1), and no contract is formed via the exchange of forms. If the parties thereafter fall into dispute before either performs, no one has liability for not performing.[48] For example, the parties in Koehring Co. v. Glowacki[49] exchanged telegrams, one with the sale "as is—where is," the other "F.O.B. our truck your plant loaded." The parties never began performing and the court held that no contract was formed since the second telegram diverged "radically."

If, on the other hand, the parties performed, we would proceed directly to subsection (3) for contract terms. There, as we have seen, the parties will get the terms on which their documents agree plus the ones that the Code offers.[50]

Sometimes courts go beyond differences between dickered terms on forms to find that the second form did not operate as an acceptance. For example, in McCarty v. Verson Allsteel Press Co.[51] the court held that a purchase order sent in response to a price quotation could not operate as an acceptance because the boilerplate language denominated it as an offer, notwithstanding that it expressly referred to itself as in accord with the price quotation.[52]

---

48. See Dorton v. Collins & Aikman Corp., 453 F.2d 1161, 10 UCC 585 (6th Cir. 1972) (*dictum*) (if the acknowledgement does not qualify as a "definite and seasonable expression of acceptance" the attempt at contract formation aborts absent conduct by the parties evidencing a contract under 2–207(3)).

49. 77 Wis.2d 497, 253 N.W.2d 64, 21 UCC 715 (1977).

50. See Alliance Wall Corp. v. Ampat Midwest Corp., 17 Ohio App.3d 59, 477 N.E.2d 1206, 41 UCC 377 (1984) (per-

formance by parties, after exchange of conflicting forms resulted in contract with terms to be supplied by 2–207(3)).

51. 89 Ill.App.3d 498, 44 Ill.Dec. 570, 411 N.E.2d 936, 30 UCC 440 (1980).

52. *Id.* See also Gord Indus. Plastics, Inc. v. Aubrey Mfg., Inc., 103 Ill.App.3d 380, 59 Ill.Dec. 160, 33 UCC 476 (1982), appeal after remand, 127 Ill.App.3d 589, 82 Ill.Dec. 855, 40 UCC 26 (1984).

We doubt the wisdom of this case. We would generally find the second form to be an acceptance unless the dickered terms are changed. Printed labels on forms are often either legally uninformative (e.g., "purchase order") or inaccurate (second form labelled "offer"); both the courts and drafters of forms should realize this.

9. Contract by Conduct

In some cases, a contract will be established by conduct.[53] In others no contract will arise.[54]

10. A Non–Merchant So 2–207(2) Not Applicable

Where the relation involves a non-merchant, 2–207(2) does not apply.[55]

Conclusion

It is unfortunate that the drafters did not more adequately design 2–207 for the terrain upon which it was ultimately to do battle. We hope that the foregoing analysis will help the lawyer and the courts apply 2–207 as intelligently as possible. We see no way to apply 2–207 that does not sometimes give an unearned and unfair advantage to the person who happens to send the first, or in some cases the second, document.

Under the present state of the law we believe that there is no language that a lawyer can put on a form that will always assure the client of forming a contract on the client's own terms. These efforts will be frustrated by a responsive document that is expressly

53. Hornell Brewing Co. v. Spry, 174 Misc.2d 451, 664 N.Y.S.2d 698, 32 UCC2d 710 (1997) (conduct of parties over many months established contract where buyer agreed to give sole Canadian distributorship and seller took all functional and legal steps to establish a distribution operation in Canada); Optical Cable Corp. v. Mass. Electric Const. Co., 35 UCC2d 773 (W.D. Va. 1998) (summary judgment denied to allow determination of whether conduct of parties created a contract under 2–207(3)); Kvaerner U.S., Inc. v. Hakim Plast Co., 74 F.Supp.2d 709, 40 UCC2d 207 (E.D. Mich. 1999) (seller's beginning work on order).

54. Transwestern Pipeline Co. v. Monsanto Co., 46 Cal.App.4th 502, 53 Cal.Rptr.2d 887, 29 UCC2d 1178 (1996) (no contract under 2–207(3) where parties met and exchanged multiple forms for years with continued disagreement over term).

55. ProCD, Inc. v. Zeidenberg, 908 F.Supp. 640, 28 UCC2d 1132 (W.D. Wis. 1996) (effectiveness of "shrink-wrap license" inside box examined under 2–209 instead of 2–207 because relationship is between merchant and consumer) (Seventh Circuit reversed on other grounds and said 2–207 did not apply because only one form was involved, 86 F.3d 1447, 29 UCC2d 1109 (7th Cir. 1996)); Hill v. Gateway 2000, Inc., 105 F.3d 1147, 31 UCC2d 303 (7th Cir. 1997) (following ProCD, arbitration clause inside box enters contract between consumer and merchant); Levy v. Gateway 2000, Inc., 1997 WL 823611, 33 UCC2d 1060 (N.Y.Sup. 1997) (2–207 does not apply since contract terms inside box are not additional, but are accepted with all other terms by failure to return within specified period); Klocek v. Gateway, Inc., 104 F.Supp.2d 1332, 41 UCC2d 1059 (D. Kan. 2000) (not merchant, so 2–207 not applicable).

conditional on assent to that document's terms, by prior oral agreement or by the document's use as an acceptance, not an offer. If one must have a term, that party should bargain with the other party for the term; a client should not get it by a lawyer's sleight of hand. If a seller must have the term to reduce its liability but cannot strike a bargain for it, the only answer may be to raise the price, buy insurance, or—as a last resort—have an extra martini every evening and do not capitalize the corporation too heavily.

§ 2–4   Attempted Revision of Sections 2–206 and 2–207

Amended Article 2 is dead. But the process of preparing an amended 2–206 and 2–207, revealed flaws in existing 2–206 and 2–207; an understanding of some of these is certain to be of value to lawyers and legal scholars who must continue to work with unrevised 2–206 and 2–207. In this section we focus on the revision process, the major proposed revisions, and the reasons for those proposals. This focus not only advances understanding of the problems involved, but also provides lawyers and scholars with materials for the construction of interpretive arguments in cases that continue to arise under these sections of the Code, in their unamended state.

a.   Offer and Acceptance in Formation of Contract, Section 2–206

Sections 2–206 and 2–207 were significantly revised in Amended Article 2. One purpose was to separate contract formation (2–206) from contract interpretation (2–207). In nearly all of the cases under existing 2–207, both parties would have conceded that a contract existed between them; they wanted to fight over the terms in that contract (mine, yours or some of each?). The drafters of Amended Article 2 sought to achieve that division in part by moving part of the last sentence of existing 2–207 (on acceptance) to 2–206(3)(a). Amended section 2–206 then read as follows:

(1) Unless otherwise unambiguously indicated by the language or circumstances:

(a) an offer to make a contract shall be construed as inviting acceptance in any manner and by any medium reasonable in the circumstances;

(b) an order or other offer to buy goods for prompt or current shipment shall be construed as inviting acceptance either by a prompt promise to ship or by the prompt or current shipment of conforming or nonconforming goods, but the shipment of nonconforming goods is not an acceptance if the seller seasonably notifies the buyer that the shipment is offered only as an accommodation to the buyer.

(2) If the beginning of a requested performance is a reasonable mode of acceptance, an offeror that is not notified of acceptance within a reasonable time may treat the offer as having lapsed before acceptance.

(3) A definite and seasonable expression of acceptance in a record operates as an acceptance even if it contains terms additional to or different from the offer.[1]

The biggest change proposed in Amended Article 2 here is the addition of subsection (3), which is a shortened version of former 2–207 (1).[2] This subsection rejects the "mirror image" rule. Before it was moved and shortened, the sentence in 2–207 (1) read as follows:

(1) A definite and seasonable expression of acceptance or a written confirmation which is sent within a reasonable time operates as an acceptance even though it states terms additional to or different from those offered or agreed upon, unless acceptance is expressly made conditional on assent to the additional or different terms.[3]

According to revised Comment 3 to 2–206 of Amended Article 2, the "unless" clause is redundant because the adjectives "definite and seasonable" already do its work:

Subsection (3) makes it clear that an expression of acceptance can operate as an acceptance (i.e., create a contract) even though it contains terms that are not identical to those in the offer. This rule applies, however, only to an expression of acceptance that is not only seasonable but also "definite." A purported expression of acceptance containing additional or different terms would not be a "definite" acceptance when the offeree's expression clearly communicates to the offeror the offeree's unwillingness to do business unless the offeror assents to those additional or different terms. This is not a definite acceptance since the offeree's expression makes it clear that the offeree is not "accepting" anything; but rather that the offeree is indicating a willingness to do business only on the offeree's terms and that the offeree is awaiting the offeror's assent to those terms. (This result is consistent with the final clause of former Section 2–207 (1).) In a situation in which the

§ 2–4

1. § 2–206 (2003).

2. UCC § 2–207 (1) (1994): A definite and seasonable expression of acceptance or a written confirmation which is sent within a reasonable time operates as an acceptance even though it states terms additional to or different from those offered or agreed upon, unless acceptance is expressly made conditional on assent to the additional or different terms.

3. § 2–207(1) (1994).

offer clearly indicates that the offeror is unwilling to do business on any terms other than those contained in the offer, and the offeree responds with an expression of acceptance that contains additional or different terms, a court could also conclude that the offeree's response does not constitute a definite expression of acceptance.[4]

In the deviant case (where the parties exchange forms, do not perform and instead, litigate over whether a contract has been formed), the new formulation would probably give the one who is trying to escape the contract a better chance. This is because under existing 2–207 (1), a party fleeing a contract must point to language in its form that makes the acceptance expressly conditional upon the other party's assent to the different or additional terms. Put differently, this requirement (expressly conditional on assent) is the only way an "acceptance" can be turned into a "counter-offer." The adjectives "definite and seasonable" would be less restrictive. Comment 2 recognized that the draft's repudiation of the mirror image rule might need some help: "any responsive record must still be reasonably understood as an 'acceptance' and not as a proposal for a different transaction."[5]

b.   Terms of Contract; Effect of Confirmation, Section 2–207

Amended 2–207 would have stated new contract rules.[6] One might call these "contract rules" to avoid the labels of contract formation and contract interpretation. One is tempted to label old section 2–207 as a contract formation provision—and to some extent that would be right—but much of the section's work was in contract interpretation, not in contract formation. Put differently, the section did not affirm the existence of a contract, rather it found work where the parties' behavior already showed a contract. Like a diligent German Shepherd, it searched among the verbal rubble for the terms of the contract.

Amended 2–207

The amended but unadopted section 2–207 reads in full as follows:

Subject to Section 2–202, if (i) conduct by both parties recognizes the existence of a contract although their records do not otherwise establish a contract, (ii) a contract is formed by an offer and acceptance, or (iii) a contract formed in any manner is confirmed by a record that contains terms additional to or

---

4. § 2–206, Comment 3 (2003).

5. § 2–206, Comment 2 (2003).

6. § 2–207 (2003). See generally, J. J. White, Contracting Under Amended 2–207, 2004 Wis. L. Rev. 723 (2004).

different from those in the contract being confirmed, the terms of the contract are:

(a) terms that appear in the records of both parties;

(b) terms, whether in a record or not, to which both parties agree; and

(c) terms supplied or incorporated under any provision of this Act.[7]

It is easy to see the footprints of the existing section's troubles in the amended 2–207. First, contract formation issues are resolved to the extent possible in 2–206[8] and elsewhere. Second, there is no advantage in having the first document, and no necessary precedence in having one's document labeled the offer; the second record has the same power as the first. Third, the amended section does not impose any condition like the one in existing 2–207(3) that the contract not be formed by the writings. Fourth, the amended section is free of much of the complexity that is found in the existing section and that carried over into the early drafts of Amended Article 2.[9]

7. § 2–207 (2003). The term "record" is defined in 1–201(b)(31) As follows: "information that is inscribed on a tangible medium or that is stored in an electronic or other medium and is retrievable in perceivable form."

8. Amended 2–206(3) reads: "A definite and seasonable expression of acceptance in a record operates as an acceptance even if it contains terms additional to or different from the offer."

9. For example, the February 1, 1999 draft of revised 2–207 read:

(a) This section is subject to Section 2–105 and 2–206.

(b) If a contract is formed by offer and acceptance and the acceptance is by a record containing terms additional to or different from the offer or by conduct of the parties that recognizes the existence of a contract but the records of the parties do not otherwise establish a contract for sale, the terms of the contract include:

(1) terms in the records of the parties to the extent that the records agree;

(2) terms, whether or not in a record, to which the parties have otherwise agreed;

(3) terms in a record supplied by a party to which the other party has expressly agreed; and

(4) terms supplied or incorporated under any provision of [the Uniform Commercial Code].

(c) If a party confirms a contract by a record received by the other party that contains terms that vary [add to or differ from] the previous agreement, the terms of the contract include:

(1) terms in the confirmations of the parties, to the extent that they agree;

(2) terms in a confirming record that vary [add to or differ from] the previous agreement to which the other party has expressly agreed; and

(3) terms supplied or incorporated under any provision of this article.

(d) If a contract for sale is formed in any manner and thereafter the seller in a record proposes terms to the buyer that vary [add to or differ from] terms previously agreed, the following rules apply:

(1) If the seller could have disclosed the varying terms to the buyer in a commercially reasonable manner at the time of contract formation and failed to do so, the terms do not become part of the contract unless expressly agreed to by the buyer;

(2) If the seller could not have disclosed the varying terms to the buyer

Finally, subsection (b) of amended 2–207 explicitly invites courts to regard terms to which the parties have otherwise "agree[d]" as part of the contract. This subsection gives courts latitude to find agreement in the verbal and nonverbal behavior of the parties even when a term to which they have agreed is not included in the records that either has sent, and even when the term agreed to is contradicted by the other's form. This would have been a battlefield under amended 2–207. And if our guess is right, it is not quite fair to say that amended 2–207 is only about interpretation and not about the contract formation because courts will also be answering contract formation questions when they decide whether the parties have "agree[d]" to a term.

Even though amended 2–207 would much simplify the law and even if it would cure some of the problems of existing 2–207, readers should not be too quick to applaud. The amended section has not been enacted in any state. It is still to be tested against the iron rule of statutory drafting: tomorrow's hard questions are rarely the same as yesterday's. To advance understanding of the basic nature of the problems that existing and amended 2–207 face, it is worthwhile to speculate on answers to some of the questions that might arise under such an amended section.

"Mine and Mine Only"

Many purchase order and confirmation forms now in use include various "mine and mine only" terms.[10] These terms state

in a commercially reasonable manner, the seller shall by conspicuous language in a record notify the buyer at the time of contract formation that additional or different terms will be proposed.

(A) If the seller gives conspicuous notice, the buyer may either accept the proposed terms by any method reasonable under the circumstances or reject the proposed terms and return the goods.

(B) If the seller fails to give conspicuous notice, the proposed terms do not become part of the contract unless expressly agreed to by the buyer.

(3) Upon returning goods to the seller, the buyer has a right to:

(A) a refund; and

(B) reimbursement of any reasonable expenses incurred related to the return and in compliance with any instructions of the seller for re-

turn or, in the absence of instructions, return postage or similar reasonable expenses in returning the goods.

(e) In this section, an express agreement to terms cannot be based upon the mere retention or use of goods.

§ 2–207 (Discussion Draft, Feb. 1, 1999), available at http://www.law.upenn.edu/bll/ulc/ucc2/ucc2299.htm.

10. For example, in Boise Cascade Corp. v. Etsco, Ltd., 1984 WL 178957, 39 UCC 410 (D. Or. 1984), the seller's "offer" contained the following language:

"ACCEPTANCE: Seller's acceptance is expressly made conditional on Buyer's assent to Seller's terms and conditions as set forth herein[,]"

and the buyer's "acceptance" read:

"ACCEPTANCE: Acceptance of this Purchase Order, whether by written acknowledgment or by performance by Seller, shall be upon the terms and conditions hereof; no other terms or condi-

that a person can form a contract with the master of the form only if this person agrees to all of the terms on the proffered form and proposes neither additional terms nor any that contradict the terms in the form. In existing 2–207 the "mine only" term mostly has the effect of forestalling a contract on the forms and of throwing the parties into subsection (3). Usually the contract formed under subsection (3) is composed of the terms that are the same on both forms and of terms implied by law.[11]

Amended 2–207 would be the same; "mine only" terms would be null except in unusual cases. In the usual case—where the parties perform even though they have exchanged documents that contain conflicting and additional terms—their behavior would form the contract under section 2–206. Under amended 2–207 the contract would be composed of the terms that appear on both records together with terms implied under Article 2.

A "mine only" term is likely to affect the parties' rights only when one party aborts the contracting process before that party's behavior amounts to the nonverbal recognition of a contract. In that case under either amended 2–206 or under the same language in existing 2–207, the mine only term converts the form that bears the term into a counter offer, not an acceptance. If that be so, no contract is formed and the master of that document is not bound. As thus amended, 2–207 and the transfer of part of existing 2–207 to amended 2–206, would be unlikely to change the law, here.

Form Hierarchy

To say that all forms are equal no matter who uses them and no matter what they say overstates the case. Consider a negotiation that is started by a buyer's sending a Request For Quotation (RFQ) to several potential suppliers. Assume that the RFQ states elaborate specifications, precisely recites the times for performance and contemplates responses by multiple sellers. Even where the winning supplier's sending its form concludes the contract, the parties probably accord a higher status to the terms in the RFQ than to those in any form that either might exchange thereafter.[12] If the terms in the RFQ have not been explicitly negotiated away, we suspect that the parties would regard those as binding on both

tions shall be binding on Buyer unless written approval thereof specifically referring to such other terms and conditions shall have been given to Seller."

11. See Boise Cascade, 39 UCC 410 (1984) ("The effect of the fact that both offer and acceptance expressly state that any contract formed must contain their terms and no others is that no contract was formed by the writings of the par-

ties. Thus [UCC § 2–207(3)] is effective and controls the present case." (citation omitted)).

12. It would appear, however, that the case law is not very supportive. See, e.g., William M. Hendrickson, Inc. v. National R.R. Passenger Corp., 2002 WL 398641, 47 UCC2d 1284 (E.D. Pa. 2002) (giving no greater weight to terms on RFQ).

because the RFQ is a noble among the commoners, the purchase orders and acknowledgments. If we are right, it is appropriate under amended subsection (b) for a court to conclude that the RFQ's terms prevail even in the face of contradictory terms in the other forms.

Oral Intervention

Sometimes the initial oral exchange is not the last; in some cases one party will make an oral objection to a term on the other's form.[13] If the other agrees to the first's oral request, there would be an agreement sufficient for a contract under amended 2–207(b), but subject to the parol evidence rule. That rule would bar this new oral agreement only if the exchange that preceded the oral request had resulted in a contract (one of the few places where one must note the moment of contracting under the amended section) and if the "confirmatory memoranda of the parties agree" or the terms are "otherwise set forth in a writing intended by the parties as a final expression of their agreement."[14] Typically, the confirmatory memoranda will not agree; one is seeking oral agreement from the other precisely because the forms do not agree.[15]

Of course, if the first party objects to the oral proposal, there is no agreement at that moment and the court will be faced with the newly complicated task of interpreting the parties' performance in light of this intermediate and often indeterminate oral exchange.

Where the oral exchange results in agreement, without more that agreement should be part of the deal. The parol evidence rule will seldom bar it, nor should section 2–209 on modification.[16] Often the oral intervention will occur before a contract has been made— even if the parties are on a trajectory to make a contract through a combination of oral agreements, exchange of forms, and perform-

---

13. See Westinghouse Elec. Corp. v. Nielsons, Inc., 647 F.Supp. 896 (D. Colo. 1986) (sustaining oral objection to seller's limitation of liability term).

14. Existing section 2–202 reads in full:

Terms with respect to which the confirmatory memoranda of the parties agree or which are otherwise set forth in a writing intended by the parties as a final expression of their agreement with respect to such terms as are included therein may not be contradicted by evidence of any prior agreement or of a contemporaneous oral agreement but may be explained or supplemented

(a) by course of dealing or usage of trade (Section 1–205) or by course of performance (Section 2–208); and

(b) by evidence of consistent additional terms unless the court finds the writing to have been intended also as a complete and exclusive statement of the terms of the agreement.

15. See Providence & Worcester R. Co. v. Sargent & Greenleaf, Inc., 802 F.Supp. 680 (D. R.I. 1992) (noting that parties' forms are seldom intended to be fully integrated agreements).

16. In most cases, 2–209 will not apply because subsections (2) and (3) refer to contracts formed by signed writings whereas the contracts contemplated here are formed by performance under section 2–207(3).

ance. In that case the oral exchange is merely further negotiation, not the modification of an existing contract.

But even if one concludes that the parties' earlier behavior had made a binding contract, can subsection (b) of amended 2–207 be read to recognize this new oral agreement as part of that contract embryo without regard to 2–209? Amended section 2–207 is built on the hypothesis that it is seldom congruent with commercial expectations in the form contract setting to ask when the contract was made. Even if the parties make an oral contract on day one, terms on which their forms agree that might have been exchanged on days 20 and 40 are part of the contract under amended 2–207(a). Should we apply similar reasoning under subsection (b) to the oral agreements that follow agreements made by exchange of forms or by earlier oral exchanges?[17]

Oral Agreement Followed by One or More Forms

Invariably, commercial contracting parties communicate with one another face to face, by telephone, or by e-mail before they conclude a contract. Sometimes there will be no contract until the exchange of forms, and sometimes none until later than that, but in some cases a contract will be reached orally before any forms are exchanged or orally in the middle of the exchange of forms.

Assume an oral agreement[18] followed by a mutual exchange of forms and performance. This is easy under amended 2–207. The contract is the terms agreed upon orally together with any terms that appear in both forms and any terms supplied by Article 2.

What if a term in one of the forms contradicts a term in the prior oral agreement? Tough. By hypothesis the parties have an oral agreement to a particular term and a later contradiction of that term by one party would not itself be an "agreement" under subsection (b) of amended 2–207, and so would not remove the term that both had agreed upon orally. Since by hypothesis this contradicting term is in only one form, it does not enter through subsection (a), and it cannot be a gap filler that finds hope in (c) because a contrary term has already been agreed upon.

And what if the term in the oral agreement is a gap filler such as the implied warranty of merchantability? Assume that the buyer's confirmation has no specific express warranty language (except to the extent that the agreed product description would be a warranty) and that the seller's form has a disclaimer of warranty.

---

17. Even if one concluded that any oral agreement would have to pass through section 2–209, its only obstacle there would be the statute of frauds (and that might be satisfied by subsequent performance).

18. Assume also that later forms or performance will satisfy the statute of frauds.

Answer: without more, the disclaimer is not in the contract because it is neither agreed upon under (b) nor in both records for (a), under amended 2–207.

Oral Discussion Without Agreement Followed by One or More Forms

The case is different under amended 2–207 where the parties do not reach agreement in their oral interchange. In that case, the forms of the parties need only be compared and the contract is the terms on both under (a) and gap fillers from (c).

Where both are to send forms, we should be slow to find agreement to another's form by performance. A priori, one would not expect one's counterpart's initial performance to be an agreement to one's terms when one knows that that party will be sending its own form, and one's counterpart would have similar expectations. One of the plausible purposes for sending a form is to forestall any inference of agreement to the other's boilerplate; one may not get one's terms by sending one's own form, but at least one cleanses one's own performance of the inference that one has accepted the other's terms by beginning to work.

Where only one party follows up an oral agreement, we think that the outcome is the same, but the passive party's inaction opens that party's performance to an enlarged risk. In the right case, a court might construe the inaction to be an agreement to the other's form. See discussion below, "If You Tie Your Shoelaces."[19]

Performance After the Exchange of One or More Forms

Performance after an incomplete or fragmentary exchange seldom has a clear, objective meaning about agreement to another's terms. Sometimes the performance shows agreement to another's terms, but more often it must mean only that the negotiated terms are okay, not that one intends to accept all of the boilerplate of the lawyer for the other party. In an era of just-in-time schedules, low inventories and emphasis on lean and quick operating, it is bad policy to punish a quick and early performer by sticking him with his counterpart's terms just because he was more diligent than another might have been.

One can think of cases where the seller's making and sending goods to the buyer should be construed as acceptance of all of the terms on the buyer's purchase order. Surely that performance signals the seller's agreement to the negotiated terms (price, quan-

---

19. See Trafalgar Square, Ltd. v. Reeves Bros., Inc., 35 A.D.2d 194, 315 N.Y.S.2d 239 (1970) (term on form becomes part of oral contract if no objection is made). But see Lemmer v. IDS Properties, 304 N.W.2d 864 (Minn. 1980) (term on form modifying oral agreement did not become part of contract).

tity, specifications and delivery and payment terms) and it would often be fair to construe it to be an agreement to other boilerplate terms such as those on risk of loss, warranty and responsibility for damages or cure.

Here the courts would earn their keep under amended 2–207. The section invites courts to interpret the parties' behavior in light of the expectations, needs and practices of the field on which they play. The inferences to be drawn from a seller's hedging of its contract for the sale of $100 million of electricity may be different from those to be drawn from a buyer's procuring a loan to buy $10 million of fertilizer, and both of those different from inferences arising from a tier one automobile supplier's shipment of coil springs to GM.

If You Tie Your Shoelaces

One of the ways that clever lawyers have tried to escape the reach of existing section 2–207 is to assert that the other party's behavior is an acceptance of all of the terms on the first party's form. For example a form might say that any action—even in preparation for performance—will be an acceptance of the offeror's terms.[20] In an act of splendid chutzpah (or unforgivable ignorance), the drafters of UCITA (law only in Maryland and Virginia) ruled that one has "manifested assent" (agreed to something) if that party "intentionally engage[s] in conduct . . . with reason to know that the other party . . . may infer from the conduct that the person assents to the term."[21] Suppose that your form asserts that intentionally tying my shoelaces tomorrow morning will be assent to all of your terms. Since I cannot tie my shoelaces unintentionally and since I have no valet, I'm stuck.

In the infamous *ProCD v. Zeidenberg* case, the Court suggests the same when it states that Mr. Z was stuck with the terms on the box because the offeror was "the master of his offer."[22] The

---

20. See Dresser Industries, Inc., Waukesha Engine Div. v. Gradall Co., 702 F.Supp. 726 (E.D. Wis. 1988); William M. Hendrickson v. Nat'l Railroad Passenger Corp., 2002 WL 398641, 47 UCC2d 1284 (E.D. Pa. 2002) (term deeming commencement of performance to be an acceptance of terms). See also Com–Corp Industries, Inc. v. H & H Mach. Tool Co. of Iowa, 1996 WL 631100 (Ohio Ct. App. 1996) (unpublished); CECG, Inc. v. Magic Software Enter., Inc., 51 Fed.Appx. 359 (3d Cir. 2002) (unpublished).

21. UCITA § 112(a) (2002) reads:

(a) A person manifests assent to a record or term if the person, acting with knowledge of, or after having an opportunity to review the record or term or a copy of it:

(1) authenticates the record or term to adopt or accept it; or

(2) intentionally engages in conduct or makes statements with reason to know that the other party or its electronic agent may infer from the conduct or statement that the person assents to the record or term.

22. 86 F.3d 1447, 1452 (7th Cir. 1996) ("A vendor, as master of the offer, may invite acceptance by conduct, and propose limitations on the kind of conduct that constitutes acceptance.").

statement is right, but the application is wrong. To say that the offeror is the master of the offer means only that the offeror may rule out certain things as acceptance, i.e., that the offeror can limit the universe of things that will be regarded as acceptances, not that the offeror can expand "acceptance" beyond the universe that a reasonable person in the offeree's shoes would believe to be acceptance.

The case is not far fetched. Two years ago one of our students brought one of us a clear plastic sleeve in which she had received the power cord to her computer. On its face was the message: "By opening this plastic sleeve, you agree to all of the terms of the seller's contract and license." Such terms should not transform behavior that would not normally be an acceptance into an acceptance, and, in general, courts have agreed.[23] If one limits section 112(a) of UCITA to the conventional case where a buyer clicks "I Agree," the rule is a tautology, for the click would be regarded by all reasonable people as an agreement, just as the oral expression of the same words would mean agreement. In our opinion one can safely tie one's shoelaces without fear of making an unfavorable contract. Conceivably there are cases near the border where such a term might push an act over the line and make something an acceptance that would otherwise fail, but we cannot identify any. If section 112 of UCITA reaches to your shoelaces, the law may be pronounced an ass.

Terms in an Invoice with the Goods

Is a seller saved by including some terms on an invoice that is delivered with the goods, long after both believed the contract had been concluded? We are not sure. This is a commercial variation of the issue that we discuss below.[24] As we point out below, the courts and drafters have long wrestled with the legal standing of terms delivered with the product, and matters require clarification. It might make a difference that the parties had dealt with one another before and that the buyer knew that seller's terms would come with the products. There is nothing in amended 2–103(1)(m) (defining "record")[25] or in 2–207(a) that keeps an invoice from

---

23. See Licitra v. Gateway, Inc., 189 Misc.2d 721, 734 N.Y.S.2d 389, 392 (Civ. Ct. 2001) ("... if the defendant, as a term and condition of filing a claim, required the consumer to sing 'O Sole Mio' in Yiddish while standing on his or her head in Macy's window, only Mandy Patinkin would qualify to object to the receipt of defective equipment. This cannot be so.").

24. Compare Klocek v. Gateway, Inc., 104 F.Supp.2d 1332 (D. Kan. 2000)

(terms in the box are not part of contract), with Hill v. Gateway 2000, Inc., 105 F.3d 1147 (7th Cir. 1997) (enforcing in-the-box terms).

25. Under § 2–103(1)(m) of Amended Article 2 (2003): "Record" means information that is inscribed on a tangible medium or that is stored in an electronic or other medium and is retrievable in perceivable form. See also § 1–201(31) of Revised Article 1.

being a record that could satisfy (a). But there is some drafting history and there is Comment 5. These show that the drafters were uneasy about terms delivered with the goods and that they were uncertain about the right outcome.

Can we distinguish terms on the invoice with the goods from terms on, or in the box, in cases like *Gateway* and *ProCD*? It is hard but perhaps possible. If, as we suggest above, terms on a record that come after the parties have reached an oral agreement become part of the contract under amended 2–207(a) without regard to 2–209—if the same terms are on the other's form—the invoice terms should make it into the contract too. By hypothesis the buyer has proposed the same terms and can hardly complain. *Gateway* and *ProCD* on the other hand must claim an "agreement" under amended 2–207(b), not just that there is a match under subsection (a).

Terms On or In the Box

Existing section 2–207 has found most of its work in industrial contracting. Most of the 2–207 cases are between industrial manufacturers and industrial buyers; the latter intend to resell or to use the products in their own manufacturing process. Yet a separate contracting practice between consumer and non-consumer end users and manufacturers has persisted even longer than the industrial contracting process. Even though the consumer and the industrial practices present similar contract issues, the two have marched in parallel with little reference in the cases from one to the similar issues in the other. The case that put Madison on the contract map, *ProCD,* has changed that.[26] The courts, the drafters of Amended Article 2, and particularly the commentators have now awakened to the common issues in the parallel tracks and to the need to reconcile the cases in the industrial forum with those in the retail forum.

Manufacturers of retail goods have long attached contract statements to or included contract documents with new goods. Early examples were warnings, disclaimers, or limitation of remedies on sacks of seed or containers of fertilizer.[27] Today, most

---

26. ProCD, Inc. v. Zeidenberg, 86 F.3d 1447 (7th Cir. 1996).

27. See Mullis v. Speight Seed Farms, Inc., 234 Ga.App. 27, 505 S.E.2d 818 (1998) (enforcing disclaimer and limitation on seed can which read: "NOTICE TO PURCHASER: [Seller] warrants that, at the time of delivery, the seeds in this container conform to the label description as required under state and federal laws. [Seller] makes no other warranties whether written, oral, statu-

tory, express or implied, including but not limited to warranty of merchantability, fitness for a particular purpose, or otherwise, that would extend beyond such descriptions contained herein. In any event, [seller's] liability for breach of any warranty with respect to such seeds shall be limited to the purchase price. Purchaser assumes the risk for results obtained from use of such seeds, including but not limited to the condition under which the seeds are planted,

appliances and other boxed electronic hardware sold new at retail include contract documents. Some terms in the box favor the buyer—the limited express warranty and the help line for computer hardware. Some favor the seller—limitations of remedy, restrictions on forum, arbitration clauses and reduction in the limitations period.[28]

Licensors and sellers of software try to protect their intellectual property interests by terms on, or in, the box, or on the software itself. They hope to make the transaction a license and not a sale so to avoid the first sale doctrine. And where the market is segmented—some will pay much and others will pay little for the same product—they badly want to keep the buyers in the less expensive market from committing arbitrage, i.e., they hope to prevent purchasers in the cheap market from reselling into the dear market.[29]

The first and still the most prominent case is ProCD v. Zeidenberg.[30] The lower court held that buyer Zeidenberg was not bound by the terms in the box because he had not seen them before the contract was made. The Circuit Court reversed; it found that Zeidenberg was bound, applied Article 2 (but not 2–207), and drew an analogy to cases like Carnival Cruise Lines,[31] where the Supreme Court found that the buyer of a cruise ticket was bound by a choice of law clause even though he had not seen the clause until long after the contract had been made.

Whatever the merit of the outcome in *ProCD* (Matthew Zeidenberg was surely a naughty boy who should have his hands slapped), Judge Easterbrook's consideration of the Article 2 issues is not as careful as it should have been. First, he applied Article 2 without considering whether the contract for the use of a database was a "transaction in goods," and so within the scope of Article 2.[32]

germinated, or grown."); Dessert Seed Co. v. Drew Farmers Supply, Inc., 248 Ark. 858, 454 S.W.2d 307 (1970) (refusing to enforce limitation of remedies on tomato seed bag which read: "Subject to the limitation of liability herein set forth, we warrant that seeds or bulbs sold are as described on the container, within recognized tolerances. Our liability on this warranty is limited in amount to the purchase price of the seeds or bulbs. In no way shall we be liable for the crop.").

28. Manufacturers of retail goods sold to consumers often do not disclaim the implied warranty of merchantability. In almost all cases, manufacturers furnish to consumers some form of express warranty of the goods. Thus, any attempt to disclaim the implied warranty of merchantability would violate the Magnuson–Moss Warranty–Federal Trade Commission Improvement Act. See 15 U.S.C. §§ 2301–12 (2003).

29. Matthew Zeidenberg's attempt at arbitrage was at issue in *ProCD*. Having purchased a consumer version of a computer telephone directory, Zeidenberg's corporation made the database (which cost over $10 million to compile) available over the Internet at a price which was much lower than ProCD charged the commercial market. See ProCD, 86 F.3d at 1449–50.

30. *Id.* at 1447.

31. See Carnival Cruise Lines v. Shute, 499 U.S. 585, 111 S.Ct. 1522, 113 L.Ed.2d 622 (1991).

32. One can argue that the ProCD contract is not for goods, and that it is governed by the common law rather

Second he dismissed section 2–207 in one sentence: "Our case has only one form; UCC 2–207 is irrelevant."[33] That statement is wrong; nothing in section 2–207, its Comments or the cases limits the section to cases with more than one form. Indeed, the second sentence in Comment 1 states a hypothetical case with only one form.[34]

A series of cases involving Gateway's arbitration clause which was contained in the computer box, have agreed with *ProCD*.[35] But one, Klocek v. Gateway, Inc.,[36] goes the other way. In *Klocek*, Judge Vratil applied section 2–207 and found that the buyer's "act of keeping the computer past five days was not sufficient to demonstrate that plaintiff expressly agreed to the Standard Terms."[37]

Before we turn to amended 2–207's treatment of terms in the box, we should give the Seventh Circuit its due. Judge Easterbrook's discussion of the economics of retail contracting and of the virtue of giving sellers easy ways to discriminate in price between sets of potential buyers deserves more respect than does his dismissal of existing 2–207. When he argues that society is well served by law that makes contracting inexpensive and easy, Judge Easterbrook is right. For a nickel or a dime almost all of us would give up our right to resell software and would agree to arbitrate. If that is so, it hardly makes sense to charge our seller a dollar in contracting costs to make that deal with us. Still the contract law and our conventional understanding deserve some respect; there must be reasons why we persist in looking for "agreement" and why courts routinely reject some behavior as inadequate to show agreement.

But these issues are not new; consider how the drafters of Article 2, now and earlier, have dealt with them. Fifty years ago Professor Llewellyn recognized the challenge to standard contract rules presented by terms that are attached to or delivered with the goods. He made only a half-hearted stab at the problem in Comment 7 to 2–313:

than by Article 2. In Hill v. Gateway 2000, 105 F.3d 1147 (7th Cir. 1997), Judge Easterbrook is saved from repeating this error, for that case deals with a contract for the sale of goods, namely a computer.

33. ProCD, 86 F.3d at 1452.

34. Comment 1 to section 2–207 stated:

"This section is intended to deal with two typical situations. The one is the written confirmation, where an agreement has been reached either orally or by informal correspondence between the parties and is followed by one or both of the parties sending formal memoranda

embodying the terms so far as agreed upon and adding terms not discussed."

35. See Westendorf v. Gateway 2000, Inc., 2000 WL 307369, 41 UCC2d 1110 (Del. Ch. 2000) (arbitration provision shipped with computer). See also Brower v. Gateway 2000, Inc., 246 A.D.2d 246, 676 N.Y.S.2d 569, 37 UCC2d 54 (1998) (warranty disclaimer included inside computer packaging); Levy v. Gateway 2000, Inc., 33 UCC2d 1060, 1997 WL 823611 (N.Y. Sup. 1997).

36. Klocek v. Gateway, Inc., 104 F.Supp.2d 1332, 41 UCC2d 1059 (D. Kan. 2000).

37. *Id.* at 1341.

The precise time when words of description or affirmation are made or samples are shown is not material. The sole question is whether the language or samples or models are fairly to be regarded as part of the contract. If language is used after the closing of the deal (as when the buyer when taking delivery asks and receives an additional assurance), the warranty becomes a modification, and need not be supported by consideration if it is otherwise reasonable and in order. (Section 2–209).[38]

In urging that the "sole question is whether the language ... [is] fairly to be regarded as part of the contract ...," Professor Llewellyn sounds like amended 2–207, rather than existing 2–207. Of course, Llewellyn was addressing express warranties where the problem is complicated by the requirement that an express warranty be "part of the basis of the bargain."

In the Article 2 amendment process the Drafting Committee dealt with these issues twice. First, it adopted 2–313A on warranties by a manufacturer to a remote buyer. Second, the committee considered and abandoned a subsection proposed for amended 2–207 specifically addressed to terms in or on the box. The poverty of our imagination is shown by the fact that no one on the Drafting Committee appears ever to have noticed that the proposed subsection to section 2–207 and proposed section 2–313A addressed the same question.

If Gateway sells through Circuit City to a consumer, Gateway's warranty in the box to the consumer (remote purchaser) would be binding and Gateway's arbitration clause and other limitation of remedies would be binding on the consumer under 2–313A(5)(a) of Amended Article 2. So far so good.

What of the same consumer's rights as a third party beneficiary of Gateway's warranty to Circuit City? Neither those warranties nor any limitation on damages for breach of them is addressed in 2–313A of Amended Article 2. Nothing in 2–313A affects the consumer's rights under the applicable alternative of 2–318 (privity rules). Any right to sue as a third party beneficiary and any bar to such suit for lack of privity are unchanged.

If Gateway sells directly to the consumer, no part of section 2–313A of Amended Article 2 would apply and the parties would be back under 2–313 and under cases interpreting that section. Ironically, a consumer who buys directly from Gateway may not be bound by Gateway's arbitration term under *Klocek*, yet if the same person buys from a retailer, he would be bound by the arbitration clause because of section 2–313A of Amended Article 2. So the

38. § 2–313, Comment 7 (1994).

attempt to codify even this small part of law on terms in the box has not distinguished the drafters of Amended Article 2.

In 2000, long after 2–313A of Amended Article 2 had been agreed upon, the Drafting Committee considered a proposed subsection in 2–207 that would have dealt with all terms in the box.[39] The subsection read as follows:

> (b) Terms to which the buyer has not otherwise agreed that are delivered to the buyer with the goods become part of the contract, subject to 2–202, only if:
>
> > (1) the buyer does not within [twenty] [thirty] days of their receipt object to the terms and offer to return the goods at the seller's expense,
> >
> > (2) the terms do not contradict the terms of the parties' agreement, and
> >
> > (3) taken as a whole, the terms do not materially alter the contract to the detriment of the buyer.[40]

The subsection was accompanied by a Comment which stated that usual terms in the box would *not* "materially alter the contract to the detriment of the buyer" if they contained an express warranty, a promise of consumer help and the like even if they also limited the buyer's remedies. Note that the word "agreement" defined in 1–201(3) and included in (b)(2) of the proposed subsection does not include gap fillers provided by Article 2; thus a limitation of remedies would not "contradict" an "agreement" that would lead to a "contract" which would include the remedies provided by part 7 of Article 2. The implied terms from part 7 would be a part of the "contract" but not part of the "agreement."

One of us thought that the proposed subsection (b) of amended 2–207 would give the sellers what they needed without subjecting the buyers to onerous terms. Wrong. The buyers (represented by Gail Hillebrand from Consumers Union) were tempted, but feared that the sellers would agree and then take the concession away in the legislatures.[41] The sellers (represented by R. Rader of Gateway) were also opposed. So the committee rejected the subsection by a

39. One of us must confess that it never occurred to him when we were considering the subsection to 2–207 that we should look back at 2–313A. We treated 2–313A as put to bed (after a big fight with sellers and advertisers several years before) and, as best as he can recall, no one suggested that the two sections might be stepping on one another's toes.

40. Amended § 2–207(b) (Discussion Draft, Mar. 2000), available at http://
www.law.upenn.edu/bll/ulc/ucc2/2300.htm.

41. In a couple of states secured creditors did not conform to the expectations of consumer debtors when Article 9 was being considered. Local bankers organizations apparently did not regard themselves bound by deals that had been struck during the negotiation of the uniform version of Revised Article 9.

vote of four to three. Of course, we will never know the true position either of the buyers and sellers or of their agents; those positions are revealed, if ever, only after a provision has been adopted. Each side may have believed that it would prevail in court. If that was their belief, one is wrong.

The proposed subsection was never adopted and was replaced by Comment 5 to amended 2–207 that reads:

> The section omits any specific treatment of terms attached to the goods, or in or on the container in which the goods are delivered. This article takes no position on whether a court should follow the reasoning in Step–Saver Data Systems, Inc. v. Wyse Technology, 939 F.2d 91 (3d Cir. 1991) and Klocek v. Gateway, Inc., 104 F.Supp.2d 1332 (D. Kan. 2000) (original 2–207 governs) or the contrary reasoning in Hill v. Gateway 2000, 105 F.3d 1147 (7th Cir. 1997) (original 2–207 inapplicable).[42]

The Comment leaves courts free to apply existing 2–207 or to decline to do so. It frees buyers to argue in and sellers to argue out.

Does amended 2–207 apply to cases like Gateway? We think so. Judge Easterbrook was mistaken about cases with only one form, and his position would be even farther from the truth under amended 2–207. The first four lines of amended 2–207 are comprehensive; they would apply to all Article 2 contracts:

> Subject to section 2–202, if (i) conduct by both parties recognizes the existence of a contract although their records do not otherwise establish a contract, (ii) a contract is formed by an offer and acceptance, or (iii) a contract formed in any manner is confirmed by a record that contains terms additional to or different from those in the contract being confirmed, the terms of the contract are . . .[43]

The difficulty is that such parties often think that they are making a binding deal at the time of the first and, often the only, conversation. They are not like industrial buyers and sellers who anticipate negotiations and perhaps a multiple exchange of documents. So it seems to us that the seller must either incorporate the terms in the box into the telephone or e-mail contract, or somehow make his term in the box into a modification.

Consider *Gateway* under amended 2–207. Since the arbitration clause appears only in Gateway's record, it does not get into the contract under (a). If there is only one record, the clause does not meet (1) for the want of a second record; if there are two records, it fails because the clause will not appear in the buyer's record.

42. § 2–207, Comment 5 (2003).   **43.** § 2–207 (2003).

The arbitration clause would make it into the contract under (b) if the parties "agree." Comment 3 to Amended 2–207 invites a court's consideration of the parties' verbal and nonverbal behavior:

> In a rare case the terms in the records of both parties might not become part of the contract. This could be the case, for example, when the parties contemplated an agreement to a single negotiated record, and each party submitted to the other party similar proposals and then commenced performance, but the parties never reached a negotiated agreement because of the differences over crucial terms. There is a variety of verbal and nonverbal behavior that may suggest agreement to another's record. This section leaves the interpretation of that behavior to the discretion of the courts.[44]

Now what behavior might do? If Gateway's agent got the buyer's agreement to the terms in the box as a part of the parties' telephone or e-mail exchange at the time of contracting, that would do. If the buyer agreed that the contract would not be binding until after the delivery—so keeping the contracting process open—that might work also.

An e-mail agreement after the initial contract discussion but before delivery might work if the seller were to condition its delivery on buyer's e-mail agreement to the terms. Of course, technically that e-mail might be a breach of the existing contract, but if the buyer accedes, the resulting e-mail deal would be an effective modification even if one thought a deal had already been struck. The e-mails would satisfy the amended statute of frauds.[45] Since consideration is not needed for modifications under 2–209 of Amended Article 2 and since the seller's good faith would arise from its legitimate need for the terms, that would work.

The seller is farther out on a limb if it must rely on a click-through agreement or on a sign on the box. For the reasons stated above, we should not permit the seller to make an act that no rational buyer would regard as an acceptance ("opening this means you agree to Gateway's terms") into an acceptance.

The buyer will have a different objection to the click-through agreement. A buyer will understand that a click on the "I agree" is a proper acceptance of the seller's terms. But now the seller's offer is coercive. The buyer has received and spent all evening setting up the computer; the buyer is sitting in a study in International Falls in underwear with a beer when called upon to decide whether to agree to the new terms or go out in the minus 30 degree tempera-

---

44. Amended § 2–207, Comment 3 (2003).

45. By substituting "record" for writing the amendments recognize e-mails as sufficient for § 2–201. See § 2– 103(1)(m) (2003). Even without the amended language, the e-mails work under UETA (see UETA § 2(13) (2000)) or E–Sign (see 15 U.S.C. § 7006(4), (9) (2000)).

ture and return the computer. Because it is coercive, this offer is more objectionable than a pre-delivery e-mail.

What about the second purchase? If the buyer buys twice from the same seller, does the buyer's knowledge of the terms from the first sale bind the buyer as to the second? We are not sure. Knowing that my opposite party's form insists on something is normally not enough to bind me if the opposite party's behavior does not back up that party's form. Remember the industrial seller whose form always demands arbitration but who always performs in the face of the buyer's silence? There, we require the seller to pull up and insist on express agreement to the seller's arbitration term if we are to find an "agreement."[46] But maybe this is different. Unlike the industrial buyer who will express terms on the buyer's own form and so implicitly reject seller's terms that are not included on the buyer's form, our Gateway buyer makes no explicit or implicit expression of discontent with the seller's terms.[47]

What about *ProCD*? Amended Article 2 might treat *ProCD* differently than it treats Gateway. First, it is probable that Amended Article 2 would not apply to *ProCD*. Even if the data are delivered on a disk that is goods, the contract is for the data and the disk is merely the temporary carrier; it can be discarded once the data are on the buyer's hard drive. So the medium that holds the data is less important than with a book where the medium is the permanent residence of the data. Amended 2–103 and its attendant Comment support that view.[48] If Amended Article 2 does

---

46. See Avedon Eng'g, Inc. v. Seatex, 112 F.Supp.2d 1090, 42 UCC2d 695 (D. Colo. 2000) (unilaterally inserted arbitration clause did not materially alter agreement and so became part of the contract where terms were clear and legible, form with clause was routinely used in parties' course of dealing, buyer had at least three chances to read clause, and custom in textile industry was to include arbitration terms in all contracts). See also Sethness–Greenleaf, Inc. v. Green River Corp., 65 F.3d 64, 27 UCC2d 360 (7th Cir. 1995) (Easterbrook, J.) (enforcing payment terms which appeared in over 200 invoices from seller but not in buyer's forms).

47. Compare ProCD, Inc. v. Zeidenberg, 908 F.Supp. 640, 654–55, 28 UCC2d 1132 (D. Wis. 1996), with ProCD, Inc. v. Zeidenberg, 86 F.3d 1447, 1452–54, 29 UCC2d 1109 (7th Cir. 1996).

48. Amended § 2–103(1)(k) (2003) reads:

"Goods" means all things that are movable at the time of identification to a contract for sale. The term includes future goods, specially manufactured goods, the unborn young of animals, growing crops, and other identified things attached to realty as described in Section 2–107. The term does not include information, the money in which the price is to be paid, investment securities under Article 8, the subject matter of foreign exchange transactions, or choses in action.

Comment 7 to 2–103 further states:

The definition of "goods" in this article has been amended to exclude information not associated with goods. Thus, this article does not directly apply to an electronic transfer of information, such as the transaction involved in Specht v. Netscape, 150 F.Supp.2d 585 (S.D.N.Y. 2001), aff'd, 306 F.3d 17 (2d. Cir. 2002). However, transactions often include both goods and information: some are transactions in goods as that term is used in Section 2–102, and some are not. For example, the sale of "smart goods" such as an automobile is a transaction in

not apply to *ProCD*, Judge Easterbrook can play all he wants in the common law without doing any harm to Amended Article 2.[49]

Even if one were to apply Amended 2–207 to *ProCD*, the result might be different from the Gateway result. Under Amended 2–207 a court could conclude that the purchase of a box with a warning on the outside about terms on the inside is an agreement to those terms under Amended 2–207(2). Unlike Gateway, this buyer would be holding the terms in hand when making the contract to buy. So here the seller avoids the doctrinal conundrum from Gateway, namely that normal rules of contracting would find that a contract existed long before the seller's terms show up in International Falls. Particularly if the box in the buyer's hand warns of terms inside, one might conclude here that the buyer's payment signifies the buyer's agreement to those terms.

If you were to sign up for a cell phone contract with AT&T Wireless, or its successor, the sales representative would read to you a "meta-term" to which you would have had to assent by pressing "1" on your phone (this is a good example of an electronic signature, by the way). This "meta-term" would reference later terms and conditions to which you also would have had to agree. You would have had 30 days to opt out if you like. Assume AT&T read to you:

> By pressing "1" at the end of this message, you are agreeing to a two-year agreement for wireless services with AT&T Wireless. The term is two-years even if another term is referenced in other materials you have received. If you cancel your service before the end of the two-year term, you will be charged a $175 early termination fee. To cancel your service, call Customer Care. You may only keep the benefits associated with a two-year agreement if you press "1" at the end of this message. This two-year agreement incorporates by reference the Service Agreement of General Terms and Conditions of service as well as the rate plan brochure and other features or promotional materials, which were provided to you. Please review the Service Agreement, General Terms and Conditions and other information carefully. By accepting this two-year agreement,

goods fully within this article even though the automobile contains many computer programs. On the other hand, an architect's provision of architectural plans on a computer disk would not be a transaction in goods. When a transaction includes both the sale of goods and the transfer of rights in information, it is up to the courts to determine whether the transaction is entirely within or out-side of this article, or whether or to what extent this article should be applied to a portion of the transaction. While this article may apply to a transaction including information, nothing in this Article alters, creates, or diminishes intellectual property rights.

49. One might even apply UCITA by analogy.

you are acknowledging receipt of and your agreement to this information. Thank you for choosing AT&T Wireless.[50]

We believe the buyer who presses "1" is bound.[51]

We lament the death of amended 2–207, for we think it does 2–207's work better than existing 2–207. Of course the drafters of amended 2–207 had the benefit of forty years of cases and knew, far better than Llewellyn, the nature of the section's work. The drafters of amended 2–207 also had knowledge of electronic and other new modes of contracting. We think the invitation of amended 2–207 to the courts to find agreement in the acts and words of the parties might also make for more sensible results than courts can achieve under existing 2–207.

§ 2–5   Firm Offers

In the long history of contract law, courts have allowed many an offeror to withdraw an offer without excuse and with impunity. Under the common law of contracts, it was frequently said "an offeror can always withdraw an offer if no consideration was received for it." But under the Code, 2–205 limits the offeror's privilege to withdraw:

> An offer by a merchant to buy or sell goods in a signed writing which by its terms gives assurance that it will be held open is not revocable, for lack of consideration, during the time stated or if no time is stated for a reasonable time, but in no event may such period of irrevocability exceed three months; but any such term of assurance on a form supplied by the offeree must be separately signed by the offeror.

50. AT&T Wireless, 2–Year Contract Automatic Phone System e-Signature FAQs, available at http://www.attwireless.com (last visited Sept. 26, 2004).

51. However, AT&T was not able to bind buyers of long-distance phone service and its pre-paid phone cards in California with this technique. The phone card package contains nine terms and conditions and states that the purchaser is also bound to the AT&T Consumer Services Agreement available either on their website or by calling their customer service number. The website contained this notice:

If you are a resident of California, please note that a court decision in a class action affects the enforceability of sections 4 and 7 of the Agreement for California customers, and you should review California Customers: Court–Ordered Notice of Class Action Judgment Regarding the AT&T Consumer Services Agreement to view the court-ordered notice in that case and related court rulings.

AT&T, AT&T Consumer Services Agreement, available at http://www.serviceguide.att.com/ACS/ext/index.cfm.

AT&T was sued by a California plaintiff and consumer advocacy group. They claimed that AT&T's limitation of liability and requirement of arbitration to settle any dispute violated California's Consumer Legal Remedies Act. The magistrate judge agreed and the 9th Circuit affirmed. Ting v. AT&T, 319 F.3d 1126 (9th Cir. 2003).

This section only applies if (1) there has actually been an offer (2) by a merchant (3) to buy or sell goods (4) in a signed writing[1] (5) which gives assurance that it will be held open. The period of irrevocability for lack of consideration is not to "exceed three months."[2] The Code does not say whether this period is to be computed from the date an offer is sent or the date it is received.[3] Nor does the Code say how "reasonable time" is to be determined.[4] Section 2–205 closes with the proviso that any firm offer on a form supplied by the offeree must be separately signed by the offeror. The purpose of this proviso is to protect "against entrapment of an offeror by a printed clause on the offeree's form, such as 'All offers are to be irrevocable for 30 days.' "[5]

Section 2–205, then, enables the offeror to make a "gift" of a firm offer. That is, the offeree need not give any consideration. The offeree need not buy an option if the offer satisfies 2–205. Section 2–205 is intended mainly to limit the power of an offeror to withdraw a firm offer when the offeree reasonably relies on the offer's firmness. In a famous pre-Code controversy,[6] a prospective prime contractor secured what it took to be a firm offer from a subcontractor, and the prime contractor used it in computing the overall prime contract bid. This prospective prime contractor won the prime contract and then sought to accept the subcontractor's bid whereupon the subcontractor withdrew. Some pre-Code courts held that the subcontractor can withdraw because an offeror can always withdraw an offer for which he received no consideration.[7] And some courts also held that the doctrine of promissory estoppel is of no avail to the prime, for this doctrine does not apply to the "formation" of contracts.[8] Section 2–205 changes the result in some of these cases. Where 2–205 is applicable and satisfied, a prime contractor's reliance is protected even though promissory estoppel does not apply. And when 2–205's terms are not met, the offeree may still be entitled to invoke 1–103 and fall back on decisions holding that promissory estoppel is applicable.[9] Or the offeree may

---

§ 2–5

1. See § 1–201(37) and § 2–205, Comment 2 (circumstances may justify something less than a formal signature).

2. See § 2–205.

3. See Mid–South Packers, Inc. v. Shoney's, Inc., 761 F.2d 1117, 41 UCC 38 (5th Cir. 1985) (three-month period began when seller tendered a letter containing price proposal).

4. E.g., Lowenstern v. Stop & Shop Cos., 1981 WL 137972, 32 UCC 414 (Mass. Super. 1981) (no reasons given in determining that 15 days is a reasonable amount of time).

5. 1 N.Y.State Law Revision Comm'n, 1955 Report 615 (1955).

6. See Schultz, The Firm Offer Puzzle: A Study of Business Practice in the Construction Industry, 19 U.Chi. L. Rev. 237 (1952).

7. 1 A. Corbin, Contracts §§ 38, 51 (1963).

8. E.g., James Baird Co. v. Gimbel Bros., 64 F.2d 344 (2d Cir. 1933).

9. Janke Constr. Co. v. Vulcan Materials Co., 386 F.Supp. 687, 16 UCC 937 (W.D. Wis. 1974), aff'd, 527 F.2d 772 (7th Cir. 1976) (manufacturer of pipe

be able to invoke the Restatement (Second) of Contracts. It provides that an "offer which the offeror should reasonably expect to induce action or forbearance of a substantial character on the part of the offeree before acceptance and which does induce such action or forbearance is binding as an option contract to the extent necessary to avoid injustice."[10] Where section 2–205 is not met, this should not be taken to prevent offerees from invoking promissory estoppel or Restatement doctrine.[11]

Section 2–205 presupposes that the offeror has made an offer. The Code does not define "offer," and courts must resort to extra-Code contract law via 1–103 to determine whether a party has made an offer. Section 2–205 merely converts a common law offer which otherwise meets 2–205 into a firm offer. As we have seen, to be a firm offer under 2–205, the offer must, among other things, give "assurance that it will be held open." An early case under the section is E.A. Coronis Associates v. M. Gordon Construction Co.[12] The appellate division of the New Jersey Superior Court held that the following language did not give the assurance required for an offer to be firm under 2–205: "We are pleased to offer * * * [goods at quoted prices] * * *. Thank you very much for this opportunity to quote."[13] It is easy enough to imagine an offer that does satisfy the 2–205 "assurance" requirement: "This offer is firm and will remain open for three months."

§ 2–6 Methods of Acceptance

The Code continues the offeror's common law right to specify that one's offer may be accepted only in a given manner. But if the offeror does not so specify, 2–206(1)(a) provides that offers generally invite acceptance "in any manner and by any medium reasonable in the circumstances." The means of communicating an acceptance need not be identical with that of the offer.[1] For example, tele-

liable under promissory estoppel even though his price quotation not firm offer).

10. Restatement (Second) Contracts § 87(2) (1981).

11. See Jenkins & Boller Co. v. Schmidt Iron Works, Inc., 36 Ill.App.3d 1044, 344 N.E.2d 275, 19 UCC 425 (1976) (court used 2–205 and promissory estoppel to hold subcontractor liable).

12. 90 N.J.Super. 69, 216 A.2d 246, 3 UCC 42 (1966).

13. *Id.* at 72, 216 A.2d at 248, 3 UCC at 43. See also Ivey's Plumbing & Electric Co. v. Petrochem Maintenance, Inc., 463 F.Supp. 543, 26 UCC 621 (N.D. Miss. 1978) (wholesaler's bid was revo-

cable since it lacked language indicating it would be held open).

§ 2–6

1. See Murray, Contracts: A New Design for the Agreement Process, 53 Cornell L. Rev. 785, 793 (1968). See e.g., Bio–Tech Pharmacal, Inc. v. International Business Connections, 86 Ark. App. 220, 184 S.W.3d 447, 53 UCC2d 476 (2004) (buyer's purchase orders which might be read to require e-mail or fax acceptance did not clearly require acceptance only by these means; home telephone call was a reasonable mode of acceptance).

graphed offers do not require telegraphed acceptances, unless reason so demands.

An offer may clearly call for acceptance by return promise or clearly call for acceptance by a specified act. When so, then the acceptance must take the specified form.[2] But an offer may also be ambiguous as to whether it calls for one or the other. Some courts have given effect to a "presumption" that such an offer calls for acceptance by return promise.[3] Section 2–206(1)(a) appears to eliminate this presumption and to permit acceptance by return promise, by performance, or by any other means reasonable under the circumstances.[4] Thus, a seller who merely ships ordered goods and so accepts, cuts off the buyer's power to revoke the offer, whereas absent 2–206(1)(a) a court might hold that the buyer has power to revoke until the seller makes a return promissory acceptance.

To form a contract, it is not even necessary under 2–206(1)(b) that the seller's shipment constituting the acceptance be of conforming goods.[5] Of course, the seller breaches if it ships nonconforming goods,[6] unless the shipment of nonconforming goods is an accommodation to the offeror, as allowed under 2–206(1)(b).[7] One authority has it that this novelty is to provide a weapon against the so-called "unilateral contract trick."[8] Under prior law a seller could play this trick by shipping nonconforming goods and, when sued by the buyer, assert "no contract" since the shipment of nonconforming goods was not the act called for by the offer. Under 2–206(1)(b) the seller's defense will fail and the buyer will have a good claim for breach of contract. Of course, not just any shipment of the goods sought will result in a contract. In Quaker State Mushroom Co. v.

2. See Smith v. Boise Kenworth Sales, Inc., 102 Idaho 63, 625 P.2d 417, 31 UCC 444 (1981) (language, "This order only becomes binding when signed" indicated signature was required for acceptance).

3. See, e.g., Davis v. Jacoby, 1 Cal.2d 370, 34 P.2d 1026 (1934).

4. See Joseph Muller Corp. Zurich v. Commonwealth Petrochemicals, Inc., 334 F.Supp. 1013, 10 UCC 1029 (S.D.N.Y. 1971) (seller's shipping propylene held acceptance of buyer's counteroffer); McAfee v. Brewer, 214 Va. 579, 203 S.E.2d 129, 14 UCC 593 (1974) (buyer's letter and enclosed check for agreed price held acceptance); Barto v. United States, 823 F.Supp. 1369, 21 UCC2d 924 (E.D. Mich. 1993) (partial performance by ordering automobile is an acceptance even without dealer's signature); Berger v. Antigone, 39 Va. Cir. 403, 32 UCC2d 413 (1997) (acceptance by delivery of payment checks was rea-

sonable). Cf. Beard Implement Co. v. Krusa, 208 Ill.App.3d 953, 153 Ill.Dec. 387, 567 N.E.2d 345, 15 UCC2d 750 (1991) (without dealer's signature, no acceptance of offer).

5. See, Dubrofsky v. Messer, 1981 Mass.App.Div. 55, 31 UCC 907 (1981) (seller's shipment of conforming and nonconforming pool covers was acceptance and buyer was entitled to accept or reject the delivery in whole or in part).

6. See 1 N.Y.State Law Revision Comm'n, 1955 Report 623 (1955).

7. See, e.g., Corinthian Pharmaceutical Sys., Inc. v. Lederle Labs., 724 F.Supp. 605, 11 UCC2d 463 (S.D. Ind. 1989) (shipment of 50 vials out of 1000 ordered was an accommodation and not an acceptance).

8. W. Hawkland, Sales & Bulk Sales 6–7 (2d ed. 1958).

Dominick's Finer Foods, Inc.,[9] the court held that a seller of mushrooms did not accept the buyer's offer even though he sent mushrooms in response to the buyer's order. The parties were proceeding under different assumptions as to price.

Section 2–206(2) provides that "[w]here the beginning of a requested performance is a reasonable mode of acceptance an offeror who is not notified of acceptance within a reasonable time may treat the offer as having lapsed before acceptance." Presumably this provision suspends the power of the offeror to revoke the offer for a period of time, a power that revives if the performing offeree does not notify the offeror within a reasonable time after the offeree commences performance.[10] Comment 3 to 2–206 suggests that under this section a bilateral contract is formed when the offeree begins performance, but that the offeror's liability thereunder is subject to the condition that the offeree duly notify the offeror of acceptance. However, the text of the section is not confined to bilateral contract possibilities, and it may also apply to explicit offers for acts—"unilateral offers"—and so protect a performing unilateral offeree against arbitrary revocation prior to completion of performance.[11] But it must be borne in mind that Article 2 does not purport to define the core of offer and acceptance doctrine. In Harper Trucks, Inc. v. Allied Welding Supply, Inc., the court said that "under 2–206(1)(b) a purchase order is presumed to be an offer * * * ".[12] This is not the law. The common law of offer and acceptance remains in force under section 1–103, except as displaced.

One federal district court case poses an interesting question concerning the overlap between sections 2–206 and 2–207 on additional terms in the acceptance. In Universal Oil Products Co. v.

---

9. 635 F.Supp. 1281, 1 UCC2d 365 (N.D. Ill. 1986).

10. See Farley v. Clark Equip. Co., 484 S.W.2d 142, 11 UCC 71 (Tex. Civ. App. 1972), error ref'd n.r.e. (assuming arguendo an offer, the court said seller did not give buyer notice of acceptance within reasonable time); Petersen v. Thompson, 264 Or. 516, 506 P.2d 697, 12 UCC 275 (1973) (trial court could have found that buyer delayed too long in communicating acceptance to seller); Nasco, Inc. v. Dahltron Corp., 74 Ill. App.3d 302, 30 Ill.Dec. 242, 392 N.E.2d 1110, 27 UCC 360 (1979) (buyer's knowledge of seller's preparation to deliver goods pursuant to buyer's purchase order sufficient to create binding contract); South Hampton Co. v. Stinnes Corp., 733 F.2d 1108, 38 UCC 1137 (5th Cir. 1984) (where buyer directly asked seller whether it intended to exercise its option to provide additional goods, and seller's response was silence, seller held not to have accepted in manner "reasonable under the circumstances.").

11. Cf. Restatement (Second) of Contracts § 45 (1979). Diskin v. J.P. Stevens & Co., 652 F.Supp. 553, 2 UCC2d 1502 (D. Mass. 1987) (where seller quoted buyer a price for a given amount of goods, and buyer wrote check to seller in that amount, with buyer noting on back of check essential and definite terms, as well as description of goods to be covered, buyer's check was clear, objective manifestation of his intent to contract), rev'd on other grounds, 836 F.2d 47, 5 UCC2d 323 (1st Cir. 1987).

12. 1986 WL 213404, 2 UCC2d 835 (D. Kan. 1986).

S.C.M. Corp.,[13] the seller sent a written offer to the buyer that did not contain a provision for arbitration of any disputes. The buyer responded with a written purchase order that did contain a provision for arbitration. The court treated the buyer's order as a counteroffer, rather than as an acceptance with a proposal for additional terms under 2–207(1) and (2). Since the seller shipped the goods pursuant to the buyer's order, the court found that the seller thereby accepted the counteroffer and became bound to arbitrate. The court purported to rely on that part of 2–206(1)(b) which provides that a seller may accept an order from a buyer for prompt shipment either by prompt shipment or by a prompt promise to ship. Although 2–206(1)(b) is broad enough to cover this case, the court's reliance on it is misplaced. The case involved a "battle of the forms" problem, and the Code drafters formulated 2–207 to deal with that problem.[14] Under 2–207(1), as generally interpreted, the buyer's order would not have been a counteroffer and the buyer's provision for arbitration would be processed via 2–207(2).[15]

On the other hand, where the buyer sends a purchase order, the seller then ships the goods, and thereafter sends a form that arrives after the goods arrive, 2–207 does not control. Rather, 2–206(1)(b) forms the contract in accord with the buyer's terms.[16]

In Hill v. Gateway 2000, Inc.,[17] customers who ordered a computer over the phone using a credit card were bound by a list of terms, including an arbitration clause that customers did not see until the terms arrived with the computer. The court emphasized that the customers had 30 days to return the computer if not satisfied and their failure to do so constituted acceptance by conduct under 2–206. The court also pointed out that customers knew in advance from seller's ads that there were additional terms. Following ProCD, Inc. v. Zeidenberg,[18] the court held that 2–207 was irrelevant because there was only one form. We believe 2–207 applies to these cases.

§ 2–7   Contract Modification, Including Waiver, Estoppel and Course of Performance

The parties to a contract may change their contract by a modifying agreement, by a course of performance or practical

---

13. 313 F.Supp. 905, 7 UCC 813 (D. Conn. 1970).

14. See § 2–207, Comment 1; but see prior drafts of § 2–207, especially the 1952 Official Draft and December 1954 Recommendations of the Editorial Board.

15. See § 2–3 *supra*, and cases cited there.

16. Wheaton Glass Co. v. Pharmex, Inc., 548 F.Supp. 1242, 35 UCC 65 (D.N.J. 1982).

17. 105 F.3d 1147, 31 UCC2d 303 (7th Cir. 1997), cert. denied, 522 U.S. 808, 118 S.Ct. 47, 139 L.Ed.2d 13 (1997).

18. 86 F.3d 1447, 29 UCC2d 1109 (7th Cir. 1996).

construction, or by conduct amounting to waiver or estoppel. Section 2–209 and supplemental general law via 1–103 together define the requirements for modification, waiver, and estoppel. Section 2–208 defines course of performance and practical construction. A court may also use section 2–302 on unconscionability and 1–203 on good faith to police modifying agreements for overreaching, as we will see.

The five subsections of unamended 2–209 provide:

(1) An agreement modifying a contract within this Article needs no consideration to be binding.

(2) A signed agreement which excludes modification or rescission except by a signed writing cannot be otherwise modified or rescinded, but except as between merchants such a requirement on a form supplied by the merchant must be separately signed by the other party.

(3) The requirements of the statute of frauds section of this Article (Section 2–201) must be satisfied if the contract as modified is within its provisions.

(4) Although an attempt at modification or rescission does not satisfy the requirements of subsection (2) or (3) it can operate as a waiver.

(5) A party who has made a waiver affecting an executory portion of the contract may retract the waiver by reasonable notification received by the other party that strict performance will be required of any term waived, unless the retraction would be unjust in view of a material change of position in reliance on the waiver.

The foregoing subsections of 2–209 and the problems with which they deal are of immense practical significance. This is partly because the occasions and pressures for contract changes are numerous and diverse. A contract modifier may be motivated by changed circumstances, unforeseen circumstances, or mere change of mind. And not all contract modifiers are honest. Extortionists, chiselers, and whiners also come to feed at 2–209.[1] As we will see, 2–209 has less to say about the problem of overreaching than about formal requirements for the validity of modifications.

----

§ 2–7

1. See generally, Levie, The Interpretation of Contracts in New York Under the Uniform Commercial Code, 10 N.Y.L.F. 350, 355–61 (1964); Murray, The Modification Mystery: Section 2–209 of the UCC, 32 Vill. L. Rev. 1 (1987); Eisler, Modification of Sales Contracts under the UCC, Section 2–209 Reconsidered, 57 Tenn. L. Rev. 401 (1990).

a. Formal Requirements of Modification

Here we consider the applicable law of consideration and any relevant writing requirements, contractual or statutory. The different ways in which a contract may be changed should be distinguished. In 2–209 an agreement that changes a prior contract is called a modification, and is to be distinguished from waivers of both the "election" and the "estoppel" variety.

There are at least three main types of modifying agreements: (1) explicit ones,[2] (2) conduct in which the other party acquiesces constituting a course of performance at variance with the terms of the contract,[3] and (3) conduct by both parties not constituting a course of performance but which may fairly be construed as a modifying agreement for purposes of 2–209.[4] In some cases the parties may modify inadvertently; it behooves contracting parties to read their mail. In Gateway Co. v. Charlotte Theatres, Inc.[5] the parties reduced their agreement to writing. The buyer then sent the contract back to the seller with a cover letter directing attention to a modifying proposal that the seller install the air conditioners by a given date. Without responding the seller performed, but not by the specified date. The court held that the parties had modified their original contract to require earlier performance, and it warned that contracting parties cannot safely follow Hearst's maxim: "Throw it in the wastebasket—every letter answers itself in a couple of weeks."[6]

Of course, a modifying agreement is one thing, an enforceable modifying agreement another. The Code reduces the formalities for a valid modification: under 2–209(1) consideration is unnecessary.

---

2. See, e.g., In re Brooks Shoe Mfg. Co., Inc., 21 B.R. 604, 34 UCC 539 (Bankr. E.D.Pa. 1982) (buyer's agreement to accept late delivery of shoes created a binding agreement modifying delivery date under the contract).

3. See T.J. Stevenson & Co., Inc. v. 81,193 Bags of Flour, 629 F.2d 338, 30 UCC 865 (5th Cir. 1980) (where contract required notice of breach via registered mail, and buyer notified seller of breach via telex and other informal communications, seller's subsequent responses to buyer's complaints established a course of performance under which contractual notice provision could be disregarded).

4. See, e.g., J.W. Goodliffe & Son v. Odzer, 283 Pa.Super. 148, 423 A.2d 1032, 31 UCC 845 (1980) (seller's attempt at modification, when combined with a course of dealing over a period of more than three years and hundreds of transactions in which buyer paid seller

rental charges not specified in written contract represented a waiver) Aero Consulting Corp. v. Cessna Aircraft Co., 867 F.Supp. 1480, 27 UCC2d 337 (D. Kan. 1994) (no modification by conduct); Weale v. Lund, 162 Vt. 622, 649 A.2d 247, 27 UCC2d 68 (1994) (course of dealing over-rode a handwritten notation); For cases on the relations between 2–207, 2–208 and 2–209, see § 3 supra.

5. 297 F.2d 483 (1st Cir. 1961).

6. But see Weisberg v. Handy & Harman, 747 F.2d 416, 39 UCC 1617 (7th Cir. 1984) (buyer's attempted modification failed where seller's contention that it never received buyer's mailgram was amply supported by the record). See also, Etheridge Oil Co. v. Panciera, 818 F.Supp. 480, 22 UCC2d 82 (D.R.I. 1993) (modification is not binding on third-party guarantor who had no knowledge of the purported modification).

Thus, the parties may modify free of the inflexibility of the so-called preexisting duty rule. According to this common law rule, the beneficiary of a modification must give or promise to give something beyond what one was under a duty to give under the original contract. Otherwise one can not enforce the prospective benefit. Reason and justice do not require this inflexible rule. Often it is neither unreasonable nor unjust to allow a party to benefit from a modification without paying anything further. For example, the parties may modify and set a date for contract performance earlier than in the prior agreement, and this may benefit one party without imposing any burden whatsoever on the other. When so, there is no reason why the beneficiary should have to pay for the change. The same is true with respect to some extensions of time for performance, some changes in place of performance, and many other possible types of modifications. Section 2–209(1) displaces the common law preexisting duty rule, and in effect permits the consideration given to support the original contract to serve also to support the modified contract.[7]

Assuming that a party can establish a modifying agreement, must this party show that it was reduced to writing? Section 2–209(3) states that "[t]he requirements of the statute of frauds section of this Article (2–201) must be satisfied if the contract as modified is within its provisions." The impact of this provision is not clear. We see at least the following possible interpretations: (1) that if the original contract was within 2–201, any modification thereof must also be in writing; (2) that a modification must be in writing if the term it adds brings the entire deal within 2–201 for the first time, as where the price is modified from $400 to $500; (3) that a modification must be in writing if it falls in 2–201 on its own; (4) that the modification must be in writing if it changes the quantity term of an original agreement that fell within 2–201; and (5) some combination of the foregoing. Given the purposes of the basic statute of frauds section 2–201, we believe interpretations (2), (3), and (4) are each justified, subject, of course, to the exceptions in 2–201 itself and to any general supplemental principles of estoppel.[8]

---

7. See Southeastern Enameling Corp. v. General Bronze Corp., 434 F.2d 330, 8 UCC 469 (5th Cir. 1970) (arbitration clause became part of contract); A & G Constr. Co. v. Reid Bros. Logging Co., 547 P.2d 1207, 19 UCC 37 (Alaska 1976) (price increase became part of contract unless buyer could show duress); Farmland Service Coop., Inc. v. Jack, 196 Neb. 263, 242 N.W.2d 624, 19 UCC 445 (1976) (accord and satisfaction enforced); Comerica Bank v. Whitehall Specialties, Inc., 352 F.Supp.2d 1077 55 UCC2d 800 (C.D. Cal. 2004) (forum selection modifier did not require new consideration).

8. Green Constr. Co. v. First Indem. of America Ins. Co., 735 F.Supp. 1254, 12 UCC2d 1034 (D.N.J. 1990), aff'd, 935 F.2d 1281 (3d Cir. 1991) (since both contract and modification are over $500, both must be in writing); Starry Constr. Co. v. Murphy Oil USA, Inc., 785 F.Supp. 1356, 17 UCC2d 353 (D. Minn. 1992), aff'd, 986 F.2d 503 (8th Cir. 1993) (statute of frauds applied to modification of a contract for the sale of asphalt

One court appears to have adopted interpretation (1) above. In ASCO Mining Co. v. Gross Contracting Co.,[9] allegedly the seller orally extended the time for the buyer to pay, and the court flatly stated that this violated 2–209(3).[10] One of us does not concur. The original deal was in writing, which alone was enough to "afford a basis for believing that the offered oral evidence rests on a real transaction."[11] Moreover, the oral change did not relate to the quantity term, the only one required to be in writing under 2–201 itself. Rather, it related to time for payment, which could have been shown through oral proof, if omitted from the original contract. The *Asco* court did recognize that the buyer might still prevail on retrial despite noncompliance with the statute of frauds, provided the buyer could prove an estoppel waiver under 2–209(4) and (5).

The parties can provide in their original agreement that its terms may be modified only in writing.[12] Section 2–209(2) specifically validates such a clause. Observe that such a clause goes far beyond 2–209(3) and 2–201, for these sections only require a writing in certain cases in which the sale involves a price of $500 or more. There are now several cases on the effect of contract clauses requiring that modifications be in writing. In one, the court ignored a stipulation that any modification not only be in writing but also be signed by both parties.[13] In a second, the court indicated that the party benefiting from the clause could (if he acted specifically with reference to it) waive it.[14] In a third the court suggested that a party could be estopped to set up such a clause, even if he did not specifically waive it. In this third case, Knutson Shipbuilding Corp. v. Rogers Construction Corp.,[15] the buyer gave an oral order for

cement oil where contract as modified exceeded $500).

9. 1965 WL 8403, 3 UCC 293 (Pa. C.P. 1965).

10. See also, LNS Inv. Co., Inc. v. Phillips 66 Co., 731 F.Supp. 1484, 12 UCC2d 113 (D. Kan. 1990) (since original contract subject to statute of frauds, any modification must be in writing).

11. § 2–201, Comment 1.

12. Marlowe v. Argentine Naval Comm'n, 808 F.2d 120, 2 UCC2d 1226 (D.C. Cir. 1986) (contract clause excluding modification except by signed writing binding where subsequent written documents did not purport to be modification); Davis v. McDonald's Corp., 44 F.Supp.2d 1251, 39 UCC2d 985 (N.D. Fla. 1998) (valid modification only by writing). Parties should be aware, however, that courts may require "magic words" such as "modification" to be in

the clause to be enforceable. See Monroc, Inc. v. Jack B. Parson Constr. Co., 604 P.2d 901, 28 UCC 18 (Utah 1979) (contract clause providing that "claims for extras positively will not be allowed unless ordered in writing" not enforceable apparently because clause did not expressly mention the word "modification"). Of course, though not a modification, a party's action can constitute a waiver under 2–209(4). See Wireless Distributors, Inc. v. Sprintcom, Inc. 2003 WL 22175607, 51 UCC2d 676 (N.D.Ill. 2003).

13. In re Upchurch's Estate, 62 Tenn.App. 634, 466 S.W.2d 886, 9 UCC 580 (1970).

14. C.I.T. Corp. v. Jonnet, 1965 WL 8370, 3 UCC 321 (Pa. C.P. 1965), aff'd, 419 Pa. 435, 214 A.2d 620, 3 UCC 968 (1965).

15. 1969 WL 11053, 6 UCC 323 (N.Y. Sup.Ct. 1969).

"extras" in the face of a clause seemingly requiring such orders to be in writing. The seller provided the extras and was awarded compensation therefor. Summers thinks this result is consistent with 2–209(4), (5), and 1–103.

Section 2–209(4) states that "[a]lthough an attempt at modification or rescission does not satisfy the requirements of subsection (2) or (3) it can operate as a waiver."[16] Moreover, 2–209(5) provides that the waiving party may not retract a waiver "affecting an executory portion of the contract" if this would be "unjust in view of a material change of position in reliance on the waiver."[17] What "consideration" and "writing" requirements are there with respect to waivers, if any? In our opinion if the elements of an estoppel waiver are present, the relying party should not be prejudiced by failure to give consideration or by the oral nature of the waiver, and we believe sections 2–209(5) and 1–103 accord with our view. But what if the elements of an estoppel are not present? There is pre- and post-Code authority that a party must give consideration in return for the waiver of a substantial right.[18] Section 2–209(1) does not in so many words change this doctrine, for 2–209 dispenses with consideration only in regard to modification agreements, not in regard to waivers. Any possible further requirement that the waiver be in writing could only derive from a contract clause, for 2–209(3) and 2–201 on the Code's statute of frauds do not apply to waivers.

Remember the parties may, as in the Asco case, provide that "no waiver * * * shall bind * * * unless in writing." This clause itself may be waived,[19] but courts should be slow to find waiver of

---

16. Double–E Sportswear Corp. v. Girard Trust Bank, 488 F.2d 292, 13 UCC 577 (3d Cir. 1973) (seller's oral agreement with buyer waived statute of frauds under 2–209(4)); Sonfast Corp. v. York International Corp. 875 F.Supp. 1099, 27 UCC2d 814 (M.D. Pa. 1995) (acquiescence in oral modification waived requirement of a writing); Smyers v. Quartz Works Corp., 880 F.Supp. 1425, 27 UCC2d 142 (D. Kan. 1995) (attempted oral modification operated as waiver). What is required for a waiver is well discussed in BMC Industries, Inc. v. Barth Industries, Inc., 160 F.3d 1322, 37 UCC2d 63 (11th Cir. 1998). See also, Palmer v. Idaho Peterbilt, Inc., 102 Idaho 800, 641 P.2d 346, 33 UCC 827 (App. 1982) (acceptance of a returned deposit did not waive other remedies); United California Bank v. Eastern Mountain Sports Inc., 546 F.Supp. 945, 34 UCC 849 (D. Mass. 1982) (acceptance of credit for defective goods did not waive other remedies), aff'd, 705 F.2d 439 (1st Cir. 1983).

17. See Double–E Sportswear Corp. v. Girard Trust Bank, 488 F.2d 292, 13 UCC 577 (3d Cir. 1973) (whether waiving party gave reasonable notice of retraction a question of fact); Nora Springs Co-op. v. Brandau, 247 N.W.2d 744, 20 UCC 909 (Iowa 1976) (seller's retraction of waiver upheld under 2–209(5)).

18. See, e.g., Rennie & Laughlin, Inc. v. Chrysler Corp., 242 F.2d 208 (9th Cir. 1957).

19. For Code cases dealing with possible waivers, see Indussa Corp. v. Reliable Stainless Steel Supply Co., 369 F.Supp. 976, 14 UCC 709 (E.D. Pa. 1974) (alleged oral agreement not a modification; nothing in parties conduct evinced waiver of "no oral modifications" clause); In PC COM, Inc. v. Proteon, Inc., 946 F.Supp. 1125, 32 UCC2d

anti-waiver provisions. When parties agree in writing that no waiver or modification shall be binding unless in writing, the one seeking a modification should get it in writing.

Section 2–209(4) says that:

Although an attempt at modification or rescission does not satisfy the requirements of subsection (2) [clauses requiring that modifications be in writing are enforceable] or (3) [statute of frauds] it can operate as a waiver.

Does this mean that just any attempt at modification can be construed as a waiver thereby nullifying a clause requiring the modification to be in writing? In Wisconsin Knife Works v. National Metal Crafters,[20] the Seventh Circuit directly confronted this question. The buyer had contracted for the purchase of spade bit blanks to use in its manufacturing process. The buyer and seller agreed that "No modification of this contract, shall be binding upon Buyer unless made in writing and signed by Buyer's authorized representative."[21] The seller failed to deliver the spade bit blanks pursuant to the deadlines specified in the contract and the buyer sued for breach of contract. The seller claimed that the buyer's conduct manifested agreement to the new dates. The court, per Judge Posner, addressed the question whether the seller could nullify the contract term requiring that modifications be in writing by labelling the buyer's conduct allegedly agreeing to new dates as a "waiver" rather than a "modification" (which would have to be in writing). In resolving the tension between 2–209(2) and 2–209(4), Judge Posner held that an attempted modification is effective as a waiver pursuant to 2–209(4) only if there is reliance.

Reliance, if reasonably induced and reasonable in extent, is a common substitute for consideration in making a promise legally enforceable, in part because it adds something in the way of credibility to the mere say-so of one party. The main purpose of forbidding oral modifications is to prevent the promisor from fabricating a modification that will let him escape his obligations under the contract; and the danger of successful fabrication is less if the promisor has actually incurred a cost, has relied. There is of course a danger of bootstrapping—of incurring a cost in order to make the case for a modification. But it is a risky course and is therefore less likely to be attempted than merely testifying to a conversation; it makes one put one's money where one's mouth is.

663 (S.D.N.Y. 1996) the court upheld a clause requiring a waiver be in writing.

20. 781 F.2d 1280, 42 UCC 830 (7th Cir. 1986).

21. 781 F.2d at 1283, 42 UCC at 831. See § 2–209 Comment, para. 2.

Thus, under this approach, if the jury found on remand that the seller had reasonably relied on assurances from the buyer that late delivery would be acceptable, then the attempted modification by conduct could operate as a waiver. If the seller did not incur any reliance costs, then the waiver would be ineffective. The *Wisconsin Knife Works* approach finds support in the wording of 2–209(4). As the court stated, 2–209(4) says that an attempted modification "can operate as a waiver"; it does not say that it "is" a waiver.[22]

b. *Policing Modifications*

Contract modifications and waivers are notorious for the policing problems they generate. While most modifications are legitimate, some are not. A party who asserts a modification may simply be a liar. And if, in fact, no modification or waiver ever occurred, then we may hope that the judge or jury will discover as much. The actuality of a modification or waiver may be conceded, but the aggrieved party may claim nonetheless that he was the victim of bad faith, extortion, chiseling, or the like, and that this conduct renders the modification or waiver invalid and of no legal force or effect. Section 2–209 is itself silent on policing problems, but the comments acknowledge them. And judges can use Code sections 1–203 and 2–302 on bad faith and unconscionability to police those who unjustly demand modifications or waivers.

The extortionist is perhaps most familiar: "Pay me more or I won't finish making the goods and you won't be able to open up your new business on the scheduled date." The seller may thus get the buyer over a barrel and extort a higher price or some other concession. The wrong is aggravated if the extortionist insists on concessions that it sought but did not get in the negotiations leading up to the contract in the first place. Aggravated or not, extorted modifications or waivers are not enforceable under the Code. Courts can hold that they are in bad faith under 1–203 or unconscionable under 2–302, or invalid under the common law of duress via 1–103. Of course, in pre-Code days, courts could use the consideration doctrine to police against extortion:[23] "You gave no new consideration for the concession and you had a preexisting duty to do everything you are to do under the modified arrangement, hence the concession is unenforceable." While 2–209(1) withdraws this weapon, sections 1–203, 2–302, and 1–103 should be

22. *Id*. See also Gold Kist, Inc. v. Pillow, 582 S.W.2d 77, 26 UCC 1078 (Tenn. App. 1979) (parol evidence was barred for the purpose of showing oral modification, but permitted to show waivers); Trad Indus., Ltd. v. Brogan, 246 Mont. 439, 805 P.2d 54, 14 UCC2d 718 (1991) (seller of elk estopped from asserting oral modification not valid because of course of conduct).

23. See generally, Patterson, An Apology for Consideration, 58 Colum. L. Rev. 929, 936–39 (1958).

adequate policing weapons.[24] Moreover, the extortionist can no longer hope to sustain a modification or waiver by giving a new consideration merely technical in character (a "horse, hawk, or robe").[25]

One party may also take unfair advantage of a market shift to exact a price adjustment that will enhance the profit on the contract. Thus when the market price falls significantly below the original contract price, the buyer may say to the seller: "Reduce the price or I will buy elsewhere and you will have to sue me if you want to recoup." Of course, a buyer's behavior is seldom so blatant as this. But blatant or not, courts should not uphold such modifications unless there is some recognized commercial practice that sanctions them in the particular trade. Here, too, courts may resort to 1–203 and 2–302.[26]

The "dishonest compromiser" is one who conjures up a dispute over the meaning of the original contract, not really believing in one's position, but hoping to secure a favorable "compromise settlement."[27] This wrong can take a variety of aggravated forms. For example, the dishonest compromiser may also seek to take advantage of the notorious "conditional check cashing rule" according to which the cashing of a check offered in settlement constitutes acceptance of the proposed settlement. (The check itself may include an inscription on it to that effect.) Courts have sought to police this and still other types of dishonest compromises by insisting that the dispute be "in good faith" and "honest" in origin.[28] Under the Code courts may similarly invoke 1–203.

To state the legal rule is easy; to distinguish justified, tough bargaining from extortion is hard. How may a contracting party rebut a charge of extortion, profiteering, chiseling, or the like? Comment 2 to 2–209 suggests one approach:

24. See A & G Constr. Co. v. Reid Brothers Logging Co., 547 P.2d 1207, 19 UCC 37 (Alaska 1976) (court notes modification would be invalid under 1–203 if duress shown); El Paso Natural Gas Co. v. Minco Oil & Gas Co., 964 S.W.2d 54, 36 UCC2d 313 (Tex. App. 1997) (bad faith modification induced by wrongfully ceasing performance).

25. Pinnel's Case, 5 Coke's Reps. 117, 77 Eng.Rep. 237 (C.P.1602). See also Ralston Purina Co. v. McNabb, 381 F.Supp. 181, 15 UCC 390 (W.D. Tenn. 1974) (buyer's attempts at modification in bad faith in light of market conditions). But see, Weisberg v. Handy & Harman, 747 F.2d 416, 39 UCC 1617 (7th Cir. 1984) (attempt to modify price

term after precipitous change in market conditions does not indicate bad faith).

26. Levie, The Interpretation of Contracts in New York Under the Uniform Commercial Code, 10 N.Y.L.F. 350, 357 (1964).

27. But see the facts of Ruble Forest Products, Inc. v. Lancer Mobile Homes, Inc., 269 Or. 315, 524 P.2d 1204, 15 UCC 35 (1974) (buyer's claim of defect resulting in compromise, held in good faith).

28. See, e.g., De Mars v. Musser–Sauntry Land, Logging & Mfg. Co., 37 Minn. 418, 35 N.W. 1 (1887); Berger v. Lane, 190 Cal. 443, 213 P. 45 (1923). On the check cashing problem, see further § 1–207; § 3–311 of Revised Article 3.

Subsection (1) provides that an agreement modifying a sales contract needs no consideration to be binding.

However, modifications made thereunder must meet the test of good faith imposed by this Act. The effective use of bad faith to escape performance on the original contract terms is barred, and the extortion of a "modification" without legitimate commercial reason is ineffective as a violation of the duty of good faith. Nor can a mere technical consideration support a modification made in bad faith.

The test of "good faith" between merchants or as against merchants includes "observance of reasonable commercial standards of fair dealing in the trade" (Section 2–103), and may in some situations require an objectively demonstrable reason for seeking a modification. But such matters as a market shift which makes performance come to involve a loss may provide such a reason even though there is no such unforeseen difficulty as would make out a legal excuse from performance under Sections 2–615 and 2–616.

The facts of Skinner v. Tober Foreign Motors, Inc.,[29] illustrate one kind of modification or waiver that will stand up under the Code. The buyers of an airplane expected to pay for it out of earnings from its use, a fact known to the seller. The engine developed difficulties not covered by the seller's warranty. The buyers told the seller they could not afford both to keep up on their monthly payments to the seller and make the repairs. The buyers even offered to return the plane in exchange for a release from any further obligations. Instead, the seller proposed a reduction in payments with an extension of the payment period, and the buyers agreed. Later the court refused to let the seller disaffirm this modification. Although the buyers gave no new consideration for the modification, they did not overreach. The buyers also had a good business reason for modification, and both sides may have benefitted—a Pareto outcome superior to default?

The case of Roth Steel Products v. Sharon Steel Corp.[30] suggests that the party seeking to uphold a modification must demonstrate two things.[31] First, he must show that a modification was consistent with commercial standards of fair dealing in the trade. To do this the would-be modifier must demonstrate that he was motivated by factors that would motivate an ordinary merchant in the trade to seek a similar modification. Second, the modifier must

---

29. 345 Mass. 429, 187 N.E.2d 669, 1 UCC 1 (1963).

30. 705 F.2d 134, 35 UCC 1435 (6th Cir. 1983).

31. 705 F.2d 134 at 145–46, 35 UCC at 1451.

have a legitimate commercial reason for seeking the modification.[32] The *Skinner* and *Roth* opinions, as well as others like them may help courts sort out modifications that are honest and just from others. There will be plenty of hard cases here; many of these depend on *a priori* moral judgments about what is fair and what is not.

c. Course of Performance

Section 2–208 provides as follows:

(1) Where the contract for sale involves repeated occasions for performance by either party with knowledge of the nature of the performance and opportunity for objection to it by the other, any course of performance accepted or acquiesced in without objection shall be relevant to determine the meaning of the agreement.

(2) The express terms of the agreement and any such course of performance, as well as any course of dealing and usage of trade, shall be construed whenever reasonable as consistent with each other; but when such construction is unreasonable, express terms shall control course of performance and course of performance shall control both course of dealing and usage of trade (Section 1–205).

(3) Subject to the provisions of the next section on modification and waiver, such course of performance shall be relevant to show a waiver or modification of any term inconsistent with such course of performance.

This section not only can operate to fill gaps in agreements or to interpret agreements (topics treated in Chapter 3). It can also modify or waive the express terms of an agreement. It is true that 2–208(2) provides that "The express terms of the agreement and any such course of performance * * * shall be construed whenever reasonable as consistent with each other; but when such construction is unreasonable, express terms shall control course of performance * * * ". This language might be read to suggest that course of performance can never modify or waive the express terms of the agreement. Certainly there can be clear cases where the express term is X, the course of performance Y, and it would be unreasonable to construe the two as consistent with each other. Here, the applicable general rule of 2–208 (set forth in 2–208(2)) is that the express term controls.[33] But 2–208(3) provides an exception to this

---

32. See also, American Exploration Co. v. Columbia Gas Transmission Corp., 779 F.2d 310, 42 UCC 1218 (6th Cir. 1985) (changed market condition provided a contractually-based justification for seeking modification).

33. Blalock Machinery & Equip. Co. v. Iowa Mfg. Co., 576 F.Supp. 774, 36 UCC 753 (N.D. Ga. 1983) (express term

general rule: "such course of performance shall be relevant to show a waiver or modification of any term inconsistent with such course of performance." As we have already seen, both waiver and modification are defined outside of section 2–208.[34] But if, in light of a "relevant" course of performance, either a waiver or a modification (so defined) is thus shown, courts sometimes say that course of performance "controls" and thus alters the express term.[35] Of course, many cases will remain subject to the general rule of 2–208(2) and not fall into the exception provided in 2–208(3). Fearing that courts may be too quick to use one party's behavior to save another from the burden of its negotiated deal, we think resort to 2–208(3) should be rare.

More fundamentally, course of performance is relevant under section 2–208(1) to determine the "meaning of the agreement" in the first place. When the section is so used, the apparent inconsistency between an express term and course of performance can melt away. After all, the very theory of course of performance, according to Comment 1, is that "[t]he parties themselves know best what they have meant by their words of agreement and their action under that agreement is the best indication of what that meaning was." When course of performance thus "controls," despite a seemingly inconsistent express term, the express term is not modified or waived. Since it is not possible to draw a sharp line between course of performance that determines the original meaning of an express contract term under 2–208(1) and course of performance that shows a waiver or modification of an express term under 2–208(3), any consideration of the general ways an agreement may be

controls under 2–208(2); requirements of 2–208(3) exception not met).

34. For a valid modifying agreement, § 2–209(1) requires only that there be an "agreement," not that there be consideration. Agreement is defined in 1–201(3). Comment 2 says a modifying agreement must also "meet the test of good faith imposed by this act." The Code does not define the requirements of a valid waiver. See 1–103. However, subsection 2–209(4) and (5) apply to waivers.

35. In a number of cases, the courts have, in effect, found course of performance relevant to waiver or modification under 2–208(3). Flood v. M.P. Clark, Inc., 319 F.Supp. 1043, 8 UCC 836 (E.D. Pa. 1970), motion denied, 335 F.Supp. 970, 9 UCC 1226 (E.D. Pa. 1971) (express term as to time of payment waived by course of performance); Farmers State Bank v. Farmland Foods, Inc., 225 Neb. 1, 402 N.W.2d 277, 3 UCC2d 902 (1987) (continued failure of secured party to object to debtor's conduct in violation of contract may amount to a waiver); Mulberry–Fairplains Water Ass'n, Inc. v. Town of North Wilkesboro, 105 N.C.App. 258, 412 S.E.2d 910, 17 UCC2d 48 (1992) (seller estopped from enforcing clause on maximum quantity after 15 years course of performance of supplying excess amounts); Wagner Excello Foods, Inc. v. Fearn Int'l, Inc., 235 Ill.App.3d 224, 176 Ill.Dec. 258, 601 N.E.2d 956, 20 UCC2d 1221 (1992) (minimum purchase requirement of concentrated juice waived by course of performance); In re McClamrock, 51 UCC2d 683 (Bankr. M.D.N.C. 2003) (high car payment waived by course of performance).

altered could not be complete without taking into account 2–208(1).[36]

There is a growing body of case law on what constitutes "course of performance" under 2–208. The section applies only when there are "repeated occasions for performance", not merely a single instance.[37] The other party must have "knowledge of the nature of the performance and opportunity for objection to it." When, for example, the other party is mistaken, the section does not apply.[38] The other party must accept, or acquiesce in the tendered performance.[39] If objection is made, it must be timely.[40]

Even when the evidence would show a course of performance as defined by 2–208(1) and applicable case law, a court may still bar the evidence by invoking a version of the plain meaning rule.[41] Arguably "plain meaning" cannot coexist with section 2–208. We suspect there are some cases when the court cannot stomach the aggrieved party's claims in the face of the words of the contract.[42]

The definition and effect that the Code drafters gave course of performance is not identical in some important respects with its common law counterpart, often called the doctrine of "practical construction".[43] Doubtless some courts will interpret 2–208 against this common law background, which is rich in some states.[44]

Most of the states adopting Revised Article 1, which includes course of performance in section 1–303, simply repealed section 2–208 on course of performance in Unamended Article 2. A few states kept 2–208 as it was.

36. Among the so-called "interpretation" cases under 2–208(1), see Blue Rock Indus. v. Raymond Int'l, Inc., 325 A.2d 66, 15 UCC 328 (Me. 1974) (meaning of "truck measure"); National Heater Co., Inc. v. Corrigan Co. Mechanical Contractors, 482 F.2d 87, 13 UCC 78 (8th Cir. 1973) (meaning of delivery terms); Lancaster Glass Corp. v. Philips ECG, Inc., 835 F.2d 652, 5 UCC2d 1306 (6th Cir. 1987) (measurements of light bulbs); Computer Network, Ltd. v. Purcell Tire & Rubber Co., 747 S.W.2d 669, 6 UCC2d 642 (Mo. App. 1988) (quantity of computers purchased).

37. See Comment 4 to 2–208. See Wilson v. Marquette Electronics, Inc., 630 F.2d 575, 29 UCC 399 (8th Cir. 1980). See also cases cited in n.37.

38. Kern Oil & Refining Co. v. Tenneco Oil Co., 792 F.2d 1380, 1 UCC2d 651 (9th Cir. 1986), cert. denied, 480 U.S. 906, 107 S.Ct. 1349, 94 L.Ed.2d 520 (1987) (mistake vitiates course of performance).

39. In re Rose Stone & Concrete, Inc. v. Broome County, 76 A.D.2d 998,

429 N.Y.S.2d 295, 29 UCC 43 (1980) (express nonacquiescence); Pennsylvania Tire Co., 26 B.R. 663, 37 UCC 410 (Bankr. N.D. Ohio 1982) (neither acceptance nor acquiescence).

40. Oskey Gasoline & Oil Co. Inc. v. OKC Refining Inc., 364 F.Supp. 1137, 13 UCC 767 (D. Minn. 1973).

41. Lemnah v. American Breeders Service, Inc., 144 Vt. 568, 482 A.2d 700, 38 UCC 1558 (1984) (contract term "unambiguous"); Island Creek Coal Co. v. Lake Shore, Inc., 636 F.Supp. 285, 2 UCC2d 59 (W.D. Va. 1986), aff'd in part, rev'd in part, 832 F.2d 274 (4th Cir. 1987) (unambiguous).

42. For a case that takes the appropriate general approach here, see Westinghouse Credit Corp. v. Shelton, 645 F.2d 869, 31 UCC 410 (10th Cir. 1981). See also, Blue Rock Indus. v. Raymond Int'l, Inc., 325 A.2d 66, 15 UCC 328 (Me. 1974).

43. See generally, Corbin on Contracts § 558.

44. New York is such a jurisdiction.

Chapter 3

STATUTE OF FRAUDS AND PAROL EVIDENCE RULE

Analysis

§ 3–1 Introduction

The year: 1676. The place: Old Marston, Oxfordshire, England. Egbert, a Marstonian, owned a fighting cock named Fiste. John sued Egbert, alleging that Egbert had orally promised to sell Fiste to him in exchange for a hundred shillings, a "deal" which John's friend, Harold, claimed he overheard. Egbert denied all this. At the end of the lawsuit John prevailed, though in truth the deal between John and Egbert never took place. But the court did not permit Egbert to testify, even to rebut the testimony of Harold, John's friend. In 1676 courts did not permit parties to a lawsuit to testify. Moreover, courts in that day had no power to throw out jury verdicts manifestly contrary to the evidence.[1] Egbert's case and

§ 3–1
1. Willis, The Statute of Frauds—A Legal Anachronism, 3 Ind. L.J. 427, 429–32 (1928).

others (real and imagined) offended the Goddess of Justice. What to do? The next year (1677), Parliament passed a famous "statute of frauds" which required that certain contracts for the sale of goods be in writing to be enforceable. All this to combat "fraude and perjurie."[2]

In Colonial America and after, state legislatures and courts followed suit. In the Twentieth Century, section four of the Uniform Sales Act became law in most states.[3] Yet the law also eventually permitted parties to lawsuits to testify on their own behalf, both in England and in America. Further, both in England and America the law eventually gave courts certain power to deal with unreasonable jury verdicts. And in 1954 the British Parliament repealed its 1877 statute of frauds for the sale of goods.[4] However, those state-side law professors who, in the 1940's and 1950's, evolved the Uniform Commercial Code did not follow suit. They kept the spirit of '77 alive in section 2–201 of the Code. Section 2–201(1) provides that "a contract for the sale of goods for the price of $500 or more is not enforceable by way of action or defense unless there is some writing sufficient to indicate that a contract for sale has been made."[5] The Code drafters kept this writing requirement largely because they saw it as a means to the end of combatting perjured testimony in contract cases.

The soundness of this basic means-end hypothesis was questioned in England early on.[6] And when English law abandoned the rules of evidence precluding "party" testimony and developed rules for judicial control of unreasonable jury verdicts, part of the original rationale for the statute of frauds for goods faded. Yet the statute remained until 1954 in England, and it is still much alive in the United States today. Tons of pre-Code and post-Code case law testify to the significance of this whole topic for lawyers.

Though the statute of frauds is still much alive in the United States today, its writing requirement has been displaced in one major realm, that of electronic transactions. In section 3–9, we will treat in general terms a new Uniform Act called the "Uniform Electronic Transactions Act" known as the "UETA", and will also briefly treat a federal statute called "E–Sign". The purpose of the

---

2. This entire history is reiterated in Thomson Printing Machinery Co. v. B.F. Goodrich Co., 714 F.2d 744, 36 UCC 737 (7th Cir.1983). See generally, Costigan, The Date and Authorship of the Statute of Frauds, 26 Harv.L.Rev. 329 (1913); Henning, The Original Drafts of the Statute of Frauds and Their Authors, 61 U.Pa.L.Rev. 283 (1913); Stephen & Pollack, Section Seventeen of the Statute of Frauds, 1 L.Q.Rev. 1 (1885).

3. Uniform Sales Act § 4.

4. Grunfeld, Law Reform (Enforcement of Contracts) Act, 1954, 17 Mod. L.Rev. 451 (1954).

5. When 2–201 is applicable, most courts hold that the more general common law Statute of Frauds is inapplicable. Rajala v. Allied Corp., 66 B.R. 582, 2 UCC2d 1203 (D.Kan.1986).

6. Child v. Godolphin, 1 Dick. 39, 21 Eng.Rep. 181 (1723).

UETA is to remove barriers to electronic commerce by validating and effectuating electronic records and signatures. E–Sign is similar in function to UETA. Thus, except for electronic commerce, the Article 2 statute of frauds (sec. 2–201) remains intact.

§ 3–2   Transactions to Which Statute Applies; Other UCC Statutes of Frauds

Section 2–201 does not apply to the sale of realty. It does not apply to construction contracts.[1] It does not apply to the rendering of services for a price.[2] It does not apply to the sale of corporate stocks and bonds or to choses in action generally.[3] It does not apply to contracts of employment, commission, or brokerage even when these look to the sale of goods.[4] It does not apply to investments[5] or to options. Nor does the section by its terms apply to leases (or the like) of personalty. Rather the section applies to a "contract for the sale of goods for the price of $500 or more." Section 2–106(1) defines a "sale" as "the passing of title from the seller to the buyer for a price," and 2–105(1) defines "goods" generally to mean "all things which are movable at the time of identification to the contract for sale." When a transaction includes both the sale of goods and the transfer of rights in information, it is up to the courts to determine whether the transaction is entirely within or without of Article 2, or whether or to what extent Article 2 should be applied to a portion of the transaction.

It is easy to imagine clear cases to which section 2–201 applies. But as with any legal language, borderline cases arise. When does property cease to be realty and become goods for purposes of 2–201? Consider a contract for the sale of a building to be removed from the land, or for the sale of minerals to be extracted. Section 2–107(1) makes it clear that these are all "contracts for the sale of goods" "if they are to be severed by the seller." Section 2–107(2)

§ 3–2

1. Arango Constr. Co. v. Success Roofing, Inc., 46 Wash.App. 314, 730 P.2d 720, 3 UCC2d 20 (1986).

2. National Historic Shrines Foundation, Inc. v. Dali, 1967 WL 8937, 4 UCC 71 (N.Y.Sup.1967), (contract to paint picture); Computer Servicenters, Inc. v. Beacon Mfg. Co., 328 F.Supp. 653, 9 UCC 851 (D.S.C.1970), aff'd, 443 F.2d 906 (4th Cir.1971) (computer services); Mallin v. University of Miami, 354 So.2d 1227, 23 UCC 864 (Fla.App.1978) (contract to publish book); Zayre Corp. v. S.M. & R. Co., 882 F.2d 1145, 9 UCC2d 465 (7th Cir.1989) (contract to design, buy, and sell jewelry at markup was primarily sale of goods).

3. See § 8–319 and § 1–206.

4. See, e.g., Stone v. Krylon, Inc., 141 F.Supp. 785 (E.D.Pa.1956); Brown v. Lee, 242 Ark. 122, 412 S.W.2d 273 (1967); Hanson Sales v. VSA, Inc., 619 N.W.2d 307, 239 Wis.2d 232, 43 UCC2d 270 (2000) (holding that an agreement to broker snack products is not a contract for the sale of goods and does not implicate the UCC because the broker did not purchase any goods—all sales were between the snack maker and the end customers).

5. Markarian v. Garoogian, 771 F.Supp. 939, 16 UCC2d 1001 (N.D.Ill. 1991) (investment in cold fusion invention without transfer or sale of invention itself).

also explicitly treats contracts for the sale of growing crops as contracts for the sale of goods. The 1972 Amendment to this section treats timber to be cut in the same way.

But experience affords many examples of borderline cases to which the Code's scope provisions do not explicitly apply. For example, when two parties bargain for several items each at a price lower than $500, but when taken together exceed $500, is there one sale to which the statute applies or several sales to which the statute does not apply?[6] When one party orally agrees to sell its business to another, including an inventory of goods as well as a franchise, goodwill and the like, does the statute apply?[7] When the arrangement is a distributorship does the statute apply?[8]

When a party transfers both goods and services in the same transaction, does the statute apply?[9]

Many courts have tended to narrow the scope of pre-Code versions of the statute by refusing to apply it in borderline cases.[10] This practice is certainly understandable if the special needs for a statute of frauds back in 1677 no longer apply today, if the very idea of the statute rests on a faulty hypothesis, and if there are still other objections to the statute.[11] Also, if all these things are true, perhaps it follows *a fortiori* that courts should not extend 2–201 by analogy.[12] Rational extension by analogy requires not merely that the reason behind a rule "extend" to a new situation but also that the quality of that reason be sound.[13] Where a rule rests on a reason

---

6. 2 A. Corbin, Contracts § 475 (1950) and cases cited therein.

7. Cf. Foster v. Colorado Radio Corp., 381 F.2d 222, 4 UCC 446 (10th Cir.1967); Crooks v. Chapman Co., 124 Ga.App. 718, 185 S.E.2d 787, 10 UCC 336 (1971) (not within statute); Wikler v. Mar–Van Indus., Inc., 39 Pa.D. & C.3d 136, 2 UCC2d 1190 (1984) (within statute).

8. The courts are not in agreement on this question. See e.g., Babst v. FMC Corp., 661 F.Supp. 82, 4 UCC2d 680 (S.D.Miss.1986) (yes); Webcor Electronics, Inc. v. Home Electronics, Inc., 231 Mont. 377, 754 P.2d 491, 7 UCC2d 683 (1988) (no); Beehive Brick Co. v. Robinson Brick Co., 780 P.2d 827, 11 UCC2d 803 (Utah App.1989) (no); United Beer Distrib. Co. v. Hiram Walker (N.Y.) Inc., 163 A.D.2d 79, 557 N.Y.S.2d 336, 12 UCC2d 38 (1990) (yes).

9. 2 A. Corbin, Contracts § 476 (1950); Robertson v. Ceola, 255 Ark. 703, 501 S.W.2d 764, 13 UCC 753 (1973)

(sale and installation of construction materials not within statute).

10. See Corbin, The Uniform Commercial Code—Sales; Should It Be Enacted?, 59 Yale L.J. 821, 832–33 (1950).

11. For further discussion of these "ifs," see §§ 3–7 and 3–8 *infra*.

12. The Official Comments to § 1–103 carry forward the spirit of unrevised § 1–102, Comment 1:

Courts * * * have recognized the policies embodied in an act as applicable in reason to subject-matter which was not expressly included in the language of the act * * *. They have done the same where reason and policy so required, even where the subject-matter had been intentionally excluded from the act in general.

13. Traynor, Statutes Revolving in Common–Law Orbits, 17 Catholic U.L.Rev. 401 (1968); Note, The Uniform Commercial Code as a Premise for Judicial Reasoning, 65 Colum. L.Rev. 880 (1965).

that is itself questionable, the case for extension is weaker. This is all the more true of a statute long under fire.

An earlier version included a writing requirement for certain sales of "personal property." The Code also includes a specific writing requirement for sale or return deals,[14] for sales of securities[15] and for most security agreements.[16] And 5–104(1) and (2) incorporated a kind of statute of frauds requirement for certain credits or letters of credit.

Finally, 2–201(1) applies not only to oral agreements that fall within its provisions in the first instance. It applies as well to future oral modifications of such contracts.[17] Section 2–209(3) states explicitly that "[t]he requirements of the statute of frauds * * * must be satisfied if the contract as modified is within its provisions."[18] Section 2–209(4) takes some of the bite out of 2–209(3), for it permits a noncomplying oral modification to "operate as a waiver."[19] Can such a modification operate to waive not only a contract term but the very requirement of a writing itself? One court has answered affirmatively.[20]

14. § 2–326. Consolidated Foods Corp. v. Roland Foods, Inc., 1973 WL 21362, 13 UCC 245 (D.C.Super.1973) (oral "or return" clause invalid). Estate of Purnell v. LH Radiologists, 90 N.Y.2d 524, 664 N.Y.S.2d 238, 686 N.E.2d 1332, 34 UCC2d 1115 (1997) (holding that 8–319 does not apply to a certificate of incorporation, even where that certificate authorizes the issuance of shares).

15. § 8–319.

16. § 9–203.

17. McCollum Aviation, Inc. v. CIM Assoc., Inc., 446 F.Supp. 511, 26 UCC 1072 (S.D.Fla.1978) (written option to purchase airplane could not be altered by oral modification extending time to exercise option); Community Bank v. Newmark & Lewis, Inc., 534 F.Supp. 456, 33 UCC 1232 (E.D.N.Y.1982) (when written sales invoice intended to be final expression of agreement, buyer precluded from introducing contradictory evidence of oral terms); Cooley v. Big Horn Harvestore Systems, Inc., 767 P.2d 740, 7 UCC2d 1051 (Colo.App.1988), aff'd in part, rev'd in part, 813 P.2d 736 (Colo. 1991) (modification of contract for sale of goods for more than $500 must be in writing and signed); Green Constr. Co. v. First Indem. of America Ins. Co., 735 F.Supp. 1254, 12 UCC2d 1034 (D.N.J. 1990) (attempted oral modification ineffective).

18. June G. Ashton Interiors v. Stark Carpet Corp., 142 Ill.App.3d 100, 96 Ill.Dec. 306, 491 N.E.2d 120, 2 UCC2d 74 (1986) (letter from seller satisfied statute of frauds requirement for modification); Wixon Jewelers, Inc. v. Di–Star, Ltd., 218 F.3d 913, 42 UCC2d 94 (8th Cir. 2000) (seller's attempted modifications, which failed for lack of a writing, did not constitute a breach where buyer's prior breach led seller to attempt to modify the contract by bringing in additional buyers).

19. Cf. C.I.T. Corp. v. Jonnet, 419 Pa. 435, 214 A.2d 620, 3 UCC 968 (1965); South Hampton Co. v. Stinnes Corp., 733 F.2d 1108, 38 UCC 1137 (5th Cir.1984) (modification may operate as waiver under 2–209(4), but no-oral-modification clause in contract precluded this). But see, Monroc, Inc. v. Jack B. Parson Constr. Co., 604 P.2d 901, 28 UCC 18 (Utah 1979) (evidence was inconsistent with buyer's claim that parties intended any modification to be effected only by a writing signed by buyer, 2–201, rather than 2–209 governed the modified agreement).

20. Double–E Sportswear Corp. v. Girard Trust Bank, 488 F.2d 292, 13 UCC 577 (3d Cir.1973).

§ 3–3   General Structure of Statute; Consequences of Compliance and Noncompliance

The entire text of 2–201 is set forth below:[1]

(1) Except as otherwise provided in this section a contract for the sale of goods for the price of $500 or more is not enforceable by way of action or defense unless there is some writing sufficient to indicate that a contract for sale has been made between the parties and signed by the party against whom enforcement is sought or by his authorized agent or broker. A writing is not insufficient because it omits or incorrectly states a term agreed upon but the contract is not enforceable under this subsection beyond the quantity of goods shown in the writing.

(2) Between merchants if within a reasonable time a writing in confirmation of the contract and sufficient against the sender is received and the party receiving it has reason to know its contents, it satisfies the requirements of subsection (1) against such party unless written notice of objection to its contents is given in a writing within 10 days after it is received.

(3) A contract which does not satisfy the requirements of subsection (1) but which is valid in other respects is enforceable

(a) if the goods are to be specially manufactured for the buyer and are not suitable for sale to others in the ordinary course of the seller's business and the seller, before notice of repudiation is received and under circumstances which reasonably indicate that the goods are for the buyer, has made either a substantial beginning of their manufacture or commitments for their procurement; or

(b) if the party against which enforcement is sought admits in the party's pleading, or in the party's testimony or otherwise in court that a contract for sale was made, but the contract is not enforceable under this provision beyond the quantity of goods admitted; or

(c) with respect to goods for which payment has been made and accepted or which have been received and accepted (Sec. 2–606).

The general rule is set forth in subsection (1) and requires that there be "some writing sufficient to indicate that a contract for sale has been made between the parties and signed by the party against which enforcement is sought." There are both statutory and nonstatutory exceptions to the foregoing general rule. The first statuto-

§ 3–3
1.   § 2–201.

ry exception is not a full-fledged one, for it merely ameliorates the writing requirement. A writing is still required, but it need not be signed by the party to be charged. The character of this exception is best understood in light of the form of fraud it was designed to combat. Assume that Orval Orfed and Len Lemhi orally agree over the telephone that Orfed will sell Lemhi 1000 bushels of wheat at $4.00 a bushel. Orfed, the seller, thereafter sends a signed confirmatory memorandum to Lemhi reciting the terms of the deal, a common practice in such transactions. That memo would be good against Orfed under 2–201 should Orfed back out and Lemhi sue him for damages. But absent 2–201(2), the confirmatory memo would not be good against Lemhi, for it is not signed by him as required by 2–201(1). Thus Lemhi would be free to sit back and "play the market." If at delivery date the cost of wheat had fallen to some level below $4.00 a bushel, and he wanted to buy elsewhere, he could back out, whereas Orfed could not back out, at least so far as the statute of frauds goes, should the market rise. Section 2–201(2) is designed to prevent the Lemhis of the world from taking advantage of the Orfeds. It says that a writing good against Orfed will also be good against Lemhi provided that (1) both are merchants,[2] (2) the writing is sent by Orfed to Lemhi within a reasonable time (after the phone call), (3) the writing by its terms "confirms" the oral contract, (4) the writing is good against Orfed under 2–201(1), (5) Lemhi receives it, (6) Lemhi has "reason to know its contents," and (7) Lemhi does not object to its contents within ten days of receipt.[3] This carefully circumscribed section thus seeks to combat one form of fraud which pre-Code versions of the statute of frauds actually facilitate. At the same time 2–201(2) itself encourages the common and wise business practice of sending writings in confirmation of oral deals, for the section obviates a disadvantage to which the sender would otherwise be subject.

Some courts have erroneously held that failure to object to a signed confirmatory memorandum renders its terms binding rather than merely removes the bar of the statute. Even when the confirmation also falls under 2–207(1) and thus operates as an acceptance, it does not follow that all terms thereon are binding. "Different" terms are not. And under 2–207(2) certain "additional" terms may not be.

---

2. § 2–104. See, e.g., Cook Grains, Inc. v. Fallis, 239 Ark. 962, 395 S.W.2d 555, 2 UCC 1141 (1965); Louis Price Paper Co. v. Federation Employment & Guidance Svc., Inc., 1994 WL 116649, 23 UCC2d 43 (Sup.Ct., N.Y. County, N.Y. 1994) (social service provider not a merchant).

3. See, e.g., Simmons Oil Corp. v. Bulk Sales Corp., 498 F.Supp. 457, 31 UCC 1236 (D.N.J.1980) (telex proposing substitution of more acceptable payment clause insufficient objection).

The second statutory exception to the writing requirement of 2–201(1) is more full-fledged. Section 2–201(3)(a) dispenses with a writing in certain cases where the seller significantly relies on an oral contract specially to manufacture goods for the buyer.

The third exception is embodied in 2–201(3)(b) and provides that an oral contract falling in 2–201(1) becomes enforceable against a party if that party admits in the party's pleading, or in the party's testimony or otherwise under oath that a contract for sale was made. The fourth statutory exception appears in 2–201(3)(c) and provides for enforceability "with respect to goods for which payment has been made and accepted or which have been received and accepted." To say that an oral contract is "enforceable" because it falls into one of the foregoing four statutory exceptions is not the same as to say that it is enforceable to the full extent of the entire terms of the actual oral contract.

If past case law is any indicator, the foregoing four statutory exceptions are not the whole story. At the time of the Code's general reception, courts had carved out other exceptions to the writing requirements of pre-Code statutes of frauds.[4] According to some courts, a party cannot invoke the statute actually to perpetrate a fraud, nor can a party invoke the statute if the elements of an equitable estoppel can be shown against him. Many of these exceptions survived enactment of the Code. Section 1–103 explicitly incorporated "supplemental general principles" on fraud and estoppel (but not where the Code itself spoke—as it did in the exceptions in 2–201(c)), and 1–203 (now 1–304) stated that "[e]very contract or duty within this Act imposes an obligation of good faith in its performance or enforcement."[5] Even so, lawyers accustomed to relying on case law under pre-Code statutes of frauds should be wary, for 2–201 makes many changes in the pre-Code statutory law.[6] Cases good under pre-Code statutes of frauds do not automatically remain good law under the Code version. Also, we will consider further changes here.

So much for the general rule of 2–201 and its various exceptions, statutory and nonstatutory. In sections 3–4, 3–5, and 3–6 of this Chapter, we explore the rule and its exceptions more fully. In section 3–9 below, we also explain how Article 2's so called "writing" requirements have also been modified by UETA and E-sign.

---

4. See, e.g., L. Vold, Law of Sales 90–93 (2d ed.1959) and cases cited therein.

5. Summers, "Good Faith" in General Contract Law and the Sales Provisions of the Uniform Commercial Code, 54 Va.L.Rev. 195 (1968).

6. Section 85, subd. 1(a) of the New York Personal Property Law was replaced by § 2–201 of the Uniform Commercial Code which amended, but did not change the substance of the law.

General Consequences of Compliance and Noncompliance

A plaintiff who wants to enforce an alleged oral contract and who has a writing satisfying 2–201(1) does not necessarily have much to write home about. A complying writing is not boon in the way a noncomplying writing is bane. Absent applicable exceptions, the plaintiff simply loses if he or she has only a noncomplying writing. But a complying writing is not equivalent to victory.[7] Of course, a complying writing might be a complete embodiment of the deal, be duly signed by both parties, and be attested by forty Bishops. If the writing is of this variety, then it is indeed boon, for a court will decide upon the existence and the terms of the alleged oral agreement merely by looking to the complying writing itself. But most statute of frauds cases are not of this kind; in most, the writing is either nonexistent or sketchy. And whether sketchy or not, the theory is that a complying writing itself is not conclusive proof of the existence of the oral contract, let alone of its terms. Beyond producing a writing "sufficient to indicate that a contract for sale has been made between the parties," the plaintiff must still persuade the trier of fact that the parties did make an oral contract and that its terms were thus and so.[8] By parity of analysis, a defendant who unsuccessfully pleads the defense of the statute of frauds may still "defend on the facts" and prevail, that is, he or she may still persuade the trier of fact that no contract was ever made.[9]

What else follows from noncompliance? The theory is that noncompliance merely renders the oral contract unenforceable, not void.[10] This distinction can be significant in various ways. A valid (not void) oral contract that is currently or was once unenforceable

---

7. See, e.g., Pecker Iron Works, Inc. v. Sturdy Concrete Co., 96 Misc.2d 998, 410 N.Y.S.2d 251, 26 UCC 1066 (1978) (denial of statute of frauds defense means that trier of fact must still determine if there was an oral contract) National Microsales Corp. v. Chase Manhattan Bank, N.A., 761 F.Supp. 304, 14 UCC2d 995 (S.D.N.Y.1991) (preclusion of statute of frauds defense does not affect burden of persuasion regarding existence of oral agreement). Cf. Continental Can Co. v. Poultry Processing, Inc., 649 F.Supp. 570, 3 UCC2d 31 (D.Me.1986) (an admission that an oral contract was made bars statute of frauds defense but does not establish terms of contract).

8. For an exemplary opinion, see Perdue Farms, Inc. v. Motts, Inc., 459 F.Supp. 7, 25 UCC 9 (N.D.Miss.1978) (§ 2–201(2) at issue).

9. See, e.g., Deardorff–Jackson Co. v. New York Fruit Auction Corp., 1978 WL 23511, 37 Agric.Dec. 1755, 25 UCC 975 (1978) and cases cited in note 11 *supra*.

10. 1 S. Williston, Sales §§ 71A, 72A (Rev.Ed.1948). See UCC § 2–201, Comment 4:

Failure to satisfy the requirements of this section does not render the contract void for all purposes, but merely prevents it from being judicially enforced in favor of a party to the contract. See Omega Engineering v. Eastman Kodak, 908 F.Supp. 1084, 30 UCC2d 194 (D Conn. 1995) (court finds that contract is unenforceable under the statute of frauds, but considers breach of warranty, promissory estoppel, and other claims).

under the statute by one or the other parties may still have value. A prospective defendant might for instance send a prospective plaintiff a letter in which he acknowledges the oral contract and signs his name! The oral contract would then become not merely "not void," but enforceable too. Moreover, from the fact that an oral contract is not enforceable by one party for lack of a required writing, it does not follow that the other party cannot enforce it, for he or she may have a complying writing. Yet prospective enforceability of an initially unenforceable oral contract does not turn solely on the production of complying writings. As we have seen, an initially unenforceable oral contract may later become enforceable to some extent if one party prepares to perform,[11] admits the contract in litigation,[12] or partly performs.[13] All this would be legally impossible if oral contracts, initially unenforceable under the statute of frauds, were void. Professor Corbin discussed a number of other ways in which an oral contract, unenforceable under the statute of frauds but not void, may be legally significant.[14] For example, this "contract" may prevent a buyer who takes control of the goods from being a trespasser. It may enable a party to the oral contract to show in a quasi-contractual action that he or she conferred a benefit on the defendant pursuant to an agreement, so that he or she was not an officious volunteer and therefore is truly entitled to quasi-contractual relief.

It is sometimes said that the statute of frauds is a rule of substantive law and not a rule of evidence. It is not clear what this means. The temptation to call the statute a rule of evidence derives from the possibility that it can operate to preclude testimony in a court case. A party may be able to convince a court that the plaintiff's writing does not satisfy the statute and that plaintiff cannot satisfy it in any other way, so that the plaintiff is precluded from offering any further oral evidence as to the existence and terms of the oral contract. But not just any rule which operates to affect the materiality and therefore the admissibility of evidence should be called a rule of evidence. For every rule of law can affect the materiality and therefore the admissibility of evidence. A true exclusionary rule of evidence operates to exclude a given type of evidence, for example hearsay, but permits the relevant legal rights to be established by still other kinds of evidence. When a statute of frauds applies to render an oral contract unenforceable, however, the theory is that no other evidence can make the contract enforceable. Consequently, some courts have remarked that "the statute is

---

11. § 2–201(3)(a).

12. § 2–201(3)(b).

13. § 2–201(3)(c).

14. 2 A. Corbin, Contracts § 279 et seq. (1950).

not a mere rule of evidence, but a limitation of judicial authority to afford a remedy."[15]

§ 3–4   Satisfying the Statute With a Writing

To satisfy the statute with a writing a party need only (1) produce a writing, (2) that shows a contract has been made (3) signed by the party to be charged, which (4) recites a quantity term. It makes no difference that the writing omits or incorrectly states a term agreed upon. The writing requirement is also satisfied by an electronic record and an electronic signature so long as the record indicates that a contract was made and includes a quantity term and so long as the parties have consented to conduct the transaction electronically.[1]

According to one pre-Code judicial doctrine, a party need not produce a complying writing if the party can prove that the writing once existed but was somehow lost, misplaced, or destroyed.[2] Section 2–201 does not expressly sanction this doctrine, but pre-Code statutes did not either. Doubtless it remains good law even under 2–201 in some states. To satisfy 2–201(1), must the writing consist of one piece of paper? In light of the statutory purpose, we believe several writings can be pieced together to satisfy the requirement, writings which taken alone would not be sufficient.[3] Moreover, it appears that the writing or writings need not be sent with intent to acknowledge a contract. Indeed, one of the writings taken together to satisfy the statute may even be disputatious. Further, a writing or writings sufficient to satisfy the statute with respect to a principal oral contract may also be sufficient with respect to a separate but ancillary oral contract.[4]

The writing must be "signed by the party against whom enforcement is sought or by his authorized agent or broker."[5] What

---

15. *Id.* § 279 n.34: "The statute is not a mere rule of evidence, but a limitation of judicial authority to afford a remedy." See Safe Deposit & Trust Co. of Pittsburg v. Diamond Coal & Coke Co., 234 Pa. 100, 83 A. 54 (1912).

§ 3–4

1. See section 3–9 *infra*.

2. See 2 A. Corbin, Contracts § 529 (1950).

3. Cf. Reich v. Helen Harper, Inc., 1966 WL 8838, 3 UCC 1048 (N.Y.Civ.Ct. 1966). See also, Waltham Truck Equip. Corp. v. Massachusetts Equip. Co., 7 Mass.App.Ct. 580, 389 N.E.2d 753, 26 UCC 613 (1979) (three separate writings read together satisfied 2–201's requirements).

4. Conner v. May, 444 S.W.2d 948, 7 UCC 185 (Tex.Civ.App.1969), error ref'd n.r.e.

5. § 2–201(1). Of course, UETA (and E–Sign) provide that an "electronic signature" is valid. See also Entertainment Sales Co. v. SNK, Inc., 232 Ga.App. 669, 502 S.E.2d 263, 36 UCC2d 308 (1998) (purchase orders were not signed by seller or his authorized agent so not enforceable against seller); Precise–Marketing Corp. v. Simpson Paper Co., 1999 WL 259518, 38 UCC2d 717 (S.D.N.Y. 1999) (internal memorandum, signed by the party against whom enforcement is sought, which lists quantity, price, and location of shipment is enforceable).

counts as a signature has generated a good deal of litigation. The Code expressly "deformalizes" the signature requirement.[6] Even a letterhead will do, provided it "authenticates" the writing.[7] A tape recording may comply as well.[8] Even a board's minutes of a meeting has been held to satisfy the signature requirement.[9]

It is not necessary that the writing state all the terms of the contract, or even that it state any of them accurately[10] or unambiguously.[11] It must state a quantity term,[12] but not a price term[13] and if that quantity term proves lower than the quantity actually agreed upon as shown in oral proof, the contract will be enforceable

6. § 2–201, Comment 1, defines "signed" as including "any authentication which identifies the party to be charged." § 1–201(37) states: " 'Signed' includes using any symbol executed or adopted with present intention to adopt or accept a writing," and § 1–201, Comment 37, further explains:

The symbol may be printed, stamped or written; it may be by initials or by thumbprint. It may be on any part of the document and in appropriate cases may be found in a billhead or letterhead. No catalog of possible situations can be complete and the court must use common sense and commercial experience in passing upon these matters. The question always is whether the symbol was executed or adopted by the party with present intention to adopt or accept the writing.

7. Automotive Spares Corp. v. Archer Bearings Co., 382 F.Supp. 513, 15 UCC 590 (N.D.Ill.1974); A & G Constr. Co. v. Reid Bros. Logging Co., 547 P.2d 1207, 19 UCC 37 (Alaska 1976) (typed name); Barber & Ross Co. v. Lifetime Doors, Inc., 810 F.2d 1276, 3 UCC2d 41 (4th Cir.1987), cert. denied, 484 U.S. 823, 108 S.Ct. 86, 98 L.Ed.2d 48 (1987) (seller's trademark on a sales brochure was a sufficient "signature"); Cloud Corp. v. Hasbro, Inc., 314 F.3d 289, 49 UCC2d 413 (7th Cir.2002) (sender's name on relevant e-mails satisfies signature requirement); Casazza v. Kiser, 313 F.3d 414, 49 UCC2d 342 (8th Cir.2002) (in action for breach of contract to sell a sailboat, signature requirement is not satisfied by a signed navigational software license transfer agreement).

8. Ellis Canning Co. v. Bernstein, 348 F.Supp. 1212, 11 UCC 443 (D.Colo. 1972). See generally, Misner, Tape Recordings, Business Transactions Via Telephone, and the Statute of Frauds, 61 Iowa L.Rev. 941 (1976). See also, Wilkerson, Comment, Electronic Commerce Under the U.C.C. § 2–201 Statute of Frauds: Are Electronic Messages Enforceable?, 41 U.Kan.L.Rev. 403 (1993).

9. Modern Machinery v. Flathead County, 202 Mont. 140, 656 P.2d 206, 36 UCC 395 (1982).

10. A number of cases construe the quantity requirement liberally. See, e.g., Fort Hill Lumber Co. v. Georgia–Pacific Corp., 261 Or. 431, 493 P.2d 1366, 10 UCC 616 (1972) ("timber is located in approximately T. 10 S., R. 11 W," and consists of all hemlock that is "within cutting lines marked").

11. Autonumerics, Inc. v. Bayer Indus., Inc., 144 Ariz. 181, 696 P.2d 1330, 39 UCC 802 (App.1984) (every possible term or contingency need not be delineated and ambiguities did not affect underlying contract).

12. All commentators say the memo must state a quantity term. However, a close reading of § 2–201 indicates that all commentators may be wrong. An alternative interpretation is that only if the writing states a quantity term is that term determinative. See Riegel Fiber Corp. v. Anderson Gin Co., 512 F.2d 784, 16 UCC 1207 (5th Cir.1975); Lohman v. Wagner, 160 Md.App. 122, 862 A.2d 1042, 54 UCC2d 1057 (2004) (no quantity term in writing).

13. Alabama Great Southern R. Co. v. McVay, 381 So.2d 607, 29 UCC 767 (Miss.1980) ("only the quantity term is crucial"); Busch v. Dyno Nobel, Inc., 40 Fed.Appx. 947, 48 UCC2d 874 (6th Cir. 2002) (lack of price term in letter of intent did not render it unenforceable).

only to the extent of the quantity specified in the writing.[14] Thus, under 2–201 the general theory is that the successful plaintiff recovers on an oral contract, not on a written one. It is not unnatural, however, for the inexperienced to inquire why, if there is to be a statute of frauds at all, it should not require all terms of a deal to be in writing. The explanations are several. First, such a requirement would be unrealistic. Business people do not and will not act by legal ritual. For convenience they often send sketchy memos and notes to one another. They may even choose to leave price and quality out of a writing. The Code itself includes "suppletive" terms on price and quality which apply in the absence of contrary agreement of the parties.[15] Second, a requirement that all or most of the terms be written can itself be easily turned into an instrument of fraud. As Karl N. Llewellyn said before the New York Law Revision Commission:

> It was pointed out that the statute of frauds provision, the number of which is 2–201, made a tremendous innovation in the law. It does, and thank God it does. It was pointed out that the statute of frauds provision—at least I presume it was; it is in Mr. Fifield's memorandum—changes the necessary memo of the transaction, where a memo is required—that is, in cases under $500. It frees the memo from the necessity of laying down every term of the agreement and indeed requires the memo only to state specifically the single term of quantity.
>
> Now, just take a look for a moment at what the statute of frauds has raised in the way of trouble and see whether this isn't a wise and at the same time a very safe provision. What you have got as a requirement under the Code is that there shall be no doubt that there was a contract for sale. That is No. 1. Secondly, that you can't enforce it beyond the quantity stated. You can be inaccurate about other things or leave them out, mostly—price, for example, you can leave out. You refer to the market—you have to keep the jury from going crazy. You can't swear too much of a price onto a guy when there is a market around to test whether or not it is likely that that was the term agreed upon.
>
> But here is the kind of thing you get under the present law, and I submit that it is something to raise any commercial man's hair. Talk about uncertainty—no matter how perfect a

14. Ivey's Plumbing & Electric Co. v. Petrochem Maintenance, Inc., 463 F.Supp. 543, 26 UCC 621 (N.D.Miss. 1978) (memorandum covered only two compressors, and number orally contracted for was five).

15. Llewellyn, Memorandum Replying to the Report and Memorandum of Task Group 1 of the Special Committee of the Commerce and Industry Association of New York, Inc., on the Uniform Commercial Code, 1 N.Y.State Law Revision Comm'n, 1954 Report 106, 117–18 (1954).

memorandum is, though signed by both sides, the law is clear, and it is clear, I think, in every state that has a statute of frauds, that the fellow who doesn't want the contract enforced can say, "Sure, we made a contract. Sure, that is the memorandum I signed. But there was a term we agreed upon which is not in that memorandum." And he can give all evidence as to that term and nobody can keep it from being given. He goes to the jury on whether it was agreed, and if it was agreed, the contract is unenforceable.

Why, nothing is safe—nothing is safe! There can always be evidence that there was not included in the memorandum an extra term, and the parol evidence rule is no protection against it.

We regard this as commercial outrage. We think that if there was ever an instrument of fraud, that strange interpretation of the old statute which has become universal is an instrument of fraud. We turn to the exact opposite and say, as long as you are sure you have got a deal, go to the jury as you would in any other case, and we say the risk is very small, and here is why the risk is very small. You can't be sued under the memo for more than the quantity stated, which puts a top limit on what you could possibly be stuck with, and the whole practice of all intelligent business is to confirm in detail or make careful written contracts so that the number of cases in which defective memos will actually come into operation not only is already almost nugatory, but is decreasing by the minute.[16]

The primary job of the writing required by 2–201(1), then, is "to indicate that a contract for sale has been made." Perhaps the clearest case of a writing that so "indicates" is one which appears on its face to incorporate all conceivable terms that such a contract might include, is signed by both parties and is dated contemporaneously with the alleged real transaction which the writing is supposed to "indicate." Very few litigated cases will be so clear. And contrary to what is sometimes assumed, even if the plaintiff produces a writing so overwhelmingly "indicative" of a contract, the defendant may still deny and prove there was no contract. For the main theory of the writing sufficient under 2–201(1) is not that it conclusively proves the existence of the contract but that it affords the trier of fact something reliable to go on in addition to the mere oral testimony of the plaintiff.

Does "sufficient to indicate" imply a standard of proof stronger than, equivalent to, or weaker than "by the balance of probabili-

16. *Id.* at 163–64.

ties?" The comments to 2–201 offer two separate elaborations which are not identical:

> All that is required is that the writing afford a reasonable basis to determine that the offered oral evidence rests on a real transaction.[17] * * * [I]t must evidence a contract for the sale of goods.[18]

Also, Professor Llewellyn, draftsman of 2–201, offered these translations at different times before the New York Law Revision Commission:

> [Plaintiff may proceed] once there is given enough of a memorandum to document the presence of a deal.[19]

> What the section does * * * is to require some objective guaranty, other than word of mouth that there really has been some deal.[20]

> There shall be no doubt that a contract was made.[21]

Plainly, this last of Llewellyn's formulations must be considered a slip of the tongue (or pen). The spirit of his other formulations and of the comments seems to be that "sufficient to indicate" is roughly equivalent to "more probable than not," rather than "no doubt."

The case law on the "sufficient to indicate" rubric is now plentiful. The cases arise from two sources: (1) direct interpretations of 2–201(1),[22] and (2) interpretations of 2–201(2) which inevitably address themselves to 2–201(1).[23] The latter interpretations are necessarily a source of relevant analogies because the writing in confirmation under 2–201(2) must satisfy 2–201(1). Courts have

---

17. § 2–201, Comment 1.

18. *Id.*

19. Llewellyn, Memorandum Replying to the Report and Memorandum of Task Group 1 of the Special Committee of the Commerce and Industry Association of New York, Inc., on the Uniform Commercial Code, 1 N.Y.State Law Revision Comm'n, 1954 Report 106, 111 (1954).

20. *Id.* at 119.

21. *Id.* at 163.

22. See Barton Chem. Corp. v. Pennwalt Corp., 79 Ill.App.3d 829, 35 Ill.Dec. 454, 399 N.E.2d 288, 28 UCC 319 (1979), appeal after remand, 106 Ill. App.3d 561, 62 Ill.Dec. 469, 436 N.E.2d 51 (1982) (letter confirming negotiations, citing new price and quantity terms agreed upon was sufficient writing) Dallas Aerospace, Inc. v. CIS Air

Corp., 352 F.3d 775, 52 UCC2d 295 (2d Cir. 2003) (modification invalid under statute of frauds); Central Illinois Light Co. v. Consolidation Coal Co., 349 F.3d 488, 52 UCC2d 75 (7th Cir.2003) (statute of frauds not satisfied by invoice prepared, but never sent by party urging enforcement; court reasoned that the fact that the invoice was never sent suggests it embodied mere wishes of the party which created it and not the terms of a contract).

23. R.S. Bennett & Co., Inc. v. Economy Mechanical Indus., Inc., 606 F.2d 182, 27 UCC 345 (7th Cir.1979) ("the clear purpose of § 2–201(2) is to make memos of a contract that would be binding on the sender under § 2–201(1) equally binding on the party receiving the memo in the absence of objection"); See also, Entertainment Sales Co. v. SNK, Inc., 232 Ga.App. 669, 502 S.E.2d 263, 36 UCC2d 308 (1998).

found writings insufficient to indicate that a contract had been made. Essentially "futuristic" language in the writing disqualifies a writing. To illustrate: in one instance the writing concluded with the language: "It is our intention to award you a contract."[24] In another, the writing recited: " * * * tentative deposit on tentative purchase."[25] The writing must indicate the *consummation* of a contract, not mere negotiations, nor a mere offer, nor a counteroffer,[26] nor a rejection or other nonacceptance.[27] Also, if it can be shown that a writing is merely preliminary to a formal document required before contract formation, such a writing cannot suffice.[28] One court has suggested that the contract so indicated must be of the same type as that proved.[29]

Of what significance is it if a writing is not admissible under the Rules of Evidence as distinguished from whether it is sufficient under 2–201? In Trebor Sportswear Co., Inc. v. The Limited Stores, Inc.,[30] the question posed was whether evidence excluded by Federal Rule of Evidence 408 because it was evidence of a settlement offer could be used to satisfy the statute of frauds. The majority answered in the negative. The dissent seems to get the better of it. The dissent focused on the proposed use of the evidence, satisfaction of the statute of frauds.

Even when the writing satisfies 2–201(1) or (2), the plaintiff cannot enforce any oral contract he or she is able to prove beyond the quantity term shown in the writing.

§ 3–5 Satisfying Statutory Exceptions to the Writing Requirement

Section 2–201(2) states:

> Between merchants if within a reasonable time a writing in confirmation of the contract and sufficient against the sender is received and the party receiving it has reason to know its contents, it satisfies the requirements of subsection (1) against

24. John H. Wickersham Eng'r & Constr., Inc. v. Arbutus Steel Co., 1962 WL 9355, 1 UCC 49, 50 (Pa.Com.Pl. 1962).

25. Arcuri v. Weiss, 198 Pa.Super. 506, 507, 184 A.2d 24, 25, 1 UCC 45, 46 (1962).

26. See, e.g., Howard Constr. Co. v. Jeff–Cole Quarries, Inc., 669 S.W.2d 221, 37 UCC 1040 (Mo.App.1983) (a "proposal could be no more than an offer").

27. See, e.g., East Europe Domestic Int'l Sales Corp. v. Island Creek Coal Sales Co., 572 F.Supp. 702, 37 UCC 1030 (S.D.N.Y.1983).

28. Barton Chem. Corp. v. Pennwalt Corp., 79 Ill.App.3d 829, 35 Ill.Dec. 454, 399 N.E.2d 288, 28 UCC 319 (1979), appeal after remand, 106 Ill.App.3d 561, 62 Ill.Dec. 469, 436 N.E.2d 51, 34 UCC 185 (1982) (contracting held not conditional on signing of formal document).

29. Artman v. International Harvester Co., 355 F.Supp. 482, 12 UCC 87 (W.D.Pa.1973).

30. 865 F.2d 506, 7 UCC2d 975 (2d Cir.1989).

such party unless written notice of objection to its contents is given within 10 days after it is received.

Section 2–201(2) may be viewed as a kind of exception to the writing requirement of 2–201(1), for while 2–201(2) requires a writing in confirmation, it need not be signed by the party to be charged. Note first that the writing must be "sufficient against the sender,"[1] that is, it must be signed by him or her or his or her agent and state a quantity.[2] Like a writing under 2–201, the confirming writing complies even if it incorrectly states or omits terms.[3] The parties must both be merchants, and some courts would do better when construing this requirement to pay more attention to Comment 2 to 2–104. A party need not produce a writing in confirmation if he can prove that the writing once existed but for some reason no longer exists.[4] While the confirmation must be received within a reasonable time, a notice of objection thereto need only be sent within ten days of receipt.[5] What if a writing in confirmation and a letter of withdrawal cross in the mail? One court has held that the latter cannot qualify as an "objection" under 2–201(2).[6]

When is a writing sent "in confirmation of the contract?" As we have seen, 2–201(1) has comparable language which requires that the writing be "sufficient to indicate" a contract. Admittedly this latter language is not identical with the former, but we believe that our earlier analysis of the meaning of the "sufficient to

§ 3–5

1. Jem Patents, Inc. v. Frost, 147 Ga.App. 839, 250 S.E.2d 547, 26 UCC 1070 (1978) ("invoices sent on printed forms bearing buyer's name and address were 'sufficient against sender' "); Automated Controls, Inc. v. Mic Enters., Inc., 1978 WL 23448, 27 UCC 661 (D.Neb. 1978), aff'd, 599 F.2d 288, 27 UCC 677 (8th Cir.1979) (purchase order with buyer's name and address, which specified three types of goods with quantity and price was sufficient against sender)See generally, Del Duca, Statute of Frauds Effect of Failure to Object to Merchant's Written Confirmation, 38 UCC Law J. 74 (2005).

2. See Mel–Tex Valve, Inc. v. Rio Supply Co., 710 S.W.2d 184, 2 UCC2d 55 (Tex.App.1986) (unsigned internal business memorandum written on a purchase order form did not satisfy the 2–202 exception).

3. Thus, if the confirming memo merely includes some additional or different terms, that alone does not dis-

qualify it. See, e.g., Leonard Pevar Co. v. Evans Products Co., 524 F.Supp. 546, 32 UCC 720 (D.Del.1981) (mere assertion of additional terms in response to confirmatory writing not an objection and 2–201(2) did not apply). But see, e.g., Frances Hosiery Mills, Inc. v. Burlington Indus., Inc., 19 N.C.App. 678, 200 S.E.2d 668, 13 UCC 759 (1973), aff'd, 285 N.C. 344, 204 S.E.2d 834, 14 UCC 1110 (1974).

4. Sebasty v. Perschke, 404 N.E.2d 1200, 29 UCC 39 (Ind.App.1980) (evidence of properly addressed and stamped letter deposited at post office is prima facie proof that it was received by the person to whom it was addressed, but this presumption of receipt is not conclusive).

5. Tiffany Inc. v. W.M.K. Transit Mix, Inc., 16 Ariz.App. 415, 493 P.2d 1220, 10 UCC 393 (1972) (notice of objection sent but not received within ten days held timely).

6. Continental–Wirt Electronics Corp. v. Sprague Electric Co., 329 F.Supp. 959, 9 UCC 1049 (E.D.Pa.1971).

indicate" language applies to the "in confirmation" language of 2–201(2).[7] An early case under 2–201(2) sets a rational standard. In Harry Rubin & Sons, Inc. v. Consolidated Pipe Co. of America,[8] the buyer sent a letter to the seller that referred to the buyer's earlier oral "order" as a closed deal rather than merely as a pending offer. The court rejected seller's argument that because the buyer used the word "order" in his letter rather than "agreement" or "contract," the letter was not what would be a writing "in confirmation of a contract sufficient to satisfy 2–201(2)."[9] The court perceived that the true test was whether "the writing offered a basis for believing that the offered oral evidence rested on a real transaction" and observed that the buyer "must still sustain the burden of persuading the trier of fact that the contracts were in fact made prior to the written confirmation."[10]

Section 2–201(3) provides:

A contract which does not satisfy the requirement of subsection (1) but which is valid in other respects is enforceable

(a) if the goods are to be specially manufactured for the buyer and are not suitable for sale to others in the ordinary course of the seller's business and the seller, before notice of repudiation is received and under circumstances which reasonably indicate that the goods are for the buyer, has made either a substantial beginning of their manufacture or commitments for their procurement; or

(b) if the party against whom enforcement is sought admits in the party's pleading, or in the party's testimony or otherwise under oath that a contract for sale was made, but the contract is not enforceable under this provision beyond the quantity of goods admitted; or

(c) with respect to goods for which payment has been made and accepted or which have been received and accepted (Section 2–606).

Subsections 2–201(3)(a), (b), and (c) all contemplate enforcement of certain oral contracts absent a writing. But in each of these exceptions, a valid oral contract must be proved, plus something more. This "something more" varies in each of the exceptions, but

---

7. See Upsher–Smith Lab., Inc. v. Mylan Lab., Inc., 944 F.Supp. 1411, 31 UCC2d 698 (D.Minn.1996).

8. 396 Pa. 506, 153 A.2d 472, 1 UCC 40 (1959). But see, Trilco Terminal v. Prebilt Corp., 167 N.J.Super. 449, 400 A.2d 1237, 26 UCC 616 (1979), aff'd, 174 N.J.Super. 24, 415 A.2d 356 (1980) ("a more stringent writing requirement under subsection (2) can be justified by the statutory language and the fact that its effect is to bind a merchant to a writing he did not sign," but "whether more is required of a writing under subsection (2) than subsection (1) is not yet clear").

9. *Id.* at 511, 153 A.2d at 475, 1 UCC at 43.

10. *Id.* at 512, 153 A.2d at 476, 1 UCC at 44.

each has this in common: it is a kind of special indicator that a contract, albeit oral, was in fact made. Sellers do not produce custom-made goods just to pass the time of day. Parties do not admit contracts lightly in open court, nor do they ordinarily confer gratuitous benefits on others, except perhaps at Christmas or during other holidays.

The 2–201(3)(a) exception to the writing requirement applies only if the plaintiff-seller can prove the valid oral contract and prove that (1) the goods are to be specially manufactured for the buyer, (2) they are not suitable for sale to others in the ordinary course of seller's business, (3) seller made either a substantial beginning of their manufacture or commitments for their procurement, (4) seller's beginnings or commitments occurred under circumstances which reasonably indicate the goods are for buyer, and (5) these beginnings or commitments occurred before seller received a notice of repudiation from the buyer.[11] Some commentators have suggested that where the oral contract calls for delivery of divisible or only apportionable units, the seller can enforce it only as to that unit (or units) with respect to which seller has made either a substantial beginning of manufacture or commitments for their procurement.[12] This view is contrary to interpretations of comparable pre-Code statutes of frauds, and judicial adherence to it would be a step backward.[13] If the seller must still prove its oral contract, and if the fact-finder is to be trusted to find or not to find the contract itself, why should the fact-finder not also be trusted to determine the quantity too, once the plaintiff has satisfied the fact-finder that a real transaction exists? True, 2–201(1) does provide that the oral contract is not enforceable beyond the quantity shown in the writing. But the theory of a statute of frauds is that a writing is somehow sacrosanct; small wonder, therefore, that the quantity term appearing in a writing is accorded some special effect. Section 2–201(3)(a) dispenses with a writing, and it does not expressly limit recovery to units on which work was begun or for which commitments were made.

A specific quantity limitation does appear in 2–201(3)(b) involving admissions in pleadings or in open court. One might reconcile

---

11. See, e.g., LTV Aerospace Corp. v. Bateman, 492 S.W.2d 703, 12 UCC 1042 (Tex.Civ.App.1973), error ref'd n.r.e.; RIJ Pharm. Corp. v. Ivax Pharmaceuticals, Inc., 322 F.Supp.2d 406, 54 UCC2d 130 (S.D.N.Y. 2004) (goods specially manufactured and not suitable for sale to others in ordinary course); Vanstar Corp. v. AT & T Solutions, Inc., 2004 WL 1664790, 54 UCC2d 335 (Ct. App. 1st D. Cal. 2004) (specially manufactured).

12. R. Nordstrom, Handbook of the Law of Sales § 27 (1970). See EMSG Systems Division, Inc. v. Miltope Corp. 37 UCC2d 39 (E.D.N.C. 1998) (not enough to start an order under 2–201(3) but must actually produce "each individual good").

13. 2A Corbin Contracts § 477 (1950).

the presence of a quantity limit in that subsection with the absence of a similar limit in 2–201(3)(a) by saying that the kind of reliance contemplated by 2–201(3)(a) is a better indicator of the existence of a real transaction than is a flustered oral admission in court that a real contract exists and that there is therefore less justification for a quantity limit in 2–201(3)(a) than in 2–201(3)(b). Finally, it is worth noting that 2–201(3)(a) is a seller's exception to the statute, although buyers have attempted to use it also.[14]

Turn now to the exception in 2–201(3)(b).[15] This subsection, like 2–201(1) and 2–201(2) reflects the desire of the Code's drafters to have their cake and eat it too—to have both a statute of frauds requirement and a requirement that cannot, in particular cases, be turned into an instrument of fraud. Comment 7 to 2–201 explains that under this subsection it is "no longer possible to admit the contract in court and still treat the statute as a defense." Some would regard it a mockery of the statute to permit the defendant to use the statute effectively as a defense, yet in pleadings or in open court admit a contract. This subsection tells the defendant that, whatever the facts, he must keep his mouth shut if he wants to rely on the statute.

Section 2–201(3)(b) requires an admission in a pleading, testimony, or otherwise under oath.[16] Admissions in pleadings are for this purpose necessarily voluntary.[17] But involuntary admissions qualify too, whether occurring during pre-trial discovery or elicited during cross examination or the like at trial.[18] Whether a mere

14. Global Truck & Equip. Co., Inc. v. Palmer Machine Works, Inc., 628 F.Supp. 641, 42 UCC 1250 (N.D.Miss. 1986) (unsuccessful).

15. See generally, Weiskopf, In–Court Admissions of Sales Contracts and the Statute of Frauds, 19 UCC L.J. 195 (1987); Shedd, The Judicial Admissions Exception to the Statute of Frauds: An Update, 12 Whittier L.Rev. 131 (1991); Herbert, Procedure and Promise: Rethinking the Admissions Exception to the Statute of Frauds Under Articles 2, 2A, and 8, 45 Okla.L.Rev. 203 (1992).

16. Most courts have held that the admission must be made in the same action in which enforcement of the contract is sought. See, e.g., International Commodities Export Co. v. Wolfkill Feed & Fertilizer Corp., 665 F.2d 1052, 32 UCC 687 (9th Cir.1981); Siam Numhong Products Co., Ltd. v. Eastimpex, 866 F.Supp. 445, 27 UCC2d 59 (N.D. Cal. 1994) (defendant admitted existence of contract in numerous pleadings and papers submitted to court).

17. See, e.g., Chrysler Corp. v. Majestic Marine, Inc., 35 Mich.App. 403, 192 N.W.2d 507, 10 UCC 130 (1971); Stalnaker v. Lustik, 1999 PA Super 346, 745 A.2d 1245, 40 U.C.C.2d 386 (1999) (admission by wife of deceased appellee, where the wife was not a party to the contract but is now substitute appellee for the deceased, does not qualify as an admission for the purposes of § 2–201(3)(b)); Wehry v. Daniels, 784 N.E.2d 532, 49 UCC2d 1070 (Ind. App. 2003) (admission in court testimony).

18. See, e.g., Quad County Grain, Inc. v. Poe, 202 N.W.2d 118, 11 UCC 720 (Iowa 1972); Nebraska Builders Products Co. v. Industrial Erectors, Inc., 239 Neb. 744, 478 N.W.2d 257, 16 UCC2d 568 (1992) (party's reference to "the contract" on cross-examination admission where evidence indicated party had not misspoken); In re Uni–Products, Inc., 153 B.R. 764, 20 UCC2d 1233 (Bankr.E.D.Mich.1993) (2–201(3)(b) satisfied where several statements in deposition, countercomplaint, and affidavit

"adverse credibility determination" may count as an admission is the subject of dispute.[19] What might be classified as "merely procedural" admissions do not qualify.[20]

As already indicated, 2–201(3)(b) makes it possible for a defendant to lose its defense of the statute of frauds via an admission at the pleading stage. Can defendant also win the case at the pleading stage by, for instance, demurring to a complaint that alleges an oral contract within 2–201(1) and by appending a sworn affidavit denying that an oral contract was ever made? Summers believes defendants should no longer prevail in this fashion. Certainly the language of 2–201(3)(b) could be stretched enough to require that all cases go to trial so far as a statute of frauds defense is concerned, for 2–201(3)(b) contemplates the possibility that an oral contract within the statute may become enforceable by virtue of an admission in "open court" on cross-examination. A number of cases concur with that interpretation.[21]

White fears that allowing trial in all of these cases will cut the heart out of the writing requirement of 2–201(1). If the plaintiff makes enough hay on cross-examination to get past defendant's motion for a directed verdict, then the case goes to the jury. Will a jury clearly divide the issues between the statute of frauds issue

"tantamount to an acknowledgement" that debtor agreed to purchase).

19. Cf. Cox v. Cox, 292 Ala. 106, 289 So.2d 609, 14 UCC 330 (1974) with Dangerfield v. Markel, 222 N.W.2d 373, 15 UCC 765 (N.D.1974), appeal after remand, 278 N.W.2d 364, 26 UCC 419 (N.D.1979); Quaney v. Tobyne, 236 Kan. 201, 689 P.2d 844, 40 UCC 37 (1984) ("It is not necessary that there be an express declaration in which the party admits the making of an oral contract. It is sufficient if his words or admitted conduct reasonably lead to that conclusion."). See generally, Malinowski, The Use of Oral Admissions to Lift the Bar of the Statute of Frauds UCC Section 2–201(3)(b), 65 Cal.L.Rev. 150, 161–2 (1977).

20. Beter v. Helman, 41 Westmoreland Co.L.J. 7 (Pa.C.P.1959); Anthony v. Tidwell, 560 S.W.2d 908, 23 UCC 561 (Tenn.1977); In re Morristown Lincoln–Mercury, Inc., 25 B.R. 377, 35 UCC 268 (Bankr.E.D.Tenn.1982) (defendant denied existence of contract in answer and claimed was buyer in ordinary course as alternative defense); Rinderknecht v. Luck, 965 P.2d 564, 38 UCC2d 740 (Utah App.1998) (purported admission does not satisfy the exception to the statute of frauds even though defen-

dant's answer admitted that he made an offer to sell and that buyer proposed a price and time and method of delivery and referred to buyer's proposal as the "contract price," the court held that fairness requires that the defendant's position be ascertained from the total posture of his defense which was that no contract existed).

21. Garrison v. Piatt, 113 Ga.App. 94, 147 S.E.2d 374, 3 UCC 296 (1966) See generally, Duesenberg, The Statute of Frauds in Its 300th Year: The Challenge of Admissions in Court & Estoppel, 33 Bus.Law. 1859, 1864–1866 (1978); Theta Products, Inc. v. Zippo Mfg. Co., 81 F. Supp. 2d 346, 39 UCC2d 670 (D.R.I. 1999), aff'd by Theta Products, Inc. v. Zippo Mfg. Co., 8 Fed.Appx. 3, 45 UCC2d 81 (1st Cir. 2001) (defendant's motion to dismiss not granted because it would defeat plaintiff's opportunity to elicit admission at trial). Note, The Application of the Oral Admissions Exception to the Uniform Commercial Code's Statute of Frauds, 32 U.Fla. L.Rev. 486 (1980); Note, U.C.C. 2–201(3)(b): The Search for the "Bargain-in–Fact" Through the Use of the Oral Admissions Exception of the U.C.C. and Its Impact on Other Contract Areas, 3 J.L. & Com. 167 (1983).

and the issue whether the oral contract was ever made? We doubt it. Instead, the jury may decide the entire case on the basis of whether it thinks the parties really made a deal, and the defendant's statute of frauds defense will lose any independent significance. At least one court has refused to let cases go to trial because of these concerns:

> [w]here defendant has answered and denied the existence of a contract, 2–201(3)(b) does not create an affirmative right to badger the defendant through discovery and trial simply because of the possibility of obtaining an admission.[22]

The exception to the writing requirement in 2–201(3)(c) provides that "a contract which does not satisfy the requirements of subsection (1) but which is valid in other respects is enforceable with respect to goods for which payment has been made and accepted or which have been received and accepted (section 2–606)."[23] This subsection expressly limits enforceability only to the apportionable part of goods that the buyer has received and accepted, or for which seller has received and accepted payment, and so changes prior law.[24] When the whole shipment is apportionable, and the whole is paid for, the oral contract is enforceable as to the whole contract.[25] In Haken v. Scheffler,[26] the buyer had not actually

---

22. See Triangle Marketing, Inc. v. Action Indus., Inc., 630 F.Supp. 1578, 1 UCC2d 36 (N.D.Ill.1986). See also Simmons Oil Corp. v. Bulk Sales Corp., 498 F.Supp. 457, 31 UCC 1236 (D.N.J.1980) (defendant not required to file answer before raising statute of frauds as a defense, on the chance it would admit the existence of an alleged contract); Hoffmann v. Boone, 708 F.Supp. 78, 9 UCC2d 474 (S.D.N.Y.1989) (summary judgment granted where defendant's affidavit stated there was no agreement). See also, DF Activities Corp. v. Brown, 851 F.2d 920, 7 UCC2d 1396 (7th Cir. 1988) (Posner, J.).

23. See generally, Note, The Doctrine of Part Performance Under UCC §§ 2–201 and 8–319, 9 B.C.Ind. & Com. L.Rev. 355 (1968).

24. 2 A. Corbin, Contracts § 482 (1950). And several courts have so held. See, e.g., Bagby Land & Cattle Co. v. California Livestock Comm. Co., 439 F.2d 315, 8 UCC 844 (5th Cir.1971) (enforceable only as to cattle delivered rather than orally contracted for); Hugh Symons Group v. Motorola, 292 F.3d 466, 48 UCC2d 67 (5th Cir. 2002) (pro forma invoice not evidence of payment and acceptance under 2–201(3)(c)).

25. Alarm Device Mfg. Co. v. Arnold Indus., Inc., 65 Ohio App.2d 256, 417 N.E.2d 1284, 31 UCC 821 (1979) (when buyer of steel screws accepted entire 10,-000 lot shipment, the entire transaction fell within the 2–201(3)(c) exception); TCP Indus., Inc. v. Uniroyal, Inc., 661 F.2d 542, 32 UCC 369 (6th Cir.1981) (where whole shipment of apportionable butadiene is paid for and accepted, the oral contract was enforceable on the whole shipment); Bowlin's, Inc. v. Ramsey Oil Co., 99 N.M. 660, 662 P.2d 661, 36 UCC 1110 (App.1983) (when written contract for sale of gasoline terminated, and consignee orally made the same contract, payment and acceptance of gasoline fell within 2–201(3)(c) exception); Battista v. Radesi, 112 A.D.2d 42, 491 N.Y.S.2d 81, 41 UCC 748 (1985) (when 1,000 cases of wine paid for with $500 deposit, deposit was a partial payment for entire shipment); Seminole Peanut Co. v. Goodson, 176 Ga.App. 42, 335 S.E.2d 157, 42 UCC 74 (1985) (whole peanut crop accepted and thus whole contract was enforceable even though quantity term unclear); Trimble v. Todd, 510 So.2d 810, 4 UCC2d 1359 (Ala.1987) (claim not barred where shipment of coal accepted and delivered); W.I. Sny-

accepted all brick, stone, and mill irons that the seller had delivered, yet the buyer's acceptance and use of part of them plainly indicated the existence of a real transaction between the parties. Accordingly, the court held that 2–201(3)(c) was satisfied.

Numerous cases deal with acceptance. In First American Farms, Inc. v. Marden Manufacturing Co.[27] the court held that a machine received for demonstration purposes was not "accepted" even though it remained stuck in a swamp on the prospective buyer's premises for eight months. Since acceptance is determined in accord with 2–606, the court might, instead, have found that the prospective buyer either acted inconsistently with seller's ownership or failed to make an effective rejection and thus accepted the goods.[28] In Dykes Restaurant Supply, Inc. v. Grimes,[29] the court held that goods could be accepted under section 2–201(3)(c) even if that acceptance was by a noncontractual third party. What constitutes receipt and acceptance of payment? One decision suggests that receipt of a check without indorsement or negotiation cannot be enough,[30] but other cases are to the contrary.[31]

der Corp. v. Caracciolo, 373 Pa.Super. 486, 541 A.2d 775, 7 UCC2d 993 (1988) ("part payment of an indivisible contract takes the entire contract outside of the requirements of the Statute of Frauds"); Bradburn v. Hagen, 1998 WL 612910, 36 UCC2d 668 (Minn. 1998) (summary judgment for lack of a writing not appropriate where purchaser made more than $32,000 in payments on equipment, had sole possession and use of the equipment for more than three years and, over that period, owner did not tend to the equipment or act in any manner that might indicate he was the owner).

26. 24 Mich.App. 196, 180 N.W.2d 206, 8 UCC 349 (1970). See also Fairley v. Turan–Foley Imports, Inc., 65 F.3d 475, 27 UCC2d 723 (5th Cir.1995).

27. 255 So.2d 536, 10 UCC 648 (Fla. App.1971), cert. denied, 261 So.2d 845 (Fla.1972). See also O'Day v. George Arakelian Farms, Inc., 24 Ariz.App. 578, 540 P.2d 197, 17 UCC 1163 (1975) (failure to make effective rejection); New Hermes, Inc. v. Adams, 125 Wash.App. 1021, 55 UCC2d 931 (2005) (goods received and accepted). For cases defining rejection, see National Steel Service Center, Inc. v. Wollin Silos & Equip., Inc., 92 Wis.2d 133, 284 N.W.2d 606, 27 UCC 1246 (1979) (physical possession of steel not acceptance until buyer has had a reasonable opportunity to inspect the goods).

28. The conduct need not "unequivocally refer" to the oral contract. Partial performance can be shown by receipt and acceptance of the goods notwithstanding other possible explanations of the conduct. See, e.g., West Central Packing, Inc. v. A.F. Murch Co., 109 Mich.App. 493, 311 N.W.2d 404, 32 UCC 1361 (1981). See also Hofmann v. Stoller, 320 N.W.2d 786, 33 UCC 1622 (N.D. 1982) (conduct need not be "exclusively referrable" to the oral contract). See also § 2–201, Comment 2 ("The overt actions of the parties make admissible evidence * * *. This is true even though the actions of the parties are not * * * inconsistent with a different transaction * * *.").

29. 481 So.2d 1149, 42 UCC 1603 (Ala.Civ.App.1985). See also In re MSR Exploration, Ltd., 147 B.R. 560, 20 UCC2d 49 (Bankr.D.Mont.1992) (company accepted "the benefits of the gas purchase contract negotiated by its agent").

30. Presti v. Wilson, 348 F.Supp. 543, 11 UCC 716 (E.D.N.Y.1972). See also, Integrity Material Handling Sys. v. Deluxe Corp., 317 N.J.Super. 406, 722 A.2d 552, 40 UCC2d 377 (1999) (plaintiff's tendering of down payment to contractor did not constitute acceptance of payment by the contractor because contractor did not subsequently cash the check).

31. See, e.g., Kaufman v. Solomon, 524 F.2d 501, 17 UCC 1159 (3d Cir.

Some courts have had to consider whether a down payment on a single nondivisible unit transaction indicates a contract and permits the party making the payment to prove and recover in full on his oral contract. A court might say that 2–201(3)(c) is not satisfied, because payment must be made in full with respect to the single unit. Williamson v. Martz,[32] a Pennsylvania lower court case, so held. Other courts (correctly, in our opinion) have gone the other way.[33] Lockwood v. Smigel[34] is illustrative. There the court held that a $100 down payment on an $11,000 Rolls Royce brought 2–201(3)(c) into play and permitted the seller to try to prove his oral contract for the whole.

Can the party who has not partially performed rely on 2–201(3)(c)? The cases appear to be in conflict,[35] but Comment 2 to the section plainly indicates "yes."

§ 3–6 Satisfying Nonstatutory Exceptions to the Writing Requirement

In pre-Code days there were judge-made exceptions to the writing requirement. There is reason to believe that many remain good law, post-Code.[1] It is not difficult to imagine oral contracts which do not satisfy the writing requirement and do not fall into any of the explicit statutory exceptions, but which nonetheless cry out for enforcement. It is well to put forth one such case, based as it is on the facts of an actual case.[2]

1975); Songbird Jet Ltd. v. Amax, Inc., 581 F.Supp. 912, 38 UCC 431 (S.D.N.Y. 1984) (check for $250,000 indorsed and proceeds kept by defendant for two months and then returned to plaintiff would be, if proven, an acceptance); Miller v. Wooters, 131 Ill.App.3d 682, 86 Ill.Dec. 835, 476 N.E.2d 11, 40 UCC 1623 (1985) (delivery of check to seller constitutes payment under 2–201(3)(c) and buyer's subsequent stop payment order of no legal significance). But mere receipt and holding of check for a brief period may not be sufficient. See also In re Uni–Products, Inc., 153 B.R. 764, 20 UCC2d 1233 (Bankr.E.D.Mich.1993) (acceptance of promissory note constitutes payment under 2–201(3)(c)).

32. 11 Pa.D. & C.2d 33 (1958). See also Jones v. Wide World of Cars, Inc., 820 F.Supp. 132, 21 UCC2d 27 (S.D.N.Y. 1993) (down payment not part performance of contract for an indivisible item; note, however, that car dealer trying to bind car purchaser; court states that case law suggests recipient may be bound, not person paying).

33. Starr v. Freeport Dodge, Inc., 54

Misc.2d 271, 282 N.Y.S.2d 58, 4 UCC 644 (1967); Sedmak v. Charlie's Chevrolet, Inc., 622 S.W.2d 694, 31 UCC 851 (Mo.App.1981) (partial payment of $500 for a single $15,000 automobile validates oral contract under 2–201(3)); The Press, Inc. v. Fins & Feathers Publishing Co., 361 N.W.2d 171, 40 UCC 33 (Minn.App.1985) (partial payment of $18,000 for two million-piece print run takes entire contract out of statute).

34. 18 Cal.App.3d 800, 96 Cal.Rptr. 289, 9 UCC 452 (1971).

35. Compare Mann v. Commissioner of Internal Revenue, 483 F.2d 673, 13 UCC 630 (8th Cir.1973) with In re Flying W Airways, Inc., 341 F.Supp. 26, 11 UCC 982 (E.D.Pa.1972).

§ 3–6

1. See also L. Vold, The Law of Sales, 94 (2d ed. 1959) and cases cited therein.

2. Mosekian v. Davis Canning Co., 229 Cal.App.2d 118, 40 Cal.Rptr. 157 (1964).

Assume that Grower raises fruit and orally contracts to sell the fruit to Canner who agrees to pick the fruit. The day for Canner to come and pick arrives, but Canner does not show up. Grower frantically seeks to induce Canner to pick, yet Canner refuses. Within two or three days Grower stops trying to procure another buyer and has a local jobber pick the fruit. Assume that Grower has acted reasonably and that while seeking another buyer, a good part of the fruit became overripe and had to be disposed of as hog-feed. In the foregoing case there was no writing, and the oral deal would not have fallen into any of the exceptions to 2–201(3). Yet there is authority that in such cases a statute of frauds will not operate as a bar, provided the plaintiff establishes the elements of an estoppel.[3] According to one view, the plaintiff establishes an estoppel when he or she shows that: (1) the defendant promised to perform, (2) the plaintiff reasonably relied on this promise, and (3) the plaintiff would suffer either an "unconscionable injury" or there would be "unjust enrichment" from refusal to enforce the contract.[4] Some courts require that the unconscionable injury or unjust enrichment be especially serious.[5] And some courts require that the defendant deceitfully promise to perform.[6] Indeed, some states refuse to

3. Note, The Doctrine of Equitable Estoppel and the Statute of Frauds, 66 Mich.L.Rev. 170 (1967); Contracts—The Availability of Promissory Estoppel to Defeat the Statute of Frauds, 14 Mem. Stat.U.L.Rev. 89 (1983). See, e.g., Esquire Radio & Electronics, Inc. v. Montgomery Ward & Co., 804 F.2d 787, 2 UCC2d 826 (2d Cir.1986) (having reneged on its promise to repurchase plaintiff's spare parts, defendant is equitably estopped from raising the statute of frauds); Trad Indus., Ltd. v. Brogan, 246 Mont. 439, 805 P.2d 54, 14 UCC2d 718 (1991) (seller who assured buyer elk available past cut-off date estopped from insisting upon enforcement of original cut-off date); Dixon v. Roberts, 853 P.2d 235, 21 UCC2d 513 (Okl.App.1993) ("estoppel by silence" where seller failed to respond to buyer's letter summarizing results of negotiations undertaken after seller failed to deliver under original contract; seller had obligation to respond if it disagreed with terms and conditions in letter); Atlantic Paper Box Co. v. Whitman's Chocolates, 844 F.Supp. 1038, 23 UCC2d 361 (E.D.Pa. 1994) (estoppel or waiver); Mass Cash Register v. Comtrex Sys. Corp., 901 F.Supp. 404, 29 UCC2d 110 (D. Mass. 1995) (estoppel theory not allowed where plaintiff cannot demonstrate detrimental reliance); Dumarc Shipping Co.

v. C.I.T. Group, 1998 WL 307258, 34 UCC2d 924 (D.N.J. 1998) (estoppel argument rejected).

4. Mosekian v. Davis Canning Co., 229 Cal.App.2d 118, 40 Cal.Rptr. 157 (1964). See also, Fairway Machinery Sales Co. v. Continental Motors Corp., 40 Mich.App. 270, 198 N.W.2d 757, 10 UCC 1405 (1972); Jamestown Terminal Elevator, Inc. v. Hieb, 246 N.W.2d 736, 20 UCC 617 (N.D.1976); Siam Numhong Products v. Eastimpex, 866 F.Supp. 445, 27 UCC2d 59 (N.D. Cal. 1994) (estoppel may operate as an exception to the statute of frauds where party asserting estoppel proves detrimental reliance and unconscionable injury).

5. E.g., Irving Tier Co. v. Griffin, 244 Cal.App.2d 852, 53 Cal.Rptr. 469 (1966).

6. E.g., Rockland Indus., Inc. v. Frank Kasmir Assoc., 470 F.Supp. 1176, 26 UCC 852 (N.D.Tex.1979) (estoppel operates only where misrepresentation was made that statute of frauds' requirements had already been complied with, or a promise was made that they would be met); Adams v. Petrade Int'l, Inc., 754 S.W.2d 696, 7 UCC2d 369 (Tex. App.1988) (party asserting estoppel must show other party promised to sign written agreement or misrepresented

recognize an estoppel exception to the statutes of frauds requirement.[7] Comment 2 to section 2–201 of Amended Article 2 (not likely to be adopted anywhere) now makes clear that Amended Article 2 would preserve the possibility that a promisor can be estopped to raise the statute of frauds defense in appropriate cases.

If the estoppel exception enters the Code, it now does so via section 1–103(b):

> Unless displaced by the particular provisions of this Act, the principles of law and equity, including the law merchant and the law relative to capacity to contract, principal and agent, estoppel, fraud, misrepresentation, duress, coercion, mistake, bankruptcy, or other validating or invalidating cause shall supplement its provisions.

At least one court has used 1–102(2) of Unrevised Article 1 to reach exactly the opposite conclusion; estoppel should not be allowed to enter the Code through then existing 1–103 because it would make commercial law less uniform and would mystify, rather than simplify, commercial law.[8] The court reasons that since the language, legislative history, and objectives of 2–201 do not indicate that estoppel is displaced, it is included in 1–103. These courts generally rejected the argument that Unamended 2–201 is a "particular provision" that "displaces" the estoppel principle. In fact 2–201(3)(a) is a form of estoppel.[9] White fears that willy nilly recognition of estoppel will diminish certainty and crush any hope of speedy and inexpensive resolution of these disputes by summary judgment. Summers is sympathetic to the estoppel defense, but even he would use it sparingly.[10]

---

that statute of frauds had been satisfied).

7. E.g., Polka v. May, 383 Pa. 80, 118 A.2d 154 (1955) ("principle of estoppel may not be invoked against the operation of the statute of frauds"); Renfroe v. Ladd, 701 S.W.2d 148, 42 UCC 547 (Ky.App.1985) (citing C.G. Campbell, *supra*, court reasons by analogy that statute of frauds is unambiguous and it will not read in exceptions); Varnell v. Henry M. Milgrom, Inc., 78 N.C.App. 451, 337 S.E.2d 616, 42 UCC 814 (1985) (no evidence of reliance); T.K. Stanley, Inc. v. Scott Paper Co., 793 F.Supp. 707, 18 UCC2d 673 (S.D.Miss.1992) ("Mississippi Supreme Court has refused to recognize fraud or promissory estoppel as an exception to the UCC statute of frauds").

8. Some prior cases did not. Lige Dickson Co. v. Union Oil, 96 Wash.2d 291, 635 P.2d 103, 32 UCC 705 (1981).

For a well-reasoned case in which the court recognizes the estoppel exception, see B & W Glass, Inc. v. Weather Shield Mfg., Inc., 829 P.2d 809, 18 UCC2d 1 (Wyo.1992).

9. See Futch v. James River–Norwalk, Inc., 722 F.Supp. 1395, 10 UCC2d 684 (S.D.Miss.1989), aff'd, 887 F.2d 1085 (5th Cir.1989); International Products & Technologies, Inc. v. IOMEGA Corp., 1989 WL 138866, 10 UCC2d 694 (E.D.Pa.1989). These courts emphasize the lead-in language of 2–201: "Except as otherwise provided *in this section* * * *." (emphasis supplied). From this language, they deduce that there can be no non-statutory exceptions to 2–201 via 1–103.

10. See generally Summers, "Good Faith" in General Contract Law and the Sales Provisions of the Uniform Commercial Code, 54 Va.L.Rev. 195, 259 (1968). See also Northwest Potato Sales,

§ 3–7 Procedural and Remedial Matters

If a defendant chooses to invoke the defense of the statute of frauds, how is he to raise it procedurally? The Code is silent. The "modern trend" is said to be that the defendant must affirmatively plead the statute.[1] It is important to consider how a disputed statute of frauds defense might be tried, for in a particular case this can make all the difference. Assume that as a matter of procedure the statute of frauds defense has been properly raised. The plaintiff then has the burden at trial of introducing evidence of a legally sufficient writing or evidence establishing that the case falls within an exception to 2–201. Absent one or both of these, the theory is that the defendant will prevail on a motion to dismiss (or on other appropriate procedural move).

As we suggested earlier, this theory may not prove out. As a part of its effort to introduce a legally sufficient writing (or evidence of an exception), plaintiff may be able to introduce convincing evidence that an oral contract was made between the parties. Certainly judges already skeptical of statutes of frauds will then be disposed to find a way to let the entire case go to the jury, especially since under the Code, the theory is that the successful plaintiff recovers on an oral contract (when enforceable) even when it produces a complying writing.[2]

But would not the defendant always be able to keep the plaintiff's evidence of the oral contract out on the ground that it is technically irrelevant on the question whether the statute of frauds is met? First, the plaintiff's order of proof in presenting the "case in chief" is discretionary with the judge.[3] Moreover, many plaintiffs will argue that proof of the oral contract is itself relevant to the

---

Inc. v. Beck, 208 Mont. 310, 678 P.2d 1138, 37 UCC 1468 (1984) (§ 1–203 requires good faith in all UCC transactions).

§ 3–7

1. F. James, Civil Procedure § 4.8 (1965). Frank Adams & Co., Inc. v. Baker, 1 Ohio App.3d 137, 439 N.E.2d 953, 34 UCC 794 (1981) (statute of frauds is an affirmative defense which defendant has burden to prove); Harvey v. McKinney, 221 Ill.App.3d 140, 163 Ill.Dec. 632, 581 N.E.2d 786, 16 UCC2d 1003 (1991) (failure to raise statute until after case is on appeal is deemed a waiver); Central Production Credit Ass'n v. Hopkins, 810 S.W.2d 108, 15 UCC2d 631 (Mo.App. 1991) (failure to object to evidence is a waiver); Mulberry–Fairplains Water Ass'n, Inc. v. Town of North Wilkesboro, 105 N.C.App. 258, 412 S.E.2d 910, 17 UCC2d 48 (1992) (defense waived where defendant failed to plead statute).

2. It is difficult to find recent cases in which the courts have upheld a statute of frauds defense in the face of convincing oral evidence of the contract itself. Cf. N. Dorman & Co. v. Noon Hour Food Products, Inc., 501 F.Supp. 294, 31 UCC 31, 37 (E.D.N.Y.1980) (court to consider writing "standing alone", but court cites pre-Code case) with Slocomb Indus., Inc. v. Chelsea Indus., 1983 WL 160582, 36 UCC 1543 (E.D.Pa.1983) (a document very similar to prior contract was signed by one party but not other, and parties continued to "perform" for five months; though evidence was conflicting, and jury must decide, evidence still "strongly suggests" a contract; hence statute of frauds satisfied).

3. C. McCormick, Law of Evidence § 58 (1954).

statute of frauds issue. To be sufficient under 2–201, the writing must be sufficient to "indicate" that a contract between the parties was made. Many a signed writing will or will not be "sufficient to indicate that a contract was made" depending on whether the alleged oral contract was simple or complex. Whether the alleged oral contract was simple or complex cannot be ascertained without hearing some of the plaintiff's evidence.

Furthermore, the plaintiff may convince the court that the oral evidence of the contract is properly admitted and heard even when plaintiff is not seeking to show a sufficient writing. The plaintiff may urge that it is entitled to put the entire case into evidence, all preliminary to calling the defendant and seeking to force an admission that a contract pursuant to 2–201(3)(b) exists.[4] Suppose the defendant still denies the contract. Can plaintiff get to the jury on the theory that defendant's denial is not credible in the face of plaintiff's overriding evidence? Subsection 2–201(3)(b) requires the defendant to admit the contract, and a denial, however incredible, cannot constitute an admission.[5]

The topic of remedies is more fully explored elsewhere in this book. Here we consider only remedial problems specially related to the statute of frauds. Section 2–201 is silent on remedial matters. Assume a court decides that the plaintiff's oral contract is unenforceable in part or in full under 2–201, yet the plaintiff shows that he conferred a benefit on the repudiating defendant. Non–Code law permits the plaintiff to recover the reasonable value in money of any benefit he has conferred.[6] Does the plaintiff have a right to restitution of the very thing conferred upon the defendant? Some pre-Code case law suggests as much.[7]

Courts may read 2–201 in ways that generate serious "apportionment" problems. Suppose a buyer agrees to an oral contract for the purchase of a used truck which seller agrees to equip with a rack and trailer, all for a total price of $5,000, with buyer to pay $2500 on delivery of the truck and $2500 on delivery of the rack and trailer. Assume also that the truck is worth significantly more than the rack and trailer. Buyer repudiates after paying the $2500 and receiving the truck. If the seller is willing to let the buyer keep the truck, but wants fair value therefor, how might it get the fair value? If the oral agreement had apportioned the price among the three items, the just thing would be for the court to use the price tag the parties had placed on the truck. Purists might object that

---

4. Cf. Garrison v. Piatt, 113 Ga.App. 94, 147 S.E.2d 374, 3 UCC 296 (1966).

5. Cf. Dangerfield v. Markel, 222 N.W.2d 373, 15 UCC 765 (N.D.1974), appeal after remand, 278 N.W.2d 364, 26 UCC 419 (1979).

6. 2A Corbin, Contracts §§ 326–27 (1950).

7. 2A Corbin, Contracts § 330 (1950).

this would involve enforcing the oral contract contrary to the statute of frauds, but if the buyer wants to keep the truck and the seller is willing, then neither party can sensibly object to this use of the price term of the unenforceable oral contract. Since the parties did not apportion the total price, the parties will be forced to use some other method for determining the amount seller receives. Market value, as determined by comparable sales of comparable vehicles, is the most likely alternative.

Suppose the buyer can show that if the seller had fully performed, it would have cost the seller a total of $6000 (valuing the truck at $4000 and assigning a cost of $2000 to the construction of the rack and trailer). Here the seller might seek $4000 for the truck (less the $2500 down payment), but the buyer might urge that the seller's recovery should not exceed the "contract rate," that is, the seller should recover no more than 4/6 of $5,000 or $3,333. This is the more defensible of the two alternatives, unless the defendant is to be punished for repudiating and setting up the statute of frauds. Under 2-201(3)(c) the oral agreement is enforceable at least to the extent of goods received and accepted, and here the defendant received and accepted the truck. If the contract is to be enforced against defendant to that extent, it should be allowed to show the oral contract price in its favor to reduce plaintiff's recovery to an amount consistent with the contract rate, pre-Code case law to the contrary notwithstanding.[8]

Occasionally, a buyer makes a down payment on an oral contract within the statute, but repudiates and sues to get the down payment back. Assume the seller does not want to invoke 2-201(3)(c), but does want to keep the down payment. Can seller do this? A few courts, in pre-Code cases, seem to have said yes,[9] but these results are inconsistent not only with the letter of contract theory, but also with the spirit of restitutionary theory. The seller has been enriched. The seller should not be allowed to retain this benefit; for it has no enforceable contract claim to the money. Moreover, the buyer is not a volunteer conferring a benefit gratuitously, rather the down payment was paid in contemplation of the performance of a contract unenforceable under the statute of frauds.

Section 2-201 of Amended Article 2 (not adopted) includes a new subsection (4) which reads that: "A contract that is enforceable under the section is not unenforceable merely because it is not capable of being performed within one year or any other period after its making."

---

8. 2A Corbin, Contracts at § 327 (1950) and cases cited therein.

9. 2A Corbin, Contracts at § 332 (1950).

§ 3–8   Statutes of Frauds—An Evaluation

There are at least four relevant forms of courtroom fraud: (1) a plaintiff might convince a fact-finder that the defendant made an oral contract when in fact it did not; (2) a plaintiff might convince a fact-finder that the terms of an admitted contract were more favorable to the plaintiff than those in fact agreed on; (3) a defendant might convince a fact-finder that the parties did not enter an oral contract when they did; or (4) the defendant might convince a fact-finder that the actual terms of an admitted contract were more favorable to it than those in fact agreed on. The motive for any such fraud is usually economic; a plaintiff wants something for less (or nothing), or a defendant wants out of a deal because of a break in the market or because of some change in his or her own plans. Occasionally the motive is not economic. One party might simply become "fed up" with the other, or come to dislike him, or to like some other supplier better, and so on. When a fraudulent party succeeds, reactions of outrage are likely. Just such reactions led to the enactment of the first statute of frauds, a development all the more understandable given that (1) a party was not then allowed to testify even to rebut perjured oral testimony of a third party ("friend" of the other party, no doubt) and (2) judges had little or no effective control over unreasonable jury findings.

Thus the primary theory of statutes of frauds, past and present, is that they are means to the end of preventing successful courtroom perjury. The means to this end is simply the requirement of a writing signed by the party to be charged. Doubtless this requirement operates in some cases to block what would otherwise be successful perjury. But, the fact that "A" may in *some* cases serve as the means to "B" is hardly sufficient to justify calling A a means to B. Of course, a legal requirement cannot be devised which would be an absolute guarantee against all perjury, but the statute of frauds writing requirement is, at least in the opinion of one of your authors, so far from any kind of guarantee against successful perjury that it is inappropriate even to call it a means to fraud prevention at all.

A "writing signed by the party against whom enforcement is sought" is not self-authenticating. Forgery is always a possibility, especially in a continuing relationship. (The possibility of forgery is real with respect to electronic records.) While forgery may be more difficult to achieve than perjury, the difference is hardly monumental. More fundamental, an admittedly authentic signed writing "sufficient to indicate that a contract for sale has been made" is commonly still far from conclusive evidence that a contract for sale was made. Such a writing can easily exist despite the fact no oral contract was ever made. For example, the party who signed the writing might have done so for convenience during preliminary negotiations in advance of the time when the parties actually contemplated an agreement. Even if the signed writing is authentic, and even if it does, in fact, "indicate" a real deal, fraud may still occur. The defendant may still persuasively lie to the jury either as to the existence of the contract or as to its terms. Further, if neither party can produce a signed writing, it does not even tend to follow that the parties did not make an oral contract. Indeed, if they did actually make an oral contract, it seems more probable than not that in the inception of the contract no signed writing would exist! Moreover, in many real deals, oral though they be, the parties might thereafter refrain from reducing terms to a writing because of a belief that a person's word is as good as his or her bond.

A true "means to an end" surely should not serve commonly as a means to disserve that end either.[1] Yet, centuries of experience and tons of case law testify that a statute of frauds can be an instrument of perjury and fraud. The possibility that plaintiffs might conjure up forged writings and perjured oral contracts out of whole cloth is unreal. These plaintiffs would be most unlikely to survive cross-examination, motions for directed verdict, and a jury's own scrutiny. But the possibility that defendants might get out of actual oral contracts simply for lack of a signed writing is not unreal at all. In sum, the "abuse potential" of a statute of frauds is great. This fact, more than any other, probably accounts for the disfavor in which many judges have held statutes of frauds. Yet some theorists have defended statutes of frauds on the basis that it is harder for a party to succeed at forgery than at perjury and that writing requirements imposed by law have the salutary effect of encouraging parties to put at least the terms of important deals into a writing. One of your authors (White) wants to take this line. He says he sees a lot of fraud in court and thinks something should be done about it.

As a matter of fact, White disagrees with most of the argument in the four foregoing paragraphs. He believes that faulty memories combine with greed and dishonesty to render much testimony by interested parties inaccurate. He believes forgery is a much less frequent occurrence and favors any rule that stimulates parties to write down their deals. Moreover he believes that the statute of frauds is consistent with laymen's ideas about serious contract, that is, no writing, no enforcement.

The aborted attempt to revise Article 2 between 1990 and 2003 featured the same debate over the statute of frauds. Driven by law teachers' hostility to the statute, the earliest draft omitted the

§ 3–8

1. Burdick, A Statute for Promoting Fraud, 16 Colum.L.Rev. 273 (1916).

statute of frauds. In response to the angry outburst of practitioners, section 2–201 was promptly reinstated and remained in the revised Article 2 thereafter.

§ 3–9 The Uniform Electronic Transactions Act (UETA) and Related Law

The Uniform Electronic Transactions Act (hereinafter "UETA") had, as of May, 2009, been adopted in forty-seven states.[1] With the advent of electronic means of communication and information transfer, ways of doing business have evolved to take advantage of the speed, efficiencies, and cost benefits of electronic technologies. A statute of frauds requiring that there be information or signatures in a "writing" posed real barriers to effective use of electronic media. Accordingly, NCCUSL prepared the Uniform Electronic Transactions Act UETA. This act removed these barriers by establishing the equivalence for legal purposes of an electronic record of the required information such as writings and signatures. See also the definition of "record" in 1–201(b)(31) which also accommodates electronic contracting.

The purpose of UETA is not to introduce a new general contracting statute. UETA does not affect the substantive rules of contract. Rather, UETA merely removes barriers to electronic commerce by validating and making electronic records and signatures legally binding. As Prefatory Note B stresses, the over-riding purpose is "to assure that records and signatures will be treated in the same manner, under currently existing law, as written records and manual signatures." Thus, substantive law is left intact, and one provision of UETA, section 8, is, according to its Comment 1, "designed to assure, consistent with the fundamental purpose of this Act, that otherwise applicable substantive law will not be overridden by this Act."

The provisions of UETA, with Official Comments, appear as Appendix to Volume One of this treatise. In what follows, we identify and discuss a number of the key provisions. The general scope of UETA is quite limited. As the Prefatory Note says, the Act "does not apply to all writings and signatures but only to electronic writings and signatures relating to a transaction." Section 2(5) of UETA defines "electronic" as "relating to technology having electrical, digital, magnetic, wireless, optical, electromagnetic, or similar capabilities." The definition of "transaction" in section 2(16) provides: "Transaction" means an action or set of actions occurring between two or more persons relating to the conduct of business,

1. Forty-seven states, the District of Columbia and U.S. Virgin Islands. See also, Robertson, Electronic Commerce on the Internet and the Statute of Frauds, 49 S.C.L. Rev. 787 (1998).

commercial, or governmental affairs. Section 5(a) of UETA provides that the Act "applies only to transactions between parties each of which has agreed to conduct transactions by electronic means." Section 5(a) adds that "whether the parties agree to conduct a transaction by electronic means is determined from the context and surrounding circumstances, including the parties' conduct."

The most basic legal effect of the UETA is merely to validate and thus effectuate electronic records and electronic signatures where parties have agreed to conduct transactions by electronic means. As section 5 stresses, the UETA does not itself require parties to so conduct transactions. Rather, the parties must agree, as above, to do so.

Thus the operative scope of the UETA depends on the existence of a specific agreement of the parties to conduct transactions by electronic means. Even with such an agreement, the UETA does not itself operate with regard to all articles of the Uniform Commercial Code. Subsection 3(b)(2) states that "This Act does not apply to a transaction to the extent it is governed by the Uniform Commercial Code *other than* Sections 1–107 and 1–206, Article 2, and Article 2A." (ital. supplied). Comment 4 adds that "This Act does not apply to the excluded UCC articles, whether in "current" or "revised" form." The comment stresses that "The Act does apply to UCC Articles 2 and 2A and to UCC Sections 1–107 and 1–206." Thus Article 2 on sales and Article 2A on leases are covered.

Why the scope exclusions for certain other Articles of the UCC? Comment A to the UETA Prefatory Note explains that the exclusion of specific Articles of the Uniform Commercial Code reflects the recognition that, particularly in the case of Articles 5, 8, and Revised Article 9, electronic transactions were addressed in the specific contexts of those revision processes. In the context of Articles 2 and 2A, the UETA provides the vehicle for assuring that such transactions may be accomplished and effected via an electronic medium. Is the UETA duly aligned with federal law on the use of electronic signatures? The answer is yes. The Congress in 2000 passed the Electronic Signatures in Global and National Commerce Act ("E–SIGN"), an act which, among other things, provides that a "signature, contract, or other record relating to" any transaction in or affecting interstate commerce may not be denied legal effect, validity, or enforceability solely because it is in electronic form.[2]

Comment B of the Prefatory Note to the UETA stresses that the scope of the UETA is "minimalist and procedural." The Act defers to existing substantive and other law such as law on the

---

2. See generally, Note, E–Sign: Paperless Transactions in the New Millennium, 51 De Paul L. Rev. 619 (2001).

meaning and effect of "sign," law on how information is to be displayed or transmitted, and the law of mistake (as explained in sec. 10). Whether a record is to be attributed to a person is left to law outside the UETA.

Various further implementive provisions of the UETA that may be noted are section 7 on legal recognition of electronic records, signatures, and electronic contracts, section 8 on satisfaction of a writing requirement by electronic record, section 9 on attribution and electronic records and signatures to a person, section 10 on changes or errors occurring in a transmission, section 11 on notarization, acknowledgment, verification, and oath taking, section 12 on recognition of electronic records, section 13 on admissibility in evidence, section 14 on automated transactions, section 15 on time and place of sending and receipt, and section 16 on transferable records.

§ 3–10   The Parol Evidence Rule—Does It Give Preference to Written Evidence of Contract Terms?

The law should give effect to the contract. The contract might be entirely oral, or it might be half and half. If the contract is not unenforceable under the statute of frauds,[1] a court will have to ascertain its terms. Partly to guard against the uncertainties of litigation over oral contract terms, parties frequently undertake to write their contracts. But there can be no magic in this. One party may later contend that the writing does not embody the terms agreed upon; a writing cannot prevent disputes over terms. A writing is only evidence to be introduced in court, should the parties go to court to resolve a dispute over terms.

Courts are frequently called on to resolve disputes over terms. The novice might expect that the process of adjudication here would be the same as in any other type of case in which facts are disputed: the parties would introduce conflicting evidence as to terms, including any other writing, and the trier of fact would then determine the terms. Also there would be the usual division of labor between judge and jury. Judges would, for example, rule on relevancy and admissibility, and they would be empowered to grant

---

§ 3–10

1. Some of the basic differences between a statute of frauds requirement and a parol evidence rule should be noted. The former requires a certain kind of agreement to be partly in writing to be legally enforceable, but the latter imposes no such requirement. The latter, in effect, gives special preference to a writing in determining the terms of the agreement where both written and oral evidence are proffered, but the former does not have this effect except in regard to any quantity term in the writing. Finally, the parties may satisfy the former requirement without ever having made a contract, but the latter presupposes a contract and is concerned only with what its terms are.

a motion for a non-suit, for a directed verdict, or for a judgement *n.o.v.* Thus, the usual protections against unreasonable jury determinations would be available to help assure that in the end, the court gives effect to the contract of the parties as actually agreed.

But Anglo–American law does not handle all disputes over contract terms in this way. Our courts apply some version of a so-called "parol evidence rule"[2] when some of the terms are written and some are not. This gives preference to the written version of those terms. Writings are more reliable than memories to show contract terms, and forgery is easier to detect and less common than is lying on the witness stand. These are the principal premises of a parol evidence rule. Early critics of the rule challenged these premises and emphasized that the rule is inconsistent with our usual processes of proof. If juries are to be "trusted" in disputes over contract terms not involving writings, then why should they not hear all the evidence, even where writings are involved, and decide accordingly? One reason is the same social Darwinist reason given above for 2–201: to train contracting parties to memorialize their agreements and so to minimize disputes between them and in the courts.[3]

Many versions of a parol evidence rule are possible; here, we focus solely on that version adopted in Article 2 of the Code.[4]

Section 2–202 provides:

Terms with respect to which the confirmatory writings of the parties agree or which are otherwise set forth in a writing intended by the parties as a final expression of their agreement with respect to such terms as are included therein may not be contradicted by evidence of any prior agreement or of a contemporaneous oral agreement but may be explained or supplemented

   (a) by course of dealing or usage of trade (section 1–303) or by course of performance (section 2–208); and

   (b) by evidence of consistent additional terms unless the court finds the writing to have been intended also as a complete and exclusive statement of the terms of the agreement.

As we earlier indicated, this rule is to assure that a court will approximate more closely the intention of the parties as to disputed

---

2. See 3A Corbin on Contracts §§ 573–96 (1950).

3. For example, compare Comment, The Parol Evidence Rule: A Conservative View, 19 U.Chi.L.Rev. 348 (1952) with Note, The Parol Evidence Rule: Is It Necessary?, 44 N.Y.U.L.Rev. 972 (1969). See generally Sweet, Contract Making and Parol Evidence: Diagnosis

and Treatment of a Sick Rule, 53 Cornell L.Rev. 1036 (1968).

4. For a discussion of 2–202's impact, see, Wallach, Declining Sanctity of Written Contracts—Impact of the Uniform Commercial Code on the Parol Evidence Rule, 44 Mo.L.Rev. 651 (1979).

terms. In substance, the "rule" says that if the court finds the writing to have been intended as a complete and exclusive statement of the terms of the agreement, then the writing alone constitutes the contract. This comes close to saying no more than if X is the contract, then X is the contract. As a corollary, the rule also says that to the extent the writing incorporates terms the parties agreed on, then the writing controls as to those terms and anything contradictory or inconsistent is of no force or effect. This comes close to repeating if X, then X.

As Professor McCormick taught, the division of functions between judge and jury in administering the rule can "give preference" to written evidence over oral evidence of contract terms.[5] So, too, can allocations of burden of proof. Section 2–202 does not state very clearly what the division of functions is supposed to be. But the way the rule is worded, the trial is certainly not to be a freewheeling affair in which the parties may introduce before the jury all evidence of terms, including the writing, with the jury then to decide on terms. Rather, it is plain from the rule and from prior history of similar rules that some of the evidence is to be heard initially only by the judge and that the judge may invoke the rule to keep this evidence from the jury. The evidence that is in this way subject to exclusion will usually be oral evidence. Indeed, before a judge can invoke a parol evidence rule at all, the judge must first admit a writing into evidence before the jury. If the judge thereafter excludes oral evidence of terms on the basis of the parol evidence rule, the judge gives preference to the writing already in evidence by prohibiting the jury from considering the oral evidence.

But when can the judge invoke 2–202 to exclude oral evidence of terms? First, the judge may exclude the evidence on finding that the parties intended the writing to be a *complete and exclusive* statement of the terms of the agreement (unless it be evidence of course of dealing, usage of trade, or course of performance introduced only to explain or supplement the writing). Code and comments both state that the question of completeness and exclusivity is for the judge.[6] Second, the judge may exclude evidence extrinsic

---

5. McCormick, The Parol Evidence Rule as a Procedural Device for Control of the Jury, 41 Yale L.J. 365 (1932).

6. § 2–202(b); Comment 3. See Whirlpool Corp. v. Regis Leasing Corp., 29 A.D.2d 395, 288 N.Y.S.2d 337, 5 UCC 94 (1968); Conner v. May, 444 S.W.2d 948, 7 UCC 185 (Tex.Civ.App.1969), error ref'd n.r.e.; Port City Constr. Co. v. Henderson, 48 Ala.App. 639, 266 So.2d 896, 11 UCC 722 (1972); Shore Line Properties, Inc. v. Deer–O–Paints and Chem., Ltd., 24 Ariz.App. 331, 538 P.2d

760, 17 UCC 353 (1975); Camargo Cadillac Co. v. Garfield Enters., Inc., 3 Ohio App.3d 435, 445 N.E.2d 1141, 35 UCC 749 (1982) (determination of exclusiveness and completeness made away from trier of fact by the judge); Morgan v. Stokely–Van Camp, Inc., 34 Wash.App. 801, 663 P.2d 1384, 36 UCC 1535 (1983) (question of whether a written contract was an integrated agreement was a question of fact for trial court); Rajala v. Allied Corp., 66 B.R. 582, 2 UCC2d 1203 (D.Kan.1986) (determination of facial completeness on summary judgment);

to terms set forth in the writing if he or she decides that the writing is a final written expression as to these terms and that the other evidence contradicts these terms. The Code does not say that this question is for the judge, but if "completeness and exclusivity" is for the judge, then whether a writing is a final written expression as to the terms it does include would be for the judge, for the greater ordinarily includes the lesser.[7] The issue of contradictoriness is also generally for the judge.[8] Third, in passing on any parol evidence rule objection, the judge may decide that the proffered evidence of terms extrinsic to the writing is not credible, and he or she may exclude it on that ground alone.[9] Section 2-202 is silent on this, but Professor McCormick thought that the "real service" of the parol evidence rule was here.[10]

The foregoing division of functions between judge and jury in the administration of 2-202 inevitably operates to favor written evidence of terms. Yet there is no necessary identity between a writing and the actual deal. Some commentators[11] and at least a few courts[12] conclude that 2-202 abolishes any presumption that a

Northwest Central Pipeline Corp. v. JER Partnership, 943 F.2d 1219, 16 UCC2d 1004 (10th Cir.1991) (integration may be viewed as question of law but more commonly characterized as question of fact); Sho–Pro of Indiana, Inc. v. Brown, 585 N.E.2d 1357, 17 UCC2d 56 (Ind.App.1992) ("an ordinary question of fact"; do not exclude relevant testimony merely because oral); Compania Sud–Americana de Vapores, S.A. v. IBJ Schroder Bank & Trust Co., 785 F.Supp. 411, 17 UCC2d 1050 (S.D.N.Y.1992) ("function of the court").

7. Intercorp, Inc. v. Pennzoil Co., 877 F.2d 1524, 9 UCC2d 454 (11th Cir. 1989) (whether final expression is question for the court); Compania Sud–Americana de Vapores, S.A. v. IBJ Schroder Bank & Trust Co., 785 F.Supp. 411, 17 UCC2d 1050 (S.D.N.Y.1992) (court determines whether final expression; looks at documents, not at parties' subjective intent); Ace, Inc. v. Maynard, 108 N.C.App. 241, 423 S.E.2d 504, 19 UCC2d 1060 (1992) (court decides); Middletown Concrete Products, Inc. v. Black Clawson Co., 802 F.Supp. 1135, 20 UCC2d 815 (D.Del.1992) (court decides whether final written expression; looks at parties' intent, writing, and circumstances).

8. Perryman v. Peterbilt, Inc., 708 S.W.2d 403, 1 UCC2d 650 (Tenn.App. 1985) (affirming trial judge's grant of summary judgment where plaintiff's

oral evidence was in contravention of defendant's written disclaimer of all warranties); Island Creek Coal Co. v. Lake Shore, Inc., 636 F.Supp. 285, 2 UCC2d 59 (W.D.Va.1986), aff'd in part, rev'd in part, 832 F.2d 274, 4 UCC2d 1067 (4th Cir.1987) (on summary judgment motion court refused to consider deposition testimony offered by plaintiff to show limitation of damages clause only applied to delivery date of contract since it contradicted language). But see, Alaska Northern Development, Inc. v. Alyeska Pipeline Service Co., 666 P.2d 33, 36 UCC 1527 (Alaska 1983), cert. denied, 464 U.S. 1041, 104 S.Ct. 706, 79 L.Ed.2d 170 (1984) (whether excluded evidence contradicts the integrated portion of the writing is left to trier of fact if there is choice between competing inferences, but is determined as a matter of law if an asserted inference cannot be reasonably derived from writing).

9. See, e.g., Norwest Bank Billings v. Murnion, 210 Mont. 417, 684 P.2d 1067, 38 UCC 1509 (1984) (trial testimony was uncorroborated and contradictory).

10. C. McCormick, Handbook of the Law of Evidence 440 (1954). See also, Annot., 10 A.L.R.2d 720 (1950).

11. 1 N.Y. State Law Revision Comm'n, 1955 Report 598 (1955).

12. Symonds v. Adler Restaurant Equip. Co., 1969 WL 11077, 6 UCC 808

writing apparently complete on its face is complete and exclusive. We are uncertain. One of us (White) would be quite quick to find completeness from elaborate writings and quite comfortable in stilling the tongues of parties claiming other terms or innovative interpretations. The other (Summers) trusts the jury more and is more suspicious of the drafter. As with 2–201, White remains a social Darwinist; Summers, a social creationist.

§ 3–11   Substantive Aspects of the Parol Evidence Rule—Problems of Interpretation

First, the parol evidence rule does not apply to evidence of *subsequent* agreements or modifications.[1] This is a fact that a few lawyers and judges continue to forget. Nor does the rule exclude evidence that the parties did not intend the writing to be binding.[2] For example in Simpson v. Milne[3] the signer of a note claimed that the note had been executed as a fiction to ease the mind of the recipient's dying wife who strongly felt a debt was owed to her. The Colorado Court of Appeals received this parol evidence on the theory that it went to the question whether the parties agreed that the note was to be enforceable.

To constitute a "writing" for parol evidence rule purposes, it is not necessary that it be the one and only "writing" in the case. Parties may express their agreement in several writings.[4] Under 2–202, if two contradictory but contemporaneous writings are involved, the judge may admit both with the jury to decide which

(Okl.1969); Michael Schiavone & Sons, Inc. v. Securalloy Co., 312 F.Supp. 801, 7 UCC 674 (D.Conn.1970); S.M. Wilson & Co. v. Smith Int'l, Inc., 587 F.2d 1363, 25 UCC 1066 (9th Cir.1978); Killion v. Buran Equip. Co., 1979 WL 30096, 27 UCC 970 (Cal.App.1979) (2–202 rejects notion that because an agreement is in writing it is considered complete and final); Amoco Production Co. v. Western Slope Gas Co., 754 F.2d 303, 40 UCC 370 (10th Cir.1985) (2–202 does not presume that parties intended writing to be a complete expression); Century Ready–Mix Co. v. Lower & Co., 770 P.2d 692, 10 UCC2d 705 (Wyo.1989) ("well-accepted doctrine" that UCC parol evidence rule "intended to liberalize rigidity of the common law and to eliminate the presumption that a written contract is a total integration").

§ 3–11

1. Gold Kist, Inc. v. Pillow, 582 S.W.2d 77, 26 UCC 1078 (Tenn.App. 1979) (parol evidence rule does not apply

to oral agreement made after written contract); Trad Indus., Ltd. v. Brogan, 246 Mont. 439, 805 P.2d 54, 14 UCC2d 718 (1991) (telephone conversations after writings not barred).

2. Pendleton Grain Growers v. Pedro, 271 Or. 24, 530 P.2d 85, 16 UCC 315 (1975); B.N.E. Swedbank, S.A. v. Banker, 794 F.Supp. 1291, 20 UCC2d 35 (S.D.N.Y.1992) (telexes in foreign currency exchange; evidence that the parties did not intend the writing to be binding).

3. 677 P.2d 365, 36 UCC 1262 (Colo. App.1983).

4. Cf. Stern & Co. v. State Loan & Finance Corp., 238 F.Supp. 901, 2 UCC 721 (D.Del.1965).

embodies the actual agreement.[5] Where one writing is prior it may not be admitted if it contradicts a subsequent writing that is either a complete and exclusive statement of all terms or a final expression of some terms.

If the judge finds that the writing is a "complete and exclusive" statement of the contract terms, then the judge may not admit evidence even of terms that do not contradict terms in the writing. Of course, some cases will be easy, as where the parties include a conspicuous merger clause stating in the very language of 2–202 that the writing is complete and exclusive.[6]

The language of 2–202 does not expressly set forth "tests" by which the judge is to determine whether the writing is a complete and exclusive statement of the terms of the contract. Over the years, courts have devised different tests. One of these is the so-called "four corners" test by which the trial judge simply looks at what is within the four corners of the writing and decides if the writing looks complete.[7] The structure of section 2–202 seems less congenial to this test than earlier versions of the parol evidence rule. The section may not adopt any presumption that the entire agreement is embodied in the writing. A four corners test thrives more readily under a rule that presumes full embodiment in the writing unless only partial embodiment is proved. Further, Comment 3 to 2–202 may reject a four corners test.[8] Usually a judge should be willing to go beyond the four corners and consider any proffered evidence on the issue of completeness and exclusivity.[9] At

---

5. See Airstream, Inc. v. CIT Financial Services, Inc., 111 Idaho 307, 723 P.2d 851, 2 UCC2d 816 (1986) (when confirmatory memoranda do not agree, 2–207 is applicable and resorting to 2–202 is improper).

6. One court has argued that the omission of a merger clause, while not creating a presumption of incompleteness, is a factor the court may properly consider in determining a document's completeness. Rajala v. Allied Corp., 66 B.R. 582, 2 UCC2d 1203 (D.Kan.1986).

7. E.g., Philipp Bros. Div. of Engelhard Minerals & Chem. Corp. v. El Salto, S.A., 487 F.Supp. 91, 28 UCC 1280 (S.D.N.Y.1980) (court looks to completeness of written instrument, not subjective intent); Happy Dack Trading Co., Ltd. v. Agro–Indus., Inc., 602 F.Supp. 986, 41 UCC 1718 (S.D.N.Y.1984) (where telexes purported to cover complete agreement and included provisions on product type, quantity, unit, price, packing requirements, manufacturer, date of shipment, loading port, payment method, and more, and were followed by

written confirmation, writings were integrated).

Of course, a four corners test is double-edged. In some cases it will be quite obvious from the writing alone that the writing is not a complete and exclusive statement of the contract terms. See, e.g., Hull–Dobbs, Inc. v. Mallicoat, 57 Tenn.App. 100, 415 S.W.2d 344, 3 UCC 1032 (1966); Mies Equipment, Inc. v. NCI Bldg. Systems, 167 F.Supp. 2d 1077, 44 UCC2d 1017 (2001).

8. § 2–202, Comment 3: Under paragraph (b) consistent additional terms, not reduced to writing, may be proved unless the court finds that the writing was intended by both parties as a complete and exclusive statement of all the terms. If the additional terms are such that, if agreed upon, they would certainly have been included in the document in the view of the court, then evidence of their alleged making must be kept from the trier of fact.

9. See, e.g., Compania Sud–Americana de Vapores, S.A. v. IBJ Schroder

minimum the judge must learn of the context and of the character of the terms not in the writing; otherwise he or she will be in the dark at least as to some of the respects in which the writing might not be complete and exclusive. Comment 3 tells us that "if the additional terms are those that, if agreed upon, they would certainly have been included in the document in the view of the court, then evidence of their alleged making must be kept from the trier of fact." Thus, in light of this comment, and all evidence of completeness and exclusivity, the judge should consider whether the alleged additional terms are such that, *if agreed upon,* they would certainly have been included in the writing. The word "certainly" is not self-defining, nor can judges rationally apply it in the dark.[10] Sometimes a judge, knowing the claim of the party wishing to add a term, can resolve the issue without evidence (this fifty-page document negotiated by New York lawyers would have included that term if it had been agreed upon). In other cases, the judge may need evidence explaining the offered term, the relevant practice on comprehensiveness of writings and the reasons for exclusion of the term from the writing.[11]

If the judge decides the writing *is* complete and exclusive, evidence even of consistent additional terms may not be admitted.[12] However, the writing may be explained or supplemented by course of dealing, usage of trade, or course of performance (on which, more later).

If the judge decides the writing *is not* complete and exclusive, then he or she may admit evidence of "consistent additional terms," unless he or she also determines that the alleged extrinsic term, if agreed upon would certainly have been included in the

---

Bank & Trust Co., 785 F.Supp. 411, 17 UCC2d 1050 (S.D.N.Y.1992) (court considers parol evidence in determining that confirmations of foreign currency transactions not complete and exclusive).

10. On the "certainty" test, see e.g., Lakeside Bridge & Steel Co. v. Mountain State Constr. Co., Inc., 400 F.Supp. 273, 17 UCC 917 (E.D.Wis.1975), rev'd, 597 F.2d 596 (7th Cir.1979), cert. denied, 445 U.S. 907, 100 S.Ct. 1087, 63 L.Ed.2d 325 (1980); Sagent Technology, Inc. v. Micros Systems, Inc., 276 F.Supp.2d 464, 51 UCC2d 59 (D.C. Md.2003).

11. See, e.g., Tigg Corp. v. Dow Corning Corp., 822 F.2d 358, 4 UCC2d 44 (3d Cir.1987) (trial court erred in granting summary judgment; should have admitted evidence that "mini-

mums" would be adjusted annually with buyer's requirements).

12. See e.g., Community Bank v. Newmark & Lewis, Inc., 534 F.Supp. 456, 33 UCC 1232 (E.D.N.Y.1982) (parol evidence cannot contradict final expression agreement); Arthur Jaffee Assoc. v. Bilsco Auto Service, Inc., 89 A.D.2d 785, 453 N.Y.S.2d 501, 34 UCC 894 (1982), aff'd, 58 N.Y.2d 993, 461 N.Y.S.2d 1007, 448 N.E.2d 792 (1983) (where writing express and unambiguous, employee's deposition could not be used to contradict it) Raj Jewelers v. Dialuck Corp., 300 A.D.2d 124, 752 N.Y.S.2d 40, 49 UCC2d 1085 (2002) (oral testimony contradicted term); TIBCO Software, Inc. v. Gordon Food Service, Inc., 2003 WL 21683850, 51 UCC2d 102 (W.D. Mich. 2003) (agreement integrated, so no parol).

writing.[13] Thus the judge could, on the basis of evidence as to the general scope of the negotiations and the basis of evidence as to the finality of the writing conclude that the writing was not complete and exclusive, yet at the same time conclude that if a given term had been agreed upon it certainly would have been in the writing, and bar its admission. When a judge decides that a writing is not complete and exclusive, and that evidence of additional terms is admissible, the familiar problem of filling genuine gaps in the agreement arises.[14]

Of course, even if the judge decides the writing is not complete and exclusive, yet decides it is a final written expression as to some terms, evidence of contradictory *prior or contemporaneous* terms may not be admitted.

What are "terms"? Section 1–201(b)(40) defines "term" to mean "a portion of an agreement which relates to a particular matter." In 1–201(b)(3) "agreement" means "the bargain of the parties in fact as found in their language or inferred from other circumstances * * *." If a writing is *silent* as to a particular matter,[15] then one can argue that it includes no "term" thereon and that extrinsic evidence of an alleged term covering the matter is not "contradictory" of anything in the writing and is admissible. In Hunt Foods & Industries, Inc. v. Doliner,[16] the writing appeared to be an unconditional option to purchase defendant's stock that the plaintiff might exercise at any time prior to its expiry. The writing said nothing at all about any condition. Defendant claimed the parties had orally agreed that the option was conditional, specifically, that it could only be exercised if the defendant used a prior offer of the plaintiff to solicit higher offers. Defendant sought to introduce extrinsic evidence to this effect. The court upheld the defendant, and proclaimed that (1) the evidence of the alleged extrinsic term (the condition) did not contradict a term of the

13. ARB (American Research Bureau), Inc. v. E–Systems, Inc., 663 F.2d 189, 30 UCC 949 (D.C.Cir.1980) (additional "no cover" provision would certainly have been included in contract).

14. Courts have admitted evidence to fill gaps of many kinds. See, e.g., MacGregor v. McReki, Inc., 30 Colo.App. 196, 494 P.2d 1297, 10 UCC 383 (1971) (time for performance); Northwest Central Pipeline Corp. v. JER Partnership, 943 F.2d 1219, 16 UCC2d 1004 (10th Cir.1991) (parol evidence admitted on whether buyer had right to cancel long-term contract if the industry was deregulated).

15. Alimenta (U.S.A.), Inc. v. Anheuser–Busch Cos., Inc., 803 F.2d 1160, 2 UCC2d 441 (11th Cir.1986) (seller's sample peanuts given to buyer to represent appearance and taste constituted additional contract terms).

16. 26 A.D.2d 41, 270 N.Y.S.2d 937, 3 UCC 597 (1966), noted in 66 Colum.L.Rev. 1370 (1966). For extended discussion of this case, see Broude, The Consumer and the Parol Evidence Rule: Section 2–202 of the Uniform Commercial Code, 1970 Duke L.J. 881, 890–99. For a case rejecting the Hunt Food's approach, see Alaska Northern Dev., Inc. v. Alyeska Pipeline Service Co., 666 P.2d 33, 36 UCC 1527 (Alaska 1983), cert. denied, 464 U.S. 1041, 104 S.Ct. 706, 79 L.Ed.2d 170 (1984).

writing, and (2) as evidence of a *consistent* additional term, the evidence was admissible inasmuch as it was not evidence of a term that would "certainly" have been included in the writing if actually agreed upon. We do not agree that the oral condition did not contradict a specific term of the writing. The written option was unconditional, the oral evidence rendered it conditional.

We believe a better way to deal with *Hunt Foods* would be to say that 2–202 does not apply unless the parties intend their writing to be a "final expression of their agreement with respect to such terms as are included therein," and they did not so intend here. Another approach—but one with its own problems—would be to say that the parol evidence rule simply does not bar evidence that the legal effectiveness of a writing was conditioned on the occurrence of an external event that did not occur.[17]

Assume that a grower contracts to sell crops to a buyer without inserting a clause that the crops are to be grown on grower's land and for some reason grower is unable to deliver. May the grower introduce evidence that the crops were to be grown on his or her land and claim an excuse for nondelivery? The grower has generally lost on the theory that the omitted term contradicts the writing.[18]

Suppose a writing says nothing of express warranties in regard to a given matter and includes no disclaimers. The plaintiff then seeks to introduce extrinsic evidence to prove an express oral warranty. May the defendant keep this evidence from the trier of fact on the ground that it contradicts a term *in the writing?* Presumably not, if the *Hunt Foods* theory of contradictoriness is followed. This would not necessarily mean that the plaintiff would be home free, for the judge might still keep the evidence out on the ground that if such an additional term had been agreed upon, it would most certainly have been embodied in the writing. On the other hand, if the writing includes an express warranty on a given matter and a party seeks to introduce evidence of a different extrinsic warranty on that matter, or if the writing includes a disclaimer and a party seeks to introduce evidence of an extrinsic

---

17. See Ketchian v. Concannon, 435 So.2d 394, 36 UCC 1259 (Fla.App.1983) (parol evidence of condition precedent admissible despite face of document to the contrary because such instrument never matured as a valid obligation); In re McFarland, 112 B.R. 906, 12 UCC2d 249 (Bankr.E.D.Tenn.1990) (oral agreement between debtors and car dealer that contracts subject to obtaining financing from Ford for both cars admissible since condition precedent; only agreements that contradict written contract are excluded). See also, 3 A. Corbin, Contracts § 590 (1950); 1 N.Y. State Law Revision Comm'n, 1955 Report 683 (1955). But see, Deck House, Inc. v. Scarborough, Sheffield & Gaston, Inc., 139 Ga.App. 173, 228 S.E.2d 142, 20 UCC 278 (1976).

18. Bunge Corp. v. Recker, 519 F.2d 449, 17 UCC 400 (8th Cir.1975). The grower prevailed in Paymaster Oil Mill Co. v. Mitchell, 319 So.2d 652, 17 UCC 1173 (Miss.1975) but the writing there included the words, "as per our conversation", thus inviting parol. Cases against the grower include Wickliffe Farms, Inc. v. Owensboro Grain Co., 684 S.W.2d 17, 39 UCC 195 (Ky.App.1984).

express warranty, one could properly bar the evidence as "contradictory." Of course, if the disclaimer is legally ineffective under 2–316, then it cannot be contradictory, for it does not "exist."[19] One court has said that a disclaimer does not exist if the parties did not specifically bargain for it,[20] but section 2–316 does not require that a disclaimer be bargained.

Sometimes a court distinguishes between an agreement and an inducement to agree. In Hull–Dobbs, Inc. v. Mallicoat,[21] the court said:

> The parol evidence rule does not apply where the parol evidence in no way contradicts or alters the terms of the written contract but the representations or statements are made as an inducement to the contract and form the basis and consideration for it.[22]

The court approved the admission of evidence of extrinsic "inducing warranties" although the security agreement included the words "accepted in its present condition." The court also said that the merely inducing "warranties" did not contradict this writing. The court explained that the language in the security agreement "accepted in its present condition" referred to acceptance. In the court's view, this language was "not synonymous with 'as is' or 'with all faults' and other like language which according to common usage call the buyer's attention to the exclusion of representations and warranties." The court added that if it was mistaken in holding the extrinsic "warranties" to be an inducement to the contract rather than a part of it "we hold that the Security Agreement as written was not intended as a final expression of the agreement of the parties." The court also went on to say that "even if it should be held that the security agreement was intended as a final statement of the terms of sale, the representations were not inconsistent

19.   Hertz Commercial Leasing Corp. v. Transportation Credit Clearing House, 59 Misc.2d 226, 298 N.Y.S.2d 392, 6 UCC 132 (City Civ.1969), rev'd on other grounds, 64 Misc.2d 910, 316 N.Y.S.2d 585 (1970).

20.   Hertz Commercial Leasing Corp. v. Transportation Credit Clearing House, 59 Misc.2d 226, 298 N.Y.S.2d 392, 6 UCC 132 (City Civ.1969), rev'd on other grounds, 64 Misc.2d 910, 316 N.Y.S.2d 585 (1970). See also, Providence & Worcester R. Co. v. Sargent & Greenleaf, Inc., 802 F.Supp. 680, 19 UCC2d 21 (D.R.I.1992) (form invoice not final expression as to preprinted, nonnegotiated terms; parol evidence of representations admissible and disclaimer not effective; but, according to Editor's Note

at 19 UCC2d 23, court ignores merger clause).

21.   57 Tenn.App. 100, 415 S.W.2d 344, 3 UCC 1032 (1966). But see Avery v. Aladdin Products Div., Nat. Service Indus., Inc., 128 Ga.App. 266, 196 S.E.2d 357, 12 UCC 628 (1973) (oral inducing warranty contradicts disclaimer).

22.   57 Tenn.App. at 104, 415 S.W.2d at 346, 3 UCC at 1033–34. See also, Mountaineer Contractors, Inc. v. Mountain State Mack, Inc., 165 W.Va. 292, 268 S.E.2d 886, 30 UCC 134 (1980) (2–202 did not preclude showing that after contract negotiations had ended, seller made oral inducements, which in effect, modified the written contract).

therewith. As consistent additional terms, these representations could be admitted." Thus whether or not the extrinsic "warranties" were an inducement or part of the contract itself, the court would have reached the same result. Although the result may be sound, the judge misreads section 2–202. It does not recognize "indirect warranties" as different from other terms and, if those warranties would be binding, they should not be treated like other terms.

Suppose a writing includes an express warranty, or disclaims express warranties. May the plaintiff introduce evidence to prove an implied warranty? Some cases indicate that the answer is yes, even where the writing is not silent on the general subject of warranties. A distinction is sometimes drawn between express and implied warranties, and it is said that an implied warranty is not a *term* of the *agreement* at all but arises by operation of law, and that the parol evidence rule excludes only evidence of extrinsic *terms.*[23]

Courts besides the *Hunt Foods* court have also had to consider what "contradicts" means in 2–202.[24] We offer a brief review of some of these cases. The usual terms of a written bill of sale are not contradicted by evidence of an oral term providing for security.[25] A writing providing for the sale of cattle is not contradicted by evidence of an oral term providing that the seller would feed the cattle in a certain manner prior to delivery.[26] Terms of the writing ("Discount and payment periods will start from the date of receipt of * * * by the Buyer * * * and no verbal modification hereof shall be effective") are contradicted by the proffered evidence of the alleged extrinsic term (the seller would "supervise installation, fully check out all equipment, provide operational training * * * and notify * * * that the plant was fully equipped, installed and opera-

---

23. Nettles v. Imperial Distribs., Inc., 152 W.Va. 9, 159 S.E.2d 206 (1968).

24. For good cases on contradiction under 2–202, see, Casper v. Metal Trades, Inc., 604 F.2d 299, 27 UCC 14 (4th Cir.1979), cert. denied, 444 U.S. 981, 100 S.Ct. 483, 62 L.Ed.2d 408 (1979) (where original contract delivery dates had penciled in different dates next to them, and some of the notations differed between plaintiff and defendant's copy, the writing was unintegrated and ambiguous and evidence clarifying the handwritten terms was admissible); Luria Bros. & Co. v. Pielet Bros. Scrap Iron & Metal, Inc., 600 F.2d 103, 26 UCC 1081 (7th Cir.1979) (agreement calling for unconditional sale was contradicted by seller's claim that obligations were conditioned upon

receiving the goods from a certain supplier); Middletown Concrete Products, Inc. v. Black Clawson Co., 802 F.Supp. 1135, 20 UCC2d 815 (D.Del.1992) (letter guaranteeing production rates in specified writings contradicted exclusion of all warranties not contained in the writings); Harry J. Whelchel Co., Inc. v. Ripley Tractor Co., Inc., 900 S.W.2d 691, 27 UCC2d 879 (Tenn. App. 1995) (testimony excluded as to oral agreement that buyer only conditionally bound).

25. McDown v. Wilson, 426 S.W.2d 112, 6 UCC 317 (Mo.App.1968).

26. Conner v. May, 444 S.W.2d 948, 7 UCC 185 (Tex.Civ.App.1969), error refused n.r.e.

tional" before the buyer would be obligated to pay the plaintiff).[27] This decision is difficult to reconcile with the *Hunt Foods* theory of contradictoriness and with those cases which permit a party to show that the legal effect of a writing was dependent upon the occurrence of a "condition precedent to the entire contract" which did not occur. An oral agreement to renegotiate a note contradicts a six month due date.[28] Twelve thousand cubic yards is more than a mere variation on "70,000 cubic yards," which appeared in the writing.[29] An oral damages limitation does not contradict a written delivery date on which damages would ordinarily be calculated.[30] A written quantity term is contradicted by oral evidence of a much lower amount.[31] An oral warranty contradicts an "as is" clause.[32] The Code itself says in 2–326(4) that an "or return" term contradicts a "sale."[33] A provision consenting to bankruptcy court jurisdiction to settle disputes between the parties is contradicted by evidence predicating that jurisdiction on a receipt of store purchase orders.[34]

A clause limiting guarantor's liability to twenty percent of the amount due under a note was contradicted by evidence that the limit was twenty percent of the principal amount.[35] An express ninety day return period was contradicted by a "reasonable" time for inspection of the goods.[36] Evidence that termination could only be for cause contradicted an automatic termination provision in the contract.[37] A contract provision calling for payment simultaneous with the arrival of goods at the warehouse was not contradicted by evidence that in practice payment was delayed until the goods were loaded on the trucks.[38] An "as is" clause did not contradict a clause

27. Whirlpool Corp. v. Regis Leasing Corp., 29 A.D.2d 395, 288 N.Y.S.2d 337, 5 UCC 94 (1968).

28. Chaplin v. Milne, 555 S.W.2d 161, 23 UCC 374 (Tex.Civ.App.1977).

29. Southern Concrete Services, Inc. v. Mableton Contractors, Inc., 407 F.Supp. 581, 19 UCC 79 (N.D.Ga.1975), aff'd, 569 F.2d 1154 (5th Cir.1978).

30. Bunge Corp. v. Miller, 381 F.Supp. 176, 15 UCC 384 (W.D.Tenn. 1974).

31. Chemetron Corp. v. McLouth Steel Corp., 381 F.Supp. 245, 15 UCC 832 (N.D.Ill.1974), aff'd, 522 F.2d 469, 17 UCC 772 (7th Cir.1975).

32. Jordan v. Doonan Truck & Equip., Inc., 220 Kan. 431, 552 P.2d 881, 19 UCC 1297 (1976); Harper v. Calvert, 687 S.W.2d 227, 39 UCC 1655 (Mo.App. 1984) (parol evidence of oral warranty not allowed to contradict "as is" clause); Ace, Inc. v. Maynard, 108 N.C.App. 241, 423 S.E.2d 504, 19 UCC2d 1060 (1992).

33. Consolidated Foods Corp. v. Roland Foods, Inc., 1973 WL 21362, 13 UCC 245 (D.C.Super.1973) (parol evidence not allowed to prove sale or return).

34. In re W.T. Grant Co., 1 B.R. 516, 28 UCC 1283 (S.D.N.Y.1979).

35. Warnaco, Inc. v. Farkas, 664 F.Supp. 738, 4 UCC2d 1651 (S.D.N.Y. 1987), aff'd in part, rev'd in part, 872 F.2d 539, 8 UCC2d 427 (2d Cir.1989).

36. Polygram, S.A. v. 32–03 Enters., Inc., 697 F.Supp. 132, 8 UCC2d 914 (E.D.N.Y.1988).

37. General Aviation, Inc. v. Cessna Aircraft Co., 915 F.2d 1038, 14 UCC2d 73 (6th Cir.1990). See also O'Neill v. United States, 50 F.3d 677, 26 UCC2d 1 (9th Cir. 1995).

38. In re Julien Co., 128 B.R. 987, 16 UCC2d 649 (Bankr.W.D.Tenn.1991).

which provided that any rights and remedies "which may arise in the future" would be exercisable.[39] The court reasoned that the waived warranty rights were not "future" rights.

Under 2–202, whenever the judge finds that evidence of the alleged extrinsic term is not evidence of a term that contradicts a term in the writing, the evidence may, if of a "consistent additional term," be used to supplement the writing, provided the judge does not find that the term, if agreed upon, would certainly have been included in the writing.[40] One court has stressed that the more complete a writing appears to be on its face, the less likely it is that any extrinsic term was agreed upon, even if consistent with the writing.[41]

Even if the writing is a "complete and exclusive" statement of the terms of the agreement, parties may still introduce course of dealing, usage of trade, or course of performance to explain, supplement, or add to the agreement[42] (but not contradict it).[43] This is so even where the language of the agreement is unambiguous on its face.

There are a few aptly illustrative decisions. In one, the court held that the words "delivery June–August" could be shown to have acquired a special meaning in the retail clothing trade that ruled out delivery of the entire lot in August.[44] In another case, the court held that the words "thirty-six inch steel" could be shown to have acquired by trade usage a special meaning such that delivery

39. Quaker Alloy Casting Co. v. Gulfco Industries, Inc., 686 F.Supp. 1319, 7 UCC2d 429 (N.D.Ill.1988).

40. See, e.g., § 2–202, Comment 3. Anderson & Nafziger v. G.T. Newcomb, Inc., 100 Idaho 175, 595 P.2d 709, 27 UCC 21 (1979) (when written contract gave no delivery date, parol evidence of oral delivery date was admissible).

41. Whirlpool Corp. v. Regis Leasing Corp., 29 A.D.2d 395, 288 N.Y.S.2d 337, 5 UCC 94 (1968).

42. See, generally, Levie, Trade Usage and Custom Under the Common Law and the Uniform Commercial Code, 40 N.Y.U.L.Rev. 1101 (1965); Note, Admissibility of Evidence of Course of Dealing and Usage of Trade Under Uniform Commercial Code § 2–202(a), 30 Wash. & Lee.L.Rev. 117 (1973); Modine Mfg. Co. v. North East Independent School Dist., 503 S.W.2d 833, 14 UCC 317 (Tex.Civ.App.1973), error ref'd n.r.e. (trade usage) Central Arizona Water Conservation Dist. v. United States, 32 F.Supp.2d 1117, 38 UCC2d 318 (D. Ariz. 1998) (usage can be used to show ambi-

guity); Allapattah Svcs., Inc. v. Exxon Corp., 333 F.3d 1248, 50 UCC2d 1047 (11th Cir. 2003) (where party is accused of violating duty of good faith in setting prices, extrinsic evidence explaining party's manner of setting prices is admissible under 2–202(1)(a)).

43. General Plumbing & Heating, Inc. v. American Air Filter Co., 696 F.2d 375, 35 UCC 364 (5th Cir.1983) (course of dealing or usage of trade on delivery dates not admissible because express term to contrary); Bib Audio–Video Products v. Herold Marketing Assocs., Inc., 517 N.W.2d 68, 24 UCC2d 455 (Minn. App. 1994) (no use of usage of trade to contradict terms). For an argument that usage of trade and course of dealing are not to be subjected to any test that they "explain, supplement, or be additional" to the writing, see Kirst, "Usage of Trade and Course of Dealing: Subversion of the UCC Theory", 1977 U.Ill.L.F. 811, 833 et seq.

44. Warren's Kiddie Shoppe, Inc. v. Casual Slacks, Inc., 120 Ga.App. 578, 171 S.E.2d 643, 7 UCC 166 (1969).

of thirty-seven inch steel constituted performance.[45] Of course, when the writing is not "complete or exclusive" or is ambiguous, there is even more of a basis for introducing course of dealing, usage of trade, or course of performance.[46]

In Division of Triple T Service, Inc. v. Mobil Oil Corp.,[47] the parties expressly agreed that a franchising arrangement would "terminate at the end of any current period (original or renewal) by notice from either party to the other, given not less than 90 days prior to such termination * * *." The franchisee claimed that trade usage therefore could not be admitted. Section 1–303(e) (and prior law) requires that express terms, trade usage, and course of performance be construed wherever reasonable as consistent with each other. Can exclusion of trade practice here be reconciled with *Hunt Foods*?[48] In *Triple T,* the court emphasized that the express agreement treated "the entire area of termination," but in *Hunt Foods* the agreement said nothing about any condition on the right to exercise the option. Also, oral testimony may be more "admissibility-worthy" than mere evidence of general trade usage. Certainly, oral testimony is less remote from the specific transaction.

In Nanakuli Paving & Rock Co. v. Shell Oil Co., Inc.,[49] the buyer and Shell agreed to a long term contract containing language that the price of asphalt would be Shell's "Posted Price" at time of delivery. After the buyer (a paving company) had agreed to supply third parties on the basis of Shell's then existing "Posted Price," Shell raised its posted price and sought to impose that price on the buyer. The buyer sued Shell for breach and prevailed by showing that the prevailing trade practice at the time of contracting was to provide "price protection" with the result that Shell's changes in the posted price could not be applied to buyers who had already made commitments based on earlier prices. In response to Shell's argument that this result impermissibly allowed trade usage to control "express terms" contrary to 1–205(4) (now 1–303), the

---

45. Decker Steel Co. v. Exchange Nat. Bank, 330 F.2d 82 (7th Cir.1964).

46. United States for Use and Benefit of Union Building Materials Corp. v. Haas & Haynie Corp., 577 F.2d 568, 27 UCC 32 (9th Cir.1978) (contract ambiguous as to amount due could be supplemented by trade usage); Mohave Valley Irrigation & Drainage Dist. v. Norton, 244 F.3d 1164, 44 UCC2d 40 (9th Cir. 2001) (to determine whether a contract's terms are ambiguous, courts may only consider evidence of course of dealing, trade usage, or course of performance).

47. 60 Misc.2d 720, 304 N.Y.S.2d 191, 6 UCC 1011 (1969), aff'd, 34 A.D.2d 618, 311 N.Y.S.2d 961 (1970). See also

Blalock Machinery and Equip. Co. v. Iowa Mfg. Co., 576 F.Supp. 774, 36 UCC 753 (N.D.Ga.1983) (while continuous dealings of parties during 27 years may have created reasonable expectation that neither would terminate without cause, the language expressly gave each the right to do so, and therefore course of dealing or performance could not contradict).

48. Hunt Foods & Indus., Inc. v. Doliner, 26 A.D.2d 41, 270 N.Y.S.2d 937, 3 UCC 597 (1966). See also Columbia Nitrogen Corp. v. Royster Co., 451 F.2d 3, 9 UCC 977 (4th Cir.1971);

49. 664 F.2d 772, 32 UCC 1025 (9th Cir.1981).

court stated that "Such a usage forms a broad and important exception to the express term but does not swallow it entirely." The court would have done better to have rested on 1–205(1) and held that the usage established a "common basis of understanding for interpreting" the contract language "Shell's Posted Price," i.e., an understanding that changes in posted price would not be retroactive as above. At least if so interpreted, no conflict would arise under 1–205(4) (1–303) between express term and trade usage.

Can evidence of course of dealing, usage of trade, or course of performance *add* a term to the writing? Section 2–202(a) is drafted broadly enough to permit this and 1–303(d) is in accord. In Provident Tradesmens Bank & Trust Co. v. Pemberton,[50] the court used evidence of trade usage to add an additional term to the writing, namely that the plaintiff-lender owed a duty to notify the defendant-dealer if the dealer's customer let the insurance lapse on the car sold to him. There was also evidence of a course of dealing between the parties that recognized this duty to give notice. Yet the written agreement between the lender and the dealer was entirely silent on the matter. If the plaintiff had wanted to negate or exclude such a term, it could easily have drafted a contract clause to that effect. In the absence of a contract clause, courts will likely permit parties to use course of dealing, usage of trade, and course of performance to establish *additional* terms.[51]

So-called "course of performance" evidence may explain or supplement language in a writing, for it shows how the parties themselves interpreted their own deal. In one important case, Associated Hardware Supply Co. v. Big Wheel Distributing Co.,[52] the court relied on "course of performance" evidence in concluding that a buyer bought at a price of "dealer catalogue less 11%." The buyer claimed that the agreed price was really "cost plus 10% on warehouse shipments and cost plus 5% on factory shipments." The buyer was billed on the basis of "dealer catalogue less 11%" and made payments at that rate. The court thought this was a course of performance which showed that the buyer acquiesced in the seller's pricing term. It is not clear from the opinion, however, whether the buyer argued that its course of performance merely constituted acquiescence in a mode of payment rather than assent to the seller's pricing term. The buyer probably should have prevailed on this argument, especially given his allegation that the seller had

---

50. 196 Pa.Super. 180, 173 A.2d 780, 1 UCC 57 (1961).

51. Levie, The Interpretation of Contracts in New York under the Uniform Commercial Code, 10 N.Y.L.F. 350, 368–72 (1964). See also C–Thru Container Corp. v. Midland Mfg. Co., 533 N.W.2d 542, 27 UCC2d 72 (Iowa 1995) (court can add consistent terms if warranted by trade usage); Heller, Inc. v. Indiana Dept. of Trans., 819 N.E.2d 140, 55 UCC2d 464 (Ind. App. 2004) (usage of trade existed and added term).

52. 355 F.2d 114, 3 UCC 1 (3d Cir. 1965).

assured him during relevant times that "dealer catalogue less 11%" would be a price equivalent to "cost plus 10%." The court did send the buyer's counterclaim back for trial on whether the seller had thus defrauded the buyer, even though the court concluded that a contract had in fact been formed between the parties on the basis of the seller's price.

A party showing a usage of trade must prove that the behavior has such regularity of observance as to justify an expectation that it will be observed with respect to the transaction in question.[53] When a trade usage is widespread, there is a presumption that the parties intended its incorporation, unless the contract language carefully negates it.[54]

Of course, parties may attach special meanings to the words they use without resort to usage of trade or course of dealing. One court allowed extrinsic evidence to show that "500 tons" really meant "up to 500 tons,"[55] and properly so. In another case, the court interpreted a covenant not to sue a defendant in the business of giving hair treatments to apply only to injuries to the plaintiff's hair and scalp but not to the plaintiff's ear, even though the covenant was broad enough to cover ear injuries.[56]

If a court invalidates a clause as unconscionable, may a court then admit parol evidence to determine what the replacement clause should look like? One court said "yes."[57]

§ 3–12　Judge–Made Exceptions to the Parol Evidence Rule

Courts have made numerous exceptions to the parol evidence rule. Each exception is canvassed in Professor Corbin's treatise,[1] and except insofar as the wording of 2–202 renders any exception redundant, each remains good law under the Code via 1–103. The

53. § 1–205(2). See, e.g., B.F. Hirsch, Inc. v. Enright Refining Co., 577 F.Supp. 339, 38 UCC 444 (D.N.J.1983), aff'd in part, vacated in part, 751 F.2d 628 (3d Cir.1984), on remand 617 F.Supp. 49 (D.N.J.1985) (retainage assessment on scrap gold deliveries to jewelry manufacturer were not so prevalent that the parties intended their agreement to be governed by it and thus was not a usage of trade); H & W Industries, Inc. v. Occidental Chem. Corp., 911 F.2d 1118, 12 UCC2d 921 (5th Cir.1990) (no credible trade usage evidence where unique contract duration and peculiar market state; when evidence of dealing with someone other than other party, must show parallelism).

54. See, e.g., Foxco Indus., Ltd. v. Fabric World, Inc., 595 F.2d 976, 26

UCC 694 (5th Cir.1979) (the term "first quality goods" had a specific definition according to Standards for Finished Knitted Fabrics of the Knitted Textile Association even though buyer unaware of the definition, usage was admissible).

55. Michael Schiavone & Sons, Inc. v. Securalloy Co., 312 F.Supp. 801, 7 UCC 674 (D.Conn.1970).

56. Ciunci v. Wella Corp., 26 A.D.2d 109, 271 N.Y.S.2d 317, 3 UCC 811 (1966).

57. Ashland Oil, Inc. v. Donahue, 159 W.Va. 463, 223 S.E.2d 433, 18 UCC 1129 (1976).

§ 3–12

1. See 3 A. Corbin, Contracts §§ 573–621 (1950).

fraud exception is the most important. It is often said that a party may not invoke the parol evidence rule in order to shield his or her own fraud.[2] Fraud may also serve as a basis for rescission or for affirmative relief. In Associated Hardware Supply Co. v. Big Wheel Distributing Co.,[3] the court sent buyer's counterclaim back for retrial on the issue of whether the seller fraudulently told the buyer that "dealer catalogue less 11%" was equivalent to "cost plus 10%" and thereby induced the buyer to enter into or go forward with the deal. Insofar as any such representations were oral, they were outside the writing which the court said constituted the contract. Of course, the buyer might try to introduce them not to show fraud, but to show the meaning of the words in the contract, and this is permissible under 2–202. Yet, the buyer might go beyond this and show fraud, too.[4]

Courts should be wary of turning the fraud exception into an exception that swallows up the entire parol evidence rule. A party should not be allowed to introduce evidence of an alleged extrinsic term merely by alleging fraud.[5] Fraud is easy to claim, but hard to prove. The judge should hold a preliminary hearing away from the jury to determine whether the party offering the evidence really is seeking to show fraudulent misrepresentation or fraudulent nondisclosure.[6] What constitutes fraud depends to some extent on local state law. For example, in Clements Auto Co. v. Service Bureau Corp.,[7] the court invoked Minnesota common law to find actionable fraud absent scienter. In states which do require an element of scienter for fraud, the judge should not invoke the fraud exception to admit extrinsic evidence where he or she concludes that a misrepresentation is wholly innocent.[8] This is not to say, however, that the judge should not admit the evidence on any ground. It may

---

2. See generally, Sweet, Promissory Fraud and the Parol Evidence Rule, 49 Calif.L.Rev. 877 (1961); George Robberecht Seafood, Inc. v. Maitland Bros. Co., 220 Va. 109, 255 S.E.2d 682, 26 UCC 669 (1979) (proof of false representations that airplane was airworthy not excludable under parol evidence rule); McMahon Food Corp. v. Burger Dairy Co., 103 F.3d 1307, 31 UCC2d 283 (7th Cir. 1996) (parol evidence to show fraud admissible).

3. 355 F.2d 114, 3 UCC 1 (3d Cir. 1965).

4. Ed Fine Oldsmobile, Inc. v. Knisley, 319 A.2d 33, 14 UCC 700 (Del.Super.1974) (misrepresentation of a used car's history).

5. See, e.g., Westfield Chem. Corp. v. Burroughs Corp., 1977 WL 25591, 21 UCC 1293 (Mass.Super.1977) ("mere

characterization of representations as fraudulent is insufficient"). See also, Kalil Bottling Co. v. Burroughs Corp., 127 Ariz. 278, 619 P.2d 1055, 30 UCC 128 (App.1980).

6. Universal Drilling Co. v. Camay Drilling Co., 737 F.2d 869, 38 UCC 1576 (10th Cir.1984) (at preliminary hearing, plaintiff was unable to establish evidence of fraud).

7. 444 F.2d 169, 9 UCC 189 (8th Cir.1971).

8. Sagent Technology, Inc. v. Micros Systems, Inc., 276 F.Supp.2d 464, 51 UCC2d 59 (D. Md. 2003) (where parol evidence contradicts the terms of the written agreement, the alleged misrepresentations must be intentional for evidence to be admissible).

still be admissible to show that the parties attached a special meaning to contract words.

Mistake is a second judge-made exception to the parol evidence rule.[9] The exception applies not only to mutual mistake but to unilateral mistake as well.[10]

It is well understood that the parol evidence rule does not bar evidence bearing on a genuine issue of interpretation arising because of ambiguity or other unclarity.[11] Some courts require that the term to be interpreted be ambiguous on its face.[12]

Here section 2–202 and the Restatement Contracts 2d part company. Where a written statement in an integrated contract shows no lack of clarity or ambiguity, 2–201 seems to allow usage of the trade, course of performance and course of dealing, but would exclude oral testimony and other extrinsic evidence to show meaning.

But section 212 of the Restatement and particularly Comment b to that section follow the lead of Justice Traynor and the California courts. Section 212 would apparently always allow the jury to hear oral testimony to show "meaning."

> Comment b reads *"Plain meaning and extrinsic evidence. It is sometimes said that extrinsic evidence cannot change the plain meaning of a writing, but meaning can almost never be plain except in a context. Accordingly the rule stated in Subsection [212](i) is not limited to cases"* of ambiguity.

So if a party is clever enough to find a word or a phrase that deals with his issue he can get his evidence in front of the jury under the Restatement by claiming that he is merely "showing the meaning" of the word or phrase. Taken to its extreme, the Restatement rule guts the parol evidence rule.

§ 3–13 "Merger" Clauses and the Parol Evidence Rule

Section 2–202 reads as follows:

Terms with respect to which the confirmatory memoranda of the parties agree or which are otherwise set forth in a writing

9. Braund, Inc. v. White, 486 P.2d 50, 9 UCC 183 (Alaska 1971).

10. General Equip. Mfrs. v. Bible Press, Inc., 10 Mich.App. 676, 160 N.W.2d 370, 5 UCC 822 (1968). See also, Continental Information Sys. Corp. v. Mutual Life Ins. Co., 77 A.D.2d 316, 432 N.Y.S.2d 952, 31 UCC 816 (1980) (parol evidence admissible to show true consideration was other than that recited in bill of sale).

11. See, e.g., Flamm v. Scherer, 40 Mich.App. 1, 198 N.W.2d 702, 11 UCC 83 (1972) ("seed" required interpretation); Sicor Ltd. v. Cetus Corp., 51 F.3d 848, 26 UCC2d 686 (9th Cir. 1995), cert. den. 516 U.S. 861, 116 S.Ct. 170, 133 L.Ed.2d 111 (1995) ("substantial ambiguity" not required to admit evidence to interpret); Hessler v. Crystal Lake Chrysler–Plymouth, 338 Ill.App.3d 1010, 273 Ill.Dec. 96, 788 N.E.2d 405, 50 UCC2d 330 (2d Dist. 2003) (where contract is ambiguous, extrinsic evidence is admissible).

12. See, e.g., Paragon Resources, Inc. v. National Fuel Gas Distrib. Corp., 723 F.2d 419, 37 UCC 1482 (5th Cir.1984).

intended by the parties as a final expression of their agreement
with respect to such terms as are included therein may not be
contradicted by evidence of any prior agreement or of a contemporaneous oral agreement but may be explained or supplemented

(a) course of dealing, or usage of trade (section 1–303) or
by course of performance (section 2–208); and

(b) by evidence[1] of consistent additional terms unless the
court finds the writing to have been intended also as a complete and exclusive statement of the terms of the agreement.

This statutory language does not bar all evidence extrinsic to a
writing already in evidence. A court may decide that the writing is
not a "final written expression" as to any terms and admit the
evidence. A court may decide that the writing is a final expression
of some terms, but not a "complete and exclusive" statement of all
terms, and admit evidence of "consistent additional terms." A court
may decide that the writing is a final written expression as to terms
and also that the writing is a "complete and exclusive statement,"
yet admit evidence of course of dealing, usage of trade, or course of
performance to "explain" the meaning of terms in the writing.
Under judge-made exceptions to 2–202 a court may also admit
evidence extrinsic to the writing. But can the parties, by contract,
preclude the introduction of evidence at trial to show terms outside
the writing? "Merger" clauses (because they "merge" the negotiation and prior tentative agreements into the writing) are generally
valid.[2] We offer the following illustrative clause which we believe
would be valid and effective (so far as it goes): "THIS AGREE-
MENT SIGNED BY BOTH PARTIES AND SO INITIALED BY
BOTH PARTIES IN THE MARGIN OPPOSITE THIS PARA-
GRAPH CONSTITUTES A FINAL WRITTEN EXPRESSION OF
ALL THE TERMS OF THIS AGREEMENT AND IS A COM-
PLETE AND EXCLUSIVE STATEMENT OF THOSE TERMS."

This language should be effective to preclude a judge from
admitting extrinsic evidence on a theory that the writing is not a
complete and exclusive statement of the contract terms. The specific initialing of the clause will defeat later claims that the clause was
inconspicuous boilerplate that can be disregarded as unconscionable

§ 3–13

1. Bank of America v. C.D. Smith
Motor Co., 353 Ark. 228, 106 S.W.3d
425, 50 UCC2d 670 (2003) (a merger
clause does not bar evidence extrinsic to
a writing already in evidence where the

writing is silent on the subject of the
extrinsic) (citing White and Summers).

2. See, e.g., General Motors Acceptance Corp. v. Grady, 27 Ohio App.3d
321, 501 N.E.2d 68, 2 UCC2d 887
(1985).

or for some other reason.[3] The foregoing clause would not, however, keep all extrinsic evidence out. It would not keep out evidence of course of dealing, usage of trade, or course of performance introduced to explain the meaning of contract terms—but a more specific clause could do this.[4] Moreover, it would not keep out evidence introduced to impose rights and duties that arise by operation of law. Implied warranties are the prime example. If the parties want to disclaim or exclude these, they must take further steps. In addition, the foregoing contract language would not normally bar evidence introduced pursuant to such judge-made exceptions to the parol evidence rule as mistake or fraud.

Merger clauses are widely used and have special value in two classic situations aptly illustrated in the cases. In the first situation, the parties negotiate over a period of time, making and withdrawing numerous proposals. They finally reach an agreement and make a writing. Here there is special need for a merger clause to protect against the risk that one party will, honestly or dishonestly, seek to resurrect some proposal that did not show up in the final writing. In the Oklahoma Court of Appeals case of Holton v. Bivens,[5] the parties had negotiated extensively over the purchase and sale of a used bulldozer. They finally entered into a written agreement that included this language: "No oral agreement, guaranty, promise, representation or warranty shall be binding." Thereafter a dispute arose, and the trial court allowed the buyer to introduce evidence of an express oral warranty.[6] The appellate court reversed.[7] It cited the foregoing merger clause and emphasized that "[e]very person should have the right to rely upon written contracts. Allowing testimony of oral agreements in contradiction thereof can only result in confusion concerning reliability of the writing"[8]

In the second classic situation, the seller's effusive salesperson makes unauthorized oral representations to the buyer who thereafter signs a written agreement that does not include these representations. Here the seller needs protection against the risks that the buyer will seek to introduce evidence of the unauthorized oral representations to enhance his or her legal rights against the seller.

---

3. See, e.g., Seibel v. Layne & Bowler, Inc., 56 Or.App. 387, 641 P.2d 668, 33 UCC 893 (1982), review denied, 293 Or. 190, 648 P.2d 852 (1982) (inconspicuous merger clause was ineffective).

4. Bank of America, N.A. v. C.D. Smith Motor Company, Inc., 353 Ark. 228, 106 S.W.3d 425, 50 UCC2d 670 (2003) (presence of merger clause does not bar evidence of course-of-dealing to supplement, as opposed to contradict, terms of agreement). However, for the opposite holding, see J.A. Indus. v. All Am. Plastics, Inc., 133 Ohio App.3d 76, 726 N.E.2d 1066, 42 UCC2d 404 (Putnam County 1999) (presence of a merger clause which says contract "constitutes the entire agreement of the parties" precludes evidence of additional consistent terms).

5. 1971 WL 17904, 9 UCC 836 (Okl. App.1971). This case was not reported officially by express order of the court.

6. Id. at 837.

7. Id. at 838.

8. Id.

Sellers can use merger clauses to protect against this risk. In addition to the usual merger language, sellers are well advised to include some such wording as this: "ANY REPRESENTATIONS, PROMISES, WARRANTIES OR STATEMENTS BY SELLER'S AGENT THAT DIFFER IN ANY WAY FROM THE TERMS OF THIS WRITTEN AGREEMENT SHALL BE GIVEN NO FORCE OR EFFECT." The standard clause in Santos v. Mid–Continent Refrigerator Co.[9] proved effective. Lessee leased a freezing unit to hold frozen foods for sale in his store. The written contract provided that the lease would terminate on certain conditions that did not include an option by the lessee to terminate at any time he determined that frozen foods would not sell at his store. Yet the lessee sought to terminate for lack of sales. On motion for summary judgment, the lessee admitted the foregoing contract but presented an affidavit in which he claimed that lessor's salesman had orally assured the lessee that he would have such an option. The trial court entered judgment for the lessor, and the Texas Court of Civil Appeals affirmed,[10] citing the following contract language: "It is expressly understood and agreed that there are no conditions of the terms of this contract other than those herein expressly carried out."[11] There was also an express disclaimer of warranties of fitness for any particular purposes.

But parties cannot always rely on merger clauses, even well drawn ones; we now consider several ways around them. First, it is often said that a merger clause will not keep out evidence of true fraud. In neither of the two cases just discussed did the party seeking to introduce the extrinsic evidence actually claim fraud. The case law as a whole is in conflict on whether merger clauses preclude such extrinsic evidence. Some courts hold not, either on the theory that "fraud vitiates all;"[12] or on the entirely different theory that fraud generates rights in tort.[13] Other courts have refused to admit evidence of fraud. These courts stress that a party should not sign a merger clause in an agreement that includes terms inconsistent with their oral agreement.[14] This is like a

---

9. 469 S.W.2d 24, 9 UCC 587 (Tex. Civ.App.1971), error ref'd n.r.e.

10. *Id.*

11. *Id.* at 26, 9 UCC at 589. Cf. Thorman v. Polytemp, Inc., 1965 WL 8338, 2 UCC 772 (N.Y.Co.Ct.1965). See also, Hoover Universal, Inc. v. Brockway Imco, Inc., 809 F.2d 1039, 3 UCC2d 46 (4th Cir.1987) (where written contract contained a merger clause and a clause limiting the warranty, evidence of additional terms in a handout given by seller to buyer was barred); Roland K. Molinet, M.D., P.A. v. Mai Basic Four, Inc., 1992 WL 454480, 19 UCC2d 401

(S.D.Fla.1992) (merger clause "disavows prior expressions of warranty as a matter of law").

12. Coson v. Roehl, 63 Wash.2d 384, 387 P.2d 541 (1963).

13. See, e.g., City Dodge, Inc. v. Gardner, 232 Ga. 766, 208 S.E.2d 794, 15 UCC 598 (1974) (tort of misrepresentation); Keller v. A.O. Smith Harvestore Products, Inc., 819 P.2d 69, 15 UCC2d 733 (Colo.1991) (tort of negligent misrepresentation).

14. E.g., 80th Division Veterans' Ass'n, to Use of Parke, Austin & Lips-

"contributory negligence" justification for upholding the merger clause against charges of fraud.

At least one of us thinks merger clauses should be fostered and that they should usually be effective even against claims of fraud. But some courts may have gone too far in permitting parties to use merger clauses as shields against alleged fraud. Where the alleged victim is sophisticated, where there is little evidence of weaseling, and where the object of the claim has a reputation for shady dealing, we think it overly harsh to deny the alleged victim of fraud a chance to prove its case. In our view, decisions like Holland Furnace Co. v. Williams[15] are questionable. There the seller was allowed to recover the price of a gas burner. The court held that it would be no defense that seller's own agent, to induce the defendant to buy a new furnace, had fraudulently represented to the defendant that the furnace he had been using would emit carbon monoxide into his house. The court reasoned that the merger clause left the defendant "bound to know" that the agent did not have authority to make any representations about the defendant's own furnace.[16] It may help to know that the Holland Furnace Company of the 1950s was allegedly notorious for its questionable sales tactics.[17]

Second, in a rare case Code rules on bad faith might be used to attack a merger clause. Consider the following partly hypothetical case.[18] Buyer butchers and sells poultry for Kosher poultry markets in the area. Buyer's competitors can produce larger volumes and therefore sell at lower prices. To meet this competition, buyer enters negotiations with seller for processing equipment which will enable buyer to produce larger volumes. Seller visits buyer's plant and learns that the equipment is to be for "Kosher operation." Yet the contract later signed says nothing of "Kosher operation" and includes the following conspicuous merger clause which buyer specifically signs: "I understand that the contract between the parties consists solely of this written agreement and that there are no implied warranties whatsoever." The equipment is delivered and it turns out not to be for a Kosher operation. If buyer refuses to pay the price or seeks damages, he or she will want to prove an express oral warranty of fitness for a particular purpose. But the court should permit buyer's evidence only on finding that the seller knew not only that "Kosher operation" had been promised but that the

comb, Inc. v. Johnson, 100 Pa.Super. 447, 159 A. 467 (1931).

15. 179 Kan. 321, 295 P.2d 672 (1956).

16. *Id.* at 324, 295 P.2d at 674.

17. Comment, Special Provisions in Contracts to Exclude Contentions Based upon Parol Evidence, 32 Ill.L.Rev. 938, 948 (1938).

18. Cf. Berk v. Gordon Johnson Co., 232 F.Supp. 682, 2 UCC 240 (E.D.Mich. 1964).

equipment delivered would not permit that operation. Mistake by the seller on this should be borne by the buyer.

Third, in the rarest of all cases, section 2–302 on unconscionability might be invoked to invalidate a merger clause.[19] For example, cases such as Champlin v. Transport Motor Co.[20] are good law under the Code. In that case, the writing, a conditional sales contract between a dealer and one of its salespersons, provided for the sale of a car to the salesperson, who was to pay certain monthly installments. The writing also provided that "[n]o warranties, representations or agreements have been made by the seller unless specifically set forth herein." Yet, the parties admitted that the sale was a device whereby the dealer would be able to procure chattel paper that he could transfer to a finance company in return for a much needed advance "owing to the almost total collapse of business generally in the automobile business in and around Spokane in 1932."[21] It was also undisputed that the dealer orally agreed to hold his salesperson harmless in the transaction so that he would not ultimately be liable for the payments.[22] The evidence also showed that the dealer had forced his salesmen either to give up their jobs or go along with the deal outlined. Plaintiff salesperson went along, but when he failed to make the payments, the finance company repossessed the car he had been forced to buy ("trading in" his own therefor), thereby leaving him carless in the end. All in all he judged he lost $500, and, despite vigorous efforts by the dealer to invoke the parol evidence rule, the court allowed the salesperson to recover this amount from the dealer under the oral extrinsic hold-harmless clause. The court stressed that "there was here undoubted business compulsion exerted upon respondent."[23] Presumably 2–302 contemplates duress as one form of procedural unconscionability.[24] Certainly 1–103 can be invoked against duress.[25]

Fourth, a court may fail to give effect to a merger clause because it concludes that the parties did not intend to form an integrated contract. In Latham & Associates, Inc. v. William Raveis Real Estate, Inc.,[26] the court admitted evidence of seller's express

19. See generally, Kerry L. Macintosh, When Are Merger Clauses Unconscionable?, 64 Denv.U.L.Rev. 529 (1988).

20. 177 Wash. 659, 33 P.2d 82 (1934).

21. *Id.* at 660, 33 P.2d at 82.

22. *Id.* at 661, 33 P.2d at 83.

23. *Id.* at 663, 33 P.2d at 84.

24. On the concept of procedural unconscionability, see Leff, Unconscionability and the Code—The Emperor's New Clause, 115 U.Pa.L.Rev. 485 (1967).

25. At least two courts have even found mistakes sufficient to let one out of a merger clause. We have doubts. See, e.g., Stephenson v. Ketchikan Spruce Mills, Inc., 412 P.2d 496 (Alaska 1966); In re Amica, Inc., 135 B.R. 534, 17 UCC2d 11 (Bankr.N.D.Ill.1992) (evidence needed to establish parties' intent; agreement drafted by layperson).

26. 218 Conn. 297, 589 A.2d 337, 14 UCC2d 394 (1991).

warranty, despite a merger clause, because the seller had misrepresented the amount of its expertise. The Latham court reasoned that, due to the misrepresentation, the parties had not intentionally adopted an integrated writing.

The court in Sierra Diesel Injection Service, Inc. v. Burroughs Corp., Inc.[27] held that there was a lack of intent to form an integrated contract and thus gave no effect to the merger clause. This case involved a form contract between an uneducated, unsophisticated computer buyer and a computer manufacturer.

The court in L.S. Heath & Son, Inc. v. AT & T Information Systems, Inc.,[28] held that the parties' "Master Agreement" was not complete and exclusive, despite the inclusion of a merger clause, because it omitted certain subject matter. The court asserted that, "[i]f the allegedly integrated writing does not, without reference to another document or other coordinating information, reveal what the basic transaction entailed, then the writing is not integrated."[29]

Do not mistake what is happening here. Even though a valid written agreement says "black," the courts are finding that the real agreement is "white." These are dangerous precedents. Only when a court finds behavior akin to fraud should it feel free to substitute its view for the parties' explicit agreement on a point.

Finally, of course, courts may use uncertain and covert tools here too—to interpret or construe a merger clause so that it does not apply to the alleged extrinsic understanding.[30] A court may torture the language of the clause.[31] Or, it may simply hold that the clause is of limited scope and silent on the matter at hand. Or, the court may conclude that the parties made two separate contracts, with the merger clause applicable only to the one at hand but not to the other. Thus, in an illustrative case,[32] the court, in referring to a merger clause, remarked:

> This paragraph is intended to buttress rights accruing under the royalty contract—to cut off defenses otherwise open. But

27. 874 F.2d 653, 8 UCC2d 617 (9th Cir.1989).

28. 9 F.3d 561, 22 UCC2d 27 (7th Cir.1993).

29. Id. at 569, 22 UCC2d at 35.

30. ARB (American Research Bureau), Inc. v. E–Systems, Inc., 663 F.2d 189, 30 UCC 949 (D.C.Cir.1980) (even with merger clause, court can look to circumstances to discover if merger clause does express genuine intention of parties to make writing complete).

31. See Hartsfield, The "Merger Clause" and the Parol Evidence Rule, 27 Tex.L.Rev. 361 (1949); Comment, Special Provisions in Contracts to Exclude Contentions Based upon Parol Evidence, 32 Ill.L.Rev. 938 (1938).

32. Champlin Refining Co. v. Gasoline Products Co., 29 F.2d 331 (1st Cir. 1928). See also Latham & Assocs., Inc. v. William Raveis Real Estate, Inc., 218 Conn. 297, 589 A.2d 337, 14 UCC2d 394 (1991) (merger clause in second contract between parties not intended to discharge seller's obligations under first contract; no accord and satisfaction).

Cf. Step–Saver Data Sys., Inc. v. Wyse Technology, 939 F.2d 91, 15 UCC2d 1 (3d Cir.1991) (integration clause invalid because contract in effect before product and writing arrived).

no defense to claims under this contract is now made; it is admitted that plaintiff is entitled to recover every dollar it claims. The issue here is solely as to defendant's right to counterclaim for damages suffered under another contract. The fact that this other contract relates to what is, in important aspects, the same transaction, does not extend this fifteenth paragraph to the destruction of that other contract. Its effect is limited to the contract sued upon.[33]

Merger clauses do not apply to modifications made after the merged agreement is signed. The parties are always free to modify their prior agreements, though they may specify that this can be done only by taking specific steps.[34] And they may even waive those steps.

33. Champlin Refining Co. v. Gasoline Products Co., 29 F.2d 331, 337 (1st Cir.1928).

34. In re Upchurch's Estate, 62 Tenn.App. 634, 466 S.W.2d 886, 9 UCC 580 (1970) (alternate holding).

Chapter 4

TERMS OF THE CONTRACT (INCLUDING THE LAW OF TENDER, EXCUSE, AND TITLE TRANSFER (2–403))

Analysis

§ 4–1   Introduction

In this chapter we use "terms" to include express and implied promises, conditions, provisos, and presuppositions that bind the parties. We will survey the nature and sources of contract terms (each section will treat a different basic source), identify the outer boundaries of freedom of contract under Article 2, and state the Code law applicable when parties do not expressly agree on delivery and payment terms, or price, or on quantity (requirements and output contracts).[1] We will also consider the Code provisions on seller's tender of delivery and buyer's tender of payment (concurrent conditions), on the defense of commercial impracticability and excuse, and on transfer of title and bona fide purchase.

§ 4–2   Terms Supplied by Express Agreement of the Parties

The general rule is that parties are free to make their own contracts for the sale and purchase of goods. Section 1–302 of Revised Article 1 is headed "Variation by Agreement" and provides:

> (a) Except as otherwise provided in subsection (b) or elsewhere in [the Uniform Commercial Code], the effect of provisions of [the Uniform Commercial Code] may be varied by agreement.

> (b) The obligations of good faith, diligence, reasonableness, and care prescribed by [the Uniform Commercial Code] may not be disclaimed by agreement. The parties, by agreement, may determine the standards by which the performance of those obligations is to be measured if those standards are not manifestly unreasonable. Whenever [the Uniform Commercial Code] requires an action to be taken within a reasonable time,

---

§ 4–1

1. For general reading, see, J. Dolan, Uniform Commercial Code: Terms and Transactions in Commercial Law (1991); R. Barnett, The Sound of Silence: Default Rules and Contractual Consent, 78 Va.L.Rev. 821 (May 1992); M. Gergen, The Use of Open Terms in Contract, 92 Colum.L.Rev. 997 (June 1992); B. Levin, Applying the UCC's Supplementary Terms to Contracts Formed by Conduct Under § 2–207(3), 24 UCC L.J. 210 (Winter 1992). On standard form contracting, see Standard–Form Contracting in the Electronic Age, Hillman and Rachlinski, 77 N.Y.U. L. Rev. 429 (2002). See also, J. J. White, Autistic Contracts, 45 Wayne L. Rev. 1693 (2000).

a time that is not manifestly unreasonable may be fixed by agreement.

(c) The presence in certain provisions of [the Uniform Commercial Code] of the phrase "unless otherwise agreed," or words of similar import, does not imply that the effect of other provisions may not be varied by agreement under this section.

The gist of the foregoing language is, of course, that freedom of contract is the rule rather than the exception.[1]

The Code defines the word "agreement." Thus, when 1–302(a) states that provisions of the Uniform Commercial Code may be varied by "agreement," this means, under 1–201(b)(3), by "the bargain of the parties in fact as found in their language or inferred from other circumstances including course of performance, course of dealing, or usage of trade as provided in section 1–303" and related provisions. The parties can generally vary or supersede Code provisions without doing so explicitly. The express agreement may be silent on a matter, yet usage of trade, course of dealing, or course of performance may fill the gap. Indeed, under 1–302 "circumstances" may fill gaps too, even when they fall short of what constitutes usage of trade, course of dealing, or course of performance. Consider this example: Section 2–308 states in part that "unless otherwise agreed the place for delivery of goods is the seller's place of business." But what if the seller contracts to sell goods to a distant buyer and nothing is expressly said about delivery terms? May the seller insist that under 2–308 the buyer must pick the goods up at the seller's place of business? Or is the buyer entitled to have the seller ship them? The "circumstance" that the buyer is in a far off city, even without other factors, may induce a court to say that the seller has contracted (1) to deliver the goods to a carrier and (2) to comply with 2–504 in so doing.

The parties will often contract expressly as to quality, quantity, price, and some aspects of delivery and payment. In general, their agreement without more will be sufficient to displace any otherwise applicable Code provisions. But to displace some Code provisions, the parties must follow specified procedures. For example, the Code implies a warranty of merchantability in 2–314. To vary this provision by contrary agreement, the parties must jump through the hoops specified in 2–316(2) and (3).

However, freedom of contract under Article 2 is not unlimited. There are several substantive provisions in the Article the effect of which parties may not vary by agreement, no matter how explicit.[2]

§ 4–2

1. See generally Bunn, Freedom of Contract Under the Uniform Commercial Code, 2 B.C.Ind. & Com.L.Rev. 59 (1960).

2. See also § 1–301 and 1–302.

§ 4–3 Terms Supplied by Course of Dealing, Usage of Trade, and Course of Performance

The agreement of the parties includes that part of their bargain that may be found in course of dealing, usage of trade, or course of performance.[1] These sources are relevant not only to the interpretation of express contract terms, but may themselves constitute contract terms. And these sources may not only supplement or qualify express terms, but in rare circumstances, may even override express terms.

The definitions of course of performance, course of dealing, and usage of trade all now appear in section 1–303. Section 1–303(b) reads:

A course of dealing is a sequence of conduct concerning previous transactions between the parties to a particular transaction that is fairly to be regarded as establishing a common basis of understanding for interpreting their expressions and other conduct.

Thus, this definition is now in Article 1 but was formerly in Article 2. If a state adopts Revised Article 1, but not Amended Article 2, what happens to old 2–208 (the old trade usage section)? We believe the courts should regard 2–208 as still applicable. Note that a single occasion cannot constitute a *sequence* and therefore cannot be a course of dealing.[2] In addition, the mere sending of terms back and forth does not, without more, create a course of dealing.[3]

§ 4–3

1. See Levie, The Interpretation of Contracts in New York Under the Uniform Commercial Code, 10 N.Y.L.F. 350 (1964); Levie, Trade Usage and Custom Under the Common Law and the Uniform Commercial Code, 40 N.Y.U.L.Rev. 1101 (1965); Carroll, New Perspectives on Usage of Trade, 12 B.C.Ind. & Com. L.Rev. 139, 154–78 (1970); Kirst, Usage of Trade and Course of Dealing: Subversion of the UCC Theory, 1977 U.Ill.L.F. 811. See generally Note, Custom and Trade Usage: Its Application to Commercial Dealings and the Common Law, 55 Colum.L.Rev. 1192 (1955); Warren, Trade Usage and Parties in the Trade: An Economic Rationale for an Inflexible Rule, 42 U.Pitt.L.Rev. 515 (1981).

2. See, e.g., Sun River Cattle Co. v. Miners Bank of Montana N.A., 164 Mont. 237, 521 P.2d 679, 14 UCC 1004 (1974), remittitur corrected, 164 Mont. 479, 525 P.2d 19 (1974) (holding and paying one check not sufficient "sequence of previous conduct"); Bowdoin v. Showell Growers, Inc., 817 F.2d 1543, 3 UCC2d 1366 (11th Cir.1987) (one transaction generally insufficient to establish course of conduct). Compare Weale v. Lund, 162 Vt. 622, 649 A.2d 247, 27 UCC2d 68 (1994) (several instances). But mere "repeated delivery of invoice terms" does not create a course of dealing. The court indicates that a course of dealing must be bilateral. See In re CFLC, Inc., 166 F.3d 1012, 37 UCC2d 475 (9th Cir. 1999).

3. Step–Saver Data Systems, Inc. v. Wyse Technology, 939 F.2d 91, 15 UCC2d 1 (3d Cir.1991) (box top disclaimer of warranty not valid as a course of dealing). In re Charter Co.; Charter Crude Oil Co. v. Exxon Co., U.S.A., 103 B.R. 302, 10 UCC2d 73 (M.D.Fla.1989) (series of invoices over two years containing interest provision constituted "course of conduct" and could be enforced, though no interest paid before). We are doubtful.

Article 1 of the Code defines usage of trade in 1–303(c):

A "usage of trade" is any practice or method of dealing having such regularity of observance in a place, vocation or trade as to justify an expectation that it will be observed with respect to the transaction in question. The existence and scope of such a usage must be proved as facts. If it is established that such a usage is embodied in a trade code or similar record, the interpretation of the record is a question of law.

Note particularly that it is not necessary for both parties to be consciously aware of the trade usage. It is enough if the trade usage is such as to "justify an expectation" of its observance.[4]

Course of performance is defined in subsections 1–303(a)(1) and (2) as follows:

(a) A "course of performance" is a sequence of conduct between the parties to a particular transaction that exists if:

(1) the agreement of the parties with respect to the transaction involves repeated occasions for performance by a party; and

(2) the other party, with knowledge of the nature of the performance and opportunity for objection to it, accepts the performance or acquiesces in it without objection.

Course of performance differs from usage of trade. For example, a party can be chargeable with a usage of trade of which it is ignorant, but the same ignorance is normally a defense to a claim arising from course of performance. Course of performance also differs from course of dealing. For example, a course of dealing is a sequence of conduct between the parties prior to entering into a particular agreement whereas course of performance arises subsequent to entry into the agreement.[5] While the difference appears clear, both courts and lawyers occasionally err.[6]

What is the legal effect of course of dealing and one or more of its cohorts, once proved? First, one or more may add to the express terms of the agreement.[7] This may occur even where the contract is

---

4. United States for Use and Benefit of Union Building Materials Corp. v. Haas and Haynie Corp., 577 F.2d 568, 27 UCC 32 (9th Cir.1978); Mieske v. Bartell Drug Co., 92 Wash.2d 40, 593 P.2d 1308, 26 UCC 262 (1979) (trade usage between film processors does not qualify agreement between film processor and commercial customer when defendant failed to prove plaintiff customer knew or should have known of trade usage); Architectural Metal Systems, Inc. v. Consolidated Systems, Inc., 58 F.3d 1227, 26 UCC2d 1047 (7th Cir. 1995) (usage of trade saved contract from fatal indefiniteness).

5. For cases discussing these distinctions, see especially Kunststoffwerk Alfred Huber v. R.J. Dick, Inc., 621 F.2d 560, 28 UCC 1371 (3d Cir.1980).

6. See, e.g., Idaho First Nat. Bank v. David Steed & Assocs., Inc., 121 Idaho 356, 825 P.2d 79, 17 UCC2d 673 (1992) (course of performance pleaded as course of dealing and refused admission on grounds that performance took place after contracting).

7. § 1–303(d). See also Figgie Int. Inc. v. Destileria Serralles, Inc., 190 F.3d 252, 39 UCC2d 275 (4th Cir. 1999) (usage of trade added term); Accord, Caul-

unambiguous and complete on its face.[8] In Columbia Nitrogen Corp. v. Royster Co.,[9] for example, buyer agreed to buy at least 31,000 tons of phosphate per year for three years from seller. When due to market changes, buyer ordered only a fraction of the minimum, the seller sued. The trial judge refused to admit evidence of course of dealing and usage of trade purportedly showing that the contract's price and quantity terms were "mere projections to be adjusted according to market forces."[10] The Fourth Circuit reversed and remanded.[11]

Course of dealing and its cohorts may also import an additional term imposing a duty on one party to give a notice to the other in a given situation, even though the express agreement is silent on the matter.[12] Or they may foreclose a particular remedy unless it is sought within a given time period, even though the express agreement is silent on remedies. They may even add a warranty under 2–314(3), or disclaim a warranty under 2–316(3)(c).[13] They may not, however, create a new contract.[14]

Second, course of dealing, usage of trade, or course of performance may give particular meaning to the language of the agreement.[15] Thus each may contradict, supersede or confirm the ordi-

kins Indiantown Citrus Co. v. Nevins Fruit Co., Inc., 831 So.2d 727, 49 UCC2d 31 (Fla. App. 2002); Hercules Machinery Corp. v. McElwee Brothers, Inc., 49 UCC2d 72 (E.D. La. 2002) (contemporaneous faxes showed course of dealing).

8. See § 2–202, Comment 2. See also 2–208. But it is often said usage of trade etc. cannot vary terms of an unambiguous contract. See Caulkins Indiantown Citrus Co. v. Nevins Fruit Co., Inc., 831 So.2d 727, 49 UCC2d 31 (Fla. App. 2002). Express terms may not be clear enough to exclude course of dealing. See Interstate Narrow Fabrics, Inc. v. Century USA, Inc., 218 F.R.D. 455, 52 UCC2d 381 (M.D.N.C. 2003) (express terms controlled); Bio–Tech Pharmacal, Inc. v. International Business Connections, 86 Ark.App. 220, 184 S.W.3d 447, 53 UCC2d 476 (2004); Abourdaram v. De Groote, 2004 WL 1242426, 54 UCC2d 1110 (D.D.C. 2004) (express terms controlled over contradictory course of dealing).

9. 451 F.2d 3, 9 UCC 977 (4th Cir. 1971).

10. 451 F.2d at 7, 9 UCC at 982.

11. See discussion in § 3–11 *supra*.

12. See Provident Tradesmens Bank & Trust Co. v. Pemberton, 196 Pa.Super. 180, 173 A.2d 780, 1 UCC 57 (1961).

13. Christenson v. Milde, 402 N.W.2d 610, 3 UCC2d 525 (Minn.App. 1987) (usage of trade created implied warranty); ITT Corp. v. LTX Corp., 926 F.2d 1258, 14 UCC2d 87 (1st Cir.1991) (course of dealing excluded warranty of merchantability).

14. Wichita Sheet Metal Supply, Inc. v. Dahlstrom & Ferrell Constr. Co., 246 Kan. 557, 792 P.2d 1043, 12 UCC2d 634 (1990) (usage of trade cannot create a contract where none had previously existed); Bespress, Inc. v. Capital Bank of Delhi, 616 So.2d 795, 22 UCC2d 640 (La.App.1993) (course of dealing cannot create an agreement to lend).

15. § 1–303(d). See also Baumgold Bros., Inc. v. Allan M. Fox Co., East, 375 F.Supp. 807, 14 UCC 580 (N.D.Ohio 1973) (diamonds sent "on memorandum" signifies sale or return contract); Amerine Nat. Corp. v. Denver Feed Co., 493 F.2d 1275, 14 UCC 885 (10th Cir. 1974) (Amerine turkeys include crossbreeds as well as purebreds); Falvey Cargo Underwriting, Ltd. v. Metro Freezer & Storage, 2002 WL 31677198, 49 UCC2d 278 (Mass. Super. 2002) (course of dealing gave notice of clause). See also Hyosung America, Inc. v. Sumagh Textile Co., Ltd., 137 F.3d 75, 34 UCC2d 930 (2d Cir. 1998) (acceptance of

nary language of words used in an agreement.[16] If the parties contract with reference to a trade usage that imports a meaning different from the ordinary lay meaning of words used, so much the worse for the lay meaning. The trade usage will control. For example, a deal for a "thousand rabbits" may actually call for delivery of twelve hundred rabbits.[17]

Third, course of dealing and one or more of its cohorts may cut down or even subtract what would otherwise be whole terms of the express agreement of the parties.[18] Section 1–303(d) says that course of dealing and usage of trade may "qualify" the express terms of the agreement. Thus, "delivery June–August" may be qualified by trade usage to require deliveries spread through these three months rather than all at once.[19] And 1–303(a) and (d) on course of performance are drafted broadly enough to allow for the same kind of effect. A major function of course of performance, together with the law of modification and waiver, is to help cut down or subtract express terms altogether.[20] Section 1–303(f) says that a course of performance "is relevant to show a waiver or modification of any term inconsistent with the course of perform-ance."[21]

Fourth, when course of dealing and its cohorts in some way become part of the agreement, they, like express terms, supersede or vary the effect of the contractually variable *Code* provisions that would otherwise govern. For example, an express contract disclaim-er is not always required to disclaim the warranty of merchantabili-ty that section 2–314 "implies" in contracts for sale of goods.[22]

non-conforming goods without objec-tion).

16. Skyline Steel Corp. v. A.J. Du-puis Co., 648 F.Supp. 360, 3 UCC2d 475 (E.D.Mich.1986) (course of dealing sup-ported giving effect to express language of contract and excluding parol evi-dence).

17. Smith v. Wilson, 3 B. & Ad. 728, 110 Eng.Rep. 266 (K.B.1832).

18. See, e.g., Brownie's Army & Navy Store, Inc. v. E.J. Burke, Jr., Inc., 72 A.D.2d 171, 424 N.Y.S.2d 800, 28 UCC 90 (1980) (plaintiff not entitled to payment of interest on delinquent ac-count or payment of attorneys fees for collection of account despite printed terms on sales slip after plaintiff had accepted late payment from defendant for 15 years; and plaintiff did not men-tion interest or placement of account with attorney for collection until 2 months before bringing suit.); Figgie In-ternational, Inc. v. Destileria Serralles,

Inc., 190 F.3d 252, 39 UCC2d 275 (4th Cir. 1999) (usage of trade precluded con-sequential damages); Pioneer/Eclipse Corp. v. Kohler Co., Inc., 113 F.Supp.2d 811, 44 UCC2d 59 (W.D.N.C. 2000) (course of dealing confirmed warranty term); Interstate Narrow Fabrics, Inc. v. Century USA, Inc., 218 F.R.D. 455, 52 UCC2d 381 (M.D.N.C. 2003) (course of performance may show express terms were modified).

19. Warren's Kiddie Shoppe, Inc. v. Casual Slacks, Inc., 120 Ga.App. 578, 171 S.E.2d 643, 7 UCC 166 (1969). Cf. Michael Schiavone & Sons, Inc. v. Secu-ralloy Co., 312 F.Supp. 801, 7 UCC 674 (D.Conn.1970).

20. Course of performance may even help form a contract.

21. See discussion in Chapter 1. To be effective, some waivers must be in writing. See § 1–306.

22. See, e.g., Kincheloe v. Geldmeier, 619 S.W.2d 272, 31 UCC 1608 (Tex.Civ.

Section 2–316(3)(c) makes plain that a usage of trade or course of performance or dealing can disclaim, too.[23] On the other hand, a course of conduct may not override the writing requirement of 2–326.[24]

Fifth, course of dealing and its cohorts may give meaning to terms of the agreement when the contract is formed through course of performance.[25] The terms may be found in the writings exchanged between the parties[26] or they may be imposed simply by the parties' conduct, or some combination of these.

Sixth, course of dealing et al. play additional, supplementary roles in defining contract terms. They may define a material alteration under section 2–207, and thus determine whether a proposed term in a "battle of the forms" will be given effect.[27] Course of dealing and its cohorts may also provide supplemental terms under section 2–207. In addition, course of performance, course of dealing, and trade usage may establish the reasonability of an express term and thus determine its unconscionability.[28]

App.1981) (trial court did not err in finding trade usage excluded or modified implied warranty of merchantability under § 2–314).

23. § 2–316(3)(c) provides "[A]n implied warranty can also be excluded or modified by course of dealing or course of performance or usage of trade."

See also Bickett v. W.R. Grace & Co., 1972 WL 20845, 12 UCC 629 (W.D.Ky. 1972) (course of dealing disclaimer re seed corn); Standard Structural Steel Co. v. Bethlehem Steel Corp., 597 F.Supp. 164, 40 UCC 1245 (D.Conn. 1984) (implied warranties of merchantability and fitness excluded through course of dealing); Figgie International, Inc. v. Destileria Serralles, Inc., 190 F.3d 252, 39 UCC2d 275 (4th Cir.1999) (usage of trade can exclude consequential damages).

24. Consolidated Foods Corp. v. Roland Foods, Inc., 1973 WL 21362, 13 UCC 245 (D.C.Super.1973).

25. Gord Indus. Plastics, Inc. v. Aubrey Mfg., Inc., 127 Ill.App.3d 589, 82 Ill.Dec. 855, 469 N.E.2d 389, 40 UCC 26, 27–28 (1984) ("[T]he parties have no written contract, but one created by their conduct, supplemented by customs and usages of the trade, if any, and by terms on which the writings agree.");

Magallanes Inv., Inc. v. Circuit Sys., Inc., 994 F.2d 1214, 20 UCC2d 765 (7th Cir.1993) (usage of trade established that telexes confirming agreement on major terms constituted a binding agreement).

26. Johnson Tire Service, Inc. v. Thorn, Inc., 613 P.2d 521, 29 UCC 774 (Utah 1980) (course of dealing added interest terms but not attorney's fees to agreement); Mid–South Packers, Inc. v. Shoney's, Inc., 761 F.2d 1117, 41 UCC 38 (5th Cir.1985) (extensive course of dealing between parties helped establish interest and collection cost terms as part of agreement when buyer's purchase orders did not contain all terms of agreement, seller's invoice sent the day after shipment included these terms, and buyer never objected to the terms either as exception to § 2–207(2)).

27. Schulze & Burch Biscuit Co. v. Tree Top, Inc., 831 F.2d 709, 4 UCC2d 641 (7th Cir.1987); Dixie Aluminum Products Co., Inc. v. Mitsubishi Int'l Corp., 785 F.Supp. 157, 17 UCC2d 1073 (N.D.Ga.1992) (arbitration agreement valid after inclusion on 10 purchase orders).

28. Southland Farms, Inc. v. Ciba–Geigy Corp., 575 So.2d 1077, 14 UCC2d 404 (Ala.1991) (limiting liability by ex-

What legal impact do course of dealing, usage of trade, and course of performance have on each other in event of conflict? Section 1–303(e) states the hierarchy:

> Except as otherwise provided in subsection (f), the express terms of an agreement and any applicable course of performance, course of dealing, or usage of trade must be construed wherever reasonable as consistent with each other. If such construction is unreasonable:
>
> (1) express terms prevail over course of performance, course of dealing, and usage of trade;
>
> (2) course of performance prevails over course of dealing and usage of trade; and
>
> (3) course of dealing prevails over usage of trade.

The provision that express terms control inconsistent course of dealing and its cohorts really cannot be taken at face value, at least in some courts.[29] But course of dealing does override usage of trade,[30] and course of performance overrides both course of dealing and usage of trade, as is now made explicit in 1–303(e).[31] Course of dealing between the parties is "closer" to their expectations than general trade usage and should prevail over it.

Though now modified by federal statute, the largest cluster of cases citing the foregoing provisions does not deal with straight sales but with a common secured transaction. These cases implicate third parties' rights. For example, suppose a farmer executes a security agreement which forbids the sale of collateral without written consent of the secured party. If, in previous deals, the secured party has allowed the debtor to sell the goods without permission and to apply the proceeds to the debt, may the secured party enforce an interest in the goods if the farmer sells them,

---

cluding consequential damages not unconscionable as it is a trade usage).

29. Celebrity, Inc. v. Kemper, 96 N.M. 508, 632 P.2d 743, 32 UCC 105 (1981) (even though court said express terms control over course of dealing, court allowed course of dealing to control so long as buyer had reason to rely on it; provision cannot be taken at face value); Nanakuli Paving & Rock Co. v. Shell Oil Co., Inc., 664 F.2d 772, 32 UCC 1025 (9th Cir.1981) (court found express term, "Shell's Posted Price at time of delivery" could be qualified by trade usage). But see, Kologel Co. v. Down in the Village, Inc., 539 F.Supp. 727, 34 UCC 12 (S.D.N.Y.1982) (when "usage and the express terms of a contract are in direct opposition, 'express terms control * * * usage of trade.' ").

30. Barliant v. Follett Corp., 138 Ill. App.3d 756, 91 Ill.Dec. 677, 483 N.E.2d 1312, 42 UCC 1206 (1985) (course of dealing that buyer was billed by seller for transportation and insurance, controlled trade usage that FOB included transportation and insurance charges).

31. Brunswick Box Co. v. Coutinho, Caro & Co., 617 F.2d 355, 28 UCC 616 (4th Cir.1980) (trial court erred in refusing to permit jury to find parties, through course of performance, had "otherwise" agreed to meaning of "FAS Norfolk" and such conduct should override the trade usage defining that term).

takes the money and fails to repay?[32] The cases are in sharp conflict. A number have said that the secured party's mere acquiescence is not sufficient to override express terms under 1–205(4) which becomes 1–303(c) in Revised Article 1 (likely to be widely adopted).[33] Other courts have said that course of dealing itself waives the security interest.[34] This last line of authority has been sharply criticized,[35] but we believe that it provides an equitable solution. Section 1–103 read in conjunction with 9–306(2), indicates that equitable waiver is still alive in this context.[36] Section 1–303, and its predecessor, however, purport to deal only with rights between the original parties.[37] Courts should not consider it determinative here.

A further question concerns matters of proof. As we have already seen, the parol evidence rule should not be a hurdle so long as the conduct merely explains rather than contradicts the writ-

---

32. § 9–315(a) provides:

[Disposition of collateral: continuation of security interest or agricultural lien; proceeds.] Except as otherwise provided in this Article and in § 2–403(2):

(1) a security interest or agricultural lien continues in collateral notwithstanding sale, lease, license, exchange, or other disposition thereof unless the secured party authorized the disposition free of the security interest or agricultural lien; and

(2) a security interest attaches to any identifiable proceeds of collateral.

See also Note, Food Security Act Supersedes Farm Products Exception of the UCC § 9–307(1), 47 U.Pitt.L.Rev. 749 (1986).

33. See, e.g., Baker Production Credit Ass'n v. Long Creek Meat Co., 266 Or. 643, 513 P.2d 1129, 13 UCC 531 (1973); First Nat. Bank of Atoka v. Calvin Pickle Co., 516 P.2d 265, 12 UCC 943 (Okl. 1973); Wabasso State Bank v. Caldwell Packing Co., 308 Minn. 349, 251 N.W.2d 321, 19 UCC 315 (1976); North Central Kansas Production Credit Ass'n v. Washington Sales Co., 223 Kan. 689, 577 P.2d 35, 23 UCC 1343 (1978); Central California Equip. Co. v. Dolk Tractor Co., 78 Cal.App.3d 855, 144 Cal.Rptr. 367, 23 UCC 1051 (1978). It should be noted that although all of these courts find mere acquiescence insufficient to waive express terms, some hint that certain types of waiver are possible.

34. United States v. Central Livestock Ass'n, Inc., 349 F.Supp. 1033, 11 UCC 1054 (D.N.D.1972); Lisbon Bank &

Trust Co. v. Murray, 206 N.W.2d 96, 12 UCC 356 (Iowa 1973) (no provision requiring written consent); Moffat County State Bank v. Producers Livestock Marketing Ass'n, 598 F.Supp. 1562, 40 UCC 314 (D.Colo.1984), aff'd, 833 F.2d 908, 4 UCC2d 1608 (10th Cir.1987) (court found bank expressly consented to sale of cattle and thus lost security interest in collateral); FDIC v. Bowles Livestock Comm'n Co., 739 F.Supp. 1364, 13 UCC2d 23 (D.Neb.1990) (failure by bank to object to sale of secured livestock without notice amounted to waiver).

35. See, e.g., Miller, Farm Collateral Under the UCC: "Those Are Some Mighty Tall Silos, Ain't They Fella?", 20 S.D.L.Rev. 514 (1975). See also, Farmers State Bank v. Farmland Foods, Inc., 225 Neb. 1, 402 N.W.2d 277, 3 UCC2d 902 (1987) (dissent argues course of performance waiver of notice of sale requirement should not also waive security interest).

36. § 1–103(b) provides:

Unless displaced by the particular provisions of the Uniform Commercial Code the principles of law and equity, including the law merchant and the law relative to capacity to contract, principal and agent estoppel, fraud, misrepresentation, duress, coercion, mistake, bankruptcy, or other validating or invalidating cause supplement its provisions.

37. Transamerica Commercial Finance Corp. v. Union Bank & Trust Co., 584 So.2d 1299, 15 UCC2d 412 (Ala. 1991) (trade usage irrelevant between parties not in privity).

ing.[38] What are the tests of admissibility of evidence of course of dealing, usage of trade, and course of performance? It is possible to glean these tests from a close review of the relevant definitional subsections.[39] The standard for admissibility may not be the same for course of performance, usage of trade and course of dealing.[40] Problems may arise with respect to the tests for admissibility of trade usage in particular, for it is likely to be confused with "custom" and the law has long encumbered proof of custom with stringent requirements.[41] The courts at common law said that a custom must be lawful, reasonable, well known, certain, precise, universal, ancient, and continuous,[42] though courts did not always apply these tests consistently. Code requirements for proof of trade usage are far less stringent.[43] Of course, the usage must be lawful. It need not be reasonable, yet it cannot be unconscionable under 2–302. A trade usage that second hand automobile dealers always set odometers back could not survive 2–302 on unconscionability.[44] A usage of trade need not be well known, let alone "universal." It is enough if it has "such regularity of observance in a place, vocation or trade as to justify an expectation that it will be observed with respect to the transaction in question."[45] Comments add these two glosses: the usage must be observed by "the great majority of decent dealers, even though dissidents ready to cut corners do not agree" and "usages may be either general to the trade or particular to a special branch of trade." The language of 1–303(c) does not require that the usage be certain and precise; it merely requires that the usage be "any practice or method of dealing." Comment 8 is more expansive:

38. See § 3–12. See, e.g., Tigg Corp. v. Dow Corning Corp., 822 F.2d 358, 4 UCC2d 44 (3d Cir.1987) (no finding of ambiguity necessary to admit course of performance et al.); Hoover Universal, Inc. v. Brockway Imco, Inc., 809 F.2d 1039, 3 UCC2d 46 (4th Cir.1987) (usage of trade not admitted to contradict express terms); Dominion Bank, N.A. v. Star Five Assocs., Inc., 1991 WL 332244, 16 UCC2d 688 (Va.Cir.1991) (evidence of course of dealing admissible under "partial integration" and "collateral contract" doctrines).

39. § 1–303(a), (b), and (c) of Article 1.

40. H & W Industries, Inc. v. Occidental Chem. Corp., 911 F.2d 1118, 12 UCC2d 921 (5th Cir.1990) (higher threshold for usage of trade than course of dealing).

41. See generally Levie, Trade Usage and Custom Under the Common Law

and the Uniform Commercial Code, 40 N.Y.U.L.Rev. 1101 (1965).

42. Id. at 1103.

43. See, e.g., Western Indus., Inc. v. Newcor Canada Ltd., 739 F.2d 1198, 38 UCC 1458 (7th Cir.1984) (the UCC has a more "hospitable approach" to trade usage and does not require the pre-Code standards of "clear and explicit" evidence).

44. See, e.g., Boise Dodge, Inc. v. Clark, 92 Idaho 902, 453 P.2d 551 (1969).

45. § 1–303(c) of Revised Article 1. See, e.g., Scott Brass, Inc. v. C & C Metal Products Corp., 473 F.Supp. 1124, 27 UCC 372 (D.R.I.1979) (insufficient evidence presented to establish trade usage); H & W Indus., Inc. v. Occidental Chem. Corp., 911 F.2d 1118, 12 UCC2d 921 (5th Cir.1990) (changed circumstances may make usage of trade inadmissible).

In cases of a well established line of usage varying from the general rules of this Act where the precise amount of the variation has not been worked out into a single standard, the party relying on the usage is entitled, in any event, to the minimum variation demonstrated. The whole is not to be disregarded because no particular line of detail has been established. In case a dominant pattern has been fairly evidenced, the party relying on the usage is entitled under this section to go to the trier of fact on the question of whether such dominant pattern has been incorporated into the agreement.

Proof of course of dealing or course of performance seldom requires resort to expert witnesses and poses no special problem under the hearsay rule in the law of evidence. This is not so of usage of trade. To prove it, a party must usually call on an expert;[46] and when a party seeks to prove a trade code,[47] hearsay problems may arise. However, exceptions to the hearsay rule permit introduction of trade codes upon proper proof.

Who has the burden of proof? The Code does not say. Yet courts are likely to impose the burden of proof on the party who seeks to benefit from evidence of course of dealing, trade usage, or course of performance.[48] It does not follow, however, that the party who has this burden of proof should also have the burden of proof on parol evidence rule issues under 2–202. Thus if the opposing party seeks to bar admission of evidence under 2–202, that party should generally shoulder the burden of proof on that issue.

§ 4–4 Terms Supplied by Gap Filler Provisions of Article 2 and General Law—Introduction

Contracts often have gaps in them, intentional or inadvertent. Gaps arise, too, out of the "battle of forms" under sections 2–204

46. See, e.g., Balfour, Guthrie & Co. v. Gourmet Farms, 108 Cal.App.3d 181, 166 Cal.Rptr. 422, 29 UCC 1144 (1980) (expert witness, a grain buyer and merchandiser for two large west coast grain companies for 18 years, testified for corporate grain broker on customs and usages of grain brokerage industry); First Nat. State Bank v. Reliance Electric Co., 668 F.2d 725, 32 UCC 1073 (3d Cir. 1981) (trial court did not err in permitting Homer Kripke, scholar and expert on UCC, to testify on bank customs and practices); H & W Indus., Inc. v. Occidental Chem. Corp., 911 F.2d 1118, 12 UCC2d 921 (5th Cir.1990) (testimony of one corporate officer of his company's practice insufficient).

47. A published trade code does not necessarily constitute a usage of trade within § 1–303. It must meet the tests of that section. Cf. Emco Mills, Inc. v. Isbrandtsen Co., 210 F.2d 319 (8th Cir. 1954) (evidence contradictory on whether grain dealer association rules actually reflect a trade custom). Even though the evidence establishes a trade code that is also a trade usage within § 1–205, it still may not be a trade code binding on both parties.

48. Generally the party who asserts the existence of a trade usage or the like and benefits from its proof has the burden of proving it. See Bigham, Presumptions, Burden of Proof and the Uniform Commercial Code, 21 Vand.L.Rev. 177 (1968).

and 2–207. Some gaps are more or less complete, others only partial. Article 2 of the Code includes numerous gap filler provisions which taken together constitute a kind of standardized statutory contract. Of course, the parties, can vary the effect of these provisions by agreement. These provisions only come into play when the agreement of the parties (including course of dealing and its cohorts) is silent. We will consider the most important gap filler provisions of Article 2 in the next six sections of this chapter.[1]

§ 4–5   Article 2 Gap Fillers on Delivery Terms (Herein, too, of Seller's Proper Tender of Delivery)

In commercial deals, a seller and buyer who reside in the same general area usually agree explicitly on the time and place of delivery. What if the parties do not agree, expressly or impliedly, on delivery terms, and there is no applicable usage of trade, course of dealing, or course of performance? In these circumstances, the Code's gap filler provisions on delivery control. These provisions also control when the parties initially agree on delivery terms but thereafter waive them.[1]

Section 2–309(1) provides that unless otherwise agreed, the time for delivery shall be a "reasonable time."[2] What is reasonable will vary with the case depending on such factors as the nature of goods to be delivered,[3] the purpose for which they are to be used,[4]

§ 4–4

1. See generally, Choi, Contracts With Open or Missing Terms Under the Uniform Commercial Code and the Common Law: A Proposal for Unification, 103 Colum. L. Rev. 50 (2003). A sales "contract" which leaves too much open cannot be valid. See Drug Line, Inc. v. Sero–Immuno Diagnostics, Inc., 217 Ga. App. 530, 458 S.E.2d 170, 27 UCC2d 77 (1995). Yet under 2–311, particulars of performance may be left to specification by one of the parties. See Allapattah Servs. v. Exxon Corp., 61 F.Supp.2d 1300, 41 UCC2d 107 (S.D. Fla. 1999).

§ 4–5

1. See, e.g., Mott Equity Elevator v. Svihovec, 236 N.W.2d 900, 18 UCC 388 (N.D.1975) (same); Shankle–Clairday, Inc. v. Crow, 414 F.Supp. 160, 20 UCC 47 (M.D.Tenn.1976) (2–309 applied where "time of the essence" clause waived).

§ 2–309 does not apply when time for performance is specifically geared to completion of a specific project, or when trade usage controls. See respectively Mishara Constr. Co. v. Transit–Mixed

Concrete Corp., 365 Mass. 122, 310 N.E.2d 363, 14 UCC 556 (1974); and United States Indus., Inc. v. Semco Mfg., Inc., 562 F.2d 1061, 22 UCC 589 (8th Cir.1977), cert. denied, 434 U.S. 986, 98 S.Ct. 613, 54 L.Ed.2d 480 (1977) (reasonableness test not needed where contract provided for delivery on "as released" basis).

2. Lundy v. Low, 200 Ga.App. 332, 408 S.E.2d 144, 16 UCC2d 292 (1991) (2–309 applied when no date set for delivery of Christmas trees).

3. E.g., Kutner–Goldstein Co. v. Workman, 112 Cal.App. 132, 296 P. 313 (1931); Mott Equity Elevator v. Svihovec, 236 N.W.2d 900, 18 UCC 388 (N.D. 1975); Alliance Wall Corp. v. Ampat Midwest Corp., 17 Ohio App.3d 59, 477 N.E.2d 1206, 41 UCC 377 (1984) (parties could not reach agreement on material term of shipment date and court filled gap by requiring it to be reasonable).

4. See, e.g., Kutner–Goldstein Co. v. Workman, 112 Cal.App. 132, 296 P. 313 (1931); Jamestown Terminal Elevator, Inc. v. Hieb, 246 N.W.2d 736, 20 UCC

the extent of seller's knowledge of buyer's intentions,[5] transportation conditions, the nature of the market,[6] and so on.[7] The timing of seller's tender of delivery must be reasonable not only as to date but as to hour.[8] Section 2–503(1)(a) states that "tender must be at a reasonable hour, and if it is of goods they must be kept available for the period reasonably necessary to enable the buyer to take possession."[9] The parties may expressly agree that one or the other has the option to specify the time for delivery. If they do not so agree, the Code makes clear that "specifications or arrangements relating to shipment are at the seller's option."[10] This does not permit seller to ship at any time it chooses; its choice must be in good faith and commercially reasonable.[11] Section 2–309(2) provides that a contract for successive performances, infinite in duration, is also valid for a reasonable time, although either party may terminate at any time.[12]

Unless it has a lawful excuse,[13] a seller breaches if it fails to make timely delivery or tender thereof.[14] On the other hand, the buyer breaches if it refuses to receive a timely tender, provided the tender is proper in other respects.[15] Under Comment 4 to 2–309, unreasonably early offers of or demands for delivery should be viewed as requests for the other party's assent but should not alone constitute breach.[16] However, the comments indicate that where the

617 (N.D.1976); Barbarossa & Sons, Inc. v. Iten Chevrolet, Inc., 265 N.W.2d 655, 23 UCC 1183 (Minn.1978); Mayflower Farms v. Tech–Mark, Inc., 64 Or.App. 121, 666 P.2d 1384, 37 UCC 25 (1983) (defendant was aware plaintiff needed delivery in time for the summer ice cream season).

5. See, e.g., R.L. Pohlman Co. v. Keystone Consolidated Indus., Inc., 399 F.Supp. 330, 17 UCC 1188 (E.D.Mo. 1975); Jamestown Terminal Elevator, Inc. v. Hieb, 246 N.W.2d 736, 20 UCC 617 (N.D.1976); Beiriger & Sons Irrigation, Inc. v. Southwest Land Co., 705 P.2d 532, 41 UCC 1621 (Colo.App.1985) (delivery of sprinkler system was reasonable when parties agreed it was to be used in conjunction with 1982 crop but no evidence was presented to show seller knew the crop was to be oats and had to be planted by June 1).

6. § 1–205(a).

7. Fast v. Southern Offshore Yachts, 587 F.Supp. 1354, 38 UCC 1569 (D.Conn.1984) (seller established reasonable time for delivery by its own conduct in delivering a non-conforming yacht seven months after the parties entered into contract).

8. See, e.g., Eades Commodities, Co. v. Hoeper, 825 S.W.2d 34, 17 UCC2d 771 (Mo.App.1992) (buyer normally accepted deliveries between 3:00 am and 3:00 pm, thus delivery during that time was reasonable).

9. But such requirement does *not* alter any contractually agreed-upon time for delivery.

10. § 2–311(2).

11. § 2–311(1).

12. See, e.g., Goldstein v. S & A Restaurant Corp., 622 F.Supp. 139, 42 UCC 81 (D.D.C.1985) (contract terminated at will under § 2–309(2) by seller after buyer breached contract). See section 4–6 *infra*.

13. As where the buyer repudiates. See e.g., § 2–610.

14. § 2–301. The breach may or may not be a total breach. See § 2–612(3).

15. §§ 2–301; 2–602, Comment 3. The breach may or may not be a total breach. See § 2–612(3).

16. Southern Utilities, Inc. v. Jerry Mandel Machinery Corp., 71 N.C.App. 188, 321 S.E.2d 508, 39 UCC 1231

time for delivery is a reasonable time, the seller must usually take steps to nail down a specific delivery date before it can put the buyer in breach for refusal to receive the goods.[17] Two kinds of cases can arise: where the deal is wholly silent as to time and where the parties originally agreed on a time (or a method for determining it) but thereafter waived it. In both cases, Comment 5 to 2–309 seems to require that the seller propose to the buyer a date after which the seller's duty to tender will expire and the buyer will be in breach for refusal to accept tender theretofore made or proposed. Comment 6 indicates that if the buyer does not respond to the seller's time proposal, this constitutes acquiescence in it and buyer defaults if it refuses to accept tender on or before then. If the buyer responds but rejects the seller's reasonable proposal and insists on undue delay, "a question of flat breach" arises. Both Comments 5 and 6 to 2–309(1) are somewhat obscure, and both go beyond the actual text of the section, yet we believe they are sound. Where time for delivery is no more specific than a "reasonable time," it is generally only just to require that the seller nail this time down and give the buyer an opportunity to go along before the seller charges the buyer with breach.

The contract of the parties may be wholly silent on the place for delivery. Section 2–308 generally fills this gap with the seller's place of business as the place for delivery.[18] Often, however, the gap will only be partial. In an important class of cases, the contract will either require or authorize the seller to ship the goods, but will not require the seller to deliver them at a particular destination. The most common of these are contracts that include the symbols "F.O.B. seller's plant" or "F.O.B. seller's city." The place of delivery in such contracts (and those that include equivalent lan-

(1984) (defendant's letters requesting payment and implicitly offering delivery were expressions of desire and not to be viewed as a breach; but plaintiff's response indicating it was unwilling to pay or accept under the contract and demanding return of its deposit constituted a breach).

17. § 2–309, Comments 5, 6. See, e.g., Kingston 1686 House, Inc. v. B.S.P. Transportation, Inc., 121 N.H. 93, 427 A.2d 9, 30 UCC 1586 (1981) (carrier did not make proper tender of delivery when carrier did not give consignee notice of delivery but just appeared at time when consignee had no employees available to unload truck); Taft–Peirce Manufacturing Co. v. Seagate Technology, Inc., 789 F.Supp. 1220, 17 UCC2d 711 (D.R.I. 1992) (failure of buyer to assert a deadline precluded breach for untimely delivery).

18. But § 2–308 reads as follows:

Unless otherwise agreed

(a) the place for delivery of goods is the seller's place of business or if it has none the seller's residence; but

(b) in a contract for sale of identified goods which to the knowledge of the parties at the time of contracting are in some other place, that place is the place for their delivery; and

(c) documents of title may be delivered through customary banking channels.

See, e.g., Franklin Pavkov Const. Co. v. Roche, 279 F.3d 989, 46 UCC2d 1011 (Fed.Cir.2002) (in absence of express designation of place of delivery, location agreed upon by both parties at which inventory was to be taken is the delivery location).

guage) is the place where the facilities of seller's carrier are located, for the seller must "put the goods into the possession of the carrier."[19] In the jargon of commercial lawyers, a contract that requires or authorizes the seller to send the goods to the buyer but does not require that the seller deliver them at any particular destination is called a "shipment contract." Generally, in shipment contracts, risk of loss passes to the buyer at the point of shipment, which is also the point of "delivery,"[20] while in "destination contracts" (seller must deliver at a particular destination) risk passes upon seller's tender at destination.[21] From the agreement of the parties and surrounding circumstances it will usually be possible to tell (1) whether the seller is authorized to send the goods (the fact the parties are at a distance will usually be enough) and (2) whether the contract is of the shipment or the destination variety. Where the contract is silent, Code comments state a presumption that the parties intended a shipment contract. The case law is not enlightening on what it takes to overcome this presumption.[22] The place of delivery in a contract that includes symbols such as "F.O.B. buyer's plant" or equivalent language is, of course, the named destination point.

In the absence of a lawful excuse the seller's failure to tender delivery at the proper place constitutes breach on its part.[23] On the other hand the buyer's refusal to take delivery at the proper place generally constitutes breach on its part, provided seller's tender is proper in other respects.[24] In addition, if buyer appoints or requires delivery to a third party and that party refuses delivery, the buyer

---

19. § 2–504(a). See, e.g., Travenol Labs., Inc. v. Zotal, Ltd., 394 Mass. 95, 474 N.E.2d 1070, 40 UCC 487 (1985) (for conflict of law purposes, delivery was in Massachusetts where goods sold F.O.B. Cambridge, Mass.); Pittsburgh Indus. Furnace Co. v. Universal Consolidated Cos., Inc., 789 F.Supp. 184, 18 UCC2d 152 (W.D.Pa.1991) ("FOB points of shipment" meant delivery took place upon delivery to carrier).

20. § 2–509(1)(a).

21. § 2–509(1)(b). Of course, so long as the parties use unequivocal language, they may vary these risk allocations by agreement. See § 2–509(4) and Chapter 6 *infra*.

22. See, e.g., Electric Regulator Corp. v. Sterling Extruder Corp., 280 F.Supp. 550, 4 UCC 1025 (D.Conn.1968) ("ship to" with address does not overcome presumption); Ninth St. East, Ltd. v. Harrison, 5 Conn.Cir.Ct. 597, 259 A.2d 772, 7 UCC 171 (1968); Eberhard Mfg. Co. v. Brown, 61 Mich.App. 268, 232 N.W.2d 378, 17 UCC 978 (1975) ("ship to" with address does not overcome presumption). But see, National Heater Co. v. Corrigan Co. Mechanical Contractors, Inc., 482 F.2d 87, 13 UCC 78 (8th Cir.1973) ("Delivered to Rail Siding" overcomes presumption); Windows, Inc. v. Jordan Panel Systems Corp., 177 F.3d 114, 38 UCC2d 267 (2d Cir. 1999) (To overcome presumption favoring shipment contracts, the parties must "explicitly" agree to such terms; " 'All windows to be shipped properly crated/packaged/boxed suitable for cross country motor freight transit and delivered to New York City' " not explicit enough to overcome presumption).

23. § 2–301. The breach may or may not be total. See § 2–612(3).

24. §§ 2–301; 2–507(1); 2–602, Comment 3. It need not be a total breach. See § 2–612(3).

has breached.[25] The seller may tender delivery both at the proper time and at the proper place, but still fail to make a proper tender under 2–503. This can be particularly important in determining when a breach of warranty has occurred under section 2–725(3), as failure to make proper tender prevents the statute of limitations from running.[26] And if the seller fails to make a proper tender, generally it not only incurs liability for breach but also deprives itself of any power to put the buyer in breach for failure to take delivery. Beyond offering to deliver at the proper time and place, what else must a seller do to make a proper tender? The parties are free to agree on what else the seller must do.[27] In the absence of such agreement, the Code fills this gap with several requirements. Section 2–503(1) states that the seller must "put and hold conforming goods at the buyer's disposition and give the buyer any notification reasonably necessary to enable the buyer to take delivery. Normally the seller's invoice will satisfy the notice requirements. In a contract to deliver "CIF Pakistan," delivery was held not complete until goods cleared customs and buyer could take physical possession."[28]

In addition, where the seller contracts to send the goods to the buyer under a shipment contract in which risk of loss passes to the buyer on seller's due delivery to the carrier,[29] unless otherwise agreed the seller must, under 2–504:

> (a) put the goods in the possession of such a carrier and make such a contract for their transportation as may be reasonable having regard to the nature of the goods and other circumstances of the case; and

25. Eades Commodities, Co. v. Hoeper, 825 S.W.2d 34, 17 UCC2d 771 (Mo. App.1992).

26. City of Willmar v. Short–Elliott–Hendrickson, Inc., 475 N.W.2d 73, 15 UCC2d 912 (Minn.1991) (tender of sewage control device not proper until installed and running); St. Anne–Nackawic Pulp Co. v. Research–Cottrell, Inc., 788 F.Supp. 729, 17 UCC2d 699 (S.D.N.Y.1992) (tender of pollution control system not valid until operational).

27. See, e.g., Evco Distrib., Inc. v. Commercial Credit Equip. Corp., 6 Kan. App.2d 205, 627 P.2d 374, 31 UCC 1544 (1981) (gap-filling tender requirements of 2–503 inapplicable where contract specifically provided equipment purchased for leasing would be delivered to and accepted by lessee); City of New York v. Pullman Inc., 662 F.2d 910, 31 UCC 1375 (2d Cir.1981), cert. denied, 454 U.S. 1164, 102 S.Ct. 1038, 71 L.Ed.2d 320 (1982) (contract specifications provided that subway cars would be required to pass a 30–day on-line inspection before they would "conform" to contract requirements).

28. Beech–Nut Nutrition v. Milupa Corp., 715 F.Supp. 1230, 10 UCC2d 1263 (S.D.N.Y.1989) (contract to deliver C I F, Pakistan, delivery not completed until goods cleared customs and buyer could take physical possession). See also, Parks Hiway Enters., LLC v. CEM Leasing, Inc., 955 P.2d 657, 40 UCC2d 678 (Alaska 2000) (title transfer at delivery); Sam and Mac, Inc. v. Treat, 783 N.E.2d 760, 49 UCC2d 1153 (Ind. App. 2003) (title did not pass until delivery at buyers home, as required under contract); Circuit City Stores, Inc. v. Commissioner of Revenue, 439 Mass. 629, 790 N.E.2d 636, 51 UCC2d 438 (2003) (tender of delivery occurred when store put and held conforming goods for buyer).

29. § 2–509(1)(a).

(b) obtain and promptly deliver or tender in due form any document necessary to enable the buyer to obtain possession of the goods or otherwise required by the agreement or by usage of trade; and

(c) promptly notify the buyer of the shipment.

Failure to notify the buyer under paragraph (c) or to make a proper contract under paragraph (a) is a ground for rejection only if material delay or loss ensues.[30]

The first of the foregoing requires the seller to make a proper contract of carriage, a requirement designed to assure that the goods will arrive not only on time, but in good condition as well. The buyer needs this protection, for in a shipment contract it has the risk of loss in transit and becomes liable for the price to the extent the goods are lost or damaged.[31] Thus if the seller does not make a proper contract of carriage, risk of loss remains on the seller, and properly so. Furthermore, if the seller does not make a proper contract of carriage, it thereby fails to make a proper tender, too. Section 2–503(2), on what constitutes proper tender, requires the seller in a shipment contract to comply with 2–504.[32] A seller can fail to comply with 2–504 in many ways. The seller might fail to select a direct route,[33] to arrange for suitable vehicles,[34] to arrange for proper loading,[35] to declare the proper valuation for insurance purposes,[36] and more.[37]

30. § 2–504. See also, Harlow & Jones, Inc. v. Advance Steel Co., 424 F.Supp. 770, 21 UCC 410 (E.D.Mich. 1976) (buyer not justified in rejecting steel shipped late but delivered on time); Rheinberg–Kellerei GmbH v. Vineyard Wine Co., 53 N.C.App. 560, 281 S.E.2d 425, 32 UCC 96 (1981), review denied, 304 N.C. 588, 289 S.E.2d 564 (1981) (risk of loss of wine never passed from seller to buyer in shipment contract because seller failed to give buyer prompt notice of the shipment as required by § 2–504(c)).

31. § 2–509(1)(a). Ninth St. East, Ltd. v. Harrison, 5 Conn.Cir.Ct. 597, 259 A.2d 772, 7 UCC 171 (1968) (seller entitled to price where goods lost or damaged in transit under F.O.B. seller's place of business).

32. § 2–503(2) says: "Where the case is within the next section respecting shipment tender requires that the seller comply with its provisions."

33. See, e.g., Rosenberg Bros. & Co. v. F.S. Buffum Co., 234 N.Y. 338, 137 N.E. 609 (1922).

34. See, e.g., Paul Blum Co., Inc. v. Daewoo International (America) Corp., 38 Bankr. Ct. Dec. 205, 46 UCC2d 1023 (S.D.N.Y.2001) (seller has no duty to ensure the seaworthiness of vessel that carried goods. Under 2–504 the seller must enter into a contract with a carrier that, given the circumstances, is reasonable. Given that the seller did not know of ship's lack of seaworthiness, the vessel was the variety typically used to haul the goods, buyer approved of choice of vessel, and that the Chinese government had inspected and approved of the ship, seller's contract with carrier was reasonable. Thus, the risk had passed to buyer).

35. Cf. Madeirense do Brasil S/A v. Stulman–Emrick Lumber Co., 147 F.2d 399 (2d Cir.1945), cert. denied, 325 U.S. 861, 65 S.Ct. 1201, 89 L.Ed. 1982 (1945).

36. See, e.g., Lopez v. Henry Isaacs, 210 App.Div. 601, 206 N.Y.S. 405 (1924); La Casse v. Blaustein, 93 Misc.2d 572, 403 N.Y.S.2d 440, 23 UCC 907 (Civ.Ct. 1978).

37. See § 2–505(2). On whether there must be a causal relation between

In a shipment contract the seller must comply with section 2–504 as part of its tender responsibilities. Where the seller does comply, its compliance should reduce the chances that anything untoward will happen to the goods in transit and will thus protect the buyer, for the buyer has the risk of loss in transit in a shipment contract.[38] The Code does not provide comparable protection for the buyer in a destination contract, however. Under the law, buyer does not need it. If nonconforming goods arrive in a destination contract, the buyer may simply reject them.[39] Buyer is not liable for the price since it does not have the risk of loss in transit.[40] Unless otherwise agreed, the seller retains this risk and has full responsibility for delivering conforming goods to buyer.

Even if the seller in a shipment contract delivers conforming goods to the carrier at the proper time and place and even if the seller makes a proper contract for their transportation, seller must, unless otherwise agreed, do more to complete its proper tender. It must see that at destination the goods are made available for inspection, for unless the buyer contracts it away buyer has a right to inspect before either payment or acceptance.[41] While this conclusion may appear contrary to the language of section 2–507, it is firmly grounded in the wording of sections 2–310 and 2–513. But if the buyer on inspection finds that the goods do not conform, it does not follow that the seller is in breach and that the buyer is entitled to reject. The seller would not be in breach and the buyer would not be entitled to reject if the seller delivered conforming goods to the carrier, and if the nonconformity on arrival is traceable to something that occurred during transit for which the seller is not responsible.

What of the buyer's obligations under a shipment contract? Section 2–503(1)(b) requires that "unless otherwise agreed the buyer must furnish facilities reasonably suited to the receipt of the goods." Thus, where a buyer of scrap metal provided a ship

---

any loss in transit and the seller's default under § 2–504, see 1 N.Y. State Law Revision Comm'n, 1955 Report 472 (1955); Cook Specialty Co. v. Schrlock, 772 F.Supp. 1532, 16 UCC2d 360 (E.D.Pa.1991) (seller in compliance with § 2–504 notwithstanding failure to ensure carrier had adequate insurance and use of a carrier with an unprofessional name).

38. Rheinberg–Kellerei GMBH v. Vineyard Wine Co., 53 N.C.App. 560, 281 S.E.2d 425, 32 UCC 96 (1981), review denied, 304 N.C. 588, 289 S.E.2d 564 (1981) ("The requirement of prompt notification by the seller, as used in [§ 2–504(c)], must be construed as taking into consideration the need of a buy-

er to be informed of the shipment in sufficient time *for him* to take action to *protect himself* from the risk of damage to or loss of the goods while in transit." (emphasis added)).

39. § 2–601. For exceptions to this principle, see §§ 2–612; 2–508.

40. § 2–509(1)(b).

41. §§ 2–310(b); 2–513(1). HCI Chem. (USA), Inc. v. Henkel KGaA v. Empresa Naviera Santa, S.A., 966 F.2d 1018, 18 UCC2d 436 (5th Cir.1992) (chemicals delivered to carrier in Chile could be inspected and rejected by buyer in New Jersey).

unsuitable for the purchased cargo, the buyer was found to be in breach.[42]

In a *shipment* contract, seller's delivery and buyer's payment are not concurrent conditions. For events to be such it must be possible for them to occur at the same time. But in a shipment contract, delivery technically occurs at the point of shipment,[43] yet payment is not due until after the goods become available for inspection at destination.[44] Delivery and payment therefore cannot be concurrent.

Even though the goods have become available for inspection the buyer is still not obligated to pay in a shipment contract unless and until it has a reasonable opportunity to inspect, and the seller tenders any documents "necessary to enable buyer to obtain possession of the goods."[45] Commonly, no such documents will be involved, for the seller will ship pursuant to a nonnegotiable bill of lading naming buyer as consignee or the like. Under such a bill the carrier may deliver to the buyer without demanding the bill. But under 2–505 the seller can have the carrier issue a negotiable bill of lading to seller's order or a nonnegotiable bill of lading naming the seller as consignee. By the terms of such a bill in either form (or in comparable form), the seller retains power over the goods, for the carrier is thereby bound to follow the seller's instructions.[46] Through this control a seller can reduce the risk that buyer will get the goods without paying or at least without making satisfactory arrangements to pay. Of course if the deal is on credit, there is no occasion for the seller to retain control. It should be added that the seller can retain control through the form of the bill of lading and yet arrange for the buyer to inspect. The seller may authorize the buyer to inspect while the goods are still in the hands of the carrier and under seller's control.[47]

So far we have only considered what the Code requires for the seller to make a proper tender of delivery when the contract calls for it to tender delivery of *goods* but is otherwise silent on one or more aspects of this tender. But sometimes the seller will contract to tender delivery through tender of *documents* covering the goods. Comment 7 to 2–503 states that tender of documents as the mode of delivery is "never required except where there is an express

---

42. Great Western Sugar Co. v. World's Finest Chocolate, Inc., 169 Ill. App.3d 949, 120 Ill.Dec. 238, 523 N.E.2d 1149, 7 UCC2d 1020 (1988) (failure of buyer to designate time and place for delivery as required by industry custom constituted breach).

43. §§ 2–503; 2–504.

44. §§ 2–310(b); 2–513.

45. § 2–504(b).

46. §§ 2–505; 7–303(1); 7–403(1). However, see Ciba–Geigy Corp. v. Flo–Lizer, Inc. (In re Flo–Lizer, Inc.), 946 F.2d 1237, 15 UCC2d 1198 (6th Cir. 1991) (§ 2–505 does not apply to disputes between seller and debtor in possession; where a seller of chemicals sent a non-negotiable bill of lading, it did not successfully create a security interest).

47. See § 2–310, Comment 2.

contract term or it is plainly implicit in the peculiar circumstances of the case or in a usage of trade." Domestic contracts calling for delivery through tender of documents are infrequent. Those contracts usually involve so-called "documentary sales" in which the buyer agrees to pay cash when seller's agent presents a sight draft and bill of lading covering the goods. To make tender of delivery through tender of documents (absent contrary agreement), the seller must deliver the documents at the buyer's city.[48] The time for delivery is a "reasonable time."[49] The seller may send the documents through customary banking channels,[50] and seller must tender "all documents" in "correct form."[51] Once the seller does all these things under a contract calling for the buyer to pay when the seller's agent presents a sight draft and documents, seller has discharged its delivery obligations and becomes entitled to payment "at the time and place at which the buyer is to receive the documents regardless of where the goods are to be received."[52] The buyer has no right to inspect the goods prior to accepting and paying for the documents, unless it has expressly reserved this right in the contract.[53]

Do not think that documents of title figure in proper tender only where the contract calls for tender of delivery by tendering *documents*. Earlier we explained that in the so-called "shipment contract," in which the seller is required to tender *goods* to the buyer, the seller must, unless otherwise agreed, "obtain and promptly deliver or tender in due form any document necessary to enable the buyer to obtain possession of the goods."[54] If documents are necessary, and seller fails to tender them, its tender will not be proper under sections 2–503(1), (2), (3) and 2–504, even though seller has already made delivery at the point of shipment. Similarly in a destination contract the seller may, as part of its overall duty to make a proper tender of goods, also be required to tender documents covering them.[55] Even after the goods are transported under either a shipment or a destination contract calling for delivery of goods, the seller, in the absence of contrary agreement, remains responsible for two things: (1) to offer the buyer a reasonable opportunity to inspect, and (2) to offer to relinquish any control seller has retained over the goods through documents of

---

48.   §§ 2–310(a); 2–310, Comment 3. See also §§ 2–308(c); 2–308, Comment 3.

49.   § 2–309(1).

50.   § 2–503(5)(b).

51.   § 2–503(5)(a). There is a tradition of strictness in regard to documentary tenders. See, e.g., Mitsubishi Goshi Kaisha v. J. Aron & Co., 16 F.2d 185 (2d Cir.1926).

52.   § 2–310(c).

53.   §§ 2–310(c); 2–513(3)(b).

54.   § 2–504(b).

55.   § 2–503(3). See, e.g., In re Production Steel, Inc., 54 B.R. 417, 42 UCC 1285 (Bankr.M.D.Tenn.1985) (where delivery was F.O.B. New Orleans, and bills of lading were not tendered to buyer until goods were in Nashville, delivery occurred in Nashville and buyer's debt was incurred at that time).

title. Not until these things are done can the seller put the buyer in breach for failure to accept and pay.[56]

Nearly all the Code law on seller's delivery and tender of delivery is gap filling law. The parties are free to agree as they wish[57] and the Code only fills gaps.[58] The Code's gap fillers may seem somewhat strict. But the Code itself also includes three distinct types of sections that modify and thus ameliorate the strictness of its gap fillers on tender. First, in some circumstances the seller's duty to tender delivery may be excused altogether. This will be so, for example, when "presupposed conditions" of the contract fail.[59] Second, in some circumstances the seller is allowed to tender through a substitute carrier or in a substitute manner. When it does so, the substitute tender is considered the real thing.[60] Third, even though the seller's noncomplying tender is not excused and is not a permissible substitute, the tender may in some circumstances still be sufficient at least to preclude rejection.[61] In section 6–2, we also discuss FOB, CIF and Incoterms.

§ 4–6 Article 2 Gap Fillers on Duration and Notice of Termination

Section 2–309 headed: "Absence of Specified Time Provisions; Notice of Termination", provides:

> (1) The time for shipment or delivery or any other action under a contract if not provided in this Article or agreed upon shall be a reasonable time.

> (2) Where the contract provides for successive performances but is indefinite in duration it is valid for a reasonable

---

56. The language of § 2–511(1) is not well chosen. It reads: "Unless otherwise agreed tender of payment is a condition to the seller's duty to tender and complete any delivery." The word delivery is inapt for shipment contracts, for in them the seller has technically already delivered at point of shipment. Thus he no longer has any delivery obligation, though he must arrange for relinquishing any control retained. See § 2–504(b).

57. Increasingly, and especially in transnational sales, parties turn to the International Chamber of Commerce Incoterms as a source for standard contract terms regarding delivery, risk of loss, and related matters. See section 6–2 for our discussion of Incoterms.

58. See, e.g., Steuber Co., Inc. v. Hercules, Inc., 646 F.2d 1093, 31 UCC 508 (5th Cir.1981) (trial court erred in directing verdict where conflict in evidence exists as to parties' agreement on delivery terms despite use of "C.I.F." term). Cf. Monte Carlo Shirt, Inc. v. Daewoo Int'l (America) Corp., 707 F.2d 1054, 36 UCC 487 (9th Cir.1983) (court accepts *arguendo* that 2–504 overrides contractual obligations finding jury instructions were not in error, but, in footnote 7, court finds literal reading of 2–504 would not allow Code to override terms).

59. § 2–615.

60. § 2–614.

61. "Failure to notify the buyer * * * or to make a proper contract * * * is a ground for rejection only if material delay or loss ensues." § 2–504.

time but unless otherwise agreed may be terminated at any time by either party.

(3) Termination of a contract by one party except on the happening of an agreed event requires that reasonable notification be received by the other party and an agreement dispensing with notification is invalid if its operation would be unconscionable.

We considered 2–309(1) in 4–5. Here we focus on issues of duration, power of termination, and notice of termination. These issues are dealt with in subsections (2) and (3) above and in Official Comments 7, 8, 9, and 10 of section 2–309.

Subsection (2) purports to fill two gaps in certain agreements. In appropriate circumstances, it fills a gap as to duration and also a gap as to the power to terminate. Thus, if the agreement provides for "successive performances" and is "indefinite as to duration", subsection (2) fills the gap as to duration with a "reasonable time". Moreover, the section makes clear that such indefiniteness as to duration does not invalidate the contract. (Cf. 2–204(3).) In addition, the subsection fills any further gap ("unless otherwise agreed") as to power of termination by stating that a contract which "provides for successive performances" yet is "indefinite in duration" may be "terminated at any time by either party." This language has been paraphrased to mean "termination at will,"[1] subject, of course, to the notice provisions of 2–309(3).

When does 2–309(2) come into play not only to fill a gap as to duration with a duration consisting of a reasonable time but also to fill a gap as to power of termination with terminability being at will, subject to notice? Two conditions must be met to bring the duration gap filler into play. First, the contract must provide for successive performances. Second, the contract must be indefinite in duration. These two conditions are also required to bring the power of termination gap-filler into play, and here there is a third as well: the agreement must not provide otherwise as to when the contract may be terminated.

In order for a contract to be subject to a gap filler provision as to duration at all, it must first provide for successive performances. Typically, a distributorship agreement where one party agrees to sell the products of the other for an indefinite period of time will fall under section 2–309(2). In a case where the distributor had an agreement with a piano manufacturer to market and sell the manufacturer's pianos, the agreement was found to call for succes-

§ 4–6

1. In re Pennsylvania Tire Co., 26 B.R. 663, 37 UCC 410 (Bankr.N.D.Ohio 1982).

sive performances in that the distributor was to continue to purchase pianos from the manufacturer as retail sales warranted. Each order under the contract constituted a separate, successive performance, and as such, it was held that the agreement was governed by section 2–309(2) and was terminable at will.[2]

Conversely, in Panhandle Agri–Service, Inc. v. Becker,[3] a farmer had agreed to sell 10,000 tons of hay and was unable to deliver the entire amount as a result of a bad harvest. The court held that a further agreement to deliver the balance from the following year's crop was not governed by section 2–309(2) because the contract called for a single performance, the delivery of 10,000 tons of hay, and the mere agreement to take delivery over a period of time did not constitute an agreement for successive performances and thus the contract was not terminable at will.

The second requirement that must be fulfilled before section 2–309(2) comes into play is that the contract in question must be indefinite in duration. Comment 1 provides that such an agreement "may be found in a term implied from the contractual circumstances, usage of trade or course of dealing or performance as well as in an express term."

As would be expected, contracts that do not expressly provide for duration, or do not entail performances which involve a definite duration, are governed by section 2–309(2). Thus a contract calling for a party to distribute a manufacturer's valves nationwide, with no provision for duration, was found to be governed by the Code in this respect. There is little in the nature of a typical distributorship agreement that implies a duration. The bulk of section 2–309(2) decisions arise out of these agreements.[4]

Where a contract called for a supplier of concrete to provide its requirements for a particular construction project, a court concluded that the project itself created a definite time for the duration of the contract, and as such it did not require a gap filler for duration and could not be terminated at will by virtue of section 2–309(2).[5] In another case, which involved a contract to supply photocopying chemicals providing for annual renewals subject to certain condi-

2. McGinnis Piano & Organ Co. v. Yamaha Int'l Corp., 480 F.2d 474, 12 UCC 265 (8th Cir.1973). See also Zidell Explorations, Inc. v. Conval Int'l, Ltd., 719 F.2d 1465, 37 UCC 466 (9th Cir. 1983); Viking Supply v. National Cart C., 310 F.3d 1092, 49 UCC2d 94 (8th Cir.2002) (absent a specific termination date, a distributorship is terminable at will); RGJ Associates, Inc. v. Stainsafe, Inc., 300 F.Supp. 2d 250, 52 UCC2d 675 (D. Mass. 2004) (accord).

3. 231 Kan. 291, 644 P.2d 413, 33 UCC 1320 (1982).

4. Sinkoff Beverage Co. v. Jos. Schlitz Brewing Co., 51 Misc.2d 446, 273 N.Y.S.2d 364, 3 UCC 733 (1966) (beer distributorship); Corenswet, Inc. v. Amana Refrigeration, Inc., 594 F.2d 129, 26 UCC 301 (5th Cir.1979) (home appliances).

5. Mishara Constr. Co. v. Transit–Mixed Concrete Corp., 365 Mass. 122, 310 N.E.2d 363, 14 UCC 556 (1974).

tions, the court held the agreement to be definite in duration and thus not governed by section 2–309(2).[6] While the contract could have conceivably continued for an indefinite duration, the renewal process created a framework for duration that precluded the application of section 2–309(2). This seems a proper reading of 2–309(2). After all, a gap filler should always give way in the face of agreement—and doubts should be resolved in favor of the agreement.

A review of even a few of the cases shows how considerable those doubts can be. In Besco, Inc. v. Alpha Portland Cement Co.[7] Portland agreed to sell Besco kiln dust produced by its operations. The contract provided for termination by Portland "solely" if either Besco failed to purchase certain minimum quantities or if Portland did not produce the dust in the ordinary course of business. The Fifth Circuit held that as Portland could only terminate on those grounds, the parties had "agreed otherwise," and section 2–309(2) did not govern.

But the same court concluded that a nearly identical arrangement, in which the contract provided for termination in the event of a distributor's failing to meet certain sales goals, did not constitute an agreement otherwise. In that case section 2–309(2) governed and the contract was terminable at will, although reasonable notice is required for contracts terminable at will.[8] In distinguishing *Delta Services* from *Portland*, the Fifth Circuit focused on the word "solely" in the earlier case, and concluded that its presence was inconsistent with a determination of terminability at will.[9] At least in the Fifth Circuit and in the absence of "solely," or language of similar effect, general provisions allowing for termination do not necessarily constitute "agreements otherwise."

In coming to this position, the Fifth Circuit stated two policy reasons for favoring the "indefinite" interpretation and so subject a contract to termination under subsection (2). First, the court asserted that parties do not normally intend to maintain their business relationships forever, and second, the UCC goal of promoting mutually beneficial dealings is not fostered if parties must continue to perform after their relationship has soured.[10] Since indefiniteness allows for termination at will, a determination to that effect conformed to the court's policies. Although we do not disagree with the

6. Copylease Corp. of America v. Memorex Corp., 403 F.Supp. 625, 18 UCC 317 (S.D.N.Y.1975).

7. 619 F.2d 447, 29 UCC 436 (5th Cir.1980).

8. Delta Services & Equip., Inc. v. Ryko Mfg. Co., 908 F.2d 7, 14 UCC2d 414 (5th Cir.1990); Viking Supply v. National Cart Co., Inc., 310 F.3d 1092, 49 UCC2d 94 (8th Cir. 2002) (no duration so terminable at will); Coburn Supply Company, Inc. v. Kohler Co., 342 F.3d 372, 51 UCC2d 80 (5th Cir. 2003) (even though at will, reasonable notice required and 105 days sufficient).

9. *Id.* at 9, 14 UCC2d at 417.

10. *Id.* at 11, 14 UCC2d at 420.

conclusion in *Besco*, we question the court's policy justifications. As we indicated above, we would err on the side of "agreements otherwise."

Finally, with respect to duration, one court has suggested that a contract must run for a reasonable time under 2–309(2) before the power to terminate even comes into play.[11] This conclusion is at odds with 2–309(2) which says "but * * * may be terminated at any time." Another court has held that an indefinite contract can be terminated prior to the passage of our initial reasonable time.[12]

We have seen that 2–309(2) makes the duration of an indefinite contract "a reasonable time." Comment 7 says that:

> The "reasonable time" of duration appropriate to a given arrangement is limited by the circumstances. When the arrangement has been carried on by the parties over the years, the "reasonable time" can continue indefinitely and the contract will not terminate until notice.

What is reasonable in a particular case is ordinarily a question of fact.[13] Beyond the cliche that it is dependent upon the nature, purpose and circumstances of the transaction,[14] the case law reveals little about how to define a reasonable duration.[15] No court seems to have reached the conclusion that an active contract exceeded a reasonable duration and thus became invalid.

Assuming a party has a power to terminate under section 2–309(2), section 2–309(3) requires that the party give notice of termination unless (1) the party has the right to cancel for breach, or (2) termination by that party is pursuant to the happening of an agreed event, or (3) the parties have validly dispensed with notice of termination.

Comment 9 states that "justifiable cancellation for breach is a remedy for breach and is not the kind of termination covered by the present section [Section 2–309]." There is no obligation to give notice when termination is so justified and Mott Equity Elevator v. Svihovec so holds.[16] There, a grain buyer breached the contract by

---

11. Superior Foods, Inc. v. Harris–Teeter Super Markets, Inc., 288 N.C. 213, 217 S.E.2d 566, 17 UCC 970 (1975).

12. Jo-Ann, Inc. v. Alfin Fragrances, 731 F.Supp. 149, 11 UCC2d 782 (D.N.J. 1989).

13. Zidell Explorations, Inc. v. Conval Int'l, Ltd., 719 F.2d 1465, 37 UCC 466 (9th Cir.1983).

14. Montana Millwork, Inc. v. Caradco Corp., 648 F.Supp. 88, 2 UCC2d 921 (D.Mont.1986).

15. As a matter of general contract, several courts indicated that a reasonable duration for either a franchise or distributorship agreement is the length of time necessary for the franchisee to recoup its initial investment. This is dubious, as it could take a very long time. McGinnis Piano & Organ Co. v. Yamaha Int'l Corp., 480 F.2d 474, 12 UCC 265 (8th Cir.1973) (6 years sufficient time for retailer of pianos to recoup investment).

16. 236 N.W.2d 900, 18 UCC 388 (N.D.1975).

refusing delivery, and the court said the seller was not obligated to notify the buyer when he resold the grain elsewhere.[17]

Comment 10 states that "the requirement of notification is dispensed with where the contract provides for termination on the happening of an agreed event." This is supported by the language of subsection (3), and is sensible, as the agreement itself provides notice of termination, and the occurrence of the agreed upon event in question does the same.

As to the power of the parties validly to dispense with notice under subsection (3), Comment 8 points out that:

> Subsection (3) recognizes that the application of principles of good faith and sound commercial practice normally call for such notification of the termination of a going contract relationship as will give the other party reasonable time to seek a substitute arrangement. An agreement dispensing with notification or limiting the time for the seeking of a substitute arrangement is, of course, valid under this subsection unless the results of putting it into operation would be the creation of an unconscionable state of affairs.

Thus, where an agreement to distribute beer included the right of the brewer to terminate without notice, the brewer was allowed to terminate on 10 days notice—despite a six-year relationship and notwithstanding the fact that the distributor had made a substantial investment in the business.[18]

Of course, as both subsection (3) and Comment 8 point out, any agreement to dispense with notification must not be unconscionable. Subsection (3) requires the invalidation of such an agreement "if its *operation* would be unconscionable," and Comment 8 calls for invalidation if "the results of *putting it into operation* would be the creation of an unconscionable state of affairs" (emphasis added). The conclusion seems inescapable that the Code intends the focus of an unconscionability determination under 2–309 be on the result of its application as seen at the time of termination. Yet courts sometimes look to the time of the making of the contract for signs of oppression or the opportunity for unfair surprise. In one case, the court confused the unconscionability provision of section 2–309(3) with the general unconscionability provision of section 2–302(1), and thus erroneously focused attention on the time of the making of the contract.[19]

17. See also Farmers Union Grain Terminal Ass'n v. Hermanson, 549 F.2d 1177, 21 UCC 61 (8th Cir.1977); Mayflower Farms v. Tech–Mark, Inc., 64 Or. App. 121, 666 P.2d 1384, 37 UCC 25 (1983).

18. Sinkoff Beverage Co. v. Jos. Schlitz Brewing Co., 51 Misc.2d 446, 273 N.Y.S.2d 364, 3 UCC 733 (1966). See also Coburn Supply Co. v. Kohler Co., 342 F.3d 372, 51 UCC2d 80 (5th Cir. 2003) (reasonable notice given).

19. In re Pennsylvania Tire Co., 26 B.R. 663, 37 UCC 410 (Bankr.N.D.Ohio

In addition to the unconscionability requirements of subsection (3), termination under section 2–309 is subject to the obligation of good faith by section 1–203 (Rev. 1–304). Certainly termination in general is covered by 1–203 (Rev. 1–304). In Baker v. Ratzlaff[20] a grower and seller of popcorn was found to have violated the good faith requirement of the Code. The seller had the express right to terminate if the buyer failed to pay on delivery. The seller exercised this right. However, the seller never requested payment from the buyer but immediately sold the popcorn that would have otherwise been committed under the contract to another buyer for nearly double the contract price. In light of these facts, the court upheld a finding of a breach of the Code's good faith provision. The court did note, however, that the agreement did not expressly allow for termination at will.[21]

In a contract explicitly terminable at will, no termination violates a duty of good faith. In Corenswet, Inc. v. Amana Refrigeration, Inc.,[22] the Fifth Circuit overturned a lower court's finding that a contract terminable "at any time and for any reason" had been terminated in bad faith. The court held that 1–203 (Rev. 1–304) could not override or strike express contract terms. As long as the provision allowing for termination was not unconscionable, the contract could be terminated even in bad faith.[23]

Where does this leave contracts that are terminable at will because of 2–309(2)? In a Ninth Circuit case,[24] there is dictum to the effect that such a termination is subject to 1–203 (Rev. 1–304), yet the cases cited by the court were decided not under the UCC, but general state contract law.[25] The conclusion that termination at will under 2–309(2) may be governed by good faith seems well supported by the language of 1–203 "*every * * * duty* within the Uniform Commercial Code imposes an obligation of good faith" (emphasis added). But we see no role for good faith here. We do not believe that ideas of good faith should be used to deprive a terminating party of the rights it would otherwise have under 2–309(2). These cases remind one of debtors' argument that payees on demand notes had to have a good faith reason to call those notes. In the lender liability cases, that argument has now been generally rejected.

1982). See also Sinkoff Beverage Co. v. Jos. Schlitz Brewing Co., 51 Misc.2d 446, 273 N.Y.S.2d 364, 3 UCC 733 (1966); Zapatha v. Dairy Mart, Inc., 381 Mass. 284, 408 N.E.2d 1370, 29 UCC 1121 (1980).

20. 1 Kan.App.2d 285, 564 P.2d 153, 21 UCC 1217 (1977).

21. *Id.*, 564 P.2d at 156, 21 UCC at 1221.

22. 594 F.2d 129, 26 UCC 301 (5th Cir.1979).

23. *Id.* at 138, 26 UCC at 313.

24. Zidell Explorations, Inc. v. Conval Int'l, Ltd., 719 F.2d 1465, 37 UCC 466 (9th Cir.1983).

25. *Id.* at 1473, 37 UCC at 472.

When notice of termination is required, what kind of notice must be given? First the notice must be reasonable as to method. Second the notice must be reasonable as to timing. Third, the notice must be "reccived". It is not enough if it is merely sent (as under 9–611 of the 1999 Official Text Article 9).

What constitutes a reasonable method? In a case involving the supply of chicken feed, a court concluded that the method of notice must afford the party affected by the termination an opportunity to make substitute arrangements.[26] Dispute arose when the supplier terminated two different pricing agreements with the buyer. The first price policy involved a 2 percent deduction for prompt payment, and notice was given to the buyer through a letter and the removal of the advice of the 2 percent policy from the standard invoice. The second pricing policy that was terminated involved a cost plus arrangement in which the supplier was to compute the price according to an agreed upon formula and bill the buyer accordingly. Here, the seller simply stopped billing according to the formula, and later claimed that as the buyer could have computed the formula price himself and discovered it was different from the invoice price, the buyer therefore received "all the notice of price changes a merchant could reasonably expect to receive." The court upheld the lower court's determination that the notice of termination of the 2 percent deduction was reasonable, and also its determination that the notice of termination of the cost plus agreement was not.[27] Clearly, the effectiveness of the notice, and the degree to which the terminating party evinces a desire to actually communicate notice of termination, plays a role in the determination of reasonableness.

As well as a reasonable method, notification of termination requires a reasonable amount of time before termination actually takes place. This is the recommendation of Comment 8, which specifically calls for time to seek a substitute arrangement. The case law is in accord.

Thus, when a supplier of beauty care products terminated an agreement with a distributor without any advance notice, it was found to be unreasonable as a matter of law. Plainly a substitute arrangement cannot be made in no time.[28] But where a new, unopened, stationery store's supplier of greeting cards terminated their agreement, the court held that there could be no question of

---

26. Agway, Inc. v. Ernst, 394 A.2d 774, 25 UCC 665 (Me.1978).

27. Id. 394 A.2d at 779.

28. Jo–Ann, Inc. v. Alfin Fragrances, Inc., 731 F.Supp. 149, 11 UCC2d 782 (D.N.J.1989). See also Maytronics, Ltd.

v. Aqua Vac Systems, Inc., 277 F.3d 1317, 46 UCC2d 379 (11th Cir. 2002) (recovery of damages for termination without adequate notice; damages equal lost profits during notice period).

reasonable notice, given that the store was able to find a new supplier before it opened.[29]

The question of reasonable timing of notice of termination takes on a special dimension when a manufacturer or supplier is supplying custom-made goods. In that case, courts have looked to the time necessary for the manufacturer or supplier to sell out the remaining inventory in determining the reasonableness of notice. Thus, when a supplier of uniforms to an airline was given a year's notice of termination, it was held not to be reasonable as a matter of law. As the question of the unsold inventory was an issue for the trier of fact, the buyer's motion for summary judgment was denied.[30]

§ 4–7 Article 2 Gap Fillers on Payment Terms (Herein, too, of Buyer's Tender of Payment)

Section 2–507(1) provides that seller's proper tender of delivery entitles it to "payment according to the contract." But as we shall see, payment has numerous aspects, and the contract of the parties may be silent on one or all of them. The Code includes several gap fillers on payment.[1] If the agreement is silent, must the buyer pay cash or is it entitled to an extension of credit? The Code fills this gap by requiring that the buyer pay cash on the barrelhead.[2] The buyer must bargain for credit. This may seem surprising, for in

29. Teitelbaum v. Hallmark Cards Inc., 25 Mass.App.Ct. 555, 520 N.E.2d 1333, 7 UCC2d 705 (1988). See Maytronics, Ltd. v. Aqua Vac Systems, Inc., 277 F.3d 1317, 46 UCC2d 379 (11th Cir. 2002) (when a terminable at will contract under 2–309 is terminated without adequate notice, the non-terminating party is entitled to recover the lost profits it would have earned during the reasonable notification period).

30. Hamilton Tailoring Co. v. Delta Air Lines, Inc., 1974 WL 21756, 14 UCC 1310 (S.D.Ohio 1974); Superior Foods, Inc. v. Harris–Teeter Super Markets, Inc., 288 N.C. 213, 217 S.E.2d 566, 17 UCC 970 (1975).

§ 4–7

1. Speedi Lubrication Centers, Inc. v. Atlas Match Corp., 595 S.W.2d 912, 29 UCC 556 (Tex.Civ.App.1980) (where parties had agreed any repudiation by buyer would entitle seller to full payment in advance of delivering remaining goods, seller's failure to deliver goods did not bar it from recovering after buy-er defaulted); St. Paul Structural Steel Co. v. ABI Contracting, Inc., 364 N.W.2d 83, 40 UCC 789 (N.D.1985) (trial court erred in applying § 2–310 to determine when payment due since only gap in agreement was regarding retainage fee; parties had agreed on when progress payments due). Of course, the parties can intend to contract even though no payment terms are specified. See, Crest Ridge Construction Group, Inc. v. Newcourt, Inc., 78 F.3d 146, 29 UCC2d 130 (5th Cir. 1996). Absent agreement on credit terms, seller is entitled to retain possession until buyer pays cash. See State of Oregon v. Alexander, 186 Or. App. 600, 64 P.3d 1148, 49 UCC2d 1134 (2003).

2. §§ 2–310(a); 2–507(1); 2–507, Comment 2. See also Koreag, Controle et Revision S.A. v. Refco F/X Associates, Inc. (In re Koreag, Controle et Revision S.A.), 961 F.2d 341, 17 UCC2d 1036 (2d Cir.1992) (unless otherwise agreed, payment due on delivery); State of Oregon v. Alexander, 186 Or.App. 600, 64 P.3d 1148, 49 UCC2d 1134 (2003) (payment due on delivery).

most commercial sales in which the parties do address this question, the seller extends credit.

When and where must the buyer pay cash? If the deal is silent, 2–310(a) states that "payment is due at the time and place at which the buyer is to receive the goods even though the place of shipment is the place of delivery."[3] Section 2–503(1)(a) suggests that the place of receipt is where the buyer is to take physical possession of the goods. Frequently the time and place for payment will be the time and place where the seller is to make delivery, for this will be the "time and place at which the buyer is to receive the goods." But frequently this will not be true, too. That is, frequently the time and place where the buyer is to receive the goods will not be the same as the time and place for seller's "delivery." In 2–504 "shipment contracts," the time and place of delivery is at seller's city or place of business, and this is obviously not where the buyer takes possession of the goods. The comments to 2–310(a) indicate that the section was drafted in light of the possibility that time and place of delivery might differ from time and place of receipt.[4] In the absence of contrary agreement, 2–513 provides that the buyer is entitled to inspect prior to payment, a right that it should not have to exercise by traveling to the seller's city to inspect at the time and place the seller delivers to the carrier. The Code drafters therefore deferred the buyer's duty to pay until the time and place of its receipt, where buyer may conveniently exercise its customary right of inspection prior to payment.

But it must not be assumed that the buyer is entitled to withhold payment until it has taken full possession and control of the goods. Absent contrary agreement, the Code theory is that the buyer is entitled to full possession and control over the goods only where it concurrently tenders payment. Accordingly, while the seller must make the goods available for inspection, "he is not required to give up possession of the goods until he has received payment,"[5] assuming, of course, that the seller has not agreed to extend credit.

3. Southwest Eng'g Co. v. Martin Tractor Co., 205 Kan. 684, 473 P.2d 18, 7 UCC 1288 (1970) (court invoked § 2–310 to fill gap with payment on delivery term). Koreag, Controle et Revision S.A. v. Refco F/X Associates, Inc., 961 F.2d 341, 17 UCC2d 1036 (2d Cir.1992) (seller of $6.9 million entitled to reclamation if a cash sale, as § 2–310(a) provides for payment on delivery, or if a credit sale, as § 2–702(2) allows if buyer received goods while insolvent and seller made its demand within 10 days); Sethness–Greenleaf, Inc. v. Green River Corp., 65 F.3d 64, 27 UCC2d 360 (7th Cir. 1995) (despite seller's leniency, invoices controlled payment due dates); Simpson Properties, Inc. v. Oexco, Inc., 916 P.2d 853, 29 UCC2d 748 (Okla. App. 1996) (custom covered finances charges on unpaid invoices).

4. See, e.g., § 2–310, Comment 1.

5. § 2–310, Comment 2. Koreag, Controle et Revision, S.A. v. Refco F/X Associates, Inc., 961 F.2d 341, 17 UCC2d 1036 (2d Cir.1992) (unpaid seller of U.S. dollars retained possession).

What if buyer discovers what appears to be a breach of warranty? Can the buyer withhold part of its payment and still insist that the seller relinquish possession of the goods? Of course, if the seller admits the breach of warranty, seller may agree to buyer's proposal to withhold part of the payment and no problem will arise. But assuming that the seller denies the breach of warranty, nothing in the Code on tender requires that seller give up the goods in return for reduced payment. Accordingly, if the buyer should refuse acceptance, except on its reduced terms, the seller would not be in breach for refusing to relinquish possession of the goods.[6] The seller should not be forced to give up the goods in return for the lower payment since more often than not the goods will prove to be conforming (most sellers perform most of the time), and if the buyer pays in full, both parties will then more often than not be in the position they expected to be in after performance.

Thus buyer's payment and seller's relinquishment of full possession and control are "concurrent conditions," absent contrary agreement.[7] Even though the time and place where the buyer is to receive the goods is in a city far away from the seller's place of business, the seller can still retain full possession and control over the goods by procuring a document of title from the carrier in appropriate form, for example, a negotiable bill of lading to the seller's own order or a nonnegotiable bill of lading naming the seller as consignee.[8] Documents in this form require the carrier to obey instructions from the seller as to disposition of goods.[9] Unless the buyer has agreed to pay against documents, the seller must be careful to assure that the carrier allows the buyer a reasonable opportunity to inspect. The buyer is entitled to inspect unless buyer explicitly gives up the right or agrees to a C.O.D. payment term or to a term which, in the language of 2–513(3)(b), calls for "payment against documents of title, except where such payment is due only after the goods are to become available for inspection." In general a buyer who agrees to pay against documents gives up the right to inspect. Section 2–310(c) reads:

> [I]f delivery is authorized and made by way of documents of title otherwise than by subsection (b) then payment is due at

6. If buyer has received the goods, § 2–717 lets buyer tender a reduced price.

7. Spikes v. Bauer, 6 Kan.App.2d 45, 626 P.2d 816, 31 UCC 498 (1981) ("In the present case delivery and payment and receipt were to be simultaneous."); State of Oregon v. Alexander, 186 Or. App. 600, 64 P.3d 1148, 49 UCC2d 1134 (2003) (tender of delivery is condition of buyer's duty to pay).

8. §§ 2–310(b); 2–505. See also, In re Ault, 6 B.R. 58, 30 UCC 1714 (Bankr. E.D.Tenn.1980) (buyer did not have the right to take possession of goods shipped C.O.D. under a straight bill of lading until buyer paid carrier).

9. §§ 2–505(1); 7–303(1)(a), (b); 7–403(1).

the time and place at which the buyer is to receive the documents regardless of where the goods are to be received....

Section 2–513(3)(b) contemplates a variation on payment against documents that is considered to preserve the right to inspect. The buyer does not give up its right to inspect before payment even when it agrees to pay against documents if "such payment is due only after the goods are to become available for inspection." The comments[10] also support this conclusion.[11]

In the absence of contrary agreement, then, the buyer must tender payment at the time and place where it is to receive the goods and must also furnish facilities reasonably suited to delivery of the goods.[12] Unless performance of these duties is excused, the buyer's failure to do any of these will put it in breach.[13] On the other hand if buyer does perform these duties, but the seller fails in its corresponding duties, the seller will be in breach.[14]

What exactly must the buyer tender as payment? Sections 2–511(2) and (3) fill any gap in the contract:

(2) Tender of payment is sufficient when made by any means or in any manner current in the ordinary course of business unless the seller demands payment in legal tender and gives any extension of time reasonably necessary to procure it.

(3) Subject to the provisions of this Act on the effect of an instrument on an obligation (Section 3–310), payment by check is conditional and is defeated as between the parties by dishonor of the check on due presentment.

Tender of a check is only a conditionally valid tender.[15] As between seller and buyer,[16] the seller is entitled to reassert domin-

10. § 2–310(b), Comment 4; § 2–513, Comment 5.

11. § 2–513 does not, however, give the purchaser the right to inspect merchandise prior to the formation of the contract of sale. Gillen v. Atalanta Systems, Inc., 997 F.2d 280, 21 UCC2d 271 (7th Cir.1993).

12. § 2–503(1)(b).

13. §§ 2–301; 2–507; 2–511. The breach may or may not be a total breach. See e.g., § 2–612(3).

14. §§ 2–301; 2–507. The breach may or may not be a total breach, as in an installment case. See, e.g., § 2–612(3). See also, Ross Cattle Co. v. Lewis, 415 So.2d 1029, 34 UCC 913 (Miss. 1982) (seller in breach when failed to make proper tender of delivery and had cattle sold at auction instead of delivering to buyer; buyer not in breach for failing to tender payment prior to deliv-

ery as requested by seller where contract made payment due on delivery; seller entitled to demand assurance under § 2–609 when insecure but seller not entitled to treat contract as breached when buyer fails to tender payment earlier upon seller's request).

15. But see Chicago Limousine Service, Inc. v. Hartigan Cadillac, Inc., 191 Ill.App.3d 886, 139 Ill.Dec. 1, 548 N.E.2d 386, 10 UCC2d 1418 (1989) (rescission of sale valid even when return payment check was later dishonored). See also Nygaard v. Continental Resources, Inc., 598 N.W.2d 851, 39 UCC2d 399 (N.D. 1999) (sight drafts instead of legal tender constituted valid tender to extend lease).

16. Western Idaho Production Credit Ass'n v. Simplot Feed Lots, Inc., 106 Idaho 260, 678 P.2d 52, 37 UCC 1748 (1984) (sellers not entitled to assert

ion over the goods if the buyer has acquired them by giving a check that bounces.[17] There is some authority that the seller must reassert dominion within ten days of buyer's receipt of the goods or delivery of goods to buyer.[18] Other courts, however, reject the 10–day limitation.[19] But, except where the buyer is insolvent, the Code does not expressly impose a ten-day limit.[20]

§ 4–8 Article 2 Gap Fillers on Price

Most contracts for the sale of goods specify a price. In this way they assign the risks of a fluctuating market. As Professor Prosser once put it (before torts became his *idée maitresse*):

> A prospective seller, who owns a thousand bushels of wheat, is necessarily subject to the risk that, before he sells, the market value of the wheat will decline, and he will receive less for it than it is now worth. A prospective buyer, who requires a thousand bushels of wheat, is correspondingly subject to the risk that before he buys the market will go up, and the wheat will cost him more than he would now have to pay. When the two agree upon a contract for the sale of the wheat at a price of one dollar per bushel, these risks are exchanged. It is now the seller who assumes the risk that the market will rise, and that he will have lost a profit; the buyer who assumes the risk that the market will go down, and the bargain prove to be a bad one. If the contract is for future delivery, the situation is the same, except that the seller doubtless feels more acutely the hardship of delivering wheat at one dollar, when its value has risen to one dollar and fifty cents, or the buyer regrets more

rights under § 2–507 against bona fide purchaser; such rights limited as between seller and buyer and do not extend to bona fide purchaser or buyer).

17. §§ 2–507(2); 2–511(2), (3). In re Mort Co., 208 F.Supp. 309, 1 UCC 166 (E.D.Pa.1962); Lawrence v. Graham, 29 Md.App. 422, 349 A.2d 271, 18 UCC 657 (1975) (seller allowed to maintain trover action against third party where buyer's check dishonored); Farmers & Merchants Bank v. Davis, 151 Ill.App.3d 929, 104 Ill.Dec. 850, 503 N.E.2d 565, 4 UCC2d 72 (1987) (with insurance contracts, when express or implied intent of the parties is that acceptance of a check is absolute, payment may not be defeated by dishonor of a check).

18. In re Helms Veneer Corp., 287 F.Supp. 840, 5 UCC 977 (W.D.Va.1968); Sorrels v. Texas Bank & Trust Co., 597 F.2d 997, 26 UCC 896 (5th Cir.1979) (assuming without deciding that Texas courts would interpret UCC to provide

reclamation rights to cash sellers, it appears that 2–507 incorporates by reference the strict 10–day limits of 2–702) See also, § 2–507, Comment 3.

19. Burk v. Emmick, 637 F.2d 1172, 29 UCC 1489 (8th Cir.1980) ("We determine that as between the seller and the buyer, where a cash seller reclaims goods sold to a breaching buyer, the only limitation imposed upon the seller's right is a reasonableness requirement", court rejects the 10–day limitation); Citizens Bank v. Taggart, 143 Cal.App.3d 318, 191 Cal.Rptr. 729, 36 UCC 529 (1983) (court rejects *Szabo* line of cases and adopts Burk v. Emmick "reasonable" limitation to seller's right of reclamation).

20. Compare § 2–702 with § 2–507. See also, In re Kirk Kabinets, Inc., 393 F.Supp. 798 (M.D.Ga.1975). Note that sellers' rights of reclamation may be subordinate to the rights of lien creditors and to perfected security interests.

poignantly his bad judgment if the market has fallen to fifty cents.[1]

Sometimes parties omit the price term or leave it to be set by formula or other procedure. Parties may do this because they recognize their inability to set an agreeable and fair price in a long term contract. Some may even hope to have their cake and eat it too; these may hope to negotiate a better price later than they can negotiate initially. And there are parties too hurried to tie up the details; in the glow of "agreement in principle" these assume that completing the price negotiation will be no problem.

Section 2–305 of the Code recognizes these economic facts of life. It reads:

(1) The parties if they so intend can conclude a contract for sale even though the price is not settled. In such a case the price is a reasonable price at the time for delivery if

(a) nothing is said as to price; or

(b) the price is left to be agreed by the parties and they fail to agree; or

(c) the price is to be fixed in terms of some agreed market or other standard as set or recorded by a third person or agency and it is not so set or recorded.

(2) A price to be fixed by the seller or by the buyer means a price to be fixed in good faith.

(3) When a price left to be fixed otherwise than by agreement of the parties fails to be fixed through fault of one party the other may at his option treat the contract as cancelled or himself fix a reasonable price.

(4) Where, however, the parties intend not to be bound unless the price be fixed or agreed and it is not fixed or agreed there is no contract. In such a case the buyer must return any goods already received or if unable so to do must pay their reasonable value at the time of delivery and the seller must return any portion of the price paid on account.

Section 2–305 has both a contract formation aspect[2] and a gap filling aspect (and it is to be noted that a good faith price may not

---

§ 4-8

1. Prosser, Open Price in Contracts for Sale of Goods, 16 Minn.L.Rev. 733, 733 (1932). See also Howard, Open Terms as to Price in Contracts for the Sale of Goods, 48 Aust.L.J. 419 (1974). Cf. 1 N.Y.State Law Revision Comm'n. 1955 Report 662–67 (1955).

2. O'Brien v. Chandler, 107 N.M. 797, 765 P.2d 1165, 7 UCC2d 1450 (1988) (buyer and seller created binding sales contract despite lack of agreement on price); Wagner Excello Foods, Inc. v. Fearn Int'l, Inc., 235 Ill.App.3d 224, 176 Ill.Dec. 258, 601 N.E.2d 956, 20 UCC2d 1221 (1992) (contractual procedure for

be the same as a reasonable price). Our focus will be on the latter, but their close relationship dictates discussion of both aspects. Whether a court is to fill a gap under 2–305 cannot even arise unless the court decides that the parties "intended" a contract under the first sentence of that section.[3] Consider the litigation between Bethlehem Steel Corporation and Litton Industries. After extensive negotiations, Litton agreed to construct a newly designed ore vessel for Bethlehem at a fixed price. Thereafter, the parties agreed in writing that Bethlehem should have an option to require Litton to construct up to five additional ore vessels for the same design at a stated base price of $20.4 million. If Bethlehem exercised an option, the base price was subject to escalation on terms to be agreed by the parties. Despite Litton's requests, Bethlehem refused to exercise the option or to negotiate the option price. After Litton closed its shipyard, Bethlehem sought to exercise the option for three additional vessels. Both parties negotiated over the escalated price but, despite apparent good faith efforts, were unable to agree. Bethlehem then sued Litton for $95,000,000 in damages, claiming that despite the failure to agree on price, the parties intended to contract for the three vessels and that the court should supply a reasonable, escalated price.

The trial court treated the intention issue as a question of fact. Given the importance of the escalation clause to the contract, the complexity of the determinations involved, and the rapid inflation underway, the court concluded that the parties did not intend to contract unless an agreement could be reached on price. On appeal, a three judge trial reversed. Bethlehem Steel Corp. v. Litton Industries, Inc.[4] On rehearing, a panel of seven judges reversed the decision of the three judge panel and reinstated the decision of the trial court to the effect that there was no contract.[5] The "panel of seven's" decision was affirmed by an equally divided Pennsylvania Supreme Court.[6] The Supreme Court justices voting to affirm the decision of the trial court stressed that (1) the writings of the parties were ambiguous and many terms were left open; (2) there was competent evidence to support the conclusion that the conduct of the parties was inconsistent with an intent to be bound; (3) there was no reasonably certain basis for giving an appropriate remedy; and (4) the "option" was not supported by consideration.

---

negotiating price sufficient to establish valid contract).

3. See, e.g., D.R. Curtis, Co. v. Mathews, 103 Idaho 776, 653 P.2d 1188, 35 UCC 1425 (App.1982) (court determines parties intended to enter into a contract before considering reasonableness of price); In re BTS, Inc., 104 B.R. 1009, 11 UCC2d 444 (Bankr.W.D.Mo.1989) (lower court misplaced reliance on § 2–305 to allow contract where there was no intent without a price agreement).

4. 1982 WL 171058, 35 UCC 1091 (Pa.Super.1982).

5. 321 Pa.Super. 357, 468 A.2d 748, 37 UCC 1059 (1983).

6. 507 Pa. 88, 488 A.2d 581, 40 UCC 1639 (1985).

Justice Zappala, on the other hand, argued that Litton's negotiation over the escalation provision was in bad faith. Despite Bethlehem's willingness to consider a number of price indices, Litton, according to Justice Zappala, "did not intend to develop any language regarding a proposed ship construction contract" and "prevented execution of a ship construction contract by failing to bargain in good faith on the open terms."[7] On his view, this was a breach for which Bethlehem was entitled to damages. The case nicely demonstrates the rotten job that awaits a court that has to interpret 2–305 in the face of bitter and well counseled litigants. In Shell Oil Co. v. HRN[8], the Supreme Court of Texas held that a price fixed by an oil refiner under an open-price-term with its dealers was in good faith under UCC 2–305. The court rejected the dealer's view that good faith incorporates a subjective test "honesty in fact" as well as an objective test "observance of reasonable commercial standards of fair dealing." Only the latter is required, said the court, citing White and Summers. The case in effect reverses Mathis v. Exxon Corp.[9]

A court's willingness to find intent to contract may turn partly upon the nature of the gap to be filled. A court cannot hold that the parties made a contract unless there is a "reasonably certain basis for giving an appropriate remedy" for breach.[10] If no price can be set, there will be no way to compute damages based either on contract-market differentials, on the difference between the contract price and the cost of cover (in the case of an aggrieved buyer), or on the difference between the contract price and a resale price (in the case of an aggrieved seller).

Price gaps may be complete or partial. A "partial" gap arises when the parties have specified how the price is to be determined but the method fails. Section 2–305(1)(a) governs complete gaps. Sections 2–305(1)(b) and (c) and 2–305(2) and (3) govern partial gaps.[11]

Whether a gap exists may itself be the subject of dispute. The case of Associated Hardware Supply Co. v. Big Wheel Distributing

---

7. *Id.* at 600. See HRN, Inc. v. Shell Oil Co., 102 S.W.3d 205, 49 UCC2d 1108 (Tex. App. 2003). See also Allapattah Services, Inc. v. Exxon Corp., 333 F.3d 1248, 50 UCC2d 1047 (11th Cir. 2003).

8. 144 S.W.3d 429, 54 UCC2d 725 (Tex. 2004).

9. 302 F.3d 448, 59 Fed. R. Evid. Serv. 1178, 48 UCC2d 1 (5th Cir. 2002), reh'g and reh'g en banc denied, 48 Fed. Appx. 919 (5th Cir. 2002) (applying Texas law).

10. § 2–204(3). Alamo Clay Products, Inc. v. Gunn Tile Co., 597 S.W.2d 388, 29 UCC 31 (Tex.Civ.App.1980) (binding contract found where parties did not mention price but evidence showed they entered into a contract on August 31, 1973 on the basis of prices prevailing on that date).

11. H.C. Schmieding Produce Co., Inc. v. Cagle, 529 So.2d 243, 7 UCC2d 676 (Ala.1988) (gap did not exist when price was "market price").

Co.[12] involved such a dispute. There the buyer proposed a price of cost plus ten percent. The seller billed the buyer for goods delivered at "dealer catalogue prices less 11%," which the seller allegedly told the buyer was equivalent to cost plus ten percent. In fact the two were not equivalent. The seller's representation was either fraudulent or mistaken. If fraudulent, the buyer would be entitled to retain the goods and pay only their reasonable value, as the court recognized.[13] But if a mistake, then although the parties failed to agree on a price, the court thought the buyer's acceptance of the goods constituted acquiescence in the seller's price proposal. Here the court seems to have erred, for on the facts alleged, the buyer only acquiesced in a method of billing, not a price, and the court could have turned to 2–305.[14]

When there is a gap, 2–305 directs the court to determine "a reasonable price," provided the parties intended to contract. Note that the section says "a reasonable price" and not "fair market value of the goods." These two would not be identical. For example, evidence of a prior course of dealing between the parties might show a price below or above what is claimed to be the proper market.[15] Without more, a court could justifiably hold in these circumstances that the course of dealing price is the "reasonable price."[16]

In the "complete" gap cases, the courts use various forms of evidence. If there is sufficient evidence of price based on course of dealing, course of performance, or usage of trade, this will determine "reasonable price." Indeed, with such evidence it may even be said that there is no "gap" at all in the agreement of the parties.

12. 355 F.2d 114, 3 UCC 1 (3d Cir. 1965). See also Propane Indus., Inc. v. General Motors Corp., 429 F.Supp. 214, 22 UCC 321 (W.D.Mo.1977) (whether there was a gap depended on the validity of a prior requirements contract).

13. 355 F.2d at 120, 3 UCC at 8–9.

14. Compare Hollywood Wholesale Elec. Co. v. Jack Baskin, Inc., 146 Cal. App.2d 399, 303 P.2d 1049 (1956) (buyer's acceptance of goods at invoiced price without objection held to bind buyer to that price), with Lamberta v. Smiling Jim Potato Co., 1966 WL 8981, 25 Agri. Dec. 1181, 3 UCC 981 (1966) (use of the reasonable price did not bind buyer to invoice price).

15. Koenen v. Royal Buick Co., 162 Ariz. 376, 783 P.2d 822, 11 UCC2d 1096 (App.1989) (course of dealing showed that price of car was to be sticker price).

16. Cf. Columbus Milk Producers' Co–op. v. Department of Agriculture, 48 Wis.2d 451, 180 N.W.2d 617, 8 UCC 481 (1970) (course of dealing held basis for price at the general going rate); TCP Indus., Inc. v. Uniroyal, Inc., 661 F.2d 542, 32 UCC 369 (6th Cir.1981) (court adds that reasonable price could be set other than pursuant to "reasonable commercial standards of fair dealing."); See Offices Togolais Des Phosphates v. Mulberry Phosphates, Inc., 62 F.Supp.2d 1316, 41 UCC2d 85 (M.D. Fla. 1999), aff'd, 228 F.3d 414 (11th Cir. 2000). To show noncompliance with 2–305, evidence must indicate whether price was set in bad faith or not commercially reasonable. See Schwartz v. Sun Co., Inc., 276 F.3d 900, 46 UCC2d 615 (6th Cir. 2002).

But in many, perhaps most, cases the court's duty is to find and choose the fair market price at the time and place of delivery.[17]

A "partial gap" occurs when a price setting method fails. It is important to distinguish complete gap from partial gap cases, for what is a reasonable price in the two cases is not necessarily the same. In complete gap cases a court is on its own, and properly so. But in some partial gap cases, a reasonable price should be influenced to some extent by the price it thinks would have been set had the parties been successful with the method to which they agreed.

Parties' price formulae are highly varied. First, parties may simply agree to agree on a price at a later date. Some courts invalidate these agreements as too indefinite.[18] But the Code validates these—provided the parties intend to contract and there is a reasonably certain basis for granting an appropriate remedy.[19] In these cases courts are to fill the gap with a reasonable price.[20] Sometimes the parties will agree that one of them is to fix the price. Here the agreed method may fail for either of two quite different reasons. The appointed party may fail to set any price, or may set a price in bad faith.[21] If the failure was owing to its own fault, 2–305 provides that the other party may "fix a reasonable price."[22] But if the failure to fix a price was not the fault of either party, the Code empowers the court to fix a reasonable price. If the party who is to fix the price fixes it in bad faith, the court can substitute a

17. See Havird Oil Co., Inc. v. Marathon Oil Co., Inc., 149 F.3d 283, 36 UCC2d 63 (4th Cir. 1998) (commercial reasonableness of price buyer/retailer was to charged by wholesale seller was determined by relevant market prices even though, due to an exceptional occurrence, wholesale prices were actually higher than retail prices).

18. See, e.g., Sun Printing & Publishing Ass'n v. Remington Paper & Power Co., 235 N.Y. 338, 139 N.E. 470 (1923).

19. §§ 2–204(3); 2–305.

20. See, e.g., Schmieder v. Standard Oil Co., 69 Wis.2d 419, 230 N.W.2d 732, 17 UCC 360 (1975) (court set price where parties could not agree on depreciation); Bethlehem Steel Corp. v. Litton Industries, Inc., 1982 WL 171058, 35 UCC 1091 (Pa.Super.1982) (majority found parties intended to enter into binding contract leaving price to be agreed later, filled gap by applying reasonable price to be calculated by escalating the agreed base by "reasonable" index; dissent felt parties did not intend to be bound until parties agreed on price— and other terms).

21. Marquette Co. v. Norcem, Inc., 114 A.D.2d 738, 494 N.Y.S.2d 511, 42 UCC 79 (1985) (seller's refusal to consider anything but maximum price in open price contract to be negotiated later, was bad faith). Bad faith requires more than proof that price is higher than the market price. TCP Indus., Inc. v. Uniroyal, Inc., 661 F.2d 542, 32 UCC 369 (6th Cir.1981) (jury could find price of long term contract reasonable and set in good faith although it was set in accord with total market prices including spot market prices as well as long term contract prices); Au Rustproofing Center, Inc. v. Gulf Oil Corp., 755 F.2d 1231, 40 UCC 802 (6th Cir.1985) (seller did not set reasonable price in bad faith simply by setting higher price than competitors).

22. But see, Weisberg v. Handy & Harman, 747 F.2d 416, 39 UCC 1617 (7th Cir.1984) (court applies reasonable price determined by course of dealing where defendant at fault; § 2–305(3) applies only when some action is required by the parties to enable a third party or external agency to set the price in accordance with the agreement).

reasonable price; 2–305(2) provides that a "price to be fixed by the seller or by the buyer means a price to be fixed in good faith."[23]

The parties may also agree to set a price by reference to costs of one of the parties.[24] For example, a seller may be empowered to charge the buyer "cost plus ten percent." When this method of pricing fails, a court under 2–305(1) may supply a reasonable price.

The parties may agree to set the price by methods that do not require either party to act further. Thus they may agree that the price will be the prevailing market price at a given time and place or that the price will be equivalent to prices charged by a competitor or group of competitors. Columbus Milk Producers' Co–op. v. Department of Agriculture,[25] was a case in which the parties had not expressly agreed that farmers would be paid the "going rate" for milk, yet their course of dealing, course of performance, and usage of trade did show such an agreement. Thus all the court had to do was grant damages accordingly, for the buyer had not paid the going rate.

Sometimes the parties agree that the contract price will be based on quotations in a trade journal or similar index[26] and the journal ceases publication or ceases publishing the needed quotation.[27] In North Central Airlines, Inc. v. Continental Oil Co.,[28] parties to a long term contract agreed that the price of aviation fuel would be determined with reference to posted crude oil prices. This formula became unworkable when the government introduced a two-tier pricing system for crude oil in 1973. The court resorted to the reasonableness standard of 2–305 to fill the gap. The parties may also agree that the price is to be set according to prevailing industry standards,[29] or according to a manufacturer's suggested retail price.[30] Contracts may also provide for arbitration of the

---

23. Allapattah Services, Inc. v. Exxon Corp., 333 F.3d 1248, 50 UCC2d 1047 (11th Cir. 2003) (in normal case, posted price or price in effect applies; what is "normal" is question of fact). Compare Shell Oil Co. v. HRN, Inc., 144 S.W.3d 429, 54 UCC2d 725 (Tex. 2004) (price set in good faith).

24. Bernina Distrib., Inc. v. Bernina Sewing Machine Co., 646 F.2d 434, 31 UCC 462 (10th Cir.1981) (importer established complex price provisions with base prices and modifications based on cost increases in invoice, duty, shipping, etc.).

25. 48 Wis.2d 451, 180 N.W.2d 617, 8 UCC 481 (1970).

26. Board of Commissioners v. Annadale Scrap Co., 14 O.O.3d 430, 60 Ohio App.2d 415, 398 N.E.2d 810, 28 UCC 52 (1978) (price for scrap metal "calculated by market formula of 57% of the highest price per ton paid for No. 1 heavy melting steel on Cleveland Market, as quoted in Iron Age magazine for week").

27. See, e.g., American Car & Foundry Co. v. East Jordan Furnace Co., 275 Fed. 786 (7th Cir.1921).

28. 574 F.2d 582, 23 UCC 581 (D.C.Cir.1978).

29. Bornstein v. Somerson, 341 So.2d 1043, 21 UCC 36 (Fla.App.1977), cert. denied, 348 So.2d 944 (Fla.1977).

30. Sedmak v. Charlie's Chevrolet, Inc., 622 S.W.2d 694, 31 UCC 851 (Mo. App.1981) (manufacturer's suggested retail price sufficient to meet price requirements of an enforceable contract);

price. Whenever the arbitration process fails to get underway or breaks down, the court may be faced with a 2–305 issue, or it may be asked only to direct that arbitration proceed.

If the court is to fill a price gap with a reasonable price consisting of a market price, when and where is this price to be ascertained? Under 2–305, this price is to be determined "at the time for delivery."[31] The defendant will want to make sure that it does not overcompensate the plaintiff. For example, if the contract calls for a buyer to pay freight costs, assume the risk of loss and so receive tender at the shipping point, seller should not be permitted to show a 2–305 price equivalent to market price at its buyer's city; that price would reflect the cost of transporting goods to that city.

The foregoing discussion presupposes that the parties intended to contract and that the facts afford a reasonably certain basis for granting an appropriate remedy.[32] But what is a "reasonably certain basis"? Comment 4 to 2–305 states:

> The section recognizes that there may be cases in which a particular person's judgment is not chosen merely as a barometer or index of a fair price but is an essential condition to the parties' intent to make any contract at all. For example, the case where a known and trusted expert is to "value" a particular painting for which there is no market standard differs sharply from the situation where a named expert is to determine the grade of cotton, and the difference would support a finding that in the one the parties did not intend to make a binding agreement if that expert were unavailable whereas in the other they did so intend. Other circumstances would of course affect the validity of such a finding.

Consider the case of Interstate Plywood Sales Co. v. Interstate Container Corp.[33] in light of the above comment. The defendant agreed to sell plywood to the plaintiff over a period of time at a contract price equivalent to market price based on prices published by five other plywood mills. Thereafter some of the mills went out

Roy Buckner Chevrolet, Inc. v. Cagle, 418 So.2d 878, 34 UCC 413 (Ala.1982) (list price sufficiently definite to create binding contract); Morris v. Perkins Chevrolet, Inc., 663 S.W.2d 785, 38 UCC 20 (Mo.App.1984) (agreed price of $250 over manufacturer's suggested retail price not so indefinite as to prevent contract from coming into existence).

31. See, e.g., Osguthorpe v. Anschutz Land & Livestock Co., 456 F.2d 996, 10 UCC 620 (10th Cir.1972) (reasonable price to be determined at time of delivery, not by what the buyer received for the goods one year later); Robinson v. Stevens Indus., Inc., 162 Ga.App. 132, 290 S.E.2d 336, 33 UCC 1251 (1982) (price determined at time of delivery and equal to federal support prices rather than substantially higher market price at time seller collected payment). But see, D.R. Curtis, Co. v. Mathews, 103 Idaho 776, 653 P.2d 1188, 35 UCC 1425 (App.1982) (reasonable price determined when buyer learned of seller's breach, absent definite delivery date).

32. See generally Note, UCC § 2–305(1)(c): Open Price Terms and the Intention of the Parties in Sales Contracts, 1 Val.U.L.Rev. 381 (1967).

33. 331 F.2d 449 (9th Cir.1964).

of business or failed to publish any relevant prices. The court defined the issue in these terms: "Whether the five-mill pricing formula was designed to be the only binding means of setting price, or whether the contract called for sales of plywood at the general market price, with the five-mill formula being merely a guide thereto?"[34] In other words, was the case more like the sale of a painting with the price to be set by an expert appraiser, than like a sale of cotton priced according to grade but with an expert to determine grade?[35] The plywood case arose prior to the effective date of the Code in California, and the court decided that the parties' intent to be bound was conditioned on the availability of a price based on the five-mill formula; since this price could not be determined, the deal could not be enforced. Consequently the seller was free to sell its plywood elsewhere.[36] In our view, the parties chose a specific means of determining price merely as a "barometer or index of a fair price" rather than as "an essential condition to the parties' intent to make any contract at all."[37] There were numerous other comparable mill prices that could have been used as an index of a fair price. We believe that under 2–305, the court should not have let the seller out. Virtually all relevant factors indicated that the parties intended an ongoing contractual relationship. Moreover, there was a reasonably certain basis for granting an appropriate remedy.

§ 4–9 Article 2 Gap Fillers on Quantity (Especially in Requirements Contracts)

Parties may create contractual obligations for the sale of goods without committing to purchase a specific quantity. This often occurs in the form of a "requirements contract," a type of agreement described by Professor Farnsworth:

> A requirements contract is one under which the seller agrees to sell and the buyer to buy all of the goods of a particular kind that the *buyer* may *require* in its business.[1]

34. *Id.* at 452.

35. § 2–305, Comment 4.

36. Interstate Plywood Sales Co. v. Interstate Container Corp., 331 F.2d 449, 452 (9th Cir.1964).

37. § 2–305, Comment 4.

§ 4–9

1. Farnsworth, Contracts 2nd 79 (1990). For earlier discussions, see Havighurst & Bearman, Requirement and Output Contracts, 27 Ill.L.Rev. 1 (1932); Note, Requirements Contracts: Problems of Drafting and Construction, 78 Harv.L.Rev. 1212 (1965); Note Requirements Contracts under the Uniform Commercial Code, 102 U.Pa.L.Rev. 654 (1954); Annot., 26 A.L.R.2d 1099 (1952). See also Wiestart, Requirements and Output Contracts: Quantity Variations Under the UCC, 1973 Duke L.J. 599; Note, Requirements Contracts, "More or Less" under the U.C.C., 33 Rutgers L.Rev. 105 (1980); Axelrod, Requirements Contract–What is Required?, 31 Drake L.Rev. 83 (1981–82).

At one end of the spectrum an open or indefinite quantity term may be completely indefinite. Thus, two parties unknown to each other may each enter a wholly new business in a wholly new trade. Here no one may be able to forecast requirements. At the other end of the spectrum, the parties may own established businesses and state maxima and minima in their agreement on the basis of past experience. Most requirements contracts fall somewhere between these extremes.[2] In one type, the seller at a specified price, agrees to supply all of the buyer's "needs" for sand and gravel, or for potatoes, or for eggs, and so on, over a given period. If the buyer's business is an established one, if the needs of that business fluctuate little, and if the seller has been dealing with the buyer over time, a court can judge after breach or repudiation what the buyer might have ordered during the remaining life of the contract, multiply this quantity by the contract price, and arrive at a total contract price to be used for computing damages. But some cases fall at that end of the spectrum where there is little basis on which to compute quantity. Yet even quite indefinite requirements contracts may be attractive to a buyer insofar as they assure it of a source of supply, allow it to meet the fluctuating needs of its business, and offer the economies and conveniences of dealing with only one supplier. To the seller, the contract may offer assurance of a market outlet, facilitate efficient scheduling of business activity, and save storage and marketing costs. The intrinsic indefiniteness of the agreement causes trouble only when a dispute arises.

As Professor Farnsworth's definition indicates, a requirements contract, in order to be valid, must (1) obligate the buyer to buy goods, (2) obligate the buyer to buy the goods exclusively from the seller, and (3) obligate the buyer to buy all goods of a particular kind from the seller.

The recognition of the validity of these agreements, and of their necessary elements, predates the UCC. In particular, the obligation of the buyer to buy, and to do so exclusively from the seller, has long been recognized as creating the mutuality necessary for a valid contract, even when the buyer may supply some of its own requirements.[3] The Code, too, validates requirements con-

---

2. See, e.g., Meuse–Rhine–Ijssel Cattle Breeders of Canada Ltd. v. Y–Tex Corp., 590 P.2d 1306, 26 UCC 292 (Wyo. 1979) (ambiguity whether contract was for given number of units, or requirements contract was material fact issue and summary judgment was inappropriate).

3. In re United Cigar Stores Co., 8 F.Supp. 243 (S.D.N.Y.1934); aff'd, 72 F.2d 673 (2d Cir.1934), Harvey v. Fear-

less Farris Wholesale, Inc., 589 F.2d 451, 25 UCC 993 (9th Cir.1979).

Many potential requirements contracts fail because the buyer does not promise to purchase *exclusively* from the seller. See, e.g., Rangen, Inc. v. Valley Trout Farms, Inc., 104 Idaho 284, 658 P.2d 955, 35 UCC 1129 (1983) (separate contracts were not requirements contracts because while seller was buyer's primary supplier, it was not exclusive supplier); Brooklyn Bagel Boys, Inc. v.

tracts. Section 2–204(3) provides that "even though one or more terms are left open a contract for sale does not fail for indefiniteness if the parties have intended to make a contract and there is a reasonably certain basis for giving an appropriate remedy." These statutory conditions are satisfied in almost all requirements contracts that contain the elements included in Professor Farnsworth's definition. Comment 2 to 2–306(1) explicitly rejects the notion that requirements contracts are too indefinite; they are "held to mean the actual good faith * * * requirements" of the particular party.[4] Certainly, the mere existence of an open quantity term does not support invalidation, since indefiniteness is inherent in requirements contracts.[5] In addition, the Code's recognition of the validity of these contracts is consistent with the existing case law.[6]

While 2–306 implies that requirements contracts are not lacking in mutuality by virtue of the absence of a specific quantity, quantity is the only gap it serves to fill. Therefore, while the Code provides that the "good faith" requirements of the buyer will serve as the contract quantity, it does not provide the required element of exclusivity.[7] Because section 2–306 depends on exclusivity to determine the quantity, there can be no valid requirements contract without it. As such, where a retailer of gasoline had an agreement to purchase its supply from a wholesaler, but was free to purchase from other suppliers, the absence of exclusivity could not be cured by 2–306, and the agreement was found unenforceable for lack of mutuality.[8]

Despite the presence of another supplier, the contract may be sufficiently "exclusive." This may occur where a purchaser agrees to purchase exclusively from a seller up to a certain quantity. Thus, where a municipality agreed to purchase its parking meter requirements from a manufacturer, the agreement was held to be a valid requirements contract even though the buyer would be free to purchase elsewhere after it had purchased an initial quantity from the manufacturer.[9]

Earthgrains Refrigerated Dough Prods., 212 F.3d 373, 41 UCC2d 445 (7th Cir. 2000).

4. Moreover, § 2–306, Comment 1, implies that contracts to supply the requirements of "dealers or distributors" are generally valid although many such buyers are just entering business or are ones whose business needs fluctuate markedly. The seller assumes the risk of all good faith variations in buyer's requirements. See, e.g., Indiana–American Water Co., Inc. v. Town of Seelyville, 698 N.E.2d 1255, 38 UCC2d 1133 (Ind. App. 1998).

5. Stacks v. F & S Petroleum Co., 6 Ark.App. 327, 641 S.W.2d 726, 35 UCC 376 (1982) (indefinite number of gasoline gallons to be purchased did not support invalidation).

6. Harvey v. Fearless Farris Wholesale, Inc., 589 F.2d 451, 25 UCC 993 (9th Cir.1979).

7. Ibid.

8. *Id.* at 461, 25 UCC at 1001.

9. City of Louisville v. Rockwell Mfg. Co., 482 F.2d 159, 12 UCC 840 (6th Cir.1973).

Although the Code will not supply the exclusivity required to validate a requirements contract, express contract provisions are not the only source of exclusivity. Exclusivity can also be established through implication, course of dealing, or extrinsic evidence. In Cyril Bath Co. v. Winters Industries,[10] the supplier was aware that the buyer was purchasing component parts to fill a particular order from General Motors, and that the buyer's estimated requirements approximated the entire amount the buyer would need. The Sixth Circuit found the agreement to be exclusive by implication.[11]

Additionally, where a manufacturer of kitchen equipment had exclusively supplied a restaurant chain with all of its pizza pans for over three years, a contract to supply a new style of pan, although apparently ambiguous, was found to be exclusive by virtue of the course of dealing.[12] Of course, course of dealing can also defeat an assertion of exclusivity. Where a purchaser of propane alleged a requirements contract and the language of the agreement was inconclusive, the court looked to the purchaser's actions under an earlier, identical agreement, and found that the purchaser had used other sources to fulfill some of its requirements. The inescapable conclusion was an absence of exclusivity.[13]

While the exclusivity promise can be supplied implicitly, the mere use of the word "requirements" in a contract is not enough to do so. As one court pointed out, "requirements" is not a term of art, and it can mean either "all needed, or, all desired from the seller."[14] In that case, the contract was held unenforceable for lack of mutuality although it called for "a possible requirement" on an "as required basis."[15]

Further, the omission of exclusivity in the agreement cannot be cured by subsequent "bootstrapping" purchases solely from the seller. Where an agreement does not establish exclusivity and is otherwise silent as to quantity, the agreement is treated as an open offer to sell.[16] While partial performance can establish mutuality when the agreement is to purchase a specific quantity, it cannot

10. 892 F.2d 465, 10 UCC2d 725 (6th Cir.1989).

11. See also, Gestetner Corp. v. Case Equip. Co., 815 F.2d 806, 3 UCC2d 1328 (1st Cir.1987) (lower court correct in allowing jury to find implied exclusivity). See Essco Geometric v. Harvard Industries, 46 F.3d 718, 25 UCC2d 661 (8th Cir. 1995) (no particular words are required to establish a requirements contract; language suggesting exclusivity, along with extrinsic evidence which supports exclusivity, establishes a requirements contract).

12. Universal Power Sys., Inc. v. Godfather's Pizza, Inc., 818 F.2d 667, 3

UCC2d 1748 (8th Cir.1987). See also Century Ready–Mix Co. v. Lower & Co., 770 P.2d 692, 10 UCC2d 705 (Wyo.1989) (summary judgment invalidating contract inappropriate as usage of trade could establish requirements contract).

13. Propane Indus., Inc. v. General Motors Corp., 429 F.Supp. 214, 22 UCC 321 (W.D.Mo.1977).

14. Id. at 329.

15. Id. at 221, 22 UCC 321, 329.

16. Billings Cottonseed, Inc. v. Albany Oil Mill, Inc., 173 Ga.App. 825, 328 S.E.2d 426, 41 UCC 398 (1985).

establish exclusivity, and therefore cannot provide the mutuality necessary in a requirements contract. As such, in an agreement where the seller promised to provide all of the buyer's cottonseed requirements, but the buyer did not agree to take all of its requirements from the seller, there was no mutuality. The court held that the buyer's performance, consisting of exclusive purchases from the seller, did not establish the absent mutuality as the buyer was not bound to continue to purchase solely from the seller.[17]

The law on requirements contracts is almost entirely judge-made. A requirements contract may simply be too indefinite to afford a basis for any remedy. But some courts have invalidated agreements that were in fact definite enough to afford a basis for computing damages.[18] In some of these cases one party had taken unfair advantage of the other, for instance, by ordering a vastly increased amount during a sharp price rise. But invalidation is a clumsy tool for policing purposes. And despite the inherent indefiniteness of requirements contracts, most courts have validated them. By the late 1950's when the Code was widely proposed for adoption, some courts had also devised policing doctrines that enabled them to curb abuses under requirements contracts without resorting to the blunderbuss of invalidation.[19] The Code leaves this case law on policing intact.[20]

Some courts have held against parties who invoked the lack of a quantity term to show noncompliance with the statute of frauds. For example, in R.L. Kimsey Cotton Co. v. Ferguson,[21] farmers who agreed to sell all the cotton from 230 acres of their land contended that the deal lacked a quantity term and was therefore not enforce-

17. *Id.* at 430, 41 UCC at 401.

18. E.g., Interstate Plywood Sales Co. v. Interstate Container Corp., 331 F.2d 449 (9th Cir.1964). But the contract must not be so indefinite that it cannot be discerned to be a requirements contract. See, e.g., W.H. Barber Co. v. McNamara–Vivant Contracting Co., 293 N.W.2d 351, 27 UCC 899 (Minn.1979) (language in letter "We * * * are looking forward to supplying your requirements for the coming season" did not indicate requirements contract because of its precatory nature); Lowenstern v. Stop & Shop Cos., Inc., 1981 WL 137972, 32 UCC 414 (Mass.Super.1981) (rain checks for records were not requirements contract when there was not an honest purpose and no mutual promise between parties to deal exclusively with each other).

19. E.g., Sylvan Crest Sand & Gravel Co. v. United States, 150 F.2d 642 (2d Cir.1945). Cf. Simons v. American Dry Ginger Ale Co., 335 Mass. 521, 140 N.E.2d 649 (1957).

20. The case law on damages provides illuminating examples. See e.g., B.B. Walker Co. v. Ashland Chem. Co., 474 F.Supp. 651, 34 UCC 561 (M.D.N.C. 1979) (buyer could not recover damages for breach of requirements contract, since all its requirements had been met by cover); Pulprint, Inc. v. Louisiana–Pacific Corp., 124 Misc.2d 728, 477 N.Y.S.2d 540, 39 UCC 426 (1984) (where requirements contract called for 3,000 tons of rayon to be shipped to buyer before any others, and seller shipped buyer 120 tons and 1730 tons to others, buyer's damages were lost profits on 1730 tons, not 2880 (3000 120 tons)).

21. 233 Ga. 962, 214 S.E.2d 360, 16 UCC 1223 (1975).

able. The Court wisely rejected this argument.[22] The parties should be certain that if they do leave a quantity term out, the contract can be positively identified as a requirements contract. In Cox Caulking & Insulating Co. v. Brockett Distributing Co.,[23] the parties were not careful enough; the court held that a contract for bags of insulating materials "for the above project." merely designated the project that was the subject of a letter.

A second class of cases also governed by 2–306(2) consists of "best efforts" contracts. In these one party promises to use its best efforts to promote the sales of the other's goods.[24] This class includes "exclusive dealing" contracts where the Code imposes a "best efforts" obligation.[25]

Validity aside, courts must still police against abuses. Abuses commonly take one of three forms: (1) unjustified increases in requirements, (2) unjustified decreases, and (3) unjustified withdrawal of either the buyer or the seller. In policing against abuses, a court will set quantities and thus fill "gaps" in the contract. In addition to the policing tools available in the case law (to which we return below), courts may invoke 2–306(1):

> A term which measures the quantity by the output of the seller or the requirements of the buyer means such actual output or requirements as may occur in good faith, except that no quantity unreasonably disproportionate to any stated estimate or in the absence of a stated estimate to any normal or otherwise comparable prior output or requirements may be tendered or demanded.

Under this section, claimed requirements may constitute an abuse if they (1) are not actual, (2) are not in good faith, or (3) are unreasonably disproportionate to any stated estimate or to any normal or otherwise comparable prior requirements. Many courts have construed 2–306(1). Some have applied it to broadly worded contracts (all the buyer's requirements for x years);[26] others have

---

22. See also, Harris v. Hine, 232 Ga. 183, 205 S.E.2d 847, 14 UCC 1101 (1974) (output contract for cotton upheld); Orchard Group, Inc. v. Konica Medical Corp., 135 F.3d 421, 35 UCC2d 454 (6th Cir. 1998).

23. 150 Ga.App. 424, 258 S.E.2d 51, 27 UCC 355 (1979).

24. See, e.g., Bloor v. Falstaff Brewing Corp., 601 F.2d 609, 26 UCC 281 (2d Cir.1979); Rocka v. Gipson, 3 Ark.App. 293, 625 S.W.2d 558, 33 UCC 1643 (1981); Tigg Corp. v. Dow Corning Corp., 962 F.2d 1119, 17 UCC2d 730 (3d Cir.1992) (best efforts includes good faith, but good faith does not require best efforts absent exclusivity).

25. Thermal Systems of Alabama, Inc. v. Sigafoose, 533 So.2d 567, 7 UCC2d 698 (Ala.1988) (agreement to distribute heat exchanger valid, mutuality provided by obligation to use "best efforts"); Jo–Ann, Inc. v. Alfin Fragrances, Inc., 731 F.Supp. 149, 11 UCC2d 782 (D.N.J.1989).

26. See, e.g., Feld v. Henry S. Levy & Sons, Inc., 37 N.Y.2d 466, 373 N.Y.S.2d 102, 335 N.E.2d 320, 17 UCC 365 (1975) (output contract); Eastern Air Lines, Inc. v. Gulf Oil Corp., 415 F.Supp. 429, 19 UCC 721 (S.D.Fla.1975); Orange & Rockland Utilities, Inc. v. Amerada Hess Corp., 59 A.D.2d 110, 397 N.Y.S.2d 814, 22 UCC 310 (1977).

used it for more narrowly defined deals (all the buyer's needs for a specific project).[27]

In a batch of pre-and post-Code cases, the buyer substantially increased its "requirements" over a relatively short time. Such action may or may not constitute an abuse. And if an abuse, a court may or may not invalidate the contract altogether. As already indicated, the Code expressly affords means of policing that do not require invalidation. In nearly all of the cases the seller contended that it was not obligated to supply the increase. In resolving these cases, courts usually take a variety of factors into account, but in some cases one factor will be decisive. For example, to avoid liability for an increase it is usually enough for a seller to show that the buyer was not buying solely for its current actual needs but was, for instance, stockpiling or having contracted goods for its own use, was buying for resale.[28] Even where the buyer's increased requirements truly reflect the current needs of its business, the case law indicates that the seller may still avoid liability for the increase by showing some combination of the following: (1) that the seller had no reasonable basis on which to forecast the requested increase;[29] (2) that the increase itself was quite substantial;[30] (3) that the market price of the goods rose considerably above the price at which the seller had been selling to the buyer; (4) that this striking market shift was itself fortuitous;[31] (5) that the contract as a whole favored the buyer;[32] and (6) that the buyer increased its "requirements" solely to take advantage of the favorable price term, rather than because of a mistaken estimate,[33] a technological breakthrough, or the like. Of course, a seller need not show *all* the foregoing factors to avoid liability for the increase, but the more the better.

---

27. See, e.g., Mishara Constr. Co., Inc. v. Transit–Mixed Concrete Corp., 365 Mass. 122, 310 N.E.2d 363, 14 UCC 556 (1974).

28. See, e.g., Massachusetts Gas & Electric Light Supply Corp. v. V–M Corp., 387 F.2d 605, 4 UCC 897 (1st Cir.1967).

29. Compare New York Cent. Ironworks Co. v. United States Radiator Co., 174 N.Y. 331, 66 N.E. 967 (1903), with Marx v. American Malting Co., 169 Fed. 582 (C.C.A.6 1909), and American Trading Co. v. National Fibre & Insulation Co., 31 Del. 258, 114 A. 67 (1921).

30. See, e.g., Asahel Wheeler Co. v. Mendleson, 180 App.Div. 9, 167 N.Y.S. 435 (1917); Moore v. American Molasses Co., 106 Misc. 263, 174 N.Y.S. 440 (1919).

31. See, e.g., Anaheim Sugar Co. v. T.W. Jenkins & Co., 274 Fed. 504 (9th Cir.1921), cert. denied, 257 U.S. 659, 42 S.Ct. 186, 66 L.Ed. 421 (1922); Smith v. Donk Bros. Coal & Coke Co., 260 S.W. 545 (Mo.App.1924).

32. Under the Code, even greater significance can be attached to this factor than before. See § 2–302. For a case which raised the 2–302 issue in a requirements contract, see Brem–Rock, Inc. v. Warnack, 28 Wash.App. 483, 624 P.2d 220, 31 UCC 860 (1981) (buyer's power to prevent third party sales of gravel by seller was not unconscionable when buyer had interest in not seeing seller's gravel pit depleted).

33. See N.S. Sherman Mach. & Iron Works v. Carey, Lombard, Young & Co., 100 Okl. 29, 227 P. 110 (1924).

The seller's own reason for refusing to supply the increase can help its case as well. For example, if seller can show that it refused to supply the increase not only because of the unprofitability of doing so, but also because of unforeseen factors that impaired its own capacity to produce, seller will strengthen its position in the eyes of a court.[34]

Are all the foregoing factors relevant under the Code? It would appear so. Certainly 2–306(1) is drafted broadly. An increase must be in good faith.[35] Among other things, this rules out increases that do not represent *genuine* increases in the buyer's requirements (but, of course, genuineness, like beauty, will be in the eye of the beholder). It also rules out increases that the buyer knows to be beyond the spirit of the deal. Further, 2–306 requires that increases not be "unreasonably disproportionate" to any stated estimate or to any normal or otherwise comparable prior requirements.[36] The word "unreasonably" allows for the interplay of almost any factor a court properly considers relevant. An increase might be in good faith, yet unreasonably disproportionate to prior requirements. This presumably changes the pre-Code law of some states in which courts sanctioned unforeseeable and very large increases within a rather short time.[37] Yet it codifies the law of certain other states.[38]

Sellers are not, however, automatically entitled to resist demands of buyers for any and all large increases. Sellers sometimes have reason to anticipate large increases. When the contract has a fixed price, the seller should anticipate increased demand from the buyer if market prices rise. Further, buyers sometimes have reasons for increased requirements in addition to or other than the desire to take advantage of the market. Finally, one *raison d'etre* of a requirements contract is to allow a buyer some flexibility in the size of its orders. In a proper case a court may sanction a sizeable

34. See, e.g., Sheesley v. Bisbee Linseed Co., 337 Pa. 197, 10 A.2d 401 (1940).

35. Homestake Mining Co. v. Washington Public Power Supply Sys., 476 F.Supp. 1162, 26 UCC 1113 (N.D.Cal. 1979), aff'd, 652 F.2d 28 (9th Cir.1981) (insistence on delivery for unneeded uranium was not good faith, even though at time order was placed the uranium was needed).

36. See, e.g., Shea–Kaiser–Lockheed–Healy v. Department of Water & Power, 73 Cal.App.3d 679, 140 Cal.Rptr. 884, 22 UCC 607 (1977): A similar construction is imposed on output contracts. See, e.g., Harry Thuresson, Inc. v. United States, 197 Ct.Cl. 88, 453 F.2d 1278, 10 UCC 345 (1972) (defendant breached where output of hyposolution

was only 1.7% of the stated estimate). But see, State, Dept. of Fisheries v. J–Z Sales Corp., 25 Wash.App. 671, 610 P.2d 390, 28 UCC 1284 (1980) (output change was unreasonably disproportionate when market was falling and buyer was asked to buy surplus fish product output of more than 3 times the estimated amount of salmon eggs and 2/3 more than estimate for salmon carcasses).

37. See, e.g., New York Cent. Ironworks Co. v. United States Radiator Co., 174 N.Y. 331, 66 N.E. 967 (1903) (court upheld buyer when his needs more than doubled in a short time and prices rose dramatically).

38. See, e.g., C.A. Andrews Coal Co. v. Board of Directors, 151 La. 695, 92 So. 303 (1922).

increase. Indeed where the increase is gradual and the buyer is not found to be acting in bad faith, a court may permit an increase that is extremely large. In one pre-Code case,[39] the court enforced a contract under which the buyer's orders for bread gradually increased from fifty or sixty loaves to three or four thousand loaves per week. Presumably the case would be decided in the same way under the Code.

A policing problem can also arise where a requirements buyer *decreases* its orders significantly over a relatively short period. Of course, if the buyer is actually procuring its requirements more cheaply elsewhere, this is bad faith, and the courts will find that it constitutes breach. Where the market price of the required goods falls below that which the buyer contracted to pay the seller, the buyer may be tempted to try to get out. Some buyers may pretend for a time not to have any requirements at all. Doubtless courts will impose liability when they discover as much.[40]

Some buyers have simply sought cheaper *substitute* products. Here the cases point in different directions, some for the buyer[41] and some not,[42] depending on whether the court finds the buyer to have purchased the substitute in good faith. If a buyer drastically reduces requirements solely to cut losses on the very requirements contract in question, a court may find breach. Certainly there is dictum to this effect.[43] Code comments are in accord; a reduction "merely to curtail loss" is not in good faith.[44] The same rule applies to output contracts as well.[45]

A court might also hold a buyer liable if it seeks to sell its entire business in a falling market without requiring its purchaser to assume any obligations under the requirements contract.[46] There is even authority that a buyer may not deliberately evade its

39. Ehrenworth v. George F. Stuhmer & Co., 229 N.Y. 210, 128 N.E. 108 (1920).

40. See, e.g., Fort Wayne Corrugated Paper Co. v. Anchor Hocking Glass Corp., 130 F.2d 471 (3d Cir.1942) (dictum). See also Simcala, Inc. v. American Coal Trade, Inc., 821 So.2d 197, 46 UCC2d 369 (Ala. 2001), and MDC Corp. v. John H. Harland Co., 288 F.Supp.2d 387, 48 UCC2d 910 (S.D.N.Y. 2002).

41. Cf. Helena Light & Ry. Co. v. Northern Pac. Ry. Co., 57 Mont. 93, 186 P. 702 (1920); Southwest Natural Gas Co. v. Oklahoma Portland Cement Co., 102 F.2d 630 (10th Cir.1939).

42. Compare Loudenback Fertilizer Co. v. Tennessee Phosphate Co., 121 Fed. 298 (6th Cir.1903), with Southwest Natural Gas Co. v. Oklahoma Portland Cement Co., 102 F.2d 630 (10th Cir. 1939).

43. M.W. Kellogg Co. v. Standard Steel Fabricating Co., 189 F.2d 629 (10th Cir.1951); HML Corp. v. General Foods Corp., 365 F.2d 77 (3d Cir.1966).

44. § 2–306, Comment 2.

45. Feld v. Henry S. Levy & Sons, Inc., 37 N.Y.2d 466, 373 N.Y.S.2d 102, 335 N.E.2d 320, 17 UCC 365 (1975). See also Atlantic Track & Turnout Co. v. Perini Corp., 989 F.2d 541, 20 UCC2d 426 (1st Cir.1993) (good faith reductions in output contracts are permissible, even if highly disproportionate).

46. See, e.g., Texas Indus. v. Brown, 218 F.2d 510 (5th Cir.1955).

obligation by simply abandoning its business.[47] Of course, if the buyer is insolvent, its legal liability is unlikely to be worth much.

We have doubt about cases that find reduction to avoid loss to be in bad faith. Surely any buyer will respond that the very purpose of the requirements term—in lieu of a fixed quantity term—was to give it the right to have *no* requirements and make no purchases.

The seller's case against a buyer who decreases or ceases its requirements is more appealing when the seller shows it was not able to anticipate the buyer's action and had even expended significant sums or otherwise relied on promises of the buyer in preparing to meet the buyer's needs. It will also help the seller if it shows that the buyer knew of this reliance.[48]

Both pre-Code cases and 2–306(1) allow "good faith" reductions and even abandonment. Thus, it is not bad faith for a buyer to reduce its orders where its own business needs have actually fallen off.[49] Similarly, it is not bad faith to reduce orders because of a decision to take advantage of a technological advance.[50] Nor is it bad faith to cut orders because of new government regulations or a strike, or some other event beyond the buyer's control, provided that the buyer did not assume the risk of its occurrence.[51] Doubtless there are other ways to negate bad faith as well. Who has the burden of proof on the issue of bad faith? One view is that the party who is to benefit from a showing of bad faith must prove it.[52] Thus a seller claiming breach would have to show that the buyer decreased his orders in bad faith.

Section 2–306(1) limits a buyer to reductions that are not "unreasonably disproportionate to * * * any normal or otherwise comparable prior * * * requirements." Are "highly" disproportionate to normal prior requirements the same as "unreasonably"

47. See, e.g., Wells v. Alexandre, 130 N.Y. 642, 29 N.E. 142 (1891).

48. See, e.g., Diamond Alkali Co. v. P.C. Tomson & Co., 35 F.2d 117 (3d Cir.1929); and Paramount Lithographic Plate Service, Inc. v. Hughes Printing Co., 1977 WL 757, 2 Pa.D. & C.3d 677, 22 UCC 1129 (Com.Pl.1977).

49. See § 2–306, Comment 2.

50. See, e.g., Southwest Natural Gas Co. v. Oklahoma Portland Cement Co., 102 F.2d 630 (10th Cir.1939).

51. See, e.g., Cragin Products Co. v. Fitch, 6 F.2d 557 (8th Cir.1925); Brewster of Lynchburg Inc. v. Dial Corp., 33 F.3d 355, 24 UCC2d 738 (4th Cir. 1994) (reduction in good faith); Indiana–American Water Co., Inc. v. Town of Seelyville, 698 N.E.2d 1255, 38 UCC2d 1133

(Ind. App. 1998) (good faith reduction must be proved by buyer).

52. See HML Corp. v. General Foods Corp., 365 F.2d 77 (3d Cir.1966); Paramount Lithographic Plate Service, Inc. v. Hughes Printing Co., 1977 WL 757, 2 Pa.D. & C.3d 677, 22 UCC 1129 (1977), aff'd 249 Pa.Super. 625, 377 A.2d 1001 (1977); Western Sign, Inc. v. State of Montana, 180 Mont. 278, 590 P.2d 141, 25 UCC 989 (1979). The other view is that the seller must always bear the burden. See, e.g., Tigg Corp. v. Dow Corning Corp., 962 F.2d 1119, 17 UCC2d 730 (3d Cir.1992); Canusa Corp. v. A & R Lobosco, Inc. 986 F.Supp. 723, 35 UCC2d 73 (E.D.N.Y.1997) (a seller under an output contract can reduce its output, but it can demonstrate that the reduction was done in good faith).

disproportionate? They are not. Even drastic good faith reductions are not unreasonably disproportionate.[53] Judge Posner, in the Empire Gas Corp. case,[54] took the view that if a requirements buyer placed no orders merely because it got a better deal elsewhere this would be bad faith, but not so if the buyer had a business reason independent of the contract such as that its own business was doing so badly it had to sell its trucks, such would be good faith.

At least one of us is skeptical of decisions that seem easily to distinguish between bad faith and good faith changes in output or requirements. He believes that a party to a requirements or output contract should bear a heavy burden if that party is to escape because of the other party's reduction or increase in output or requirements. If a requirements seller wants a guaranteed minimum or maximum, the seller can and should bargain for it. The same is true for an output buyer. A seller who believes that the buyer's requirements will not fluctuate with market price and with the profitability of buyer's business is a fool.

§ 4–10 Article 2 Gap Fillers and Mandatory Terms Relating to Excuse, Commercial Impracticability, and the Like—Herein Mainly of 2–615

The parties to a sale of goods contract often include elaborate clauses—commonly called *force majeure* clauses—in their contracts allocating the risk that performance will be impossible, impracticable, or that the value of a performance will be frustrated. These terms may enter the agreement via Section 1–302(a) and via usage of trade, course of dealing, and course of performance, too. See also 1–303 and 2–208. See especially Comment 8 to 2–615. The last sentence of Comment 8 indicates that the agreed upon excusing contingencies must be stated or identifiable with sufficient specificity and their occurrence must have been prejudicial. Comment 8

---

53. In Wilsonville Concrete Products v. Todd Bldg. Co., 281 Or. 345, 574 P.2d 1112, 23 UCC 590 (1978), the court allowed the buyer to stop accepting goods entirely when the state terminated buyer's contract to build a hospital. See also, R.A. Weaver & Assoc., Inc. v. Asphalt Constr., Inc., 587 F.2d 1315, 25 UCC 388 (D.C.Cir.1978); Atlantic Track & Turnout Co. v. Perini Corp., 989 F.2d 541, 20 UCC2d 426 (1st Cir.1993) (good faith reductions in outputs contracts are permissible, even if highly disproportionate).

54. Empire Gas Corp. v. American Bakeries Co., 840 F.2d 1333, 5 UCC2d 545 (7th Cir.1988). For a different interpretation of the role of reduction under 2–306, see Dienes Corp. v. Long Island Railroad Co., 2002 WL 603043, 47 UCC2d 941 (E.D.N.Y.2002) (the "unreasonably disproportionate" language of 2–306 does not apply to decreases in demand). See also, Northern Indiana Public Service Co. v. Colorado Westmoreland, Inc., 667 F.Supp. 613, 5 UCC2d 564 (N.D.Ind.1987) (decrease in demand subject only to good faith); Aventis Environmental Science v. Scotts Co., 383 F.Supp.2d 488, 55 UCC2d 776 (S.D.N.Y. 2005) (good faith imposed certain marketing and sales obligations on buyer).

also makes it clear that: "Agreement can also be made in regard to the consequences of exemption as laid down in paragraphs (b) and (c) and the next section on procedure on notice claiming excuse."

But what if there is a gap in the contract? Here, the Code fills this gap mainly with 2–615 and 2–616. In some instances, 2–613, 2–614, and general contract law via 1–103(b) must also be consulted.

The doctrines of impossibility, commercial impracticability or as the Uniform Commercial Code knows it, Excuse by Failure of Presupposed Conditions, comprise unclimbed peaks of contract doctrine. Clearly, all of the famous early and mid-twentieth century mountaineers, Corbin, Williston, Farnsworth and many lesser persons have made assaults on this topic but none has succeeded in conquering the very summit. The topic inheres in 2–615 of the UCC, in section 261 of the Restatement (Second) of Contracts and in a series of Anglo–American cases. In spite of attempts by all of the contract scholars and even in the face of eloquent and persuasive general statements, it remains impossible to predict with accuracy how the law will apply to a variety of relatively common cases. Both the cases and the Code commentary are full of weasel words such as "severe" shortage, "marked" increase, "basic" assumptions, and "force majeure".[1]

Students who have concluded a first year contracts course in confusion about the doctrine of impossibility and have since had difficulty mastering 2–615 or have found that the cases somehow slip through their fingers when they try to apply them to new situations, may take some comfort in knowing that they are in good company.[2]

In this discussion we have three modest goals. First, we state the general principles of commercial impracticability. Second, we consider those principles as applied by the courts to a variety of circumstances since adoption of the Code. Third, we discuss the consequences of a finding of commercial impracticability. Under the third heading we consider the principles of allocation in 2–615(b).

---

§ 4–10

1. See InterPetrol Bermuda Ltd. v. Kaiser Aluminum Int'l Corp., 719 F.2d 992, 37 UCC 1134 (9th Cir.1983) (standard oil industry force majeure clause covers seller and its supplier); Nissho–Iwai Co. v. Occidental Crude Sales, Inc., 729 F.2d 1530, 38 UCC 1237 (5th Cir. 1984) ("force majeure" implies a reasonable effort requirement, whereby the party takes all reasonable steps to ensure performance notwithstanding the force majeure).

2. For general reading, see, J. J. White and David Peters, A Footnote for Jack Dawson, 100 Mich. L. Rev. 1954 (2002); S. Halpern, Application of the Doctrine of Commercial Impracticability: Searching for "The Wisdom of Solomon," 135 U.Pa.L.Rev. 1123 (1987); J. Wladis, Impracticability as Risk Allocation: The Effect of Changed Circumstances Upon Contract Obligations for the Sale of Goods, 22 Ga.L.Rev. 503 (Spring 1988); S. Walt, Expectations, Loss Distribution and Commercial Impracticability, 24 Ind.L.Rev. 65 (1990).

Our focus is on 2–615(a) which reads in full as follows:

Delay in delivery or non-delivery in whole or in part by a seller who complies with paragraphs (b) and (c) is not a breach of his duty under a contract for sale if performance as agreed has been made impracticable by the occurrence of a contingency the non-occurrence of which was a basic assumption on which the contract was made or by compliance in good faith with any applicable foreign or domestic governmental regulation or order whether or not it later proves to be invalid.

We begin with a few preliminary interpretive difficulties. The section covers "impracticability" and thus expands prior law in states that formerly required that performance be rendered objectively "impossible." Implicit in 2–615(a) and explicit in the language of some of the cases is the proposition that the impracticability must not be the fault of the seller. If one of the links in the causal chain that renders performance impracticable is the seller's fault (as for example where the seller fails to pick fruit before a hard freeze injures it), the seller cannot claim the protection of 2–615.[3]

If performance is rendered impracticable by a governmental regulation or order, the seller is freed from its obligation without reference to the language of 2–615 concerning contingency and basic assumption.[4] Of course it is still necessary that the regulation itself and not the seller's fault cause the impracticability. If, for example, the seller could have escaped the effect of a government regulation, it will not be freed by 2–615.[5] One seller claimed excuse due to its compliance with a federal regulation, but conveniently failed to mention that its representatives had lobbied for the regulation in the first place.[6]

As a final preliminary one should note that 2–615 expressly frees only sellers. Yet the last sentence in Comment 9 states that in certain circumstances "the reason of the present section may well

---

3. Luria Bros. & Co. v. Pielet Bros. Scrap Iron & Metal, Inc., 600 F.2d 103, 26 UCC 1081 (7th Cir.1979) (seller failed to respond to buyer's invitation to deliver substitute goods when originals became unavailable, and thus, 2–615 defense was not available); Nissho–Iwai Co. v. Occidental Crude Sales, Inc., 729 F.2d 1530, 38 UCC 1237 (5th Cir.1984) (embargo which stopped oil supply was caused by seller's own refusal to pay back taxes, royalties and oil costs owed to Libyan government).

4. Harriscom Svenska, AB v. Harris Corp., 3 F.3d 576, 37 UCC2d 665 (2d Cir.1993) (when seller complies with a government regulation banning the sale of an item, in the absence of evidence of seller's bad faith, issue of seller's good faith does not raise enough of an issue of fact to preclude summary judgment).

5. See Washington Mfg. Co. v. Midland Lumber Co., 113 Wash. 593, 194 P. 777 (1921).

6. Northern Illinois Gas Co. v. Energy Cooperative, Inc., 122 Ill.App.3d 940, 78 Ill.Dec. 215, 461 N.E.2d 1049, 38 UCC 1222 (1984).

apply and entitle the buyer to the exemption."[7] Otherwise, a buyer who seeks to be freed from its obligation because of excuse by failure of presupposed conditions will have to look to the common law and will have to escape from Article 2 under the provisions of 1-103 on supplementary principles of common law and equity. Unlike the text of 2-615, neither the cases nor the Restatement distinguish between buyers and sellers as such. Indeed, one of the famous frustration cases, Krell v. Henry,[8] freed a buyer (renter) from his obligation to pay rent because the coronation pageant had been cancelled as a result of the King's illness.

Initially, it is worth noting that the burden of proof on an impracticability claim rests with the party making the claim.[9] Some courts have also interpreted impracticability as a question of law, and thus fit for summary judgment,[10] although almost all others have considered the issue more suitable for the trier of fact.[11] A seller who wishes to escape from liability for its failure to deliver must show that its performance (1) has been made impracticable (2) by the occurrence of a contingency the nonoccurrence of which was a basic assumption on which the contract was made or, by compliance in good faith with any foreign or domestic governmental regulation or order. One court has summarized the statute as follows:

> Three elements must be proven before excuse becomes available under § 2-615: (1) the seller must not have assumed the risk of some unknown contingency; (2) the nonoccurrence of the contingency must have been a basic assumption underlying the contract; and (3) the occurrence of that contingency must have made performance commercially impracticable.[12]

Of course determining whether the seller has "assumed the risk" is often very much like trying to determine whether or not the occurrence was foreseeable. Obviously if a seller has explicitly assumed the risk, it has foreseen it.[13] But if a seller has foreseen a

7. See, e.g., Nora Springs Co-op. Co. v. Brandau, 247 N.W.2d 744, 20 UCC 909 (Iowa 1976) (applies to buyers).

8. 2 K.B. 740 (1903).

9. Louisiana Power & Light Co. v. Allegheny Ludlum Industries, Inc., 517 F.Supp. 1319, 32 UCC 847 (E.D.La. 1981) (burden is on raiser of issue).

10. Ibid.

11. See, e.g., Meuse–Rhine–Ijssel Cattle Breeders of Canada Ltd. v. Y–Tex Corp., 590 P.2d 1306, 26 UCC 292 (Wyo. 1979) (impossibility of performance is most suitable for determination by trier of fact); Nissho–Iwai Co., Ltd. v. Occi-

dental Crude Sales, Inc., 729 F.2d 1530, 38 UCC 1237 (5th Cir.1984) (issue of reasonable effort was one for jury).

12. Iowa Electric Light & Power Co. v. Atlas Corp., 467 F.Supp. 129, 23 UCC 1171 (N.D.Iowa 1978), rev'd on other grounds, 603 F.2d 1301 (8th Cir.1979), cert. denied, 445 U.S. 911, 100 S.Ct. 1090, 63 L.Ed.2d 327 (1980).

13. For an example of a greater assumption being treated as an issue of foreseeability, see, Harper & Assoc. v. Printers, Inc., 46 Wash.App. 417, 730 P.2d 733, 3 UCC2d 594 (1986) (printer assured performance despite technical hurdles, contingency foreseeable).

risk that its performance will be impracticable, it does not follow necessarily that seller has assumed it. Its failure to include a specific contract proviso against it may be weighty evidence that seller has assumed it, but other factors may point the other way. Comment c to section 261 of the Restatement of Contracts, Second, identifies a number of relevant factors:

> A party may, by appropriate language, agree to perform in spite of impracticability that would otherwise justify his non-performance under the rules stated in this Section. He can then be held liable for damages although he cannot perform. Even absent an express agreement, a court may decide, after considering all the circumstances, that a party impliedly assumed such a greater obligation. In this respect the rule stated in this Section parallels that of the Uniform Commercial Code § 2–615, which applies "Except so far as a seller may have assumed a greater obligation...." Circumstances relevant in deciding whether a party has assumed a greater obligation include his ability to have inserted a provision in the contract expressly shifting the risk of impracticability to the other party. This will depend on the extent to which the agreement was standardized, the degree to which the other party supplied the terms, and, in the case of a particular trade or other group, the frequency with which language so allocating the risk is used in that trade or group. The fact that a supplier has not taken advantage of his opportunity expressly to shift the risk of a shortage of his supply by means of contract language may be regarded as more significant where he is a middleman, with a variety of sources of supply and an opportunity to spread the risk among many customers on many transactions by slight adjustment of his prices, than where he is a producer with a limited source of supply, few outlets, and no comparable opportunity. A commercial practice under which a party might be expected to insure or otherwise secure himself against a risk also militates against shifting it to the other party. If the supervening event was not reasonably foreseeable when the contract was made, the party claiming discharge can hardly be expected to have provided against its occurrence. However, if it was reasonably foreseeable, or even foreseen, the opposite conclusion does not necessarily follow. Factors such as the practical difficulty of reaching agreement on the myriad of conceivable terms of a complex agreement may excuse a failure to deal with improbable contingencies. See comment b to this Section and comment a to § 285.

Another rub comes in determining which "nonoccurrences" were "basic" assumptions and which were not.[14] In some cases this interpretative difficulty is compounded by the necessity of also deciding whether the performance has been made "impracticable" or not. Assume for example that seller has entered into a long-term contract to deliver fuel oil of a specified grade to buyer. The seller argues that its performance has been made impracticable because its cost of oil has gone out of sight. The language of the Code does not carry one far in determining whether this seller's performance has been made "impracticable", and if so, whether the "basic assumptions" of the parties extended to the nonoccurrence of the Arab Oil Embargo, the Iranian revolution and attendant general market disruptions.

To assist in answering such questions, it may be helpful to follow an analysis suggested by Professor Farnsworth.[15] In his view, impracticability cases are really cases where the parties have failed adequately to state their intentions. If in our foregoing case the seller had agreed that it would provide the oil or pay damages notwithstanding war, embargo or any other disruption, there would be no impracticability problem. The seller would be liable for breach. Our problem arises because the parties did not foresee the eventuality or if they foresaw it, did not incorporate a governing clause. Professor Farnsworth suggests that a court faced with our problem should first attempt to determine whether the contingency was one that was in fact foreseen by the parties. If it was foreseen by them, he suggests that the courts should then attempt to determine the parties' actual expectations. Their expectations might be revealed by the course of the negotiations, including the various proposals that the seller may have made concerning differ-

---

14. Tallackson Potato Co. v. MTK Potato Co., 278 N.W.2d 417, 26 UCC 929 (N.D.1979) (where payment schedule was designed after third party's payment schedule to buyer, but not explicitly made an assumption of the contract, buyer was still liable on payment schedule to seller, even though third party failed to pay buyer); Federal Pants, Inc. v. Stocking, 762 F.2d 561, 41 UCC 110 (7th Cir.1985) (seller did not breach by nondelivery where manufacturer of goods had terminated seller as an authorized dealer); Red River Commodities, Inc. v. Eidsness, 459 N.W.2d 805, 13 UCC2d 1076 (N.D.1990) (excuse clause including "acts of God" implies non-occurrence of drought was basic assumption).

15. Farnsworth, Disputes Over Omission in Contracts, 68 Colum.L.Rev. 860 (1968). See also Hurst, Freedom of Contract in an Unstable Economy: Judi-cial Reallocation of Contractual Risks Under UCC § 2–615, 54 N.C.L.Rev. 545 (1976); Note, Schwartz, Sales Law and Inflations, 50 So.Calif.L.Rev. 1 (1976); Duesenberg, Contract Impracticability: Courts Begin to Shape § 2–615, 32 Bus. Law. 1089 (1977); Contractual Flexibility in a Volatile Economy: Saving UCC § 2–615 from the Common Law, 72 N.W.U.L.Rev. 1032 (1978); Wallach, Excuse Defense in the law of Contracts: Judicial Frustration of the U.C.C. Attempt to Liberalize the Law of Commercial Impracticability, 55 Notre Dame L.Rev. 203 (1979); Huffmire, § 2–615 and Corporate Accountability, 13 UCC L.J. 256 (Winter 1981); Black, Sales Contracts and Impracticability in a Changing World, 13 St. Mary L.J. 247 (1981); Marcantonio, Unifying the Law of Impossibility, 8 Hastings Int'l & Com. L.Rev. 41 (1984).

ent prices based upon different contingencies, or by trade usage. If any of these sources adequately reveals the parties' expectations, it should govern.

More commonly, however, the contingency will be one not foreseen by the parties and about which they had no expectations. In that case it would be fictional to purport to carry out their expectations. Here the court is not called upon to interpret the contract; its job is to direct a just and reasonable result. In light of the terms on which the parties did agree, what would reasonable persons have further agreed if they had contemplated this contingency?

Perhaps the most significant factor in this analysis is the foreseeability of the contingency that actually occurred.[16] If it was foreseeable that soybeans would be in short supply because of bad summer weather, that the Suez Canal would be closed because it had been closed once ten years earlier when the Arabs and Israelis were at war, or that copper would be hard to buy because of continuous political unrest in Peru and Chile, the parties should be held to have foreseen those contingencies and to have made their contract with the expectation that these contingencies might occur. In that case it is usually appropriate to hold the seller liable notwithstanding the occurrence. But in Code terms, if the parties made the contract with the understanding that the Peruvian mines might well be closed, the closing of the mines is not a "contingency the nonoccurrence of which was a basic assumption * * * " thus 2–615 does not apply, and the seller is liable in damages notwithstanding its inability to deliver Peruvian copper. Put another way, the seller's agreement to a fixed quantity, fixed price contract allocates the risk of shortages to the seller.

The analysis may be illustrated by example four from § 460 of the first Restatement of Contracts; that example reads in full as follows:

> A contracts in the spring with B to raise on a specific tract of land a crop of potatoes and to sell 200 tons of the crop to B at a stated price. The land would ordinarily produce 1000 tons. A's duty is discharged if owing to seizure of the land by eminent domain, he cannot raise the crop, or if owing to blight or to the destruction of the growing plants by a malicious neighbor there is no crop, where the planting and cultivation were properly done. If 100 tons were obtained by A from the land, A's

---

16. See, especially, Note, Rate of Foreseeability in Allocation of Risk under UCC 2–615, Excuse by Failure of Presupposed Conditions, 21 S.Tex.L.J. 441 (1981). See also, Upsher–Smith Laboratories, Inc. v. Mylan Laboratories, Inc., 944 F.Supp. 1411, 31 UCC2d 698 (D. Minn. 1996) (defendant not excused where knew its orders nearly double available supply three weeks before entering contract).

contractual duty would be modified to a duty to sell that amount. If the land habitually produced only 250 tons, and owing to unfavorable weather only 175 were raised in the season to which the contract related, A's duty would not be discharged or modified. The risk was obvious and the possibility of shortage should have been anticipated. B, however, would be under no duty to accept this amount. He could refuse the potatoes and nevertheless recover damages.

Why do the drafters of the Restatement take the position that failure of a 1000 ton crop frees the seller from a contract to deliver 200 tons, but that a less drastic failure of a considerably smaller crop does not free seller from its contract obligation? Perhaps they reached the conclusion in the latter case by finding that a modest crop failure is a foreseeable consequence and by inferring that it is a risk the seller has undertaken by entering the contract. One can discharge the seller in the former case by finding such catastrophic destruction of the crop to have been an unforeseeable event.

a. Increased Cost as a Basis for a Finding of Commercial Impracticability

The most persistent problem under 2–615 in the last forty years has been the question whether a radical rise in a seller's costs frees seller from its obligation to perform. This was the issue with respect to uranium in the famous *Westinghouse* case;[17] it was raised by Gulf Oil in Eastern Air Lines, Inc. v. Gulf Oil Corp.[18] concerning aviation fuel; by Atlas Corporation in Iowa Electric Light and Power Co. v. Atlas Corp.;[19] by Alcoa in Aluminum Co. of America v. Essex Group, Inc.[20] and by others in similar circumstances.[21] Many of these cases were somehow related to the radical increase in the price of crude oil that has occurred since 1972.[22] With rare excep-

17. Virginia Electric & Power Co. v. Westinghouse Electric Corp., Civ. No. 75–0677–R (E.D.Va.1978). See also, Tennessee Valley Authority v. Westinghouse Electric Co., 69 F.R.D. 5, 18 UCC 945 (E.D.Tenn.1975).

18. 415 F.Supp. 429, 19 UCC 721 (S.D.Fla.1975).

19. 467 F.Supp. 129, 23 UCC 1171 (N.D.Iowa 1978), rev'd on other grounds, 603 F.2d 1301 (8th Cir.1979), cert. denied, 445 U.S. 911, 100 S.Ct. 1090, 63 L.Ed.2d 327 (1980).

20. 499 F.Supp. 53, 29 UCC 1 (W.D.Pa.1980) (non-occurrence of extreme deviation of Wholesale Price Index was basic assumption on which contract was made).

21. See, e.g., Maple Farms, Inc. v. City School Dist., 76 Misc.2d 1080, 352 N.Y.S.2d 784, 14 UCC 722 (1974); Publicker Indus. v. Union Carbide Corp., 1975 WL 22890, 17 UCC 989 (E.D.Pa. 1975); Resources Investment Corp. v. Enron Corp., 669 F.Supp. 1038, 5 UCC2d 616 (D.Colo.1987) (increased costs reason for fixed price contracts).

22. A number of cases raised the Arab oil embargo as a defense. See, e.g., Missouri Public Service Co. v. Peabody Coal Co., 583 S.W.2d 721, 27 UCC 103 (Mo.App.1979), cert. denied, 444 U.S. 865, 100 S.Ct. 135, 62 L.Ed.2d 88 (1979) (possibility of embargo was common knowledge, having been discussed by government, media, economists, and business, and thus was foreseeable);

tions the courts have rejected the sellers' 2–615 arguments. For example, in the Sabine case, the court held a two-fold increase in cost of performance no excuse.[23]

To begin the analysis of these cases, consider the language of Comment 4 to 2–615. That Comment is devilishly coy. First it seems to stand four square for the proposition that increased cost is *not* enough: "Increased cost alone does not excuse performance * * *." But it continues: "unless the rise in cost is due to some unforeseen contingency which alters the essential nature of the performance." No plaintiff and defendant are likely to agree on the question whether the change in cost has altered the "essential nature" of the performance. The seller will argue that it has and the buyer that it has not. The Comment returns to the buyer's defense:

> Neither is a rise or a collapse in the market in itself a justification, for that is exactly the type of business risk which business contracts made at fixed prices are intended to cover.

The Comment concludes with an overture to the seller:

> But a severe shortage of raw materials or of supplies due to a contingency such as war, embargo, local crop failure, unforeseen shutdown of major sources of supply or the like, which either causes a marked increase in cost or altogether prevents the seller from securing supplies necessary to his performance, is within the contemplation of this section.

The Comment leaves one baffled about the appropriate outcome in a case in which the seller is arguing that it should be freed from the contract because of an unforeseen but radical rise in its costs. The courts have been less coy; they have favored buyers.

The strongest authority for the proposition that increased costs alone can render performance commercially impracticable is probably a 1916 California case, Mineral Park Land Co. v. Howard.[24] There the court freed a buyer from his obligation to quarry below the water table because of greatly increased costs. That case and a handful of others favor the defense of increased costs.[25] Against

Helms Constr. & Dev. Co. v. State, ex rel. Dept. of Highways, 97 Nev. 500, 634 P.2d 1224, 32 UCC 859 (1981) (Arab oil embargo was reasonably foreseeable, and only increased cost overruns by 2.7%, which was not commercially impracticable).

23. See, Sabine Corp. v. ONG Western, Inc., 725 F.Supp. 1157, 11 UCC2d 83 (W.D.Okl.1989).

24. 172 Cal. 289, 156 P. 458 (1916). But see, City of Albertville, Alabama v.

United States Fidelity and Guar. Co., 272 F.2d 594 (5th Cir.1959).

25. See Gay v. Seafarer Fiberglass Yachts, Inc., 1974 WL 21674, 14 UCC 1335 (N.Y.Sup.Ct.1974). See also, Northern Corp. v. Chugach Electric Ass'n, 518 P.2d 76 (Alaska 1974), vacated on reh'g., 523 P.2d 1243 (1974); Asphalt International, Inc. v. Enterprise Shipping Corp., S.A., 667 F.2d 261, 33 UCC 570 (2d Cir.1981) (when tanker was severely damaged, and cost of repair was prohibitive, far exceeding fair market value of

these slender reeds blows a gale of judicial opinions.[26] Representative of those opinions are Transatlantic Financing Corp. v. United States[27] involving a carrier that had to go around the Cape of Good Hope upon the closing of the Suez Canal at an added expense of approximately $44,000 over a contract price of approximately $300,000; Maple Farms, Inc. v. City School Dist.,[28] involving a radical increase in milk costs; Publicker Industries v. Union Carbide,[29] in which there was a rapid rise in the costs of ethylene; and Iowa Electric Light and Power Co. v. Atlas Corp.[30] In the last, Atlas had agreed to deliver uranium for approximately $9 per pound. The cost of uranium to Atlas had risen to approximately $14 per pound, yet the court held that Atlas was not freed from its obligation to deliver.

Few of the cited cases address the question whether an unforeseen rise in costs of a certain percentage renders contract performance impracticable. Without exception the aggrieved buyer argues not only that the rise in prices was insufficient to render performance impracticable but also that the rise was foreseeable. Thus arguments about foreseeability are typically intertwined with discussion of impracticability.[31]

As commerce grows more sophisticated and multinational it becomes more vulnerable to disruption from embargoes, wars, revolutions, and terrorism in countries producing natural resources. It is paradoxical that with each disruption, subsequent disruptions become more foreseeable and therefore less likely to provide a basis for escape from a contract under 2–615. No one remotely related to the petroleum or uranium industry will be able to argue persuasively for the foreseeable future that it should be freed from its contract obligation because of an unforeseen rise in price or cost. If anything is certain and foreseeable, it is that prices in those markets will experience periodic radical changes.

tanker, lessor could plead impracticability against lessee's claim for breach of rental contract).

26. See, e.g., Alamo Clay Products, Inc. v. Gunn Tile Co., 597 S.W.2d 388, 29 UCC 31 (Tex.Civ.App.1980) (economic burden of $11,000 does not make tile manufacture impracticable, especially where the seller manufactured such tiles before); Lawrance v. Elmore Bean Warehouse, Inc., 108 Idaho 892, 702 P.2d 930, 41 UCC 358 (App.1985) (rise or fall in market is not a justification for nonperformance when it does not alter the essential nature of the performance).

27. 363 F.2d 312, 3 UCC 401 (D.C.Cir.1966).

28. 76 Misc.2d 1080, 352 N.Y.S.2d 784, 14 UCC 722 (1974).

29. 1975 WL 22890, 17 UCC 989 (E.D.Pa.1975).

30. 467 F.Supp. 129, 23 UCC 1171 (N.D.Iowa 1978), rev'd on other grounds, 603 F.2d 1301 (8th Cir.1979), cert. denied, 445 U.S. 911, 100 S.Ct. 1090, 63 L.Ed.2d 327 (1980).

31. Sabine Corp. v. ONG Western, Inc., 725 F.Supp. 1157, 11 UCC2d 83 (W.D.Okl.1989) (could not be a basic assumption that prices would not fluctuate).

We would not argue that a seller should never be excused from its obligations because of cost increases, however we agree with the thrust of the cases discussed above. In our judgment an increase in price, even a radical increase in price, is the thing that contracts are designed to protect against. Because of that and because the experience of the last forty years has made these cost changes more foreseeable than formerly, we do not oppose the hard nosed decisions.

We reserve for more detailed discussion here Alcoa's successful attempt to escape an onerous long-term contract, an attempt that produced the most deviant—Professor Dawson called it grotesque[32] —impracticability decision of the last thirty years. In Aluminum Company of America v. Essex Group Inc.[33] Alcoa sought to be freed from a contract that had been signed in 1967 and was to run to 1983 with an option by Essex to extend it to 1988. Although Alcoa is sometimes cast in the role of the seller of goods, in fact, it was merely selling a service, for it took the raw material provided by Essex, converted it into molten aluminum and returned it to Essex for further processing.

Because the contract had a potential term of 20 years, the parties seemed well aware of the need to maintain a flexible price. They worked out a complex price escalator under which the labor portion of Alcoa's price would fluctuate in one way and the price attributable to non-labor production costs in another. The non-labor portion fluctuated with the Wholesale Price Index of Industrial Commodities. The price term also included a "cap" and various other features. According to the opinion, Alcoa was assisted in devising this complex escalation clause by the eminent economist Alan Greenspan. Because of material cost increases attributable to the oil shock in the mid–1970's and to pollution control requirements, and despite the escalator, the contract became unprofitable for Alcoa in the late 1970's. At trial it maintained that it would lose in excess of $75,000,000 between the time of trial and the expiration of the contract.

Alcoa asserted a right to be free of the contract. First it argued that the contract should be reformed on the ground that the parties suffered "mutual mistake" in selecting the wholesale price index with the belief that it would yield "a return of around 4 cents a pound" to Alcoa. Alcoa also argued that performance of the contract was commercially impracticable, and that the increase in costs was unforeseeable and unallocated. Finding for Alcoa on nearly all counts, the court did not free Alcoa from performance, but rather

---

32. Dawson, Judicial Revision of Frustrated Contracts: The United States, 64 B.U.L.Rev. 1, 26 (1984). Cf. Speidel, Court–Imposed Price Adjust-ments Under Long–Term Supply Contracts, 76 Nw.U.L.Rev. 369 (1981).

33. 499 F.Supp. 53, 29 UCC 1 (W.D.Pa.1980).

rewrote the contract to provide a series of alternative price terms the court thought more appropriate than those provided in the contract.

The court was wrong in concluding that the contract should be avoided or modified because of mistake. In the words of Professor Palmer, "In a lay sense the word 'mistake' is commonly used to describe an erroneous prediction of the future course of events, but this is not mistake in the legal sense. If any relief from the terms of a contract is available in such circumstances, it must be in accordance with contract doctrines relating to impossibility, impracticability, or frustration of purpose."[34]

More to the point of the present discussion, we also have doubts about the court's judgment on the alternative ground, namely, that the Alcoa contract's performance had become impracticable. The hiring of Alan Greenspan to assist in devising a complicated escalator clause makes it obvious the parties foresaw the possibility of cost fluctuations and foresaw the need to adjust the price. Should not the court have recognized this elaborate clause and extensive negotiation as an explicit allocation of the risks of increased cost fluctuation? We think it should have.

The parties negotiated a contract with a specific escalated price over a fixed term. They had many other options open to them. They could have negotiated a flat cost-plus contract or a shorter contract renewable from time to time. They could have entered into a joint venture under which each shared costs and the profits. In short, they rejected many devices that would not have allocated the potential cost increases in the way in which a long-term fixed-price contract invariably does. By rejecting those alternatives, alternatives surely known to the executives of both parties and to experts such as Mr. Greenspan, we believe the parties should be understood to have allocated the risks that are associated with contracts carrying fixed prices, even escalated fixed prices.

b.   *Crop Failure as a Basis for a Finding of Commercial Impracticability*

Contracts for the sale of agricultural commodities have been the second fertile area for 2–615 disputes. These cases typically follow on the heels of floods, drought or general crop failures. Comment 9 speaks to these cases as follows:

> The case of a farmer who has contracted to sell crops to be grown on designated land may be regarded as falling either within the section on casualty to identified goods or this section, and he may be excused, when there is a failure of the specific crop, either on the basis of the destruction of identified

34. G. Palmer, The Law of Restitution, 1986 Supp. p. 200.

goods or because of the failure of a basic assumption of the contract.

In conformity with that comment, courts have routinely freed farmers from contracts of sale where it appeared that the parties contemplated that the crops to be sold would be grown on the farmer's land and when there was no expectation that the farmer would go to the market for replacements. Dunavant Enterprises, Inc. v. Ford[35] is representative. There the court freed the farmer from his obligation to deliver cotton to the buyer when high water had prevented the seller from planting his full acreage in the spring. The court discussed the contemplation of the parties and correctly relied on Comment 9. Representative of those cases in which crop failure has been rejected as a defense is Bliss Produce Co. v. A.E. Albert & Sons, Inc.[36] In that case a middleman seller asserted that the general failure of Arizona potatoes freed him from his obligation. The court rejected that argument on the ground that Comment 9 speaks only of farmers who have contracts with respect to specific pieces of land. It seems to us that the courts are correct in focusing upon the question whether the parties contemplated that the seller would grow the crop on his own land. If that is the contemplation, neither party would expect the seller to replace the ungrown crops by purchases on the market. In those cases the buyer is usually a professional purchaser who can buy substitutes more easily than the seller. Conversely if the seller is a middleman or a farmer who sells crops other than those or in addition to his own, one can conclude that the seller has assumed a greater obligation than simply to attempt to grow the crops on a specific piece of land.[37]

c. Failure of a Source of Supply as a Basis for a Finding of Commercial Impracticability

An area of impracticability posing issues similar to those presented in cases of crop failure is that of failure of a source of supply. The official comments of the Code, the Restatements, and the cases all authorize excuse when a mutually contemplated source of supply becomes unavailable. Comment 5 to 2–615 states:

> In the case of failure of production by an agreed source for causes beyond the seller's control, the seller should, if possible, be excused since production by an agreed source is without more a basic assumption of the contract.

---

35. 294 So.2d 788, 20 UCC 667 (Miss.1974).

36. 35 Agric.Dec. 742, 20 UCC 917 (1976).

37. See e.g., Semo Grain Co. v. Oliver Farms, Inc., 530 S.W.2d 256, 18 UCC 668 (Mo.App.1975). Compare, Alamance County Bd. of Ed. v. Bobby Murray Chevrolet, Inc., 121 N.C.App. 222, 465 S.E.2d 306, 28 UCC2d 1220 (1996) (seller could have acquired goods from other sources).

While Comment 5 explicitly recognizes this type of excuse, the courts—consistent with the spirit of the impracticability doctrine—impose strict requirements for its availability. Thus, the source of supply must not only fail,[38] it must have (1) been mutually contemplated by the parties as the sole source of supply,[39] (2) the failure must not have been foreseeable at the time of the contracting[40] and (3) the party seeking to be excused must have employed "all due measures" to insure that the source did not fail.[41] In addition, a seller seeking excuse must of course comply with 2–615(b) & (c) of the Code with regard to notice and allocation.

The case of Selland Pontiac–GMC, Inc. v. King[42] involved a contract to supply an automobile dealer with four school bus bodies. The writing itself indicated that the bodies were to be manufactured by a particular supplier. Thus, there was a single, mutually contemplated, source of supply. The supplier encountered financial difficulties and could not fulfill its obligations. The seller had no reason to know of its supplier's troubles, and notified its buyer as soon as it learned that it would not be able to complete performance. Hence, 2–615 was applicable, and the seller was excused from performance.

d. A Strike as a Basis for a Finding of Commercial Impracticability

In the modern business world, it is difficult to conceive of a strike as a totally unforeseen contingency.[43] Indeed, many contracts allocate the risk of strikes in force majeure clauses. Further, since strikes can usually be resolved by undertaking additional costs, it is

38. Neal–Cooper Grain Co. v. Texas Gulf Sulphur Co., 508 F.2d 283, 16 UCC 7 (7th Cir.1974) (where supplier of potash had producing mines in another country, no failure of supply despite increased cost).

39. Center Garment Co. v. United Refrigerator Co., 369 Mass. 633, 341 N.E.2d 669, 18 UCC 672 (1976); Inter-Petrol Bermuda Ltd. v. Kaiser Aluminum Int'l Corp., 719 F.2d 992, 37 UCC 1134 (9th Cir.1983) (where seller contemplated particular source for petroleum but did not communicate that to the buyer, that source not basic assumption of parties).

40. Heat Exchangers, Inc. v. Map Constr. Corp., 34 Md.App. 679, 368 A.2d 1088, 21 UCC 123 (1977) (where seller experienced difficulty with a particular supplier prior to contracting, failure foreseeable); Record Corp. v. Logan Constr. Co., 22 Pa.D. & C.3d 358, 34 UCC 1579 (Com.Pl.1982) (foreseeability

of strike at supplier precluded excuse). Cf. Paul T. Freund Corp. v. Commonwealth Packing Co., 2004 WL 2075427, 54 UCC2d 966 (W.D.N.Y. 2004).

41. § 2–615, Comment 5. See, e.g Roth Steel Products v. Sharon Steel Corp., 705 F.2d 134, 35 UCC 1435 (6th Cir.1983) (seller continued to accept more orders than it could fill after it knew of shortage of raw materials).

42. 384 N.W.2d 490, 1 UCC2d 463 (Minn.App.1986). See also, SCA Int'l, Inc. v. Garfield & Rosen, Inc., 337 F.Supp. 246, 10 UCC 1062 (D.Mass. 1971) (raw materials and factories damaged by unprecedented flooding); Federal Pants, Inc. v. Stocking, 762 F.2d 561, 41 UCC 110 (7th Cir.1985) (termination of status as authorized dealership by supplier).

43. See, Carroll, Dan L. & Edwards, Mark C., Labor Strife and U.C.C. 2–615: One Strike and You're Out? 14 U.C.Davis L.Rev. 669 (Spring 1981).

all the more unlikely that a strike will qualify as an excusing condition. On top of this, the failure of the party seeking excuse to take steps necessary to avoid a strike in the first place may preclude excuse on the basis that this party was at fault.

Nevertheless, in Glassner v. Northwest Lustre Craft Co.,[44] an action brought against a seller of china dishes who failed to perform as a result of a labor dispute, the Oregon Court of Appeals reversed a summary judgment for the plaintiff. The court held that a strike could have rendered defendant's performance impracticable and therefore must be submitted to a trier of fact. Further, in Mishara Construction Co. v. Transit–Mixed Concrete Corp.,[45] where a defendant supplier failed to deliver concrete as promised, the Massachusetts Supreme Judicial Court held that a jury could take into account labor difficulties in finding that performance by the defendant was excused. But here the strike was not against the defendant seeking to be excused. The court merely held that the trial judge did not err in refusing to charge the jury that defendant was required to make deliveries regardless of picket lines, strikes, or labor difficulties at the job site.

e. Compliance With Governmental Regulation as a Basis for a Finding of Commercial Impracticability

After death and taxes, few things are more foreseeable than the prospect of government regulation. Yet 2–615(a) provides:

> Delay in delivery or non-delivery is * * * not a breach * * * if performance as agreed has been made impracticable ... by compliance in good faith with any applicable foreign or domestic governmental regulation or order whether or not it later proves to be invalid.

The Restatement of Contracts also asserts that any government regulation that makes performance impracticable "is an event the non-occurrence of which was a basic assumption on which the contract was made."[46] This suggests that the foreseeability may even be irrelevant here.

Thus, when a supplier of potatoes contracted to deliver them at a specific time, performance was excused when the state police ordered the delivery truck off the road due to adverse weather conditions.[47] The tribunal noted that while poor weather may have been foreseeable, and that this particular risk may have been allocated to the supplier who promised delivery, the risk of the

---

44. 39 Or.App. 175, 591 P.2d 419, 26 UCC 416 (1979).

45. 365 Mass. 122, 310 N.E.2d 363, 14 UCC 556 (1974).

46. Restatement of Contracts 2d, § 264.

47. Process Supply Co., Inc. v. Sunstar Foods, Inc., 1979 WL 30091, 27 UCC 122 (U.S.Dept.Ag.1979).

resulting government interference was not allocated and 2–615 was applicable.[48] It should be noted that this was a decision by an administrative official. But the 5th Circuit, in Eastern Air Lines, Inc. v. McDonnell Douglas Corp., even excused delayed delivery of aircraft when McDonnell Douglas gave military orders priority over commercial orders at the mere request, but not the order of, the federal government.[49]

While excuse on the grounds of impracticability by virtue of government regulation may be easier to earn than others, it is far from an open floodgate. Parties must still demonstrate that performance is forestalled not just inhibited,[50] and as comment 10 suggests, the party must not have induced the governmental regulation that it complains of.[51] While active lobbying for the regulation may preclude excuse, mere cooperation and early compliance with the regulation will not. Thus, in International Minerals & Chemical Corp. v. Llano, Inc., the Tenth Circuit excused a potash miner's obligation to buy natural gas when the buyer could no longer burn natural gas in the quantities anticipated at the time the contract was made and still comply with new state emission standards.[52] The court excused the buyer despite its ready cooperation with the state in implementing the new emission standards and its early compliance. Noteworthy is the fact that the buyer was excused from a "take or pay" contract. Other courts have ruled that when the actual purchasing and taking of goods sold under a "take or pay" contract becomes impracticable, excuse is not normally available.[53]

A complicated set of regulations and deregulations of prior rules disrupted the natural gas market in the 1980s. These changes increased the costs of buyer-pipelines (or destroyed their resale

---

48. *Id.* at 124–25.

49. 532 F.2d 957, 19 UCC 353 (5th Cir.1976). See also, Harriscom Svenska, AB v. Harris Corp., 3 F.3d 576, 37 UCC2d 665 (2d Cir. 1993).

50. Florida Power & Light Co. v. Westinghouse Electric Corp., 517 F.Supp. 440, 31 UCC 930 (E.D.Va.1981) (regulation of reprocessing of spent nuclear fuel made performance more costly, but not impracticable); Northern Indiana Public Service Co. v. Carbon County Coal Co., 799 F.2d 265, 1 UCC2d 1505 (7th Cir.1986) (buyer electric utility could still purchase coal despite refusal of rate commission to grant higher rates to cover the contract price); Engel Indus., Inc. v. First American Bank, N.A., 798 F.Supp. 9, 18 UCC2d 832 (D.D.C.1992) (bank could have applied for exemption from Presidential order freezing Iraqi assets during Gulf War).

51. § 2–615, Comment 10.

52. 770 F.2d 879, 41 UCC 347 (10th Cir.1985). See also, Harriscom Svenska, AB v. Harris Corp., 3 F.3d 576, 37 UCC2d 665 (2d Cir. 1993) (defense available where complying with U.S. informal ban on sales to Iran).

53. See, e.g., Sabine Corp. v. ONG Western, Inc., 725 F.Supp. 1157, 11 UCC2d 83 (W.D.Okl.1989) (no factual showing that payment was impracticable); Kaiser–Francis Oil Co. v. Producer's Gas Co., 870 F.2d 563, 8 UCC2d 1048 (10th Cir.1989) (payment still viable alternative when taking impracticable).

markets) and many sought court relief. In rejecting the buyers' claims, one court found that (1) a twofold increase in the cost of performance did not materially alter the essential nature of the contract, (2) the purchaser had assumed the risk of higher prices, and (3) that governmental regulation is foreseeable as a matter of law and was in fact foreseen by the parties.[54]

f. Destruction or Loss of Goods as a Basis for a Finding of Commercial Impracticability

A party might seek to be excused from performance on the grounds of impracticability where the goods are destroyed or lost before the seller could deliver them. Such a seller might seek excuse under either 2–613 or 2–615. While 2–613 deals specifically with the destruction or loss of goods, it requires that those goods be identified at the time the contract was made.[55] If they were not so identified, the seller must turn to 2–615.

While 2–615 sweeps more broadly than 2–613, the familiar hurdles of foreseeability, impracticability, assumption of a greater obligation, and fault remain, and the case law results themselves are mixed. In what may appear to be a particularly lenient decision, the Second Circuit held that a shipowner was excused from performance under a charter-party agreement when the ship in question was substantially damaged in a collision.[56] The ship owner recovered nearly the entire cost of repair from its insurance company, thus rendering performance only slightly more burdensome than originally anticipated.

Not all courts are so willing to dispense excuse. In Bende & Sons, Inc. v. Crown Recreation, Inc., the court held that delivery of 11,000 combat boots destined for Ghana was not excused despite their destruction in a train derailment.[57] The court held that the prospect of derailment was foreseeable, and that had they wished an alternative allocation of risks, the parties could have expressed that desire in the contract.[58]

---

54. Sabine Corp. v. ONG Western, Inc., 725 F.Supp. 1157, 11 UCC2d 83 (W.D.Okl.1989). See also, Resources Investment Corp. v. Enron Corp., 669 F.Supp. 1038, 5 UCC2d 616 (D.Colo. 1987); Golsen v. ONG Western, Inc., 756 P.2d 1209, 5 UCC2d 605 (Okl.1988).

55. § 2–613. See Bende & Sons, Inc. v. Crown Recreation, Inc., 548 F.Supp. 1018, 34 UCC 1587 (E.D.N.Y.1982).

56. Asphalt Int'l, Inc. v. Enterprise Shipping Corp., S.A., 667 F.2d 261, 33 UCC 570 (2d Cir.1981).

57. 548 F.Supp. 1018, 34 UCC 1587 (E.D.N.Y.1982).

58. See, Arabian Score v. Lasma Arabian Ltd., 814 F.2d 529, 3 UCC2d 590 (8th Cir.1987) (purchaser of promotional services for a race horse not excused from performance upon death of horse since this was a foreseeable contingency).

g. Consequences of a Finding of Commercial Impracticability

Section 2–615(a) tells that a finding of commercial impracticability prevents seller's failure of performance from being a "breach of his duty". The basic result of 2–615 is to give the seller or, by analogy the buyer, freedom from suit for breach of the contract notwithstanding the fact that seller does not fully perform.

To receive the benefits of sub-section (a), the seller must comply with subsections (b) and (c). These subsections require first that seller allocate "in any manner which is fair and reasonable," and secondly that it give seasonable notification to the buyer of any delay, non-delivery, or allocation quota.[59] Section 2–616 sets forth the buyer's options on receipt of notification of impracticability. If the delay or the deficiency substantially impairs the value of the whole contract, the buyer may terminate the contract as to the affected installments or it may agree to take its allocable share in modification of the contract. One court has held that a partial failure of a source of supply does not excuse performance.[60]

Two questions remain. First when is the impracticability such that it voids the whole contract as opposed to one part of it? Second, by what standard does one determine when the seller has a right to allocate, not just to delay? One must answer the first question by reference to the common law of contracts and in the case of installment contracts by referring to 2–612. We know of no good answer to the second question. Sections 2–615 and 2–616 seem to contemplate allocation or delay in delivery as alternatives in certain circumstances, but neither section tells which cases are appropriate for delay and which for allocation. Often seller's interests will be served by allocating, for by doing so seller satisfies its obligation at the contract price by less than a full delivery. Seller can then sell any newly acquired stock at a higher non-contract "shortage" price. We see no explicit restrictions on seller's discretion here. Of course, seller must act in good faith, and seller should be held to any trade practice.

When the seller chooses to allocate, the Code says only that it must do so in a "fair and reasonable" way. Comment 11 to 2–615 breathes some life into those two words as follows:

59. Glassner v. Northwest Lustre Craft Co., 39 Or.App. 175, 591 P.2d 419, 26 UCC 416 (1979) (seasonability of notice is an issue of fact, so summary judgment is improper); Red River Commodities, Inc. v. Eidsness, 459 N.W.2d 805, 13 UCC2d 1076 (N.D.1990) (actual knowledge sufficient notice); Lambert v. City of Columbus, 242 Neb. 778, 496 N.W.2d 540, 20 UCC2d 176 (1993) (partial failure of a source of supply does not excuse performance).

60. Lambert v. City of Columbus, 242 Neb. 778, 496 N.W.2d 540, 20 UCC2d 176 (1993).

An excused seller must fulfill his contract to the extent which the supervening contingency permits, and if the situation is such that his customers are generally affected he must take account of all in supplying one. Subsections (a) and (b), therefore, explicitly permit in any proration a fair and reasonable attention to the needs of regular customers who are probably relying on spot orders for supplies. Customers at different stages of the manufacturing process may be fairly treated by including the seller's manufacturing requirements. A fortiori, the seller may also take account of contracts later in date than the one in question. The fact that such spot orders may be closed at an advanced price causes no difficulty, since any allocation which exceeds normal past requirements will not be reasonable. However, good faith requires, when prices have advanced, that the seller exercise real care in making his allocations, and in case of doubt his contract customers should be favored and supplies prorated evenly among them regardless of price. Save for the extra care thus required by changes in the market, this section seeks to leave every reasonable business leeway to the seller.

Comment 11 and the direction that the allocation should be "fair and reasonable" are descended from more than 100 years of American cases on contract allocation.[61] For the most part those cases ratify the seller's choice of pro rata allocation methods. An examination of them tells us that the typical seller will be held to have acted fairly and reasonably if it does a general pro rata allocation among all of its contract customers. It may include itself and non-contract customers but not new buyers who are not "customers". However it need not include non-contract customers. Seller may prefer certain buyers over others in certain circumstances.[62] In Cliffstar Corp. v. Riverbend Products,[63] plaintiff was allocated 319, other customers up to 859, and this was not unreasonable as a matter of law. If for example the injury to one buyer will be particularly great, the seller may also allocate a greater than pro rata share to that buyer. The seller may treat itself as a customer but it may not deviate too far from the pro rata scheme in order to maximize its profits.[64]

61. See e.g., Oakman v. Boyce, 100 Mass. 477 (1868); McKeefrey v. Connellsville Coke & Iron Co., 56 Fed. 212 (3d Cir.1893). For post-UCC allocation cases see, e.g., Intermar, Inc. v. Atlantic Richfield Co., 364 F.Supp. 82 (E.D.Pa. 1973); Mansfield Propane Gas Co., Inc. v. Folger Gas Co., 231 Ga. 868, 204 S.E.2d 625, 14 UCC 953 (1974).

62. See McKeefrey v. Connellsville Coke & Iron Co., 56 Fed. 212 (3d Cir. 1893).

63. Cliffstar Corp. v. Riverbend Products, Inc., 750 F.Supp. 81, 13 UCC2d 392 (W.D.N.Y.1990).

64. For cases in which courts pulled up on a seller who was too kind to itself, see Davison Chem. Co. v. Baugh Chem. Co., 133 Md. 203, 104 A. 404 (1918);

One should note that a direction to allocate pro rata is far from an explicit and rigid set of allocation rules. Seller may choose to prorate based upon historic deliveries, historic contract amounts, current needs, current contract amounts and possibly other grounds. By choosing one or another scheme to establish its proration, the seller may be able to favor one set of customers over another to a considerable extent. Moreover if we allow further deviations in the pro rata scheme based upon appropriate priority rules either because of the social utility of certain uses or because of the more serious injuries that some buyers would suffer if they did not receive more than a pro rata share, we leave the seller with a great deal of flexibility. We believe that the seller should have considerable flexibility and that courts will not often improve things by putting their oar in. The seller's selfish long-term interest in maintaining a cadre of customers will usually induce a seller to treat most of its customers as it should.

The foregoing discussion assumes a straightforward application of 2–615 and 2–616. Aluminum Co. of America v. Essex Group,[65] discussed above, shows that these sections contain only a small part of the universe of remedies that might be applied upon a finding of commercial impracticability. In that case the judge ordered neither an allocation nor a cancellation, rather he devised and imposed his own alternative price schedule. At page 80 of the *Alcoa* opinion, one comes upon a detailed set of price terms that look as though they belong in an elaborate contract, not in a court's opinion. Apparently without consulting the parties, and clearly without their consent, Judge Teitelbaum wrote a seven-year contract for the parties.

Professor Dawson describes this portion of the opinion as "the only instance in which an American judge has tried to dictate entirely different substantive terms in a contract that was still being actively performed."[66] Professor Dawson suggests, first, that there is nothing in judges' training that might "qualify them to invent variable new designs for disrupted enterprises * * *."[67] He also challenges the *Alcoa* decision on the grounds of civil liberty by raising the question where the court finds the power not merely to excuse further performance, but "to impose on them a new contract without the free assent of both * * *."[68]

We share Professor Dawson's reservations about the court's act in *Alcoa*.[69] It is one thing for the court to say the parties should be freed from the contract, or that there should be allocation under 2–

ACME Mfg. Co. v. Arminius Chem. Co., 264 Fed. 27 (4th Cir.1919).

65. 499 F.Supp. 53, 29 UCC 1 (W.D.Pa.1980).

66. Dawson, Judicial Revision of Frustrated Contracts: The United States, 64 B.U.L.Rev. 1, 35 (1984). See also, J. White, A Footnote for Jack Dawson, 100 Mich. L. Rev. 1954 (2002).

67. *Id*. at 35.

68. *Id*. at 35.

69. *Id*. at 37.

615 and 2–616 as the legislature has directed; it is something else to redraft a contract that still has seven years to run. We are skeptical, therefore, of the arguments of our colleague Speidel that the courts can and should make such specific adjustments in long-term contracts.

There is a final point in all this that should not be overlooked: parties negotiating long-term contracts do so "in the shadow of the law." If one can rely upon activist judges to modify onerous price terms, a clever negotiator may be motivated to play all its cards on other terms (such as price over the short term) in the hope that the judge will change the rules of the game before the opponent can play its cards if the price term later turns. Making *Alcoa* the norm would not remove the problem; it might even increase the rewards of strategic behavior during the negotiation of the contract.

§ 4–11 Mandatory Terms Under Article 2—General Limits on Freedom of Contract

By agreement, the parties can displace most provisions of Article 2. This is true of most gap filler provisions. But certain other provisions cannot be modified. Section 1–302(b) provides that the parties may not "disclaim" their Code obligations of "good faith, diligence, reasonableness and care." Some provisions explicitly state that they cannot be varied by contrary agreement.[1] A number of others explicitly state they are variable.[2] The latter pose no problem. But what of the sections that are not specifically flagged as variable or nonvariable?

It is clear that some of these provisions cannot be varied by agreement, despite the general green light in section 1–302(a) and the statement in the comments that the "residual rule is that the effect of all provisions of the act may be varied by agreement."[3] An obvious example is 2–201 on the Statute of Frauds; the comments state that this section is not variable even though the text is silent.[4] An equally obvious example of a nonvariable provision not so flagged is 2–302 on unconscionability. Section 2–719(3) on unconscionable remedy limitations is also unflagged. Not all unflagged provisions are obviously nonvariable. On the contrary, most are obviously variable. Yet if the unflagged provisions include some that are variable and some that are not, and if the unflagged provisions are not all obviously one or the other, then it becomes necessary to articulate criteria for deciding the less obvious cases.

§ 4–11

1. See, e.g., §§ 1–301(g); 1–205; 2–210(1)(2); 2–318; 2–718(1); 2–719(3).

2. See, e.g., §§ 2–206; 2–305; 2–306(2); 2–307; 2–308; 2–309; 2–310; 2–311; 2–503; 2–504; 2–507; 2–509; 2–511.

3. § 1–302, Comment 3.

4. § 1–302, Comment 1.

For example, can the parties dispense with the notice of breach required by 2–607(3)(a)? May they vary the burden of proof imposed by 2–607(4)? There is little case law on this general problem, and we can only offer a general approach. Article 2 embodies a general presumption that, absent a strong countervailing policy, the contract language of the parties should prevail.[5] But what should count as a strong countervailing policy? One clue would be to consider whether the explicitly nonvariable provisions of Article 2 reflect any general policies which the drafters considered strong enough to override any provisions of the parties to the contrary. Several general policies are immediately apparent. For example, several of the nonvariable provisions of Article 2 are intended to prevent one party from taking undue advantage of the other, as by striking an unconscionable bargain,[6] unfairly upsetting justifiable reliance,[7] or acting in bad faith.[8]

But the category of strong overriding policies includes more than just those policies that groups of explicitly nonvariable provisions have in common. Some unflagged provisions are doubtless nonvariable quite without regard to whether they manifest a policy reflected in a group of explicitly nonvariable provisions. For example, several Code sections purportedly protect the interests of third parties.[9] In earlier drafts of 1–102, a subsection provided that "[e]xcept as otherwise provided by this Act the rights and duties of a third party may not be adversely varied by an agreement to which he is not a party or by which he is not otherwise bound."[10] This subsection was eventually deleted only because it was thought unnecessary. Thus, while most of Article 2's specific third party protection provisions are unflagged and while their modification should be permissible between parties to the modification, their effect on third parties should not be changed without the agreement of those parties.

It should be added that section 1–302(b) states that the "obligations of good faith, diligence, reasonableness and care prescribed by this Act may not be disclaimed by agreement." Thus the Code imposes these obligations in every contract for the sale of goods. But 1–302(b) goes on to say that "the parties may by agreement determine the standards by which the performance of such obligations is to be measured if such standards are not manifestly unreasonable."

5.   § 1–302.

6.   § 2–302.

7.   See, e.g., § 2–609(1).

8.   § 1–304.

9.   E.g., §§ 2–210(1); 2–403; 2–502; 2–702.

10.   A case decided under this section is Girard Trust Corn Exch. Bank v. Warren Lepley Ford, Inc., 12 Pa.D. & C.2d 351, 1 UCC 495 (Com.Pl.1957).

We should not forget that the strength of the market economy and the very efficiency of sales contracts depends on determined loyalty to the parties' agreement. Courts should not look for ways to restrict agreement; quite the opposite, courts should be unreceptive to claims of nonvariability. They should demand strong reasons from anyone who claims that the legislature in adopting Article 2 set out a better rule for all cases than the parties can set out for themselves.

§ 4–12 Mandatory Terms—Transfer of Title Under 2–403

Section 2–401(1) allows the parties to control passage of title, *as between them* by contract terms. Section 2–403, however, governs title *vis à vis third parties,* except for cases covered by 2–403(4), 9–320, and the like.

Section 2–403 deals with three related topics—the general powers of a transferor of goods to transfer title or interests, the title of a good faith purchaser of goods, and the rights of a buyer in ordinary course from a merchant to whom goods have been entrusted. Section 2–403 applies generally to owners of an interest in goods; the rights of others with more specific claims such as secured creditors and lessees are generally governed by other parts of the Code.[1]

a. *General Powers of Transferor*

The general powers of a transferor to transfer title to goods are set out in subsection (1) of 2–403:

A purchaser of goods acquires all title which his transferor had or had power to transfer except that a purchaser of a limited interest acquires rights only to the extent of the interest purchased.

This rule seems simple enough. At minimum, Bert Buyer, at least if he does not purchase a limited interest, acquires whatever interest his seller had in the goods. The requirement of "purchase" poses no hurdles since 1–201(29) and (30) define purchase broadly to include: "taking by sale, discount, negotiation, mortgage, pledge, lien, issue or re-issue, gift or any other voluntary transaction creating an interest in property."[2] Also, there are no good faith or lack of notice requirements for such "mere purchasers."

§ 4–12

1. See, e.g., McConnell v. Barrett, 154 Ga.App. 767, 270 S.E.2d 13, 31 UCC 565 (1980) (bank which held note on mobile home was not an entrustor, since mobile home was in principal debtor's name only); United Carolina Bank v. Sistrunk, 158 Ga.App. 107, 279 S.E.2d 272, 31 UCC 1731 (1981) (2–403 applies only to owners of goods, and secured party is not owner).

2. Farmers Livestock Exch., Inc. v. Ulmer, 393 N.W.2d 65, 2 UCC2d 1194

Beyond stating the obvious, that is, whatever Sam Seller actually had, Bert Buyer gets, the foregoing provision accomplishes two things that may not be so obvious. First, the phrase "or had power to transfer" makes clear that the law of agency, apparent agency and estoppel apply. Thus, under this language, Bert Buyer may get a better title than his transferor actually had.[3]

Second, the opening sentence of 2–403 embodies a "shelter" principle. That is, once a transferor has acquired title through 2–403 or otherwise,[4] its transferees generally benefit accordingly—even when the transferees have knowledge that would keep them from achieving bona fide purchaser status in their own right. Section 2–403 does not use the word "shelter," but we so read the language granting a transferee "all title" of the transferor. Moreover, prior law did recognize the principle,[5] cognate Code provisions embody the principle,[6] courts in Code cases have so interpreted 2–403,[7] and appropriate protection of a transferee's "market" for retransfer requires some recognition of a shelter principle.[8]

Two examples will make the shelter idea clearer. First, assume Sam buys in the ordinary course of business a stereo from Crazy Joe's Stereo Store. Crazy Joe had been purchasing from a supplier and paying with "rubber checks." Even so, Sam gets good title against the supplier through 2–403(1)(b) and 2–403(2). Second, when Sam trades in his stereo to Bob's Stereo shop, Bob, too, gets good title even though Bob happens to know the details of his competitor's shady operations. Thus although Bob himself would not be a good faith purchaser if he were buying from Crazy Joe, Bob still acquires "all title which his transferor had"—all of Sam's title—under 2–403(1). Section 2–403(1) thus provides "shelter" protection even to a party who is a "mere purchaser."

(N.D.1986) (mere possession of cattle by auctioneer not a purchase).

3. Comment 1 to § 2–403 makes this proposition clear. See, e.g., Humphrey Cadillac & Oldsmobile Co. v. Sinard, 85 Ill.App.2d 64, 229 N.E.2d 365, 4 UCC 640 (1967) (apparent authority); Locke v. Arabi Grain & Elevator Co., Inc., 197 Ga.App. 854, 399 S.E.2d 705, 13 UCC2d 1058 (1990) (finding that the owner of a grain silo had "entrusted" its contents to his own manager, who was therefore able to pass good title when he sold the contents as his own); Morgold, Inc. v. Keeler, 891 F.Supp. 1361, 27 UCC2d 315 (N.D. Cal. 1995) (agency, at least).

4. For example, through another Code BFP provision, e.g., § 9–307.

5. See generally, L. Vold, Handbook of the Law of Sales § 79 (2d ed.1959).

6. The concept of a shelter principle is recognized in § 3–203(b) and in Comment 2 to § 3–203.

7. See, e.g., Linwood Harvestore, Inc. v. Cannon, 427 Pa. 434, 235 A.2d 377, 4 UCC 920 (1967); Aircraft Trading & Services, Inc. v. Braniff, Inc., 819 F.2d 1227, 3 UCC2d 1297 (2d Cir.1987); Toyota Motor Credit Corp. v. C.L. Hyman Auto Wholesale, Inc., 256 Va. 243, 506 S.E.2d 14, 37 UCC2d 1022 (1998). But to get any title, a transferee must take "under a transaction of purchase". See Met–Al, Inc. v. Hansen Storage Co., 844 F.Supp. 485, 23 UCC2d 1135 (E.D. Wis. 1994).

8. Compare § 3–201, Comment 1.

The shelter which 2–403 provides is not unlimited (although no limitations are spelled out in the section). For example, does a purchaser who buys at a "distress" sale get the benefit of the shelter principle? There is a dispute about this.[9] It will be left to the courts to evolve limitations on the 2–403 shelter principle.

b. Good Faith Purchasers

Section 2–403(1) enhances the title that transferors with "voidable title" give when their transferees are good faith purchasers for value. The section provides: "A person with voidable title has power to transfer a good title to a good faith purchaser for value." Several issues arise. What constitutes voidable title? Who qualifies as a good faith purchaser? What constitutes value? Some of these answers lie outside of the Code.

Section 1–204 defines value broadly. Almost any purchaser[10] (as defined in sections 1–201(29) and 1–201(30)), except a donee, gives value. Satisfaction of an antecedent debt is value. Value itself is rarely a hurdle.[11] The amount of value given, however, may be relevant to the purchaser's good faith. For example, in Hollis v. Chamberlin,[12] an individual bought a camper from a dealer in one city (with a check that eventually bounced) and resold the camper to another dealer in a different town a few days later. The court considered the value given by the second dealer ($500 for a new camper worth at least $1000) and the buyer's failure to observe dealer standards (he did not ask for a certificate of title) and concluded that as a matter of law the second dealer did not qualify as an "innocent purchaser for value."

Good faith is defined in section 1–201(20) and in 2–103(1)(b). The meaning of good faith has been the subject of litigation in

9. Compare In re Dennis Mitchell Indus., Inc., 419 F.2d 349, 6 UCC 573, 7 UCC 112 (3d Cir.1969) (shelter principle applies to sale by bankruptcy trustee) with R. Anderson, Uniform Commercial Code § 2–403:9 (2d ed.1970) (no shelter principle at judicial sales). We favor the Third Circuit view.

10. While § 1–201(29) and (30) include mortgagees, lien holders and pledgees as purchasers, at least one court has reached the questionable conclusion that a fraudulent purchaser cannot grant a good security interest to a good faith lender against the property, in part because of the sufficient rights in collateral requirement of 9–203. See South Mississippi Finance Co. v. Mississippi State Tax Comm'n, 605 So.2d 736, 17 UCC2d 766 (Miss.1992). Contra, Evergreen Marine Corp. v. Six Consignments of Frozen Scallops, 806 F.Supp.

291, 19 UCC2d 449 (D.Mass.1992), rev'd on other grounds, 4 F.3d 90, 21 UCC2d 502 (1st Cir.1993) (fraudulent purchaser of scallops transferred enforceable property rights to secured creditor).

11. Werhan v. Pinellas Seafood Co., 404 So.2d 570, 31 UCC 1320 (Ala.1981) (partial satisfaction of pre-existing debt is value); Lavonia Mfg. Co. v. Emery Corp., 52 B.R. 944, 41 UCC 1172 (E.D.Pa.1985) (secured parties give value when they take after-acquired security interest in property in exchange for pre-existing debt).

12. 243 Ark. 201, 419 S.W.2d 116, 4 UCC 716 (1967). See also Kotis v. Nowlin Jewelry, Inc., 844 S.W.2d 920, 19 UCC2d 1067 (Tex.App.1992) (purchaser of Rolex watch worth $8,000 paid $3,550, not acting in good faith).

every branch of commercial law where it applies. We set out only a handful of cases here,[13] and we caution anyone who is confident about the meaning of good faith to reconsider.

Under 2–403, voidable title should be distinguished from void title. A thief, for example, "gets" only void title and without more cannot pass any title to a good faith purchaser.[14] "Voidable title" is a murky concept. The Code does not define the phrase. The comments do not even discuss it. Subsections (1)(a)–(d) of 2–403 clarify the law as to particular transactions which were "troublesome under prior law." Beyond these, we must look to non-Code state law.[15] In general voidable title passes to those who lie in the middle of the spectrum that runs from best faith buyer at one end to robber at the other. These are buyers who commit fraud, or are otherwise guilty of naughty acts (bounced checks), but who conform to the appearance of a voluntary transaction; they would never pull

13. See, e.g., In re Samuels & Co., 510 F.2d 139, 16 UCC 577 (5th Cir. 1975), rev'd 526 F.2d 1238, 18 UCC 545 (1976) (bad faith because knew financial status; decision on this point doubtful); Ellsworth v. Worthey, 612 S.W.2d 396, 31 UCC 897 (Mo.App.1981) (buyer who takes car without certificate of title has not acted in good faith and cannot be BOC). But see In re Tom Woods Used Cars, Inc., 21 B.R. 560, 34 UCC 518 (Bankr.E.D.Tenn.1982) (buyers of used cars who did not demand title certificates were still acting in good faith);

See also, Liles Bros. & Son v. Wright, 638 S.W.2d 383, 34 UCC 1174 (Tenn. 1982) (not good faith purchase when purchaser of backhoe knew true market price and paid only half of that, bill of sale was blank purchase order, and purchaser received no warranty papers which he knew were standard on a new machine); Shell Oil Co. v. Mills Oil Co., 717 F.2d 208, 37 UCC 116 (5th Cir.1983) (contention that bank knew that plaintiff had not been paid for products sold to its debtor was not sufficient to raise good faith issue); Richter v. United States, 663 F.Supp. 68, 4 UCC2d 722 (S.D.Fla.1987) (buyer in bad faith where seller, a complete stranger, required payment in nine separate checks made payable to a third party unknown to buyer); Hodges Wholesale Cars v. Auto Dealer's Exchange, 628 So.2d 608, 24 UCC2d 482 (Ala. 1993) (purchaser in good faith under 2–403(1)); Creggin Group, Ltd. v. Crown Diversified Ind., 113 Ohio App.3d 853, 682 N.E.2d 692,

34 UCC2d 980 (1996) (purchaser in good faith under 2–403(1)).

14. See, e.g., Allstate Ins. Co. v. Estes, 345 So.2d 265, 21 UCC 1032 (Miss.1977); Marvin v. Connelly, 272 S.C. 425, 252 S.E.2d 562, 26 UCC 370 (1979) (defendant sold stolen vehicle to plaintiff; no title passed even though defendant himself did not know that vehicle was stolen when he brought foreclosure action on his mechanic's lien and received title that way); Candela v. Port Motors Inc., 208 A.D.2d 486, 617 N.Y.S.2d 49, 25 UCC2d 681 (1994) (purchaser from thief); Ryan v. Patterson & Son Motors, 726 So.2d 667, 38 UCC2d 793 (Ala. App. 1998) (no transaction of purchase under 2–403(1) so no title acquired thereby).

15. See, e.g., Inmi–Etti v. Aluisi, 63 Md.App. 293, 492 A.2d 917, 40 UCC 1612 (1985) (when court found no 2–403(1)(a)–(d) situations, it turned to state law of Maryland; court found, on unclear records, that owner never voluntarily transferred car to Y, irrespective of the fact that X obtained titled certificate from state authorities); Green v. Arcadia Financial Ltd., 174 Misc.2d 411, 663 N.Y.S.2d 944, 36 UCC2d 89 (1997) (seller of car who forged release of lien conveyed void title). Compare Creggin Group, Ltd. v. Crown Diversified Industries Corp., 113 Ohio App.3d 853, 682 N.E.2d 692, 34 UCC2d 980 (1996) (purchaser with bad check gets voidable title under 2–403); Allan Nott Enterprises, Inc. v. Nicholas Starr Auto, 2005 WL 696839, 56 UCC2d 820 (Ohio App. 2005)

a gun or crawl in through a second story window. Presumably these fraudulent buyers get voidable title from their targets, but second story men get only void title because the targets of fraud are themselves more culpable than the targets of burglary. In Kenyon v. Abel, the court held that voidable title cannot arise under 2–403(1) where the goods were wrongfully taken.[16]

Subsection (1)(a) of 2–403 deals with impersonation. Where the transferor is deceived as to the identity of the purchaser, voidable title passes to the "deceiver" and the "deceiver" thus acquires power to pass good title to a good faith purchaser for value.[17]

Subsection (1)(b) of 2–403 deals with a more common occurrence: the "rubber check." Even when Bert Buyer pays Sam Seller with a check that returns to Sam marked "NSF," a good faith purchaser from Bert takes good title.[18]

Subsection (1)(c) of 2–403 deals with "cash sales." Thus, even where Bert and Sam agree that no title will pass to Bert until Sam gets paid, Bert, under 2–403(1)(c), acquires voidable title and power to pass good title to a good faith purchaser.[19]

Subsection (1)(d) of 2–403 provides that even where delivery was procured through criminal fraud, voidable title passes. Thus if Bert acquired goods from Sam with a forged check, a good faith purchaser from Bert would obtain good title.[20]

(person with voidable title can transfer good title).

16. Kenyon v. Abel, 36 P.3d 1161, 46 UCC2d 660 (Wyo. 2001). See also, Moore Equipment Co. v. Halferty, 980 S.W.2d 578, 37 UCC2d 1008 (Mo. App. 1998) (thief did not have voidable title or power to transfer title to good faith purchaser).

17. See, e.g., Phelps v. McQuade, 220 N.Y. 232, 115 N.E. 441 (1917). But see Met–Al, Inc. v. Hansen Storage Co., 828 F.Supp. 1369, 21 UCC2d 1107 (E.D.Wis. 1993) (where possession is obtained by the fraudulent representation that the defrauder is acting as an agent for a third party, goods are treated as obtained by theft, and void, not voidable, title is obtained).

18. See, e.g., Central Bank, N.A. v. American Charms, Inc., 149 Ga.App. 218, 253 S.E.2d 857, 26 UCC 377 (1979); Los Angeles Paper Bag Co. v. James Talcott, Inc., 604 F.2d 38, 27 UCC 394 (9th Cir.1979); Burk v. Emmick, 637 F.2d 1172, 29 UCC 1489 (8th Cir.1980); Rufenacht v. Iowa Beef Processors, Inc., 492 F.Supp. 877, 29 UCC 1522

(N.D.Tex.1980), aff'd, 656 F.2d 198 (5th Cir.1981), cert. denied, 455 U.S. 921, 102 S.Ct. 1279, 71 L.Ed.2d 462 (1982); Mitchell Motors v. Barnett, 249 Ga.App. 639, 549 S.E.2d 445, 46 UCC2d 655 (2001) (bad check).

19. See, e.g., Matter of Samuels & Co., 526 F.2d 1238, 18 UCC 545 (5th Cir.1976), cert. denied, 429 U.S. 834, 97 S.Ct. 98, 50 L.Ed.2d 99 (1976); Big Knob Volunteer Fire Co. v. Lowe & Moyer Garage, Inc., 338 Pa.Super. 257, 487 A.2d 953, 40 UCC 1691 (1985) (seller who ordered and received, but did not pay for chassis of fire truck, had power to transfer all rights to buyer).

20. See, e.g., Atlantic Mut. Ins. Co. v. A–Leet Leasing Corp., 1976 WL 23719, 18 UCC 1199 (N.Y.Sup.1976); Paccar Financial Corp. v. J.L. Healy Constr. Co., 561 F.Supp. 342, 36 UCC 639 (D.S.D.1983) (distinguishes between fraudulently obtained certificate of title and fraudulent conveyance of vehicle); Marlow v. Conley, 787 N.E.2d 490, 50 UCC2d 712 (Ind. App. 2003) (dealer got voidable title and transferred good title).

In determining voidable title, some courts have focused on 2–403(1)'s phrase "transaction of purchase."[21] Thus, in Paschal v. Hamilton,[22] a wrongdoer acquired a car with a forged check. The court considered the transfer a "transaction of purchase" and thus distinguished it from theft and the like.[23] In another case, the court treated a lease that was a disguised conditional sales contract as a transaction of purchase.[24] Where the one purporting to give good title is a lessee, the governing rule is section 2A–305. Under that section a defrauded buyer usually gets only the lessee's interest and takes subject to the lease.

c. *Entrustment*

Subsections (2) and (3) of 2–403 deal with "entrusting."[25] The provisions are relatively straightforward. In the words of the official Comment: "The many particular situations in which a buyer in ordinary course of business from a dealer has been protected against reservation of property or other hidden interest are gathered by subsections (2)–(4) into a single principle protecting persons who buy in ordinary course out of inventory." This principle runs throughout the Code and explicitly appears in 2–403, 2A–305, 7–205 and 9–320.

Subsection 2–403(2) of Unamended Article 2 provides:

Any entrusting of possession of goods to a merchant who deals in goods of that kind gives him power to transfer all rights of the entruster to a buyer in ordinary course of business.

Four questions are raised by the entrustment provisions. First, what constitutes "entrusting of possession of goods?" Second, who qualifies as a "merchant" dealing in goods of that kind? Third, what "rights" are transferred? And finally, who is a "buyer in ordinary course of business?"

Section 2–403(3) broadly defines entrustment to include "any delivery[26] and any acquiescence in retention of possession."[27] In

21. Alabama Great Southern RR. Co. v. McVay, 381 So.2d 607, 29 UCC 767 (Miss.1980) (where oil dealer A made unsolicited fuel delivery to RR, but oil dealer B billed and received payment from RR for that delivery, there was no "transaction of purchase" between A & B, and B therefore passed no title to RR; thus, RR could not assert 2–403 defense against A).

22. 363 So.2d 1360, 25 UCC 154 (Miss.1978).

23. § 2–403 does not operate to pass good title to stolen goods.

24. See, e.g., United Road Machinery Co. v. Jasper, 568 S.W.2d 242, 24 UCC 610 (Ky.App.1978).

25. See generally, Levy, Outer Limits of Entrusting, 35 Ark.L.Rev. 50 (1981).

26. A mistaken donation of the family silver to Goodwill does not constitute entrustment because there can be no delivery without awareness. Kahr v. Markland, 187 Ill.App.3d 603, 135 Ill. Dec. 196, 543 N.E.2d 579, 10 UCC2d 355 (1989).

27. § 2–403(3) states in full:

addition, the subsection incorporates 2–403(1)(a)–(d).[28] Entrusting usually falls into one of four common fact patterns. First, Ernie Entruster turns his car over to Dave Dealer so that Dave can sell it for Ernie.[29] A buyer in ordinary course takes free of Ernie's ownership rights.[30] Second, a wholesaler gives Dealer the goods "on consignment" or under a "floor planning" agreement. A buyer in ordinary course from Dealer is not bound by any "title retention" agreement between Dealer and the wholesaler as to passage of title.[31] Third, George leaves goods to be repaired with Dealer who resells them to a buyer in ordinary course.[32] Finally, Edgar buys goods from Dealer but leaves the goods in Dealer's hands. A buyer in ordinary course cuts off George's and Edgar's interests.[33] Of course, not every case falls into one of these four "standard" fact patterns.[34]

(3) "Entrusting" includes any delivery and any acquiescence in retention of possession regardless of any condition expressed between the parties to the delivery or acquiescence and regardless of whether the procurement of the entrusting or the possessor's disposition of the goods have been such as to be punishable under the criminal law.

28. The language of subsection (3) as well as Comment 2 to § 2–403 imports § 2–403(1)(b)–(d) into the entrustment provisions. As for § 2–403(1)(a), although one case requires that the entrustor know the person is a merchant, Atlas Auto Rental Corp. v. Weisberg, 54 Misc.2d 168, 281 N.Y.S.2d 400, 4 UCC 572 (1967), the better view holds that there can be valid entrustment even if the entrustor was deceived as to the acquiring party's identity. See also Heinrich v. Titus–Will Sales, Inc., 73 Wash. App. 147, 868 P.2d 169, 23 UCC2d 1143 (1994) (entrustment of car).

29. The UCC transfer of title scheme occasionally, but by no means always, runs up against state motor vehicle registration laws. See Hicks v. Thomas, 516 So.2d 1344, 6 UCC2d 105 (Miss.1987) (failure of owner to endorse title certificate precluded "innocent purchaser" from obtaining good title); Dugdale of Nebraska, Inc. v. First State Bank, 227 Neb. 729, 420 N.W.2d 273, 6 UCC2d 111 (1988) (bank entrusted floor planned cars to dealer, purchaser gets good title though bank held title certificates).

30. See, e.g., Palmer v. Booth & Cowley, Ltd., 1970 WL 12564, 7 UCC 182 (N.Y.Sup.1970); Byrne Fund Management, Inc. v. Jim Lynch Cadillac,

Inc., 922 S.W.2d 434, 29 UCC2d 821 (Mo. App. 1996) (entrustment to merchant).

31. See, e.g., In re Novak, 1969 WL 11107, 7 UCC 196 (Md. Cir.Ct. 1969); Williams v. Western Surety Co., 6 Wash. App. 300, 492 P.2d 596, 10 UCC 122 (1972).

32. See, e.g., General Electric Credit Corp. v. Western Crane & Rigging Co., 184 Neb. 212, 166 N.W.2d 409, 6 UCC 67 (1969); Litchfield v. Dueitt, 245 So.2d 190, 9 UCC 244 (Miss.1971); Perez–Medina v. First Team Auction, Inc., 206 Ga. App. 719, 426 S.E.2d 397, 20 UCC2d 473 (1992) (tractor delivered to dealer for repairs, entrusted and purchaser received good title).

33. See, e.g., Simson v. Moon, 137 Ga.App. 82, 222 S.E.2d 873, 18 UCC 1191 (1975); Shacket v. Roger Smith Aircraft Sales, Inc., 497 F.Supp. 1262, 30 UCC 148 (N.D.Ill.1980), aff'd, 681 F.2d 506, 33 UCC 1648 (7th Cir.1982) (sale of aircraft to third party by dealer, when dealer had never paid for aircraft); DeWeldon, Ltd. v. McKean, 125 F.3d 24, 33 UCC2d 835 (1st Cir. 1997) (buyers in ordinary course); Bank One, Milwaukee v. Loeber Motors, Inc., 293 Ill.App.3d 14, 227 Ill.Dec. 629, 687 N.E.2d 1111, 35 UCC2d 482 (1997) (failed observe standards of fair dealing in trade so not buyer in ordinary course). Consider, too, §§ 2–326 and 9–307.

34. E.g., Gallagher v. Unenrolled Motor Vessel River Queen, 475 F.2d 117, 12 UCC 131 (5th Cir.1973) (renting a stall at a marina not entrusting); Mer-

In addition, problems arise because the Code does not define "possession."[35] In determining whether there is possession for the purpose of entrustment the court should look to the dealer's appearances of control over the goods. The Comments to both 2–403 and 9–320 refer to "inventory", but nothing in the sections themselves or the Code definition of "buyer in ordinary course" requires the goods to be physically located in a seller's inventory.[36]

The 2–403 requirement of a "merchant that deals in goods of that kind" restricts the Code definition of merchant in 2–104. Unlike the 2–104 definition, which turns on the person's skill or knowledge, the concern of 2–403 is with a narrower class based on appearances.[37] An individual buying a product from an apparent dealer in such goods expects to get good title. This expectation facilitates exchange. One cannot ascertain the seller's title without slowing commerce. One expects to get good title when buying a shiny new car from a General Motors dealer. On the other hand, one buying goods from a mere warehouseman trying to recover storage costs knows that the seller is dealing with somebody else's goods.[38] Similarly, a buyer is expected to know that a broker deals with goods that are not the broker's own.[39]

Section 2–403(2) gives to the merchant the power to transfer all of the entruster's rights to the goods and to transfer the goods free of any interest of the entruster to a buyer in ordinary course.[40]

cedes–Benz Credit Corp. v. Johnson, 110 Cal.App.4th 53, 1 Cal.Rptr.3d 396, 51 UCC2d 168 (2003) (lessor does not "entrust" to lessee).

35. California, for example, has limited a merchant's power to entrust by adding the words "for the purpose of sale, obtaining offers to purchase, locating a buyer, or the like" following the words "retention of possession" in 2–403(3).

36. See, e.g., Fuqua Homes, Inc. v. Evanston Bldg. & Loan Co., 52 Ohio App.2d 399, 370 N.E.2d 780, 23 UCC 19 (1977) (dealer need not have physical possession). Cf., DePaulo v. Williams Chevrolet–Cadillac, Inc., 1965 WL 8372, 3 UCC 600 (Pa.C.P.1965) (broker's lack of possession a factor in denying purchaser BOC status); Schneider v. J.W. Metz Lumber Co., 715 P.2d 329, 42 UCC 1648 (Colo.1986) (goods need not be physically located in seller's inventory).

37. Comment 2 to § 2–104, third paragraph, speaks of a restricted class of merchants for § 2–403(2).

38. See, e.g., Mercantile Financial Corp. v. Bloom, 1971 WL 17928, 63 Berks 180, 9 UCC 1216 (Pa.C.P.1971); Chartered Bank of London v. Chrysler Corp., 115 Cal.App.3d 755, 171 Cal.Rptr. 748, 30 UCC 1438 (1981) (boat in possession of owner's warehouse agent was not entrusted). But entrusting includes leaving goods with a dealer for repair. See Alamo Rent–A–Car v. Mendenhall, 113 Nev. 445, 937 P.2d 69, 34 UCC2d 664 (1997). See also, Jones v. Mitchell, 816 So.2d 68, 46 UCC2d 1000 (Ala. App. 2001) (entrustment to dealer).

39. See, e.g., Toyomenka, Inc. v. Mount Hope Finishing Co., 432 F.2d 722, 8 UCC 21 (4th Cir.1970); Kusler v. Cipriotti v. Darling Yacht Sales, Inc., 221 N.J.Super. 654, 535 A.2d 567, 5 UCC2d 492 (1987) (pleasure boat not part of inventory when dealer was owner's broker).

40. Sunnyland Employees' Federal Credit Union v. Fort Wayne Mortgage Co., 182 Ga.App. 5, 354 S.E.2d 645, 3 UCC2d 1383 (1987) (repossessing bank could not entrust mobile home to dealer where title certificate indicated that original defaulting debtors were owners).

Also, section 2–403(1) converts voidable title to good title and in conjunction with the "shelter principle" expands the merchant's power to transfer title. In addition, sections like 9–317(b), 9–320 and 2–326 provide for priority over security interests in some cases.

A particularly thorny issue arises where a buyer in the ordinary course purchases an item subject to a security interest not created by the seller. In re Sunrise R.V., Inc.[41] was such a case. There, the dealer sold a used motor home to a good faith purchaser that was still subject to a security interest granted by the previous owner who had traded the motor home into the dealer. The court correctly found that 9–307(1) (now 9–320) only frees a buyer in the ordinary course from security interests granted by the seller (here, the dealer). Since the secured party had not "entrusted" the motor home to the dealer, section 2–403 did not apply and the purchaser did not take free of the security interest.

Possible conflict between 2–403 and sections like 9–320 is considerable; so beware. The interplay (and potential for conflict) between relevant sections can be readily illustrated: Stereo Manufacturer, sells compact disc players to Jobber, for a check that later bounces. Jobber, well aware of risks in credit transactions, in turn sells the compact disc players to Wholesaler, for "cash on the barrelhead." Wholesaler consigns the compact disc players to Retailer, retaining a perfected security interest. Retailer then sells a compact disc player to a buyer in ordinary course of business. Buyer gets good title. When Wholesaler purchased the compact disc player from Jobber, Wholesaler received good title under 2–403(1)(b). The ultimate sale in ordinary course of business to the consumer cut off the Wholesaler's security interest (9–320) and gave the buyer the rights of Retailer, namely a clear title. Of course, Manufacturer has a right of action against Jobber for the bum check, and Wholesaler can go after the Retailer for violating their consignment agreement, but our buyer can listen in peace.

Sections 2–403(1) and (2) could play havoc with the more narrow and precise rules in 2A–305 and 9–320. A court should respect the fences between these articles; it does that by applying 2A–305 whenever the seller is a lessee and by applying 9–320 whenever the buyer's competitor is a perfected secured creditor.

Finally, who qualifies as a "buyer in ordinary course of business?" The Code, in section 1–201(9), sets forth a definition.[42] That

---

41. 105 B.R. 587, 10 UCC2d 210 (Bankr.E.D.Cal.1989).

42. § 1–201(9) provides:

"Buyer in ordinary course of business" means a person who in good faith and without knowledge that the sale violates the rights of another person in the goods, and in the ordinary course from a person, other than a pawnbroker, in the business of selling goods of that kind. A person buys goods in the ordinary course if the sale to the person comports with the usual or customary practices in the kind of business in which the seller is engaged or with the seller's own usual

definition is fairly straightforward and the cases so indicate. Cases interpreting "good faith purchaser" under 2–403(1) and "buyer in ordinary course of business" under 2–403(2) and 9–320 deal with similar policy issues—the cutting off of third party property interests. Judicial glosses on the definitions often apply equally under Articles 9 and 2.[43]

Whether a purchaser qualifies as a buyer in ordinary course is said to be a mixed question of fact,[44] and the circumstances surrounding the purchase are, of course, relevant.[45] Additionally, if the purchaser is a merchant, it must meet a higher standard with regard to imputed knowledge.[46] Generally, however, to disqualify the purchaser, it is necessary to show that the purchaser had "knowledge that the sale to him [was] in violation of the ownership rights * * * of a third party,"—not just knowledge that a third party had some interest.[47]

or customary practices. A person that sells oil, gas, or other minerals at the wellhead or minehead is a person in the business of selling goods of that kind. A buyer in ordinary course of business may buy for cash, by exchange of other property, or on secured or unsecured credit, and may acquire goods or documents of tile under a pre-existing contract for sale. Only a buyer that takes possession of the goods or has a right to recover the goods from the seller under Article 2 may be a buyer in ordinary course of business. "Buyer in ordinary course of business" does not include a person that acquires goods in a transfer in bulk or as securityfor or in total or partial satisfaction of a money debt.

43. See generally, Skilton, Buyer in Ordinary Course of Business under Article 9 of the Uniform Commercial Code (and Related Matters), 1974 Wis.L.Rev. 1.

44. See, e.g., Associates Discount Corp. v. Rattan Chevrolet, Inc., 462 S.W.2d 546, 8 UCC 117 (Tex.1970); Cosid, Inc. v. Bay Steel Products Co., 252 So.2d 274, 9 UCC 690 (Fla.App.1971).

45. See, e.g., DePaulo v. Williams Chevrolet–Cadillac, Inc., 1965 WL 8372, 3 UCC 600 (Pa.C.P.1965) (buyer required to pay prior to delivery and dealer not in possession—held not BOC); Madrid v. Bloomington Auto Company, Inc., 782 N.E.2d 386, 49 UCC2d 795 (Ind. App. 2003) (failure of buyer to request certificate of title at time of sale did not preclude BOC status); Brasher's Cascade Auto Auction v. Valley Auto Sales and Leasing, 119 Cal.App.4th

1038, 15 Cal.Rptr.3d 70, 53 UCC2d 990 (2004) (buyer who is merchant must observe reasonable commercial standards to be BOC).

46. See, e.g., Mattek v. Malofsky, 42 Wis.2d 16, 165 N.W.2d 406, 6 UCC 277 (1969); Sherrock v. Commercial Credit Corp., 277 A.2d 708, 9 UCC 294 (Del.Super.1971), rev'd 290 A.2d 648, 10 UCC 523 (1972); Swift v. J.I. Case Co., 266 So.2d 379, 11 UCC 190 (Fla.App.1972), cert. denied, 271 So.2d 147 (Fla.1972) Aircraft Trading & Services, Inc. v. Braniff, Inc., 819 F.2d 1227, 3 UCC2d 1297 (2d Cir.1987) (seller generally not in the business of selling its own capital equipment; airline, though frequent seller of its used aircraft engines, was not a seller in the ordinary course).

47. See, e.g., Correria v. Orlando Bank & Trust Co., 235 So.2d 20, 7 UCC 937 (Fla.App.1970); Dowell v. Beech Acceptance Corp., 4 Cal.App.3d 748, 84 Cal.Rptr. 654, 7 UCC 545 (1970), rev'd, 3 Cal.3d 544, 91 Cal.Rptr. 1, 476 P.2d 401, 8 UCC 274 (1970), cert. denied, 404 U.S. 823, 92 S.Ct. 45, 30 L.Ed.2d 50 (1971); Blackhawk Pontiac Sales, Inc. v. Orr, 84 Ill.App.3d 456, 39 Ill.Dec. 746, 405 N.E.2d 499, 29 UCC 838 (1980) (licensed used car dealer who accepted cars knowing they were not paid for by seller was not good faith purchaser); The requirement of knowledge of a violative sale arises under the § 1–201(9) definition. That it is reiterated in § 9–320 should not affect its application in § 2–403. But see, Exxon Company, U.S.A. v. TLW Computer Indus., Inc.,

In addition to good faith, 1–201(9) sets forth other require-ments. A purchaser from a pawnbroker cannot qualify as a buyer in ordinary course of business. Unlike 2–403(1) which requires only that the purchaser give "value," the buyer in ordinary course of business provision restricts the allowable consideration. For exam-ple, a foreclosing creditor or a party transferring security for a money debt[48] does not qualify as a buyer in ordinary course.[49]

§ 4–13 Assignment and Delegation

The assignment of rights and the delegation of duties in sales contracts is treated in section 2–210. Section 2–210 favors free assignability of rights and delegation of duties except where the rights and duties of the contracting parties are significantly altered. Case law under 2–210 is not plentiful, but the Restatement of Contracts (Second) offers guidance.

Free assignability of contractual rights[1] was contrary to early common law.[2] Historically, contractual rights, as well as all other choses in action, were not assignable. They were considered person-al rights that by their nature could not be assigned. The assign-ment of contractual rights was also prohibited at early common law because it was thought to commit "maintenance"—the offense of tending to spur litigation. With the rise of commercial business in the seventeenth century, these rules began to erode. With the Uniform Commercial Code, outright sales of contractual rights are common. Former Comment 4 to old § 9.318 explained "as accounts and other rights under contracts have become the collateral which secure an ever increasing number of financial transactions, it has been necessary to reshape the law so that these intangibles * * *

1983 WL 160563, 37 UCC 1052 (D.Mass. 1983) (customer was aware that comput-er was not in seller's inventory at time of sale, and $310,000 price should have signalled to commercial customer that seller-broker's license was necessary—thus no BOC).

48. See § 1–201(9).

49. See, e.g., Wesgo Division of GTE Products Corp. v. Harrison, 648 F.2d 252, 31 UCC 887 (dicta) (5th Cir.1981) (secured creditor cannot be BOC under 2–403(3), although he can be good faith purchaser under 2–403(1)); In re Sitkin Smelting & Refining, Inc., 639 F.2d 1213, 30 UCC 1566 (5th Cir.1981) (transfer of security for money debt was not "buying" and thus, no BOC).

§ **4–13**

1. Despite the frequent use of term "contract right" in the literature to re-fer to a right arising under a contract,

this discussion will employ the phrase "contractual right." This is because the term "contract right" had a special meaning under the 1962 version of Arti-cle 9 and Comment 3 to § 2–210 specifi-cally remarks that the scope of § 2–210 does not extend to "contract rights." Since "contract rights" were subsumed in "accounts" in the 1972 version of Article 9, we are not sure of the remain-ing significance of the statement.

2. For the history of assigning and delegating choses in action see W.S. Holdsworth, The History of the Treat-ment of Choses in Action by the Com-mon Law, 33 Harv.L.Rev. 997, 1016–1030 (1920); Farnsworth, Contracts § 11.2 (1982).

can be freely assigned."[3] Section 2–210, thus, reflects the requirements of modern commercial business.[4]

Section 2–210 does not state all the law on the assignment and delegation of contractual rights and duties.[5] It clarifies those areas that were especially unclear or where there were splits in the case law.[6]

The section does not even define its basic terms. To some extent the Restatement (Second) of Contracts fills this void by defining both "assignment" and "delegation" in reference to section 2–210.[7] Although the term "assignment" is often used to mean both transfer of rights and the delegation of performance, the Restatement and section 2–210 draw a sharp distinction between "assignment" and "delegation." According to the Restatement, an "assignment" is the transfer of a *right* (only) by its owner (sometimes "the obligee" or "assignor") to another person (the "assignee") whereby the assignee acquires a right to performance by the obligor and the assignor's right to that performance is extinguished.[8] A duty, in contrast, cannot be "assigned" because a person subject to a duty, an obligor, does not have the power to extinguish the duty and transfer it to someone else without the consent of the obligee.[9] The performance of a duty, however, can be "delegated." A delegation, as the Restatement explains, is the transfer of the performance of a duty to another, a delegatee, with the expectation that the delegatee will perform in lieu of the obligor. The obligor remains liable to perform until the duty has been discharged.[10] Below we consider the legal consequences of "assignments" and "delegations" more fully.

Section 2–210 addresses three topics: (1) rules concerning the assignment of rights, 2–210(2); (2) rules about the delegation of the performance of duties, 2–210(1) and (5); and (3) rules of construction to resolve ambiguity, 2–210(3) and (4).

---

3. § 9–318 Comment 4 (referring to § 9–318(4), which addresses the same issue as § 2–210(2) second sentence within the context of Article 9—making ineffective terms of contracts which prohibit certain types of assignments). The same idea is now expressed in 9–406(d).

4. § 2–210 Comment 1. See generally Baxter Healthcare v. O.R. Concepts, Inc., 69 F.3d 785, 27 UCC2d 1185 (7th Cir. 1995).

5. § 2–210 Comment 7.

6. § 2–210 Comment 7. In the words of the drafters, "neither this section nor this Article, touches directly on such questions as the need or effect of notice of the assignment, the rights of succes-sive assignees, or any question of the form of an assignment, either as between the parties or as against any third parties." *Id.*

7. Restatement (Second) of Contracts § 316 Comment c; § 9–406.

8. Restatement (Second) of Contracts § 316 Comment c; § 9–402.

9. Restatement (Second) of Contracts § 316 Comment c; § 9–406. Such consent is called a novation. The necessity of a novation to relieve the obligor of its duty is discussed later in this section.

10. Restatement (Second) of Contracts § 316 Comment c; § 9–406.

a. Assignment of Rights

The assignment of rights is generally allowed under section 2–210.[11] This reflects the code's underlying assumption that "limitations on the power to transfer contract rights restricts commercial activity."[12] The most noteworthy example of mercantile transfer is accounts receivable financing. By allowing account receivables to be used to secure loans, business people turn dormant accounts into working capital.[13] Sections 9–404, 9–405 and 9–406 of Article Nine generally reinforce this mode of financing (and are discussed extensively in volume 4 of the fifth edition of this treatise).

But overriding reasons may prohibit assignment. Section 2–210(2) appears to state four exceptions to free assignability; as we will see, three of these exceptions seem really to be only variations on a single theme. The first is "where the assignment would materially change the duty of the other party."[14] To determine what "materially changes the duty of the other party," the Restatement states that one must look to the nature of the contract and to the circumstances surrounding it.[15] Notwithstanding the ad hoc nature of this inquiry, one can generalize to some extent about when a duty is or is not materially changed. For instance, when the duty of the other party is to pay money, an assignment will usually not materially change this duty.[16] An illustration that the Restatement gives is that if B contracts to support A for the remainder of A's life, A cannot assign to C a right to have B support C for the rest of C's life.[17] A and C are different people with different life spans and needs, and assignment would materially change B's (the *other* party's) duty.

Before the Code was widely enacted, the assignment of a requirements contract would have often fallen under the "material change of duty" exception. The textbook case of Crane Ice Cream Co. v. Terminal Freezing and Heating,[18] decided in 1925, is illustrative. In *Crane*, Frederick assigned his rights under a requirements contract with the defendant.[19] The contract required the defendant to provide Frederick with all the ice he needed in his business with a 250 ton ceiling.[20] The court, reacting to the fact that the assign-

---

11. § 2–210(2), first sentence. See Baxter Healthcare Corp. v. O.R. Concepts, Inc., 69 F.3d 785, 27 UCC2d 1185 (7th Cir. 1995). See also, § 9–404.

12. Traffic in Contract Rights and Duties—Assignment and Delegation, 105 U.Pa.L.Rev. 906, 907 (1957). See also UCC § 9–318 Comment 4.

13. *Id.* at 909–910.

14. § 2–210(2), first sentence. Accord, Restatement (Second) of Contracts § 317(2)(a).

15. Restatement (Second) of Contracts § 317 Comment d.

16. *Id.*

17. Restatement (Second) of Contracts § 317 Comment d, illus. 3.

18. 147 Md. 588, 128 A. 280 (1925).

19. *Id.* at 281.

20. *Id.*

ment "set up a new measure of ice to be supplied and so a new term in the agreement,"[21] held that the contract was too personal to be assigned and, thus, that the assignment was ineffective.[22]

The result might be different under the Code. Comment 4 to section 2–210 suggests that section 2–306(1) sets limits to what can be demanded under requirement contracts. It holds that only "actual * * * requirements as may occur in good faith" may be requested, and further that "no quantity unreasonably disproportionate to any stated estimate or in the absence of a stated estimate to any normal or otherwise comparable prior * * * requirements may be * * * demanded."[23] Because an assignee cannot demand an amount of goods that unreasonably strays from the assignor's estimated or actually required amount, absent other considerations, the result should be that the buyer's rights under most requirements contracts are assignable.[24]

Continental Can Co. v. Poultry Processing, Inc.[25] involved a requirements contract that was assigned under section 2–210. The court found an assignment of rights to receive "those cans necessary for the canning season then underway" to be effective and, thus, the assignee's promise to pay for those cans to be enforceable.[26] The court reasoned that the quantity term of the contract would be sufficiently definite to enforce unless the demanded quantities were unreasonably disproportionate to either stated estimates or to prior or normal requirements.[27] Since disproportion was not alleged, the court found the assignee liable to pay for the cans it promised to purchase.[28]

The second exception to free assignability is similar to the prohibition of assignments that cause "material changes in duty" of the other party. The second exception prevents effective assignments where the assignment would "increase materially the burden or risk imposed on [the other party] by his contract."[29] Although it is listed as a separate exception, it is unclear when an assignment of a right would cause a "material increase of the burden or risk imposed by the obligor's contract" and would not bring about a "material change in duty."[30] A case that has prohibited assignment

21. *Id.* at 283.

22. *Id.* at 284.

23. § 2–306(1).

24. For more on this point see § 2–210 Comment 4.

25. 649 F.Supp. 570, 3 UCC2d 31 (D.Me.1986).

26. *Id.* at 575.

27. *Id.*

28. *Id.*

29. § 2–210(2), first sentence. Accord Restatement (Second) of Contracts

§ 317(2)(a). See In re Clark v. BP Oil Co., 137 F.3d 386, 35 UCC2d 440 (6th Cir. 1998) (assignment did not materially increase risk); Nedwick Steel Company, Inc., 289 B.R. 95, 50 UCC2d 736 (Bankr. N.D. Ill. 2003) (invalid because materially increased risk); Compare Clapp v. Orix Credit Alliance, Inc. 192 Or. App. 320, 84 P.3d 833, 52 UCC2d 1016 (2004).

30. With a delegation of the performance of a duty, it is clearer when an increased burden or risk need not be a material change in duty. For example,

under the exception is Kaiser Aluminum & Chemical Corp. v. Ingersoll–Rand Co.[31] *Kaiser* held that warranties are not assignable in Georgia because any assignment of warranty would "materially change the risks and burdens of the original seller."[32] The *Kaiser* court could have prohibited the assignment also because it would have "materially changed the duty of the other party."

The third exception to free assignability of contractual rights in section 2–210 arises when the assignment would "impair materially [the other party's] chance of obtaining return performance."[33] The exact meaning of this exception is not clear. One interpretation is that an assignment is prohibited when it increases the other party's risk (of not receiving return performance) under the contract. According to this interpretation, however, the third exception is merely a replay of the second.[34] A case on the third exception is Tennell v. Esteve Cotton Co.[35] The court, in dicta, explained that a mere failure of the assignor to give the obligor notice of the assignment did not constitute a "material impairment of the chance of receiving return performance."[36] *Tennell* does not cast light on when an assignment would be prohibited under the third exception.

Comment d to section 317 of the Restatement notes that material impairment is most likely to occur where there is also an "improper delegation":[37]

> The clause on material impairment of the chance of obtaining return performance operates primarily in cases where the assignment is accompanied by an improper delegation under section 318 or section 319: If the obligor is to perform in exchange for the promise of one person to render a return

the performance delegated could be the repaying of a loan. While the duty of the other party may remain the same, that party's risk under the contract (the loan) might change materially. With an assignment of a right, however, it is unclear how the other party (the obligor) could have an increased burden or risk with regard to the assigned right unless the associated duty is somehow affected.

31. 519 F.Supp. 60, 32 UCC 1369 (S.D.Ga.1981).

32. *Id.* at 73–74. In contrast see Clark v. BP Oil Co., 137 F.3d 386, 35 UCC2d 440 (6th Cir.1998) (Franchisor assigned its contract with franchisee, and assignee raised price of gas, which harmed franchisee; this did not "materially increase the franchisee's risks and burdens under 2–210" because original

franchisor could have raised prices to same levels).

33. § 2–210, first sentence. Restatement (Second) of Contracts § 317(2)(a).

34. And, accordingly, encounters the above criticisms of the second exception.

35. 546 S.W.2d 346, 21 UCC 978 (Tex.Civ.App.1976).

36. *Id.* at 352 n.3.

37. Restatement (Second) of Contracts § 317 Comment d. See also, In re Nedwick Steel Company, Inc., 289 B.R. 95, 50 UCC2d 736 (Bankr. N.D. Ill. 2003) (party should not be forced to accept performance from a competitor); Clapp v. Orix Credit Alliance, Inc., 192 Or.App. 320, 84 P.3d 833, 52 UCC2d 1016 (2004) (contractual prohibition of transfer construed to bar only delegation of performance).

performance at a future time, substitution of the return performance of another impairs the obligor's expectation of counterperformance.

The final instance where section 2–210 prohibits assignment is when the parties have "otherwise agreed."[38] In other words, when the parties agree that the obligee cannot assign its rights, it cannot. But several courts have enforced assignments in the face of anti-assignment agreements. For example, some courts have distinguished between rights to money and other contractual rights, and have held only the latter to be restricted by the contract provisions.[39] Other courts drew a line between rights arising under a contract and rights arising from a breach of a contract.[40]

Section 2–210(2) broke from most earlier contract law[41] by allowing assignment "despite agreement otherwise": "A right to damages for breach of the whole contract or a right arising out of the assignor's due performance of his entire obligation can be assigned despite agreement otherwise."[42] To see how a right for breach of the whole might be assigned, suppose that A holds an industrial insurance policy issued to A by Insurance Company; the policy lapses because A fails to pay premiums. Insurance Company then refuses to pay the cash surrender value still due under the policy. Because Insurance Company breached the entire contract by refusing to repay the cash value, A and others in the same position can assign their claims to C for collection without regard to any contractual prohibition of assignment.[43] Similar examples can be imagined arising from the sale of goods.

38. § 2–210(2). Accord Restatement (Second) of Contracts § 317(2)(c).

39. See, e.g., Omaha v. Standard Oil Co., 55 Neb. 337, 75 N.W. 859 (1898); Dixon–Reo Co. v. Horton Motor Co., 49 N.D. 304, 191 N.W. 780 (1922); Trubowitch v. Riverbank Canning Co., 30 Cal.2d 335, 182 P.2d 182 (1947). See generally Traffic in Contract Rights—Assignment and Delegation, 105 Pa.L.Rev. 906 (1957).

40. See, e.g., Trubowitch v. Riverbank Canning Co., 30 Cal.2d 335, 182 P.2d 182 (1947); Fuller v. Favorite Theaters Co., 119 Utah 570, 230 P.2d 335 (1951).

41. See Restatement of Contracts § 151(c) (1932) ("A right may be the subject of effective assignment unless * * * the assignment is prohibited by the contract creating the right."). In the original Restatement there was no section equivalent to Restatement (Second) of Contracts § 322 creating exceptions to § 151(c).

See also, e.g., Crane Ice Cream Co. v. Terminal Freezing & Heating Co., 147 Md. 588, 128 A. 280 (1925) ("[T]he law accords to every man freedom of choice in the party with whom one deals, and the terms of his dealing. He cannot be forced to do a thing which he did not agree to do because it is like and no more burdensome than something which he did contract to do.").

42. § 2–210(2), second sentence. Accord Restatement (Second) of Contracts § 322(2)(a) But an assignee may be subject to an arbitration provision in the underlying contract. Cone Constructors, Inc. v. Drummond Community Bank, 754 So.2d 779, 41 UCC2d 82 (Fla.App. 1st Dist, 2000).

43. Restatement (Second) of Contracts § 322 Comment b, illus. 1 (based on the case National Life & Acc. Ins. Co. v. Magers, 319 S.W.2d 53 (Mo.App. 1958), aff'd, 329 S.W.2d 752 (Mo.1959)).

Second, one cannot restrict the assignability of "a right arising out of the assignor's due performance of his entire obligation." Suppose buyer agrees to buy 200 fruitcakes from seller. Suppose further that buyer fully performs under the contract by paying $600, the full price. When seller refuses to deliver the fruitcakes, buyer assigns its rights to C. Regardless of any contractual prohibition of assignment, the assignment to C is effective.[44]

The power of obligees to disregard the terms of their contracts and assign their rights troubled one court that had to address this Code provision frontally. In Mingledorff's, Inc. v. Hicks[45] the Air Conditioning and Heating Service Company contracted with the defendant Hicks to provide and install a heating and air conditioning system in an apartment complex.[46] After fully performing under the contract, Air Conditioning assigned the part of the money due to Mingledorff's without the consent of Hicks. The contract prohibited the assignment of the contract or any part of it. Mingledorff's sued and alleged that the anti-assignment clause was invalid under section 2–210(2). The court declined to apply section 2–210(2) to the assignment. Finding that the contract at issue was one for "services and labor with [only] an incidental furnishing of equipment and materials," it held that Article 2 did not apply and found that the rights were not assignable.[47] Under section 9–406(d) of Article 9, important terms in agreements are ineffective that prohibit, restrict, or require the consent of the account debtor or person obligated on a note to the assignment or transfer or the creation, attachment, perfection or enforcement of a security interest in the account, chattel paper, payment intangible, or promissory note or impose various other limits.

What are the consequences of assigning rights when their assignment is prohibited by contract? Section 2–210(2) says that the assignment can be effective. Does the assignment break the contract? One might argue that the Code strikes the prohibition out of the contract.[48] On the other hand, one might attribute a smaller chore to 2–210—to bless the assignment's effectiveness (i.e., recognizing the assignee's rights) without nullifying any other effect of the prohibition (i.e., simultaneously treating the assignor as in breach because of the assignment). We have found no cases squarely in point. The Restatement appears to take the second approach. Section 322(2) of the Restatement states that:

44. The example is adapted from Restatement (Second) of Contracts § 322 Comment b, illus. 2 (similar facts except in the illustration the object of sale was land).

45. 133 Ga.App. 27, 209 S.E.2d 661, 15 UCC 763 (1974).

46. 209 S.E.2d at 662.

47. Id.

48. As in § 2–302(1) where the court "may enforce the remainder of the contract without the unconscionable clause".

A contract term prohibiting assignment of rights under the contract, unless a different intention is manifested,

    (a) does not forbid assignment of a right to damages for breach of the whole contract or a right arising out of the assignor's due performance of his entire obligation;

    (b) gives the obligor a right to damages for breach of the terms forbidding assignment but does not render the assignment ineffective.

If subsections (a) and (b) are read conjunctively, then the Restatement appears to espouse the second approach—that even an effective assignment is a breach. In effect the Restatement is saying to the obligor: you must pay the assignee, but if you can prove damages, recover them from the obligee.[49]

b. Delegation of the Performance of Duties

Assignment of rights is one thing, delegation of duties is another. As long as work is performed by the person who has agreed to perform it, the person who has agreed to pay may be indifferent whether he pays to that person, to that person's bank, or some other assignee. The obligee is more likely to be concerned when Michelangelo delegates the painting to an assistant, a heart surgeon brings in an intern, or when a tested and trusted mechanic assigns the repair of a car to a third person. In many cases one chooses a contracting party because of that person's particular skill, reliability, or reputation. Unless that person or one under his supervision is to perform the contract, the obligee will be denied what has been promised. On the face of it, section 2–210 treats assignment and delegation as more or less the same, but in reality they are different.

Subsection (1) to 2–210 reads in full as follows:

A party may perform his duty through a delegate unless otherwise agreed or unless the other party has a substantial interest in having his original promisor perform or control the acts required by the contract. No delegation of performance

---

49. Assignments of express warranties have troubled the courts. While the courts agree that the breach of warranty claims are assignable, they differ as to whether the assignment of the express warranty rights themselves are assignable. In Kaiser Aluminum & Chemical Corp. v. Ingersoll–Rand Co., 519 F.Supp. 60, 32 UCC 1369 (S.D.Ga.1981) the court held that all assignments of express warranty rights are prohibited.

Several other courts, however, have either permitted their assignment or have held that the assignment of express warranty rights is not per se invalid. These latter courts have treated express warranty rights like any other right to assign. See Gold'n Plump Poultry, Inc. v. Simmons Eng'g Co., 805 F.2d 1312, 2 UCC2d 1232 (8th Cir.1986) (assignments of warranty rights are authorized under 2–210, however, for an effective assignment there must be a contract of assignment and not just the sale of the warranted item).

relieves the party delegating of any duty to perform or any liability for breach.

Note two things about subsection (1). First, the test is whether the obligee had a "substantial interest" in having the original promisor perform or control the acts required by the contract. Obviously, the more performance depends upon the particular skill and talent of the promisor the more likely the promisee "has a substantial interest" in having that person perform the act. It is obvious, too, that people can differ about when and under what circumstances there is that kind of reliance on the promisor.

Note the second sentence; delegation does not discharge the original party. If things work out badly, the original party will be a proper defendant—small satisfaction if the wedding pictures have been bungled or the heart was installed backwards.

The reasons why a promisee might have a substantial interest in the promisor's performance are many and varied. For example, in Aslakson v. Home Savings Association[50] the lender was held to "have a substantial interest" in having the obligor perform its mortgage. This was true despite the fact that the original mortgagor would have remained liable and the performance involved no particular skill but was simply the payment of money. In another case the assignee was a subsidiary of a direct competitor, and the court found a substantial interest in having the assignor perform instead.[51]

Under section 2–210(1) an agreement not to delegate is binding. Here too the drafters recognize the obligee's concern about delegation to be different from its concern about assignment. Section 2–210 and other law overrides some prohibitions on assignment. Prohibitions on delegation are treated differently; they are valid and not overridden by the law.

Note, finally, the protection in Unamended section 2–210(6):

> The other party may treat any assignment which delegates performance as creating reasonable grounds for insecurity and may without prejudice to his rights against the assignor demand assurances from the assignee (Section 2–609).

In this section the delegation is an *ipso facto* basis for insecurity and gives a right to demand assurances.

In summary, section 2–210 continues the common law's suspicion of delegation of duties. It proceeds on the hypothesis that most contracts are made with a particular party for a particular purpose and that the duties under those contracts should not lightly be

---

50. 416 N.W.2d 786, 6 UCC2d 35 (Minn.App.1987).

51. Sally Beauty Co. v. Nexxus Products Co., 801 F.2d 1001, 2 UCC2d 82 (7th Cir.1986).

delegated. Some might argue that this law and the cases under it reflect a pre-industrial suspicion of third parties and that they should be cast aside in modern industrial society where many— with the aid of modern technology—can perform the same act with the same ability. We are not sanguine about the many. Our experience tells us that performance even as simple as a plumber's changing a pipe or an electrician's changing a switch may depend upon reliability and skill of the tradesman. Neither consumers nor business persons routinely accept delegation—even of simple tasks of that sort. Thus we share the courts' and the Code's suspicion of delegation and anticipate that delegation of duties will continue to be treated quite differently from assignment of rights.

c. Rules of Construction

What if the contract does not use the technical language of the Code and the Restatement? Careful lawyers will speak of assignment of rights and delegation of duties, but lay persons may not. Unamended section 2–210(5) construes general language to be both an assignment of rights and a delegation of duties:

> An assignment of "the contract" or of "all my rights under the contract" or an assignment in similar general terms is an assignment of rights and unless the language or the circumstances (as in an assignment for security) indicate the contrary, it is a delegation of performance of the duties of the assignor and its acceptance by the assignee constitutes a promise by him to perform those duties. This promise is enforceable by either the assignor or the other party to the original contract.

There are several useful tidbits in the language of subsection (4). First, acceptance of the duty by the assignee "constitutes a promise to perform." Thus, the original party need not look further for a promise from the assignee and need not look to the common law dealing with third party beneficiaries; the assignee is liable as though the assignee signed the contract. Either the assignor or the assignee may enforce the contract.[52]

Circumstances may show no intention to delegate the duty, the parenthetical phrase gives an example—an assignment for security. Both the statute and the comment segregate assignments for security. Many courts have relied on the security aspect of assignment in holding performance of the assignor's duties were not delegated.[53] Finally, section 2–210(3) reads a prohibition against assign-

---

52. See Hyosung America, Inc. v. Sumagh Textile Co., Ltd., 137 F.3d 75, 34 UCC2d 930 (2d Cir. 1998) (party that accepted assignment of X's rights and interests also assumed X's duties under the contract).

53. Pendarvis v. General Motors Corp., 1969 WL 11059, 6 UCC 457

(N.Y.Sup.1969); Richter, S.A. v. Bank of America Nat. Trust and Sav. Ass'n, 939 F.2d 1176, 16 UCC2d 681 (5th Cir.1991); BAII Banking Corp. v. UPG, Inc., 985 F.2d 685, 20 UCC2d 155 (2d Cir.1993).

ment of "the contract" to bar only delegation and not an assignment of rights.

Section 2–210 and the related sections of the Restatement Contracts sections 316, 317, and 318 set out a comprehensive body of rules that will answer many lawyer questions. In general they indorse assignment. They are more skeptical of delegation and they have a variety of presumptions and rules of construction to help us deal with ambiguous terms.

Chapter 5

UNCONSCIONABILITY

Analysis

§ 5–1 Introduction

In preparing this chapter we had once attempted to discuss all of the legal doctrines courts use in policing sales. By "policing" we meant a court's refusal to enforce all the terms of a contract, or its award of damages against the allegedly over-reaching party to the contract either because that party engaged in fraud or kindred conduct in procuring the other party's agreement or because the terms as agreed upon were oppressive, contrary to public policy, or illegal. We soon realized that a radically diverse array of legal doctrine fits under the "policing" umbrella. Not only do fraud and unconscionability fit there, but so do the tort of misrepresentation, some warranty liability, illegality, and various statutory duties that the federal Consumer Credit Protection Act,[1] the Retail Installment Sales Acts, and the Uniform Consumer Credit Code impose, as well as much more. Despite our best efforts, we were unable to tame all of this doctrine—certainly not for purposes of a single chapter in this book. The task demands a book of its own. Here we can only catalog most of the policing doctrines as a prelude to digging into

§ 5–1

1. Act of 1968, Pub.L. No. 90–321, 82 Stat. 151 et seq.; 15 U.S.C.A. §§ 1601–1681 (1974).

253

the UCC unconscionability section at length.[2] These opening paragraphs on several cognate policing doctrines will remind the reader that unconscionability is only one member of a large family of doctrines that restricts unbridled freedom of contract and protects against numerous forms of advantage taking.

Fraud is a most ancient and well-recognized doctrine[3]—one that is at least a first cousin to the doctrine of unconscionability—but today law schools, treatise writers, lawyers, and courts are in their own way sometimes neglectful of fraud theory. Indeed it is now commonplace for lawyers to sue for breach of warranty and negligence, and entirely omit a count in fraud even when that theory might be the most plausible avenue of relief. Unlike unconscionability, the gist of which is often said to be *defensive,* fraud is often a plaintiff's weapon as well as a defendant's. Presumably most fraud is more heinous than unconscionable conduct and would also constitute unconscionable behavior that could be attacked under 2–302, but the reverse is not necessarily true. To prove fraud, one typically must show that the misstatement or other behavior of the defendant (1) related to a material matter of fact, (2) was made deceitfully with intent to induce reliance, (3) induced justifiable reliance (4) as a result of which the relying party suffered damages.[4] Fraud is a case law doctrine that varies from state to state and our four part list of elements will not hold true in all states or in all circumstances.

Closely allied to fraud is liability for misrepresentation and for breach of an express warranty. Depending upon local law, the plaintiff's case in fraud or misrepresentation may be identical but this is not necessarily so. The plaintiff may find that it can prove misrepresentation without proof of some of the factors that it must prove in order to sustain a case of fraud.[5] Likewise, express warran-

---

2. For a sample of the voluminous literature on § 2–302, see Leff, Unconscionability and the Code—The Emperor's New Clause, 115 U.Pa.L.Rev. 485 (1967); Murray, Unconscionability: Unconscionability, 31 U.Pitt.L.Rev. 1 (1969); Ellinghaus, In Defense of Unconscionability, 78 Yale L.J. 757 (1969); Spanogle, Analyzing Unconscionability Problems, 117 U.Pa.L.Rev. 931 (1969); Braucher, The Unconscionable Contract or Term, 31 U.Pitt.L.Rev. 337 (1970); Leff, Unconscionability and the Crowd—Consumers and the Common Law Tradition, 31 U.Pitt.L.Rev. 349 (1970); Dawson, Unconscionable Coercion: The German Version, 89 Harv.L.Rev. 1041 (1976); Schwartz, Re-examination of Nonsubstantive Unconscionability, 63

Va.L.Rev. 1053 (1977); Hillman, Debunking Some Myths About Unconscionability: A New Framework for U.C.C. Sections 2–302, 67 Cornell L.Rev. 1 (1981). See also Swanson, Unconscionable Quandary: UCC Article 2 and the Unconscionability Doctrine, 31 N.M.L.Rev. 359 (2001); Brown, The Uncertainty of U.C.C. Section 2–302: Why Unconscionability has Become a Relic, 105 Comm.L.J. 287 (2000); Barnhizer, Inequality of Bargaining Power, 76 Colo. L. Rev. 139 (2005). See also articles cited in § 5–9 *infra.*

3. See W. Prosser et al., Prosser and Keeton on Torts § 105 (5th ed.1984).

4. *Id.* at 728.

5. *Id.* at 727–29.

ty liability flows much more readily from a merely inaccurate statement than does fraud liability.[6]

The Code also offers section 1–304, which imposes a general obligation of good faith, as a weapon against various forms of advantage taking.[7] We have sought elsewhere to corral that complex obligation.[8] It goes without saying that a lawyer may also invoke various notions long recognized in general contract law, such as undue influence, duress, and mistake to combat contractual over-reaching. Finally, a contract term may be illegal because it violates the usury statutes or the provisions in the Uniform Consumer Credit Code or other statutes which explicitly outlaw certain terms. Finally, a contract term may simply be invalid as contrary to public policy.

No lawyer who seeks to undo a contract or to recover damages on the basis of unconscionability should rely exclusively on that doctrine until he or she has considered and rejected each of the foregoing possibilities. A careful lawyer who asserts that a contract or term is unconscionable will also test the facts against the various cognate doctrines we have just cataloged.

§ 5–2   Unconscionability in General

For at least two hundred years equity courts have refused to grant specific enforcement of, or have rescinded, contracts so unconscionable "as no man in his senses and not under delusion would make on the one hand, and as no honest and fair man would accept on the other."[1] The doctrine of unconscionability is enshrined in case law and in the statutory law of forty-nine states.[2]

Section 2–302 reads in full as follows:

(1) If the court as a matter of law finds the contract or any clause of the contract to have been unconscionable at the time it was made the court may refuse to enforce the contract, or it may enforce the remainder of the contract without the uncon-

---

6. *Id.* at 729.

7. § 1–201(b)(20) supplies a general definition of good faith.

8. Summers, "Good Faith" in General Contract Law and the Sales Provisions of the Uniform Commercial Code, 54 Va.L.Rev. 195 (1968).

§ 5–2

1. Earl of Chesterfield v. Janssen, 2 Ves.Sr. 125, 28 Eng.Rep. 82, 100 (Ch. 1750).

2. California omits § 2–302. Though California omitted § 2–302 when adopting the Code, the doctrine is part of the

state's common and statutory law. See, e.g., A & M Produce Co. v. FMC Corp., 135 Cal.App.3d 473, 186 Cal.Rptr. 114, 34 UCC 1129 (1982). The court in this case also relied on the general unconscionability statute incorporated in 1979 into the California Civil Code as § 1670.5 (West 1985).

Louisiana has not adopted any of Article 2, of the Code, but the doctrine is applied through various sections of the state's Civil Code.

scionable clause, or it may so limit the application of any unconscionable clause as to avoid any unconscionable result.

(2) When it is claimed or appears to the court that the contract or any clause thereof may be unconscionable the parties shall be afforded a reasonable opportunity to present evidence as to its commercial setting, purpose and effect to aid the court in making the determination.

Most courts do not confine section 2–302 to sales of goods.[3] But some do.[4]

For a case applying 2–302 by analogy consider Waters v. Min Ltd.,[5] where the court struck down as unconscionable the assignment of an annuity policy for $50,000. The policy was worth $189,000 at the time of assignment and it would ultimately return $694,000. The twenty-one-year-old plaintiff was influenced by her boyfriend to assign the policy to defendants. The boyfriend, who had introduced the plaintiff to drugs, acted as the defendants' agent and benefitted from the assignment.

Many of the cases that apply 2–302 by analogy arise from leases. Those are now governed by section 2A–108. It adopts the basic concept of 2–302, but it has some important additions too.

As a preamble let us lay out the battlefield upon which the 2–302 battles are fought. Most who assert 2–302 and most who have used it successfully in reported cases have been consumers. Most of these successful consumer litigants have been poor or otherwise disadvantaged. Since much literature suggests that the low-income consumer is often the victim of sharp practices,[6] it is not surprising that the targets of the unconscionability doctrine are usually plaintiff-creditors and credit sellers. The courts have not generally been receptive to pleas of unconscionability by one merchant against another. Presumably, few business persons and middle-class cash purchasers are victims of the kinds of gross advantage-taking that

---

3. See, e.g., Murphy v. McNamara, 36 Conn.Sup. 183, 416 A.2d 170, 27 UCC 911 (1979) (even if agreement was a true lease rather than conditional sale, it was a "transaction in goods" and hence 2–302 applies); All–States Leasing Co. v. Ochs, 42 Or.App. 319, 600 P.2d 899, 27 UCC 808 (1979) (where lease was intended as security transaction, unconscionability of lease provision could be raised under 2–302); Gonzalez v. A–1 Self Storage, Inc., 350 N.J.Super. 403, 795 A.2d 885, 41 UCC2d 1119 (Ct. Law Div. 2000) (applied 2–302 to rental of storage space).

See also Honey Dew Associates, Inc. v. M & K Food Corp., 81 F. Supp. 2d 352, 41 UCC2d 149 (D.R.I. 2000) (2–302 is applicable to "all aspects of a franchise agreement by analogy").

4. See, e.g., Troy Mining Corp. v. Itmann Coal Co., 176 W.Va. 599, 346 S.E.2d 749, 2 UCC2d 1248 (1986) (2–302 does not apply to contracts for services, although the common law concept of unconscionability may).

5. 412 Mass. 64, 587 N.E.2d 231, 17 UCC2d 381 (1992). See also Arthur v. Microsoft Corp., 267 Neb. 586, 676 N.W.2d 29, 53 UCC2d 195 (2004).

6. See, e.g., H. Black, Buy Now Pay Later (1967); W. Magnuson & J. Carper, The Dark Side of the Marketplace (1968); D. Caplovitz, The Poor Pay More (1979).

usually calls forth 2–302.[7] In the next six sections of this chapter our treatment focuses mainly on the bearing of unconscionability on the rights of consumers. We turn in Section 5–9 to its impact in commercial settings.

§ 5–3 Procedure and Procedural Unconscionability

Before exploring the substance of the unconscionability doctrine, consider some of its procedural facets. Subsection (1) assigns the issue of unconscionability exclusively to the judge.[1] Although it would be useful for the defendant to plead unconscionability as an affirmative defense, the words of 2–302(1) also seem to permit a court to raise the issue *sua sponte*.[2] Furthermore, the party raising the issue has the burden of proof—at least according to most courts[3]—and must show that the contract or term was unconscionable at the time of contracting. That it appear unconscionable at the time of performance is irrelevant. The test is not by hindsight.[4]

The section specifically authorizes three forms of relief: (1) the court may refuse to enforce the entire contract, (2) or a part of it, or (3) the court may limit the application of a particular term to prevent an unconscionable result. The doctrine generally dresses as an affirmative defense and is not usually intended as a basis for damage recovery.[5] (There are other and as yet undeveloped possibilities for other remedies such as injunction and punitive damages.)

---

7. See, e.g., Buettner v. Super Laundry Machinery, 857 F.Supp. 471, 23 UCC2d 79 (E.D. Va. 1994), aff'd 47 F.3d 116, 25 UCC2d 1086 (4th Cir. 1995). See however, American General Financial Services Inc. v. Griffin, 327 F.Supp.2d 678, 54 UCC2d 408 (N.D. Miss. 2004). See, Mallor, Unconscionability in Contracts between Merchants, 40 Sw.L.J. 1065 (Nov.1986).

§ 5–3

1. Mieske v. Bartell Drug Co., 92 Wash.2d 40, 593 P.2d 1308, 26 UCC 262 (1979) (matter of law, error harmless that jury was not instructed that exclusionary clause not binding.); Rite Color Chem. Co. v. Velvet Textile Co., 105 N.C.App. 14, 411 S.E.2d 645, 18 UCC2d 384 (1992) (question of law); Krupp PM Engineering, Inc. v. Honeywell, Inc., 209 Mich.App. 104, 530 N.W.2d 146, 26 UCC2d 742 (1995) ("matter of law" for court). See generally Price, Conscience of Judge and Jury: Statutory Unconscionability as a Mixed Question of Law and Fact, 54 Temp.L.Q. 743 (1981). UCCC § 5.108 similarly reserves these

issues for the court, but the Consumer Credit Protection Act, of 1968, Pub. L.No. 90–321, 82 Stat. 146 et seq., 15 U.S.C.A. §§ 1601–81, 1640 (1974), leaves questions concerning nondisclosure of credit terms to the jury.

2. Cf. Kohlenberger, Inc. v. Tyson's Foods, Inc., 256 Ark. 584, 510 S.W.2d 555, 14 UCC 1281 (1974); Barco Auto Leasing Corp. v. PSI Cosmetics, Inc., 125 Misc.2d 68, 478 N.Y.S.2d 505, 39 UCC 840 (1984) (while party did not plead unconscionability as affirmative defense, court deemed matter at issue).

3. Geldermann & Co. v. Lane Processing, Inc., 527 F.2d 571, 18 UCC 294 (8th Cir.1975).

4. For a case providing a model of systematic analysis, see Bruce v. ICI Americas, Inc., 933 F.Supp. 781, 29 UCC2d 796 (S.D. Iowa 1996) (assent, unfair surprise, notice, disparity of bargaining power, and substantive unfairness.)

5. See, e.g., W.L. May Co., Inc. v. Philco–Ford Corp., 273 Or. 701, 543 P.2d 283, 18 UCC 599

Subsection (2) permits the alleged oppressor to show that the contract or term was reasonable in light of the commercial setting. On several occasions appellate courts have reversed findings of unconscionability because the trial court failed to offer such an opportunity to the alleged oppressor.[6] Exactly what a seller proves that might persuade a skeptical judge is not so clear. As Professor Leff so cleverly suggested, seller's reason for using the clause—to "have an extra hook in buyer" or the like—is unlikely to win approval of a judge who mistrusts the market and favors judicial regulation.

Neither the Code nor the comments define the word *unconscionable*. Comment 1 to 2–302 suggests a litmus test for unconscionability which seems reasonably workable at first glance:

> [W]hether, in the light of the general commercial background and the commercial needs of the particular trade or case, the clauses involved are so one-sided as to be unconscionable under the circumstances existing at the time of the making of the contract.

The comment also says:

> The principle is one of the prevention of oppression and unfair surprise ... and not of disturbance of allocation of risks because of superior bargaining power.

Experimentation with even a single case shows this test to be nearly useless; in no sense is the Comment an objective definition of the word. It is simply a string of subjective synonyms covered with heavy and conclusory value gravy: "oppression," "unfair," or "one-sided." To the extent that the comment gives a message, it is an ambiguous one, for it acknowledges that the court in some circumstances has the power to overturn various terms in a contract, but it assures us that the purpose is not to disturb the allocation of risks. How a court can refuse to enforce certain contracts or terms that were formerly enforceable and not at the same time disturb the allocation of the risk because of superior bargaining power, is difficult to see.

It is not possible to *define* unconscionability. It is *not a concept, but a determination* to be made in light of a variety of factors not unifiable into a formula.[7] We now suggest a very general framework

---

6. In re E.F. Lynch, Inc. v. Piccirilli, 28 Mass.App.Dec. 49, 5 UCC 830 (1964); Elkins–Dell Mfg. Co., 253 F.Supp. 864, 3 UCC 386 (E.D.Pa.1966) (remanded to referee in bankruptcy); Toy Co. Salem, Inc. v. Wood, 109 Or.App. 265, 819 P.2d 312, 16 UCC2d 264 (1991) (trial court erred in concluding contract was unconscionable when issue was not pleaded or litigated; parties must have opportunity to argue and present evidence).

7. See Mieske v. Bartell Drug Co., 92 Wash.2d 40, 593 P.2d 1308, 26 UCC 262 (1979) (unconscionability not defined and numerous factors enter into its determination, but no one element is controlling).

for analysis. Professor Leff distinguished between "bargaining naughtiness" (procedural unconscionability) and overly harsh terms (substantive unconscionability).[8] Substantive unconscionability involves those one-sided terms of a contract from which a party seeks relief (for instance, "I have the right to cut off one of your child's fingers for each day you are in default"), while procedural unconscionability deals with the process of making a contract— "bargaining naughtiness" (for instance, "Just sign here; the small print on the back is only our standard form").[9] Each of these branches of unconscionability has common-law cousins; procedural unconscionability looks like fraud or duress during contract formation, and substantive unconscionability reminds us of contracts or clauses contrary to public policy or illegal. The two branches of unconscionability can be illustrated in the facts of Williams v. Walker–Thomas Furniture Co.,[10] an early, and still one of the preeminent cases under 2–302.

Although *Walker–Thomas* arose in the District of Columbia before the UCC had become effective in that jurisdiction, Judge Wright noted that Congress had enacted 2–302 to govern contracts in the District of Columbia, and he relied upon it in his decision. The appellant Mrs. Williams was a welfare mother with seven children and a monthly income of $218; she had purchased $1800 of merchandise from Walker–Thomas over a period of several years. For each purchase Mrs. Williams signed an installment contract which included a complex cross-collateral agreement. This device provided that each payment would be credited pro rata to all purchases which Mrs. Williams had ever made from the store and which she had not paid for in full.[11] In other words, until the customer reduced her balance to zero, the store retained a security

---

8. Leff, Unconscionability and The Code—The Emperor's New Clause, 115 U.Pa.L.Rev. 485, 487 (1967). For cases invoking this analysis, see Industralease Automated & Scientific Equip. Corp. v. R.M.E. Enters., Inc., 58 A.D.2d 482, 396 N.Y.S.2d 427, 22 UCC 4 (1977); Constr. Assocs., Inc. v. Fargo Water Equip. Co., 446 N.W.2d 237, 10 UCC2d 821 (N.D. 1989).

9. See generally, Dugan, Standardized Forms: Unconscionability and Good Faith, 14 N.Eng.L.Rev. 711 (1979) which lays a foundation for a good faith unconscionability definition in standard form contracts. See also, Murray, The Standardized Agreement Phenomena in the Restatement (Second) of Contracts, 67 Cornell L.Rev. 735 (1982).

10. 350 F.2d 445, 2 UCC 955 (D.C.Cir.1965). See Colby, What did the Doctrine of Unconscionability do to the

Walker–Thomas Furniture Company? 34 Conn.L.Rev. 625 (2002).

11. The cross-collateral clause read as follows:

The amount of each periodical installment payment to be made by [purchaser] to the Company under this present lease shall be inclusive of and not in addition to the amount of each installment payment to be made by [purchaser] under such prior leases, bills or accounts; *and all payments now and hereafter made by [purchaser] shall be credited pro rata on all outstanding leases, bills and accounts* due the Company by [purchaser] at the time each such payment is made.

Id. at 447, 2 UCC at 956 (emphasis added by the court).

interest in every item it had sold her, no matter how long ago. Mrs. Williams' last purchase was a stereo set which cost $514.95. After she had paid the store more than $1400, Mrs. Williams defaulted, and the store filed an action to replevy all the items it had sold her. The trial court granted the judgment, and the Municipal Court of Appeals affirmed. The Circuit Court of Appeals reversed and remanded for findings on the issue of unconscionability.[12]

In discussing the standards courts must apply to determine whether a contract is unconscionable, Judge Wright touched upon both aspects of unconscionability:

> Unconscionability has generally been recognized to include an absence of meaningful choice on the part of one of the parties together with contract terms which are unreasonably favorable to the other party.[13]

A "meaningful choice" or its absence presumably bears upon procedural unconscionability; to characterize a term as "unreasonably favorable" to one party is probably to say that it is substantively unconscionable to the other party. Numerous cases include useful general discussions of the nature of unconscionability.[14] Nearly all are consistent with the foregoing analysis. Some emphasize disparity in sophistication of the parties. Others do not.

A judicial finding of lack of "meaningful choice," that is, of procedural unconscionability, is usually founded upon a recipe consisting of one or more parts of assumed consumer ignorance and several parts of seller's guile. For example in *Walker–Thomas*, Judge Wright emphasized the defendant's lack of education and the use of fine print by the seller in its contract form.[15] The cross-collateral clause the seller used in that case is so hard to understand that it regularly baffles first year law students who read it in

---

12. *Id.* at 450, 2 UCC at 960.

13. *Id.* at 449, 2 UCC at 958.

14. See, e.g., Geldermann & Co. v. Lane Processing, Inc., 527 F.2d 571, 18 UCC 294 (8th Cir.1975) ("inequality of bargaining power"). See also, Siemens Credit Corp. v. Marvik Colour, Inc., 859 F.Supp. 686, 24 UCC2d 705 (S.D.N.Y. 1994) (factors considered by New York courts in considering unconscionability are "disparity of bargaining power, an atmosphere of haste and pressure, and lack of understanding by one of the parties" which result in terms unreasonably favorable to one party); Pig Improvement Co., Inc. v. Middle States Holding Co., 943 F.Supp. 392, 31 UCC2d 422 (D. Del. 1996) ("experienced attorney and businessman" lost unconsciona-bility claim); Deminsky v. Arlington Plastics Machinery, 259 Wis.2d 587, 657 N.W.2d 411, 50 UCC2d 53 (2003) (conspicuous references to back of form, on back, not unconscionable).

See also American General Financial Services, Inc. v. Griffin, 327 F.Supp.2d 678, 54 UCC2d 408 (N.D. Miss. 2004) (not procedural unconscionability just because one party not sophisticated and so did not know what word "arbitration" meant).

15. Williams v. Walker–Thomas Furniture Co., 350 F.2d 445, 2 UCC 955 (D.C.Cir.1965). See also Tinsman v. Moline Beneficial Finance Co., 531 F.2d 815, 18 UCC 1056 (7th Cir.1976) (language in loan agreement did not describe type of security interest).

their contracts course. In Jefferson Credit Corp. v. Marcano,[16] a buyer who had "at best a sketchy knowledge of the English language"[17] signed an automobile installment sales contract which waived the implied warranties of merchantability and fitness for a particular purpose. The court found "it can be stated with a fair degree of certainty"[18] that the buyer neither knew nor understood that he had made such waivers, even though they were printed in large black type. In Seibel v. Layne & Bowler, Inc.[19] the court nullified an inconspicuous merger clause which effectively excluded oral warranties since unfair surprise made it unconscionable. Many of the cases are form contract cases.

The assumption of consumer ignorance may be based upon the consumer's proven inability to read the language in which the contract was printed, upon the consumer's proven lack of education or status as a poor person. We question whether these middle-class assumptions of the ignorance of poor people are warranted, but some courts seem willingly to indulge in these assumptions. Seller's guile often takes the form of a term difficult to understand and placed in fine print on the rear of the contract. But it may also take the form of fraud, high pressure sales tactics, and so on.

Explicit in this recipe of procedural unconscionability, of course, is the proposition that a clause procedurally unconscionable with respect to one person may not be unconscionable with respect to another who is better endowed with intelligence and education, or with the monetary trappings from which courts will infer such intelligence and education.

Several troublesome points lay just beneath the surface in the opinions that discuss procedural unconscionability. The opinions often emphasize the lack of bargaining power on the part of the consumer-debtor. Although these statements have usually been made in opinions dealing with consumers who are ignorant, poor, or both, the courts have not limited their discussion of bargaining power to such circumstances, and of course, even an intelligent middle-class consumer may have little bargaining power in a one-on-one situation against a sizeable organization.[20] The middle-class consumer's bargaining power presumably derives from his or her

16. 60 Misc.2d 138, 302 N.Y.S.2d 390, 6 UCC 602 (Civ.Ct.1969).

17. *Id.* at 141, 302 N.Y.S.2d at 393, 6 UCC at 605.

18. *Id.* at 141, 302 N.Y.S.2d at 393–94, 6 UCC at 605.

19. 56 Or.App. 387, 641 P.2d 668, 33 UCC 893 (1982), review denied, 293 Or. 190, 648 P.2d 852 (1982).

20. Cf. Henningsen v. Bloomfield Motors, Inc., 32 N.J. 358, 161 A.2d 69 (1960), in which the New Jersey Supreme Court held that a middle-class automobile purchaser had no real bargaining power when all auto manufacturers disclaim warranties on form contracts. This was a pre-Code case. Of course, it is much harder for a large and sophisticated entity to show unconscionability. See, e.g., Siemens Credit Corp. v. American Transit Ins. Co., 2001 WL 40775, 43 UCC2d 1180 (S.D.N.Y. 2001).

ability to shop and, if necessary, to whipsaw the sellers by using the offer of one as a bargaining lever against another. One can hope that courts will not be carried away by the "bargaining power" and "fine print" language of some of the opinions and so strike down the terms of garden variety contracts signed by middle-class consumers.[21] Certainly, the drafters did not intend 2–302 to invalidate these contracts wholesale. Although there may be good reason for departure from the fiction that a consumer who signs a long contract knows its terms, that departure should be made by the legislatures after due consideration of the consequences and not by judicial stretching of the unconscionability doctrine.

§ 5–4 Substantive Unconscionability

Passing to the question of substantive unconscionability, what do the cases disclose? Most of the cases in which the courts have found clauses to be substantively unconscionable can still be lumped under one of two headings: excessive-price cases and cases in which the creditor unduly restricted the debtors' remedies or unduly expanded its own remedial rights. Thus, substantive unconscionability alone can be enough. Here we consider only the cases falling under these headings.

§ 5–5 Substantive Unconscionability—Excessive Price

The leading case holding that excessive price can render a contract unconscionable continues to be American Home Improvement, Inc. v. MacIver.[1] MacIver, who may well have been a skinflinted New England Scot, signed an installment contract for the installation of windows and home siding. When the seller sued for payment, the court held that the contract was unenforceable because the seller had failed to comply with a state disclosure statute[2] and, alternatively, because the excessive price rendered the contract unconscionable. The court accepted the defendant's allegation that the goods sold and services rendered were worth $959 and concluded that the additional $800 of commission and $809 of finance charge resulted in an excessive price.[3] The court also noted that the

---

21. See Block v. Ford Motor Credit Co., 286 A.2d 228, 10 UCC 139 (D.C.App.1972) (plaintiff a "Ph.D. business executive"; lengthy agreement enforceable); Moorer v. Hartz Seed Co., 120 F.Supp.2d 1283, 43 UCC2d 295 (M.D. Ala. 2000) (sophisticated parties validly allocated risk).

§ 5–5

1. 105 N.H. 435, 201 A.2d 886, 2 UCC 235 (1964). See generally, Darr,

Unconscionability and Price Fairness, 30 Hous. L. Rev. 1819 (1994).

2. *Id*. at 438–39, 201 A.2d at 888, 2 UCC at 237.

3. *Id*. at 439, 201 A.2d at 888, 2 UCC at 237.

buyer "received little or nothing of value" since the plaintiffs did not perform the contract.[4]

In the second price case, Frostifresh Corp. v. Reynoso,[5] a Spanish-speaking consumer purchased a freezer for a total time price of $1,145.88. The defendants signed an installment contract written in English, but the salesperson neither translated nor explained the contract to them. The cash sales price for the freezer was $900 and its wholesale cost to the plaintiff had been $348. Without citing either *Walker–Thomas* or *MacIver,* the court found under 2–302 "that the sale of the appliance at the price and terms indicated in this contract is shocking to the conscience."[6] The court was also influenced by the fact that the salesperson had advised the buyers that the appliance would cost them nothing because they would be paid bonuses or commissions of $25 on each of the sales which were made to their friends.

Other New York cases have reaffirmed the *Frostifresh* decisions, and New Jersey and Connecticut cases have followed it. In State ex rel. Lefkowitz v. ITM, Inc.,[7] the court enjoined a comprehensive referral sales scheme which included price-value disparities comparable to those in the *MacIver* case. The prices charged in the retail installment contracts varied from two to six times the seller's unit costs, and the purchase price-market value ratio ranged to 2 1/2.[8] Jones v. Star Credit Corp.[9] held that:

> under the circumstances of this case, the sale of a freezer unit having a retail value of $300 for $900 ($1,439.69 including credit charges and $18 sales tax) is unconscionable as a matter of law.[10]

The purchaser had very limited financial resources and that fact was known to the door-to-door salesperson. According to the court this difference in financial status of seller and buyer caused a "gross inequality of bargaining power."[11] In a third case, Central Budget Corp. v. Sanchez,[12] because "[e]xcessively high prices may constitute unconscionable contractual provisions within the meaning of Sec. 2–302,"[13] the plaintiff-assignee was denied summary

---

4. *Id.* at 439, 201 A.2d at 886, 2 UCC at 238.

5. 52 Misc.2d 26, 274 N.Y.S.2d 757, 3 UCC 1058 (Dist.Ct.1966), rev'd on issue of relief, 54 Misc.2d 119, 281 N.Y.S.2d 964, 4 UCC 300 (1967). See Bender, Consumer Protection for Latinos: Overcoming Language Fraud and English–Only in the Marketplace, 45 Am. U.L. Rev. 1027 (1996).

6. 52 Misc.2d at 27, 274 N.Y.S.2d at 759, 3 UCC at 1059.

7. 52 Misc.2d 39, 275 N.Y.S.2d 303, 3 UCC 775 (1966).

8. *Id.* at 53, 275 N.Y.S.2d at 320, 3 UCC at 792.

9. 59 Misc.2d 189, 298 N.Y.S.2d 264, 6 UCC 76 (1969).

10. *Id.* at 191–92, 298 N.Y.S.2d at 266, 6 UCC at 78–79.

11. *Id.* at 192, 298 N.Y.S.2d at 267, 6 UCC at 79.

12. 53 Misc.2d 620, 279 N.Y.S.2d 391, 4 UCC 69 (Civ.Ct.1967).

13. *Id.* at 621, 279 N.Y.S.2d at 392, 4 UCC at 70.

judgment on his automobile sales contract action so that the defendant might present evidence showing unconscionability of price.[14]

The New Jersey case of Toker v. Westerman[15] follows the familiar pattern of a defendant who purchased an appliance from a door-to-door salesperson at a very high price. In that case the defendant had purchased a refrigerator-freezer for a cash price of $899.98. The total price including interest, insurance, *etc.* was $1,229.76. At trial an appliance dealer had testified that the freezer in question was known in the trade as a "stripped unit" and that a reasonable retail price at the time of the sale would have been between $350.00 and $400.00. The holding of the court rests exclusively on excessiveness of the price, and it reads as follows:

> Suffice it to say that in the instant case the court finds as shocking and therefore unconscionable, the sale of goods for approximately two and one-half times their reasonable retail value. This is particularly so where, as here, the sale was made by a door-to-door salesman for a dealer who therefore would have less overhead expense than a dealer maintaining a store or showroom.[16]

In the Connecticut case of Murphy v. McNamara,[17] the court held that a contract requiring a welfare recipient to pay $1248 on time for a television set which retailed at $499 called for an excessive price and violated the public policy of the State as embodied in UCC 2–302. The seller had not informed the buyer of the full-time price (again over 2 1/2 times the regular retail sales price) and was also guilty of an unscrupulous collection practice, having threatened the buyer with arrest.

In Sho–Pro of Indiana, Inc. v. Brown,[18] the Indiana Court of Appeals affirmed the trial court's decision that a contract for the sale of replacement windows which required buyer to pay four times the seller's cost was unconscionable. Buyer had responded to

14. *Id.* at 622, 279 N.Y.S.2d at 393, 4 UCC at 71. A trial court in New Jersey found an excessive price to be unconscionable in a case in which the price charged for a freezer was more than 2 ½ times its fair market value. Toker v. Perl, 103 N.J.Super. 500, 247 A.2d 701, 5 UCC 1171 (1968), aff'd, 108 N.J.Super. 129, 260 A.2d 244, 7 UCC 194 (1970). However, this was an alternative holding since the court also found that the contract was unenforceable because it had been procured by fraud—the buyers believed that they were contracting only for food, but in fact the salesperson procured their signatures on a contract for a freezer also. On appeal, the Appellate Division affirmed solely on the ground of fraud and refused to express an opinion on the unconscionability question. 108 N.J.Super. 129, 260 A.2d 244, 7 UCC 194 (1970).

15. 113 N.J.Super. 452, 274 A.2d 78, 8 UCC 798 (Dist.Ct.1970).

16. *Id.* at 454, 274 A.2d at 80, 8 UCC at 799–800.

17. 36 Conn.Sup. 183, 416 A.2d 170, 27 UCC 911 (1979).

18. 585 N.E.2d 1357, 17 UCC2d 56 (Ind.App.1992). See also, Maxwell v. Fidelity Financial Services, Inc., 184 Ariz. 82, 907 P.2d 51, 28 UCC2d 806 (1995).

a contest offered by seller and was subjected to a four-to-five hour demonstration of the replacement windows by seller's representatives. After this demonstration, buyer signed the contract, which had been prepared by seller, without reading it.

Clearly the foregoing cases do not mark the end of the development of the idea that excessive price can render a contract unconscionable. This idea is also embodied in the UCCC,[19] and one suspects that it may be the unarticulated premise that explains cases such as *Walker–Thomas*.

Determining which prices are excessive and which are not is an uncertain task since a court may use any one of several possible standards to measure "excess." The price might be said to be excessive because it returns too great a profit to the seller, or because it yields too great a return on the seller's invested capital, or because it is a substantially higher price than other merchants similarly or unsimilarly situated charge for like items. The courts in *MacIver* and *Frostifresh* used the crudest of all suggested tests: a price may be excessive merely because the mark-up is very large.[20] In *MacIver* the court determined that the price was excessive simply because the defendants were obligated to pay $2,568.60 for goods and services whose wholesale value was $959.00.[21] The New Hampshire court apparently did not consider whether the seller made any profit or what other merchants charged for comparable siding.

In other cases, for example, State ex rel. Lefkowitz v. ITM, Inc.,[22] Jones v. Star Credit Corp.,[23] and Toker v. Westerman,[24] courts have found prices to be excessive because they were higher than those charged by other merchants for the same or similar goods.[25] In *Westerman* the buyer proved that prices of competitors were lower. In *Jones* the court noted that the consumers were obligated to pay $1,439.69 ($539.60 of which was finance charges) for a refrigerator which was sold for $300 by W.T. Grant stores.[26]

---

19. UCCC § 6.111(3)(c).

20. In *Frostifresh* the court stated that "[t]he service charge, which almost equals the price of the appliance is in and of itself indicative of the oppression which was practiced on these defendants." 52 Misc.2d at 27, 274 N.Y.S.2d at 759, 3 UCC at 1059.

21. 105 N.H. at 439, 201 A.2d at 888, 2 UCC at 238. The court's method of determining the value of the goods and services was questionable. The sloppiness of the decision can perhaps be explained partially by the failure of plaintiff's attorney to file a brief.

22. 52 Misc.2d 39, 275 N.Y.S.2d 303, 3 UCC 775 (1966).

23. 59 Misc.2d 189, 298 N.Y.S.2d 264, 6 UCC 76 (1969).

24. 113 N.J.Super. 452, 274 A.2d 78, 8 UCC 798 (Dist.Ct.1970).

25. A lower court in a third case, Toker v. Perl, 103 N.J.Super. 500, 247 A.2d 701, 5 UCC 1171 (1968), aff'd on other grounds, 108 N.J.Super. 129, 260 A.2d 244, 7 UCC 194 (1970), also found a price to be excessive by comparing it to prices charged by other stores. See notes 15–16 and accompanying text *supra*.

26. 59 Misc.2d at 190, 298 N.Y.S.2d at 265, 6 UCC at 77; interview with George Nager, attorney for plaintiffs, March, 1970. This was a suit for declaratory relief by the buyers.

Similarly, in *ITM* it was shown that appliances were being sold by the door-to-door salespersons at two to three times the prices charged at stores in the same shopping center in which defendant's offices were located.[27]

If section 2–302 is not to run merchants out of low income locations, it is unfair to compare the ghetto seller's prices to those of the suburban seller without some adjustment for the substantially different costs, terms and conditions.[28] Any standard which is adopted must give the merchant with a lower income clientele due consideration for its added credit risks and for other legitimate expenses which are greater than those experienced by the suburban merchant. Thus, some have suggested that a court should only compare the prices of similar goods sold by similar sellers under similar circumstances.[29] Indeed, section 6.111(3)(c) of the 1968 UCCC (modified somewhat in section 5.108(4)(c) of the 1974 UCCC) has set up the following test:

> gross disparity between the price of the property or services sold or leased and the value of the property or services measured by the price at which similar property or services are readily obtainable in credit transactions by like buyers or lessees * * *.

The difficulty with this test is that both the defendant seller and the one whose prices set the standard may be making monopoly profits. By establishing some permissible net return on invested capital or net profit on each sale after taxes as the standard, the courts could enable low-income merchants to charge prices high enough to make a living without exploiting unsophisticated shoppers. Of course, that standard would have its drawbacks. In the first place the low-income merchant might make its net profit appear to be less than it really is by paying excessive salaries to its owner-employees or by otherwise distorting expenses. Second, the party asserting the unconscionability defense would be required to bear a nearly impossible factual burden if that person had to prove that the opposing party made an excessive profit on the sale.

The case of Patterson v. Walker–Thomas Furniture Co.[30] well illustrates the difficulties facing a defendant-buyer who attempts to sustain a claim of excessive price. In that case, the court affirmed the trial court's denial of defendant's request for interrogatories, for a subpoena *duces tecum,* and for the appointment of a special

---

27. Interview with Mark Walsh, Office of the Attorney General, New York State, March, 1970. See also, Klock, Unconscionability and Price Discrimination, Tenn. L. Rev. 317 (2002).

28. It should be noted that only two of the excessive price cases, *Jones* and *Frostifresh*, involved low income neighborhoods.

29. It appears that in *Jones, ITM,* and *Toker* the courts employed this narrower comparison.

30. 277 A.2d 111, 9 UCC 27 (D.C.App.1971).

master or expert witness to establish the value of the goods. The appellate court found that excessive price would be an element of unconscionability and that certain aspects about the price were discoverable, but it held:

> An unsupported conclusory allegation in the answer that a contract is unenforceable as unconscionable is not enough. Sufficient facts surrounding the "commercial setting, purpose and effect" of a contract at the time it was made should be alleged so that the court may form a judgment as to the existence of a valid claim of unconscionability and the extent to which discovery of evidence to support that claim should be allowed.[31]

The court goes on to discuss "fraud, duress or coercion" at the time of making the contract and states that such facts must be alleged to permit discovery of matters having to do with excessive price. If those are not the necessary allegations, it is unclear from the opinion what the defendant must allege in his or her answer in order to entitle him or her to discovery on the question of excessive price.

A reasonable alternative to placing the entire burden of establishing excessive price on the party asserting unconscionability would be for the court to allow that party to make out a *prima facie* case either by showing a markup of two or three times, or by showing that the price at which the product was sold was two or three times greater than at least one other available price—in the low income neighborhood or elsewhere. Indeed, in four of the cases in which courts have found prices to be unconscionably excessive under section 2–302, the contract price to "market value" ratio has varied from 2:1 to 3:1.[32] After the buyer makes out his or her *prima facie* case, then the plaintiff-merchant would be permitted under 2–302(2) to rebut the buyer's case by showing that the net return or net profit was not excessive.

In a free market economy where a seller sets his prices and a buyer must decide if he will negotiate, buy, or walk away, it should not be surprising that courts are reluctant to overturn decisions on price. The reported litigation based on excessive price has dwindled

---

31. *Id.* at 114, 9 UCC at 31.

32. The *Frostifresh* case did not discuss market value but did show that there was a $552 mark-up from the $348 seller's cost, 52 Misc.2d at 27, 274 N.Y.S.2d at 759, 3 UCC at 1059. It is reasonable to assume that the market value of the refrigerator was no more than $450, half of the $900 purchase price.

Students of comparative law may be struck by the similarity of this 2:1 ratio

to the Roman civil law doctrine of laesio enormis. This Christian moralistic doctrine, which goes back to the days of Diocletian (Corpus Juris Civilis, C. 4.44.2), allowed rescission of a contract whenever the value of an item equalled less than half the price. See Dawson, Economic Duress and the Fair Exchange in French and German Law, 11 Tul. L.Rev. 345, 364–66 (1937).

to a trickle. In one case, a lower New York court refused to enforce a promise to pay $67,000 for jade carvings with a fair market value of $14,750.[33] The seller was an expert and knew the buyers were not. In an Arkansas case, timber worth over $50,000 was purchased for far less by a buyer who represented himself as an expert in such matters and opined that the value was between $18,000 and $30,000. The court set aside the deed.[34] In both cases, there were also elements of procedural unconscionability. In a Connecticut case, a lower court found a clause calling for a buyer of a television set to pay 2 1/2 times the regular retail price to be unconscionable.[35] In an Arizona case, the Supreme Court sent the case back for hearing on excessiveness of price.[36]

§ 5–6   Substantive Unconscionability—Remedy Meddling

Allegedly unconscionable remedy meddling has been another battleground in the case law. A creditor-seller's contractual meddling with its own and the buyer's rights and remedies upon default can take a variety of forms. Typically, a credit seller will attempt to set liquidated damages for nonacceptance,[1] limit the liability for consequential damages,[2] and disclaim some or all of its warranty liability.[3] Seller may also include a waiver of defense clause,[4] and if the sale is on secured credit, may include a clause that gives the seller a right to repossess if it "deems itself insecure." In addition there are various other examples such as consent to jurisdiction of a court far distant from the buyer's home.

The Code invites judicial scrutiny of liquidated damages clauses. Section 2–718(1) provides, in part, "A term fixing unreasonably large liquidated damages is void as a penalty." In an early Code

33. Vom Lehn v. Astor Art Galleries, Ltd., 86 Misc.2d 1, 380 N.Y.S.2d 532, 18 UCC 861 (1976). See, however, Maxwell v. Fidelity Financial Services, Inc., 184 Ariz. 82, 907 P.2d 51, 28 UCC2d 806 (1995) (grossly excessive price alleged).

34. Davis v. Kolb, 263 Ark. 158, 563 S.W.2d 438, 23 UCC 887 (1978). See also, Mobile America Corp. v. Howard, 307 So.2d 507, 16 UCC 625 (Fla.App. 1975).

35. Murphy v. McNamara, 36 Conn. Sup. 183, 416 A.2d 170, 27 UCC 911 (1979).

36. Maxwell v. Fidelity Financial Services, Inc., 184 Ariz. 82, 907 P.2d 51, 28 UCC2d 806 (1995).

§ 5–6

1. See § 2–718. See also, Rassa v. Rollins Protective Services Co., 30 F.Supp.2d 538, 37 UCC Rep. Serv.2d 298

(D. Md. 1998) (court held that a limitation of damages is not unconscionable when a fire alarm system fails if the price charged by the system provider does not include a premium for insurance losses).

2. See § 2–719(3) discussed in Chapter 13.

3. See § 2–316 discussed in Chapter 13.

4. See § 9–206(1). See Chemical Bank v. Rinden Professional Ass'n, 126 N.H. 688, 498 A.2d 706, 41 UCC 1035 (1985) (waiver of defense clause not unconscionable since it did not deprive buyer of all remedies, was not obscurely worded, and was reviewed by major law firm).

case, the trial court struck down a liquidated damages clause on the ground that it was unconscionable.[5] One court dismissed a car dealer's action to recover liquidated damages for nonacceptance amounting to twenty percent of the contract price. Among other things, the court found that the liquidated damages clause was unconscionable under section 2–302 because the parties had unequal bargaining power arising from the fact that most car dealers impose similar clauses and thus eliminate the buyer's freedom of choice.

The Code also explicitly incorporates the unconscionability concept into 2–719(3) as follows:

> Consequential damages may be limited or excluded unless the limitation or exclusion is unconscionable. Limitation of consequential damages for injury to the person in the case of consumer goods is prima facie unconscionable but limitation of damages where the loss is commercial is not.[6]

There are even cases that uphold exclusion of consequential damages for personal injuries.[7]

There are also cases holding that warranty disclaimers are to be tested against 2–302.[8] Judicial hostility to disclaimers is, of course, understandable. What is somewhat surprising is that some courts have felt free to analyze these cases under 2–302 and without any reference whatsoever to section 2–316.[9] Section 2–316 could easily be construed as an explicit and statutory definition of unconscionability in the disclaimer area which the drafters carved

---

5. Denkin v. Sterner, 10 Pa.D. & C.2d 203, 1 UCC 173 (C.P.1956). While the court applied the Code and used the word "unconscionable," it did not refer to § 2–302. See also, Bogatz v. Case Catering Corp., 86 Misc.2d 1052, 383 N.Y.S.2d 535, 19 UCC 755 (1976) (clause holding plaintiffs liable for full contract price in the event of cancellation of wedding found unconscionable).

6. See, e.g., Rassa v. Rollins Protective Services Co., 30 F.Supp.2d, 538, 37 UCC2d 298 (D. Md. 1998) ($500 limit clause not unconscionable); Antz v. GAF Materials Corp., 719 A.2d 758, 36 UCC2d 726 (Pa. Super. Ct. 1998) (producer of roofing tiles limited liability to replacing the defective tiles; cost of replacing the tiles was far less than the cost of labor of removing and replacing tile and thus terms were unconscionable); Mullis v. Speight Seed Farms, Inc., 234 Ga.App. 27, 505 S.E.2d 818, 37 UCC2d 88 (1998) (limiting damages for defective seeds to cost of replacing them

unconscionable because the seeds have little value themselves, but have value only after large sums of money have been spent cultivating them); Southwest Pet Prods. v. Koch Indus., 89 F.Supp.2d 1115, 41 UCC2d 520 (D. Ariz. 2000) (court doubtful sophisticated buyer on remand could show unconscionability).

7. Blevins v. New Holland, 97 F.Supp.2d 747, 42 UCC2d 97 (W.D.Va. 2000). Compare Northern States Power v. ITT Corp., 550 F.Supp. 108, 35 UCC 1124 (D.Minn. 1982).

8. For a discussion of warranty disclaimers and 2–302, see Chapter 13. See, e.g., Hewlett–Packard Co. v. Intergraph Corp., 2004 WL 1918892, 54 UCC2d 783 (N.D. Cal. 2004) (disclaimers conspicuous etc., so not unconscionable).

9. Evans v. Graham Ford, Inc., 2 Ohio App.3d 435, 442 N.E.2d 777, 34 UCC 50 (1981) (warranty disclaimer found unconscionable with no reference to 2–316).

out and set down in some detail because they well realized that this would be an area of dispute between buyers and sellers, and they did not wish to leave courts free to make inconsistent and nonuniform judgments on their own under 2–302.

It is frequently not clear from the cases whether counsel for sellers have argued that 2–316 applies to the exclusion of 2–302, but it is clear from the cases cited in the comments to 2–302 that the drafters envisioned the possibility that 2–302 would apply. Moreover many courts have so far applied 2–302 here. Indeed, the court in Electronics Corporation v. Lear Jet Corp.[10] held that even business buyers must be given the right to present proof that a complete disclaimer was unconscionable. In Jefferson Credit Corp. v. Marcano[11] the court said that a disclaimer that arguably complied with 2–316 was ineffective because of 2–302:

> It is my opinion that the lack of equality between the bargaining parties, the contract clauses under which the defendants unwittingly and unknowingly waived both the warranty of merchantability and the warranty of fitness for the purpose for which the motor vehicle was purchased and the defective condition of the motor vehicle, are sufficient to render the contract unenforceable under the provisions of the Uniform Commercial Code, Sec. 2–302 as between Francisco and Maria Marcano and the Fiesta Motors Corp.[12]

In that case the defendants, who could read only Spanish, had signed a printed form of a retail installment contract which limited all warranties to a thirty-day guarantee. The car was defective but the dealer managed to persuade the buyers to keep the car for thirty days. After that time he denied any further responsibility. Of course the court could have reached the same result on the basis of 2–316 by holding that the disclaimer of implied warranty of merchantability was not sufficiently "conspicuous" to a non-English reading party and was therefore ineffective under 2–316.[13] In Koch

10. 55 Misc.2d 1066, 286 N.Y.S.2d 711, 4 UCC 647 (1967). The New York court was applying Massachusetts law in this case, but the Code was in effect in both states.

11. 60 Misc.2d 138, 302 N.Y.S.2d 390, 6 UCC 602 (Civ.Ct.1969).

12. Id. at 142, 302 N.Y.S.2d at 394–95, 6 UCC at 606. Buettner v. R.W. Martin & Sons, Inc., 47 F.3d 116, 25 UCC2d 1086 (4th Cir. 1995) (held that warranty limitation clause that limited liability of seller to employee harmed by machine purchased by buyer wasn't unconscionable).

13. For other cases resorting to § 2–302 whether or not § 2–316 is satisfied,

see, e.g., Chrysler Corp. v. Wilson Plumbing Co., 132 Ga.App. 435, 208 S.E.2d 321, 15 UCC 78 (1974); Industralease Automated & Scientific Equip. Corp. v. R.M.E. Enters., Inc., 58 A.D.2d 482, 396 N.Y.S.2d 427, 22 UCC 4 (1977); Butcher v. Garrett–Enumclaw Co., 20 Wash.App. 361, 581 P.2d 1352, 24 UCC 832 (1978); A & M Produce Co. v. FMC Corp., 135 Cal.App.3d 473, 186 Cal.Rptr. 114, 34 UCC 1129 (1982) (warranty disclaimer on standardized form found unconscionable under 2–302 even though satisfied 2–316); Martin v. Joseph Harris Co., 767 F.2d 296, 41 UCC 315 (6th Cir.1985) (warranty disclaimers which comply with 2–316 are limited by 2–

Supplies, Inc. v. Farm Fresh Meats, Inc.,[14] the Fifth Circuit noted in dicta the desirability of evidence, such as initialing a warranty exclusion clause, which indicated that the buyer understood he was paying $57,000 for a smokehouse which was not required to be operable.

In Unico v. Owen[15] the New Jersey Supreme Court used 2–302 to strike down a waiver of defense clause in a retail installment sale contract which had been assigned to a finance company. Defendants had signed a contract to purchase 140 stereo albums and a stereo set from the Universal Stereo Corporation for a total price of $849.72. The seller immediately assigned the contract and note to Unico, but delivered only twelve albums and the stereo before it became insolvent. When the buyers refused to make any additional payments, the assignee, Unico, sued them on the note and on the contract. The court construed the text of 9–206(1)—"subject to any statute or decision which establishes a different rule for buyers or lessees of consumer goods"—to authorize its determination that waiver-of-defense clauses are unconscionable.[16]

A series of New York cases refuses to enforce clauses in consumer sales contracts which grant exclusive jurisdiction to a court distant from the consumer's home.[17] Another New York case, Robinson v. Jefferson Credit Corp.,[18] found unconscionable conduct on the part of the seller which took place after contract formation. Because it deemed itself insecure, the assignee of a retail installment contract refused to return a repossessed car after collecting past due payments, late charges, and repossession fees from the buyer. The court held that this refusal was unconscionable because

302); Northrup King Co. v. Ammons, 883 F.2d 69, 9 UCC2d 836 (4th Cir. 1989) (seed seller's limitation of liability which complied with 2–316(2) was not unconscionable under 2–302).

14. 630 F.2d 282, 30 UCC 68 (5th Cir.1980); Antz v. GAF Materials Corp., 719 A.2d 758, 36 UCC2d 726 (Pa. Super. Ct. 1998) (court held warranty limitation, which was alluded to but whose terms were only available if consumer sent away for them, was unconscionable because buyer had no meaningful choice and the terms of the warranty "unreasonably favor" the seller); Brower v. Gateway 2000, Inc., 246 A.D.2d 246, 676 N.Y.S.2d 569, 37 UCC2d 54 (1998) (a clause that required arbitration before the International Chamber of Commerce, which would entail thousands of dollars of expenses for the buyer plus the risk of paying seller's fees if the buyer lost, unconscionable due to the cost).

15. 50 N.J. 101, 232 A.2d 405, 4 UCC 542 (1967).

16. *Id.* at 125, 232 A.2d at 418, 4 UCC at 560. But some courts uphold waiver of defense clauses in appropriate circumstances and in light of § 9–206 (now 9–403). Holt v. First Nat. Bank, 297 Minn. 457, 214 N.W.2d 698, 13 UCC 547 (1973); Personal Finance Co. v. Meredith, 39 Ill.App.3d 695, 350 N.E.2d 781, 20 UCC 198 (1976). See § 5–9 *infra.*

17. Paragon Homes, Inc. v. Carter, 56 Misc.2d 463, 288 N.Y.S.2d 817, 4 UCC 1144 (1968), aff'd per curiam, 30 A.D.2d 1052, 295 N.Y.S.2d 606, 5 UCC 991 (1968), relied solely on § 2–302. Bruch, Forum Selection Clauses in Consumer Contracts: An Unconscionable Thing Happened on the Way to the Forum, 23 Loy. U. Chi.L.J. 329 (1992).

18. 1967 WL 8820, 4 UCC 15 (Sup. Ct.1967).

it did not meet the standard of commercially reasonable conduct. The idea of reasonable conduct was explored in Rassa v. Rollins Protective Services Co.,[19] where the court held that a firm which provided burglar alarms at a price that did not reflect the costs of insuring the homes it serviced, and which offered insurance which covered the losses to the homeowner if its alarms failed, was acting in a commercially reasonable way when it limited consequential damages stemming from its alarm's failure. Another relevant case is Bruce v. ICI Americas, Inc.[20] in which the court held that a producer of agricultural pesticide was reasonable in limiting consequential damages because so much of what determines a pesticide's effectiveness is dependent upon factors outside the firm's control. In neither instance was the limitation term found to be unconscionable. Both decisions can also be seen as an attempt by the court to force those who want insurance to buy it from somebody who is in a better position to evaluate and bear the risks.

One case has held that a disclaimer, if intended to exclude tort liability, is unconscionable.[21]

A clause requiring the buyer to test the product before accepting it or waive any claims of defects is not unconscionable.[22]

It is hardly surprising that the Code provisions on remedies and limitations of remedies have caused so much conflict.[23] It is here that the seller's lawyer does her work. At sale no one—at least no one but a pathological person like a lawyer—contemplates default.

19. 30 F.Supp.2d 538, 37 UCC2d 298 (D. Md. 1998).

20. 933 F.Supp. 781, 29 UCC2d 796 (S.D. Iowa 1996).

21. Reibold v. Simon Aerials, Inc., 859 F.Supp. 193, 24 UCC2d 496 (E.D.Va. 1994).

22. Metalized Ceramics for Electronics, Inc. v. National Ammonia Co., 444 Pa.Super. 238, 663 A.2d 762, 27 UCC2d 1271 (1995).

23. See, e.g., Eckstein v. Cummins, 41 Ohio App.2d 1, 321 N.E.2d 897, 16 UCC 373 (1974); Majors v. Kalo Labs., Inc., 407 F.Supp. 20, 18 UCC 592 (M.D.Ala.1975); J.D. Pavlak, Ltd. v. William Davies Co., 40 Ill.App.3d 1, 351 N.E.2d 243, 20 UCC 394 (1976) (no violation of 2–302 or 2–719 found); Tuttle v. Kelly–Springfield Tire Co., 585 P.2d 1116, 24 UCC 1070 (Okl.1978); Spring Hope Rockwool, Inc. v. Industrial Clean Air, Inc., 504 F.Supp. 1385, 30 UCC 1008 (E.D.N.C.1981) (no violation of 2–302 or 2–719 when choice of forum clause was not burdensome and arbitration proceeding in that forum did not fail of essential purpose); Johnson v. John Deere Co., 306 N.W.2d 231, 31 UCC 992 (S.D.1981) (failure of essential purpose is determined after making of the contract; unconscionability determined at time of contracting); Dowty Communications, Inc. v. Novatel Computer Sys. Corp., 817 F.Supp. 581, 19 UCC2d 73 (D.Md.1992) (failure of essential purpose of limited remedies clause and unconscionability of clause excluding liability for consequentials must be analyzed separately).

For more on §§ 2–316 and 2–719, see Chapter 13.

Doubtless other patterns of substantive unconscionability will also develop; we do not suggest that price and remedies are the end of the story.[24]

§ 5–7　Relation of Procedural to Substantive Unconscionability

Almost all of the foregoing cases exhibit creditor behavior that may be regarded as both procedurally and substantively unconscionable. At the very least the term upon which the seller or creditor relies is printed on its own form, often on the back in small print, and the seller rarely calls it to the buyer's attention. Frequently, as in Jefferson Credit Corp. v. Marcano,[1] the consumer is poorly educated, and sometimes the contract is not even in his or her own language.

Two problems not yet resolved by existing case law are these: First, it is not clear whether some form of procedural unconscionability must be present for a court to find a term or contract unconscionable at all within the meaning of 2–302. On the other hand, it is not clear whether "superconscionable" procedural conduct (that is, big print or different colored print for tough clauses) will take the curse off what would otherwise be a substantively unconscionable contract term under 2–302.

It is at least arguable that the courts in American Home Improvement, Inc. v. MacIver[2] and Toker v. Westerman[3] found contracts unconscionable without any evidence of procedural unconscionability. In *MacIver* the buyers were apparently middle-class homeowners living in New Hampshire. Although an alternative holding relies on the fact that there were blanks in the contract at the time the party signed, there is no suggestion that the buyer was misled by these blanks or that the blanks were improperly filled in at a later time. In *Toker v. Westerman* there is no suggestion of procedural unconscionability whatever.[4]

Most courts take a "balancing approach" to the unconscionability question, and to tip the scales in favor of unconscionability, most courts seem to require a certain quantum of procedural, plus

---

24. See, e.g., Kosches v. Nichols, 68 Misc.2d 795, 327 N.Y.S.2d 968, 10 UCC 147 (1971) (unlimited right to repossess from debtor's residence); Fairfield Leasing Corp. v. Techni–Graphics, Inc., 256 N.J.Super. 538, 607 A.2d 703, 18 UCC2d 713 (1992) (clause waiving the right to a jury trial).

§ 5–7

1. 60 Misc.2d 138, 302 N.Y.S.2d 390, 6 UCC 602 (Civ.Ct.1969). See other cases cited in § 5–3.

2. 105 N.H. 435, 201 A.2d 886, 2 UCC 235 (1964).

3. 113 N.J.Super. 452, 274 A.2d 78, 8 UCC 798 (Dist.Ct.1970).

4. See also Andover Air Ltd. Partnership v. Piper Aircraft Corp. v. Kladstrup, 13 Fed.R.Serv.3d 734, 7 UCC2d 1494 (D.Mass.1989) (even in absence of procedural unconscionability, court must consider oppressiveness of terms and whether buyer is left without adequate remedy); Basselen v. General Motors Corp., 341 Ill.App.3d 278, 275 Ill.Dec. 267, 792 N.E.2d 498, 51 UCC2d 698 (2003) (procedural and substantive required).

a certain quantum of substantive, unconscionability. Some cases suggest that excessive price alone is insufficient. After denying defendant's appeal, the court in Patterson v. Walker–Thomas Furniture Co., Inc.,[5] concluded as follows:

> It cannot be said that the goods were grossly overpriced merely from an examination of the prices which appear on the face of the contracts. No other term of the contract is alleged to be unconscionable, nor is an absence of a meaningful choice claimed. *We hold that the two elements of which unconscionability is comprised; namely, an absence of meaningful choice and contract terms unreasonably favorable to the other party, must be particularized in some detail before a merchant is required to divulge his pricing policies* through interrogatories or through the production of records in court. An answer, such as the one here, asserting the affirmative defense of unconscionability only on the basis of the stated conclusion that the price is excessive is insufficient.[6]

It is not clear from the quoted holding whether excessive price alone is never enough. The court might only be saying that the allegations and the proof were insufficient. In our view the court holds that one must show some procedural unconscionability and that a high price, no matter how excessive, is not sufficient in and of itself.[7] The court in Mobile America Corp. v. Howard[8] refused to strike down a contract providing for an annual interest rate of 11.75 percent stating:

> Of those cases dealing with price at all, most require in addition to a grossly excessive price, some element of nondisclosure, fraud, overreaching or manifestly unequal bargaining position.[9]

Finally it appears that a contract that is ninety-eight parts substantively unconscionable may require only two parts of procedural unconscionability to render it unenforceable and vice versa. As the court said in Tacoma Boatbuilding Co., Inc. v. Delta Fishing Co.,[10]

---

5. 277 A.2d 111, 9 UCC 27 (D.C.App. 1971).

6. *Id.* at 114, 9 UCC at 32 (emphasis added).

7. See In re Colin, 136 B.R. 856, 17 UCC2d 873 (Bankr.D.Or.1991) (court can not conclude unconscionable on basis of price alone; not appropriate for court to interfere with judgment of "buyers and sellers in a free market"). Branco v. Norwest Bank Minnesota, 381 F.Supp.2d 1274, 57 UCC2d 909 (D. Hawaii 2005) (both required).

8. 307 So.2d 507, 16 UCC 625 (Fla. App.1975).

9. *Id.* at 508, 16 UCC at 626.

10. 1980 WL 98403, 28 UCC 26, 37 n. 20 (W.D.Wash.1980). See also Murphy v. McNamara, 36 Conn.Sup. 183, 416 A.2d 170, 27 UCC 911 (1979); Carboni v. Arrospide, 2 Cal.App.4th 76, 2 Cal. Rptr.2d 845, 16 UCC2d 584 (1991) (substantive unconscionability, 200% interest rate on a secured loan of $99,000 severe enough to overcome weaker procedural unconscionability, borrower acting under emotional distress because

"The substantive/procedural analysis is more of a sliding scale than a true dichotomy. The harsher the clause, the less 'bargaining naughtiness' that is required to show unconscionability." If our interpretation of *Patterson v. Walker–Thomas*, on the one hand, and *MacIver* and *Westerman*, on the other, is accurate, the cases are in conflict. We favor the former interpretation, namely, that excessiveness of the price is alone insufficient for finding a contract unconscionable.

The courts have not yet given a general answer to the question whether a creditor can make a substantively harsh clause enforceable by prominently placing it in the contract or by having the purchaser separately initial it. Certainly there is support in the Code (for instance, sections 2–316 and 2–209) for validating a clause that would be unenforceable if buried in fine print by making it conspicuous or by specifically focusing the consumer's attention on it.[11] But it is unlikely that any device in a form can really capture the consumer's attention. Given buyers' unwillingness to read the contracts and given that the consumer-buyer will often see the contract for the first time after deciding to buy the product, it seems most unlikely that big print and contrasting colors will do much to change consumers' behavior. If our only goal is to reveal the sad state of the consumer's rights at the outset, but not actually to afford relief from that status, then separate initialling should be sufficient to remove the curse from an otherwise unconscionable contract. Courts probably delude themselves when they assume that the prominence of a printed clause brings it to the buyer's attention and thus gives buyer a more "meaningful choice."

§ 5–8   Form of Relief

When the equity courts found contracts to be unconscionable, they refused specific enforcement,[1] or granted rescission. Affirmative recovery in damages was not given.[2] The remedial tools avail-

---

borrowing to pay for parents' medical expenses).

11. See, e.g., Raybond Electronics, Inc. v. Glen–Mar Door Mfg. Co., 22 Ariz. App. 409, 528 P.2d 160, 16 UCC 121 (1974) (limitation of liability upheld where the warranty was a dickered term). See also, Brunsman v. DeKalb Swine Breeders, Inc., 138 F.3d 358, 35 UCC2d 69 (8th Cir. 1998).

§ 5–8

1. See Earl of Chesterfield v. Janssen, 28 Eng.Rep. 82 (Ch.1750). Cf. Syncsort, Inc. v. Indata Services, 14 Conn. App. 481, 541 A.2d 543, 7 UCC2d 642 (1988) (where seller sought equitable

remedy of specific performance, court focused on the equities and refused to enforce computer program licensing contract which required seller to pay for three years of service when seller had program for only two months and used it only once).

2. W.L. May Co. v. Philco–Ford Corp., 273 Or. 701, 543 P.2d 283, 18 UCC 599 (1975); Vom Lehn v. Astor Art Galleries, Ltd., 86 Misc.2d 1, 380 N.Y.S.2d 532, 18 UCC 861 (1976); Super Glue Corp. v. Avis Rent A Car Sys., Inc., 132 A.D.2d 604, 517 N.Y.S.2d 764, 4 UCC2d 385 (1987) (2–302 not a basis for affirmative recovery because unconscionability is "a shield, not a sword");

able to a modern court under section 2–302 are of a similarly equitable nature: the court may refuse to enforce the entire contract, it may refuse to enforce an unconscionable term, or it may limit the application of the terms so as to avoid an unconscionable result. Since the cases which have held contracts to be unconscionable have so far involved mostly buyers, the most common obligation the courts have refused to enforce has been the payment of the contract price.

Courts occasionally have refused in terms to enforce contracts *in toto.* In Hertz Commercial Leasing Corp. v. Dynatron, Inc.,[3] for example, the great number of individually unconscionable clauses in a lease empowered the court to void the entire contract. However in one of these cases, Jefferson Credit Corp. v. Marcano,[4] the defendants had already partially performed by making payments. Two other cases involved anticipatory repudiation. In Kabro Construction Corp. v. Carire[5] and Hult Chevrolet, Inc. v. Meier,[6] the sellers sought to enforce liquidated damages clauses against consumers who breached retail installment contracts before any goods or services had been provided. Thus, while some courts have refused to require obligees of unconscionable contracts to pay the full contract price, these obligees have not received the benefit of the contracts without expense.[7]

In State ex rel. Lefkowitz v. ITM, Inc.,[8] a whole series of retail installment contracts which were part of a comprehensive scheme were declared unenforceable under 2–302 through an action brought by the Attorney General pursuant to a New York statute.[9] This type of injunctive decree, in which a seller is enjoined from enforcing unconscionable contracts, can be useful to buyers since they need only plead as a defense facts showing that the particular transaction conforms to the circumstances involved in the injunc-

Arthur v. Microsoft Corp., 267 Neb. 586, 676 N.W.2d 29, 53 UCC2d 195 (2004) (not a basis for award of money damages).

Cf. Tanner v. Church's Fried Chicken, Inc., 582 So.2d 449, 15 UCC2d 1155 (Ala.1991) (breach of express promise to "act in good faith" does not give rise to claim because 1–203 is "directive, not remedial").

3. 37 Conn.Sup. 7, 427 A.2d 872, 30 UCC 770 (1980).

4. 60 Misc.2d 138, 302 N.Y.S.2d 390, 6 UCC 602 (Civ.Ct.1969).

5. [1968–71 Transfer Binder] Pov. L. Rep. (CCH) ¶ 10,808 (N.Y.Civ.Ct. 1970). This case also involved a construction of 2–718.

6. [1968–71 Transfer Binder] Pov. L. Rep. (CCH) ¶ 10,283 (No. 124–489) (Wis. Cir. Ct. 1969).

7. While the seller did not perform at all in American Home Improvement, Inc. v. MacIver, 105 N.H. 435, 201 A.2d 886, 2 UCC 235 (1964), it is not clear whether the buyers had made any payments.

8. 52 Misc.2d 39, 275 N.Y.S.2d 303, 3 UCC 775 (1966). See also, State ex rel. Lefkowitz v. Colorado State Christian College of Church of Inner Power, Inc., 76 Misc.2d 50, 346 N.Y.S.2d 482 (1973) (enjoined deceptive practices of "in name only" college which sold honorary Ph.D. degrees).

9. 52 Misc.2d at 41, 275 N.Y.S.2d at 309, 3 UCC at 776.

tive proceeding. In many instances, of course, the buyers will have already made a significant number of payments under the contract.

In a few cases, courts have limited relief to nullifying only a single term of a contract. Thus in Unico v. Owen,[10] a waiver of defense clause was not enforced, and in Paragon Homes, Inc. v. Carter[11] a clause subjecting the parties to a foreign jurisdiction was nullified. The result in each case, however, was that the court refused to enforce any part of the contract. In *Unico,* without the waiver of defense clause the assignee was left subject to a valid defense to the entire obligation. Finding itself without jurisdiction in Paragon Homes, the New York court dismissed the entire action. Thus, relief from a single term can be a totally effective remedy for the defendant.

In 1663 an English court had before it a party who had been tricked into agreeing to pay one hundred pounds for a horse worth only eight. The court required him only to pay the reasonable value.[12] Under 2–302 a few courts have likewise reformed contracts in order to avoid unconscionable results. In one case, the court reduced the interest rate on a secured loan from 200% to 24%.[13] The trial court in Frostifresh Corp. v. Reynoso[14] ruled that because the total price of $1,145.88 for a refrigerator-freezer was unconscionable, the buyer would only be obligated to pay $348, the seller's cost. However the appellate court ruled that the seller was entitled to the net cost plus a reasonable profit, necessary expenses, and reasonable finance charges.[15] Jones v. Star Credit Corp.[16] took a slightly different approach. Finding that the buyers had already paid over $600 towards a freezer with a retail value of $300, the court "reformed and amended" the contract "by changing the payments called for therein to equal the amount of payment actually so paid."[17] The result is thus similar to that achieved in cases where courts have refused to enforce contracts on which payments

---

10. 50 N.J. 101, 232 A.2d 405, 4 UCC 542 (1967). See also Jones Leasing, Inc. v. Gene Phillips & Assoc., 282 S.C. 327, 318 S.E.2d 31, 39 UCC 422 (App. 1984) (if certain provisions of contract are unconscionable, the rest of the contract is still enforceable).

11. 56 Misc.2d 463, 288 N.Y.S.2d 817, 4 UCC 1144 (1968), aff'd, 30 A.D.2d 1052, 295 N.Y.S.2d 606, 5 UCC 991 (1968).

12. James v. Morgan, 83 Eng.Rep. 323 (K.B.1663). The defendant had agreed to pay a barley corn for each nail in the horse's shoe, doubling the number of grains with each nail. The 32 nails resulted in an obligation for four thousand bushels, equal to one hundred pounds sterling.

13. See Carboni v. Arrospide, 2 Cal. App.4th 76, 2 Cal.Rptr.2d 845, 16 UCC2d 584 (1991) (court reduced interest rate on secured loan from 200% to 24%).

14. 52 Misc.2d 26, 274 N.Y.S.2d 757, 3 UCC 1058 (Dist.Ct.1966), rev'd on issue of relief, 54 Misc.2d 119, 281 N.Y.S.2d 964, 4 UCC 300 (1967).

15. Frostifresh Corp. v. Reynoso, 54 Misc.2d 119, 281 N.Y.S.2d 964, 4 UCC 300 (1967).

16. 59 Misc.2d 189, 298 N.Y.S.2d 264, 6 UCC 76 (1969).

17. 59 Misc.2d at 193, 298 N.Y.S.2d at 268, 6 UCC at 80.

have already been made. What are the proper limits on judicial power to reform contract terms? We believe there are some limits here, and would argue some courts have gone over the line.

An occasional reformation or denial of the price is not an effective method of deterring a seller bent on a pattern of unconscionable behavior. As the New York Court of Appeals stated in relation to sales practices involving actual fraud:

> In the calculation of his expected profits, the wrongdoer is likely to allow for a certain amount of money which will have to be returned to those victims who object too vigorously, and he will be perfectly content to bear the additional cost of litigation as the price for continuing his illicit business.[18]

That court's solution was to allow punitive damages.[19] For the same reasons, it might be desirable to impose punitive damages in certain unconscionability cases.

There are two main barriers to such a policy. First, punitive damages are generally not available in an action for breach of contract.[20] This rule, however, relates only to actions seeking compensation for breach. Unconscionability is not a breach, but rather conduct analogous to fraud that renders the agreement void and unenforceable. The rule is well established that punitive damages are appropriate in cases involving malicious, wanton, or reckless fraud.[21] For example, punitive damages were awarded in District Motor Co. v. Rodill[22] when a salesperson set back the odometer on a used car and sold it as new. It would be a natural extension of these principles to grant punitive damages where one party engages in behavior that is a first cousin to fraud and knowingly enters into a contract which unconscionably benefits him or her (as when a refrigerator dealer leads an unsophisticated buyer to believe that the price for the item is a "good deal" when in reality it is two or three times the going market price).[23] Arguably, therefore, the doctrine which bars punitive damage recoveries to contract litigants ought not to bar a counterclaim for such recovery even though

---

18. Walker v. Sheldon, 10 N.Y.2d 401, 406, 223 N.Y.S.2d 488, 179 N.E.2d 497, 499 (1961).

19. *Id.* at 406, 179 N.E.2d at 500. But see Vom Lehn v. Astor Art Galleries, Ltd., 86 Misc.2d 1, 380 N.Y.S.2d 532, 18 UCC 861 (1976).

20. C. McCormick, Law of Damages § 137 (1935); 5 A. Corbin, Contracts § 1077 (1964).

21. See C. McCormick, Law of Damages § 81 (1935); Walker v. Sheldon, 10 N.Y.2d 401, 223 N.Y.S.2d 488, 179 N.E.2d 497 (1961); Rice, Exemplary

Damages in Private Consumer Actions, 55 Iowa L.Rev. 307 (1969). The Rice article provides a fine background to the use of punitive damages in cases involving simple fraud.

22. 88 A.2d 489 (D.C.Mun.App. 1952).

23. For arguments opposing the use of exemplary damages in consumer protection cases, see Rice, Exemplary Damages in Private Consumer Actions, 55 Iowa L.Rev. 307, 340 (1969).

defendant asserts unconscionability as a defense to a contract claim.

Section 1–305(a) presents a second obstacle:

[N]either consequential or special damages nor penal damages may be had except as specifically provided in [the UCC] or by other rule of law.

Section 2–302 does not explicitly provide any damage remedy for victims of unconscionable contracts. For that reason various courts have denied punitive damage recoveries under 2–302.[24] Thus, any court wishing to award punitive damages for unconscionable conduct will have to rely on section 1–103[25] and the last phrase in section 1–305(a) allowing punitive damages when they are authorized by "other rule of law."[26] The court will have to find or make up the "other rule of law," by extrapolation from the fraud cases. Indeed, the New Jersey Supreme Court in Unico v. Owen[27] used language similar to 9–206(1)[28] to provide consumer protection in addition to that specifically delineated by the Code. At least one of us is hesitant to turn loose the punitive damage dogs. After all, this is a commercial, not a consumer code.

But a court is clearly empowered to enforce the contract without the unconscionable clause. Such enforcement may itself lead to the award of compensatory damages in a particular case.[29]

Occasionally a court has remarked that a finding of unconscionability affords no basis for a recovery on a restitutionary theory.[30] But 2–302 does not so provide. Moreover, if money or property has been transferred to a party pursuant to a clause later held unconscionable, a restitutionary recovery would be precisely the appropriate remedy.[31]

24. See, e.g., Pearson v. National Budgeting Sys., Inc., 31 A.D.2d 792, 297 N.Y.S.2d 59, 6 UCC 81 (1969).

25. § 1–103(b) reads as follows:

Unless displaced by the particular provisions of [the UCC], the principles of law and equity, including the law merchant and the law relative to capacity to contract, principal and agent, estoppel, fraud, misrepresentation, duress, coercion, mistake, bankruptcy, and other validating or invalidating cause shall supplement its provisions.

26. Again, the pertinent part of § 1–305(a) reads as follows: "neither consequential or special nor penal damages may be had except as specifically provided in this Act or by other rule of law."

27. 50 N.J. 101, 232 A.2d 405, 4 UCC 542 (1967).

28. § 9–206(1) then read as follows:

Subject to any statute or decision which establishes a different rule for buyers or lessees of consumer goods, an agreement by a buyer or lessee that he will not assert against an assignee any claim or defense which he may have against the seller or lessor is enforceable * * *. This section has been replaced in the 2003 Official Text. See § 9–403.

29. See, e.g., Langemeier v. National Oats Co., Inc., 775 F.2d 975, 41 UCC 1616 (8th Cir.1985).

30. See e.g., Best v. United States Nat. Bank, 78 Or.App. 1, 714 P.2d 1049, 1 UCC2d 6 (1986), aff'd, 303 Or. 557, 739 P.2d 554, 4 UCC2d 8 (1987); Arthur v. Microsoft Corp., 267 Neb. 586, 676 N.W.2d 29, 53 UCC2d 195 (2004).

31. For cases on unconscionability and personal injury, see 2–719 and Collins v. Uniroyal, Inc., 64 N.J. 260, 315

§ 5–9　Unconscionability in Commercial Settings

Can procedural unconscionability be determinative in a commercial case? Is mere substantive unconscionability ever sufficient for invalidation of a business person's contract?[1] As we remarked earlier, courts have not generally been solicitous of business persons in the name of unconscionability. Indeed, many courts have stressed that it is improper to borrow concepts developed to protect consumers and employ them in favor of one commercial party over another.[2]

But a few courts may have found mere procedural unconscionability determinative, even in commercial settings. For example, in Weaver v. American Oil Company,[3] the Indiana Supreme Court held that clauses exculpating an oil company from liability for its negligence and obligating the station operator to indemnify the oil company for damages attributable to the company's negligence were unconscionable:[4]

> The facts reveal that Weaver had left high school after one and a half years and spent his time, prior to leasing the service station, working at various skilled and unskilled labor oriented jobs. He was not one who should be expected to know the law or understand the meaning of technical terms. The ceremonious activity of signing the lease consisted of nothing more than the agent of American Oil placing the lease in front of Mr. Weaver and saying "sign", which Mr. Weaver did. There is nothing in the record to indicate that Weaver read the lease; that the agent asked Weaver to read it; or that the agent, in any manner, attempted to call Weaver's attention to the "hold harmless" clause in the lease. Each year following, the procedure was the same * * *. The evidence also reveals that *the*

A.2d 16, 14 UCC 294 (1974); McCarty v. E.J. Korvette, Inc., 28 Md.App. 421, 347 A.2d 253, 18 UCC 14 (1975); Tuttle v. Kelly–Springfield Tire Co., 585 P.2d 1116, 24 UCC 1070 (Okl.1978). See Chapter 13.

§ 5–9

1. On the general subject of unconscionability in commercial settings, see Mallor, Unconscionability in Contracts Between Merchants, 40 SW.L.J. 1065 (1986); Goldberg, Unconscionability in a Commercial Setting: The Assessment of Risk in a Contract to Build Nuclear Reactors, 58 Wash.L.Rev. 343 (1983).

2. See, e.g., Stanley A. Klopp, Inc. v. John Deere Co., 510 F.Supp. 807, 31 UCC 454 (E.D.Pa.1981), aff'd, 676 F.2d 688 (3d Cir.1982). See further, Earman

Oil Co. v. Burroughs Corp., 625 F.2d 1291, 30 UCC 849 (5th Cir.1980) (when both parties are well-established businesses, there is a presumption of arms-length dealing). See as well, Colonial Life Insurance Co. of America v. Electronic Data Systems Corp., 817 F.Supp. 235, 20 UCC 2d 753 (D. N.H. 1993) (limitation of damages clause conscionable because party trying to invoke unconscionability was large business with experience in purchasing similar services and which had independent consultants and legal counsel work on the contract). See also cases cited at end of n. 15 in section 5–3.

3. 257 Ind. 458, 276 N.E.2d 144 (1971).

4. *Id.* at 460–62, 276 N.E.2d at 145–147.

clause was in fine print and contained *no title heading* which would have identified it as an indemnity clause * * *.

The court stated that it did not base its findings of unconscionability on the alleged substantive unfairness of the clauses.[5]

In Maxon Corp. v. Tyler Pipe Industries, Inc.,[6] an Indiana Court of Appeals reaffirmed the Weaver decision by declaring that an indemnification clause in a contract between commercial parties was procedurally unconscionable and against public policy. As in *Weaver*, the clause was written in fine print with no title heading. It was also at the end of a long paragraph on the reverse side of an invoice that Tyler received after accepting delivery of the products from Maxon. The Court also imposed an affirmative obligation on the seller to make the buyer, even an experienced businessperson, aware of such clauses and to avoid any procedural and *substantive* unconscionability.[7]

In Johnson v. Mobil Oil,[8] a federal district court struck down a clause in a dealer contract limiting the company's liability for consequential damages, a clause the court noted was "not prima facie unconscionable in a commercial setting".[9] Like the plaintiff in Weaver, Johnson was a high school drop out. He could not read, a fact of which Mobil was ignorant. Still, the court found that Mobil had "an affirmative duty to obtain the voluntary knowing assent of the other party. This could easily have been done in this case by explaining to plaintiff in laymen's terms the meaning and possible consequences of the disputed clause."[10]

In Moscatiello v. Pittsburgh Contractors Equipment Co.,[11] a Pennsylvania Superior Court upheld the trial court's finding that remedy-limiting clauses in a contract for the sale of a paving machine were unconscionable. The clauses were inconspicuous. The buyer was inexperienced in the industry and unfamiliar with the business practices of the seller. The court stated that the seller had failed to take advantage of "numerous opportunities throughout the purchase negotiations to notify the [buyer] of the exclusion of warranties and the limitation on potential remedies set forth on the reverse side of the contract".

The *Johnson* court, too, claims to be resting its decision entirely on procedural unconscionability. Moreover, the *Weaver, Maxon, Johnson* and *Moscatiello* courts impose novel duties of explanation

---

5. *Id.* at 464–65, 276 N.E.2d at 148.

6. 497 N.E.2d 570, 3 UCC2d 52 (Ind. App.1986).

7. *Ibid.*

8. 415 F.Supp. 264, 20 UCC 637 (E.D.Mich.1976).

9. *Id.* at 268, 20 UCC at 641.

10. *Id.* at 269, 20 UCC at 643. See also, Sunbeam Farms Inc. v. Troche, 110 Misc.2d 501, 442 N.Y.S.2d 842, 32 UCC 733 (1981); A & M Produce Co. v. FMC Corp., 135 Cal.App.3d 473, 186 Cal.Rptr. 114, 34 UCC 1129 (1982).

11. 407 Pa.Super. 363, 595 A.2d 1190, 16 UCC2d 71 (1991).

and disclosure in commercial settings. A decision that extends the defendant's "duty to disclose" beyond terms contained in the contract to facts about the plaintiff's own business is Langemeier v. National Oats Co., Inc.[12] The defendant sold popcorn seed to plaintiff, agreeing to buy plaintiff's grown crop as well, subject to a clause allowing rejection for frost damage. The plaintiff was an agronomist and financier but new at growing popcorn. The defendant failed to explain that the popcorn needed not only ninety-nine days to grow to maturity but also an additional twenty days to field dry. Plaintiff planted in late May with defendant's approval but defendant later rejected the crop because it was badly damaged due to freezing weather in September and October. The Eighth Circuit upheld a finding of unconscionability because of the nondisclosure. If this case is correct, it is on the borderline. Farmers ought to know their own businesses.

What if there is no non-disclosure and no high pressure or the like, yet the clause involved is of a type that is not likely to be understood by the other party? There is now authority in the commercial context indicating that a confession of judgment clause may fall in this category, and be unconscionable.[13]

It is too early to say that cases described here signify a trend. In general, it remains far more difficult for a business person to establish procedural unconscionability than for an ordinary consumer to do so. Nonetheless, one moral of the foregoing cases is that when a business person is poorly educated, "over a barrel," or the victim of fine print, a court may invalidate a clause that otherwise would stand up between ordinary business persons.[14]

But some courts go too far. In Allen v. Michigan Bell,[15] the Michigan Court of Appeals held unconscionable a clause limiting liability for failure to include advertising in the yellow pages:

> We believe the law in Michigan to be that, where goods or services used by a significant segment of the public can be obtained from only one source, or from limited sources on no more favorable terms, an unreasonable term in a contract for

12. 775 F.2d 975, 41 UCC 1616 (8th Cir.1985). See also Industralease Automated & Scientific Equipment Corp. v. R.M.E. Enterprises, Inc., 58 A.D.2d 482, 396 N.Y.S.2d 427, 22 UCC 4 (1977).

13. Sunbeam Farms Inc. v. Troche, 110 Misc.2d 501, 442 N.Y.S.2d 842, 32 UCC 733 (Civ.1981) (other elements of unconscionability present). See also Architectural Cabinets, Inc. v. Gaster, 291 A.2d 298 (Del.Super.1971).

14. See Northwest Acceptance Corp. v. Almont Gravel, Inc., 162 Mich.App. 294, 412 N.W.2d 719, 4 UCC2d 1352 (1987) (procedural unconscionability where lessee faced losing leased equipment and thus had no realistic alternative but to accept terms of additional lease agreements unreasonably favorable to lessor).

15. 18 Mich.App. 632, 171 N.W.2d 689 (1969).

such goods or services will not be enforced as a matter of public policy.[16]

Here, the court did not rest its decision on procedural unconscionability alone. It said that the limitation was "substantively unreasonable."[17] In Gianni Sport, Ltd. v. Gantos, Inc.,[18] the Michigan Court of Appeals upheld a finding that a termination clause was unconscionable. The court stressed several factors of procedural unconscionability: there was no evidence the termination clause was negotiable—large retailers imposed it on small manufacturers with no clout; the small manufacturer whose contract had been terminated had made the goods specifically to order, and these goods could not merely be returned to stock to await another buyer, given fast-changing styles; the termination took place at the last minute just prior to the delivery date and after the manufacturer had finished the goods. The court also suggested the clause was substantively unreasonable, but it merely provided that buyer may terminate the contract as to any part of the purchase order with respect to goods that have not actually been shipped by the seller.

We question these two Michigan cases. The *Allen* case (yellow pages) was not decided under the Code. We believe that business parties should be able to allocate liability risks as in the Allen contract. Nearly all other courts agree with us.[19] We would say the same of the *Gianni* case if this were all that was involved. Actually, the case may be right in result but wrong in rationale. A termination clause is not itself unconscionable in substantive terms.[20] And we do not think, as between business persons, it should be viewed as procedurally unconscionable. But when the dust settled in this case, the buyer ended up with the goods anyway, and at 50 percent off the price. The manufacturer had nothing else it could do with them when it received the termination notice—a fact not lost on the buyer. We think the bargain there was a de facto modification of the contract under 2–209. As such, it had to be in good faith,[21] but it was not. Moreover, the termination under 2–309(3) may have been invalid because reasonable notification was not given. The notice here did not enable the manufacturer to avoid incurring serious reliance losses.[22]

---

16. *Id.* at 640, 171 N.W.2d at 694.

17. *Id.* at 640, 171 N.W.2d at 694.

18. 151 Mich.App. 598, 391 N.W.2d 760, 1 UCC2d 1433 (1986).

19. See e.g., Southwestern Bell Telephone Co. v. FDP Corp., 811 S.W.2d 572, 15 UCC2d 765 (Tex.1991).

20. See § 2–309.

21. See Comment 2 to 2–209.

22. To be distinguished on its facts is the case of Cardinal Stone Co. v. Rival Mfg. Co., 669 F.2d 395, 32 UCC 1313 (6th Cir.1982). See also Discount Fabric House, Inc. v. Wisconsin Telephone Co., 113 Wis.2d 258, 334 N.W.2d 922, 36 UCC 1128 (App.1983), rev'd, 117 Wis.2d 587, 345 N.W.2d 417 (1984).

In general, then, in the absence of procedural unconscionability, courts will not invalidate commercial contracts in the name of unconscionability.[23] Yet businesses continue to litigate![24] A great many courts, however, continue to emphasize that well-educated and sophisticated persons with equal bargaining power may not invoke the unconscionability doctrine.

A few courts, however, have struck down clauses in commercial contracts in the absence of procedural unconscionability.[25] In one of these, Shell Oil Co. v. Marinello,[26] the court held that a clause giving an oil company the right to terminate a dealer agreement on

23. See also K & C, Inc. v. Westinghouse Electric Corp., 437 Pa. 303, 263 A.2d 390, 7 UCC 679 (1970) (the owners—an attorney who had practiced law for eleven years and a rooming house landlord—entered into agreement after long and careful study). See further, Bernina Distrib., Inc. v. Bernina Sewing Machine Co., 646 F.2d 434, 31 UCC 462 (10th Cir.1981) (where commercial equals negotiated with no unfair surprise or superior bargaining power, ignorance of exchange note fluctuation did not make contract unconscionable); Angus Medical Co. v. Digital Equip. Corp., 173 Ariz. 159, 840 P.2d 1024, 17 UCC2d 724 (App.1992) (clause establishing eighteen month limitation period for bringing an action not unconscionable where no overreaching or unequal bargaining power); In re Chateaugay Corp., 162 B.R. 949, 22 UCC2d 1012 (Bankr. S.D.N.Y.1994) (both substantive and procedural unconscionability required).

24. See, e.g., Phillips Machinery Co. v. LeBlond, Inc., 494 F.Supp. 318, 31 UCC 445 (N.D.Okl.1980); Harper Tax Services, Inc. v. Quick Tax Ltd., 686 F.Supp. 109, 6 UCC2d 408 (D.Md.1988) (term in adhesion contract excluding liability for consequentials not unconscionable where party free to reject contract or offer to pay more for more financial security); Polygram, S.A. v. 32–03 Enters., Inc., 697 F.Supp. 132, 8 UCC2d 914 (E.D.N.Y.1988) (90–day return period not unconscionable where buyer had experience dealing with seller and experience in the industry in general); MacDonald v. First Interstate Credit Alliance, Inc. (In re MacDonald), 100 B.R. 714, 10 UCC2d 1057 (Bankr.D.Del.1989) (cross-collateralization clause not unconscionable, even though lender had superior bargaining power and clause hidden in "boilerplate", because use of clause common in the industry, debtor knew of

clause, and clause repeated in six security arrangements). But see A & M Produce v. FMC Corp., 135 Cal.App.3d 473, 186 Cal.Rptr. 114, 34 UCC 1129 (1982) ("even large business entities may have little bargaining power, depending on the identity of the other contracting party and the commercial circumstances surrounding the agreement.") We think this language in the A & M Produce and other similar cases goes too far.

25. Fairfield Lease Corp. v. Marsi Dress Corp., 60 Misc.2d 363, 303 N.Y.S.2d 179 (Civ.Ct.1969) (acceleration clause in lease unconscionable); Fairfield Lease Corp. v. Umberto, 1970 WL 12608, 7 UCC 1181 (N.Y.City Civ.Ct. 1970) (lease allowing lessor to accelerate all unaccrued rent upon lessee's failure to perform any condition of the lease no matter how trivial was unconscionable); Majors v. Kalo Labs., Inc., 407 F.Supp. 20, 18 UCC 592 (M.D.Ala.1975) (exclusion of liability for consequential damages unconscionable; manufacturer knew product's effectiveness questionable; farmer left without recovery for large and foreseeable consequential damages); Ashland Oil, Inc. v. Donahue, 159 W.Va. 463, 223 S.E.2d 433, 18 UCC 1129 (1976) (in contract between an oil company and dealer, clause giving only oil company right to terminate on 10 days notice was unconscionable on its face); Trinkle v. Schumacher Co., 100 Wis.2d 13, 301 N.W.2d 255, 31 UCC 39 (App.1980) (limitation of consequential damages clause which left no effective remedy so one-sided as to be unconscionable); Pittsfield Weaving Co. v. Grove Textiles, Inc., 121 N.H. 344, 430 A.2d 638, 32 UCC 421 (1981) (limitation of remedy clause which prevented buyer from obtaining damages was unconscionable where parties were both businesses, but seller had considerably more bargaining power).

26. 63 N.J. 402, 307 A.2d 598 (1973).

10 days' notice was simply void as against public policy. Unlike the plaintiffs in the Johnson and Weaver cases, Marinello knew and understood the terms of his lease.[27] Nevertheless, the court found the termination clause grossly unfair. The court reasoned that if the oil company terminated the contract it could always get another dealer; it "is the incumbent dealer who has everything to lose, since, even if he had another location to go to, the going business and trade he built up would remain with the old station."[28] The court here ignores the business rationale for termination clauses.[29] When an oil company allows a dealer to use its trademark, it must exercise some control to protect its name and goodwill. That protection is actually in the interest of dealers, too. Thus, in our view, a general right to terminate a dealership is commercially reasonable.[30] This is not to say that every particular exercise of such a right is conscionable, however.

27. Shell Oil Co. v. Marinello, 120 N.J.Super. 357, 294 A.2d 253 (1972), mod., 63 N.J. 402, 307 A.2d 598 (1973).

28. Shell Oil Co. v. Marinello, 63 N.J. 402, 409, 307 A.2d 598, 602 (1973).

29. Jordan, Unconscionability at the Gas Station, 62 Minn.L.Rev. 813, 837–840 (1978). On termination clauses, see also, Corenswet, Inc. v. Amana Refrigeration, Inc., 594 F.2d 129, 26 UCC 301 (5th Cir.1979), cert. denied, 444 U.S. 938, 100 S.Ct. 288, 62 L.Ed.2d 198 (1979) (clause permitting unilateral termination of distributorship without cause was not unconscionable because party had meaningful choice); Zapatha v. Dairy Mart, Inc., 381 Mass. 284, 408 N.E.2d 1370, 29 UCC 1121 (1980) (clause providing for termination of franchise without cause was not unconscionable).

30. See § 2–302, Comment 1.

Chapter 6

RISK OF LOSS

Analysis

§ 6–1   Introduction

It is not news that the travel of goods from seller to buyer today is a perilous one in the United States and even more perilous when the goods must travel overseas. The carrier may lose the goods; its employees may injure or destroy them; thieves may steal them and, of course, fire, storm, shipwreck, or other acts of God may take their toll. When goods are lost or damaged without the fault of the buyer or seller, the law might allocate the loss between them in a variety of ways. First, the law might simply put the loss on the one who happened to suffer it in the first instance, and foreclose that person from suing the other party. Such a rule would be crude, for it would mean the seller would bear the loss in one case and the buyer in another although the circumstances of both were identical, except, for example, that the buyer's check had arrived a little sooner in one case than in the other. A second possibility would be always to prorate the loss between the parties and ask each to bear part of it. The final possibility, and the one the Code has adopted, is to allocate the entire loss to one party depending upon: (1) the parties' agreement, (2) whether one party or the other is in breach, and (3) the moment in the transaction when the loss occurred.[1]

§ 6–1

1. Useful examinations of the Code's risk of loss provisions include: Note, Risk of Loss Under Section 2509 of the California Uniform Commercial Code, 20 UCLA L.Rev. 1352 (1973); Note, Risk of

At the outset one should understand the legal consequences of casting risk of loss on one party or the other. To say that buyer had the risk of loss at the time the goods were destroyed is to say that buyer is liable for the price under 2–709. To say that seller had the risk of loss at the time the goods were destroyed is to say that seller is liable in damages to the buyer for nondelivery unless seller tenders a performance in replacement for the destroyed goods.[2]

a. Agreement Allocating Risk

Sections 2–509 and 2–510 are the basic risk of loss provisions in Article 2. The wise lawyer will enter those sections first through 2–509(4) which states in part: "The provisions of this section are subject to contrary agreement of the parties * * *."

The Code invites any lawyer who drafts a contract for the sale of goods to include a clause that specifically allocates the risk of loss between the buyer and the seller. There is no magic in 2–509 and 2–510, and there is no reason why the parties cannot agree to some other allocation. Consequently, all variations under 2–509(4) should be clearly stated, especially where the parties seek to shift the risk of loss to the buyer before it takes possession of the goods.[3] As we will see, the parties may specifically allocate risk by a clause which specifies the allocation in so many words or they may do so by the selection of symbols such as "C.I.F." and "F.O.B.," which under the Code have special risk of loss meaning. "Incoterms", discussed in section 6–2, may govern.

Whether the parties have made a contrary agreement under 2–509(4) is a question that has arisen in various special contexts, too. It is not uncommon for sellers to do something further to goods after delivery to buyer. In general, it seems unlikely that the

Loss Under the Uniform Commercial Code, 7 Ind.L.Rev. 711 (1974); Note, Uniform Commercial Code—Risk of Loss, 28 Ark.L.Rev. 508 (1975); Howard, Allocation of Risk of Loss Under the UCC: A Transactional Evaluation of Sections 2–509 and 2–510, 15 UCC L.J. 334 (1983); Note, Risk of Loss in Commercial Transactions: Efficiency Thrown into the Breach, 65 Va.L.Rev. 557 (1979).

2. § 2–613 states an exception for goods damaged without fault of either party before risk of loss passes to the buyer and when "the contract requires for its performance goods identified when the contract is made * * *." In those narrow circumstances § 2–613 frees the seller from his obligation "if the loss is total," and if the loss is partial, it gives the buyer the option to treat the contract as void or to accept the goods with due allowance for the deterioration. That limited exception to the risk of loss rule applies only in the case of "goods whose continued existence is presupposed by the agreement." § 2–613, Comment 1. It has no application to the typical case in which the seller is selling garden variety goods to a buyer under a usual sale of goods contract.

3. Hayward v. Postma, 31 Mich.App. 720, 188 N.W.2d 31, 9 UCC 379 (1971).

parties intend the risk of loss to remain with the seller in these cases for it no longer has control and is unlikely to have insurance.[4]

Secured sales contracts frequently include risk of loss language, e.g., that debtor (the buyer) shall carry insurance "at all times." Is this a "contrary agreement" under 2–509(4) so that the buyer has the risk even before delivery? Without more, we doubt that the parties so intended, and at least one case so holds, but that term must mean that the insurance should be written to cover the loss— no matter who bears the risk.[5] When goods are sold at auction, the registration form may place "full responsibility" on the buyer from the moment of sale. Courts have held this to be a contrary agreement.

b. History

The rules on risk of loss laid down in 2–509 and 2–510 may not only be varied by agreement, they may also be affected by 1–103 on supplemental general principles, including estoppel. In the well-known case of Mercanti v. Persson,[6] the Connecticut Supreme Court used the doctrine of equitable estoppel to impose the risk of loss on a party who otherwise would not have borne the risk.

In some ways the basic provisions of 2–509 and 2–510 are the most radical departure from prior law in Article 2. The prior law, section 22 of the Uniform Sales Act, provided in general that the party who had title or property in the goods also had the risk of loss.[7] The usual job of the court in a risk of loss case under the Uniform Sales Act was therefore to determine whether buyer or seller had title to the goods at the time they were lost, stolen, or destroyed. If the seller still had title, in general the seller had to bear the loss and could not recover the price from the buyer; if title had passed, the buyer usually was liable for the price and thus bore the risk. Who had title and what caused title to pass from the seller to the buyer were often mysteries to both the lawyers and the courts. These questions were bountiful sources of litigation and controversy.[8] Speaking before the New York Law Revision Commis-

---

4. Snider v. Berea Kar Co., 65 Ohio App.3d 552, 584 N.E.2d 1248, 16 UCC2d 1056 (1989) (buyer assumed risk when possession taken of car, although title transfer not completed). But see, Lynch Imports, Ltd. v. Frey, 200 Ill.App.3d 781, 146 Ill.Dec. 521, 558 N.E.2d 484, 13 UCC2d 750 (1990) (buyer took new car home, risk of loss did not pass as matter of law as car was not conforming; creation of buyer's insurable interest does not pass risk of loss).

5. Hayward v. Postma, 31 Mich.App. 720, 188 N.W.2d 31, 9 UCC 379 (1971).

6. 160 Conn. 468, 280 A.2d 137, 8 UCC 969 (1971).

7. One who retraced risk of loss through the Uniform Sales Act had to go first to § 22, then to § 18, and finally to § 19.

8. A cursory search for cases turned up more than 100 pre-Code reported appellate opinions in which a main issue of controversy was the risk of loss question.

sion, Professor Llewellyn summarized the status of the law under the Uniform Sales Act and set forth his hopes for Article 2:

> May I say one other thing in that connection, and say it without any hesitancy at all for the record? The number of lawyers who have an accurate knowledge of sales law is extremely small in these United States. My brother Bacon has taught sales law for 28 years. When he says it isn't too difficult to determine where the court will decide the title is or isn't or is going to be or should be, he is speaking a truth within limits for people who have taught sales law for 28 years. I submit to you, sir, that there are not many of them.[9]

In Llewellyn's eyes the drafters' chief task here was to make the law certain. Above all, 2–509 and 2–510 were to be certain to lawyers and to courts. We believe the drafters succeeded admirably. Sections 2–509 and 2–510 have so far generated only a small fraction of the litigation produced under the Uniform Sales Act during a comparable period, and the decisions under 2–509 and 2–510 are generally sound and accurate interpretations of the drafters' intent.[10]

Subsidiary policies in 2–509 and 2–510 place the loss upon the one most likely to have insured against it and most likely to take precautions to protect against loss. Usually this will be the party who controls possession of the goods.[11] Consistent with this, courts have concluded, for example, that risk of loss in a shipment contract does not move to the buyer on mere completion of the goods or the like by the manufacturer-seller, but rather upon placement with the carrier.[12] Under the Uniform Sales Act, however, title—and therefore risk—would often jump to the buyer after

---

9. 1 N.Y. Sate Law Revision Comm'n 1954 Report 160–61 (1954). Despite speculation that internet retailing would cause increased litigation over Article 2's risk of loss provisions, this has not happened.

10. See Commonwealth Propane Co. v. Petrosol Int'l, Inc., 818 F.2d 522, 3 UCC2d 1778 (6th Cir.1987) (agreement as to passage of title no bearing on risk of loss); Snider v. Berea Kar Co., 65 Ohio App.3d 552, 584 N.E.2d 1248, 16 UCC2d 1056 (1989) (possession of title irrelevant to risk of loss; damaged automobile). See also, McKenzie v. Olmstead, 587 N.W.2d 863, 37 UCC2d 1027 (Minn. Ct.App. 1999) (finding "contrary agreement" shifting risk of loss to buyer found where buyer and seller orally agreed to leave trailer outside seller's fenced-in and secured area for buyer to pick up); Windows, Inc. v. Jordan Panel Systems Corp., 177 F.3d 114, 38 UCC2d

267 (2d Cir. 1999) (finding shipment contract existed despite language in confirmation stating "All windows to be shipped properly ... and delivered to New York City."); Jordan v. Kentshire Galleries, Ltd., 282 A.D.2d 319, 723 N.Y.S.2d 456, 45 UCC2d 806 (App.Div. 2001) (finding pursuant to 2–509(1)(a) that risk of loss shifted to buyer after seller delivered goods to carrier where evidence suggested parties intended shipment contract).

11. See, e.g., Snider v. Berea Kar Co., 65 Ohio App.3d 552, 584 N.E.2d 1248, 16 UCC2d 1056 (1989) (title irrelevant to risk of loss, buyer in possession better bearer of risk, being in control of goods).

12. GMAC Business Credit v. Ford Motor Co., 271 B.R. 534, 47 UCC2d 747, 755 (Bank.E.D. Mich. 2002).

the goods had become identified to the contract even though they were still in the seller's possession. Thus, despite the fact that the goods might still be in the seller's warehouse, guarded by the seller's watchman, and covered by the seller's insurance, the risk would often be on the buyer under the Uniform Sales Act. The Code drafters altered this rule; in Comment 3 to 2–509 they explained: "[Our] underlying theory ... is that a merchant who is to make physical delivery at his own place continues meanwhile to control the goods and can be expected to insure his interest in them. The buyer, on the other hand, has no control of the goods and it is extremely unlikely that he will carry insurance on goods not yet in his possession." The drafters' intent to place the loss on the insurance company itself is further evidenced by the anti-subrogation provisions in 2–510.

Section 2–509 divides sales contracts into three basic categories and provides rules for the allocation of risk of loss in each case.[13] Subsection (1) covers those cases in which the "contract requires or authorizes the seller to ship the goods by carrier." Most business contracts for the sale of goods fall within subsection (1). Subsection (2) covers the less frequent cases in which "goods are held by a bailee to be delivered without being moved * * *." Subsection (3) is the residuary clause which covers all other cases. Important among the cases covered by subsection (3) are those in which the buyer is, by the contract, to pick up the purchased goods at the seller's place of business. Below we will consider each of these categories separately and will dwell on some of the interpretative difficulties that may arise under them. Some of the issues we treat below are law school questions only; others pose real practical difficulties. An analysis of appellate opinions indicates that 2–509 and 2–510 are fulfilling the fondest hopes of the drafters.

§ 6–2 Section 2–509(1), Contracts Contemplating Transportation by Carrier

Section 2–509(1) reads in full as follows:

Where the contract requires or authorizes the seller to ship the goods by carrier

> (a) if it does not require him to deliver them at a particular destination, the risk of loss passes to the buyer when the goods are duly delivered to the carrier even though the shipment is under reservation (§ 2–505); but

> (b) if it does require him to deliver them at a particular destination and the goods are there duly tendered while

---

13. § 2–509 went through only modest change from its appearance in the early drafts to its present form. In the 1956 draft, the section took substantially its present form.

in the possession of the carrier, the risk of loss passes to the buyer when the goods are there duly so tendered as to enable the buyer to take delivery.

One should read 2–509(1) in conjunction with 2–319 on F.O.B. and F.A.S. terms and 2–320 and 2–321 on C.I.F. and C. & F. terms. Some of the provisions of 2–319 and 2–320 are more explicit statements of the generalized terms of 2–509(1). See also the upcoming discussion of Incoterms.

A purchase order and confirmation will frequently contain a statement that the shipment is to be made "F.O.B. seller's place of business," a shipment contract, or "F.O.B. the buyer's place of business," a destination contract. By incorporating trade terms as code symbols in 2–319 and stating their risk of loss consequences in 2–319 and 2–509, the drafters have given us a simple solution to most risk of loss problems. If the contract reads "F.O.B. seller's place of business," 2–319(1)(a) indicates that the seller must there "ship the goods in the manner provided in this Article (2–504) and bear the expense and risk of putting them into the possession of the carrier." Section 2–319(1)(b) tells us that under an "F.O.B. the place of destination" contract, the seller must "at his own expense and risk transport the goods to that place and there tender delivery of them * * *." The negative implication of the quoted provision from 2–319(1)(a), Comment 1 to 2–504,[1] and the decided cases make it clear that the F.O.B. seller's place of business contract is one in which the seller is *not* obliged to deliver at a "particular destination" but rather that such a contract is a "shipment" contract in which the seller's only obligations are to make an appropriate contract for shipment and to get conforming goods into the possession of the carrier. Thus under the provisions of 2–509(1)(a) the risk in such a case passes to the buyer when the goods are "duly delivered to the carrier." Conversely, when the contract reads "F.O.B. *buyer's* place of business," both 2–509(1)(b) and 2–319(1)(b) make it clear that the risk does not pass to the buyer until the goods are tendered to the buyer at the place of destina-

---

§ 6–2

1. § 2–504, Comment 1 reads:

The section [2–504] is limited to "shipment" contracts as contrasted with "destination" contracts or contracts for delivery at the place where the goods are located. The general principles embodied in this section [2–504] cover the special cases of F.O.B. point of shipment contracts and C.I.F. and C. & F. contracts. Under the preceding section [2–503] on manner of tender of delivery, due tender by the seller requires that he comply with the requirements of this section [2–504] in appropriate cases.

Under 2–321, one court has held that risk passage is not affected even if CIF contract provides for payment after delivery. Alaska Russian Salmon Caviar Co. v. M/V Marit Maersk, 45 Fed. R.Serv.3d 754, 41 UCC2d 158 (S.D.N.Y. 2000).

tion. However, the parties can agree otherwise under 2–319(1) so that seller would bear risk to place of destination.[2]

Since the Code has adopted the trade symbols already in use in business, one will find only infrequent cases where business people who contemplate transportation have not used those symbols and have left their lawyers and the courts without a clear legal principle under 2–509 and 2–319 or 2–320. Section 2–509(1)(a) requires that the seller "duly" deliver the goods to the carrier. In order for the risk of loss to pass to the buyer, subsection 2–503(1) on manner of seller's tender of delivery generally requires that (1) the goods be conforming, (2) the seller put and hold the goods at the buyer's disposition, and (3) the seller give the buyer any notification reasonably necessary to enable it to take delivery. Subsection 2–503(2) adds that where the case is within 2–504, "tender requires that the seller comply with its provisions." Subsection 2–504(a) requires that the seller "make such a contract for [the goods'] transportation as may be reasonable having regard to the nature of the goods and other circumstances of the case." Under this subsection, what constitutes an "unreasonable" contract of transportation? Egregious cases do arise. For example, in La Casse v. Blaustein,[3] the package was underinsured, misaddressed, shipped by fourth class mail, and bore a "theft-tempting" inscription. Accordingly, the court held that 2–504(a) was not met, and that the risk of loss did not pass.[4]

Section 2–504 not only requires that the seller properly load and make a reasonable contract of transportation with the carrier, it also requires that the seller under subsection (b) "obtain and promptly deliver or tender in due form any document necessary to enable the buyer to obtain possession of the goods or otherwise required by the agreement or by usage of trade", and requires that the seller under subsection (c) "promptly notify the buyer of the shipment." Are these requirements also conditions of passage of risk to the buyer under 2–509(1)(a) and 2–319(1)(a)? The sections are not wholly clear, and the case law has not yet yielded a clear answer. One case indicates that if the seller's failure to notify deprived the buyer of an opportunity to insure that it would

---

2. Clark v. Messer Indus., Inc., 222 Ga.App. 606, 475 S.E.2d 653, 31 UCC2d 93 (1996). See also, McKenzie v. Olmstead, 587 N.W.2d 863, 37 UCC2d 1027 (Minn. App. 1999) (court applied 2–509(4), given contrary agreement of parties as to risk).

3. 93 Misc.2d 572, 403 N.Y.S.2d 440, 23 UCC 907 (Civ.Ct.1978).

4. *Id.* 23 UCC at 909. See also, Merchants Acceptance, Inc. v. Jamison, 752 So.2d 422, 40 UCC2d 171 (Miss.Ct.App. 1999) (under 2–509(1)(b) risk of loss remains with seller who ships the goods to the wrong address until the buyer receives the goods; court also suggests that even under 2–509(1)(a) the risk of loss remains with the seller who delivers goods addressed to a destination different than agreed upon in the contract to a carrier).

otherwise have taken advantage of, the buyer does not bear the risk.[5]

The F.O.B. term in a sales contract controls risk of loss even where another term in the contract instructs the seller to "ship to Omaha." Assume for example a contract between a North Dakota seller and a New York buyer which provides: "F.O.B., N.D. * * * ship to 145 Bank Ave., New York, N.Y. 10001." In these cases buyers have occasionally argued that the "ship to N.Y." term made the contract into a destination contract or, at minimum rendered it ambiguous. The courts have properly rejected these arguments; all shipment contracts must contain a term that tells the seller where it is to ship the goods. Seller cannot make an appropriate contract for a shipment if the buyer has not told it the place to which to ship them. Thus virtually all contracts properly regarded as shipment contracts because they provide for a term "F.O.B. place of shipment" will also include the name of the destination to which seller is to make a contract for shipment; they remain "shipment" contracts.

A more serious problem under 2–509 is presented by the unusual case where the sales contract does not contain an F.O.B. term, but contains language that arguably substitutes for that term. Consider, for example, the case in which there is no F.O.B. term but the contract states "seller shall pay freight". The buyer can argue that such a payment term is consistent with an F.O.B. destination contract and that the court should find the contract to be an F.O.B. destination contract. Although the buyer's argument might have prevailed under the Uniform Sales Act,[6] there is ample evidence that the drafters of the Code intended a different result. Comment 5 to 2–503 states that the contract in question would normally be regarded as a shipment, not a destination contract, and goes on as follows:

> For the purposes of subsections (2) and (3) there is omitted from this Article the rule under prior uniform legislation that a term requiring the seller to pay the freight or cost of transportation to the buyer is equivalent to an agreement by the seller to deliver to the buyer or at an agreed destination. This

---

5. Rheinberg–Kellerei GMBH v. Vineyard Wine Co., 53 N.C.App. 560, 281 S.E.2d 425, 32 UCC 96 (1981), review denied, 304 N.C. 588, 289 S.E.2d 564 (1981) (notice gives buyer choice to protect self against risk in transit).

6. Under the Uniform Sales Act § 19, Rule 5, the seller was presumed to have retained title and thus the risk if he was obliged to pay the freight. See, e.g., Pulkrabek v. Bankers' Mortg. Corp., 115 Or. 379, 238 P. 347 (1925) (where seller is required to prepay freight, title does not pass until arrival at destination). See also Madeirense do Brasil S/A v. Stulman–Emrick Lumber Co., 147 F.2d 399 (2d Cir.1945), cert. denied, 325 U.S. 861, 65 S.Ct. 1201, 89 L.Ed. 1982 (1945) (C. & F. contract an exception to ordinary rule that payment of freight by seller implies that parties intend no passage of title until goods reach destination to which freight is paid).

omission is with the specific intention of negating the rule, for under this Article the "shipment" contract is regarded as the normal one and the "destination" contract as the variant type. The seller is not obligated to deliver at a named destination and bears the concurrent risk of loss until arrival, unless he has specifically agreed so to deliver or the commercial understanding of the terms used by the parties contemplates such delivery.

Thus a contract which contains neither an F.O.B. term nor any other term explicitly allocating loss is a "shipment" contract.[7] This is so although the seller has agreed to pay the shipment cost. Of course there will still be cases in which it will be unclear whether the parties have used terms tantamount to "F.O.B. place of destination" or which otherwise constitute an agreement with respect to risk of loss.[8] In those cases the buyer must show that the included language deviates from the presumed shipment contract. The allocation of risk in contracts that use language equivalent to "F.O.B. destination" but fail to employ those words is difficult to predict.

The New York Law Revision Commission considered the case where the seller agrees to absorb only part of the transportation expense. When a seller seeks to meet the competition of another seller nearer to the buyer, this problem may arise as follows: a Gary, Indiana seller competes with a Pittsburgh seller for the east coast market. The Gary seller may quote a price plus freight from Pittsburgh. The commissioners concluded that although the seller's price absorbs part of the transportation expense, he has not agreed to deliver at a particular destination and consequently, under subsection (1)(a) risk passes to the buyer when the goods are "duly delivered to the carrier."[9]

In sum, the parties, in a contract contemplating carriage, must *explicitly* agree to a destination contract by using "F.O.B. buyer's place of business" or equivalent language. Otherwise, the contract will be a "shipment" contract.

A remaining problem of minimal significance in 2–509(1) is that of defining the word "carrier." Section 2–509(1) covers only cases where the contract "requires or authorizes the seller to ship the goods by *carrier*." If the contract obliges the seller to ship the

7. See, e.g., Windows, Inc. v. Jordan Panel Systems Corp., 177 F.3d 114, 38 UCC2d 267 (2d Cir. 1999) (finding a shipment contract existed despite language in the confirmation stating "All windows to be shipped properly ... and delivered to New York City.").

8. One court found a "shipment" contract where the parties had agreed that the goods would be shipped to the buyer's residence. The agreement contained no F.O.B. term. The court relied on Comment 5 to 2–503 which states that a contract should normally be regarded as a "shipment" contract. Morauer v. Deak & Co., 1979 WL 30079, 26 UCC 1142 (D.C.Sup.Ct.1979).

9. 1 N.Y. State Law Revision Comm'n 1955 Report 488 (1955).

goods in its own truck, the risk of loss would be governed by subsection (3) not by subsection (1), for there would be no shipment by carrier. We can conceive of highly ambiguous contracts which would lie on the borderline between subsection (1) and subsection (3). Consider for example a contract that provides "F.O.B. place of shipment" but also states that the seller would ship in his own truck. If one interprets that contract to mean that the seller has an option to ship in its own truck, or by carrier, then the contract is under subsection (1) since it is one which at least "authorizes" shipment by carrier. If one decides that the contract obliges the seller to carry the goods itself and prohibits shipment by carrier, the seller might still argue that the "F.O.B. shipping point" term is an agreement by the parties (authorized by 2–509(4)) that risk shifts to the buyer when goods are loaded on seller's truck. If we are to follow the policy of 2–509(3) discussed below we would reject seller's argument.

Since the Code does not define "carrier" it is unclear how far the term reaches.[10] Surely it covers railroads, commercial air carriers, and truckers. Does it also cover the United States mail? Although the United States mail does not normally come to mind when one speaks of a "carrier," we can see no reason why it should not be regarded as a carrier for this purpose. One mailing a package has given up possession and control as fully as one who has shipped by rail; his insurance coverage is not likely to differ greatly in the two cases, and we see no other reason to distinguish them. A New York case supports our view.[11]

Commercial lawyers should also be aware that trading partners, especially when located in different countries, frequently use the International Chamber of Commerce (ICC) Incoterms (an abbreviation for "international commercial terms") as a source of standard contract terms apportioning risk of loss as well as other matters.[12] According to the ICC, "Incoterms are international rules that are accepted by governments, legal authorities and practitioners worldwide for the interpretation of the most commonly used terms in international trade. They either reduce or remove altogether uncertainties arising from differing interpretations of such terms in different countries."[13] Incoterms are periodically revised by the ICC to conform to changes in international commercial

---

10. Other definitions to which one might turn include those in the Interstate Commerce Act, Revised Interstate Commerce Act of 1978, Pub.L.No. 95–473, 92 Stat. 1338, 49 U.S.C.A. § 10102(4) (1979 Supp.).

11. La Casse v. Blaustein, 93 Misc.2d 572, 403 N.Y.S.2d 440, 23 UCC 907 (1978).

12. See the ICC's official Incoterms website at http://www.iccwbo.org/incoterms (last visited May 28, 2009).

13. *Id.* at http://www.iccwbo.org/incoterms/id3038/index.html (last visited May 28, 2009).

practice. The current version is referred to as "Incoterms 2000." (In domestic transactions parties may use only F.O.B. or other UCC terms.)

The thirteen Incoterms[14] are limited in scope to defining the rights and obligations of the parties to a contract for sale of goods insofar as these rights and obligations pertain to the delivery of those goods. The rights and obligations relate to considerations such as: which party is responsible for loading and unloading of the goods, which party bears the risk of loss or damage during transport, which party is to pay the costs and freight of delivery, and which party is responsible for clearing the goods through customs. The ICC does not consider "intangibles" such as computer software as "goods" within the scope of the Incoterms.

A potential source of confusion is that an ICC Incoterm may differ from its Uniform Commercial Code counterpart.[15] For example, under 2–319, the F.O.B. term may be used for any means of transport including rail or air; the ICC FOB Incoterm however, is restricted to sea or inland waterway transport. Because the ICC recommends that the phrase "Incoterms 2000" be explicitly used in conjunction with Incoterms (e.g., FOB Amsterdam Incoterms 2000), it should usually be apparent when the parties have chosen to use Incoterms rather than the definitions in the Uniform Commercial Code. However, parties to an international sale of goods may be bound by the ICC definitions even though they do not explicitly reference "Incoterms". For example, this might arise if the parties' choice of law clause selects the law of a state which by default applies the U.N. Convention on Contracts for the International Sale of Goods (CISG), which itself implicitly incorporates Incoterms as trade usage.[16]

§ 6–3 Section 2–509(2), Goods Held by a Bailee

Section 2–509(2) reads in full as follows:

Where the goods are held by a bailee to be delivered without being moved, the risk of loss passes to the buyer

14. EXW ex works (named place); FCA free carrier (named place); FAS free alongside ship; FOB free on board (named port of shipment); CFR cost and freight (named port of destination); CIF cost, insurance and freight (named port of destination); CPT carriage paid to (named place of destination); CIP carriage and insurance paid to (named place of destination); DAF delivered at frontier (named place); DES delivered ex ship (named port of destination); DEQ delivered ex quay (named port of destination); DDU delivered duty unpaid (named place of destination); DDP delivered duty paid (named place of destination).

15. See generally, John Spanogle Jr., Incoterms and UCC Article 2 Conflicts and Confusion, 31 Int'l Law 111 (1997); Neil Gary Oberman, Thesis, Transfer of Risk From Seller to Buyer in International Commercial Contracts: A Comparative Analysis of Risk Allocation Under the CISG, UCC and Incoterms (1997) at http://www.cisg.law.pace.edu/cisg/thesis/Oberman.html (last visited May 28, 2009).

16. See St. Paul Guardian Ins. Co. v. Neuromed Med. Sys. & Support, 2002 WL 465312 (S.D.N.Y. 2002), aff'd, 53 Fed. Appx. 173 (2002) (applying Incoterms definition of CIF where parties selected German law).

    (a) on his receipt of a negotiable document of title covering the goods; or

    (b) on acknowledgment by the bailee of the buyer's right to possession of the goods; or

    (c) after his receipt of a non-negotiable document of title or other written direction to deliver, as provided in subsection (4)(b) of Section 2–503.

Problems do not arise as frequently under subsection (2) as under subsection (1), and the courts that have dealt with 2–509(2) have experienced relatively little difficulty.[1] In one case, the court emphasized that to satisfy 2–504(2)(b), a bailee must actually notify the buyer; a seller's mere acknowledgment to bailee that buyer has the right of possession is not enough.[2]

The only important interpretive difficulties concern the word "bailee" and the interpretation of (2)(c). If one limits his consideration to (2)(c), it will appear that the risk of loss passes to a buyer upon "receipt" (the acquisition of physical possession) of a non-negotiable document. However, one who takes care to follow out the cross-reference to (4)(b) of 2–503 finds that "risk of loss of the goods and of any failure by the bailee to honor the non-negotiable document of title or to obey the direction remains on the seller until the buyer has had a reasonable time to present the document or direction * * * ".[3]

The most common circumstance under which subsection (2) will be applied is that in which the goods are in the hands of a professional bailee (for instance, a warehouseman) and the seller passes a negotiable or a non-negotiable document of title covering the goods to the buyer. That case is simple enough. One question remains, however. Can the seller ever be a "bailee" as the word is

---

§ 6–3

1. For a case involving two sales of the same goods held at all times by one bailee, where the Sixth Circuit reversed the district court's ruling on both sales, see, Commonwealth Propane Co. v. Petrosol Int'l, Inc., 818 F.2d 522, 3 UCC2d 1778 (6th Cir.1987). See also Commonwealth Petroleum Co. v. Petrosol Int'l, Inc., 901 F.2d 1314, 11 UCC2d 852 (6th Cir.1990).

2. O.C.T. Equipment, Inc. v. Shepherd Machinery Co. and Caterpillar Redistribution Systems, Inc., 95 P.3d 197, 54 UCC2d 327 (Okla.Civ.App. 2004) (no acknowledgment of right to possession).

3. One minor interpretive question arose with respect to subsection (2)(c). The Seventh Circuit had to decide whether "acknowledgment" by the bailee could be made to the seller instead of to the buyer. See the opinion of Judge Posner in Jason's Foods, Inc. v. Peter Eckrich & Sons, Inc., 774 F.2d 214, 41 UCC 1287 (7th Cir.1985). After performing an extensive textual analysis and discussing Code policy, the court concluded that acknowledgment could only be made to the buyer.

used in subsection (2)?[4] The facts in a pre-Code case, Courtin v. Sharp,[5] illustrate the problem. There the seller had reached agreement with buyer for the sale of a colt. The parties had agreed that the seller would hold the colt for the buyer and, depending upon the terms of the payment of the price, would or would not charge him a fee for stabling the colt. The colt was killed without any fault of the seller, and the seller sued the buyer for the purchase price. In that case the seller could certainly argue that he was a bailee and that risk had passed since he had acknowledged the buyer's "right" to possession of goods under (2)(b). The case would be a particularly appealing one for that argument if the seller were receiving payment from the buyer for the boarding of the horse.

We believe that such an interpretation of the word bailee should be rejected by the courts, and except where there is a formed, explicit bailment, a seller should not ever be regarded as a bailee.[6] To allow sellers in possession of goods already sold to argue that they are bailees and that the risk of loss in those cases is governed by subsection (2) would undermine one of the basic policies of the Code's risk of loss scheme. As we have pointed out, the drafters intended to leave the risk on the seller in many circumstances in which the risk would have jumped to the buyer under prior law. The theory was that a seller in possession should have the burden of taking care of the goods and is more likely to insure them against loss.

If we accept such sellers' arguments, that is, that they are bailees under subsection (2) because of their possession of the goods sold or because of a clause in the sale's agreement, we will be back where we started from, for in bailee cases risk jumps under (2)(b) on the bailee's "acknowledgment" of the buyer's right to possession. By hypothesis our seller has acknowledged the buyer's right

---

4. Consider this definition in § 7–102(a)(1):

'Bailee' means a person that by a warehouse receipt, bill of lading or other document of title acknowledges possession of goods and contracts to deliver them.

The choice of the word "bailee" in a section full of references to buyers and sellers and the presence of subsection 2–509(3) to deal with the case in which seller possesses goods already bought by buyer both suggest that the word "bailee" does not include sellers in possession. Similarly, the word 'bailee' does not include those who are, in fact, agents of the buyer. See Oakland Gin Co., Inc. v. Marlow (In re Julien Co.), 44 F.3d 426, 26 UCC2d 117 (6th Cir. 1995)

(finding no bailment resulted when seller delivered cotton to warehouse where warehouse was owned by buyer's affiliate, the buyer and warehouse shared officers and shareholders, and warehouse was operated under a management agreement that was mainly for buyer's benefit.)

5. 280 F.2d 345 (5th Cir.1960), cert. denied, 365 U.S. 814, 81 S.Ct. 693, 5 L.Ed.2d 692 (1961).

6. See, e.g., Silver v. Wycombe, Meyer & Co., 124 Misc.2d 717, 477 N.Y.S.2d 288, 39 UCC 467 (Civ.Ct.1984), aff'd, 130 Misc.2d 227, 498 N.Y.S.2d 334 (1985) (sellers cannot transform sale of goods into a bailment "simply because they acceded to the buyer's request to postpone delivery").

and is simply holding the goods at buyer's disposal. Thus, to accomplish the drafter's purpose and leave risk on the seller in possession, we believe that one should find only non-sellers to be "bailees" as that term is used in 2–509(2). Notwithstanding the fact that a seller retains possession of goods already sold and has a term in the sale contract which characterizes seller as a "bailee," we would argue that seller is not a bailee for the purposes of subsection (2) of 2–509 and would analyze his situation under subsection (1) or subsection (3) of 2–509.[7]

§ 6–4   Section 2–509(3), The Residue

Section 2–509(3) reads in full as follows:

In any case not within subsection (1) or (2), the risk of loss passes to the buyer on his receipt of the goods if the seller is a merchant; otherwise the risk passes to the buyer on tender of delivery.

The subsection sets out two rules: one for merchant sellers and another for nonmerchant sellers.[1] In the former case, the risk remains on the seller until the buyer "receives" the goods.[2] Receipt in this case means taking physical possession of the goods (2–103(1)(c)), and thus a merchant seller who retains physical possession may bear the risk of loss long after title has passed and the seller has received its money. Note that this would also cover the case where the seller ships in its own truck and does not use a carrier. Although 2–103(1)(c) defines receipt as "taking physical possession," one may still find interpretative difficulties if he digs

---

7. In Conway v. Larsen Jewelers, Inc., 104 Misc.2d 872, 429 N.Y.S.2d 378, 29 UCC 842 (Civ.Ct.1980), the defendant jeweler argued that placing an item on "lay-away" created a bailor-bailee relationship. Thus, by placing the item aside until he received full payment, the seller acknowledged the buyer's ultimate though conditional "right" to possession. The court properly rejected the seller's argument. In reaching its conclusion, the court reasoned that sellers in possession are more likely to insure against loss.

§ 6–4

1. § 2–104(1) defines merchant as follows:

(1) 'Merchant' means a person who deals in goods of the kind or otherwise by his occupation holds himself out as having knowledge or skill peculiar to the practices or goods involved in the transaction or to whom such knowledge or

skill may be attributed by his employment of an agent or broker or other intermediary who by his occupation holds himself out as having such knowledge or skill.

2. See Rheinberg Kellerei GmbH v. Brooksfield Nat. Bank of Commerce Bank, 901 F.2d 481, 11 UCC2d 1214 (5th Cir.1990) (risk passed to buyer when containers of wine arrived at destination); Merchants Acceptance v. Jamison, 752 So.2d 422, 40 UCC2d 171 (Miss. Ct. App. 1999) (risk remained with merchant seller who failed to deliver to buyer's home address as specified); Ganno v. Lanoga Corp., 199 Wash.App. 310, 80 P.3d 180, 52 UCC2d 144 (2003) (when seller merchant placed lumber in buyer's truck bed, buyer had taken receipt of goods and thus risk of loss passed to buyer; seller had no further duty of care and was not liable for buyer's injuries suffered when lumber fell out of buyer's truck).

deeply enough into that language. For example, could one argue in Courtin v. Sharp[3] that when the seller agreed to board the horse for a fee, he had commenced to act as the buyer's agent and had so "received" the goods? Clearly a buyer could receive goods through an agent; presumably all corporate buyers can only receive through the acts of their human agents. *Courtin v. Sharp* presents such an appealing case for that argument that we are afraid to predict how it might come out. Courts considering these questions should keep in mind the policy of the Code to retain the risk on the insured seller, and except in extraordinary cases—as, for example, those when the buyer and seller formally change their relationship and the buyer pays the seller to keep an item—should not find receipt on behalf of the buyer in the acts of the seller.

In the case of a non-merchant seller, the risk passes to the buyer upon tender of delivery as defined in 2–503.[4] Under this section, tender of delivery requires that (1) the goods be conforming, (2) the seller put and hold the goods at the buyer's disposition and (3) the seller give the buyer notification reasonably necessary to enable buyer to take delivery. The section, however, poses several interpretive questions. For example, when are the goods at the buyer's disposition? What notification is reasonably necessary to enable the buyer to take delivery? If the loss occurs before the buyer has had time to take delivery, should this preclude the seller from shifting the risk to the buyer? A court might be tempted to place the risk on the seller because of that party's control over the goods. The Code, however, specifically establishes a separate rule for merchant and nonmerchant sellers. If the drafters had intended the nonmerchant seller to bear the risk of loss whenever he controls the goods, they could have made the risk pass on receipt. Section 2–503 should be read to shift the risk of loss to the buyer at the point when the seller has done everything in his power to make conforming goods available,[5] and the buyer has had a reasonable time to take possession.

3. 280 F.2d 345 (5th Cir.1960), cert. denied, 365 U.S. 814, 81 S.Ct. 693, 5 L.Ed.2d 692 (1961).

4. See, e.g., Mitchell v. Highway Equip. Co., 1976 WL 23670, 21 UCC 1034 (Pa.C.P.1976). See also, Martin v. Melland's Inc., 283 N.W.2d 76, 27 UCC 94 (N.D.1979) (even though seller had given buyer certificate of title, risk remained with the seller because he had not tendered delivery); St. Paul Fire and Marine Ins. Co. v. Toman, 351 N.W.2d 146, 39 UCC 394 (S.D.1984) (no "tender of delivery" of house that was to be severed from the land); Rickmyer v. Merry Maker Sales, Inc., Minn. St.Sec.

480a.08(3), 2000 WL 1015830, 42 UCC2d 724 (App. 2000) (tender of delivery was sufficient under 2–509(3) to shift risk of loss to buyer where nonmerchant seller placed goods on porch of buyer).

5. This is supported by Comment 1:

"due tender * * * contemplates an offer coupled with a present ability to fulfill all the conditions resting on the tendering party and must be followed by actual performance if the other party shows himself ready to proceed."

See also, St. Paul Fire and Marine Ins. Co. v. Toman, 351 N.W.2d 146, 39 UCC

Given the existence of separate rules for merchant and non-merchant sellers, the definition of merchant is important. Section 2–104(1) defines merchant as:

[A] person who deals in goods of the kind or otherwise by his occupation holds himself out as having knowledge or skill peculiar to the practices or goods involved in the transaction or to whom such knowledge or skill may be attributed by his employment of an agent or broker or other intermediary who by his occupation holds himself out as having such knowledge or skill.

Thus, either of two attributes signifies that a person is a merchant: experience and special knowledge.

Finally, we reiterate that 2–509 is subject "to contrary agreement of the parties" and to the provisions "on sale on approval."[6] The parties will often wish to spell out their rights with respect to loss in their sales contracts. These attempts at private legislation should be recognized and carried out by the courts.

§ 6–5   Section 2–510, Effect of Breach on Risk of Loss

Section 2–509 sets forth the primary rules allocating risk of loss. Section 2–510, which has produced relatively little litigation,[1] is headed "Effect of Breach on Risk of Loss," and includes three subsections, the first two of which deal with breach by the seller and the third with breach by the buyer.

Section 2–510 reads as follows:

(1) Where a tender or delivery of goods so fails to conform to the contract as to give a right of rejection the risk of their loss remains on the seller until cure or acceptance.

(2) Where the buyer rightfully revokes acceptance he may to the extent of any deficiency in his effective insurance coverage treat the risk of loss as having rested on the seller from the beginning.

394 (S.D.1984) (no "tender of delivery" of house that was to be severed from the land).

6.   § 2–509(4) reads as follows:

"The provisions of this section are subject to contrary agreement of the parties and to the provisions of this Article on sale on approval (§ 2–327) and on effect of breach on risk of loss (§ 2–510)."

§ 6–5

1.   See, e.g., Graaff v. Bakker Bros. of Idaho, Inc., 85 Wash.App. 814, 934 P.2d

1228, 35 UCC2d 126 (1997) (risk of loss remained on seller of seed found non-conforming after customary germination tests were performed); Spirit of Excellence v. Intercargo Insurance Co., 334 Ill.App.3d 136, 267 Ill.Dec. 857, 777 N.E.2d 660, 48 UCC2d 1354 (2002) (seller does not retain risk of loss under 2–510 for goods non-conforming when received by buyer but for which buyer nevertheless manifested acceptance).

(3) Where the buyer as to conforming goods already identified to the contract for sale repudiates or is otherwise in breach before risk of their loss has passed to him, the seller may to the extent of any deficiency in his effective insurance coverage treat the risk of loss as resting on the buyer for a commercially reasonable time.

Comment 1 to 2–509 says that 2–509 applies "[w]here there has been no breach by the seller." Thus if, for example, the goods the seller tenders are nonconforming, 2–509(1) does not pass the risk to the buyer. Section 2–510(1) renders this result explicit.[2] But the text of 2–510(1) is somewhat misleading. It indicates that the language "so fails to conform" suggests that the degree of nonconformity is generally relevant. But at least in "one-shot" deals,[3] any significant degree of non-conformity is enough to justify rejection and preclude passage of the risk to the buyer. (See especially 2–601). Presumably the result is to be different where the nonconformity is in an installment contract. Of course, under 2–510(1), a seller can cure a nonconforming tender and thus pass the risk to the buyer.[4] Also, a buyer can, under that section, accept a nonconforming tender and thereby incur the risk of loss.[5] A number of cases treat what constitutes acceptance for this purpose.[6]

Two quirks of significance remain in 2–510(1). The subsection leaves the risk with seller only when seller's nonconformity is

2. Goosic Constr. Co. v. City Nat. Bank, 196 Neb. 86, 241 N.W.2d 521, 19 UCC 117 (1976); Graaf v. Bakker Bros. of Idaho. Inc., 85 Wash.App. 814, 934 P.2d 1228, 35 UCC2d 126 (1997) (risk of loss remained on seller of seed found to be nonconforming after customary germination tests were performed).

3. William F. Wilke, Inc. v. Cummins Diesel Engines, Inc., 252 Md. 611, 250 A.2d 886, 6 UCC 45 (1969); Jakowski v. Carole Chevrolet, Inc., 180 N.J.Super. 122, 433 A.2d 841, 31 UCC 1615 (1981) (new car but without undercoating and finish as promised); In re Thomas, 182 B.R. 347, 26 UCC2d 774 (Bankr. S.D. Fla. 1995) (placement of pool heater in the driveway of buyer who contracted for an "installed" pool heater constituted delivery that so failed to conform to the contract as to give the buyer the right of rejection and left the risk of loss on the seller. The seller retains the risk of loss of goods until such contracted-for services like installation and set-up occur).

4. See, e.g., Southland Mobile Home Corp. v. Chyrchel, 255 Ark. 366, 500 S.W.2d 778, 13 UCC 617 (1973).

5. § 2–510(1) so states, and see Comment 2.

6. § 2–606 treats what constitutes acceptance here. See, T.J. Stevenson & Co., Inc. v. 81,193 Bags of Flour, 629 F.2d 338, 30 UCC 865 (5th Cir.1980) (acceptance did not occur until buyer had a "reasonable opportunity to inspect."); Spirit of Excellence v. Intercargo Insurance Co., 334 Ill.App.3d 136, 151 n.3, 267 Ill.Dec. 857, 777 N.E.2d 660, 673 n.3, 48 UCC2d 1354 (2002) (stating that buyer by failing to communicate a rejection and by repairing the damage to the goods had accepted the damaged goods); Fabrica De Tejidos Imperial, S.A. v. Brandon Apparel Group, Inc., 218 F. Supp. 2d 974, 48 UCC2d 960 (N.D. Ill. 2002) (holding buyer's redecoration and resale of goods established their acceptance); Franklin Pavkov Construction Co. v. Roche, 279 F.3d 989, 997, 46 UCC 2d 1011, 1021 (Fed.Cir. 2002) (holding acceptance had occurred after contractor/buyer had reasonable time to inspect and reject the goods even though no inspection was actually completed within that reasonable time).

serious enough to give the buyer a right of rejection. Nonconformities that do not substantially impair installment contracts and defects in tender which result from the seller's having made an improper shipment contract but which do not cause substantial delay (2–504) do not give a right of rejection and are therefore not sufficient to cause the risk of loss to remain on the seller.[7] That is simple enough until one compares the language of 2–510 with that in 2–709 on the action for the price. Above we have suggested that 2–709 must be read together with the risk of loss provisions since if the risk has passed to the buyer and the goods are destroyed, the buyer is then liable for the price under 2–709(1)(a). To pose our problem, assume seller ships goods that are part of an installment contract and contain an insubstantial defect under an F.O.B. shipment contract. Since the buyer has no right to reject (2–612), the risk passes to him under 2–509, and 2–510(1) does not interfere with that passage. The seller would have a cause of action for the price against the buyer if the goods were destroyed *en route*. Unfortunately, however, 2–709(1)(a) gives a cause of action only in the case in which "conforming goods" are lost or damaged. By hypothesis the goods in question were not conforming, and there's the rub. Sections 2–509 and 2–510 say that the risk is on the buyer, but 2–709 deprives seller of the usual mode of recovery.[8] The proper result is for a court to bend 2–709(1)(a) to conform to the apparent intention of the drafters and allow the seller to recover the price in cases in which nonconforming goods are destroyed, provided the nonconformity is not one which would give rise to a right to reject.

The second quirk can be illustrated by modifying the hypothetical. Assume, instead that the goods conform to the contract, but that the carrier holds the goods for a commercially unreasonable time before the goods are destroyed *en route*. As before, under section 2–509(1), the risk of loss passes to the buyer. The seller's cause of action for the price under section 2–709, however arises only if the loss occurs within a "commercially reasonable time." By hypothesis, the goods in question were destroyed *after* a commercially reasonable time. Once again section 2–709 deprives the seller of the usual mode of recovery.

Clearly the seller should have a cause of action against the buyer who in turn should have a cause of action against the carrier. The carrier is the one who has defaulted on its obligation. The drafters did not intend that the seller should bear the risk of the

---

7. Note that § 2–510(1) comes into action only upon a breach such as "to give a right of rejection."

8. This ellipsis apparently resulted when § 2–510 was modified in response to New York Law Revision Commission criticism; thus the risk remained on seller only when the nonconformity was serious enough to give a right to reject. See 1 N.Y.State Law Revision Comm'n, 1955 Report 494 (1955). Section 2–709 should have been modified to accommodate this change.

carrier's default. The seller should have the risk of loss only when his actions cause the delay, i.e. he is in control of the goods.[9]

Section 2–510(2) throws the risk back upon the seller's shoulders when the buyer "rightfully revokes acceptance."[10] The section seems simple enough, but one should note that it will not help the buyer where it accepts defective goods and attempts to revoke acceptance only after they have been lost or stolen or otherwise injured. Transfer of the risk back to the seller occurs only when there is rightful revocation of acceptance.[11] Section 2–608(2) requires that a buyer revoke acceptance "before any substantial change in condition of the goods which is not caused by their own defects." Thus, if the goods are destroyed after acceptance but before revocation, the buyer's power to revoke and so use 2–510(2) is foreclosed.[12]

Section 2–510(3) will cause the risk to jump to a buyer who repudiates or "is otherwise in breach." The risk jumps, however, only if the following four additional conditions are met: (1) goods are conforming, (2) they are "already" identified to the contract, (3) to the extent that the loss is not covered by seller's insurance, and (4) loss occurs within a commercially reasonable time (presumably from the repudiation or other breach). The application of this subsection may be somewhat more troublesome because the lawyer must determine whether a "commercially reasonable time has passed"; one will have to determine not only that the goods are conforming, but also that the buyer has breached. Still, subsection (3) seems a rather unremarkable provision.

A question of at least passing interest presented by both subsection (2) and subsection (3) of 2–510 is the effect of the language in those sections "to the extent of any deficiency in his effective insurance coverage." These are essentially antisubrogation clauses which place the loss on any insurance company. For a discussion of those clauses see section 6–7.

---

9. This second quirk also derives from New York Law Revision Commission criticism. The Commission was concerned with the way the 1952 rule left the risk of loss on the buyer when the seller retained control of the goods, no matter when the loss occurred. The Commission did not want the buyer to forever bear the risk of loss under those circumstances. The drafters responded to this criticism by inserting the "commercially reasonable time" requirement in § 2–709 and 2–510(3). See 1 N.Y.State Law Revision Comm'n Report 489 (1955).

10. For a discussion of rejection and revocation, see Chapter 9.

11. See, e.g. Design Data Corp. v. Maryland Cas. Co., 243 Neb. 945, 503 N.W.2d 552, 21 UCC2d 230 (1993) (buyer's rejection of goods damaged in transit, several days after receipt, shifted risk of loss back to the seller).

12. See, e.g., Meat Requirements Coordination, Inc. v. GGO, Inc., 673 F.2d 229, 33 UCC 917 (8th Cir.1982) (buyer has duty to conduct inspection within a reasonable time "to discover defects in the product and to revoke acceptance before a substantial change in the condition of the goods occurs").

At the beginning of the discussion of 2–510, we raised the question whether buyer's or seller's fault (that is, its breach of the contract) ought to be relevant in determining who bears the risk of loss. Note that other kinds of fault, namely those causally connected with the destruction of the goods, will sometimes determine who bears the loss and may take the transaction entirely out of the 2–509, 2–510 scheme. If, for example, risk has passed from seller to buyer under 2–509(3) because the seller had tendered delivery to the buyer, and the goods are then destroyed because of the negligence of the seller, at minimum buyer should be freed from the obligation to pay the price, and it would be appropriate to give buyer a cause of action for damages as well. Note also that a seller's misbehavior can affect the risk in other ways. If, for example, a seller loads conforming goods on a railway car but loads them in a negligent fashion so that they will inevitably be destroyed, the risk does not pass to the buyer under 2–509(1) because seller fails to "duly" deliver.[13] Cases governed by 2–509 and 2–510 are rarely those in which there is a causal connection between the buyer's or seller's act and the destruction of the goods. For the most part we are concerned in this chapter with cases in which neither party is at fault except to the extent that he may be in breach of contract.

We close our discussion with some general criticisms of 2–510. The drafters never clearly articulated why the party in breach should bear the loss in certain circumstances when he would not bear that risk were he not in breach. Apart from the curbstone equity of the provision and a limited statutory and case law tradition of placing loss on the one who was in breach,[14] it is not clear why breach by one party dictates a deviation from the rules of 2–509. Note that 2–510 is considerably out of step with the policies of 2–509. First, it places the risk of loss on the one who does not have possession, who does not have control, and who, in the circumstances there covered, would be least likely to insure. To some extent this result under 2–510 is mitigated by the fact that it will not operate in certain circumstances when the party seeking to invoke it has insurance to cover the loss.[15] Second, because 2–510's

---

13. See Graaff v. Bakker Bros. of Idaho, 85 Wash.App. 814, 934 P.2d 1228, 35 UCC2d 126 (1997) (F.O.B. term allocating risk of loss to buyer does not come into play unless seller tenders conforming goods).

14. The Uniform Sales Act made breach specifically relevant only when delivery was delayed by the fault of a party. Section 22(b) of the Sale Act read:

Where delivery has been delayed through the fault of either the buyer or the seller the goods are at the risk of the

party in fault as regards any loss which might not have occurred but for such fault.

15. See § 6–7 infra.

Professor John Honnold discussed the matter before the New York Law Revision Commission:

Subsection (3) of § 2–510 is much more revolutionary. It reads as follows:

(3) Where the buyer as to conforming goods already identified to the contract for sale repudiates or is otherwise in breach before risk of their loss has

application turns on such difficult legal judgments as whether the goods conform, and whether there has been a repudiation, it conflicts with the basic policy of 2–509, to set down clear and certain rules.

§ 6–6   Subrogation

Insurers often attempt to subrogate themselves to the claims of their insureds against third parties. Although the Code deals only incidentally with insurance, subrogation is a topic of great concern for merchants who store or ship goods. Our focus in this section will be on subrogation in the sales context, on cases in which the insurer of buyer or of seller is acting as the claimant.

For our purposes subrogation is the insurer's assertion of his insured's right against a third party (the carrier, the other party to the sales transaction, or some third party) for the loss for which it has reimbursed its insured. At the outset one should understand certain conditions which must be met before the insurer will have any right to subrogation. It must have reimbursed the insured for the loss.[1] The insured must in fact have a cause of action somehow related to the insured's loss against a third party.[2] The subrogation right is equitable, and it normally need not be stated in the agreement between the insured and the insurer.[3] However, as we

passed to him, the seller may to the extent of any deficiency in his effective insurance coverage treat the risk of loss as resting on the buyer.

This provision would drastically change present law and to a substantial extent would undercut other provisions of the Code which were designed to place the risk of loss on the person who is in possession of the goods. Its scope is enhanced by the ease with which the Code permits goods to be "identified" to a contract prior to delivery or shipment. Unlike present law, under § 2–501 of the Code identification can be performed by seller alone and without assent by buyer. Under the Code, seller's setting goods aside for buyer prior to shipment or delivery and without notification to or other contact with buyer would constitute "identification".

Section 2–510(3) contains the crucial provision that after such identification, if buyer "repudiates or is otherwise in breach," buyer will bear the risk of loss to the extent that seller is uninsured. The impact of this provision can best be seen with the aid of concrete examples.

1 N.Y.State Law Revision Comm'n, 1955 Report 496 (1955).

§ 6–6

1. See, e.g., Fidelity & Cas. Co. v. First Nat. Bank, 397 F.Supp. 587 (D.N.J.1975) ("subrogation is based on payment and not on liability"); Barnes v. Independent Auto. Dealers Ass'n of California Health & Welfare Benefit Plan, 64 F.3d 1389 (9th Cir. 1995) (holding that insurer's subrogation rights did not arise until the insured was paid).

2. See, e.g., Lumber Mut. Ins. Co. v. Clarklift, Inc., 224 Mich.App. 737, 569 N.W.2d 681, 33 UCC 1105 (1997) (warranty disclaimer effective against insured also effective against subrogation claim of insurer); Minnesota Trust Co. v. Yanke (In re Yanke), 230 B.R. 374 (B.A.P.) (8th Cir. 1999) (subrogee's rights against the third party debtor are no greater than those of the subrogor); Bakowski v. Mountain States Steel, 52 P.3d 1179 (Utah 2002) (insured's and third party's waiver of subrogation clause blocked insurer's subrogation claim against the third party despite insurer's lack of notice of this waiver).

3. See Great Northern Oil Co. v. St. Paul Fire and Marine Ins. Co., 291 Minn. 97, 189 N.W.2d 404 (1971) (subro-

will see, a clause that details the right will often be helpful and occasionally necessary if the insurer is to have a right to be subrogated to all of the rights of his insured.[4]

The law of subrogation has enjoyed an irregular and episodic growth in sales law and in analogous areas. The unsatisfactory state of the law is well illustrated by the English and American cases discussing subrogation of an insurer to the rights of a seller of real property on the one hand and a mortgagee on the other against a buyer and a mortgagor respectively. Assume that the mortgagee or the seller has insurance on the land and buildings, that the policy protects only those interests, the property is destroyed while part of the mortgage debt or purchase price remains unpaid, and the insured mortgagee or seller collects the insurance. If there were no insurance, destruction of the property would not discharge the mortgagor from the mortgage debt, nor, in the land contract case, would it discharge the buyer's obligation to pay the price.[5] When there is insurance the large majority of the American courts treat the two cases differently. They find that the buyer of real property is entitled "to the benefit" of the seller's insurance and therefore that the insurer is not entitled to be subrogated to the seller's suit against the buyer for the price of the real estate which has been

---

gation is normal incident of insurance contract, which does not depend on contract terms); New Hampshire Ins. Co. v. Kansas Power & Light Co., 212 Kan. 456, 510 P.2d 1194 (1973) (subrogation right is a "creature of equity" arising without regard to policy provisions). Cf. Underwriters at Lloyds v. Shimer (In re Ide Jewelry Co.), 75 B.R. 969, 4 UCC2d 451 (Bankr.S.D.N.Y.1987) (consignor of diamonds, stolen from consignee, must subrogate its insurer with regard to claims against consignee).

4. The insurance clause set out below is illustrative of a specific provision binding the insured to cooperate in the company's assertion of a right to subrogation:

Company's Right of Recovery: In the event of any payment under this policy, the Insured shall execute and deliver instruments and papers and do whatever else is necessary to secure the subrogation rights of the Company. The Insured shall do nothing after loss to prejudice such rights. However, the Company specifically waives its rights of subrogation against all the subsidiary and affiliated companies of the Insured. Any release from liability, other than as provided in Section 19, entered into pri-

or to loss hereunder by the Insured shall not affect this policy or the right of the Insured to recover hereunder. At the option of the Company, the Insured will execute a loan agreement, to the extent of any loss collectible under this policy. Said loan will bear no interest and will be repayable only in the event and to the extent of the net recovery affected from any party believed to be liable for said loss, the Insured will at the Company's request and expense make claim upon and institute legal proceedings against any party which the Company believes to be liable for such loss, and will use all proper and reasonable means to recover the same, under the exclusive direction and control of the Company.

5. At least five different theories allocating the burden of fortuitous losses between seller and buyer have been advanced in real property law. The view most widely accepted was first enunciated in Paine v. Meller, 6 Ves. Jr. 349 (Ch.1801), that from the time the seller-buyer relation arises the burden of loss is on the buyer even though the seller may be in possession. 3 American Law of Property Section 11:30 (A. Casner ed.1952).

destroyed.[6] On the other hand the American courts find that a
mortgagor is not entitled to "the benefit" of the mortgagee's
insurance and that the mortgagee's insurer is subrogated to the
mortgagee's rights against the mortgagor on the debt.[7] The financing seller on the one hand and the financing mortgagee on the
other are often in identical economic positions; risk to the insurer
may be identical in both cases. Why the courts distinguish the two
cases is a mystery. With that kind of confusion as to real property
where the law is "mature and well developed," one can hardly
rejoice at the prospect of a swim in the turbulent waters of sale of
goods law. We will do our best to keep the reader afloat.

The general classes of rights to which the insurer may wish to
be subrogated in a sales contract can be divided into two groups.
The first are the rights of the insured to recover from the carrier or
some other party for his negligence or other destruction of the
goods in question. Second are rights, commonly called collateral
rights, against third parties who did not necessarily have anything
to do with the destruction of the goods. An illustration of the
second class is the seller's cause of action against the buyer for the
price of goods destroyed at a time when the risk of loss was on the
buyer's shoulders.[8]

A court faced with a subrogation situation in the sales transaction has three alternates for dividing the loss. Consider a case in
which the insurance company has paid a seller-insured for conforming goods destroyed after risk had passed to buyer. If the insurer
seeks to be subrogated to the seller's right to the price against the
buyer, what outcome? The court could: (1) permit the insurance
company to recover from the buyer and so place the loss on the
buyer; (2) deny the insurance company the right to recover from
the buyer, but permit the seller (who had already received the
insurance proceeds) to recover from him and so be doubly compensated; or (3) bar both the insurance company and the seller from
recovery and so place the loss on the insurance company. Although

---

6. See, e.g., Williams v. Lilley, 67
Conn. 50, 34 A. 765 (1895) (lessee, on
subsequently exercising option of purchase, entitled to have balance of insur
ance money in lessor's hands credited as
payment on price).

7. See, e.g., Carpenter v. Providence
Washington Ins. Co., 41 U.S. (16 Pet.)
495, 10 L.Ed. 1044 (1842) (payment of
insurance does not discharge debt and
insurer is entitled to be subrogated to
rights of mortgagee under the mortgage). See generally W. Vance, Insurance Section 130 (3d ed. 1951); 16 G.
Couch, Cyclopedia of Insurance Law
Section 61:360 (2d Rev. ed. 1983).

8. In view of the fact that most
courts allow subrogation to collateral as
well as rights for the direct recovery for
the injury caused, one normally need not
worry about distinguishing the two classifications. However there is a third
class of cases which may cause lawyers
trouble. These are causes of action so far
removed from the insured injury that
they are not even "collaterally" attached
to it. For example, is an insurer subrogated to a buyer's cause of action under
§ 2–714 for breach of contract as to
goods which were destroyed after buyer
incurred some expenses in attempted repair?

outcome two is the one apparently reached in a number of automobile accident cases, it has nothing to commend it, and it has been regularly rejected by the courts in sales and analogous cases.[9]

This leaves the choice between outcomes one and three: to put the loss on the buyer or on the insurance company? The argument in favor of denying subrogation and so leaving the loss on the insurance company, runs as follows: the insurance company has calculated its risk and has received its premium for taking that risk. Now that the feared event has come to pass, the insurer should not be permitted to cast its loss on another's shoulders when it has already received payment for bearing that loss.

An answer to that argument is that the contract between the insured and the insurer is a "personal" one and that the court should not interfere with their agreement. If the insurer agreed to pay the insured but only on the understanding that the insurer would have the right to assert the insured's claims against third persons, then the courts should not interfere. A less doctrinal but possibly persuasive answer to the argument is that the insurer is not receiving a windfall but that its rates will be affected and ultimately set by reference not just to its losses, but to its net losses after subrogation recoveries—but for the subrogation rights its premium would have been higher. Whether there is empirical support for this argument that the premium will vary in relation to the subrogation right, we cannot say.[10] Except for the modest inroads made by the 2–510 antisubrogation clause and by cases like In re Future Manufacturing Cooperative, Inc.,[11] discussed below, the insurer in sales transactions usually is successfully subrogated to its insured's rights. When the insurer is seeking to be subrogated to so-called *noncollateral* rights, that is, to the cause of action in negligence or otherwise against the one who in fact caused the injury, the courts unanimously allow subrogation.[12] Why the courts

---

9. See generally King, Subrogation Under Contracts Insuring Property, 30 Texas L.Rev. 62, 71 (1951); Note, Subrogation of the Insurer to Collateral Rights of the Insured, 28 Colum.L.Rev. 202 (1928).

10. Data is unavailable and no uniformity exists among the subrogation practices of insurers. See R. Horn, Subrogation in Insurance Theory and Practice, 149 (1964). See also Case Note, 72 Harv.L.Rev. 1380, 1382 (1959).

11. 165 F.Supp. 111 (N.D.Cal.1958).

12. See, e.g., Tokio Marine & Fire Ins. Co., Ltd. v. M/V L. Jalabert Bontang, 624 F.Supp. 402 (S.D.N.Y.1985), aff'd, 800 F.2d 1128 (2d Cir.1986) (court assumed that insurer had right to recov-er its subrogated claim against carrier; issue in dispute was whether insurer had established carrier's negligence); Clarys v. Ford Motor Co., 592 N.W.2d 573, 39 UCC2d 72 (N.D. 1999) (assuming insurer could be subrogated to insured's claims against manufacturer of a defective product; issue in dispute was whether economic loss doctrine barred recovery under tort claim); Steiner v. Ford Motor Co., 606 N.W.2d 881 (N.D. 2000) (assuming insurer could be subrogated to insured's claims against manufacturer of a defective product; issue in dispute was whether economic loss doctrine barred recovery under tort claim); Commercial Union Ins. Co. v. M.V. Bremen Express, 16 F.Supp.2d 403 (S.D.N.Y. 1998) (holding insurer was

have found these cases so easy is not clear. Perhaps we are seeing only the desire to punish the wrongdoer; perhaps the courts' actions arise from the hope that the wrongdoer can be made to act with greater care if he knows he will have to bear the loss. In any event the cases agree; the insurer is subrogated to the insured's rights to recover for the injury caused.

Although the courts are not unanimous in permitting an insurer to be subrogated to the so-called *collateral* rights of the insured (for instance, price of goods destroyed, indebtedness secured by goods destroyed), the large majority of these cases permit subrogation.[13] These cases are well illustrated by Home Insurance Co. v. Bishop,[14] a case in which the court concluded that the insurance company was "substituted for the mortgagee and in legal effect has purchased its rights." After the debtor destroyed the insured automobile, the court authorized the insurance company of the creditor to be subrogated to the creditor-insured's rights on the buyer's note. The minority position, denying subrogation to collateral rights, is best articulated by Judge Goodman in In re Future Manufacturing Cooperative, Inc.[15] In that case the insurance company paid the unpaid portion of the purchase price to the seller and then sought to enforce the seller's right to the price against the estate of the bankrupt buyer. The sales contract provided that the bankrupt buyer would insure the equipment in favor of the seller against fire. After a thorough discussion of the policy and a careful

rightfully subrogated to the insured's claim against the carrier where carrier was found to have failed to properly guard goods); Farm Bureau Mut. v. Combustion Research Corp., 255 Mich. App. 715, 662 N.W.2d 439, 50 UCC2d 67 (2003) (assuming insurer could be subrogated to insured's claims against manufacturer of defective product; issue was whether economic loss doctrine barred recovery). A shipper who, under a C.I.F. contract, agrees to procure insurance for the shipment is obliged to pay the buyer in case of loss, and thus becomes the insurer of the shipment. In this situation, there is a split of authority as to whether the shipper or his insurer will be subrogated to the rights of the buyer against the carrier.

13. In Royal Zenith Corp. v. Citizens Publications, Inc., 179 N.W.2d 340 (Iowa 1970) (pre-Code), Justice Uhlenhopp of the Supreme Court of Iowa commented on the problem in dictum as follows:

In a particular case the task is to divine, from what the parties said and did and the nature of the transaction, which one of them they intended should

be the ultimate risk taker—who should be primarily and who secondarily responsible if loss occurred. A salient fact may demonstrate what that intention was. In the seller-buyer situation, if the buyer is to obtain insurance at his own expense for the seller's protection, and does so, plainly that insurer is intended to bear the loss as among the three parties. In the consignment situation, if the consignment contract recites as to the consignee, "Risks of loss or damage from all hazards of any kind, with or without negligence on your part is yours," manifestly the consignee has the burden of loss as opposed to the consignor and his insurer. In the bailment situation, if the storage contract provides the storage company guarantees against loss by fire to the extent it receives payment from its insurer, clearly that insurer bears the ultimate loss to the extent of its limits, though the depositor also maintains insurance. 179 N.W.2d at 346 (citations omitted).

14. 140 Me. 72, 77, 34 A.2d 22, 24 (1943).

15. 165 F.Supp. 111 (N.D.Cal.1958).

consideration of the real property precedents described above, the court concluded, "While a rule giving the vendee the benefit of the vendor's insurance may run counter to the normal concept of an insurance policy as a personal contract between the insurer and the assured, this theoretical objection does not weigh as heavily as the equitable considerations in favoring the vendee."[16] The court denied the subrogation claim.

But for the large body of real property case law which prohibits subrogation and gives one party the "benefit" of the other's insurance and but for the praise such cases have received from the commentators,[17] one could dismiss *Future Manufacturing* and the few other cases like it as aberrations. The care and persuasiveness with which Judge Goodman writes adds substantially to the weight of his decision. Nevertheless, we regard the *Future Manufacturing* outcome as undesirable. We believe that the court's premise, namely that the insurance company would get a windfall if, having received its premium, it also had a right to subrogation may be inaccurate. We find little authority to support Professor Gilmore's assertion that the current "case law trend has been to give the uninsured contract obligor the benefit of the other party's insurance."[18]

Moreover, Harper and James' assumptions about "overtaxing"[19] the court with subrogation cases are not supported by any data known to us and seem naive in a day and age when the bulk of all cases and the large bulk of all sales cases are settled, not tried. We think that the rights of insured and insurer to transfer assets (such as claims against third parties) between them should not be

16. *Id.* at 116.

17. Several commentators have criticized the doctrine of subrogation. Professor Gilmore observed:

The argument for insurer's subrogation seems, when first put forward, extremely plausible. Only on reflection does the argument become suspect. That seems to be, in a nutshell, the common law history. When the subrogation argument was first put forward, in the early days of insurance law, it was accepted almost without question. The nineteenth century cases, English and American, consistently accepted the subrogation rule with respect not only to tort claims but also to various types of contract claims. The twentieth century story has been quite different. The rule of subrogation to tort claims has maintained itself in the case law, but has been subjected to increasingly hostile and effective criticism. The recent cases which have considered insurer's claims to be subrogated to contract rights have, on the whole, been unsympathetic to the claims. Although there has been some diversity of result, it seems fair to say that the case law trend has been to give the uninsured contract obligor the benefit of the other party's insurance. In sum, the history which the proponent of the subrogation rule could point to is mostly ancient history; current history lets him down.

2 G. Gilmore, Security Interests in Personal Property § 42.7.2 at 1149–50 (1965). See generally Case Note, 72 Harv.L.Rev. 1380 (1959); Case Note, 20 Md.L.Rev. 161 (1960).

18. 2 G. Gilmore, Security Interests in Personal Property § 42.7.2 at 1150 (1965).

19. 2 F. Harper & F. James, The Law of Torts § 25.23 at 1360 (1957).

disturbed except in cases such as 2–510(2) and (3) where the legislature has made the judgment that there should be no subrogation.

There are at least two important situations in which even Judge Goodman might permit subrogation. First the court states that the insurer could save his right to subrogation "by including a clause in the policy specifically subrogating it to the vendor's right to recover the purchase price from the vendee."[20] Until one examines the policy at issue in *Future Manufacturing,* that seems a safe and certain out for the insurer. The policy in that case contained a clause which provided that upon "payment under this policy, the Company shall be subrogated to all the Assured's rights of recovery therefor against any person or organization * * *."[21] It appears to us that the insurer in *Future Manufacturing* had already done exactly what Judge Goodman states that an insurer must do in order to preserve his rights of subrogation. One familiar with that line of 20th Century pre-Code cases[22] in which courts repeatedly stated that parties could disclaim their warranty liability but found they had simply "not chosen the right language" in the case before the court might accuse Judge Goodman of speaking with forked tongue. A wise insurance counsel will now include a careful and detailed subrogation clause in the policy, but a cautious counsel will read Judge Goodman's statement as the gratuitous dictum it is and will not warrant to his client that the clause will preserve the insurer's right to be subrogated to the collateral rights of the insured.

Secondly, Judge Goodman states that the insurer did not seek to be subrogated to seller's cause of action for buyer's breach of his promise to insure. He does not indicate what the outcome would have been had the insurer sought to be subrogated to that claim, but it is conceivable that he would have classified that right as a "noncollateral" right to which the insurer could have been subrogated.

In summary, the insurer's right of subrogation to a cause of action against one who wrongfully destroyed goods is universally recognized. *Future Manufacturing* to the contrary notwithstanding, the majority of cases dealing with personal property finds that insurers are subrogated to the collateral rights of the insured as well. However, there are a variety of limits and restrictions upon the doctrine with which the lawyer should be familiar.

---

20. In re Future Mfg. Co–op., Inc., 165 F.Supp. 111, 116 (N.D.Cal.1958).

21. *Id.* at 112.

22. See, e.g., Bekkevold v. Potts, 173 Minn. 87, 216 N.W. 790 (1927); Wade v. Chariot Trailer Co., 331 Mich. 576, 50 N.W.2d 162 (1951).

§ 6–7   Restrictions and Limitations Upon the Doctrine of Subrogation

An important restriction upon the application of the subrogation doctrine, and one easily overlooked, is the case in which the third party against whom the insured would have a cause of action is also a beneficiary of the insurance policy. Consider, for example, United States Fidelity & Guaranty Co. v. Slifkin.[1] Slifkin was a diamond merchant who held goods of others on consignment for resale. His insurance policy covered not only his own interest in the goods, but also those "in trust or on commission," and those "held by him in any capacity whether or not the insured is liable for the loss thereof." The court found that the consignors of the stolen diamonds were third-party beneficiaries of Slifkin's policy. In such circumstances Slifkin's insurer had no cause of action against the consignors because those persons in effect were insured under the same policy.[2]

Subsections 2–510(2) and (3) throw the risk of loss back upon the breaching seller and forward on to the repudiating or breaching buyer in certain circumstances. However, they transfer that risk only "to the extent of any deficiency in [the aggrieved party's] effective insurance coverage." The effect of the language is to deprive the insurance company of certain of the subrogation rights which the insured buyer or seller would have had but for the language in subsections (2) and (3) of 2–510.[3] Since 2–510(2) and

§ 6–7

1. 200 F.Supp. 563 (N.D.Ala.1961).

2. Similarly, an insurer cannot subrogate against a party that it insures under an unrelated liability policy. This would be to allow the insurer to subrogate against its own insured. This has not been permitted on public policy grounds.

Such action, if permitted would (1) allow the insurer to expend premiums collected from its insured to secure a judgment against the same insured on a risk insured against; (2) give judicial sanction to the breach of the insurance policy by the insurer; (3) permit the insurer to secure information from its insured under the guise of policy provisions available for later use in the insurer's subrogation action against its own insured; (4) allow the insurer to take advantage of its conduct and conflict of interest with its insured; and (5) constitute judicial approval of a breach of the insurer's relationship with its own insured.

Royal Exch. Assur. v. S.S. President Adams, 510 F.Supp. 581, 584 (W.D.Wash.1981) (quoting from Home Ins. Co. v. Pinski Bros., Inc., 160 Mont. 219, 500 P.2d 945, 949 (1972)).

3. See generally Professor Honnold writing for the New York Law Revision Commission:

Subsections (2) and (3) of § 2–510 in the Code have a common provision which is unique in the treatment of risk of loss. The essence of the provision is that if one of the parties is in breach of the contract, the aggrieved party "may, to the extent of any deficiency in his effective insurance coverage, treat the risk of loss as resting on" the defaulting party. It will be noted that this section has no impact on the rules of § 2–509 which control risk in the absence of breach. Only if risk would be thrown on the party in breach by § 2–510 does this provision operate to hold risk on the innocent party to the extent of his insurance.

The result has some resemblance to decisions giving to one party with risk of

(3) give the aggrieved *but fully insured* party no claim, the aggrieved party's insurer who only steps into the insured's shoes finds that the party too has no cause of action. In short the proper analysis is to say that there is no cause of action to which the insurer can be subrogated.

Assume, for example, that a seller has a contract to sell $10,000 of goods to a buyer. The goods are identified under the contract, but they are in the possession of the seller and are covered by seller's insurance. Buyer repudiates the contract and shortly thereafter the goods are destroyed. Under the terms of 2–510(3), the seller could treat the buyer as having the risk of loss if the seller were uninsured. Since the seller is fully insured, there is no deficiency in the seller's effective insurance coverage, and subsection (3) does not operate at all. Thus, seller's insurance company pays the entire loss to seller and has no cause of action against buyer.

But what of the insurer whose policy is specifically designed to counteract 2–510(2) and (3) or of the party who is only partially insured? In the former case, the insurance contract might provide that the insurance coverage is "ineffective as long as the buyer or the seller, as the case may be, has a cause of action for the price or for contract damages against the other party." The policy might also provide that the insurer would lend the insured the amount of his loss pending the outcome of the litigation. Under such circumstances, is there a "deficiency" in the "effective insurance coverage"? Professor Gilmore has argued (we think persuasively) that 2–510(2) and (3) set down rules of public policy which cannot be varied by the agreement of the parties.[4] That we believe to be the most probable meaning of the last sentence of Comment 3 to 2–510: "This section merely distributes the risk of loss as stated and is not intended to be disturbed by any subrogation of an insurer."

Thus we believe that attempts to deprive one party to the sales transaction of the benefits of the other's insurance in the circumstances covered by 2–510(2) and (3) should be rejected by the courts whether those attempts take the form of fancy footwork in the policy or of fictional loans.[5]

loss the benefit of insurance taken by the other party. The theory is, however, quite different. Instead of transferring the proceeds of the policy to the party who has risk of loss, the Code transfers risk to the party with insurance. This difference in approach avoids any possibility that the insurer, after paying on the insurance, will seek subrogation to the insured's rights on the sales contract against the party in breach. Since, under the Code the insured party has the risk of loss, he has no contract rights against the other party to which the insurer can be subrogated.

1 N.Y. State Law Revision Comm'n, 1955 Report 499 (1955).

4. 2 G. Gilmore, Security Interests in Personal Property § 42.7.2 at 1150–51 (1965).

5. Insurers sometimes advance the insured the amount of loss to the extent of the insurer's liability. The loan is

Consider the second case, one in which the seller has an insurance contract with policy limits of $10,000 and a contract for the sale of $20,000 worth of goods. The goods are destroyed in the seller's hands shortly after the buyer repudiates the contract. Clearly there is a deficiency in the effective insurance coverage to the extent of $10,000 and to that extent the seller should recover from the buyer. May insurer step forward and claim that $10,000 under his subrogation rights? If he does, seller has a "deficiency in his effective insurance" of yet another $10,000. But to allow him to take a second $10,000 out of the buyer's skin would violate the purpose of 2–510 (to give one party the "benefit" of the other's insurance). If on the other hand we allow the insurer to have the $10,000 but do not allow seller to sue buyer for a second $10,000, the seller will be in a worse position for having insured than he would have been in had he had no insurance but had contracted with a solvent-buyer defendant; in the latter case he would collect $20,000 from buyer and keep it all.

The correct outcome in these circumstances is to find that the seller has a cause of action against the buyer for the difference between the price and his insurance coverage, and to deny the insurer's plea for subrogation to that claim. Quite logically the insurer can claim subrogation to the claim for the first $10,000, the amount paid to the insured, but there is no cause of action against the buyer on that part since it is fully insured. To put it another way, we think the transaction should be regarded as two separate claims. Part one is a loss of $10,000 as to which the seller carries full insurance, has no deficiency, and therefore has no claim under 2–510(3) against the buyer. Part two is a loss of $10,000 as to which there is no insurance. Since this claim is uninsured, the insurer has no more right to be subrogated to it than he has to an infinite variety of other claims unrelated to losses he has insured. Any other outcome produces inconsistencies with the outcomes in analogous cases under 2–510 and conflicts with the policy of 2–510(2) and (3).

One finds an analogous limitation on subrogation in 9–207(b)(2) which reads in part as follows:

> [T]he risk of accidental loss or damage is on the debtor to the extent of any deficiency in any effective insurance coverage * * *.

The negative implication of the quoted language is that when goods which have been pledged to a creditor are destroyed, the loss is on his insurance company. If there is no insurance, then the loss is on

repayable only in the event and to the extent of any net recovery by the insured. See generally 16 G. Couch, Cyclopedia of Insurance Law Section 61:75 (2d ed. (Rev.) 1983).

the debtor. As in 2–510, absent an agreement to the contrary, the insurance company has no right of subrogation because there is no cause of action on the part of the debtor to which the insurance company can be subrogated. Whether the parties can change this outcome by contract is unclear. Under 2–510 one at least gets the help of the last sentence in Comment 3 which, with a little stretching, seems to be a statement of public policy against subrogation in that circumstance.[6] We find Professor Gilmore's argument that the "unless otherwise agreed" language of the original 9–207 refers to other parts of subsection (2) to be plausible but not persuasive.[7] We conclude that the insured and the insurer should not be permitted to alter the antisubrogation outcome in 9–207, but we are not confident of the intention of the drafters here.

An intriguing limitation upon the subrogation right is found in bills of lading commonly used by railroads and other common carriers. When one reads the insurance policy provisions that the insurer "shall have all causes of action under the sun which belong to the insured and shall not be obliged to 'benefit' any third party" and compares that language with the bill of lading which states that the carrier shall "under all circumstances without fail, until hell freezes over, have the benefit of all insurance purchased by anyone with whom he deals," he is put in mind of two young boys trying to determine who gets first at bat by going up the bat hand-over-hand until finally one of them cannot get all four fingers on the top of the bat and so loses. The question becomes whose medicine is more powerful, the railroad's which says it benefits from the shipper's insurance or the insurer's which says it may recover from the railroad? In general the shipper's insurance seems to have prevailed.[8]

---

6. § 2–510, Comment 3 reads as follows:

In cases where there has been a breach of the contract, if the one in control of the goods is the aggrieved party, whatever loss or damage may prove to be uncovered by his insurance falls upon the contract breaker under subsections (2) and (3) rather than upon him. The word "effective" as applied to insurance coverage in those subsections is used to meet the case of supervening insolvency of the insurer. The "deficiency" referred to in the text means such deficiency in the insurance coverage as exists without subrogation. This section merely distributes the risk of loss as stated and is not intended to be disturbed by any subrogation of an insurer.

7. 2 G. Gilmore, Security Interests in Personal Property § 72.7.2 at 1152 (1965).

8. See, e.g., Hartford Fire Ins. Co. v. Payne, 199 Iowa 1008, 203 N.W. 4 (1925) (absent contrary stipulation, shipper's insurer is subrogated to shipper's claim against carrier). See also Luckenbach v. W.J. McCahan Sugar Refining Co., 248 U.S. 139, 39 S.Ct. 53, 63 L.Ed. 170 (1918) (upholding validity of loan receipt device by which insurer made advance to insured as a loan is repayable only to extent of recovery from carrier).

Chapter 7

BUYER'S REMEDIES FOR REPUDIATION, FOR NONDELIVERY AND FOR FAILURE TO DELIVER CONFORMING GOODS (WHICH THE BUYER REFUSED TO KEEP)

Analysis

§ 7–1 Introduction

Buyer's and seller's remedies for breach of contract have been a source of student puzzlement and lawyer argument since long before the Code. Generations of students have wrestled with the problems of the proper time and place for measuring the market and with the baffling opinion in Hadley v. Baxendale.[1] The Uniform

§ 7–1

1. 9 Ex. 341, 156 Eng.Rep. 145 (1854).

Commercial Code combines ancient learning with some ideas of Professor Llewellyn to produce the most comprehensive set of buyer's and seller's remedies found in the law. In the cases in this chapter the seller has usually repudiated, or has otherwise wrongfully failed to deliver, or has delivered nonconforming goods which the buyer has properly refused to keep. Section 2–711[2]—an index of the buyer's remedies—tells us that the aggrieved buyer, after recovering any money paid to the seller, may cover (2–712)[3] or obtain damages for nondelivery (2–713). In addition, 2–711(2) notes that in certain cases, the buyer may recover goods identified to the contract (2–502)[4] or secure specific performance or replevin (2–716). Two important buyer's remedies that we have treated in Chapter 9 rather than here are rejection (2–601) and revocation of acceptance (2–608). Also, we will not treat damages for breach in regard to accepted goods (2–714) here; we deal with that important remedy in Chapter 11 on warranty damages. Our main focus in this chapter is on unamended Article 2.

2. § 2–711 provides (emphasis added):

(1) Where the seller fails to make delivery or repudiates or the buyer rightfully rejects or justifiably revokes acceptance then with respect to any goods involved, and with respect to the whole if the breach goes to the whole contract (Section 2–612), the buyer may cancel and, whether or not he has done so, may in addition to recovering so much of the price as has been paid—

(a) "cover" and have damages under the next section as to all the goods affected whether or not they have been identified to the contract; or

(b) recover damages for non-delivery as provided in this Article (Section 2–713).

(2) Where the seller fails to deliver or repudiates the buyer may also

(a) if the goods have been identified recover them as provided in this Article (Section 2–502); or

(b) in a proper case obtain specific performance or replevy the goods as provided in this Article (Section 2–716).

(3) On rightful rejection or justifiable revocation of acceptance a buyer has a *security interest* in goods in his possession or control for any payments made on their price and any expenses reasonably incurred in their inspection, receipt, transportation, care and custody and may hold such goods and resell them in

like manner as an aggrieved seller (Section 2–706).

3. See PEB Study Group for the Uniform Commercial Code Article 2 (hereinafter "Study Group"); Preliminary Report on Revisions to Article 2, 3–1–90 (hereinafter "Study Group Report"); and Task Force of the ABA, Subcommittee on General Provisions, Sales, Bulk Transfers, and Documents of Title Committee on the UCC (hereinafter "Task Force"), An Appraisal of the March 1, 1990, Preliminary Report of the Uniform Commercial Code Article 2 Study Group (hereinafter "Task Force Report"), 16 Del.J.Corp.L. 981 (1991).

The Study Group recommended addition of a test for breach of the whole contract. Study Group Report at 222. The Task Force concurred with this recommendation. Task Force Report, at 1228.

4. § 2–502, "Buyer's Right to Goods on Seller's Insolvency," indicates that if the seller becomes insolvent within ten days after receiving the first installment on their price, the buyer may recover those goods identified to the contract (under § 2–501) if the buyer tenders the unpaid balance of the price. Subsection (2), however, restricts the application of 2–502 in the situation where the buyer identifies the goods to the contract. Section 2–502 is discussed more fully in conjunction with specific performance (2–716) in 7–6 *infra*.

§ 7–2 Repudiation, Nondelivery, and Other Occasions for Resort to a Remedy

Although a variety of factors may explain nondelivery, its occurrence is simple enough. Some breaches are easy to prove; if without excuse the seller fails to deliver at all or fails to deliver on time, his breach is clear. On the other hand, if the seller delivers arguably non-conforming goods or if he makes pre-delivery rumblings which might be interpreted as a repudiation of the contract, the task of the buyer's lawyer will be harder. In this section we consider what constitutes an anticipatory repudiation. Although our principal concern in this chapter is buyer's remedies, in this section we treat not only seller's but also buyer's repudiation. The Code provisions on anticipatory repudiation and on the damages arising from repudiation are pure joy to Contracts teachers (and doubtless pure hell to many students). The complexity of these provisions intimidates judges too.

The first issue in an anticipatory repudiation case is whether the words or acts of the prospective defendant constitute an anticipatory repudiation. If the lawyer incorrectly advises the client that the other party has repudiated and instructs the client that he may turn elsewhere for cover or that he may cease his own performance, the client may be liable for anticipatory repudiation or for breach of the contract at the time performance becomes due.[1] A clever and well advised prospective defendant, who does not wish to forfeit the contract but is currently unable to perform, is likely to send thoroughly ambiguous signals to the other party. Such a party may, for example, be a seller begging for but not demanding some form of increased payment for performance, or may be a buyer suffering a severely restricted cash flow who wants the seller to continue performance and who fully hopes to be able to pay despite the gathering clouds of bankruptcy. The lawyer must often decide whether the seller's chiseling for a higher price or the buyer's equivocal expression of inability to perform constitutes anticipatory repudiation.[2]

Before we try to define anticipatory repudiation, consider a Code innovation designed to mitigate the lawyer's anxiety in these circumstances. Section 2–609[3] authorizes one party upon "reason-

§ 7–2

1. Harlow & Jones, Inc. v. Advance Steel Co., 424 F.Supp. 770, 21 UCC 410 (E.D.Mich.1976) (buyer's premature rejection held breach); National Farmers Org. v. Bartlett & Co., Grain, 560 F.2d 1350, 22 UCC 658 (8th Cir.1977) (seller's suspension of performance held anticipatory repudiation); In re Beeche Systems Corp., 164 B.R. 12, 24 UCC2d

1132 (N.D.N.Y. 1994) (seller's mere filing for bankruptcy not anticipatory repudiation).

2. Reliance Cooperage Corp. v. Treat, 195 F.2d 977 (8th Cir.1952).

3. § 2–609:

(1) A contract for sale imposes an obligation on each party that the other's expectation of receiving due perform-

able grounds for insecurity" to "demand adequate assurance of due performance and until he receives such assurance * * * if commercially reasonable suspend any performance for which the party has not already received the agreed return."[4] Subsection (4) of 2–609 provides that a prospective repudiator's "failure to provide within a reasonable time not exceeding thirty days such assurance of due performance" constitutes a "repudiation of the contract." All this makes the job of the lawyer somewhat easier. In some cases at least, the lawyer need no longer trust solely in the efforts of courts to grapple with the fictions of implied promises[5] or to apply notions of insolvency.[6] For example, if the client is in a position to wait a month after receipt of an ambiguous statement that might constitute a repudiation, the client need only demand adequate assurance of performance and wait out the month. But in other cases 2–609 is not so helpful. Among other things, it incorporates numerous problematic concepts: What are "reasonable grounds for insecurity"? When has a party given an "adequate assurance" of due performance? When is it commercially reasonable to suspend performance while awaiting assurance?[7] Partly as a result of the uncertain application of the concepts involved, section 2–609 sometimes does little more than extend the minuet between the weaseling party and the contractual counterpart and add a couple of new moves.

Whether a party has reasonable grounds for insecurity depends upon many factors including the seller's exact words or actions, the course of dealing or performance between the particular parties and the nature of the industry. What constitutes reasonable grounds for

ance will not be impaired. When reasonable grounds for insecurity arise with respect to the performance of either party the other may demand adequate assurance of due performance and until he receives such assurance may if commercially reasonable suspend any performance for which he has not already received the agreed return.

(2) Between merchants the reasonableness of grounds for insecurity and the adequacy of any assurance offered shall be determined according to commercial standards.

(3) Acceptance of any improper delivery or payment does not prejudice the aggrieved party's right to demand adequate assurance of future performance.

(4) After receipt of a justified demand failure to provide within a reasonable time not exceeding thirty days such assurance of due performance as is adequate under the circumstances of the particular case is a repudiation of the contract.

4. § 2–609(1).

5. Hochster v. De La Tour, 2 El. & Bl. 678, 118 Eng.Rep. 922 (1853). Cf. Frost v. Knight, L.R. 7 Ex. 111 (1872); Restatement (First) of Contracts § 318, comment a (1932).

6. Rock–Ola Mfg. Corp. v. Leopold, 98 F.2d 196 (5th Cir.1938).

7. The repudiatee must remember that 2–609(1) only authorizes the suspension of any performance "for which [this party] has not already received the agreed return." It does not terminate the liability to pay for goods once in hand.

insecurity in one case might not in another. Consequently, the trier of fact must normally answer whether grounds for insecurity exist.[8]

The clearest case for insecurity arises when one party—declaring the contract invalid or at an end—accuses the other of materially breaching the contract, and states that it no longer will do any business with the other party.[9] Case law illustrations of reasonable grounds for insecurity include: a seller that stops producing the machines to be delivered under the contract;[10] goods like those contracted for but delivered to other buyers fail to work as anticipated;[11] seller of a boat defaults on a mortgage thereby creating a cloud on the title;[12] seller fails to deliver goods on schedule and prompt delivery is essential;[13] and, where the seller states that the contract price is too low to guarantee performance.[14] In several cases, courts have concluded that no reasonable grounds for insecurity existed; consequently no assurances had to be given.[15]

In addition to comparing the facts of the case at hand to those already decided, the lawyer should analyze the various Code policies before giving advice on whether grounds for insecurity are "reasonable" and whether any assurances provided are "adequate". Not surprisingly, subsection (2) defines both "reasonableness" and

---

8. See AMF, Inc. v. McDonald's Corp., 536 F.2d 1167, 19 UCC 801 (7th Cir. 1976); Kaiser–Francis Oil Co. v. Producer's Gas Co., 870 F.2d 563, 8 UCC2d 1048 (10th Cir.1989)

9. Cf. Copylease Corp. of America v. Memorex Corp., 403 F.Supp. 625, 18 UCC 317 (S.D.N.Y.1975). See Hess Energy, Inc. v. Lightning Oil Co., Ltd., 276 F.3d 646, 46 UCC2d 668 (4th Cir. 2002) (buyer's assignment not a material breach; if felt insecure, could have demanded assurances).

10. AMF, Inc. v. McDonald's Corp., 536 F.2d 1167, 19 UCC 801 (7th Cir. 1976) (prototype cash register did not perform adequately during one year trial; seller stopped manufacturing the remaining machines).

11. Creusot–Loire Int'l, Inc. v. Coppus Engineering Corp., 585 F.Supp. 45, 39 UCC 186 (S.D.N.Y.1983) (buyer of burners for ammonia plant in Yugoslavia justified in seeking assurances when similar equipment installed in plants in Syria and Sri Lanka failed to function properly).

12. Clem Perrin Marine Towing, Inc. v. Panama Canal Co., 730 F.2d 186, 38 UCC 490 (5th Cir.1984), cert. denied, 469 U.S. 1037, 105 S.Ct. 515, 83 L.Ed.2d 405 (1984)(purchaser was a renter of boat with an option to buy who was informed of owner's default).

13. Universal Builders Corp. v. United Methodist Convalescent Homes, Inc., 7 Conn.App. 318, 508 A.2d 819, 1 UCC2d 763 (1986).

14. Erwin Weller Co. v. Talon Inc., 295 N.W.2d 172, 29 UCC 1302 (S.D. 1980) (mounting debt owed by buyer to seller was reasonable ground for insecurity); Kaiser–Francis Oil Co. v. Producer's Gas Co., 870 F.2d 563, 8 UCC2d 1048 (10th Cir.1989) (seller had reasonable grounds for insecurity *as a matter of law* because buyer of natural gas clearly refused to continue performance unless seller agreed to modify a "take-or-pay" provision).

15. In Cole v. Melvin, 441 F.Supp. 193, 22 UCC 1154 (D.S.D.1977), the seller of exotic cattle sent a letter demanding 2–609 assurance from the buyer. The buyer justifiably refused to answer since the seller had no "reasonable grounds for insecurity." See also In re Pacific Gas and Electric Co., 271 B.R. 626, 47 UCC2d 598 (N.D. Cal. 2002) (no reasonable grounds for insecurity if seller's non-performance contemplated by agreement of parties); Koch Materials Co. v. Shore Slurry Seal, Inc., 205 F.Supp. 2d 324, 48 UCC2d 157 (D.N.J. 2002) (buyer told seller it selling out to third party; this was grounds for seller's insecurity).

"adequacy" by "commercial standards," and Comment 3 reminds us of the pervasive obligation of good faith. The cases provide some hints about the meaning of "commercial standards." Thus, in Kunian v. Development Corp. of America[16] the seller of plumbing and heating materials made an installment contract with the buyer. Several months later the buyer was $38,000 behind in payments for installments of goods delivered. After the seller demanded assurance of performance from the buyer, the buyer promised that he would pay the outstanding indebtedness if the seller would continue his performance. When a month passed and the buyer had made no further payments, the seller informed the buyer that further deliveries would not be made unless the buyer deposited in escrow a sufficient amount of cash to pay for the delivered goods. The buyer did not escrow. The court held that the seller had "reasonable grounds for insecurity" and that his suspension of performance was justified under 2–609.[17]

The grounds for insecurity need not arise from circumstances directly related to the parties or the contract itself. Thus, where the market price of a commodity is rising, the buyer may be justified in seeking assurances of performance from the seller even though the seller did nothing to cause buyer's insecurity.[18]

---

16. 165 Conn. 300, 334 A.2d 427, 12 UCC 1125 (1973).

17. See also In re Amica, Inc., 135 B.R. 534, 17 UCC2d 11 (Bankr.N.D.Ill. 1992) (the seller was within its rights to cancel a contract for the sale of software to the buyer and refuse to ship remaining software ordered by the buyer, after the buyer failed to make payment to the seller and sent the seller several dishonored checks). Professor Honnold comments that 2–609 gives the court broad discretion to determine what are reasonable grounds and that the comments provide guidelines for a properly conservative application of the section to balance two conflicting interests: (1) providing certainty that the promisor will not breach, and (2) flagrant use of 2–609 as a weapon to avoid unprofitable contracts. 1 N.Y. State Law Revision Comm'n, 1955 Report 537 (1955).

On "reasonable grounds" and "adequate assurance," Comment 4 cites two pre-Code cases which together illustrate the intended commercial standards. According to Comment 4, reasonable grounds for insecurity would exist in a case like Corn Products Refining Co. v. Fasola, 94 N.J.L. 181, 109 A. 505 (1920), where a buyer who customarily took advantage of a ten-day payment discount

failed to make his usual ten-day payment. As to the adequacy of assurance, the Comment states that in the absence of such a failure to pay within the customary period, that sending a good credit report from a banker and expressing an ability and willingness to pay within thirty days should be satisfactory. Comment 4 also expressly requires that the satisfaction of a party requesting "assurance" must be based on reason and not caprice. Of course, a seller must show it demanded assurances either orallly or in writing to show breach arising from failure to provide assurance. Cumberland County Improvement Authority v. GSP Recycling Co., Inc., 358 N.J.Super. 484, 818 A.2d 431, 49 UCC2d 1186 (A.D. 2003).

18. See Ford Motor Credit Co. v. Ellison, 334 Ark. 357, 974 S.W.2d 464, 36 UCC2d 995 (1998) (FMC did not have reasonable ground for insecurity where buyer's willingness and ability to perform obligations under contract were not in question; car had been impounded after third party was arrested while driving it, and insecurity instead arose from fear that lien would not be protected if vehicle were impounded again. Note, however, that other party's filing for bankruptcy, without more, is not

Once the buyer correctly determines that he has reasonable grounds for insecurity, he must properly request assurances from the seller.[19] Although the Code requires this request to be in a record,[20] the cases and commentators have generally been more generous.[21] All that is required is a demand upon the other party for adequate assurances of performance.

But an ambiguous request is not enough.[22] In Alaska Pacific Trading Co. v. Eagon Forest Products, Inc.,[23] Alaska agreed to sell Argentinean logs to Eagon, a Korean buyer. When the price of logs fell, the parties had a prolonged negotiation over Eagon's willingness to take the logs and pay the agreed price. When the negotiation lasted beyond the delivery date without performance by the seller, Eagon claimed the right to cancel for non performance. Alaska claimed that its oral demands during the negotiation were demands for assurance under 2–609. Acknowledging that oral statements could qualify for 2–609 treatment, the court found that Alaska's "demands" were merely part of the negotiation and so too ambiguous to qualify for treatment under 2–609. It concluded: "the section requires a clear demand so that all parties are aware that, absent assurances, the demanding party will withhold performance. An ambiguous communication is not sufficient."[24]

Once one has properly made a demand for assurances, he still has the difficult task of determining the proper "adequate assurances." If the assurances he demands are more than "adequate" and the other party refuses to accede to the excessive demands, the court may find that the demanding party was in breach, a repudiator. The Code gives no clear guidelines, but courts should follow common sense and reasonable business practices in determining which assurances are adequate and which are not.[25] Pittsburgh–Des

reasonable ground for insecurity). In re Beeche Sys. Corp., 164 B.R. 12, 24 UCC2d 1132 (N.D.N.Y. 1994).

19. A party may only request assurances when it anticipates or suspects the other party will breach; a demand cannot be made after the breach has occurred. Chronister Oil Co. v. Unocal Refining and Mktg., 34 F.3d 462, 24 UCC2d 485 (7th Cir.1994).

20. See UCC § 2–609(1); § 1–201(31).

21. Although § 2–609(1) speaks of a demand made in writing, the courts have not required such formality in all cases.

22. Kunian v. Development Corp. of America, 165 Conn. at 312, 313, 334

A.2d at 433, 12 UCC at 1133. See also In re Beeche Sys. Corp., 164 B.R. 12, 24 UCC2d 1132 (N.D.N.Y. 1994) (letter expressing concern about other party's financial ability without referencing UCC or tracking 2–609 language is not sufficient to indicate a demand for assurances).

23. 85 Wash.App. 354, 933 P.2d 417, 34 UCC2d 672 (1997).

24. Id. at 363.

25. S & S, Inc. v. Meyer, 478 N.W.2d 857, 17 UCC2d 137 (Iowa App.1991) (whether assurances adequate is question of fact); Enron Power Marketing, Inc. v. Nevada Power Co., 2004 WL 2290486, 55 UCC2d 31 (S.D.N.Y. 2004) (to be adequate, assurances need not equal sum of all prospective damages).

Moines Steel Co. v. Brookhaven Manor Water Co.,[26] misconstrues the language of 2–609. The aggrieved seller insisted that the buyer place the entire purchase price in escrow and that the buyer's president give a personal guarantee of payment. The court found that the seller had repudiated. It concluded that the seller had no reasonable grounds for insecurity. In dictum, the court stated that even if seller had had reasonable grounds for insecurity, its demand was excessive because it called for more than seller was entitled to have under the contract. Read literally, the court is incorrect. All demands for adequate assurance call for more than was originally promised under the contract, and that is precisely what 2–609 authorizes.[27] If, for example, it was appropriate to sell on open credit at the outset of a contract but subsequent events cause insecurity, 2–609 calls for modification of the contract to provide greater security to the seller than the seller could have demanded, absent such insecurity. Thus it is the very purpose of 2–609 to authorize one party to insist upon more than the contract gives. Of course there are limits. One can demand only "adequate" assurances.[28] If a party demands and receives specific assurances, then absent a further change of circumstances, if the assurances demanded and received are adequate, the party who has demanded the assurances is bound to proceed.[29] Of course, the party receiving assurances is entitled to conforming performance.[30]

It is also possible that the one threatening breach gives assurances that are not adequate. For example, in Land O'Lakes, Inc. v. Hanig,[31] a farmer gave assurances of his production and sale of grain under several "hedge-to-arrive" contracts by promising to perform the contracts only if the contracts "are determined to be enforceable." Since the seller promised performance only if the contracts proved enforceable, the court found the proposal to be inadequate. In addition, the court noted that it would be impossible

---

26. 532 F.2d 572, 18 UCC 931 (7th Cir.1976).

27. However, as the *Pittsburgh–Des Moines* court correctly noted, § 2–609 is not a pen for rewriting the contract to include terms previously waived by the party seeking the modification. In that case, the payment terms demanded by the seller in its 2–609 request had been specifically rejected by the buyer during preliminary negotiations between the parties. The court's reluctance to insert such terms into the contract is understandable.

28. The Task Force recommended requiring some assurances even if the insecure party makes excessive demands. Task Force Report, at 1170–71.

29. American Bronze Corp. v. Streamway Products, 8 Ohio App.3d 223, 456 N.E.2d 1295, 37 UCC 687 (1982) (buyer agreed to assurances of prompt payment and tendered a check for outstanding debts; seller became obligated to perform). Of course, the demanding party need not proceed with his own performance when received assurances are inadequate.

30. ARB, Inc. v. E–Systems, Inc., 663 F.2d 189, 30 UCC 949 (D.C.Cir.1980) (buyer properly rejected nonconforming tender).

31. 610 N.W.2d 518, 41 UCC2d 512 (Iowa 2000).

for the condition (a judicial determination of enforceability) to occur within the 30 days allowed by 2–609.

In some cases clients will not wait for 2–609 to run its course and will call upon the lawyer to decide whether the other party has "repudiated." Section 2–610[32] does not introduce any new tests, but Comment 1 to 2–610 summarizes the general common law definition:

> * * * anticipatory repudiation centers upon an overt communication of intention or an action which renders performance impossible or demonstrates a clear determination not to continue with performance.[33]

Like the common law, the Code allows for nonverbal repudiation by "action which reasonably indicates a rejection of the continuing obligation,"[34] and is consistent with section 250 of the Restatement (Second) of Contracts.[35]

What kind of statement or conduct is a repudiation? The easiest case is where a party irretrievably makes its own performance impossible, as where a seller resells unique goods to another before time for performance.[36] However, Comment 2 to 2–610 indicates that repudiation may occur short of actual impossibility. Where on the spectrum between impossibility and inconvenience is the line which divides "repudiation" from "non-repudiation"? Comment 2 to 2–610 does little more than paraphrase the question; it states that a demand for greater performance than agreed constitutes a repudiation "when under a fair reading it amounts to

---

32. § 2–610:

When either party repudiates the contract with respect to a performance not yet due the loss of which will substantially impair the value of the contract to the other, the aggrieved party may

(a) for a commercially reasonable time await performance by the repudiating party; or

(b) resort to any remedy for breach (Section 2–703 or 2–711), even though he has notified the repudiating party that he would await the latter's performance and has urged retraction; and

(c) in either case suspend his own performance or proceed in accordance with the provisions of this Article on the seller's right to identify goods to the contract notwithstanding breach or to salvage unfinished goods (Section 2–704).

33. See also 4 A. Corbin, Contracts, § 973 (1951); 11 S. Williston, Contracts, §§ 1322–23 (3d ed. 1968).

34. § 2–610, Comment 2.

35. Restatement (Second) of Contracts § 250 (1979):

A repudiation is

(a) a statement by the obligor to the obligee indicating that the obligor will commit a breach that would of itself give the obligee a claim for damages for total breach under § 243, or

(b) a voluntary affirmative act which renders the obligor unable or apparently unable to perform without such a breach.

36. See generally, Allen v. Wolf River Lumber Co., 169 Wis. 253, 172 N.W. 158 (1919) (defendant sold a limited amount of peeled bark which plaintiff had previously arranged to purchase); Oloffson v. Coomer, 11 Ill.App.3d 918, 296 N.E.2d 871, 12 UCC 1082 (1973) (defendant informed plaintiff he was not going to plant the corn contracted for by plaintiff because ground was too wet); White, Eight Cases and Section 251, 67 Cornell L.Rev. 841 (1982).

a statement of intention not to perform except on conditions which go beyond the contract."

Suppose, for example, that a seller contracts to sell 10,000 bushels of soybeans at $2.00/bushel and then phones to tell the buyer that he is not sure he can perform unless the buyer can meet the current price of $2.15/bushel. There are hundreds, perhaps a thousand, ways in which a clever chiseler might communicate his proposition. If he is foolish enough to say, "I won't ship unless you pay me $2.15," he has repudiated. If, on the other hand, all he does is to carry on at great length about how others are now getting $2.15 and about the financial difficulties that he will suffer if he is forced to deliver at $2.00, he probably has not repudiated.[37] In Neptune Research & Development, Inc. v. Teknics Industrial Systems, Inc.,[38] a seller failed to deliver a precision drill by mid-June, as ordered. After frequent evasive responses, the seller notified the buyer in late August that the drill would definitely be ready for pickup on September 5. Because there was no "time-of-the-essence" clause in the contract and nothing in the surrounding circumstances to indicate that the initial time of performance was essential, the court held that the non-delivery in mid-June was not a repudiation.

In Tradax Energy, Inc. v. Cedar Petrochemicals, Inc.,[39] the value of the contract for 10,000 barrels of methanol had apparently increased by more than $180,000. Buyer, Tradax, called seller, Cedar, to insist that Cedar prepare a Texas sales tax certificate (necessary to free the Texas buyer from paying sales tax on goods to be resold to others). In the phone conversation with a clerical employee at Cedar, the Tradax representative said that he would not pay unless he got the certificate and the Cedar employee promised to prepare one and send it. Later Cedar claimed that the threat not to pay was repudiation. Noting that the Cedar employee had agreed to provide the certificate and that producing it was a "trivial" requirement, the court found no repudiation. In fact, the court noted that the parties' behavior better fit the model of a contract modification under 2–209. Regrettably, we have no test to tell when the seller's demands for additional pay or other performance or his refusal to perform become sufficiently unequivocal to amount to repudiation.

37. See, e.g., Unique Systems, Inc. v. Zotos Int'l, Inc., 622 F.2d 373, 28 UCC 1340 (8th Cir.1980) (request for modification without threat of nonperformance is not a repudiation); Lantec, Inc. v. Novell, Inc., 306 F.3d 1003, 49 UCC2d 147 (10th Cir. 2002) (e-mail merely stating a party "wanted to terminate" not a repudiation).

38. 235 N.J.Super. 522, 563 A.2d 465, 10 UCC2d 107 (1989).

39. 317 F.Supp. 2d 373, 53 UCC2d 243 (S.D.N.Y. 2004).

A second kind of repudiation occurs when one of the parties simply announces an intention not to perform.[40] Comment 1 to 2–610 appears to retain the common law requirement that a statement of intention not to perform must be positive and unequivocal.[41] An indefinite statement as to future contingencies will not alone constitute a repudiation. In T & S Brass and Bronze Works v. Pic–Air, Inc.,[42] buyer's statement after extended difficulties with the seller's performance that it "could not make any further payments . . . until such time as this entire matter is cleared up" was not a repudiation, but merely a demand for assurance. An old case on the requisite is Dingley v. Oler,[43] where a defendant-seller declined to deliver ice to the plaintiff-buyer because of an increase in the market price but instead suggested two alternative courses of action.[44] Refusing to find a repudiation, the court explained:

> [a]lthough * * * they decline to ship the ice that season, it is accompanied with the expression of alternative intention, and that is, to ship it, as must be understood, during that season, if and when the market price should reach the point which, in their opinion, the plaintiffs ought to be willing to accept as its fair price between them * * *.

> This, we think, is very far from being a positive, unconditional, and unequivocal declaration of fixed purpose not to perform the contract in any event or at any time. In view of the consequences sought to be deduced and claimed as a matter of law to follow, the defendants have a right to claim that their expressions, sought to be converted into a renunciation of the contract, shall not be enlarged by construction beyond their strict meaning.[45]

---

40. See BarclaysAmerican/Business Credit, Inc. v. E & E Enterprises, Inc., 697 S.W.2d 694, 42 UCC 706 (Tex.App. 1985) (seller's oral notice that it was closing its plant was anticipatory repudiation). However, see Lantec, Inc. v. Novell, Inc. 306 F.3d 1003, 49 UCC2d 147 (10th Cir.2002) (voice mail merely stating desire to terminate not anticipatory repudiation).

41. Diamond Gateway Coal Co. v. LTV Corp. (In re Chateaugay Corp.), 104 B.R. 637, 11 UCC2d 506 (S.D.N.Y. 1989) (because seller always assured full performance as understood by buyer, seller of coal did not express intention to repudiate even though he continuously asserted an erroneous interpretation of contract in talks with buyer); Lantec, Inc. v. Novell, Inc., 306 F.3d 1003, 1014–15, 49 UCC2d 147, 153–54 (10th Cir. 2002) (voice mail message stating that two executives "want to terminate the relationship" too indefinite to be an anticipatory repudiation, as it did not state they would not perform their duties under the agreement).

42. 790 F.2d 1098, 1 UCC2d 433, 441 (4th Cir.1986).

43. 117 U.S. 490, 6 S.Ct. 850, 29 L.Ed. 984 (1886).

44. Plaintiff shipped a load of ice to defendant (1879) in return for a promise to deliver a like amount by the end of the next season (September 1880). At the time plaintiff delivered the ice to defendant it was priced at about 50 cents per ton. In the following July, however, the price had climbed to $5.00 a ton.

45. 117 U.S. at 501–502, 6 S.Ct. at 853, 854.

Dingley v. Oler was decided before the Supreme Court had fully adopted the doctrine of anticipatory repudiation, but the case reflects a longstanding judicial preference for "saving the contract."[46]

Not only must the repudiation be unequivocal; it must also "substantially impair the value of the contract to the other."[47] Thus even a clear repudiation of part of a contract may not be a repudiation of the whole and so give rise to 2–610 remedies unless the value of the whole contract is substantially impaired.[48] Comment 3 to 2–610 characterizes the test as "the same as that in the section on breach in installment contracts * * *, whether material inconvenience or injustice will result if the aggrieved party is forced to wait and receive an ultimate tender minus the part or aspect repudiated."[49]

46. The alleged repudiation consisted of a written communique from defendant to plaintiff, stating in part: "We must therefore decline to ship the ice for you this season, and claim, as our right, to pay you for the ice, in cash, at the price you offered it to other parties here [fifty cents a ton], or give you ice when the market reaches that point."

Id. at 501.

47. § 2–610.

48. See Cargill, Inc. v. Storms Agri Enterprises, Inc., 46 Ark.App. 237, 878 S.W.2d 786, 26 UCC2d 127 (1994) (buyer's repudiation of 14 out of 17 cottonseed loads substantially impaired value of contract to seller). The question of "substantial impairment" under § 2–610 is a question of fact. Bill's Coal Co. v. Board of Public Utilities of Springfield, Mo., 887 F.2d 242, 9 UCC2d 1238 (1989).

49. Consider § 2–612:

(1) An "installment contract" is one which requires or authorizes the delivery of goods in separate lots to be separately accepted, even though the contract contains a clause "each delivery is a separate contract" or its equivalent.

(2) The buyer may reject any installment which is non-conforming if the non-conformity substantially impairs the value of that installment and cannot be cured or if the non-conformity is a defect in the required documents; but if the non-conformity does not fall within subsection (3) and the seller gives adequate assurance of its cure the buyer must accept that installment.

(3) Whenever non-conformity or default with respect to one or more installments substantially impairs the value of the whole contract there is a breach of the whole. But the aggrieved party reinstates the contract if he accepts a non-conforming installment without seasonably notifying of cancellation or if he brings an action with respect only to past installments or demands performance as to future installments.

Subsection 2–612(3) is most relevant to a consideration of anticipatory repudiation, since when there is a material breach of an installment contract such that it "substantially impairs the value of the whole contract," there will also be an anticipatory repudiation as to the remaining installments. Thus it is not surprising that the Code drafters have elected to use an interchangeable test.

Comments 4, 6, and 7 to 2–612 provide some aid (1) to define *beforehand* what kind of nonconformity will be acceptable and (2) to predict the result of a battle in court *after* a nonconforming installment has been tendered.

See In Superior Derrick Services, Inc. v. Anderson, 831 S.W.2d 868, 18 UCC2d 706 (Tex.App.1992), the buyer wrongfully cancelled an installment contract for workover rig masts. Defects in the masts were curable, and the court held that under 2–612 an installment is nonconforming only if the value to buyer is substantially impaired and the defects are incurable. But in Tennessee Gas Pipeline Co. v. Lenape Resources Corp., 870 S.W.2d 286, 24 UCC2d 45 (Tex. App. 1993), judgment rev'd 925 S.W.2d

A third distinguishable kind of repudiation occurs when a defendant willing to perform finds itself unable to do so. Perhaps out of charity to the earnest but incompetent defendant, courts have been more hesitant to find anticipatory repudiation here than in cases where the prospective defendant expressed an unwillingness to perform.[50] But we believe that the aggrieved party's position here is no different than in the situation described above[51] and think it should have the same rights as a repudiatee there.[52]

A fourth type of repudiation occurs when a party fails to give adequate assurances of performance when required to do so under section 2–609(4).[53] Of course, repudiation only occurs where there were reasonable grounds for insecurity necessitating the requested assurances. The party failing to provide adequate assurances is treated as a repudiator.

One party's cancellation of a contract after the other's material breach is not repudiation. Once the contract has been materially breached, there is nothing to repudiate.[54] For example, where a seller of gasoline had delivered gasoline that contained too much water, that gasoline had been rejected and the time for delivery had passed, the contract had been terminated and talk of assurances was irrelevant.[55]

Section 2–611(1) recognizes that an anticipatory repudiation may be revocable. Under 2–611(1), the repudiator may retract until his next performance is due.[56] However, he may retract only if the

---

565 (Tex. 1996), (the court held that buyer's consistent underpayment for each contract period was not anticipatory repudiation).

50. 4 A Corbin, Contracts § 974 (1951). For example, a party who invoked contract's force majeure clause provision to delay performance—rather than indicating that it did not intend to perform at all—did not repudiate. Blue Creek Farm, Inc. v. Aurora Co-op. Elevator Co., 259 Neb. 1032, 614 N.W.2d 310, 42 UCC2d 172 (2000). See also, Dawley v. La Puerta Architectural Antiques, Inc., 133 N.M. 389, 62 P.3d 1271, 49 UCC2d 1207 (App. 2002).

51. *Id.*; 11 S. Williston, Contracts § 1324 (3d ed.1968).

52. See Bliss Produce Co. v. A.E. Albert & Sons, Inc., 35 Agric.Dec. 742, 20 UCC 917 (1976) (seller of potatoes held to have repudiated contract; seller's defense of adverse weather conditions rejected).

53. Creusot–Loire Int'l, Inc. v. Coppus Engineering Corp., 585 F.Supp. 45, 39 UCC 186 (S.D.N.Y.1983) (seller's fail-

ure to provide adequate assurances by extension of contractual guarantee and providing letter of credit held a repudiation); Colorado Interstate Gas Co. v. Chemco, Inc., 854 P.2d 1232, 23 UCC2d 433 (Colo. 1993) (failure to provide adequate assurances); Koch Materials Co. v. Shore Slurry Seal, Inc., 205 F.Supp.2d 324, 48 UCC2d 157 (D.N.J. 2002) (failure to provide assurances on valid demand was repudiation).

54. See, e.g., Mayflower Farms v. Tech–Mark, Inc., 64 Or.App. 121, 666 P.2d 1384, 37 UCC 25 (1983) (after time for performance expired buyer's refusal to pay pending resolution of its suit for breach was not repudiation).

55. Chronister Oil Co. v. Unocal Refining and Marketing, 34 F.3d 462, 24 UCC2d 485 (7th Cir.1994).

56. § 2–611:

(1) Until the repudiating party's next performance is due he can retract his repudiation unless the aggrieved party has since the repudiation cancelled or materially changed his position or other-

aggrieved party has not (1) cancelled, (2) materially changed his position, or (3) otherwise indicated that he considers the repudiation final.[57] This section is consistent with the approach taken by the leading commentators on pre-Code law.[58] Pre–Code law defines "material change." For example, pre-Code cases generally hold that bringing suit for anticipatory breach constitutes a material change.

Section 2–611(2) allows the repudiator to retract by "any method which clearly indicates to the aggrieved party that the repudiating party intends to perform * * *." While a verbal communication would be the most direct method of retracting, the section allows any other method that clearly evidences intent to comply with the contract.[59] Thus if a party regains the ability to perform or experiences other relevant changes of circumstances and these facts are communicated to the repudiatee before a material change of position, both pre-Code law and 2–611 favor reinstating the contract.[60] If the repudiation occurred because of a failure to give adequate assurance of performance (2–609), then 2–611(2) requires that retraction include any assurance so demanded. Even when repudiation clearly has occurred, the aggrieved party may

wise indicated that he considers the repudiation final.

(2) Retraction may be by any method which clearly indicates to the aggrieved party that the repudiating party intends to perform, but must include any assurance justifiably demanded under the provisions of this Article (Section 2–609).

(3) Retraction reinstates the repudiating party's rights under the contract with due excuse and allowance to the aggrieved party for any delay occasioned by the repudiation.

This led Professor Patterson to question whether a retraction might be given as to any future performance even if the repudiator had committed a "present material breach." 1 N.Y.State Law Revision Comm'n, 1955 Report 676 (1955).

57. § 2–611, Comment 1.

58. 4 A Corbin, Contracts § 980 (1951); 11 S. Williston, Contracts § 1335 (3d ed.1968).

59. See, e.g., Wahnschaff Corp. v. O.E. Clark Paper Box Co., 166 Ga.App. 242, 304 S.E.2d 91, 36 UCC 1186 (1983) (conduct of the parties in ignoring a repudiation served as a retraction); Fast v. Southern Offshore Yachts, 587 F.Supp. 1354, 38 UCC 1569

(D.Conn.1984) (execution of escrow agreement for remaining 10% of payment price retracted previous repudiation) (alternative holding). But see BarclaysAmerican/Business Credit, Inc. v. E & E Enterprises, Inc., 697 S.W.2d 694, 42 UCC 706 (Tex.App.1985) (continuing negotiations alone do not constitute retraction).

60. Cf. Restatement (Second) of Contracts § 256 (1979) provides:

(1) The effect of a statement as constituting a repudiation under § 250 or the basis for a repudiation under § 251 is nullified by a retraction of the statement if notification of the retraction comes to the attention of the injured party before he materially changes his position in reliance on the repudiation or indicates to the other party that he considers the repudiation to be final.

(2) The effect of events other than a statement as constituting a repudiation under § 250 or the basis for a repudiation under § 251 is nullified if, to the knowledge of the injured party, those events have ceased to exist before he materially changes his position in reliance on the repudiation or indicates to the other party that he considers the repudiation to be final.

choose to ignore the anticipatory repudiation, in hopes that the repudiator will retract and perform.[61]

§ 7–3 Cover, Section 2–712

Once the "seller fails to make delivery or repudiates or the buyer rightfully rejects or justifiably revokes acceptance * * *," the buyer may resort to the remedies identified in 2–711. Chief among those, and a remedy that enables the buyer "to obtain the goods" and thus meet its "essential need", is its right to cover embodied in 2–712. So states Comment 1.

Section 2–712 reads as follows:

(1) After a breach within the preceding section the buyer may "cover" by making in good faith and without unreasonable delay any reasonable purchase of or contract to purchase goods in substitution for those due from the seller.

(2) The buyer may recover from the seller as damages the difference between the cost of cover and the contract price together with any incidental or consequential damages as hereinafter defined (Section 2–715), but less expenses saved in consequence of the seller's breach.

(3) Failure of the buyer to effect cover within this section does not bar him from any other remedy.[1]

In most cases, the operation of 2–712 is simple and easy to understand. After seller breaches and the buyer "covers" under 2–712(1), the buyer can recover the difference between the cost of the substitute goods and the original contract price, plus any incidental or consequential damages allowable under 2–715, but less expenses saved as a result of seller's breach. In the typical case a timely "cover" purchase by an aggrieved buyer will preclude any 2–715 damages.

In Laredo Hides Co., Inc. v. H & H Meat Products Co., Inc.,[2] the court applied this basic formula. At trial the aggrieved buyer introduced uncontroverted evidence of its replacement purchases. After setting out the relevant portions of 2–712, the court concluded that the buyer was entitled to:

The difference between the cover price and the contract price * * * a total of $142,254.48. In addition, Laredo Hides offered

---

61. Pittsburgh Industries Furnace Co. v. Universal Consol. Companies, Inc., 789 F.Supp. 184, 18 UCC2d 152 (W.D.Pa.1991). This choice is not without risks. See *infra* 7–7 for consequences of waiting for performance.

er, "Remedying Anticipatory Repudiation—Past, Present, and Future," 52 SMU L. Rev. 1787 (1999).

2. 513 S.W.2d 210, 16 UCC 78 (Tex. Civ.App.1974).

§ 7–3

1. Many cases affirm that cover is not mandatory. See generally, DeNooy-

evidence of increased transportation costs of $1,435.77, and increased handling charges of $2,013.18. These are clearly recoverable as incidental damages where the buyer elects to "cover." [There was no evidence offered by H & H * * * to "establish expenses saved in consequence of the seller's breach," as permitted by 2–712.][3]

Since 2–712 measures buyer's damages by the difference between his actual cover purchase and the contract price, the formula will often put buyer in the identical economic position that performance would have.[4] (The buyer may be in a better position if he covers before performance was due, since he then might resell earlier, at a better price, or might start using the goods sooner.)

Section 2–712 was a significant departure from the prior law. Under prior law, if an aggrieved buyer made a cover purchase, there was no assurance that the court would measure the market at or near the time when buyer made the purchase,[5] and accordingly, the court's contract-market differential formula might over or under compensate buyer. His actual cost of cover and the market price at the time and place of the cover were, at least in theory, irrelevant to the damage suit.[6] If for example, seller repudiated a $20,000 contract for shoes and buyer promptly covered for $24,000, and the market price at the time for performance was $22,000 buyer could recover only $2,000. Except in the rare case in which the buyer could prove that the requisition of substitute goods was in the contemplation of the parties at the time the contract was made, the buyer was forced to bear the extra $2,000 cost.[7]

There are several interpretive problems under 2–712. What are "expenses saved in consequence of the seller's breach" when the buyer has covered? This problem appears when the shipping terms of the cover contract differ from those in the original contract.[8]

3.   513 S.W.2d at 221–22, 16 UCC at 91.

4.   Where the buyer has made a number of purchases which exceed the volume involved in the breach, it may be appropriate to determine the cover price by averaging. See Bigelow–Sanford, Inc. v. Gunny Corp., 649 F.2d 1060, 31 UCC 968 (5th Cir.1981).

5.   An exception to this proposition was discussed by Professor Honnold, 1 N.Y. State Law Revision Comm'n, 1955 Report 570 (1955). He noted one context where pre-Code decisions found buyer's substitute purchase binding: "If buyer purchases substitute goods for *less* than market price, this repurchase price may be the maximum amount on which damages can be measured."

6.   See Uniform Sales Act § 67.

7.   The outlandish results produced by the failure of the courts to recognize substitute purchases were evident in common law times and continued under the Uniform Sales Act. See, e.g., Missouri Furnace Co. v. Cochran, 8 F. 463 (W.D.Pa.1881).

8.   For different fact situations involving this problem, see Melms v. Mitchell, 266 Or. 208, 512 P.2d 1336, 13 UCC 223 (1973) ("cover" damages reduced by buyer's savings from not having to cut the "cover" wood); Terex Corp. v. Ingalls Shipbuilding, Inc., 671 So.2d 1316, 31 UCC2d 134 (Miss. 1996) (buyer covered seller's breach of contract for two forklifts with a contract for four forklifts; buyer's cover damages re-

Assume for example, that a Washington, D.C. buyer contracts to purchase food blenders from a Seattle seller for $10,000, F.O.B. shipping point (Seattle), with shipping costs totaling $500. Further, assume a breach by seller, and that buyer covers in Kalamazoo for $12,000, F.O.B. buyer's plant (Washington, D.C.). What are the "expenses saved in consequence of the seller's breach"? Bearing in mind the goal of placing the buyer in the position he would have been in had no breach occurred, one sees that the buyer's cost of putting the blenders in his hands in Washington, D.C. under the original contract was $10,500.[9] Under the substitute contract the analogous cost is $12,000, and the proper recovery is $1,500. Collating the hypothetical figure with the 2–712(2) formula leads to the same result: cost of cover ($12,000) less the contract price ($10,000) plus other damages ($0) less expenses saved ($500 shipping charges from Seattle). $12,000 − 10,000 + 0 − 500 = $1,500.[10]

Assume the seller's breach takes the form of delayed delivery, and the buyer, on learning of the impending delay, covers at a price above the contract price, yet later also accepts the delayed delivery too and resells it at a profit. Must the buyer deduct this profit from his cover damages? On principle and authority, we think so.

In Fertico Belgium S.A. v. Phosphate Chemicals Export Ass'n, Inc.,[11] the New York Court of Appeals reversed a lower court that had answered "yes"[12] and held that no such deduction is required. *Fertico* is a close case and we are not sure about the proper outcome. The real question for us is to compare the plaintiff's economic status at the end of all the relevant transactions with the economic status that the plaintiff would have enjoyed had the defendant not breached the contract. In *Fertico* the majority assumes that if the contract had been performed, the plaintiff would have made the intended resale to the Iraqi buyer, and also a second resale to the other buyer. The dissent suggests that is only speculation. The dissent indicates that it is likely that if the American seller had not breached, the European buyer would not have sought substitute goods in Lebanon to fulfill its contract with the Iraqis and in fact would only have had one sale. If that is what would have

duced by per-unit cost-savings achieved due to seller's breach). S.N.A. Nut Co., 247 B.R. 7, 41 UCC2d 834 (Bankr. N.D. Ill. 2000) (buyer cannot seek damages for cover when substitute goods are obtained at lower price).

9. $10,000 contract price plus $500 shipping charges.

10. The problem of interpreting the phrase expenses "saved in consequence of the seller's breach" is discussed more fully in 7–4 *infra*.

11. 70 N.Y.2d 76, 510 N.E.2d 334, 517 N.Y.S.2d 465, 3 UCC2d 1812 (1987), reargument denied, 70 N.Y.2d 694, 512 N.E.2d 556, 518 N.Y.S.2d 1030 (1987).

12. Fertico Belgium S.A. v. Phosphate Chemicals Export Ass'n, 120 A.D.2d 401, 501 N.Y.S.2d 867, 1 UCC2d 771 (1986). Of course, the effect of this approach is to measure overall damages in light of the buyer's special circumstances. Compare 7–5 *infra*.

happened, the dissent is correct. If, on the other hand, the European reseller would have had both resales, then the majority seems correct. Contrary to our conclusion in the last edition, we are now more doubtful of the majority's opinion. It is clear that the market for phosphate was rising in the period between the signing of the contract and its performance. It may be true that Fertico could have made two sales, but if it did not have the first shipment from defendant Phoschem, Fertico would have had to buy additional phosphate on the market at a price that probably would have been higher than its contract price with Phoschem. By entirely ignoring the profit on the resale, the majority almost certainly gives Fertico more than it could have had by full performance. So in our view, there should be an offset from Fertico's recovery equal to the difference between the price at which Fertico would have purchased phosphate on the market for the second contract and the contract price for that phosphate between it and Phoschem.

In these circumstances we believe it should be the responsibility of the defendant (who seeks to reduce the plaintiff's damages) to show that it is more probable than not that the plaintiff would *not* have had both sales, would not have enjoyed the second resale profit, and thus that the second resale profit (as a child of the breach) should be used to reduce the plaintiff's recovery.[13]

A second interpretative difficulty lies in defining the phrases "good faith" and "goods in substitution." Good faith will always be a slippery phrase, but this does not mean it is devoid of meaning, and it is no more slippery here than elsewhere. Section 1–201(b)(20)[14] has established both a subjective standard for measuring good faith (honesty in fact) and an objective one (observance of reasonable commercial standards). In addition, under 2–103(1)(b), a merchant buyer always had to observe "reasonable commercial standards of fair dealing in the trade." Even without the adoption of Revised Article 1, merchants under Article 2 are subject to both a subjective and an objective test of good faith.[15] Presumably the covering buyer acts in good faith unless it knowingly and without reason avoids a less expensive market in favor of a more expensive one. If the cover remedy is to work to the benefit of an aggrieved buyer, the court should give buyer wide latitude to reject the least expensive cover when there is any reasonable basis for choosing a

---

13. For more on these questions, see the discussion of 2–708(2) in Chapter 8.

14. § 1–201(b)(20) provides: " 'Good faith' . . . means honesty in fact and the observance of reasonable commercial standards of fair dealing." It appears that some states will not include the new definition of good faith in their adoption of Article 1. Nevertheless the invocation of reasonable commercial standards of fair dealing applies not just to merchants in Article 2 but to all transactions in Articles 3, 4, 4A and 9.

15. § 2–103(1)(b) provides: " 'Good faith' in the case of a merchant means honesty in fact and the observance of reasonable commercial standards of fair dealing in the trade."

more expensive cover (for instance, the goods are of better quality or the seller more reliable).

It is a more difficult task to assign substance to the standard of reasonableness in 2–712. Section 2–712 indicates that cover must be made without "unreasonable delay," and that it must be a "reasonable purchase." Among other things, Comment 2 to 2–712 says:

> The test of proper cover is whether at the time and place the buyer acted in good faith and in a reasonable manner, and it is immaterial that hindsight may later prove that the method of cover used was not the cheapest or most effective.

Thus, the unreasonable delay requirement is not intended to limit the time necessary for the buyer to decide how best to cover. Section 1–205(a) defines reasonable time as follows:

> Whether a time for taking an action required . . . is reasonable depends on the nature, purpose and circumstances of the action.

The drafters have hardly left us with a solid basis to predict whether a given act was or was not "reasonable"; each addition in the Comment is like an additional bucket of muck thrown into a quagmire.

Of course the drafters were not dummies, and their vagueness may have been purposeful. One aid to which floundering courts and lawyers may turn is the Code's Revised 1–305 basic remedial injunction: put the plaintiff in the position performance would have. If 2–712 is to be the remedy used by more aggrieved buyers than any other remedy, then the courts should be slow to find a buyer's good faith acts unreasonable. The courts should not hedge the remedy with restrictions in the name of "reasonableness" that render it useless or uncertain for the good faith buyer. Indeed, one may argue that the courts should read very little substance into the reasonableness requirement and insist only that the buyer proceed in good faith. A lawyer might test a client's good faith under 2–712 by asking: "How, where, and when would you have procured these goods if you had not been covering and had no prospect of a court recovery from another?" If the client can answer truthfully that he would have spent his own money in the same way, the court should demand no more.

For the most part the courts have adopted sensible interpretations of the buyer's action when buyer covers. In one case the court held the purchases made nine and twenty-two days after the seller's breach were "commercially reasonable;"[16] in another case the court

---

16. Farmers Elevator Co. v. Lyle, 90 S.D. 86, 238 N.W.2d 290, 18 UCC 1143 (1976).

approved the buyer's act of waiting until its delivery of contract goods to a third party was due before it covered.[17] Still another court upheld a finding of reasonableness where the cover occurred 42 days after an anticipatory repudiation.[18] Whether a buyer's delay is reasonable may also turn on the seller's behavior.[19] It may also be wise for the buyer to build a record that shows it made reasonable inquiries of alternative sources of supply before making its cover purchase.[20]

In apparent contrast to the foregoing cases is Oloffson v. Coomer.[21] There a farmer agreed to sell 40,000 bushels of corn at $1.12 a bushel to his merchant buyer. The contract was made on April 16th; on June 3rd the farmer unequivocally informed the buyer that he, the farmer, was not going to plant corn because the season had been too wet. The merchant already had made a contract for the resale of the corn and ultimately satisfied that obligation by buying corn at $1.35 and $1.49 a bushel late in the fall. Buyer sued seller for the difference between the $1.12 contract price and the $1.35 and $1.49 cover price. The court found that in these circumstances the buyer should have covered the same day the seller repudiated and that to wait longer under those circumstances was not reasonable. The court approved damages equal to the difference between the market price and the contract price on June 3rd but refused to grant any other recovery. So put, the court's conclusion is wrong on several counts in our judgment. We discuss the interpretation of 2–713 elsewhere. Even though there was a readily available market and even if the farmer's repudiation was as unequivocal as he could make it, one should not insist that cover be achieved on the same day that repudiation is received. At minimum we should grant the buyer a few days in which to see if

17. Jamestown Terminal Elevator, Inc. v. Hieb, 246 N.W.2d 736, 20 UCC 617 (N.D.1976). The aggrieved buyer was a middleman who had made both his purchase contract and a contract to resell on July 3rd. The delivery date for his resale contract was August 31st. The seller arguably repudiated on July 19th. In these circumstances the court found that the jury was justified in finding the buyer's cover on September 4th to be reasonable.

18. Mason Distributors, Inc. v. Encapsulations, Inc., 484 So.2d 1275, 42 UCC 1307 (Fla.App. 1986). See also Dangerfield v. Markel, 278 N.W.2d 364, 26 UCC 419 (N.D.1979) (38 days).

19. Compare Erie Casein Co. v. Anric Corp., 217 Ill.App.3d 602, 577 N.E.2d 892, 160 Ill.Dec. 567, 15 UCC2d 1240 (1991), appeal denied, 142 Ill.2d 653, 584 N.E.2d 128, 164 Ill.Dec. 916 (1991) (buyer not guilty of unreasonable delay in covering when buyer relied on seller's continued assurances that the goods would eventually be delivered) with Bockman Printing & Services, Inc. v. Baldwin–Gregg, Inc., 213 Ill.App.3d 516, 157 Ill.Dec. 630, 572 N.E.2d 1094, 15 UCC2d 490 (1991) (buyer's cover unreasonable where buyer did not buy until well after seller's behavior made it clear seller would not perform).

20. Damages cases, of course, require a proper record. See, e.g., Productora e Importadora de Papel, S.A. de C.V. v. Fleming, 376 Mass. 826, 383 N.E.2d 1129, 25 UCC 729 (1978).

21. 11 Ill.App.3d 918, 296 N.E.2d 871, 12 UCC 1082 (1973).

the seller is going to change his mind or in which to search for the better market or to consider alternatives.[22]

The outcome of the case can be defended only on the ground that the contract was implicitly modified by the trade usage that prevailed in the corn market in that part of Illinois. According to testimony at trial the buyer Oloffson "adhered to a usage of trade that permitted his customers to cancel the contract for a future delivery of grain by making known to him a desire to cancel and paying to him the difference between the contract and the market price on the day of cancellation."[23] If the court had held only that this trade usage modified the plaintiff's rights under part 7 of Article 2, we could not disagree. However the opinion says much more than that; read as narrowly as we suggest, the opinion is tolerable.[24]

To comply with 2–712, buyer must purchase goods "in substitution for those due from the seller." Comment 2 to 2–712 says that the section "envisages * * * goods not identical with those involved but commercially usable as reasonable substitutes under the circumstances of the particular case; and contracts on credit or delivery terms differing from the contract in breach, but again reasonable under the circumstances."[25] For example, a buyer that used package labels that were the wrong size and the wrong color in a stop gap measure, did not "cover" even though this use was in partial substitution for conforming labels.[26] The "substitution" requirement may pose two problems. First, how does one determine which of several contracts are in substitution when the buyer makes a series of purchases? Second, how does one adjust the damage formula when the cover purchase is "in substitution" but differs significantly from the goods contracted for (e.g., A.M./F.M. radios in substitution for A.M. radios)?

When the relevant market prices are subject to abrupt and significant variation, a buyer who continually goes into the market

22. But see Saboundjian v. Bank Audi (USA), 157 A.D.2d 278, 556 N.Y.S.2d 258, 11 UCC2d 1165 (1990) (buyer's cover within 30 days after bank's failure to execute a currency transaction unreasonable when buyer could have covered on day he learned of breach when bank informed buyer of inability to place transaction the previous day and market was extremely volatile).

23. Oloffson v. Coomer, 11 Ill.App.3d 918, 922, 296 N.E.2d 871, 875, 12 UCC 1082, 1087 (1973).

24. On the "reasonableness" of an aggrieved buyer's cover purchases, see also Transammonia Export Corp. v.

Conserv, Inc., 554 F.2d 719, 22 UCC 301 (5th Cir.1977).

25. See Valley Die Cast Corp. v. A.C.W. Inc., 25 Mich.App. 321, 181 N.W.2d 303, 8 UCC 488 (1970) (no "cover" where buyer purchased entirely different type of goods); International Cosmetics Exchange, Inc. v. Gapardis Health & Beauty, Inc., 303 F.3d 1242, 48 UCC2d 621 (11th Cir. 2002) (no "cover" damages in a distributorship agreement, where cover would require obtaining counterfeit goods).

26. Credit Institute v. Veterinary Nutrition Corp., 133 N.M. 248, 62 P.3d 339, 49 UCC2d 1160 (Ct.App. 2002).

for new purchases may have a wide range of possible alternatives for a cover contract. Though it seems unlikely that a buyer in reliance upon the outcome of an always uncertain law suit will spend more than necessary to cover, some buyer somewhere might select the contract that most significantly enhances its damage recovery. For example, if a buyer knows of four potential cover sellers whose prices for substantially identical goods range from $10,000 to $6,000 and if he buys from the seller charging the highest price, a court should deny his cover claim because he did not cover in good faith.[27] Moreover, the court may also limit the bad faith buyer to proper cover damages (denying any resort to 2–713).[28]

Further, where, following the seller's breach, the buyer for his own business purposes makes a number of purchases at various prices above the contract price and these exceed the quantity involved in the seller's breach, may the buyer, without more, charge off against the seller the differential between the contract price and the highest priced purchases on the theory that *these* purchases were of goods bought "in substitution" under 2–712(1)? We think not, and in the absence of special circumstances, would, in light of 2–712's good faith and reasonableness requirement limit the buyer to no more than the average costs of the purchases in the relevant time period.[29]

What of the buyer who covers by purchasing goods of superior quality for use as a commercial substitute? Suppose, for example, that seller breaches a sales contract for four-speed food blenders. Desiring to take advantage of the Code's cover provision, buyer procures a substitute contract for more expensive eight-speed food blenders. If comparable four-speed machines were available, it is clear that buyer should not recover the full difference between the cover price and the contract price. Although Comment 2 instructs that the substitute need not be the least expensive cover, nothing in the Code indicates that the buyer is free to pass over an identical substitute and to select his own windfall. Indeed section 1–305 and its predecessors aim at matching performance, nothing more.

If the eight-speed blenders were the only available substitute, then what? One can argue that the buyer should recover the full difference between the price of the superior eight-speed and the contract price. Unlike the former case, here the buyer has not elected to increase his damage recovery. If the added quality of the

---

27. Peters, Remedies for Breach of Contracts Relating to the Sale of Goods Under the Uniform Commercial Code: A Roadmap for Article 2, 73 Yale L.J. 199, 256 (1963).

28. See Study Group Report, at 223–24 (recommendation of some members); Task Force Report, at 1228–29 (agree-ing, but relegating the suggestion to the comments due to potential proof problems).

29. Support for an averaging approach is to be found in Bigelow–Sanford, Inc. v. Gunny Corp., 649 F.2d 1060, 31 UCC 968 (5th Cir.1981).

cover item will not benefit the buyer in any way, then he should be allowed to claim the full differential from the breaching seller. However, if because of the added quality the seller can prove that the buyer stands to make a greater profit on resale, then the buyer's damage recovery under 2–712 should be reduced sufficiently to put him in the same position as performance would have.[30]

If the aggrieved buyer will itself consume the cover goods, as for example by the use of furniture or equipment in a business, the problem is more difficult. Should the damage recovery under 2–712 be reduced because the cover machinery which the aggrieved buyer purchased is marginally more efficient? Because the waiting room furniture is slightly more attractive than that contracted for? We think the damage recovery should not be reduced unless the seller comes forward with persuasive evidence that the buyer will reap added profits because of the superior quality of the cover merchandise.

Where the buyers' cover and other events put the buyer in as good as or better position than performance, the courts have disagreed. In KGM Harvesting Co. v. Fresh Network,[31] buyer purchased cover lettuce at a price well above the contract price. Apparently buyer then passed on that price increase (under cost plus contracts with buyer's buyers) but was still able to recover the difference as cover from its seller. To the contrary is Terex Corporation v. Ingalls Shipbuilding, Inc.[32] There, Ingalls covered when Terex broke its contract to deliver several large forklifts for use on Navy ships. When it was disclosed that Ingalls' cover contract ultimately resulted in a savings of more than $100,000, the judgment against Terex was reduced. We favor the outcome in Terex as more true to the model of contract damages, but we can understand the sentiment that a clear breacher should be made to pay if there is a real loss that must be borne by someone who is not before the court. One might argue that it is better to give a windfall to a plaintiff than to leave the defendant who broke the contract without a proper incentive to behave himself.

---

30. See also Martella v. Woods, 715 F.2d 410, 36 UCC 1200 (8th Cir.1983) (where seller breached contract to provide certain heifers, and buyer covered by purchasing heifers of superior condition, i.e., pregnant and heavier, buyer is in better position than had the contract been performed, and therefore not entitled to full difference between the cost of cover and contract price). However, see KGM Harvesting Co. v. Fresh Network, 36 Cal.App.4th 376, 42 Cal.Rptr.2d 286, 26 UCC2d 1028 (1995) (buyer, who covered at a price higher than contract price was able to pass most of the in-

creased cost on to its customers; despite risk of windfall, buyer was entitled to collect full difference between cover and contract price). This case follows numerous New York decisions allowing similar recoveries (e.g. G.A. Thompson & Co., Inc. v. Wendell J. Miller, Mortg. Co., Inc., 457 F.Supp. 996, 24 UCC 1285 (S.D.N.Y. 1978)).

31. 36 Cal.App.4th 376, 42 Cal. Rptr.2d 286, 26 UCC2d 1028 (1995).

32. 671 So.2d 1316, 31 UCC2d 134 (Miss. 1996).

Sometimes the exigencies of the market necessitate further dealings between the aggrieved buyer and the breaching seller. In B.B. Walker Co. v. Ashland Chemical Co.,[33] Ashland and Harrelson (Walker's subsidiary) had been doing business since 1969 and by 1973 Ashland was Harrelson's exclusive supplier of masterbatch, a basic material used in Harrelson's manufacturing process. In October 1973, when masterbatch producers nationwide began allocating their production and declining new customers because of the shortage in petrochemicals, Harrelson was in a precarious position. Ashland breached the contract on November 1, 1973 as part of an effort to force Harrelson to agree to higher prices. Because no other sources of supply were available, and because Harrelson required the masterbatch to avoid going out of business, Harrelson agreed to Ashland's demands. Walker and Harrelson later sued Ashland for breach of contract seeking to recover the amount paid above the contract price as cover damages. The court held that Ashland had breached the contract and that because of the circumstances of the case Harrelson's purchases from Ashland thereafter during the contract period constituted cover.[34] Another and more appropriate avenue to the same result would be to allow the buyer recovery on the ground that the seller in effect exacted a bad faith modification of the agreement.

But not every request for a price increase constitutes bad faith—particularly where there are extended dealings. In Kelsey–Hayes Co. v. Galtaco Redlaw Castings Corp.,[35] a three-year requirements contract provided that the defendant was to be the plaintiff's sole source of supply of certain types of castings at fixed prices for the first year, and scheduled price reductions for the next two years. By the end of 1989, the defendant had been losing money for several years, and decided to discontinue production of castings. To insure its customers enough castings while they attempted to cover, it offered to maintain production for several months in exchange for a price increase of 30%. The plaintiff accepted the offer in order to keep its own clients' businesses running. The defendant asked for another 30% increase a few months later. When the plaintiff sued for breach of the contract, the court held that buying the same goods from the same seller at a higher price could qualify as "cover."

To see that the buyer gets full measure under 2–712 we think courts should construe 2–712 as a generous and relatively unfettered remedy for the aggrieved buyer. Of course it is possible that 2–712 will overcompensate an occasional buyer because, for exam-

---

33. 474 F.Supp. 651, 34 UCC 561 (M.D.N.C.1979).

34. 474 F.Supp. at 661, 34 UCC at 573–74.

35. 749 F.Supp. 794, 14 UCC2d 469 (E.D.Mich.1990).

ple, the seller will be unable to prove that the buyer specifically benefitted from the added quality of the cover, but it seems equally likely that nonrecoverable legal fees and other costs of litigation will offset any such benefit and that the more likely and more common consequence of 2–712's application is to leave the buyer short of the economic position that full and timely performance offered.

Although section 2–712 does not explicitly recognize what might be called "internal cover," the case law does. For example, in Dura–Wood Treating Co. v. Century Forest Industries, Inc.,[36] the Fifth Circuit allowed an aggrieved buyer to recover the difference between contract price and the cost to the plaintiff of manufacturing substitute goods in house. The Maine Supreme Judicial Court has arrived at a similar result.[37] An important question in these cases is how to measure cost of such internal cover. Should the internally covering buyer be held to its actual historic costs of components? May the buyer charge current market prices if those are higher? So far the cases do not address these issues.

A similar question arises when the aggrieved buyer uses existing inventory to replace the goods expected from the breaching seller. Can purchases made prior to the breach constitute cover? In Commonwealth Edison Co. v. Allied Chemical Nuclear Products, Inc.,[38] the defendant breached its contract to reprocess the plaintiff's spent nuclear fuel. When the plaintiff sued for 2–713 contract-market damages, the defendant argued that the buyer had covered out of its own inventory that had been purchased from other sellers before the breach. The court held that if the buyer had built up the inventory as a backup to protect against loss of other sources (such as the defendant) the inventory could constitute cover.

A final question is whether a buyer who has covered may disregard 2–712 and sue for the contract-market differential in 2–713. We will discuss that problem below.

In sum, the importance of 2–712 cannot be overstated. Not only does the damage formula in 2–712 come close to putting the aggrieved buyer in the same economic position as actual performance would have, but it also enables a buyer to achieve its prime objective, namely that of acquiring needed goods.[39]

§ 7–4 Contract–Market Damages, Section 2–713

Section 2–713 gives the buyer the contract-market differential. If people in business behave as the Code drafters believed, 2–713

36. 675 F.2d 745, 33 UCC 1201 (5th Cir.1982), cert. denied, 459 U.S. 865, 103 S.Ct. 144, 74 L.Ed.2d 122 (1982).

37. Cives Corp. v. Callier Steel Pipe & Tube, Inc., 482 A.2d 852, 39 UCC 1705 (Me.1984).

38. 684 F.Supp. 1434, 6 UCC2d 434 (N.D.Ill.1988).

39. § 2–712, Comment 1.

would be much less significant and would be invoked much less often than 2–712.[1] Presumably, the typical aggrieved buyer will persist in his desire to get the goods that the breaching seller did not deliver; accordingly the buyer will cover. If so, 2–713 will come into play only in the aberrational case in which the buyer decides not to cover or finds that he is unable to do so. Of course, a buyer need not show an unsuccessful attempt to cover as a condition to resorting to 2–713.[2] Section 2–713 provides:

> (1) Subject to the provisions of this Article with respect to proof of market price (Section 2–723), the measure of damages for non-delivery or repudiation by the seller is the difference between the market price at the time when the buyer learned of the breach and the contract price together with any incidental and consequential damages provided in this Article (Section 2–715), but less expenses saved in the consequence of the seller's breach.

> (2) Market price is to be determined as of the place for tender or, in cases of rejection after arrival or revocation of acceptance, as of the place of arrival.[3]

The formula in 2–713 can be expressed as follows:

market price (at the time buyer learned of the breach)

− contract price

− expenses saved as a result of seller's breach

+ incidental and consequential damages (2–715)

= 2–713 damage recovery

§ 7–4

1. The fact is that neither section is much cited in reported cases and one cannot say with certainty how each is used in negotiations or in trial courts. See White, Evaluating Article 2 of the Uniform Commercial Code: A Preliminary Empirical Expedition, 75 Mich. L.Rev. 1262 (1977). See generally Childres, Buyer's Remedies: The Danger of Section 2–713, 72 Nw.U.L.Rev. 837 (1978).

2. See § 2–712(3), and Kashi v. Gratsos, 790 F.2d 1050, 1 UCC2d 768 (2d Cir.1986). See also Kneale v. Jay Ben, Inc., 527 So.2d 917, 6 UCC2d 1492 (Fla. App.1988) (when buyer purchased chairs at a sale price, and the seller oversold and failed to deliver, buyer entitled, not to refund, but to market value of the goods).

3. In Egerer v. CSR West, 116 Wash. App. 645, 67 P.3d 1128, 50 UCC2d 479 (2003), the court stated that there is "reasonable leeway" in measuring market price for purposes of 2–713 damages. A prior draft of § 2–713 appeared in 1949 and 1952 as follows:

(1) The measure of damages for non-delivery is the difference between the price current at the time the buyer learned of the breach and the contract price together with the incidental and consequential damages as provided in this Article (Section 2–715), but less any expense saved in consequence of the seller's breach.

(2) Current price is to be determined as of the place for tender or, in cases of rejection after arrival or revocation of acceptance, as of the place of arrival.

Abstractly stated, the damage formula is deceptively easy to understand. However, understanding the formula and putting it into operation are two different things. Consider the following questions:

(1) When and where does one measure the market price? Does "tender" occur when goods are given to the carrier or only when the carrier delivers them to the buyer?

(2) Has a buyer "saved expenses" when seller fails to ship and so frees buyer from paying the shipping costs on the contract goods? Or has such a buyer not "saved" these expenses because it will have to pay similar costs on any replacement contract?

(3) What is the time for measuring the market in the special case of an anticipatory repudiation? Does "learned of the breach" mean the time buyer learned of the "repudiation," or the time of tender, or something else?

(4) What proof of the market price must the aggrieved buyer show in order to prove its damage claim?

(5) Can an aggrieved buyer "cover" under 2–712, yet receive a larger contract-market differential under 2–713?

(6) Are buyer's 2–713 damages to be limited to no more than what the buyer stood to gain had seller delivered the goods?

Before proceeding to these questions, one should search the section and its history for principles to guide the trip through the thickets. Surely the drafters did not intend for this section to put the buyer in the same position as performance would have (pursuant to the general principle of Section 1–305 and its predecessors, "in as good a position as if the other party had fully performed"). Performance would have given the buyer certain goods for consumption or resale. The consequence of that consumption or resale might have been a net economic gain for the buyer or a net economic loss. The contract-market differential is not a function of the change in the buyer's economic status caused by the breach. It is possible that the 2–713 differential might be large even though the breach actually saved the buyer money (as for example when a middleman buyer's resale markets dry up after the breach). It is also possible that the buyer's lost profit from resale or consumption would exceed the contract-market difference. Assume, for example, that seller breaches a $50,000 contract for overalls. Assume further that the market price at the time used for the purposes of measuring 2–713 damages was $55,000 and that 2–713 would have yielded a $5,000 recovery for buyer.

Consider two separate hypothetical cases. Upon learning of the breach, the buyer decides not to cover, for he believes that the market in overalls is going cold. In case 1 the buyer proves correct; had seller delivered, buyer's gross receipts on resale of the contracted for goods would have been only $40,000. Carrying out the contract would have cost him more than $10,000. In that case the $5,000 difference money recovery under 2–713 puts buyer in a better position than performance would have.

In case 2 the buyer also does not cover, but here his judgment is faulty. Here overalls are in short supply and can be sold at higher prices than the buyer ever imagined so that the net profit on the contract would have exceeded $20,000. In that case the $5,000 recovery would leave the buyer in a substantially worse economic position than performance would have. So putting the buyer in the same place as performance would have cannot be the purpose of 2–713.

A second but no more happy explanation for the existence of 2–713 is that it is an historical anomaly. Since cover under 2–712 was not a recognized remedy under pre-Code law, it made sense under that law to say that the contract-market formula put buyer in the same position as performance would have *on the assumption that the buyer would purchase substitute goods.* If things worked right, the market price would approximate the cost of the substitute goods and buyer would be put "in the same position." But under the Code, 2–712 does this job with greater precision, and 2–713 reigns over only those cases where the buyer does not purchase a substitute. Perhaps the drafters retained 2–713 not out of a belief in its appropriateness, but out of fear that they would be dismissed as iconoclasts had they proposed that the court in noncover cases simply award the buyer any economic loss proximately caused by seller's breach pursuant to 1–305.

A third, and perhaps the best, explanation of 2–713 is that it is a statutory liquidated damage clause, a breach inhibitor the payout of which need bear no close relation to plaintiff's actual loss.[4] This explanation conflicts with the policy in 1–305 (only as good a position as performance and no more), but is consistent with the belief that plaintiffs recover too little and too infrequently for the threat of damages to be an optimal deterrent.

Which of these analyses actually explains the presence of 2–713 in Article 2? The drafters unquestionably intended that 2–713 take a backseat to 2–712 and certainly did not intend to offer an incentive (in the form of a higher damage award) which would influence buyers not to use 2–712. It appears that the drafters

---

4. See Allied Canners & Packers, Inc. v. Victor Packing Co., 162 Cal. App.3d 905, 209 Cal.Rptr. 60, 39 UCC 1567 (1984) (finding 2–713 to be a liquidated damages provision but refusing to apply it on the facts of that case).

intended 2–713's formula to yield approximately the same judgment in noncover cases against the seller as the 2–712 formula would have yielded had the buyer covered. Comment 1 to 2–713 expresses the idea as follows:

> The general baseline adopted in this section uses as a yardstick the market in which the buyer would have obtained cover had he sought that relief.

Section 2–713's statutory ancestor is section 67 of the Uniform Sales Act: "Action for Failing to Deliver Goods." The only important departure in 2–713 from USA § 67 is the choice of the "time when the buyer learned of the breach" as the time for measuring the market. The Uniform Sales Act, in the absence of special circumstances, used "the time or times when they ought to have been delivered, or, if no time was fixed, then at the time of the refusal to deliver." Except in the anticipatory repudiation cases (see 7–7 *infra*) where the "learned of the breach" language contributes to confusion, this difference in the time when one measures the market is not likely to be significant since the buyer will usually learn of the breach at the time of tender or shortly thereafter. In fact, under the Code, there has not been much change in the law as applied by the courts.[5] Thus in Perkins v. Minford,[6] plaintiff contracted to purchase sugar from the defendant, F.O.B. shipping point (Cuba). Defendant breached by sending too small a quantity, and plaintiff was unaware of this until receipt of the bill of lading. By the time of receipt prices had risen sharply. The court concluded that since the buyer neither knew nor had the means of discovering the breach and so could not protect against a rising market by buying from others:

> special circumstances are present showing "proximate damages of a greater amount" than those provided for by the general rule. The time as to when the damages are measured is shifted. It is now the date when the buyer knew or should have known of the default.[7]

The "learned of breach" language of 2–713 appears in part to be a codification of the USA's "special circumstances" exception. Amended Article 2 would have removed the language and used the time of tender in the basic case and explicitly adopted a "reasonable time after the buyer learned of the repudiation" where there is repudiation. The Study Committee agreed with the law as the

---

5. For that law in New York, see 1 N.Y. State Law Revision Comm'n, 1955 Report 698 (1955).

6. 235 N.Y. 301, 139 N.E. 276 (1923).

7. *Id.* at 305, 139 N.E. at 277. A similar case relied on by the Perkins court was Boyd v. L.H. Quinn Co., 18 Misc. 169, 41 N.Y.S. 391 (1896).

courts have applied it, and, at least as regards breach from nonde-livery, recommended no changes to 2–713.[8]

The basic operation of 2–713's formula in non-discriminatory cases under 2–713(1) is well illustrated by Deardorff–Jackson Co. v. National Produce Distributors, Inc.,[9] a reparation proceeding under the Perishable Agriculture Commodities Act of 1930. Defendant entered into a written contract as the exclusive marketing agent for plaintiff's potatoes. Defendant contracted to purchase fifty carloads of potatoes from the plaintiff, a local grower in Wasco, California. Only twenty carloads of potatoes were ever delivered. The court concluded that notice of the breach was first given on June 14, the date the first carload was shipped. The grower brought suit for the price of the potatoes delivered and the buyer counterclaimed for the damages suffered because he was not able to fulfill his own resale obligations. Acknowledging the applicability of the 2–713 formula, the court took official notice of the prices quoted in the Federal Market News Report for June 14, 1965, for the type of potatoes specified under the contract. The court first ascertained the market value for the undelivered thirty carloads as $5.87½ per 100 pound sack or a total of $84,600. The contract price for the undelivered thirty carloads equalled $39,600. Applying the formula of market price less contract price, the court found damages in the amount of $45,000. However, because the defendant still owed $39,075 for potatoes delivered, his net recovery was $5,925. In this case defendant did not claim any additional incidental or consequential damages (2–715), nor did he claim the benefit of any expenses saved in consequence of the breach.

An initial and at least superficially thorny problem in the 2–713 formula concerns the place of tender—the place where the market may be measured. Section 2–713 measures the market at "the place for tender or, in cases of rejection after arrival or revocation of acceptance * * * the place of arrival." Thus in all cases where the seller breaches or repudiates before delivery the relevant market will be the place for tender. Nowhere does the Code precisely define place of tender, but a good starting point in a search for a definition is 2–503: "Manner of Seller's Tender of Delivery."[10] Section 2–503(1) at least half-heartedly defines tender in the "across the counter" sale, but only in the most oblique

---

8. See also Study Group Report, at 224–25 (recommending retention of the "learned of the breach" language for non-delivery situations, because it "protects a buyer who does not learn that a seller has failed to deliver on a promised date until after that date has passed"); see also Task Force Report, at 1231 (agreeing with Study Group). The Study Group recommended changes when the breach is by repudiation.

9. 1967 WL 8815, 26 Agri.Dec. 1309, 4 UCC 1164 (1967).

10. § 2–503 in part:

(1) Tender of delivery requires that the seller put and hold conforming goods at the buyer's disposition and give the buyer any notification reasonably necessary to enable him to take delivery. The manner, time and place for tender are

fashion does it deal with place of tender in the common commercial contract in which seller ships to buyer via common carrier. Does tender occur when seller delivers goods to the carrier or only when the carrier delivers to buyer? Section 2–503(2) provides:

> Where the case is within the next section respecting shipment tender requires that the seller comply with its provisions.

If the section had gone on to say "and when a seller has complied with 2–504[11] he has tendered," our prayers would be answered. But only by implication does one get the message that a seller who complies with 2–504 has thus tendered. The implicit meaning of 2–503(2) is that a seller who is bound to ship goods to a buyer but not required to deliver them at a particular destination (that is, one who has contracted to ship "F.O.B. seller's plant," not "F.O.B. buyer's plant") properly tenders by delivering the goods to the carrier and contracting for proper shipment.[12] It follows that tender in a "destination" contract in which seller undertakes the obligation not just to ship but to deliver "F.O.B. buyer's plant" occurs only upon carrier's tender in buyer's city.[13]

That the foregoing analysis is consistent with the terms of the analogous risk of loss provisions enhances its plausibility.[14] Sections 2–509 and 2–319 indicate that risk of loss in a destination contract

determined by the agreement and this Article, and in particular

    (a) tender must be at a reasonable hour, and if it is of goods they must be kept available for the period reasonably necessary to enable the buyer to take possession; but

    (b) unless otherwise agreed the buyer must furnish facilities reasonably suited to the receipt of the goods.

11. § 2–504:

Where the seller is required or authorized to send the goods to the buyer and the contract does not require him to deliver them at a particular destination, then unless otherwise agreed he must

    (a) put the goods in the possession of such a carrier and make such a contract for their transportation as may be reasonable having regard to the nature of the goods and other circumstances of the case; and

    (b) obtain and promptly deliver or tender in due form any document necessary to enable the buyer to obtain possession of the goods or otherwise required by the agreement or by usage of trade; and

    (c) promptly notify the buyer of the shipment.

Failure to notify the buyer under paragraph (c) or to make a proper contract under paragraph (a) is a ground for rejection only if material delay or loss ensues.

12. See In re Ault, 6 B.R. 58, 30 UCC 1714 (Bankr.E.D.Tenn.1980) (delivery of goods to the carrier constitutes tender in a shipment contract).

13. See In re Production Steel, Inc., 54 B.R. 417, 42 UCC 1285 (Bankr. M.D.Tenn.1985) (destination contract requires seller to tender at destination).

14. § 2–509:

(1) Where the contract requires or authorizes the seller to ship the goods by carrier

    (a) if it does not require him to deliver them at a particular destination, the risk of loss passes to the buyer when the goods are duly delivered to the carrier even though the shipment is under reservation (Section 2–505); but

    (b) if it does require him to deliver them at a particular destination and the goods are there duly tendered while in the possession of the carrier, the risk of loss passes to the buyer

passes to the buyer when the goods arrive at the particular destination, and in a shipment contract when the seller duly delivers the goods to the carrier.[15] Consider for example, a shipment contract (F.O.B. shipping point) for pills from seller in Kalamazoo to buyer in East Liverpool. Section 2–509(1)(a) indicates that the risk of loss passes to the buyer when the pills are delivered to the carrier in Kalamazoo. If the pills are destroyed *en route* and tender occurred when risk of loss passed on delivery to the carrier, buyer must bear the risk and cannot shift it by responding with a suit for damages for breach, for seller's conforming "tender" in Kalamazoo fulfilled its obligations. If, on the other hand, we conclude that tender under 2–503 and 2–504 occurred only on arrival in East Liverpool, we would have open warfare between 2–509 (buyer bears the risk in shipment) and 2–507 (seller's tender in East Liverpool must conform to the contract). Our conclusion that tender in a "shipment" contract occurs when goods are duly delivered to the carrier and that in a "destination" contract it occurs only upon tender to the buyer by the carrier harmonizes these sections.

when the goods are there duly so tendered as to enable the buyer to take delivery.

(2) Where the goods are held by a bailee to be delivered without being moved, the risk of loss passes to the buyer

(a) on his receipt of a negotiable document of title covering the goods; or

(b) on acknowledgment by the bailee of the buyer's right to possession of the goods; or

(c) after his receipt of a non-negotiable document of title or other written direction to deliver, as provided in subsection (4)(b) of Section 2–503.

(3) In any case not within subsection (1) or (2), the risk of loss passes to the buyer on his receipt of the goods if the seller is a merchant; otherwise the risk passes to the buyer on tender of delivery.

(4) The provisions of this section are subject to contrary agreement of the parties and to the provisions of this Article on sale on approval (Section 2–327) and on effect of breach on risk of loss (Section 2–510).

§ 2–319(1):

(1) Unless otherwise agreed the term F.O.B. (which means "free on board") at a named place, even though used only in

connection with the stated price, is a delivery term under which

(a) when the term is F.O.B. the place of shipment, the seller must at that place ship the goods in the manner provided in this Article (Section 2–504) and bear the expense and risk of putting them into the possession of the carrier; or

(b) when the term is F.O.B. the place of destination, the seller must at his own expense and risk transport the goods to that place and there tender delivery of them in the manner provided in this Article (Section 2–503);

(c) when under either (a) or (b) the term is also F.O.B. vessel, car or other vehicle, the seller must in addition at his own expense and risk load the goods on board. If the term is F.O.B. vessel the buyer must name the vessel and in an appropriate case the seller must comply with the provisions of this Article on the form of bill of lading (Section 2–323).

15. See §§ 2–509(1)(a) and 2–319(1)(a) note 15 *supra.* See also, Ladex Corp. v. Transportes Aereos Nacionales, S.A., 476 So.2d 763, 42 UCC 133 (Fla. App.1985) ("In the normal shipment contract, the title to the goods and the risk of loss passes to the buyer when the goods are properly delivered to the carrier for shipment to the buyer").

Our analysis of place of tender in 2–713 is consistent with pre-Code case law. The Uniform Sales Act specified no particular place for the measurement of damages, and many courts relied on Judge Cardozo's holding in Standard Casing Co. v. California Casing Co.,[16] where plaintiff-buyer in New York contracted for twenty casks of salted pig guts F.O.B. shipping point from a California seller:

> The damages are to be estimated according to the conditions prevailing at the place where the final act of performance was due from the vendor [California].[17]

In Bliss Produce Co. v. A.E. Albert & Sons, Inc.,[18] an Arizona seller breached its contract to deliver potatoes to a North Carolina buyer. The contract called for delivery "Arizona, F.O.B., grade guaranteed to destination."[19] Is such a contract a shipment or destination contract? If the former, is it nevertheless a shipment contract under which "tender" occurs in North Carolina? Without discussing tender, the court chose North Carolina as the proper place to measure damages. It might have justified that conclusion by referring to the "grade guaranteed to destination" language, but it did not do so. Rather the court relied upon Comment 1 to 2–713 and made the following point:

> UCC section 2–713 comment No. 1 states that the prices to be used in calculating damages come from "the market in which the buyer would have obtained cover had he sought that relief." Since potatoes were unobtainable in the Arizona market * * * it appears that North Carolina is a reasonable market from which cover could have been obtained.[20]

The court's use of Comment 1 was intriguing but incorrect. In many of the cases in which sellers breach on shipment contracts, they do so because there are no conforming goods at the sellers' place of business. Had the drafters intended that a place other than the place of shipment be used to measure the market in all such cases, they surely would have said so. In the interest of certainty and consistent interpretation we suggest that the court's analysis here be rejected and that the place of shipment under a "shipment" contract is the proper market for measuring damages despite the lack of goods there.

What of the case in which seller holds the goods for buyer? The place of tender under the Code would be seller's place of business, but it still may be difficult to determine the time for tender. The pre-Code cases decided under the USA reflect a substantial concern

---

16. 233 N.Y. 413, 135 N.E. 834 (1922).

17. *Id.* at 419, 135 N.E. at 836.

18. 35 Agric.Dec. 742, 20 UCC 917 (1976).

19. *Id.* at 744, 20 UCC at 918.

20. *Id.* at 747, 20 UCC at 922.

with the elusive concept of property and title. In Sadler Machinery Co. v. Ohio National, Inc.,[21] a machine manufacturer in Upper Sandusky, Ohio, who had contracted to sell equipment to a dealer in Detroit, Michigan, agreed to retain and store the machinery at his plant for a week or two beginning about January 26, 1951. On January 30, 1951, the machinery was destroyed by fire. The court framed the issue as follows: "Did title to the machine pass to the plaintiff prior to the loss?"[22] The court set out USA § 18 and USA § 19[23] and decided that title had passed.[24] Unlike the situation where the goods are shipped via a carrier, 2–503 and 2–509(3) of the Code indicate that where the seller holds goods for the buyer, tender and risk of loss are not inextricably intertwined.[25] Subsection (1) of 2–503 requires the tendering seller to put conforming goods at the buyer's disposition and that the buyer be given reasonable notice.[26] Applying the Code to the *Sadler Machine Co.* facts, a court should probably find that Ohio National had put the goods at buyer's disposition, and the several communications passing between the parties served as adequate notice. Thus, under the Code too, tender probably occurred before the fire. (Note, however, that risk probably would have passed upon receipt and not upon tender in this case under 2–509(3)).[27]

a. Expenses Saved

A second interpretative problem in 2–713 concerns the meaning of "expenses saved in consequence of the seller's breach."[28]

21. 102 F.Supp. 652 (N.D.Ohio 1952), aff'd, 202 F.2d 887 (6th Cir.1953).

22. 102 F.Supp. at 653.

23. USA § 18:

(1) Where there is a contract to sell specific or ascertained goods, the property in them is transferred to the buyer at such time as the parties to the contract intend it to be transferred.

(2) For the purpose of ascertaining the intention of the parties, regard shall be had to the terms of the contract, the conduct of the parties, usages of trade and the circumstances of the case.

USA § 19:

Rule 5. If the contract to sell requires the seller to deliver the goods to the buyer, or at a particular place, or to pay the freight or cost of transportation to the buyer, or to a particular place, the property does not pass until the goods have been delivered to the buyer or reached the place agreed upon.

24. Then relying on USA § 22, the court concluded that risk of loss was also on the buyer.

25. Thus, in the case of a merchant seller, § 2–509(3) and Comment 3 thereto indicate that risk of loss will not pass to the buyer until actual receipt of the goods.

26. Hunt–Wesson Foods, Inc. v. Marubeni Alaska Seafoods, Inc., 23 Wash. App. 193, 596 P.2d 666, 26 UCC 704 (1979) (section 2–503 requires seller to keep the goods available for the period reasonably necessary to enable buyer to take possession and the fact that seller is required to hold the goods after they have been tendered does not alter the time of tender).

27. Under § 2–509(3) tender and the passage of risk of loss are not synonymous.

28. § 2–713:

(1) Subject to the provisions of this Article with respect to proof of market price (Section 2–723), the measure of damages for non-delivery or repudiation by the seller is the difference between the market price at the time when the

There are at least three common contracts in which this problem may arise with respect to transportation costs: (1) an F.O.B. shipment contract under which goods are shipped and eventually rejected, (2) an F.O.B. shipment contract under which goods are never shipped, and (3) an F.O.B. destination contract. In the first (goods are shipped F.O.B. seller's plant but rejected by buyer before it pays the shipping cost), the 2–713 damage formula measures the market for the contract-market differential as of the place of arrival.[29] Comment 1 to 2–713 states the philosophy as follows:

> [T]his section uses as a yardstick the market in which the buyer would have obtained cover had he sought that relief. So the place for measuring damages is the place of tender (or the place of arrival if the goods are rejected or their acceptance is revoked after reaching their destination) * * *.[30]

The assumption is that in cases of rejection after arrival the buyer will eventually (or would have) covered at the place of arrival. In a shipment contract (F.O.B. seller's place of business or shipping point) the buyer would have borne the expenses in the replacement contract. As a result of the breach the buyer would pay that much less or save that amount "in consequence of the seller's breach." Therefore the shipping cost should be subtracted from the contract-market differential and any incidental and consequential damages recovered under 2–715.

To illustrate, assume a Chicago seller ships $20,000 of nonconforming goods, F.O.B. seller's plant, to a San Diego buyer who rejects the goods upon their arrival. Assume that the market value in California is $25,000 at the time buyer learned of the breach and that buyer's shipping expenses would have been $4,000. Damages under 2–713 should be the market-contract differential, ($25,000 − $20,000) less expenses saved ($4,000), or total damages of $1,000. Note that $1,000 puts buyer in the same position as buyer would have been in had he covered in San Diego on the date he learned of the breach.

When the goods are never shipped as under an F.O.B. shipping point contract, market price is measured as of the place for tender, the seller's place of business. The general assumption, expressed in Comment 1 to 2–713, is that the buyer will search for a replacement contract at the shipping point.[31] If buyer seeks a replacement

---

buyer learned of the breach and the contract price together with any incidental and consequential damages provided in this Article (Section 2–715), but less expenses saved in consequence of the seller's breach.

29. § 2–713(2):

Market price is to be determined as of the place for tender or, in cases of rejection after arrival or revocation of acceptance, as of the place of arrival.

30. § 2–713, Comment 1.

31. Thus the Code makes contradictory assumptions in the cases where the "shipping market" or the "delivery mar-

at the shipping point, he would incur replacement shipping costs roughly equivalent to those on the original contract. Thus by comparison with such a replacement contract there would be no expenses "saved" in consequence of the seller's breach because we are assuming that the buyer must pay the expenses for shipping under the new contract as well.

A final case is a destination contract (F.O.B. buyer's plant). In this situation the place for tender and the place of arrival are identical. The buyer bears no shipping cost, and there are no shipping expenses to be saved in consequence of the seller's breach.[32]

In general, the time when breach occurs is unproblematic; the time when performance is due (except for repudiation cases to be discussed in 7–7 *infra*) is occasionally problematic. Thus where the delivery date is definite yet waived by negotiations, or is indefinite to begin with, a court will have to decide when the breach occurred.[33]

b. *Proof of Market Price*

Assuming that an aggrieved buyer can find the proper time and place at which to measure the market price, what proof of the market is necessary? What is sufficient? Comment 2 to 2–713 suggests one should turn first to the "general market price" for goods of the same kind.[34] Commodity and securities markets of

ket" is used to measure market price. Is the distinction well founded? Conceding that the shipping market may be the norm, in a case of rejection the buyer may be pressed for time and therefore be unable to return to the usual market. However, there is little reason to assume that this basis is sufficiently widespread to justify transforming an exception into a rule. The facts in some cases suggest that when a buyer is faced with a repudiation by a distant seller, he will choose to seek replacement locally rather than return to the "shipping market" as the drafters assumed. See, e.g., Neal–Cooper Grain Co. v. Texas Gulf Sulphur Co., 508 F.2d 283, 16 UCC 7 (7th Cir.1974).

32. For two cases misinterpreting the "expenses saved" clause in 2–713, see Pendleton Grain Growers v. Pedro, 271 Or. 24, 530 P.2d 85, 16 UCC 315 (1975) (breaching seller successfully argued that, on remand, the jury should be instructed to view certain handling costs and taxes incurred by the seller as possible "expenses saved;" there was no evidence that the buyer was to pay these costs under the contract); Ralston Puri-

na Co. v. McFarland, 550 F.2d 967, 21 UCC 136 (4th Cir.1977) (where aggrieved buyer did not attempt to recover incidental or consequential damages, the breaching seller is not entitled to present evidence of expenses allegedly saved by the buyer as a result of the breach). See Hess Energy, Inc. v. Lightning Oil Co., 338 F.3d 357, 51 UCC2d 1 (4th Cir. 2003) ("when seller learned of breach" refers to the date seller was to tender, not earlier date on which seller communicates his repudiation to buyer).

33. D.R. Curtis, Co. v. Mathews, 103 Idaho 776, 653 P.2d 1188, 35 UCC 1425 (App.1982). See also Buford v. Wilmington Trust Co., 841 F.2d 51, 5 UCC2d 621 (3d Cir.1988) (applying 2–713 by analogy to failure to deliver investment securities, court held that breach occurred on date securities should have been delivered).

34. § 2–713, Comment 2:

The market or current price to be used in comparison with the contract price under this section is the price for

course fit this description. It would also seem that one could usually find a general market for widely sold goods such as new and used cars. For those who cannot find such a market the Code offers 2–723. That section allows reasonable leeway in time, in place, and in kinds of substitutes.[35] Comment 3 to 2–713 goes even further; it approves the use of evidence of spot sale prices where there is no available market price.[36] The Code directs the courts to accept virtually any evidence—even evidence of marginal relevance. For example, in Egerer v. CSR West, LLC,[37] seller, CSR, broke a contract to deliver fill material at $.50 per cubic yard. Six months later, Egerer could have purchased fill material of similar but not identical quality for $8.25 to $9.00. More than two years after the breach, Egerer bought the needed fill for $6.39. In accepting the $8.25 figure, the court explicitly relied on Comment 3 to 2–713. The $.50 contract had been lucky—fill available from the shoulders of a widened interstate highway—and the best substitute in the period right after the breach would have been the slightly different fill at $8.25. Of course, aggrieved buyers and sellers can still argue that some evidence is too uncertain to be received in a court of law. And not all courts will be as fortunate as the *Deardorff–Jackson* court which simply picked the relevant price of potatoes from the Federal Market News Report.

Indeed in a remarkable number of cases parties appear to have lost their cases by failing to offer adequate evidence of market price. In several cases[38] the buyers lost either because there was no evidence whatsoever of the market price or because none was offered for the appropriate time. Surely the plaintiff can usually produce an expert in each case who could have presented some plausible evidence about a timely market price.

goods of the same kind and in the same branch of trade. See also, Hess Energy, Inc. v. Lightning Oil Co., Ltd., 338 F.3d 357, 51 UCC2d 1 (4th Cir. 2003) (court based market price on price of superior goods six months after breach where such most reasonable substitute).

35. § 2–723 in part:

(2) If evidence of a price prevailing at the times or places described in this Article is not readily available the price prevailing within any reasonable time before or after the time described or at any other place which in commercial judgment or under usage of trade would serve as a reasonable substitute for the one described may be used, making any proper allowance for the cost of transporting the goods to or from such other place.

(3) Evidence of a relevant price prevailing at the time or place other than the one described in this Article offered by one party is not admissible unless and until he has given the other party such notice as the court finds sufficient to prevent unfair surprise.

See, e.g., Chappell Chevrolet, Inc. v. Strickland, 4 Ark.App. 108, 628 S.W.2d 25, 33 UCC 1327 (1982).

36. See, e.g., Kirkwood Agri–Trade v. Frosty Land Foods Int'l, Inc., 650 F.2d 602, 31 UCC 1360 (5th Cir.1981).

37. 116 Wash.App. 645, 67 P.3d 1128, 50 UCC2d 479 (2003).

38. See, e.g., Three–Seventy Leasing Corp. v. Ampex Corp., 528 F.2d 993, 19 UCC 132 (5th Cir.1976); Maxwell v. Norwood Marine, Inc., 58 Mass.App.Dec. 59, 19 UCC 829 (1976).

In Burgess v. Curly Olney's, Inc.[39] the buyer was attempting to prove the market price of three combines. At trial the buyer's lawyer offered the appropriate pages from the " 'Official Guide Tractors and Farm Equipment,' Spring 1974" providing average values for the type of combines under contract. The court rejected such proof as insufficient because the actual value depended upon the condition of the individual machine and upon its location. No competent evidence was offered on those matters. These cases are fair warnings that every lawyer should be prepared with expert opinion or with some other form of acceptable evidence of the market price on the relevant dates.

c. Relation Between 2–712 and 2–713

We come now to the problem of a buyer who has covered but who seeks to ignore 2–712 and sue for a larger contract-market differential under 2–713. On first reading, it seems that the buyer can disregard 2–712; section 2–711 tells buyers that they can "cover" or they can recover damages for nondelivery under 2–713. Commenting on the relationship between 2–712 and 2–713, Judge Peters argued that an aggrieved buyer who purchases goods "in substitution" may disregard 2–712 and seek recovery under the contract-market differential of 2–713.[40] However, this interpretation allows a buyer to learn of a breach on September 2 when the market is at $25,000, wait until September 15 to cover, when the market is at $23,000, and then sue under 2–713 for the higher damages of contract-market differential, all contrary to the general principle of Revised 1–305(a) and its predecessor, 1–106, (in as good a position as if the other party had performed and no more). Moreover Comment 5 to 2–713 indicates that a buyer who has covered may not use 2–713:

> The present section provides a remedy which is *completely alternative* to cover under the preceding section and applies only *when and to the extent that the buyer ha*s̲ *not covered.* (Italics added.)

If the Code's goal is to put the buyer in the same position as though there had been no breach,[41] and if 2–712 will accomplish that goal

---

39. 198 Neb. 153, 251 N.W.2d 888, 21 UCC 794 (1977).

40. Peters, Remedies for Breach of Contracts Relating to the Sale of Goods Under the Uniform Commercial Code: A Roadmap for Article 2, 73 Yale L.J. 199, 260 (1963).

41. Revised § 1–305(a) and its predecessor § 1–106(1). The "same position" would include as badly off as though there had been no breach. See L.

Albert & Son v. Armstrong Rubber Co., 178 F.2d 182 (2d Cir.1949) (Learned Hand, C.J.). Buyer was given a set-off, against seller's damages, in the amount of $3,000 buyer spent building the foundation for the "Refiners." But buyer's set-off was "subject to the seller's privilege to deduct from that amount any sum which upon a further hearing it can prove would have been the buyer's loss upon the contract, had the 'Refiners'

but 2–713[42] will do so only by coincidence, why not force the covering buyer to use 2–712? There is no room for punitive damages here. Nor is it analogous to the similar case on the seller's side when an aggrieved seller who resells under 2–706 to one of his customers loses volume and thus needs an additional remedy to put him in the same position as performance would have. Notwithstanding Judge Peters' arguments concerning the statutory history and her pleas for identical rules on the buyer's and seller's side, both the message of Comment 5 to 2–713 and the policy of the Code properly deny the covering buyer any use of 2–713.[43] Amended Article 2 agrees; proposed Comment 7 to Amended Section 2–713 restricts a covering buyer to cover damages.[44] Of course, whether

been delivered on or before May 1st, 1945." 178 F.2d at 191. See also Keller v. Inland Metals All Weather Conditioning, Inc., 139 Idaho 233, 76 P.3d 977, 51 UCC2d 303 (2003), where seller contractor breached when the contracted 7.5–ton dehumidifier turned out to be too small and thus was not fit for its intended purpose; buyer was not entitled to damages for its cover with a larger, 10–ton dehumidifier, because the larger size was not contemplated by the agreement, and buyer presented no evidence that the contract price for the 7.5–ton unit was less than the market price. The dissent believed buyer should be able to recover the difference between the prices of the 10–ton and the 7.5–ton units unit and condemned the majority's emphasis on the size of the humidifier as specified in the contract, noting that buyers relied on seller's expertise and skill in determining the appropriate size for the unit. See also Professor Palmer's incisive analysis of "same position" in, The Contract Price as a Limit on Restitution for Defendant's Breach, 20 Ohio State L.J. 264 (1959).

42. § 2–713(1) states:

[T]he measure of damages for nondelivery or repudiation by the seller is the difference between the market price * * * and the contract price together with any incidental and consequential damages provided in this Article (Section 2–715), but less expenses saved in consequence of the seller's breach.

43. § 2–712(3) provides that "failure of the buyer to effect cover within this section does not bar him from any other remedy." However, as Comment 3 candidly admits, failing to cover when such

is possible can have ramifications. First, 2–715(2)(a) limits consequential damages from seller's breach to:

any loss resulting from general or particular requirements and needs of which the seller at the time of contracting had reason to know *and which could not reasonably be prevented by cover* or otherwise. (emphasis added)

Thus failing to cover when a reasonable substitute is available will preclude recovery of consequential damages. Secondly, cover possibilities may foreclose specific performance which "may be decreed where the goods are unique or in other proper circumstances." (2–716) Rejecting uniqueness as the singular requirement for specific relief, Comment 2 to 2–716 explicitly recommends that "inability to cover is strong evidence of 'other proper circumstances'." Finally, speaking for itself as to the effect of the possibility of cover on the remedy of replevin, § 2–716(3) provides in part:

The buyer has a right of replevin for goods identified to the contract if after reasonable effort he is unable to effect cover for such goods or the circumstances reasonably indicate that such effort will be unavailing * * *.

44. Comment 7: A buyer that has covered under Section 2–712 may not recover the contract price market price difference under this section, but instead must base the damages on those provided in Section 2–712. To award an additional amount because the buyer could show the market price was higher than the contract price would put the buyer in a better position than performance would have. Of course, the seller would bear the burden of proving that

purchases following seller's breach are cover purchases may be disputed.[45] If the facts prove cover, 2–712 applies. If the facts do not show cover, 2–713 applies.[46] The burden of proof rests with the seller.[47]

d. Capping 2–713 Recoveries

Finally is the question whether a buyer's 2–713 contract-market differential should ever be limited by proof that the buyer's expectation of gain from performance was less than the 2–713 differential. This issue is not new to the law. However, for the first time under the Code, two courts have held—on the basis of proof of limited expectations—that some buyers are not entitled to the full contract-market differential despite the unqualified language of 2–713. In H–W–H Cattle Co. v. Schroeder,[48] the Court of Appeals for the Eighth Circuit limited the buyer to anticipated commissions on resale of cattle; these commissions were less than the contract-market differential. In a longer, and more fully reasoned opinion, Allied Canners and Packers, Inc. v. Victor Packing Co.,[49] a California intermediate appellate court agreed.

In the latter case the seller, Victor, was a packer and processor of dried fruits. Victor had made a contract to sell a quantity of natural Thompson seedless raisins to Allied. Allied, in turn, had made resale contracts with two Japanese buyers for the raisins. Victor's sale price to Allied was $.2975 per pound with a discount of 4%. Allied's resale contracts with the Japanese buyers were also at $.2975 per pound, but without any discount. Thus Allied's expectancy was a 4% profit on its resale of the raisins. Heavy rain during the night of September 9, 1976 severely damaged the California

cover had the economic effect of limiting lifting the buyer's actual loss to an amount less than the contract price-market price difference.

See also Study Group Report, at 223 ("[A] buyer who effects a proper cover under § 2–712 should be barred from a remedy under § 2–713."); Task Force Report, at 1228.

45. Bigelow–Sanford, Inc. v. Gunny Corp., 649 F.2d 1060, 31 UCC 968, 972 (5th Cir.1981) (Whether buyer covered was "a question of fact submitted to jury. In the event that it had not, alternative damages were available * * * under 2–713.").

46. Cosden Oil & Chemical Co. v. Karl O. Helm Aktiengesellschaft, 736 F.2d 1064, 38 UCC 1645, reh'g denied, 750 F.2d 69 (5th Cir.1984) (post-breach purchases not cover; 2–713 available).

47. Koenen v. Royal Buick Co., 162 Ariz. 376, 783 P.2d 822, 11 UCC2d 1096 (App.1989) (one year after seller failed to deliver a limited edition Buick to a rare car collector, buyer bought another car of the same make from another dealer; but, because the buyer indicated he was still "in the market for another one," and seller presented no contrary evidence indicating buyer's intent to cover, seller had failed to carry his burden of proving that the purchase constituted cover).

48. 767 F.2d 437, 41 UCC 832 (8th Cir.1985). See also, Unlimited Equipment Lines, Inc. v. Graphic Arts Centre, Inc., 889 S.W.2d 926, 25 UCC2d 744 (Mo. App. 1994) (no proof existing resale contract would be less than market contract price differential).

49. 162 Cal.App.3d 905, 209 Cal. Rptr. 60, 39 UCC 1567 (1984).

raisin crop which was then drying on the ground. Victor breached its contract of sale. Because the raisin market is controlled by the Raisin Administrative Committee, neither party was able to buy raisins on the market until October of 1976 when "reserve raisins" that had been restricted for sale in the overseas market were put on the "free market." The price then rose to between $.80 and $.87 per pound.

Allied did not cover, and so never made any deliveries under its resale contracts with the Japanese buyers. One buyer released Allied from its contract; the other never sued Allied and may have been dissuaded from doing so by a force majeure clause in the contract.

At the time the case between Allied and Victor went to trial, the statute of limitations had run on the second Japanese party's claim. It was conceded that Allied was not liable to its Japanese buyers. Victor apparently conceded liability of $4,462.52 (the 4% commission Allied had expected to realize on the resales); Allied argued instead for $150,281.25 (the contract-market differential).

Noting that section 2–713 was merely "hypothetical cover," and that the 2–713 formula might have to be justified as a kind of statutory liquidated damages clause, the court rejected plaintiff's claim for the $150,281.25 recovery. The court relied substantially on the policy of 1–106(1) (as good a position as if the other had performed) in deciding that the plaintiff should recover only its expected resale profits of $4,462.52, not the contract-market differential. (Again, 1–106 has been replaced by 1–305.)

Having already taken the general position that a defendant should be able to use the plaintiff's post breach behavior and circumstances to limit the plaintiff's damages, we are inclined to endorse the *Allied* and *H–W–H* decisions. If, as we argue in Chapter 8, the *seller* under 2–708 should receive only expected profit when that is lower than the contract-market differential, and if the buyer under 2–712 should receive only the difference between cover and the contract price when the buyer covers (and that difference is less than the contract price differential), why should a different rule govern here? Although one might distinguish *Allied* and *H–W–H* from the 2–708 and 2–712 cases based upon the language of the Code, we see no way on principle to distinguish them. Thus we are at least tentatively persuaded that *Allied* and *H–W–H* should be followed.

Courts should take care to apply the *Allied* and *H–W–H* limitation narrowly. First, it should be applied only when the defendant proves that the plaintiff's expected resale profit was less than the 2–713 differential; we would not impose the burden of proving the negative on the plaintiff as part of its case in chief. Second, in any case in which the buyer's resale purchaser will likely insist upon performance, the buyer's damages should not be limited to the buyer's expected resale profit, for in that case the buyer will be liable in damages to its own purchaser equal to the difference between the buyer's resale contract price and the market price (or will have to cover at market price in order to make delivery).

What if the buyer actually settles with its resale purchaser at something less than the contract-market differential? In TexPar Energy, Inc. v. Murphy Oil USA, Inc.,[50] the seller, Murphy, repudiated the contract to sell at $53 per ton. Buyer, Texpar, had made a resale contract at $56. When Murphy repudiated, Texpar renegotiated its contract with its buyer to $68.50. The court awarded Texpar, $386,370—the difference between the market ($80) and the contract price ($53). It refused to reduce the number even though it acknowledged that the recovery put the plaintiff in a much better position than performance would have done. Should the buyer's damages against its own seller be reduced accordingly? This is a complex question and we are uncertain of the right answer. On the one hand the general principle of *Allied* and *H–W–H* seems to apply here, for the rights of the plaintiff have been as fully determined as they were in *Allied*. On the other hand, routine reduction in the buyer's recovery could cause undesirable strategic behavior by the buyer-reseller who might lose his incentive to negotiate a settlement with its buyer (out of the knowledge that such a settlement would limit his right to recover from his own buyer). So we tend to think that the plaintiff-middleman should be limited by the negotiated settlement he makes with his purchaser, but we are not certain.

At another time it would be appropriate to think more generally about the extent to which post-breach behavior and circumstances should properly be used in measuring the plaintiff's damages. We recognize that the prospect of a reduction in damages may have some impact upon a seller's willingness to perform, and may make the security of a buyer's expectations somewhat smaller than would otherwise be the case. Arguably, too, our position will unjustly enrich an occasional seller, and may also make the trial more complicated. Even so, we think our overall position is more faithful to the idea that the contract plaintiff should recover only his lost expectancy. That idea is deeply entrenched in Anglo–American common law and is adopted in section 1–305 and its predecessor section 1–106 of the UCC.[51] Limiting the plaintiff to expectation

---

50. 45 F.3d 1111, 25 UCC2d 759 (7th Cir. 1995).

51. Early proposals for the revision of 2–701 might have had an impact on the cases in this section. These proposals would have made mitigation principles explicitly applicable in Article 2 and would have limited an aggrieved party's remedy to one that does not exceed its expectation interest nor fundamentally conflict with other remedies. See Study Group Report at 194–196.

damages also preserves the possibility of what economists call efficient breach, an idea endorsed by one of your authors.

§ 7–5 Buyer's Incidental and Consequential Damages

Sections 2–711 through 2–714 allow the buyer to recover "incidental and consequential damages" where the seller repudiates, fails to deliver the goods, rightfully rejects delivery of nonconforming goods, revokes acceptance of nonconforming goods, or accepts nonconforming goods and sues for breach of warranty. Both here and in sections 11–3 and 11–4, *infra*, we deal with incidental and consequential damages of a buyer who accepts nonconforming goods and sues for breach of warranty. Our emphasis here is on cases where the buyer does not accept; our emphasis in Chapter 11 is on cases of acceptance.

Section 2–715 addresses incidental and consequential damages as follows:

(1) Incidental damages resulting from the seller's breach include expenses reasonably incurred in inspection, receipt, transportation and care and custody of goods rightfully rejected, any commercially reasonable charges, expenses or commissions in connection with effecting cover and any other reasonable expense incident to the delay or other breach.

(2) Consequential damages resulting from the seller's breach include

(a) any loss resulting from general or particular requirements and needs of which the seller at the time of contracting had reason to know and which could not reasonably be prevented by cover or otherwise; and

(b) injury to person or property proximately resulting from any breach of warranty.

It is standard to distinguish between "general" or "direct" damages, on the one hand, and "incidental or consequential" damages on the other. In the Code's scheme, the damages recoverable by a buyer under 2–712, 2–713, and 2–714 qualify as general or direct damages. Other recoverable damages under 2–715 are "incidental or consequential."

Section 2–714(1) most explicitly incorporates the concept of general or direct damages for nonconformities as "the loss resulting in ordinary course of events from the seller's breach," i.e., the rule as general or direct damages set forth in the first rule stated in *Hadley v. Baxendale*. Sections 2–711, 2–712, 2–713, and 2–714(2) largely set forth special measures of that loss. It is by contrast with this concept of directness that the concept of consequential damages is to be understood. According to the second rule in *Hadley v. Baxendale*, consequential damages are those which do not flow in ordinary course from the seller's breach, and even then they are not recoverable if, as per 2–715(2), they do not result from general or particular requirements and needs of the buyer which the seller had reason to know of at time of contracting. Nor are they recoverable if the buyer could have prevented them by cover or otherwise. Nor are they recoverable if a "no consequential damages" clause excludes them. For more on consequential damages see section 10–4.

The court in Petroleo Brasileiro, S.A., Petrobras v. Ameropan Oil Corp.[1] distinguished between incidental and consequential damages in this way:

> While the distinction between the two is not an obvious one, the Code makes plain that incidental damages are normally incurred when a buyer (or seller) repudiates the contract or wrongfully rejects the goods, causing the other to incur such expenses as transporting, storing, or reselling the goods. On the other hand, consequential damages do not arise within the scope of the immediate buyer-seller transaction, but rather stem from losses incurred by the non-breaching party in its dealings, often with third parties, which were a proximate result of the breach, and which were reasonably foreseeable by the breaching party at the time of contracting.

To recover incidental damages, the buyer must show (1) that they were incurred incident to the breach, and (2) that they were reasonable. For example, a buyer who rightfully rejects nonconforming goods should be able to recover, as incidental damages, the costs of inspecting the goods as well as storage and transportation expenses.[2] The limitations on recovery of incidental damages exist to further the Code's general policy expressed in 1–305, the successor of section 1–106, which provided that the aggrieved party be placed "in as good a position as if the other party had fully performed." Thus, in Productora E Importadora De Papel, S.A. De

---

§ 7–5

1. 372 F.Supp. 503, 508, 14 UCC 661, 667 (E.D.N.Y.1974). For a discussion of incidental and consequential damages, see generally Special Project, Article 2 Warranties in Commercial Transactions—An Update, 72 Cornell L.Rev. 1159, 1232–1244 (1987).

2. See, e.g., AFA Corp. v. Phoenix Closures, Inc., 501 F.Supp. 224, 230, 30 UCC 81, 88–89 (N.D.Ill.1980) (cost of returning nonconforming goods to the seller recoverable even though some of the goods were only suspected of being defective); Mitsui O.S.K. Lines, Ltd. v. Consolidated Rail Corp., 327 N.J.Super 343, 743 A.2d 362, 43 UCC2d 897 (2000) (buyer's survey expenses are analogous to inspection expenses, and are recoverable); Mitchell Family Development Co., Inc. v. Universal Textile Technologies, 268 Ga.App. 869, 602 S.E.2d 878, 54 UCC2d 402 (2004) (testing expenses incurred in inspecting and covering are recoverable as incidental).

C.V. v. Fleming,[3] the court correctly denied recovery of a claim for incidental damages consisting of import fees and freight charges from Boston to Mexico. Because the seller did not deliver all it had agreed to deliver, the fees and charges associated with the undelivered amount were expenses saved because of the breach. In addition to showing that it incurred the expenses because of the breach, the buyer must show that the incidental damages were reasonable. Thus, in Industrial Graphics, Inc. v. Asahi Corp.,[4] the court denied the buyer's claim for additional overhead and interest expenses incurred in its unsuccessful attempt to resell defective citizens-band radios because it had maintained high prices in a declining market.[5]

Consequential Damages

Consequential damages may include sums for lost profits, loss of goodwill, losses resulting from interruption of buyer's production process, lost interest, and much else. To recover consequential damages, the buyer must establish: (1) causation, (2) foreseeability, (3) reasonable certainty as to amount, and (4) that it is not barred by mitigation doctrines.[6]

Courts are alert to the possibility that the buyer did not suffer any loss whatsoever. For example, in Wilson v. Marquette Electronics, Inc.[7] the court denied the corporate buyer recovery for losses its employee-doctor suffered when he had to spend time away from his private practice to work on a computer system that failed to function as warranted. The evidence showed only a loss to the doctor's private practice, not a loss to the buyer.

3. 376 Mass. 826, 383 N.E.2d 1129, 25 UCC 729 (1978).

4. 485 F.Supp. 793, 28 UCC 647 (D.Minn.1980).

5. But see District Concrete Co., Inc. v. Bernstein Concrete Corp., 418 A.2d 1030, 1037, 30 UCC 201, 210–11 (D.C. 1980) (buyer "need not bear the burden of unanticipated costs that were actually incurred because the selected method proved more expensive"). See also Task Force Report, at 1234. Consequential damages already must meet these restrictions. At least one court has read in the requirement of foreseeability for incidental damages. Magnum Press Automation, Inc. v. Thomas & Betts Corp., 325 Ill.App.3d 613, 259 Ill.Dec. 384, 758 N.E.2d 507, 46 UCC2d 97 (2001) (buyer cannot recover incidental damages for costs of repair when seller could not have foreseen that buyer would expend over $11,000—almost 25% of the machine's value—hiring a third party to attempt to repair defective machinery,

rather than involving seller in the repairs).

6. City Nat. Bank of Charleston v. Wells, 181 W.Va. 763, 384 S.E.2d 374, 10 UCC2d 798 (1989). But see Task Force Report at 1235. Consequential damages do not, however, include time value of money. See M.S. Distrib. Co. v. Web Records, Inc., 2003 WL 21788988, 51 UCC2d 716 (N.D. Ill. 2003). The Code does not explicitly provide for consequential damages to a seller. See Atlantic Paper Box Co. v. Whitman's Chocolates, 844 F.Supp. 1038, 23 UCC2d 361 (E.D. Pa. 1994) (looking to state common law to determine availability of consequential damages to seller); Roan v. Murray, 219 Mich.App. 562, 556 N.W.2d 893, 31 UCC2d 562 (1996) (refusing to award attorney fees as consequential damages to seller because the UCC does not allow consequential damages upon a buyer's breach).

7. 630 F.2d 575, 29 UCC 399 (8th Cir.1980).

When the plaintiff is a consumer, sometimes courts are generous. In Elmore v. Doenges Brothers Ford, Inc.[8] the court upheld a jury verdict of $25,000 for the buyer of a car that had an incurable defect in the title. According to the plaintiff's testimony, that defect reduced the value of the car to $100 to $200 as "salvage" from the plaintiff's purchase price of $10,500. Since he could not use the car, the plaintiff testified that he lost eight months of work at $2,500 per month. So with his testimony and little else, Elmore won a jury verdict for $25,000 that withstood appeal.

In a conventional commercial controversy between RIJ a contract manufacturer of generic pharmaceuticals (seller here) and Ivax a seller of generics (buyer here), the court in RIJ Pharmaceutical Corp. v. Ivax Pharmaceuticals, Inc.[9] showed a more skeptical eye after an audit that allegedly uncovered unsanitary conditions in RIJ's plant (if you have a weak stomach and consume generic drugs you may not want to read this case) and after some controversy about the quality of RIJ's performance, Ivax cancelled its contract with RIJ. In its counterclaim Ivax claimed consequential damages for lost profits while it was finding a substitute supplier, and damages for its lost market share of several products that RIJ had supplied.

Emphasizing that "it must be demonstrated with certainty that such damages have been caused by the breach ..." the court acknowledged that IVAX had apparently suffered a loss because of the breach, but found that evidence was necessary to confirm the losses. It found Ivax's deposition testimony inadequate and declined to award summary judgment on most of the counterclaims.

The buyer must also prove that the claimed consequential damages were caused by the seller's breach.[10] It is familiar that the buyer must show: 1) a causal link between the seller's breach and each item of claimed damages; and 2) that the seller's breach was a cause in fact of the loss. Sellers can sometimes show that the

---

8. 21 P.3d 65, 44 UCC2d 522 (Okla. App. 2000).

9. 322 F.Supp.2d 406, 54 UCC2d 130 (S.D.N.Y. 2004).

10. Compare J & J Farms, Inc. v. Cargill, Inc., 693 F.2d 830, 836 (8th Cir. 1982) (buyer of contaminated seed not entitled to consequential damages from subsequent disruption of marketing program because such project "too remote and speculative") and Kirby v. Chrysler Corp., 554 F.Supp. 743, 754, 35 UCC 497, 511–12 (D.Md.1982) (automobile dealer failed to prove that investment losses arose from manufacturer's breach where dealer had lost money in preceding years and unordered vehicles could not account for the magnitude of the claimed losses) with Cottonwood Elevator Co. v. Zenner, 105 Idaho 469, 470, 670 P.2d 876, 877 (1983) (buyer of spring wheat seed in business of resale could recover losses sustained in reimbursing customers for their subsequent damages proximately resulting from seller's breach). See Indiana Glass Co. v. Indiana Michigan Power Co., 692 N.E.2d 886, 37 UCC2d 332 (Ind. App. 1998); Hangzhov Silk Import and Export v. P.C.B. Int. Ind., Inc., 2002 WL 2031591, 48 UCC2d 1367 (S.D.N.Y. 2002) (start up company could not get consequential damages for loss of goodwill).

damages in fact resulted from some intervening concurrent cause, partially or in toto. When the buyer's own negligence is the proximate cause of the damages, the buyer may recover no consequential damages. But in some cases comparative fault rules may apply[11] to apportion the loss, particularly where there is personal injury or property damage.

The buyer must also show foreseeability to recover consequential damages. A loss is foreseeable where the parties, at the time of contracting, knew or had reason to know facts that made the loss a foreseeable result of the breach. This "relaxed" interpretation of foreseeability enhances the buyer's duty to "mitigate" damages. It is also basic that the buyer must prove the amount of damages with reasonable certainty.[12]

The Code does not use the word mitigation but that is the meaning of the phrase in 2–715(2)(a) that bars recovery for losses that could have been prevented by cover or otherwise.[13]

The most common consequential damages arising from goods never accepted are lost profits. Where the seller knows, or has reason to know that the buyer is in the business of resale, lost profits resulting from breach are foreseeable and usually recoverable.[14] Courts have also awarded damages to buyers arising out of interruptions of their production processes caused by a seller's breach. In Hawthorne Industries, Inc. v. Balfour Maclaine International, Ltd.[15] the court awarded a carpet manufacturer damages for lost efficiencies in its carpet-production process arising when seller failed to deliver conforming jute.

---

11. Indust–Ri–Chem Laboratory, Inc. v. Par–Pak Co., 602 S.W.2d 282, 290, 29 UCC 794, 804–05 (Tex.Civ.App. 1980) (buyer's consequential damages reducible to the extent damages resulted from buyer's unreasonable conduct).

12. Givan v. Mack Truck, Inc., 569 S.W.2d 243, 24 UCC 1077 (Mo.App. 1978) ("substantial basis," not mathematical certainty required, but buyer failed to prove that business opportunities were available to him while his truck was being repaired, so claim of lost profit not allowed). Various Code cases allow recovery of lost profit to buyers starting new businesses. See, e.g., Parker Tractor & Implement Co. v. Johnson, 819 So.2d 1234, 1239–40, 48 UCC2d 1025, 1031 (Miss. 2002) (noting that "damages are speculative only when the cause is uncertain, not when the amount is uncertain"; reasonable to find that defective farm equipment would reduce productivity and cause a loss of profits); RIJ Pharmaceutical Corp. v. Ivax Phar-

maceuticals, Inc., 322 F.Supp.2d 406, 54 UCC2d 130 (S.D.N.Y. 2004).

13. See, e.g., cf. Chatlos Systems, Inc. v. National Cash Register Corp., 479 F.Supp. 738, 746, 27 UCC 647, 657 (D.N.J.1979), aff'd in part, rev'd in part, 635 F.2d 1081, 30 UCC 416 (3d Cir. 1980) (buyer in no position to cover by obtaining alternate computer system). Landmark Motors, Inc. v. Chrysler Credit Corp., 662 N.E.2d 971, 31 UCC2d 1026 (Ind. App. 1996) (consequential recovery rejected because buyer failed to show seller had reason to know of, and that wouldn't have been prevented by cover).

14. "In the case of sale of wares to one in the business of reselling them, resale is one of the requirements of which the seller has reason to know within the meaning of subsection (2)(a)." § 2–715, Comment 6.

15. 676 F.2d 1385, 33 UCC 1339 (11th Cir.1982).

Claims for lost goodwill are more troublesome.[16] In theory goodwill losses should be recoverable. In practice lost goodwill may be hard to prove and even harder to quantify. In Hangzhou Silk Import and Export Co. v. P.C.B. Int'l Industries, Inc.[17] an American start up company contracted to buy various garments of its design from a Chinese manufacturer. When several shipments proved to be defective, P.C.B. sought to recover for harm done to its reputation and goodwill. Noting that P.C.B. had failed to show that the cancellation of several of its accounts had been caused by defects in goods purchased from Hangzhou, and that it had not offered testimony or communications from its customers to show that their cancellations were so caused, the court denied P.C.B.'s claim for injury to its goodwill. The court reached this conclusion despite evidence that the Chinese seller had committed fraud by representing to one of the principals of P.C.B. that a manufacturing plant that belonged to another company was its own.

Section 2–715 is a set of rules under which contracting parties may assess potential damages and allocate risks. When courts mislabel incidental and consequential damages, they may frustrate those allocations. As the Seventh Circuit stated in AES Technology Systems, Inc. v. Coherent Radiation,[18] before a court awards consequential damages, it should:

> carefully examine the individual factual situation including the type of goods involved, the parties and the precise nature and purpose of the contract. The purpose of the courts in contractual disputes is not to rewrite contracts by ignoring parties' intent; rather, it is to interpret the existing contract as fairly as possible when all events did not occur as planned.[19]

Comment 4 to Section 2–715 provides that "[t]he burden of proving the extent of loss incurred by way of consequential damage is on the buyer." However, the buyer's burden of proof on the amount of loss may be easier to carry because the level of certainty

---

16. Compare, e.g., Consolidated Data Terminals v. Applied Digital Data Systems, Inc., 708 F.2d 385, 36 UCC 59 (9th Cir.1983) (allowed) *with* Argo Welded Products, Inc. v. J.T. Ryerson Steel & Sons, Inc., 528 F.Supp. 583, 33 UCC 1349 (E.D.Pa.1981) (too speculative); Step–Saver Data Systems, Inc. v. Wyse Technology, 912 F.2d 643, 12 UCC2d 343 (3d Cir.1990) (discussing circumstances under which goodwill losses are certain enough to be recoverable as consequential damages, and holding that consequential damages to buyer's goodwill may be demonstrated by amounts that buyer paid out to customers to maintain customers' satisfaction, even where buyer not legally obligated to pay out such amounts).

17. 48 UCC2d 1367 (S.D.N.Y 2002).

18. 583 F.2d 933, 24 UCC 861, 25 UCC 473 (7th Cir.1978).

19. *Id.* at 941, 24 UCC at 871–72. See also Piper Jaffray & Co. v. SunGard Systems Int'l, Inc., 2004 WL 2222322, 54 UCC2d 1088 (D.Minn. 2004) (contractual waiver of damages remains intact even though an exclusive or limited remedy fails of essential purpose).

required to establish the *amount* of a loss may be lower than that required to establish the *fact* or *cause* of a loss.

§ 7–6   Specific Performance

When the seller of five-penny nails defaults on its contract, its buyer will purchase nails from another supplier and may or may not think it worth the legal fees, time, and grief to sue under 2–712. If, however, the buyer can readily procure five-penny nails only from the breaching seller, it may try to force the seller to deliver. If in addition, the aggrieved buyer has prepaid the price to a shaky seller who may not be good for a money judgment, the buyer's interest in specific performance will intensify. To accommodate buyers who want the goods and not money, the Code offers sections 2–716 and 2–502.[1] Section 2–716 provides:

(1) Specific performance may be decreed where the goods are unique or in other proper circumstances.

(2) The decree for specific performance may include such terms and conditions as to payment of the price, damages, or other relief as the court may deem just.

(3) The buyer has a right of replevin for goods identified to the contract if after reasonable effort he is unable to effect cover for such goods or the circumstances reasonably indicate that such effort will be unavailing or if the goods have been shipped under reservation and satisfaction of the security interest in them has been made or tendered * * *.[2]

Of course the Code drafters did not write on a *tabula rasa* here but upon a slate already crowded with centuries of judicial and legislative markings.[3] The most familiar of these is the requirement that for a court to grant specific performance, the plaintiff's remedy at law must be inadequate to put him in the same position as performance would have. Section 68 of the Uniform Sales Act

---

§ 7–6

1. § 2–502:

(1) Subject to subsections (2) and (3) and even though the goods have not been shipped a buyer who has paid a part or all of the price of goods in which he has a special property under the provisions of the immediately preceding section may on making and keeping good a tender of any unpaid portion of their price recover them from the seller if ... the seller becomes insolvent within ten days after receipt of the first installment on their price....

(3) If the identification creating his special property has been made by the buyer he acquires the right to recover the goods only if they conform to the contract for sale.

2. On specific performance generally, compare Kronman, Specific Performance, 45 U.Chi.L.Rev. 351 (1978) *and* Schwartz, The Case for Specific Performance, 89 Yale L.J. 271 (1979).

3. For a detailed history of § 2–716, see Greenberg, Specific Performance Under Section 2–716 of the Uniform Commercial Code: "A More Liberal Attitude" in the "Grand Style," 17 New. Eng.L.Rev. 321 (1982).

sought to liberalize that requirement by inviting a court to grant specific performance as to "specific or ascertained goods" whenever it "thinks fit."[4] However, the pre-Code decisions (both under the USA and general equity powers) did not much expand the use of specific performance in sale of goods cases.[5]

Like the Uniform Sales Act, the Code (2–716(1)) omits any express proviso that the remedy at law be inadequate; moreover it deletes the Uniform Sales Act's requirement that the goods be "specific" and instead authorizes specific performance "where the goods are unique or in other proper circumstances."[6] Comment 1 to 2–716 shows that the drafters intended to continue "prior policy as to specific performance and injunction against breach," but it also "seeks to further a more liberal attitude than some courts have shown" toward specific performance. Under the Code some courts have granted specific performance where it might not have been available under the USA, but the changes are modest (and often well disguised).

a. Unique Goods

What are "unique or in other proper circumstances"? Surely treasured heirlooms remain "unique," but Comment 2 to 2–716 suggests a broader meaning:

> The test * * * must be made in terms of the total situation which characterizes the contract. Output and requirements contracts involving a particular or peculiarly available source or market present today the typical commercial specific performance situation * * *.

The courts are thus encouraged to take notice of current market sources and commercial realities in determining whether goods are "unique."[7] The case of Fast v. Southern Offshore Yachts was a

---

4. See also 1 N.Y. State Law Revision Comm'n, 1955 Report 575.

5. See Fortner v. Wilson, 202 Okla. 563, 216 P.2d 299 (1950). Cf. Curtice Bros. Co. v. Catts, 72 N.J.Eq. 831, 66 A. 935 (1907); Manchester Dairy System v. Hayward, 82 N.H. 193, 132 A. 12 (1926); Eastern Rolling Mill Co. v. Michlovitz, 157 Md. 51, 145 A. 378 (1929).

6. USA § 68:

Where the seller has broken a contract to deliver specific or ascertained goods, a court having the powers of a court of equity may, if it thinks fit, on the application of the buyer, by its judgment or decree direct that the contract shall be performed specifically, without giving the seller the option of retaining the goods on payment of damages. The

judgment or decree may be unconditional, or upon such terms and conditions as to damages, payment of the price and otherwise, as to the court may seem just.

7. In re Tennecomp Systems, Inc., 12 B.R. 729, 735, 31 UCC 1307, 1316 (Bankr.E.D.Tenn. 1981) ("The test of uniqueness under [§ 2–716] would be made in terms of the total situation which characterizes the contract."). See in re Bullet Jet Charter, Inc., 177 B.R. 593, 27 UCC2d 1256 (Bankr. N.D. Ill. 1995) (goods "unique" and buyer unable to cover); In re Surplus Furniture Liquidators, Inc. of High Point, 199 B.R. 136, 31 UCC2d 396 (Bankr. M.D.N.C. 1995) (type of furniture not unique).

classic case.[8] There the plaintiff obtained specific performance of a contract to sell a custom-made yacht.

Still, the decisions put relatively little flesh on the bones of "unique." In McCormick Dray Line, Inc. v. Lovell,[9] the court granted specific performance of a contract to sell a trucking business. The court found that the rights under the certificates issued by the Interstate Commission and the Public Utility Commission were unique and, therefore, the decree should issue. In another case, Hilmor Sales Co. v. Helen Neushaefer Division of Supronics Corp.,[10] the plaintiff sought to enjoin the defendant from disposing of lipstick and nail polish which were the subject of a sales contract. According to the court the only unique aspect of the contract was the "closeout" price. The buyer could not purchase similar goods at such a favorable price elsewhere, but he did not claim that replacement was impossible. In a similar case, Duval & Co. v. Malcom,[11] where the price of cotton rose dramatically, the buyer sought specific enforcement of the contract solely on the ground that the price increase made the cotton unique. The courts in both *Hilmor* and *Duval* denied specific performance.

A fourth case, Division of Triple T Service, Inc. v. Mobil Oil Corp.,[12] also resulted in a denial of plaintiff's claim for injunction. There the plaintiff sought to enjoin the defendant from ending his service station franchise. In a long opinion containing dictum to the effect that a franchise agreement is analogous to an output contract and therefore an appropriate subject for injunctive relief, the court denied the injunction on the ground that the contract contained a clause allowing the franchisor to cancel and that in doing so it did not breach its franchise obligations.

I.Lan Systems, Inc. v. Netscout Service Level Corp.[13] deals with the claim that a software system is unique, so as to entitle the buyer/licensee to an order that the licensor continue to update and service for some indefinite period. The licensee argued that the software was unique for two reasons: 1) it was copyrighted and took years to produce; and 2) the licensee had "tailored" its business to fit the software. The court rejected the claim. It noted that many things which are not unique are copyrighted and took great cost and effort to produce. The court concluded that several competing

---

8. 587 F.Supp. 1354, 38 UCC 1569 (D.Conn.1984). See also Sedmak v. Charlie's Chevrolet, Inc., 622 S.W.2d 694, 31 UCC 851 (Mo.App.1981) (specific performance of limited production automobile). With Sedmak, compare Scholl v. Hartzell, 20 Pa. D. & C.3d 304, 33 UCC 951 (1981) (1962 Corvette might be collector's item, but not unique, so no specific performance).

9. 13 Pa. D. & C.2d 464 (1958).

10. 1969 WL 11054, 6 UCC 325 (N.Y.Sup.1969).

11. 233 Ga. 784, 214 S.E.2d 356, 16 UCC 1217 (1975).

12. 60 Misc.2d 720, 304 N.Y.S.2d 191, 6 UCC 1011 (1969), aff'd, 34 A.D.2d 618, 311 N.Y.S.2d 961 (1970).

13. 183 F.Supp.2d 328, 46 UCC2d 287 (D.Mass.2002).

software packages could and did perform the same functions as the software in the case. It suggested that the licensee was confusing reliance with uniqueness. So, at least in Massachusetts, not much software is unique, and surely the court is right to focus on function, not on a program's elegance or unusual technical features.

The outcomes in these cases are correct under the Code, but the direction in which they point is unclear. The analogy drawn in the *Mobil Oil* case between an output contract and a franchise agreement is sound and, in the absence of a specific clause authorizing termination, the court could properly have granted the franchisee's request for an injunction. One certainly cannot quarrel with the holdings in the *Hilmor* and *Duval* cases if the buyers showed only that they had contracts at very favorable prices. However, the dictum in *Hilmor* comes straight from the nineteenth century: it is never appropriate to award specific performance where the "plaintiff can be adequately compensated * * * by an award of money damages."[14]

b. Other Proper Circumstances

Even if goods are not unique, specific performance may be granted if a buyer can show "other proper circumstances." Comment 2 to 2–716 gives this cryptic phrase some meaning:

> [T]he relief may also be granted "in other proper circumstances" and inability to cover is strong evidence of "other proper circumstances."

Perhaps this phrase was added to preserve the traditional power of an equity court to provide or withhold specific relief in its sound discretion and subject to such traditional defenses in equity as clean hands, laches, etc. The perimeters of uniqueness *vis à vis* "other proper circumstances" remain undefined. If "uniqueness" equals "not available elsewhere," then what is left for the category "other proper circumstances"? An opinion that shows the independent significance of "other proper circumstances" is Stephan's Machine & Tool, Inc. v. D & H Machinery Consultants, Inc.[15] There, plaintiff bought a machine from defendant, borrowing $96,000 to pay for it. The machine failed to function. Defendant agreed to replace it but failed to do so. Plaintiff was unable to raise the money to buy a replacement elsewhere although such machines

---

14. 6 UCC at 325. For still other Code cases dealing with "unique" goods and 2–716(1), see I.Lan Systems, Inc. v. Netscout Service Level Corp., 183 F.Supp.2d 328, 46 UCC2d 287 (D.Mass. 2002) (software which is mass-produced is not unique, even when buyer has designed operations in reliance on a particular program).

15. 65 Ohio App.2d 197, 417 N.E.2d 579 (1979).

were available. The court granted specific performance of the replacement agreement because of plaintiff's financial position.[16]

In Laclede Gas Co. v. Amoco Oil Co.,[17] the buyer, a distributor of propane, received an injunction against his seller's breach of a long-term contract for the supply of that gas. The breach occurred in the midst of the 1973–74 energy crisis. In view of the long-term nature of the contract, the uncertain future of energy supplies and the uncontroverted testimony that the buyer probably could not find another seller willing to enter into such a long-term contract, the court found that:

> [E]ven if * * * [the buyer] * * * could obtain supplies of propane for the affected developments through its present contracts or newly negotiated ones, it would still face considerable expense and trouble which cannot be estimated in advance.[18]

In a similar case Gulf Oil was enjoined from breach of its jet fuel contract with Eastern Airlines.[19] The court enjoined breach of a large jet fuel contract on the ground that interruption would cause "chaos and irreparable damage."[20]

In another case the federal District Court in Colorado awarded specific performance based on a combination of uniqueness and other circumstances. In Colorado–Ute Electric Ass'n, Inc. v. Envirotech Corp.,[21] Colorado–Ute sued for specific performance when a hot-side electrostatic precipitator, purchased from Envirotech for pollution control at a coal-burning electricity generating plant, failed to operate according to specific warranties. In awarding specific performance, the court first found the precipitator to be unique. The court then noted that awarding monetary damages based on the cost of Colorado–Ute's use of a chemical additive to

---

16. But see Klein v. PepsiCo, Inc., 845 F.2d 76, 6 UCC2d 728 (4th Cir. 1988), appeal after remand, 875 F.2d 315 (4th Cir.1989) (court denies specific performance; that cover price has risen does not signify "other proper circumstances"). We would read the "other proper circumstances" language of 2–716 to allow specific performance here.

17. 522 F.2d 33, 17 UCC 447 (8th Cir.1975), rev'd on other grounds, 531 F.2d 942 (8th Cir.1976).

18. Id. at 40, 17 UCC at 452; Bander v. Grossman, 161 Misc.2d 119, 611 N.Y.S.2d 985, 23 UCC2d 1159 (1994) (establishes that an unduly lengthy delay in asserting a claim for specific performance can result in an otherwise valid claim for specific performance being denied).

19. Eastern Air Lines, Inc. v. Gulf Oil Corp., 415 F.Supp. 429, 19 UCC 721 (S.D.Fla.1975). See also, In re Surplus Furniture Liquidators, Inc. of High Point, 199 B.R. 136, 31 UCC2d 396 (Bankr.M.D.N.C. 1995). The court in the latter case denied specific performance to the buyers, who had paid in full for furniture from a dealer who declared bankruptcy before delivery. The goods were not unique, and the fact that the seller was in bankruptcy did not give rise to "other proper circumstances." Furthermore, the buyer had an adequate remedy at law, namely the right to collect from the seller, even though full recovery might not be possible.

20. Id. at 442, 19 UCC at 739.

21. 524 F.Supp. 1152, 33 UCC 965 (D.Colo.1981).

bring the precipitator up to state pollution-control levels would not be a satisfactory solution because of the uncertainty that the state would continue to allow the use of chemical additives. The award of damages based on the use of the chemical additives would also be speculative because of deregulation and fluctuations in the market. Colorado–Ute would also be irreparably harmed in case of a shutdown resulting from clean air violations.

Perhaps *Laclede*, *Gulf*, and *Colorado–Ute* could have been decided under the "unique" rubric and thus may add little to our understanding about the distinction between "uniqueness" and "other proper circumstances." Or are the courts accepting the drafters' invitation to apply the "other proper circumstances" language in cases in which the uniqueness does not arise from traditional factors (e.g., heirloom) but arises because of economic circumstances? At least in the *Eastern* and *Colorado–Ute* cases, the courts may have been influenced by the quasi-public utility status of an airline and a power company and by the disruption and inconvenience that would be caused to the public by interrupting the service of either.

There are various defenses to specific performance. The remedy is granted only in the equitable discretion of the court. Among other things, specific performance is generally not granted if the party seeking the remedy did not perform fairly, equitably and honestly.[22]

c. The Law and Economics Debate Over Specific Performance

There has been a lively debate in the law and economic literature about the virtues of a specific performance regime (such as the civil law countries have) by comparison with the damage regime (such as the common law countries have).[23] In contract cases traditional common law says that specific performance is not available unless damages are inadequate to put the aggrieved party in the same position as performance would have. The civil law generally allows specific performance of a contract whenever the aggrieved party chooses.

22. Slidell, Inc. v. Millennium Inorganic Chemicals, Inc., 2004 WL 1447921, 53 UCC2d 829 (D.Minn. 2004).

23. For arguments to limit specific performance on economic grounds, see Posner, Economic Analysis of Law (2d ed.1987); Kronman, Specific Performance, 45 U.Chi.L.Rev. 351 (1978); Muris, The Costs of Freely Granting Specific Performance, 1982 Duke L.J. 1053; Yorio, In Defense of Money Damages for Breach of Contract, 82 Colum.L.Rev. 1365 (1982). For proponents of specific performance, see Schwartz, The Case for Specific Performance, 89 Yale L.J. 271 (1979); Ulen, The Efficiency of Specific Performance: Toward a Unified Theory of Contract Remedies, 83 Mich.L.Rev. 341 (1984).

The earliest law and economic academic writers defended common law restrictions. At its crudest and most simplistic level the efficiency argument against specific performance says that the granting of specific performance to an aggrieved party might cause the goods to go to that party when there is another who values them more highly and would pay more highly for them. If, for example, a seller contracts with Buyer One, who values the good at $10, and then finds Buyer Two, who is willing to pay $15, there will be an inefficiency if Buyer One uses the goods. Arguably it would be more efficient to give the goods to Buyer Two, and to pay Buyer One's expected profit, thereby making him whole.

Passing for a moment a series of assumptions about efficiency that lie under the statements in the foregoing paragraph, consider the response of the specific performance advocates to this crude example.[24] The specific performance advocates will first point out that Buyer One may value the goods at more than $10 perhaps even at $15. That he has contracted to pay only $10 tells little about his true value. Second, they will note that if Buyer One values the goods at $10 and Buyer Two at $15, the goods can still end up in the hands of Buyer Two under a specific performance regime, but that the $5 surplus will go to Buyer One, not to Seller, a better result. Money damages advocates may reply that the latter transaction (giving Buyer One the right to the goods via specific performance) exaggerates the transaction costs (Seller must negotiate with Buyer One to be able to sell to Buyer Two) by comparison with the damage regime and thus produces inefficiencies.[25]

Proponents of damage regimes make other more subtle arguments too. For example, they argue that the presence of specific performance may cause a promisee to fabricate subjective value and so force a settlement that gives him more than the contract was really worth to him.[26] Some assert that the uniqueness rule in section 2–716 correctly describes the only circumstances under which money damages provide inadequate compensation.[27] When a different buyer is willing to pay more for the same goods than the original buyer, forcing the seller to perform the original contract is inefficient and, at best, will require the seller to incur additional transaction costs negotiating for a release from the first buyer—so conclude the opponents of expanded specific performance.

Proponents of specific performance start with the unquestioned proposition that current damage rules often undercompensate an injured party.[28] If for no other reason, undercompensation occurs because a winning American plaintiff does not recover attorneys

---

24. Schwartz and Ulen, *supra*, n. 23.

25. See Posner, Kronman, Muris, and Yorio, *supra*, n. 23.

26. See Muris, *supra* n. 23.

27. Kronman, *supra*, n. 23 at 354–59.

28. Schwartz and Ulen, *supra*, n. 23.

fees. Advocates of specific performance argue that an injured party would not choose specific performance unless damages undercompensated him.[29] They suggest that promisees would otherwise want to avoid dealing with a hostile promisor and so save the expense of monitoring a reluctant performer.[30] Moreover, proponents of specific performance argue that the costs of cover are likely to be the same for buyers and sellers and therefore that seller—who would be required to perform—could procure substitute goods to satisfy the contract or negotiate with the buyer to purchase the right to require specific performance. Consequently, post-breach transaction costs would be no higher in a specific performance regime than in a damage regime—so argue the proponents of specific performance.[31]

Specific performance also provides its own efficiency gains. In a regime that undercompensates a promisee (by awarding damages), a promisor may breach more often than if specific performance were available. Because such a breach leaves the promisee worse off than performance, the result is not Pareto-superior.[32] The availability of specific performance minimizes this inefficient result. Additionally, expanded availability reduces the frequency of parties' attempts to avoid 2–716 restrictions with liquidated damages clauses. Thus, specific performance might eliminate the strategic behavior and negotiation costs associated with liquidated damages clauses.[33]

As we indicate above, proponents of specific performance do not rely exclusively on efficiency arguments. They point out that the right to specific performance carries with it the potential allocation of the "surplus" that arises from the new transaction. To understand that point consider the following hypothetical. Assume that Seller has a contract to sell to Buyer One for $10 when Buyer Two, willing to pay $15 appears. If the damage regime permits Seller to pay Buyer One's potential expectancy (assume it is $1) and get rid of him, Seller then captures the entire $5 surplus (net $4) that is available in the second transaction because Buyer Two is willing to pay $15. If, on the other hand, Buyer One has a right to specific performance, he has the power to enjoy the surplus by getting the goods and, himself, reselling them to Buyer Two. Of course, this does not necessarily cause an efficiency gain, but causes

29. Schwartz, *supra* n. 23, at 274–77; Alan Schwartz, The Myth That Promisees Prefer Supracompensatory Remedies: An Analysis of Contracting for Damages Measures, 100 Yale L.J. 369, 388–89 (1990) (asserting that a buyer must pay more for a specific performance right, so will avoid it unless buyer deems it worth the price).

30. *Id.* at 277.

31. Macneil, Efficient Breach of Contract: Circles in the Sky, 68 Va.L.Rev. 947 (1982); Schwartz, *supra*, n. 23 at 287.

32. Schwartz, *supra* n. 23 at 291.

33. *Id.* at 291–92; Ulen, *supra* n. 23 at 376–77.

a wealth transfer or allocation from the original seller in a damage regime to aggrieved buyers in a specific performance regime.[34]

Whether one is persuaded by this argument for specific performance may depend upon his or her conclusion about the "right" to the surplus arising out of the original contract. If the parties' expectations at the time of signing the original contract are that the buyer should and would have a right to any surplus upon the appearance of a second buyer, then specific performance should be granted. If their expectation is the opposite, the argument carries no weight and specific performance may produce a dead weight loss.

Although they disagree on the appropriate scope of court-imposed specific performance, most law-and-economics scholars agree that parties should be able to choose specific performance by contract.[35] Efficiency assumes that parties know their interests better than the legislature does, and a system that allows free choice is more efficient than one that denies it.[36] Because promisees usually have better information about the costs of monitoring and the adequacy of damages they may make more informed and efficient decisions.[37] Moreover, allowing contractual choice might reduce the number of lawsuits and breaches.[38] If parties could be encouraged to negotiate most issues before the breach, post-breach costs would be less for both the parties and the courts.[39]

In considering changes to section 2–716, the Article 2 Study Committee evaluated the arguments of the law-and-economics scholars and reached two conclusions. Although the Committee agreed that the uniqueness test was probably too restrictive, it was unwilling to give complete discretion to award specific perform-

---

34. Ulen, *supra* n. 23 at 383 ("[S]trategic behavior is most likely to arise where there is a surplus to be distributed, [but] the most that can be said against it is that it will frustrate redistribution of that surplus, not that it will frustrate an efficient exchange."). See also Macneil, *supra* n. 31.

35. Kronman, *supra* n. 23 at 370–73; Schwartz, *supra* n. 23 at 278; Schwartz, *supra* n. 29 at 371; Ulen, *supra* n. 23 at 346.

36. Kronman, *supra* n. 23 at 370:

[E]x ante arguments for the efficiency of a particular legal rule assume that individuals remain free to contract around that rule, and a legal system that denies private parties the right to vary rules in this way will tend to be less efficient than a system that adopts the same rules but permits contractual variation.

See also Schwartz, *supra* n. 29 at 406 (suggesting that the courts' current refusal to enforce contractually chosen remedies "restrict[s] party efforts to contract out of statutory rules that were explicitly meant to be defaults").

37. Schwartz, *supra* n. 23 at 278; Ulen, *supra* n. 23 at 365–66 (commenting that, when enforced, specific performance requires the parties to conduct valuations, not the court).

38. *Id.* at 373.

39. *Id.* at 365, 371, 379; see also Linzer, On the Amorality of Contract Remedies—Efficiency, Equity, and the Second Restatement, 81 Colum.L.Rev. 111 (1981) (suggesting that parties already include costs of specific performance in initial negotiations).

ance.[40] Consequently, the Committee recommended that 2–716(1) remain as is.[41] The Committee did agree that parties should have the right to choose specific performance by agreement.[42] Accordingly, the second recommendation was to require enforcement of specific performance when the agreement so provides.[43]

The Amended Article 2 includes a provision that directs a court to allow specific performance when a non-consumer contract provides specific performance as a remedy. The Amended Article retains the language of uniqueness and other proper circumstances. Even if the Amended Article were adopted, we doubt the authorization for specific performance where the contract so provides would have real impact. That is because we have never seen a contract that specifies specific performance as a remedy, and we doubt that many exist.

In general we side with Alan Schwartz and other advocates of specific performance. We believe the world would be a slightly better place if the courts were to grant specific performance more often and were to relax the traditional Anglo–American condition (absence of adequate remedy at law). We doubt that granting specific performance would cause any significant inefficiencies and, like the law and economics advocates of specific performance, we suspect that specific performance might even promote efficiency. We believe that the principal economic consequence of more readily granting specific performance would not be a change in efficiency but a wealth redistribution from the breaching party to the aggrieved party. By giving the latter instead of the former an implicit claim to the surplus from resale to a third party, a specific performance regime might modestly enrich the plaintiff compared to the current regime. We take comfort from the fact that the civil law countries have traditionally allowed specific performance without regard to the adequacy of damages. We see no evidence that their legal systems or economies have suffered from these rules.

d.   Sections 2–716(3) and 2–502

Sections 2–716(3) and 2–502 give buyer a *right* to goods in seller's hands in certain limited circumstances when the goods have

---

40. PEB Study Group Report, at 231 (1993); Task Force Report, 16 Del. J.Corp.L. 981 (1991).

41. Study Group Report, at 231 ("[T]he Study Group recommends no revision that would clarify or expand the power of a court to grant specific performance."). See also Task Force Report, at 1236 (agreeing with the Study Committee).

42. Study Group Report, at 232; see also Task Force Report, at 1236.

43. Study Group Report, at 232 ("We recommend, however, that § 2–716(1) [allowing specific performance] be revised * * * to expand the power of the parties to agree in advance for specific performance."); see also Task Force Report, at 1236 ("We agree * * * with the recommendation to expand the party's ability to agree in advance to specific performance.").

been "identified" to the contract. The court must grant a decree of replevin if the buyer's case fits the narrow limits of 2–502 or the somewhat more generous terms of 2–716(3). Still, the principal condition for application of 2–716(3) ("cover" unavailable) looks suspiciously like "uniqueness" in new attire.

Section 2–502(1)(b) reads in part as follows:

> Subject to subsections (2) and (3) and even though the goods have not been shipped a buyer who has paid a part or all of the price of goods in which he has a special property under the provisions of the immediately preceding section may on making and keeping good a tender of any unpaid portion of their price recover them from the seller if . . . the seller becomes insolvent within ten days after receipt of the first installment on their price.

Section 2–502 gives the buyer a right to get goods identified to the contract and at least partly paid for if the seller becomes insolvent within ten days after receipt of the first installment on their price.[44] Thus in a limited number of cases the Code resolves the perplexing problem whether insolvency alone is a sufficient ground for specific relief.[45]

However, the Code limits this right to reach the goods in several ways. First, the buyer must have a special property interest under 2–501(1).[46] Second, the buyer's right is limited to the situation in which the seller becomes insolvent "within ten days after receipt of the first installment on their price." The period is short, and the contract goods must be identified within or prior to those ten days. At least in the case of the buyer who advances capital to finance manufacture of its goods, identification will often come too late. When one considers not only the ten-day limitation but also the possibility (if not probability) that buyer's 2–502 rights will be subordinate to the rights of the trustee in bankruptcy and to the rights of secured creditors, the importance of this section diminishes even further. Worse, at least one court has held that 2–502 rights are unenforceable in bankruptcy proceedings, finding 2–502 to be inconsistent with and preempted by section 365 of the Bankruptcy Code, which allows trustees to accept or reject executory contracts—rendering 2–502 all but useless to the unfortunate buyer whose seller's insolvency sends it into bankruptcy.[47]

---

44. § 2–502, Comment 1.

45. See 5 A Corbin, Contracts § 1156 (1964).

46. See, e.g., In re CSY Yacht Corp., 42 B.R. 619, 39 UCC 879 (Bankr. M.D.Fla.1984).

47. In re G. Paoletti, Inc., 205 B.R. 251, 34 UCC2d 987 (Bankr. N.D.Cal.

1997). The court also held that 2–716 does not apply when the seller is insolvent—only 2–502. The court thus suggests that, to have 2–502 available to him, the buyer must hope that his insolvent seller does not file for bankruptcy protection.

When 2–502 is not available, buyer can fall back on 2–716(3) as a second line of defense. Under this section the buyer may replevy (or the like) goods identified to the contract when (1) cover is or reasonably appears to be foreclosed, or (2) goods are shipped under reservation (for instance, shipment under a negotiable bill of lading to seller's order) and satisfaction of the security interest is at least tendered. Of course, the buyer's rights under this section are subject to attack by the trustee in bankruptcy with the same weapons the trustee will use against 2–502.

One would expect 2–716(3) to be used most commonly where "cover" is unavailable. However, even here the section may be of limited use since if the goods are unique the buyer can get specific performance; if they are not unique, then reaching the goods may be unnecessary. However, even if the bare inability to cover proves neither "uniqueness" nor "other proper circumstances," the aggrieved buyer faces a difficult burden to prove that he was "unable to effect cover" for the goods. Not only must the buyer prove that a market did not exist (or at least was inaccessible), he must also convince the court that a breaching seller who is willing to sell to the buyer at a price over the contract price should not be considered an available source for cover. Also, equity is by tradition unwilling to order specific performance where it would force parties to work together, especially for any sustained period.[48] It may be crucial here to consider the relative bargaining positions of the parties, good faith, changes in market conditions, etc. Because there have been so few decisions interpreting 2–716(3), it is hard to predict how the courts will resolve these issues. The judicial silence bespeaks the unimportance of 2–716(3).

§ 7–7 The Buyer's Possible Responses to Repudiation

We have so far attempted to define "repudiation" and have discussed buyer's remedies in general.[1] Here we turn to the most difficult interpretative problems that face the buyer who desires a remedy for anticipatory repudiation.

The basic alternatives are indexed in 2–610:

* * * the aggrieved party may

(a) for a commercially reasonable time await performance by the repudiating party; or

(b) resort to any remedy for breach (section 2–703 or section 2–711), even though he has notified the repudiating

---

48. See generally 5 A. Corbin, Contracts §§ 1204, 1206 (1964).

1. See 7–2 *supra*.

party that he would await the latter's performance and has urged retraction; and

(c) in either case suspend his own performance * * *.

Section 2–610(b) thus provides a remedy for breach of contract before the time for performance has arrived, or, in the context of an installment contract, any time during the period of the contract.[2] Yet several questions remain under the 2–610 option of treating a repudiation as an immediate breach. When does the breach occur? Are damages measured as of the time for performance, time of repudiation, or some other time?

The buyer who chooses to treat the repudiation as a breach may, under 2–610(b), proceed to 2–711. Under section 2–711(1), the buyer may:

(1) cancel[3]

(2) recover any portion of the price paid to seller,[4] and

(3) seek damages either for "cover" (2–712) or the contract-market differential (2–713).[5]

If "cover" is unavailable (as where the goods are unique), 2–610, 2–711 and 2–716 indicate that specific performance may be available.[6] One significant problem arises with specific relief in the context of anticipatory breach: when should the repudiator perform? Although 2–610(b) authorizes the aggrieved buyer immediately to "resort to any remedy for breach," the Code does not

2. See, e.g., Missouri Public Service Co. v. Peabody Coal Co., 583 S.W.2d 721, 27 UCC 103 (Mo.App.1979), cert. denied, 444 U.S. 865, 100 S.Ct. 135, 62 L.Ed.2d 88 (1979) (buyer sued for specific performance of the remainder of the 10-year installment contract during period of contract).

3. Distinguish true cancellation from rescission for anticipatory breach coupled with a right of action on the contract. See Carvage v. Stowell, 115 Vt. 187, 55 A.2d 188 (1947); Baird v. Barton, 163 Cal.App.2d 502, 329 P.2d 492 (1958); Gordon v. Southgate Park Corp., 341 Mass. 534, 170 N.E.2d 691 (1960); Graulich Caterer, Inc. v. Hans Holterbosch, Inc., 101 N.J.Super. 61, 243 A.2d 253, 5 UCC 440 (App.Div.1968).

4. Throughout Chapters 7 and 8 we generally maintain that the plaintiff should never recover more than enough to put him in the same position as performance would have put him (1–106). Section 2–711 allows a buyer to recover "so much of the price as has been paid"

whether or not he recovers other damages. If the buyer had paid $5,000 of the contract price and the contract would have lost him $5,000 or more because his resale market price was lower than the contract price, our theory would say that buyer could not recover damages since that would exceed the value of performance. Nevertheless 2–711 seems to allow buyer to recover the full amount he paid. An old restitution case, Bush v. Canfield, 2 Conn. 485 (1818), specifically rejects the seller's argument that the buyer's potential loss of $3,000 on 2,000 barrels of flour should be deducted from the recovery of a $5,000 down payment made on the contract.

For an illuminating and useful discussion of limitations on damages, see Palmer, The Contract Price as a Limit on Restitution for Defendant's Breach, 20 Ohio State L.J. 264 (1959).

5. See 7–3 (§ 2–712) and 7–4 (§ 2–713) supra.

6. See 7–6 supra (§ 2–716).

answer the "when." Is it fair to accelerate the contractual obligations of the repudiator? Pre–Code law resolved this issue by allowing the repudiatee to bring an immediate action for a decree of specific performance, but it postponed the effectiveness of the decree itself until the date for performance specified in the contract.[7] Section 2–610(b) can be read the same way. The aggrieved party will have immediate recourse against the repudiator (as 2–610(b) directs in order to provide relief for an injured party to a contract). However, absent unusual circumstances the decree of specific relief should require performance in accordance with the contract and not at an accelerated pace.

Measuring buyer's damages under 2–713 upon an anticipatory repudiation presents one of the most impenetrable interpretive problems in the entire Code. Section 2–713(1) says:

> Subject to the provisions of this Article with respect to proof of market price (section 2–723), the measure of damages for non-delivery or repudiation by the seller is the difference between the market price at the time when the *buyer learned of the breach* and the contract price * * *. (emphasis added).

The italicized language might be interpreted to have any one of at least three possible meanings in the anticipatory repudiation context:

(1) When the buyer learns of the repudiation,

(2) When the buyer learns of the repudiation plus a commercially reasonable time thereafter,

(3) When actual performance by the seller is due under the contract.

Besides 2–713, sections 2–610, 2–711 and 2–723 entangle here to make an impossible legal thicket. We favor the third interpretation—time of performance. But the "plain meaning" of 2–713—the one you would probably get from your spouse if you presented an anticipatory repudiation case to him or her—is the first, namely that "learned of the breach" in the repudiation context is the equivalent of "learned of the repudiation," and therefore, the 2–713(1) market-contract differential should be measured at repudiation, not at performance.[8] Sad to say, most courts have adopted this

---

7. See, e.g., Brackenbury v. Hodgkin, 116 Me. 399, 102 A. 106 (1917).

8. Consider § 2–723(1):

(1) If an action based on anticipatory repudiation comes to trial before the time for performance with respect to some or all of the goods, any damages based on market price (§ 2–708 and § 2–713) shall be determined according to the price of such goods prevailing at the time when the aggrieved party learned of the repudiation.

This section explicitly applies to any case of anticipatory repudiation coming to trial before the time for performance named in the contract. In that situation the market is to be measured "at the time when the aggrieved party learned of the repudiation." Although the con-

obvious, if pedestrian, interpretation of the "learned of the breach" language.[9] In defense of those courts one must concede the language is powerful and that reading obvious. Indeed the reading is so obvious that several courts have entirely overlooked the other plausible readings.

Having considered the issue, some courts have rejected the interpretation that "learned of the breach" means "learned of the repudiation." But these courts do not agree on which of the other two plausible readings is correct. There is authority for our view that "when the buyer learned of the breach" means when performance is due under the contract.[10] There is also authority that this language means when the buyer learns of the repudiation plus a commercially reasonable time thereafter.[11]

We have taken heart from a decision by Judge Niemeyer who writes for the Court of Appeals for the Fourth Circuit in Hess Energy, Inc. v. Lightning Oil Co., Inc.[12] In that case seller, Lightning, found a buyer who would pay a higher price for natural gas that Lightning had contracted to sell to Hess. The court found that the seller had repudiated in July of 2000. The time for delivery was later in 2000 or in 2001 when the market price for natural gas was much higher than it was in July of 2000. In affirming Hess' jury verdict of $3,052,571, the Fourth Circuit agrees with our interpretation and arguments set out below for the proposition that 2–713 measures the contract market difference at the time of delivery not at time of repudiation in a repudiation case. Hurray for Judge Niemeyer.

flicting provisions affecting repudiation might more easily be reconciled by finding that 2–723 applies only to sellers (and thus does not conflict with 2–713, 2–712, etc.), two important facts make such an argument untenable: (1) 2–723, in terms refers to 2–713 and thus was probably intended to be used by buyers and (2) 2–713 as well refers specifically to 2–723.

The importance of 2–723 can be exaggerated, however. In a world of clogged dockets and long delays before trial, only the long term installment contracts will confront 2–723(1). In all others, trial will be after performance would have occurred.

9. For cases adopting this obvious interpretation, see Oloffson v. Coomer, 11 Ill.App.3d 918, 296 N.E.2d 871, 12 UCC 1082 (1973) (buyer of corn under a contract calling for fall delivery limited to contract-market damages as of June 3rd, date of seller's repudiation); Fredonia Broadcasting Corp. v. RCA Corp.,

481 F.2d 781, 12 UCC 1088 (5th Cir. 1973) (Fifth Circuit said in calculating contract-market damages resulting from seller's repudiation, 2–713(2) specifies that the measuring market price is price at time buyer learned of breach);

10. Cargill, Inc. v. Stafford, 553 F.2d 1222, 21 UCC 707 (10th Cir.1977) (normal measure is time performance due); Trans World Metals, Inc. v. Southwire Co., 769 F.2d 902, 41 UCC 453 (2d Cir. 1985) (dictum). This is the interpretation which the Fifth Circuit gave the language in Cosden Oil & Chemical Co. v. Karl O. Helm Aktiengesellschaft, 736 F.2d 1064, 38 UCC 1645 (5th Cir. 1984), a case which gives the issue its most elaborate treatment so far.

11. Cosden Oil, 736 F.2d 1064, 38 UCC 1645 (5th Cir.1984) (court stressed 2–610 allowing buyer a reasonable time to await performance; acknowledges that 2–723(1) points other way).

12. 338 F.3d 357, 51 UCC2d 1 (4th Cir. 2003).

Why should the "obvious" interpretation—i.e., that time one learns of the breach in a repudiation case is the time of the repudiation—be rejected? In the first place, if they intended repudiation why didn't the drafters use the word "repudiation" instead of "breach" in 2–713? (Of course, one could argue that since the drafters used the "time and place for tender" in 2–708(1), they would have used the same words in 2–713(1) had they intended the same result.)

Secondly, if the buyer's damages are to be measured at the time the buyer learned of the repudiation, then the buyer cannot do what 2–610(a) seems to give him the right to do, namely await performance for a "commercially reasonable time"—at least not without risking loss as a result of post repudiation market shifts. Assume, for example, that a buyer of skis learns of a seller's repudiation of the contract on August 2 when the market is $225 per pair. The buyer exercises his right to wait a reasonable time and waits for performance until September 2 (when the market has risen to $250 a pair). Under the "plain meaning" interpretation of 2–713(1) the buyer would be forced to compute the damages based upon the August 2 market price, and would be deprived of the right to wait that 2–610 apparently offers. (Of course if the buyer can and does cover within a "reasonable" time, he will not be affected by section 2–713.)

A third argument which explains use of the language "learned of the breach" is that the drafters intended the language in 2–713 to apply only to the case in which there had been no anticipatory repudiation but only where the buyer had learned of the breach after performance had come and gone. It appears that Professor Patterson in his report to the New York Law Revision Commission adopted this interpretation of the language "learned of the breach" and did not consider that it could also apply to a time prior to the time of tender. Professor Patterson commented that 2–713 was "*apparently* a change in New York law; but actually it probably is not a change in the law as applied by New York courts."[13] He was referring to the "special circumstances" exception to section 67 of the Uniform Sales Act which allowed the court in special circumstances to measure the market at a time other than that scheduled for performance. However, the two cases cited[14] for this proposition indicate that the "special circumstances" exception (and thus the Code "learned of the breach" rule) was used to delay the time to measure the market past the date scheduled for performance; the section was not intended to accelerate the time to measure the

13. 1 N.Y. State Law Revision Comm'n, 1955 Report 698 (1955) (emphasis in original).

14. Boyd v. L.H. Quinn Co., 18 Misc. 169, 41 N.Y.S. 391 (1896); Perkins v. Minford, 235 N.Y. 301, 139 N.E. 276 (1923). See also 7–4 *supra*.

market in a repudiation case. In Perkins v. Minford,[15] defendant (seller) breached a contract by shipping too little sugar; the plaintiff (buyer) was unaware of the breach until he received the bill of lading. It was in this setting that the court declared that special circumstances warranted measuring the market at a date *later* than performance, not *earlier*:

> The reason is clear. Usually, knowing of the breach of contract, the buyer may protect himself against the consequences of a rising market by buying from others. * * * What if the delivery [is] being made at a distance [and] the buyer neither knows nor has means of knowledge that the contract has not been completed until he actually receives the goods or a bill of lading stating the amount shipped to him? * * * The time as to when the damages are measured is shifted. It is now the date when the buyer knew or should have known of the default.[16]

Similarly in Boyd v. L. H. Quinn Co.,[17] the court recognized an extraordinary situation existed where the seller breached a contract to ship goods by rail (from Illinois to New York), but buyer was unaware of the breach until he questioned seller and received his refusal. Thus *Boyd*, as well as *Perkins*, illustrates the intent in 2–713 to delay the time to measure the market after the time for performance has passed in cases where the buyer does not learn of the breach at the time it actually occurs.

Other and unchallenged statements in the New York Law Revision Commission reports include this comment of Professor Patterson:

> The measure of damages for the anticipatory repudiation of a duty to deliver, or to accept, goods under a contract of sale, is to be determined as of the date when performance was due, rather than the date of repudiation, under New York law.[18]

Also, when he reviewed 2–723 for the Commission, Professor John Honnold agreed that the rule at common law and under the USA based "market value on the date for performance prescribed in the contract." He recognized that 2–713 could be read to change this result, but he said that this "incongruity probably must be avoided by excluding 'repudiation' from the concept of breach employed in section 2–713, so that after anticipatory repudiation damages are measured under that section as of the date of performance."[19]

15. 235 N.Y. 301, 139 N.E. 276 (1923).

16. *Id.* at 305, 139 N.E. at 277.

17. 18 Misc. 169, 41 N.Y.S. 391 (1896).

18. 1 N.Y. State Law Revision Comm'n, 1955 Report 669, 672 (1955).

Professor Patterson cites two New York cases to support his position; Goldfarb v. Campe Corp., 99 Misc. 475, 164 N.Y.S. 583 (City Ct.1917); Segall v. Finlay, 245 N.Y. 61, 156 N.E. 97 (1927).

19. 1 N.Y. State Law Revision Comm'n, 1955 Report 590 (1955).

A fourth and more elegant argument against the "plain meaning" interpretation of 2–713 is that it conflicts with, and would render useless, a part of 2–723(1) which reads as follows:

> If an action based on anticipatory repudiation comes to trial before the time for performance with respect to some or all of the goods, any damages based on market price (section 2–708 or section 2–713) shall be determined according to the price of such goods prevailing at the time when the aggrieved party learned of the repudiation.

Every interpreter of statutes knows the doctrine that one should interpret in such a way as to give some meaning to all the words. If "learned of the breach" means "learned of the repudiation," then the court would always look to the time when the aggrieved party learned of the repudiation to measure damages whether or not the time for performance had passed when the case came to trial.[20] Thus the "plain meaning" construction makes the portion of 2–723(1) which refers to 2–713 superfluous. Consequently, the drafters in writing section 2–723(1) must have thought "learned of the repudiation" had a different meaning than "learned of the breach."

A fifth argument against the "obvious" interpretation of 2–713 in anticipatory repudiation cases is that, if the "learned of the breach" language is construed to mean "learned of the repudiation," 2–713 will be inconsistent with the analogous section on seller's damages, 2–708. Section 2–708(1) measures an aggrieved seller's damages for repudiation as the "difference between the market price *at the time and place for tender* and the unpaid contract price * * *." Thus, under our interpretation of 2–713, a court would always measure repudiation damages from the date of performance under contract except in those few cases under 2–723(1).

A final and most persuasive argument in favor of reading "learned of the breach" to mean "time for performance" in antici-

---

20. Note that the drafters used "repudiation" in 2–723 and "breach" in 2–713. Any argument that the word "breach" in 2–713 does not include "repudiation" falters on two counts. First, "breach" is used in 2–713 to refer to anticipatory repudiation and to failure to perform at the time of tender. Second, although the pre-Code law relying on Lord Chief Justice Cockburn's opinion in Frost v. Knight, L.R. 7 Ex. 111 (1872), continued the obscure distinction between "repudiation" and "breach" by requiring the repudiatee to manifest an election to treat repudiation as a breach in order to pursue an immediate cause of action, even the pre-Code trend was toward abolishing the attenuated distinctions between repudiation and breach. See 11 S. Williston, Contracts §§ 1302–1322 (3d ed.1968); 4 A. Corbin, Contracts § 959 (1951); Restatement (First) of Contracts § 318 (1932). To this end the first Restatement of Contracts stated that any of the various acts described above "constitutes an anticipatory repudiation which is a total breach of contract." It appears that 2–610 continues this idea since after repudiation the buyer is given resort to any remedy for breach. See also Restatement (Second) Contracts § 253(1) (1979).

patory repudiation cases is the history upon which the Code was built. Pre–Code common law, the Restatement (First) of Contracts, and the Uniform Sales Act all permitted the buyer in an anticipatory repudiation case to recover the contract-market differential at the date for performance.[21] Before we permit the drafters to upset such uniform and firmly entrenched doctrine, we can rightfully ask for at least a sentence or two of comment and more explicit statutory language than "learned of the breach."

In summary we stick to our conclusion that "learned of the breach" means "time of performance" in the anticipatory repudiation cases. That interpretation makes 2–708 and 2–713 symmetrical; gives some meaning to the language in 2–723; is consistent with the pre-Code law, and carries forward the desirable policy of not forcing the aggrieved party to choose instantly at his peril. We concede that there are strong arguments to read "learned of the breach" to mean "learned of the repudiation" and to measure the market at the time of the repudiation. The most powerful argument of course is the language itself, and we grant that the drafters could have said it more clearly had they agreed with us and foreseen the problem. While we concede that the many cases have gone against us,[22] we find hope for our arguments from Cargill, Inc. v. Stafford[23] in the Tenth Circuit and the *Roth Steel* case in the Sixth Circuit.[24] We cite the *Cosden Oil* case in the Fifth Circuit as rejecting the majority view,[25] and we are particularly pleased with *Hess* in the Fourth Circuit.[26]

21. Restatement (First) of Contracts § 318 (1932); USA §§ 64(3), 67(3).

22. See n.9 *supra*.

23. 553 F.2d 1222, 21 UCC 707 (10th Cir.1977). The *Cargill* case agrees with us at least in the circumstances where the buyer has a "valid reason * * * for failure or refusal to cover." *Id*. at 1227, 21 UCC at 714. But one might argue, for example, that the language in 2–610, depriving him of damages resulting from his waiting beyond the commercially reasonable time means that the contract-market differential should be measured at the end of such "commercially reasonable time" after the buyer learns of the repudiation. See the Cargill case itself. Such an argument, of course, does more violence to the language of 2–713 than does the one which we have suggested above. Moreover, it lacks the weight of tradition and rests almost exclusively upon an implication drawn from a comment. For discussion of the American courts' rejection of the "election" theory, see 1 N.Y. State Law Revision Comm'n, 1955 Report 673 (1955).

Consider, too, the applicability of notions of mitigation or avoidable consequences. 11 S. Williston, Contracts § 1302 (3d ed.1968); 4 A. Corbin, Contracts § 983 (1951).

24. Roth Steel Products v. Sharon Steel Corp., 705 F.2d 134, 156, 35 UCC 1435, 1465 (6th Cir.1983). See also, Hess Energy, Inc. v. Lightning Oil Co., 338 F.3d 357, 51 UCC2d 1 (4th Cir. 2003).

25. Cosden Oil & Chemical Co. v. Karl O. Helm Aktiengesellschaft, 736 F.2d 1064, 38 UCC 1645 (5th Cir.1984).

26. We do admit that Amended Article 2 language went against our arguments. That result is particularly distasteful to White, who was a member of the Study Committee and, in the later stages, the Drafting Committee.

Post Repudiation Behavior

Even after one has settled upon the proper time for measuring damages, troublesome questions about cover and buyer's other behavior after the repudiation remain. Section 2–610(a) provides that the aggrieved party "may for a commercially reasonable time await performance by the repudiating party." Several difficult questions are:

(1) How long is a commercially reasonable time?

(2) What rights does the aggrieved party lose by waiting too long? Does it lose only the right to cover? The right to have damages measured at the time of performance? Consequential damages which the defendant proves could have been avoided? Or some combination?

(3) Is there any duty to mitigate while the aggrieved party suspends performance?

There has been even less case law development under the Code in the situation where the buyer exercises his option to await performance "for a commercially reasonable time"[27] than where buyer resorts at once to his remedies for breach.[28] Our three questions do not have certain answers.

First, how long can the aggrieved party wait without forfeiting rights?[29] The pre-Code cases are in conflict on the question.[30] One can see from 2–610 that the repudiatee is not to be forced into making a hurried decision. Even though during this period, he urges the repudiator to retract and tells the repudiator he will await performance, the aggrieved party may, under 2–610(b), still "resort to any remedy for breach." But if the aggrieved party does not cancel, or materially change his position, or tell the repudiator that he regards the repudiation to be final, the repudiator may, under 2–611 withdraw its repudiation and reinstate the contract.[31]

The Code consistently disclaims setting specific time periods, and 2–610 is no exception. Comment 1 simply reiterates that the test of a reasonable time is judged by a commercial standard. The

---

27. § 2–610(a).

28. § 2–610(b).

29. Comment 1 implies that an aggrieved party is entitled to await performance for a reasonable time and then resort to his remedies for breach. A similar implication arises from section 2–610(b) which allows an action for breach "even though he has notified the repudiating party that he would await the latter's performance * * *." Presumably if such a notification was given, the buyer will have waited a short time, however

minimal it may have been. Comment 4 further supports this view.

30. See Roehm v. Horst, 178 U.S. 1, 20 S.Ct. 780, 44 L.Ed. 953 (1900); Skeele Coal Co. v. Arnold, 200 Fed. 393 (2nd Cir.1912), cert. denied, 226 U.S. 612, 33 S.Ct. 219, 57 L.Ed. 381 (1912).

31. See, e.g., Wahnschaff Corp. v. O.E. Clark Paper Box Co., 166 Ga.App. 242, 304 S.E.2d 91, 36 UCC 1186 (1983); Gibbs, Nathaniel (Canada) Ltd. v. International Multifoods Corp., 804 F.2d 450, 2 UCC2d 1312 (8th Cir.1986).

only other limitation is that the repudiatee pursue his remedy in good faith.[32] One court directly faced the timing issue in Aura Orchards v. A. Peltz & Sons, Inc.[33] where plaintiff contracted on October 12, 1965 for the sale of apples to be stored until receipt of shipping instructions no later than April 15, 1966. Sometime between mid-November and mid-December, 1965, buyer repudiated. Plaintiff waited until April, 1966 to resell after which it brought suit for the contract-market differential, resale expenses, and storage charges. The court interpreted 2–610 as follows:

> Under section 2–610 of the Uniform Commercial Code, complainant was not required to recognize respondents' anticipatory breach of the contract but could await the time for performance by respondents under the contract.[34]

This language is sweeping; it is reminiscent of Lord Cockburn.[35] Yet sweeping as the opinion may be, the total waiting period between repudiation and time for performance was only four or five months.[36] It is difficult to imagine that it is always commercially reasonable to wait until the scheduled time for performance. First, if that was the drafters' intention, it was unnecessary to define the time period as commercially reasonable at all. Waiting until the time for performance in a long-term installment contract—where the waiting period could be several years—seems unreasonable. Although it is hard to define the outer limits, the date of performance can and sometimes should be regarded as beyond a reasonable time.[37]

Assume that the aggrieved party waits too long. What rights does he lose? The Code is silent. However, the drafters probably intended that an aggrieved party who awaits performance for more than a commercially reasonable time should lose the right to cover.[38] Although 2–610 fails to set definite limits for what will be considered a commercially reasonable time, it does parallel the

---

32. Comment 4 to § 2–610 explicitly refers to § 1–203.

33. 1968 WL 9291, 27 Agri.Dec. 1546, 6 UCC 149 (1968).

34. *Id.* at 1553, 6 UCC at 152.

35. Frost v. Knight, L.R. 7 Ex. 111 (1872).

36. For a similar case, see Carson v. Mulnix, 263 N.W.2d 701, 23 UCC 1162 (Iowa 1978) (buyer of corn held to have waited for commercially reasonable time where, after sending buyer a notice to deliver on August 14th and receiving no answer, he waited until December 28th).

37. See Oloffson v. Coomer, 11 Ill. App.3d 918, 296 N.E.2d 871, 12 UCC

1082 (1973) (buyer of corn waited beyond commercially reasonable time where, after seller unequivocally repudiated contract on June 3rd, he waited until after October contract delivery date before effecting alleged "cover"); First Nat. Bank v. Jefferson Mortgage Co., 576 F.2d 479, 23 UCC 1282 (3rd Cir.1978) (buyer of Government National Mortgage Association securities waited beyond commercially reasonable time where, after seller unequivocally repudiated contract on October 1st, it waited until October 5th before effecting alleged "cover"; 2–713 applied by analogy).

38. §§ 2–610(b); 2–711; 2–712. In addition, see 7–3 *supra.*

Code description of the time allowed for "cover" under 2–712. Section 2–712(1) allows the buyer to cover if he proceeds "without unreasonable delay." Comment 2 to 2–712 reveals the intention not to limit:

> the time necessary for him to look around and decide as to how he may best effect cover. The test here is similar to that generally used in this Article as to reasonable time and seasonable action.

The time periods should be roughly equivalent. This analysis is consistent with the philosophy underlying the "cover" option. It is intended to be a shield—a means by which an aggrieved buyer can obtain substituted goods without suffering any loss. The buyer is given a "reasonable time" to cover instead of any specific time period to allow him to find "how he may best effect cover." It is not a sword to be used to punish the seller for breaching.

In addition, consequential damages that could have been avoided will not be allowed when the buyer has delayed too long. If the aggrieved buyer waits an unreasonable length of time to cover, the buyer should not recover the profits on the resale contracts as consequential damages. Section 2–715(2)(a) allows the buyer to collect only losses "which could not reasonably be prevented by cover or otherwise." In this context section 2–610 is but a specific application of 2–715 and 2–712 to an anticipatory repudiation.

Does delaying too long affect the right to have damages measured as of the time for performance? There are only a few reported cases, but we think that delaying for more than a commercially reasonable time should not affect the damage recovery. First, no real harm is done to the repudiating seller since the contract-market differential is measured at a time generally unrelated to the plaintiff's act. (Contrast the effect of increasing consequential damages by delay as described in the preceding paragraph.) Second, consider the unappealing nature of the alternatives available. One alternative might be to bar the buyer from any recovery under 2–713 at all, but since the function of 2–713 is probably to serve as a type of statutory liquidated damages clause,[39] total elimination of this remedy seems unwarranted. Another option is to go back to the time when the buyer learned of the repudiation.[40] But the drafters probably did not intend that. A third alternative is to measure the market at the end of the "commercially reasonable time."[41] The difficulties of pinpointing this time, however, especial-

---

39. See 7–4 *supra* (§ 2–713).

40. See Oloffson v. Coomer, 11 Ill. App.3d 918, 296 N.E.2d 871, 12 UCC 1082 (1973).

41. See Cargill, Inc. v. Stafford, 553 F.2d 1222, 21 UCC 707 (10th Cir.1977) (if "cover" is readily available and no valid reason exists for not "covering," 2–713 damages are calculated from end

ly in a rapidly fluctuating market, may outweigh the advantages of using this time. One should remember, too, that contract-market damages equal actual damages suffered only by the remotest of chances.[42] Perhaps the major purposes of 2–713 in the repudiation context are *not* accurately to compensate for profits and losses, but are instead (1) to provide a minimum recovery in all cases and (2) induce the repudiatee to return quickly to the market[43] and then recover the contract-cover differential.[44] Hence, to seek an alternative to measuring the market at the time for performance may be a foolish exercise.

Both at common law[45] and under section 2–610(c), the repudiatee may at least suspend his own performance. But what of the reverse, that is, can the aggrieved party continue readying himself for performance, must he take affirmative steps to mitigate his damages, or must he just refrain from taking affirmative steps that might further increase his damages?

Even though some pre-Code courts spoke of treating the repudiation as totally inoperative until the time for performance,[46] they also recognized that a repudiatee should not continue with his own performance if doing so would increase his damages.[47] The decisions fail to distinguish between an affirmative duty to cover or resell and the less demanding duty not to take affirmative action that increases damages. Probably the pre-Code courts wished only to prohibit the affirmative acts that would increase damages.[48] The contract-market differential remedy[49] in the normal breach situation (because the market price is set in time and place) is unaffected by mitigation;[50] mitigation directly affects consequential damages.[51] Two early Code cases deal with mitigation of incidental damages of repudiatees. In Aura Orchards v. A. Peltz & Sons, Inc.,[52] the seller of apples (under a contract repudiated by the buyer four to five months before the last possible time for performance had

---

of commercially reasonable time after buyer learned of seller's repudiation).

42. See 7–4 *supra* (§ 2–713).

43. §§ 2–610(b); 2–713.

44. But if this was the goal, why allow the option of awaiting performance at all? Is it the remnant of history?

45. 4 A. Corbin, Contracts §§ 975, 977–78 (1951).

46. Hochster v. De La Tour, 2 El. & Bl. 678, 118 Eng.Rep. 922 (1853); Frost v. Knight, L.R. 7 Ex. 111 (1872); Bu-Vi-Bar Petroleum Corp. v. Krow, 40 F.2d 488 (10th Cir.1930); Carvage v. Stowell, 115 Vt. 187, 55 A.2d 188 (1947).

47. See Roth & Co. v. Taysen, Townsend & Co., 8 Asp.M.C. 120 (Queen's

Bench 1895); Mays Mills v. McRae, 187 N.C. 707, 122 S.E. 762 (1924).

48. "Cover," of course, is a term new in the Code. What is meant here is whether there is a duty to seek a replacement contract, etc. This is directly relevant when considering the position of a seller (manufacturer) confronted with buyer's repudiation and the question whether to complete manufacture.

49. § 2–713.

50. See 7–4 *supra* (§ 2–713).

51. § 2–715(2) limits consequential damages to those "which could not reasonably be prevented by cover."

52. 1968 WL 9291, 27 Agri.Dec. 1546, 6 UCC 149 (1968).

arrived) was allowed to await performance until the date specified in the contract. In awarding damages, the court included storage charges of $1,570 and did not mention mitigation. A New York Supreme Court, in E–Z Roll Hardware Mfg. Co. v. H & H Products & Finishing Corp.,[53] was not as generous. A manufacturer (seller) in the process of making 10,000 sets of special folding door hardware received buyer's repudiation after 3,010 sets had been shipped. Seller elected not to complete manufacture and instead brought suit (within a reasonable time) under 2–709(3) and for storage costs as incidental damages.[54] The court refused compensation for storage costs:

> The plaintiff's claim for storage is rejected. To qualify for incidental damages as contemplated by UCC § 2–710, there must be compliance with the statutory provisions (UCC §§ 2–709, 2–706) designed to minimize damages. No such action was taken in this case.[55]

We find these cases impossible to reconcile. We favor *Aura Orchards.* (See also sections 11–3 and 11–4 on incidental and consequential damages.)

§ 7–8   Special Issues in Breach of Long Term Contracts

The simplest and most prevalent sales contract is for delivery of a fixed quantity of goods at a fixed price in one or more installments. The term might be one month or a few months; in rare cases it might be longer than a year but almost never longer than five years. Calculating damages upon breach of such a contract is straight-forward.

Compare this typical short term contract with the atypical long-term contract to which Article 2 also applies. Likely the latter is a contract for the sale of coal, natural gas, oil, uranium fuel or the like. Its term might be 20 years, or conceivably for the life of a natural gas reservoir. The market against which any loss would most accurately be measured is far in the future.

The givens in a short-term contract—quantity and price—will be in serious dispute here. With rare exception the contract price in a long-term contract will be variable: it may have a fixed escalator (8% per year) or it may be at a fixed premium over a spot price (spot price + 5%) but more likely the contract price will vary in accordance with an index like the CPI, the GDP or with the prices in other contracts (under a "most favored nation" clause the seller

53. 1968 WL 9138, 4 UCC 1045 (N.Y.Sup.1968).

54. § 2–710.

55. E–Z Roll Hardware Mfg. Co., Inc. v. H & H Products & Finishing Corp., 1968 WL 9138, 4 UCC 1045, 1048 (N.Y.Sup.1968).

may get no less than certain others selling a similar commodity in the same location).

The contract quantity in a remote year will be as uncertain as the contract price; in a gas contract it may be a function of both the seller's ability to deliver from a particular gas reservoir and the buyer's needs. The quantity may have a ceiling, a floor or both.

Finally, any calculation of damages on a long-term contract requires discounting to present value. One dollar of damages to be suffered twenty years hence can be satisfied by a much smaller sum today.

Every one of these complications—market, price, quantity, discount—introduces uncertainty into the damage calculation on breach of a long term contract. Drafters of the UCC anticipated these issues only dimly; the more remote in time are the events to be measured, the more inherently uncertain is the calculation of damages.

In a perfect world it would be easy to determine damages. Assume, for example, that a purchaser of natural gas breaks a contract in year one that calls for delivery of gas for 20 years. To measure the damages precisely one would need to know the contract price for each of the 20 years, the appropriate market price for each of those years, the quantity of gas to be delivered in each and the appropriate discount rate. If one knew each of those factors he could calculate the damages with precision and order the buyer to pay a specific dollar amount in year one that would exactly compensate the seller.

But the courts cannot know the future, and the UCC gives them only wobbly proxies for the data described in the preceding sentence. Section 2–723 instructs a court to measure damages as of the time when "the aggrieved party learned of the repudiation" if the case comes to trial before the time for performance. Ignoring the considerable technical difficulties with section 2–723 itself, understand first how crude the proxy is. Presumably the drafters are telling the court to measure contract-market difference on the date of repudiation and then to project that differential forward for the 19 years of our contract. Necessarily, such a projection ignores changes in the market price, changes in the contract price and it gives no help in estimating the quantity. Because it does not even mention discount, it gives no clue about the rate to be chosen or the basis for the choice.

Section 2–723

The drafters of the 1950's probably did not contemplate 20 or 30 year contracts, but they clearly contemplated contracts where performance would occur after the time for trial. Section 2–723 is designed to deal with at least one issue in such cases. It instructs the court to base damages on the "market price" at the date that the aggrieved party learns of the repudiation.

What of the contract price? Section 2–723 does not in terms say that the "contract price" at the time buyer learns of the repudiation should be the other part of the damage formula. But surely the contract price must also be measured at the time the aggrieved party learned of the repudiation. To choose any other price deprives the contract-market differential of its legitimacy. Damages are measured by comparing the market price with the contract price at a particular time and place on the ground that the aggrieved party will turn to that market for purchase or sale. To select a contract price remote in time from the date of repudiation is to ignore that basic principle upon which the contract market differential formula is based.

In *Columbia Gas*,[1] certain gas producers acknowledged that 2–723 set the time to measure the market price but argued for use of the (escalated) contract price at the time of trial more than two years after the repudiation. Gas had been deregulated after repudiation but before trial; on deregulation some contract prices doubled and even quadrupled. By comparing a 1993 contract price with a 1991 market price these sellers would have greatly magnified their damages. To split the dates at which one measures the market price and contract price makes no sense; it magnifies any distortions that otherwise occur in the contract market differential because it allows one (contract) to escalate while the other (market) is held steady. That is exactly what would have happened in the *Columbia Gas* case if certain sellers had had their way. The market price, (about $1.20 at time of repudiation) would have been held steady whereas the contract price, (between $2.00 and $3.00 at time of repudiation would have jumped as much as four or five dollars). In that same time the spot market had itself doubled.

In our opinion section 2–723 must be read to measure both the contract and the market price at the time the aggrieved party learned of the repudiation. We suspect that section 2–723 does not mention contract price because the drafters in the Forties were dealing with contracts that had fixed prices, not with today's long term commitment contracts with variable contract prices.

Section 2–723 poses a second difficulty. Quite clearly, one is to measure the market (and we think the contract price) as of the date of repudiation for periods after the trial, but what about the contract/market differential for the period after repudiation but before the trial? The plain language of 2–723(1) says that "any

§ 7–8

1. Matter of Columbia Gas Transmission, Inc., No. 91–804 (Bankr.D.Del. 1991).

damages"—apparently including those in that gap period—are to be measured at the time the aggrieved party learned of the repudiation. But why ignore the actual and known market and contract prices that prevailed before trial?

We would twist the language of 2–723 slightly to allow parties to use the actual market and the actual contract prices to measure damages in the gap between repudiation and trial. With crowded dockets and extensive discovery that is commonly practiced in large commercial law suits, trial might not occur for five years or longer after the repudiation. When so, the damages for the intervening time may be a substantial portion of the plaintiff's recovery and we see no reason to ignore these data. Of course, choosing the actual contract and the market prices in the interim period produces the irony that damages later in time (after trial) are measured by an earlier market (time of repudiation) than is used to measure damages suffered earlier (before trial).

Whether one chooses the time of repudiation, the time of trial or some other time to measure damages, there is always the possibility that one or both parties may engage in strategic behavior to minimize damages or to maximize recovery. For example, it would be in the interest of a purchaser of natural gas to repudiate his contract shortly before decontrol if the contract price then prevailing is lower than the likely price would be after decontrol. Conversely, if prices were likely to fall after decontrol, the buyer might wait until after decontrol to repudiate. If damages are measured at the time of trial, one party has an incentive to put off trial—to make additional motions and take additional discovery in the hope that passage of time will reduce or increase his damage claim. We see no way completely to avoid strategic behavior in breaches of long term contracts. We hope that the courts will be alert to this possibility and will respond to appropriate pleas by the other party in circumstances where one is engaging in strategic activity.

What Market?

Should one use a spot market, a long term market, or some variation to find market price when a long term contract is breached? In *Manchester Pipeline*[2] the Court of Appeals for the Tenth Circuit remanded a suit for breach of a long term gas contract with instructions that the proper market was not the spot market but instead the market for long term gas. Initially, one of us was persuaded by that case and requested that it be cited in the Article 2 Study Group Report. On reflection, we think the Tenth Circuit is

2. Manchester Pipeline Corp. v. Peoples Natural Gas Co., 862 F.2d 1439, 7 UCC2d 1000 (10th Cir.1988).

sending the trial court on a goose chase. In the case of 20 year contracts for the sale of commodities such as gas, coal or oil, there is unlikely ever to be a "long term market" that can be used as a reliable damage reference. Any long term market will not be at a fixed price posted daily on a commodities exchange; it will be at a variable price tied to unknowable events. Assuming that such contracts signed at or near the time of repudiation were available to the parties (and ignoring that the price terms in those contracts may not be public knowledge), they would not give any better basis for establishing a market than the spot market. Even when there are forward contracts, those contracts will be for one year or less and they will be no better than the spot price. Although we think the court should look to the most comparable market available, we doubt that there will ever be a long term market that will be suitable for use in establishing the market in the 2–723 formula.

Still, one could do slightly better than spot price in these circumstances. The spot price for certain commodities (such as natural gas) may rise and fall systematically during the year because of seasonal factors. It does not offend the language of 2–723 to use a "smoothed" spot price that is deseasonalized. Nor does 2–723 rule out the averaging of several months of spot prices or the like. We believe that a court should be willing to hear arguments for modified spot prices, and when it seems sensible to do so, adopt those prices. Yet one should not feel too sorry for a seller who is stuck with a low spot price or a buyer who is stuck with a high one. In many cases the breaching party will have chosen the date of repudiation. Moreover section 2–723 also sticks the seller with his contract price at that "spot" and so deprives seller of escalation terms that might outrun increases in the spot price.

Volume

With no exceptions that we know of, long term contracts for the sale of commodities such as oil, gas, coal, nuclear fuel and the like do not have fixed quantities for remote time periods. In the natural gas industry it would be common to limit the seller's obligation to some percentage of the amount "deliverable". The amount that would be deliverable would be a function of the pressure in the field and of other operating circumstances that might influence that amount. These contracts are also likely to have restrictions on the buyer's duty to take. For example, there are the take or pay contracts that we discuss *infra* at 8–18. The contract might have a ceiling and a floor and such a contract might have a variety of "outs" for buyers who experience a decline in their need for a particular commodity. Where there are minimum quantities those amounts can provide a floor on the quantities to be delivered. Every one of these potential fluctuations compounds the plaintiff's proof problem. We think a court should be generous in listening to an aggrieved party's expert testimony about projections.

The Discount Rate

Although Article 2 nowhere discusses discounting future damages to present value, its modern sister, Article 2A, does contemplate discounting.[3] Despite the silence in Article 2, damages for future failure to perform must be discounted. As early as 1916 the Supreme Court recognized the need to discount damages awarded for future benefits to present value. In Chesapeake & Ohio Railway Co. v. Kelly[4] the court noted:

> So far as a verdict is based upon the deprivation of future benefits, it will afford more than compensation if it be made up by aggregating the benefits without taking account of the earning power of the money that is presently to be awarded. It is self evident that a given sum of money in hand is worth more than the like sum of money payable in the future. * * * [A]s a rule, and in all cases where it is reasonable to suppose that interest may safely be earned upon the amount that is awarded, the ascertained future benefits ought to be discounted in the making up of the award. * * * [T]he verdict should be made up on the basis of their present value only.

Today, the court's statement is a platitude. In even the simplest personal injury case it is now common place to discount damages to present value. The hard part is not to understand that damages for future losses should be discounted but to understand what rate.

The following formula is the one commonly given for calculating present value:

$$\frac{X}{(1 + d)^N}$$

Where X equals the amount of money to be discounted, d is the discount rate and N equals the number of years hence when the money is to be available. Thus, if one were to discount $1,000 at 10% for one year, the formula would read as follows:

$$\frac{1,000}{(1 + .1)\,1} = 909$$

3. Article 2A of the Code, recognizing that leases by their nature are long term, uses formulas similar to those in Article 2, but specifically requires courts to discount to present value. See UCC 2A–518, 2A–519, 2A–527, 2A–528, 2A–529.

4. 241 U.S. 485, 489–90, 36 S.Ct. 630, 631–32, 60 L.Ed. 1117 (1916).

If one were to discount $1,000 at 10% for two years, it would be:

$$\frac{1,000}{(1 + .1)\,2} = 826$$

One should note some assumptions about the formula used here and about the formula that would normally be used in the calculation of long term damages on a sales contract. We assume that X is fixed. It is found by use of 2–723 or by some other means. In that respect, this formula is not like the formulae that are sometimes used in calculating personal injury recoveries of lost wages where the numerator of the fraction (X) is itself increased with time to reflect inflation even as the denominator is used to reduce the amount because of its discount to present value. Here we assume that the dollar figure to be paid is known; the formula takes no account of any changes that should be made in that number because of change in markets, contract prices or any other factors.

Of course, present value is inversely related to the magnitude of the discount rate. For example, $1,000 payable two years hence has a present value of $961 if the discount rate is 2% but only $826 discounted at 10%.

Also obvious is the fact that the more remote the payment, the greater the impact of the discount rate. Thus the difference between a 2% and a 10% discount over only two years is $135 on $1,000 ($961 = $826) but that difference grows to $434 for a payment due ten years from the time of calculation. Assume a case in which a defendant owes the plaintiff $1,000,000 for each of seven years. The present value of those damages at a 6% discount is $5,582,000; their present value at a 10% discount rate is almost $1,000,000 less, $4,868,000. As the dollar amounts grow and the prospective time of payment becomes more remote, discount rates have a growing importance, merit careful examination and can engender bitter argument.

Although there is wide agreement about the need to discount, there is not wide agreement about the theory or the principle that should guide one in selecting the proper discount rate.[5] One possibility is to pick a "risk free" rate.[6] This would be a rate such as

---

5. Some states have statutory discount rates, e.g. Pennsylvania. Another possibility which comes to mind is using the aggrieved party's expected after-tax profit margin. This presumably equals what the entity earns by using the funds available to it. However, as a matter of fairness the breaching party perhaps should not be saddled with the success (or lack thereof) with which the aggrieved party runs its business.

6. In this discussion, we rely in part on discussions and explanations of various economists in the claim estimation proceedings in the Columbia Gas Transmission Co. bankruptcy. The suggested discount rates in that proceeding ranged from 6–30%.

that earned on U.S. Treasury Bonds. Using such a small discount rate is likely to overcompensate every plaintiff except those who are quite risk averse (and who would therefore invest any damages at a low and safe rate). Sometimes these rates have been used with personal injury plaintiffs on the assumption that they would be risk averse and quite conservative. Sometimes such rates are also justified for use in the denominator on the ground that other risks are incorporated in the numerator (our X) of the present value fraction.

With a typical business plaintiff, we do not believe that the risk free rate is appropriate. It seems to us that such a rate would almost always overstate a risk neutral plaintiff's damages by failing to discount them adequately.

A second possibility is to use the borrowing rate of the defendant as the discount rate. This treats the damage transaction as though the aggrieved party were borrowing money from the defendant. Of course, in a sense, that is what a long term contract is—a promise of distant performance by each party to the other. Whether or not the defendant would be technically regarded as a debtor of the plaintiff in such a contract, in effect each is both a debtor and a creditor in a long term bilateral deal. Arguably, therefore, the long term contract is analogous to a loan by the plaintiff to the defendant and should take account of the probability that the defendant might not perform. Arguably this is the "bargained for" risk and it can be estimated by looking at the price (interest rate) that a bank would require to loan money to an entity with a similar type of business and a similar credit rating to the breaching party. The defendant's credit rating, of course, should be determined at the time the contract was entered into, not at the time of breach and then it should be carried forward to estimate the cost of borrowing.

The consequence of such a choice would be a large discount (and therefore comparatively smaller damages) if the defendant had a comparatively low credit rating, but a small discount (and therefore comparatively large damages) if the defendant were a blue-chip company. In any event, we are doubtful of the legitimacy here of raising and lowering the present value based upon the creditworthiness of the defendant.

A third way of setting the discount rate is to try to estimate the return that persons in the shoes of the aggrieved party, the plaintiff, would earn on money given to him at the time of judgment. If this amount could be precisely estimated, it would give the plaintiff exactly the amount of money in year two, three and later years that has been calculated as the appropriate amount in the numerator. Thus, if one knew for certain that the plaintiff would earn a 10%

return compounded, then a 10% discount rate would be the appropriate rate.

Of course there are complications here too. One needs to make assumptions about a plaintiff's probable behavior. A good guess is to assume that the plaintiff will invest in his own business. Having assumed an investment in the business, one needs to calculate the rate of return in the business or its cost of capital. Calculating the cost of capital itself requires some art, for one would need to consider the cost of borrowing together with the cost of equity. Those two would have to be weighted in accordance with the debt-equity ratio at the time of breach. Moreover, economists will differ on how to calculate the cost of equity. One way to do it would be to use a capital asset pricing model under which a risk-free rate is added to a risk premium that is calculated on the basis of a financial "beta". The financial beta is a sensitivity index that measures the volatility of a stock relative to the stock market as a whole. Therefore even if one accepts our suggestion that one should look at the plaintiff and not at the defendant and should attempt to estimate the return that that plaintiff will make on the money given him at judgment, finding that return and calculating it even with relative precision will be a hard task.

Use of the particular behavior of a plaintiff or of the plaintiff's return on equity has an ironic consequence similar to the one described above with respect to the credit-worthiness of the defendant. If the plaintiff is a particularly efficient company or is engaged in an industry where the return on capital is relatively high it will be punished for that efficiency because the high rate of return produces a high discount rate and gives correspondingly lower damages.

We wonder whether the lucky and efficient should be so penalized. Perhaps that argues for the proposition that one should not look just at the return on equity of the particular plaintiff or of a particular industry but rather at the return investors in such businesses generally expect.

Chapter 8

SELLER'S REMEDIES

Analysis

---

§ 8–1 Introduction, Section 2–703

Section 2–703 catalogues the seller's principal remedies under the Code.[1] It lists the following options open to an aggrieved seller:

(a) withhold delivery of such goods;

§ 8–1

1. See also § 2–721 which reconciles common law remedies for fraud with the remedies under the Code.

(b) stop delivery by any bailee as hereafter provided (Section 2–705);

(c) proceed under the next section respecting goods still unidentified to the contract;

(d) resell and recover damages as hereafter provided (Section 2–706);

(e) recover damages for non-acceptance (Section 2–708) or in a proper case the price (Section 2–709);

(f) cancel.[2]

In this chapter we will consider four of these options:

(1) recovery of the price under 2–709;

(2) resale and recovery of damages under 2–706;

(3) recovery of damages under 2–708(1) and (2) (particularly by the lost volume seller); and

(4) proceeding under 2–704.

Some of the same words discussed in the foregoing chapter on buyer's remedies (for instance, "tender") appear here; we will not repeat that discussion. Nor will we repeat our discussion of the Code's remedial philosophy embodied in section 1–305 to the effect that "the aggrieved party" should be put "in as good a position as if the other party had fully performed," or how courts can best fulfill that policy when they deal with long-term contracts.[3] We will emphasize the interpretive problems found in the seller's provisions that do not appear in the buyer's remedy provisions.

§ 8–2 Action for the Price, Section 2–709

In limited circumstances 2–709[1] gives an aggrieved seller a

2. L & M Enterprises, Inc. v. BEI Sensors & Systems Co., 45 F.Supp.2d 879, 38 UCC2d 1181 (D. Kan. 1999) (cancellation, unlike termination, does not require reasonable notice); Ergonomic Systems Philippines Inc. v. CCS Intern. Ltd., 7 A.D.3d 412, 777 N.Y.S.2d 446, 53 UCC2d 789 (1st Dept. 2004) (a seller who is first to commit material breach, cannot withhold delivery). The Article 2 Revision Study Group wanted to clarify that the seller may cancel for the buyer's failure to pay on time, Study Committee Report at 202.

3. The Article 2 Revision Study Group recommended that the remedial philosophy of the Code be restated in a redrafted section 2–701. Study Committee Report at 194. For further analysis

of this same remedial policy under the common law, see Restatement (Second) of Contracts § 344 (1979). Of course, this remedial philosophy is contractual, not tort-based. See Dinsmore Instrument Co. v. Bombardier, Inc., 999 F.Supp. 968, 37 UCC2d 605 (E.D. Mich. 1998) aff'd 199 F.3d 318 (6th Cir. 1999).

§ 8–2

1. Section 2–709 reads as follows:

(1) When the buyer fails to pay the price as it becomes due the seller may recover, together with any incidental damages under the next section, the price

(a) of goods accepted or of conforming goods lost or damaged within a

right to recover the contract price.[2] He may recover the price:

(1) when the goods have been "accepted" by the buyer, or

(2) when the risk of loss has passed to the buyer and the goods have been lost or damaged within a reasonable time after risk has passed, or

(3) when goods have been identified to the contract and the seller is unable to resell them.

Only by meeting one of these three conditions can the seller recover the price and any incidental damages as defined in 2–710.[3]

Before considering 2–709 in detail we outline its scope and explain the policies which shaped it. The seller can recover the price of goods "accepted," but, with important exceptions, he cannot recover the price of goods not yet accepted. Why the buyer should have to pay the price for accepted goods is not hard to understand. The buyer has possession of them, they have started to depreciate, and any number of things may have happened to them after the buyer's acceptance. In such circumstances it would be unfair to limit the seller's recovery to the contract-market differential and thus impose on him the burden of redisposing of the goods in order to be made whole.[4] Here, the seller ought to get the price, and he does.[5]

commercially reasonable time after risk of their loss has passed to the buyer; and

(b) of goods identified to the contract if the seller is unable after reasonable effort to resell them at a reasonable price or the circumstances reasonably indicate that such effort will be unavailing.

(2) Where the seller sues for the price he must hold for the buyer any goods which have been identified to the contract and are still in his control except that if resale becomes possible he may resell them at any time prior to the collection of the judgment. The net proceeds of any such resale must be credited to the buyer and payment of the judgment entitles him to any goods not resold.

(3) After the buyer has wrongfully rejected or revoked acceptance of the goods or has failed to make a payment due or has repudiated (Section 2–610), a seller who is held not entitled to the price under this section shall nevertheless be awarded damages for non-acceptance under the preceding section.

2. The action for the price is, of course, the analogue to the buyer's action for specific performance.

3. See HPS, Inc. v. All Wood Turning Corp., 21 N.C.App. 321, 325, 204 S.E.2d 188, 190, 14 UCC 949, 952 (1974) ("An acceptance of the goods entitles the aggrieved seller to recover the contract price of the goods as well as any expenses reasonably incurred as a result of the breach."). A seller has no duty to mitigate by accepting returns. See Siemens Energy & Automation, Inc. v. Coleman Electrical Supply Co., Inc., 46 F.Supp.2d 217, 38 UCC2d 418 (E.D.N.Y. 1999).

4. Conversely, if the seller is entitled to the price under 2–709, it would be unfair for the seller to recover a higher contract-market differential under 2–708(1) because this would put the seller in a better position than if the buyer had performed. The court in Commonwealth Edison Co. v. Decker Coal Co., 653 F.Supp. 841, 3 UCC2d 601 (N.D.Ill. 1987) so held.

5. This policy is also expressed in § 2–607(1) of the Code: "(1) The buyer must pay at the contract rate for any goods accepted."

Siemens Energy & Automation, Inc. v. Coleman Electrical Supply Co., Inc.[6] nicely illustrates the relationship among acceptance, the action for the price and the duty to mitigate. Coleman had accepted goods sold by Siemens but had failed to pay the price. Coleman offered to return the goods, but Siemens declined to take them back. In response to Siemens' action for the price, Coleman argued that Siemens had a duty to mitigate by taking the products back. The court held otherwise; it found that a seller had no duty to take back conforming, accepted goods. We believe that this is a proper interpretation of the Code and that it conforms to the policy behind the rules on acceptance (2–606), revocation (2–608) and price (2–709). At some point in every completed sale of conforming goods, the goods become irrevocably the responsibility of the buyer; by delivering conforming goods that have been accepted, the seller has fully discharged his responsibility. On the other hand, the Code drafters have generally denied the price to a seller of goods not yet accepted because the seller is usually in the business of selling those goods, is likely to have better market contacts, and is therefore in a better position to salvage by redisposing of the goods through normal channels. Although it is easy to think of circumstances in which the buyer has better redisposition opportunities than the seller (for instance, Sears, Roebuck as a buyer), the drafters' general hypothesis seems accurate.

There are two exceptions to the general rule that a seller cannot recover the price of unaccepted goods. First, 2–709(1)(a) permits recovery of the price of "conforming goods lost or damaged within a commercially reasonable time after risk of their loss has passed to the buyer." Here, since the goods are at least damaged, often missing or destroyed, the seller's presumptively superior resale opportunity is diminished and may be nonexistent.

Subsection 2–709(1)(b) permits the seller to recover the price if the seller is "unable after reasonable effort to resell them at a reasonable price or the circumstances reasonably indicate that such effort will be unavailing." By hypothesis, that seller is no better able than the buyer to resell the goods. To illustrate: assume Slalom, the operator of a local ski shop, orders one hundred pairs of hand-made wooden skis from seller, Vadel, at a cost of $10,000. Upon arrival of the skis, Slalom refuses to accept because a new fiberglass ski has been introduced which makes wooden skis obsolete. Assuming that the demand for wooden skis has fallen so far that the market no longer exists, Vadel can recover the contract price under 2–709(1)(b), and buyer will be left with the goods. Since

Although the buyer is liable for the price of all goods it accepts, it may still sue the seller for all damages caused as a consequence of seller's breach of warranty. In re Repco Products Corp., 100 B.R. 184, 8 UCC2d 950 (Bankr.E.D.Pa. 1989).

6. 46 F.Supp.2d 217, 38 UCC2d 418 (E.D.N.Y. 1999).

there is no market for the goods and seller could not resell, the outcome is consistent with the policy behind 2–709. However, if the availability of fiberglass skis merely reduced the demand for wooden skis, our seller could not resort to the price remedy but would have to be content with a damage action and would have to resell the wooden skis to be made whole.

Section 2–709(2) leaves a few matters to conjecture. The section requires a seller suing for the price to "hold for the buyer any goods which have been identified to the contract and are still in his control * * *." That the breaching buyer is entitled to the goods upon payment of a 2–709 judgment, is left to implication. Several courts have ruled that the buyer is entitled to unsold goods upon payment to the seller. Without inquiring as to the mechanics of such an exchange, this result still leaves many questions. What of the breaching buyer who pays part of the judgment for the price? We can imagine cases where the buyer might then be entitled to part of the goods, but this solution breaks down when there is partial payment for indivisible goods. Presumably in the case of indivisible goods partially paid for, such as a Boeing 747, for example, one could grant the buyer a security interest in the goods to the extent of the buyer's payment but subordinate that interest to the seller's right to receive the remainder of the price. If the seller were required to reimburse the buyer to the extent of the buyer's security interest and before the seller is satisfied by a resale, then the seller would never be made whole unless the seller could obtain at least the original contract price on resale.

Section 2–709(2) also allows the seller to resell the goods prior to collection of a judgment. The Code states that the "net proceeds" of that resale must be credited to the buyer.[7] But what happens in the rare case where the seller makes a profit on the resale? Must seller turn the profits over to the buyer? Arguably section 2–709(2) conflicts with section 2–706(6). Section 2–709(2) states that "[w]here the seller sues for the price" and decides to resell the goods, "net proceeds of any resale must be credited to the buyer." Yet 2–706(6) stipulates that "[t]he seller is not accountable to the buyer for any profit made on any resale."

The potential area of conflict between 2–709 and 2–706 is smaller than first appears. In the cases posed the seller plaintiff still possesses the goods. Since the seller possesses the goods the principal ground for recovering the price—for goods "accepted"— will not apply since a buyer who does not have possession will almost never have "accepted." In the lion's share of these cases, even though the plaintiff may state a cause of action in his

---

7. See Rheinberg Kellerei GmbH v. Brooksfield Nat. Bank of Commerce Bank, 901 F.2d 481, 11 UCC2d 1214 (5th Cir.1990) (buyer is entitled to a credit for the net proceeds of any resale of the damaged goods).

complaint for the price, he has no right to the recovery of the price and will never get a judgment for it. Therefore, the area of conflict between 2–709(2) and 2–706(6) is reduced to the cases in which the seller has a claim under 2–709(1)(b) because the seller is unable "to resell at a reasonable price or circumstances reasonably indicate that such effort will be unavailing."

Comparing the conditions for recovery under 2–709(1)(b) with the facts in these cases shows that the area of potential conflict is yet smaller than suggested; by hypothesis, we are here concerned with the case in which the seller finds a market and resells. Only the most bizarre concatenation of events is likely to produce a conflict between 2–709 and 2–706—the plaintiff seller, in possession of the goods, must claim that he cannot resell them and must recover a judgment on that basis only to find that the basis for the judgment was invalid because the seller can and does resell them.

We suggest the following solution. First, cases where a plaintiff-seller alleges a proper cause of action for the price but has not received a judgment at the time of resale of the goods should be treated under 2–706, not under 2–709. In that rarest of cases where the seller gets a judgment for the price and later resells (contrary to the assumptions upon which the original judgment was based), we would read 2–706(6) to give seller the profit (after all, 2–706(6) says the seller is "not accountable for *any* profit made on *any* sale"). We would make 2–706(6) consistent with 2–709(2) by reading "net proceeds" in 2–709(2) to mean only the amount up to the claim that the seller has against the buyer but not including the part of the resale price in excess of the judgment against the original buyer.

§ 8–3 Action for the Price—Goods Accepted

Under the first clause of 2–709(1)(a) when the buyer fails to pay the price as it becomes due, the buyer is liable for the price of "goods accepted." Acceptance is a term of art in the Code, and both luck and lawyer skill are required to pinpoint the time of acceptance. Some lawyers will be tempted to equate "acceptance" with "passage of title" to the goods from seller to buyer. But acceptance is unrelated to passage of title; its occurrence is more dependent upon the buyer's possession or control and opportunity to inspect.

Needless to say, a principal legal issue in nearly every suit under 2–709(1)(a) is whether the buyer has accepted under 2–606.[1]

§ 8–3

1. § 2–606:

(1) Acceptance of goods occurs when the buyer

(a) after a reasonable opportunity to inspect the goods signifies to the seller that the goods are conforming or that he will take or retain them in spite of their non-conformity; or

For more extensive discussion of "acceptance," see Chapter 8. Here we limit our consideration to the relationship among acceptance and rejection and revocation; this relationship is important and complex.[2] Note at the outset that if a buyer has accepted under 2–606, he may not reject under 2–602, though he may still be entitled to revoke his acceptance under 2–608. Distinguish too between possible "substantive" grounds for rejection or revocation (nonconformity as to quality, delay, etc.) and possible "procedural" requirements for a rejection or revocation (timely action and notice).

Under 2–602(1) and 2–608(2), procedurally effective rejections and revocations generally require timely action and proper notice.[3] First, under 2–602 a procedurally effective rejection for which there are substantive grounds forecloses acceptance and eliminates any possible claim by the seller for the price under the first clause of 2–709(1)(a).[4] Likewise under 2–608 a procedurally effective revocation of acceptance for which there are substantive grounds will bar a seller's recovery of the price under the first clause of 2–709(1)(a).[5]

(b) fails to make an effective rejection (subsection (1) of Section 2–602), but such acceptance does not occur until the buyer has had a reasonable opportunity to inspect them; or

(c) does any act inconsistent with the seller's ownership; but if such act is wrongful as against the seller it is an acceptance only if ratified by him.

(2) Acceptance of a part of any commercial unit is acceptance of that entire unit.

For cases where goods accepted, see, e.g., Connor v. Bogrett, 596 P.2d 683, 26 UCC 902 (Wyo.1979); Weil v. Murray, 161 F.Supp.2d 250, 44 UCC2d 482 (S.D.N.Y. 2001) (seller entitled to price where buyer had opportunity to accept and did not reject).

2. The Code drafters have described three distinct types of rejection. First, § 2–606(1)(b) notes that acceptance will occur unless the buyer makes a rejection that is "effective." Second, § 2–703 indexes the seller's various remedies that are to be available when the buyer's rejection is "wrongful." Finally, § 2–711 contemplates the available remedies to the buyer when his rejection is "rightful."

Revocation of acceptance is also described in three different ways. First, § 2–608(2) requires that notice be given to the seller in order that the revocation be "effective." Next, the index of remedies suggested by § 2–703 are triggered

by a "wrongful" revocation of acceptance. Finally, in two places the Code refers to a "justified" revocation. Comment 5 to § 2–709 defines "goods accepted" as used in § 2–709(1)(a) as "goods as to which there has been no justified revocation of acceptance." And § 2–711 refers to justifiably revoking acceptance as a ground to invoke the various buyer's remedies.

3. § 2–602(1):

Rejection of goods must be within a reasonable time after their delivery or tender. It is ineffective unless the buyer seasonably notifies the seller.

§ 2–608(2):

Revocation of acceptance must occur within a reasonable time after the buyer discovers or should have discovered the ground for it and before any substantial change in condition of the goods which is not caused by their own defects. It is not effective until the buyer notifies the seller of it.

4. See Hayes v. Hettinga, 228 N.W.2d 181, 16 UCC 983 (Iowa 1975) (trial court properly dismissed the seller's 2–709 price action where seller failed to show that the buyer accepted the goods).

5. Comment 5 to § 2–709 states: " 'Goods accepted' by the buyer under subsection (1)(a) include only goods as to which there has been no justified revocation of acceptance * * *."

In both cases there is no binding acceptance and *a fortiori* there can be no recovery for the price of "goods accepted."

But what of a rejection or revocation that is not "procedurally" effective because it is not timely, or the like? Here 2–606(1)(b) provides that acceptance occurs and that the buyer is liable for the price under 2–709(1)(a) (subject to a potential setoff for damages because of the nonconformity).[6] Thus a procedurally effective rejection or revocation for which there are substantive grounds bars acceptance; a rejection or revocation which is not effective—has a procedural flaw—does not bar acceptance, even though the goods are actually nonconforming and the rejection or revocation therefore substantively rightful.

The most troubling case is the one in which the buyer has no substantive basis on which to reject or revoke but nevertheless effectively rejects or revokes, that is, he acts in time and properly communicates the rejection or revocation to the seller. Commentators[7] agree that the Code drafters contemplated effective rejections which might be substantively wrongful and intended that all such rejections forestall acceptance without regard to their substantive wrongfulness. Writing for the New York Law Revision Commission, Professor Honnold stated: "buyer may have the power to make an 'effective' rejection even though his action is in breach of contract and subjects buyer to liability for damages."[8] Professor Honnold's judgment is consistent with the implication of 2–606(1)(b) which provides that failure to make an "effective rejection" results in acceptance. The implication of that subsection is that *any* effective rejection bars acceptance. We conclude, therefore, that a procedurally proper (effective) rejection forestalls acceptance whether or not the rejection is rightful. This conclusion is consistent with the policy behind 2–709, which normally imposes the burden of redisposing of the goods upon the seller.[9]

In Brandeis Machinery & Supply Co., LLC v. Capitol Crane Rental, Inc.,[10] the court explicitly recognized the distinction be-

---

6. See Euroworld of California, Inc. v. Blakey, 613 F.Supp. 129, 41 UCC 403 (S.D.Fla.1985), aff'd, 794 F.2d 686 (11th Cir.1986) (where buyer did not inspect goods for 4 months and did not send notice of revocation for 9 months, both rejection and revocation were ineffective for not being within reasonable time; held: seller may maintain action for the price).

7. See Peters, Remedies for Breach of Contracts Relating to the Sale of Goods Under the Uniform Commercial Code: A Roadmap for Article 2, 73 Yale L.J. 199, 241 (1963); Nordstrom, Handbook of the Law of Sales 544 (1970). But

see Cochran v. Horner, 121 Ga.App. 297, 173 S.E.2d 448, 7 UCC 707 (1970).

8. 1 N.Y. State Law Revision Comm'n, 1955 Report 520 (1955).

9. See Zhong Ya Chemical (USA) Ltd. v. Industrial Chemical Trading, Inc., 2001 WL 69438, 43 UCC2d 879 (S.D.N.Y. 2001), amended in part, 2001 WL 1491378 (S.D.N.Y. 2001) (when buyer's rejection is procedurally correct but substantively baseless, no acceptance and seller not entitled to price).

10. 765 N.E.2d 173, 47 UCC2d 200 (Ind. App. 2002). See also, Purina Mills,

tween an effective but wrongful rejection and an ineffective rejection. Capitol first leased and then agreed to buy a crane. Shortly after the purchase agreement was signed, Capitol's business was sold and Capitol returned the crane to Brandeis. Capitol appears never to have claimed that the crane was defective. Brandeis sued for the price and Capitol maintained that its rejection, even if wrongful, was effective to forestall acceptance. The court agreed and allowed only difference money damages of $19,273.46 not the price of $291,773.46.

Whether the buyer is entitled to make "effective" but wrongful *revocations*, and if so whether they free the buyer from "acceptance" and therefore from liability for the price under 2–709(1)(a) is unclear. On the one hand, section 2–607(2) states that a buyer cannot revoke an acceptance made with knowledge of a nonconformity unless the buyer accepted on the reasonable assumption that the nonconformity would be seasonably cured. It would seem to follow *a fortiori* from this and from the grounds for revocation of acceptance stated in 2–608 that a buyer cannot revoke acceptance of conforming goods.[11] At least one reading of Comment 5 to 2–709 supports the interpretation that a procedurally flawless but substantively wrongful revocation does not undo acceptance.[12] That comment seems to mean that goods accepted remain accepted unless the buyer "justifiably" revokes. On the other hand, 2–709(3) seems to contemplate at least some circumstances in which a buyer who has "wrongfully * * * revoked" will *not* be liable for the price. If only justified revocations free the buyer from liability under 2–709(1)(a), then there would be no need to mention wrongful revocations in 2–709(3), for one who wrongfully revoked would always be liable for the price as one who "accepted" the goods. Moreover, 2–703 refers to wrongful revocation and rejection in tandem without apparent distinction.

Finally, one may argue that there is no reason to distinguish here between rejection and revocation and that if the Code lets a naughty buyer escape liability for the price when the buyer effectively but wrongfully rejects, then it must do the same for the

---

L.L.C. v. Less, 295 F.Supp.2d 1017, 52 UCC2d 310 (N.D. Iowa 2003).

11. § 2–608(1) reads:

The buyer may revoke his acceptance of a lot or commercial unit whose nonconformity substantially impairs its value to him if he has accepted it

    (a) on the reasonable assumption that its non-conformity would be cured and it has not been seasonably cured; or

    (b) without discovery of such nonconformity if his acceptance was rea-

sonably induced either by the difficulty of discovery before acceptance or by the seller's assurances.

12. § 2–709, Comment 5:

"Goods accepted" by the buyer under subsection (1)(a) include only goods as to which there has been no justified revocation of acceptance, for such a revocation means that there has been a default by the seller which bars his rights under this section.

buyer who revokes "effectively" but wrongfully. This parallel construction argument is unpersuasive, however. In almost all sales transactions there is a continuum of control running from the seller's initial ownership and absolute control of the goods to the buyer's ownership, absolute control, and use of the goods at the end. All agree that we must draw the line somewhere and say to the buyer, "you are liable for the price, no matter what you do hereafter." Logic does not dictate that this line be drawn after the time for revocation. Indeed, we believe that revocation of acceptance is generally a more drastic remedy than rejection and therefore should not be as readily available. It is appropriate to say to a buyer who attempts to revoke acceptance: "All right, you may revoke acceptance, but beware, for if your revocation is found to be substantively wrongful, you will be liable for the full price, and you'd better think twice before you allow those accepted goods to rot in a warehouse or on a railroad siding." Moreover, to leave the burden on the buyer with respect to goods which might have depreciated, which he might have used to his benefit, and which he might actually have misused or otherwise damaged, is consistent with the policy of 2–709 and with the idea that the buyer should normally have to pay the price of accepted goods. Despite the language of 2–709(3) and notwithstanding the parallel references to rejection and revocation in 2–703, we would argue that any buyer who accepts goods is liable for the price unless he makes a procedurally effective *and* substantively *rightful* revocation of acceptance; we believe that a procedurally effective but substantively wrongful revocation should not free the buyer from price liability under 2–709(1)(a).

The mitigation principle should not apply to actions for the price under 2–709 and therefore absent a procedurally effective rejection or a justifiable revocation, the seller has no duty to retrieve the goods and attempt to sell them to limit its damages. This result holds true even when the buyer has requested the seller to pick up the goods because the buyer cannot pay for them.[13] As noted in Section 8–2 *supra*, the policies of 2–709 are advanced by placing the burden of reselling the goods on the buyer once the buyer has accepted control over them.

13. See Industrial Molded Plastic Products, Inc. v. J. Gross & Son, Inc., 263 Pa.Super. 515, 398 A.2d 695, 26 UCC 1154 (1979); Lupofresh, Inc. v. Pabst Brewing Co., Inc., 505 A.2d 37, 42 UCC 1651 (Del.Super.1985), aff'd, 510 A.2d 487 (Del.Supr.1986); F & P Builders v. Lowe's of Texas, Inc., 786 S.W.2d 502, 11 UCC2d 549 (Tex.App.1990). See also Siemens Energy & Automation, Inc. v. Coleman Electrical Supply Co., Inc., 46 F.Supp.2d 217, 38 UCC2d 418 (E.D.N.Y. 1999) (seller tendered conforming goods accepted by buyer and had no duty to mitigate by accepting goods in return because buyer had experienced financial difficulties). However, see Zhong Ya Chemical (USA) Ltd. v. Industrial Chemical Trading, Inc., 2001 WL 69438, 43 UCC2d 879 (S.D.N.Y. 2001) (even a seller that recovers the price under 2–709 has a duty to mitigate damages by reselling returned goods).

On a related issue, a buyer's return of accepted goods (in circumstances which do not constitute an effective rejection or revocation) does not deprive seller of his 2–709 right to the price. In one case[14] a seller repossessed the goods from the buyer and in another[15] the seller took the goods back after the buyer used them for a period of time. In both cases the plaintiff seller's right to the price was upheld by the court. These cases seem consistent with the general theory that the buyer should be responsible for the price once he has accepted the goods. Indeed, one of them was the work of an old Code drafter himself, Judge Braucher.

§ 8–4   Action for the Price—Lost or Damaged Goods

Under the second clause of 2–709(1)(a) the seller can recover the price of "conforming goods lost or damaged within a commercially reasonable time after risk of their loss has passed to the buyer." To apply this clause of 2–709(1)(a), a court must resort to Article 2's complex risk of loss provisions (which we discuss in Chapter 6). Except for possible difficulty in defining "commercially reasonable," the second clause of 2–709(1)(a) offers few problems worthy of lawyer concern. A routine case under the second clause of 2–709(1)(a) is Ninth Street East, Ltd. v. Harrison.[1] A Los Angeles seller shipped goods F.O.B. Los Angeles to a Connecticut buyer. After the carrier attempted to deliver the goods to the buyer's place of business (an attempt frustrated by a dispute between the buyer's wife and the carrier's agent) the goods disappeared. The court found that risk of loss had passed to the buyer in Los Angeles under the F.O.B. term and properly held the buyer liable for the price under the second clause of 2–709(1)(a).

In a more recent but equally unremarkable case,[2] a New York Court held for a seller of plants who had shipped them under a contract that specified "No risk to supplier" and "NOTICE: ALL SHIPMENTS TRAVEL AT RISK AND COST OF PURCHASER." The court awarded the seller the full price by relying on Section 2–509(4) (on right of parties to govern risk by agreement) and without specific reference to 2–709, which must have been the basis of the suit.

14. Weil v. Murray, 161 F.Supp.2d 250, 44 UCC2d 482 (S.D.N.Y. 2001) (citing White and Summers, the court held that once buyer accepts goods, seller is entitled to price, even if buyer subsequently returns goods).

15. Akron Brick and Block Co. v. Moniz Engineering Co., Inc., 365 Mass. 92, 310 N.E.2d 128, 14 UCC 563 (1974).

§ 8–4

1. 5 Conn.Cir.Ct. 597, 259 A.2d 772, 7 UCC 171 (1968).

2. Forest Nursery Co. v. I.W.S., Inc., 141 Misc.2d 661, 534 N.Y.S.2d 86, 8 UCC2d 923 (1988).

§ 8–5 Action for the Price—Goods Not Reasonably Resalable

Section 2–709(1)(b) also permits the seller to recover the price of goods "identified to the contract" which seller cannot reasonably unload. Since here the seller can recover the price only as to goods "identified to the contract," he must resort to 2–501 for definition of "identified."[1] In general these are goods already shipped to the buyer, labeled as buyer's, or "otherwise designated by the seller as goods to which the contract refers."[2]

Next, and more difficult, the seller must show that the goods are not resalable at "a reasonable price" after "reasonable effort" or circumstances that "reasonably indicate" that an effort to resell will be unavailing. Elsewhere we have despaired of interpreting sentences which contain only one "reasonable." Who can interpret a sentence with three "reasonables"?

Courts have not agreed on the proof of unsalability necessary to activate section 2–709(1)(b). In Hammond v. Streeter[3] the court merely noted that the goods had "some value" and therefore "efforts to resell * * * might not have been unavailing." In contrast, in Great Western Sugar Co. v. Pennant Products, Inc.,[4] the

---

§ 8–5

1. § 2–501:

(1) The buyer obtains a special property and an insurable interest in goods by identification of existing goods as goods to which the contract refers even though the goods so identified are nonconforming and he has an option to return or reject them. Such identification can be made at any time and in any manner explicitly agreed to by the parties. In the absence of explicit agreement identification occurs

(a) when the contract is made if it is for the sale of goods already existing and identified;

(b) if the contract is for the sale of future goods other than those described in paragraph (c), when goods are shipped, marked or otherwise designated by the seller as goods to which the contract refers;

(c) when the crops are planted or otherwise become growing crops or the young are conceived if the contract is for the sale of unborn young to be born within twelve months after contracting or for the sale of crops to be harvested within twelve months or the next normal harvest season after contracting, whichever is longer.

(2) The seller retains an insurable interest in goods so long as title to or any security interest in the goods remains in him and where the identification is by the seller alone he may until default or insolvency or notification to the buyer that the identification is final substitute other goods for those identified.

(3) Nothing in this section impairs any insurable interest recognized under any other statute or rule of law.

2. See Draper v. Minneapolis–Moline, Inc., 100 Ill.App.2d 324, 241 N.E.2d 342, 5 UCC 972 (1968) (dealer identified tractor to contract by showing it to buyer in store, and buyer recalled last three digits of tractor's serial number which coincided with number on purchase agreement); City of Louisville v. Rockwell Mfg. Co., 482 F.2d 159, 12 UCC 840 (6th Cir.1973) (seller identified 1,000 parking meters to the contract by manufacturing them, packaging them, and holding them pending delivery instructions).

3. 225 Neb. 491, 406 N.W.2d 633, 4 UCC2d 758 (1987).

4. 748 P.2d 1359, 4 UCC2d 1080 (1987), cert. denied, 12 Brief Times Rep. 178 (Colo.1988).

seller made no effort to resell the sugar, yet recovered under 2–709(1)(b) on a showing that the market price declined drastically and although the seller sold some sugar, it always had enough available to fill the buyer's contract.

As additional guideposts for sellers who invoke 2–709(1)(b) we offer three early Code cases. In two, the courts found that the seller was unable to resell at a reasonable price, but in the third the court rejected the argument. The first case, Walter Balfour & Co. v. Lizza & Sons, Inc.,[5] is straightforward enough. There the plaintiff sued for $16,000, the price of several specially manufactured, "tailor-made," rolling steel doors. The plaintiff proved that the doors were not stocked but were "tailor-made" for each job as the contract for it was awarded. The doors in question would have had a scrap value of $630, could not have been adapted to any other job, and would have cost $75 to $100 to deliver to a scrap dealer. Here the court held that buyer was liable for the price. In similar circumstances the Massachusetts Court of Appeals held a buyer liable for the price of a mink jacket of "petite size" that had been further altered to make it even smaller in the neck and shoulders. In Ludwig, Inc. v. Tobey,[6] the court found that the plaintiff had been "ready and willing to sell the coat at any time it received a good offer" but that efforts to resell were unavailing. Accordingly the court held that the seller could recover the price.

In In re Bacon's Estate,[7] a Pennsylvania court rejected the seller's plea for the price on a contract for a dining room suite, a bedroom suite, two sofas, a cocktail table, and assorted chairs. Although it acknowledged that the merchandise might be quite difficult to sell at the prices the deceased buyer had agreed to pay (apparently because of the buyer's bizarre choice of fabric colors), the court found that the plaintiff had not proved his inability to sell the goods at "reasonably marked down prices."

The first of the foregoing cases is soundly decided and largely unremarkable; if the steel doors would fit on defendant's building and no other, the goods are not reasonably resalable. But why the furniture was resalable at a reasonable price yet the mink coat not, is hard to explain. Neither case offers guidelines about the kind of search for purchasers the seller must undertake, nor about what a "reasonable price" might be in terms of the original price, the resale market, the seller's cost, or any other objective basis. Indeed, we suspect that the real difference between the cases is the Pennsylvania court's unwillingness to allow a seller to reap the benefits of a decedent's profligacy out of the heirs' legacies.

5. 1969 WL 11070, 6 UCC 649 (N.Y.Sup.1969).

6. 28 Mass.App.Dec. 6, 13, 5 UCC 832, 836 (1964).

7. 45 Pa. D. & C.2d 733 (Orphan's Ct.1968).

Later decisions have confirmed our suspicions that these two cases were but the beginning of apparently random interpretations of 2–709(1)(b). In one case, W.I. Snyder Corp. v. Caracciolo,[8] the court accepted seller's claim that efforts to resell surplus equipment would have been unavailing where the seller proved only that available auctioneers demanded a guaranteed fee, but would not guarantee a return. We disagree with this result and believe that the court should require the seller to produce at least some evidence of market conditions. A court should determine what inquiries the seller made, at what price he attempted to sell the goods, and how long he placed them on what markets.[9]

Adding to the uncertainty is the likelihood that issues regarding whether the seller made reasonable efforts to resell or whether any efforts would be fruitless will be left largely to the jury.[10]

In some cases the evidence is straightforward and persuasive. For example, in Indeck Energy Services, Inc., et al. v. NRG Energy, Inc., et al.,[11] defendant Waukesha had manufactured several transformers and Indeck had agreed to purchase them. Later Indeck attempted to assign its purchase contract to NRG, a utility that was having financial problems. The transformers were to be used at a power project in Bourbonnais, Illinois where they were to be matched up with certain generators that had unusual voltage requirements. The generators had been built in Germany according to "European standards" for voltage and the transformers had been designed to accommodate that particular and unusual voltage. Waukesha completed the transformers and attempted to deliver them to NRG or to Indeck. Indeck directed that it take the generators to its plant in Wisconsin and hold them. Ultimately, Waukesha counterclaimed in the lawsuit against Indeck for the price. The court found Indeck liable for the price of approximately $3 million holding first that it had accepted the goods and by finding alternatively that the goods had been "identified to the

---

8. 373 Pa.Super. 486, 541 A.2d 775, 7 UCC2d 993 (1988).

9. For cases where the seller proved the contract goods could not be reasonably resold, see, e.g. Emanuel Law Outlines, Inc. v. Multi–State Legal Studies, Inc., 899 F.Supp. 1081, 28 UCC2d 842 (S.D.N.Y. 1995) (when seller prepared goods to buyer's specifications which had "no value" to other buyers, seller was entitled to price under 2–709(1)(b)).

For cases where seller fails to show inability to resell, see, e.g., In re Narragansett Clothing Co., 138 B.R. 354, 17 UCC2d 786 (Bankr.D.R.I.1992) (action for the price not allowed where seller made no commercially reasonable efforts to resell clothing fixtures and was unable to prove that such an attempt would be unavailing); Data Documents, Inc. v. Pottawattamie County, 604 N.W.2d 611, 40 UCC2d 713 (Iowa 2000) (attempt at resale not reasonable where only one potential purchaser was contacted and that purchaser would have purchased the goods for a lower price than offered by the seller, which seller refused; also, there was market for the goods).

10. See W.I. Snyder Corp. v. Caracciolo, 373 Pa.Super. 486, 541 A.2d 775, 7 UCC2d 993 (1988).

11. 2004 WL 2095554, 54 UCC2d 990 (N.D. Ill. 2004).

contract and any efforts to resell the transformers are unavailing given their highly specialized and unique configuration." There was ample evidence in the record that the transformers would not work with conventional American generators and that there were no available foreign generators other than those at Bourbonnais where apparently the project was stalled. If the generators had been specifically constructed according to specifications provided by Indeck, they had clearly been identified to the contract. Extensive testimony on available alternative uses showed persuasively they could not be reasonably resold.

As a final supplement to our discussion of 2–709(1)(b), consider the case of a seller who receives an anticipatory repudiation from its buyer before the seller has completed the manufacture of the contract goods. If the seller chooses not to complete the manufacture, the goods could never be "identified to the contract" under 2–709(1)(b) nor be "accepted" or conforming under 2–709(1)(a),[12] accordingly the seller could have no action for the price. If instead the seller chooses to complete the manufacture after the repudiation, it is conceivable though unlikely that the seller may recover the price. As we will see, 2–704 authorizes the seller to complete manufacture "in the exercise of reasonable commercial judgment for the purposes of avoiding loss." It will require very careful navigation to achieve a finding that the completion was commercially reasonable under 2–704(2) but that the goods, when completed, were not reasonably resalable under 2–709(1)(b). Of course the two findings are not logically inconsistent, for the one is made at the time of the decision to complete and the other only after the goods have been completed. Conceivably the picture could be rosy at the time of the repudiation but disastrous at the time of the actual completion. It will take a persuasive lawyer to convince a court that it should not measure the 2–704 decision by hindsight when the plaintiff, having completed, finds himself unable to resell.[13]

Some sellers have completed manufacture under 2–704 and then prevailed on an action for the price under 2–709(1)(b). In Foxco Industries, Ltd. v. Fabric World, Inc.,[14] Fabric World placed an order with Foxco for 12,000 yards of fabric. Foxco's operation was limited to manufacturing fabric to fill orders placed by customers for the spring and fall buying seasons. When the price of yarn dropped sharply, Fabric World cancelled its order. Foxco finished

12. See Detroit Power Screwdriver Co. v. Ladney, 25 Mich.App. 478, 181 N.W.2d 828, 8 UCC 504 (1970) (§ 2–709(1) not applicable where the machine under contract was never completed but instead was stored in a partially finished state).

13. For a general discussion of § 2–704, see 8–15 *infra*.

14. 595 F.2d 976, 26 UCC 694 (5th Cir.1979).

manufacturing the already "substantially completed" order and managed to sell 7,000 yards of it during the next spring buying season. By that time, however, the fair market value had dropped to half of the original contract price. Foxco's failure to notify Fabric World of the resale precluded it from recovering damages under 2–706. The Fifth Circuit upheld a jury determination which found Foxco's completion commercially reasonable under 2–704 and awarded Foxco damages under 2–709(1)(b) less the value of the resale. The court concluded that, under 2–709(1)(b), Foxco "was required only to use reasonable efforts to resell its goods at a *reasonable* price" and that the jury was entitled to give Foxco "the full benefit of its original bargain."[15] Since Foxco specially manufactured each order, it was difficult to resell fabric for one customer to other buyers. Further, there was little market for spring fabric after the spring buying season had ended. Thus Foxco was unable to resell until prices had dropped precipitously.

§ 8–6   Seller's Resale, Section 2–706

The analogue to the buyer's right to cover under 2–712 is the seller's right to resell under 2–706.[1] This section authorizes an

---

15. *Id.*, at 984, 26 UCC at 701.

§ 8–6

1. § 2–706:

(1) Under the conditions stated in Section 2–703 on seller's remedies, the seller may resell the goods concerned or the undelivered balance thereof. Where the resale is made in good faith and in a commercially reasonable manner the seller may recover the difference between the resale price and the contract price together with any incidental damages allowed under the provisions of this Article (Section 2–710), but less expenses saved in consequence of the buyer's breach.

(2) Except as otherwise provided in subsection (3) or unless otherwise agreed resale may be at public or private sale including sale by way of one or more contracts to sell or of identification to an existing contract of the seller. Sale may be as a unit or in parcels and at any time and place and on any terms but every aspect of the sale including the method, manner, time, place and terms must be commercially reasonable. The resale must be reasonably identified as referring to the broken contract, but it is not necessary that the goods be in existence or that any or all of them have been identified to the contract before the breach.

(3) Where the resale is at private sale the seller must give the buyer reasonable notification of his intention to resell.

(4) Where the resale is at public sale

(a) only identified goods can be sold except where there is a recognized market for a public sale of futures in goods of the kind; and

(b) it must be made at a usual place or market for public sale if one is reasonably available and except in the case of goods which are perishable or threaten to decline in value speedily the seller must give the buyer reasonable notice of the time and place of the resale; and

(c) if the goods are not to be within the view of those attending the sale the notification of sale must state the place where the goods are located and provided for their reasonable inspection by prospective bidders; and

(d) the seller may buy.

(5) A purchaser who buys in good faith at a resale takes the goods free of any rights of the original buyer even though the seller fails to comply with

aggrieved seller to resell the contract goods and to measure his damages by the difference between the contract price and the resale price.[2] Like the "cover" provision for the buyer, 2–706 is an important Code innovation. If the buyer is solvent, 2–706 will usually put the seller in the same position as performance would have. Resale is not mandatory.[3] When the seller does resell, he may resell privately or at a public sale. The Code nowhere defines public sale. It is clear enough that an auction sale open to the public is a public sale, but what of a nonauction to which the public may come or an auction sale (such as a dealer's used car auction) from which some of the public is excluded? Comment 4 to 2–706 states that "[b]y 'public' sale is meant a sale by auction," but the courts have yet to work out the precise dividing line between public and private resales. We would classify most sales open only to a limited segment of the public, such as dealer auctions, as public sales on the theory that competitive forces are usually at work at such sales similar to those usually at work at public sales to which all of the public is invited.

For private resales, section 2–706 sets out three comparatively simple steps for the seller to follow:

(1) identify the resale contract to the broken contract;

(2) give the buyer reasonable notification of the seller's intention to resell; and

(3) resell in good faith and in a commercially reasonable manner.

If the seller resells publicly, he must:

(1) identify the resale contract to the broken contract;

(2) resell only identified goods, except where there is a recognized market for goods of the kind in question;

(3) conduct the resale at the usual place for a public sale, if there is such a place;

---

one or more of the requirements of this section.

(6) The seller is not accountable to the buyer for any profit made on any resale. A person in the position of a seller (Section 2–707) or a buyer who has rightfully rejected or justifiably revoked acceptance must account for any excess over the amount of his security interest, as hereinafter defined (subsection (3) of Section 2–711).

2. Cook Composites, Inc. v. Westlake Styrene Corp., 15 S.W.3d 124, 40 UCC2d 703 (Tex. App.–Houston 14th Dist.

2000) (court held that satisfying 2–706's three requirements requires "strict," not merely substantial compliance).

3. See, e.g., Berg v. Hogan, 322 N.W.2d 448, 34 UCC 505 (N.D.1982). Although the text of § 2–703 and Comment 1 thereto indicate that resale is not mandatory, our discussion of 2–708(2) indicates that where a seller has completed goods on hand and brings an action under 2–708(2), the court should treat him as though he had resold. See 8–11 *infra*.

(4) give the buyer reasonable notice of the time and place of resale, except in the case of perishable goods or of goods which threaten to decline in value rapidly;

(5) keep the goods on display at the time of resale, or provide for their reasonable inspection by potential bidders at the place where the goods are located; and

(6) resell in good faith and in a commercially reasonable manner.

Failure to comply deprives the seller of the measure of damages stated in 2–706 and relegates the seller to the measure provided in 2–708.[4] Even if the seller does not resell properly, any purchaser at the resale who buys in good faith still takes the goods free of any claims of the original buyer.[5]

The application of 2–706 in a simple contract case is not difficult. Assume, for example, that a New York seller sells 1,000 embroidered pot holders at a contract price of $1,000, F.O.B. buyer's plant, to a New York buyer. The buyer breaches and the seller resells to another New York party for $900, F.O.B. buyer's plant. The costs of shipping ($60) are the same under both contracts. If seller incurs no additional costs in reselling the pot holders, the seller will recover $100 (the difference between the resale price and the contract price). If the seller incurs $50 additional resale costs, the recovery is $150 (the difference between the resale price and the contract price together with incidental damages under 2–710).[6] However if the resale contract is F.O.B. seller's plant and the seller thus saves the $60 shipping costs which it would have incurred under the original contract, then the seller's recovery will be only $90, that is, the difference between the resale price and the contract price, plus incidental damages, but less expenses saved as a consequence of buyer's breach.

In Section 8–7 we deal with the most difficult question under 2–706, the effect of resale upon the seller's 2–708 claim for damages. Does resale foreclose a later claim for damage under 2–708 or may the seller who has resold nevertheless elect a more generous damage recovery under 2–708?

In a case of multiple post breach sales of goods like those contracted for, which is the 2–706 resale? The seller's incentive is to identify the resale contract with the lowest price to the broken

---

4. See B & R Textile Corp. v. Paul Rothman Indus., Ltd., 1979 WL 30097, 27 UCC 996 (N.Y.Sup.1979); Cook Composites, Inc. v. Westlake Styrene Corp., 15 S.W.3d 124, 40 UCC2d 703 (Tex. App.–Houston 14th Dist. 2000) (seller that fails to comply with 2–706 can still collect damages under 2–708).

5. See § 2–706(5).

6. See, e.g., Cohn v. Fisher, 118 N.J.Super. 286, 287 A.2d 222, 10 UCC 372 (1972).

contract. In Apex Oil Co. v. Belcher Co. of New York, Inc.,[7] the buyer breached a contract to buy oil. The oil had been identified to the contract and seller resold this oil the next day at a higher price than oil it later purported to identify to the contract and sell. The seller sought to use the later figure to measure its damages under 2–706. The court refused to award the higher damage amount, holding that while a seller could "de-identify" fungible goods and identify other goods to the original contract under 2–501 and 2–103(2), the 2–706 resale price of such newly identified substitute goods must "accurately reflect the market value" of the contract goods. Here the delay prevented the resale from accurately reflecting the value of the contract goods. We believe the court reached the correct result. Whenever the seller de-identifies goods once identified to a contract in order to substitute goods sold at a lower price, a court may rightfully question whether the resale was "made in good faith" as 2–706(1) requires. Courts do not permit an unscrupulous seller to manipulate resales in order to apply the lowest possible resale to the broken contract, but some courts may want to be more lenient toward the seller's identification of the resale contract in the absence of obvious switching tactics.

Section 2–706 basically requires that resale be made in a commercially reasonable fashion and that the seller act in good faith.[8] In Larsen Leasing, Inc. v. Thiele, Inc.,[9] the court found that the sale of trucks to a sister company of the seller was not in good faith and not done in a commercially reasonable manner where there was no evidence about the efforts that the seller made to achieve a different sale or one for a higher price. What we have said in Chapter 7 on the comparable 2–712 requirements applies here as well.

In certain circumstances the courts must adjust the resale contract price to put it on a footing comparable to the original contract.[10] If, for example, the original contract called for payment

---

7. 855 F.2d 997, 6 UCC2d 1025 (2d Cir. 1988).

8. Sales to related entities are suspect, but not necessarily unreasonable. See Afram Export Corp. v. Metallurgiki Halyps, S.A., 772 F.2d 1358, 41 UCC 1709 (7th Cir.1985) (resale of scrap iron to an affiliated company not in good faith; resale by affiliated company set price under 2–706); Allied Grape Growers v. Bronco Wine Co., 203 Cal.App.3d 432, 249 Cal.Rptr. 872, 6 UCC2d 1059 (1988) (the court upheld a 2–706 sale to a subsidiary. However, the sale apparently had the effect of reducing seller's damages).

9. 749 F.Supp. 821, 13 UCC2d 407 (W.D.Mich.1990).

10. See, e.g., Islamic Republic of Iran v. Boeing Co., 771 F.2d 1279, 41 UCC 1178 (9th Cir.1985), cert. dismissed, 479 U.S. 957, 107 S.Ct. 450, 93 L.Ed.2d 397 (1986). Iran repudiated a contract for a Boeing 747. The contract price was $54.7 million less a credit memorandum for $2.8 million. Upon Iran's breach, Boeing resold the 747 to a third party for $55.7 million less a credit memorandum for $12.7 million. "Credit memorandum" was a credit term which the court determined to be normal business practice in most Boeing aircraft sales.

of $20,000 (including interest) in semi-annual installments over three years but the resale contract required total payment of $12,000 in cash, the court could not simply subtract the price received in the second case from the total time price in the first case and get a fair result. The court must adjust for the credit factor in the original contract.[11] The present value of $20,000 to be paid in six semi-annual payments over three years would be much less than $20,000. The cash resale price should be subtracted from the present value of the $20,000 in order to get the correct damage figure. No case to date has encountered such a problem and nothing indicates that these problems will be grave. They should be less grave than analogous problems respecting "cover" under 2–712.

Section 2–706 differs from 2–712 in one important respect: it lives in the shadow of a large body of case law on resales by secured creditors under old 9–504(3) (new 9–610(b)). Under Article 9 a seller or creditor who has repossessed collateral and chosen to resell must do so in "a commercially reasonable manner." The same phrase appears in 2–706, and courts will surely look to decisions under Article 9 for guidance in determining what is "commercially reasonable."[12] One should be wary of undue reliance upon Article 9 decisions in Article 2 cases. The Article 9 cases are influenced by a most skeptical judicial attitude about the fairness of "deficiency judgment sales." The ignorant, ill represented, and foolish consumer-debtor calls forth the milk of judicial kindness in these cases. If one assumes that the typical deficiency judgment case is GMAC v. Pitiful Wretch but that the typical 2–706 case is Sears Roebuck v. General Electric, the courts need not and should not be as finicky about commercial reasonability under 2–706 as they have been under Article 9. Inevitably the debtor under Article 9 is down at the heel or he would not be in default. The same is not necessarily true of the business defendant under 2–706.

In the cases under 2–706 to date, the courts have found little difficulty with the section. Five of the reported cases have been

Iran argued that its credit memorandum should be included in damages calculations while the resale credit memorandum should not. The court concluded that Boeing's damages should reflect the credit memoranda issued to both Iran and the resale purchaser.

11. For example, the buyer may have contracted to pay $100,000 a year for five years for an inventory to be placed in the buyer's new store. Upon the buyer's breach the seller enters into a proper resale contract for $350,000 cash. If one assumes that the seller complied with the requirements of 2–706, a mechanical application of 2–706 would yield $150,000 damages. However, in our hypothetical, seller expected the use of only $100,000 cumulatively each year for five years. Thus a recovery of $500,000 cash in one year will give it a windfall. Somehow the courts must discount the $150,000 damage figure to reflect the actual contract situation.

12. However, as case law under 2–706 grows, courts should look increasingly to 2–706 for guidance, not to resales under 9–504. For a case in which the court looked to Article 9 for guidance, see Larsen Leasing, Inc. v. Thiele, Inc., 749 F.Supp. 821, 13 UCC2d 407 (W.D.Mich.1990).

before the hearing boards of the Department of Agriculture. In each case the board allowed sellers who resold lettuce, onions and the like, and cattle to recover their difference money.[13] In a number of other decisions, the courts have refused to apply 2–706 either as a final matter or on summary judgment on the ground that the seller failed to give the breaching buyer the required notice of resale. Representative of these cases is Cook Composites v. Westlake Styrene Corp.[14] In that case the plaintiff not only failed to plead that all the conditions of 2–607 had been met, but also failed to give notice of its intention to resell the product. Presumably many of these cases arise from the fact that the parties resell the goods and only later go to a lawyer who opens up the Code book. In a smaller group of cases courts have held that the seller's manner of resale was not commercially reasonable and, therefore, no 2–706 recovery was possible.[15] In one case the court refused a 2–706 recovery because the seller failed to identify the resold goods to the broken contract.[16] Finally, a large group of non-farm sellers has recovered at least some measure of 2–706 damages in an assorted lot of cases dealing with everything from investment securities (applied by analogy) to precision-made rocket components.[17] In most of these cases 2–706 worked like a well-oiled machine, and from all indications, the courts reached appropriate decisions.

Two subsections tucked away at the bottom of 2–706 merit a word. Section 2–706(5), like 9–617, is designed to enhance the resale market by protecting a good faith buyer even in circumstances in which the seller fails to comply with 2–706. Subsection (6) establishes the right to the excess over the contract price in the rare case in which the person reselling realizes a higher price than would have been realized on the original sale. Presumably because the seller is the "owner", the basic rules in 2–706 allow the seller to keep the resale proceeds. The meaning of that subsection will never be litigated in a 2–706 case, because the resale above the

---

13. See I. Kallish & Sons v. Jarosz Produce Farms, Inc., 1967 WL 9022, 26 Agric.Dec. 1285, 4 UCC 1168 (U.S.Dept. Agric. 1967).

14. 15 S.W.3d 124, 40 UCC2d 703 (Tex. App. 2000).

15. See Uganski v. Little Giant Crane & Shovel, Inc., 35 Mich.App. 88, 192 N.W.2d 580, 10 UCC 57 (1971).

16. Hunt–Wesson Foods, Inc. v. Marubeni Alaska Seafoods, Inc., 23 Wash. App. 193, 596 P.2d 666, 26 UCC 704 (1979). But cf. Servbest Foods, Inc. v. Emessee Industries, Inc., 82 Ill.App.3d 662, 403 N.E.2d 1, 37 Ill.Dec. 945, 29 UCC 518 (1980). After buyer breached a contract for meat trimmings, seller re-

sold on the market. The goods resold were not, in fact, those identified to the breached contract. The court held that where a contract involves fungible goods, a seller may recover 2–706 damages based on a resale of goods other than those identified to the contract since such a sale would not affect the price received for the goods.

17. See, e.g., Wurlitzer Co. v. Oliver, 334 F.Supp. 1009, 10 UCC 367 (W.D.Pa. 1971); Cohn v. Fisher, 118 N.J.Super. 286, 287 A.2d 222, 10 UCC 372 (1972); American Nat. Bank & Trust Co. of Chicago v. Weyerhaeuser Co., 692 F.2d 455, 34 UCC 1335 (7th Cir.1982).

contract price means that the aggrieved seller is no longer "aggrieved" and has no claim against the buyer under 2–706.

The buyer who has rightfully rejected or justifiably revoked and who thus holds the goods for the seller but decides to sell them to satisfy his claim in accordance with the terms of 2–711(3) receives different treatment. That buyer is treated as the holder of a "security interest," not as the owner of the goods. Thus, when that buyer resells for more than his damages, he merely recovers his damages and must remit the proceeds to the breaching seller. Several unremarkable cases have applied 2–706 to the aggrieved buyer's exercise of the similar rights under 2–711(3).

In sum, courts seem to be using 2–706 in proper ways. And *mirabile dictu,* courts do not seem disposed to restrict it by narrow definitions of good faith or commercial reasonability.[18]

§ 8–7 Damages for Nonacceptance or Repudiation, Section 2–708(1)

Section 2–708(1) states the seller's right to the traditional contract-market differential recovery. It reads:

> Subject to subsection (2) and to the provisions of this Article with respect to proof of market price (Section 2–723), the measure of damages for non-acceptance or repudiation by the buyer is the difference between the market price at the time and place for tender and the unpaid contract price together with any incidental damages provided in this Article (Section 2–710), but less expenses saved in consequence of the buyer's breach.

The provision is among the least novel and least remarkable of the Code's damage sections,[1] and the principal questions that 2–708(1) leaves unanswered are these: May a seller who has resold under 2–706 elect to use 2–708(1)? May a seller who could not have benefitted by completing the contract, and who would get no damages under 2–708(2) (lost profit), nevertheless recover under 2–708(1)?

---

18. For an extensive discussion of § 2–706, see Nordstrom, Seller's Damages Following Resale Under Article 2 of the Uniform Commercial Code, 65 Mich. L.Rev. 1299 (1967); Peters, Remedies for Breach of Contracts Relating to the Sale of Goods Under the Uniform Commercial Code: A Roadmap for Article 2, 73 Yale L.J. 199, 253–57, 260–61 (1963).

§ 8–7

1. Section 2–708(1)'s immediate ancestor is Uniform Sales Act § 64, which reads in part as follows:

(3) Where there is an available market for the goods in question, the measure of damages is, in the absence of special circumstances, showing proximate damage of a greater amount, the difference between the contract price and the market or current price at the time or times when the goods ought to have been accepted, or, if no time was fixed for acceptance, then at the time of the refusal to accept.

Before we consider these lawyer questions we should put 2–708(1) in perspective.[2] Here, as on the buyer's side, the contract-market differential will seldom be the same as the seller's actual economic loss from breach. Consider a contract to sell 5,000 pairs of sandals F.O.B. seller's plant for $5,000. If it cost the seller $2,000 to manufacture the sandals, seller's expectation would be a profit of $3,000. Only if the seller resells the sandals at the market price prevailing on the date of tender and the collection of damages is cost free will 2–708(1) put him in the same economic position as performance would have.[3] If seller resells for less than the market price at the date of tender, his profit on the resale and his damage recovery under 2–708(1) will not equal the $3,000 profit seller would have had. On the other hand, if he resells for more than the market price at the time of tender, his resale profit and 2–708(1) damages will total more than $3,000, and he will get a windfall. Of course one may view 2–708(1) and the buyer's counterpart, 2–713, as statutory liquidated damage clauses. For a fuller discussion of that view of 2–708 and 2–713, see the discussion of 2–713 in Chapter 7.

For one understanding the formula in 2–713, section 2–708(1) has no mysteries.[4] The market is measured at "the time and place for tender," and the seller is entitled to the difference between the contract price and the market price. If no market exists for the product with which to measure damages, an action for the price under 2–709 (or in some cases for lost profits under 2–708(2) rather than an action under 2–708(1)) is appropriate.[5] Even a first year

---

2. The scope of 2–708 is explored in Colorado Interstate Gas Co. v. Chemco, Inc., 854 P.2d 1232, 23 UCC2d 433 (Colo. 1993) (2–708 is not necessarily the remedy for a breach; parties can contract for a measure of damages and when they do, the court will generally enforce the contracted for damages, not 2–708); Caraustar Industries, Inc. v. Georgia–Pacific Corp., 2001 WL 34000141, 44 UCC2d 517 (N.C. Super. 2001) (under UCC 2–708, equitable remedies are not available in the absence of contractual agreement to contrary).

3. Note that, unlike the usual 2–708(1) recovery, a resale and damage recovery under 2–706 will put most sellers except those with the lost volume problem back into the same economic position as performance would have.

For a discussion of 2–706, see 8–6 *supra*.

4. For judicial consideration of 2–708(1), see Jagger Bros., Inc. v. Technical Textile Co., 202 Pa.Super. 639, 198

A.2d 888, 2 UCC 97 (1964); Bache & Co. v. International Controls Corp., 339 F.Supp. 341, 10 UCC 248 (S.D.N.Y. 1972), aff'd, 469 F.2d 696, 11 UCC 936 (2d Cir.1972); Wendling v. Puls, 227 Kan. 780, 610 P.2d 580, 28 UCC 1362 (1980); Buchsteiner Prestige Corp. v. Abraham & Straus, 107 Misc.2d 327, 433 N.Y.S.2d 972, 30 UCC 1006 (1980); Publicker Industries, Inc. v. Roman Ceramics Corp., 652 F.2d 340, 32 UCC 449 (3d Cir.1981); Klockner, Inc. v. Federal Wire Mill Corp., 663 F.2d 1370, 32 UCC 1097 (7th Cir.1981).

5. See Rheinberg Kellerei GmbH v. Brooksfield Nat. Bank of Commerce Bank, 901 F.2d 481, 11 UCC2d 1214 (5th Cir.1990). The court states that 2–708 is applicable only when a reasonable market resale is possible and has no application when the market value of the goods at the time and place of tender has deteriorated. The first statement has merit, but the second goes too far. It is precisely when the market price

law student knows when and where tender has occurred in an "across the counter" sale. Less clear is the case when the seller ships goods to the buyer "F.O.B. buyer's plant" or "F.O.B. seller's plant." In the former case we believe tender occurs at buyer's plant, in the latter at seller's plant. Under 2–708(1) the aggrieved seller may recover any incidental damages flowing from the breach (2–710)[6] but the seller must subtract any "expenses saved in consequence of the buyer's breach."

Although seller's 2–708(1) is almost a twin of buyer's 2–713, section 2–708(1) varies in one puzzling respect. Under 2–713 the aggrieved buyer measures the market at the time he "learns of the breach."[7] Section 2–713(2) fixes the crucial place as "the place for tender or, in cases of rejection after arrival or revocation of acceptance, as of the place of arrival." Apparently the drafters used the place of rejection and the time buyer learned of the breach to measure the market at the time and place where buyer would be most likely to cover. Section 2–708(1), however, directs the aggrieved seller to measure the market at the time and place for tender, and this is not the time and place where the seller is most likely to resell. The significance of this difference between 2–708 and 2–713 can be illustrated by an example. Suppose that a New York buyer contracts to purchase 5,000 sandals from a Los Angeles seller, F.O.B. seller's plant. Assume the contract price was $5,000. Seller correctly crates and ships the sandals, and two weeks after the shipping date they arrive in New York. There the buyer, who has since found a less expensive source, wrongfully rejects the goods and thus breaches the contract. If the market prices are as follows, what is the proper measure of recovery under 2–708(1)?

(1) Los Angeles market price at the time the goods were shipped, $3,000.

falls that the buyer will be tempted to breach, and the seller will need the protection of the market/contract price differential. See Northwest Airlines, Inc. v. Flight Trails, 3 F.3d 292, 24 UCC2d 94 (8th Cir. 1993) (in determining damages under 2–708, the court rejected both parties' evidence "in view of the limited and declining market for the goods" and arrived at a "fair price" by reference to "comparable markets" even though "the record did not directly support the figure." The court conceded that such an analysis was fraught with uncertainty and held such uncertainty should be resolved against breaching party).

6. See § 2–710:

Incidental damages to an aggrieved seller include any commercially reason-

able charges, expenses or commissions incurred in stopping delivery, in the transportation, care and custody of goods after the buyer's breach, in connection with return or resale of the goods or otherwise resulting from the breach.

See also Bache & Co. v. International Controls Corp., 339 F.Supp. 341, 10 UCC 248 (S.D.N.Y.1972), aff'd, 469 F.2d 696, 11 UCC 936 (2d Cir.1972) (stockbroker recovered brokerage commissions due on resale of securities as incidental damages).

7. For discussion of the confusion which the quoted language has caused, see Chapter 7.

(2) Los Angeles market price at the time the goods were wrongfully rejected, $2,500.

(3) New York market price when the goods were shipped and when they were rejected, $2,000.

Since the contract was F.O.B. Los Angeles, tender occurs upon delivery to the carrier in Los Angeles. Therefore the seller's damages are measured in the Los Angeles market on the date of shipment. This is true even though the goods are in New York and the seller did not learn of the breach until well after the time for tender. Why the philosophy exhibited in section 2–713 (to choose the most likely cover market) should not apply to the seller's contract-market differential with respect to the most likely resale market is unclear. In our case the seller will doubtless resell in the New York market. If the seller fails to qualify for a 2–706 recovery (because, for example, it did not give the buyer notice of the resale), the seller will then recover $1,000 less under 2–708(1) than it would have recovered if it could have used the New York market at the time it learned of the breach.

A more significant and troublesome question about 2–708(1) is its relationship to the other seller's remedies. May the seller's lawyer use 2–708(1) anytime it increases the damage award, irrespective of the client's resale or other behavior? First consider the relationship with 2–706. When the seller is not a "lost volume" seller,[8] the 2–706 remedy will put it in precisely the same position as performance would have. Yet a greedy seller may seek a windfall in the form of a larger 2–708(1) recovery. Assume, for example, this seller resells goods with a contract price of $6,000 for $4,000. Assume that the contract-market differential under 2–708(1) was $3,000. May the seller recover the $3,000 and thus gross $7,000? Or is the seller limited to a $2,000 recovery and a $6,000 gross? The courts could avoid this conflict by fiddling with the "expenses saved in consequence of the buyer's breach" part of the 2–708(1) formula. However, nothing in the pre-Code law or in the statutory history of the Code suggests that "expenses saved" were intended to include profits made on resale.[9]

Whether the drafters intended a seller who has resold to recover more in damages under 2–708(1) than he could under 2–706 is not clear. We conclude that a seller should not be permitted

---

8. "Lost volume" occurs when the seller resells to a buyer who would have bought from the seller even if there had been no breach of the original contract. The result is the seller's total volume of sales by year's end is reduced by one, and the seller's damages are the profit the seller would have made on that additional sale. For a more detailed discussion, see Harris, A Radical Restatement of the Law of Seller's Damages: Sales Act and Commercial Code Results Compared, 18 Stan. L. Rev. 66, 80–87 (1965).

9. "Expenses saved" are dealt with more fully in connection with Buyer's Remedies. See Chapter 7.

to recover more under 2–708(1) than under 2–706, but we admit we are swimming upstream against a heavy current of implication which flows from the comments and the Code history. Section 1–305 of Revised Article One indicates that a seller who has resold may not invoke 2–708(1). That section states that Code remedies are to put the aggrieved party in as good a position as performance would have, but no better. By hypothesis our seller would recover more under 2–708(1) than the seller "needs" to make himself whole. Section 1–305 derives some faint assistance from the third sentence in Comment 1 to 2–703: "Whether the pursuit of one remedy bars another depends entirely on the facts of the individual case." The comment at least suggests that the seller's use of one remedy may foreclose his use of another. Yet, the immediately preceding sentence in the same comment says: "This Article rejects any doctrine of election of remedy as a fundamental policy and thus the remedies are essentially cumulative in nature and include all of the available remedies for breach."[10]

Some Code history supports the proposition that a seller who has resold under the provisions of 2–706 may nevertheless sue under 2–708(1). One writer for the New York Law Revision Commission recommended that section 2–703 be rewritten to make it clear that an aggrieved seller who had resold could use 2–708(1).[11] In response to that recommendation the Editorial Board deleted the language "so far as any goods have not been resold" from 2–703(e), stating its purpose as being to "make it clear that the aggrieved seller was not required to elect between damages under 2–706 and damages under 2–708."[12]

The Restatement (Second) of Contracts has not enlightened us. Section 350 on avoidability as a limitation on damages might be regarded as illuminating our ignorance, nothing more.[13] Comment C to section 350 discusses the obligation of one whose employment

---

10. B & R Textile Corp. v. Paul Rothman Indus. Ltd., 101 Misc.2d 98, 420 N.Y.S.2d 609, 27 UCC 994 (City Civ.Ct.1979), aff'd, 1979 WL 30097, 27 UCC 996 (N.Y.Sup.1979).

11. 1 N.Y. State Law Revision Comm'n, 1955 Report 550–52 (1955).

12. The comparable remedies on the buyer's side are sections 2–712 (Cover) and 2–713 (Damages for Non–Delivery or Repudiation). However, the drafters clearly indicated their essentially "elective" intention in Comment 3 to § 2–712:

Subsection (3) expresses the policy that cover is not a mandatory remedy for the buyer. The buyer is always free to choose between cover and damages for non-delivery under the next section.

13. Restatement (Second) of Contracts § 350 reads in full:

Avoidability as a Limitation on Damages

(1) Except as stated in Subsection (2), damages are not recoverable for loss that the injured party could have avoided without undue risk, burden or humiliation.

(2) The injured party is not precluded from recovery by the rule stated in Subsection (1) to the extent that he has made reasonable but unsuccessful efforts to avoid loss.

contract has been broken to find a substitute transaction. It goes on as follows:

> In the case of the sale of goods, this principle has inspired the standard formulas under which a buyer's or seller's damages are based on the difference between the contract price and the market price on that market where the injured party could have arranged a substitute transaction for the purchase or sale of similar goods.

By holding out 2–708 and 2–713 as the relevant "substitute transactions" the drafters of the Restatement overlook the possibility of alternative plausible "substitutes"—a hypothetical sale under 2–708 and an actual sale under 2–706. Its indorsement of substitute transactions might be read to point to the actual substitute transaction as the proper measure of damages, but its choice of the hypothetical 2–708 formula as a substitute casts doubt on that outcome.[14] On the other hand, Comment E to section 347[15] states that a party's damages are limited "[i]f he makes an especially favorable substitute transaction, so that he sustains a smaller loss than might have been expected * * *." Read alone, Comment E to section 347 seems to suggest that a court should award damages based upon the actual substitute transaction, not upon the hypothetical substitute. Yet each of the four illustrations under E deals with personal service contracts; none is a sale of goods contract. That omission becomes important when we are confronted with the discussion quoted above in section 350 that indicates that the drafters of the Restatement regard the hypothetical resale under 2–708 or 2–713 as a "substitute" and apparently do not mean to distinguish between that hypothetical substitute and the actual substitute in a case where there is a true resale.

Where does this leave us? Note first that the current Code and comments are equivocal; though they may bend in the direction of permitting the seller to choose at will, they stop well short of clearly authorizing this. It is possible that the New York Law Revision Commission had in mind the seller who would not receive

---

14. The confusion is carried into the illustration. See, e.g., illustration 7. In that case, an aggrieved seller refuses an alternative sale. The Restatement indicates that the seller is limited by the price at which it could have sold the commodity. The citation following the example is to 2–708(1) which is apparently to lead one to the conclusion that a potential resale price is the market price.

15. Restatement (Second) of Contracts § 347 reads in full:

Measure of Damages in General

Subject to the limitations stated in §§ 350–53, the injured party has a right to damages based on his expectation interest as measured by

(a) the loss in the value to him of the other party's performance caused by its failure or deficiency, plus

(b) any other loss, including incidental or consequential loss, caused by the breach, less

(c) any cost or other loss that he has avoided by not having to perform.

a windfall by suing under 2–708(1) and simply wanted to make it clear that a seller who makes a good faith attempt to comply with 2–706 but fails may then resort to 2–708(1). Nothing in their report suggests that they considered the case in which 2–706 recovery would be small because the seller sold at a price very near to the contract price yet the contract-market differential under 2–708 would be large. Despite the powerful arguments of Professor Peters[16] and the broad implications from the statutory history, we conclude that a seller who has resold at the time of trial should not be permitted to recover more under 2–708(1) than he could recover under 2–706. However, we would not cast the burden on the seller who sues under 2–708(1) to prove that 2–706 was less advantageous. Rather we would make it the buyer's burden to show that the seller had in fact resold, that this was not a lost volume case, and that 2–708(1) recovery would be greater than 2–706 recovery.[17] Of course this burden may be so heavy that every seller will have the option to use 2–706 or 2–708 because the buyer will be unable to prove the facts necessary to keep the seller out of 2–708.

All of the foregoing discussion assumes that the buyer who wishes to limit the seller to the difference between the contract and the resale price can show that the goods resold were the goods contracted for. If the seller could have fulfilled the buyer's contract by its own purchase on the market or by a choice among a variety of fungible goods in inventory, the buyer will be unable to limit the seller to 2–706 damages. The buyer will not be able to prove that any resale is "reasonably identified as referring to the broken contract." Put another way, the difference between the contract and a specific resale price is not the proper measure of the seller's expectation damages unless that resale is a substitute for the one actually conducted.

Consider one case in which the court rejected buyer's attempt to limit the seller to the resale, a case that is incorrect in our judgment. In Wendling v. Puls,[18] Wendling offered 103 head of cattle to Puls and Watson. It appears that the farmer had raised the cattle, and in fact Puls and Watson (a veterinarian), came to Wendling's farm to inspect the cattle. After the inspection, the

---

16. See Peters, Remedies for Breach of Contracts Relating to the Sale of Goods Under the Uniform Commercial Code: A Roadmap for Article 2, 73 Yale L.J. 199, 260–61 (1963).

17. For cases dealing with 2–708 and the burden of proof, see Dehahn v. Innes, 356 A.2d 711, 19 UCC 407 (Me. 1976) (in using resale price as evidence of 2–708 market value, seller has burden to prove (1) that a price change between the dates of the breach and the resale was unlikely, and (2) that the resale was

fair and in good faith); B & R Textile Corp. v. Paul Rothman Indus. Ltd., 101 Misc.2d 98, 420 N.Y.S.2d 609, 27 UCC 994 (City Civ.Ct.1979), aff'd, 1979 WL 30097, 27 UCC 996 (N.Y.Sup.1979) (in using resale price as evidence of 2–708 market value, seller has burden of proving resale price accurately reflects market price).

18. 227 Kan. 780, 610 P.2d 580, 28 UCC 1362 (1980).

parties agreed to the terms of a sale at $.61 per pound for 98 head and $.59 per pound for the remaining five. When the time for performance came, Puls and Watson dragged their feet. After several unsuccessful attempts to get the buyers to take possession and pay the money, Wendling invited three qualified livestock dealers to make a bid on the cattle and offered them for sale. The only bidder bid $.42 per pound, a price that would have produced $34,849.08 as compared to the $50,533.50 contract price. For reasons that are not explained, Wendling did not sell to the bidder but sold at some later date at a higher price of $39,978.49.

Wendling then sued Puls and Watson for the difference between the $.42 bid and the $.61 contract price. Despite the fact that he had sold them for $4,000 more than the bid, he recovered the difference between the contract and the bid price under 2–708(1). The case seems wrong. Wendling was not a cattle dealer with unlimited animals to sell. He was a farmer who had raised 103 head that he had for sale, not more and not less. That he was not free to substitute other cattle is suggested by the fact that the prospective buyers, one of whom was a veterinarian, in fact inspected and bid upon these very cattle. Presumably Wendling could not have lost volume because he could not have raised replacements in the time available to him and he was not a trader. For all of these reasons it appears to us that the difference between the actual resale price, $39,978.49 and the contract was the correct, indeed, the exact measure of his expectations.

If Wendling bought and sold cattle and if he could have satisfied the contract with cattle other than those inspected at his farm, the court's outcome would be justifiable. In that case we should not give the buyers the benefit of his resale. Wendling's expectation in that case might well have been to satisfy Puls and Watson by the purchase and resale of another 103 head, saving for himself the second sale at a higher value.

Despite *Wendling v. Puls* and despite the arguments of Judge Peters, we hold to our view that a seller who resells goods reasonably identified to the broken contract for a price above the 2–708(1) market price should be limited to the difference between the contract price and the actual resale price. We believe that this is an exact measure of the seller's expectation and that the seller should not recover more than that. Two cases have agreed with our analysis.[19]

The Article 2 Revision Study Group accepted this analysis, including the allocation of the burden of proof to the buyer.[20] The

19. See Tesoro Petroleum Corp. v. Holborn Oil Co., Ltd., 145 Misc.2d 715, 547 N.Y.S.2d 1012, 10 UCC2d 814 (1989); Eades Commodities, Co. v. Hoe-per, 825 S.W.2d 34, 17 UCC2d 771 (Mo. App.1992).

20. See Study Committee Report at 207–08.

Study Group recommended that the Comments clarify that the seller who has actually resold the contract goods in compliance with 2–706(1) should be limited to damages as measured by 2–706(1) (provided the seller is not a lost volume seller), and that the seller who in bad faith failed to comply with 2–706 not be permitted to recover 2–708 damages that would put him in a better position than performance would have. The Task Force of the ABA assigned to study the Study Group's recommendations agrees with this conclusion.[21]

We will consider the relationship between 2–708(1) and 2–708(2) in Sections 8–11 and 8–12 below. Except for the questions concerning its relationship to 2–706 and 2–708(2), section 2–708(1) deserves comparatively little of the student's or the lawyer's time. It is a contract-market formula that the drafters assembled from old and familiar parts.

§ 8–8   Lost Profits, Section 2–708(2)

Section 2–708(2) says:

> If the measure of damages provided in subsection (1) is inadequate to put the seller in as good a position as performance would have done then the measure of damages is the profit (including reasonable overhead) which the seller would have made from full performance by the buyer, together with any incidental damages provided in this Article (Section 2–710), due allowance for costs reasonably incurred and due credit for payments or proceeds of resale.

This section addresses a group of problems that the drafters did not well formulate or well understand. In light of Professor Harris' writings[1] on seller's damages it is easy to be critical of the

---

21. Task Force Report, 16 Del. J.Corp.L. 1205, 1215 (1991).

§ 8–8

1. See Harris, A General Theory for Measuring Seller's Damages for Total Breach of Contract, 60 Mich.L.Rev. 577 (1962), Harris, A Radical Restatement of the Law of Seller's Damages: Michigan Results Compared, 61 Mich.L.Rev. 849 (1963); Harris, A Radical Restatement of the Law of Seller's Damages: New York Results Compared, 34 Fordham L.Rev. 23 (1965); Harris and Graham, A Radical Restatement of the Law of Seller's Damages: California Results Compared, 18 Stan.L.Rev. 553 (1965); Harris, A Radical Restatement of the Law of Seller's Damages: Sales Act and Commercial Code Results Compared, 18 Stan.L.Rev. 66 (1965).

For other articles on 2–708(2), see Childres and Burgess, Seller's Remedies: The Primacy of 2–708(2), 48 N.Y.U.L.Rev. 833 (1973); Goetz and Scott, Measuring Seller's Damages: The Lost–Profits Puzzle, 31 Stan.L.Rev. 323 (1979); Speidel and Clay, Seller's Recovery of Overhead Under UCC Section 2–708(2): Economic Cost Theory and Contract Remedial Policy, 57 Cornell L.Rev. 681 (1972); Schlosser, Construing UCC Section 2–708(2) to Apply to the Lost–Volume Seller, 24 Case W.Res.L.Rev. 686 (1973); Shanker, The Case for a Literal Reading of UCC Section 2–708(2) (One Profit for the Reseller), id. at 697; Comment, A Theoretical Postscript: Microeconomics and the Lost–Volume Seller, id. at 712; Goldberg, An Economic Analysis of the Lost Volume Retail Sell-

drafters' work in 2–708(2). It is as though the drafters were spent after producing one novel and admirable seller's remedy, 2–706. The drafters incorporated the standard contract-market formula in 2–708(1) without questioning it and then proceeded by fits and starts to build 2–708(2). In the pages to follow we will deal with two general questions under 2–708(2). First, what cases does it cover? This is a question of considerable complexity with no certain answer. Second, when it applies, what do its various parts mean, and what kind of evidence must the plaintiff or the defendant bring forward to satisfy their burden in each case?

§ 8–9   Lost Profits, Section 2–708(2)—The Lost Volume Seller

Judges in pre-Code cases, writers, and Code drafters[1] perceived that a contract-market formula would not even grossly approximate the proper damage recovery for certain sellers. The drafters early labeled one such class as those who sell "standard priced" goods.[2] Apparently the theory on "standard priced" goods was that the absence of a contract-market differential must necessarily mean in

er, 57 S.Cal.L.Rev. 283 (1984); Schlosser, Damages for the Lost Volume Seller: Does an Efficient Formula Already Exist?, 17 U.C.C.L.J. 238 (1985); Note, Lost Profits Damage Awards Under Uniform Commercial Code Section 2–708(2), 37 Stan.L.Rev. 1109 (1985); Anderson, Damages for Sellers Under the Code's Profit Formula, 40 Sw.L.J. 1021 (1986).

§ 8–9

1. The statutory history begins with the Joint Editorial Committee of the American Law Institute and the National Conference of Commissioners on Uniform State Laws. Their product was a revision of the Uniform Sales Act and became the proposed draft of the Uniform Revised Sales Act (Sales Article of the proposed Commercial Code). Section 110 of the Uniform Revised Sales Act reads as follows:

Damages for Non–Acceptance. The measure of damages for non-acceptance is the difference between the unpaid contract price and the price current at the time and place for tender together with any incidental damages under Section 112 but less any expense saved in consequence of the buyer's breach, except that if the foregoing measure of damages is inadequate to put the seller in as good a position as performance would have done then the measure of damages is the profit the seller would

have made from full performance by the buyer.

Uniform Revised Sales Act, Proposed Final Draft No. 1 at 58 (1944). Of course, it is the "except * * * if" clause that is of prime concern here. Unfortunately, no notes or comments to § 110 in the Proposed Final Draft of 1944 explain what kind of "profit" cases the drafters meant to accommodate. However, the section is useful if only to note the early belief in inadequacy of the general damage formula which now appears in § 2–708(1).

2. In May, 1949, when § 110 became § 2–708 in the 1949 draft of the Uniform Commercial Code, official comments were added. The "except" clause was explained in Comment 2 to 2–708 as follows (emphasis added):

The provision of this section permitting recovery of expected profit where the standard measure of damages is inadequate, together with a new requirement that price actions may be sustained only where resale is impractical, are designed to eliminate the unfair and economically wasteful results arising under the older law when *fixed price articles* were involved. This section permits the recovery of lost profits in all appropriate cases, which would include *all standard priced goods.*

such cases that some other measure of recovery was needed. At a later stage the drafters made room in 2–708(2) for a seller who had ceased manufacture and sold the goods for salvage or who had never purchased the goods.[3] Unfortunately, the drafters never identified or articulated any principle to unite these cases. In fact it appears that they did not identify the relevant characteristic of the "standard priced" class. That characteristic is not the "standard pricedness" of the goods the seller is selling but the fact that the seller will lose one sale when Buyer No. 1 breaches and, if seller resells Buyer No. 1's goods to Buyer No. 2, it still will not be made whole by difference money because one sale will have been lost, one profit foregone.

To illustrate, assume a contract for the sale of a washing machine with a list price of $500. Assume further that the seller has or can obtain more machines than it can sell. The buyer breaches, and the seller resells the washing machine destined for the breacher at the same list price to another. However, the resale buyer is one of seller's regular customers who had intended to purchase a washing machine from seller anyway. If the seller's total cost per machine was $300, seller stood to gain an aggregate profit of $400, that is, $200 profit from each of two sales. Clearly the 2–708 contract-market differential formula is inadequate in this situation since it gives no damages to the seller who has lost a $200 profit because of the breach. In such a case the damage award should be the lost profit, that is, $200, for this will place the seller "in as good a position as performance would have done."[4] For an elaborate and well informed discussion of the application of 2–708 to a dairies seller against its purchaser, consider New England Dairies, Inc. v. Dairy Mart Convenience Stores, Inc.[5] In that case Dairy Mart had a requirements contract to purchase all of its requirements of certain dairy products from New England Dairies.

3. 1954 Recommendations of the Enlarged Editorial Board to § 2–708 at 14.

4. For cases applying 2–708(2) to lost volume sellers, see R.E. Davis Chemical Corp. v. Diasonics, Inc., 924 F.2d 709, 13 UCC2d 1094 (7th Cir.1991) (seller's lost volume upheld although seller did not specify the particular unit buyer had agreed to buy nor "trace the exact resale buyer for that unit"); Unique Designs, Inc. v. Pittard Machinery Co., 200 Ga. App. 647, 409 S.E.2d 241, 16 UCC2d 116 (1991),cert. denied (1991) (seller entitled to lost volume recovery where it proved it had unlimited supply of the standard priced goods); Sons of Thunder, Inc. v. Borden, Inc., 148 N.J. 396, 690 A.2d 575, 32 UCC2d 66 (1997) (court gave lost profits based on one year estimate).

For cases denying 2–708(2) to sellers claiming lost profits, see Malone v. Carl Kisabeth Co., Inc., 726 S.W.2d 188, 4 UCC2d 1075 (Tex.App.1987) (seller waived lost profit recovery where jury instructions did not ask whether resale buyer would have purchased a unit absent the breach); Bill's Coal Co., Inc. v. Board of Public Utilities of Springfield, Mo., 887 F.2d 242, 9 UCC2d 1238 (10th Cir.1989) (seller not entitled to lost profits where it did not have sufficient production capacity to perform buyer's contract and other contracts).

5. 2002 WL 229900, 47 UCC2d 480 (D. Conn. 2002).

When it sold off its New England convenience stores, it canceled the contract. The court held that the sale and cancellation was a repudiation and that New England had a right to damages under 2–708. The court carefully examined New England's capacity to fulfill the contract as well as to perform its existing contracts with other purchasers of dairy products. The court then calculated the amount of the lost profits during the year and one half period after the breach, until the time at which the court found the seller no longer to be a lost volume seller because its sales to other buyers had increased to the extent that it could no longer have satisfied the defendant, Dairy Mart. The case contains a good analysis of 2–708(2) and a detailed calculation of the lost profits that might have been incurred in a business such as New England Dairies.

A seller is not a "lost volume seller" unless the seller would have made the sale to the breaching buyer *and* the sale to the party who purchased the buyer's goods. Courts that look only at whether the seller had excess capacity ask only whether the seller *could* have made an additional sale, not whether it *would* have. If the additional sale would be unprofitable, under every profitability measurement, the seller would not have made it.[6] Mindful of this distinction, the Seventh Circuit adopted a four-part test for manufacturers that seek lost profits: (1) the seller must have had the capacity to produce the additional unit, (2) this would have been profitable so that manufacturer would have produced the additional unit, (3) the party who bought the breached unit would have been offered an additional unit had buyer not breached, and (4) that party would have accepted such an offer.[7] We support the first three parts of this test with some modification. If the seller presents evidence of the first part, the second part should be presumed. If, however, the buyer presents enough evidence to question the profitability of the second sale, the seller should then have to prove that the second sale would have been economically beneficial. This information should normally be in the possession of seller.[8] However, we would suggest that courts interpret the term "profitability" loosely so that if the seller demonstrates any basis for finding that the second sale would be beneficial, that should suffice. The fourth part, which apparently requires testimony from the third party,

6. See Scullin Steel Co. v. PACCAR, Inc., 748 S.W.2d 910, 6 UCC2d 433 (Mo. App.1988) (court denied lost profit award where evidence indicated sale would be unprofitable).

7. See R.E. Davis Chemical Corp. v. Diasonics, Inc., 826 F.2d 678, 4 UCC2d 369 (7th Cir.1987).

8. Compare Anderson, Damages for Sellers Under the Code's Profit Formu-la, 40 Sw.L.J. 1021, 1060 (1986) who would shift to the buyer the burden of going forward with evidence that seller was not "left at lost volume" once the seller made "a basic showing of lost volume status." However, the ultimate burden of persuasion remains with the seller. This approach is consistent with the Restatement (Second) of Contracts § 347, comment f.

seems unnecessary absent some evidence that the third party would not have accepted the offer.

Return to our seller of washing machines. If the seller is in a market in which the demand for the product exceeds the available supply (as for example the car market immediately after World War II), seller will lose nothing (except for incidental damages) when one party breaches, and should recover no damages on breach even if the goods are "standard priced." By the same token when the goods are not standard priced but seller loses one sale as a result of one buyer's breach, seller needs more than the contract-market differential on the resale to put it in the same economic position as performance would have; seller needs the profit on the lost sale that year. (If in the foregoing example the price of washing machines fluctuated between $450 and $550 and the seller could prove a contract-market difference of $100 to $150, seller still would not be made whole by that difference.)[9]

§ 8–10   Lost Profits, Section 2–708(2)—Components and Jobber Sellers

In the later stages of the drafting process the drafters identified a second class of sellers who deserved special treatment. These are sellers who can be said to lose volume not because they resell completed goods to another regular customer but because they either resell uncompleted goods for scrap or are jobbers who never purchase the contract goods at all. These are Professor Harris' "components" and "jobber" sellers.[1] The "components seller" is one who agrees to manufacture or assemble the contract goods. Regardless of whether the seller itself produces all of the necessary components or instead acquires them from a third party, the seller's final task is assembly. If the buyer breaches before final assembly and the seller elects to cease manufacture,[2] the seller will have lost one sale since no sale of completed goods will occur. Unless the seller substantially completes it cannot pursue an action for the price under 2–709. And while 2–708(1) and 2–706 both refer to market price, those sections suggest the use of the finished product as the subject of the market price. However, our seller can

---

9. Two further points are made in New England Dairies, Inc. v. Dairy Mart Convenience Stores, Inc., 2002 WL 229900, 47 UCC2d 480 (D. Conn. 2002): (1) under 2–708(2) lost profits are net profit plus overhead or gross profit including overhead and (2) assuming that but for the breach there would be a continuing contract, a lost volume seller can collect damages for period between breach and time at which it secures enough alternate business.

1. See Harris, A Radical Restatement of the Law of Seller's Damages: Sales Act and Commercial Code Results Compared, 18 Stan.L.Rev. 66, 68–72, 97–98 (1965) [hereafter cited as Harris].

2. § 2–704(2) allows an aggrieved seller who has not yet completed the contract goods to cease manufacture in the exercise of reasonable commercial judgment.

at least tally up the value of the components on hand. Professor Harris has argued that:

> where plaintiff stops production after breach and seeks *components-valued* damages, the court should side with him unless defendant shows that (1) plaintiff knew or should have known this decision would enhance damages and (2) a decision to complete would not have unreasonably imperiled or harmed plaintiff's other interests.[3]

And previously, Professor Harris had noted:

> To calculate what plaintiff saved or should have saved as a result of the breach, the court must add the total value of the various goods on hand at the time of repudiation that were to be used in plaintiff's performance to the costs of completing performance that were saved because of breach.[4]

The drafters apparently had similar intentions, for in December 1954, the Recommendations of the Enlarged Editorial Board inserted an additional phrase at the end of what was then 2–708 (emphasis added):

> * * * except that if the foregoing measure of damages is inadequate to put the seller in as good a position as performance would have done then the measure of damages is the profit, (including reasonable overhead,) which the seller would have made from full performance by the buyer *with due allowance for costs reasonably incurred and due credit for any resale.*

The additional phrase at the end of section 2–708 was added "to clarify the privilege of the seller to realize junk value when it is manifestly useless to complete the operation of manufacture."[5] Thus the drafters indicated a second situation as appropriate for the profit remedy of 2–708, namely the situation where a seller-manufacturer learns of the buyer's breach while in the process of manufacturing the contract goods.[6]

The "jobber" is yet another kind of seller who can look to 2–708(2) for recovery of lost profits. By "jobber" we refer to a seller who satisfies two conditions. First, it is a seller who never acquires (or never manufactures) the contract goods. Second, its decision not

---

3. Harris, *supra* note 1, at 72.

4. *Id.* at 68.

5. 1954 Recommendations of the Enlarged Editorial Board to § 2–708 at 14.

6. For cases dealing with various components sellers and 2–708(2), see Detroit Power Screwdriver Co. v. Ladney, 25 Mich.App. 478, 181 N.W.2d 828, 8 UCC 504 (1970) (manufacturer of highly technical industrial machine entitled to lost profits where no market existed for the machine following the buyer's breach); City of Louisville v. Rockwell Mfg. Co., 482 F.2d 159, 12 UCC 840 (6th Cir.1973) (manufacturer of parking meters entitled to lost profits on meters not completed following buyer's breach).

to acquire those goods after learning of the breach is commercially reasonable under 2–704. In these circumstances the seller's actions for the price or resale are inapplicable. And a recovery of damages under 2–708(1) will place it in the same position as performance only by chance. Since the jobber has no goods on hand to resell, seller cannot even resell on the market at the time of tender and so recoup the amount necessary to make it whole by adding such proceeds to its 2–708(1) recovery. Thus the only recovery which grossly approximates the "jobber's" economic loss is a recovery based on lost profits.[7]

Of course the jobber is not functionally different from the components seller, and as Professor Harris notes:

> In this situation a components approach is more appropriate— that is, plaintiff should abandon efforts to acquire the goods. Valuation of the yet-to-be-acquired goods should be at cost of acquisition ("components valuation") even if there is only a single component to be valued—the goods themselves.[8]

§ 8–11   Lost Profits, Section 2–708(2)—Other Cases

If the drafters had simply identified the above two classes of plaintiffs and had told us that 2–708(2) should apply to them and to no others, the law would be simple if not necessarily fair. However, the drafters left us with the troublesome preamble to 2–708(2):

> If the measure of damages provided in subsection (1) is inadequate to put the seller in as good a position as performance would have done then the measure of damages is * * * [that set out in subsection (2)].

Literally this principle covers a multitude of plaintiffs who are neither lost volume sellers, nor jobbers, nor components sellers. As Professor Peters has pointed out,[1] only by happenstance does the contract-market differential of 2–708(1) put the seller in the same economic position as performance would have. When the seller who sues under 2–708(1) resells the goods at a lower price than the market price on the date of tender, 2–708(1) will always leave the

---

7. For cases dealing with jobbers and 2–708(2), see Blair Int'l Ltd. v. LaBarge, Inc., 675 F.2d 954, 33 UCC 1242 (8th Cir.1982) (seller with contracts to buy and resell steel oil well casings entitled to lost profits where it never acquired the goods and its decision not to acquire them was commercially reasonable); Stamtec, Inc. v. Anson Stamping Co., LLC, 346 F.3d 651, 51 UCC2d 1048 (6th Cir. 2003) (a jobber's measure of damages under 2–708(2) when it has no responsibility for delivery costs to buyer is gross profits with no reduction for over-

head; when the jobber must pay for delivery to buyer, the measure of damages under 2–708(2) is gross profits (no reduction) for overhead minus the saved delivery cost).

8. Harris, *supra* note 1, at 77.

§ 8–11

1. Peters, Remedies for Breach of Contracts Relating to the Sale of Goods Under the Uniform Commercial Code: A Roadmap for Article 2, 73 Yale L.J. 199, 259 (1963).

seller short of the economic position in which performance would have put it. If, on the other hand, the seller resells the goods at a higher price than the market price on the date of tender, 2–708(1) overcompensates; it gives the seller a larger profit than performance would have. Since history tells us, and presumably all agree, that the lost volume seller, the components seller (who ceases manufacture and sells for salvage), and the jobber are entitled to enter through the Pearly Gates to 2–708(2), the question arises: what if a seller—who is not one of those—argues that 2–708(1) will not leave it in the same economic condition as would performance? More puzzling yet, what of the defendant buyer who argues that plaintiff seller should be forced to use 2–708(2) because 2–708(1) would put the seller in a *better* economic position than performance would have?

a. Section 2–708(2), Not Enough Compensation

In answer to the first question we believe that any plaintiff who is hardy enough to prove that the 2–708(1) measure of damages will not put it in the same position performance would have, should be permitted to prove what performance would have done and should recover that amount under 2–708(2). We take the position with a healthy respect for the problems it poses for the plaintiff and the court. Asking a court to put a plaintiff in the same economic position as performance would have done is asking for a much more subtle and difficult judgment than is asked when the court must find only the difference between a contract price and a market price.

Before examining the complexities of these cases, we consider the kinds of cases, apparently now excluded from 2–708(2), which we argue ought to be included in 2–708(2). If the seller has resold to one of its regular customers and so lost volume, it is already within 2–708(2) as a lost volume seller. Moreover a seller who is a jobber or a manufacturer and has incurred no costs falls within the Harris jobber category and is included in 2–708(2). Likewise if the seller is a manufacturer who ceases manufacture in midstream, it is already within the confines of 2–708(2) as one of Harris' components sellers.

That leaves only two cases for addition to 2–708(2). The first arises when the seller resells a finished product but is unable to prove lost volume as a result of the breach. The second is the seller who holds completed goods on hand and unsold at the time of trial. Because the contract-market differential at the time of tender would grossly approximate the damage which these sellers would have suffered—if they had resold in the relevant market at or shortly after the breach—standard doctrine would send each of these sellers to 2–708(1). These sellers differ, then, from the lost volume seller in that they cannot prove that they lost a profit on one sale during the year. They differ from the jobber or salvage seller in that they have a completed product which they could have sold on the market at or near the time of tender, thereby reducing their damages.

In both cases (completed goods on hand at time of trial; completed goods resold prior to trial) the 2–708(2) formula is easy to apply in a mechanical fashion. The art comes in establishing the figure which the court will allow as "due credit for payments or proceeds of resale." If the seller has resold, the due credit should never be less than the amount for which the goods have been resold (remember the seller is not a lost volume seller), but conceivably it should be more than that figure if the court finds, for example, that the seller lacked commercial reasonability in waiting as long as it did in the falling market. If the seller still holds the goods at time of trial, the court will still have to determine a figure to include as due credit for a putative resale even though the seller has not yet resold. If the court does not deduct some amount for due credit for resale, 2–708(2) will simply become a back door action for the price, and quite clearly the drafters did not intend that. That result would also violate the mitigation principle which is still alive and well in the UCC.[2]

To sharpen our focus on the problem, consider the following hypothetical case. Assume that Boeing has a contract for the sale of two used 727's at a price of $2 million each. The buyer breaches at a time when the used 727 market is $1.7 million per aircraft (give or take $100,000). After breach, seller resells one aircraft for $1.6 million, and at the time of trial Boeing has not sold the other 727. At the time of trial the fair market value of used 727's has fallen to $1.4 million because many more aircraft have come onto the market with the introduction of widebody jets. Note that 2–708(1) will not put Boeing in the same position that performance would have. Under 2–708(1) Boeing will recover $300,000 on each aircraft (the difference between the $2 million contract price and the $1.7 million market price at the time and place for tender). However, Boeing did not receive the market price (at the time of tender) of $1.7 million for the aircraft which it resold, and it appears that Boeing will receive $1.4 million or less for the aircraft still on hand. Consequently, the damages obtained under 2–708(1) will be inadequate to put Boeing in the same economic position as performance would have, that is, performance = $4 million in pocket, but 2–708(1) = $600,000 (damages) + $1.6 million (proceeds of resale) + $1.4 million (probable proceeds of resale) = $3.6 million.

2. See § 1–103.

Assume that Boeing's direct cost of purchasing the used aircraft and refurbishing them was $1.3 million per aircraft and that the remaining $700,000 between the figure and the contract price would have been net profit and reimbursement for overhead. With respect to the aircraft which it resold for $1.6 million, Boeing will argue for a 2–708(2) recovery as follows:

	$ 700,000	(profit plus overhead)
plus	1,300,000	(costs reasonably incurred)
minus	1,600,000	(due credit for resale)
	$ 400,000	Damage

In the second case it will argue for:

	$ 700,000	(profit plus overhead)
plus	1,300,000	(costs reasonably incurred)
minus	1,400,000	(due credit for resale)
	$ 600,000	Damage

Buyer's first line of defense will be to argue that Boeing may not use 2–708(2) since it can show no lost volume and is neither a jobber nor a manufacturer who ceased manufacture. If the court rejects that argument, the buyer's second line of defense will be to argue that it should be given a greater "due credit" in each case. The buyer may maintain that Boeing should have resold for $1.7 million at the time of tender and that its failure to do so was commercially unreasonable. Unless the buyer can show that Boeing's failure to resell was commercially unreasonable, that is, that Boeing knew the market would fall and could have resold but did not, we would reject the buyer's contention and permit Boeing to recover under 2–708(2). Since Boeing's recovery under 2–708(1) would be $300,000 per aircraft, their use of 2–708(2) would net it an additional $400,000. (Were the court dealing with simply the first transaction, that is, the actual resale, the same result could be reached through the application of 2–706).

Some argue that this opportunity to receive a more ample recovery under 2–708(2) than would be available under 2–708(1) will encourage the Boeings of this world to forego resale and to stand around waiting in hopes of a sizeable recovery under 2–708(2) and a later lucky resale at a higher price. It is true that escape from the mandatory "mitigation" price in 2–708(1) (i.e., market price at time of tender) can reduce a seller's incentive to resell promptly. As we have said before, we suspect that business people seldom forego dollars in the pocket from a reasonably satisfactory resale in hope of recovering a larger amount through litigation, the outcome of which is unpredictable at best and disastrous, if the court finds no breach. We would give the courts a somewhat freer reign than they have had heretofore to award the seller its economic benefit. We appreciate that such cases will present novel and difficult questions both to the parties' lawyers and to the judges, but we believe the benefits to be gained outweigh these costs.[3]

The UCC Study Group, concerned with the likelihood that 2–708(1) either overcompensates or undercompensates the seller, favored increased use of 2–708(2) by the courts. It would have limited 2–708(1)'s application to three situations where the goods have been resold or remain available for resale:

> (1) the seller has resold in compliance with 2–706 but has lost volume;

> (2) the seller has resold in good faith but otherwise has failed to comply with the conditions of 2–706; and

> (3) the seller has not resold in fact, but has identified goods on hand or goods that were intended for the contract.[4]

The ABA Task Force agreed that application of 2–708(1) should be limited in favor of 2–708(2), but suggested that the first subset be narrowed further to read:

> The Seller has resold in compliance with section 2–706 and has "lost volume," but either cannot adequately prove damages under 2–708(2) or damages under section 2–708(1) would be less than damages under section 2–708(2).[5]

The focus of the suggested revision would have been to put the seller in the position performance would have done—no better, no worse.

To see how the proposed revision would have changed things consider Tigg Corp. v. Dow Corning Corp.[6] Tigg and Dow Corning

---

3. For cases in which an aggrieved seller recovered lost profits under 2–708(2) although it probably did not fall within any of our above-listed categories, see Paramount Lithographic Plate Service, Inc. v. Hughes Printing Co., 2 Pa. D. & C.3d 677, 22 UCC 1129 (Com. Pl. 1977), aff'd, 249 Pa.Super. 625, 377 A.2d 1001 (1977) (buyer of lithographic plates breached an exclusive requirements contract before it was operative; seller entitled to lost profits because the only available proof of seller's damages was a reconstruction of the work which was to be done under the contract); Colorado Interstate Gas Co. v. Natural Gas Pipeline Co. of America, 661 F.Supp. 1448, 4 UCC2d 668 (D.Wyo.1987), aff'd in part, rev'd in part, 885 F.2d 683 (10th Cir.1989) (court allowed recovery under

2–708(2) where a market price could not be determined under 2–708(1)). One court partially relied on 2–708 for awarding damages to a buyer caused by seller's breach of warranty. AGF, Inc. v. Great Lakes Heat Treating Co., 51 Ohio St.3d 177, 555 N.E.2d 634, 11 UCC2d 859 (1990).

These cases confirm our view that 2–708(2) is an elastic section that will accommodate considerable growth and development.

4. Study Committee at 211.

5. Task Force Report, 16 Dela. J.Corp.L. 981, 1222–23 (1991).

6. 962 F.2d 1119, 17 UCC2d 730 (3d Cir.1992), cert. dismissed, 506 U.S. 1042, 113 S.Ct. 834, 122 L.Ed.2d 111 (1992).

entered into a joint development agreement to create a new product (Retrosil) capable of removing PCBs from electrical transformers. Subsequently, the parties entered into a five-year (1982–86) supply agreement whereby Dow Corning agreed to purchase all of its requirements of Retrosil control stations and absorber units from Tigg, and Tigg agreed to supply only to Dow Corning, provided Dow Corning purchased the minimum quantities specified in the agreements. Dow Corning purchased the minimum quantity in 1982, but failed to do so in 1983, and suspended purchases altogether in April 1984. Dow Corning eventually terminated the contract.

The jury found that Dow Corning had breached the contract by failing to purchase the minimum quantities and awarded lost profits of $10 million under 2–708(2). The Third Circuit remanded for a new trial on damages, holding that the trial judge improperly instructed the jury. The instructions failed to state that the jury could award lost profits only if it determined that damages under 2–708(1) were inadequate. According to the court, damages under 2–708(1) would be inadequate *only* if the seller proved either that it had lost volume or that the product was a specialty product. Tigg argued that no market existed for Retrosil from which to calculate a market price.[7] Dow Corning had also argued (on another issue) that Retrosil was a failed product, rejected by the market. Nevertheless, the court held that neither it nor the trial court could determine that damages under 2–708(1) were inadequate as a matter of law.

This case is precisely the type that concerns the Study Group because of the risk that 2–708(1) would grossly over or under compensate Tigg. Retrosil was developed by the parties for the exclusive sale to Dow Corning. Dow Corning presumably influenced the final product to a great extent under the joint development agreement. (For instance, Retrosil was intended to be used with Dow Corning's chemicals.) Retrosil certainly seems to fit the description of a specialty product. Moreover, Retrosil never effectively penetrated the market. Therefore, to calculate damages under 2–708(1), the court could either conclude that no market existed for the product—so a market price of $0 and a windfall for Tigg—or perhaps use the cost of a similar device which performed the same function as Retrosil in a different manner to set the market price. The latter scheme might result in a finding of no damages to Tigg. The Study Group's recommendation would direct the use of 2–708(2) in this situation. Section 2–708(2) would award Tigg the minimum amount it anticipated earning from this venture—its per unit profit multiplied by the minimum quantities for each year.

7. The court also found that under an exclusive dealing arrangement such as that between Tigg and Dow Corning, Dow Corning assumed responsibility to use best efforts to develop the market.

Following existing law, the Third Circuit had to remand the case for Tigg to prove that 2–708(1) damages would be inadequate.[8]

Amended 2–708(2) omitted the last two phrases in subsection 2: "due allowance for costs reasonably incurred," and "due credit for payment or proceeds of resale." Those phrases work fine when the seller is quitting and selling off a partially completed project for scrap, but impede the route to the right result when the seller completes and sells completed goods to a third party. The comments to Amended 2–708(2) explain the reason for the changes and noted that the changes were merely a repair project to take account of the case where the seller has completed goods on hand. Comment 5 makes clear that a seller who would be incapable of making or, for any reason, would not have made both the sale contracted for and the replacement sale in the absence of breach, does not have lost volume and that a recovery under 2–706 or 2–708(1) would be adequate. Thus, the Drafters of Amended 2–708 did not accept the invitations of the Study Committee or the Task Force to make significant changes in 2–708(2).

§ 8–12 Lost Profits, Section 2–708(2)—Is 2–708(1) Ever Too Generous?

Can the defendant ever restrict the plaintiff to 2–708(2)? The case might arise when the defendant argues that the seller's direct costs (all saved) would have equalled the contract price and argues therefore that the seller should recover none of the contract-market differential. We believe that the defendant should be permitted to restrict the plaintiff to 2–708(2) in those circumstances in which the defendant-buyer can show that 2–708(1) will overcompensate the plaintiff. This position is consistent with the basic damage philosophy of the Code at least insofar as it is stated in 1–106: to put the plaintiff in the same economic position performance would have and not in a better one.[1]

8. Another instance in which 2–708(2) is used to award lost profit is Sons of Thunder, Inc. v. Borden, Inc., 148 N.J. 396, 690 A.2d 575, 32 UCC2d 66 (1997), rev'ing Sons of Thunder, Inc v. Borden, Inc., 285 N.J.Super. 27, 666 A.2d 549, 29 UCC 2d 33 (1995) (lost profits under 2–708(2) appropriate when breaching party breached the implied covenant of good faith and fair dealing); section 2–708(2) is available when the goods are so specialized that they have no resale value. See Purina Mills, L.L.C. v. Less, 295 F.Supp.2d 1017, 52 UCC2d 310 (N.D. Iowa 2003).

§ 8–12

1. This position was supported by both the UCC Study Group and the ABA Task Force.

An analogous damage problem occurs when a plaintiff sues on a losing contract in the construction industry. Assume that a builder sues for breach of a $50,000 contract. He estimated his profit at $10,000 when he began the project and spent $30,000 toward completion. If the cost to finish the project was $10,000, the damages that the builder should receive are his out of pocket expenses plus the profit he would have made ($30,000 + $10,000 = $40,000). But if the cost to finish the project is

Most damaging to the proposition that a seller may be forced into 2–708(2) are arguments from the language and from the statutory history of 2–708(2). In the first place the preamble to 2–708(2) states that it is available when the measure of damage in subsection (1) is "inadequate" to put the seller in as good a position, etc. On its face it does not consider the possibility that the measure in subsection (1) may be more than adequate. Secondly, it is clear from Code history that the plaintiffs foremost in the drafters' minds were those not sufficiently compensated by 2–708(1);[2] we find no mention in the New York Law Revision Commission Reports or elsewhere of the plaintiff to whom 2–708(1) is too generous.

It is possible that the drafters believed that plaintiffs in general are too little rewarded and breachers too little deterred. If that was their philosophy, it is conceivable that they regarded 2–708(1) as a liquidated damage clause available to the plaintiff irrespective of its actual damage. That position of course is inconsistent with the philosophy stated in 1–305. We prefer Comment 1 to 1–305 of Revised Article 1 (formerly Comment 1 to 1–106):

> * * * compensatory damages are limited to compensation. They do not include consequential or special damages, or penal damages; and the Act elsewhere makes it clear that damages must be minimized.[3]

We are unpersuaded by the need to have a liquidated damage clause; we suspect that damage formulas play a minimal part in the decisions of business people who are deciding whether to break a contract. For that reason we reject breach deterrence as an impor-

---

$25,000, then he would have lost $5,000 ($50,000 (contract price) − $55,000 (cost)) if no breach had occurred. In our view the damages the builder should receive with a losing contract should be limited by the total contract price minus the estimated cost to finish the structure ($50,000 − $25,000 = $25,000). This would leave the builder $5,000 in the red ($30,000 (costs already incurred) − $25,000 (damages awarded)) which is where he would be if the other party had not breached. For more detailed discussion, see Jones, Farnsworth & Young, Cases and Materials on Contracts 669–73 (1965); Patterson, Builder's Measure of Recovery for Breach of Contract, 31 Colum.L.Rev. 1286 (1931).

2. Patterson, 1 N.Y.State Law Revision Comm'n, 1955 Report 694 (1955).

3. Consider the seller's consequential damages problem. Suppose seller has a contract with buyer under which the buyer agrees to distribute the seller's goods. Buyer-distributor breaches the contract, and seller loses profits because it takes a year to find another distributor in the same market to sell the goods. In some ways the problem resembles an aggravated version of the lost volume problem considered in 8–9 *supra*. So far as we are able to tell, the Code does not contemplate a seller's recovery of consequential damages. (See § 1–305, Comment 1.) But see discussion 8–16 *infra*. However, it seems only fair that in the case posed the seller should receive consequential damages. One possible way to give consequential damages to the seller is to interpret the "profit" language in 2–708(2) very broadly. Doubtless, though, this stretches 2–708(2) well beyond the intention of the drafters.

tant factor in choosing damage formulae and would choose that formula which best approximates the actual economic loss.

We believe that the plaintiff seller, having proved the contract-market differential, should not be ousted from that recovery unless the defendant proves that it overcompensates the seller. Putting that burden on the defendant will doubtless foreclose any chance of buyer's victory in many cases. In the first place, the defendant will have to prove its case largely from the records of the plaintiff and out of the mouths of the plaintiff's employees. In the second place, the best available evidence in many cases will still not demonstrate that the contract-market differential under 2–708(1) is too generous, for such a finding would depend upon acts not done and decisions never made.

Consider two major cases. In the first, Nobs Chemical, USA, Inc. v. Koppers Co., Inc.,[4] Koppers contracted to buy 1,000 metric tons of cumene, an additive for high octane motor fuel, at $540 per ton. Nobs, an intermediary, arranged to purchase this cumene from a Brazilian supplier at $445 per ton. Apparently Nobs had a requirements contract with its Brazilian supplier. When Koppers breached the contract, Nobs did not buy cumene from its Brazilian supplier (its requirements were reduced) and it sued Koppers for the contract-market differential under 2–708(1).

At the time of breach the market price had dropped from $264 to $220 per ton. Thus the damage award under 2–708(1) could have been as high as $320,000, compared with $95,000 of lost profit. In an opinion that squarely confronts the conflict between 2–708(1) and (2) and deals with the language that would appear to prohibit the outcome, the Fifth Circuit concluded that Nobs' recovery should be limited to $95,000. Consistent with old 1–106, the lost profits recovery placed Nobs in the position it would have been in had the parties fully performed the contract:

> Had the transaction been completed, their "benefit of the bargain" would not have been affected by the fall in market price, and they would not have experienced the windfall they otherwise would receive if the market price-contract price rule [contained in 2–708(1) were] followed.[5]

We concur with the court's analysis. Two recent cases, Diversified Energy, Inc. v. Tennessee Valley Authority[6] and Purina Mills v. Less[7] agree with our analysis and follow the Nob's Chemical case.

---

4. 616 F.2d 212, 28 UCC 1039 (5th Cir.1980), reh'g denied, 618 F.2d 1389 (5th Cir.1980). Accord Union Carbide Corp. v. Consumers Power Co., 636 F.Supp. 1498, 1 UCC2d 1202 (E.D.Mich. 1986).

5. 616 F.2d at 215, 28 UCC at 1043.

6. 339 F.3d 437 (6th Cir. 2003).

7. 295 F.Supp.2d 1017, 52 UCC2d 310 (N.D. Iowa 2003).

The second major case, Trans World Metals, Inc. v. Southwire Co.,[8] more fully reveals the complexity of the problem and the weight of the defendant's burden. There the buyer broke its contract to purchase a large quantity of aluminum when the market price dropped. The Second Circuit affirmed the district court's award under 2–708(1) of damages in excess of $7,000,000. On appeal, the buyer had argued that seller's lost profits were less than the 2–708(1) award would be and that the seller should be restricted to its recovery under 2–708(2). The court rejected that argument first by expressing skepticism about whether 2–708(2) was ever designed to restrict the recovery under 2–708(1) and second by concluding there was no evidence that the plaintiff had been overcompensated by its 2–708(1) award. The court distinguished *Nobs Chemical* by pointing out that

> Nobs had entered into a second fixed price contract with its own supplier for purchase of the goods to be sold under the contract sued upon; its "market price" thus had been fixed in advance by contract * * *. [I]t would have been unfair to permit the seller to reap a riskless benefit.[9]

Without endorsing all of the reasoning in *Trans World v. Southwire* and unaware of facts not reported in the appellate opinion, it is easy to agree with the court's conclusion. There is no indication in the appellate opinion that the buyer had proved or offered to prove that the inevitable, or even most probable, consequence of performance would have been a profit less than the contract-market differential. We do not know whether the seller is a manufacturer or merely a middleman. Nor do we know what arrangements the seller had with upstream suppliers. Given such uncertainty, it would hardly be fair to the seller for the court to conclude that 2–708(1) overcompensated.

Consider some variation based on *Trans World*. First, the seller might already have owned the goods, and thus would have had to resell them at the lower prevailing price. The subsections 2–708(1) and 2–708(2) produce almost identical outcomes. That is to say, if the contract were at $5 per unit, the market at $2 per unit and the buyer had purchased or produced at $3 per unit, it could recover $3 under 2–708(1) (5 minus 2) or it could recover its lost profit of $3 under 2–708(2): $2 (5 minus 3) plus the cost expended, $3, minus resale ($2, current market).

The second possibility is that the seller neither produced nor purchased the goods nor made a contract to do so. Then the seller is entitled to the 2–708(1) recovery because it could have purchased at the lower market price ($2) and resold at its contract price ($5).

---

8. 769 F.2d 902, 41 UCC 453 (2d Cir.1985).

9. *Id.* at 908, 41 UCC at 461.

The court suggests that this scenario is the correct one. It found in *Trans World* that buyer had accepted the risk that the market price would fall while the seller took the risk that the market price would rise. Thus, the seller was entitled to the benefit of its bet as well as its bargain.

To summarize, the plaintiff-seller should be denied 2–708(1) recovery only when the buyer is able to show that events had foreclosed the seller's use of the lower market price to satisfy the contract. In a case such as *Nobs Chemical* the market is not the true substitute price because Nobs' requirements contract foreclosed its use of the lower market price as a means of satisfying its contract with Koppers (or with any other party during the relevant time). That does not appear to have been the case with the seller in *Trans World*. Absent such a showing by the buyer, the case is correct.[10]

We agree that 1–305 favors application of 2–708(2) if 2–708(1) truly overcompensates. However, we would caution courts to analyze all the circumstances surrounding the transaction before concluding that 2–708(1) overcompensates. We would place the burden on the buyer's shoulders. If the buyer accepted the risk that market prices would fall, it ought fully to compensate the seller for winning the bet if market prices rise.

§ 8–13   Lost Profits, Section 2–708(2)—The Formula

In explaining how the formula of 2–708(2) actually works we focus mainly on the two sellers traditionally entitled to 2–708(2) treatment: (1) the lost volume seller and (2) the components seller and the jobber. The formula for the third group of sellers, those we have elegantly labeled "Other Cases," has been considered in our discussion above.

Since the statutory history of the Code and Comment 2 to 2–708 indicate that 2–708(2) was intended to provide an adequate remedy for the lost volume seller, it is surprising to find that the 2–708(2) formula strictly applied will not yield the correct recovery in many lost volume cases. That formula reads as follows:

> If the measure of damages provided in subsection (1) is inadequate to put the seller in as good a position as performance

10. See Purina Mills, L.L.C. v. Less, 295 F.Supp.2d 1017, 52 UCC2d 310 (N.D. Iowa 2003) (seller entered into agreement with third party to procure hogs at a fixed priced to resell to buyer; buyer breached and a few days later third party supplier extended an offer to buyer to buy out the remainder of the contract; buyer declined and sought contract/market differential under 2–708(1), which was larger than lost profits under 2–708(2) from buyer, which sought to limit seller to lost profits; court limited seller to lost profits, holding that UCC limits the non-breaching party's recovery to loss occasioned by breach and that non-breaching party cannot be put in a better position than he would have been had the breaching party performed).

would have done then the measure of damages is the profit (including reasonable overhead) which the seller would have made from full performance by the buyer, together with any incidental damages provided in this Article (Section 2–710), due allowance for costs reasonably incurred and due credit for payments or proceeds of resale.

Assume that Boeing has contracts for the sale of fifty 747's during the coming year. TWA, who had contracted to buy the third aircraft off the line, breaches its contract and Boeing sells that particular plane to UAL who had agreed to buy the fourth. Because of the breach Boeing sells only 49 aircraft during the year and loses one $3 million profit (its unit profit and overhead allocation per aircraft).

Boeing computes its 2–708(2) damages as follows:

	$2 million	(profit)
plus	1 million	(overhead)
plus	0	(incidental)
plus	0	(costs reasonably incurred)
		(all allocated to UAL and so saved)
minus	0	(credit for resale)
	$3 million	Damage

Ignoring the problems of defining "reasonable overhead" and "cost reasonably incurred," how does one answer TWA's argument: "You resold the 747 which you had manufactured for us and which you had labeled with our name to UAL for the same price which you were going to charge us. Therefore, we have the right under the 2–708(2) formula to 'due credit for payments or proceeds of resale.' "? Of course if one gives TWA due credit for the resale, the 2–708(2) formula produces a zero, and it will misfire in every other lost volume case.

TWA figures the damages as follows:

	$2 million	(profit)
plus	1 million	(overhead)
plus	0	(incidental)
plus	17 million	(costs reasonably incurred)
minus	20 million	(credit for resale)
	0	Damage

How does one meet this problem? Unfortunately there is no explanation for it, and there is no polished solution. As the formula is now written, it simply will not yield the recovery which all right-minded people would agree the lost volume seller should have.

Gross errors of the kind here committed by the drafters call for extraordinary solutions. We agree with Professor Harris: courts should simply ignore the "due credit" language in lost volume cases.[1] Only by ignoring that language can they apply 2–708(2) to put the Boeings of this world in the same position as performance would have. Note that the omission of part of the language from existing 2–708(2) in Amended 2–708 would have solved this problem.

What must a lost volume seller prove in order to win under 2–708(2)? First, the seller must prove that it is in fact a lost volume seller. In the words of Professor Harris:

> Resale results in loss of volume only if three conditions are met: (1) the person who bought the resold entity would have been solicited by the plaintiff had there been no breach and resale; (2) the solicitation would have been successful; and (3) the plaintiff could have performed that additional contract.[2]

Second, the seller must establish "the profit (including a reasonable overhead)." This phrase is likely to be the scene of bloody battles between the accountants of the various parties. One can expect no unanimity among accountants about what is overhead and what is not or about how the overhead is to be allocated to the seller's various contracts. We can give no assistance with those highly practical problems; we hope only to shed some light upon the principles embodied in the phrase. Presumably the Code gives the seller net profit after taxes plus that part of its fixed costs which the seller would have satisfied out of the proceeds from this contract. Courts should not be hesitant to award more than the plaintiff's net profit; a contract with a theoretical net profit of zero may nevertheless carry a substantial economic benefit to the contracting party.

Assume for example, that Boeing owes rent, state and local property taxes, and executive salaries. It will incur all of these costs whether it sells 50 airplanes or 100 airplanes. Any contract whose additional direct costs are less than the contract price will produce some cash flow to pay a share of the property taxes, salaries, and rent. Therefore any such contract has an economic benefit to Boeing even though there is a zero or negative "net profit" on it. Therefore, it is logical and also consistent with the policy of 1–305 to award the seller not only its net profit but also that pro rata

---

§ 8–13

1. Harris, A Radical Restatement of the Law of Seller's Damages: Sales Act and Commercial Code Results Compared, 18 Stan.L.Rev. 66 at 99. The Study Group recommends that this language be dropped in the redraft of lost profit for lost volume sellers. See Study Committee Report at 218.

2. Harris, A Radical Restatement of the Law of Seller's Damages: Sales Act and Commercial Code Results Compared, 18 Stan.L.Rev. 66, at 82. See also § 8–9.

share of its fixed costs which the broken contract would have satisfied.[3]

The 2–708(2) formula has three remaining parts. It permits the seller to recover "incidental damages" (2–710). This should offer no difficulty.[4] It authorizes "due credit for payments or proceeds of resale," a phrase which we have said above must be ignored if we are to reach the right outcome in lost volume cases. And it gives the seller "due allowance for costs reasonably incurred." This latter phrase will apparently give the seller, in addition to its profit and overhead, an amount equal to what it has expended for performance of the contract that will now be valueless. If, for example, Boeing had made a contract with a supplier for some equipment which TWA wished to have installed in the airplane but which was of no use to UAL, and Boeing had to pay a fee to be freed from that contractual obligation, that fee would be a cost reasonably incurred which it could charge against TWA.

The use of the 2–708(2) formula by the components seller can be illustrated by the "junk value, partially manufactured goods" situation, and here the formula set forth in subsection (2) works like a charm. One begins with the "profit," including reasonable overhead. To this add incidental damages as authorized by section 2–710. Then add "costs reasonably incurred" in the manufacturing, less the "payments or proceeds of resale" or salvage. In Chicago Roller Skate Manufacturing Co. v. Sokol Manufacturing Co.,[5] the court handled this problem with great facility although neither party argued the Code correctly. The buyer of skateboard wheel assemblies without commercial resale value repudiated its contract. Seller rebuilt the assemblies for use on roller skates and credited the buyer with the reasonable value of the salvaged goods. At trial the seller recovered the balance of the price ($4,285.00). On appeal by the buyer, however, the court recognized that under 2–708(2) the proper recovery should have been lost profits (determined by subtracting the salvage value) of $2,572.00 plus salvage expenses of

---

3. See Vitex Mfg. Corp. v. Caribtex Corp., 377 F.2d 795, 4 UCC 182 (3d Cir.1967) (overhead allowed in recovery of lost profit on contract to process imported cloth; although UCC was not controlling in the Virgin Islands when contract was formed, court stated its opinion based on Code's language); Nederlandse Draadindustrie NDI B.V. v. Grand Pre–Stressed Corp., 466 F.Supp. 846, 26 UCC 406 (E.D.N.Y.1979) (overhead allowed in recovery of lost profit on sale of steel), aff'd, 614 F.2d 1289 (2nd Cir.1979); Unique Systems, Inc. v. Zotos Int'l, Inc., 622 F.2d 373, 28 UCC 1340 (8th Cir.1980) (overhead allowed in recovery of lost profits on sale of hair spray even though product not successfully marketed at the time of trial); Automated Medical Laboratories, Inc. v. Armour Pharmaceutical Co., 629 F.2d 1118, 30 UCC 996 (5th Cir.1980) (overhead allowed in recovery of lost profit on sale of plasma).

4. See Neri v. Retail Marine Corp., 30 N.Y.2d 393, 285 N.E.2d 311, 334 N.Y.S.2d 165, 10 UCC 950 (1972) (seller's costs of storage, upkeep, finance charges and insurance allowed as incidental damages; attorney fees excluded).

5. 185 Neb. 515, 177 N.W.2d 25, 7 UCC 804 (1970).

$3,540.76 for a total of $6,112.76. However, since only the buyer had appealed, the court felt bound to affirm the lower court's finding of damages in the amount of $4,285.00.[6]

The jobber has no particular problems in using the formula set out in 2–708(2). There can be no resale, because by definition the jobber is without any goods to resell.[7]

Finally, how precise must a plaintiff's proof be if seller is to recover under section 2–708(2)? Although a number of courts have denied plaintiffs' claims under 2–708(2) because they did not prove their damages, neither these cases nor those that permit recovery treat the precision with which a plaintiff must prove lost profits or discuss the various attacks on a plaintiff's proof that defendant can mount. By and large these cases are joustings between the plaintiff's and the defendant's accountants. When the plaintiff has lost, it usually appears from the opinion that it simply offered no proof whatsoever from which the court could determine its damages.[8] But

6. A components seller might encounter problems under 2–708(2), if the aborted contract would have been a losing one. Assume, for example, that a seller has a contract that would cost $120,000 to complete and that the contract price is $100,000. Buyer breaches when seller has incurred $20,000 in costs, but seller is able to save all additional costs thanks to the breach. Seller then sues buyer under 2–708(2) and seeks to recover the $20,000 as "due allowance for costs reasonably incurred." Buyer responds that the contract would have been a loser (let us assume that there are no fixed costs such as depreciation, taxes, etc.) and that the "profit" term in 2–708(2) should be interpreted as including losses, as negative profits, and that the $20,000 which the seller would have lost had the contract been performed must be subtracted. Thus the buyer argues the damages ($0 in this case) will put seller in the same position as performance would have put it. Buyer's argument finds some support from the theory that the damage formula is only meant to put the seller in the position that performance would have and no better. (See § 1–106(1)). For another statement of the problem, see Peters, Remedies for Breach of Contracts Relating to the Sale of Goods Under the Uniform Commercial Code: A Roadmap for Article 2, 73 Yale L.J. 199, 274 (1963). Reynolds Metals Co. v. Electric Smith Constr. & Equip. Co., 4 Wash.App. 695, 483 P.2d 880 (1971), lends some support

to buyer's argument, although the damages were computed under Restatement of Contracts § 333 (1932) rather than under 2–708(2). Electric Smith had a contract to build a bus assembly for a Reynolds aluminum plant at a price of approximately $1.4 million. Reynolds cancelled because of production delays, but the court found that Reynolds had "substantially and materially" contributed to the delay. The damages awarded by the trial court and affirmed by the Washington Court of Appeals were computed as approximately: $376,000 (net costs incurred by Electric Smith less credit for buyer's payments and resale of materials and equipment) minus $30,000 ($50,000 projected loss on contract, prorated on an "apportionment of fault" theory). Seller's total award for damages was thus $346,000.

7. The jobber formula is explored in Stamtec, Inc. v. Anson Stamping Co., LLC, 346 F.3d 651, 51 UCC2d 1048 (6th Cir. 2003) (jobber's measure of damages under 2–708 (2) when it has no responsibility for delivery costs to buyer is gross profits with no reduction for overhead, when jobber must pay for delivery to buyer, the measure of damages under 2–708(2) is gross profits (no reduction) for overhead minus saved delivery cost).

8. Cf., Roboserve, Ltd. v. Tom's Foods, Inc., 940 F.2d 1441, 20 U.S.P.Q.2d 1321, 16 UCC2d 987 (11th Cir.1991) (seller must prove "track record" of profitability before it can seek future profits; other evidence, however,

when the plaintiff has offered such proof, the courts have not been unduly finicky[9] about the sufficiency of the proof, although they sometimes quibble about the method of calculation.[10]

Although they have not yet been discussed in appellate opinions, fine spun burden of proof and causation issues can arise in 2–708(2) cases. In these cases each side is armed with the testimony of accountants, economists, and other experts, to prove profit, overhead, due credit, etc. Here, as in the proof of 2–708(1) damages, there are limits on the burden we would impose upon sellers. In some circumstances a plaintiff seller may be such a large player in a limited market that its lost volume—its ceasing production of the commodity—would have a measurable effect upon the general market for that product or for downstream products composed of or derived from that product.

Assume, for example, that a large and long-term purchaser from U.S. Steel broke its contract and that U.S. Steel closed down a major line for a specialty steel. If U.S. Steel had other plants that produced that same product or a derivative product, it is conceivable that its lost profit would be less than the loss attributable to the loss of the single contract. That could be so because of the value of its continuing supply and of the derivative products from that supply would increase because the overall supply had been reduced by the closing of the single plant. We suspect such consequences are so remote that the courts should rarely take them into account. As we indicate in section 8–14 below, we would put the burden on the defendant buyer to prove these consequences.

So ends the saga of 2–708(2). It is a section of great promise. It began life as a graft on 2–708(1), bloomed before it was enacted into law, and was finally enacted in such a weird mutation that it now barely accommodates some of the cases for which it was originally designed.

§ 8–14 Lost Profits and the Economists

Section 2–708(2) and the prospect of a seller's recovery of lost profits have attracted the attention of a fair number of lawyer

may be admissible if it establishes a reasonable means for calculating future profits). See P.F.I., Inc. v. Kulis, 363 N.J.Super. 292, 832 A.2d 931, 51 UCC2d 926 (App. Div. 2003) (in absence of evidence of lost profits, seller's own testimony of lost profits not sufficient proof).

9. See Anchorage Centennial Development Co. v. Van Wormer & Rodrigues, Inc., 443 P.2d 596, 5 UCC 811 (Alaska 1968) (recovery of lost profits allowed for breach of contract to purchase specially manufactured gold coins for municipal celebration).

10. See, e.g., Cyril Bath Co. v. Winters Industries, 892 F.2d 465, 10 UCC2d 725 (6th Cir.1989). Seller calculated lost profits by taking the total manufacturing costs and dividing by the units shipped, including units from inventory which had been expensed in another period. The court affirmed the district court's method of dividing the manufacturing costs for two quarters by the number of units manufactured during those quarters.

economists. Some defend 2–708(2);[1] others are mostly critical.[2] Although these arguments have not yet found their way into the cases to any substantial degree, they merit the lawyer's attention. Some assume facts that seem so unlikely to exist that they can be dismissed in most cases. Others involve a misconstruction of 2–708(2). Still others suggest modifications of the section.

For the most part the arguments set out below come from Goetz and Scott, Measuring Seller's Damages: the Lost Profits Puzzle.[3] That article is the most comprehensive statement of the criticisms one might make of the lost profits recovery from the economists' viewpoint, where the recovery is based on loss of volume. In general, Goetz and Scott argue that routine awards of lost profits on this basis will overcompensate the plaintiff. They point to several reasons why that might be so.

Initially, section 2–708(2) may overcompensate because the court computes the lost profit by assuming that the buyer (but for the breach) would have taken the goods and then disappeared from the seller's market. That assumption is not necessarily true. Assume, for example, that the aggrieved seller is Boeing and the subject of the sale was a 747. Having no need for the 747, the buyer nevertheless went through with the contract in the face of Boeing's threat of suit. The buyer might then resell the 747 in competition with Boeing itself. If that happened, Boeing might lose a sale or alternatively it might be forced to sell its remaining 747s at a lower price than would otherwise prevail. If the 2–708(2) formula assumes that, but for the breach, the buyer would have taken the 747 and put it in use in a market unrelated to the one in which Boeing was selling, allowing a full lost profit recovery overcompensates. At least in the setting such as Neri v. Retail Marine Corp.[4] where the subject of the lost sale was a boat to be sold in a retail sale, Professor Goldberg points out that it is unlikely that the consumer-buyer could have taken the boat and competed effectively in the seller's market.

§ 8–14

1. Goldberg, An Economic Analysis of the Lost Volume Retail Seller, 57 S.Cal.L.Rev. 283 (1984); Cooter & Eisenberg, Damages for Breach of Contract, 73 Cal.L.Rev. 1432 (1985) (Cooter and Eisenberg argue that lost volume formula is appropriate for sellers operating by "the fishing model," but a much smaller measure is appropriate for sellers who sell off the lot goods to consumers.).

2. Goetz & Scott, Measuring Seller's Damages: The Lost–Profits Puzzle, 31 Stan.L.Rev. 323 (1979).

3. 31 Stan.L.Rev. 323 (1979). Later Professor Scott argued that courts awarding lost profits unduly focus on contractual expectations at the time for performance rather than at the time of contracting. He urges courts not to decide that 2–708(1) over or under compensates, but determine how the parties expressly or impliedly allocated market risks at the time of contracting. See Scott, The Case for Market Damages: Revisiting the Lost Profits Puzzle, 57 U.Chi.L.Rev. 1155 (1990).

4. 30 N.Y.2d 393, 334 N.Y.S.2d 165, 285 N.E.2d 311, 10 UCC 950 (1972).

On the other hand, where the breaching buyer is both a buyer and seller of a commodity and where there are a limited number of players in the market, the Goetz and Scott argument carries more weight. There it is conceivable, even likely, that had the contract gone through, the use by the particular buyer of the commodity would have affected the availability of other buyers and the price at which they would have been willing to buy.

Assume that our seller is a steel manufacturer who sells sheet steel but who also sells fabricated steel parts. The buyer is a fabricator who buys steel from our seller and from others. After the buyer fabricates the steel, it competes with the seller for the market in fabricated goods. Assume furthermore that there are only five sellers of these products in the country. Because of a change in the market, the buyer wishes to get out of the contract but the seller refuses to let the buyer do so.

Assume the buyer either goes through with the contract despite its lack of enthusiasm, or it breaches. If the buyer goes through with the contract, presumably, it buys the steel, pays the contract price, fabricates and sells it on the market in competition with the original seller. The presence of that steel in the market attracts potential buyers away from the original seller's fabricated steel and reduces the price the original seller can obtain for its fabricated steel.

If, on the other hand, the buyer breaches the contract (does not buy the sheet steel), the original seller's loss would probably be less than its total lost profit on the contract. Why is that? That is because buyer will no longer be competing in the fabricated steel market, at least to the same extent that it would otherwise. Thus, presumably, our seller will find more buyers at a higher price for its fabricated steel. In this circumstance one can argue that a routine application of 2–708 will overcompensate the seller. It will give the seller more dollars in its pocket than the seller would have had if the contract had been performed.

There is a second way in which blind application of the lost profit formula might overcompensate the aggrieved seller. The lost sales could possibly have been at significantly lower profit margins than earlier ones. This could be so where the marginal cost of the foregone sales would have been higher than those of the sales made. Assume, for example, that seller can produce 100,000 tons of steel at $4 per ton. Starting with the 100,001 tons, the cost per ton jumps to $6 per ton because the seller has to put on an overtime crew and use obsolete facilities. If, in computing lost profit, one assumed that the lost volume would produce a profit on the tonnage after the first 100,000 identical to the profit produced on the first 100,000, we would overcompensate the plaintiff and give it more as damages than it would have lost as a result of the breach.

A third possibility is that the breach will cause no lost volume at all, particularly in circumstances where there is a relatively flat demand curve. Assume a case in which there is a demand for 100,000 tons of steel at the price of $12 per ton. If the price were lowered to $11 the demand would increase by another 200,000 tons. If the seller's marginal costs rise gradually and pass above $11 just after the 100,000th ton, the seller may lose no volume. That is to say, tonnage that would have gone to the last breaching buyer will now go to the next person in line at $11 not at $12. What the seller will lose is the difference between $11 and $12, the proper measure of compensation under 2–706.

Why will the seller make the sale to this last buyer when there has been a breach but not otherwise? Presumably the seller does so because the original breach now made available on one order of low-cost steel that could be sold profitably to a buyer at $11, but if that steel could have been sold to the original breaching buyer, and if the next 100,000 tons would have been produced at a cost higher than $11 yet could not be sold at a profit to one who is willing to pay $11 but not $12.

All of the above economic theories make sense in some settings and no sense in others. How should the court deal with these arguments? How should lawyers and courts handle them? We believe that courts should handle most of these arguments in much the same way as we suggested in regard to *Nobs Chemical*, namely, by allocating the burden of proof. Because we are persuaded that lost profits under 2–708(2) is the proper and best measure of damages in the large majority of cases, we would demand only that the plaintiff prove its basic case under 2–708(2). If the defendant is then able to prove that the lost profits are overstated because the breaching buyer would have sold the goods in competition with the seller, or because the marginal cost curve was rising rapidly at the point of breach,[5] or that there was no lost volume because of the flat demand curve and because a sale was made that would not have been made because of the breach, then the damages should be reduced accordingly.

In general, we believe the burden of proving these possible limitations on 2–708(2) should be on the defendant. Only the defendant will know its behavior in the absence of breach and what facts can be raised as a defense. We think it is inappropriate to ask

---

5. The ABA Task Force apparently would place the burden on the lost volume seller to prove it would have made the second sale absent the breach. The seller, under this approach would be required to prove that the next sale would be profitable. We are not opposed to this approach once buyer successfully raises the unprofitability of the sale as an issue. For a case which adopts this approach see R.E. Davis Chemical Corp. v. Diasonics, Inc., 826 F.2d 678, 4 UCC2d 369 (7th Cir.1987).

the plaintiff to prove the absence of every single potential defense suggested by the economic literature.

§ 8–15　Seller's Rights and Obligations With Respect to Unidentified and Incomplete Goods, Section 2–704

Some of the most trying moments in a commercial lawyer's practice are likely to occur when her best client, a seller who has received a repudiation, asks what his rights and obligations are with respect to the uncompleted goods. One can hear the questions of the client who expects and deserves a clear and accurate response: "Am I legally obliged to complete? If I choose not to complete, what damages may I recover? If I complete, can I get my added costs out of the buyer's hide? If I choose to complete, will I lose any rights that I would otherwise have? If I choose not to complete, will I lose any rights I would otherwise have?" Section 2–704 gives some answers, though not necessarily certain ones, to these important practical questions. It reads in full as follows:

> (1) An aggrieved seller under the preceding section may
>
> > (a) identify to the contract conforming goods not already identified if at the time he learned of the breach they are in his possession or control;
> >
> > (b) treat as the subject of resale goods which have demonstrably been intended for the particular contract even though those goods are unfinished.
>
> (2) Where the goods are unfinished an aggrieved seller may in the exercise of reasonable commercial judgment for the purposes of avoiding loss and of effective realization either complete the manufacture and wholly identify the goods to the contract or cease manufacture and resell for scrap or salvage value or proceed in any other reasonable manner.[1]

Subsection (1) is comparatively free of difficulty. Subsection (1)(a) authorizes identification of conforming goods on hand on the date the seller learns of the breach, and (1)(b) authorizes resale of unfinished goods. Upon resale the seller will be permitted to recover the difference between the contract price and the resale price plus 2–710 incidental damages but less any expenses which it saved because it did not complete.

The questions which challenge the lawyer's skill lurk in subsection (2). Consider the troublesome language: "[S]eller may in the

§ 8–15

1. Restatement (Second) of Contracts § 350(2) reflects the policy underlying 2–704 of encouraging the injured party to make reasonable efforts to avoid loss. Like 2–704, § 350 protects the injured party if such reasonable efforts fail.

exercise of reasonable commercial judgment * * * either complete the manufacture * * * or cease manufacture and resell for scrap or salvage value * * *." The quoted language suggests at least three lawyer-questions: (1) By what standard does one measure "reasonable commercial judgment," and when does one make that judgment? (2) If the seller completes pursuant to a decision which is later found to be commercially unreasonable, what ill consequences will it suffer? (3) Does the section ever oblige a seller to complete?

The comments give some assistance on the first question. First, they make clear that the burden is on the buyer to prove that seller failed to use reasonable commercial judgment.[2] Second, they point out that the decision is to be measured according "to the facts as they appear at the time he learns of the breach,"[3] not by hindsight after the market has changed in an unforeseen way. Third, the comments offer "damages suffered" as a preliminary litmus test to determine which alternative is the way of reasonable commercial judgment.[4] Hence, if a seller is confronted with a repudiation after very little work under the contract and would, if he then sued, recover a $2,000 profit under 2–708(2), the seller acts unreasonably if he completes manufacture at a total cost of $10,000 when he knows that the finished goods will bring less than $8,000. By completing with such knowledge the seller has inflated his damages from $2,000 to an amount greater than $2,000 and, presumptively at least, has acted in a commercially unreasonable manner.

Therefore, the first question which the lawyer should ask is what damages the seller may recover from the buyer if he ceases manufacturing at once and sues under 2–708(2) for lost profit. Next, how do those damages compare with the damages the seller is likely to recover under 2–706 upon completion of the manufacture and the resale of the goods? It is not enough to do good legal analysis. One must also make careful empirical judgments about the current and future market and about the seller's lost profit. And the lawyer and client should preserve evidence which formed the basis for the decision and document by letter or contemporaneous memoranda when and why the decision to complete or not to complete was made.

Additional factors may occasionally complicate the decision about the commercial reasonableness of completion. Suppose the

2. § 2–704, Comment 2:

* * * The burden is on the buyer to show the commercially unreasonable nature of the seller's action in completing manufacture.

3. § 2–704, Comment 2:

Under this Article the seller is given express power to complete manufacture or procurement of goods for the contract unless the exercise of reasonable commercial judgment as to the facts as they appear at the time he learns of the breach makes it clear that such action will result in a material increase in damages.

4. *Id.*

client says the damages on this contract will probably be enhanced by completing, but that he cannot afford to cease manufacture, lay off skilled employees, and lose many of them to other employers. Surely such a seller is making an intelligent and commercially reasonable judgment to complete even though he may increase the damages to this particular buyer. In such circumstances we should permit the seller to complete and should not find his action commercially unreasonable.[5]

In summary, the general standard, though not the exclusive one, is to compare two quantities: "What are my damages if I stop now?" against "What are my damages if I complete and resell?" If the former is greater than the latter, completion is commercially reasonable. Recall that the burden is on the buyer to show the absence of commercial reasonableness and that the test is to be applied at the time of the repudiation, not by hindsight at the time of trial.

Recognizing that section 2–704 gives the seller a right to complete in certain circumstances, does it also oblige the seller to do so when a commercially reasonable seller would complete? The title to 2–704 speaks of the seller's "right" to complete or to cease manufacture, but subsection (2) simply says that the seller may in the exercise of reasonable commercial judgment complete or not complete. The comments, on the other hand, deal principally with the problem of the seller who has completed, and who is faced by the buyer who argues that the completion was commercially unreasonable. Thus one who reads just 2–704 and its comments is left in doubt about whether the drafters intended ever to oblige a seller to complete manufacture; the body of the Code points toward an obligation to complete in some cases, while the comments do not.

Reading 2–704 as consistent with the general rules of mitigation, we interpret it to mean that the seller must exercise commercially reasonable judgment not only when he decides to complete, but also when he decides not to. That is, if it is not commercially reasonable to cease manufacture, we would find that 2–704 obliges the seller to complete manufacture or to suffer the consequences. Although we have found no cases in which a seller ceased manufacture and was later denied recovery of damages initially suffered on the ground he could have avoided those damages by completing, the

---

5. The court agreed with this proposition in O'Hare v. Peacock Dairies, 26 Cal.App.2d 345, 79 P.2d 433 (1938). Plaintiff agreed to sell all of the milk he produced for ten years to the defendant. However, when the market price dropped after four years the defendant breached. Although continuing to produce milk enhanced damages, the court held that plaintiff was not obliged to sell his herd and stop production. A similar case was presented in Northern Helex Co. v. United States, 197 Ct.Cl. 118, 455 F.2d 546, 10 UCC 353 (1972), and 207 Ct.Cl. 862, 524 F.2d 707 (1975), cert. denied, 429 U.S. 866, 97 S.Ct. 176, 50 L.Ed.2d 146 (1976).

general doctrine of mitigation would oblige the seller to continue manufacture when it was clear that he could minimize his losses by doing so and when there was no other reason to justify stopping.[6]

Perhaps because the drafters thought it self-evident, the Code does not spell out the consequences to a seller acting in a commercially unreasonable way under 2–704. It would appear that the consequences under the Code are the same as those under the common law for failure to behave properly in mitigating damages.[7] In most circumstances even a seller who has made a foolish choice to complete should be entitled to the contract-market difference under 2–708(1). In effect that formula is a substitute for mitigation; it indulges in an assumption of resale, even in circumstances where seller did not complete.

However, there might be circumstances in which a plaintiff who completed unreasonably should be denied the damages he might otherwise enjoy. Assume a case in which the contract price is $5.00 and the market is $2.00. Seller completes the goods and resells them for $1.00. If the seller's completion is commercially unreasonable, presumably he should not recover the difference between $5.00 and $1.00 under 2–706, but should be limited to the difference between $5.00 and $2.00.

By the same token it is conceivable that some sellers should be limited to even smaller amounts when they complete. Assume a case in which a seller with a contract price of $5.00 completes at a cost of $6.00. Upon completion, the seller finds the goods cannot be sold, but must be scrapped for $.50. If the completion were commercially unreasonable, the seller, by his bullheaded behavior, has proved that the contract had a negative value. Here we would allow the defendant buyer to force the seller into 2–708(2) and to limit the seller's recovery to his realistically expected profit, $0. See Section 8–12 *supra*. Of course to preserve the usefulness of 2–704, the courts will have to be careful to place the burden on the buyer and to insist that the buyer come forward with persuasive evidence that the seller acted in a commercially unreasonable way before they foreclose seller from the right to complete or not to complete. Otherwise sellers, and particularly their lawyers, will grow even more timid than they are now, and 2–704 could become a dead letter. In Young v. Frank's Nursery & Crafts, Inc.,[8] Frank's had a contract to buy 360 tons of pine boughs from Young. In June

---

6. See Bead Chain Mfg. Co. v. Saxton Products, Inc., 183 Conn. 266, 439 A.2d 314, 31 UCC 91 (1981) (when buyer wrongfully rejected specially manufactured goods, seller had right to cease manufacture and sell materials for scrap value or to proceed in any commercially reasonable manner).

7. 11 S. Williston, Contracts § 1353 at 274–78 (3d ed.1968); 5 A. Corbin, Contracts § 1039 at 241–43 (1964).

8. 58 Ohio St.3d 242, 569 N.E.2d 1034, 14 UCC2d 463(1991), reh'g denied, 60 Ohio St.3d 705, 573 N.E.2d 673 (1991)

Frank's sent a new purchase order that reduced the total amount to 70 tons. Young estimated that the reduction would have had the effect of cutting the contract price from approximately $240,000 to less than $60,000. At the time he received the reduction, Young had already begun some preparations for the year's cutting. After the repudiation he contacted various alternative buyers but was unable to find anyone who would take anything like the quantity that Frank's had previously purchased. Young found that most of the other parties had already made contracts with other sellers by the time he contacted them in the summer of 1987. At trial the jury awarded damages of $132,902. The intermediate appellate court reversed on the ground that the trial court had erred in putting the burden of proving Young's decision commercially unreasonable on defendant Frank's. Citing White and Summers (with uncommon grace, as "respected commentators"), the Supreme Court reversed the intermediate appellate court, relying upon our argument to conclude that the burden is and should be on defendant to show that the plaintiff did not act in a commercially reasonable way when he proceeded under section 2–704. It is a good decision.

§ 8–16   Seller's Incidental and Consequential Damages, Section 2–710

Section 2–710 defines a seller's incidental damages and sections 2–706, 2–708 and 2–709 specifically provide for recovery of incidental damages by a seller. There are no comparable provisions allowing a seller to recover consequential damages.[1] One might think that the definition and recovery of incidental damages are completely ancillary to the other questions discussed in this chapter and so doctrinally straightforward as to merit no more than a moment's consideration. Were there separate provisions authorizing the seller's recovery of consequential damages, that would likely be true. But the absence of a provision allowing sellers to recover consequential damages has turned the question of when sellers may recover incidental damages into a difficult and hotly disputed issue. Knowing that a seller may be denied any recovery for damages labeled "consequential," a lawyer may dress the seller's consequential damages in the clothes of incidental damages to recover them.

a.   Incidental Damages

Before we examine the incidental-consequential problem, consider the routine and uncontroversial incidental damage cases. The list of items "incidental" to other recovery in 2–710 is merely

§ 8–16

1.   Sonfast Corp. v. York Int'l Corp.,
875 F.Supp. 1088, 24 UCC2d 811 (M.D.
Pa. 1994) (no consequentials for sellers).

illustrative, not exhaustive. In a straightforward application of 2–710, courts have allowed sellers to recover the cost of care and custody of unsold goods,[2] the cost of transporting goods after buyer's breach, and commissions paid on resale of contracted-for goods.[3] Each is either explicitly mentioned in 2–710 or an easy analogue of the categories in that section.

In Mexamerican Hides v. Central International Co.,[4] the seller of cow hides whose contract had been broken had a claim under 2–710 for interest. He lost for several reasons. First, he failed to show that the interest charges related "in any way" to the breach of the contract for 1500 cow hides. Second, he failed to show that any interest charges were incurred after the breach and not before; interest charges incurred before the breach would not constitute damages for breach. Third, any lost interest would in reality have been a consequential damage and consequential damages may not be recovered by sellers under Article 2.

Section 2–710 presents a few straightforward interpretive difficulties. Such damages must "result from the breach." Presumably that means, among other things, that items of expense incurred prior to the defendant's breach ordinarily cannot be caused by and therefore are not recoverable as incidental damages. For example, in Serna, Inc. v. Harman,[5] the seller sought incidental damages for the cost of feeding and maintaining several fancy Charolais cattle that were the subject of the contract. The court denied costs incurred prior to the time of breach. In a similar case, a seller of steel sought to recover the cost of moving the steel from place to place in its warehouse when its buyer failed to take delivery. To the extent the movement was dictated by special terms in an earlier lease of the steel warehouse to a third party, the court denied the added costs.[6]

---

2. See, e.g., Connor v. Bogrett, 596 P.2d 683, 26 UCC 902 (Wyo.1979); Cesco Mfg. Corp. v. Norcross, Inc., 7 Mass.App. Ct. 837, 391 N.E.2d 270, 27 UCC 126 (1979); Indeck Energy Services, Inc. et al. v. NRG Energy, Inc. et al., 2004 WL 2095554, 54 UCC2d 990 (N.D. Ill. 2004) (breaching buyer liable for transportation, storage, and maintenance costs incurred by seller after breach).

3. See, e.g., Peoria Harbor Marina v. McGlasson, 105 Ill.App.3d 723, 434 N.E.2d 786, 61 Ill.Dec. 431, 33 UCC 448 (1982); Berg v. Hogan, 322 N.W.2d 448, 34 UCC 505 (N.D.1982).

4. 2000 Mass.App.Div. 327, 43 UCC2d 587 (2000).

5. 742 F.2d 186, 39 UCC 481 (5th Cir.1984). See also, Smyers v. Quartz

Works Corp., 880 F.Supp. 1425, 27 UCC2d 142 (D. Kan. 1995) (seller not entitled to recover under 2–710 the cost of shipping goods to third party warehouse when the goods were sent there as a means of self help because the seller had yet to receive payment from buyer and was apprehensive about ever receiving payment; seller was not entitled to recover because the shipping charges "were not incident" to the buyer's repudiation). See Stamtec, Inc. v. Anson Stamping Co., LLC, 346 F.3d 651, 51 UCC2d 1048 (6th Cir. 2003) (seller cannot get storage costs incurred before buyer's breach under 2–710, but may recover such costs under 2–708).

6. Ernst Steel Corp. v. Horn Constr. Div., 104 A.D.2d 55, 481 N.Y.S.2d 833, 40 UCC 145 (1984).

More problematical is the limitation imposed in Associated Metals and Minerals Corp. v. Sharon Steel Corp.[7] In that case the buyer, Sharon, ultimately paid the entire contract price, but only after much jawboning and a long delay. The seller sought to recover interest for the delayed payment. Correctly pointing out that 2–710 does not itself authorize recovery but merely defines incidental damages, the court denied the recovery on the grounds that there were no damages in 2–706, 2–708 or 2–709 to which these damages could be "incidental." This may be an impeccable reading which leads to an unjust result. Presumably if the plaintiff had suffered one dollar of damage recoverable under 2–708, it could have attached $2,000,000 of interest costs "incidental" to that, but having lost no "general damage" dollars, it recovers no incidental damages. Perhaps the solution to the problem lies in the discussion below where we consider the possibility of granting consequential damage recoveries to sellers. But putting aside the consequential damages argument, we would read 2–706 and 2–708 more broadly to authorize the recovery of such damages even in which the main recovery under 2–708 might be zero.

In American law, attorneys' fees are a special problem. Any economist or accountant readily recognizes that the attorneys' fees a seller incurs when recovering his basic damage award are an incidental expense that ought to be recoverable. But any American lawyer would point to the traditional American rule under which a victorious party is not permitted to recover his attorneys' fees. In general, courts have concluded that the Code drafters did not intend to override the American rule through 2–710. Only when an otherwise effective agreement with the buyer grants such fees to the victorious side, or when a separate statute provides for their recovery, have the courts allowed them under 2–710.[8]

b. Consequential Damages

May the seller ever recover consequential damages for the breach of a sales contract? The answer in all appellate opinions that have discussed that question to date—at least the superficial answer—is "no." Consequential damages are specifically granted to the buyer under section 2–715. Section 1–305 states that consequential or other such damages are not available unless they are specifically provided for "in this Act or by other rule of law." Reading the explicit grant in 2–715 together with the restriction in 1–305, courts have concluded that the drafters did not intend to

7. 590 F.Supp. 18, 39 UCC 892 (S.D.N.Y.1983), aff'd, 742 F.2d 1431 (2d Cir.1983).

8. See Brownie's Army & Navy Store, Inc. v. E.J. Burke, Jr., Inc., 72 A.D.2d 171, 424 N.Y.S.2d 800, 28 UCC 90 (1980).

give the seller consequential damages.[9] The courts seem also to have concluded that the words "or otherwise resulting from the breach" in 2–710 itself do not authorize recovery of consequential damages.

We are not so certain of these conclusions. The drafters were far from perfect. In this very chapter we have seen how confused the drafters seem to have been about the proper aim and scope of 2–708(2) and how the various drafts vacillated from one idea to another. It is conceivable that an omission of any reference to a seller's consequential damages is attributable not to any intention to prohibit, but to a failure to contemplate their possibility. After all, seller's consequential damages are relatively rare. It is the buyer who routinely suffers consequential damages arising out of undelivered or defective products (in the form of lost resale profits, personal injury or worse). Usually, a seller can be made whole via a resale recovery under 2–706 or one of the recoveries under 2–708 or 2–709.

Yet the experience of the last 30 years has shown many instances in which the seller can and does suffer consequential damages. Consider, for example, Nobs Chemical, U.S.A., Inc. v. Koppers Co., Inc.[10] In that case the plaintiff seller was entitled to receive quantity discounts from its seller. When the buyer breached the contract, the total quantity for the year declined; thus the seller failed to achieve the quantity discount on other purchases that it would have enjoyed had the contract been performed. This seems clearly to be an item of damages attributable to the buyer's breach that should have been recovered by the seller. The court summarily denied the recovery.[11]

A second and commonplace item of damage that strains the incidental-consequential distinction is the seller's claim for added interest costs borne by him because the buyer did not make prompt payment. In that case, the seller may have specific and provable costs of money borrowed that he would not otherwise have borrowed. In other cases the seller's loss may be simply the lost opportunity to reinvest the money and so earn a return on it.

9. See, e.g., Petroleo Brasileiro, S.A., Petrobras v. Ameropan Oil Corp., 372 F.Supp. 503, 14 UCC 661 (E.D.N.Y. 1974); Nobs Chemical, U.S.A., Inc. v. Koppers Co., Inc., 616 F.2d 212, 28 UCC 1039, reh'g denied, 618 F.2d 1389 (5th Cir.1980); Firwood Mfg. Co. v. General Tire, Inc., 96 F.3d 163, 30 UCC2d 789 (6th Cir. 1996) (sellers do not get consequentials); Mexamerican Hides v. Central Int. Co., 2000 Mass.App.Div. 327, 43 UCC2d 587 (2000) (sellers no consequentials).

10. 616 F.2d 212, 28 UCC 1039, reh'g denied, 618 F.2d 1389 (5th Cir. 1980).

11. A harder case may be Colorado Interstate Gas Co. v. Natural Gas Pipeline Co. of America, 661 F.Supp. 1448, 4 UCC2d 668 (D.Wyo.1987), aff'd in part, rev'd in part, 885 F.2d 683 (10th Cir. 1989) (seller entitled to recover premium bill payments "to its supplier for goods that buyer refused to take").

A direct consequence of the uniform judicial stonewall of sellers' claims for consequential damages is that sellers seek to dress their large and hairy consequential damage claims into the petite garb of "incidental damages" so that they will fit under the categories in 2–710. This has now occurred in many cases involving interest costs resulting from the buyer's breach. Some courts, recognizing such claims for the large and hairy consequential damage claims they are, deny their recovery.[12] Other courts casting a blind eye on their true nature, or perhaps truly fooled by their new attire, have found these to be incidental.[13]

In one case, an able judge indicated that a payment (which could have been as large as $20,000,000) might constitute incidental damages. In Union Carbide Corp. v. Consumers Power Co.,[14] Union Carbide made payments to its seller to be freed from the obligation to purchase oil that its buyer, Consumers Power, refused to take. Quaere whether the drafters intended payments of that type and magnitude to be regarded as merely "incidental" to the main contract action? Since the seller in that case presumably could have recovered the same amount under 2–708(2) no damage was done. The case, however, is but another that poses the inevitable classificatory problems arising under the Code's damage categories; direct, incidental, or consequential. Sadly, the drafters' error in not expressly providing for seller's consequential damages leads to exactly the kind of practice that the principal draftsman, Karl Llewellyn, so despised—the resort to "covert" legal tools. It will be obvious to good judges that sellers in these circumstances deserve these recoveries if justice is to be done. Given nothing better, we suspect many judges will grant consequential recoveries under the rubric "incidental."

How should the courts confront the seller's consequential damages claim? The courts might use Section 1–305 and 1–103 as vehicles to allow sellers overtly to recover consequential damages. Section 1–103 incorporates general rules of contract law. Section 1–305 allows recovery of consequential damages if they are authorized

12. S.C. Gray, Inc. v. Ford Motor Co., 92 Mich.App. 789, 286 N.W.2d 34, 29 UCC 417 (1979). That case relied on the distinction between incidental and consequential damages made in Petroleo Brasileiro, S.A., Petrobras v. Ameropan Oil Corp., 372 F.Supp. 503, 14 UCC 661 (E.D.N.Y.1974). There the court defined consequential damages as those arising outside the "scope of the immediate buyer-seller transaction." Id. at 508, 14 UCC at 667. See also, Bill's Coal Co., Inc. v. Board of Public Utilities of Springfield, Mo., 887 F.2d 242, 9 UCC2d 1238 (10th Cir.1989) (seller not entitled to recover interest expense: "Incidental expenses include commercially reasonable expenses incurred in stopping delivery in the transportation, care, and custody of goods after the buyer's breach.").

13. See Atlas Concrete Pipe, Inc. v. Roger J. Au & Son, Inc., 467 F.Supp. 830, 26 UCC 395 (E.D.Mich.1979), rev'd sub nom. In re Atlas Concrete Pipe, Inc., 668 F.2d 905 (6th Cir.1982).

14. 636 F.Supp. 1498, 1 UCC2d 1202 (E.D.Mich.1986).

by this act or "by other rule of law." That general contract law now allows such recovery on behalf of a seller seems clear. The Restatement (Second) of Contracts section 347(b) allows any "injured party" to recover "any other loss, including incidental or consequential loss, caused by the breach." Comments to that section note that the policy is to put the injured party in as good a position as if the parties had performed. The comments specifically point out that the terms incidental or consequential are not "controlling," but that the principle is for "all losses, however described, [to be] recoverable." Moreover section 351 on consequential damages makes no distinction between buyer and seller, and refers to the "party in breach."[15]

At least one court has followed exactly that route. In Associated Metals and Minerals Corp. v. Sharon Steel Corp.,[16] Judge Motley concluded that the seller could not recover interest costs under the Uniform Commercial Code since they were consequential damages. The judge followed 1–103 into the common law of Pennsylvania where she found that such damages were recoverable. We would merely reformulate her statement of the conclusion, namely to find that such damages are recoverable under the Uniform Commercial Code on the ground that 1–103 makes the common law rules part of the Code.[17] Section 2–710 of Amended Article 2 would explicitly grant consequential as well as incidental damages to sellers.

c. Cost of Lost Opportunity

Inevitably the buyer's breach consists of or includes his failure to pay some or all of the price in a timely manner. It is therefore equally inevitable that seller will have lost the opportunity to use those funds. The seller may merely lose the return he would have achieved by an investment of the funds in his business, or the seller may incur a specific interest cost from having to replace the funds

---

15. Restatement (Second) of Contracts § 351 reads in part:

Unforeseeability and Related Limitations on Damages

(1) Damages are not recoverable for loss that the party in breach did not have reason to foresee as a probable result of the breach when the contract was made.

(2) Loss may be foreseeable as a probable result of a breach because it follows from the breach

   (a) in the ordinary course of events, or

   (b) as a result of special circumstances, beyond the ordinary course of events, that the party in breach had reason to know.

16. 590 F.Supp. 18, 39 UCC 892 (S.D.N.Y.1983), aff'd, 742 F.2d 1431 (2d Cir.1983).

17. See also Study Committee Report 203, 221. The ABA supports this recommendation. Task Force Report 16 Dela.J.Corp.L. 981, 1227 (1991). The UCC Study Group incorporates the foreseeability standard of Hadley v. Baxendale, 9 Ex. 341, 156 Eng.Rep. 145 (1854). For an argument that courts should move away from the strict foreseeability standard at the time of contracting to a regime based on contractual allocation of loss, fair disclosure, and proximate cause, or foreseeability at the time of breach, see Eisenberg, The Principle of Hadley v. Baxendale, 80 Cal. L.Rev. 563 (1992).

by a loan. In either case there is a direct and measurable cost arising out of the buyer's breach; in some cases it is more direct and easily measurable, but it is always present. This, of course, is a variant of the problem discussed above. A few courts have dealt with the question of how interest should be treated, as incidental or consequential.

In Afram Export Corp. v. Metallurgiki Halyps, S.A.,[18] Judge Posner deals with these and other questions concerning damages in the form of interest costs. A Wisconsin seller of scrap steel sued a Greek buyer who had repudiated the contract when the price fell. Among its specific items of damage, the seller sought to recover interest of approximately $40,000 on a bank loan in excess of $2,000,000 for the period between the time of breach and the time it resold the goods after the breach. Concluding that consequential damages are not recoverable, the court considered how one distinguishes incidental and consequential damages. Never at a loss for an economist's argument, Judge Posner suggests that some interest costs (very large ones) should be regarded as consequential damages and others (very small ones) should be regarded as incidental. He arrives at that conclusion by surmising that the seller is the least cost-risk avoider of the disastrous consequences (bankruptcy), that might follow from "back-breaking" interest expense. The buyer can therefore expect the seller to conduct its business in such a way that a single breach of contract does not cause bankruptcy unless the buyer has notice to the contrary. On the other hand, in Judge Posner's view, the seller cannot be expected to go wholly without credit. The seller's resort to such credit is always foreseen in those circumstances, and is the cost most easily avoided by the buyer's performance of the contract.

In *Afram*, the seller did not show that he repaid the loan after the resale to the third party or indeed that the loan (which was for an amount in excess of the total contract price), was directly related to this particular contract. Given that lack of connection, Judge Posner concluded that "interest on a general business loan not tied to the subject matter of the sale"[19] would not have been recoverable either as incidental or as consequential damages under Wisconsin law.[20]

What of the lost opportunity for the reinvestment of the money not timely paid where the seller is not in debt at all?[21] Why should the buyer not be made to pay such imputed, as well as actual,

---

18.   772 F.2d 1358, 41 UCC 1709 (7th Cir.1985).

19.   *Id*. at 1370, 41 UCC at 1715.

20.   In a case decided a few years after *Afram*, Judge Posner denied 2–710 prejudgment interest where "right up to the jury's verdict it was entirely unclear

what * * * [the] loss had been." See Empire Gas Corp. v. American Bakeries Co., 840 F.2d 1333, 5 UCC2d 545 (7th Cir.1988).

21.   For an answer to this question, see Firwood Mfg. Co., Inc. v. General Tire, Inc., 96 F.3d 163, 30 UCC2d 789

interest? We believe that the buyer should. We would argue that such a recovery should be included as an element of the seller's consequential damages recoverable under 1–103, at least in circumstances in which the applicable common law does not prevent it.[22]

§ 8–17 Seller's Remedies on Buyer's Insolvency

As a general proposition, a seller who sells goods on unsecured credit has no greater claim to the goods sold than he has to any other goods of his debtor-buyer, nor does the seller have a greater right to the goods sold than do other unsecured creditors of the common debtor. Section 2–702 is an exception to that rule. It not only authorizes the seller to refuse to deliver if he discovers the buyer to be insolvent, but, in certain circumstances, permits the seller to reclaim the goods from the hands of the insolvent buyer.

Since the seller's rights under 2–702 exist only when his buyer has become insolvent, it is not surprising that the reclaiming seller finds himself competing not only with his buyer but also with its buyer's trustee in bankruptcy and with his buyer's secured creditors. Indeed we would bet a considerable sum that far more than half of all the 2–702 cases are bankruptcy cases and that the bankruptcy judges are likely to become much more familiar with 2–702 than are any other judicial officers. For those reasons we have chosen only to mention 2–702 under Seller's Remedies. We have discussed section 2–702 and the cases under 2–702 in Chapter 32 of the 4–volume Treatise. That Chapter is devoted generally to bankruptcy and the secured creditor; we believe it better to catalog 2–702 as a quasi security claim and not as a standard Article 2 remedy.[1]

§ 8–18 Applying Section 2–708 to Mutant Sales Contracts, Take or Pay

A series of cases decided since 1985 has confronted the "take-

---

(6th Cir. 1996) (seller not allowed to collect interest stemming from buyer's breach because lost interest is consequential and consequential damages are not available to sellers under the UCC); Stamtec, Inc. v. Anson Stamping Co., LLC, 346 F.3d 651 51 UCC2d 1048 (6th Cir. 2003) (UCC does not allow aggrieved seller to collect damages for interest stemming from either lost use of money or interest paid third parties because such costs are consequential damages, and not allowed to sellers under the UCC).

22. Where the law grants a victorious plaintiff interest on a judgment from the date of breach or from the time of

trial, that amount must, of course, be offset against any interest awarded as incidental or consequential damages. Where there is a generous and early award of interest on the amount of the judgment, conceivably that amount could equal or even exceed the lost opportunity cost of the plaintiff.

§ 8–17

1. See, e.g., In re Kellstrom Industries, Inc., 282 B.R. 787, 48 UCC2d 613 (Bankr. D. Del. 2002) (stoppage of delivery to insolvent buyer); In re Trico Steel Co., 282 B.R. 318, 48 UCC2d 1004 (Bankr. D. Del. 2002) (same).

or-pay" clause in contracts for the sale of natural gas.[1] In a take-or-pay clause the buyer, generally a pipeline, agrees either to take a particular quantity of gas (typically seventy to eighty percent of the quantity the pipeline had a right to take) or to pay for that quantity.[2] A makeup provision typically allows the pipeline a period of time, such as five years, in which to take the quantity for which it had previously paid, but had not taken. These terms were offered by the pipelines during a period of short supply in the late 1960's and 1970's as a means to provide gas producers with a steady flow of income while affording the pipelines some flexibility in the volume of gas purchased. The parties apparently believed that the market price would rise upon deregulation because the contracts typically contained detailed price redetermination clauses which would pass on to producers the benefits of the increased price, but no provisions to protect the buyer if the market price fell during the deregulation process.[3] They also frequently contained a species of most favored nation treatment which guaranteed the producers the highest price or a price as high as the price the pipeline paid other producers.[4]

Instead of lifting the lid on gas prices all at once, Congress decided to let the steam out slowly when it enacted the Natural Gas Policy Act of 1978.[5] The phased-in deregulation coupled with the most favored nation clauses had the effect of increasing contract prices to supramarket levels.[6] Pipelines were contractually required

§ 8–18

1. See Medina, et. al., Take or Litigate: Enforcing the Plain Meaning of the Take or Pay Clause in Natural Gas Contracts, 40 Ark.L.Rev. 185, 187 (1986) (The authors, attorneys representing producers, report well over 100 cases involving take-or-pay clauses.).

2. See R. Pierce, Jr., Natural Gas Regulation, Deregulation, and Contracts, 68 Va.L.Rev. 63 (1982) for a detailed discussion of natural gas contracts in the period prior to deregulation. See also Prenalta Corp. v. Colorado Interstate Gas Co., 944 F.2d 677, 15 UCC2d 854 (10th Cir.1991) (discussing the incipience of take or pay clauses). See generally 4 H. Williams, Oil & Gas Law § 724.54 (discussing take-or-pay clauses in gas contracts).

3. See Koch Hydrocarbon Co. v. MDU Resources Group, Inc., 988 F.2d 1529 (8th Cir.1993); Golsen v. ONG Western, Inc., 756 P.2d 1209, 5 UCC2d 605 (Okla.1988). See also Barnes & Wood, The Allocation of Risk in Gas Purchase Contracts After *Golsen v.*

ONG Western, 13 Okla.City U.L.Rev. 503 (1988); Crump, Natural Gas Price Escalation Clauses: A Legal and Economic Analysis, 70 Minn.L.Rev. 61, 63 (1985) (During the 1970s, "it became clear to all informed observers that the market price of gas would rise.").

4. The most favored nation provisions were of two types. A two party clause required the pipeline to pay the producer a price as high as the pipeline paid to other producers in the region. A third party clause required the pipeline to pay a price at least as high as the producer received from any other pipeline. See Edward J. Neuner, The Natural Gas Industry 91 (1960).

5. Pub.L. No. 95–621, 92 Stat. 821, (codified at 15 U.S.C.A. §§ 3301–3432).

6. See S. Williams, The Natural Gas Revolution of 1985 (1985) for an extensive discussion of the natural gas industry and the effect of regulation and deregulation. See also D. Crump, Natural Gas Price Escalation Clauses: A Legal and Economic Analysis, 70 Minn.L.Rev. 61, 73 (1985).

to purchase gas above prices for which they could resell to their customers.[7] Further exacerbating the situation, FERC revised its regulations to require the pipelines to transport gas for competing sellers who had bought cheaper gas on the spot market. In addition, demand for gas fell as many users, particularly industrial users, switched to alternative fuels.[8] Faced in the 1980s with high cost of gas and low resale prices for gas, pipelines attempted to renegotiate their long term contracts. Many pipelines, who were unsuccessful at this endeavor, eventually repudiated the contracts, and the litigation began.

In these cases, the buyers of natural gas refused to accept the contracted quantity and, by one means or another, sought to avoid the contractual obligation to pay for the gas under the "take-or-pay" clauses. The arguments of the pipelines have taken many forms. First, they have claimed that the clauses are unenforceable liquidated damages clauses. Second, they have argued that such clauses are unconscionable.[9] Third, they have argued that they are freed of their contract obligations because of partial impracticability, frustration of purpose, or impossibility—all argued more or less under 2–615.[10] Fourth, they have urged common law doctrines such as mutual mistake[11] or that enforcement of the clause would violate public policy.[12] Finally, various defendants have argued that terms

7. Government regulations required pipelines to resell gas based on the weighted average cost of its gas.

8. See Williams, The Natural Gas Revolution of 1985 at 10 (he reports that in the twelve months following July 1982, the quantity demanded by industrial users fell by 20%); Crump, Natural Gas Price Escalation Clauses: A Legal and Economic Analysis, 70 Minn.L.Rev. 61, 73 (1985).

9. Courts have been quite hostile to defendants' unconscionability arguments, noting that 2–302 requires that the contract be found unconscionable "at the time of making the contract," and finding that an increase in price is not normally a basis for unconscionability. See Kerr–McGee Corp. v. Northern Utilities, Inc., 673 F.2d 323, 33 UCC 440 (10th Cir.1982), cert. denied, 459 U.S. 989, 103 S.Ct. 344, 74 L.Ed.2d 385 (1982).

10. The arguments under 2–615 or analogous doctrines have been equally unavailing for defendants.

11. Courts also rejected defendants' arguments that the parties made a mutual mistake concerning the industry and the conditions under which the

take-or-pay clause would operate. The pipelines claimed that the parties entered into the contracts with the expectation that pipelines would continue to buy and resell gas in a market which was continually expanding. Matter of Columbia Gas System, Inc., 133 B.R. 174 (Bankr.D.Del.1991), Memorandum of Columbia Gas Transmission Corp. pursuant to Phase III(A)(c) of the Claims Estimation Schedule at 15 (Jan.11, 1993). While it is true that the parties failed to predict gas surpluses and the disparity that would arise between market prices and contract prices, the courts correctly note that "[m]istaken predictions of future economic conditions * * * will not facilitate relief from contractual obligations." Resources Inv. Corp. v. Enron Corp., 669 F.Supp. 1038, 1042, 5 UCC2d 616 (D.Colo.1987) (citations omitted); accord Sabine, 725 F.Supp. at 1178–79.

12. Defendants claimed that the contracts were against public policy because they imposed unjustifiable burdens on defendants, increased the price of gas to consumers, and contravened the policy of the NGPA. These arguments likewise lacked merit. One court noted that the

in their contracts (such as force majeure clauses) free them from responsibility.[13] These arguments for the most part have failed.

A court must first decide whether the take-or-pay contract provides for "alternative performance" or for a single mode of performance together with a remedy for breach. Most have held that these contracts provide for alternative performance.[14]

In finding that the take-or-pay contract provides for performance in the alternative rather than for liquidated damages, the Tenth Circuit relied on Corbin which states:

> It is evident that some alternative contracts giving the power of choice between the alternatives to the promisor can easily be confused with contracts that provide for the payment of liquidated damages in case of breach, provided that one of the alternatives is the payment of a sum of money. * * * If, upon a proper interpretation of the contract, it is found that the parties have agreed that either one of the two alternative performances is to be given by the promisor and received by the promisee as the agreed exchange and equivalent for the return performance rendered by the promisee, the contract is a true alternative contract. This is true even though one of the alternative performances is the payment of a liquidated sum of money, that fact does not make the contract one for the rendering of a single performance with a provision for liquidated damages in case of breach.[15]

The court found the take-or-pay contract to be "clearly an alternative contract" under which the pipeline could either "purchase the contract quantity or * * * pay the value of the contract quantity" in exchange for the producer's tender of the makeup gas at a later time.

It is sometimes difficult to distinguish between a provision for alternative performance and an agreed remedy. In the case of take or pay clauses familiar to us, we generally agree with the courts' view that they are for alternative performance and are not agreed remedies, i.e., not liquidated damage clauses. Certainly it would be

public interest in holding parties to their contracts outweighs any interest in protecting defendants from unwise contracts. Resources Inv. Corp., 669 F.Supp. at 1040.

13. Courts have not been shy in holding that the buyer's inability to resell the gas at a profit was not "in the contemplation of the law a force majeure event." Golsen v. ONG Western, Inc., 756 P.2d 1209, 1211–12, 5 UCC2d 605, 608 (Okla.1988); accord Sabine, 725 F.Supp. at 1169.

14. See Superior Oil Co. v. Transco Energy Co., 616 F.Supp. 98 (W.D.La. 1985); International Minerals & Chemical Corp. v. Llano, Inc., 770 F.2d 879, 41 UCC 347 (10th Cir.1985), cert. denied, 475 U.S. 1015, 106 S.Ct. 1196, 89 L.Ed.2d 310 (1986); Roye Realty & Developing, Inc. v. Arkla, Inc., 863 P.2d 1150, 22 UCC2d 183 (Okla.1993).

15. *Prenalta*, 944 F.2d at 689 (quoting 5A Corbin, Corbin on Contracts § 1082, at 463–64 (1964)).

possible to write a cousin to the take or pay clause that could qualify as a liquidated damage clause and would have to be analyzed under 2–718 and 2–719.

Courts that have correctly found these contracts to be for alternative performance have not always understood the legal consequence of that finding. That conclusion means that neither part of the contract is an agreed remedy. If the alternatives are to pay now and take now, or pay now and take later, each is a command to perform in a particular way and neither is a liquidated damage provision for failure to perform. Therefore, the conclusion that a clause is for alternative performance necessarily means that the remedy for breach of that clause must be found elsewhere. Put another way, agreed remedies and contracts for alternative performance are mutually exclusive categories; a clause cannot be both an agreed remedy and for alternative performance. Both the Tenth Circuit in *Prenalta* and the Colorado Supreme Court failed to appreciate that fact.[16] Despite our best efforts to convince the courts otherwise, the Tenth Circuit in *Prenalta* found that the parties had agreed on a specific remedy (as permitted by 2–719) but, oblivious to the inconsistency in its finding, then found that it was not a liquidated damage clause but rather a provision for "alternative performance." Finding that only the "money alternative" remained, the court awarded the entire deficiency payment as an agreed remedy!

We disagree with the reasoning of the Tenth Circuit. First, the clause is either a remedy clause or an alternative performance clause; it cannot be both. Second, even if the clause was a remedy under 2–719, it would be subject to the requirements of 2–718 on liquidated damages. The Tenth Circuit did not put the clause to the 2–718 test. Contrary to the Court's opinion, you cannot get there from here. If the clause is an agreed remedy, it must pass under 2–718; if it is for alternative performance, *a fortiori* not an agreed remedy, the remedy must be found in part 7 of Article 2.

Other courts have awarded specific performance of one of the alternative performances.[17] This approach, unlike the Tenth Circuit's, is internally consistent, but the Code allows specific performance of a buyer's obligations to pay only in the very limited circumstances specified in 2–709. An action for the price *is* seller's

---

16. See Prenalta Corp. v. Colorado Interstate Gas Co., 944 F.2d 677, 15 UCC2d 854 (10th Cir.1991); Colorado Interstate Gas Co. v. Chemco Inc., 854 P.2d 1232, 23 UCC2d 433 (Colo.1993).

17. Superior Oil Co. v. Transco Energy Co., 616 F.Supp. 98 (W.D.La.1985) (applying Louisiana law); Universal Resources Corp. v. Panhandle Eastern Pipe Line Co., 813 F.2d 77, 3 UCC2d 988 (5th Cir.1987) (awarding the entire deficiency payment), reh'g denied, 821 F.2d 1097, 4 UCC2d 490 (1987). Under Louisiana law, according to the court, when the obligor fails to make an election and perform one of two alternatives, the obligee can choose the alternative. The seller chose, and was granted, specific performance of the take option.

claim for specific performance. Under 2–709, the buyer must have accepted the goods or the seller must be unable to sell them at reasonable prices after reasonable effort. The producers cannot meet these conditions. The action for the price under 2–709(1)(a) is not available because the buyer has not accepted the goods; they are still in the possession of the seller. The buyer fails the requirements of 2–709(1)(b) because the gas commingled in the underground reservoir has not yet been identified to the contract and, furthermore, the seller would invariably be able to resell the gas at a reasonable price with reasonable effort. For policy and other reasons discussed above, the seller cannot and should not recover the price under 2–709.

Recognizing that the law and policy forecloses the peculiar kind of specific performance available to a seller under Article 2 (i.e., action for the price, 2–709) one might hope that a self-respecting seller would abandon its specific performance argument. Not so. Sellers have tried to circumvent section 2–709 by arguing that the "or pay" alternative is not a payment for the sale of goods.[18] But this argument ignores the realities of the contract—the buyer's option under the contract (prior to breach) is to pay for the gas now and take delivery now or pay now and take later.[19]

A few courts have awarded sellers damages under 2–708(1).[20] Once the court has concluded that the take-or-pay contract provides for alternative performances, we believe this is the appropriate response. Remember, the buyer has repudiated *both* alternatives. If the "or pay" clause is not a remedy clause, it cannot determine damages. Rather, a court must then look to the Code for remedies upon repudiation. Section 2–708 contains the Code's remedy for a buyer's repudiation.[21] The pay alternative is a promise to make deficiency payments in return for the seller's promise to deliver makeup gas. Upon the buyer's repudiation, the seller is free to sell the gas to other customers, and the buyer is liable for damages.[22]

---

18. The Tenth Circuit seems to have accepted this argument. See *Prenalta*, 944 F.2d at 689.

19. Even if the courts accept seller's argument that the pay option does not involve the sale of goods, specific performance must still pass muster under common law requirements. See e.g., Restatement Second on Contracts § 359 (remedy at law must be inadequate).

20. Koch Hydrocarbon Co. v. MDU Resources Group, Inc., 988 F.2d 1529 (8th Cir.1993). In this case, the contract price could not be readily ascertained because of the redetermination clauses which envisioned market price increases not decreases upon deregulation. The

court remanded the case to the trial court to admit parol evidence concerning the intent of the parties in the event of a price decrease.

21. Of course, if the case comes to trial before the time of performance, § 2–708(1) damages must be calculated with reference to the snapshot approach of § 2–723. See *supra* 7–8.

22. This is the reasoning adopted by the court in Roye Realty & Developing, Inc. v. Arkla, Inc., 863 P.2d 1150 (Okla. 1993). The *Roye* court cites 5A Corbin on Contracts § 1081, at 461–62 (1964) for its conclusion that if the second alternative is a payment of money, special treatment is required; the more appro-

Courts that have rejected 2–708(1) as a proper measure of damages for take-or-pay contracts sometimes justify their conclusions on equitable grounds. They believe the pipelines were sophisticated buyers who accepted the risk of a decline in market demand and the resulting decline in market price. Further, they find the pipelines used the "or pay" provision as a bargaining chip during a period of short supply.[23] They claim to award the seller the full extent of its bargain which they believe to be the full deficiency payment without a deduction for the market value of the still unsold gas as would be required under 2–708(1).

We have no doubt that the take-or-pay contracts were a bargaining chip,[24] but we are not convinced that the parties bargained for the buyer's obligation to make deficiency payments upon repudiation when the seller would no longer have the obligation to deliver makeup gas. The parties can quibble about whether the producers in each case had sufficient capacity to deliver substantial quantities of makeup gas. But there is a distinction between a buyer's assuming a risk that if it made a large prepayment, it would not be able to take all the gas during the makeup period and a buyer's assuming an obligation to pay for *all* the contract gas upon repudiation while the seller is free to sell that very gas to others.

We find the latter result (seller keeps the gas for later resale and also gets its price) particularly incongruous because it appears to us that the take-or-pay contract was a concession granted by the buyers to the sellers from the former requirements contracts which existed in the industry.[25] Under a requirements contract, the buyer

priate measure of damages should be in accordance with the less valuable of the two alternatives which is usually the market value of the specific alternative.

23. See Universal Resources Corp. v. Panhandle Eastern Pipe Line Co., 813 F.2d 77, 3 UCC2d 988 (5th Cir.1987); Prenalta Corp. v. Colorado Interstate Gas Co., 944 F.2d 677, 15 UCC2d 854 (10th Cir.1991). See also Brooke, Note, Great Expectations: Assessing the Contract Damages of the Take-or-Pay Producer, 70 Tex.L.Rev. 1469, 1476–77 (1992) (rejecting 2–708(1) because it gives the seller what it would normally get "giving no effect to the negotiated risk allocation.") "Intuitively," he argues, the seller deserves something more. The producer is a lost volume seller because, under the contract, the producer would sell some of the gas twice.

24. See, e.g. Williams, The Natural Gas Revolution of 1985 at 7–8 (1985)

(Under a price control regime, take-or-pay clauses were "a device by which interstate pipelines could compete for scarce supply."); Pierce, Reconsidering the Roles of Regulation and Competition in the Natural Gas Industry, 97 Harv. L.Rev. 345, 355 (1983).

25. Professor Pierce has written that the gas industry during the 1930s–1950s was characterized by monopsony conditions. The pipelines enjoyed the better bargaining position and often provided the sole market outlet for a number of competing producers. See Pierce, Natural Gas Regulation, Deregulation, and Contracts, 68 Va.L.Rev. 63, 79 (1982). He reports that historically, purchase contract took the form of a purchase or lease of a right to take the gas. The pipeline paid only for the quantity taken. *Id*. at 79 n.63.

There seems to be considerable consensus that natural gas contracts were

takes and pays for only what it needs. Under the take-or-pay, the buyer agrees to pay a minimum amount each year and to take the gas that year or to take it later. At the time of contracting the sellers would have preferred take *and* pay obligations which would require the buyer to take and pay for a minimum quantity annually rather than take-or-pay contracts which gave the buyer the option to take quantities at a later date.[26] Damages for breach of a take *and* pay obligation would be based on 2–708(1). Yet for breach of a provision less favorable (take *or* pay), the courts are granting the seller the full price.[27] We believe that the seller is being awarded more than its bargain.[28]

a. Liquidated Damages

If contrary to our judgment a court were to conclude that a take-or-pay clause was a remedy provision, could it be upheld under 2–718(1)? The payment amount might be "reasonable" in light of the "anticipated or actual harm" under 2–718(1), but this case would not present "difficulties of proof of loss" nor would it necessarily present any inconvenience or nonfeasibility of otherwise obtaining an adequate remedy. Finally, of course, a take or pay clause might be regarded as a term fixing an unreasonably large liquidated damage and thus unenforceable under the last sentence of 2–718(1).

Particularly in cases among highly sophisticated and well represented business entities such as these, we believe courts should

originally requirements contracts. It is far less clear whether the take-or-pay clause fell between requirements contracts and take and pay contracts or were considered to be improvements on take and pay clauses from the seller's standpoint. Mosburg, writing in 1964, recommends take-or-pay over what he terms "take-or-breach" provisions. However, he does so because of the uncertainty of legal damages under a take or breach clause. *Id.* at 263–63. The uncertainty may have arisen because the Code was still in its infancy.

Take-or-pay clauses have been characterized by pipelines as better than take and pay clauses because of the flexibility of being able to refuse to take gas in a given period without losing the source of supply. See Matter of Columbia Gas System, Inc., 133 B.R. 174 (Bankr.D.Del. 1991), Memorandum of Columbia Gas Transmission Corp. pursuant to Phase III(A)(c) of the Claims Estimation Schedule at 28–29 (Jan. 11, 1993). See also, Pierce, Natural Gas Regulation, Deregulation, and Contracts, 68 Va. L.Rev. 63, 78–79 (1982).

26. Contracts frequently included take and pay provisions for a smaller portion of the well's output which implies they were more onerous than take-or-pay provisions. See Matter of Columbia Gas System, Inc., 133 B.R. 174 (Bankr.D.Del.1991), Memorandum of Columbia Gas Transmission Corp. pursuant to Phase III(A)(c) of the Claims Estimation Schedule at 30 (Jan. 11, 1993).

27. The mitigation principle also precludes awarding the full price for all contract quantities.

28. Lest we sob too much, one commentator reports that the pipelines enjoyed a fair degree of success in liquidating take-or-pay contracts, typically paying only 10–15 cents on the dollar. See Williams, The Natural Gas Revolution of 1985 at 43 (1985). FERC Order 500 established a mechanism by which pipelines will pass some of their buy-out costs through to their customers.

be respectful of such clauses if they are found to be liquidated damages clauses. Because the parties can always negotiate to a more efficient outcome, there is no necessary waste in a liquidated payment. Why should the court substitute its view for the proper outcome of a dispute when well represented and knowledgeable parties specify their own remedy? We doubt the court should do that.[29]

29. If they conclude the clause is a remedy provision, the courts must then address the gas makeup provision. Is this right forfeited upon repudiation?

Chapter 9

BUYER'S REJECTION OR REVOCATION OF ACCEPTANCE, AND SELLER'S RIGHT TO CURE

Analysis

---

§ 9–1　Introduction

Section 2–601 and the sections following define "goods oriented" remedies: rejection and revocation of acceptance.[1] The Code drafters also attempted to bring some order out of that confusing body of law that had previously passed under the title "rescission," and they sought to codify the concept of cure for the first time. The drafters made important advances in the doctrine of cure, but the provisions on cure and revocation of acceptance have raised nearly as many questions as they have answered.

Rejection and revocation are self-help remedies. Although the Code describes the procedure one must follow in order to make an effective and rightful rejection, the Code nowhere defines the verb "reject." Somewhat simplified, rejection is a combination of the buyer's refusal to keep delivered goods and the buyer's notification

§ 9–1
1. See generally, Travilio, The UCC's Three "R's": Rejection, Revocation, and (The Seller's) Right to Cure, 53 U.Cinn.L.Rev. 931 (1984).

to the seller that the buyer will not keep them. Revocation of acceptance is a similar refusal on the buyer's part to keep goods, but it comes at a later time in the transaction, after the buyer has "accepted" by allowing the time for rejection to pass, or by some act with respect to the goods. As we will see, in certain circumstances a seller who learns of an alleged defect in the goods has the right under 2–508 to "cure" and thus foreclose the buyer's rejection. Whether the right to cure limits revocation of acceptance is not fully settled. Courts are divided, but Amended Article 2 would have allowed cure to forestall revocation in certain circumstances. See Section 9–7.

At the outset one should understand the significance of a self-help remedy which permits the buyer to return the goods to the seller, (that is, rejection or revocation of acceptance). In these cases the buyer is freed from its obligation to pay the price, and the buyer has a right to recover that part of the price already paid.[2] Moreover, except in unusual circumstances, the buyer need not resell the goods.[3] One should understand the economic difference between the status of the buyer who has rejected and the status of the buyer who has accepted and sued for breach of warranty. The typical buyer who accepts and sues for breach of warranty under 2–714 will recover only for injury proximately resulting from defects in the goods at the time of sale. If, for example, the purchased automobile had a cracked piston that will cost $500 to repair (and the value of the car is so diminished by $500), buyer will recover that $500. On the other hand, if buyer rejects the goods, buyer is first recompensed for the losses resulting from the seller's failure to perform his end of the contract (for example, by a suit under 2–713 or 2–712); more important, buyer escapes the bargain, and throws any loss resulting from depreciation of the goods back upon the seller.[4]

---

2. § 2–711(1) grants the right to a return of money paid (emphasis added):

Where the seller fails to make delivery or repudiates or the buyer rightfully rejects or justifiably revokes acceptance then with respect to any goods involved, and with respect to the whole if the breach goes to the whole contract (§ 2–612), the buyer may *cancel* and whether or not he has done so may *in addition to recovering so much of the price as has been paid* * * *.

3. In the usual case, the rejecting or revoking buyer in possession of the goods need only "hold them with reasonable care at the seller's disposition for a time sufficient to permit the seller to remove them." See 2–602(2)(b). Only if the more limited facts in 2–603 are

present (merchant buyer, seller not present at market of rejection, etc.) need the buyer do more. For general discussion of the buyer's obligations with respect to rejected goods, see Integrated Circuits Unlimited, Inc. v. E.F. Johnson Co., 691 F.Supp. 630, 7 UCC2d 1478 (E.D.N.Y.1988), damages calculation reversed, 875 F.2d 1040, 8 UCC2d 695 (2d Cir.1989).

4. However, some courts have awarded sellers a sum for the value the buyers derived from their use before rejection or revocation. See Selectouch Corp. v. Perfect Starch, Inc., 111 S.W.3d 830, 51 UCC2d 1070 (Tex. App. 2003), for a discussion of the distinction between the buyer who sues for breach of contract after rejecting or revocation of

The importance of goods oriented remedies can be illustrated by an example from a commodity market. Assume that the seller delivers 10,000 bushels of potatoes and that 100 of those bushels are rotten. If the buyer accepts the potatoes, he will have a cause of action under 2–714, and he will recover money approximately equivalent to the value of those 100 bushels. If, on the other hand, the buyer rejects the entire delivery, if the seller cannot cure, and if the price of the potatoes has fallen substantially, the buyer's rejection may save him thousands of dollars by allowing the purchase of conforming goods on the market at a much lower price than specified in the contract. Rejection avoids the economic injury of a bad bargain as well.

A word should be devoted to that ambiguous action called "rescission." Some use the word rescission to encompass what the Code defines as a rejection or revocation of acceptance;[5] others use it to mean simply the buyer's act in returning the goods;[6] still others use it to cover the buyer's cancellation of the executory terms of the contract;[7] and finally some might call it the buyer's cause of action for fraud,[8] (including presumably the return of the goods, cancellation of the executory portion of the contract and the return of money paid). The drafters apparently intended to restrict the word rescission to a limited number of cases, those involving a mistake or in which the seller has committed fraud, duress, or the like. Comment 1 to 2–608 on revocation states: "The section no longer speaks of 'rescission,' a term capable of ambiguous application either to transfer of title to the goods or to the contract of sale and susceptible also of confusion with cancellation for cause of an executed or executory portion of the contract.'"[9] If the seller has not

acceptance and the buyer who accepts and sues for breach of warranty. See also Jaramillo v. Gonzales, 132 N.M. 459, 50 P.3d 554, 49 UCC2d 159 (2002).

5. See, e.g., Woods v. Van Wallis Trailer Sales Co., 77 N.M. 121, 419 P.2d 964 (1966). Courts sometimes use "rescission" to mean "revocation." See Aluminum Line Products Co. v. Rolls–Royce Motors, Inc., 66 Ohio St.3d 539, 613 N.E.2d 990, 21 UCC2d 626 (1993).

6. See, e.g., Leveridge v. Notaras, 433 P.2d 935, 4 UCC 691 (Okl.1967).

7. Some cases limit "rescission" to cancellation of the executory portion of the contract; others require a full restoration by both parties to the *status quo ante*. See, e.g. Colton v. Decker, 540 N.W.2d 172, 30 UCC2d 206 (S.D. 1995) (recission not possible because very difficult to return parties to condition they were in before the sale).

8. See, e.g., In re Mosely v. Johnson, 90 Ga.App. 165, 82 S.E.2d 163 (1954); Woerderhoff Shoe Co., 184 F.Supp. 479 (N.D.Iowa 1960), aff'd, 297 F.2d 1 (8th Cir.1961); Hayes v. Equine Equities, Inc., 239 Neb. 964, 480 N.W.2d 178, 18 UCC2d 452 (1992).

9. § 2–721 states that all of the Article 2 remedies are available to a defrauded party to a sales transaction. It continues, "Neither rescission or a claim for rescission of the contract * * * shall bar or be deemed inconsistent with a claim for damages or other remedy." Although their meaning is not crystal clear, it appears that the drafters contemplate a cause of action for fraud in which the buyer would have a right to return the goods purchased and get its money back. Presumably this right to return the goods and get its money back is a right to "rescission" which exists outside the Code.

committed fraud, or the like, we believe that the Code preempts the field and that the buyer's only rights to return the goods are those stated in Article 2.[10]

§ 9–2 Acceptance, Section 2–606

"Acceptance" is a term of art that must be distinguished from a variety of other acts which the buyer might commit. Note first that whether the buyer has "accepted" the goods is unrelated to the question whether title has passed from seller to buyer.[1] Second, acceptance is only tangentially related to buyer's possession of the goods. Often the buyer will have had possession of the goods for some time before he has "accepted" them, however, actual possession by the buyer is not necessarily a prerequisite to acceptance.[2]

Under section 2–606(1) "[a]cceptance of goods occurs when the buyer

(a) after a reasonable opportunity to inspect the goods signifies to the seller that the goods are conforming or that he will take or retain them in spite of their non-conformity; or

(b) fails to make an effective rejection (subsection (1) of section 2–602), but such acceptance does not occur until the buyer has had a reasonable opportunity to inspect them; or

(c) does any act inconsistent with the seller's ownership; but if such act is wrongful as against the seller it is an acceptance only if ratified by him."

Section 2–607 states the general legal consequences of acceptance. Upon acceptance, (1) the buyer must pay at the contract rate for the goods accepted, (2) the buyer loses its right to reject, (3) time starts to run within which buyer must complain of breach or be barred from any remedy, and (4) the burden shifts to the buyer to "establish * * * breach."[3] In addition, under 2–201(3)(c), acceptance takes the contract out of the statute of frauds.[4] Apart from

---

10. Absent fraud, we believe the drafters intended to limit the buyer to the rights specified in the Code. See 1 N.Y. State Law Revision Comm'n, 1955 Report 528 (1955) where Professor Honnold said, "Under the Code, 'revocation of acceptance' takes the place of 'rescission.'"

§ 9–2

1. § 2–401. See also Unlaub Co. v. Sexton, 568 F.2d 72, 23 UCC 69 (8th Cir.1977).

2. See, e.g. Commonwealth Propane Co. v. Petrosol Int'l, Inc., 818 F.2d 522, 3 UCC2d 1778 (6th Cir.1987) (buyer had

accepted propane though it remained in seller's storage tank).

3. Furthermore, many government contracts provide that acceptance forecloses the buyer from all remedies for nonlatent defects. See, e.g., Appeal of Mazur Bros. & Jaffe Fish Co., 1965 WL 230, 65–2 BCA 4932, 3 UCC 419 (V.A.B.C.A.1965).

4. See, e.g. Johnson v. Holdrege Co-op. Equity Exchange, 206 Neb. 568, 293 N.W.2d 863, 29 UCC 764 (1980) (valid delivery and acceptance under 2–201 where grain tested by single load then co-mingled with other wheat so as to make particular wheat unrecoverable);

the case where the contract explicitly renders acceptance "final" and bars all goods oriented remedies thereafter so that the legal consequences of acceptance to the buyer are clearly substantial, it is difficult to calculate the real significance of acceptance. Absent an explicit contract term so providing, even explicit acceptance does not foreclose buyer's suit for breach of warranty.[5] And, where acceptance is not final by contract, the buyer may still have the right to revoke acceptance.

Presumably, one needs a more serious complaint to support revocation of acceptance than one needs to support rejection; theoretically, in the case of revocation, the buyer's burden of proving breach is more difficult, and conceivably the "reasonable time" specified in 2–607(3) may be shorter. Despite these theoretical legal consequences, we think it is an unusual case when acceptance changes the outcome very much—unless considerable time intervenes between acceptance and revocation. The cases give little support to the proposition that the buyer may freely reject but only rarely revoke acceptance; neither do the cases make plain that buyer carries a heavier burden of proof in revocation than in rejection cases.[6]

Some of the circumstances to which 2–606(1)(a) applies after an opportunity to inspect are easy to identify; others are not. Certainly when a professional purchaser inspects goods bought for use in its business and then states orally or in writing to the seller that buyer will take the goods or "retain them in spite of the nonconformity," we have an acceptance.[7] According to Comment 3 to

Frank Adams & Co. v. Baker, 1 Ohio App.3d 137, 439 N.E.2d 953, 34 UCC 794 (1981) (contract excepted from statute of frauds where buyer received and accepted goods by failing to reject within a reasonable time); Hofmann v. Stoller, 320 N.W.2d 786, 33 UCC 1622 (N.D. 1982) (trial court's finding that feed had been "received and accepted" not clearly erroneous; thus oral contract excepted from statute of frauds); Joseph Heiting & Sons v. Jacks Bean Co., 236 Neb. 765, 463 N.W.2d 817, 13 UCC2d 336 (1990) (commingling of seller's beans with others constituted acceptance by buyer thereby excepting sale contract from statute of frauds); Winston American Transp., Inc. v. Motorola Communications and Electronics, 229 A.D.2d 1033, 645 N.Y.S.2d 185, 32 UCC2d 1077 (1996) (buyer's receipt and acceptance of radios and other equipment eliminated writing requirement under statute frauds); Regal Custom Clothiers, Ltd. v. Mohan's Custom Tailors, Inc., 1997 WL 370595 (S.D.N.Y. 1997) (to extent that

buyer received and accepted suits and paid seller for suits, oral contract was enforceable); Power Press Sales Company v. MSI Battle Creek Stamping, 238 Mich.App. 173, 604 N.W.2d 772, 39 UCC2d 964 (1999) (oral sales agreement for power presses was enforceable under statute of frauds where buyer had accepted and retained presses 5 years earlier).

5. § 2–714 is designed to recompense one who has accepted defective goods.

6. Miron v. Yonkers Raceway, Inc., 400 F.2d 112, 5 UCC 673 (2d Cir.1968), is a case in which the buyer lost nominally because he did not carry his burden. There the court found that the burden had shifted to the buyer and found that his proof did not show that the horse in question was defective at the time of sale.

7. Sessa v. Riegle, 427 F.Supp. 760, 21 UCC 745 (E.D.Pa.1977), aff'd, 568 F.2d 770 (3d Cir.1978) (§ 2–606(1)(a) ac-

2–606, payment is another "circumstance tending to signify acceptance," but it is ambiguous and not—according to the comment—"conclusive."[8] A reasonable opportunity to inspect is essential to a finding of acceptance under 2–606(1)(a).[9]

Suppose a purchaser signs a contract which contains a clause to the effect that she has inspected the automobile or other merchandise and found it to be conforming. A few cases to the contrary notwithstanding,[10] the prevailing view is that one who buys complex goods such as an automobile and signs a contract for purchase after only a short demonstration ride should not be held to have had "a reasonable opportunity to inspect" and therefore not be held to have accepted the goods.[11]

Section 2–606(1)(b) provides that one has accepted when one "fails to make an effective rejection * * *." An effective rejection under 2–602 must occur "within a reasonable time after * * * delivery or tender," and there must be seasonable notification of rejection by the buyer to the seller.[12] While an ineffective and

ceptance found where buyer's agent inspected the horse and both buyer and agent indicated to seller that buyer would take horse); Beaver Valley Alloy Foundry Co. v. Therma–Fab, Inc., 814 A.2d 217, 49 UCC2d 507 (Pa. Super. 2002) (finding that where the buyer asks the seller to deliver the goods despite their defects and then keeps the goods upon delivery, the buyer accepted the goods).

8. For cases where payment was held to constitute a § 2–606(1)(a) acceptance, see Atlantic Aluminum & Metal Distrib. v. Adams, 123 Ga.App. 387, 181 S.E.2d 101, 9 UCC 63 (1971) (payment for aluminum with knowledge of defects); Konitz v. Claver, 287 Mont. 301, 954 P.2d 1138, 36 UCC2d 688 (1998) (noting that buyer's payment, "although not determinative, signifies his acceptance of the goods").

9. See, e.g., Columbia Can Co. v. Africa–Middle East Marketing, Inc., 188 N.J.Super. 45, 455 A.2d 1143, 36 UCC 137 (1983) (buyer's request that goods be trans-shipped from one location to another cannot be construed as signifying acceptance under § 2–606(1)(a) since seller should have known buyer had not inspected goods prior to request); Salt Lake City Corp. v. Kasler Corp., 842 F.Supp. 1380, 24 UCC2d 81 (D. Utah 1994) (even if non-conforming buyer should have discovered breach much earlier before incorporation in concrete; hence acceptance); Gragg Farms &

Nursery v. Kelly Green Landscaping, 81 Ohio Misc.2d 34, 674 N.E.2d 785, 32 UCC2d 1119 (1996) (acceptance generally contemplates opportunity to inspect; payment under C.O.D. contract not acceptance).

10. Rozmus v. Thompson's Lincoln–Mercury Co., 209 Pa.Super. 120, 224 A.2d 782, 3 UCC 1025 (1966); Bicknell v. B & S Enters., 160 Ga.App. 307, 287 S.E.2d 310, 33 UCC 263 (1981) (since buyer given "ample opportunity to inspect the car to ascertain whether it had an operating air-conditioner and radio before she took possession of it and signed bill of sale" and financing agreement, buyer accepted car "as is", and unable to reject following day after mechanic checked car and found worth half what buyer paid).

11. See, e.g. Palladino v. Dunn, 361 Pa.Super. 99, 521 A.2d 946, 3 UCC2d 98 (1987) (buyer was killed on auto test drive; despite all conditions in conformity with sales agreement, buyer retained right to inspect; seller's, not buyer's, insurance should cover).

12. For cases dealing with § 2–606(1)(b) see, e.g., Pioneer Peat, Inc. v. Quality Grassing & Services, Inc., 653 N.W.2d 469, 49 UCC2d 440 (Minn. App. 2002) (rejection one month after delivery not timely); Franklin Pavkov Const. Co. v. Roche, 279 F.3d 989, 46 UCC2d 1011 (Fed.Cir.2002) (where a party failed to inspect goods delivered and did

wrongful rejection may constitute an acceptance under 2–606(1)(b), an effective yet *wrongful* rejection does not.[13] An effective rejection is procedurally proper under 2–602(1) (assuming buyer has had a reasonable opportunity to inspect); if there is no breach, it will be wrongful. In *Brandeis Machinery*[14], because the trial court could have concluded that the buyer of a crane made a wrongful, yet effective rejection, seller's action for the price had to fail. Fighting issues in 2–606(1)(b) cases are discussed in section 9–3 on rejection.

The final and most obstreperous subsection is 2–606(1)(c) which provides that a buyer has accepted when he has done "any act inconsistent with the seller's ownership."[15] Assume, for example, that a buyer purchases 1400 feet of cast iron pipe. On the day after the purchase the buyer discovers that the sections of pipe are not of uniform length. Thereafter buyer makes a contract to resell the pipe, and still later—after the resale contract has fallen through for other reasons—the buyer attempts to reject. Without more, we think the attempt to resell at a time buyer was aware of the alleged defect in the goods is an act inconsistent with the seller's ownership and an acceptance.

We think it vital to an intelligent interpretation of section 2–606(1)(c) that one consider the buyer's act in the context of buyer's knowledge and behavior prior to that act.[16] An act may have a different meaning when done by a buyer in ignorance of a defect than it would have if the buyer knew of the defect. Assume, for example, that Judas Construction Company purchases a large truck. No one would regard its use of that truck on the day after

not inform government that delivery was non-conforming for six months after delivery, that party deemed to have accepted goods).

13. A wrongful rejection is a rejection of conforming goods. Integrated Circuits Unlimited, Inc. v. E.F. Johnson Co., 691 F.Supp. 630, 7 UCC2d 1478 (E.D.N.Y.1988), rev'd on other grounds, 875 F.2d 1040, 8 UCC2d 695 (2d Cir. 1989) (even if buyer's rejection of microprocessors was wrongful, it met the requirements of 2–602 and was therefore effective); Zhong Ya Chemical (USA) Ltd. v. Industrial Chemical Trading, Inc., 2001 WL 69438, 43 UCC2d 879 (S.D.N.Y. 2001).

14. Brandeis Machinery & Supply Co., LLC v. Capitol Crane Rental, Inc., 765 N.E.2d 173, 47 UCC2d 200 (Ind. App.2002).

15. See, Ford v. Starr Fireworks, Inc., 874 P.2d 230, 25 UCC2d 699 (Wyo. 1994) (acts of resale inconsistent).

16. See e.g., Lloyd v. Classic Motor Coaches, Inc., 388 F.Supp. 785, 17 UCC 761 (N.D.Ohio 1974); Cardwell v. International Housing, Inc., 282 Pa.Super. 498, 423 A.2d 355, 31 UCC 512 (1980) (buyer reaccepted mobile home after revocation by continuing to reside there, using it for storage after moving out, and continuing to make payments); Fabrica de Tejidos Imperial, S.A. v. Brandon Apparel Group, Inc., 218 F.Supp.2d 974, 48 UCC2d 960 (N.D. Ill. 2002) (decorating and reselling inconsistent); Ask Technologies, Inc. v. Cablescope, Inc., 2003 WL 22400201, 51 UCC2d 1028 (S.D.N.Y. 2003) (continued use of goods for nine months after installation, notification of seller of defects, and seller's substantial repair of defects, constituted acceptance); Indeck Energy Services, Inc. v. NRG Energy, Inc., 2004 WL 2095554, 54 UCC2d 990 (N.D.Ill.2004) (buyer accepted transformers where it sought another owner for them and other uses for them).

purchase and before any defect was discovered as the kind of act encompassed in 2–606(1)(c), despite the fact that any use is theoretically inconsistent with the seller's ownership. One might draw a different conclusion if the buyer discovered a defect, attempted unsuccessfully to reject the truck, and then took it back to the job site and used it on a regular basis. To give meaning to 2–606(1)(c), buyers' acts ought to be divided into at least three categories: (1) acts done in ignorance of the defect; (2) acts done with knowledge that the goods are defective, but before any attempt is made to reject; and (3) acts done with knowledge that the goods are defective and after an attempt to reject. We would argue that acts done in ignorance of the defects which buyer could not have discovered are never covered by 2–606(1)(c).[17] The use of the goods and passage of time might constitute an acceptance under 2–606(1)(a) or 2–606(1)(b). But if any use (and all use is possibly inconsistent with seller's ownership) constitutes an inconsistent act as that term is used in 2–606(1)(c), then there will always be acceptance the minute the buyer uses the goods notwithstanding the fact the buyer has not yet had a "reasonable opportunity to inspect" under 2–606(1)(a) and still has a "reasonable time" to reject under 2–602 (and therefore has not accepted under 2–606(1)(b)). The only reading of 2–606(1)(c) which is consistent with the Code policy[18] and which leaves any elbow room for the other subsections of 2–606 is to find that use of goods in justifiable ignorance of the defective nature of the goods is not, as such, "inconsistent" under 2–606(1)(c).[19]

The other end of the spectrum includes acts done after an attempted rejection and with knowledge of the defect. These are contemplated by 2–606(1)(c). Comment 4 to 2–606 specifically refers to them as follows: "[A]ny action taken by the buyer, which is inconsistent with his claim that he has rejected the goods, consti-

---

17. Defects which are not discovered because of the buyer's failure to take advantage of his opportunity to inspect are covered by § 2–606(1)(c). See, e.g., Trinity Industries, Inc. v. McKinnon Bridge Co., Inc., 77 S.W.3d 159, 46 UCC2d 119 (Tenn.Ct.App.2001) (goods could have been inspected prior to their use in construction of bridge and buyer's failure to inspect prior to use constituted acceptance).

18. One policy of the Code is to encourage the parties to work out their differences and so to minimize losses resulting from defective performance. A rule which makes any use tantamount to acceptance will make the buyer understandably nervous about attempting to use the goods while the buyer works

out the bugs with the seller and may so cause the buyer to reject more quickly than otherwise.

19. See Lloyd v. Classic Motor Coaches, 388 F.Supp. 785, 17 UCC 761 (N.D.Ohio 1974) (no acceptance found where buyer made minimal use of the car after receipt, placed it in garage on seller's refusal to repair, and waited five days before rejecting); In re H.P. Tool Manufacturing Corp., 37 B.R. 885, 38 UCC 110 (Bankr.E.D.Pa.1984) (no acceptance where buyer placed goods in inventory and sold without knowledge of their defects; was reasonable for buyer not to inspect and discover defect; effective rejection when rejected immediately upon learning from customers that goods were nonconforming).

tutes an acceptance." Any buyer who goes more than a very small step beyond the acts which the buyer is obliged and permitted to take under 2–603 and 2–602 takes a risk that he will have accepted the goods.[20] Of course, there may be cases where continued use is inevitable (for instance, use of a carpet nailed to the floor), and in these cases use should seldom be regarded as inconsistent with seller's ownership.[21]

Nonetheless, the most difficult case arises when the buyer uses the goods in his business with the knowledge that they are defective but before buyer has attempted to reject. These circumstances often prevail when the buyer and the seller are attempting to work the bug out of a complex piece of machinery. In these cases courts should be hesitant to find that buyer's acts to be "inconsistent with the seller's ownership." The parties should be encouraged to engage in this kind of bargaining and adjustment, and the buyer should not be made to engage in it at his peril.[22] In Steinmetz v. Robertus,[23] there was no 2–606(1)(c) acceptance where buyer's 10–12 day use was a reasonable effort to determine why a pump failed to work and to cure the defect. We conclude that 2–606(1)(c) is designed principally, perhaps exclusively, for the case where the buyer has attempted to reject and then has done some act with respect to the goods. Rarely should an act of the buyer in justifiable ignorance of the defective nature of the goods be held "inconsistent with the seller's ownership."[24]

20. See, e.g., Fred J. Miller, Inc. v. Raymond Metal Products Co., 265 Md. 523, 290 A.2d 527, 10 UCC 959 (1972) (buyer accepted when continued to use goods after notifying seller about half would have to be returned).

21. See, e.g., Garfinkel v. Lehman Floor Covering Co., 60 Misc.2d 72, 302 N.Y.S.2d 167, 6 UCC 915 (Dist.Ct.1969) (carpet on floor of buyer's house). Of course one may have trouble drawing a line between those cases where the buyer must use the goods (e.g., a rug) and those where it would be very convenient but not necessary for him or her to do so (e.g., commuting by "rejected" car rather than by bus). Cases involving the rejection or revocation of acceptance of mobile homes, or both, have been especially difficult to classify.

22. See, e.g., Can–Key Indus., Inc. v. Industrial Leasing Corp., 286 Or. 173, 593 P.2d 1125, 26 UCC 675 (1979) (no acceptance by use inconsistent with seller's ownership where buyer continued to use equipment after notifying seller it was unacceptable and use approved by

seller in attempt to solve problems with equipment).

But see, e.g., Atlantic Aluminum and Metal Distrib. v. Adams, 123 Ga.App. 387, 181 S.E.2d 101, 9 UCC 63 (1971) (buyer accepted when he used and paid for goods with knowledge of defects); In our view, none of these cases truly falls under § 2–606(1)(c) and can better be explained as § 2–606(1)(a) acceptances where the buyer notifies the seller that the buyer will accept the goods in spite of nonconformity.

23. Steinmetz v. Robertus, 196 Mont. 311, 637 P.2d 31, 32 UCC 1441 (1981).

24. Where acceptance is found when buyer retained and used goods for a long period of time with knowledge of their defective condition, acceptance should be based on § 2–606(1)(b), not § 2–606(1)(c). But see Danjee, Inc. v. Addressograph Multigraph Corp., 44 N.C.App. 626, 262 S.E.2d 665, 28 UCC 689 (1980) (court finds 2–606(1)(c) acceptance where plaintiff retained machines, and had ample opportunity to reject them

The cases have not painted a consistent pattern here. They have not focused with any consistency upon the status of the buyer's knowledge or upon the question whether the buyer has attempted to reject. One suspects in fact that some courts have first decided upon the merits of the buyer's claim and then reasoned backwards to the determination whether there has been an acceptance because of an inconsistent act. Acts which courts find inconsistent with the seller's ownership are many and varied. They include making payments, taking possession of the goods, use of the goods, repairing, working on them, attempts to resell them, and dealing with them in other ways.[25] Continued use with knowledge of defects appears to be common. In Ask Technologies v. Cablescope, Inc.,[26] this use constituted acceptance, seller having done substantial repairs, too.

Section 2–606(2) provides that "acceptance of part of any commercial unit is acceptance of that entire unit." Section 2–105(6) defines "commercial unit":

> "Commercial unit" means such a unit of goods as by commercial usage is a single whole for purposes of sale and division of which materially impairs its character or value on the market or in use. A commercial unit may be a single article (as a machine) or a set of articles (as a suite of furniture or an

while aware of their defects); In Bell v. Red Ball Potato Co., 430 A.2d 835, 32 UCC 1427 (Me.1981) (buyer tested potatoes upon delivery and found them nonconforming, yet immediately combined them with other potatoes and gave seller an inspection receipt, an act inconsistent with seller's ownership which constituted acceptance under § 2–606(1)(c)).

25. Regarding payment as evidence of acceptance, see § 2–606, Comment 3. Regarding modifying the goods, see Park County Implement Co. v. Craig, 397 P.2d 800, 2 UCC 379 (Wyo.1964). Taking possession of the goods contributed to a finding of acceptance in Campbell v. Pollack, 101 R.I. 223, 221 A.2d 615, 3 UCC 703 (1966); Connor v. Bogrett, 596 P.2d 683, 26 UCC 902 (Wyo.1979) (buyer accepted dog by treating as own in every respect, particularly by using own training methods, entering dog in competition, and offering services for breeding); Bacchus Indus., Inc. v. Frontier Mechanical Contractors, 36 S.W.3d 579, 42 UCC2d 1011 (Tex.App.2000) (repairing of goods after effectively rejecting constitutes reacceptance of goods); Weil v. Murray, 161 F.Supp.2d 250, 44 UCC2d 482 (S.D.N.Y. 2001) (cleaning and restoring of painting constituted ac-

ceptance, even though it may have increased painting's value, because such actions were inconsistent with the seller's ownership); China Nat'l Metal Products Import/Export Co. v. Apex Digital, Inc., 141 F.Supp. 2d 1013, 45 UCC2d 492 (C.D.Cal.2001) (buyer continued to order and market non-conforming goods to consumers even after telling seller goods were non-conforming, was inconsistent with seller's ownership and constituted acceptance); Olson v. Ford Motor Co., 258 Ga.App. 848, 575 S.E.2d 743, 50 UCC2d 166 (2002) (buyer reaccepted goods after refusing to allow seller to obtain repairs for truck, using implied ownership of truck in negotiations with credit union over final disposition of truck, paying taxes on truck and carrying insurance on truck); Keller v. Inland Metals All Weather Conditioning, Inc., 139 Ida. 233, 76 P.3d 977, 51 UCC2d 303 (2003) (buyer's rejection seasonable in light of seller's attempts to cure).

26. Ask Technologies, Inc. v. Cablescope, Inc., 2003 WL 22400201, 51 UCC2d 1028 (S.D.N.Y. 2003).

assortment of sizes) or a quantity (as a bale, gross, or carload) or any other unit treated in use or in the relevant market as a single whole.

If a buyer receives a commercial unit of goods in which some of the goods are conforming and others are nonconforming, the buyer must either accept or reject the entire commercial unit.[27] If the buyer accepts the conforming goods, he also accepts the nonconforming goods within the commercial unit. Section 2–606(2) is quite explicit: "Acceptance of a part of any commercial unit is acceptance of that entire unit." Section 2–608 does, however, permit revocation with respect not only to a commercial unit, but also a "lot."[28]

Buyers should take care when faced with a commercial unit containing a mix of conforming and nonconforming goods.[29] On occasion, an unsuspecting buyer who accepts the conforming goods in a commercial unit may find himself stuck with the nonconforming goods. Even if the buyer cannot revoke, he should still have a breach of warranty claim.[30]

§ 9–3 The Buyer's Right of Rejection, Sections 2–601, 2–602, 2–612

The Code differentiates between two goods oriented remedies of the buyer: a right of "rejection" and a "right to revoke acceptance". The second presupposes acceptance. (The law on acceptance was treated in the preceding section.) Of course, in some cases it will be difficult to know whether an acceptance has occurred and thus difficult to know whether a buyer may have a right to reject or a right to revoke (or neither). But in many cases, an acceptance either plainly will have occurred or plainly will not have occurred, and the buyer will know with certainty which goods oriented remedy it is claiming. The remedies do differ and separate bodies of law have now grown up around them. We consider rejection here, and revocation of acceptance in 9–4 *infra*. Both remedies generally free the buyer from paying the price under 2–709. In a proper case, a buyer who rightfully rejects or who properly revokes acceptance

---

27. See § 2–601.

28. A "lot" is narrowly defined in 2–105(5) as a "parcel or a single article which is the subject matter of a separate sale or delivery, whether or not it is sufficient to perform the contract."

29. See, e.g., A.W. Fabrizio & Son, Inc. v. Fort Lauderdale Produce, Inc., 1980 WL 98446, 39 Agric.Dec. 60, 28 UCC 680 (1980) (buyer who accepted portion of truckload of mixed agricultural commodities, accepted entire truckload); Unipay, Inc. v. Lynk Systems, Inc., 251 Ga.App. 674, 555 S.E.2d 78, 45

UCC2d 808 (2001) (buyer accepting an underdelivery was only obligated to pay contract rate per item delivered, suggesting that commercial unit was the individual item, not the shipment).

30. See Salinas Lettuce Farmers Co-op. v. Larry Ober Co., 1980 WL 98447, 39 Agric.Dec. 65, 28 UCC 684 (1980) (buyer who accepted entire truckload by accepting part, successfully maintained breach of warranty claim for nonconforming portion of delivery).

may also cancel under 2–711(1), and either recover damages for non-delivery under 2–713 or cover and collect cover damages under 2–712 (See Chapter 7). Neither rejection nor revocation is an "election" and neither forecloses buyers' damage remedies. Moreover, as we have seen, a buyer need not reject or revoke an entire amount but may confine such remedies to parts of the whole constituting "any commercial unit or units".

Section 2–601 confers the right to reject as follows:

Subject to the provisions of this Article on breach in installment contracts (Section 2–612) and unless otherwise agreed under the sections on contractual limitations of remedy (Sections 2–718 and 2–719), if the goods or the tender of delivery fail in any respect to conform to the contract, the buyer may

(a) reject the whole; or

(b) accept the whole; or

(c) accept any commercial unit or units and reject the rest.

a. Substantive Requirements

From sections 2–601, 2–602, 2–508, and 2–612, one can distill at least the following general substantive requirements for the right to reject: (1) absence of acceptance, (2) goods that do not conform or a tender of delivery that does not conform, (3) absence of an effective and rightful cure by the seller under 2–508 and (4) absence of a contract term prohibiting rejection.

Absence of acceptance is dealt with in the immediately preceding section of this chapter. Absence of cure is dealt with in section 9–5 *infra*. We concentrate on the requirement of nonconformity, on absence of bad faith, and on the procedural requirements of an effective rejection.

The road to rejection is often easy; if the goods or the tender depart in any important way from the contract, the buyer may reject if the seller does not exercise a right to cure under 2–508 and if the buyer satisfies the procedural requirements of an effective rejection. At least in theory, the standards of non-conformity which authorize rejection in one-shot contracts differ from those in installment contracts.

b. Perfect Tender

Section 2–601, the only section applicable to one-shot contracts, states a "perfect-tender" rule; seller must conform perfectly to its obligation, for the buyer may reject at any time "the goods or the tender of delivery fail *in any respect* to conform to the contract." We are skeptical of the real importance of the perfect tender rule. Even before enactment of the Code, the perfect tender rule was in decline,[1] and the Code erodes the rule.[2] First of all, Section 2–601 renders the perfect tender rule inapplicable to installment contracts, and 2–612 permits rejection only if "the non-conformity substantially impairs the value of that installment * * *." The seller's right to cure a defective tender, in 2–508 and discussed in the following section, is a further restriction upon the buyer's apparent right to reject for insubstantial defects under 2–601. Additional restrictions upon the perfect tender rule in 2–601 may be found in 2–504 (an improper shipment contract which causes a late delivery is grounds for rejection only if "material delay or loss ensues")[3] and in the Code's general invitations to use trade usage, course of dealing, and course of performance in the interpretation of contracts.[4] If trade usage states that nineteen or twenty-one items are the equivalent of twenty items, a buyer who receives nineteen on a contract calling for twenty has received a perfect tender—one conforming in every respect—and may not reject.

Further, the Code case law in regard to one-shot contracts indicates that section 1–304 (former 1–203) may sometimes be invoked to bar rejections by a buyer acting in bad faith. In T.W. Oil, Inc. v. Consolidated Edison Co.,[5] the buyer sought to reject in a falling market because of insubstantial nonconformity, and despite an offer of a monetary allowance by the seller. The New York Court of Appeals cited 1–203 to find the buyer's rejection improper. The court stressed that the buyer was really trying to take advantage of a market break and was invoking a minor nonconformity to do that. In an alternative holding, the court decided that this was in

§ 9–3

1. Of course, where goods are purchased for resale, the intermediate buyer cannot rightfully reject merely because the ultimate buyer fails to complete the transaction. See Electrical Power Systems, Inc. v. Argo International Corp., 864 F.Supp. 1080, 27 UCC2d 94 (N.D. Okla. 1994).

2. See E. Peters, Commercial Transactions 33–37 (1971). The classic early article on rejection is Honnold, Buyer's Right of Rejection, 97 U.Pa.L.Rev. 457 (1949). See D.P. Technology Corp. v. Sherwood Tool, Inc., 751 F.Supp. 1038, 13 UCC2d 686 (D.Conn.1990) (exceptions to perfect tender rule found in 2–508 and 2–612).

3. § 2–504 reads in part as follows:

Failure to notify the buyer under paragraph (c) or to make a proper contract under paragraph (a) is a ground for rejection only if material delay or loss ensues.

4. §§ 2–208; 1–303. See Continental Forest Products, Inc. v. White Lumber Sales, Inc., 256 Or. 466, 474 P.2d 1, 8 UCC 178 (1970) (buyer of plywood not entitled to cancel after receipt of a nonconforming shipment, because trade code allowed seller to reject only nonconforming load).

5. 57 N.Y.2d 574, 35 UCC 12 (1982). See also Neumiller Farms, Inc. v. Cornett, 368 So.2d 272, 26 UCC 61 (Ala. 1979); D.P. Technology Corp. v. Sherwood Tool, Inc., 751 F.Supp. 1038, 13 UCC2d 686 (D.Conn.1990) (the court states, "A rejection of goods that have been specially manufactured for an insubstantial delay where no damage is caused is arguably not in good faith."). But see Alaska Pacific Trading Co. v. Eagon Forest Products, Inc., 85 Wash. App. 354, 933 P.2d 417, 34 UCC2d 672 (1997) (buyer may reject goods due to late delivery under 2–601 where facts suggest buyer may have been looking for a way to avoid acceptance due to a softening of the market for goods).

bad faith and not permissible. The other holding of the court, one which the court emphasized somewhat more, was that the case fell within 2–508(2). Of course, *T.W. Oil* relies on a proposition that does not have universal acceptance: that rejections justified on one ground (e.g., insignificant delay) but motivated by another (e.g., price change) are in bad faith. Harder heads might find rejection of defective goods to be in good faith even when the defect is of no consequence to buyer.

The courts may also deny rejection for what they regard as insubstantial defects by manipulating the procedural requirements for rejection. That is, if the court concludes that a buyer ought to be denied his right to reject because he has suffered no or only minor damage, the court might arrive at that conclusion by finding that the buyer failed to make an effective rejection (for example, because his notice was not timely).

We conclude, and the cases decided to date suggest, that the Code changes and the courts' manipulation have so eroded the perfect tender rule that the law would be little changed if 2–601 gave the right to reject only upon "substantial" non-conformity. Of the reported Code cases on rejection, few actually grant rejection on what could fairly be called an insubstantial nonconformity, despite language in some cases allowing such rejection.

In the face of the campaign against perfect tender, both the Article 2 Study Committee and the proposals of the Article 2 Revision Committee would retain the perfect tender rule. The consumer representatives on those committees argued for its retention. One of us asks: are consumers asking for the right to return the dress with a single stitch out of place because they have found the same dress elsewhere at a lower price? For shame.

The basic test in the installment case under 2–612(3) is that the goods be "substantially" nonconforming. The Code gives no guidelines to determine which performances are substantially nonconforming and which are only insubstantially so. The common law concept of "material breach" is at least a first cousin to the concept of "substantial non-conformity," and it offers a fruitful analogy to one who seeks to determine whether seller's performance substantially fails to conform. The factors which section 241 of the Restatement (Second) of Contracts lists in determining whether the breach has been material are the following:

> (a) the extent to which the injured party will be deprived of the benefit which he or she reasonably expected,

> (b) the extent to which the injured party can be adequately compensated for the part of that benefit of which he or she will be deprived,

(c) the extent to which the party failing to perform or to offer to perform will suffer forfeiture,

(d) the likelihood that the party failing to perform or to offer to perform will cure his failure, taking account of all the circumstances including any reasonable assurances,

(e) the extent to which the behavior of the party failing to perform or to offer to perform comports with standards of good faith and fair dealing.

Whether the listed factors will carry the lawyer much further on the question of substantiality of a breach as to a given installment than his or her common sense[6] will, we are unsure. To date, there is little case law under 2-612(2). The judicial activity has been under 2-612(3) where the standard is not "substantially [impairing] the value of that installment" but "substantially [impairing] the value of the whole contract". We will turn to that issue shortly. First we must consider just what an installment contract is. Section 2-612(1) defines an installment contract as follows:

An "installment contract" is one which requires or authorizes the delivery of goods in separate lots to be separately accepted, even though the contract contains a clause "each delivery is a separate contract" or its equivalent.

Comment 1 explains that the definition is broad "so as to cover installment deliveries tacitly authorized by the circumstances or by the option of either party." Section 2-612(2) gives the buyer the right to reject an installment when there is a substantial impairment in the installment that cannot be cured.

When the breach of one installment of the contract gives the buyer the right to reject subsequent installments and to cancel executory portions of the contract is another question. That question is covered by section 2-612(3) which reads in full as follows:

Whenever non-conformity or default with respect to one or more installments substantially impairs the value of the whole contract there is a breach of the whole. But the aggrieved party reinstates the contract if he accepts a non-conforming installment without seasonably notifying of cancellation or if he brings an action with respect only to past installments or demands performance as to future installments.

Whether a specific default or non-conformity substantially impairs "the value of the whole" is often hard to answer. In Continen-

---

6. Though not in reference to an installment contract, at least one court has stated that substantiveness is "a common sense determination." Hem-mert Agric. Aviation, Inc. v. Mid-Continent Aircraft Corp., 663 F.Supp. 1546, 4 UCC2d 726 (D.Kan.1987).

tal Forest Products, Inc. v. White Lumber Sales, Inc.,[7] there was an installment contract for the sale of twenty carloads of plywood. The first carload did not conform to the contract because nine percent of the plywood in the car deviated from the thickness specifications. The trade standard authorized deviations of five percent. The second and third carloads which arrived at buyer's place of business after buyer had purportedly canceled the contract did conform. The court held that the deviation did not substantially impair the value of the whole contract and found moreover that the non-conformity could be cured by an adjustment in the price.

We continue to believe that the best judicial analysis of the general question, "When does a breach of part of an installment contract constitute a breach of the whole?," appears in the pre-Code case, Plotnick v. Pennsylvania Smelting & Refining Co.[8] In that case seller had delivered a carload of lead but had not received his payment. Seller then refused to make further deliveries except for cash and declined the buyer's offer even to pay by sight draft against a bill of lading. In analyzing section 45 of the Uniform Sales Act from the seller's standpoint, Judge Hastie observed:

> First, non-payment for a delivered shipment may make it impossible or unreasonably burdensome from a financial point of view for the seller to supply future installments as promised. Second, buyer's breach of his promise to pay for one installment may create such a reasonable apprehension in the seller's mind concerning payment for future installments that the seller should not be required to take the risk involved in continuing deliveries.[9]

One could apply a similar analysis to the problem that faces the buyer. If the first shipment constitutes a part of a machine that will be delivered in subsequent installments, and if the part is not repairable but is necessary for the operation of the machine, then the failure of the first installment will be a breach of the whole contract. Likewise if the defect in the first shipment gives "reasonable apprehension" in the buyer's mind about the ability or willingness of the seller to complete the other installments, it is a breach of the whole. By defining installment contracts broadly, and limiting rejection to cases of substantial nonconformity the drafters have removed a significant part of all cases from perfect tender.

The relation between a right to cancel or reject the whole on substantial nonconformity in installment contracts under 2–612(3) and on the right to adequate assurance of performance in the face of reasonable grounds for insecurity under 2–609 arose in Cher-

---

7. 256 Or. 466, 474 P.2d 1, 8 UCC 178 (1970).

8. 194 F.2d 859 (3d Cir.1952).

9. *Id.* at 862.

well–Ralli, Inc. v. Rytman Grain Co., Inc. Professor (later Judge) Peters of the Connecticut Supreme Court analyzed the problem in these terms:[10]

> The buyer argues that the seller in an installment contract may never terminate a contract, despite repeated default in payment by the buyer, without first invoking the insecurity methodology of * * * 2–609. That is not the law. If there is reasonable doubt about whether the buyer's default is substantial, the seller may be well advised to temporize by suspending further performance until it can ascertain whether the buyer is able to offer adequate assurance of further payments. * * * But if the buyer's conduct is sufficiently egregious, such conduct will, in and of itself, constitute substantial impairment of the value of the whole contract and a present breach of the contract as a whole. An aggrieved seller is expressly permitted * * * [under 2–703(f)] upon breach of a contract as a whole, to cancel the remainder of the contract "with respect to the whole undelivered balance."

The aggrieved party who wishes to invoke 2–612(3) should take care. Section 2–612(3) also provides that if a party accepts nonconforming performance or brings an action only for *past* installments and not the entire contract, the contract is reinstated despite any breach by the other party that may have been a substantial impairment of the value of the whole contract.[11]

c. *Procedural Requirements*

The Code imposes two procedural requirements for rejections. Under 2–602, a rejection must be "within a reasonable time" after delivery or tender of the goods, and it is "ineffective unless the buyer seasonably notifies the seller." We discuss these in reverse order. The policies for speedy notification are not mysterious. The obvious policies behind the notice provisions are to give the seller an opportunity to cure, to permit the seller to assist the buyer in minimizing the buyer's losses, and to return the goods to seller early—before they have depreciated, rotted or worse. If the seller can cure the difficulty and so save the sale and prevent lost profits that the buyer might otherwise suffer, the policy has been fulfilled. Even if the seller's inspection discloses that the goods are defective and the seller agrees to take them back, the entire loss from the

---

10. 180 Conn. 714, 433 A.2d 984, 29 UCC 513, 516–17 (1980). For further discussion on the relationship between §§ 2–612 and 2–609, see Hudson Feather & Down Products, Inc. v. Lancer Clothing Corp., 128 A.D.2d 674, 513 N.Y.S.2d 173, 3 UCC2d 1804 (1987) (seller's refusal to give adequate assur-ance was a substantial impairment of the whole contract).

11. See BOC Group, Inc. v. Chevron Chemical Co., LLC, 359 N.J.Super. 135, 819 A.2d 431 (2003) (buyer's continued acceptance of late deliveries that buyer had alleged substantially impaired contract reinstated the contract).

transaction may be minimized by early action, because the seller may be able to resell the goods to another party and at a higher price than the goods would command after they had depreciated.[12] The U.N. Convention on International Sale of Goods, CISG, includes provision for a more demanding notice. On CISG, see further note 2 at Section 9–5 *infra*.

The Code and case law on the requirement of notice tell us a number of things. Although the Code does not require written notice, those who have depended on non-written notice, or on equivocal notice, have not fared well in the courts.[13] We counsel that notice be written and unequivocal, and sufficiently detailed. In Imex v. Wires Engineering, a simple statement that the goods "do not work" was not enough.[14] Moreover, under 2–605, the buyer's failure to state a particular defect which is ascertainable by reasonable inspection precludes buyer from relying on the unstated defect to justify rejection or establish breach where the seller could have cured the defect had the buyer stated the defect seasonably.

Finally, 2–602 requires that the buyer "seasonably" notify the seller of rejection. This requirement of seasonable notice serves the same policy objectives as the requirement of timely rejection as such. Consequently, the same four factors we articulate below for judging the timeliness of rejection are also relevant here, and since notice is meant to give the seller a chance to cure, courts frown upon "notice through legal papers."[15]

12. See Julian C. Cohen Salvage Corp. v. Eastern Electric Sales Co., 205 Pa.Super. 26, 206 A.2d 331, 2 UCC 432 (1965) (court required notice in writing); Steinmetz v. Robertus, 196 Mont. 311, 637 P.2d 31, 32 UCC 1441 (1981) (emphatic disapproval is notice); Oda Nursery, Inc. v. Garcia Tree & Lawn, Inc., 103 N.M. 438, 708 P.2d 1039, 42 UCC 163 (1985) (telephone call that goods did not look "up to snuff" not notice of rejection). Two cases holding oral notice valid are Western Conference Resorts, Inc. v. Pease, 668 P.2d 973, 36 UCC 131 (Colo.App.1983) and National Fleet Supply, Inc. v. Fairchild, 450 N E.2d 1015, 36 UCC 480 (Ind.App.1983).

13. See, e.g., Uchitel v. F.R. Tripler & Co., 107 Misc.2d 310, 434 N.Y.S.2d 77, 30 UCC 933 (App.Term 1980); Oda Nursery, Inc. v. Garcia Tree & Lawn, Inc., 103 N.M. 438, 708 P.2d 1039, 42 UCC 163 (1985) (buyer merely referred to "deterioration" of plants; not sufficient particularity); China Nat'l Metal Products Import/Export Co. v. Apex Digital, Inc., 141 F.Supp.2d 1013, 45 UCC2d 492 (C.D. Cal. 2001) (mere complaints of nonconformity are not unequivocal enough to constitute rejection); Fabrica De Tejidos Imperial, S.A. v. Brandon Apparel Group, Inc., 218 F. Supp. 2d 974, 48 UCC2d 960 (N.D. Ill. 2002) (buyer's mere complaint about quality of goods not sufficient to constitute rejection); Sutter Insurance Co. v. Applied Systems, Inc., 2004 WL 161508, 52 UCC2d 548 (N.D. Ill. 2004) (buyer's telephone call to seller qualified as sufficient notice of breach, as was a letter expressing desire for compensation and referencing seller's failure to perform).

14. Imex Int'l, Inc. v. Wires Engineering, 261 Ga.App. 329, 583 S.E.2d 117, 50 UCC2d 448 (2003).

15. See e.g., Western Conference Resorts, Inc. v. Pease, 668 P.2d 973, 36 UCC 131 (Colo.App.1983) (notice must let seller know that transaction is troublesome so seller has opportunity to correct defects and prepare for negotiations and litigation through timely investigation); Keller v. Inland Metals, Inc., 139 Idaho 233, 76 P.3d 977, 51 UCC2d 303 (2003) (rejection seasonable in light of

A persistently litigated yet perpetually confused question in rejection (and revocation) cases is whether the buyer's action in rejecting was timely. Rejection of goods must occur "within a reasonable time after their delivery or tender" (2-602(1)). Both the cases and the Code are full of disheartening platitudes on timeliness. Section 1-205(a) tells us, "Whether a time for taking an action required by [the UCC] is reasonable depends on the nature, purpose and circumstances of the action;" one hardly needs to read the Code to find that out. At the risk of peddling a few of our own platitudes, we suggest at least four "circumstances" which will always have relevance to the determination whether a reasonable time has passed before the buyer took action to reject:[16]

(1) the difficulty of discovering the defect,

(2) the terms of the contract,

(3) the perishability of the goods, and

(4) the course of performance after the sale and before the formal rejection.

Although 2-602 does not make explicit reference to the difficulty of discovery, the comments, the statutory history, and the cases suggest that this factor is relevant.[17] The nature of the defect,[18] the complexity of the goods, and the sophistication of the buyer may all influence the difficulty of discovery. Quite clearly one needs more time to discover the defect in an automobile or an airplane than in an axe or a wedge.

Although the cases do not make clear the extent to which the buyer's sophistication is to be considered in determining whether a particular defect was difficult to discover, at least in a gross sense, the buyer's skill should be relevant to this question. For example, a defect in an automobile may be "more difficult to discover" when the purchaser is a consumer than when the purchaser is the Yellow

---

seller's attempts to cure); Business Communications, Inc. v. KI Networks, Inc., 157 N.C.App. 710, 580 S.E.2d 77, 50 UCC2d 799 (2003) (can buy contract set time for rejection). See also, Saffire Corp. v. Newkidco, 286 F.Supp.2d 302, 52 UCC2d 147 (S.D.N.Y. 2003).

16. Our analysis here has been adopted in a number of cases. See, e.g., Keller v. Inland Metals All Weather Conditioning, Inc., 139 Idaho 233, 76 P.3d 977, 51 UCC2d 303 (2003) (noting that the trial court used the four factors laid out by White & Summers in determining whether rejection occurred within a reasonable time after delivery).

17. In discussing what is a reasonable time for rejection under 2-602(1),

Comment 1 to that section states, "The sections of this Article dealing with inspection of goods must be read in connection with the buyer's reasonable time for action under this subsection."

How much time is acceptable is a "question of fact."

18. One commentator has written that "[i]f any pattern is emerging it is that the more severe the defect, the greater the time within which the buyer has the right to invoke the remedy, particularly where efforts have been made to compel the seller to repair or replace." Duesenberg, General Provisions, Sales, Bulk Transfers and Documents of Title, 28 Bus.Law. 805, 827 (1973).

Cab Company. We believe it will be a rare case where a business buyer is given substantial additional time in which to reject because the defect was "difficult to discover," and the courts will be more willing to listen to that argument when it is made by a consumer purchaser of a complex machine.[19]

A second factor is the contract itself. If the contract provides that the buyer must inspect and report all complaints within a specified period of time, the court will give effect to such a contract term under section 1–302(2)—provided the time set is not "manifestly unreasonable."[20] Not surprisingly, in the *Xuchang* case, a 30 day contractual notification period for non-conformities was reasonable given buyer's knowledge and experience.[21] Similarly, if a contract reserved the right to reject at "any time", timeliness would no longer be a factor unless the contract clause is manifestly unreasonable.[22] Even if the time appears to be manifestly unreasonable and the court finds that the term is not part of the contract, it may still hold that the term puts the buyer on notice that it must inspect with reasonable promptness. As one court put it:

> The court attaches no significance to the caveat [about time for rejection] announced in the seller's invoice. It was unilateral and the court finds it not to be binding upon the purchaser. Its only probative value was to activate the purchaser to a reasonably timely inspection of the goods purchased.[23]

19. See, e.g., Jatco, Inc. v. Charter Air Center, Inc., 527 F.Supp. 314, 33 UCC 240 (S.D.Ohio 1981) (buyer who was an airplane mechanic who thoroughly inspected airplane prior to purchase could not reject two months later when crack was discovered by FAA inspection); Quaker Alloy Casting Co. v. Gulfco Indus., Inc. v. Consolidated Foundries & Mfg. Corp., 686 F.Supp. 1319, 7 UCC2d 429 (N.D.Ill.1988) (merchants held to higher standard for notice than consumers).

20. See, e.g., Bowlin's, Inc. v. Ramsey Oil Co., 99 N.M. 660, 662 P.2d 661, 36 UCC 1110 (App.1983) (two day notification provision in contract for supply of gasoline, not unreasonable). (Note that the court sought to analyze the rejection under White and Summers' four part test; recognition that the contract term was not manifestly unreasonable probably should have ended the inquiry, however); Saffire Corp. v. Newkidco. LLC, 286 F.Supp.2d 302, 52 UCC2d 147 (S.D.N.Y. 2003) (seventeen days, as specified in contract, was reasonable); Business Communications, Inc. v. KI Networks, Inc., 157 N.C.App. 710, 580

S.E.2d 77 (2003) (where contract provision required rejection within 3 weeks of delivery and buyer discovered defect 1 day after delivery, rejection 5 months after delivery was not timely).

21. Xuchang Rihetai Human Hair Goods Co., Ltd. v. Hanyu Int'l USA Inc., 2001 WL 883646, 45 UCC2d 1077 (S.D.N.Y. Aug. 7, 2001).

22. See Bevel–Fold, Inc. v. Bose Corp., 9 Mass.App.Ct. 576, 402 N.E.2d 1104, 28 UCC 1333 (1980) (buyer of stereo cabinets could reject them for defects at any time; actual time of rejection unclear from case).

23. Michael M. Berlin & Co. v. T. Whiting Mfg., Inc., 1968 WL 9236, 5 UCC 357, 359–360 (N.Y.Sup.1968). Cf. § 2–513, Comment 7. Premier Mountings, Inc. v. Clyde Duneier, Inc., 2003 WL 21800082, 51 UCC2d 1033 (S.D.N.Y. 2003) also suggests that a contract term specifying time within which rejection must occur can be implied from course of performance between the parties during prior transactions. This use of course of performance to determine reasonable time for rejection should be dis-

A third circumstance is the relative perishability of the goods. If the goods are potatoes that may rot, a live horse that may injure itself, shrimp that will spoil, the buyer had better get things in gear if he wishes to reject or revoke acceptance.[24]

A final factor, sometimes articulated in court opinions, is the course of performance between the parties after the sale but before the formal rejection or revocation. If the principal policy of the notice requirements of 2–602 and 2–608 is to give sellers an opportunity to cure and to permit them to assist in minimizing buyers' losses, that policy is met if there has been a continuing series of complaints, negotiations, and attempted repairs prior to the formal rejection or revocation. This is so even though the formal notice comes a considerable time after the sale.[25] In Sarnecki v. Al Johns Pontiac,[26] the court allowed a jury verdict permitting rejection to stand even though the rejection of the automobile did not occur until five months and more than 3,000 miles after the purchase. A noteworthy fact reported in the opinion without comment is that the buyer first complained about the defect in the automobile only four days after the purchase. From that time until the rejection five months later there was an almost continuous series of negotiations and repairs. In those circumstances it came as no surprise that the buyer rejected; certainly the principal purpose of a timely rejection requirement was fulfilled by the continuous complaints of the buyer.[27]

Of course, the course of performance between the parties can cut both ways. Thus, where the buyer continues to buy products from the seller after discovering a continuing nonconformity and fails to inform the seller of the nonconformity until a month later, he cannot then reject, for buyer's actions indicated that the goods were conforming.[28]

tinguished from considerations of course of performance between the parties with regard to the specific transaction in question, as under the fourth "circumstance," which we suggest has relevance in determining a reasonable time for rejection.

24. Appeal of Mazur Bros. & Jaffe Fish Co., 1965 WL 230, 65–2 BCA P 4932, 3 UCC 419 (VABCA 1965) (shrimp; five days too late); Miron v. Yonkers Raceway, Inc., 400 F.2d 112, 5 UCC 673 (2d Cir.1968) (race horse; twenty-four hours too late).

25. E.g., Yates v. Clifford Motors, Inc., 283 Pa.Super. 293, 423 A.2d 1262, 30 UCC 967 (1980) (filing of complaint held sufficient to reject goods where there was course of communications between parties complaining of truck's de-

fects); Latham & Assocs., Inc. v. William Raveis Real Estate, Inc., 218 Conn. 297, 589 A.2d 337, 14 UCC2d 394 (1991) (buyer reasonably delayed right to reject computer systems while seller attempted to cure).

26. 1966 WL 8826, 3 UCC 1121 (Pa. C.P.1966).

27. See also Hayes v. Hettinga, 228 N.W.2d 181, 16 UCC 983 (Iowa 1975).

28. See, e.g., Bowlin's, Inc. v. Ramsey Oil Co., Inc., 99 N.M. 660, 662 P.2d 661, 36 UCC 1110 (App.1983) (short deliveries of gasoline noticed in mid-April but no notification until mid-May buyer continued to purchase gasoline after noticing shortages); Hyosung America, Inc. v. Sumagh Textile Co., Ltd., 137 F.3d 75, 34 UCC2d 930 (2nd Cir. 1998) (buy-

We realize that this modest accumulation of four factors: (1) difficulty of discovery, (2) contract terms, (3) perishability, and (4) course of performance between the parties after the sale and before rejection, will sometimes take the lawyer only a short distance toward a reliable judgment about whether a buyer's rejection was timely. However, we despair of doing more than citing a few of the many reported cases and acknowledging that we will gratefully bow to those of more powerful insight or greater wisdom who can distill useful principles from the Code and the decided cases.

It is important to distinguish between "wrongful" rejections and "ineffective" rejections. If timely notice is sent and if the buyer lives up to its post rejection obligations under section 2–602 et seq., a rejection—though possibly "wrongful"—would be "effective." As such it would preclude acceptance of the goods and forecloses a liability for the price under 2–709(1)(a). (The buyer, of course, might be liable to the seller for breach of contract under 2–708 or 2–706.) On the other hand, a rejection of nonconforming goods which is procedurally defective (for instance, notice was given too long after tender) will be "ineffective." Even if the goods are nonconforming, the parties to an ineffective rejection will be treated as though no rejection has occurred; in that case, the buyer will have accepted the goods and will be liable for the price. However, in at least one case, even though the buyer failed effectively to reject the nonconforming goods, the court allowed the buyer to offset its liability for the contract price to the seller because of the nonconforming goods where the seller clearly acted in bad faith and took advantage of the buyer's lack of business experience.[29]

d. Post Rejection Procedures

After effective rejection there is but one hurdle to clear. Sections 2–602, 2–603, and 2–604 instruct the buyer on proper post-rejection procedure. If the buyer has taken "physical possession" of the goods, the buyer is obliged to hold them under 2–602(2)(b) for a time sufficient to permit the seller to remove them.[30] In Huntsville

---

er, who accepts 3 shipments of nonconforming textile without objection, cannot reject later shipments on ground nonconforming); Zhong Ya Chemical (USA) Ltd. v. Industrial Chemical Trading, Inc., 2001 WL 69438, 43 UCC2d 879 (S.D.N.Y. 2001) (seller could not maintain action under 2–709 against buyer who failed to establish goods were nonconforming, but did establish rejection was seasonable, buyer seasonably notified seller, and buyer held goods in reasonable care for seller to remove).

29. Gulf Trading Corp. v. National Enterprises of St. Croix, Inc., 912 F.Supp. 177, 24 UCC2d 478 (D. V.I. 1996).

30. But the buyer is not obligated to return the goods to make his or her rejection effective. See Paramount Sales Co., Inc. v. Stark, 690 S.W.2d 500, 41 UCC 441 (Mo.App.1985). Credit Institute v. Veterinary Nutrition Corp., 133 N.M. 248, 62 P.3d 339, 49 UCC2d 1160 (App. 2002) (buyer's use of properly rejected non-conforming goods pursuant to seller's instructions is not inconsistent with seller's ownership).

Hospital v. Mortara Instrument,[31] the 11th Circuit held that the buyer was not required to physically return the goods after rejection, especially since the seller did not instruct the buyer on how to package the goods for return or on which carrier to use. Under 2–603 the buyer has an obligation to do more than merely hold the goods, e.g., resell them, only if the following conditions are met: (1) the seller has no agent or place of business at the market of rejection; (2) the buyer is a merchant, and (3) the goods are in the buyer's possession or control. If those conditions are met, the buyer must follow reasonable instructions of the seller and in the absence of instructions, sell the goods for the seller's account if they are "perishable or threaten to decline in value speedily."[32] The buyer has the same obligations under 2–608(3) (with respect to goods for which it has revoked acceptance). In Credit Institute v. Veterinary Nutrition Corp.[33], the court said where buyer effectively rejects goods, holds them for a reasonable time, and seller refuses to pick up goods, buyer has no further obligation regarding the goods.

After rejection the buyer should use care not to take actions "inconsistent with the seller's ownership" for fear of accepting goods that the buyer has attempted to reject or invalidating an otherwise effective rejection. In Borges v. Magic Valley Foods, Inc.[34] the buyer, who had received nonconforming potatoes that he was entitled to reject, was instructed by the seller to blend the potatoes with others to bring them up to grade. The buyer did so without success. Thereafter and without authorization from the seller, buyer made the potatoes into flakes and resold them. The Idaho Supreme Court held that the buyer had accepted the goods under 2–606(1)(c) and had become liable for the contract price rather than for the lower amount received on resale. The court stressed that 2–603(1) is triggered by an absence of instructions from the seller. Here the seller had given instructions and the buyer was not justified in his actions without further instructions from the seller. Section 2–603(3) provides that a buyer is "held only to good faith, and good faith conduct * * * [under 2–603] * * * is neither acceptance nor conversion nor the basis of an action for damages."[35]

31. Huntsville Hospital v. Mortara Instrument, 57 F.3d 1043, 27 UCC2d 435 (11th Cir. 1995).

32. See Integrated Circuits Unlimited, Inc. v. E.F. Johnson Co., 691 F.Supp. 630, 7 UCC2d 1478 (E.D.N.Y.1988), rev'd on other grounds, 875 F.2d 1040, 8 UCC2d 695 (2d Cir.1989) (despite later market shift, value did not threaten to decline when dispute arose; buyer not required to sell rejected goods); sale by buyer pursuant to 2–603, absent instructions from seller, is not an act inconsistent with the seller's ownership and cannot be considered acceptance under 2–606(1)(c).

33. 133 N.M. 248, 62 P.3d 339, 49 UCC2d 1160 (App. 2002).

34. 101 Idaho 494, 616 P.2d 273, 29 UCC 1282 (1980).

35. A buyer was not liable for refusal to follow the seller's instructions to return the goods (accompanied by offer of freight expenses) where the buyer acted for what he thought were good reasons,

Fortunately the buyer may look to the goods and their proceeds for some purposes. Section 2–603(2) specifies that the merchant buyer is entitled to reimbursement from the seller out of the proceeds for reasonable expenses incurred in caring for and reselling goods. Section 2–711(3) gives the buyer "a security interest in goods in his possession or control for any payments made on their price and any expenses reasonably incurred in their inspection, receipt, transportation, care and custody and may hold such goods and resell them in like manner as an aggrieved seller (Section 2–706)."[36] Note that the security interest does not secure the buyer's damage claim under 2–713.[37]

Perhaps because they did not contemplate long use followed by rejection or revocation, the drafters included no provision in Article 2 to deal with the *seller's* right to an offset for the buyer's use of the goods before—and, in some cases, after—such rejection or revocation. The cases cited in this chapter include many buyers who have been long in possession of goods before rejection or revocation. In many of those cases the buyer received an undisputed benefit from using the goods. In these cases the buyer should be made to pay the seller the value of the use; in fact "payment" will frequently come in the form of a setoff by the seller against the buyer when the buyer sues for return of the purchase price.[38] Of course that result can be reached only by reference to the common law—probably the law of restitution—incorporated in the Code under 1–103. Congress also thought that sellers are entitled to such a setoff; in the Magnuson–Moss Warranty Act, it specifically authorized an award to the seller for the value of the depreciation resulting from the dissatisfied buyer's use.[39] Amended Article 2 would also grant the seller a right to reimbursement for a buyer's use of goods that are returned.

though he may have made an error of judgment.

36. See, e.g. Northrop Corp. v. Litronic Industries, 29 F.3d 1173, 24 UCC2d 407 (7th Cir. 1994) (noting that purchaser of defective goods obtains a security interest in them when it pays for them).

37. Comment 2 to § 2–711 contains the following limitation on the buyer's security interest:

The buyer's security interest in the goods is intended to be limited to the items listed in subsection (3), and the buyer is not permitted to retain such funds as he might believe adequate for his damages.

38. See, e.g., Page v. Dobbs Mobile Bay, Inc., 599 So.2d 38, 18 UCC2d 720

(Ala.Civ.App.1992) (seller entitled to offset for buyer's continued use of van after revocation).

39. Act of 1975, Pub.L.No 93–637, Title I § 101, 88 Stat. 2183, 15 U.S.C.A. § 2301(12) (Supp.1979):

The term "refund" means refunding the actual purchase price (less reasonable depreciation based on actual use where permitted by rules of the Commission).

In 1976, the Federal Trade Commission proposed a rule to implement the offset for buyer's use envisioned in the statute. Due to the public response against such a rule, the Commission decided to delay promulgation. For a full description, see 41 Fed.Reg. 22,099 (1976).

To say that the seller should be paid for this benefit conferred on the buyer sidesteps the two significant questions, namely, which are the appropriate cases for such an award and what is the value of the benefit conferred? One case[40] offers a uniquely appropriate example for a payment by the buyer to the seller, or perhaps to a third party. In *American Container* the buyer "rescinded" the contract for the purchase of a truck, after using the truck for sixteen months. The vehicle was stolen property. The buyer had no difficulty with the truck; according to the court it operated quite satisfactorily. In that case, the seller—or perhaps the true owner—should be entitled to payment for the buyer's use. Moreover, the value of the use in that case could easily be estimated by a reference to the rental value of similar trucks. We believe that the seller—or the true owner if not the seller—should enjoy that amount as an offset or as a recovery from the buyer.

The typical case is more difficult. There the goods are defective and they fail somehow to perform properly. If they confer a benefit at all, it is a lesser benefit than the buyer expected to receive. Moreover, the buyer may be able to claim that he suffered the psychic cost associated with the uncertainty about whether the goods would work and the aggravation associated with unsuccessful attempts to cure. In a typical contract suit we would not allow the buyer to recover for such psychic injuries but perhaps they should be worked into the valuation scheme where the breaching party is claiming recourse. In any event the principle is the same, namely that the buyer should pay for the benefit conferred; the difficulty arises only in valuing that benefit. Presumably, since the breaching party (the seller) is the "bad guy" the court should not be generous to the seller but should leave the seller the burden of coming forward with credible evidence to show that it is entitled to an offset by proving the value of the benefit conferred on the buyer. In a number of cases, the seller has been granted an offset for the buyer's use *prior* to rejection or revocation.[41] In Mercedes Benz Credit Corp. v. Lotito,[42] the court held that a buyer is not required to prove the credit the seller is entitled to for the value of the buyer's use of the car prior to revoking acceptance. In some cases the seller was granted an offset for use *after* rejection or revocation as well.[43]

---

40. American Container Corp. v. Hanley Trucking Corp., 111 N.J.Super. 322, 268 A.2d 313, 7 UCC 1301 (1970) (reasonable value of possessory interest of buyer offset against return of purchase price).

41. See, e.g., North American Lighting, Inc. v. Hopkins Manufacturing, Corp., 37 F.3d 1253, 24 UCC2d 1061 (7th Cir. 1994).

42. 328 N.J.Super. 491, 746 A.2d 480, 40 UCC2d 1012 (App. Div. 2000).

43. See, e.g., Huntsville Hospital v. Mortara Instrument, 57 F.3d 1043, 27 UCC2d 435 (11th Cir. 1995) (affirming trial court's grant of offset for value of buyer's use of goods after rejecting them).

§ 9–4 The Buyer's Right to Revoke Acceptance, Sections 2–607, 2–608

Section 2–608 presupposes acceptance, a topic treated in section 9–2 *supra*. Section 2–608 sets forth the buyer's right to revoke acceptance as follows:

(1) The buyer may revoke his acceptance of a lot or commercial unit whose non-conformity substantially impairs its value to him if he has accepted it

    (a) on the reasonable assumption that its non-conformity would be cured and it has not been seasonably cured; or

    (b) without discovery of such non-conformity if his acceptance was reasonably induced either by the difficulty of discovery before acceptance or by the seller's assurances.

(2) Revocation of acceptance must occur within a reasonable time after the buyer discovers or should have discovered the ground for it and before any substantial change in condition of the goods which is not caused by their own defects. It is not effective until the buyer notifies the seller of it.

(3) A buyer who so revokes has the same rights and duties with regard to the goods involved as if he had rejected them.

Why is it necessary to have both a right of rejection and a right to revoke acceptance? After one has dug through the detail in 2–601 and sections following, detail necessitated in part by the distinction between rejection and revocation, one may have even more doubt about the need for the two distinct rights. In general the right to reject is more readily available, and one wishing to exercise that right has fewer hurdles to jump.

Wisely the drafters believed that a buyer who has had goods for a long time should have to make a better case in order to throw the goods back on the seller. A variety of policies support the proposition that a buyer who has had possession for any considerable period of time or has otherwise accepted should only rarely have the right to return the goods to the seller. In the first place, the longer the buyer has the goods, the higher the probability that the alleged defect was caused by the buyer or aggravated by its failure properly to maintain the goods. Secondly, the longer the buyer holds the goods, the greater the benefit the buyer may have derived from their use. Finally the longer the delay, the greater the depreciation and the greater the loss to society. These factors support a rule that makes it more difficult for the buyer who has once accepted to cast the goods and attendant loss from depreciation and market factors back on the seller.

When the Code was introduced, the term "revocation of acceptance" was new, and during the early years of the Code the courts did not take to it. What the drafters would call revocation of acceptance and would analyze under 2–608, the courts would sometimes define as rescission or rejection and discuss without reference to the provisions of 2–608. In recent years, however, this trend has reversed itself.[1]

Since revocation of acceptance always occurs after acceptance and may occur long after the seller regarded the transaction as closed, a buyer who might have rejected with ease before acceptance must—in theory at least—meet several additional conditions to revoke acceptance. Section 2–608 of the Code sets up the following substantive and procedural conditions for the buyer who wishes to revoke acceptance: (1) a nonconformity which substantially impairs the value of the "lot or commercial unit"; (2) acceptance (a) (with discovery of the defect) on the reasonable assumption that the nonconformity would be cured or (b) (without discovery) reasonably induced by the difficulty of the discovery or by seller's assurances; (3) revocation within a reasonable time after the nonconformity was discovered or should have been discovered; (4) revocation before a substantial change occurs in the condition of the goods not caused by their own defects; and (5) due notice of revocation to the seller.[2]

The road to revocation for the lawyer in advising a revoking buyer may not be easy. First, our lawyer must decide whether the acceptance was made with or without discovery of the defect. Second, he must consider whether it was made on "the reasonable assumption of cure" or whether it was induced by the "difficulty of discovery" or the "seller's assurances." Finally, the lawyer must determine whether the attempted revocation will occur within a reasonable time after discovery (or time when the buyer should have discovered) and, last of all, whether there has been a substantial deterioration in the goods. Consider all of the difficult judgments: When did the acceptance occur? Was the buyer's assumption of cure reasonable? Was the acceptance "reasonably" induced by the difficulty of discovery or by seller's assurances? Has more than a reasonable time passed since the discovery of the nonconformity? Have the goods undergone a substantial change? Does the noncon-

---

§ 9–4

1. For judicial treatment of revocation as it displaces rescission, see Sudol v. Rudy Papa Motors, 175 N.J.Super. 238, 417 A.2d 1133, 29 UCC 1290 (1980); Cissell Mfg. Co. v. Park, 36 P.3d 85, 43 UCC2d 889 (Colo. App. 2001).

2. See generally New Pacific Overseas Group (USA) Inc. v. Excal Int'l

Development Corp., 2001 WL 40822, 43 UCC2d 1149 (S.D.N.Y. 2001); MacSteel Int'l USA Corp. v. Superior Products Co., Inc., 2002 WL 472288, 47 UCC2d 468 (N.D. Ill. 2002); Cuesta v. Classic Wheels, Inc., 358 N.J.Super. 512, 818 A.2d 448, 50 UCC2d 791 (App. Div. 2003).

formity substantially impair? A search for that rare form of certainty which soothes the student's anxiety and warms the heart of the corporate lawyer is fruitless here. We can do little more than footnote some of the relevant cases and advise the lawyer dealing with 2–608 to charge a handsome fee.

The buyer who would revoke its acceptance must show that the nonconformity in the goods accepted "substantially impairs" the value of the goods "to him." As Comment 2 to 2–608 states: "Revocation of acceptance is possible only where the nonconformity substantially impairs the value of the goods to the buyer." Thus there must be (1) a "nonconformity," i.e., a respect or respects in which the goods do not conform to the contract, and (2) this nonconformity must substantially impair the value of the goods "to the buyer." A determination of the existence or non-existence of a nonconformity requires reference to the terms of the contract, including the law of warranty.[3] As we will see in Chapter 13, the courts do not look with favor on disclaimers that purport to disclaim responsibility for what the seller has in essence agreed to sell.[4] But if the only relevant language in the agreement as to quality has been effectively disclaimed, no nonconformity in the goods sufficient for revocation can exist.[5] If the goods are sold "as is," Comment 7 of 2–316 states the "buyer takes the entire risk as to the quality of the goods."[6]

The value of the goods must be substantially impaired. Earlier we suggested that a fruitful source of factors on substantiality is the general contract law on material breach. But there is now a body of case law under 2–608(1) itself. Many of these cases involve efforts by the seller to repair. Where the seller can and does readily

3. Blankenship v. Northtown Ford, Inc., 95 Ill.App.3d 303, 50 Ill.Dec. 850, 420 N.E.2d 167, 31 UCC 480 (1981); Cissell Mfg. Co. v. Park, 36 P.3d 85, 43 UCC2d 889 (Colo. App. 2001) (using jury's determination that goods were "as warranted," "suitable," and "merchantable" for purposes of buyer's breach of warranty claim as determinative that goods value was not substantially impaired with regard to buyer's revocation of acceptance claim); Parsley v. Monaco Coach Corp., 327 F.Supp.2d 797, 54 UCC2d 301 (W.D. Mich. 2004) (buyer could not revoke acceptance where dealer effectively disclaimed all warranties). See also Herring v. Home Depot, Inc., 350 S.C. 373, 565 S.E.2d 773, 48 UCC2d 984 (App. 2002) (breach of warranty allows revocation only if substantially impairs value of goods to buyer); Ramos v. Ford Motor Co., 655

N.W.2d 447, 49 UCC2d 1174 (S.D. 2002) (accord).

4. Seekings v. Jimmy GMC, Inc., 130 Ariz. 596, 638 P.2d 210, 32 UCC 1450 (1981).

5. Crume v. Ford Motor Co., 60 Or. App. 224, 653 P.2d 564, 35 UCC 144 (1982). But see Advanced Computer Sales, Inc. v. Sizemore, 186 Ga.App. 10, 366 S.E.2d 303, 6 UCC2d 18 (1988) holding 2–608 "is an available remedy even where the seller has attempted to limit its warranties." Compare majority and dissenting opinions in Esquire Mobile Homes, Inc. v. Arrendale, 182 Ga.App. 528, 356 S.E.2d 250, 3 UCC2d 1798 (1987).

6. See Schneider v. Miller, 73 Ohio App.3d 335, 597 N.E.2d 175, 18 UCC2d 764 (1991).

repair there is no substantial impairment.[7] But a seller usually cannot bar revocation where its "repairing" constitutes substituting a major new integral part in the whole—such as an engine in a *new* car.[8] Moreover, where a whole series of defects arises seriatim, the seller cannot bar revocation indefinitely simply by repairing, and standing by to repair every defect that has or will emerge. As one court put it, there comes a time when "enough is enough."[9] And even if the repairs are not so numerous as to fall in the "enough is enough" category, they may justify revocation when the buyer loses confidence in the goods, or, as it is sometimes put, the buyer's "faith is shaken."[10] But if the buyer agrees to a reduction in the price of the goods, this may compensate for any impairment and bar revocation.

The buyer may revoke only if there is substantial impairment of the value "to him." The use of "to him" suggests that the court is to measure the impairment by reference to the buyer's particular needs. That suggestion is confirmed by the last clause in the last sentence of Comment 2 of 2–608: "[T]he question is whether the non-conformity is such as will in fact cause a substantial impairment of value to the buyer though the seller had no advance knowledge as to the buyer's particular circumstances." It is theoretically possible, therefore, for the seller to deliver goods which a buyer of conventional tastes would find satisfactory (though non-conforming in insubstantial details) and yet find that because of the particular needs or taste of this buyer, the buyer has a right to revoke acceptance.

The cases seem to require both subjective and objective elements. The buyer must provide objective evidence that the value of the goods was substantially impaired, but this value is to be viewed

---

7. Pratt v. Winnebago Indus., Inc., 463 F.Supp. 709, 26 UCC 68 (W.D.Pa. 1979); Hardy v. Winnebago Industries, Inc., 120 Md.App. 261, 706 A.2d 1086, 34 UCC2d 1007 (1998); Ask Technologies, Inc. v. Cablescope, Inc., 2003 WL 22400201, 51 UCC2d 1028 (S.D.N.Y. 2003).

8. See, e.g., Zabriskie Chevrolet, Inc. v. Smith, 99 N.J.Super. 441, 240 A.2d 195, 5 UCC 30 (1968).

9. Oberg v. Phillips, 615 P.2d 1022, 29 UCC 846 (Okla.App.1980); Bland v. Freightliner LLC, 206 F.Supp.2d 1202, 49 UCC2d 524 (M.D. Fla. 2002) (while each of the 21 defects individually may not have been a substantial impairment, taken together they may be).

10. Welch v. Fitzgerald–Hicks Dodge, Inc., 121 N.H. 358, 430 A.2d 144, 31 UCC 1336 (1981) (car); Lathrop v.

Tyrrell, 128 Ill.App.3d 1067, 84 Ill.Dec. 283, 471 N.E.2d 1049, 39 UCC 1653 (1984) (satellite dish); Haverlah v. Memphis Aviation, Inc., 674 S.W.2d 297, 40 UCC 1263 (Tenn.App.1984) (airplane); Kelynack v. Yamaha Motor Corp., USA, 152 Mich.App. 105, 394 N.W.2d 17, 2 UCC2d 166 (1986) (motorcycle). But see Ramos v. Ford Motor Co., 655 N.W.2d 447, 49 UCC2d 1174 (S.D. 2002) (buyer attempted to revoke on the basis that a series of defects caused him to lose confidence in his car, but court rejected this because no defect was detectable at the time he rejected the car. Also, if a revoking buyer refuses to allow the seller to repair, a court may hold that the buyer "reaccepted." Olson v. Ford Motor Co., 258 Ga.App. 848, 575 S.E.2d 743, 50 UCC2d 166 (2002).

through the unique needs and circumstances of that particular buyer and not those of the average buyer. However we dress it, this concept looks goofy. How can something be objective and, at the same time, subjective? Perhaps the courts are asking us to listen to *this* buyer's complaint—but not too closely.

Assuming discovery of a defect, when is it reasonable for the buyer to believe that the nonconformity would be cured? The most obvious case is where the seller states that it will cure.[11] But it has been held the seller does not get a second chance to cure.[12] A past course of dealing or usage of trade may also make it reasonable to conclude that the seller will cure.[13] Still other factors, including the nature of the goods (as, for example, goods requiring some post-delivery adjustment or adaptation), may make that assumption reasonable.[14]

If the buyer accepted the goods without discovering the nonconformity, the buyer can still revoke under 2–608(1)(b) if his failure to discover the nonconformity was "reasonably induced either by the difficulty of discovery before acceptance or by the seller's assurances." Thus, if the buyer failed to make a reasonable inspection and that would have revealed the nonconformity, buyer is barred from revocation.[15] In a number of cases, courts have found that the buyer's investigation could not have revealed the nonconformity because of the "difficulty of discovery."[16]

A residual substantive question under 2–608 is the meaning of "assurances" in 2–608(1)(b):

> [Revocation is permitted if acceptance occurred] without discovery of such non-conformity if his acceptance was reasonably induced * * * by the seller's assurances.

11. Automated Controls, Inc. v. Mic Enters., Inc., 1978 WL 23448, 27 UCC 661 (D.Neb.1978), aff'd, 599 F.2d 288, 27 UCC 677 (8th Cir.1979); Polycon Indus., Inc. v. Hercules Inc., 471 F.Supp. 1316, 26 UCC 917 (E.D.Wis.1979); Berg Chilling Systems, Inc. v. Hull Corp., 2002 WL 31681955, 49 UCC2d 189 (E.D. Pa. 2002) (buyer is barred from revoking acceptance where it knew of non-conformity at the time of acceptance and there was no evidence that it accepted on assumption that nonconformities would be cured).

12. Steele v. Pacesetter Motor Cars, Inc., 267 Wis.2d 873, 672 N.W.2d 141, 52 UCC2d 405 (2003).

13. Gindy Mfg. Corp. v. Cardinale Trucking Corp., 111 N.J.Super. 383, 268 A.2d 345, 7 UCC 1257 (1970).

14. Ybarra v. Modern Trailer Sales, Inc., 94 N.M. 249, 609 P.2d 331, 28 UCC 1329 (1980). See also Berg Chilling Systems, Inc. v. Hull Corp., 2002 WL 31681955, 49 UCC2d 189 (E.D. Pa. 2002) (however, buyer who knew of nonconformities when accepting could not revoke, given no evidence buyer assumed cure was possible). But if cost of replacement high, this might not nullify right to revoke. See, e.g., Deere & Co. v. Johnson 271 F.3d 613, 46 UCC2d 433 (5th Cir. 2001).

15. Hummel v. Skyline Dodge, Inc., 41 Colo.App. 572, 589 P.2d 73, 26 UCC 46 (1978).

16. Atlan Indus., Inc. v. O.E.M., Inc., 555 F.Supp. 184, 35 UCC 795 (W.D.Okl. 1983).

The buyer's failure to discover nonconformities may be attributable to assurances of the seller. Thus the seller may say things that throw the buyer off guard or otherwise reasonably induce the buyer not to discover the nonconformity.[17] But mere puffing on the part of the seller does not constitute assurances under 2–608(1)(b).[18]

Under 2–608(2) a revocation of acceptance must take place "within a reasonable time after the buyer discovers or should have discovered the ground for it." The policies which support this requirement are similar to those requiring a timely rejection, discussed earlier, and include affording some opportunity for adjustment or settlement. Thus, the time period begins to run when the buyer discovers or should have discovered the ground for revocation. The courts have considered several basic factors to answer when the buyer should have discovered—including the difficulty of discovering the defect, the terms of the contract, the perishability of the goods, and the course of performance after the sale and before revocation. All of these were discussed earlier in connection with rejection.[19] Of course, the time allowed for revocation may be limited by agreement.[20]

Especially where the delay is attributable to efforts to repair the goods, the revocation may even come long after sale and still be timely.[21] But in a number of cases, courts have found or held that the revocation was not timely.[22] Of course, the longer the buyer

17. Morrisville Comm'n Sales, Inc. v. Harris, 142 Vt. 9, 451 A.2d 1092, 34 UCC 1190 (1982).

18. Scaringe v. Holstein, 103 A.D.2d 880, 477 N.Y.S.2d 903, 38 UCC 1595 (1984). And, of course, a defect may be latent at time of acceptance. Cissell Mfg. Co. v. Park, 36 P.3d 85, 43 UCC2d 889 (Colo. App. 2001).

19. For a thoughtful opinion applying our multi-factor analysis, see EPN–Delaval, S.A. v. Inter–Equip, Inc., 542 F.Supp. 238, 34 UCC 130 (S.D.Tex. 1982). Eggl v. Letvin Equipment Co., 632 N.W.2d 435, 45 UCC2d 538 (N.D. 2001) (trial court's determination that over 160 hours and 6 months use of tractor prior to revocation of acceptance was within reasonable time for discovery was not clearly erroneous); Jaramillo v. Gonzales, 132 N.M. 459, 50 P.3d 554, 49 UCC2d 159 (2002) (affirming that five years and 8 months was a reasonable time in which to revoke acceptance of a mobile home with defective plumbing where defect was latent and not discovered for 5 years and buyers spent 8 months attempting to find someone to repair the plumbing); Imex Int'l, Inc. v.

Wires Engineering, 261 Ga.App. 329, 583 S.E.2d 117, 50 UCC2d 448 (2003) (holding that revocation of acceptance is not effective where buyer notifies seller of revocation six months after delivery and where buyer knew of defect within one month of delivery).

20. In re East Coast Brokers and Packers, Inc., 120 B.R. 221, 14 UCC2d 461 (Bankr.M.D.Fla.1990).

21. Solomon Refrigeration, Inc. v. Osburn, 148 Ga.App. 772, 252 S.E.2d 686, 26 UCC 73 (1979); Steele v. Pacesetter Motor Cars, Inc., 267 Wis.2d 873, 672 N.W.2d 141, 52 UCC2d 405 (Ct. App. 2003) (after repeated unsuccessful attempts of seller to repair, buyer allowed to revoke acceptance). See, however, China Nat. Metal Prod. v. Apex Digital, Inc., 141 F.Supp. 2d 1013, 45 UCC2d 492 (C.D. Calif. 2001) (buyer's four month effort to work out defects signified non-revocable acceptance).

22. See, e.g., Euroworld, Inc. v. Blakey, 613 F.Supp. 129, 41 UCC 403 (S.D.Fla.1985), aff'd, 794 F.2d 686 (11th Cir.1986) (four month delay by expert buyer in inspecting airplane engines and

keeps and uses the goods, the greater the likelihood that some conduct on its part itself accounts for any nonconformity. Comment 4 to Section 2–608 states that the time period "should extend in most cases beyond the time in which notification of breach must be given, beyond the time for discovery of nonconformity after acceptance and beyond the time for rejection after tender."

The buyer's right to revoke acceptance automatically expires under 2–608(2) if the goods undergo a substantial change in condition "which is not caused by their own defects". According to Comment 6, a buyer ought not to be allowed to revoke its acceptance of goods that have "materially deteriorated" in the buyer's hands except insofar as this is attributable to original "defects" in the goods. Examples of such "deterioration" not attributable to original defects are: buyer's cutting of a fabric,[23] buyer's use of the goods after modifying them and improperly maintaining them,[24] buyer's manufacture of goods into parts,[25] buyer's resale of the goods without recalling them,[26] buyer's cutting of goods into narrow strips in accord with specifications of sub-purchaser,[27] buyer's knitting defective yarn.[28] But reasonable changes due to good faith efforts by the buyer to make the goods usable generally do not bar revocation;[29] neither do changes (e.g. accident damage to a car) which the buyer has fully repaired,[30] nor "changes" in the form of liens for repairs.[31] Continued use while awaiting an attempted cure does not necessarily equate to a substantial change.[32] If the buyer makes a reasonable inspection and does not discover a defect, then effects a substantial change to the goods unwittingly, revocation

notice of revocation nine months after delivery). But one court allowed revocation of acceptance of a mobile home where buyer had lived in it for more than five years. Jaramillo v. Gonzales, 132 N.M. 459, 50 P.3d 554, 49 UCC2d 159 (App. 2002). But see Basselen v. General Motors Corp., 341 Ill.App.3d 278, 275 Ill.Dec. 267, 792 N.E.2d 498, 51 UCC2d 698 (2003).

23. Trinkle v. Schumacher Co., 100 Wis.2d 13, 301 N.W.2d 255, 31 UCC 39 (App.1980).

24. Royal Typewriter Co. v. Xerographic Supplies Corp., 719 F.2d 1092, 37 UCC 429 (11th Cir.1983).

25. Intervale Steel Corp. v. Borg & Beck Div., Borg–Warner Corp., 578 F.Supp. 1081, 38 UCC 805 (E.D.Mich. 1984).

26. Eaton Corp. v. Magnavox Co., 581 F.Supp. 1514, 39 UCC 152 (E.D.Mich.1984); China Nat'l Metal Products Import/Export Co. v. Apex Di-

gital, Inc., 141 F.Supp.2d 1013, 45 UCC2d 492 (C.D. Ca. 2001).

27. Toyomenka (America), Inc. v. Combined Metals Corp., 139 Ill.App.3d 654, 94 Ill.Dec. 295, 487 N.E.2d 1172, 42 UCC 1267 (1985).

28. Calvert Knit Corp. v. Glendale Textiles, Inc., 1987 WL 257439, 3 UCC2d 585 (N.Y.Sup.1987).

29. ARB (American Research Bureau), Inc. v. E–Systems, Inc., 663 F.2d 189, 30 UCC 949 (D.C.Cir.1980); J.F. Daley Int'l, Ltd. v. Midwest Container & Indus. Supply Co., 849 S.W.2d 260, 20 UCC2d 1259 (Mo.App.1993).

30. Preston Motor Co. v. Palomares, 133 Ariz. 245, 650 P.2d 1227, 34 UCC 1184 (App.1982).

31. Sumner v. Fel–Air, Inc., 680 P.2d 1109, 38 UCC 91 (Alaska 1984).

32. Smith v. Navistar Int'l Transp. Corp., 714 F.Supp. 303, 10 UCC2d 790 (N.D.Ill.1989).

may not be available, but the buyer may still have a valid breach of warranty claim.[33]

In addition, section 2–608(2) states that a buyer's revocation is not effective until the buyer "notifies the seller of it". Comment 5 to 2–608 is frequently quoted in the cases.[34] It states:

> The content of the notice under subsection (2) is to be determined in this case as in others by considerations of good faith, prevention of surprise, and reasonable adjustment. More will generally be necessary than the mere notification of breach required under the preceding section [2–607]. On the other hand the requirements of the section on waiver of buyer's objections [2–605] do not apply here. The fact that quick notification of trouble is desirable affords good ground for being slow to bind a buyer by his first statement. Following the general policy of this Article, the requirements of the content of notification are less stringent in the case of a non-merchant buyer.

Mere notification of breach under 2–607(3) then is not enough.[35] One line of cases between merchants holds that the essential content of the notice of revocation must set forth "the nonconformity in the goods materially impairing their value to the buyer."[36] The notice must inform the seller that the buyer does not wish to keep the goods.[37] If the buyer equivocates in word[38] or in deed,[39] his purported revocation may be invalid.[40] While the buyer's

---

33. Western Paper Co. v. Bilby, 783 P.2d 980, 11 UCC2d 503 (Okl.App.1989). But, for both sides of this question, see majority and concurring opinions in Roy Burt Enters., Inc. v. Marsh, 328 N.C. 262, 400 S.E.2d 425, 15 UCC2d 486 (1991).

34. Cardwell v. International Housing, Inc., 282 Pa.Super. 498, 423 A.2d 355, 31 UCC 512 (1980).

35. Connecticut Inv. Casting Corp. v. Made–Rite Tool Co., 382 Mass. 603, 416 N.E.2d 966, 31 UCC 531 (1981).

36. See e.g., Lynx, Inc. v. Ordnance Products, Inc., 273 Md. 1, 327 A.2d 502, 15 UCC 1040 (1974); Solar Kinetics Corp. v. Joseph T. Ryerson & Son, Inc., 488 F.Supp. 1237, 29 UCC 85 (D.Conn. 1980).

37. Allis–Chalmers Corp. v. Sygitowicz, 18 Wash.App. 658, 571 P.2d 224, 22 UCC 1151 (1977); Connecticut Inv. Casting Corp. v. Made–Rite Tool Co., 382 Mass. 603, 416 N.E.2d 966, 31 UCC 531 (1981); Agrarian Grain Co., Inc. v.

Meeker, 526 N.E.2d 1189, 7 UCC2d 786 (Ind.App.1988).

38. Atlantic Building Sys., Inc. v. Alley Constr. Corp., 1981 WL 138027, 32 UCC 1414 (D.Mass.1981); Agrarian Grain Co. v. Meeker, 526 N.E.2d 1189, 7 UCC2d 786 (Ind.App.1988) (seller's knowledge of buyer's dissatisfaction does not unequivocally equate to notice of revocation); HCI Chemicals (USA) v. Henkel KGaA, 966 F.2d 1018, 18 UCC2d 436 (5th Cir.1992) (must be clear and unambiguous). See also Mitcham v. First State Bank of Crossett, Arkansas, 333 Ark. 598, 970 S.W.2d 267, 40 UCC2d 468 (1998).

39. Hays Merchandise, Inc. v. Dewey, 78 Wash.2d 343, 474 P.2d 270, 8 UCC 31 (1970); Gilbert v. Caffee, 293 N.W.2d 893, 29 UCC 1299 (S.D.1980); Konicki v. Salvaco, Inc., 16 Ohio App.3d 40, 474 N.E.2d 347, 41 UCC 103 (1984).

40. But see Cardwell v. International Housing, Inc., 282 Pa.Super. 498, 423 A.2d 355, 31 UCC 512 (1980).

notice of revocation needs to be unequivocal, it need not be "formal."[41] And if the buyer after sending a valid notice of revocation thereafter "reaccepts" the goods, his earlier revocation notice will be superseded.[42] Such a "reacceptance" need not be explicit but may be implied from conduct such as continued use of the goods.

The question whether the buyer's continued use of the goods after giving an otherwise valid notice of revocation constitutes a reacceptance or waiver has been litigated in numerous cases. The cases tell that this use is risky by a buyer who wants to claim revocation. In McCullough v. Bill Swad Chrysler–Plymouth, Inc.[43] the Ohio Supreme Court took the view that whether the buyer's post revocation use constitutes reacceptance or waiver depends on whether that use was reasonable. According to the court, the trier of fact should divine the answers to the following questions:[44]

> (1) Upon being apprised of the buyer's revocation of his acceptance, what instructions, if any, did the seller tender the buyer concerning return of the now * * * [revoked] goods? (2) Did the buyer's business needs or personal circumstances, compel the continued use? (3) During the period of such use, did the seller persist in assuring the buyer that all nonconformities would be cured or that provisions would otherwise be made to recompense the latter for the dissatisfaction and inconvenience which the defects caused him? (4) Did the seller act in good faith? (5) Was the seller unduly prejudiced by the buyer's continued use?

Some generalizations are possible. If, because of limited financial resources or for other reasons such as the unavailability of any substitutes, a buyer is compelled to continue using the goods after giving notice of revocation, a court may rule—even as a matter of law—this continued use does not bar revocation.[45] However, revocation may be barred as a remedy if, after revoking, the buyer continues to use the goods while not seeking out replacements with which to "cover" with adequate dispatch.[46] If the seller refuses to acknowledge the buyer's notice of revocation and declines to accept a tender of the goods, courts are less likely to view some continued

---

11. Cissell Mfg. Co. v. Park, 36 P.3d 85, 43 UCC2d 889 (Colo. App. 2001).

42. See, e.g., Hutchinson Utilities Commission v. Curtiss–Wright Corp., 775 F.2d 231, 42 UCC 396 (8th Cir. 1985).

43. 5 Ohio St.3d 181, 449 N.E.2d 1289, 36 UCC 513 (1983). See also Basselen v. General Motors Corp., 341 Ill. App.3d 278, 275 Ill.Dec. 267, 792 N.E.2d 498, 51 UCC2d 698 (2003) (revoking buyer has burden of proving continued use reasonable, and driving car 19,000

more miles after revoking acceptance was not reasonable).

44. See also, McCullough v. Bill Swad Chrysler–Plymouth, Inc., 5 Ohio St.3d 181, 184, 449 N.E.2d 1289, 1293, 36 UCC 513, 518–19 (1983).

45. Fablok Mills, Inc. v. Cocker Machine & Foundry Co., 125 N.J.Super. 251, 310 A.2d 491, 13 UCC 449 (1973).

46. L.S. Heath & Son, Inc. v. AT & T Information Sys., Inc., 9 F.3d 561, 22 UCC2d 27 (7th Cir.1993).

use of the goods by the buyer as a reacceptance or a waiver.[47] On the other hand, in one case the buyer never attempted to procure substitute goods despite their availability, continued to make payments despite protests as to defects, permitted additional service calls and repairs after notice of revocation, and continued to use the goods throughout litigation. The court refused to permit revocation.[48]

Timeliness of a *notice* of revocation is not really separate from the timeliness of the actual revocation itself. Thus the cases on timeliness of a revocation apply here. A buyer has a longer period in which to notify of revocation under 2–608(2) than to notify of breach under 2–607.[49] And, of course, the time frame for a notice of rejection and for a notice of revocation may differ greatly.[50] Although the cases hold that an oral notice of revocation is enough,[51] unequivocal written notice is better.[52] Several courts—for reasons we do not understand—have found a notice is invalid if it is contained in legal papers initiating a lawsuit.[53]

The cases generally hold that a buyer may only revoke acceptance of goods as against his own seller. In Neal v. SMC Corp., the Texas court held the buyer could not revoke against the manufacturer in the absence of a contractual relationship.[54] One court has expressed a willingness to allow revocation against a third party if an agency relationship exists between that party and the seller.[55]

However, where a distributor not in privity with the buyer has expressly warranted the goods to a remote buyer, courts have allowed the buyer to revoke acceptance against that party.[56] At least one state has codified this rule, but only regarding motor vehicles.[57]

47. McGregor v. Dimou, 101 Misc.2d 756, 422 N.Y.S.2d 806, 28 UCC 66 (1979); Deere & Co. v. Johnson, 271 F.3d 613, 46 UCC2d 433 (5th Cir. 2001) (buyer's continued use of defective combine not unreasonable where seller refused tender of combine upon revocation).

48. Fargo Machine & Tool Co. v. Kearney & Trecker Corp., 428 F.Supp. 364, 21 UCC 80 (E.D.Mich.1977).

49. Gasque v. Mooers Motor Car Co., 227 Va. 154, 313 S.E.2d 384, 38 UCC 120 (1984). See also Lanners v. Whitney, 247 Or. 223, 428 P.2d 398, 4 UCC 369 (1967).

50. Rutland Music Service, Inc. v. Ford Motor Co., 138 Vt. 562, 422 A.2d 248, 31 UCC 536 (1980) (stresses several major differences between rejection and revocation).

51. Royal Lincoln–Mercury Sales, Inc. v. Wallace, 415 So.2d 1024, 33 UCC 1262 (Miss.1982).

52. At least one court has expressly agreed with our approach. See DeVoe Chevrolet–Cadillac, Inc. v. Cartwright, 526 N.E.2d 1237, 7 UCC2d 792 (Ind. App.1988).

53. Ybarra v. Modern Trailer Sales, Inc., 94 N.M. 249, 609 P.2d 331, 28 UCC 1329 (1980).

54. 99 S.W.3d 813, 49 UCC2d 1179 (Tex. App. 2003).

55. Funk v. Montgomery AMC/ Jeep/Renault, 66 Ohio App.3d 815, 586 N.E.2d 1113, 18 UCC2d 446 (1990).

56. Durfee v. Rod Baxter Imports, Inc., 262 N.W.2d 349, 22 UCC 945 (Minn.1977).

57. N.C. Gen. Stat. § 25–2–103(d) (1986). See Alberti v. Manufactured

Another court decided that where the manufacturer's warranty and the seller's sales contract were "so closely linked that they blended into a single unit" at the time of sale,[58] the buyer could revoke against both. Finally, where a manufacturer's dealer had gone out of business, the Eighth Circuit allowed the buyer to revoke as against the manufacturer.[59] The first two of these cases can be explained on the ground that the distributor and the manufacturer had warranty liability to the ultimate buyer. The third case is not so easy. The Eighth Circuit allowed the buyer not only to revoke against the manufacturer but also to recover its down payment from the manufacturer. On the question whether the manufacturer had warranty liability to the buyer, the court remarked that although the Code "eliminates the defense of privity in suits for damages for breach of warranties it is silent as to revocation of acceptance." The court went on to say that remedies should, however be administered "liberally". In our view, the court's decision is not authorized by the Code. Section 2–608 twice uses the words "the seller." Here the manufacturer was not the seller. Absent warranty liability between the manufacturer and the seller, we would not go so far as the court in this case.

Once a buyer has jumped through all the correct hoops for a valid revocation, may the seller under 2–508 insist on a right to cure? The language of the Code text and nearly all of the cases also say "no".[60] However, many recent cases show the willingness of courts to find an implied right to cure before revocation in the language of 2–508 and 2–608.[61] More on this in the next section.

Section 2–608(3) provides that a buyer who revokes has the same rights and duties with regard to accepted goods as if the buyer had rejected them. We have already discussed these rights and duties. Here the buyer need not return the goods or even tender them back.[62] Nor must the buyer tender any sum for rental or beneficial use. In fact, the buyer may retain the goods to protect its security interest.[63] The only duty the buyer has is to hold the goods for the seller.[64] The buyer must be cautious, though, to avoid

Homes, Inc., 329 N.C. 727, 407 S.E.2d 819, 15 UCC2d 1184 (1991).

58. Volkswagen, Inc. v. Novak, 418 So.2d 801, 34 UCC 1150 (Miss.1982). See also Royal Lincoln–Mercury Sales, Inc. v. Wallace, 415 So.2d 1024, 33 UCC 1262 (Miss.1982).

59. Ford Motor Credit Co. v. Harper, 671 F.2d 1117, 33 UCC 921 (8th Cir. 1982).

60. See e.g., Head v. Phillips Camper Sales & Rental, Inc., 234 Mich.App. 94, 593 N.W.2d 595, 37 UCC2d 1033 (1999).

61. See Web Press Services Corp. v. New London Motors, Inc., 203 Conn. 342, 525 A.2d 57, 3 UCC2d 1386 (1987).

62. Art Hill, Inc. v. Heckler, 457 N.E.2d 242, 37 UCC 697 (Ind.App.1983);

63. See, e.g., Vista Chevrolet, Inc. v. Lewis, 704 S.W.2d 363, 1 UCC2d 1165 (Tex.App.1985), aff'd in part and rev'd in part, 709 S.W.2d 176 (1986). State "lemon laws" may also provide for such "set off." See e.g., Chapter 444, Laws of New York (1987) (General Business Law sec. 198a).

64. Bryant v. Prenger, 717 S.W.2d 242, 3 UCC2d 582 (Mo.App.1986).

any use of the goods that may be construed as inconsistent with the seller's ownership interest and thereby a re-acceptance by the buyer. What of the seller's right to an *offset* for the buyer's use of the goods before or after revocation? The issues here are the same as those already discussed in regard to rejection.

A buyer who rightfully revokes acceptance can be entitled to return of the full purchase price.[65]

§ 9–5   Seller's Right to Cure, Section 2–508

Section 2–508 had no antecedent in the Uniform Sales Act. The section is a restriction upon the buyer's right to reject; it offers many significant but unanswered questions. Although it was a novel legal doctrine, it was not new to business practice; it does no more than give legal recognition to a practical right that many sellers have exercised over the years. Professor Macaulay has informed us that legal sanctions are neither the only nor the most important sanctions of an aggrieved party, and it seems likely that 2–508 simply recognizes a general pattern of business behavior and adds a legal sanction to those economic and nonlegal sanctions which the parties had and have.[1] Amended section 2–508, would have expanded the right.[2]

It is clear that the seller's right to cure under 2–508 limits the buyer's right to reject under 2–602; whether 2–508 limits the buyer's right to revoke acceptance under 2–608 is less clear. Until recent years, most courts held against the applicability of the right to cure in revocation cases; these courts relied mostly on a strict reading of the text of the Code.[3] Section 2–508 speaks only of

65. See, e.g., Fryatt v. Lantana One, Ltd., 866 So.2d 158, 53 UCC2d 543 (Fla. App. 2004). See also, Cuesta v. Classic Wheels, Inc., 358 N.J.Super. 512, 818 A.2d 448, 50 UCC2d 791 (2003).

§ 9–5

1. Macaulay, Non–Contractual Relations in Business: A Preliminary Study, 28 Am.Soc.Rev. 55 (1963). On the right to cure, see Travilio, The UCC's Three "R's": Rejection, Revocation and (The Seller's) Right to Cure, 53 U.Cinn.L.Rev. 931 (1984); Lawrence, Cure After Breach of Contract Under the Restatement (Second) of Contracts: An Analytical Comparison with the Uniform Commercial Code, 70 Minn.L.Rev. 713 (1986).

2. As of May 28, 2009, seventy-four nations including the U.S., are parties to the U.N. Convention on International Sale of Goods (CISG), which, in the absence of contract terms to the contrary, governs sales between these participating countries. For example, CISG articles 34, 37, and 48 specify the seller's right to cure, which varies only slightly from the seller's right under the Uniform Code. See also Catherine Piché, The Convention on Contracts for the International Sale of Goods and the Uniform Commercial Code Remedies in Light of Remedial Principles Recognized Under U.S. Law: Are the Remedies of Granting Additional Time to the Defaulting Parties and of Reduction of Price Fair and Efficient Ones?, 28 N.C. J. Int'l L. & Com. Reg. 519 (2003); Eric C. Schneider, The Seller's Right to Cure Under the Uniform Commercial Code and the United Nations Convention on Contracts for the International Sale of Goods, 7 Ariz. J. Int'l & Comp. L. 69 (1989).

3. See, e.g., Pavesi v. Ford Motor Co., 155 N.J.Super. 373, 382 A.2d 954, 23 UCC 929 (1978); Head v. Phillips Camper Sales & Rental, Inc., 234 Mich.

rejection. The word "revocation" does not appear in either the text of 2–508 or in its official comments. Proponents of this approach argue that this was intended by the Code's drafters and that the act of acceptance draws the line where the right to cure ends.

Newer case law and commentary show an increased willingness to allow the seller to cure after acceptance and before allowing the buyer to exercise the right to revoke.[4] Certainly, a case can be made for this approach. The Code itself says that it is to "be construed liberally" in order "to promote its underlying purposes and policies."[5] A stated policy of the Code is to incorporate commercial practices and custom.[6] A reading of the cases indicates most buyers allow, or even desire, an opportunity to cure by the seller before resorting to the more drastic action of revocation. Two policies not stated in the Code but clearly evident in its provisions are to facilitate the settlement of disputes by the parties themselves, and to minimize economic waste.[7] Allowing the seller the chance to cure might go further toward these goals than permitting the buyer unilaterally to revoke and sending the parties to court to see if the revocation is justified. A recent Mississippi Supreme Court decision with four justices in dissent in effect applied UCC 2–508 to preclude a finding of breach.[8] Amended Article 2, section 2–508(1), would have permitted cure against buyers, other than consumers, who are attempting to revoke.

Some courts have held that the applicability of the 2–508 right to cure to 2–608 revocation is implied in the language of the Code. This is usually done by applying 2–608(1)(a) (either correctly or incorrectly) or finding a buyer's "duty" to allow cure implied in 2–608(3).[9]

Courts wishing to preserve a seller's right to cure can also skirt the issue. For example, courts may misapply 2–608(1)(a) to a 2–608(1)(b) situation or decide the buyer had not yet had a "reason-

App. 94, 593 N.W.2d 595, 37 UCC2d 1033 (1999) (discussing policy reasons for disallowing right to cure in case of revocation of acceptance under 2–608(1)(b)).

4. See, e.g., Erling v. Homera, Inc., 298 N.W.2d 478, 30 UCC 181 (N.D. 1980); Jackson v. Rocky Mountain Datsun, Inc., 693 P.2d 391, 39 UCC 885 (Colo.App.1984) (court treats 2–608(1)(b) case as 2–608(1)(a) case); Magnum Press Automation, Inc. v. Thomas & Betts Corp., 325 Ill.App.3d 613, 259 Ill.Dec. 384, 758 N.E.2d 507, 46 UCC2d 97 (2001) (applying 2–508(1) to a revocation situation). See also Foss, The Seller's Right to Cure When the Buyer Re-

vokes Acceptance: Erase the Line in the Sand, 16 S. Ill.U.L.J. 1 (1991).

5. See § 1–102(1).

6. § 1–102(2)(b).

7. Fitzner Pontiac–Buick–Cadillac, Inc. v. Smith, 523 So.2d 324, 328, n.1, 6 UCC2d 396, 401, n.1 (Miss.1988). See also Mercury Marine v. Clear River Const. Co., Inc., 839 So.2d 508, 49 UCC2d 989 (Miss. 2003).

8. Mercury Marine v. Clear River Const. Co., Inc., 839 So.2d 508, 49 UCC2d 989 (Miss. 2003).

9. § 2–608(3) reads: "A buyer who so revokes has the same rights and duties with regard to the goods involved as if he had rejected them."

able opportunity to inspect" so that acceptance had not yet occurred.

Under the text of 2–608(1)(a), if the buyer accepted the goods on the reasonable assumption that the nonconformity would be cured, the buyer cannot revoke acceptance before giving the seller a reasonable opportunity to cure.[10] We suspect that the drafters failed to envision an important type of revocation case where cure should be allowed and that the drafters might have allowed cure here had they thought about it. This is the case where the seller tenders early, buyer accepts and then later discovers the defect and revokes acceptance, whereupon the seller tenders a conforming delivery still before expiration of the contract period.

Once one finds that the seller has a right to cure and that seller has cured, the legal rights of the parties under 2–508 and the other provisions are clear. Upon proper exercise by seller of his right to cure, the buyer loses any right to reject, although he retains the right to sue under 2–714 if buyer has suffered any injury because the original tender was nonconforming.[11]

Section 2–508(1) gives the seller an unfettered right to cure "within the contract time." That section offers few interpretive difficulties. Beyond the "contract time"—after the time for performance has passed—the seller has the right to cure only if (1) the seller had reasonable grounds to believe that a nonconforming tender would be acceptable, (2) the seller seasonably notifies the buyer of its intention to cure, and (3) the seller cures within a "further reasonable time."

Combing through the words of the section and applying them to the wide variety of cases to which they could conceivably apply, one can find a host of questions lurking in 2–508(2).[12] Here we will consider only four interpretive difficulties: (1) When does the seller have "reasonable grounds to believe" that tender would have been acceptable? (2) What constitutes seasonable notification of intent to cure? (3) What is a further reasonable time to cure? (4) What constitutes an effective cure? Section 2–508 reads in full as follows:

> (1) Where any tender or delivery by the seller is rejected because non-conforming and the time for performance has not

---

10. See e.g., United States Roofing, Inc. v. Credit Alliance Corp., 228 Cal. App.3d 1431, 279 Cal.Rptr. 533, 14 UCC2d 746 (1991).

11. Comment 2 to § 2–714 states, "The 'non-conformity' referred to in subsection (1) includes not only breaches of warranties but also any failure of the seller to perform according to his obligations under the contract." See also § 2–715 on buyer's incidental and consequential damages. Thus where the buyer incurs, for example, transportation expenses to return nonconforming goods to the seller, the buyer can recover these expenses from the seller notwithstanding a subsequent cure and acceptance.

12. See generally Peters, Remedies for Breach of Contracts Relating to the Sale of Goods Under the Uniform Commercial Code: A Roadmap for Article 2, 73 Yale L.J. 199 (1963).

yet expired, the seller may seasonably notify the buyer of his intention to cure and may then within the contract time make a conforming delivery.

(2) Where the buyer rejects a non-conforming tender which the seller had reasonable grounds to believe would be acceptable with or without money allowance the seller may if he seasonably notifies the buyer have a further reasonable time to substitute a conforming tender.

Comment 2 to 2–508 gives some direction to one's search for the meaning of the "reasonable grounds to believe" language; it indicates that:

> Such reasonable grounds can lie in prior course of dealing, course of performance or usage of trade as well as in particular circumstances surrounding the making of the contract. The seller is charged with commercial knowledge of any factors in a particular sales situation which require him to comply strictly with his obligations under the contract as, for example, strict conformity of documents in an overseas shipment or the sale of precision parts or chemicals for use in manufacture. Further, if the buyer gives notice either implicitly, as by a prior course of dealing involving rigorous inspections, or expressly, as by the deliberate inclusion of a "no replacement" clause in the contract, the seller is to be held to rigid compliance. If the clause appears in a "form" contract evidence that it is out of line with trade usage or the prior course of dealing and was not called to the seller's attention may be sufficient to show that the seller had reasonable grounds to believe that tender would be acceptable.

Under the comment, an understanding in the trade that a one percent deviation in quantity or a course of performance under which a seller has always been permitted to adjust machines after they have been sold or an explicit provision in the contract which authorized or prohibited post-delivery adjustments would have powerful and probably controlling influence on the question of whether the seller had reasonable grounds to believe that his or her tender would be acceptable with or without money allowance. In Continental Forest Products, Inc. v. White Lumber Sales, Inc.[13] the court did not explicitly discuss the question whether the seller had reasonable grounds to believe his tender would be acceptable, but it had no difficulty in finding that a seller who gave a price allowance made an effective cure on a shipment of plywood which contained a nine percent deviation from the contract specifications under trade usage which permitted a five percent deviation. The court found that a contract term requiring the buyer to "accept the balance of

---

13.   256 Or. 466, 474 P.2d 1, 8 UCC 178 (1970).

the shipment as invoiced" meant that the buyer could not reject but was obliged to accept the reduction of price as a method of cure.

The cases decided under 2–508(2) indicate that the seller has "reasonable grounds" when seller delivers what it believes to be a newer and better model than the hearing aid called for in the contract.[14] Likewise the seller may cure when it delivers a sewing machine "not shown to be of lesser quality than that contracted for" but of a different brand than that called for in the contract.[15] Thus, presumably, in the absence of special circumstances, when the seller delivers goods which are not identical to those called for in the contract but which are the functional equivalent, the seller has reasonable cause to believe they will be acceptable. When a retailer receives goods from a wholesaler or a manufacturer and simply sells them off the shelf, the retailer too has reasonable cause to believe that the goods will be acceptable and is so entitled to further reasonable time in which to cure.[16] Thus, for example, a retailer of Sony merchandise who sells a television set without opening the shipping container has reasonable cause to believe that the set will be acceptable and should have the right to cure if the set proves defective. That reasonable cause will arise from the retailer's past dealings with the manufacturer.

How one generalizes from the foregoing cases and the above quoted comment is not clear. It is apparent, of course, both in the cases and the comments, that the seller can have knowledge of the "defect" and yet have reasonable grounds to believe that the goods will be acceptable. The seller's ignorance of a defect should not *ipso facto* mean that the seller has reasonable grounds to believe that the goods will be acceptable. We should burden the seller not only with the knowledge which it has but also with knowledge which a reasonable, prudent seller would have had. If that knowledge would have deprived the seller of reasonable grounds to believe that the goods would be acceptable, then we should deny the seller the right to cure under 2–508(2). If we did not impute this knowledge to the seller, then any seller could preserve its right to cure simply by convincing the court that it had no knowledge that the goods would be unacceptable—and irrespective of the fact that any nonnegligent business person in the seller's shoes would have known that the goods would not have been acceptable. This seems an appropriate stopping point between charging a seller only with its knowledge and attributing to seller full knowledge of the status of the goods.

14. Bartus v. Riccardi, 55 Misc.2d 3, 284 N.Y.S.2d 222, 4 UCC 845 (1967).

15. Appleton State Bank v. Lee, 33 Wis.2d 690, 148 N.W.2d 1 (1967).

16. Wilson v. Scampoli, 228 A.2d 848, 4 UCC 178 (D.C.App.1967). See also, Mercury Marine v. Clear River Construction Co., Inc., 839 So.2d 508, 49 UCC2d 989 (Miss. 2003) (seller of boat engines should have been given reasonable chance to cure defect).

If ignorance of a defect does not always entitle a seller to cure, does ignorance foreclose cure? If a seller must have "reasonable grounds to believe that goods will be acceptable with or without money allowance," then seller must also know of a defect, otherwise seller would have no reason to have an opinion about goods' acceptability, not so? Put another way, is knowledge of a defect implicit in the quoted description of seller's necessary state of mind? We think the answer is no and the cases—without directly confronting the argument—seem to agree. If the Sony dealer who sells in ignorance of Sony's defect can cure, knowledge of the defect is not necessary.

We believe that cure is a remedy which should be carefully cultivated and developed by the courts. To that end we would argue that a seller should be found to have had a reasonable belief that its tender would have been acceptable any time it can convince the court that (1) the seller would have had such reasonable belief had it not been ignorant of the defect, or (2) the seller had some reason, such as prior course of dealing or trade usage, which in fact reasonably led seller to believe that the goods would be acceptable.[17]

The New York Court of Appeals adopted this general approach in T.W. Oil, Inc. v. Consolidated Edison Co.[18] There the seller contracted to deliver oil with a .50 percent sulfur content. Acting without knowledge of any defect, the seller tendered oil with a .92 percent sulfur content which the buyer rejected. The seller thereafter offered to cure with a substitute conforming shipment of oil that would arrive in a few days. The buyer refused. The seller resold the original oil and, given the buyer's refusal to permit cure, was allowed to recover the difference between the amount received on resale of the original cargo and the contract price. On appeal, the buyer argued that 2–508(2) is limited to cases in which a seller *knowingly* made a nonconforming tender which the seller had reason to believe the buyer would accept. But the Court of Appeals affirmed, stating that the only real question was whether the seller should be viewed as having had reasonable grounds to believe that the initial nonconforming tender would be acceptable. The court stressed that "the reasonableness of the seller's belief that the original tender would be acceptable was supported * * * by testimony that, by the time the contract was made, the * * * [seller] knew * * * [that the buyer] burned fuel with a content up to 1 percent so that, with appropriate price adjustment, * * * the oil would have suited its needs even if, at delivery, it was, to the * * *

17. See Note, Uniform Commercial Code—Sales—Sections 2–508 and 2–608—Limitations on the Perfect Tender Rule, 69 Mich.L.Rev. 130, 135 (1970). See also Johannsen v. Minnesota Valley Ford Tractor Co., 304 N.W.2d 654, 31 UCC 558 (Minn.1981) (suggesting cure applies only where defects are minor).

18. 57 N.Y.2d 574, 457 N.Y.S.2d 458, 443 N.E.2d 932, 35 UCC 12 (1982).

[seller's] surprise to test out at .92 per cent.''[19] The court went on to remark that the case law and the mainstream of scholarly commentary demonstrates that "courts have been concerned with the reasonableness of the seller's belief that the goods would be acceptable rather than with the seller's pretended knowledge or lack of knowledge of the defect".[20] In thus holding that an entire substitute shipment could constitute cure, the Court of Appeals also correctly rejected the notion that a seller has no right to cure at all unless the defects are "minor."

The seller, on proper notice to the buyer, has a "further reasonable time" to substitute a conforming tender. In the *T.W. Oil* case, the New York Court of Appeals held that a delay of a month was reasonable. But the case law on "further reasonable time" is neither plentiful nor revealing. From the seller's point of view, this further reasonable time is the heart of his 2–508(2) cure rights. The subsection really offers the seller little beyond an extension of time. The seller still must provide a conforming tender. What constitutes a "further reasonable time" is a question of fact; the New Jersey Supreme Court has provided a useful inventory of relevant factors:[21]

> The determination of what constitutes a further reasonable time depends on the surrounding circumstances, which include the change of position by and the amount of inconvenience to the buyer * * *, the length of time needed by the seller to correct the nonconformity and his ability to salvage the goods by resale to others.

The cases hold that where the seller delivers goods that are supposed to be operational but are not, the seller does not have an unlimited period in which to make the goods operational by repair or replacement. Thus, eventually enough will be enough, and the buyer will be entitled to reject.[22]

What constitutes "seasonable notification" by the seller of its intent to cure? Of course, any notification must itself be clear and unequivocal.[23] And if the seller gives that notification at the time

19. *Id.* at 583, 457 N.Y.S.2d at 464, 443 N.E.2d at 938, 35 UCC at 20.

20. *Id.* at 585, 457 N.Y.S.2d at 465, 443 N.E.2d at 939, 35 UCC at 21. See also, Sinco, Inc. v. Metro–North Commuter R. Co., 133 F.Supp.2d 308, 44 UCC2d 137 (S.D.N.Y. 2001). The California Song–Beverly Consumer Warranty Act is treated in Mocek v. Alfa Leisure, Inc., 114 Cal.App.4th 402, 7 Cal. Rptr.3d 546, 52 UCC2d 414 (2003).

21. Ramirez v. Autosport, 88 N.J. 277, 285–86, 440 A.2d 1345, 1349, 33 UCC 134, 140 (1982).

22. General Motors Acceptance Corp. v. Grady, 27 Ohio App.3d 321, 501 N.E.2d 68, 2 UCC2d 887 (1985). The same is true with respect to cure under 2–608(1)(a). See, e.g., Rester v. Morrow, 491 So.2d 204, 1 UCC2d 751 (Miss. 1986).

23. T & S Brass and Bronze Works, Inc. v. Pic–Air, Inc., 790 F.2d 1098, 1 UCC2d 433 (4th Cir.1986).

the buyer informs the seller of the rejection, it will usually be seasonable.[24] But notification will not be seasonable where the seller does not give it at time of rejection, the buyer thereafter reasonably arranges for substitute goods, and the seller then claims a right to cure.[25] Also, where "time is of the essence" and the contract so provides, a court will be much less tolerant of what appears to be tardy notice,[26] especially where seller's declared intent to cure does not appear credible because of an apparent inability to do so. Otherwise, the case law tells little, and courts remark that the issue is "one of fact."

Finally, what constitutes effective cure? To one ignorant of the cases and unburdened with any consideration of the policy of 2–508, the definition of effective cure is simple. Section 2–508(2) tells us that the seller has a further reasonable time to "substitute a conforming tender." Arguably that is both the most and the least that the seller can and must do: substitute a second and conforming tender.[27] The courts generally permit repair here as well as substitution of an entirely new tender (i.e., replacement).[28] There is also authority that a seller does not make an effective cure unless it both tenders conforming goods and a sum of money to compensate for the damage the buyer sustained as a result of the earlier, nonconforming tender.[29]

However, if one accepts the proposition that 2–508 is a case of Muhammad coming to the mountain—of the drafters accommodating the law to what they believed to be business behavior, then one

24. Traynor v. Walters, 342 F.Supp. 455, 10 UCC 965 (M.D.Pa.1972) (same time); T.W. Oil, Inc. v. Consolidated Edison Co., 57 N.Y.2d 574, 457 N.Y.S.2d 458, 443 N.E.2d 932, 35 UCC 12 (1982) (notification one day after rejection).

25. National Fleet Supply, Inc. v. Fairchild, 450 N.E.2d 1015, 36 UCC 480 (Ind.App.1983).

26. June G. Ashton Interiors v. Stark Carpet Corp., 142 Ill.App.3d 100, 96 Ill.Dec. 306, 491 N.E.2d 120, 2 UCC2d 74 (1986).

27. Professor Honnold took the position that a curative tender must conform to the contract requirements in all respects other than time. 1 N.Y. State Law Revision Comm'n, 1955 Report 484 (1955). See Worldwide RV Sales & Service, Inc. v. Brooks, 534 N.E.2d 1132, 8 UCC2d 386 (Ind.App.1989) (offer to install two contracted for air conditioners while leaving hole in roof of motor home was not conforming); Travelers Indem. Co. v. Maho Machine Tool Corp., 952 F.2d 26, 16 UCC2d 369 (2d Cir.1991)

(option to cure merely extends time for seller to meet contract obligations); Allied Semi–Conductors Intern., Ltd. v. Pulsar Components Intern., Inc., 907 F.Supp. 618, 28 UCC2d 543 (E.D.N.Y. 1995) (seller must not only unequivocally and clearly communicate an intent to cure, but must actually tender the conforming delivery as it is not enough merely to offer to make conforming goods available without more).

28. See, e.g., Wilson v. Scampoli, 228 A.2d 848, 4 UCC 178 (D.C.App.1967) (repairs); Wright v. Vickaryous, 611 P.2d 20, 28 UCC 1177 (Alaska 1980) (cure of title defect possible merely by "explanation"); T.W. Oil, Inc. v. Consolidated Edison Co., 57 N.Y.2d 574, 457 N.Y.S.2d 458, 443 N.E.2d 932, 35 UCC 12 (1982) (replacement).

29. Moulden & Sons, Inc. v. Osaka Landscaping & Nursery, Inc., 21 Wash. App. 194, 584 P.2d 968, 25 UCC 454 (1978) (court required both replacement and reimbursement for extra costs incurred due to nonconforming tender).

can argue for the acceptance of other behavior by the seller as cure. Price adjustments sufficient to recompense the buyer for deficiency in quantity or quality must certainly be the most common form of cure by business people. The seller delivers 995 bushels of potatoes on a contract calling for 1,000, and if 995 are sufficient for the buyer's purposes, should we permit the seller to cure by offering a reduction in price equal to the value of the five bushels which were not delivered? Business people do and we should, even though it appears that 2–508(2) does not recognize this behavior as a form of cure. In the first place it refers to "money allowance" as something which the seller might offer the buyer which would not constitute cure and which if not accepted by the buyer, would require the seller to substitute a fully conforming tender. Second, Comment 4 to 2–508 specifies that "trade usages permitting variations without rejection but with price allowance * * * are not covered by this section."

Despite the modest violence it does to the language of 2–508(2), we believe that the buyer who complains of some insubstantial nonconformity which can be recompensed by a reduction in the price should be made to accept a reduction as cure even if there is no usage in the trade to accept such reductions.[30] We note that in one case, the court refused to recognize a price reduction as a cure.[31] The case, however, involved more than an insubstantial nonconformity.[32] A more recent case, in which an installment contract was involved, allowed price adjustment as a cure, citing Comment 5 to 2–612 as authority.[33]

To what extent does "shaken faith" limit cure? Zabriskie Chevrolet, Inc. v. Smith[34] illustrates the problem. In that case the purchasers had difficulty with the transmission in a new Chevrolet. The seller offered to cure by substituting another transmission which the court described as one "not from the factory and of unknown lineage from another vehicle in [seller's] possession."[35] The court found that the offer of this substitute transmission was

---

30. One case has allowed just such a cure. See Oral–X Corp. v. Farnam Cos., Inc., 931 F.2d 667, 16 UCC2d 111 (10th Cir.1991) (credit given to buyer for defect in one fourth of one percent of product was effective cure).

31. In Continental Forest Products, Inc. v. White Lumber Sales, Inc., 256 Or. 466, 474 P.2d 1, 8 UCC 178 (1970), the court saw and sidestepped the "price as cure" question. The court found that the parties had agreed upon a price reduction as a permissible method of cure and so did not decide whether other methods "may have existed or should be required."

32. McKenzie v. Alla–Ohio Coals, Inc., 1979 WL 30087, 29 UCC 852 (D.D.C.1979).

33. Superior Derrick Services, Inc. v. Anderson, 831 S.W.2d 868, 18 UCC2d 706 (Tex. App.1992). The applicable part of Comment 5 reads: "Cure of non-conformity of an installment in the first instance can usually be afforded by an allowance against the price."

34. 99 N.J.Super. 441, 240 A.2d 195, 5 UCC 30 (1968).

35. Id. at 458, 240 A.2d at 205, 5 UCC at 42.

not an effective cure, and it commented as follows about the state of the purchasers' mind: "Once their faith is shaken, the vehicle loses not only its real value in their eyes, but becomes an instrument whose integrity is substantially impaired and whose operation is fraught with apprehension. The attempted cure in the present case is ineffective." Of course one may argue that the court was applying an objective standard and that any reasonable purchaser in the Smiths' shoes would not have accepted the automobile with the substitute transmission. If that is the meaning of the case, the outcome is not remarkable; it is simply a recognition that "cure" cannot be defined unilaterally but must be defined with respect to the reasonable expectations of both parties. However, the court may have been speaking of the state of mind of the particular purchasers before it. If the case means that a cure must satisfy not just the reasonable expectations of the purchaser but the actual expectations of *these* purchasers, the holding is extraordinary. Surely the drafters did not intend to reopen the subjective-objective contract interpretation question under 2–508, and the case is wrong if it stands for the proposition that the only acceptable cure is one which meets the subjective desires of the particular purchaser in the case in question.

Section 2–508 is an important addition to our law. It substantially restricts the right of the buyer to reject, and it substantially complicates the job of the lawyer who represents the buyer who wishes to reject. Although it raises almost as many problems as it answers, in wise judicial hands it offers the possibility of conforming the law to reasonable expectations and of thwarting the chiseler who seeks to escape from a bad bargain.

§ 9–6 Consequences to Buyer of Wrongful Refusal to Permit or Accept Cure After Rejection

To a buyer who wrongfully refuses to permit or accept cure after rejection, the consequences may be dire. The buyer's wrongful refusal to allow cure nullifies the seller's breach and deprives the buyer of all remedies against the seller for breach arising from the contract.[1] At the same time the buyer may become liable for the price of the nonconforming goods under 2–709, or for the contract-market differential as to conforming goods under 2–708(1),[2] or for the difference between the resale price of those goods and the

§ 9–6

1. Traynor v. Walters, 342 F.Supp. 455, 10 UCC 965 (M.D.Pa.1972); Ritz–Craft Corp. v. Stanford Management Group, 800 F.Supp. 1312, 19 UCC2d 987 (D.Md.1992) (seller offered to cure, but buyer had work done by another; buyer not entitled to offset cost of cure in contract price); Mercury Marine v. Clear River Const. Co., Inc., 839 So.2d 508, 49 UCC2d 989 (Miss. 2003).

2. Carnes Constr. Co. v. Richards & Conover Steel & Supply Co., 1972 WL 20888, 10 UCC 797 (Okl.App.1972).

contract price under 2–706, less the amount attributable to the nonconformity.[3]

3. T.W. Oil, Inc. v. Consolidated Edison Co., 57 N.Y.2d 574, 457 N.Y.S.2d 458, 443 N.E.2d 932, 35 UCC 12 (1982) allowed recovery of the difference between the resale price of the rejected goods and the contract price. The oil resold was inferior to the oil the seller agreed to deliver. Thus the measure applied improperly inflated the damages. The appellate court allowed this to stand only because the defendant had not objected to this proposed method of calculation at trial.

Chapter 10

WARRANTY

Analysis

§ 10–1 Introduction

It is difficult to know how much or how little one should say about warranty liability under the Code. Others have written books and articles on the topic, and the personal-injury cases in particular tend to present a seamless web running from express warranty through the implied warranty of merchantability to strict tort liability or negligence. Only because our space is limited do we omit strict tort liability and negligence, for we well appreciate that those claims are often difficult to distinguish from liability for breach of warranty. We know that a plaintiff will sometimes be able to state a cause of action on the basis of the same facts under either theory, and in succeeding chapters we point to some of the legal consequences of choosing one or the other theory. But a plaintiff is not always free to choose. Sometimes a buyer of defective or damaged goods sues in negligence or strict liability in tort rather than for breach of warranty or breach of contract in order to secure greater recovery (particularly punitive damages), or to avoid defenses such as lack of privity, failure to give notice, disclaimers, or remedy limitations, etc.

On the other hand, "economic loss", usually cannot be recovered in tort. We consider the topic of tort claims for "economic loss" in Chapter 11, section 5. If the buyer is to recover at all, this can only be on a warranty or a breach of contract theory. Not all courts define economic loss in the same way. A frequently cited definition is that of the Illinois Supreme Court in Moorman Mfg. Co. v. National Tank Co:[1]

> "Economic loss" has been defined as damages for inadequate value, costs of repair and replacement of the defective product, or consequent loss of profits—without any claim of personal injury or damage to other property, as well as the diminution in value of the product because it is inferior in quality and does not work for the general purposes for which it was manufactured and sold.

Our discussion in the following pages will focus primarily on the meaning of: 2–313, 2–314, 2–315, 312, and also proposed 2–313A and 2–313B of Amended Article 2. Section 2–313 deals with express warranties and remedial promises made by the seller to a

1. Moorman Mfg. Co. v. National Tank Co., 91 Ill.2d 69, 435 N.E.2d 443, 61 Ill.Dec. 746, 33 UCC 510 (1982).

buyer with which the seller has a contractual relationship. Section 2–314 states the implied warranty of merchantability. Section 2–315 states the implied warranty of fitness for a particular purpose. Section 2–312 states the warranty against infringement. Proposed section 2–313A deals with the obligation of the seller of new goods to a remote purchaser created by a record packaged with or accompanying the goods. Proposed section 2–313B also deals with a type of obligation to a remote purchaser of new goods but only one created by communication with the public. After treating these sections, we will consider the changes in state warranty law brought about by the enactment of the Magnuson–Moss Warranty—Federal Trade Commission Improvement Act.[2] Chapter 11 treats the applicable Code damage sections (2–714 and 2–715).

At the outset, one should understand how a warranty lawsuit looks to a plaintiff's lawyer and how it differs from a suit against an "insurer" on the one hand or against an allegedly negligent defendant on the other. If an insurance company insures against the loss of an arm, all the claimant need do to recover is show the bloody stump. If the same claimant wishes to recover in warranty from the seller of the offending chain saw, this will be a much tougher case to prove. Proof of injury—the loss of his arm—is just the beginning. First, the claimant must prove that the defendant made a warranty, express or implied, and so incurred an obligation under 2–313, 2–314, or 2–315. Second, the claimant must prove that the goods did not comply with the warranty. Third, the claimant must prove that the injury was caused, proximately and in fact, by the defective nature of the goods (and not, for example, by his careless use of the saw). Fourth, damages must be proved. Finally, the claimant must fight off all sorts of affirmative defenses such as disclaimers, statute of limitations, privity, lack of notice, and assumption of the risk.[3]

Although the plaintiff under 2–313, 2–314 and 2–315 need not prove negligence, liability under these sections has much more in common with negligence liability than it does with a life, collision, or health insurer's liability. The two causes of action pose common problems for the plaintiff's lawyer. In both the lawyer must prove cause in fact and proximate causation on the part of a specific defendant. Too much should not be made of the fact that in a negligence suit the plaintiff must also prove that the defendant was negligent. Professor Whitford has suggested that the *res ipsa loquitur* doctrine will often carry the plaintiff to the jury and that the

---

2. Act of Jan. 4, 1975, Pub.L.No. 93–637, Title I, § 101, 88 Stat. 2183, 15 U.S.C.A. §§ 2301–2312 (1982).

3. If the seller has given an express written warranty, the Magnuson–Moss Act curtails his ability to disclaim any implied warranties or take advantage of a privity defense

jury will find defendant negligent even absent explicit proof of negligence.[4]

One should also distinguish between warranty (particularly express warranty) and fraud or misrepresentation. Typically, only a naughty seller is guilty of misrepresentation or fraud, but a seller can be Simon pure and yet break an express warranty. The former cases usually require at least that the defendant be negligent in making the representation and in some cases that it intentionally states a mistruth.[5] There is no such requirement of evil doing on the part of a warranty defendant. A seller can fully believe that the representations it makes are accurate and yet be liable for the breach of an express warranty.

§ 10–2   The Scope of Article 2 Warranties and Related Obligations

Article 2 applies to "transactions in goods." Under 2–105(1) "goods" is defined as meaning "all things (including specially manufactured goods) which are moveable at the time of identification to the contract for sale. . . . " This definition specifies that it includes "the unborn of animals, and growing crops, and other identified things attached to reality as described . . . in Section 2–107."

Code provisions on warranties and related obligations do not apply to contracts which are purely for services.[1] Unfortunately, not every transaction can be neatly classified as involving either goods or services. Many dealings, such as the purchase and installation of a water heater, are made up of both goods and services. Judges and litigants frequently face difficulty and uncertainty in determining whether the Code applies to such hybrid transactions.[2] Areas of continuous dispute include construction contracts, repairs and installations (particularly on real estate),[3] medical treatments, and

---

4. See Whitford, Strict Products Liability and the Automobile Industry: Much Ado About Nothing, 1968 Wis. L.Rev. 83.

5. Under 2–721, all of the Article 2 remedies for nonfraudulent breach are available for fraud or material misrepresentations. An aggrieved buyer may have different remedies against different defendants, as when, for example, the buyer of a car may revoke acceptance against a dealer but not get damages for breach of warranty against the car manufacturer.

§ 10–2

1. Federal law may preempt application of state law warranties to some goods.

2. Petroleo Brasileiro, S.A., Petrobras v. Nalco Chem. Co., 784 F.Supp. 160, 18 UCC2d 61 (D.N.J.1992) (determination of predominant thrust in hybrid contract irrelevant, as New Jersey does not treat contracts for services differently).

3. Osterholt v. St. Charles Drilling Co., 500 F.Supp. 529, 30 UCC 807 (E.D.Mo.1980) (contract to install a well and water system on plaintiff's property was not governed by the Code)

also software.[4] Some cases involving health care providers include sweeping language. Thus, in In re TMJ Implants Products Liability Litigation,[5] the court proclaimed that the UCC warranty provisions do not apply where an allegedly defective device was implanted in plaintiff because physicians and other health care providers are not "sellers" or "manufacturers".

Some courts have insisted on separating the goods and services components of a contract and have applied the Uniform Commercial Code only to the goods portion of the transaction.[6] Most courts, however, use the "predominant factor" test in deciding whether the Code applies to a particular contract. This test simply asks which aspect of a goods-services contract is the most important to the overall transaction. If the hybrid transaction is predominately for the sale of goods, then the UCC will apply to the entire transaction, including the services portion. If the contract primarily furnishes services, the Code will not govern any portion of the transaction.

In a leading case applying the predominant factor test, Bonebrake v. Cox,[7] the court held that the UCC was applicable to a contract for the sale and installation of bowling equipment in a bowling alley. In order to replace equipment destroyed when a fire swept through their bowling alley, the Cox brothers contracted for the purchase and installation of used lane beds, ball returns, chairs, a bubble-ball cleaning machine, lockers, house balls, storage racks, shoes, and foundation materials. The court noted that the language of the contract which warranted the lanes and equipment to be free from defects in workmanship and materials was language peculiar to sale of goods, not to sale of services. Emphasizing that all of the things sold were items of tangible property which were movable at the time of identification to the contract, the court rejected arguments that the transaction was a construction contract because it involved objects which became immovable upon installation. The court added that the used lane beds had not been constructed on the site but had come in three prefabricated sections after having been used in another bowling alley; their previous installation had not rendered them immovable. Since the contract was clearly for the replacement of equipment (i.e., "goods," destroyed by fire) the court decided that it would be inappropriate to deny Code application simply because the sale of goods necessarily included installa-

---

4. Carroll v. Grabavoy, 77 Ill.App.3d 895, 33 Ill.Dec. 309, 396 N.E.2d 836, 27 UCC 940 (1979) (dentures prepared by a dentist for his patient were not governed by Code warranties).

5. 872 F.Supp. 1019, 27 UCC2d 774 (D. Minn. 1995), aff'd, 97 F.3d 1050 (8th Cir. 1996).

6. See Stephenson v. Frazier, 399 N.E.2d 794, 28 UCC 12 (Ind.App.1980), transfer den., 425 N.E.2d 73 (1981) (Code applied to sale of a modular home, but not to construction of foundation and installation of septic system).

7. 499 F.2d 951, 14 UCC 1318 (8th Cir.1974).

tion services. Instead, it held that the test for inclusion or exclusion from UCC coverage is not whether the contracts are mixed, but "whether their predominant factor, their thrust, their purpose, reasonably stated, * * * is a service, with goods incidentally involved, or whether they are a transaction of a sale, with labor incidentally involved * * *."

In classifying the predominant factor of a hybrid transaction, most courts rely on the relative costs of the services and goods. Decisions frequently focus on the question whether an undifferentiated price was charged or the goods and labor were separately billed. Contractual language also may provide a clue to determining the predominant thrust. The terms used in an agreement or receipts, such as "purchase," "seller," and "merchandise," will often indicate a contract which is primarily for goods.

For the most part buyers seek Article 2 coverage because they wish to assert breach of the Code's warranty of merchantability. Other reasons might influence either a plaintiff or a defendant; a litigant may want to take advantage of the statute of frauds, rules on unconscionability, good faith provisions, statute of limitations, or the rules of contract construction. Whether the court applies the Code depends to some extent on the area of coverage at issue. Sympathetic plaintiffs often bring breach of warranty suits, and these litigants may have greater success in invoking Code protection than parties to non-warranty disputes. Consider a Maryland case[8] where the plaintiff recovered in warranty even though services predominated; the plaintiff was injured when he slipped and fell from the defectively-positioned diving board of his new backyard swimming pool. After reasoning that the diving board still retained its character as "goods" after being installed, the court allowed UCC warranties to be applied against the defendant who had designed and built both the pool and diving board.

A substantial number of courts have declined to bring the sale of real estate under the scope of the UCC. Those courts which arguably apply the Code to real estate transactions do so primarily in sales of mobile or modular homes. Here, of course, the courts are not called upon to distinguish between goods and services, but rather between goods and real estate. Once a modular home is attached to the real estate it may well pass with a deed and not be merely a fixture but actually a part of the real estate. On the other hand, the sale of a modular home before installation and while it is resting on a truck bed is clearly a sale of goods. One must examine the definition of goods in Article 2 and consider the facts in a particular case with care. Goods sold separately and prior to attach-

8. Anthony Pools v. Sheehan, 295 Md. 285, 455 A.2d 434, 35 UCC 408 (1983).

ment should surely be covered by the warranties. The same should not necessarily be true when a single contractor agrees to install the modular or mobile home on a piece of property and then to sell the real estate, including the home, to the buyer. Courts usually do not hesitate to apply the UCC to prefabricated homes as long as they are still movable, but outcomes may be different when foundations or other "immovables" are included in the sales package. For example, in Stephenson v. Frazier,[9] the court was willing to apply the Code to the sale of a modular home but not to the part of the contract relating to the construction of the foundation and installation of the septic system.

In the first several of the following subsections, we have grouped many of the hybrid transaction cases according to the type of goods and services involved. If we had a more pervasive and reliable principle to distinguish the cases than merely to examine the underlying subject matter, we would suggest it. To the extent there is a principle at work, we suspect it cuts across the following cases. We subdivide the cases according to the type of contract only to satisfy the lawyer's inherent urge to identify a case "on all fours with mine," (and perhaps to persuade a judge unwilling to accept a broader principle). In the last two subsections, we treat hybrids of goods and information.

a. Construction Contracts

Most courts find construction contracts to be primarily for services. But in Consolidated Edison Co. of New York, Inc. v. Westinghouse Elec. Corp.,[10] the court emphasized that there must be a careful analysis of the underlying contract. When neither the goods nor the services aspects of a contract to furnish and construct a nuclear power plant could be reasonably characterized as incidental, the UCC's applicability could not be decided on a motion for summary judgment.

Although a handful of decisions has applied the Code to construction contracts, those cases holding that the UCC does not govern such contracts are in the clear majority. Various courts have held that the Code did not apply to any of the following situations: the construction of a postal facility, a poured concrete swimming pool, a chimney intended to be permanently affixed to a house, the construction of a roof, and the construction and erection of a primary containment liner for a nuclear power station.

Parties to construction contracts can adopt the UCC by agreement. In one case, the Code governed the construction of a roller

---

9. 399 N.E.2d 794, 28 UCC 12 (Ind. App.1980), transfer den., 425 N.E.2d 73 (1981).

10. 567 F.Supp. 358, 36 UCC 1496 (S.D.N.Y.1983), motion den., 594 F.Supp. 698 (1984).

coaster by the terms of the contract.[11] The court noted that the parties to a contract may agree as to the applicable law, at least where they are dealing at arm's length and on an equal basis. In another case, the court applied the Code to the construction of a coal preparation plant because both parties had treated the transaction as a sale of goods.[12]

b. Installations and Repairs

In cases involving both the sale of goods and their installation, most courts apply the Code since the goods are usually the predominant factor. This is particularly true with goods in a hybrid transaction with goods that could have been identified to the contract before installation. Where the seller is not required to use specified items of goods, courts are most likely to find the contract not covered by the UCC. In Osterholt v. St. Charles Drilling Co., Inc.,[13] a contract for the purchase and installation of a well and water "system" of indefinite description but with a certain warranted capacity was not covered by the Code. The contract was held to be essentially for services since there was no hint of specific items to be installed and the goods did not become identified to the contract until they were actually installed.

The courts have no trouble deciding those cases in which the title to the goods is in and never passes from the one seeking the particular repair or installation service. The UCC never applies to these situations. For example, in Gentile By and Through Gentile v. MacGregor Mfg. Co.,[14] the court held that Code warranty provisions did not apply to the reconditioning of football equipment owned by a local board of education when no passage of title occurred. Since the reconditioners were primarily responsible for providing a service, certain replacement parts supplied in the course of reconditioning were incidental to that service.

c. Medical Treatments and Personal Services

Traditionally the courts have been hesitant to impose liability on hospitals. This reluctance was first challenged directly in a series of blood transfusion cases stretched across more than two decades where plaintiffs sought warranty recoveries from the "sale" of blood. While the outcomes varied, these warranty cases opened up the entire area of medical transactions to persistent litigation. The courts no longer hesitate to allow recoveries against

---

11. Intamin, Inc. v. Figley–Wright Contractors, Inc., 595 F.Supp. 1350, 40 UCC 766 (N.D.Ill.1984).

12. Wellmore Coal Co. v. Powell Constr. Co., Inc., 600 F.Supp. 1042, 40 UCC 362 (W.D.Va.1984).

13. 500 F.Supp. 529, 30 UCC 807 (E.D.Mo.1980).

14. 201 N.J.Super. 612, 493 A.2d 647, 41 UCC 15 (1985).

hospitals. In fact, a reader of recent decisions might conclude that courts now give the benefit of the doubt to the patient, not to the non-profit hospital.

The plaintiff's best line of argument in a medical case is to divide the treatment into several contracts, some for goods and some for services. For example, in Providence Hosp. v. Truly,[15] the court applied UCC warranty provisions to a contaminated drug which was injected into plaintiff's eye as part of a cataract operation. The regular practice of the hospital was to charge the patient for all drugs used in the operating room. Since the plaintiff had been billed for "drugs" used on the day of the operation, the court held this to be sufficient evidence to establish a "sale" of the drug by the hospital despite the fact that the overall operation could be classified as a medical service.

The court in Skelton v. Druid City Hosp. Bd.,[16] held that Code warranties were applicable to a suturing needle which broke off in plaintiff's body during an operation. Although there was not an actual "sale" of the needle, the hospital's use of it was a transaction akin to a lease or a rental of equipment to which the UCC applied. The court rejected arguments that the use of the needle was incidental to the provision of a service.

The courts have also opened the door to increased liability for the provision of other personal services. In the classic case of Newmark v. Gimbel's, Inc.,[17] the court relied on Code warranties when a beauty shop patron suffered hair loss and scalp injuries due to a defective permanent wave solution that was applied by her hairdresser. The opinion emphasized that it would be illogical to deny the patron recovery since the hairdresser could have brought an action in warranty if he had applied it to his own hair.

d. Intangibles

Some courts have considered whether Code warranties can be applied to transactions in "intangibles." Anything from a promise to pay money or a contract assignment to a sale of electricity might be considered an intangible. Although the case law is still rather limited, a growing number of litigants have urged the courts to apply the Code to intangibles either directly or by analogy. Some

---

15. 611 S.W.2d 127, 30 UCC 785 (Tex.Civ.App.1980); Rosci v. AcroMed., Inc., 447 Pa.Super. 403, 669 A.2d 959, 30 UCC2d 141 (1995).

16. 459 So.2d 818, 39 UCC 369 (Ala. 1984). In Medtronic, Inc. v. Lohr, 518 U.S. 470, 116 S.Ct. 2240, 135 L.Ed.2d 700, 29 UCC2d 1077 (1996), the Supreme Court decided that none of the plaintiff's common law claims were pre-empted by the Medical Devices Amendments to the Food, Drug, and Cosmetics Act. See also. In Breast Implant Product Liability Litigation, 331 S.C. 540, 503 S.E.2d 445, 38 UCC2d 49 (1998), the court held that UCC warranties do not apply to health care providers of services.

17. 54 N.J. 585, 258 A.2d 697, 6 UCC 1205 (1969).

decisions have applied the UCC to the sale of electricity while others have refused. In Navarro County Elec. Coop., Inc. v. Prince,[18] a plaintiff brought a warranty suit after electricity jumped from a high tension power line to the aerial of his mobile home and injured him. The court declined to label electricity as a good to which the UCC applied and reasoned that the legislature had not indicated affirmatively that the UCC was to apply to the rendering of electrical services.

e. Rights in Information, Software, and the Like

As Comment 7 to 2–103(1)(k) of Amended Article 2 recognized, "transactions often include both goods and information: some are transactions in goods as that term is used in 2–102, and some are not." Comment 7 was an attempt to resolve the conflict between those who wanted software contracts to be outside Article 2 and those who wanted them in. Since Amended 2 will never be enacted, it is now up to the courts to decide whether contracts for the sale and license of software are covered by Article 2. At this writing it is not clear what will happen. Many courts have summarily applied Article 2 to such contracts with little or no consideration of the question. At its final meeting in 2009, the members of the ALI approved the proposed final draft of the Principles of the Law of Software Contracts. The Principles will be published in their final form before the end of 2009. Then there will be a competing body of law, andcourts are likely to be forced at least to address the question.

§ 10–3   Contractual Express Warranties, Section 2–313

Section 2–313, which governs express warranty liability under the Code, reads in full as follows:

(1) Express warranties by the seller are created as follows:

(a) Any affirmation of fact or promise made by the seller to the buyer which relates to the goods and becomes part of the basis of the bargain creates an express warranty that the goods shall conform to the affirmation or promise.

(b) Any description of the goods which is made part of the basis of the bargain creates an express warranty that the goods shall conform to the description.

(c) Any sample or model which is made part of the basis of the bargain creates an express warranty that the whole of the goods shall conform to the sample or model.

(2) It is not necessary to the creation of an express warranty that the seller use formal words such as "warrant" or "guarantee" or that the seller have a specific intention to make

18. 640 S.W.2d 398, 34 UCC 1521 (Tex.App.1982).

a warranty, but an affirmation merely of the value of the goods or a statement purporting to be merely the seller's opinion or commendation of the goods does not create a warranty.

Before stepping more than ankle deep into this section, note several obvious but important facts. The section gives a cause of action only against "the seller."[1] The prospective defendant, then, must be a "seller." If the prospective defendant is a bailor or lessor, one may have a cause of action against that person only under Article 2A or by analogy to 2–313. The pre-Code requirement that the plaintiff must specifically rely on the warranty is gone. In its place is a much diluted reliance requirement that the warranty be "part of the basis of the bargain * * *." Finally, 2–313 implies that the plaintiff must satisfy other requirements: for example, that he prove an injury that resulted from a breach that occurred with the sale.

One who reads many express warranty cases gets the uneasy feeling that one is seeing the same play enacted again and again with different props. Sometimes the question is whether the seller's statement was a "puff" or an express warranty. At other times the question is whether the statement formed part of the "basis of the bargain." Although one may fit the cases into a variety of legal cubbyholes—for example, "description" cases, "basis-of-the-bargain" cases, and "puffing" cases—one is left with the concern that sometimes the trial judge or jury approach all cases with a single undifferentiated question: should the plaintiff recover because the goods did not do what the defendant said they would do? With that warning, we divide our discussion of express warranties into three segments:

(1) What seller's words or symbols constitute an express warranty?

(2) What reliance must buyer-plaintiff show? Where and when?

(3) Samples and models.

§ 10–4   Contractual Express Warranties, Section 2–313—What Words or Symbols?

In many cases, the seller makes an explicit oral or written representation that is unquestionably an "affirmation of fact or promise * * * which relates to the goods * * *." Such was the case

---

§ 10–3

1. Note that the Code provisions can be and with increasing frequency are extended by analogy to non-sale-of-goods cases. For a discussion of express war-ranties, see Special Project, Article 2 Warranties in Commercial Transaction: An Update. 72 Cornell L.Rev. 1159, 1170–1190 (1987).

in Rhodes Pharmacal Co. v. Continental Can Co.,[1] in which the seller stated "that the use of rustproof linings in the cans would prevent discoloration and adulteration of the Perform solution."[2] Subsection (2) of 2–313 makes clear that a seller need not use words such as "warrant" or "guarantee." Most courts would agree that a statement as explicit and relevant as that in Rhodes was an express warranty.

The "what" difficulty arises largely in two contexts: "puffing" cases and "description" cases. The law recognizes that some seller's statements are only puffing, not express warranties. Thus, 2–313(2) provides: "[A]n affirmation merely of the value of the goods or a statement purporting to be merely the seller's opinion or commendation of the goods does not create a warranty." But the recognition that some statements are not warranties tells one nothing about where the line should be drawn between puffs and warranties, and anyone who claims to be able always to tell a "puff" from a warranty is a fool or a liar. Stating that a seller's representation is only a puff and not a warranty is but a conclusory label. Indeed, one who reads a few cases gets the strong impression that the puff or warranty conclusion is only the product of an unobserved and subtle analysis that has to do with the reasonableness of the plaintiff's reliance, the seriousness of the plaintiff's injury, and other similar factors.

Of course, one can single out some factors that suggest that a statement is only an "opinion" as opposed to a warranty. Certainly the specificity of the statement is important: "this is a top-notch car" versus "this truck will give not less than 15.1 miles to the gallon when it is driven at a steady 60 miles per hour." Certainly a written statement is less likely to pass as a puff than an oral one, and a written statement in the contract of the parties is less likely to pass as a puff than a written statement in an advertisement. It is familiar contract doctrine that the context in which words are spoken influences the listener's understanding and thus their legal effect. Professor Honnold[3] well demonstrated the intractability of the puffing-warranty distinction to generations of students by his casebook's juxtaposition of the Wat Henry Pontiac[4] case and Frederickson v. Hackney.[5] In the former, a used car salesman stated that a car was in "A–1 shape" and "mechanically perfect."[6] In the

§ 10–4

1. 72 Ill.App.2d 362, 219 N.E.2d 726, 3 UCC 584 (1966). See Knapp Shoes, Inc. v. Sylvania Shoe Mfg. Corp., 72 F.3d 190, 28 UCC2d 430 (1st Cir. 1995).

2. *Id.* at 364, 219 N.E.2d at 728, 3 UCC at 585.

3. E. Farnsworth & J. Honnold, Cases and Materials on Commercial Law 456–60 (1965).

4. Wat Henry Pontiac Co. v. Bradley, 202 Okl. 82, 210 P.2d 348 (1949).

5. 159 Minn. 234, 198 N.W. 806 (1924).

6. 202 Okla. at 83, 210 P.2d at 350–51.

Frederickson case, the seller stated that a bull calf would "put the buyer on the map" and that "his father was the greatest living dairy bull."[7] When the car broke down and when the bull proved sterile, the buyers sued. While the Oklahoma court found that the used car salesman's statements were express warranties,[8] the Minnesota court was made of sterner stuff: the palaver about the bull was only trade talk, not a warranty of reproductive capacity.[9] One can dig about in the cases for distinguishing features, but the most persuasive difference is that the plaintiff in *Wat Henry* was a woman who bought the car to make a trip with her seven-month old child in 1944 to visit her husband in the army. The car broke down *en route*. Except by reference to the natural compassion one feels for a World War II service wife who is stranded with a seven-month old child, the cases are difficult to distinguish. It is true that the plaintiff in the *Frederickson* case was a farmer, not just an uninformed consumer; but, on the other hand, oral statements by used-car salesmen are notoriously unreliable—archetypal puffs, some might say.

The lesson for a lawyer from these cases and others like them is obvious. Only a foolish lawyer will be quick to label a seller's statement as puffs or not puffs, and only a reckless one will label a seller's statement at all without carefully examining such factors as the nature of the defect (was it obvious or not) and the buyer's and seller's relative knowledge.[10] The cases also suggest that the nature of the plaintiff's reliance is not as irrelevant as the Code and comments appear to say it is. To some courts the puff-warrant question is a backdoor means of examining the nature and reasonableness of the plaintiff's reliance.[11] For example, in Roscher v. Band Box Cleaners,[12] the seller of a plastic telephone attachment stated that he did not think that the telephone company would

---

7. 159 Minn. at 235, 198 N.W. at 806.

8. 202 Okla. at 84, 210 P.2d at 351. See also Felley v. Singleton, 302 Ill. App.3d 248, 235 Ill.Dec. 747, 705 N.E.2d 930, 37 UCC2d 586 (1999).

9. 159 Minn. at 235, 198 N.W. at 806.

10. See General Supply & Equip. Co., Inc. v. Phillips, 490 S.W.2d 913, 12 UCC 35 (Tex.Civ.App.1972) (test of whether a representation is a warranty or a mere expression of opinion: Did seller assume to assert a fact of which buyer was ignorant, or did he merely express a judgment on something as to which each of them might be expected to have an opinion?).

11. This approach was adopted by the Sixth Circuit in Price Bros. Co. v. Philadelphia Gear Corp., 649 F.2d 416,

31 UCC 469, 474 (6th Cir.1981), cert. denied, 454 U.S. 1099, 102 S.Ct. 674, 70 L.Ed.2d 641 (1981): "In order to determine whether the precontract statements * * * were in fact a basis of the bargain and thus an express warranty, or whether they were merely a seller's 'puffing', the court should consider the reasonableness of the buyer in believing the seller, and the reliance placed on the seller's statements by the buyer." (Citations omitted). Also on the importance of reliance, see Austin v. Will–Burt Co., 232 F.Supp.2d 682, 50 UCC2d 121 (N.D. Miss. 2002), aff'd, 361 F.3d 862 (5th Cir. 2004).

12. 90 Ohio App. 71, 103 N.E.2d 404 (1951).

object to the use of the attachment. In refusing to construe this statement as an express warranty, the court emphasized that the buyer could easily have determined the phone company's true position. This seems tantamount to finding that buyer loses because his reliance was not reasonable.[13]

A related problem involves the degree to which the seller hedges in making an affirmation or promise. For example, in Hupp Corp. v. Metered Washer Service,[14] a buyer discovered that the clothes dryers he had purchased from the seller were defective. The seller then sold the buyer some parts and stated, " '[M]aybe' or 'we think that this might solve your problem.' "[15] Apparently because the language was so uncertain, the Oregon Supreme Court held that this language was not an express warranty that the parts would correct the defects.[16] Would the remedial promise language of 2–313(4) of Amended Article 2 change this result? Not if the court thought no firm promise was made.

A second class of cases that presents difficulty for those who seek to determine what words and symbols constitute express warranties is the "description" cases. Section 2–313(1)(b) states the Code rule on descriptions as follows:

> Any description of the goods which is made part of the basis of the bargain creates an express warranty that the goods shall conform to the description.

In one application[17] of the predecessor of 2–313(1)(b), the Georgia Court of Appeals found that the description of an aircraft as "Aero Commander, N–2677B, Number 135, FAA, Flyable"[18] was an express warranty that the aircraft complied with Federal Aviation Regulation Part 135, concerning instrument and visual flight. More difficult are description cases when the plaintiff argues that a generic title such as "auto" or "haybaler"[19] is an express warranty that the machine described will carry passengers on the highway or

---

13. For a fuller discussion of whether reliance on the seller's representations is required to create an express warranty under 2–313, see § 10–5 infra.

14. 256 Or. 245, 472 P.2d 816, 8 UCC 42 (1970).

15. Id. at 247, 472 P.2d at 818, 8 UCC at 44.

16. Id. at 247, 472 P.2d at 817–18, 8 UCC at 44.

17. Hill Aircraft & Leasing Corp. v. Simon, 122 Ga.App. 524, 177 S.E.2d 803, 8 UCC 474 (1970). HDM Flugservice GmbH v. Parker Hannifin Corp., 332 F.3d 1025, 50 UCC2d 1053 (6th Cir.

2003) (a maintenance manual which lists "mandatory" maintenance of a helicopter part at 3,500 hours of flight time did not create an express warranty that part would last for 3,500 hours).

18. Id. at 526–27, 177 S.E.2d at 805, 8 UCC at 475.

19. Moss v. Gardner, 228 Ark. 828, 310 S.W.2d 491 (1958). In applying § 71 of the Uniform Sales Act, the Arkansas court held that the description "hay baler" in a sales contract did not constitute an express warranty that the hay baler could bale hay because express warranties in the contract excluded all other warranties.

bale hay.[20] Comment 4 to 2–313 urges courts to reject a literal reading of blanket disclaimers and to recognize "that the probability is small that a real price is intended to be exchanged for a pseudo obligation." What are the reasonable expectations of a buyer who has paid money and signed a document that disclaims all warranties but promises to deliver a new "automobile"? We believe that the buyer can reasonably believe that the word "automobile" is an express warranty by description under 2–313(1)(b) that the machine purchased will behave in a certain way, namely, that it will carry him around town for at least a few thousand miles. Finding the meaning of such one-word descriptions is much like defining the meaning of the implied warranty of merchantability in various contexts. (Is a cigarette not merchantable because it causes cancer in some smokers?) Likewise, the court must decide whether the use of the noun "automobile" conveys the meaning that the machine would propel itself about on its four wheels in a certain way or whether that word promises only a machine with the external characteristics of a car. We consider those problems below.

§ 10–5 Contractual Express Warranties, Section 2–313—When and Where? Basis of the Bargain

Under the Uniform Sales Act, the plaintiff in an express warranty case had to prove that he "relied" on the warranty. Section 12 of the Uniform Sales Act provided:

> Any affirmation of fact or any promise by the seller relating to the goods is an express warranty if the natural tendency of such affirmation or promise is to induce the buyer to purchase the goods, and if the buyer purchases the goods relying thereon * * *.

The Code omits any explicit mention of reliance and requires only that the promise or affirmation become "part of the basis of the bargain." The extent to which the law has so been changed is thoroughly unclear.[1] It is possible that the drafters did not intend to change the law, or that they intended to remove the reliance

---

20. Of course, such a warranty will not normally promise more than an implied warranty of merchantability would give. However, when defendant has disclaimed all implied warranties, the proof of an express warranty may be crucial to plaintiff's case

§ 10–5

1. For a general critique of the "basis of the bargain" requirement, see White, Freeing the Tortious Soul of Express Warranty Law, 72 Tulane L. Rev.

2089 (1998). See also, Murray, "Basis of the Bargain": Transconding Classical Concepts, 66 Minn.L.Rev. 283 (1982). Murrin v. Ford Motor Co., 303 A.D.2d 475, 756 N.Y.S.2d 596, 50 UCC2d 745 (2003) (complaint dismissed for failure to state a claim when plaintiff failed to allege: a) that he understood, or was even aware of, advertisements which promised truck features that were not included in plaintiff's truck, and b) that representations made in advertisements were part of bargain).

requirement in all but the most unusual case, or that they intended simply to give the plaintiff the benefit of a rebuttable presumption of reliance. In his analysis of this section for the New York Law Revision Commission, Professor Honnold well stated the prior law and the confusion inherent in the basis of the bargain test:

> The extent to which the Code's "basis of the bargain" test would change present law is less than clear. The Comments hardly solve the problem; Comment 3 to 2–313 states by way of explanation:
>
> > In actual practice affirmations of fact made by the seller about the goods during a bargain are regarded as part of the description of those goods; hence no particular reliance on such statements need be shown in order to weave them into the fabric of the agreement. Rather, any fact which is to take such affirmations, once made, out of the agreement requires clear affirmative proof. The issue normally is one of fact.
>
> But what is the issue by which the facts are to be measured? One must suppose that the "basis of the bargain" test has some meaning: this test is made an integral part of the three express warranties in Section 2–313(1) of the Code. Presumably, buyers must plead and prove that the requirement is met. But the ultimate standards by which buyers will satisfy, or fail to satisfy this test are not disclosed.
>
> One ground for confusion is the fact that the word "basis" has no generally understood legal or psychological meaning. The term does have a well understood physical meaning, but with connotations of breadth and importance. Thus, Section 2–615(a), in dealing with impossibility of performance, excuses the parties from the contractual obligations on failure of "a basic assumption" on which the contract was made.
>
> To limit buyer's legal protection to seller's representations and promises which are basic, in the sense employed in Section 2–615, would radically restrict the present scope of buyer's warranty protection. Such a change undoubtedly was not intended by the draftsmen. Buyer is entitled to legal protection for compliance of the goods with *all* of seller's promises and representations on which buyer relies, even though some may be of relatively small import.
>
> There remains the central question: What is the meaning of "basis of the bargain"? Possibly for lack of any other meaningful standard, courts must employ the test of whether buyer relied on the affirmation or promise, the test employed in Section 12 of the Uniform Sales Act.

It might be suggested that the pre-Code law required change because it was too burdensome to require buyers to prove that they relied on seller's representation or promise. Professor Williston wrote:

> There is danger of giving greater effect to the requirement of reliance than it is entitled to. Doubtless the burden of proof is on the buyer to establish this as one of the elements of his case. But the warranty need not be the sole inducement to the buyer to purchase the goods; and as a general rule no evidence of reliance by the buyer is necessary other than the seller's statements were of a kind which naturally would induce the buyer to purchase the goods and that he did purchase the goods.

* * *

The problem is posed by the facts of Hellman v. Kirschner, 191 N.Y.Supp. 202 (1921). Buyer purchased a used automobile which the memorandum of sale described as a "Cadillac sedan, model 57–V". Buyer sued seller for breach of warranty on the ground that the car was not model 57–V, but was model 57–J. Seller proved that buyer had inspected the car before the purchase so that the actual type and model of the car were then apparent. Judgment for the buyer was reversed on the ground that the trial court's instruction implied that buyer was entitled to receive a model 57–V, regardless of buyer's lack of reliance on the statement of the model number in the sales memorandum.

The same result would follow under the Code, if we assume that the "basis of the bargain" test incorporates the present reliance requirement. But this assumption cannot be made with confidence since (i) "basis of the bargain" does not convey a definite meaning, and (ii) the Code's rejection of the present reliance language might well imply an intent to modify present law.[2]

Comment 5 to 2–313 arguably means that any affirmation is presumed to be part of the basis of the bargain and that the plaintiff need put in no evidence unless the defendant offers evidence of the buyer's nonreliance: "no particular reliance on [a seller's affirmations during a bargain] need be shown * * *. Rather, any fact which is to take these affirmations or promises once made, out of the agreement requires clear affirmative proof."[3] If a

---

2. 1 N.Y. State Law Revision Comm'n. 392–93 (1955).

3. As previously noted, the extent to which prior law was changed by 2–313

(and Comment 3 to 2–313) is unclear. Some courts have held that reliance on the seller's affirmations by the buyer is not required for an express warranty to

plaintiff is suing on a seller's statement made orally during the negotiation or in writing as part of the contract, a lazy lawyer can likely pass the basis-of-the-bargain test at least initially without any proof of buyer's reliance. We would so define the "presumption" here: even though plaintiff has not put on proof of reliance, defendant's motion for a directed verdict will be denied.[4] A careful lawyer, however, will allege some reliance and offer some proof.

When the plaintiff sues on a representation far removed in time or space from the actual sales negotiation and agreement, what the plaintiff must prove is totally unclear. Can an advertisement form the basis of the bargain? What of a representation made to plaintiff's doctor, a representation that the plaintiff himself never saw or heard? What of a representation made after the sale has been consummated?

It is clear that an advertisement can be a part of the basis of the bargain,[5] and it is only fair that it be so. (See also 10–10 *infra* where 2–313B is discussed.) However, the language in Comment 3, from which some have found a presumption, is limited to "affirmations of fact made by the seller about the goods during a bargain * * *." In the usual case one would not regard an advertisement as

arise. See, e.g., Hawkins Constr. Co. v. Matthews Co., Inc., 190 Neb. 546, 209 N.W.2d 643, 12 UCC 1013 (1973) (sale of scaffolding; express warranty even though buyer did not rely on statements in seller's brochure); Martin v. American Med. Sys., Inc., 116 F.3d 102, 32 UCC2d 1101 (4th Cir.1997) (Virginia UCC variation does not require plaintiff to show reliance on defendant's representations in a breach of warranty case involving personal injury; court held "any description of the goods, other than the seller's mere opinion about the product constitutes part of the basis of the basis of the bargain and is therefore an express warranty. It is unnecessary that the buyer actually rely upon it.").

In another group of cases courts have ruled that reliance is required. See e.g. Wojcik v. Empire Forklift, Inc., 14 A.D.3d 63, 783 N.Y.S.2d 698, 55 UCC2d 190 (3d Dept. 2004) (no recovery where neither injured party nor supervisor could remember seeing statement in literature); Yurcic v. Purdue Pharma, 343 F.Supp.2d 386, 55 UCC2d 10 (M.D. Pa. 2004) (similar).

Upon analyzing these cases, one senses that the courts, though divided, are loath to give up the reliance requirement and continue it via the "basis of bargain" test of 2–313(1).

4. Under our theory, once the seller presents evidence of non-reliance, it is doubtful that the buyer can get to the jury on proof of seller's affirmation alone. The presumption (that is, the likelihood for a mechanical ruling in plaintiff's favor) arising from proof of seller's affirmation alone is gone. Plaintiff has left only an inference of reliance against which the court, in ruling on a directed verdict motion, will weigh defendant's evidence of non-reliance. Plaintiff may survive the motion if defendant's evidence is weak enough but we doubt this is the usual case. Plaintiff would be well-advised to bolster his proof of seller's affirmation with evidence of reliance if he wants to create enough doubt in the judge's mind to get to the jury. See C. McCormick, Laws of Evidence §§ 310–11 (1954).

5. See, e.g., Harris v. Belton, 258 Cal.App.2d 595, 65 Cal.Rptr. 808 (1968) (advertisement for skin cream created express warranty); Triple E, Inc. v. Hendrix & Dail, Inc., 344 S.C. 186, 543 S.E.2d 245, 43 UCC2d 533 (App. 2001) (advertisement could create express warranty); Murrin v. Ford Motor Co., 303 A.D.2d 475, 756 N.Y.S.2d 596, 50 UCC2d 745 (2003) (failed to allege aware of advertisements).

being made "during a bargain," and therefore no statement in an advertisement would normally qualify for the presumption that may be authorized in Comment 3.[6] At minimum a plaintiff in such a case should have to testify that he or she knew of and relied upon the advertisement in making the purchase. A Missouri Court of Appeals adopted just this requirement in the case of Interco, Inc. v. Randustrial Corp.[7] The court eventually held that the language in seller's catalogue which stated that a floor-covering product would "absorb considerable flex without cracking" created an express warranty under 2–313.[8] After stating that a catalogue, brochure or advertisement may constitute an express warranty, the court cautioned that for such a warranty to arise, " * * * the catalogue, advertisement or brochure must have at least been read * * * as the UCC requires the proposed express warranty be part of the basis of the bargain."[9] We approve of the court's logic and concur in the judgment. Of course, in addition to showing that an express warranty created by an advertisement was a basis of the bargain, the successful plaintiff must show that the warranty was breached. Thus, in Semowich v. R.J. Reynolds Tobacco Co.,[10] the court held that even if an express warranty had been created that defendant's low tar products were less harmful than other cigarettes, there would be no breach as this was true.

With the fall of the privity barriers, many plaintiffs have been enabled to sue defendants with whom they had no direct contact. Such suits may be justified when the plaintiff has read the defendant's advertisement. But what of the cases in which the express warranty is made to the plaintiff's employer, his doctor, or his seller?[11] In Putensen v. Clay Adams, Inc., a California appellate court had no difficulty in finding the plaintiff's doctor to be an agent for the purpose of receiving and relying on a manufacturer's

---

6. Roxalana Hills, Ltd. v. Masonite Corp., 627 F.Supp. 1194, 42 UCC 1330 (S.D.W.Va.1986) (advertisement proclaiming durability of siding fell short of factual affirmation; not warranty); Boud v. SDNCO, Inc., 54 P.3d 1131, 48 UCC2d 532 (Utah 2002) (photograph of yacht in brochure, with caption reading 'best ... in its class' did not create any express warranty because photograph and caption were not definite or objective enough to be considered facts or promises and photograph made no assertions as to mechanical or electrical problems complained of by buyer).

7. 533 S.W.2d 257, 19 UCC 464 (Mo. App.1976).

8. *Id.* at 263, 19 UCC at 471.

9. *Id.* at 262, 19 UCC at 470. See also, In re Bridgestone/Firestone, Inc.

Tires Products Liability Litigation, 205 F.R.D. 503, 47 UCC2d 140 (S.D.Ind. 2001), order rev'd in part, 288 F.3d 1012 (7th Cir.2002) (consumer was aware of written warranty language before purchase; hence, it was part of basis of bargain).

10. 1988 WL 123930, 8 UCC2d 976 (N.D.N.Y.1988).

11. And see generally, Reitz Manufacturer's Warranties of Consumer Goods, 75 Wash. L. Q. 357 (1997). See also, J.J. White, Consumer Protection and the Uniform Commercial Code, 75 Wash. U.L.Q. 219 (1997) and J.J. White, Freeing the Tortious Soul of Express Warranty, 72 Tulane L. Rev. 2089 (1998).

warranty that its plastic tubing was suitable for heart catheterization.[12]

Statements made by a seller to the buyer after the sale has been concluded are another source of reliance dispute.[13] So, too, are "warranties" in the box that includes the product sold. And what of brochures read after the sale? Some cases say no warranty.[14] It would be hard to reconcile these with finding of warranties in the box. One may argue most persuasively that once a legally binding contract of sale exists, no additional statements of the seller can be made part of the basis of that bargain. Since the buyer has already agreed to the deal, seller cannot plead that it relied on any additional statement in making its deal. To that argument one may respond that in the merchandising world a buyer, even one already legally obligated to buy, has greater rights while still standing at the seller's counter than he does two weeks later.[15] For example, suppose a camper purchases a sleeping bag, which is advertised as suitable for winter use, and right after handing over his money the seller states that it can be used when the temperature goes below zero. The camper relies on that statement and suffers frostbite one night when the temperature reaches two below. If back in the camp store the seller had told the camper that the bag could not be used in sub-zero weather, the camper probably could have returned the bag immediately and received a full refund. But after the camper has used the bag in reliance on the seller's statement, the bag may have acquired some holes and mud, and the seller will be less willing to rescind. In these circumstances it seems reasonable to make the seller's post-sale statement an express warranty.

It is noteworthy that Comment 9 to 2–313 of Amended Article 2 offered a novel solution to the post-agreement puzzle:

12.   12 Cal.App.3d 1062, 91 Cal.Rptr. 319, 8 UCC 449 (1970). See also Certain-Teed Corp. v. Russell, 883 So.2d 1266, 51 UCC2d 418 (Ala.Civ.App. 2003) (privity required for warranty claims of economic and property damage); Goodman v. PPG Industries, Inc., 849 A.2d 1239, 2004 PA Super 151, 53 UCC2d 186 (Pa.Super.2004) (defendant/manufacturer warranted to retailer that its wood preservative would keep wood from rotting for 26 years; plaintiffs purchased from retailer a product treated with the wood preservative, but were never informed of the promise manufacturer made retailer; court held there was no express warranty because 2–313 requires that the warranting party expressly communicate terms of warranty to party asserting a warranty, which never occurred in this case).

13.   See, e.g., Terry v. Moore, 448 P.2d 601 (Wyo.1968) (statement by a driller, made after contract made and drilling completed, that a well would produce a certain output held not express warranty; not part of the basis of the bargain).

14.   See, e.g., Global Truck & Equip. Co. v. Palmer Mach. Works, Inc., 628 F.Supp. 641, 42 UCC 1250 (N.D.Miss. 1986).

15.   For example, § 2–607(2) provides that acceptance of goods precludes their later rejection, and § 2–608(2) provides that "[r]evocation of acceptance must occur within a reasonable time after the buyer discovers or should have discovered grounds for it and before any substantial change in condition of the goods which is not caused by their own defects."

The precise time when words of description or affirmation are made or samples are shown is not material. The sole question is whether the language or samples or models are fairly to be regarded as part of the contract. If language that would otherwise create an obligation under this section is used after the closing of the deal (as when the buyer taking delivery asks and receives an additional assurance). An obligation will arise if the requirements for a modification are satisfied. See Downie v. Abex Corp., 741 F.2d 1235 (10th Cir. 1984).

If one accepts the analysis of Comment 9, the buyer may have a new bargain, which is based in part upon the modified warranty—the seller's description or affirmation after the time of contracting modifies the deal.[16]

Note, however, that section 2–209 and the modification analysis validate only a handful of all the possible post-deal warranties. First, section 2–209(1) contemplates an "agreement modifying a contract * * *." It is far from self-evident that a seller's post-sale words uttered during delivery are an "agreement of modification," and one can hardly attribute that bilateral connotation to an advertisement that is not published until after the sale. Indeed, Comment 9 seems to contemplate only the cases of face-to-face dealings that occur while the deal is still warm. Second, any oral modification of a contract for goods costing more than $500 must somehow meet the statute of frauds under 2–209(3) or constitute a waiver of the statute under 2–209(4). As we point out elsewhere, the statute of frauds and waiver provisions of 2–209 are ambiguous, and one might read them as prohibiting oral modification on items costing more than $500.[17] Of course, the agreement of the parties may preclude certain types of modification as well. In McDermott, Inc. v. Clyde Iron,[18] the Fifth Circuit found that a post sale warranty by modification could not be established as the contract's integration agreement required the signature of both parties to create an effective modification.

In our judgment it would be reasonable for a court to find that the "deal" had not been concluded despite the payment of money at least until the buyer had passed the seller's threshold. Until that time (or until some other necessarily arbitrary limit) the buyer, as a matter of empirical fact, will have the power to get the seller to

---

16. Phillips Petroleum Co. v. Bucyrus–Erie Co., 131 Wis.2d 21, 388 N.W.2d 584, 1 UCC2d 667 (1986) (incorporation into approval drawings, after sale, of specification for grade of steel, created express warranty by modification of original contract).

17. Cooley v. Big Horn Harvestore Sys., Inc., 767 P.2d 740, 7 UCC2d 1051 (Colo.App.1988), aff'd in part, rev'd in part on other grounds, 813 P.2d 736, 14 UCC2d 977 (Colo.1991) (jury finding of modification of warranty set aside as statute of frauds not satisfied).

18. 979 F.2d 1068, 19 UCC2d 465 (5th Cir.1992), rev'd in part on other grounds, 511 U.S. 202, 114 S.Ct. 1461, 128 L.Ed.2d 148 (1994).

take the goods back and undo the sale. To say that statements made after the payment of the cash but before the expiration of this short period are express warranties recognizes the practical realities even though it does some violence to normal contract doctrine. We would urge a different rule for seller's statements made more than a short period beyond the conclusion of the agreement.

We find enough vitality and merit in the reliance requirement that we would not find such post-deal representations to be warranties under 2–313 unless they could be proved as modifications under the terms of 2–209, but we would recognize warranties that are delivered with the goods even if the delivery came well after the deal had been made. However, a buyer would not necessarily be deprived of all recourse against his seller on a post-deal statement that misled him but did not qualify as a warranty. Like any advertiser, the seller might be liable in tort to those he misleads by his advertising.[19] In most cases we would send the buyer who had relied on a post-sale representation down the tort road.

What the Code does to the pre-Code reliance requirement is quite unclear. One may argue that the exchange of the "basis of the bargain" language for the old "reliance" language will not change the outcome in any cases. Others apparently believe that the Code dilutes and perhaps even emasculates the pre-Code reliance requirement. For most cases, we favor the former interpretation. Why should one who has not relied on the seller's statement have the right to sue? That plaintiff is asking for greater protection than one would get under the warranty of merchantability, far more than bargained for. We would send this party to the implied warranties.

In the Amendment Process, some attempts were made to dilute the reliance requirement, but Amended Article 2 leaves 2–313 unchanged in this respect. Whatever the Code or the courts say, we suspect that the requirement that buyers rely on the seller's representation will live on in the juries' minds and will sometimes function as an unarticulated but important part of the puffing doctrine.[20]

---

19. For example, Restatement, Second, Torts § 402B (1965), provides a cause of action when a seller, in the course of advertising, makes an innocent misrepresentation of a material fact concerning the character or quality of an item sold to a consumer who suffers physical harm caused by justifiable reliance on the misrepresentation.

See, e.g., Hensley v. Colonial Dodge, Inc., 69 Mich.App. 597, 245 N.W.2d 142, 20 UCC 329 (1976) (sign on premises stating "Colonial Dodge USED CARS 1 YEAR WARRANTY" did not create an

express warranty; buyer might have claim for misrepresentation).

20. Janssen v. Hook, 1 Ill.App.3d 318, 272 N.E.2d 385, 9 UCC 846 (1971), illustrates the continuing vitality of the reliance requirement. The court found as follows:

The defendant testified that the plaintiff advised him that one of the trucks was in "good condition" when, in fact, it needed extensive repair. The defendant admitted, however, that he had inspected and worked with the trucks prior to his purchase of them and was aware

§ 10–6 Contractual Express Warranties, Section 2–313—Basis of the Bargain—The Article 2 Amendment Process

For several years, the drafters of Amended Article 2, through many drafts, tried to replace or refine the phrase "basis of the bargain." Like all students of existing Article 2, they well understood that the phrase had been subject to commentators' criticisms and had caused puzzlement and frustration in the courts. In the end they gave up, and returned to the old formulation.

One may still learn something about the meaning of "basis of the bargain" in existing Article 2 by tracing the steps of the purported revisers. In their February 10, 1995 draft, the express warranties section (section 2–1302[1]) removed the language of "becomes part of the basis of the bargain" and provided that,

(a) Except as otherwise provided in subsection (b):

(1) An affirmation of fact or promise by the seller ... *presumptively becomes part of the agreement* between the seller and buyer and creates an express warranty that the goods will conform to the affirmation or promise.

(2) A description of the goods *presumptively becomes part of the agreement* between the seller and buyer and creates an express warranty that the goods will conform to the description.

(3) A sample or model that is made part of the agreement *presumptively* creates an express warranty that the whole of the goods will conform to the sample or model.

(b) An express warranty is not created under subsection (a) if the seller establishes by clear and convincing evidence that the buyer was unreasonable in concluding that an affirmation, promise, description, or sample *became part of the agreement*. (Emphasis added.)[2]

This section was revised in the May 1, 1995 Draft of Amended Article 2 as follows,

(a) An express warranty is an affirmation of fact or promise that relates to the goods, a description of the goods, or an affirmation that the whole of the goods conforms to any sample

that they needed repairs. Under the circumstances, the finding of the trial court that an express warranty, as defined by the Code, had not been made was not against the manifest weight of the evidence.
Id. at 320, 272 N.E.2d at 388, 9 UCC at 849.

§ 10–6

1. The February 10, 1995 Draft followed the "hub and spokes" approach and rearranged the sections in original Article 2. See § 2–1302 (Draft, Feb. 10, 1995) (on file with one of the authors).

2. *Id*.

or model made by a seller, including a manufacturer, to a buyer, *which becomes part of an agreement with the buyer under subsection (d)* * * *.

* * *

(d) Any description, sample, affirmation, promise, or statement that relates to the goods made by the seller under subsection (a) ... *presumptively* become part of an agreement with the seller and creates an express warranty that the goods will conform to the affirmation, promise, or statement. However, an obligation is not created if the seller establishes by a preponderance of the evidence that a reasonable person in the position of the buyer would conclude that ... or that any affirmations of fact or promises *did not become part of the agreement*. (Emphasis added.)[3]

This section (renumbered as section 2–313) was revised again in the March 1, 1996 Draft of Amended Article 2 and its subsection (b) provides,

(b) An affirmation of fact or promise that relates to the goods or a description of the goods made, or any sample or model of the goods furnished by the seller to the immediate buyer *that becomes part of the agreement* creates an express warranty that the goods will conform to the affirmation of fact, promise, or description or that the whole of the goods will conform to the sample or model.[4] (Emphasis added.)

Note 3 to section 3–313 of the March 1, 1996 Draft of Amended Article 2 explains what many would not have understood from the language of the text, namely that any vestigial reliance requirement was gone:

Subsection (b) states the general principles applicable to an "immediate" buyer who claims a breach of express warranty by the seller. They cover any case where there is privity of contract between the seller and buyer. Subsection (b) follows 2–313(1) of the 1990 Official Text except that the phrase *"becomes part of the agreement" is substituted for "becomes part of the basis of the bargain."* The change is intended to clarify that an express warranty is treated like any other term of the agreement and that the buyer need not prove reliance to establish an express warranty.[5] (Emphasis added.)

3. § 2–1302 (Draft, May 1, 1995) (on file with one of the authors).

4. § 2–313(b) (Working Draft, Mar. 1, 1996), available at http://www.law.upenn.edu/bll/ulc/ucc2/textm96.htm.

5. § 2–313, Note 3 (Working Draft, Mar. 1, 1996), available at http://www.law.upenn.edu/bll/ulc/ucc2/textm96.htm.

Only by reading the note is one likely to understand that the change of these few words would completely excise the reliance requirement from the law of express warranty.

Stealthy as it was, complete removal of reliance by the substitution of a few words was too much for the drafting committee (or possibly for its observers). In the March 1, 1998 draft the "basis of the bargain" returned:

§ 2–403. Express Warranty To Immediate Buyer.

(a) Express warranties by a seller to an immediate buyer are created [only] as provided by this section. Any representation or promise made by the seller to the immediate buyer, including those made in any medium of communication to the public, which relates to the goods and *becomes part of the basis of the bargain* creates an express warranty that the goods will conform to the representation or promise or, with respect to a sample, that the whole of the goods will conform to the sample . . . .[6] (Emphasis added.)

This draft was not quite as opaque as the earlier one. It acknowledged what was going on, and attempted to get to the same place as the earlier language by weakening the reliance concept further:

(c) *A representation or promise made under subsection (a) becomes part of the basis of the bargain unless:*

(1) a reasonable person in the position of the immediate buyer would not believe that the representation or promise was part of the agreement;

(2) the immediate buyer knew of the representation or promise and did not believe that it was true; or

(3) where the representation or promise was made in a medium for communication to the public, including advertising, the immediate buyer did not know of it at the time of the agreement.[7] (Emphasis added)

These are the seeds of what became 2–313B of Amended Article 2 discussed infra at sec. 9–10. Note that here a promise is part of the basis of the bargain unless one of the conditions occurs; in effect, it is a presumption that the basis of the bargain requirement is satisfied.

A note in this draft explains the reasons for restoring the "basis of the bargain" language:

6. § 2–403 (Discussion Draft, May 1, 1998), available at http://www.law. upenn.edu/bll/ulc/ucc2/ucc2598.htm.

7. *Id.*

The "part of the basis of the bargain" test was restored in subsection (a). Unlike current 2–313, however, subsection (c) states when a representation or promise becomes part of the basis of the bargain. This should help to clarify disagreement over what that phrase means. See e.g., Holdych & Mann, *The Basis of the Bargain Requirement: A Market and Economic Based Analysis of Express Warranties*, 45 De Paul L. Rev. 781 (1996); Buettner v. R.W. Martin & Sons, Inc., 47 F.3d 116 (4th Cir. 1995) (Virginia law); Tolmie Farms, Inc. v. J.R. Simplot Co., 862 P.2d 299 (Idaho 1993); Weng v. Allison, 678 N.E.2d 1254 (Ill. App. 1997).[8]

There is also this short but revealing Note:

"Agreement" is defined as the "bargain of the parties in fact." 1–201(3). So "basis of the bargain" is another way of saying "basis of the agreement." Since agreements can be made both before and after a contract is formed, there is no artificial time at which an express warranty must be made. They may be made to modify a contract if 2–209(1) is satisfied.[9]

Apparently the drafters were influenced by the Holdych & Mann article, in which the authors argue for a market test (i.e., an objective test) to determine what affirmations or promises become express warranties. Things that the market as a whole (buyers in general) would consider to be part of the basis of the bargain would lead to express warranties even if it could be shown that the plaintiff-buyer could not have relied. This, of course, was a redefinition of the basis of the bargain, for most had thought "basis of the bargain" to be a requirement of individual reliance on the warranty by the buyer.

After that long trip, the drafters arrived back where they started; the final version of Amended section 2–313 included the basis of the bargain language and no restricting definition.

§ 10–7   Contractual Express Warranties, Section 2–313—Samples, Models and More

We commonly conceive of warranties as verbal representations, but such a view is much too narrow. What could be a better representation than the sample or model that is to represent the very thing that the seller is selling? Section 2–313(1)(c) recognizes these symbolic statements as express warranties:

Any sample or model which is made part of the basis of the bargain creates an express warranty that the whole of the goods shall conform to the sample or model.

---

8. § 2–403, Note 2 (Discussion Draft, May 1, 1998), available at http://www.law.upenn.edu/bll/ulc/ucc2/ucc2598.htm.

9. *Id.*, Note 6.

Much of what we have said above about the basis of the bargain and about the other aspects of express warranty litigation applies equally to sample or model express warranties. We see only two significant, clear questions that have elements unique to samples or models. First, was the item under consideration in fact a "sample" or a "model?" Second, what does the sample or model mean?

There is little post-Code appellate litigation that deals with the question whether an item under consideration by the parties constitutes a sample or model.[1] Perhaps we can learn from Comment 8 to Amended 2–313 which distinguished between the two terms as follows:

> The basic situation as to statements affecting the true essence of the bargain is no different when a sample or model is involved in the transaction. This section includes both a "sample" actually drawn from the bulk of goods which is the subject matter of the sale, and a "model" which is offered for inspection when the subject matter is not at hand and which has not been drawn from the bulk of the goods.

The comment then gives some indication of the scope of the definitions of the two terms (emphasis added):

> [T]he facts are often ambiguous when something is shown as *illustrative,* rather than as a straight sample. In general, the presumption is that *any* sample or model just as any affirmation of fact is intended to become a basis of the bargain.

Although it is not free from doubt, the second quoted passage appears to mean that anything illustrative that the seller holds out to the buyer is at least presumptively a sample or model. Surely a buyer can make a plausible argument on this basis that anything that remotely resembled the goods in question and that was pointed out by the seller constitutes a sample or model and therefore that the burden should be upon the seller to show that the goods considered did not constitute a sample or model.

Nevertheless, there must be circumstances where an item considered by the parties is not a sample or model. For example, when a seller presents a "sample" of coal to a buyer but makes it clear that the coal actually being sold is of inferior quality, it seems reasonable to conclude that the previewed coal is not a sample or model for purposes of 2–313(1)(c).[2] Similarly, one can see why a

§ 10–7

1. Under section 16 of the Uniform Sales Act, it was generally held that the mere fact that a sample was exhibited did not create a warranty that the bulk would conform to the sample. Thus, if the deal was made in terms that exclud-ed the possibility that the buyer relied on the sample as conforming to the bulk, there was no warranty to that effect.

2. The West Virginia Supreme Court held that these facts did not create an express warranty in Sylvia Coal Co. v. Mercury Coal & Coke Co., 151 W.Va.

demonstration of a 42 foot boom lift did not create a warranty of performance for an 80 foot boom lift.[3] A more difficult situation can easily be imagined. Assume that buyer wishes to purchase two tons of coal from seller. Seller sends buyer into the yard where a pile of coal of several thousand tons is located. He makes no representation either oral or written about the nature of the coal, nor does he do anything to indicate that the coal in the pile is a "sample or model." If the two reach a deal and seller delivers coal which differs from that which the buyer inspected in the pile, has seller made and breached an express warranty? We find this a close case, but absent some statement by buyer or seller to indicate that the coal sold was somehow to conform to the coal in the pile, we believe that there would be no express warranty.

In general, the presumption suggested in Comment 8 to Section 2–313 of Amended Article 2 would have made the definition of samples and models less troublesome under the Code than it was under the Uniform Sales Act. It is a rare circumstance in which the seller is able to convince a court that an item inspected by him and the buyer or by the buyer at seller's suggestion does not constitute either a sample or model. Of course, the buyer would still have to show that the sample or model was made a part of the basis of the bargain. Thus, even if a court found that the previewed items in the coal and siding cases were in fact samples or models, it could reasonably hold, for the reasons discussed above, that the sample or model was not a part of the bargain.[4]

If one decides that the goods inspected are a sample or model made a part of the basis of the bargain, he must still determine exactly what characteristics the goods must display in order to conform to the sample or model. Comment 8 to Amended Article 2 would again give some help and suggests that the kind of meaning that a sample transmits may differ from that which a model transmits:

> If the sample has been drawn from an existing bulk, it must be regarded as describing values of the goods contracted for unless it is accompanied by an unmistakable denial of such responsibility. If, on the other hand, a model of merchandise not on

818, 156 S.E.2d 1, 4 UCC 650 (1967). However, the court appeared to say that the previewed coal was a sample but that the sample did not create an express warranty because it was not a part of the basis of the bargain. *Id.* at 826–27, 156 S.E.2d at 7, 4 UCC at 656.

3. Logan Equip. Corp. v. Simon Aerials, Inc., 736 F.Supp. 1188, 12 UCC2d 387 (D.Mass.1990).

4. For cases where 2–313(1)(c) express warranties were held to arise from a sale by "sample" or "model," see, e.g., Regina Grape Prods. Co. v. Supreme Wine Co., 357 Mass. 631, 260 N.E.2d 219, 7 UCC 1168 (1970) (express warranty created by samples of dry, red wine); Zion Temple First Pentecostal Church of Cincinnati, Ohio, Inc. v. Brighter Day Bookstore & Gifts, 2004 WL 2315032, 55 UCC2d 41 (Ohio App. 2004) (swatch of cloth served as sample).

hand is offered, the mercantile presumption that it has become a literal description of the subject matter is not so strong, and particularly so if modification on the buyer's initiative impairs any feature of the model.

This portion of Comment 8 tells us that a seller showing a model— something not drawn out of an existing bulk—has more leeway than when it shows a sample. Beyond this conclusion the quoted language begs the fundamental question. We know that no sample or model is truly a literal reproduction of the good itself. Just as no snowflake is the literal reproduction of any other, so no Chevrolet is the literal reproduction of any other of its particular species. In most cases, therefore, it will take at least some expert testimony about trade usage and understanding to put sufficient meat on the bones of the sample or model to enable the court or the jury to make a judgment whether the goods lived up to that sample or model.[5]

An obvious example of the inherent ambiguity in a sample or model is given in Washington Fruit & Produce Co. v. Ted Mirski Co.[6] In that case, the seller warranted that his cherries would be "twelve row larger."[7] The boxes used by the seller were capable of holding exactly twelve rows of cherries 56/64 inches in diameter. The seller also sent the buyer a sizing card with a hole, shaped like a perfect circle 56/64 inches in diameter, punched in it to indicate the size of the cherries. The buyer maintained that the warranty was to the effect that each of the cherries would be at least 56/64 inches in diameter, but the seller argued that the warranty meant that the average diameter of the cherries offered would be 56/64 of an inch. The court agreed with the seller, but in the absence of proof of trade usage, the buyer's argument was equally plausible. Although the court here held that the sizing card was not a sample or a model, it would have faced the same interpretative problem if it had held otherwise or if the seller had displayed an actual cherry exactly 56/64 inches in diameter. Incidentally, the lawyer's job in ferreting out the meaning of a sample or a model is similar to the work that one must undertake in finding what is "merchantable" under section 2–314, and we direct the lawyer to our discussion of that task in the next section.

A sample or model is frequently the visual and tangible ele ment upon which the parties conclude their bargain. In highly

---

5. One might assume that difficult proof problems would be encountered in determining whether the taste of catered food lived up to samples. The appellate court in Graulich Caterer, Inc. v. Hans Holterbosch, Inc., 101 N.J.Super. 61, 243 A.2d 253, 5 UCC 440 (App.Div. 1968), apparently recognized this prob-

lem, because it deferred to the original trier of fact's judgment of the witnesses' demeanor and credibility.

6. 1965 WL 8363, 24 Agri.Dec. 1559, 3 UCC 175 (1965).

7. Id. at 1561–62, 3 UCC at 176.

technical transactions, a contract based on a physical representation may be the best method of avoiding a misunderstanding and insuring that the parties are in agreement about their respective obligations.

A sample is actually drawn from the bulk of the goods which are for sale. In Printing Center of Texas, Inc. v. Supermind Publishing Co.,[8] the buyer was shown a sample of white newsprint to be used in the books he ordered. When the completed books had gray pages, a Texas appellate court held that the goods did not conform to the sample so that there was a breach of express warranty. In another case, AFA Corp. v. Phoenix Closures, Inc.,[9] a bottle cap manufacturer relied on the seller's specifications and samples when he ordered cap liners. When the purchased cap liners did not conform to the seller's representations and samples, the court held that the seller breached his express warranty by sample. In Indust–Ri–Chem Laboratory, Inc. v. Par–Pak Co.,[10] the buyer relied on samples when ordering specially-lined steel drums to be used in the shipping of a highly corrosive chemical, and the express warranty was breached when the linings did not correspond to the samples.

A model is offered for inspection when the goods are not at hand, but unlike a sample, a model is not drawn from the bulk of goods for sale. In Mileham & King, Inc. v. Fitzgerald,[11] the seller of interior window shutters breached an express warranty that the shutters he sold to the plaintiff would fit her window frames as tightly as the model he showed her prior to purchase. Since the shutters did not fit tightly enough after installation to prevent light from entering the interior when closed, the court found nonconformity. In Barton v. Tra–Mo, Inc.,[12] polyethylene tanks which had been manufactured for another customer and were shown to the plaintiff as an example of the strength and diversity of the material were models to which the tanks manufactured for the plaintiff would conform. When the plaintiff's tanks broke under circumstances where the models did not, the court held that there was a breach of an express warranty by model.

Not every item examined by the buyer in a transaction will give rise to an express warranty. First one must ask what characteristics are to be represented by the item. For example, in Thrall v. Renno,[13] the buyers of a brick patio selected a sample of brick solely as an example of the color to be used in the patio. Since there was

8.   669 S.W.2d 779, 39 UCC 127 (Tex. App.1984) (assuming Article 2 governed the sale).

9.   501 F.Supp. 224, 30 UCC 81 (N.D.Ill.1980).

10.   602 S.W.2d 282, 29 UCC 794 (Tex.Civ.App.1980).

11.   1982 WL 171056, 33 UCC 208 (D.C.Super.1982).

12.   69 Or.App. 295, 686 P.2d 423, 38 UCC 1601 (1984), review denied, 299 Or. 732, 705 P.2d 1157 (1985).

13.   695 S.W.2d 84, 41 UCC 1232 (Tex.App.1985).

no representation of that particular brick's quality, the court held that the specific brick inspected was a sample only for purposes of the brick's color and did not expressly warrant the quality or performance of the bricks used in the patio. Note well that not all exemplifying items constitute either samples or models. Some items may be shown to the buyer merely as representative in a general way without an implicit promise that the goods to be sold will conform in a specific way to those items. Whether something is a model depends partly upon the words spoken by the parties to the transaction. It must also depend upon the degree to which the item shown conforms to the end product. In Meredith Corp. v. Design & Lithography Center, Inc. v. Old World Arts, Inc.,[14] the buyer sued for breach of an express warranty by sample when the catalogue pages which he ordered from the printer were rejected because of "ghosting" (color variations on the borders of the same sheet) and did not conform to the sample which the buyer had been shown by the printer. The court held that the samples of the work done by the printer's "four-color process" were shown to the buyer merely as an illustration of the process and quality obtainable and, therefore, did not give rise to an express warranty that the final work would conform to the particular features of the sample.

In summary, the Code has made express warranties out of samples and models and thus strengthened the hand of the buyer somewhat. All other things being equal, we suspect that a buyer is more likely to be victorious in a suit on an express warranty than in a suit on an implied warranty. This is so because an express warranty, once made, is harder to disclaim[15] and because it is easier to prove breach of an explicit express warranty than it is to prove breach against a more general standard of "merchantability" or "fitness for a particular purpose." Beyond that 2–313(2)(c) does little to disturb the pre-Code law, and so far it has produced only a handful of cases, none of which is remarkable.

a. *Affirmations of Fact or Promise*

Under section 2–313(2)(a) "[a]ny affirmation of fact or promise made by the seller which relates to the goods and becomes part of the basis of the bargain creates an express warranty that the goods shall conform to the affirmation or promise." Promises and affirmations of fact may be in regard to any aspect of the goods in question, from their condition to their performance capabilities. We have already indicated that we believe the key distinction between factual affirmations or promises and mere "puffing" may be little

14. 101 Idaho 391, 614 P.2d 414, 29 UCC 450 (1980).

15. For the effect that the recently enacted Magnuson–Moss Act has on sell-ers' attempts to disclaim express and implied warranties, see § 10–18 *infra*.

more than the specificity of the statement. The following decisions are a sample of "typical" cases which the courts often confront. In a dispute involving roofing material, the court in Board of Directors of the City of Harriman School Dist. v. Southwestern Petroleum Corp. found that statements as to the appropriateness of the material had created an express warranty.[16] In concluding that the statements had formed a basis of the bargain, the court noted:

> Had SWEPCO * * * informed the Board of Education that the Topcoat System would be ineffective to patch the roof and in fact would increase substantially the number and volume of leaks and thus cause significant damage to the building and its contents, [they] undoubtedly would not have entered into the contract.[17]

A number of courts have addressed the issue whether expressions of future capacity or performance can constitute an express warranty. In Royal Business Machs., Inc. v. Lorraine Corp.,[18] the Court of Appeals for the Seventh Circuit held that statements by the seller that the maintenance costs of copy machines would remain low and that service calls would be required no more often than every 7,000 to 9,000 copies were express warranties. Likewise, in Crest Container Corp. v. R.H. Bishop Co.,[19] an Illinois appellate court held that affirmations of performance in the manufacturer's catalogue which were relied upon by the buyer in purchasing heating coils for a commercial heating system constituted express warranties.

Other decisions hold that seller's affirmations of fact concerning the condition of goods for sale give rise to express warranties. For example, in Wiseman v. Wolfe's Terre Haute Auto Auction, Inc.,[20] when a seller repeatedly referred to a truck as "road ready" in response to buyer's statements that he did not want to buy a vehicle with mechanical problems, the court held that seller's assertions were express warranties that were breached when the truck stopped functioning because of a cracked engine block soon after it was purchased. Similarly, the Nebraska Supreme Court found a statement by the seller in Fricke v. Hart[21] that a loader was "in good shape and ready to go to work" to be an express warranty that was breached when the buyer discovered defects in the steering cylinder after driving the loader for the first time.

16. 757 S.W.2d 669, 7 UCC2d 386 (Tenn.App.1988).

17. *Id.* at 7 UCC2d 391.

18. 633 F.2d 34, 30 UCC 462 (7th Cir.1980).

19. 111 Ill.App.3d 1068, 67 Ill.Dec. 727, 445 N.E.2d 19, 35 UCC 1498 (1982).

20. 459 N.E.2d 736, 37 UCC 1486 (Ind.App.1984).

21. 206 Neb. 590, 294 N.W.2d 737, 29 UCC 1224 (1980).

Occasionally even factors which are only indirectly related to the condition of the goods are held to be expressly warranted. In view of the fact that the buyer in Miller v. Hubbard–Wray Co.,[22] had specifically indicated to the seller that he wanted to purchase a haybaler newer than the six-year-old machine which he already owned, a seller's statement that a used haybaler which he sold the buyer was two years old was an express warranty that was breached when the buyer later discovered that the machine was actually six years old.

Affirmations of fact or promises often concern the quality of the goods being sold. In England v. Leithoff,[23] a seller's representations that breeding sows did not come from a public market where diseases abound was an affirmation giving rise to an express warranty that was breached when the pigs were found to have contracted leptospirosis from a public sale barn. A court also found a quality-related express warranty in T. J. Stevenson & Co., Inc. v. 81,193 Bags of Flour[24] when bags of flour warranted to be "of merchantable quality" were found to contain substantial amounts of live infestation. Under the prevailing standards, the court explained, the insect-infested flour was not merchantable even if it could have been eaten without causing sickness.

Promises or factual affirmations may sometimes concern the safety of the goods in question. In Drayton v. Jiffee Chem. Corp.,[25] the court held that television and newspaper advertisements which stated that a liquid drain cleaner was "safe" and showed a hand swishing water around a kitchen sink created an express warranty that the product was safe for human contact. With the buyer's testimony that he had seen and relied upon the advertisements, the court found that the express warranty had been breached when the buyer's child was injured by the liquid drain cleaner.

Obviously, not everything a seller says about the goods will rise to the level of an express warranty. For example, in Guess v. Lorenz,[26] a private seller's statements that a car was in "good shape" and that noises in the rear were "just something the car does" did not qualify as express warranties. Since the seller was not a car dealer or a person who appeared to be knowledgeable about cars, the court held that her statements were only puffs and did not expressly guarantee the condition of the car. Other statements from a variety of decisions which did not qualify as express warranties include a seller's advice that a particular airplane engine was

22. 52 Or.App. 897, 630 P.2d 880, 32 UCC 1378 (1981), mod., 53 Or.App. 531, 633 P.2d 1 (1981).

23. 212 Neb. 462, 323 N.W.2d 98, 34 UCC 453 (1982).

24. 629 F.2d 338, 30 Fed.R.Serv.2d 661, 30 UCC 865 (5th Cir.1980).

25. 591 F.2d 352, 26 UCC 865 (6th Cir.1978).

26. 612 S.W.2d 831, 30 UCC 1529 (Mo.App.1981).

"more suitable" than another,[27] a seller's statement that furnace-welded pipe was "just as good" as seamless pipe,[28] and a tire salesman's advice about the use of truck tires two years after the plaintiff began to buy tires regularly from the seller.[29]

b. Descriptions

When the seller's description of the goods becomes part of the basis of the bargain, the seller creates an express warranty that the goods will conform to the description. The specificity of the statement is once again an important factor in determining whether the description rises to the level of an express warranty. Descriptions are a particularly important subset of factual affirmations. It is not uncommon for a court to label an express warranty both an affirmation of fact under 2–313(1)(a) and a description under 2–313(1)(b).

Express warranties based on descriptions often guarantee that a specific type or brand of goods will be delivered. For example, in Select Pork, Inc. v. Babcock Swine, Inc.,[30] the contract was for the sale of two specific kinds of pigs, "Midwestern Gilts" and "Meatline Boars." A brochure entitled "Meet the Midwestern Gilt" included language defining such animals became part of the basis of the bargain and thus a warranty by description. When defendants failed to deliver Midwestern Gilts and Meatline Boars, they therefore breached their express warranty.

Technical specifications are frequently an important element of warranty descriptions. In Capital Equipment Enterprises, Inc. v. North Pier Terminal Co.,[31] an Illinois appellate court held that the seller's description of a used crane as a "30–ton McMyler Crane" in "very good condition" gave rise to an express warranty. When the crane failed to lift more than 10 tons at one time and was not in good condition but merely operable, the express warranty was breached. Similarly, the Eighth Circuit held in Limited Flying Club, Inc. v. Wood[32] that a logbook description and certification of an airplane as "airworthy" which was based on the repair and inspection history of the airplane was an express warranty that the plane was flyable. The court noted that certification records of the airplane were much like a description that is provided by a blueprint,

---

27. Patron Aviation, Inc. v. Teledyne Indus., Inc., 154 Ga.App. 13, 267 S.E.2d 274, 29 UCC 445 (1980).

28. Ingram River Equip., Inc. v. Pott Indus., Inc., 573 F.Supp. 896, 37 UCC 88 (E.D.Mo.1983).

29. Byrd Motor Lines, Inc. v. Dunlop Tire and Rubber Corp., 63 N.C.App. 292, 304 S.E.2d 773, 36 UCC 1169 (1983), review denied, 310 N.C. 624, 315 S.E.2d 689 (1984).

30. 640 F.2d 147, 30 UCC 839 (8th Cir.1981).

31. 117 Ill.App.2d 264, 254 N.E.2d 542, 7 UCC 290 (1969). See also, Northern States Power Co. v. ITT Meyer Industries, 777 F.2d 405, 42 UCC 1 (8th Cir.1985) (technical specifications, screw anchors, could create express warranty).

32. 632 F.2d 51, 29 UCC 1497 (8th Cir.1980).

and Comment 5 to 2–313 recognizes that blueprints may constitute express warranties.

Descriptions give rise to express warranties concerning condition and quality in much the same way that affirmations of fact or promises do under 2–313(1)(a). In American Honda Motor Co., Inc. v. Boyd,[33] the buyers expressed an interest in purchasing a "new car" and were then shown a car by the seller which had the appearance of a "new car," including a new car sticker and a "new car smell." After purchasing this car, however, the buyers discovered that the car had been damaged and was in need of major repair work. The court found that the evidence supported the buyer's claim for breach of warranty that the car was "new." Another court held in Wullschleger & Co. v. Jenny Fashions, Inc.,[34] that a fabric salesman's promise to supply "first quality" fabric to a manufacturer of women's dresses was an express warranty by description that was breached when the fabric proved to be skewed far beyond the maximum skew accepted by the industry. In Slyman v. Pickwick Farms,[35] the buyer purchased a horse at auction after a veterinarian's opinion was read over a loudspeaker which indicated that the horse's breathing was normal despite the unusual noise the horse made while breathing. Since he had no other knowledge of the horse and could be expected to train and race the horse, the buyer could reasonably have relied on the veterinarian's description to indicate that the horse was physically capable of racing. When the horse was found to have a breathing problem that would prevent it from racing, there was a breach of an express warranty. In Balog v. Center Art Gallery–Hawaii, Inc., the court held that an art dealer's representations that a particular work was a genuine Dali created an express warranty.[36] While the court noted that ordinarily a dealer's representation's of authenticity might be considered mere opinion, where the buyer is unsophisticated and justifiably relies on the representations, a warranty is indeed created.

Misreading a description may be one of the easiest ways to fail on an express warranty claim. In Davis v. Siloo Inc.,[37] the plaintiff argued that cautionary language on the label of a solvent cleaner which read "Avoid prolonged contact with skin. While Petisol 202 permits the immersion of hands, some dryness of skin may be noticed after prolonged exposure" created an express warranty that the product would not be harmful to the skin. Although the user of

---

33. 475 So.2d 835, 41 UCC 410 (Ala. 1985).

34. 618 F.Supp. 373, 41 UCC 1213 (S.D.N.Y.1985).

35. 15 Ohio App.3d 25, 472 N.E.2d 380, 39 UCC 1630 (1984).

36. 745 F.Supp. 1556, 12 UCC2d 962 (D.Haw.1990).

37. 47 N.C.App. 237, 267 S.E.2d 354, 29 UCC 492 (1980). Cf. Beyette v. Ortho Pharmaceutical Corp., 823 F.2d 990, 4 UCC2d 403 (6th Cir.1987) (seller's statement "more than a million women * * * have used this method successfully" not a warranty of effectiveness).

the cleaner died of aplastic anemia allegedly caused by exposure to the product, the court held that the statements on the label were not an express warranty that the product was not harmful. Likewise, in Szajna v. General Motors Corp.,[38] the court held that a description of a car as a "1976 Pontiac Ventura" did not expressly warrant that the car's transmission would be of a particular type or quality. To hold otherwise, reasoned the court, would unreasonably extend the description of the car to encompass a "description" of the transmission. Finally, in Safeway Stores, Inc. v. Certainteed Corp.,[39] the court held that an advertisement's description of a roof as "bondable up to 20 years" was not to be interpreted as a guarantee that the roof would be of sufficient quality to allow the buyer to obtain a 20–year bond on it. The description did not expressly warrant the future performance of the roof.

Descriptions that are only "sales talk" will not constitute an express warranty. For example, in Hall v. T.L. Kemp Jewelry, Inc.,[40] the seller showed the buyer a gold, emerald, and diamond bracelet priced at $1900 and stated that the gold and stones were of "excellent quality," and the buyer responded by saying, "If I have $2000 worth of jewelry, let's wrap it up." The seller later sent a letter of appraisal to the buyer which stated that the bracelet had a value of $2650. When subsequent appraisals placed the value of the bracelet at $900 and $595, the buyer sued the seller for breach of express warranty by description. The court held that the seller's statement as to the value of the goods was not an express warranty when no special circumstances existed to indicate that the statements and conduct were anything but ordinary sales talk.

As we indicate above, the distinction between express oral warranties and puffing or between sales talk and warranty are often easier to make after the fact than before. Invariably the plaintiff buyer will argue that he or she received a warranty and the seller will argue that all statements in advertising are nothing more than sales talk. In theory, at least, the *Hall* case is a particularly easy one for it deals with subjective value. Very little jewelry has utilitarian value the way that food, water, and clothing do. Its value depends upon the aesthetic reaction of the owner and those in the owner's culture. In such circumstances it is difficult to make out any assertion of value as an express warranty. The same is true, but to a lesser degree, of assertions of value about more utilitarian items such as automobiles. Clearly the less dependent an assertion is upon the idiosyncratic judgment of one of the parties the more likely it is to be found to be an express warranty and not

38. 130 Ill.App.3d 173, 85 Ill.Dec. 669, 474 N.E.2d 397, 40 UCC 77 (1985), aff'd, 115 Ill.2d 294, 104 Ill.Dec. 898, 503 N.E.2d 760, 2 UCC2d 1268 (1986).

39. 687 S.W.2d 22, 41 UCC 46 (Tex. App.1984), rev'd, 710 S.W.2d 544, 1 UCC2d 1237 (Tex.1986).

40. 71 N.C.App. 101, 322 S.E.2d 7, 39 UCC 1648 (1984).

merely sales talk. It is important, therefore, to examine not just the words that are spoken but also the context in which they are spoken, the relative knowledge of the parties, their expectations, and other factors.

The puffing problem was much discussed during the process of creating Amended Article 2. Comment 10 to Amended 2–313 identifies the relevant factors:

> For example, the relevant factors may include whether the seller's representations taken in context, (1) were general rather than specific, (2) related to the consequences of buying rather than the goods themselves, (3) were "hedged" in some way, (4) were related to experimental rather than standard goods, (5) were concerned with some aspects of the goods but not a hidden or unexpected nonconformity, (6) were informal statements made in a formal contracting process, (7) were phrased in terms of opinion rather than fact, or (8) were not capable of objective measurement.

§ 10–8 Proposed "Remedial Promise"

Section 2–313 of Amended Article 2 introduced the concept of a "remedial promise." Subsection (4) provided that "any remedial promise made by the seller to the immediate buyer creates an obligation that the promise will be performed upon the happening of the specified event." Comment 11 stated that the "concept of a remedial promise is dealt with in [subsection (4)] to make clear that it is a concept separate and apart from express warranty and that the elements of an express warranty, such as basis of the bargain, are not applicable." Comment 11 further articulates the distinction between "a promise about the quality or performance characteristics of the goods" creating an express warranty on the one hand (if the other elements of a warranty are present) and a "promise by which the seller commits itself to take remedial action upon the happening of a specified event"—a remedial promise. Comment 11 goes on to illustrate the distinction as well.

Courts have disagreed on the question whether promises to repair and replace are to be treated for the purpose of the statute of limitations as "warranties" that are unenforceable four years after the sale, or whether they should be treated as separate remedial promises that might have a longer life.

§ 10–9 Proposed Section 2–313A. Obligation to Remote Purchaser Created by Record Packaged With or Accompanying Goods, "Warranties in the Box" and the Like

Section 2–313 of Article 2 is addressed to immediate purchasers as such. Proposed Sections 2–313A and 2–313B of Amended Article

2 addressed the rights of remote purchasers. These sections will probably never be adopted in any state, but they make clear some of the limitations of 2–313, and it is likely that an understanding of these sections will be of value to lawyers and legal scholars.

§ 2–313A.   Obligation to Remote Purchaser Created by Record Packaged With or Accompanying Goods.

(1) In this section:

(a) "Immediate buyer" means a buyer that enters into a contract with the seller.

(b) "Remote purchaser" means a person that buys or leases goods from an immediate buyer or other person in the normal chain of distribution.

(2) This section applies only to new goods and goods sold or leased as new goods in a transaction of purchase in the normal chain of distribution.

(3) If in a record packaged with or accompanying the goods the seller makes an affirmation of fact or promise that relates to the goods, provides a description that relates to the goods, or makes a remedial promise, and the seller reasonably expects the record to be, and the record is, furnished to the remote purchaser, the seller has an obligation to the remote purchaser that:

(a) the goods will conform to the affirmation of fact, promise, or description unless a reasonable person in the position of the remote purchaser would not believe that the affirmation of fact, promise, or description created an obligation; and

(b) the seller will perform the remedial promise.

(4) It is not necessary to the creation of an obligation under this section that the seller use formal words such as "warrant" or "guarantee" or that the seller have a specific intention to undertake an obligation, but an affirmation merely of the value of the goods or a statement purporting to be merely the seller's opinion or commendation of the goods does not create an obligation.

(5) The following rules apply to the remedies for breach of an obligation created under this section:

(a) The seller may modify or limit the remedies available to the remote purchaser if the modification or limitation is furnished to the remote purchaser no later than the time of purchase or if the modification or limitation is contained in the record that contains the affirmation of fact, promise or description.

(b) Subject to a modification or limitation of remedy, a seller in breach is liable for incidental or consequential damages under Section 2–715, but not for lost profits.

(c) The remote purchaser may recover as damages for breach of a seller's obligation arising under subsection (3) the loss resulting in the ordinary course of events as determined in any reasonable manner.

(6) An obligation that is not a remedial promise is breached if the goods did not conform to the affirmation of fact, promise, or description creating the obligation when the goods left the seller's control.[1]

Even thought it will probably never be adopted by any state, the proposed section may influence the case law. The basic principle of 2–313A is not new to the case law of sales. The new section would have codified for the first time a large body of case law on what are commonly called "pass-through warranties." As Comment 1 stated: "The usual transaction in which this obligation arises is when the manufacturer sells goods in a package to a retailer and includes in the package a record that sets forth the obligations that the manufacturer is willing to undertake in favor of the final party in the distributive chain, who is the party that buys or leases the goods from the retailer." Because there is no direct contact between the seller and the remote purchaser, the obligation of the seller here is not contractual and is not stated as an express warranty. In general we believe that the rule stated in 2–313A are sensible and in accordance with the expectations of both buyers and sellers. We suspect that the courts, on their own, will soon bring the law to the same place that 2–313A would have brought it.

§ 10–10 Proposed Section 2–313B. Obligation to Remote Purchaser Created by Communication to Public

§ 2–313B. Obligation to Remote Purchaser Created by Communication to the Public.

(1) In this section:

(a) "Immediate buyer" means a buyer that enters into a contract with the seller.

§ 10–9

1. § 2–313A (2003). See generally, Flechtner, Enforcing Manufacturers' Warranties, "Pass Through" Warranties, and the Like: Can The Buyer Get a Refund? 50 Rutgers L. Rev. 397 (1998);

Akseli, Advertising and Pass Through Warranties Under Revised Article 2, 106 Comm. L.J. 65 (2001); J. J. White, Warranties in the Box, 46 San Diego L. Rev. ___ (forthcoming Aug/Sept 2009).

(b) "Remote purchaser" means a person that buys or leases goods from an immediate buyer or other person in the normal chain of distribution.

(2) This section applies only to new goods and goods sold or leased as new goods in a transaction of purchase in the normal chain of distribution.

(3) If in an advertisement or a similar communication to the public a seller makes an affirmation of fact or promise that relates to the goods, provides a description that relates to the goods, or makes a remedial promise, and the remote purchaser enters into a transaction of purchase with knowledge of and with the expectation that the goods will conform to the affirmation of fact, promise, or description, or that the seller will perform the remedial promise, the seller has an obligation to the remote purchaser that:

(a) the goods will conform to the affirmation of fact, promise, or description unless a reasonable person in the position of the remote purchaser would not believe that the affirmation of fact, promise, or description created an obligation; and

(b) the seller will perform the remedial promise.

(4) It is not necessary to the creation of an obligation under this section that the seller use formal words such as "warrant" or "guarantee" or that the seller have a specific intention to undertake an obligation, but an affirmation merely of the value of the goods or a statement purporting to be merely the seller's opinion or commendation of the goods does not create an obligation.

(5) The following rules apply to the remedies for breach of an obligation created under this section:

(a) The seller may modify or limit the remedies available to the remote purchaser if the modification or limitation is furnished to the remote purchaser no later than the time of purchase. The modification or limitation may be furnished as part of the communication that contains the affirmation of fact, promise, or description.

(b) Subject to a modification or limitation of remedy, a seller in breach is liable for incidental or consequential damages under Section 2–715, but not for lost profits.

(c) The remote purchaser may recover as damages for breach of a seller's obligation arising under subsection (3) the loss resulting in the ordinary course of events as determined in any reasonable manner.

(6) An obligation that is not a remedial promise is breached if the goods did not conform to the affirmation of fact, promise, or description creating the obligation when the goods left the seller's control.[1]

The basic principle of Section 2–313B is not new. The section codifies for the first time a body of case law extending a seller's obligations for new goods to remote purchasers. A well known leading case that the section follows is Randy Knitwear, Inc. v. American Cyanamid Co.[2] Still, the case law there is not plentiful. The obligation under section 2–313B arises from an advertisement or similar communication to the public. As Comment 1 stated, the "normal situation where this obligation will arise is when a manufacturer engages in an advertising campaign directed towards part or all of the market for its product and will make statements that if made to an immediate buyer would amount to an express warranty or remedial promise under Section 2–313. The goods, however, are sold to someone other than the recipient of the advertising [with the result that no express warranty could arise under 2–313] and are then resold or leased to the recipient."

Although Sections 2–313A and 2–313B have almost the same words, their foundations in the cases and in the expectations of buyers and sellers are different. In our view, Section 2–313A was wise and its foundation in the cases and in parties' expectations was strong. As we indicate above, we think it will become the law by courts' extension of 2–313. But we think that Section 2–313B was of doubtful wisdom and its foundation, weak. We expect it to have much less influence and we predict that advertisements will rarely be found to state express warranties.

§ 10–11 The Implied Warranty of Merchantability; Usage of Trade; Section 2–314—Introduction

The implied warranty of merchantability in 2–314 is important. It is a first cousin to strict tort liability, and "products liability" cases are often tried under the merchantability banner.[1] Section 2–

---

§ 10–10

1. § 2–313A (2003).

2. 11 N.Y.2d 5, 226 N.Y.S.2d 363, 181 N.E.2d 399 (Ct. App.1962).

§ 10–11

1. In First Nat. Bank of Dwight v. Regent Sports Corp., 803 F.2d 1431, 2 UCC2d 458 (7th Cir.1986), the 7th Cir-

cuit found that as strict liability in tort is essentially the liability of implied warranty without the attached contract doctrines a plaintiff could not bring a successful implied warranty action where a strict liability action had failed. According to the economic loss doctrine, a plaintiff can recover only in warranty and not in tort where the only damage is

314 is not revolutionary; it is a modernized version of the comparable Uniform Sales Act provision.[2]

In a merchantability lawsuit a plaintiff must prove that the defendant deviated from the standard of merchantability and that this deviation caused the plaintiff's injury both proximately and in fact. These make a merchantability claim a first cousin to a negligence claim. Under 2–314, a plaintiff must prove that (1) a merchant sold goods,[3] (2) which were not "merchantable" at the time of sale, (3) there was damage to the plaintiff or its property (4) caused proximately and in fact by the defective nature of the goods, and (5) notice to seller of injury. The plaintiff can fail on any of the points listed;[4] the non-privity buyer also cannot recover for economic loss from a remote manufacturer.[5] It can also succumb to any of the affirmative defenses that the defendant may raise, for instance,

to the product itself and the plaintiff has thus only lost the benefit of the bargain. See, e.g., Naporano Iron & Metal Co. v. American Crane Corp., 79 F.Supp.2d 494, 41 UCC2d 483 (D.N.J. 1999), Wausav Tile, Inc. v. County Concrete Corp., 226 Wis.2d 235, 593 N.W.2d 445, 40 UCC2d 417 (1999). Moreover, there is no implied UCC warranty as to services. See Easley v. Day Motors, Inc., 796 So.2d 236, 44 UCC2d 407 (Miss. App. 2001); HDM Flugservice GmbH. v. Parker Hannifin Corp., 332 F.3d 1025, 50 UCC2d 1053 (6th Cir. 2003).

2. Uniform Sales Act § 15(2) provided:

Where the goods are bought by description from a seller who deals in goods of that description (whether he be the grower or manufacturer or not), there is an implied warranty that the goods shall be of a merchantable quality.

3. "Sold" is important here. See Neuhoff v. Marvin Lumber and Cedar Co., 370 F.3d 197, 53 UCC2d 711 (1st Cir. 2004) (gifts are not subject to implied warranty of merchantability; thus, when windows were replaced gratuitously, they were not under the implied warranty of merchantability). See also, Steele v. Ellis, 961 F.Supp. 1458, 35 UCC2d 56 (D. Kan. 1997) (only a seller is merchant). Thus there can be no implied warranty without a sale. See Evans v. Chrysler Financial Corp., 13 Mass. L.Rptr. 156, 44 UCC2d 1003 (Super.2001) (Plaintiff was hurt while trying out a car). See also Draleau v. Center Capital Corp., 432 Mass. 1110, 738 N.E.2d 750, 36 UCC2d 129 (2000) (finance lessor is not a merchant); Chase

v. Kawasaki Motors Corp., U.S.A., 140 F.Supp.2d 1280, 45 UCC2d 782 (M.D.Ala.2001) (dealer who made fitness statements but was independent dealer could not bind manufacturer); Certain-Teed Corp. v. Russell, 883 So.2d 1266, 51 UCC2d 418 (Ala.Civ.App.2003) (when defendant sells goods it manufactured to plaintiff through a third party seller, plaintiff who is seeking damages for only economic injury and property damage cannot recover from manufacturer/defendant for a breach of 2–314 because he lacks privity with manufacturer-defendant).

4. See, e.g., Simpson v. Hyundai Motor America, Inc., 269 Ga.App. 199, 603 S.E.2d 723, 54 UCC2d 634 (2004) (implied warranty of merchantability covers only defects present at time of sale; when plaintiff drove car for more than 5,000 miles before she made any complaints, there was no breach of implied warranty of merchantability); Industrial Steel Service Center v. Praxair Distribution, Inc., 2004 WL 2005832, 54 UCC2d 871 (N.D.Ill.2004) (while implied warranty of merchantability requires that defects exist at the time of sale, it is not required that they be discovered at time of sale; a gap between sale and discovery does not defeat a claim for breach of implied warranty of merchantability when buyer alleges goods were defective when sold).

5. See e.g., Hamdan v. Land Rover North America, Inc., 2003 WL 21911244, 51 UCC2d 1024 (N.D.Ill.2003). See also Buford v. Toys R' Us, Inc., 217 Ga.App. 565, 458 S.E.2d 373, 27 UCC2d 123 (1995).

warranty disclaimed, notice of breach not timely, assumption of risk, or statute of limitations expired. Recall too that a merchantability case is likely to be somewhat more difficult for the plaintiff than an express warranty case, for implied warranties are more easily disclaimed than are express warranties, and proof of breach of an explicit express warranty is likely to be easier than is proof of breach of the more diffuse standard of merchantability.

Under 2–314, there must be a contract for the sale of goods,[6] and the seller must be a "merchant." In the normal case, proving the existence of a "contract for sale" will pose no problem. The buyer will usually have some evidence of a completed transaction: some written documentation or, at the very least, the defective goods themselves. However, where a purchaser is injured by defective goods before actually paying for them (for example, where a pop bottle explodes and injures a buyer waiting in the checkout line at a grocery store), no such evidence exists and proving that a "sale" occurred may be more difficult. Pre–Code cases, concerned with whether title had passed to the buyer, usually held that the "sale" of an article in a self-service store is not completed until payment has been made. Under the Code, however, passage of title is not determinative.[7] Several cases have held that the "sale" occurs, and the implied warranty protection arises, once the buyer takes physical possession of the goods with the intent to purchase.[8] We are willing to concede that the manufacturer and probably the retailer of the exploding bottle should have liability to a consumer injured by the bottle. We are less certain that a court should recognize a warranty cause of action in the consumer's hands at the time when no sale has occurred according to normal indicia. So bending the warranty law may be unnecessary where the consumer would have strict tort and negligence theories to rely on and where such a distortion may have untoward effects in other circumstances.

6. § 2–314 does not apply to the provision of services. Many states have established through case law or enacted statutes to the effect that the provision of blood to a patient is a service, and thus carries no implied warranties. See generally, Kozup v. Georgetown Univ., 663 F.Supp. 1048, 4 UCC2d 701 (D.D.C. 1987), aff'd in part, vac'd in part, 851 F.2d 437, 6 UCC2d 1080 (C.A.D.C.1988).

7. See § 2–401:

Each provision of this Article with regard to the rights, obligations and remedies of the seller, the buyer, purchasers or other third parties applies irrespective of title to the goods except where the provision refers to such title.

But see Oscar Mayer Corp. v. Mincing Trading Corp., 744 F.Supp. 79, 14 UCC2d 83 (D.N.J.1990) (spice broker not a seller as it never had title to goods).

8. See, e.g., Barker v. Allied Supermarket, 596 P.2d 870, 26 UCC 597 (Okl. 1979) (exploding bottle; contract existed at time of explosion because of buyer's possession and intent to pay for bottles of soda). But see McQuiston v. K–Mart Corp., 796 F.2d 1346, 1 UCC2d 1115 (11th Cir.1986) (customer injured by glass jar while lifting top to check price not protected by 2–314 as there was no sale).

Only rarely will one have occasion to wonder whether a potential defendant is a "merchant." If the seller is not a merchant, seller cannot give the warranty under 2–314. Section 2–104(1) of unamended Article 2 defines merchant as follows:

"Merchant" means a person who deals in goods of the kind or otherwise by his occupation holds himself out as having knowledge or skill peculiar to the practices or goods involved in the transaction or to whom such knowledge or skill may be attributed by his employment of an agent or broker or other intermediary who by his occupation holds himself out as having such knowledge or skill.

The section deserves some explanation. Note first that one can be a merchant by (1) "dealing in goods" or (2) "otherwise by occupation" holding itself out as having "knowledge or skill peculiar to the practices or goods involved." The first phrase captures the jeweler, the hardware store owner, the haberdasher, and others selling from inventory. The second description, having to do with occupation, knowledge, and skill, includes electricians, plumbers, carpenters, boat builders, and the like.[9] The comment points out that a "bank" or "even universities" through their agents can have the necessary knowledge or skill to make them merchants. Under 2–314, the merchant must be a merchant with respect to "goods of that kind," that is, goods of the kind that are the subject of the transaction in question.[10] Relying on pre-Code law, one court has held—incorrectly in our view—that a farmer selling soybeans he has raised is not a merchant.[11] But one should understand that the 2–104 definition of "merchant" includes a considerably broader class than the man on the street might think.

Elsewhere we deal with the question whether a buyer must rely on certain representations made by the seller in order for an express warranty to arise. No such reliance is required under 2–314; unless the implied warranty is effectively disclaimed, it attaches to the goods at the time of the "sale." In a pre-Code case, the New Mexico Supreme Court noted that "[t]he warranty is implied because the manufacturer holds himself out as being skilled

9. See, e.g., Frantz, Inc. v. Blue Grass Hams, Inc., 520 S.W.2d 313, 15 UCC 1022 (Ky.1974) (mechanical contracting firm held "merchant" with respect to cooling equipment it installed).

10. Foley v. Dayton Bank & Trust, 696 S.W.2d 356, 42 UCC 92 (Tenn.App. 1985) (bank selling repossessed truck not a merchant).

11. Cook Grains, Inc. v. Fallis, 239 Ark. 962, 395 S.W.2d 555, 2 UCC 1141 (1965). But see Woodruff v. Clark Coun-

ty Farm Bureau Co-op. Ass'n, 153 Ind. App. 31, 286 N.E.2d 188, 11 UCC 498 (1972); Dotts v. Bennett, 382 N.W.2d 85, 42 UCC 1273 (Iowa 1986) (farmer who regularly sold hay was a merchant; dissent argued farmer an expert in growing, not selling). See also, Hillinger, The Article 2 Merchant Rules: Karl Llewellyn's Attempt to Achieve the Good, the True, the Beautiful in Commercial Law, 73 Georgetown L.J. 1141 (1985).

in the construction of his products and as being able to manufacture them without latent defects in materials or workmanship."[12] We think that the same logic applies equally well to all of the other "merchants" under 2–314.

§ 10–12 The Implied Warranty of Merchantability; Usage of Trade; Section 2–314—Merchantability Defined

Most of the elements of the merchantability cause of action are familiar to any tort lawyer; we deal with only two of the elements here and in the following section. The two questions that give ulcers to plaintiffs' and defendants' lawyers are:

(1) How does one define merchantability?

(2) How does one prove causation?

There are thousands, perhaps tens of thousands, of cases in which the plaintiff's lawyer has had to convince the jury or a judge that the goods his client purchased were not merchantable, not "fit for the ordinary purposes" for which such goods are purchased.

The cigarette cases are illustrative. On the one hand, American Tobacco will argue that its Lucky Strikes are merchantable since they are fit for the ordinary purposes for which such goods are used, namely, smoking. They will admit that their cigarettes would not be merchantable if they contained some foreign object such as a toenail or a mouse's ear, but they will maintain that the goods are merchantable as long as they are essentially identical to other goods that pass in the trade under the label "cigarettes." The plaintiff will argue, on the other hand, that the proper measure of merchantability is whether the cigarette causes cancer, and he will maintain that if the cigarette causes cancer, *ipso facto* it is not suitable for the ordinary purposes for which it is sold, and it is not merchantable. Thus arises the question: to be merchantable must cigarettes be noncancer causing, or is it sufficient that they be like all other cigarettes despite the fact that they might contribute to lung cancer in some users? In Green v. American Tobacco Co., a fascinating case that must have put the plaintiff's lawyers in bankruptcy and the defendant's lawyers on easy street, just that question was passed upon in some way or other by the Florida Supreme Court,[1] by two trial courts,[2] and by the United States

---

12. Vitro Corp. of America v. Texas Vitrified Supply Co., 71 N.M. 95, 105–6, 376 P.2d 41, 49 (1962). See also Kassab v. Central Soya, 432 Pa. 217, 246 A.2d 848, 5 UCC 925 (1968) (seller of tainted cattle feed liable for breach of implied warranty of merchantability regardless of buyer's reliance). But see Transamerica Leasing Corp. v. Van's Realty

Co., 91 Idaho 510, 427 P.2d 284 (1967) (implied warranties depend on buyer's reliance; case apparently rejected when Idaho adopted the UCC on December 31, 1967).

§ 10–12

1. 154 So.2d 169 (Fla.1963). See generally, Note, "Fit for Its Ordinary Pur-

Fifth Circuit Court of Appeals[3] on four different occasions. Ultimately, the Fifth Circuit concluded as follows:

> We are not dealing with an obvious, harmful, foreign body in a product. Neither do we have an exploding or breaking bottle case wherein the defect is so obvious that it warrants no discussion. Instead, we have a product (cigarettes) that is in no way defective. They are exactly like all others of the particular brand and virtually the same as all other brands on the market.[4]

To those who would reject the Fifth Circuit's conclusion out of hand, let us suggest the case of whiskey or butter. One might want to argue that butter is unmerchantable because it contains cholesterol, and cholesterol causes heart disease. Is whiskey or are automobiles not merchantable because they may cause injury or even death when they are used improperly and contribute to injury or death even when they are used properly?[5] Surely we have not seen the last case where the parties argue about the meaning of "fit for the ordinary purposes." A new wave of cigarette litigation has arisen. The *Green* case will offer interesting study for courts and lawyers who must decide those cases.[6]

pose? Tobacco, Fast Food, and the Implied Warranty of Merchantability," 63 Ohio St. L.J. 1165 (2002).

2. CCH 1963–65 Product Liability Rep. ¶ 5341 (S.D.Fla.1964) (second trial).

3. 304 F.2d 70 (5th Cir.1962), aff'd on rehearing, 325 F.2d 673 (5th Cir. 1963), cert. denied, 377 U.S. 943, 84 S.Ct. 1349, 12 L.Ed.2d 306(1964) and, 377 U.S. 943, 84 S.Ct. 1351, 12 L.Ed.2d 306 (1964); 391 F.2d 97 (5th Cir.1968); 409 F.2d 1166 (1969), cert. denied, 397 U.S. 911, 90 S.Ct. 912, 25 L.Ed.2d 93 (1970).

4. 391 F.2d at 110 (dissenting opinion of Simpson, J., adopted as majority opinion in 409 F.2d 1166). See also Semowich v. R.J. Reynolds Tobacco Co., 1988 WL 123930, 8 UCC2d 976 (N.D.N.Y.1988) (as carcinogenic quality is common to all cigarettes it is not a breach of implied warranty of merchantability); Wright v. Brooke Group, Ltd., 114 F.Supp.2d 797, 43 UCC2d 275 (N.D. Iowa 2000) (smoker stated valid claim for implied warranty when alleged that manufacturer knowingly designed, manufactured and distributed a product it knew was not fit for ordinary purpose). On the relation between breach of warranty of merchantability and strict liability in tort, see Lee v. General Motors

Corp., 950 F.Supp. 170, 34 UCC2d 315 (S.D. Miss. 1996) and Castro v. QVL Network, Inc., 139 F.3d 114, 34 UCC2d 946 (2nd Cir. 1998).

5. Similar questions regarding cars were presented when the Ford Pinto gas tank cases came to trial. When the buyers alleged a breach of a 2–314 implied warranty of merchantability, the trial court had to decide if such warranty was breached by the gas tank design which allegedly caused them to explode on impact. In Morris v. Adolph Coors Co., 735 S.W.2d 578, 5 UCC2d 288 (Tex.App. 1987) the parent of a teenager killed in a drunk driving accident could not persuade the court that regular, untainted beer could breach an implied warranty of fitness for human consumption and driving an automobile.

6. The allergy cases present the analogous question of seller's liability for products that injure some of the people all of the time. If an appreciable class of buyers (but less than all buyers) are allergic to the product, seller is liable. See Zirpola v. Adam Hat Stores, 122 N.J.L. 21, 4 A.2d 73 (1939) (4–5% of population constitutes an appreciable class). Seller is not liable for a one-in-a-million allergic reaction. See Ray v. J.C. Penney Co., 274 F.2d 519 (10th Cir.

Most of the 2–314 cases in which courts found breaches of the warranty of merchantability involved goods that, because of defects, either did not work properly or were unexpectedly harmful.[7] Such defects may arise from improper manufacturing, incorrect labeling, or the presence of unexpected objects.[8] Holowka v. York Farm Bureau Cooperative Association[9] presents the merchantability issue in terms analogous to the cigarette cases. There a farmer purchased an insecticide called Malathion to rid his alfalfa of boll weevils. The insecticide succeeded in eliminating the bugs, but it also managed to kill and injure his livestock. In imposing liability, the court observed, "It would appear to us that the use of a material which as a by-product causes death or injury to property is a classic example of a breach of warranty that the material was safe to use."[10] Perhaps butter, whiskey, and cigarettes are distinguishable from Malathion only because the injury to butter eaters, whiskey drinkers, and smokers is farther removed in time and probability than the injury to Malathion users. Since the injury to butter eaters, cigarette smokers, or whiskey drinkers is so remote, the product may be viewed as merchantable. Also, judge and jury may be unsympathetic to cigarette plaintiffs because of traditional distaste for paternalistic laws, a distaste that can be expressed by finding that the product in question was risky but merchantable.

1959). See also Case Note, 46 Cornell L.Q. 465 (1960).

7. Latent defects "are the very evil that the implied warranty of merchantability was designed to remedy." Willis Mining, Inc. v. Noggle, 235 Ga.App. 747, 509 S.E.2d 731, 38 UCC2d 98 (1998). Scheibe v. Fort James Corp., 276 F.Supp.2d 246, 52 UCC2d 138 (D.Del. 2003) (no implied warranty of merchantability when "the purchaser knows the dangers of a product, or where that danger is obvious.").

8. See, e.g., DeGraff v. Myers Foods, Inc., 19 Pa.D. & C.2d 19, 1 UCC 110 (1958) (chicken bone in pot pie); Maze v. Bush Bros. & Co., 1971 WL 17927, 9 UCC 1201 (Tenn.App.1971) (1–1/2 inch worm in can of peas); Feingold v. Town Lyne House, Inc., 1983 Mass.App.Div. 126, 36 UCC 453 (1983) (shell in crab casserole). Compare Wentling v. 85–87 Wilson Ave., Inc., 46 Fed. R. Evid. Serv. 485, 31 UCC2d 1016 (D.N.J.) (salmonella from food prepared by restaurant breach of warranty).

But see Flippo v. Mode O'Day Frock Shops of Hollywood, 248 Ark. 1, 449 S.W.2d 692, 7 UCC 282 (1970) (bite by a spider concealed in trousers was not breach of implied warranty of merchantability because spider was not part of the goods).

9. 1963 WL 8528, 2 UCC 445 (Pa. C.P.1963).

10. *Id.* at 448. Dean Prosser suggested that inherently dangerous products, such as dynamite, rabies vaccine, and presumably Malathion, should be regarded as defective if sold without adequate warning. Prosser, The Fall of the Citadel, 50 Minn.L.Rev. 791, 808 (1966). For cases much like Holowka v. York, see Simchick v. I.M. Young & Co., 47 A.D.2d 549, 363 N.Y.S.2d 619 (1975), aff'd, 38 N.Y.2d 921, 382 N.Y.S.2d 980, 346 N.E.2d 818, 19 UCC 459 (1976) (insecticide breached 2–314 warranty where buyer's crops were destroyed by an illegal chemical residue); R. Clinton Constr. Co. v. Bryant & Reaves, Inc., 442 F.Supp. 838, 23 UCC 310 (N.D.Miss. 1977) (antifreeze containing chlorine and causing radiator corrosion breached implied warranty of merchantability); Stephens v. G.D. Searle & Co., 602 F.Supp. 379, 40 UCC 441 (E.D.Mich. 1985) (failure to warn of dangers of prescription drugs may constitute breach of warranty).

In the usual case the lawyer's job is considerably less dramatic than in the cigarette cases but it is still the same job. The buyer may be called on to convince the jury, for example, that merchantable wine must be of a certain color,[11] that merchantable cherries must be of a certain diameter,[12] or that a merchantable logging chain must be able to pull a certain weight without breaking.[13]

In the log chain case, the seller cut the last link and, at plaintiff's request, inserted a hook and rewelded the link. The chain link broke while it was being used to tow a truck uphill on a dirt road. The truck was considerably damaged. Plaintiff sued defendant on the theory that the chain was not merchantable. How does plaintiff's lawyer prove the case? First the lawyer will need testimony from the client and, if possible, from others about the normal purposes for which log chains are used. Second is testimony from the client and also from a metallurgical expert that the log chain in this case was not (at time of sale) capable of withstanding the strain which would normally be experienced in such operations. Typically, expert testimony is required to prove the causal connection between the breach and the injury.[14] But establishing the standards of merchantability is likely to be a joint task shared in part by those expert in the trade but not necessarily technical experts, and by the technical experts.

The lawyer is given some slight help in the task of defining merchantability by section 2–314(2):

Goods to be merchantable must be at least such as

(a) pass without objection in the trade under the contract description; and

(b) in the case of fungible goods, are of fair average quality within the description; and

(c) are fit for the ordinary purposes for which goods of that description are used; and

(d) run, within the variations permitted by the agreement, of even kind, quality and quantity within each unit and among all units involved; and

(e) are adequately contained, packaged, and labeled as the agreement may require; and

11. Regina Grape Prods. Co. v. Supreme Wine Co., 357 Mass. 631, 260 N.E.2d 219, 7 UCC 1168 (1970).

12. See Washington Fruit & Produce Co. v. Ted Mirski Co., 1965 WL 8363, 24 Agri.Dec. 1559, 3 UCC 175 (1965), which dealt only with express warranties under 2–313.

13. Robert H. Carr & Sons, Inc. v. Yearsley, 31 Pa.D. & C.2d 262, 1 UCC 97 (1963).

14. See Falcone v. Chrysler Motors Corp., 1990 WL 211282, 13 UCC2d 734 (D.Md.1990) (where inference of defect is beyond the understanding of the average layman, expert testimony required).

(f) conform to the promises or affirmations of fact made on the container or label if any.

The first three paragraphs make it clear that if the product conforms to the quality of other brands in the market, it will normally be merchantable. Judge Simpson's dissenting opinion in *Green*, which eventually became the majority opinion,[15] was strongly guided by this no-worse-than-anybody-else ethic.[16] An item can "pass without objection" and yet be considerably short of perfection. For example, if a contract called for "4,000 dozen Baghdad goatskins dry salted," a certain small percentage of the goatskins can be rotted, but if the lot contains "more than 3% of rotted skins," it may be abnormal and therefore not a merchantable lot.[17]

The most widely quoted of the synonyms in subsection (2) is paragraph (c), which provides that goods must be "fit for the ordinary purposes for which such goods are used." However, in most cases, to say that goods are fit for the ordinary purposes does little to advance the analysis; it simply substitutes one synonym for another. For example, it does not tell a lawyer whether the protective guards around the sides of a rotary lawn mower are sufficient to make it fit for the ordinary purposes or whether the design is fatally defective.[18] Even forged art might be merchantable.[19]

In these pages we cannot hope to summarize the thousands of cases that deal with the question of merchantability. We can only suggest where a frustrated lawyer might look for help in determining whether the goods involved ought to be classified as merchantable or nonmerchantable.

15. Green v. American Tobacco Co., 409 F.2d 1166 (5th Cir.1969), cert. denied, 397 U.S. 911, 90 S.Ct. 912, 25 L.Ed.2d 93 (1970).

16. 391 F.2d at 110. See also Shell v. Union Oil Co., 489 So.2d 569, 1 UCC2d 692 (Ala.1986) (where a chemical containing cancer causing benzene conformed to the purchaser's requirements there was no breach of the merchantability warranty; the question of inherent unreasonable danger does not arise under 2–314).

17. Agoos Kid Co. v. Blumenthal Import Corp., 282 Mass. 1, 6, 184 N.E. 279, 281 (1932). Cf. Bickett v. W.R. Grace & Co., 1972 WL 20845, 12 UCC 629 (W.D.Ky.1972) (seed corn did not breach 2–314 warranty even though the buyer's corn was ruined by the "blight"); Carlson v. General Motors Corp., 883 F.2d 287, 11 UCC2d 14 (4th Cir.1989) (2–314 warranty not breached simply because car does not meet consumer expecta-

tions as to resale value); Peerless Wall & Window Coverings, Inc. v. Synchronics, Inc., 85 F.Supp.2d 519, 41 UCC2d 462 (W.D. Pa. 2000) (computer software—no breach of warranty).

Note that paragraph (2)(f) makes conformity to affirmation on the container or label into an implied warranty. Thus, one who sues on the basis of a statement on the label need not prove that the label was part of the basis of the bargain and thus an express warranty. Rather he can sue under 2–314.

18. In this situation the Maryland Court of Appeals found no breach of warranty. Myers v. Montgomery Ward & Co., 253 Md. 282, 252 A.2d 855, 6 UCC 493 (1969).

19. Balog v. Center Art Gallery–Hawaii, Inc., 745 F.Supp. 1556, 12 UCC2d 962 (D.Hawaii 1990) (dictum).

Certainly the first place one should look is to the usage in the trade. In a Pennsylvania case,[20] the seller sold some cattle feed that contained the female hormone stilbestrol. It appeared that much of the feed for cattle being fattened for slaughter contained stilbestrol and that stilbestrol causes cattle to grow more rapidly than would otherwise be the case. However, stilbestrol also causes, or at least contributes to, abortions in pregnant cows and sterility in bulls. Unfortunately, plaintiff's cattle were used for breeding rather than slaughter, and he sued. Now a city kid might think that cattle feed is cattle feed and that since stilbestrol was an additive commonly found in cattle feed, the feed was fit for the ordinary purposes for which such goods were used. However, an investigation of the trade usage disclosed that the hormones were normally excluded from the food of breeding cattle[21] and that they were not included in feed unless specifically ordered and disclosed on the feed label.

Comment 7 to 2–314 suggests another source of information about the parties' intention:

> In cases of doubt as to what quality is intended, the price at which a merchant closes a contract is an excellent index of the nature and scope of his obligation under the present section.

If, for example, there is a dispute on the question whether an airplane that is the subject of a sale must be flyable to be merchantable, it would be revealing to find that the agreed price fell precisely within the price range charged for flyable airplanes and twenty to thirty per cent above the price normally charged for nonflyable airplanes.[22] In that case, the price is an objective manifestation of the intention of the parties to deal over a flyable aircraft.[23] Moreover, a used car with 24,000 miles on it can still be subject to the implied warranty of merchantability.[24]

Obviously, one should also look at the characteristics exhibited by goods of the same class that are manufactured by persons other than the seller in question.[25]

20. Kassab v. Central Soya, 432 Pa. 217, 246 A.2d 848, 5 UCC 925 (1968). See also, Dixon Dairy Farms, Inc. v. Conagra Feed Co., 239 Ga.App. 233, 519 S.E.2d 729, 39 UCC2d 980 (1999).

21. *Id.* at 221, 224, 226, 246 A.2d at 849, 851, 857, 5 UCC at 927, 928, 935.

22. The warranty of merchantability applies to used goods, though the merchantability standard is somewhat lower as suggested by Comment 3.

23. In Sylvia Coal Co. v. Mercury Coal & Coke Co., 151 W.Va. 818, 156 S.E.2d 1, 4 UCC 650 (1967), the court stated that an excellent guide to the nature and scope of the implied warranty of merchantability was the fact that the contract price of coal was one-half the standard price for coal used for the buyer's intended purpose.

24. See State Farm Mut. Auto Ins. Co. v. Ford Motor Co., 736 So.2d 384, 41 UCC2d 783 (Miss.Ct.App.1999).

25. Such a comparison was made in Green, 391 F.2d at 110. See also Pritchard v. Liggett & Myers Tobacco Co., 295 F.2d 292, 302 (3d Cir.1961) (another cigarette case).

One might get some idea about merchantability in cases from government standards and regulations which are now published by an increasing number of federal and state agencies.[26] If, for example, a used car lacks shoulder harnesses, which are required under federal law for a car made in that year, that fact is powerful evidence that the car is not merchantable.

Traditionally the merchantability standard was equivalent to the defect standard, however a Second Circuit case stated that the two standards are not necessarily the same. In Denny v. Ford Motor Co.[27] Mrs. Denny sued Ford after her Ford SUV had rolled over while she attempted to avoid a deer. Mrs. Denny sought to recover in tort and under a breach of warranty claim. The jury found that the vehicle was not defective, and Mrs. Denny lost the tort claim, however she was successful on the breach of warranty of merchantability claim, and allowed to recover on that claim.

On appeal the Second Circuit certified several questions to the Court of Appeals of New York. The crucial question being: whether the strict products liability claim and the breach of implied warranty claim are identical.[28] The Court of Appeals ruled that the terms "defective" and "unmerchantable" are not necessarily identical, therefore the warranty claim may succeed while the tort claim fails.[29] Comment 7 to Amended Article 2[30] attempts to resolve the discrepancy between "defective" and "unmerchantable" by foreclosing one claim when the other is unfounded. In other words a good can neither be defective, yet merchantable, nor the reverse.

As *Denny* indicates, a court may think the merchantability standard differs from the comparable strict tort standard "defective condition, unreasonably dangerous * * *." The most obvious difference between the two is that the strict tort standard is narrower in scope. It does not purport to reach all defective goods but only those that are not only defective but also "unreasonably dangerous," that is, those that have the capacity to cause personal injury or property

---

26. See, e.g., Woodbury Chem. Co. v. Holgerson, 439 F.2d 1052, 8 UCC 999 (10th Cir.1971), in which the existence of federal specifications concerning the effectiveness of weed killers helped create express and implied warranties. Cf. Handrigan v. Apex Warwick, Inc., 108 R.I. 319, 275 A.2d 262, 8 UCC 1247 (1971) (fact that a ladder met the American Standard Safety Code specifications did not automatically bar claim).

27. 42 F.3d 106 (2d Cir. 1994).

28. Denny v. Ford Motor Co., 87 N.Y.2d 248, 639 N.Y.S.2d 250, 662 N.E.2d 730, 733, 28 UCC2d 15 (1995).

29. *Id.* at 734–39.

30. Nat'l Conference of Commissioners of Uniform State Law, Amendments to Uniform Commercial Code Article 2—Sales 70 (Draft, Aug. 10, 2001) (proposing changes to U.C.C. 2 314, cmt. 7). See further, J. White & R. Summers, Revised Article 1 and Amended Article 2—Substance and Process—Supplement to Accompany Uniform Commercial Code, Practitioner Treatise Series, vols. 1–4, sec. 4–5 (West Group 2005). See also, James J. White, Reverberations from the Collision of Tort and Warranty, 53 S.C.L.R. 1067, 1072–75 (2002).

damage as opposed to those which cause only economic loss.[31] Apart from that difference, we find the terms nearly synonymous. The drafters of 402A of the Restatement, (Second) Torts, however, added comments which indicated their opinion that cigarettes and similar products are not in a defective condition unreasonably dangerous. Presumably, these comments caused the plaintiffs' lawyers in the cigarette cases to try those cases exclusively as warranty claims. Notwithstanding the drafters' statements, we see no reason why there should be a different rule with respect to an item such as cigarettes under strict tort than under warranty. Except in these areas which the drafters have given rather explicit meaning to 402A by their comments, and except for the fact that 402A would not normally apply to economic losses, we believe that the two standards are interchangeable.

In several places in the remaining chapters, we draw on, or refer to, as above, the Restatement of Torts, especially Section 402A of the Restatement (Second) Torts, which deals with "Special Liability of Seller of Product for Physical Harm to User or Consumer". In 1998, the American Law Institute replaced Section 402A and related sections of the Restatement (Second) Torts, by adopting Sections 1 and 2 and related sections of the Restatement of the Law (Third) of Torts: Products Liability. The provisions of the Restatement (Third) of Torts: Products Liability, of most relevance here are Sections 1 and 2. Section 1 is headed, "Liability of Commercial Seller or Distributor for Harm Caused by Defective Products", and reads as follows: "One engaged in the business of selling or otherwise distributing products who sells or distributes a defective product is subject to liability for harm to persons or property caused by the defect." Section 2 is headed: "Categories of Product Defect", and differentiates several major categories of product defects. However, as of 2009, most states still recognize Section 402A of the Restatement (Second) of Torts. Moreover, Sections 1 and 2 and related provisions of the Restatement (Third) of Torts: Products Liability, do not differ substantially from Sections 402A and related provisions of the Restatement Second. We make no attempt here to take account of any changes wrought by the Third Restatement. However, readers should consult the product liability law of their own jurisdictions.

Below we present a more extensive account of the litigation over the merchantability definition. We have organized our discussion around the 2–314(2) criteria.

---

31. But see Santor v. A & M Karagheusian, Inc., 44 N.J. 52, 207 A.2d 305,   16 A.L.R.3d 670, 2 UCC 599 (1965).

a. Fitness for Ordinary Purposes

Most merchantability cases are litigated under the "fit for ordinary purpose" criterion. Paragraph 2–314(2)(c) provides that merchantable goods must be "fit for the ordinary purposes for which such goods are used."[32] Amended Article 2 inserted "of that description" after the word "goods." Comment 1 explained that the phrase "goods of that description" rather than the language from the Unamended Article 2 "for which such goods are used" was inserted in subsection(2)(c) to "emphasize the importance of the agreed description in determining fitness for ordinary purposes". Some of the cases are easily decided in a summary manner. For example, in Pronti v. DML of Elmira, Inc.,[33] buyers ordered dining room furniture which was delivered with minor defects, but refused to allow the seller to cure the defects. When the buyer sued for breach of the implied warranty of merchantability, the court refused to allow recovery on that claim because the furniture was fit for the ordinary purposes for such goods are used and did not have to be in "perfect" condition to avoid a 2–314 breach. Similarly, in Fellows v. USV Pharmaceutical Corp.,[34] when the manufacturer of a prescription had given warnings of possible risks associated with the drug, plaintiff could not recover on a breach of warranty action for injuries suffered as a result of "side effects" from using the drug. Since he failed to prove that the product was not fit for its ordinary purpose, the plaintiff had no cause of action.

Many cases which allow recovery for the breach of the ordinary purpose warranty are also resolved simply. A pressure gauge which did not measure pressure building up in an expansion joint was held to be unfit for ordinary purposes and unmerchantable.[35] A haystacking machine which caught fire on the first day the buyer used it was not fit for the ordinary purpose of stacking hay.[36] Insulation foam which gave off noxious fumes causing property and business damages would not be merchantable.[37]

---

32. Ordinary use is defined at the time the sale is made. Further, goods can be fit for their ordinary purposes even if there are no willing buyers. See, e.g., Pleasurecraft Marine Engine Co. v. Thermo Power Corp., 272 F.3d 654, 46 UCC2d 977 (4th Cir. 2001).

33. 103 A.D.2d 916, 478 N.Y.S.2d 156, 39 UCC 455 (1984).

34. 502 F.Supp. 297, 30 UCC 1261 (D.Md.1980). Whitson v. Safeskin Corp., 313 F.Supp.2d 473, 53 UCC2d 216 (M.D.Pa.2004) (implied warranty of merchantability requires fitness for ordinary purposes; when nurse sued glove manufacturer because latex gloves caused her to develop allergy, there was no breach of implied warranty of merchantability because the ordinary purpose of the gloves was to prevent transmission of blood-borne illness, which they did).

35. Bernard v. Dresser Indus., Inc., 691 S.W.2d 734, 41 UCC 776 (Tex.App. 1985).

36. Nerud v. Haybuster Mfg., Inc., 215 Neb. 604, 340 N.W.2d 369, 37 UCC 703 (1983).

37. Shooshanian v. Wagner, 672 P.2d 455, 37 UCC 55 (Alaska 1983).

Obviously, a fitness for the ordinary purposes warranty could conceivably apply to virtually any goods that have an ordinary purpose. For example, in Two Rivers Co. v. Curtiss Breeding Service,[38] the court indicated in dicta that the warranty of merchantability guaranteed that the bull semen would be fit for the ordinary purpose for which it was sold. Similarly, in Alpert v. Thomas[39] the court found that custom and usage of trade established that a merchantable Arabian horse sold for breeding purposes must be fertile.

Some goods—particularly those specially manufactured—have no ordinary purpose. When so, a warranty of merchantability will not attach. In Binks Mfg. Co. v. National Presto Indus., Inc.,[40] a court held that there was no ordinary purpose for an aluminum casting "system" designed and manufactured at buyer's request for use in its electrical appliance factory. Since both parties were sophisticated business entities with equal skill and knowledge concerning the transaction, no warranty of merchantability arose.

As we have said before, "merchantable" is not synonymous with "perfect." Likewise, fitness for ordinary purposes does not mean that the product will fulfill buyer's every expectation. For example, in Skelton v. General Motors Corp.,[41] the fact that automobiles purchased by plaintiffs had transmissions which were inferior to those listed in the express warranty did not give rise to an implied warranty of merchantability claim. The court stated that the implied warranty of merchantability required only a minimum level of quality. Since there was no evidence that the automobiles were unfit for driving, they were fit for their ordinary purpose.

b. Pass Without Objection in the Trade

Under 2–314(2)(a), goods must "pass without objection in the trade under the contract description."[42] Although more or less a synonym of "fit for ordinary purposes," the "pass without objection" phrase focuses more clearly on trade usage, similar goods, and

38. 624 F.2d 1242, 29 UCC 1169 (5th Cir.1980), cert. denied, 450 U.S. 920, 101 S.Ct. 1368, 67 L.Ed.2d 348 (1981).

39. 643 F.Supp. 1406, 2 UCC2d 99 (D.Vt.1986). Of course, ordinary purpose may not include prolonged use. See, e.g., Whitson v. Safeskin Corp., 313 F.Supp.2d 473, 53 UCC2d 216 (M.D. Pa. 2004).

40. 709 F.2d 1109, 36 UCC 14 (7th Cir.1983). See also Makripodis v. Merrell–Dow Pharmaceuticals, Inc., 361 Pa.Super. 589, 523 A.2d 374, 3 UCC2d 1362 (1987) (nature of prescription drugs precludes a warranty of fitness for "ordinary purposes;" warranty of merchantability cannot be breached if prescription is properly filled).

41. 500 F.Supp. 1181, 30 UCC 846 (N.D.Ill.1980), rev'd, 660 F.2d 311, 32 UCC 1118 (7th Cir.1981), cert. den., 456 U.S. 974, 102 S.Ct. 2238, 72 L.Ed.2d 848 (1982).

42. UCC 2–314(2)(a). See, e.g., Gulf Trading Corp. v. National Enterprises of St. Croix, Inc., 912 F.Supp. 177, 29 UCC2d 478 (D. Virgin Islands 1996) (warped doors did not pass).

on the seller's conduct.[43] For example, in Printing Center of Texas, Inc. v. Supermind Publishing Co., Inc.,[44] the court held that a breach of warranty occurred when books printed for the plaintiff had off-center cover art, crooked pages, wrinkled pages, and inadequate perforation on a pull-out page. Although the contract for the books did not expressly address these conditions, the books could not pass without objection in the trade and were, therefore, unmerchantable.

Other cases litigated under the pass-without-objection requirement demonstrate its wide applicability. The court in Thomas v. Ruddell Lease–Sales, Inc.,[45] concluded that an automobile that had been wrecked and rebuilt would not even pass as a "used car" without objection in the trade and was therefore not merchantable. In Martin v. Joseph Harris Co., Inc.,[46] the court held that seed carrying a fungus known as "black leg" was not merchantable and that arguments that the seed would pass without objection in the trade were without merit. Another court held in Delano Growers' Co-op. Winery v. Supreme Wine Co., Inc.[47] that the presence of Fresno mold in sweet California wine made the wine unmerchantable, because it would not pass without objection in the trade. Since other such wines had been sold without complaints occurring, the court reasoned that even if all California sweet wine contained Fresno mold, it was not allowed to go unchecked by other wine merchants. In Dempsey v. Rosenthal,[48] the buyer purchased a pedigreed poodle which she assumed would be suitable for breeding. The buyer later discovered that the dog had an undescended testicle. This permanent condition is genetic and can be passed on to the dog's progeny. The court allowed buyer to recover on the claim that such a pedigreed dog would not pass without objection in the trade.

c. Fungible Goods of Fair Average Quality

Fungible goods must be of "fair average quality within the description" in order to be merchantable. Only a few cases have addressed this definition, and the leading examples also rely on either the failure of the goods to pass "without objection in the trade" or to be "fit for ordinary purposes." When a buyer pur-

---

43. See, e.g., Morrison v. Sears, Roebuck & Co., 319 N.C. 298, 354 S.E.2d 495, 3 UCC2d 1764 (1987) (failure of shoes to meet American footwear industry standards sufficient to support claim for breach of 2–314 warranty).

44. 669 S.W.2d 779, 39 UCC 127 (Tex.App.1984) (assuming that Article 2 governed the sale).

45. 43 Wash.App. 208, 716 P.2d 911, 1 UCC2d 394 (1986).

46. 767 F.2d 296, 41 UCC 315 (6th Cir.1985). See also the case law on reasonable expectations of the buyer of foods, e.g., Carreiro v. 99 West, Inc., 2002 WL 999475, 46 UCC2d 583 (Mass. Dist. Ct. 2002).

47. 393 Mass. 666, 473 N.E.2d 1066, 40 UCC 93 (1985).

48. 121 Misc.2d 612, 468 N.Y.S.2d 441, 37 UCC 1091 (City Civ.Ct.1983).

chased linoleum floor tiles that became discolored shortly after installation, the court held in Mindell v. Raleigh Rug Co.[49] that the tile was not of "fair average quality that would pass without objection in the trade."[50] In order to be merchantable, the court added, the tile must be durable and must hold its pattern and color for a reasonable length of time consistent with the quality selected. In a similar case, the court held in Jetero Construction Co. v. South Memphis Lumber Co.[51] that warped and discolored lumber was unmerchantable because the seller did not send building studs which were of fair average quality within the description or sample agreed upon. The court also held that the lumber studs as delivered were not fit for the ordinary purpose of building construction and would not meet general construction standards.

d. Adequately Contained, Packaged and Labelled

Section 2–314(2)(e) requires merchantable goods to be "adequately contained, packaged, and labeled as the agreement may require." In the classic packaging case of Pugh v. J.C. Whitney & Co. v. Republic Products Co.,[52] the buyer's employee injured his hand on a sharp projection when he placed his hand inside a package of automobile parts. The court held that the packaging which left potentially dangerous parts of the product uncovered and failed to warn of them breached the warranty of merchantability. In Shaffer v. Victoria Station, Inc.,[53] the court held that a restaurant breached the warranty of merchantability when a customer's wine glass shattered in his hand and caused permanent injuries. Since the wine which the customer had ordered could not be consumed without a container, there was an implied warranty that the wine would be adequately "contained, packaged, and labeled."

In the case of improper labeling, the court held in Reid v. Eckerds Drugs, Inc.[54] that the manufacturer of a deodorant breached the warranty of merchantability when it failed to warn on the label that the deodorant was highly flammable. The plaintiff in that case accidentally ignited the deodorant while lighting a cigarette and suffered a severe burn.

49. 1974 WL 21750, 14 UCC 1124 (Mass. Housing Ct.1974).

50. Id. at 1125

51. 531 F.2d 1348, 21 Fed.R.Serv.2d 642, 19 UCC 478 (6th Cir.1976).

52. 1971 WL 17939, 9 UCC 229 (E.D.N.Y.1971). See also Greene v. A.P. Products, Ltd., 264 Mich.App. 391, 691 N.W.2d 38, 55 UCC2d 410 (2004) (triable issue as to suitability of label).

53. 91 Wash.2d 295, 588 P.2d 233, 25 UCC 427 (1978). See also, Keaton v. A.B.C. Drug Co., 266 Ga. 385, 467 S.E.2d 558, 29 UCC2d 468 (1996), on remand 221 Ga.App. 778, 472 S.E.2d 721 (1996) (requirement that goods be adequately contained and packaged, extended to shelving at a height not dangerous).

54. 40 N.C.App. 476, 253 S.E.2d 344, 26 UCC 20 (1979), cert. denied, 297 N.C. 612, 257 S.E.2d 219 (1979).

e. Conform to Representations on Container or Label

Paragraph (f) requires that merchantable goods "conform to the promises or affirmations of fact on the container or label if any." This is a kind of bootstrap express warranty—but different. Under paragraph (f), it is not necessary for the buyer to show reliance on such representations or to prove that they were the basis of the bargain. After the buyer's son was injured through normal use of a golf training device in Hauter v. Zogarts[55] the court held that the machine was unmerchantable because it did not conform to the representation on the label that the machine was "completely safe." In Farmers Union Co-op. Gin v. Smith,[56] a buyer purchased seed labeled as "Shoghum Sudangrass Hybrid" for the purpose of growing pasturage for his cattle. When the grass failed to replace itself as "Shoghum Sudangrass Hybrid" normally does, the court held that the seller breached both the express warranty and the implied warranty of merchantability because the seed did not conform to the affirmations of fact on the labels.

If statements on the label are generally to be treated like express warranties, a court should also invoke the various interpretive rules that are applied to express warranties. As we have indicated above, courts often have difficulty distinguishing between "mere puffing" that is not a warranty and a statement in sales literature or during the sale process which does constitute a warranty. The assertion that an item is "completely safe" would seem to us to fall on the side of puffing, and thus we have some doubt about the merit of the decision in Hauter v. Zogarta.

The *Farmers' Cooperative* case presents the same interpretive problem that one faces in generic express warranty descriptions. What exactly does one infer from a description of a product? If, for example, a seller describes an implement as a "hay baler," is that a warranty that this particular model will bale hay? Certainly it seems possible that the seed purchased was Shoghum Sudangrass Hybrid, even though it did not have one of the characteristics commonly associated with that hybrid. Presumably an item contained in the package must have at least the dominant characteristics of the things described, but it does not follow that it must have the characteristic of a "perfect model" of such an item.

§ 10–13 The Implied Warranty of Merchantability; Usage of Trade; Section 2–314—Causation

Plaintiff's proof of causation deserves at least a word in passing. To prove that the plaintiff died of lung cancer caused by

55. 14 Cal.3d 104, 534 P.2d 377, 120 Cal.Rptr. 681, 16 UCC 938, 74 A.L.R.3d 1282 (1975).

56. 1971 WL 17902, 9 UCC 823 (Okla.App.1971).

smoking the defendant's cigarettes or that the plaintiff's scalp rash was caused by the defendant's hair dye will often be tricky and difficult. Not only must the plaintiff disclose that the breach of warranty was the cause "in fact," but—in the words of Comment 13 to 2–314—show that the "breach of the warranty was the proximate cause of the loss sustained." It takes a better Ouija board than your authors possess to define "proximate."

Post hoc ergo propter hoc is not enough, and the plaintiff normally must show more than that the goods injured the plaintiff in a certain way.[1] However, it is not always necessary that the plaintiff offer expert testimony or explicit proof to disclose the precise chain of causation. One court has held that a plaintiff stated a claim against a seller of applesauce when she alleged that her children, ages eight and ten, ate the applesauce, complained of its "funny taste," and were then so discomforted that they had to have their stomachs pumped.[2] Likewise, one need not prove exactly how the fuel in the carburetor of a Corvette caught fire and burned the car to a cinder; it is sufficient to prove a continuing source of carburetor trouble and offer an expert to opine that the carburetor probably caused the difficulty.[3] Of course, other courts have required plaintiffs to go to greater lengths to rule out rival plausible hypotheses, and it appears that in most cases the plaintiff will wish to procure expert testimony. However, when the connection be-

§ 10–13

1. See Procter & Gamble Mfg. Co. v. Langley, 422 S.W.2d 773 (Tex.Civ.App. 1967) (plaintiff failed to follow instructions when using permanent wave product); Gillespie v. American Motors Corp., 69 N.C.App. 531, 317 S.E.2d 32, 39 UCC 869 (1984) (buyer was aware of noxious fumes in passenger area of car but continued to drive the car for three years).

2. Martel v. Duffy–Mott Corp., 15 Mich.App. 67, 166 N.W.2d 541, 6 UCC 294 (1968).

3. McCrossin v. Hicks Chevrolet, Inc., 248 A.2d 917 (D.C.App.1969).

Accord, Martineau v. Walker, 97 Idaho 246, 542 P.2d 1165, 18 UCC 354 (1975) (buyer met burden of proof in a case involving breach of 2–314 warranty of 22 calves where his expert testified that disease was present in the calves, he thought the disease came from seller's ranch, the disease was the cause of death and the incubation period of the disease was consistent with the buyer's

theory; expert did not have to "scientifically identify" seller's ranch as source). See also Nevada Contract Services, Inc. v. Squirrel Companies, Inc., 119 Nev. 157, 68 P.3d 896, 50 UCC2d 1066 (2003) (buyer need not prove specific cause of defect or negate alternative sources of causation in order to prove defect, especially when product is technical and complex; when a product malfunctions, buyer must only show that product's malfunction was "likely caused" by breach of warranty); Razor v. Hyundai Motor America, 349 Ill.App.3d 651, 286 Ill.Dec. 190, 813 N.E.2d 247, 54 UCC2d 737 (2004) (a party alleging breach must prove defect existed at time of sale; defect may be proved by "direct or circumstantial evidence" and prima facie case of defect exists when there is proof that product failed to perform in a reasonably expected manner and there was no abnormal use or other cause for failure to so perform).

tween the product and the injury is reasonably obvious even to a layman, expert proof and explicit analysis of the chain of causation should not be necessary.[4]

§ 10–14 Fitness for Particular Purpose, Section 2–315

Those unfamiliar with the differences between the warranty of merchantability (fitness for the *ordinary* purposes for which such goods are used) and the warranty of fitness for a *particular* purpose often confuse the two; one can find many opinions in which the judges used the terms "merchantability" and "fitness for a particular purpose" interchangeably.[1] Such confusion under the Code is inexcusable. Sections 2–314 and 2–315 make plain that the warranty of fitness for a particular purpose is narrower, more specific, and more precise. Section 2–315 reads in full as follows:

> Where the seller at the time of contracting has reason to know any particular purpose for which the goods are required and that the buyer is relying on the seller's skill or judgment to select or furnish suitable goods, there is unless excluded or modified under the next section an implied warranty that the goods shall be fit for such purpose.

Note the conditions that are not required by the implied warranty of merchantability but that must be present if a plaintiff is to recover on the implied warranty of fitness for a particular purpose:

---

4. See, e.g., Lucchesi v. H.C. Bohack Co., 1970 WL 12553, 8 UCC 326 (N.Y.Sup.1970) (no further proof needed to hold supermarket liable when pop bottle exploded in shopping basket).

§ 10–14

1. An increasing number of courts have held that the 2–315 warranty as to fitness for a particular purpose may arise when the buyer's "specific use" is the same as the "general use" to which the goods under contract are usually put. See, e.g., Soaper v. Hope Indus., Inc., 309 S.C. 438, 424 S.E.2d 493, 20 UCC2d 101 (1992) (also merging 2–314 and 2–315). We are wary of such cases. They apparently enlarge the scope of the 2–315 warranty beyond the intent of the drafters.

We fail to see why a buyer would wish to convert his 2–314 case into a 2–315 case. If the court were willing to concede the product breached the standards of 2–314 the usual buyer would seem to gain nothing by an additional finding of a breach of 2–315. It might be in the buyer's interest to pursue a 2–315 cause

of action if he believed that a contractual disclaimer under 2–316 was effective against the warranty of merchantability but ineffective against the warranty of fitness for a particular purpose because such disclaimer did not mention "fitness." Without such a reason for pleading 2–315 we would view these "general use" cases as falling under 2–314.

For cases adopting the view that 2–315 does not apply where the buyer's "specific use" coincides with the "general use" of the goods, see, e.g., DiIenno v. Libbey Glass Div., Owens–Illinois, Inc., 668 F.Supp. 373, 4 UCC2d 706 (D.Del. 1987) (buyer's claim that failure of jar to open and close without breaking was a breach of a 2–315 warranty was "ridiculous" because opening and closing are a jar's ordinary purpose). See generally, Covington and Medved, The Implied Warranty of Fitness For a Particular Purpose: Some Persistent Problems, 9 Ga.L.Rev. 149 (1974); Note, Commercial Law—Implied Warranties Under the Uniform Commercial Code—The Implied Warranty of Fitness for a Particular Purpose, 10 Wake Forest L.Rev. 169 (1974).

(1) The seller must have reason to know the buyer's particular purpose.

(2) The seller must have reason to know that the buyer is relying on the seller's skill or judgment to furnish appropriate goods.

(3) The buyer must, in fact, rely upon the seller's skill or judgment.

Many goods that are perfectly merchantable will not meet the implied warranty of fitness for a particular purpose. David Epstein, used to make the point in bar review lectures by noting that bright, white loafers could be perfectly *merchantable* but would hardly be *fit* for *the purpose* of a job interview at a Wall Street law firm. In Kobeckis v. Budzko,[2] a pre-Code case, pork infected with trichinosis was not unmerchantable since cooking of even infected meat renders it safe for human consumption. If the plaintiff, who contracted trichinosis after eating the seller's raw pork, had succeeded in proving that the seller knew he was a sausage maker and that sausage makers customarily taste raw pork, he might nevertheless have made out a cause of action for breach of warranty of fitness for a particular purpose.[3]

The most common circumstance in which one meets the warranty of fitness for a particular purpose is where a business buys goods that have to be specially selected or particularly manufactured and assembled for its business. A typical case is Kokomo Opalescent Glass Co. v. Arthur W. Schmid International, Inc.,[4] in which the buyer offered to buy a new glass rolling machine if the defendant "thought it could be used in plaintiff's operation."[5] The seller visited the buyer's plant and advised it about the kind of machine to use. Ultimately, the machine did not roll glass of the particular kind that the buyer wished to roll, and the court found that the warranty had been breached. In these cases, the "particular purpose" of the buyer is communicated to the seller in the course of the negotiations and occasionally through the contract itself. The buyer's reliance is disclosed by its request for assistance. These cases fit neatly within 2–315; most 2–315 cases are business versus business not consumer versus business.

---

2.   225 A.2d 418 (Me.1967).

3.   The court, however, emphasized that the seller could not be held liable because Uniform Sales Act § 15(1) only requires that goods "be reasonably fit" for a particular purpose made known to the seller. Since there is no practical manner of determining whether raw pork is free of trichinae, the court concluded that the pork was reasonably fit for consumption, even when raw. 225 A.2d at 422–23.

4.   371 F.2d 208 (7th Cir.1966). The case was decided under the Uniform Sales Act.

5.   371 F.2d at 214.

How does one prove that the seller knew or had reason to know of the "buyer's purpose"? Comment 1 to 2–315 states "that the buyer need not bring home to the seller actual knowledge of the particular purpose for which the goods are intended or of the buyer's reliance on the seller's skill and judgment, if the circumstances are such that the seller has reason to realize the purpose intended or that the reliance exists." As noted, in most cases the buyer discloses the purpose in the early negotiations, and the buyer may incorporate it into the contract. But the circumstances or form of disclosure must be reasonably explicit.[6] In the *Ford Motor* case,[7] the manufacturer did not know the vehicle would ultimately be used as a tow truck, so not liable for breach of warranty of fitness for this particular purpose. In Kobeckis v. Budzko,[8] the Maine court found that the fact the buyer had a Polish name was not a sufficient basis to give the seller "reason to know" that the buyer was going to be making Polish sausage and eating the pork raw. When specifications go beyond an expression of requirements, however, the buyer tends to establish that there is no reliance upon the seller. In In re Repco Products Corp. v. Reliance Electric Co.[9] the purchaser supplied the manufacturer with detailed plans for castings to be used its boilers. The manufacturer deviated from those plans and as a result the boilers malfunctioned. The court found that the purchaser "[D]id not rely upon the [manufacturer] to select or furnish the model of the castings to be used in its boilers. Rather, the [purchaser] supplied the blueprints and expected the [manufacturer] to use its skills to provide what the [purchaser] had selected as an appropriate model for castings."

How does one prove a buyer's reliance (or lack of it) on the seller's skill and judgment? If the seller is a manufacturer and the buyer has initiated the contract negotiations by the request for a product that will do certain things, the seller is unlikely to win the reliance argument.[10] There are some circumstances, however, that give the seller some hope of winning the reliance argument. If, for example, the buyer "insists on a particular brand," buyer is not relying on the seller's skill and judgment, and, in the words of Comment 5, "no warranty results." Moreover, the relative state of

6. Global Truck & Equip. Co., Inc. v. Palmer Mach. Works, Inc., 628 F.Supp. 641, 42 UCC 1250 (N.D.Miss.1986) (2–315 warranty not breached where use made was different from that specified).

7. Ford Motor Co. v. General Acc. Ins. Co., 365 Md. 321, 779 A.2d 362, 45 UCC2d 319 (App.2001).

8. 225 A.2d 418, 421 (Me.1967).

9. 100 B.R. 184, 8 UCC2d 950 (Bankr.E.D.Pa.1989).

10. See, e.g., Whitehouse v. Lange, 128 Idaho 129, 910 P.2d 801, 31 UCC2d 78 (1996) (although plaintiffs themselves selected particular horse for purchase from defendant, their implied warranty claim based upon horse's inability to conceive could stand based upon plaintiff's reliance upon defendant to furnish horse suited to their express particular purpose—breeding). See also, State of Kansas ex rel. Stovall v. DVM Enterprises, Inc., 275 Kan. 243, 62 P.3d 653, 49 UCC2d 782 (2003).

the knowledge of the two parties about the product is highly relevant, and in the unusual case in which the buyer is more knowledgeable than the seller, the seller may win on the grounds that the buyer did not rely. In Sylvia Coal Co. v. Mercury Coal & Coke Co.,[11] for example, the seller showed that he was simply a coal miner and was ignorant of the process by which one makes coke, but that the buyer was an experienced coke maker. The court found that these circumstances did not give rise to justifiable reliance, and it therefore held that there was no warranty under 2–315 despite the fact that the coal was not satisfactory for making coke.[12]

a. Cases

We now turn to some cases that typify the role of the 2–315 warranty in the sale of goods. In Massey–Ferguson, Inc. v. Evans,[13] buyer, who had never farmed, relied on a salesman's explanation and his assistance in selecting the appropriate farm equipment. When the equipment failed to operate and was never sufficiently repaired, the buyer sued for breach of warranty. Since the seller was aware that the buyer was relying on seller's skill and expertise, and the salesman asserted that the machine equipment would be "field ready" at the time of the purchase, the court held that the seller breached its implied warranty of fitness for a particular purpose. Similarly, the buyers informed the seller in O'Shea v. Hatch[14] that they wanted to purchase a show horse which would be suitable for their teenage daughter to ride and safe around children. The seller sold them what he said was a gelding, but buyers were surprised by the aggressive, rather than gentle, temperament of the horse and soon learned that the horse was an improperly castrated ridgeling. The court held that there was a breach of the 2–315 warranty, because the horse was unfit for the young children to ride, and that had been the particular purpose of the buyers. In Tyson v. Ciba–Geigy Corp.[15] a salesman told a farmer looking to control weeds what kind of herbicide he should use and that the product should be mixed in a manner contrary to the manufacturer's instructions. When the herbicide failed to work properly, the court found a breach of the 2–315 warranty. Other sales which found a breach of the fitness warranty have involved produce boxes

---

11. 151 W.Va. 818, 156 S.E.2d 1, 4 UCC 650 (1967).

12. *Id.* at 828, 156 S.E.2d at 7, 4 UCC at 657. See also Gilbert & Bennett Mfg. Co. v. Westinghouse Elec. Corp., 445 F.Supp. 537, 22 UCC 920 (D.Mass. 1977) (no 2–315 warranty air pollution device where seller's agent disclaimed knowledge or skill and buyer used machine to remove particles which he knew it was not designed to control); Lesnefsky v. Fischer & Porter Co., 527 F.Supp.

951, 33 UCC 529 (E.D.Pa.1981) (no reliance where buyer had designed goods which seller produced).

13. 406 So.2d 15, 32 UCC 424 (Miss. 1981).

14. 97 N.M. 409, 640 P.2d 515, 33 UCC 561 (App.1982).

15. 82 N.C.App. 626, 347 S.E.2d 473, 2 UCC2d 452 (1986).

which seller selected for shipping of buyer's tomatoes,[16] lids for buyer's salad dressing bottles which seller knew were inappropriate,[17] a low ash oil which buyer asked seller to recommend for use in his irrigation engines,[18] and a steam coil heating system to be fabricated and installed by the seller in which the buyer was "interested only in the results obtained."[19]

Buyer's reliance on the seller's expertise is important too. For example, in O'Keefe Elevator Co. v. Second Ave. Properties, Ltd.,[20] the buyer purchased a wheelchair lift which could not be operated by a handicapped person in a wheelchair because of an improper landing supplied by the buyer. The court held that the buyer did not rely on the seller's expertise, because the buyer obtained its own approval from the state for the installation and was provided with exactly the goods it had ordered. Of course, where plaintiff did not purchase from seller, it could not rely on seller's skill or knowledge, and 2–315 did not apply.[21]

If a buyer is relying on the skill and judgment of the seller but the seller is not aware of this reliance or of buyer's particular purpose, no 2–315 warranty exists. One leading case illustrating this rule is Wisconsin Electric Power Co. v. Zallea Brothers, Inc.[22] in which the buyer purchased expansion joints to absorb the contraction and expansion in steam pipes. Since the buyer never communicated to the seller that strong resistance to corrosion was a particular purpose for which the joints were required and the seller could not be expected to infer from the circumstances that buyer was relying upon seller to select such joints, the court held that the expansion joints were not sold with an implied warranty of fitness for the buyer's particular purpose.

The relative knowledge between the parties is often of crucial importance in determining reliance for a particular purpose. In Price Brothers Co. v. Philadelphia Gear Corp.,[23] buyer purchased a special machine used in the wrapping of concrete pipe with wire which was made from specifications arrived at by both parties'

---

16. International Paper Co. v. Farrar, 102 N.M. 739, 700 P.2d 642, 41 UCC 54 (1985).

17. Addis v. Bernardin, Inc., 226 Kan. 241, 597 P.2d 250, 27 UCC 80 (1979).

18. Circle Land and Cattle Corp. v. Amoco Oil Co., 232 Kan. 482, 657 P.2d 532, 35 UCC 403 (1983).

19. Ingram River Equip., Inc. v. Pott Indus., Inc., 573 F.Supp. 896, 37 UCC 88 (E.D.Mo.1983), dism'd without op., 732 F.2d 160 (8th Cir.1984).

20. 216 Neb. 170, 343 N.W.2d 54, 37 UCC 1100 (1984).

21. Austin v. Will–Burt Co. 232 F.Supp.2d 682, 50 UCC2d 121 (N.D.Miss.2002).

22. 606 F.2d 697, 27 UCC 923 (7th Cir.1979); W.A. Davis Realty, Inc. v. Wakelon Agri–Products, Inc., 84 N.C.App. 97, 351 S.E.2d 816, 3 UCC2d 507 (1987) (as seller knew purchaser required wheat for human consumption, delivery of "sick wheat" was a breach of 2–315 warranty).

23. 649 F.2d 416, 31 UCC 469 (6th Cir.1981), cert. den., 454 U.S. 1099, 102 S.Ct. 674, 70 L.Ed.2d 641 (1981).

engineers. Since buyer had a high degree of knowledge regarding its own mechanical requirements and its expertise was at least equal to that of the seller, the Court of Appeals for the Sixth Circuit held that reliance on the seller was so unlikely that no warranty of fitness arose in the sale of the pipe-wrapping machine.

Sophisticated business buyers should rarely prevail under 2–315. A right under 2–315 is but a substitute for the express warranties that ought to arise out of the buyer's specifications stated in the contract. A suit under 2–315 is a tacit admission of fault by the buyer's purchasing managers. Moreover, sophisticated buyers rarely rely upon seller's skill in selecting the proper product. That, too, should be taken care of by the purchasing agents of the buyer, who in most circumstances can be expected to develop their own specifications and to write those specifications into the agreement. Because a sophisticated buyer will normally take care of such matters by express warranty, Those buyers can rarely state a meritorious 2–315 case.

In general, the implied warranty of fitness for a particular purpose is a mature legal doctrine, little changed by the Code. Unlike the warranty of merchantability, it is not beset by the tides and winds of personal-injury lawsuits brought by consumers against manufacturers; its modest place in our jurisprudence has been carefully carved out for it by the drafters and the case law.

§ 10–15 The Warranties of Title and Against Infringement, Section 2–312—Cause of Action

Among the warranties that ride along with the contract for the sale of goods is an implied warranty[1] that the seller has good title. In the words of unamended section 2–312(1), the seller warrants, subject to subsection (2), that:

> (a) the title conveyed shall be good, and its transfer rightful; and

> (b) the goods shall be delivered free from any security interest or other lien or encumbrance of which the buyer at the time of contracting has no knowledge.

If a seller sells a stolen car or one that is burdened with an unsatisfied perfected security interest, he has almost certainly breached section 2–312 and will be liable in damages to the buyer.[2]

---

§ 10–15

1. Comment 6 to § 2–312 states that the warranty of title "is not designated as an 'implied' warranty," but the purpose of the comment is to make clear that the 2–312 warranty is not subject to the disclaimer provision of 2–316. In practical effect, the warranty of title may be regarded as implied since it need not be expressed.

2. See Kruger v. Bibi, 1967 WL 9023, 3 UCC 1132 (N.Y.Sup.1967); Candela v.

We deal with damage and statute of limitations questions elsewhere.

In the following sections we focus on two questions peculiar to section 2–312:

(1) In what way must the buyer's title or possession be interfered with, and who must cause such interference for the buyer to have a cause of action under 2–312?

(2) What language will disclaim and what circumstances will foreclose the warranty of title?

a. *Title*

If the object of a sale is subject to a valid security interest or a valid claim of title in a third person, clearly the warranty in 2–312(1) has been breached, and the seller is liable in damages. Moreover, the seller need not be a merchant, and is not saved by ignorance of the defect in title.[3] Thus, if the plaintiff buyer proves the defective title or the presence of a lien or encumbrance of which the buyer had no *knowledge* at the time of the sale, the buyer will win.[4]

Courts are split on the issue of whether privity is required. In Universal C. I. T. Credit Corp. v. State Farm Mut. Auto. Ins. Co.,[5] the court held that "a warranty of title on personal property runs only to the immediate buyer". This case involved a car which the dealer purchased from an auction company and then resold to the buyer. The buyer could not pursue a claim directly against the auction company. The court distinguished situations in which the requirement of privity has been relaxed as those involving personal injury or some element of tort.

In Mitchell v. Webb,[6] the Mitchells allegedly switched serial numbers and obtained forged title to a truck before transferring title to Schults. Schults subsequently transferred title to Webb. Webb filed suit for breach of warranty of title. The Mitchell court

Port Motors, 208 A.D.2d 486, 617 N.Y.S.2d 49, 25 UCC2d 681 (1994) (vehicle stolen). See also, Midway Auto Sales, Inc. v. Clarkson, 71 Ark.App. 316, 29 S.W.3d 788, 45 UCC2d 1062 (2000).

3. For a case on who is a "seller" see, Mid–East Servs. v. Enterprise Ford Tractor, Inc., 260 Va. 398, 533 S.E.2d 618, 42 UCC2d 685 (2000) (tractor company that facilitates exchange between buyer and seller in order to pay off lien is not a "seller" and does not warrant good title).

4. Comment 1 states that the "knowledge" referred to in 2–312(1)(b) is "actual knowledge as distinct from notice." Thus, the mere fact that a financing statement is filed does not relieve the seller of his warranty.

It is not necessary to establish reliance to recover for breach under 2–312. See, Kirby Forest Indus., Inc. v. Dobbs, 743 S.W.2d 348, 5 UCC2d 1321 (Tex. App.1987).

5. 493 S.W.2d 385, 12 UCC 648 (Mo. App.1973). See also, Crook Motor Co. v. Goolsby, 703 F.Supp. 511, 8 UCC2d 363 (N.D.Miss.1988) (warranty doesn't run with chattel).

6. 591 S.W.2d 547, 28 UCC 58 (Tex. Civ.App.1979).

held that, as privity was not required, the Mitchells were liable to Webb. We are not certain about privity. In general we are suspicious of proposals to abandon privity, as the section does speak of "buyer" and "seller." On the other hand, there might be some judicial efficiency in allowing direct suit here.

An actual cloud on the title is not required for breach of the warranty. The title may be good but the transfer not rightful. Comment 1 cites an illustrative situation that arose in Sumner v. Fel Air, Inc., where a merchant bailee to which goods were entrusted for repair sold them without authority to a buyer in ordinary course.

b. Quiet Possession

What of the case in which the seller's title is good, but it is subject to a colorable claim of title in the third party or colorable claim of encumbrance on the part of some financier? Assume, for example, that a buyer purchases an automobile, that a third party subsequently claims a security interest in the automobile, but that the third party is mistaken and the security interest proves to be in another automobile. Is it the buyer's or the seller's obligation to incur the expense of defending the suit by the third party? Put another way, does the seller warrant against claims by third persons that prove to be invalid?

The courts have long recognized, still additional protection for the buyer is needed when the title is "burdened by colorable claims that affect the value of the goods." Various cases give the buyer a remedy against the seller here.

There is some point at which the third party's claim against the goods becomes so attenuated that we should not regard it as an interference against which the seller has warranted. The problem lies in defining that point. While the courts have yet to work out this problem, there are at least two plausible alternatives. A court might hold a seller liable for expenses incurred in successfully defending against an inferior claim only if the seller knew or had reason to know that such a claim was likely to be asserted. Or a court could analogize to the standards used to determine whether title to real property is marketable, specifically, whether the claim is of such a substantial nature to subject the buyer to serious litigation.[7] While this statement of the standard is vague, it at least makes clear that frivolous claims or those arising only long after

---

7. See, e.g., Kay v. Carter, 243 La. 1095, 150 So.2d 27 (1963); Chere Amie, Inc. v. Windstar Apparel Corp., 2003 WL 22056935, 51 UCC2d 969 (S.D.N.Y. 2003) (seller warrants that goods are free from any claim of copyright or trademark infringement).

sale should not give rise to warranty of title liability, and it provides reference to a well-developed body of case law.[8]

Even if courts refuse to expand the warranty of title beyond its pre-Code scope, a buyer faced with an unfounded claim does have a remedy against the seller. At common law and under the Uniform Sales Act, a buyer whose title to purchased personal property was challenged in court could give notice to the seller and request that the seller defend. If the seller then failed to defend and the challenger prevailed, even if by default judgment, the seller would be liable for breach of warranty of title.[9] Sections 2–607(3)(b) and 2–607(5) give the buyer a similar right to offer the litigation to the seller and to hold the seller liable if the seller does not defend.

c. *Infringement*

Section 2–312(3) creates a warranty "that the goods shall be delivered free of the rightful claim of any third person by way of infringement or the like * * *." The warranty applies only to merchants dealing regularly in the kind of goods sold. Besides requiring that the seller protect the buyer against patent, trademark, and similar claims, this section provides that a buyer who furnishes a seller with specifications "must hold the seller harmless" against infringement claims arising from compliance with the specifications. Thus, 2–312(2) is unique in imposing a warranty on the *buyer*.

Although this section has not been heavily litigated, there are three issues that deserve notice. First, the provision only requires that goods "be *delivered* free" (emphasis added) of infringement claims. It could be argued that this language does not protect the buyer against claims arising out of its use or resale of the goods. In the words of one commentator "where the normal, anticipated use of the product infringes a patent, the buyer is entitled to protection."[10] However, in Motorola, Inc. v. Varo, Inc.,[11] the court held

---

8. See, e.g., Wesley v. Eells, 177 U.S. 370, 20 S.Ct. 661, 44 L.Ed. 810 (1900); McCubbin v. Urban, 247 Iowa 862, 77 N.W.2d 36 (1956); Clarke v. Title Guar. Co., 44 Haw. 261, 353 P.2d 1002 (1960). See generally 4 American Law of Property § 18.7 (A. Casner ed.1952). In one case involving a frivolous claim which did not give rise to a breach of the 2–312 warranty, the court emphasized that there must be an interference with buyer's right of ownership to constitute a warranty of title claim; a mere inconvenience is not enough. Compare Saber v. Dan Angelone Chevrolet, Inc., 811 A.2d 644, 49 UCC2d 352 (R.I. 2002) (breach if

is a "substantial shadow," even if later shown valid).

9. See, e.g., Thomas v. Ferris, 113 Conn. 539, 155 A. 829 (1931); 8 S. Williston, Contracts § 980 (3d ed.1964).

10. Remarks of Professor Pasley in 1 N.Y.State Law Revision Comm'n, 1955 Report 740 (1955). See, Dolori Fabrics, Inc. v. Limited, Inc., 662 F.Supp. 1347, 4 UCC2d 393 (S.D.N.Y.1987).

11. 656 F.Supp. 716, 2 UCC2d 437 (N.D.Tex.1986). See also Chemtron, Inc. v. Aqua Prods., Inc., 830 F.Supp. 314, 21 UCC2d 550 (E.D.Va.1993) (seller not liable where buyer used "non-infringing

that a buyer whose use of the goods infringed a process patent could not recover here because the warranty was as to goods, not conduct. The *Motorola* court stated, "This sort of allegation, that the buyer was induced by the seller to purchase the good and then use it to infringe a process patent is wholly outside the language of 2–312." We think the extent of the warranty should depend on the implicit and explicit deal between the parties. Where the only known—and therefore intended—use of the product had to violate a patent, we think the warranty has been broken. We can easily imagine cases on the other side of the line too—cases where a buyer uses a product in an unanticipated or novel way and so violates another's patent.

Second, Comment 4 states that the section "rejects the cases which recognize the principle that infringements violate the warranty of title but deny the buyer a remedy unless he has been expressly prevented from using the goods." Is the warranty against infringement breached when the buyer incurs litigation expenses in successfully defending against an infringement claim? One commentator has opined: "A rightful claim is one where the buyer or seller reasonably believes that a third party's infringement charge would probably be upheld by the courts."[12] In any event, these problems will have to be worked out by the courts, which have hardly been inundated with such 2–312 cases.

A final area of uncertainty concerns whether buyers of software may have recourse to 2–312 when it is later discovered that the seller's software infringes the rights of another software developer or some other third party. At least two courts have found 2–312 to apply.[13]

§ 10–16   The Warranties of Title and Against Infringement, Section 2–312—Disclaimer

Unlike the warranties in sections 2–314 and 2–315, the warranty of title and against infringement is not governed by the disclaimer provision of 2–316. Subsection (2) to 2–312 is the section's own disclaimer provision:

component goods in an infringing device").

12. Dudine, Warranties Against Infringement Under the Uniform Commercial Code, 36 N.Y.S.B.F. 214, 219 (1964).

13. Camara v. Hill, 157 Vt. 156, 596 A.2d 349, 15 UCC2d 1216 (1991) (seller of computer system found to have breached 2–312 in regard to two software programs which were not original

copies as agreed upon); Microsoft Corp. v. Logical Choice Computers, Inc., 42 UCC2d 727 (D. Ill. 2000) (recognizing the viability of a 2–312 claim where defendant, accused of distributing infringing software, files third-party complaints against supplier of the software, but court ultimately dismissing the third-party complaints for lack of proper notice of breach under 2–607).

A warranty under subsection (1) will be excluded or modified only by specific language or by circumstances which give the buyer reason to know that the seller does not claim title in himself or that he is purporting to sell only such right or title as he or a third person may have.

Comment 6 to Amended Article 2 casts some light. It says its counterpart comment "recognizes that sales by sheriffs, executors, foreclosing lienors and persons similarly situated are so out of the ordinary commercial course that their peculiar character is immediately apparent to the buyer and therefore no personal obligation is imposed upon the seller that is purporting to sell only an unknown or limited right."[1] Insurance companies, who often purchase the rights of owners of cars that have been stolen from their insured owners and ultimately resell those cars when they are discovered, have argued that they fit within the terms of 2–312(2); that is, that they do not "claim title" in themselves and therefore make no warranty under 2–312. The only two cases that we have found on the point have rejected that argument and have found that the insurance companies are not "situated like" sheriffs and others in such circumstances.[2] Another party who closely resembles the sheriff and executor is the auctioneer. The Uniform Sales Act expressly excepted auctioneers professing to sell by virtue of authority in fact or in law from the warranty of title,[3] and at common law an auctioneer who disclosed the fact of his agency was not liable for the failure of title of goods auctioned off.[4] This background plus Comment 6 to section 2–312 of Amended Article 2 indicate that auctioneers should be absolved from any warranty of title—if they make it clear that they are selling someone else's goods.[5] However, basic principles of agency law do impose on auctioneers a warranty of their authority to act for a principal,[6] and there is no reason why an auctioneer should not be held to warrant the title of goods he sells on his own behalf. In the Landmark Motors case,[7] the seller at

§ 10–16

1. Cf. Uniform Sales Act § 13(4). But, this does not seem to run with the chattel.

2. John St. Auto Wrecking v. Motors Ins. Corp., 56 Misc.2d 232, 288 N.Y.S.2d 281, 5 UCC 112 (Dist.Ct.1968); Spillane v. Liberty Mut. Ins. Co., 65 Misc.2d 290, 317 N.Y.S.2d 203, 8 UCC 332 (City Civ. Ct.1970), aff'd, 68 Misc.2d 783, 327 N.Y.S.2d 701 (1971).

3. USA § 13(4).

4. See, e.g., Mercer v. Leihy, 139 Mich. 447, 102 N.W. 972 (1905) (principal was present at auction).

5. See Gaito v. Hoffman, 1968 WL 9270, 5 UCC 1056 (N.Y.Sup.1968)

(agent-salesman without interest in goods was not liable for the principal's breach of the 2–312 warranty).

6. 8 S. Williston, Contracts § 979 (1964).

7. Landmark Motors, Inc. v. Chrysler Credit Corp., 662 N.E.2d 971, 31 UCC2d 1026 (Ind. App. 1996). See also, Landis and Staefa (UK) Ltd. v. Flair Int'l Corp., 60 F.Supp.2d 14, 39 UCC2d 364 (E.D.N.Y. 1999) (disclaimer valid because conspicuous). Compare State Farm Mut. Auto. Ins. Co. v. Ford Motor Co., 736 So.2d 384, 41 UCC2d 783 (Miss. App. 1999) (limited warranty with several exclusions).

auction of a used carwash system had only leased the system from the manufacturer and so did not have title to sell; hence manufacturer won in suit to recover system from buyer also in part because the auctioneer expressly and repeatedly disclaimed all warranties.

Whether "circumstances" gave the buyer "reason to know" is a question of fact.[8] In Spoon v. Herndon,[9] the court held that a jury could conclude that warranty of title was excluded where seller gave buyer a certificate of title listing another person as seller.

Of course, not only "circumstances" but also "specific language" can give the buyer reason to know that the person selling does not claim title or that he or she is purporting to sell only the right that a third person may have.[10] Neither the Code, the comments, nor the cases tell us exactly what specific language is sufficient to disclaim the warranty of title. Certainly one can think of language that would suffice, for example, "I do not claim title to these goods." What of the seller who uses the real property quitclaim language: "Seller hereby forsakes and quit claims all of his right, title, and interest in X to buyer." Is that statement "specific language" sufficient to put the buyer on notice that the seller is not claiming to have title? Several older cases decided under the common law held such language sufficient. In Jones v. Linebaugh,[11] however, the Michigan Court of Appeals reached a different result. The buyer in that case offered to purchase two Bugatti automobiles possessed by the seller. The seller explained that he did not have title to the cars, but the buyer asked him to obtain title. The seller later said that his attorneys were in the process of obtaining title. The sale was completed, and the buyer received a bill of sale, which provided that the seller sold and assigned all his "right, title and interest" in the cars and that to the "best of [his] knowledge there [was] no title in existence by way of registration with the State of Michigan or with any other State or with any Nation."[12] The court followed an old Michigan case,[13] which it found to be in accord with 2–312, and held that the quoted language was "not precise and free from ambiguity" and then, "as a matter of law, [was] not sufficient

8. Shelly Motors, Inc. v. Bortnick, 4 Haw.App. 265, 664 P.2d 755, 36 UCC 39 (1983).

9. 167 Ga.App. 794, 307 S.E.2d 693, 37 UCC 928 (1983). See also Rockdale Cable T.V. Co. v. Spadora, 97 Ill.App.3d 754, 423 N.E.2d 555, 33 UCC 167 (1981); National Business Sys., Inc. v. Borg–Warner Acceptance Corp., 792 F.2d 710, 1 UCC2d 907 (8th Cir.1986).

10. § 2–312(2).

11. 34 Mich.App. 305, 191 N.W.2d 142, 9 UCC 1187 (1971).

12. *Id.* at 309, 191 N.W.2d at 144, 9 UCC at 1189; see also Kel–Keef Enters. v. Quality Components Corp., 316 Ill. App.3d 998, 250 Ill.Dec. 308, 738 N.E.2d 524, 42 UCC2d 125 (1st Dist.2000) (a contract provision that expressly stated no opinion with regard to outcome of a lawsuit does not, of itself, exclude implied warranties that would adversely affect buyer were suit to come out against seller).

13. Croly v. Pollard, 71 Mich. 612, 39 N.W. 853 (1888).

to exclude the warranty of title."[14] We prefer the approach taken in this case over the older view, which apparently was influenced by real property law.[15]

Like section 2–315, 2–312 is an unremarkable and relatively mature provision. It provides a persistent trickle of litigation, but most of the cases do not offer difficult or novel points of law. To the extent that the doctrine is still growing, that growth concerns two questions: (1) what disturbance is sufficient to give the plaintiff a cause of action, and (2) what are the damages?

§ 10–17 The Warranties of Title and Against Infringement, Section 2–312—Remedies

An aggrieved buyer has several options under 2–312. First, he may rescind the contract or revoke acceptance of the goods. In American Container Corp. v. Hanley Trucking Corp.,[1] the court reasoned that the breach "results in a failure of consideration". Thus, the buyer could rescind. Hanley Trucking had sold a semitrailer to American Container. Sixteen months later, the state police impounded the trailer. The court permitted American Container to rescind the contract, but made an adjustment for the value of the possessory interest. In Wright v. Vickaryous,[2] the court held that a buyer was not required to complete a purchase when there were apparently valid security interests on file covering the goods.

Another option is to recover damages. But what damages?[3] The issue is often whether the buyer should recover the purchase price of the goods or the value of the goods at the time of dispossession. This determination has the most impact where the goods have appreciated or depreciated in value.[4]

---

14. 34 Mich.App. at 309, 191 N.W.2d at 144, 9 UCC at 1190. A dissenting opinion argued that the case presented "circumstances which give the buyer reason to know that the person selling does not claim title in himself or that he is purporting to sell only such right or title as he or a third person may have." See § 2–312(2).

15. But see Menzel v. List, 24 N.Y.2d 91, 298 N.Y.S.2d 979, 246 N.E.2d 742, 6 UCC 330 (1969), a non-Code case in which the court suggests in dicta that the sellers of a painting could have avoided liability under the warranty of title by selling "subject to any existing lawful claims unknown to them at the time of the sale."

The warranty against infringement in § 2–312(3) is applicable "[u]nless otherwise agreed." This phrase does not appear to be as stringent as the "specific language" requirement in 2–312(2).

§ 10–17

1. 111 N.J.Super. 322, 268 A.2d 313, 7 UCC 1301 (1970).

2. 611 P.2d 20, 28 UCC 1177 (Alaska 1980).

3. No damage, no recovery. See Martin–Kahill Ford Lincoln Mercury, Inc. v. Skidmore, 62 N.C.App. 736, 303 S.E.2d 392, 36 UCC 779 (1983) (buyer failed to prove payment of tax liens).

4. See, Menzel v. List, 24 N.Y.2d 91, 298 N.Y.S.2d 979, 246 N.E.2d 742, 6 UCC 330 (1969) (appreciating; value at time of trial); Jeanneret v. Vichey, 693 F.2d 259, 35 UCC 75 (2nd Cir.1982)

According to section 2–714(2), the general measure of damages for breach is the difference at the time and place of acceptance between the value of the goods accepted and the value of the goods if title were as warranted. This may translate into the purchase price where the value of goods at delivery is zero and the purchase price indicates the value of the goods if title were as warranted. Thus, in McDonald's Chevrolet, Inc. v. Johnson,[5] the buyer of a mobile home recovered the purchase price when the home was seized by the state police as stolen property.

Section 2–714(2) states that damages may be measured differently if there are "special circumstances". In Ricklefs v. Clemens,[6] the court reasoned that the buyer's undisturbed possession of the auto for nine months was a special circumstance and held that the buyer was entitled to recover the value of the auto at the time possession was disturbed. Presumably the same result could be reached by allowing damages as of the time of sale, but less a setoff for buyer's nine months' use.

The buyer may also recover consequential damages[7] to the extent that they are foreseeable.[8] The buyer has a duty to use reasonable care to mitigate damages.[9] Under the rubric of consequential damages, buyers have recovered the amount paid to maintain possession of a car,[10] the expenses incurred in putting a car into saleable condition,[11] the costs of hiring an auto to return home when the police seized the buyer's car,[12] and the damages arising from loss of bargain on re-selling a car.[13] Courts have awarded attorneys' fees as consequential damages where the fees were incurred in dealing with a secured party,[14] in defending title,[15] and

(appreciating; value at time of trial); Metalcraft, Inc. v. Pratt, 65 Md.App. 281, 500 A.2d 329, 42 UCC 14 (1985) (depreciating; value at date of dispossession even though less than purchase price).

5. 176 Ind.App. 399, 376 N.E.2d 106, 24 UCC 331 (1978).

6. 216 Kan. 128, 531 P.2d 94, 16 UCC 322 (1975).

7. Bill Branch Chevrolet, Inc. v. Redmond, 378 So.2d 319, 28 UCC 56 (Fla. App.1980). Seller may be held to have warranted that goods are free from any claim of copyright or trademark infringement. Chere Amie, Inc. v. Windstar Apparel Corp., 2003 WL 22056935, 51 UCC2d 969 (S.D.N.Y. 2003).

8. Schneidt v. Absey Motors, Inc., 248 N.W.2d 792, 21 UCC 536 (N.D.1976) (plaintiff assumed rental costs for third party to whom it had resold auto; not entitled to recover these from original

seller because original seller did not have reason to know).

9. Catlin Aviation Co. v. Equilease Corp., 626 P.2d 857, 31 UCC 1581 (Okl. 1981) (no recovery for lost resale where buyer failed to pay $1,167 lien on a $160,000 airplane).

10. Gaito v. Hoffman, 1968 WL 9270, 5 UCC 1056 (N.Y.Sup.1968).

11. John St. Auto Wrecking v. Motors Ins. Corp., 56 Misc.2d 232, 288 N.Y.S.2d 281, 5 UCC 112 (Dist.Ct.1968).

12. Itoh v. Kimi Sales, Ltd., 74 Misc.2d 402, 345 N.Y.S.2d 416, 13 UCC 64 (1973).

13. Mitchell v. Webb, 591 S.W.2d 547, 28 UCC 58 (Tex.Civ.App.1979).

14. Gaito v. Hoffman, 1968 WL 9270, 5 UCC 1056 (N.Y.Sup.1968).

15. Universal C. I. T. Credit Corp. v. State Farm Mut. Auto. Ins. Co., 493

in defending against criminal charges for possession of stolen property.[16]

In Chere Amie, Inc. v. Windstar Apparel Corp.,[17] the court held that UCC 2–312 also applies to claims for copyright and trademark infringement, and permits recovery of costs and fees.

§ 10–18 The Magnuson–Moss Warranty Act Coverage

In the Magnuson–Moss provision[1] of the Federal Trade Commission Improvement Act, Congress has created a limited federal consumer warranty law. The Act does not generally supplant the Code provisions that we have discussed above but it has a direct impact upon manufacturers, sellers, and consumers of consumer products.[2] Generally the Act is limited to consumer buyers[3] and to "consumer products." In section 101, the Act defines consumer products to mean "tangible personal property * * * distributed in commerce * * * normally used for personal, family, or household purposes * * *."[4] Although the Act limits the kinds of disclaimers that one may use with respect to implied warranties of merchantability and fitness, it does not otherwise deal with implied warranties.[5] It is designed principally to require certain disclosures with respect to written warranties, to provide consumers certain remedies in the case of failure of disclosure or nonconformity,[6] and to

S.W.2d 385, 12 UCC 648 (Mo.App.1973); Standing v. Midgett, 850 F.Supp. 396, 22 UCC2d 472 (E.D.N.C.1993) (buyer entitled to attorney's fees incurred in bankruptcy proceeding which determined lien unenforceable).

16. De La Hoya v. Slim's Gun Shop, 80 Cal.App.3d Supp. 6, 146 Cal.Rptr. 68, 24 UCC 45 (1978).

17. 2003 WL 22056935, 51 UCC2d 969 (S.D.N.Y. 2003).

§ 10–18

1. Act of Jan. 4, 1975, Pub.L. No. 93–637, Title I, § 101, 88 Stat. 2183, 15 U.S.C.A. § 2301–2312 (1982).

2. Automobile Importers of America, Inc. v. State of Minn., 871 F.2d 717 (8th Cir.1989) (Magnuson–Moss does not preempt recovery under state lemon laws).

3. See Ismael v. Goodman Toyota, 106 N.C.App. 421, 417 S.E.2d 290, 18 UCC2d 101 (1992) (determination regarding whether the parties are "consumers" and "suppliers" for purposes of the Magnuson–Moss Act to be made by the court); Voelker v. Porsche Cars North America, Inc., 353 F.3d 516, 52 UCC2d 450 (7th Cir.2003).

4. Act of Jan. 4, 1975, Pub.L. No. 93–637, Title I, § 101, 88 Stat. 2183, 15 U.S.C. § 2301(1) (1982). Whether goods at issue in an action under the Magnuson–Moss Act are consumer goods is determined by the courts in light of the above language. For examples of goods that were not considered consumer goods, see, Kemp v. Pfizer, Inc., 835 F.Supp. 1015 (E.D.Mich.1993) (prosthetic heart valves) and Clark v. Jim Walter Homes, Inc., 719 F.Supp. 1037 (M.D.Ala. 1989) (prefabricated or modular homes); Essex Ins. Co. v. Blount, Inc., 72 F.Supp.2d 722 (E.D.Tex.1999) (heavy timber equipment designed for the logging industry).

5. With respect to some aspects of implied warranties, state law governs.

6. Congress's intent in creating the Magnuson–Moss Act was to create a federal private cause of action for consumers injured as a result of a violation of a warranty under the Act. See, e.g., Skelton v. General Motors Corp., 660 F.2d 311, 32 UCC 1118 (7th Cir. 1981) cert. denied 456 U.S. 974, 102 S.Ct. 2238, 72 L.Ed.2d 848. Congress also sought to establish standards for the form and content of written warranties beyond

force warrantors to use certain common adjectives to describe their written warranties.

Anyone who represents a manufacturer of consumer products or a retailer of those products needs to know considerably more about the Magnuson–Moss Act than we will set forth here. We have space only to suggest some of the ways in which the Act will mesh or conflict with the Uniform Commercial Code. Those who need to be experts on the Magnuson–Moss Act must look elsewhere.[7] We deal with three questions: (1) What are the minimum disclosure requirements? (2) What is the significance of labeling a warranty "full" or "limited"? (3) What remedies are available to an aggrieved buyer under the Act?

a. Disclosure Requirements

Section 102[8] includes a series of warranty disclosure suggestions and then authorizes the Federal Trade Commission to establish specific rules with respect to such disclosures. Those rules are set forth in 16 CFR § 701.3 of the FTC regulations. They require any warrantor who warrants a consumer product "actually costing the consumer more than $15" to include in any written warranty the following information:

> (1) The identity of the party or parties to whom the written warranty is extended, if the enforceability of the written warranty is limited to the original consumer purchaser or

what appears in Article 2 of the UCC. See Lysek v. Elmhurst Dodge, Inc., 325 Ill.App.3d 536, 259 Ill.Dec. 454, 758 N.E.2d 862 (2001). See also S.Rep. No.93–151, 93d Cong., 1st Sess. 6–9 (1973) and H.R.Rep.No.93–1107, 93d Cong., 2d Sess. 22–29, reprinted in (1974) U.S.Code Cong. & Ad.News 7702, 7705–11.

7. See generally, Clark and Davis, Beefing Up Product Warranties: A New Dimension In Consumer Protection, 23 Kan.L.Rev. 567 (1975); Eddy, Effects of the Magnuson–Moss Act Upon Consumer Product Warranties, 55 N.C.L.Rev. 835 (1977); C. Smith, The Magnuson–Moss Warranty Act: Federal Regulation of Written Consumer Product Warranties, in Consumer Credit 1978, 38 (H. Mortimer ed., Prac.L.Inst.1978); J. White, Warranties Under the UCC and the Magnuson–Moss Act, An Update '76, 499 (Prac.L.Inst.1976); Note, Consumer Product Warranties Under the Magnuson–Moss Warranty Act and the Uniform Commercial Code, 62 Cornell L.Rev. 738 (1977); Note, The Mag-

nuson–Moss Warranty—Federal Trade Commission Improvement Act: Should the Consumer Rejoice?, 15 J.Fam.L. 77 (1976); P. Lester, The Magnuson–Moss Warranty Act: The Courts Begin To Talk, 16 UCC L.J. 119 (1983). R. Coffinberger and L. Samuels, Legislative Responses to the Plight of New Car Purchasers, 18 UCC L.J. 168 (1985); R. Riegert, An Overview of the Magnuson–Moss Warranty Act and the Successful Consumer–Plaintiff's Right to Attorney's Fees, 95 Com.L.J. 468 (1990); A Deviance, Magnuson–Moss Act: Substitution for UCC Warranty Protection?, 95 Com.L.J. 323 (1990); A. Squillante, Remedies Provided by the Magnuson–Moss Warranty Act, 92 Com.L.J. 366 (1987). There are also procedural issues in bringing a Magnuson Moss warranty action, including amount in controversy, and jurisdiction. These issues are further complicated in class action suits.

8. Act of Jan. 4, 1975, Pub.L. No. 93–637, Title I, § 103, 88 Stat. 2187, 15 U.S.C. § 2302 (1982).

is otherwise limited to persons other than every consumer owner during the term of the warranty;

(2) A clear description and identification of products, or parts, or characteristics, or components or properties covered by and where necessary for clarification, excluded from the warranty;

(3) A statement of what the warrantor will do in the event of a defect, malfunction or failure to conform with the written warranty, including the items or services the warrantor will pay for or provide, and, where necessary for clarification, those which the warrantor will not pay for or provide;

(4) The point in time or event on which the warranty term commences, if different from the purchase date, and the time period or other measurement of warranty duration;

(5) A step-by-step explanation of the procedure which the consumer should follow in order to obtain performance of any warranty obligation, including the persons or class of persons authorized to perform warranty obligations. This includes the name(s) of the warrantor(s), together with: the mailing address(es) of the warrantor(s), and or the name or title and the address of any employee or department of the warrantor responsible for the performance of warranty obligations, and/or a telephone number which consumers may use without charge to obtain information on warranty performance;

(6) Information respecting the availability of an informal dispute settlement mechanism elected by the warrantor in compliance with Part 703 of this subchapter;

(7) Any limitations on the duration of implied warranties, disclosed on the face of the warranty as provided in Section 108 of the Act, accompanied by the following statement:

> Some states do not allow limitations on how long an implied warranty lasts, so the above limitation may not apply to you.

(8) Any exclusions of or limitations on relief such as incidental or consequential damages, accompanied by the following statement, which may be combined with the statement required in sub-paragraph (7) above:

> Some states do not allow the exclusion or limitation of incidental or consequential damages, so the above limitation or exclusion may not apply to you.

(9) A statement in the following language:

> This warranty gives you specific legal rights, and you may also have other rights which vary from state to state.

Section 701.3(b), however, contains an exception to the foregoing requirements:

> Paragraph (a)(1)–(9) of this Section shall not be applicable with respect to statements of general policy on emblems, seals or insignias issued by third parties promising replacement or refund if a consumer product is defective, which statements contain no representation or assurance of the quality or performance characteristics of the product; provided that (1) the disclosures required by paragraph (a)(1)–(9) are published by such third parties in each issue of a publication with a general circulation, and (2) such disclosures are provided free of charge to any consumer upon written request.

Note that the disclosure requirements apply only to a "warrantor or warranty of a consumer product." Subsection (b) of the regulation makes the rules inapplicable to "statements of general policy on emblems, seals or insignia issued by third parties promising replacement or refund if a consumer product is defective * * *," at least if these statements contain no "representation or assurance of the quality or performance characteristics of the product * * *." Those statements raise interesting questions about the meaning of written warranty under the Magnuson–Moss Act. Written warranty is defined as follows in section 101(6):[9]

> (A) any written affirmation of fact or written promise made in connection with the sale of a consumer product by a supplier to a buyer which relates to the nature of the material or workmanship and affirms or promises that such material or workmanship is defect free or will meet a specified level of performance over a specified period of time, or

> (B) any undertaking in writing in connection with the sale by a supplier of a consumer product to refund, repair, replace, or take other remedial action with respect to such product in the event that such product fails to meet the specifications set forth in the undertaking, * * * which written affirmation, promise, or undertaking becomes part of the basis of the bargain between a supplier and a buyer for purposes other than resale of such product.

It is obvious that the drafter of the quoted definition was aware of section 2–313 of the Uniform Commercial Code, but it is also obvious that the definition is not co-extensive with the 2–313 definition of express warranty. For example, 101(6)(B) includes promises to repair as warranties, but these promises may not be warranties under section 2–313 if not affirmations of fact or prom-

---

9. Act of Jan. 4, 1975, Pub.L. No.   U.S.C. § 2301(6) (1982).
93–637, Title I, § 101, 88 Stat. 2183. 15

ises with respect to the product. Moreover, one can argue from section 101(6)(A) that a variety of affirmations would not constitute warranties under the Magnuson–Moss Act since they must affirm or promise that the product is "defect-free or will meet a specified level of performance over a specified period of time." Would the statement "top-notch used car" be a warranty under the Magnuson–Moss Act? Arguably such an affirmation of fact would qualify as an express warranty under 2–313 of the Code. (But see 2–313(2).) It takes greater imagination to see that the statement is an assertion that the product is defect free or that it will meet a specified level of performance over a specified period of time. So beware; what may be an express warranty under 2–313 is not necessarily an express warranty under the Magnuson–Moss Act. However the converse seems not true, that is, it would appear that anything that would qualify as an express warranty under section 101(6)(A) of the Magnuson–Moss Act would also be an express warranty under 2–313 of the Code.

We leave for others to consider how required disclosures must be made—whether by brochure as part of the sale of a product or by some other method.[10] We also will not consider whether the hardware store owner as well as his wholesaler and the manufacturer of a particular product is a warrantor under the Magnuson–Moss Act.[11] Apparently the hardware retailer is not a warrantor under the Act but one can surely argue that by putting a product on his shelves he is a "warrantor warranting a consumer product" and by doing so in a defective way is himself violating the Magnuson–Moss Act. Counsel for large retailers and for manufacturers of consumer products should beware; there are many problems lurking in the words of the Magnuson–Moss Act and in the regulations promulgated under it.

b. "Full" and "Limited" Warranties

Except with respect to certain low-priced items and unless the FTC has exempted the transaction, each "warrantor warranting a consumer product by means of a written warranty" must conspicuously identify the warranty as a "limited warranty" or "full war-

---

10. On "written warranties" under the Magnuson–Moss Act and resultant causes of action, see Skelton v. General Motors Corp., 500 F.Supp. 1181, 30 UCC 846 (N.D.Ill. 1980), reversed 660 F.2d 311, 32 UCC 1118 (7th Cir.1981), cert. denied 456 U.S. 974, 102 S.Ct. 2238, 72 L.Ed.2d 848 (1982). Lysek v. Elmhurst Dodge, Inc., 325 Ill.App.3d 536, 259 Ill. Dec. 454, 758 N.E.2d 862 (2001) (service contracts, in addition to written and im-

plied warranties, may give rise to causes of action under the Act).

11. For the definition of "warrantor" under the Act, see Act of 1975, Pub.L. No. 93–637, Title I, § 101(5), 88 Stat. 2183, 15 U.S.C. § 2301(5) (1982):

The term "warrantor" means any supplier or other person who gives or offers to give a written warranty or who is or may be obligated under an implied warranty.

ranty.''[12] Apparently the Congress believed that consumers' percep-
tions of the substance of written warranties would be sharpened by
forcing all sellers to fit within one of the two categories. The Act
does not require that a seller give any written warranty but, if
seller does so then (with insignificant exceptions) it must label the
warranty "full" or "limited." In theory at least, over time these
adjectives will achieve a fixed meaning in this context in the minds
of consumers and they will thus be able to make more intelligent
decisions. If the seller's written warranty satisfies section 104 of
the Act it is a "full warranty" and must be so labeled; if it fails to
satisfy section 104, it is a "limited warranty" and must be so
labeled. The standards in Section 104[13] are as follows:

(a) In order for a warrantor warranting a consumer product by means of a written warranty to meet the Federal
minimum standards for warranty—

(1) such warrantor must as a minimum remedy such
consumer product within a reasonable time and without
charge, in the case of a defect, malfunction, or failure to
conform with such written warranty;

(2) notwithstanding section 108(b), such warrantor
may not impose any limitation on the duration of any
implied warranty on the product;

(3) such warrantor may not exclude or limit consequential damages for breach of any written or implied
warranty on such product, unless such exclusion or limitation conspicuously appears on the face of the warranty;
and

(4) if the product (or a component part thereof) contains a defect or malfunction after a reasonable number of
attempts by the warrantor to remedy defects or malfunctions in such product, such warrantor must permit the
consumer to elect either a refund for, or replacement
without charge of, such product or part (as the case may
be). The Commission may by rule specify for purposes of
this paragraph, what constitutes a reasonable number of
attempts to remedy particular kinds of defects or malfunctions under different circumstances. If the warrantor replaces a component part of a consumer product, such
replacement shall include installing the part in the product
without charge.

12. Act of Jan. 4, 1975, Pub.L. No.
93–637, Title I, § 103, 88 Stat. 2187, 15
U.S.C. § 2303(a) (1982).

13. Act of Jan. 4, 1975, Pub.L. No.
93–637, Title I, § 105, 88 Stat. 2188, 15
U.S.C. § 2304(a) (1982).

Under subsection 104(e), the mere designation of the warranty as "full" is deemed to incorporate "at least the minimum requirements of this section and rules prescribed under this section." That rule applies both in actions under the Magnuson–Moss Act itself and in state warranty actions under the Code. Under the quoted language the maker of a "full" warranty may neither impose a limitation on the duration of an implied warranty nor may it limit its liability for consequential damages unless it does so by a conspicuous statement on the face of the warranty. If the seller gives any form of warranty under the Magnuson–Moss Act, whether full or limited, section 108[14] substantially limits the seller's power to disclaim or modify the implied warranties that would arise under the UCC as follows:

> (a) No supplier may disclaim or modify (except as provided in subsection (b)) any implied warranty to a consumer with respect to such consumer product if (1) such supplier makes any written warranty to the consumer with respect to such consumer product, or (2) at the time of sale, or within 90 days thereafter, such supplier enters into a service contract with the consumer which applies to such consumer product.

Any manufacturer of consumer products and his counsel have a complex set of decisions to make with respect to the Uniform Commercial Code and the Magnuson–Moss Act. First, the manufacturer or seller must make the business decisions about the warranties that it wishes or must make in order to compete in the market place. These decisions must be made on the basis of the lawyer's advice about the various combinations of implied warranties, express warranties, limitation of remedies, and disclaimers that are now possible under the Magnuson–Moss Act. Some of the combinations of express warranties and limitations that were formerly in vogue are explicitly outlawed by the Magnuson–Moss Act. One who would comply with the Act and yet compete effectively needs to give careful consideration to the Act.

c. *Remedies*

The Act grants twofold enforcement power. On the one hand, section 110(b)[15] provides that any person who violates the Act commits a violation of Section 5 of the Federal Trade Commission Act and is thus subject to sanctions applied by the FTC via that Act. In addition, Section 110(d) grants a private right of recovery to

---

14. Act of Jan. 4, 1975, Pub.L. No. 93–637, § 108, 88 Stat. 2189, 15 U.S.C.A. § 2308 (1982).

15. Act of Jan. 4, 1975, Pub.L. No. 93–637, § 110, 88 Stat. 2189, 15 U.S.C.A. § 2310(b) (1982).

consumers who are damaged by violation of the Act. Section 110(d)[16] reads in full as follows:

(1) Subject to subsections (a)(3) and (e), a consumer who is damaged by the failure of a supplier, warrantor, or service contractor to comply with any obligation under this title, or under a written warranty, implied warranty, or service contract, may bring suit for damages and other legal and equitable relief—

(A) in any court of competent jurisdiction in any State or the District of Columbia; or

(B) in an appropriate district court of the United States, subject to paragraph (3) of this subsection.

(2) If a consumer finally prevails in any action brought under paragraph (1) of this subsection, he may be allowed by the court to recover as part of the judgment a sum equal to the aggregate amount of cost and expenses (including attorneys' fees based on actual time expended) determined by the court to have been reasonably incurred by the plaintiff for or in connection with the commencement and prosecution of such action, unless the court in its discretion shall determine that such an award of attorneys' fees would be inappropriate.

(3) No claim shall be cognizable in a suit brought under paragraph (1)(B) of this subsection—

(A) if the amount in controversy of any individual claim is less than the sum or value of $25;

(B) if the amount in controversy is less than the sum or value of $50,000 (exclusive of interests and costs) computed on the basis of all claims to be determined in this suit; or

(C) if the action is brought as a class action, and the number of named plaintiffs is less than one hundred.

One should not forget that every warranty covered by the Magnuson–Moss Act may also be a warranty under state law—the Code. Breach of the warranty will thus give a private right of action under the Code as well as any right that might be granted by section 110.

Note that section 110 gives the winning consumer costs and expenses "including attorney's fees based on actual time expended * * *," unless such award would be "inappropriate." Note too that section 110 has a series of rules on class actions. It has a final

---

16. Act of Jan. 4, 1975, Pub.L. No.   U.S.C.A. § 2310(d) (1982).
93–637, § 110, 88 Stat. 2189, 15

subsection that makes "only the warrantor actually making a written affirmation of fact or promise" liable. Apparently this last subsection is designed to free the hardware store owner from liability when he simply passes on a manufacturers' defective warranty. However, the language could be read more broadly to mean that the retailer who sells the product containing the defective warranty is himself "actually making it."

The last three decades have not witnessed a flood of litigation under this Act, and we have doubts about whether the act substantially changes the consumer's right to collect in warranty disputes. Courts do seem willing to allow Magnuson–Moss actions along with Article 2 actions, although Magnuson–Moss actions may in some circumstances preempt Article 2 actions.

Chapter 11

DAMAGES FOR BREACH
OF WARRANTY

Analysis

---

§ 11–1 Introduction

At the outset, we should distinguish the cases treated in Chapter 7 on buyer's remedies and Chapter 9 on acceptance, rejection, and revocation from the cases to be covered here. In the former chapters we treated buyer's rights under 2–712 (cover) and 2–713 (contract-market damages) when the seller failed to deliver or when the buyer rightly rejected or revoked acceptance of delivered goods. This chapter is mostly concerned with cases when the buyer accepts the goods, does not reject or revoke acceptance, but sues for damages because the accepted goods are not as warranted. The principal section that governs the rights of a buyer who has accepted nonconforming goods is 2–714. We believe that only buyers who have accepted and neither rightfully rejected nor effectively revoked can use 2–714.[1] Thus, in our view, sections 2–713 and 2–712 on the one hand and 2–714 on the other are mutually exclusive.[2] Section 2–714 reads in full as follows:

> (1) Where the buyer has accepted goods and given notification (subsection (3) of Section 2–607) he may recover as damages for any non-conformity of tender the loss resulting in the ordinary course of events from the seller's breach as determined in any manner which is reasonable.

> (2) The measure of damages for breach of warranty is the difference at the time and place of acceptance between the value of the goods accepted and the value they would have had if they had been as warranted, unless special circumstances show proximate damages of a different amount.

> (3) In a proper case any incidental and consequential damages under the next section may also be recovered.

In the concluding portions of this chapter, we consider section 2–715 on buyer's incidental and consequential damages. That discussion treats not only the buyer who accepts goods and neither rejects nor revokes but also the buyer who has rejected, revoked, or who has never received the goods that the seller promised. In that portion, we offer a taste of that bitter pill from first-year contracts, Hadley v. Baxendale.[3]

§ 11–2 Damages for Breach of Warranty—The Basic Formula, Section 2–714(1) and (2)

Section 2–714(1) states the general rule for recovery of direct damages—the buyer may recover any damages "resulting in the ordinary course of events from the seller's breach as determined in any manner which is reasonable." But 2–714(2) states the time honored and most commonly applied formula,[1] namely, that the

---

§ 11–1

1. See Selectouch Corp. v. Perfect Starch, Inc., 111 S.W.3d 830, 51 UCC2d 1070 (Tex.App.2003) ("Only after the buyer finally accepts and can no longer revoke his acceptance, is he limited to recovering under section 2–714.").

2. See Gawlick v. American Builders Supply, Inc., 86 N.M. 77, 519 P.2d 313, 13 UCC 1031 (App.1974) (2–714 not applicable when buyer has effectively revoked acceptance); Kirby v. NMC/Continue Care, 993 P.2d 951, 40 UCC2d 368 (Wyo.1999) (buyer who rightfully rejected defective custom wheelchair could not seek damages under 2–714).

3. 156 Eng.Rep. 145 (Ex.1854).

§ 11–2

1. Of course, the buyer can deduct damages even after accepting goods, knowing of their defects. See, e.g., Kingston Pipe Industries, Inc. v. Champlain Sprinkler, Inc., 177 Vt. 484, 857 A.2d 767, 54 UCC2d 109 (2004). The difference-in-value formula of 2–714(2) is, of course, not exclusive. Subsection (1) may be invoked to justify an alternative measure. See, e.g., Acme Pump Co., Inc. v. National Cash Register Co., 32 Conn. Supp. 69, 337 A.2d 672, 16 UCC 1242 (Com.Pl. 1974) (buyer's damages include

buyer gets the difference at the time of acceptance between "the value of the goods accepted and the value they would have had if they had been as warranted * * *."[2] One should first note an important element of damages that the buyer will not recover under 2–714 but that the buyer might recover under 2–713 or 2–712. That is the cost of a bad bargain. Assume, for example, that a buyer has agreed to purchase tomatoes for a total price of $5,000 but that the market price is only $4,000 at the time of delivery. If the buyer accepts the tomatoes despite the fact that they are not as warranted and then sues under 2–714, the buyer will recover the difference between $4,000 (their value had they been as warranted) and their actual value. If, on the other hand, the buyer rejects the tomatoes, revokes acceptance, or never receives the tomatoes, the buyer would have an opportunity to cover in the $4,000 market and so escape the $1,000 loss attributable to its bad bargain.

The converse is not true. By accepting the goods, the buyer captures the benefit of a good bargain. Assume in our hypothetical case that the price of tomatoes has risen at the time of delivery such that the agreed upon tomatoes would have had a fair market value of $7,000 had they been as warranted. Because they are somewhat defective, the actual value on resale of these tomatoes is only $6,500. Under the formula set out in 2–714(2), our buyer could recover the difference between the value of the goods accepted ($6,500) and the value they would have had if they had been as warranted ($7,000). Because, by hypothesis, the buyer keeps the goods, he enjoys the increase in value.

Replacement cost may be the proper measure, as with a unique customized computer system even though such cost exceeds the contract price.[3]

In the usual case, section 2–714(2) will determine plaintiff's damages. However, one should not overlook the invitation in 2–714(1) to measure damages "in any manner which is reasonable." Where damages are arguably excluded by a clause that prohibits recovery of "consequential" damages or where such damages are prohibited by the rule of Hadley v. Baxendale, a plaintiff may wish to seek recovery through 2–714(1).[4] Of course the courts should

---

deficiency judgment flowing from seller's breach of warranty).

2. Damages for breach of warranty, or any other breach of contract, may be asserted as an affirmative defense to an action brought by the seller for the purchase price. § 2–717 provides:

The buyer on notifying the seller of his intention to do so may deduct all or any part of the damages resulting from any breach of the contract from any part

of the price still due under the same contract.

3. Hospital Computer Sys., Inc. v. Staten Island Hosp., 788 F.Supp. 1351, 18 UCC2d 140 (D.N.J. 1992).

4. Students of 2–714(1) should note that some courts are willing to use the "in any manner which is reasonable" language to achieve anomalous results. See Note, UCC § 2–714(1) and the Lost–

reject such attempts if the damages are truly consequential, and the contract or other rules would prohibit their recovery. Even so, reasonable persons often differ whether an item of damage is "consequential" or not. In those cases the plaintiff may successfully argue for recovery under 2–714(1).

In the following pages we deal with three questions, all generally related to the definition of the formula contained in 2–714(2):

(1) How does one measure the "value" of the goods accepted and their "value" if they had been as warranted?

(2) To what extent is the measurement of value subjective (that is, determined by the particular need of the plaintiff buyer as opposed to the general market measurement)?

(3) What are the "special circumstances" that might show proximate damages of a different amount?

a. Measure of Value

The 2–714(2) formula (difference between the value of goods as accepted and the value of goods as warranted) is essentially the same as the pre-Code formula.[5] A common objective measurement of the difference in value as is and as warranted is the cost of repair or replacement.[6] If a buyer accepts a truck with a defective radiator, a good measure of the difference between the value of the truck as warranted and its value as delivered is the price of a new radiator.[7] Of course, the repair or replacement may not bring the goods to their full value as warranted. In a proper case, the buyer should then be able to recover any further difference between the value as warranted and the value as repaired.[8]

Despite the utility of repair or replacement cost as a measure of value differential, the technique has limitations. One problem arises when the buyer seeks the cost of repair or replacement that occurs well beyond the time of acceptance. If the buyer's automo-

---

Volume Theory: A New Remedy for Middlemen?, 77 Ky. L.J. 189 (1989).

5. C. McCormick, Law of Damages § 176, at 672 (1935).

6. In general, courts will not permit recovery under the 2–714(2) formula if the cost of successful repairs or replacement produces lesser damages. See, e.g., General Supply & Equip. Co. v. Phillips, 490 S.W.2d 913, 12 UCC 35 (Tex.Civ. App.1972), writ ref'd n.r.e. (cost of replacing greenhouse paneling less salvage value of defective paneling controlled rather than diminution in value of greenhouse).

7. Sales contracts frequently make repair or replacement of defective parts

the buyer's exclusive remedy. Assuming the seller complies with the sales obligation, the contract ensures the buyer goods of warranted value.

8. See Soo Line R. Co. v. Fruehauf Corp., 547 F.2d 1365, 20 UCC 1181 (8th Cir.1977) (approving charge that "if you find that the repair of the cars did not restore them to substantially the same condition as they would have been if properly manufactured, then the difference or diminution in value is the reasonable cost of repair, plus the difference between the fair market value [as warranted], and the fair market value of the repairs").

bile engine functions satisfactorily for a year before defects appear, and the buyer receives the cost of replacing the engine, the buyer will reap a windfall to the extent that the car may now function longer than even a car of warranted value would have. A federal district court recognized this problem when the buyer sought the cost of replacing a television tower that had collapsed during a blizzard. The court observed "that an injured party should be fully compensated for losses suffered through the fault of another, but that he should not be allowed a windfall."[9] Accordingly, the court subtracted from the cost of replacement a reasonable depreciation for the use the buyer had enjoyed before the defect appeared. Even where repair or replacement cost provides an appropriate measure of recovery, special problems of proof may arise where the buyer made the repairs[10] or had to rely on estimated costs of future repairs.

There are many cases in which the goods will be irreparable or not replaceable and therefore the costs of repair or replacement cannot serve as a yardstick of the buyer's damages. In those cases, the court will have to find some other way to measure the difference between the value of the goods *as warranted* and the value of the goods as accepted. The fair market value at the time of acceptance is the most appropriate measure of the value of the goods as warranted.[11] For goods such as commodities traded on an open market, price quotations will be available.[12] Of course, the

9. See Community Television Servs., Inc. v. Dresser Indus., Inc., 435 F.Supp. 214, 217, 22 UCC 686, 688 (D.S.D.1977), aff'd, 586 F.2d 637 (8th Cir.1978), cert. denied, 441 U.S. 932, 99 S.Ct. 2052, 60 L.Ed.2d 660 (1979); Criscuolo v. Mauro Motors, Inc., 58 Conn.App. 537, 754 A.2d 810, 42 UCC2d 968 (2000) (allowing seller to offset damages for buyer's use of the defective car for 14 months, but awarding only nominal offset because of seller's failure to sufficiently specify value of use she received).

10. See Custom Automated Mach. v. Penda Corp., 537 F.Supp. 77, 33 UCC 856 (N.D.Ill.1982) (time and parts used by buyer's maintenance people to repair machine were part of difference in value between machine as accepted and as warranted). But see, In re Empire Pac. Indus., Inc., 71 B.R. 500, 3 UCC2d 1337 (Bankr.D.Or.1987) (vague estimate of how carpenter's services reflected actual cost of repair prevented full recovery).

11. Section 2–714(2) requires that the value of goods as warranted be measured "at the time and place of acceptance." See Mayberry v. Volkswagen of America, Inc., 271 Wis.2d 258, 678 N.W.2d 357, 52 UCC2d 912 (2004). Since the contract price is often negotiated long before the time of acceptance, fair market value at the time of acceptance provides the more accurate measure of value as warranted under 2–714(2). Use of fair market value at the time of acceptance gives a buyer the benefit of a good bargain (when the market price has risen above the contract price), but prevents the buyer from recovering the cost of a bad bargain (when the market price has fallen below the contract price).

12. Jerome Kantro Co. v. Summers Bros., Inc., 27 Agric.Dec. 129, 5 UCC 135, 1968 WL 9177 (1968) (lettuce price quotations from Federal Market News Service). In the case of defective fruit trees, one recognized way to measure the difference between the value of the trees as warranted and the value of the trees as accepted is to measure the difference in the market value of the land if conforming trees were planted and the market value of the land with the accepted trees planted. Serian Brothers,

purchase price of the damaged goods may be the best evidence of the value of the goods as warranted.[13]

When repair or replacement is not possible, determining the value of defective goods *as accepted*—i.e., their value in damaged condition—may be more difficult than ascertaining the value as warranted. Several courts have used the price received on a prompt resale as the appropriate measure.[14] Others have accepted the appraisal testimony of expert witnesses as evidence of actual market value at the time of acceptance.[15] In a few cases, courts have found (or allowed the jury to find) that the value of accepted goods was zero and permitted the buyer to recover the purchase price.[16]

In sum, the general application of the 2–714(2) formula poses a variety of problems[17] but few that are unique or legally difficult. In many cases the court can refer to the cost of repair or replacement to determine the difference in value of the goods as warranted and as delivered. In other cases it will have to rely upon the usual and often unsatisfactory evidence of market value.[18] For a discussion of the problem of defining "market value," see Section 7–4 *supra*.

Inc. v. Agri–Sun Nursery, 25 Cal. App.4th 306, 30 Cal.Rptr.2d 382, 24 UCC2d 99 (1994).

13. See, e.g., Puritan Mfg., Inc. v. I. Klayman & Co., 379 F.Supp. 1306, 15 UCC 1055, 1064 (E.D.Pa.1974) (court noted that value as warranted "is not necessarily the purchase price" but accepted this indicator of value because "both parties felt the value of the [goods] was the purchase price"); Tacoma Athletic Club, Inc. v. Indoor Comfort Systems, Inc., 79 Wash.App. 250, 902 P.2d 175, 30 UCC2d 219 (1995); JHC Ventures, L.P. v. Fast Trucking, Inc., 94 S.W.3d 762, 49 UCC2d 167 (Tex.App. 2002). But see, Samual–Bassett v. KIA Motors America, Inc., 357 F.3d 392, 52 UCC2d 909 (3d Cir. 2004) (overturning adoption of purchase price as award to 2–714(2) apply difference-in-value formula).

The contract price used as evidence of value as warranted should be the cash price of the goods, not a "credit price" that includes finance charges.

14. See, e.g., Bergenstock v. Lemay's G.M.C., Inc., 118 R.I. 75, 372 A.2d 69, 22 UCC 958, 966 (1977) (resale price of defective truck at auction is "some evidence" of value as accepted); JHC Ventures, L.P. v. Fast Trucking, Inc., 94 S.W.3d 762, 49 UCC2d 167 (Tex.App.

2002) (permitting use of price quotes from commercial vendors for the defective dump truck to serve as evidence of the defective trucks value as delivered).

15. See, e.g., Soo Line Railroad Co. v. Fruehauf Corp., 547 F.2d 1365, 20 UCC 1181 (8th Cir.1977) (defective railroad hopper cars); Carlson v. Rysavy, 262 N.W.2d 27, 23 UCC 353 (S.D.1978) (defective mobile home).

16. See, e.g., W & W Livestock Enters., Inc. v. Dennler, 179 N.W.2d 484, 8 UCC 169 (Iowa 1970) (diseased pigs).

17. Even when the facts appear to fit neatly within § 2–714(2), courts should be careful not to overcompensate a buyer with a double recovery. For example, the buyer of poisonous cattle feed should not recover both the cost of the worthless cattle feed and the value the cows would have had if the feed had nourished the cows as warranted. See Walker v. American Cyanamid Co., 130 Idaho 824, 948 P.2d 1123, 36 UCC2d 76 (1997) (court properly reduced buyer's award for damages to its potato crop by amount it received from its crop loss insurance so to avoid double recovery).

18. Subject to the limitations of § 2–719 the parties may alter the measure of damages by agreement.

b. Subjective or Objective?

Occasionally, the value of the goods to a particular buyer may not be the same as their value to a class of buyers in general. For example, a seller might deliver steel of a different gauge than called for in the contract. The value of that steel on the market might be ten percent lower than the value of the steel for which the contract called, yet this difference in gauge of steel might render it wholly unsuitable for the buyer's purposes; on the other hand, the lesser-gauge steel might be ninety-eight percent effective for the buyer's purposes. When the value of the steel to this buyer (the subjective value) differs from its value to a general class of buyers (the objective value), to what extent does one adjust the formula to take account of the individual needs of the buyer? Professor Peters once suggested that the value of the goods accepted is intended to be "a personalized criterion designed to allow the buyer * * * to show that the goods accepted are less valuable to him than their market price would otherwise indicate."[19] Likewise, one may argue that the other part of the formula, the value of the goods as warranted, should be subjectively measured because the drafters failed to use the objective term "market price," the term the drafters did use in 2–713(1). As we have indicated, the value of goods as warranted will seldom be in dispute, for the contract price will be a powerful measure of that end of the formula.[20] On the other end, the outcome is not so clear. Section 1–305 which states that the aggrieved party should get only those damages necessary to put one "in as good a position as if the other party had fully performed," suggests use of a subjective measure in those cases in which an objective measure would overcompensate. Where the buyer subjectively values the defective goods more highly than does the market, an objective measure for value as accepted may overcompensate the buyer. Where the buyer's subjective valuation of the goods is lower than the market, an award based upon objective value may under-compensate the buyer.[21]

Of course when the buyer has access to those markets, it is hard to see how that buyer's value could deviate significantly from

19. Peters, Remedies for Breach of Contract Relating to the Sale of Goods Under the Uniform Commercial Code: A Roadmap for Article 2, 73 Yale L.J. 199, 269 (1963).

20. See Special Project, Article 2 Warranties in Commercial Transactions, 64 Cornell L.Rev. 30, 114 (1978) (rejecting the use of a subjective measure of value as warranted). See also Special Project, Article 2 Warranties in Commercial Transactions—An Update, 72 Cornell L.Rev. 1159, 1220–29 (1987).

21. See Special Project, Article 2 Warranties in Commercial Transactions, 64 Cornell L.Rev. 30, 124 (1978) (buyer's § 2–714(2) damages should be measured by the extent that the maximum realizable value of the goods—determined either by resale value or the subjective utility of the goods to the buyer—falls short of their warranted value).

the market value. Basic economics suggests that one should move to meet the other.

c.   Special Circumstances

We would arrive at the "subjective" outcome not by bending the word "value" in the formula but by an expansive definition of the last clause in 2–714(2). That clause authorizes a different amount of damages when "special circumstances show proximate damages of a different amount."

Most of the cases used objective criteria for determining market value, and none discussing special circumstances addresses itself to our problem.[22] Even if one accepts the proposition that special circumstances should be expansively construed,[23] one will have interpretive difficulties in measuring the appropriate amount of buyer's damages. Assume, for example, that a buyer purchases a truck that proves to be subject to a $2,000 tax lien in the State of New York. The buyer operates only in California, and the buyer's operations will therefore be unaffected by the presence of the New York lien, which can be enforced only in that state. The seller will argue that this special circumstance renders the $2,000 tax lien irrelevant and that the buyer has suffered no damages because of the lien. Yet the buyer's resale value may be marginally reduced because of the lien. On that basis, we argue that the buyer should receive some recovery because of the presence of the lien.

In a further case, Colton v. Decker,[24] the court calculated direct damages as the difference in value of vehicle prior to state's impoundment and dismantling and after state's impoundment and dismantling, and being left unprotected during an entire winter.

In many cases, courts will find a ready measure of damages by using the cost of repair that the buyer has incurred or will incur in order to bring the goods delivered up to snuff. In other cases the courts will have to turn to the familiar but difficult standards for measuring value. In all these cases the courts should give due concern to the particular needs of the buyer.

22. Occasionally even the seller would argue "special circumstances" in order to diminish the damage award. See Shavers v. Massey–Ferguson, Inc., 834 F.2d 970, 5 UCC2d 106 (11th Cir. 1987) (seller unsuccessfully argued that buyer's use of defective tractor was a "special circumstances" that should mitigate seller's damages).

23. The general rule of § 2–714(2) requires courts to compute the differ-

ence between the value of goods as warranted and their value as accepted "at the time and place of acceptance." It may be that the Code drafters intended "special circumstances" to allow a shifting of the time frame for assessing damages under 2–714.

24. 540 N.W.2d 172, 30 UCC2d 206 (S.D. 1995).

§ 11-3　Damages for Breach of Warranty—Incidental Damages, Section 2-715(1)

In Chapter 7 we discussed the buyer's remedies in regard to goods that the buyer does not retain (because they are never delivered or because buyer rejects or revokes acceptance). This chapter has thus far dealt only with breaches of warranty involving goods accepted. Since sections 2-712(2) (cover), 2-713 (buyer's damages for nondelivery or repudiation), and 2-714(3), all permit the buyer to recover incidental and consequential damages (the subjects of 2-715), the remainder of the discussion in this chapter is applicable to any kind of seller's breach. Section 2-715(1) provides:

> Incidental damages resulting from the seller's breach include expenses reasonably incurred in inspection, receipt, transportation and care and custody of goods rightfully rejected, any commercially reasonable charges, expenses or commissions in connection with effecting cover and any other reasonable expense incident to the delay or other breach.

What are incidental damages? The Code does not define incidental damages; rather 2-715(1) lists many expenses that are included as incidental damages. However, Comment 1 to 2-715 stresses that those listed "are not intended to be exhaustive" but are merely illustrative of the typical kinds of incidental expenses that can be recovered under 2-715: (1) those associated with rightful rejection[1] (for instance, inspection and storage); (2) those associated with a proper revocation of acceptance;[2] and (3) those involved in effecting cover.[3]

The courts have not been grudging in awarding damages under 2-715(1) provided the buyer's expenses were "reasonably incurred" and "incidental" to the seller's breach.[4] For example, in Grandi v. LeSage,[5] the buyer purchased a race horse for breeding purposes. The seller had represented the horse to be a stallion; in fact the horse was a gelding. The buyer revoked acceptance under 2-608 and brought suit to recover the purchase price and incidental damages.[6] The final award included incidental damages for the care,

---

§ 11-3

1. See § 2-602.

2. See § 2-608.

3. See § 2-712.

4. Even a disclaimer of "special, indirect, or consequential damages" did not exclude incidental damages for the storage of defective goods. S & R Metals, Inc. v. C. Itoh & Co. (America), 859 F.2d 814, 7 UCC2d 61 (9th Cir.1988).

5. 74 N.M. 799, 399 P.2d 285, 2 UCC 455 (1965).

6. This is one of the relatively few contract cases in which a court acknowledged the applicability of punitive damages. The court found that since § 2-711 "permits recovery of damages in an action for rescission, punitive damages may likewise be recovered in such action where the breach is accompanied by fraudulent acts which are wanton, malicious and intentional." *Id*. at 810, 399 P.2d at 293, 2 UCC at 463.

feeding, and maintenance of the horse for about three months at $1.50 per day.[7] The Oregon court, in Lanners v. Whitney,[8] granted a similar recovery. The buyer revoked acceptance of an airplane that the seller had misrepresented as airworthy. The court approved the buyer's return of the aircraft and allowed "expenses reasonably incurred as a result of seller's breach, including those incurred in the care and custody of the goods."[9] Included in the recovery were "the amounts spent in repair on the aircraft on the Chicago trip, amounts spent to preserve the craft after the Chicago trip, including cost of removal of the radio and battery, installation of storage oil, ground insurance and storage charges."[10] An example of an award of incidental damages in a breach-of-warranty case is Lewis v. Mobil Oil Corp.,[11] in which the seller supplied unsuitable oil to the buyer's hydraulic sawmill system. The oil caused the system to work improperly for two and one-half years. The court found that the seller had breached its warranty of fitness for a particular purpose,[12] and it held that the buyer was entitled to incidental damages for amounts spent on excessive quantities of oil used and on repairs and replacement of mechanical parts damaged by the failure of the oil to function as warranted.[13] In a recent Georgia case, the court gave a buyer of carpeting mats resale testing expenses reasonably incurred to determine possible defectiveness of goods.[14]

Some courts have viewed finance charges incurred from the date of sale as properly recoverable incidental damages. For example, in Hart Honey Co. v. Cudworth,[15] the buyer recovered interest

7. *Id.* at 803, 399 P.2d at 288, 2 UCC at 457–58.

8. 247 Or. 223, 428 P.2d 398, 4 UCC 369 (1967).

9. *Id.* at 236, 428 P.2d at 404, 4 UCC at 379. See also Home Shopping Club, Inc. v. Ohio Intern. Ltd., 1994 WL 861509, 27 UCC2d 433 (Fla.Cir.Ct.1994) (awarding buyer cost of handling and storing defective goods).

10. *Id.* at 236–37, 428 P.2d at 404, 4 UCC at 379.

11. 438 F.2d 500, 8 UCC 625 (8th Cir.1971).

12. *Id.* at 507, 8 UCC at 636.

13. *Id.* at 508, 8 UCC at 636–37. It may be that the *Lewis* court mislabeled both items of damage. The cost of nonconforming oil can be recovered as a primary or direct damage under 2–714(2) and the cost of equipment repairs made necessary by the breach qualify as consequential damages under 2–715(2)(b). See Keller v. Inland Metals

All Weather Conditioning, Inc., 139 Idaho 233, 76 P.3d 977, 51 UCC2d 303 (2003) (allowing buyer to recover as incidental damages the cost of labor by buyer's employees gathering data about conditions in pool area after non-conforming dehumidifier was installed).

14. Mitchell Family Development Co., Inc. v. Universal Textile Technologies, 268 Ga.App. 869, 602 S.E.2d 878, 54 UCC2d 402 (2004).

15. 446 N.W.2d 742, 10 UCC2d 405 (N.D.1989). But see International Financial Services, Inc. v. Franz, 534 N.W.2d 261, 26 UCC2d 1137 (Minn. 1995) (refusing to grant finance charges as incidental damages and noting that such damages, if "recoverable at all, ... are recoverable as consequential damages"). At least one court has characterized finance charges reasonably and foreseeably incurred by buyer as consequential damages. Bobb Forest Products, Inc. v. Morbark Industries, Inc., 151 Ohio App.3d 63, 783 N.E.2d 560, 50 UCC2d 106 (2002).

payments made on a loan financing the purchase of equipment. Other courts have awarded the costs of returning the defective goods to the injured purchaser. In Gaynor Electric Co. v. Hollander,[16] the parties had entered into a contract which barred recovery of consequential damages and also limited seller's liability on the contract to the cost of correcting defects in the goods. Upon discovering massive defects in about 29,000 electromagnetic switches, the buyer packed up and returned all of the switches to be repaired. The court held that the unpacking, packing, and shipping expenses were properly recoverable as incidental damages, notwithstanding seller's argument that the parties had excluded such damages as consequential.

A greedy plaintiff might interpret the liberal recovery of incidental damages allowed by the Code as an invitation to seek recovery of expenses remotely connected to the breach. For example, an aggrieved buyer might purchase a substitute that does not qualify as a cover because its purchase occurred beyond a "reasonable time."[17] If buyer then sues for contract-market damages under 2–713, can buyer also recover the charges incurred in finding the substitute on the grounds that they were a "reasonable expense incident to the delay or other breach"? Comment 1 to 2–715 indicates that such charges should not be recovered, since the expenses were not incurred "in connection with the handling of rightfully rejected goods or goods whose acceptance may be justifiably revoked, or in connection with effecting cover where the breach of the contract lies in non-conformity or non-delivery of the goods."[18] Moreover, since the substitute was not purchased within a reasonable time, its purchase price should not be deemed a "reasonable expense."[19] We are clear that the causal link between the breach and the damages becomes so attenuated at some point that the damages are no longer "incidental to the breach."[20] We cannot predict where one should draw the line in the thousands of fact situations that can present themselves.

16. 29 Conn.App. 865, 618 A.2d 532, 19 UCC2d 791 (1993).

17. § 2–712(1) requires that cover be made "without unreasonable delay." Or a buyer might seek incidental damages not linked causally to the breach, as in Colton v. Decker, 540 N.W.2d 172, 30 UCC2d 206 (S.D. 1995).

18. One might argue that expenses in addition to those "in connection with effecting cover" must have been intended by the language "any other reasonable expense incident to the delay or other breach," but Comment 1 to 2–715

suggests that the drafters did not so intend.

19. Another way to limit incidental damages in this situation would be to determine that damages caused by purchasing a substitute that is not a cover are per se unreasonable.

20. Insurance costs, for example, seem to be properly recoverable, but courts often have difficulty categorizing insurance as incidental to the breach. See, e.g., Bair v. A.E.G.I.S. Corp., 523 So.2d 1186, 6 UCC2d 1487 (Fla.App. 1988) (insurance as consequential).

§ 11–4   Damages for Breach of Warranty—Consequential Damages, Section 2–715(2) and Related Sections

a.   Hadley v. Baxendale

Most of the law regarding consequential damages can be traced back to the classic English case, Hadley v. Baxendale.[1] For those readers who somehow missed that crucial day (or week) in first-semester contracts when Hadley's depths were plumbed, we briefly restate the facts. An employee of the plaintiff brought a shaft, which was vital to the operation of the plaintiff's mill, to the defendant-carrier. The defendants' clerk agreed to carry it to Greenwich, where the shaft was needed in order to serve as a model for producing a replacement. The defendants neglectfully delayed delivery of the shaft, and the plaintiff sued for lost profits that resulted from the extended incapacity of the mill. After reviewing these facts, the Court of the Exchequer announced The Rule, knowledge of which has become a *sine qua non* to second-year standing in law school:

> Where two parties have made a contract which one of them has broken, the damages which the other party ought to receive in respect of such breach of contract should be such as may fairly and reasonably be considered either arising naturally, i.e., according to the usual course of things, from such breach of contract itself, or such as may reasonably be supposed to have been in the contemplation of both parties, at the time they made the contract, as the probable result of the breach of it. Now, if the special circumstances under which the contract was actually made were communicated by the plaintiffs to the defendants, and thus known to both parties, the damages resulting from the breach of such a contract, which they would reasonably contemplate, would be the amount of injury which would ordinarily follow from a breach of contract under these special circumstances so known and communicated. But, on the other hand, if these special circumstances were wholly unknown to the party breaking the contract, he, at the most, could only be supposed to have had in his contemplation the amount of injury which would arise generally, and in the great

§ 11–4

1.   156 Eng.Rep. 145 (Ex.1854). See also § 7–5 *supra*. In all this, we must bear in mind that an aggrieved party may be held to have waived the right to consequential damages. See, e.g., Piper Jaffray & Co. v. SunGard Systems Int.

Inc., 2004 WL 2222322, 54 UCC2d 1088 (D. Minn. 2004). Also an aggrieved party may lose because not in privity with defendant. Beard Plumbing & Heating, Inc. v. Thompson Plastics, Inc., 152 F.3d 313, 36 UCC2d 286 (4th Cir. 1998).

multitude of cases not affected by any special circumstances, from such a breach of contract.[2]

In regard to the particular facts before it, the court concluded that lost profits due to the non-operation of the mill

> * * * cannot reasonably be considered such a consequence of the breach of contract as could have been fairly and reasonably contemplated by both the parties when they made this contract. For such loss would neither have flowed naturally from the breach of this contract in the great multitude of such cases occurring under ordinary circumstances, nor where the special circumstances, which, perhaps, would have made it a reasonable and natural consequence of such breach of contract, communicated to or known by the defendants.[3]

An aggrieved buyer will often seek general or direct damages for seller's breach of warranty under 2–714(1) and (2). The buyer may also sue for seller's breach of collateral promises of timely performance or the like (as contemplated under Comment 2 to 2–714). At the same time the buyer may seek consequential damages under 2–714(3) and 2–715(2). A lawyer for the buyer must be clear about what must be proved to establish each basic type of damages. The basic requirements for proof of general or direct damages are set forth in 2–714(1). Thus the buyer must prove that the non-conformity of tender caused loss that resulted "in the ordinary course of events from the seller's breach." If the nonconformity was a breach of warranty, 2–714(2)—a subset of 2–714(1)—provides a measure that will adequately compensate the accepting buyer in many, but not all cases. When not, the buyer is told in Comment 2 that 2–714(2) is not an exclusive measure and the buyer may recover under the "unless" clause of 2–714(2) or under 2–714(1) itself. An example is where the goods had been rendered conforming by the time of acceptance, but the buyer had contributed some of the costs of repair. Here, the formula in 2–714(2) would yield no damages, yet the buyer could recover either under the 2–714(2) "unless" clause or under 2–714(1) itself.

General or direct damages, then, flow "in the ordinary course" from the seller's breach, as specified in 2–714(1), and in cases where the buyer accepts the goods, the lawyer begins with 2–714(1) and (2). If the damages fit there, they are general or direct. But damages may not fit there. Or some of the buyer's damages may fit there, and others not. In either case, a question will arise whether section 2–714(3) applies. It reads: "In a proper case any incidental

---

2. *Id.* at 151.

3. *Id.* Many modern cases state or elaborate this formulation. See, e.g., Jet-

pac Group, Ltd. v. Bostek, Inc., 942 F.Supp. 716, 30 UCC2d 1109 (D. Mass. 1996).

and consequential damages under the next section may also be recovered."

To recover consequential damages under 2–715(2), what must the buyer prove? Some but not all of what the buyer must show is set forth in 2–715(2). Contrary to what some courts have assumed, section 2–715(2) is not an exhaustive specification of the necessary and sufficient conditions for application of the concept of consequential damages. In short, it is not a full definition. As Comment 3 to 1–305 makes clear, the concept of consequential damages is "not defined in terms in the Code" but is used "in the sense given * * * by the leading cases on the subject." The leading case of all, Hadley v. Baxendale, specifies as one necessary condition for application of the concept of consequential damages that the damages *not* be damages that flow in the ordinary course. Thus, in Hadley v. Baxendale and in the Code, direct damages and consequential damages are mutually exclusive categories. Damages cannot both be in the ordinary course and not in the ordinary course at the same time.

Yet 2–715(2) silently presupposes that damages claimed thereunder as consequential damages, are *not* in ordinary course. This further condition for application of the concept of consequential damages is not explicitly stated in 2–715(2) (though it is inferable not only from the leading cases on the subject but (by contrast) from 2–714(1), the wording of 2–714(3), and the sequence of 2–714 and 2–715). This lack of explicitness leaves a trap for the unwary. Among other things, it is an invitation for a court merely to go to what is stated in 2–715(2), treat that as a complete definition, and then apply a "no consequential damages" clause to exclude all of the damages satisfying the incomplete definition in 2–715(2). This would exclude not only damages not in the ordinary course, but also damages in the ordinary course. That is, general or direct damages as well as consequential damages would be excluded. This is because general or direct damages might satisfy the incomplete "definitional" requirements of 2–715(2) and so be erroneously classified as consequential. These damages would obviously be ones the seller had "reason to know" of (because flowing in ordinary course), would result from seller's failure to meet "general or particular requirements or needs of the buyer," and could also be damages not preventable by cover or otherwise.

Of course, parties may seek by contract to exclude liability for consequential damages. Such provisions are sometimes not effective, however. In one of many cases, the court disregarded such a provision because an alternative remedy which failed "materially altered the balance of risk set by the parties."[4]

4. Bishop Logging Co. v. John Deere Indus. Equipment Co., 317 S.C. 520, 455 S.E.2d 183, 28 UCC2d 190 (1995). A party may also waive rights to consequential or incidental damages. See, e.g., Piper Jaffray & Co. v. SunGard Systems Int. Inc., 2004 WL 2222322, 54 UCC2d 1088 (D. Minn. 2004).

b. *Differentiating Between Elements of Damage*

In many cases, the consequential damages that appear to be recoverable under 2–715(2) may overlap with the direct "difference-in-value" damages recoverable under 2–714(2). Courts often award lump sum damages without identifying the general and consequential damage components that comprise the lump sum figure.[5] This approach is justified only if courts are careful not to award both the integrated whole and any of its component parts. In R. Clinton Construction Co. v. Bryant & Reaves, Inc.,[6] the court failed to differentiate between elements of damage and the buyer secured double recovery. The buyer purchased anti-freeze to protect its equipment against damage from engine freezing during idle winter months. The seller's anti-freeze proved defective. The court awarded the buyer damages consisting of "the reasonable cost of the labor and parts necessary to repair the damaged machinery and of loss of income to [buyer] during the down-time occasioned by the period of repairs."[7] This award put the buyer in the position buyer would have been in had the anti-freeze performed effectively. The court, however, also allowed the buyer to recover "the purchase price of the [anti-freeze] since [it] was without value as delivered," citing 2–714(2).[8]

Had the anti-freeze performed effectively, the buyer would have had undamaged equipment, but no anti-freeze; the anti-freeze would have been "consumed" by the machine or used up at the end of the winter season. Thus, award of the purchase price of the anti-freeze in addition overcompensated the buyer.[9] Although the court properly characterized the purchase price as difference-in-value damage ordinarily recoverable under 2–714(2), in this case the purchase price was an element of damage subsumed by the other two damage elements—cost of repair and lost profits.

Even where there is no possibility of double recovery, courts must sometimes distinguish between consequential damages under 2–715(2) on the one hand and incidental damages under 2–715(1) or direct damages under 2–714 on the other. When a sales contract

---

5. See, e.g., Russo v. Hilltop Lincoln–Mercury, Inc., 479 S.W.2d 211, 10 UCC 768 (Mo.App.1972).

6. 442 F.Supp. 838, 23 UCC 310 (N.D.Miss.1977).

7. 442 F.Supp. at 846, 23 UCC at 320. See also, IMI Norgren Inc. v. D & D Tooling & Manufacturing, Inc., 247 F.Supp.2d 966, 50 UCC2d 1072 (N.D. Ill. 2002) (cost of repair and replacement was part of buyer's direct damages).

8. 442 F.Supp. at 846, 23 UCC at 319. See also, Fournier Furniture, Inc. v. Waltz–Holst Blow Pipe Co., 980 F.Supp. 187, 36 UCC2d 347 (W.D. Va. 1997).

9. This double recovery problem is likely to arise anytime the defective product is a consumable item, or a product whose useful life is very short. See, e.g., Swenson v. Chevron Chem. Co., 89 S.D. 497, 234 N.W.2d 38, 18 UCC 67 (1975) (insecticide).

prohibits the buyer from recovering "consequential damages" but allows the recovery of other forms of damage, the court must draw the distinction to honor the intention of the parties. In Russo v. Hilltop Lincoln–Mercury, Inc.,[10] defective wiring caused a fire which destroyed the buyer's new automobile. The court awarded the buyer the full purchase price of the automobile without identifying that portion of the price which represented recovery for consequential damages. Only the difference between the automobile's warranted and actual value at the time of acceptance could be recovered as general damages under 2–714(2). The defective wiring system reduced the actual value of the automobile at the time of acceptance below the purchase price, but the defect did not render the auto worthless as of the acceptance date. A large part of the fire damage was therefore consequential. Had the parties excluded consequentials by contract, the court would have had to identify the value differential component of the buyer's total loss.[11]

Sometimes the courts seem to be stretching the definition of incidental damages to favor a buyer who has improvidently signed a contract that excludes consequential but not incidental damages. In Carboline Co. v. Oxmoor Center[12] a shopping mall landlord had contracted with a roofing products manufacturer to install a liquid polyurethane cover to the mall's roof to remedy severe leakage problems. When the product proved defective, the Kentucky appellate court held that the cost of the product as well as the expenses of applying the roofing material and installing the *new* roof were all recoverable as expenses incident to the seller's breach of warranty. Even the court that was willing to stretch the idea of incidental damage as far as that, found some limits. The court concluded that reimbursement of the mall's tenant for losses resulting from injury to property and interest expense from funds borrowed to finance the roofing project were consequential damages that could not be recovered.

c. The Foreseeability Test

The immediate result of Hadley v. Baxendale was two-fold: (1) the rule placed a limit on the recoveries that juries could grant for breach of contract and thus reduced business risk somewhat,[13] yet at the same time (2) it provided a mechanism by which victims of contract breaches could recover damages peculiar to their special

10. 479 S.W.2d 211, 10 UCC 768 (Mo.App.1972). In IMI Norgren Inc. v. D & D Tooling & Manufacturing Inc., 247 F.Supp.2d 966, 50 UCC2d 1072 (N.D. Ill. 2002), the court classified cost of repair and replacement as direct, not consequential.

11. Whenever a defective component part causes an accident that damages the entire product, a large part of the total damage may be consequential.

12. 1985 WL 185466, 40 UCC 1728 (Ky.App.1985).

13. See C. McCormick, Law of Damages § 138 (1935).

circumstances.[14] The language of the opinion was sufficiently vague that courts in England and America have struggled for more than a century with the question: How much notice of the special circumstances must the breacher have in order to hold the breacher liable for consequential (as opposed to direct) loss?[15] Is it necessary that the parties actually discuss buyer's special circumstances and that the seller consciously assume the risk of consequent loss in case of seller's breach? Or is it enough that the seller know of the buyer's general situation?

The courts have adopted two approaches to this question. The more restrictive or "tacit-agreement" test permits the plaintiff to recover consequential damages arising from special circumstances only if "the defendant fairly may be supposed to have assumed consciously, or to have warranted the plaintiff reasonably to suppose that it assumed, [such liability] when the contract was made."[16] In effect, this test requires the plaintiff to prove that the parties had specifically contemplated that consequential damages might result and that the defendant actually assumed the risk of such damages.[17] The other cases, and certainly the recent trend of authority, have rejected this test. As Professor Corbin said:

> All that is necessary, in order to charge the defendant with a particular loss, is that it is one that ordinarily follows the breach of such a contract in the usual course of events, or that

---

14. See 11 S. Williston, Contracts § 1356 (3d ed. 1968).

15. This interpretive problem may have stemmed from the statement of facts preceding Baron Alderson's opinion which said, "The plaintiff's servant told the [defendant's] clerk that the mill was stopped, and that the shaft must be sent immediately * * *." 156 Eng.Rep. at 147. Authorities have differed over the effect of that statement. Professor McCormick concluded that the court decided that this information did not constitute notice to the defendant of the plaintiff's special circumstances sufficient to hold the defendant liable for the special loss. C. McCormick, Law of Damages § 140, at 573 (1935). The English courts, however, have now recognized that the *Hadley* court either rejected or was unaware of such evidence. Victoria Laundry (Windsor) Ltd. v. Newman Indus. Ltd., [1949] 2 K.B. 528, 537.

Obviously, a court's view of the facts in *Hadley* will color its opinion regarding the effect of the rule announced in the case. On the basis of the facts, as reported, it is not surprising that Justice

Holmes concluded from his reading of *Hadley v. Baxendale* that "mere notice to a seller of some interest or probable action of the buyer is not enough necessarily and as a matter of law to charge the seller with special damage on that account if he fails to deliver the goods." Globe Ref. Co. v. Landa Cotton Oil Co., 190 U.S. 540, 545, 23 S.Ct. 754, 756, 47 L.Ed. 1171 (1903) (breach of contract to sell and deliver crude oil). According to Holmes, the extent of a defendant's liability "should be worked out on terms which it fairly may be presumed he would have assented to if they had been presented to his mind." *Id.* at 543.

16. Globe Ref. Co. v. Landa Cotton Oil Co., 190 U.S. 540, 544, 23 S.Ct. 754, 755, 47 L.Ed. 1171 (1903).

17. The tacit-agreement test is discussed and criticized in 5 A. Corbin, Contracts §§ 1008–12 (1964); C. McCormick, Law of Damages § 176 (1935); 11 S. Williston, Contracts § 1357 (3d ed.1968).

reasonable men in the position of the parties would have foreseen as a probable result of breach.[18]

The Code drafters agreed with this view and stated: "The 'tacit agreement' test for the recovery of consequential damages is rejected."[19] Section 2–715(2)(a) holds the defendant liable for "any loss resulting from general or particular requirements and needs for which the seller at the time of contracting *had reason to know* * * *." (emphasis added). In other words, "the test is one of reasonable foreseeability of probable consequences."[20] This objective formulation is wholly consistent with the language used by Baron Alderson himself, "[The defendant is liable for such loss] as may *reasonably be supposed* to have been in the contemplation of both parties."[21] The Baron went on to say that if the buyer communicated "special circumstances" to the seller, the loss that would ordinarily follow in such circumstances should be compensable because the parties should reasonably have contemplated it, that is, because such loss would have been foreseeable. Similarly, under the Code, the seller is liable for consequential damages when the seller had reason to know of the buyer's general or particular requirements at the time of contracting, regardless of whether the seller consciously assumed the risk of such loss.[22]

With this knowledge of the common law ancestry of 2–715(2), we turn to judicial interpretation of the section itself.[23] The majority of jurisdictions, including a number of recent cases, have followed the Code's command and rejected the tacit-agreement test in favor of the less restrictive objective approach.[24] Even Pennsylvania,

18. 5 A. Corbin, Contracts § 1010, at 79 (1964).

19. § 2–715, Comment 2.

20. Gerwin v. Southeastern Cal. Ass'n of Seventh Day Adventists, 14 Cal. App.3d 209, 220, 92 Cal.Rptr. 111, 118, 8 UCC 643, 653 (1971).

21. 156 Eng.Rep. at 151 (emphasis added).

22. § 2–715, Comment 3. The Code therefore rejects the oft-suggested rationale that the rule of Hadley v. Baxendale protects the seller against insuring risks for which, had the seller been aware of them, the seller would have demanded a greater compensation. See 5 A. Corbin, Contracts § 1008, at 74 (1964).

23. Mel Eisenberg argues that the *Hadley v. Baxendale* principle of reasonable foreseeability traditionally has been applied in an excessively demanding fashion, and that a new formulation is in order. See Eisenberg, The Principle of

Hadley v. Baxendale, 80 Calif. L. Rev. 563 (1992). Perhaps the "reason to know" language of 2–715(2) codifies a more liberal application of the foreseeability standard. Calls for the overthrow of the regime of *Hadley v. Baxendale*, though, may be premature.

24. See, e.g., Lewis v. Mobil Oil Corp., 438 F.2d 500, 8 UCC 625 (8th Cir.1971) (seller of goods to manufacturing enterprise should know that defective goods will disrupt production); Best Buy Co., Inc. v. Fedders North America, Inc., 202 F.3d 1004, 40 UCC2d 666 (8th Cir.2000) (applying foreseeability test to determine whether trial court's award of consequential damages was proper); Leanin' Tree, Inc. v. Thiele Technologies, Inc., 43 Fed.Appx. 318, 48 UCC2d 991 (10th Cir.2002) (labor costs from hand packing foreseeable when seller failed to deliver cartoner); Mississippi Chemical Corp. v. Dresser–Rand Co., 287 F.3d 359, 47 UCC2d 244 (5th Cir. 2002) (allowing buyer to recover lost

which had long adhered to the restrictive test despite adoption of the Code, changed its judicial mind and buried the tacit-agreement test. Finally, we again stress that the Code calls for liberal application of the foreseeability test: "It is not necessary that there be a conscious acceptance of an insurer's liability on the seller's part, nor is his obligation for consequential damages limited to cases in which he fails to use due effort in good faith."[25]

d. Types of Consequential Damages

Finding that one qualifies for consequential damages is only the beginning of the story; one next needs to know what kinds of loss can be recouped as consequential damages. As we will ultimately explain, however, the distinction between general or direct damages on the one hand and consequential damages on the other is relative not absolute. The most commonly litigated and doubtless the most often sought after type of consequential damages is lost profits. Most courts have permitted recovery of lost profits under the Code provided the buyer can meet judicially imposed foreseeability and certainty requirements. In fact, the recovery of lost profits is becoming commonplace in at least one important area. The United States Court of Appeals for the Eighth Circuit, applying the Arkansas Code, has held:

> Where a seller provides goods to a manufacturing enterprise with knowledge that they are to be used in the manufacturing process, it is reasonable to assume that he should know the defective goods will cause a disruption of production, and loss of profits is a natural consequence of such disruption. Hence, loss of profits should be recoverable under those circumstances.[26]

In the *Lewis* case, the defendant had supplied the wrong kind of oil for the plaintiff's hydraulic sawmill system. As a result, the mill did not work properly for two and one-half years. The court held it was permissible to compute lost profits for that period on the basis of past profits, since the plaintiff had an established business.[27] How-

profits where seller knew if compressor train malfunctioned, buyer's plant would have to be shut-down); Parker Tractor & Implement Co. v. Johnson, 819 So.2d 1234, 48 UCC2d 1025 (Miss. 2002) (lost profits foreseeable where seller knew buyer needed the combine for his business of custom harvesting); Egerer v. CSR West, LLC, 116 Wash.App. 645, 67 P.3d 1128, 50 UCC2d 479 (2003) (buyer could not recover lost rents as consequential damages where seller never knew about prospective tenants); M.S. Distributing Co. v. Web Records,

Inc., 2003 WL 21788988, 51 UCC2d 716 (N.D. Ill. 2003) (pre-judgment interest not allowed under 2–715).

25. § 2–715, Comment 3.

26. Lewis v. Mobil Oil Corp., 438 F.2d 500, 510–11, 8 UCC 625, 641 (8th Cir.1971).

27. *Id.* at 511–12, 8 UCC at 642, citing 5 A. Corbin, Contracts § 1023 (1964), and 11 S. Williston, Contracts § 1346A (3d ed. 1968). See also Jetpac Group, Ltd. v. Bostek, Inc., 942 F.Supp. 716, 30 UCC2d 1109 (D. Mass. 1996)

ever, the court denied damages for loss of profits during the two
and one-half years *following* correction of the problem. The plaintiff had argued that he was entitled to those damages because the
burden caused by the malfunctioning hydraulic system had so hurt
plaintiff's capital situation that plaintiff could not operate at full
capacity. In rejecting that argument, the court said that if there
was a market available for the plaintiff's full-capacity production,
plaintiff could have obtained the necessary financing to see the
company through the period.[28]

Numerous other items besides lost profits are recoverable as
consequential damages. These include, *inter alia,* legal fees of
buyers incurring liability to third parties,[29] the cost of unsuccessful
attempts to repair the warranted goods,[30] and physical injuries to
person or property.[31] Many courts have indicated a willingness to
allow any recognizable loss as consequential damages, if such loss
can be translated into monetary terms.[32] In one case, an appellate
court stated that if the plaintiff could convince a jury that applesauce sold by the defendant and eaten by the plaintiff was inedible,
that as a result the plaintiff no longer enjoyed eating it, and that
there was a true loss measurable in a dollar amount, then plaintiff
could recover consequential damages for loss of enjoyment.[33]

Consequential damages may also arise in the form of liability to
third persons incurred as a result of the use or resale of the seller's
product. Suppose, for example, that a shipowner buys a bottle of
ketchup, which explodes at sea and injures a seaman. Compensation paid the seaman by the shipowner should be recoverable as
consequential damages from the seller of the ketchup.[34] Some
courts have limited the buyer's recovery in this area to payments
made to third persons under legal obligation. But one court held
that when evidence showed it was the accepted practice in the
aerial insecticide spray business to respray if the first spray was

(lost profits foreseeable and reasonably
certain and thus recoverable).

28. 438 F.2d at 508, 8 UCC at 637.

29. See, e.g., Addressograph–Multigraph Corp. v. Zink, 273 Md. 277, 329
A.2d 28, 15 UCC 1025 (1974).

30. Some courts have labeled the
costs of unsuccessful repair attempts as
incidental damages.

31. See, e.g., Federal Ins. Co. v. Village of Westmont, 271 Ill.App.3d 892,
208 Ill.Dec. 626, 649 N.E.2d 986, 28
UCC2d 184 (1995).

32. Some courts attempt to categor-
ize interest as an element of consequential damages even when there has been
acceptance. See, e.g., Metropolitan

Transfer Station, Inc. v. Design Struc-
tures, Inc., 328 N.W.2d 532, 36 UCC 860
(Iowa App.1982) (company borrowed
money to repair facility damaged by
breach). If the interest arose from the
purchase contract, and the buyer accepted the goods and elected 2–714 and 2–
715 as the vehicles for recovery, interest
should not be recoverable as consequential. See Nachazel v. Miraco Mfg., 432
N.W.2d 158, 7 UCC2d 469 (Iowa 1988).

33. Martel v. Duffy–Mott Corp., 15
Mich.App. 67, 166 N.W.2d 541, 6 UCC
294 (1968).

34. In Gambino v. United Fruit Co.,
48 F.R.D. 28, 6 UCC 1056 (S.D.N.Y.
1969), a shipowner was allowed to im-
plead the manufacturer of the ketchup.

ineffective, the plaintiff could recover the cost of respraying as consequential damages from the seller of substandard weedkiller even if the plaintiff was not legally obligated to respray.[35] This latter holding has the virtue of recognizing practical obligations that require business persons to conform to custom and usage in their trade in order to stay in business.

If there is an appropriate causal connection, consequential damages can reach well beyond direct injury caused by the product itself. For example, in R.W. Murray Co. v. Shatterproof Glass Corp.[36] plaintiff recovered not only the cost of replacement of defective exterior glass, but also of other glass that would not match the new panels in reflectivity and color tint.

Even in the world of the exotic plaintiff there are some limits on consequential damages. In Bazzini v. Garrant,[37] Ms. Bazzini sought to recover from the Sexy Sadie's Bird House not only the $1,200 purchase price of her dead Toco Toucan bird, but also the veterinarian's fee for the autopsy. Although the court found the bird was not fit for the ordinary purpose ("at least one purpose is to stay around as a live bird") and found the disclaimer not mentioning merchantability to be invalid, (* * * "All entrepreneurs in the tropical bird business realize, it is a jungle out there."), the court summarily rejected the cost of the autopsy as incidental or consequential damage.

Some cases suggest that types of damages to a buyer—such as those arising from delay—are inherently consequential.[38] This is a fallacy. Damages that might be consequential under one contract can be direct or ordinary under another. Among the circumstances most relevant to the classification is the scope of the broken promise itself. If the requirements or needs of the buyer are explicitly incorporated into the subject matter of the promised performance, then at least the immediate damages from breach will be direct because they flow in the ordinary course of events from the breach. It follows that even the damages for loss of profits in *Hadley* itself could have been direct, assuming that the carrier made an explicit promise to return the shaft without delay in order that the mill could operate and generate profits. As Judge Cardozo once observed, the distinction between direct and consequential damages is not absolute but relative to circumstances, including the scope of the promise itself. A type of damages, such as delay

---

35. Woodbury Chem. Co. v. Holgerson, 439 F.2d 1052, 8 UCC 999 (10th Cir.1971). For an extensive discussion of the liability of an independent supplier whose product might precipitate a recall by an automobile manufacturer, see B. Stone, Product Recall and Consequential Damages (1971).

36. 758 F.2d 266, 40 UCC 1283 (8th Cir.1985).

37. 116 Misc.2d 119, 455 N.Y.S.2d 77, 34 UCC 1550 (Dist.Ct.1982).

38. See, e.g., American Elec. Power Co. v. Westinghouse Elec. Corp., 418 F.Supp. 435, 460 n.44 (S.D.N.Y.1976).

damages, will be consequential in some circumstances, but direct in others.[39]

e. Degree of Certainty Required in Measurement of Consequential Damages

Even if a buyer can show the losses sustained were reasonably foreseeable at the time of contracting, buyer will not prevail unless buyer can prove consequential damages with reasonable certainty. A seller can defeat a claim for consequential damages—especially lost profits[40]—by showing that they are too speculative or uncertain.[41] Comment 4 to 2–715 indicates the Code's attitude toward the certainty problem:

> The burden of proving the extent of loss incurred by way of consequential damage is on the buyer, but the section on liberal administration of remedies [1–305] rejects any doctrine of certainty which requires almost mathematical precision in the proof of loss. Loss may be determined in any manner which is reasonable under the circumstances.

Nevertheless, it is obvious that a defendant is not liable for one million dollars merely because the plaintiff testifies: "If this machine hadn't broken down, I might have made a million dollars last year." Gerwin v. Southeastern California Ass'n of Seventh Day Adventists,[42] offers some guidance on the degree of certainty necessary for a plaintiff to recover. The seller breached its contract by failing to deliver used bar equipment to the buyer, who intended to use it for a hotel with restaurant and cocktail lounge. Because the proposed business was new, the buyer was new to the business, and no evidence of comparable businesses in the area had been presented, the court concluded that future profits had not been established with reasonable certainty.[43]

The so-called "new business rule," under which defendants claim that a new business entity's lost profits are too remote and speculative to be recoverable, was pared back by the Third Circuit

---

39. See Kerr S.S. Co. v. Radio Corp. of America, 245 N.Y. 284, 157 N.E. 140, 141(1927), cert. denied, 275 U.S. 557, 48 S.Ct. 118, 72 L.Ed. 424 (1927).

40. Some commentators contend that the certainty doctrine has little or no impact outside the realm of lost profits. See C. McCormick, Handbook on the Law of Damages § 28, at 105–06 (1935).

41. Some courts are more than willing to participate in "liberal administration" of remedies when it comes to consequential damages. A West Virginia plaintiff recovered damages for the impairment of his credit rating "resulting" from the breach. City Nat. Bank v. Wells, 181 W.Va. 763, 384 S.E.2d 374, 10 UCC2d 798 (1989).

42. 14 Cal.App.3d 209, 92 Cal.Rptr. 111, 8 UCC 643 (1971).

43. Id. at 222, 92 Cal.Rptr. at 119, 8 UCC at 655. The courts have been reluctant to award lost future profits in the case of new enterprises. See, e.g., Fredonia Broadcasting Corp. v. RCA Corp., 481 F.2d 781, 12 UCC 1088 (5th Cir. 1973) (new television station).

in In re Merritt Logan, Inc.[44] The court reasoned that a grocery store which operated for a year and a half falls outside of the new business rule. The grocery did not turn any profit during the year and a half period complained of. The new business rule is in decline.

Of course, there are many situations where lost profits can be computed with considerable certainty. For example, when a buyer has purchased for resale, buyer's lost profits will equal the amount of profit that the buyer would have realized on resale; that amount may readily be ascertained by reference to a subcontract or the buyer's normal resale mark up.[45] In the case of commodities, the buyer can prove lost profits with ease and certainty by invoking the resale market price at the time of intended resale.[46]

Traditionally, most courts have not been willing to grant recovery under the Code for lost profits resulting from a loss of customer good will. These courts reasoned that alleged damage to business reputation is too speculative to be recoverable. However, several courts, including the Southern District of New York applying New York law, have now recognized that a buyer may be able to show injury to business reputation with a sufficient degree of certainty and have allowed recovery for loss of good will.[47] Because

44. 901 F.2d 349, 12 UCC2d 421 (3d Cir.1990).

45. Ease of computation may explain why out of 200 cases decided from 1946–1955, plaintiffs recovered lost profits in 75% of the resale cases but in only 50% of the buyer-manufacturer cases. Comment, Lost Profits as Contract Damages: Problems of Proof and Limitations on Recovery, 65 Yale L.J. 992, 1016 n.137 (1956). However, the buyer must prove that the reason why the resale contract fell through was, in fact, proximately caused by the seller's breach of warranty. Rogath v. Siebenmann, 129 F.3d 261, 34 UCC2d 63 (2d Cir.1997).

46. See, e.g., National Farmers Org., Inc. v. McCook Feed & Supply Co., 196 Neb. 424, 243 N.W.2d 335, 19 UCC 821 (1976) (nondelivery of corn).

In granting a buyer lost profits because buyer is unable to resell a product, a court must be careful not to overcompensate the buyer. Assume for example, that a buyer sues wholesaler for nondelivery of a shipment of fiberglass skis under § 2–713. The buyer might ask for the market-contract differential (assume it is $10,000—$8,000) plus consequential damages which are lost resale profits. If the buyer could resell the shipment of skis at $15,000 but buyer cannot cover, buyer's lost profits will be $7,000 ($15,000 − $8,000). Should a court allow a recovery of $9,000 (the market-contract differential plus lost profits)? First, 2–715(2)(a) requires cover if it is at all reasonable, and that principle would eliminate lost profits in most cases. Secondly, in the unusual case where cover is impossible the court should award only $7,000 since that amount will put the wholesaler in the same position the wholesaler would have been in if the manufacturer had sent the skis. If a court gives the buyer the market-contract differential of $2,000 under 2–713, then the "loss resulting" from the wholesaler's inability to resell under 2–715(2)(a) is only $5,000.

47. See, e.g., R.E.B., Inc. v. Ralston Purina Co., 525 F.2d 749, 18 UCC 122 (10th Cir.1975) (applying Wyoming law); Westric Battery Co. v. Standard Elec. Co., 522 F.2d 986 (10th Cir.1975) (applying Colorado law); Hangzhou Silk Import and Export Corp. v. P.C.B. Intern. Industries, Inc., 2002 WL 2031591, 48 UCC2d 1367 (S.D.N.Y.2002) (applying New York law).

Pennsylvania overruled its precedents which prohibited a plaintiff from claim-

the legal principle of certainty in the plaintiff's case is indivisible from factual questions about the amount and probity of plaintiff's evidence, it is difficult to make sensible and useful generalizations about that principle. Often cases cited under the certainty rubric could be as easily explained by saying that the "plaintiff merely failed to prove damages" or "failed to prove plaintiff's case" or "failed to prove causation." So stated, the principle is reduced to a homily and that may be what it is.

f. Mitigation

Section 2–715(2)(a) explicitly imposes a third restriction on the recovery of consequential damages: There can be recovery only for losses "which could not reasonably be prevented by cover or otherwise." In what circumstances should a court find that the loss could have been prevented? In Columbia Novelty Co. v. Leslie Dawn, Inc.,[48] the seller brought an action for the price of goods delivered and used by the buyer-manufacturer. The buyer counterclaimed for consequential damages caused by the defective goods. The court, in a terse opinion, affirmed a dismissal of the counterclaim, commenting:

> [I]t was undisputed that the defendant, an experienced manufacturer, knew of the defect but used the goods and took a chance that its customers would not complain. No recovery may be had for damages which could reasonably have been prevented * * *.[49]

The mitigation principle has also been applied in the consumer context. For example, when a consumer used a color television set and left it plugged in all night despite the fact that it had twice previously given off sparks and smoke and that its "instant-on" device had previously turned the set on spontaneously, the consumer could not hold the television dealer for $62,000 worth of damages caused when the television caught fire and burned the consumer's house down.[50]

More difficult cases arise. For example, in Bevard v. Howat Concrete Co.,[51] preliminary tests by the buyer indicated that purchased concrete might be too weak, but it was impossible to ascertain for certain whether the concrete was defective until

---

ing damage to good will in breach of warranty actions, stating "we believe that the rationale for precluding prospective profits under the rubric of 'too speculative' ignores the realities of the marketplace and the science of modern economics." See AM/PM Franchise Ass'n v. Atlantic Richfield Co., 526 Pa. 110, 584 A.2d 915, 14 UCC2d 11, 23 (1990).

48. 1969 WL 11074, 6 UCC 679 (N.Y.Sup.1969).

49. Id. at 679.

50. Erdman v. Johnson Bros. Radio & Television Co., 260 Md. 190, 271 A.2d 744, 8 UCC 656 (1970).

51. 433 F.2d 1202, 7 UCC 966 (D.C.Cir.1970).

twenty-eight days after its pouring. Under these circumstances, the District of Columbia Circuit Court of Appeals held that when the buyer immediately used the concrete, the buyer did not fail to take action that would reasonably have prevented loss. The buyer was entitled to recover consequential damages.[52]

To determine which damages could "reasonably be prevented by cover or otherwise" in the words of 2–715(2)(a), consider the Restatement (Second) of Contracts formulation of the rule contained in § 350:

Avoidability: Avoidability as a Limitation on Damages

(1) Except as stated in Subsection (2), damages are not recoverable for loss that the injured party could have avoided without undue risk, burden or humiliation.

(2) The injured party is not precluded from recovery by the rule stated in Subsection (1) to the extent that he has made reasonable but unsuccessful efforts to avoid loss.

The Restatement may be regarded as an articulation of the rules embodied in the adverb "reasonably" in 2–715. For example, the buyer in Larry Goad & Co. v. Lordstown Rubber Co.[53] successfully reduced the plaintiff's damages because of the plaintiff's failure to mitigate. In that case the buyer of a product for resale breached the contract by reselling the defective product. When the resale contract was cancelled, the buyer who canceled offered payment for the value of the work done, but the plaintiff refused it. The court reduced the plaintiff-buyer's award against the original seller by the amount of the payment plaintiff-buyer had refused from their buyer.

In Barry & Sewall Industrial Supply Co. v. Metal–Prep of Houston, Inc.,[54] the buyer of an infrared oven was not allowed to recover lost profits for the year during which the buyer chose not to replace a defective oven. This case reviews a number of limitations courts place upon plaintiffs who sit on their hands while damages accrue.

On the other hand, the buyer in Barnard v. Compugraphic Corp.[55] recovered their full claim despite the failure to mitigate. In that case the defendant argued that the buyer should have pur-

---

52. *Id.* at 1203, 7 UCC at 968–69; cf. Streeks, Inc. v. Diamond Hill Farms, Inc., 258 Neb. 581, 605 N.W.2d 110, 40 UCC2d 1024 (2000) (holding that the jury instruction on mitigation was warranted where seller presented evidence that buyer could nonetheless have sold potatoes grown from defective seed sooner at lower price, but failed to mitigate in this way).

53. 560 F.Supp. 583, 36 UCC 167 (E.D.Mo.1983).

54. 912 F.2d 252, 12 UCC2d 708 (8th Cir.1990).

55. 35 Wash.App. 414, 667 P.2d 117, 37 UCC 141 (1983).

chased a dual disk drive to duplicate the storage information recorded on the floppy disks. Buyer argued that the dual disk would not necessarily remedy the malfunction and moreover the purchase and installation of the additional part would have required them to waive their right to repair work and to a replacement machine. This case may be regarded as an application of the principle that the injured party need not undertake "undue risk or burden" in its effort to mitigate.

The second paragraph of § 350 of the Restatement is nicely illustrated by Waters v. Massey–Ferguson, Inc.[56] In that case the farmer had to hire the neighbors to plant their soybeans when the defective Massey–Ferguson tractor failed. Because of the delay, the crop yield was low and was not a fully effective mitigation. In recognition of the farmer's attempt to mitigate, the court awarded consequential damages to the farmer. One seeking to breathe more life into the words of 2–715(2) should consider not only section 350 of the Restatement, but also the comments, examples and cases that are cited in the Restatement to support § 350.

g. Injuries to Person or Property

The color television case also involves the second variety of consequential damages mentioned in 2–715(2). Paragraph (b) allows recovery for "injury to person or property proximately resulting from any breach of warranty." The issues raised by the term "proximately" are discussed in 11–8 *infra;* consequently, little needs to be said about this provision now. Note that an action brought under 2–715(2)(b) has one major advantage over actions brought under paragraph (a): paragraph (b) contains no foreseeability requirement. Thus, a seller is liable for injury to person or property even if the seller did not know of or have reason to know of the buyer's intended use.

h. Conclusion

To sum up what we have said about consequential damages, 2–715(2) codifies the more generous reading of Hadley v. Baxendale. Most of the courts have recognized that a seller is liable for all damages resulting from their breach if they arise from circumstances that the seller knew about or had reason to know about, even if the seller did not consciously assume the risk of such liability. The plaintiff can recover lost profits if the seller had reason to know at the time of contracting that if the seller breached the contract the plaintiff would be deprived of those profits. But

---

56.   775 F.2d 587, 41 UCC 1553 (4th Cir.1985). See also Federal Signal Corp. v. Safety Factors, Inc., 125 Wash.2d 413, 886 P.2d 172, 25 UCC2d 795 (1994) ("Reasonable but unsuccessful efforts to mitigate do not preclude an injured party from recovery.").

subsection (2) imposes two restrictions on the recovery of consequential damages in addition to the foreseeability requirement: they must be reasonably ascertainable, and the plaintiff cannot recover for losses it reasonably could have prevented. While damages for injuries to person and property may be recovered under 2–715(2)(b) even if they were not foreseeable, the requirement that injuries proximately result from a breach of warranty probably embraces the mitigation restriction.

Section 2–715(2) is remarkably brief in light of its impact; whether or not consequential damages are allowed can mean the difference between a fifty-cent and a million-dollar damages award. For example, if a defective fifty-cent bolt snaps, it may cause the deaths of thirty children riding a school bus or the break-down for several months of a giant generator needed to operate a factory.[57] The consequential damages provisions provide the only Code remedy that can compensate plaintiffs in these cases. Because of the brevity and significance of 2–715, it is important to remember that it draws on over a century of common law development, which began with *Hadley v. Baxendale.*

§ 11–5   Recovery of Economic Loss in Tort

In a classic law review article, Professor Marc Franklin foresaw the coming collision between warranty and contract on the one hand and the torts of strict liability, negligence, fraud and misrepresentation on the other. The collision has produced even more chaos and has had more significant reverberations than Professor Franklin anticipated.[1]

Clearly many warranty cases are also potential tort cases. When a defective product injures its purchaser or a third party, the purchaser will routinely have a warranty claim, and under the expanded versions of 2–318 a person in the purchaser's family or

---

57. In such circumstances a seller might argue that they should not be held liable for damages vastly disproportionate to the purchase price. The seller could find some support in pre-Code cases, which held that lost profits greatly out of proportion to the price paid may not be recovered. These cases reflect a somewhat inhospitable attitude toward the recovery of lost profits (see Farnsworth, Legal Remedies for Breach of Contract, 70 Colum.L.Rev. 1145, 1206–09 (1970)), and they do not seem to be based on a decision that the greatly disproportionate damages were not foreseeable.

An argument can be made that such disproportionate damage awards should be limited by courts as unconscionable. See Kniffin, A Newly Identified Contract Unconscionability: Unconscionability of Remedy, 63 Notre Dame L. Rev. 247 (1988). This "unconscionability of remedy" argument is more persuasive when examined with the aid of the Restatement (Second) of Contracts § 351(3), which allows courts some discretion when limiting damages.

§ 11–5

1. Franklin, When Worlds Collide: Liability Theories and Disclaimers in Defective Product Cases, 18 Stan.L.Rev. 974 (1966).

even an unrelated person is likely to have a warranty claim. In modern law each of them is also likely to have a cause of action in negligence or strict tort for personal injury so suffered. When the damages are not personal injury, but for damage to property, or for economic losses not associated with an "accident," plaintiffs' standard cause of action is in warranty or contract and they will have more trouble stating a cause of action in strict tort or negligence. However, even when they are shut out of strict tort or negligence, plaintiffs can sometimes state a tort cause of action for fraud or negligent misrepresentation—causes of actions that look, smell and sound like express warranty.

The overlap of warranty, on the one hand, and tort on the other, has brought all the problems Professor Franklin anticipated and more. As courts expanded the idea of torts throughout the decades after World War II, this conflict has become more aggravated and the difficulties in unsnarling contract from tort more intractable despite valiant efforts in the tort Restatements, Second and Third.

Consider why it might be in the interest of a particular plaintiff to state a cause of action in warranty or in tort. First is the statute of limitations. Section 2–725 has a four year statute—longer than most tort statutes—but the statute commences to run from the time of sale. On the other hand, tort statutes typically run from the time of discovery. Depending, therefore, on the time of discovery, Article 2 or alternatively the state statute on tort may be more favorable to the plaintiff. Second are the defenses available to a defendant who is sued in warranty. Among these might be a disclaimer, a limitation of remedies, plaintiff's failure to give notice, lack of privity or other defenses based upon the knowledge of the plaintiff or plaintiff's contributory behavior. Some but not all of those defenses exist under other rubrics in tort law, but they tend to have less bite in tort. To escape from many of the contract defenses was one of Professor Prosser's justifications for the expansion of tort; the very idea of tort expansion was to protect the plaintiff from being cast out of court because of disclaimer, lack of privity, or because of other "contract" defenses.

According to our ad hoc and unscientific observation, tort liability seemed to enjoy almost unrestricted growth in the appellate courts between 1950 and 1980. This growth was led by academics such as Professor Prosser who wrote with approval in The Fall of the Citadel.[2] Only from later empirical studies[3] and with the rise of the law and economics school, did it become clear that

---

2.   50 Minn.L.Rev. 791 (1966).

3.   See, e.g., A. Conard, J. Morgan, R. Pratt, Jr., C. Voltz, and R. Bombaugh,

Automobile Accident Costs and Payments (1964).

unchecked growth of tort liability carried substantial costs—costs that might outweigh the benefits.

One way the courts have attempted to draw a line between tort and warranty is to bar recovery in tort for "economic loss". In some states this now bourgeoning common law doctrine has achieved the status of the "economic loss doctrine", meaning that once loss is defined as "economic" it cannot be recovered at least in negligence or strict tort and perhaps not in fraud or misrepresentation.[4] Some losses (i.e., lost profits, loss of good will and the like) are indisputably economic losses. Others (i.e., loss of life and personal injury) clearly are not economic losses at least as the term is used here. Whether injury to the particular property sold or injury to other property with or without suddenness is economic loss has been a matter of dispute in the courts.

Perhaps out of recognition of the costs and inefficiencies of the tort system, courts seem to have grown more willing than before to label loss as economic, and thus not recoverable in tort. An example is the recognition of the economic loss doctrine as a limitation on tort recovery by the New Jersey Supreme Court in Spring Motors Distributors, Inc. v. Ford Motor Co.[5] Notorious for *Henningsen*[6] and *Karagheusian*,[7] we would have labelled that court as the plaintiff's Valhalla before *Spring Motors*. In the last decade, more courts have seemed to recognize injury to property that arose out of a defect in goods as "economic" even in circumstances in which the culminating event might have been described as an "accident."

Many of these cases rely upon the Supreme Court case, East River Steamship Corp. v. Transamerica Delaval, Inc.[8] In a setting analogous to Article 2, the Supreme Court there denied economic

4. See generally, Silverstein, On Recovery in Tort for Pure Economic Loss, 32 U.Mich. J. L. Ref. 403 (1999).

5. 98 N.J. 555, 489 A.2d 660, 40 UCC 1184 (1985). See also, Cyberco Holdings v. American Express Travel Related Services Corp., 2002 WL 31324028, 48 UCC2d 1324 (S.D.N.Y. 2002); Full Faith Church of Lone West, Inc. v. Hoover Treated Wood Products, Inc., 224 F.Supp.2d 1285, 48 UCC2d 1331 (D. Kan. 2002); Higgenbotham v. Dryvit Systems, Inc., 2003 WL 1528483, 50 UCC2d 128 (M.D.N.C. 2003); Grynberg v. Questar Pipeline Co., 70 P.3d 1, 50 UCC2d 171 (Utah 2003); Superior Kitchen Designs, Inc. v. Valspar Industries (U.S.A.), Inc., 263 F.Supp.2d 140, 50 UCC2d 748 (D. Mass. 2003); Ramapery v. Novastis Consumer Health, Inc., 867 So.2d 1079, 2003 WL 21246560, 51 UCC2d 117 (Ala. 2003); Holden Farms,

Inc. v. Hog Slat, Inc., 347 F.3d 1055, 51 UCC2d 986 (8th Cir. 2003).

See, however, State of Hawaii by Bronster v. United States Steel Corp., 82 Hawai'i 32, 919 P.2d 294, 32 UCC2d 118 (1996); Mainline Tractor & Equip. Co., Inc. v. Nutrite Corp., 937 F.Supp. 1095, 32 UCC2d 763 (D. Vt. 1996); Lim Enterprises v. Sears Roebuck & Co., 912 F.Supp. 478, 31 UCC2d 773 (D. Kan. 1996); Republic Ins. Co. v. Broan Mfg. Co., Inc., 960 F.Supp. 1247, 34 UCC2d 964 (E.D. Mich 1997).

6. Henningsen v. Bloomfield Motors, Inc., 32 N.J. 358, 161 A.2d 69 (1960).

7. Santor v. A & M Karagheusian, Inc., 44 N.J. 52, 207 A.2d 305, 2 UCC 599 (1965).

8. 752 F.2d 903 (3d Cir.1985), aff'd, 476 U.S. 858, 106 S.Ct. 2295, 90 L.Ed.2d 865, 1 UCC2d 609 (1986).

loss recovery to a plaintiff who failed to prove a warranty claim. Representative of the cases that have followed *East River* is Ark-wright–Boston Manufacturers Mutual Insurance Co. v. Westinghouse Electric Corp.[9] The case arose out of a broken blade in an electric turbine. When the blade broke it caused extensive damage to the remainder of the turbine and the buyer suffered more than $800,000 in damages. The plaintiff (an insurance company subrogated to the buyer's claim) sued Westinghouse in warranty and in tort. The Court of Appeals affirmed a summary judgment for the defendant.

Apparently the failure was caused by a row of turbine blades running near their resonance point. This problem had arisen in other turbines and Westinghouse had disclosed it to El Paso Electric, who intended to replace the fourth row of blades at the turbine's next scheduled maintenance outage. Unfortunately the accident occurred before that replacement.

Despite the plaintiff's argument that the loss should not be considered economic because it was "sudden and catastrophic," the court found that the loss was economic and could not be recovered in a tort action. Westinghouse had expressly warranted the turbine as "free from defects and faults in workmanship and material," but provided that the "warranty shall terminate 12 months [after acceptance] or 21 months after shipment, whichever is earliest." Pointing out that the one-year limitation was common in the industry and that the buyer, El Paso, knew of it, the court rejected the argument that the limitation was unconscionable or that it failed of its essential purpose. Realizing that the section was in fact a proper allocation of risk, El Paso purchased insurance. The court found that the time limitation was simply a mode of allocating risk and not therefore necessarily a limitation of remedy at all. Reading the entire document, disclaimers and other terms, the court concluded that the other statements alleged to be warranties in the various documents that passed between the parties were not warranties.[10]

In general we indorse the idea that these losses should not be recovered in tort. For tort to intrude willy nilly into the system of liability that has been quite carefully constructed in Part 3 of Article 2 is to upset that balance. Tort permits recoveries in

---

9. 844 F.2d 1174, 6 UCC2d 73 (5th Cir.1988).

10. Accord, Public Service Co. v. Westinghouse Elec. Corp., 685 F.Supp. 1281, 7 UCC2d 1422 (D.N.H.1988). For other cases denying economic loss in tort, see Cyberco Holdings v. American Express Travel Related Services Corp., 2002 WL 31324028, 48 UCC2d 1324 (S.D.N.Y. 2002); Quest Diagnostics, Inc. v. MCI WorldCom, Inc., 254 Mich.App. 372, 656 N.W.2d 858, 49 UCC2d 469 (2002); Rampey v. Novartis Consumer Health Inc., 867 So.2d 1079, 2003 WL 21246560, 51 UCC2d 117 (Ala. 2003); Holden Farms, Inc. v. Hog Slat, 347 F.3d 1055, 51 UCC2d 986 (8th Cir. 2003).

circumstances where the legislature—by indorsing disclaimers, particular statutes of limitations, rules on privity, and lack of notice—has concluded that none should be permitted. We accept the economic loss doctrine as a crude proxy for the dividing line between what is tort and what is not. It awaits the legislatures and the courts of the 21st century to make a more refined and careful division.

Putting aside injury to third parties that arises out of conventional tortious behavior and ignoring personal injury to the buyer, we see no reason why all other liability arising out of defective goods ought not be under Article 2. By hypothesis the parties to these suits negotiate with one another. If the buyer does not protect its own interest adequately, adequate backup protection is given by Article 2 doctrines such as unconscionability in 2–302, restriction of disclaimers under 2–316, and limitation on disclaimer of remedy under 2–719. Courts should be particularly skeptical of business plaintiffs who—having negotiated an elaborate contract or having signed a form when they wish they had not—claim to have a right in tort whether the tort theory is negligent misrepresentation, strict tort, or negligence.

Chapter 12

DEFENSES TO WARRANTY ACTIONS

Analysis

§ 12–1 Introduction

In this chapter we examine four leftover parts of warranty theory that fit nowhere else. They are privity, plaintiff's misbehavior,—e.g., contributory negligence and assumption of the risk, statute of limitations and plaintiff's failure to give timely notice of a broken warranty. Unfortunately much of the law on these issues is ad hoc and diffuse, especially as regards contributory negligence and plaintiff's failure to give notice. We do not canvas the cases. In the pages to follow we highlight pitfalls and, where possible, offer answers. For the most part the legal concepts that we discuss in this chapter are not precise or cut and dried. Inevitably these issues depend more on actions than on written agreement, more on fact than law. We will try to identify relevant factors.

Before turning to the substance of the defenses to be considered here, we first consider which party has the burden of pleading and the burden of going forward with the evidence on each defense. In most jurisdictions, the defendant has the burden of pleading and

630

going forward with evidence on the defenses of contributory negligence, assumption of the risk, and the statute of limitations.[1] The courts generally characterize these as affirmative defenses.[2]

On the other hand, courts generally hold that the plaintiff has the burden of pleading and going forward with proof on the issues of privity and notice. That is, plaintiff's complaint is demurrable if it fails to allege privity or notice. In most cases the placing of the burden will have little effect upon the outcome of the suit, but in some it will be crucial. For example, if a court were to hold that a corporate defendant may assert the notice defense only by proving that none of its agents ever received notice, in practical effect the notice defense would become unavailable to a large corporate defendant.

§ 12–2   Lack of Privity as a Defense to a Warranty Cause of Action

It may be impossible to write briefly but not superficially about privity. Then, too, the subject itself may be crumbling away. We will begin with some remarks on usage. Parties who have contracted with each other are said to be "in privity." Those who have not contracted are not in privity. There are two basic kinds of "non-privity" plaintiffs. The "vertical" non-privity plaintiff is a buyer within the distributive chain who did not buy directly from the defendant. For example, a man who buys a lathe from a local hardware store and then later sues the manufacturer is a "vertical" non-privity plaintiff. The "horizontal" non-privity plaintiff is not a buyer within the distributive chain but one who consumes or uses or is affected by the goods. For example, a woman poisoned by a bottle of beer that her husband purchased from a local grocer is a horizontal non-privity plaintiff. So, too, is a son who is injured by the new lawnmower his father bought, and the employee hurt by equipment purchased by her employer, and so on.

The 1962 version of 2–318 took no position on the rights of a vertical non-privity plaintiff.[1] That section, which is now Alterna-

§ 12–1

1. See F. James and G. Hazard, Jr., Civil Procedure, 195–201 (4th ed.1992).

2. *Id.* at 198–201. The statute of limitations is called an affirmative defense in the Federal Rules of Civil Procedure (Fed.R.Civ.P. 8(c)) and in the procedural law of most states. The Federal Rules nevertheless permit a party to raise the statute of limitations by a motion to dismiss for failure to state a claim where the complaint shows the statute to have run. See Wilburn v. Pepsi–Cola Bottling Co., 492 F.2d 1288 (8th Cir.1974); F.

James and G. Hazard, Jr., *supra* note 1 at 200. Some states, however, do not permit a defendant to assert the statute of limitations by demurrer.

§ 12–2

1. See § 2–318, Comment 3. On privity, see generally Special Project, Article Two Warranties in Commercial Transactions: An Update, 72 Cornell L.Rev. 1159, 1310–17 (1987); Clifford, Express Warranty Liability of Remote Sellers, 75 Wash. U.L.Q. 413 (1997). On who is a buyer, see Guy Trucking, Inc. v. Domer,

tive A of the 1972 (and 1978) Official Text of the Code, did extend a seller's warranty to "any natural person who is in the family or household of his buyer or who is a guest in his home" who suffers personal injury provided such person could reasonably be expected to use, consume, or be affected by the goods. As we note in section 12–3 *infra*, Alternatives B and C and various nonstandard versions of 2–318 affect the vertical as well as the horizontal privity issue.

Today, courts are not yet fully agreed on whether the Code or judge-made doctrines of strict liability control the rights of non-privity plaintiffs. Many courts seem more willing to allow recovery to non-privity plaintiffs when they characterize their cause of action as one in tort than when they characterize it as one in warranty. The most thorough judicial analyses of the warranty vs. tort question still appear in the celebrated California case, Seely v. White Motor Co.,[2] and in the less celebrated but more informative Oregon case, State ex rel. Western Seed Production Corp. v. Campbell.[3] Justice Traynor, who wrote for the majority in *Seely*, had previously held that a remote purchaser could sue the manufacturer of a lathe which caused the purchaser to suffer personal injury.[4] In *Seely*, a purchaser of a truck sued the manufacturer, White Motor, to recover that part of the price he had paid, his lost profits, and certain damages sustained in an accident involving the truck. The trial court denied the plaintiff any damages arising out of the accident (since he failed to prove causation), but ordered the defendant to return that part of the price the plaintiff had paid and awarded him more than $9,000 in lost profits. The California Supreme Court upheld the lower court, and Justices Traynor and Peters offered lengthy dicta on the rights of non-privity plaintiffs in warranty and in strict tort. Justice Traynor stated that a remote purchaser should not recover economic loss (here, lost profits) in strict tort, for no seller undertakes that his goods will meet *all* needs of *all* of his potential purchasers and sub-purchasers. It appears that Justice Traynor would also deny relief to a remote purchaser seeking similar recovery on an implied warranty theory.[5] Justice Peters, concurring and dissenting in *Seely*, thought Justice Traynor was unduly concerned that strict tort might authorize unfair consequential damages against remote sellers. According to Justice Peters, remote sellers are liable in strict tort only for damages flowing from the failure of their goods to conform to the ordinary purposes for which such goods are used. Also, in Justice

2004 WL 1802983, 54 UCC2d 516 (Ohio App. 2004).

2. 63 Cal.2d 9, 45 Cal.Rptr. 17, 403 P.2d 145, 2 UCC 915 (1965).

3. 250 Or. 262, 442 P.2d 215, 5 UCC 584 (1968), cert. denied, 393 U.S. 1093, 89 S.Ct. 862, 21 L.Ed.2d 784 (1969).

4. Greenman v. Yuba Power Products, Inc., 59 Cal.2d 57, 27 Cal.Rptr. 697, 377 P.2d 897 (1963).

5. 63 Cal.2d at 16–18, 403 P.2d at 150–51.

Peters's world, any plaintiff who is an "ordinary consumer" can sue a remote seller in strict tort but other plaintiffs must resort to the Code.

A comparison of Justice Traynor's opinion with those in the Campbell case reveals complexity dear to the heart and mind of the law professor. In *Campbell* Justice Goodwin held that "[w]here the purchaser of an unmerchantable product suffers only loss of profits, his remedy for the breach of warranty is against his immediate seller unless he can predicate liability upon some fault on the part of a remote seller."[6] Put another way, sellers have liability to remote buyers only for negligence and not for implied warranty.[7] Justice O'Connell, a dissenter in *Campbell*, argued that implied warranty liability runs to remote buyers even when the breach of that warranty causes a loss of profits. In *Seely* and *Campbell* we have articulate spokesmen for at least three different positions, and possibly four. Presumably all dispense with privity when the plaintiff is a consumer who has suffered a personal injury or property damage. Justice O'Connell dispenses with privity in nearly all circumstances, but Justice Goodwin and possibly Justice Traynor would require that a plaintiff who seeks lost profits always be in privity with his or her defendant. Justice Peters would not require "ordinary consumer" plaintiffs to be in privity. In our efforts to summarize the arguments in these cases, we have doubtless overgeneralized somewhat, but the point should be clear: privity cases can be complex and confusing.

The foregoing cases also illustrate some ways in which it is possible to divide fact patterns into manageable packages. A division into five groupings is consistent with the cases and should be helpful to those who must predict outcomes for their clients. The first four classifications are by type of injury:

(1) Personal injury,

(2) Property damage,

(3) Direct economic loss (e.g., loss of bargain), and

(4) Consequential economic loss (e.g., loss of profits).

Our fifth classification cuts across the first four, and involves a *plaintiff suing on an express warranty.*

§ 12–3　Privity—Personal Injury

Cases in which the plaintiff suffers personal injury are largely beyond the scope of this work. However, these cases are occasional-

---

6. 250 Or. at 268, 442 P.2d at 218.

7. Justice O'Connell's dissent in *Campbell* points out that the majority's reasoning would also require privity for express warranties (since privity is nec- essary for "consensual" transactions and such consent is a "matter for bargaining" and necessary to impose contractual liability). *Id.* at 279, 442 P.2d at 224.

ly tried as warranty actions, and they intersect with the Code in two ways. First, courts have evolved much of the non-privity case law in these cases, and courts sometimes cite them in cases in which a non-privity plaintiff seeks damages for other kinds of injuries. Second, although 2–318 in its 1962 form (now Alternative A) had little impact on privity doctrine in personal injury cases, Code Alternatives B and C can have substantial impact.

In most states non-privity personal injury claims can be brought under the rubric of strict tort liability, a liability that finds its most authoritative statement in section 402A of the Restatement (Second) Torts, and its successor. That section of the Restatement gives a cause of action to the "ultimate user or consumer," and applies even though "the user or consumer has not bought the product from or entered into any contractual relations with the seller" (402A(2)(b)). The Reporter states in a comment that the American Law Institute does not express any opinion as to whether 402A applies to persons other than users or consumers.[1] Under 402A, therefore, lack of privity is no defense to a cause of action in strict tort where the plaintiff is a user or consumer. Comments to 402A and cases decided on strict tort theory expand the user and consumer classes greatly. For example, Comment *l* to section 402A states that the class of consumers may include "the housewife who contracts tularemia while cooking rabbits for her husband * * * also the husband who is opening a bottle of beer for his wife to drink."

Are there any cases where a non-privity plaintiff would be denied recovery because he is not an "ultimate consumer or user"? Writing in 1965, the draftsmen of 402A suggested some possibilities in Comment *o*: "[c]asual bystanders * * * employees of the retailer, or a passer-by injured by an exploding bottle, or a pedestrian hit by an automobile * * *." Comment *o* is now forty years old, however, and a number of courts have gone far beyond it and allowed parties to recover who are not "consumers or users."

Personal injury plaintiffs in most jurisdictions will thus seek recovery on a theory of strict tort liability under 402A, under the local tort variant of 402A, or under the successor to 402A (see 10–12 *supra*). Whatever its title. If a jurisdiction has not adopted, or later abandons, strict tort liability however, a personal injury plaintiff must look to the Code.[2] The 1962 version of 2–318, entitled "Third Party Beneficiaries of Warranties Express or Implied," read as follows:

§ 12–3

1. Restatement (Second) of Torts § 402A, Comment *o* (1965). Compare, Restatement (Third) of Torts: Products Liability §§ 1–2 (1998).

2. See Swartz v. General Motors Corp., 375 Mass. 628, 378 N.E.2d 61, 24 UCC 1161 (1978).

A seller's warranty whether express or implied extends to any natural person who is in the family or household of his buyer or who is a guest in his home if it is reasonable to expect that such person may use, consume or be affected by the goods and who is injured in person by breach of the warranty. A seller may not exclude or limit the operation of this section.

This section, now Alternative A of the 1972 Official Text of the Code, is law in most states,[3] and extends warranty liability *horizontally* to natural persons in the family or household of the buyer and to his guests, but only where it is "reasonable to expect that such persons may use, consume or be affected by the goods." Would this section (Alternative A) be of any value to a *vertical* non-privity buyer who suffered personal injury? Comment 3 to 2–318 says that Alternative A is silent on the issue of vertical non-privity and is not intended to inhibit case law growth allowing such plaintiffs to recover on a warranty theory. Thus, whether a vertical non-privity plaintiff can recover for personal injuries depends on how far the case law has developed outside Alternative A to permit such recovery on a Code warranty theory.[4] Some jurisdictions do have case law that permits such recovery.[5] Note that rights so premised may still be less attractive to a plaintiff than rights based on strict tort, for recovery under a Code warranty theory may be subject to defenses which do not attend a strict tort theory.

3. As of July 2006, the following jurisdictions had adopted Alternative A or a similar provision: Alaska, Arizona, Arkansas, Connecticut, District of Columbia, Florida (extends to employees), Georgia, Idaho, Illinois, Indiana, Kentucky, Maryland, Michigan, Mississippi, Missouri, Montana, Nebraska, Nevada, New Jersey, New Mexico, North Carolina, Ohio, Oklahoma, Oregon, Pennsylvania, Tennessee, Washington, West Virginia, and Wisconsin.

4. Comment 3 to 2–318 reads in part: "The first alternative [i.e., Alternative A] expressly includes as beneficiaries within its provisions the family, household and guests of the purchaser. Beyond this, the section * * * is neutral and is not intended to enlarge or restrict the developing case law on whether the seller's warranties, given to his buyer who resells, extend to other persons in the distributive chain." Some cases do not enlarge here. See e.g., Barnett v. Leiserv, Inc., 968 F.Supp. 690, 34 UCC2d 972 (N.D. Ga. 1997). See also Bryant v. Hoffmann–La Roche, Inc., 262 Ga.App. 401, 585 S.E.2d 723, 51 UCC2d 422 (2003).

5. See, e.g., Berry v. G.D. Searle & Co., 56 Ill.2d 548, 309 N.E.2d 550, 14 UCC 346 (1974) (Illinois law); Reid v. Volkswagen of America, Inc., 512 F.2d 1294, 16 UCC 743 (6th Cir.1975) (Michigan law); Reed v. City of Chicago, 263 F.Supp.2d 1123, 50 UCC2d 146 (N.D.Ill. 2003) (under Alternative A of 2–318, privity is no longer an absolute requirement, and the list of privity exceptions here is not exhaustive; paper gowns were intended for potentially suicidal detainees, and therefore a beneficiary of a warranty made by the manufacturer of the gowns would necessarily be a detainee, and the safety of such detainee was necessarily part of bargain between manufacturer and buyer; therefore, privity was not required). The court admits that it expands Berry v. G.D. Searle & Co., 56 Ill.2d 548, 309 N.E.2d 550, 14 UCC 346 (1974); K–Tel International, Inc. v. Tristar Products, Inc., 2004 WL 212840, 52 UCC2d 654 (D. Minn. 2004). Compare Frank v. Edward Hines Lumber Co., 327 Ill.App.3d 113, 260 Ill.Dec. 701, 761 N.E.2d 1257, 46 UCC2d 419 (2001).

Either on a strict tort or warranty theory, many courts have gone well beyond the original version of 2–318 (Alternative A) in permitting horizontal (and vertical) non-privity plaintiffs to recover.[6] Moreover, 2–318 was amended in 1966 to include Alternatives B and C, and the minority of states that have adopted either of these have carried developments even further. The two Alternatives provide:

Alternative B

A seller's warranty whether express or implied extends to any natural person who may reasonably be expected to use, consume or be affected by the goods and who is injured in person by breach of the warranty. A seller may not exclude or limit the operation of this section.

Alternative C

A seller's warranty whether express or implied extends to any person who may reasonably be expected to use, consume or be affected by the goods and who is injured by breach of the warranty. A seller may not exclude or limit the operation of this section with respect to injury to the person of an individual to whom the warranty extends.

Eight states have adopted Alternative B[7] and at least eight have adopted Alternative C[8] or a similar provision. Seven other states have enacted their own expansive provisions.[9] Under Alternatives B and C, courts may expand liability even beyond that contemplated by 402A or its successor (see 10–12 *supra*). Section 402A provides a cause of action to the ultimate user or consumer

---

6. Some courts have taken Comment 3 to 2–318 to be a license to exceed the limits of Alternative A's language on *horizontal* privity, and to provide a cause of action to parties other than those specifically mentioned.

7. As of July 2006, Alabama, Colorado, Delaware, Kansas, South Carolina, South Dakota, Vermont and Wyoming had enacted Alternative B to § 2–318 or a similar provision.

8. As of July 2006, Hawaii, Iowa, Minnesota, North Dakota, Utah, and the Virgin Islands had enacted Alternative C to § 2–318 or a similar provision.

9. Maine, Massachusetts, New Hampshire, and Virginia once enacted expansive provisions similar to Alternative C that *expressly* abolished the *vertical* privity requirement, without regard to the nature of the plaintiff's injury. Tennessee enacted a provision similar to Alternative A which abolished the privi-

ty requirement in actions for personal injury and property damage. See, Tenn. Code Ann. § 29–34–104. Mississippi enacted Alternative A but has also enacted a statute abolishing any privity requirement in actions for personal injury, property damage, or economic loss. See, Miss.Code Ann. § 11–7–20. Texas enacted a statute which left the issue of privity to the courts; California omitted § 2–318 altogether; and Louisiana has not yet adopted Article 2 of the UCC. New York's section provides: "A seller's warranty whether express or implied extends to any natural person it if is reasonable to expect that such person may use, consume, or be affected by the goods and who is injured in person by breach of the warranty. A seller may not exclude or limit the operation of this section."

for physical harm caused to the user or consumer, or to his or her property by a defective product. Alternatives B and C, however, extend a seller's warranty not only to users and consumers, but also to any party "who may reasonably be expected to * * * be affected * * * by the goods * * *." Courts in states that have adopted Alternative B or C are therefore free to extend a seller's warranty beyond the ultimate user or consumer of the product. Moreover, Alternative C, unlike 402A does not expressly limit recovery to damages for physical harm to person or property. A few courts have even read Alternative C to abolish the requirement of *vertical* privity when a party seeks recovery for merely economic loss, such as loss of bargain. Thus, lawyers should consider the Code as well as strict tort or negligence when injury or damages result from a defective product.

But a plaintiff's lawyer must remember that in pursuing recovery on a Code warranty theory under Alternatives B or C, the lawyer may run into Code defenses that do not confront a plaintiff seeking recovery under 402A, its successor, or some other version of strict liability in tort.

§ 12–4   Privity—Property Damage

In this discussion we use the terms "property damage" on the one hand and "economic loss" on the other to describe different kinds of damages a plaintiff may suffer. An action brought to recover damages for inadequate value, costs of repair, and replacement of defective goods or consequent loss of profits is one for "economic loss." Property damage, on the other hand, is the Restatement's "physical harm * * * to [user's] property."[1] If one purchases a new truck and finds that the radiator has to be replaced at a cost of $300, one would suffer an economic loss of at least $300 rather than property damage. If, in addition, one should lose $1,000 in profits while one's truck was out of commission, that too would be an "economic" loss. Of course, borderline cases can arise that do not fit comfortably in either the property damage or the economic loss category. Consider a car that throws a rod after a thousand miles of normal use. Is the loss property damage because the injury occurred suddenly? Or is the loss an economic one because the suit will be for replacement of the engine?

Many non-privity plaintiffs who today seek recovery for property damage now find themselves in much the same position as those who seek recovery for personal injury.[2] Although the cases which

§ 12–4

1. Restatement (Second) of Torts § 402A (1965). See also Restatement (Third) of Torts: Products Liability § 21 (1998) (discusses damage to property and recovery for economic loss).

2. W. Prosser & W. Page Keeton, Handbook of the Law of Torts, § 101, at 707–10 (5th Ed.1984). See, e.g., Dixie

first struck down the privity doctrine were personal injury cases, and although recovery in those cases was sometimes limited to harm from "intimate body products" (for instance, food and cosmetics), the distinction between property damage and personal injury has now largely disappeared in many states. As we have noted, 402A of the Restatement provides a cause of action for physical harm caused to the "ultimate user or consumer, *or to his property.*" (emphasis added). Alternatives A and B of Code section 2–318, however, retain the distinction between personal injury and property damage and remove the privity bar only when the plaintiff is "injured in person." Alternative C has no "in person" limitation.

§ 12–5   Privity—Direct Economic Loss

May a non-privity buyer recover for "direct economic loss" against a wholesaler or manufacturer up the distributive chain? We define that loss as damage flowing directly from insufficient product quality. Direct economic loss includes ordinary loss of bargain damages: under 2–714(2), the difference between the actual value of the goods accepted and the value they would have had if they had been as warranted. Courts will also frequently measure direct economic loss by the purchaser's cost of replacement or cost of repair. "Consequential economic loss," on the other hand, encompasses all economic harm a purchaser suffers beyond direct economic loss as defined above. Thus, consequential economic loss includes loss of profits resulting from failure of the goods to function as warranted, loss of goodwill and loss of business reputation. Because the policies relevant to limiting a non-privity purchaser's recovery for consequential economic loss do not similarly apply to recovery for direct economic loss, we will treat recovery for consequential economic loss separately in the next section.

The Code does not state whether a non-privity buyer may recover for direct economic loss. Because Alternatives A and B of 2–318 are limited to cases where the plaintiff is "injured in person," they do not *authorize* recovery for such loss. But neither do they *bar* a non-privity plaintiff from recovery against such a remote manufacturer for direct economic loss. Alternatives A and B expressly refer to certain individuals, including non-purchasers as beneficiaries of a seller's warranty. The Official Comment 3 to 2 318 explains, however, that "[b]eyond this, the section * * * is neutral and is not intended to enlarge or restrict the developing case law on whether the seller's warranties, given to his buyer who

McFadden et al. v. Dryvit Systems, Inc., 2004 WL 2278542, 54 UCC2d 934 (D.Or. 2004) (purchasers who fell within manufacturer's normal distribution chain could seek property damages from manufacturer based on implied warranty even though they were not in privity).

resells, extend to other persons in the distributive chain."[1] Thus, Alternatives A and B of 2–318 do not prevent a court from abolishing the *vertical* privity requirement even when a non-privity buyer seeks recovery for direct economic loss. Alternative C, moreover, does not include the "injured in person" language. But even Alternative C does not expressly authorize recovery for direct economic loss. Indeed, the notes of the Permanent Editorial Board suggest that the Code drafters may have intended Alternative C merely to extend as far as 402A of the *Restatement,* which abolishes the privity requirement only in cases of property damage and personal injury.[2]

Given the Code's failure to address the direct economic loss issue, we may look to the courts. As we explain in section 12–7 *infra,* the law permits a non-privity buyer to recover for direct economic loss if the remote seller has breached an *express* warranty. Where the buyer cannot show reliance on express representations by the remote seller, however, the case law is in conflict. Many courts still hold that absent that reliance, a non-privity buyer cannot recover for direct economic loss on either an express or implied warranty theory. But a number of courts now allow non-privity plaintiffs to recover for direct (and even consequential) economic loss.

A minority of courts, however, permits "warranty" recovery for direct economic loss by non-privity buyers who are ordinary *consumers.* Recall that 402A authorizes recovery in strict tort only for personal injury and property damage. Most of the courts allowing non-privity consumers to recover for direct economic loss limit the consumer purchaser to an action based on a Code warranty. Moreover, as several courts have recognized, remote manufacturers should have the opportunity to avail themselves of the Code's disclaimer (2–316), remedy modification or limitation (2–719), and notice (2–607) protections when a non-privity purchaser seeks recovery only for direct economic loss.

Whatever the legal theory, most courts allowing recovery rely on one of two rationales to justify allowing non-privity consumers to recover for direct economic loss. First, some reason that manufacturers induce consumers to purchase their products by representations of quality. Merely putting the product on the market is to represent to all who might ultimately buy the product that it is at

---

§ 12–5

1. See § 2–318, Comment 3.

2. See Perm.Ed.Bd. UCC Report No. 3 at 14 (1966) for a discussion of the distinction between property damage and economic loss. See Falcon for Import and Trade Co. v. North Central Commodities, Inc., 2004 WL 224676, 52

UCC2d 896 (D.N.D. 2004) (commercial entity sustaining only economic damages not an "injured person" under Act C). See, however, Dixie McFadden v. Dryvit Systems, Inc., 2004 WL 2278542, 54 UCC2d 934 (D.Or.2004) (non-privity plaintiff in normal distribution chain could recover property damages).

least merchantable.[3] Second, some courts reason that even absent extensive advertising, manufacturers are the "real" sellers upon whom the consumers rely. The buyer's immediate dealer acts merely as a "conduit" between the manufacturer and the consumer purchaser. We are doubtful.

The easiest cases are those where a manufacturer's express warranty that is explicitly directed to the "end user" is included with the product-such as a computer. In those cases the buyer and the manufacturer intend legal consequences, and the law should honor those expectations by allowing the remote buyer to enforce the warranty.

A number of problems remain for courts that allow recovery to non-privity plaintiffs for direct economic loss. In our view, the remote seller's standard of responsibility (and, therefore, the appropriate measure of recovery) cannot be set solely in light of the terms of the transaction between the ultimate buyer and the immediate seller. In some cases it would plainly be unfair to hold the remote seller to the terms between the plaintiff and his seller. To cite an obvious case, assume that a remote seller who sells second hand goods to a dealer who passes them off as new to the plaintiff. The remote seller should not be held to have warranted the goods as new. Similarly, a manufacturer should not be held answerable for the difference between the *retail* price and the value of the goods delivered.

Another unresolved issue involves the *extent* to which a remote seller may employ warranty disclaimers and remedy limitations. Several courts that allow recovery to a non-privity consumer buyer for direct economic loss have indicated that such devices continue to be available to remote sellers.[4] The terms and conditions of their availability remain to be worked out. If the plaintiff is truly a third party beneficiary of the remote seller's promise, the plaintiff should get only what his own seller got from the remote seller.

§ 12–6   Privity—Consequential Economic Loss

Consequential economic loss includes loss of profits, loss of good will or business reputation, and other loss proximately resulting from a defective product beyond direct economic loss as defined in the preceding section (loss of bargain, cost of repair or replacement, and the like). Recall that the Code neither authorizes nor bars recovery by a non-privity purchaser for economic loss—whether consequential or direct. Many courts do not allow non-privity

---

3. See generally, Shapo, Representational Theory of Consumer Protection: Doctrine, Function and Legal Liability for Product Disappointment, 60 Va. L.Rev. 1109 (1974).

4. See, e.g., Morrow v. New Moon Homes, Inc., 548 P.2d 279, 285–86, 19 UCC 1, 10–11 (Alaska 1976); Nobility Homes, Inc. v. Shivers, 557 S.W.2d 77, 82, 22 UCC 621, 629 (Tex.1977).

consumer purchasers to recover for consequential economic loss. Even courts that allow these purchasers to recover for direct economic loss are in conflict on whether consequential loss may also be obtained.[1] Note that *consumer* buyers ordinarily do not suffer any consequential economic loss and only seek recovery for direct economic losses such as loss of bargain or costs of repair.[2]

We agree with the courts that have refused to allow recovery of consequential economic loss by remote buyers. Even if relevant policies justify non-privity consumers' recovery for direct economic loss, there can be no justification in the usual case for allowing non-privity consumer buyers to recover for consequential economic losses they sustain. Remote buyers may use a seller's goods for unknown purposes from which enormous losses might ensue. Since the remote seller cannot predict the purposes for which the goods will be used that seller faces unknown liability and may not be able to insure.[3] Insurers are hesitant to insure against risks they cannot measure.

Moreover, here more than in personal injury and property damage cases, it is appropriate to recognize the traditional rights of parties to make their own contract. If remote sellers wish to sell at a lower price and exclude liability for consequential economic loss to sub-purchasers, why should we deny them that right? Why should we design a system that forces a seller to bear the unforeseeable consequential economic losses of remote purchasers? Indeed, by forcing the buyer to bear such losses we may save costly law suits and even some economic losses against which buyers, knowing they have the responsibility, may protect themselves. In short, we believe that a buyer should pick its seller with care and recover any

§ 12–6

1. For some cases allowing recovery of consequential loss, see Groppel Co. v. United States Gypsum Co., 616 S.W.2d 49, 32 UCC 35 (Mo.App.1981) (subcontractor could recover against manufacturer of fireproofing material); Pulte Home Corp. v. Parex, Inc., 265 Va. 518, 579 S.E.2d 188, 50 UCC2d 766 (2003) (contractor's damages arising from its liability to homeowners created by its use of defective product of manufacturer were consequential, not direct; since contractor not in privity with manufacturer, it was not entitled to recover damages from manufacturer). See also, Beyond the Garden Gate, Inc. v. Northstar Freeze–Dry Mfg., Inc., 526 N.W.2d 305, 26 UCC2d 140 (Iowa 1995) (following White and Summers, the court concludes that a non-privity plaintiff can recover for breach of express warranty no more than direct economic loss damages; these are defined as difference between value of the goods as accepted and their value had they been as warranted; no recovery of lost profits or goodwill, i.e., no recovery of consequential damages is allowed).

2. See §§ 12–3 and 12–4.

3. Most products liability insurance policies do not cover economic loss. This means that not only are lost profits not covered but damage to insured's own products or work project is not covered either. The comprehensive general liability policies, as they are called, only include personal and property damage of others caused by insured's defective product. See Arnold, Products Liability Insurance, 25 Ins. Counsel J. 42, 44–46 (1958); Sorensen, Initial Investigation of Products Liability Claims, 1974 Ins.L.J. 255, 280–81.

economic loss from that seller and not from parties remote from the transaction. Put another way, we believe the user is often the "least cost avoider." By placing the loss on the users or by forcing them to bargain with their immediate sellers about the loss, we may minimize the total loss to society. If manufacturers are not the least cost risk avoiders, but must nevertheless bear the loss, we may cause them to spend more of society's resources than optimal to avoid the loss and may unnecessarily increase the cost of the commodity sold.

§ 12–7   Privity—Express Warranty

When the non-privity plaintiff's suit is not based upon 402A or its successor, or implied warranty, but upon the defendant's express representation made to the particular plaintiff in advertising or otherwise, courts generally hold that the plaintiff need not be in privity with the defendant. Usually courts characterize these cases as express warranty cases, though in some jurisdictions they are classed as misrepresentation cases.[1] The misrepresentation may come through the defendant's advertising, through labels attached to the product, or through brochures and literature about the product.[2] The plaintiff must be a party whom the defendant could expect to act upon the representation and must rely on it.[3] Of course, any plaintiff must also state the other elements of its cause of action.

Conceding that privity is dead, or nearly so, in tort, what remains in warranty?. We have hope that courts and legislatures may understand the costs of ever expanded liability. Where the manufacturer makes a direct warranty to a remote buyer (e.g., a warranty "in the box") the warranty should be enforced. In other cases (e.g., warranties by advertisement) the courts should tread cautiously.

§ 12–8   Defenses Based Upon Plaintiff's Contributory Behavior

Whether plaintiffs should be foreclosed from recovery because their own action or inaction or something peculiar to them contrib-

§ 12–7

1. See Cooper v. R.J. Reynolds Tobacco Co., 234 F.2d 170 (1st Cir.1956); Ford Motor Co. v. Lonon, 217 Tenn. 400, 398 S.W.2d 240 (1966).

2. See e.g., Greenman v. Yuba Power Products, Inc., 59 Cal.2d 57, 27 Cal. Rptr. 697, 377 P.2d 897 (1963); Whitaker v. Farmhand, Inc., 173 Mont. 345, 567 P.2d 916, 22 UCC 375 (1977).

3. Prosser, The Fall of the Citadel (Strict Liability to the Consumer), 50 Minn.L.Rev. 791, 837–38 (1966). But see Mainline Tractor & Equipment Co. v. Nutrite Corp., 937 F.Supp. 1095, 32 UCC2d 763 (D.Vt.1996) (plaintiff was allowed to proceed despite lack of evidence that plaintiff had relied on defendants representations). See also, Sebago, Inc. v. Beazer East, Inc., 18 F.Supp.2d 70, 37 UCC2d 963 (D. Mass. 1998).

uted to their injury is a question that wears many costumes. It appears in the clothing of comparative or contributory negligence, assumption of risk, and lack of proximate cause in the standard tort cases. In the vernacular of strict tort liability, it is likely to be called misuse, abnormal use, or hypersensitivity. In each case the question whether something about the plaintiff or the plaintiff's behavior should bar him or her from recovery may also be part of the larger, ultimate question whether the causal connection between the defendant's act and the plaintiff's injury is sufficiently close to justify liability. It seems to us that courts should view the plaintiff's behavior and any peculiarities only as factors that may sufficiently attenuate the causal connection between defendant's act and plaintiff's injury to bar recovery. Some courts steadfastly maintain that contributory negligence is no defense to a warranty cause of action or to a strict tort cause of action. Others state that contributory negligence is a defense to a warranty or strict tort cause of action. Some courts maintain that contributory negligence is no defense but hold that the defendant may parade the same misconduct of the plaintiff before the jury to show a lack of proximate cause.[1]

a. Assumption of Risk

The courts agree that the more specific form of contributory misconduct called "assumption of the risk" bars a plaintiff's recovery in either strict tort or warranty.[2] Predictably, one court's assumption of risk may be another's contributory negligence and vice versa. Because of this conflicting nomenclature, it is difficult to identify real differences among courts of different jurisdictions on these questions, and it is beyond the scope of our work to catalogue the cases. It suffices to say that the lawyer must review the relevant cases carefully. Conduct that should be offered to the court as contributory negligence in one jurisdiction may have to be presented as assumption of risk or absence of proximate cause in another. We limit our efforts to a summary of the relevant Restatement language and to a brief analysis of the pertinent Code language and comments.

Comment *g* of 402A of Restatement (Second) of Torts states the obvious, namely that "subsequent mishandling" which makes a product harmful or defective bars recovery against the seller. In a

---

§ 12–8

1. See, e.g., Imperial Die Casting Co. v. Covil Insulation Co., 264 S.C. 604, 609–10, 216 S.E.2d 532, 534, 17 UCC 728, 730–31 (1975); Ford Motor Co. v. Lee, 137 Ga.App. 486, 487, 224 S.E.2d 168, 170, 18 UCC 1184, 1185 (1976), aff'd in part, rev'd in part, 237 Ga. 554, 229 S.E.2d 379 (1976) ("In an action predicated on a breach of warranty, there is no defense per se of contributory negligence, but such defense presents a jury question as to whether the injuries resulted from the breach.").

2. See generally, Owen, Products Liability: User Misconduct Defenses, 52 S.C.L. Rev. 1–80 (2000). David G. Owen, Products Liability Law § 13.4 (2005).

similar vein Comment *h* warns that for injuries which result from abnormal handling (as where a beverage bottle is knocked against a radiator to remove the cap), or from abnormal preparation for use (as where too much salt is added to food), or from abnormal consumption (as where a child eats too much candy and falls ill), the seller is not liable. Likewise, Comment *i* states that goods harmful only if "over-consumed" are not unreasonably dangerous.[3] Comment *j* implies that the seller may reasonably assume that buyers will read directions and warnings on containers. Comment *n* states explicitly:

> [C]ontributory negligence of the plaintiff is not a defense when such negligence consists merely in a failure to discover the defect in the product, or to guard against the possibility of its existence. On the other hand the form of contributory negligence which consists in voluntarily and unreasonably proceeding to encounter a known danger, and commonly passes under the name of assumption of risk, is a defense under this Section as in other cases of strict liability. If the user or consumer discovers the defect and is aware of the danger, and nevertheless proceeds unreasonably to make use of the product and is injured by it, he is barred from recovery.

This distinction between "mere" contributory negligence (no defense) and assumption of risk (a defense) has been adopted by courts in warranty actions in addition to actions brought in strict tort.[4]

b. Proximate Cause

The Uniform Commercial Code includes only a few words about the effect of plaintiff's behavior on his right to recover in warranty. These appear in Comment 13 to 2–314, Comment 5 to 2–715, and in section 2–715(2). Section 2–715(2)(b) authorizes recovery for "injury to person or property proximately resulting from any breach of warranty." The crucial word is "proximately," a word that imports into the Code the many pre-Code warranty cases and the many tort cases on proximate cause which courts turn out in every jurisdiction of the United States every year. Comment 5 to 2–715 elaborates:

> Where the injury involved follows the use of goods without discovery of the defect causing the damage, the question of

---

3. Comment *i* of section 402A indicates that the seller will not be liable to the hypersensitive plaintiff. See also, on the successor to 402A, section 10–12 *supra*.

4. See, e.g., Broce–O'Dell Concrete Products, Inc. v. Mel Jarvis Constr. Co.,

6 Kan.App.2d 757, 634 P.2d 1142, 32 UCC 762 (1981) (contributory negligence is not a defense in an express warranty action but use of a product after discovery of a defect is a defense).

"proximate" cause turns on whether it was reasonable for the buyer to use the goods without such inspection as would have revealed the defects. If it was not reasonable for him to do so, or if he did in fact discover the defect prior to his use, the injury would not proximately result from the breach of warranty.

The drafters do not say whether they intended this comment as a definition, as an exclusive statement of the meaning of "proximately," or only as an illustration. In view of the traditional expansiveness of the word and the absence of any language in Comment 5 which purports to make it a definition we regard Comment 5 as only illustrative.[5]

Note that 2–715(2)(b) applies only to injury to persons and property and not to loss of bargain or loss of profits. In the Code scheme, loss of bargain can be recovered under 2–714(2) and loss of profits under 2–715(2)(a). One may ask, therefore, whether a plaintiff who seeks recovery only for loss of bargain or loss of profits must prove proximate causation. Comment 13 to 2–314 indicates that proximate causation is an element of proof at least in all implied warranty cases, whatever the relief sought. In pertinent part it reads as follows:

> In an action based on breach of warranty, it is of course necessary to show not only the existence of the warranty but the fact that the warranty was broken and that the breach of the warranty was the proximate cause of the loss sustained. In such an action an affirmative showing by the seller that the loss resulted from some action or event following his own delivery of the goods can operate as a defense.

The quoted comment is artfully vague about the kinds of conduct that may negate proximate cause. It does reiterate the illustrative case in the comments to 2–715 about a buyer's use of goods he knows to be defective. And certainly it also includes misuse and overuse by the plaintiff-buyer. The lawyer may resort to cases for further illustrations.

c. *Comparative Negligence*

By statute or case law many states have now adopted some form of comparative fault in traditional tort cases. Comparative fault principles have begun to seep from negligence actions into strict tort and, recently, into warranty actions.

Some have welcomed comparative fault as a way of eliminating the harshness of contributory negligence rules under which a plaintiff was turned out of court if any part of the fault was his.

---

5. Although Comments 5 and 13 to 2–314 suggest that a failure to inspect or to discover a defect will act as a bar, the courts have not always agreed.

Because so many personal injury decisions are the unexplained result of the jury process, it is dangerous to predict the consequences of changes in the law such as the adoption of comparative negligence rules. Moreover, the comparative negligence rules themselves differ from state to state. Under some rules the plaintiff's damage recovery is reduced in direct proportion to his or her fault. Thus, if the fact finder determines that the plaintiff was 40 percent at fault and defendant was 60 percent at fault and that the plaintiff's damages were $50,000, plaintiff will recover $30,000. On the same findings in a contributory negligence state, the plaintiff would receive nothing. To say that the plaintiff would receive nothing however, is to make certain assumptions about jury behavior that may not be accurate. In the first place, the jury in the contributory negligence state may turn a blind eye to plaintiff's contributory negligence in circumstances where the plaintiff's case was particularly appealing. On the other hand, in the comparative state, the jury might increase the $50,000 to a number that would grant the plaintiff the figure the jury thought proper after the percentage of fault had been applied to that number. The jury, therefore, is itself an immeasurable variable in the equation in almost all of these cases, and its presence makes it difficult to predict the consequences of adopting these rules.

The problem is complicated further. For example, in some states the plaintiff's recoveries are reduced in proportion to their fault but are barred entirely if their contributory negligence constitutes a certain percentage of the whole.[6] Thus, plaintiffs might recover no damages if their fault were equal to or greater than the defendants'.

How do and should these comparative fault principles apply in strict tort and applied warranty actions? To some extent the court's reaction to an argument for comparative fault in strict liability will depend upon the statute that has been enacted. If the legislature enacts a statute that provides "all products liability actions brought [for] personal injury or property damage" are covered by the comparative rules, presumably the legislature intended to include some warranty actions, and the courts have the responsibility to work comparative fault principles into personal injury, or property damage warranty actions. That was the conclusion of the Michigan Supreme Court applying such a statute in Karl v. Bryant Air Conditioning Co.[7] If, on the other hand, the statute provides only that comparative fault applies in "negligence actions," the courts would have no such responsibility to work comparative fault princi-

---

6. See e.g., Mass.General Laws c. 231, § 85 (1986).

7. 416 Mich. 558, 331 N.W.2d 456, 35 UCC 382 (1982). See also Fiske v. MacGregor, Div. of Brunswick, 464 A.2d 719, 36 UCC 1128 (R.I. 1983).

ples into other schemes. In Correia v. Firestone Tire & Rubber Co.,[8] the Massachusetts Supreme Court declined to apply a statute that spoke only of recovery of "damages for negligence."

In Signal Oil and Gas Co. v. Universal Oil Products,[9] the Texas Supreme Court imported comparative fault into warranty actions using "proximate cause" as the vessel. It relied on 2–715 and Comment 5 to 2–715 to produce what is essentially a comparative fault system. Under that case the rules would apply not merely to property damage and personal injury, but presumably to economic loss as well.

Ironically the use of comparative fault ideas sometimes seems to favor the plaintiff and sometimes the defendant. In the Michigan and Massachusetts cases, the defendants were arguing for the application of comparative fault as a way to reduce their liability. In those cases the conventional strict liability rule would have imposed the entire liability on the defendant and would have disregarded the substantial negligence of the plaintiffs. In *Karl v. Bryant Air Conditioning*, the jury found the plaintiff to be 95% at fault. If that fault were to be disregarded, the defendants would have been liable for the entire $52,000 damage claim.[10] If, on the other hand, comparative fault rules applied, defendants would have been liable for only $2,600. Compare that outcome to Sun Valley Airlines, Inc. v. Avco–Lycoming Corp.[11] There the plaintiff had "misused the aircraft in a manner unforeseeable to the manufacturers." Absent comparative fault, the plaintiff would have received nothing, even in strict liability. Because the court applied the comparative statute, it gave the plaintiff the chance of recovering damages equal to 10% of the injury upon a finding that manufacturers were 10% at fault.

In the long run, we suspect that ideas of comparative fault will inevitably be the rule and not the exception—at least in personal injury cases. It probably makes little sense to apply comparative fault to the negligence claim and fail to do that in a warranty or strict tort claim tried before the same jury, in the same courtroom simultaneously. Still, we have some doubt about the wisdom of applying comparative fault and particularly about the wisdom of extending it to conventional cases of economic loss.

We have two concerns. First, in general, we think it important that the system have the grit to put the loss on the least cost-risk avoider in the hope that all the rest of us do not pay the price for

8.   388 Mass. 342, 446 N.E.2d 1033 (1983). But see, Kennedy v. Sawyer, 228 Kan. 439, 618 P.2d 788 (1980).

9.   572 S.W.2d 320, 24 UCC 555 (Tex. 1978). See also Cipollone v. Liggett Group, Inc., 893 F.2d 541, 10 UCC2d 625 (3d Cir.1990) (comparative fault is available in an express warranty action).

10.   416 Mich. 558, 331 N.W.2d 456, 35 UCC 382 (1982) (answering certified questions of law from Sixth Circuit).

11.   411 F.Supp. 598 (D.Idaho 1976).

another's foolishness. To some extent, ideas of comparative fault may diminish that possibility by freeing the courts of the hard tasks of deciding who really is the least cost-risk avoider. Second, we are concerned that ideas of comparative fault may encourage lawsuits that should not be brought. These principles may improve the chances of a jury verdict even for those who do not deserve one.

But we confess that our views are based on no solid data, and we recognize the possibility that we might be quite wrong. Comparative fault is but a single input in a large and complicated "products liability" formula. The cases show that its use may produce completely contradictory results depending upon the other factors in the formula. It would be foolhardy for us to predict with assurance the outcomes under comparative fault schemes. Our society is far from agreement on the proper place of comparative fault in the strict liability sphere. Indeed, the cases suggest that the diversity may be increasing, not subsiding.

Plainly it is wrong to say that under doctrines of strict liability the defendant seller or manufacturer of a defective product is liable for all injuries caused by the product without regard to plaintiff's fault. What costume plaintiff's fault is to wear is a much more difficult question. For now the principal ones are proximate cause and assumption of risk. Comparative fault may become the costume of tomorrow.

§ 12–9   Statute of Limitations

Section 2–725 is the basic Article 2 statute of limitations. Subsection (1) provides that "[a]n action for breach of any contract for sale must be commenced within four years after the cause of action has accrued." Subsection (2) specifies that a cause of action for breach of warranty ordinarily accrues when "tender of delivery is made." The application of this statute presents no difficulty to the lawyer or the judge in most cases. Suits for damages for failure to pay or failure to tender accrue on the date that *payment* or *tender* is due.[1] Similarly uncomplicated is the usual business warranty case where the machine proved not to work properly and buyer sues the seller under 2–714 for the difference in value between the machine as warranted and the machine as delivered.

---

§ 12–9

1. See 4 A. Corbin, Contracts § 989 (1951). See generally, Garvin, Uncertainty and Error in the Law of Sales: the Article 2 Statute of Limitations, 83 Boston U. L. Rev. 345 (2003). Of course, the transaction must be a transaction in goods. See, e.g., DiIorio v. Structural Stone & Brick Co., Inc., 368 N.J.Super. 134, 845 A.2d 658, 53 UCC2d 249 (A.D. 2004) (only incidentally a transaction in goods, so not applicable). See also, Gannett v. Pettegrow, 2005 WL 217036, 55 UCC2d 936 (D. Me. 2005) (predominantly a contract for services).

Unless our buyer falls within the exception to the general rule of 2–725(2),[2] it must sue within four years after delivery of the machine.

Most of the interpretative difficulties in 2–725 arise out of the continuing friction between strict tort liability on the one hand and warranty liability under the Code on the other. The Code statute of limitations generally does not apply to strict tort cases, only to warranty cases. If the case is strict tort, the appropriate statute will be one dealing with tort claims. Tort statutes are typically two years or less in duration, but most tort statutes do not commence to run until the defect causes an injury, or in some cases, until the plaintiff has or should have discovered the injury. Depending upon the length of time between the sale and the injury, whether the injury is "latent," and the duration of the appropriate tort statute, a particular cause of action may be barred by 2–725 but not by the tort statute, or it may be barred by the tort statute but not by 2–725.

The courts, however, have not clarified when a cause of action should be classified as warranty rather than tort for purposes of the statute of limitations.[3] In New York, for example, the Court of Appeals squarely held in Mendel v. Pittsburgh Plate Glass Co.[4] that an action "arising from a breach of warranty," even if for personal injury, is governed by the contract rather than the tort statute of limitations. Yet confusion and conflicting decisions persist in New York and other states as to the applicable limitations period in products liability actions that are partly dependent on warranty but involve personal injury.[5]

2. The second sentence of § 2–725(2) provides:

A breach of warranty occurs when tender of delivery is made, except that where a warranty explicitly extends to future performance of the goods and discovery of the breach must await the time of such performance the cause of action accrues when the breach is or should have been discovered.

3. See the discussion in Annot., 20 A.L.R. 4th 915 (1983), Annot., 4 A.L.R.3d 821 (1965) and Annot., 37 A.L.R.2d 698 (1954) for an extensive compilation of cases on the choice of the applicable statute of limitations in warranty actions. See generally, Phillips, An Analysis of Proposed Reform of Products Liability Statutes of Limitations, 56 N.C.L.Rev. 663 (1978); Note, When the Product Ticks: Products Liability and Statutes of Limitations, 11 Ind.L.Rev. 693, 705–726 (1978).

4. 25 N.Y.2d 340, 305 N.Y.S.2d 490, 253 N.E.2d 207 (1969).

5. See, e.g., DeCrosta v. A. Reynolds Constr. & Supply Corp., 49 A.D.2d 476, 375 N.Y.S.2d 655 (1975), aff'd, 41 N.Y.2d 1100, 396 N.Y.S.2d 357, 364 N.E.2d 1129 (1977) (confusion as to the applicable statute of limitations in suit against swimming pool builder); Infante v. Montgomery Ward & Co., 49 A.D.2d 72, 371 N.Y.S.2d 500, 17 UCC 788 (1975) (section 2–725 held not applicable in products liability action for personal injuries); Gladhart v. Oregon Vineyard Supply Co., 164 Or.App. 438, 994 P.2d 134, 40 UCC2d 722 (1999) (action for seller's claim that grape vines were phylloxera-free based in warranty, not product liability); Spain v. Brown & Williamson Tobacco Corp., 230 F.3d 1300, 50 UCC2d 1082 (11th Cir. 2000) (claim that cigarettes are unreasonably dangerous is a product liability claim); Galletta v. Stryker Corp., 283 F.Supp.2d 914, 51 UCC2d 735 (S.D.N.Y. 2003) (claim concerning defective knee implant barred under 2–725).

In determining the applicable statute of limitations, most courts consider at least three factors: the nature of the injury, the language of the complaint, and whether the parties are in privity of contract. As we have noted in section 12–2, characterization as tort is more likely in cases of personal injury and property damage than in cases of economic loss.[6] Although neither the defendant nor the court is bound by the plaintiff's characterization of the cause of action, the language of the complaint may influence the court. A complaint explicitly couched in terms of strict tort liability is more likely to incline a court to decide that 2–725 does not apply. Similarly, a court is more likely to apply 2–725 when the complaint explicitly refers to Code warranty sections than when it merely invokes a "warranty" theory without reference to the Code. Finally, many courts say that 2–725 does not apply when the plaintiff and defendant are not in privity of contract.[7] Courts holding 2–725 inapplicable to non-privity plaintiffs reason that a non-privity plaintiff, like the ordinary tort plaintiff, will not be aware of the time the goods were tendered or delivered by the remote seller and will have had no opportunity to inspect the goods at time of delivery.

Once a court determines that 2–725 or, alternatively, a tort statute applies, it must still determine when the statute commences to run. Section 2–725(2) provides:

> A cause of action accrues when the breach occurs, regardless of the aggrieved party's lack of knowledge of the breach. A breach of warranty occurs when tender of delivery is made, except that

6. See, e.g., Evans v. GMC, 314 Ill. App.3d 609, 247 Ill.Dec. 363, 732 N.E.2d 79, 42 UCC2d 485 (2000) (injured minors under Illinois tolling law may file suit two years after reaching majority); Fine v. Huygens, 57 Mass.App.Ct. 397, 783 N.E.2d 842, 49 UCC2d 1218 (2003).

Some courts have ruled that § 2–725 governs personal injury actions under appropriate circumstances.

7. See, e.g., Southgate Community School Dist. v. West Side Constr. Co., 399 Mich. 72, 247 N.W.2d 884, 20 UCC 1202 (1976) (tort statute of limitations governs school district's economic loss claim against remote manufacturer of floor tiles: "By its terms, UCC § 2–725 applies only to an 'action for breach of any contract for sale,' and was not meant to apply to actions between consumers and manufacturers who were never in any commercial relationship or setting").

Some cases do not apply the Code because the contract is for services and not goods. Richard A. Rosenblatt & Co.

v. Davidge Data Systems Corp., 295 A.D.2d 168, 743 N.Y.S.2d 471, 47 UCC2d 1390 (2002); DaimlerChrysler Services North America v. Ouimette, 175 Vt. 316, 830 A.2d 38, 50 UCC2d 1121 (2003) (hybrid sale-security action governed by Article 2).

In deciding that the two year tort statute of limitations rather than § 2–725 applies to a non-privity plaintiff, one court reasoned as follows: "[T]he four-year statute in the Uniform Commercial Code expressly allows the parties to reduce the period to not less than one year by original agreement * * *. Because a seller has not had an opportunity to bargain for a shorter limitation period with persons who lack privity of contract with him, it would be inappropriate to give such persons the benefit of the same longer statute of limitations governing those persons who have bargained and contracted with the seller." Anderson v. Fairchild Hiller Corp., 358 F.Supp. 976, 979, 12 UCC 655, 659 (D.Alaska 1973).

> where a warranty explicitly extends to future performance of the goods and discovery of the breach must await the time of such performance the cause of action accrues when the breach is or should have been discovered.

Apart from the case in which the warranty "explicitly extends to future performance," the section is quite clear. The statute normally commences to run upon tender of delivery, and the clock *ticks even though the buyer does not know the goods are defective*. This is quite different from the usual interpretation of tort statutes. If, for example, a wheel on an automobile were defective the cause of action would not arise until the wheel caused some injury.[8] If the injury is difficult to discover (as when a drug causes a personal injury discoverable only long after the drug is purchased and used), many cases hold that the statute does not begin to run until the plaintiff discovered or reasonably should have discovered the injury.[9]

One of the main reasons to fight over the true genus of plaintiff's cause of action is because one statute will have run when the other has not. Most courts now foreclose the plaintiff's use of the tort "discovery" rule by denying tort claims for economic loss. The cases in New Jersey are representative. In Santor v. A & M Karagheusian, Inc.,[10] the plaintiff sued in strict tort and warranty for the diminution in value of a rug which after a period, commenced to show unusual lines. In that case there was no accident or sudden event which revealed the defect and "caused injury"; presumably the deterioration of the rug was gradual. In such cases the courts could apply the tort standard for latent defects and find that the statute did not commence to run until the plaintiff should have known of the defect. *Santor* might be the highwater mark for tort recovery of economic loss. In Spring Motors Distributors, Inc. v. Ford Motor Co.,[11] the New Jersey Supreme Court declined to extend *Santor* into a commercial setting and held that a truck leasing company suing for both direct (repair, replacement parts) and consequential (lost profits due to lost leasing contracts) damages could not recover in strict tort. Limiting *Santor's* application to actions by a consumer buyer who has suffered direct economic loss, the court held that the Code preempted strict tort in cases involv-

---

8. W. Prosser & W. Keeton, Handbook of the Law of Torts, § 30 at 165 (5th Ed.1984) (statute of limitations does not begin to run against a negligence claim until some damage has occurred).

9. See, W. Prosser & W. Page Keeton, Handbook of the Law of Torts, § 30 at 165 (5th Ed.1984) (many courts now construe tort statutes as commencing to

run only when the plaintiff has in fact discovered that he has suffered injury, or by the exercise of reasonable diligence should have discovered it).

10. 44 N.J. 52, 207 A.2d 305, 2 UCC 599 (1965).

11. 98 N.J. 555, 489 A.2d 660, 40 UCC 1184 (1985).

ing a commercial buyer. As a result, the four-year statute of limitations applied.

Although the time of accrual under 2–725 is ordinarily clear— "when tender of delivery is made"—the exception to this general rule poses interpretive difficulties. The second sentence of 2–725(2) provides that the statute does not begin to run upon tender of delivery where "a warranty explicitly extends to future performance of the goods and discovery of the breach must await the time of such performance." In such cases 2–725(2) states that the cause of action accrues when "the breach is or should have been discovered." First, it should be clear that this extension of the normal warranty period does not occur in the usual case, even though all warranties in a sense apply to the future performance of goods. The quoted portion of 2–725(2) applies only in a case in which the warranty "explicitly extends to future performance." Presumably such a case would be one in which the seller gave a "lifetime guarantee" or one in which the seller, for example, expressly warranted that an automobile would last for 24,000 miles or four years whichever occurred first.[12] If the automobile failed in the 20,000th mile and after three years of driving, the buyer (if she had no notice or knowledge of the defect prior to the failure) would have four years from that date to commence her suit notwithstanding that her suit would then be brought seven years after the sale had occurred. Two cases illustrate the difficulty that the courts have had in determining which warranties "explicitly extend."

In Perry v. Augustine[13] the allegedly defective product was a heating system. The seller had warranted the system would be able to maintain the temperature at 75 degrees inside at a −20 degree outside temperature. The time of tender was July, 1961. The court decided that the statute did not begin to run as of that date because

---

12. See Rempe v. General Electric Co., 28 Conn.Supp. 160, 254 A.2d 577, 6 UCC 647 (1969); R. Nordstrom, Handbook of the Law of Sales § 185, at 563–64 (1970) ("if the seller warranted the goods for (say) two years, the four-year period does not begin until the buyer discovered or should have discovered the breach"). See also Marvin Lumber & Cedar Co. v. PPG Indus., 223 F.3d 873, 42 UCC2d 15 (8th Cir. 2000); Donatelle Plastics Inc. v. Stonhard, Inc., 2002 WL 31002847, 48 UCC2d 1399 (D. Minn. 2002); Controlled Environmentalists Construction, Inc. v. Key Industrial Refrigeration Co., 266 Neb. 927, 670 N.W.2d 771, 51 UCC2d 1079 (2003).

Further "no extension" cases include: Selzer v. Brunsell Bros., Ltd., 257 Wis.2d 809, 652 N.W.2d 806, 48 UCC2d 629 (App. 2002) (builder's statement that "wood is deep-treated to permanently protect against rot" not warranty of future performance); Lee v. R & K Marine, Inc., 165 N.C.App. 525, 598 S.E.2d 683, 54 UCC2d 248 (2004); Sandy Springs Toyota v. Classic Cadillac Atlanta Corp., 269 Ga.App. 470, 604 S.E.2d 303, 54 UCC2d 844 (2004).See also Meron v. Ward Lumber Company, Inc., 8 A.D.3d 805, 779 N.Y.S.2d 597, 54 UCC2d 55 (2004) (repair and replacement of shingles for 20 years); PPG Industries, Inc. v. JMB/Houston Centers Partners LP, 146 S.W.3d 79, 54 UCC2d 166 (Tex. 2004) (five-year warranty for windows extended to future performance).

13. 37 Pa.D. & C.2d 416, 3 UCC 735 (C.P.1965).

the warranty explicitly extended to future performance of the goods. The court stated:

> Here the warranty in question relates to what the heating system sold and delivered in June and July 1961, would do in the future, i.e., when it was tested under subzero temperature conditions. Discovery of a breach of that kind of a warranty in this climate would necessarily have to await winter weather.[14]

Whether this warranty in fact extended to the future performance of the goods is unclear. The court's rationale is that *discovery* of breach would have to await the future performance of the goods, and therefore the warranty was explicitly prospective. The reasoning is not persuasive. The same could be said of all warranties and in the *Perry* case the temperature might never reach − 20 degrees.

In Rempe v. General Electric Co.,[15] the court assumed that section 2–725 did not govern. The opinion, however, included dictum that were the Code statute of limitations applicable, the case would have fallen within the exception in section 2–725 regarding future warranties. In purchasing the defective product, the plaintiff received a "lifetime" warranty. The court properly found that this warranty was prospective, that is, that it promised performance of the product not merely at the moment of purchase but at some future date as well. The cause of action, therefore, did not accrue until "the breach is or should have been discovered."[16] The court suggested, however, that because of the ambiguity of the warranty (how long is a "lifetime"?), the defendant should have the opportunity to persuade the trier of fact that the warranty had expired more than four years before commencement of the action.

In many cases, a casual reading of an agreement that apparently promises future performance leaves one in considerable doubt about its true meaning. Consider the case in which the manufacturer promises to repair any defect in a car's drive-train that occurs within two years or 24,000 miles, whichever occurs first. As we suggest above, many courts would interpret this as a warranty that explicitly extends to future performance and would therefore grant four years from the time of the occurrence of the defect. On the other hand, one might read the agreement to mean simply that the seller will repair any defect that comes to light within that period irrespective of its cause, but that seller's liability ends at the earlier 24,000 miles and does not extend for four years beyond that time. The seller (and buyer if the truth be known) may construe such agreement not as a warranty at all but as an agreement to repair

14. *Id*. at 418, 3 UCC at 737.

15. 28 Conn.Supp. 160, 254 A.2d 577, 6 UCC 647 (1969).

16. § 2–725(2).

unrelated to any defect in the goods (as, for example, a wheel that breaks when it hits a pothole).

In summary, we can do little more than warn the lawyer not to make hasty judgments about the applicable statute of limitations or about when it will commence to run. Section 2–725 offers a sane and workable statutory scheme,[17] but it is one the courts will infrequently follow when the plaintiff's blood has been spilled or when the defendant is a remote seller. To courts, these cases look like tort, not contract, particularly when the tort statute of limitations favors the plaintiff. For other consideration of the collision of tort and warranty, see Chapter 11, section 5 on the economic loss doctrine.

§ 12–10   Buyer's Failure to Give Notice as a Defense to an Action for Breach of Warranty

A buyer who accepts nonconforming goods must notify the seller that the goods are nonconforming, "or be barred from any remedy." Section 2–607(3)(a) of the Code provides:

Where a tender has been accepted

(a) the buyer must within a reasonable time after he discovers or should have discovered any breach notify the seller of breach or be barred from any remedy * * *.

"Any remedy" within the meaning of section 2–607(3)(a) includes ancillary rights such as the right to revoke acceptance under 2–608 as well as the right to damages. Of course, if plaintiff's cause of action is in strict tort, 2–607(3)(a) does not apply.

Does the statute dispense with notice where, as in late delivery cases, the seller already has full and actual knowledge of the breach? There is a split of authority.[1]

---

17.   Comment 2 to 2–312 makes clear the drafters' opinion that the implied warranty of title and its corollary of quiet possession is breached if at all, at the time of sale. It reads as follows:

§ 2–725 provides that the cause of action accrues when the breach occurs. Under the provisions of that section the breach of the warranty of good title occurs when tender of delivery is made since the warranty is not one which extends to "future performance of the goods."

§ 12–10

1.   The majority of cases find actual notice to suffice. See, e.g., Crest Container v. R.H. Bishop Co., 111 Ill.App.3d 1068, 445 N.E.2d 19, 35 UCC 1498 (1982) (notice satisfied when heating

coils malfunctioned in presence of manufacturer's employee); Malawy v. Richards Mfg. Co., 150 Ill.App.3d 549, 103 Ill.Dec. 355, 501 N.E.2d 376, 3 UCC2d 511 (1986) (actual observance by seller's employees of product failure qualifies as notice); Myers v. Koop, 757 P.2d 162, 7 UCC2d 461 (Colo.App.1988); M.K. Associates v. Stowell Products, Inc., 697 F.Supp. 20, 7 UCC2d 775 (D.Me.1988); Agrarian Grain Co. v. Meeker, 526 N.E.2d 1189, 7 UCC2d 786 (Ind.App. 1988) (seller's knowledge of buyer's dissatisfaction with buckled storage bin extensions met notice requirement); Chemtrol Adhesives, Inc. v. American Mfrs. Mut. Ins. Co., 42 Ohio St.3d 40, 537 N.E.2d 624, 9 UCC2d 88 (1989); Cheyenne Mountain Bank v. Whetstone

The most vexatious and frequently litigated 2–607(3)(a) question is: what constitutes a "reasonable time" within which the buyer "should have discovered any breach" and have notified the seller? On reading the cases one is tempted to say that a reasonable time in this context has as many meanings as there are fact patterns in the cases. Although we are tempted to leave it at that, the situation may not be quite that dismal. A lawyer cognizant of the policies behind the notice requirement may be able to predict how a court will apply "reasonable time," and may be able to argue convincingly that a specific time was or was not reasonable in light of those policies. One can identify at least four policies behind 2–607. The first and most important reason for requiring notice is to enable the seller to make adjustments or replacements or to suggest opportunities for cure to the end of minimizing the buyer's loss and reducing the seller's own liability to the buyer. For example, purchasers of trucks should tell their seller at once of any defects and procure any necessary replacements and adjustments. They should not allow the truck to sit in their yard for a year and then sue for the profits that they would have made during that year had the truck worked properly. The second policy behind the notice requirement is to afford sellers an opportunity to arm themselves for negotiation and litigation. For example, our sources tell us that

Corp., 787 P.2d 210, 11 UCC2d 64 (Colo. App.1990); AGF, Inc. v. Great Lakes Heat Treating Co., 51 Ohio St.3d 177, 555 N.E.2d 634, 11 UCC2d 859 (1990); Laird v. The Scribner Coop., Inc., 237 Neb. 532, 466 N.W.2d 798, 14 UCC2d 433 (1991) (buyer of tainted corn notified seller months after purchase once veterinarian confirmed suspicion that hogs' illness was caused by the corn); Arcor, Inc. v. Textron, Inc., 960 F.2d 710, 17 UCC2d 475 (7th Cir.1992) (notice deemed satisfied when seller observed problems of electrical discharge machine); Hospital Computer Sys., Inc. v. Staten Island Hospital, 788 F.Supp. 1351, 18 UCC2d 140 (D.N.J.1992).

Several cases, however, require more than actual notice. Eastern Air Lines, Inc. v. McDonnell Douglas Corp., 532 F.2d 957, 19 UCC 353 (5th Cir.1976) (buyer must make clear he considers seller in breach so there can be settlement negotiations); Stamper Black Hills Gold Jewelry, Inc. v. Souther, 414 N.W.2d 601, 5 UCC2d 340 (N.D.1987) (no notice when seller merely knew buyer needed timely shipment and knew that such shipment was delayed); Quaker Alloy Casting Co. v. Gulfco Industries, Inc. v. Consolidated Foundries & Manufacturing Corp., 686 F.Supp. 1319, 7 UCC2d 429 (N.D.Ill.1988); Southeastern Steel v. W.A. Hunt Constr. Co., 301 S.C. 140, 390 S.E.2d 475, 12 UCC2d 103 (1990) (actual notice does not satisfy since seller needs to know buyer is making legal claim of breach); American Bumper & Manufacturing Co. v. Transtechnology Corp., 252 Mich.App. 340, 652 N.W.2d 252, 48 UCC2d 607 (2002) (buyer told seller was problem but did not assert breach).

One case left the question for the jury, but ruled that actual notice alone was not unreasonable as a matter of law. Cheyenne Mountain Bank v. Whetstone Corp., 787 P.2d 210, 11 UCC2d 64 (Colo. App.1990) (when actual notice could be found failure to give formal notice of defective equipment was not necessarily unreasonable); Cambridge Technologies, Inc. v. Argyle Industries, Inc., 146 Md. App. 415, 807 A.2d 125, 48 UCC2d 966 (2002) (UCC did not require buyer of parts to give notice to seller of seller's breach where seller did not deliver by agreed upon deadlines).

Notice to an immediate seller may be sufficient against remote seller. Sullivan v. Young Bros. & Co., Inc., 893 F.Supp. 1148, 30 UCC2d 106 (D.Me. 1995).

the Henningsens notified Chrysler so late in their famous case that Chrysler was not even able to find and inspect the automobile in which Mrs. Henningsen was injured.[2] Had Chrysler been able to find the allegedly defective car, it might have been able to present certain defenses or at least have been able to limit the jury's speculation. A third reason to cut off a claimant who does not promptly give notice of a defect is our disbelief of tardy claims. That many American consumers of products toil on in stoic silence in the face of known defects is not credible. We are properly skeptical of tardy claims of defect and the notice requirement of 2–607 is a proper expression of that skepticism.

A final policy behind the notice requirement is to give defendants that same kind of mind balm they get from the statute of limitations.[3] There is some value in allowing sellers, at some point, to close their books on goods sold in the past and to pass on to other things.

In cases resting mostly on the first policy, the courts are not at all hesitant to find that commercial buyers failed to live up to the notice requirements and thus forfeited their Code remedies. Comment 4 states that in these cases 2–607 defeats "commercial bad faith," and if the court senses that merchant buyers are lying in the grass with the thought of increasing their damages, it will not hesitate a moment to cut them off. A case in point is A.C. Carpenter, Inc. v. Boyer Potato Chips.[4] In that case the buyer sent a "breach" letter to the seller eight days after receiving nonconforming potatoes. The seller received the letter four days after it was sent. The hearing officer held that the notice was not timely; twelve days was too long for parties dealing in perishables. The hearing officer might have suspected that the buyer was not acting in good faith, for the buyer did not call the seller although he knew the seller's address and the telephone number. In G. & D. Poultry Farms, Inc. v. Long Island Butter & Egg Co.,[5] the court found a delay unreasonably long because, in part, the buyer had ordered and paid for additional goods without notifying the seller that the goods were in any way unsatisfactory. In short, a merchant buyer who receives defective goods and who expects to reject, revoke acceptance, or sue under 2–714 and 2–715 should act fast.

The cases which rest mostly on the second policy, that is, the policy affording sellers a fair opportunity to arm themselves to defend against a suit arising out of an injury caused by the defect, reflect greater judicial willingness to permit the buyer to dilly dally. Indeed, the drafters of the comments went out of their way to

---

2. Henningsen v. Bloomfield Motors, Inc., 32 N.J. 358, 161 A.2d 69 (1960).

3. See § 2–607, Comment 4.

4. 1969 WL 10993, 28 Agri.Dec. 1557, 7 UCC 493 (1969).

5. 33 A.D.2d 685, 306 N.Y.S.2d 243, 6 UCC 1258 (1969).

encourage courts not to close the door too quickly on a "retail consumer," and one suspects that the drafters (and many courts) would tolerate an even longer delay on the part of a retail consumer whose blood has been spilled.[6] Comment 4 to 2–607 states that "[a] 'reasonable time' for notification from a retail consumer is to be judged by different standards so that in his case it will be extended, for the rule of requiring notification is [not designed] to deprive a good faith consumer of his remedy." Not only the drafters but also the commentators and the courts seem to disfavor the lack of notice defense when invoked against an injured consumer. Indeed, one of the oft cited virtues of strict tort theory is that it does not require notice.[7] The defendant's lawyer whose client is sued not by a merchant-buyer but by a consumer, especially by a consumer who suffered personal injury or property damage, should not rely heavily on a lack of notice defense. Here the notice policies collide with a countervailing policy that unsophisticated consumers who suffer real and perhaps grievous injury at the hands of the defendant-seller ought to have an easy road to recovery.

To what extent may the parties to a sales contract legislate for themselves with regard to notice and its timeliness? Section 1–302(b) of Revised Article 1 (that is, prior 1–204(1)) validates a contractual time limit within which a buyer must notify his seller, provided that the agreed time period is not "manifestly unreasonable". In Q. Vandenberg and Sons, N.V. v. Siter,[8] the goods were tulip bulbs which the seller warranted to be capable of flowering at the time of shipment. Months after delivery, the buyer discovered they would not flower. The buyer alleged that the inability of the bulbs to flower was due to a defect existing at the time of delivery. However, the contract provided that the buyer waived any claim for breach of warranty unless he asserted such claim within eight days after delivery. The buyer argued that such a provision, insofar as it applied to defects which were latent and impossible to discover within the eight-day period, was "manifestly unreasonable". The court held that the buyer succeeded in raising a jury question.

---

6. Bonker v. Ingersoll Prods. Corp., 132 F.Supp. 5 (D.Mass.1955) (notice of bone in can of "Boneless Chicken" given to manufacturer four months after injury was not unreasonable delay under Uniform Sales Act); Downey v. Mahoney, 25 Mass.App.Dec. 196, 4 UCC 661 (1962) (notice of unfit pork given 32 days after plaintiff fell ill was held reasonable notice of breach of warranty). See also Maldonado v. Creative Woodworking Concepts, Inc., 296 Ill.App.3d 935, 230 Ill.Dec. 743, 694 N.E.2d 1021, 35 UCC2d 501 (1998) (plaintiff's filing of complaint sufficient notice to defendant seller of a breach of warranty where plaintiff a consumer who suffered personal injury).

7. See W. Prosser, Handbook of the Law of Torts § 97, at 690 (5th ed. 1984) (2–607(3) is a "booby-trap for the unwary"). Remember Dean Prosser was a member of the plaintiffs' booster club.

8. 204 Pa.Super. 392, 204 A.2d 494, 2 UCC 383 (1964).

Two questions remain. First, does anyone other than a buyer have a duty to give notice of breach? Second, must a buyer give notice to any seller other than the one from whom he actually purchased the goods? Tomczuk v. Town of Cheshire,[9] a personal injury action, raised both questions. The plaintiff was a playmate of a girl whose parents had purchased a bicycle. While riding the bicycle, plaintiff sustained injuries allegedly caused by defects in the bicycle. Section 2–318 indicated that plaintiff would have the same rights under the seller's warranties as an actual purchaser would. The question was whether plaintiff had the same or similar duties under section 2–607. Comment 5 to 2–607 answers this question affirmatively:

> Under this Article various beneficiaries are given rights for injuries sustained by them because of the seller's breach of warranty. Such a beneficiary does not fall within the reason of the present section in regard to discovery of defects and the giving of notice within a reasonable time after acceptance, since he has nothing to do with acceptance. However, the reason of this section does extend to requiring the beneficiary to notify the seller that an injury has occurred. What is said above, with regard to the extended time for reasonable notification from the lay consumer after the injury is also applicable here; but even a beneficiary can be properly held to the use of good faith in notifying, once he has had time to become aware of the legal situation.

The court, however, ignored the quoted comment and absolved the plaintiff of any duty to give notice to the manufacturer. The court reasoned that the notice requirement applied only to buyers, and since the plaintiff was not a buyer,[10] she had no duty to give notice.[11] Although it was a moot question in view of the court's position that the requirements of 2–607(3)(a) did not apply to the plaintiff in this case, the court went on to opine that the words "the seller" in 2–607(3)(a) should be read "his immediate seller." In short the court indicated that a consumer need not notify a manufacturer provided the consumer did not purchase directly from him.[12]

9. 26 Conn.Supp. 219, 217 A.2d 71, 3 UCC 147 (1965).

10. See § 2–103(a).

11. See also, Taylor v. American Honda Motor Co., 555 F.Supp. 59, 35 UCC 391 (M.D.Fla.1982) (notice requirement not applicable to a 2–318 beneficiary in a personal injury action when he is not a buyer under 2–103(1)(a)); Lariviere v. Dayton Safety Ladder Co., 525 A.2d 892, 4 UCC2d 433 (R.I.1987)

(plaintiff as beneficiary of product, as opposed to buyer, need only act in good faith in notifying seller or manufacturer of injury incurred while using a defective ladder).

12. Cf. Ruderman v. Warner–Lambert Pharmaceutical Co., 23 Conn.Supp. 416, 184 A.2d 63 (1962); Cole v. Keller Industries, Inc., 132 F.3d 1044, 34 UCC2d 401 (4th Cir.1998), appeal after remand, 342 Ill.App.3d 1028, 277 Ill.Dec.

In more recent decisions, however, the courts indicate that a non-privity consumer buyer must timely notify a remote manufacturer of alleged defects, at least when the buyer seeks recovery under the Code for economic loss. We concur in this view. If the manufacturer is to be held responsible for the buyer's losses, it needs the protection of timely notice at least as much as the buyer's immediate seller.

Finally, what constitutes sufficient notice under 2–607(3)(a)? How explicit must it be? May it be oral? Must it threaten litigation? Quite clearly the drafters intended a loose test; a scribbled note on a bit of toilet paper will do:

> The content of the notification need merely be sufficient to let the seller know that the transaction is still troublesome and must be watched. There is no reason to require that the notification which saves the buyer's rights under this section must include a clear statement of all the objections that will be relied on by the buyer, as under the section covering statements of defects upon rejection (Section 2–605). Nor is there reason for requiring the notification to be a claim for damages or of any threatened litigation or other resort to a remedy. The notification which saves the buyer's rights under this Article need only be such as informs the seller that the transaction is claimed to involve a breach, and thus opens the way for normal settlement through negotiation.[13]

Under this comment, it is difficult to conceive of words which, if put in writing, would not satisfy the notice requirement of 2–607. Indeed, a letter containing anything but the most exaggerated encomiums would seem to tell that the transaction "is still troublesome and must be watched."

The law seems well established now that oral notification satisfies the notice requirement of 2–607(3)(a). Section 2–607(3)(a) uses the verb "notify;" that word is defined in 1–202(d) (old 1–201(26)) in a way that permits an oral statement to constitute notice. That other Code sections impose writing requirements by using the word "sent" supports this interpretation of 2–607(3)(a).[14] Moreover, the most authoritative interpretation of 2–607 to date indicates that a *variety of acts* other than a formal written notice

---

576, 796 N.E.2d 662 (2003) (plaintiff was injured on a ladder purchased by his employer; he waited three and a half months after receiving an expert's report indicating design and manufacturing faults in the ladder before giving manufacturer notice of his claim; District Court dismissed claim for failure to give reasonable notice of a claim under 2–607; the 4th Circuit reversed, holding that a non-purchaser is never required to give notice to the manufacturer under 2–607).

13. § 2–607, Comment 4.

14. Compare, e.g., § 9–406 (notice must "be sent," i.e., presumably by letter or telegram).

may satisfy 2–607. In Boeing Airplane Co. v. O'Malley,[15] the buyer purchased a helicopter which was delivered on December 1, 1959. The seller did not receive formal notice of dissatisfaction until February, 1961. The court held that certain events well prior to February, 1961 were sufficient to constitute notice to the seller. The first of these was the failure of the helicopter to function properly in the presence of one of the seller's experts. After the demonstration, but before February, 1961, the buyer had informed the seller that the buyer was closing down operations because of inadequacies in the helicopter and was moving the helicopter elsewhere in order to take care of it.

In conclusion, we draw attention to differences between the notice specified in 2–607(3)(a) and discussed in this chapter and that specified in 2–602(1) and discussed in Chapter 9. The former is a condition to any remedy; the latter is a condition only to the remedy of rejection. The rejection notice should normally come earlier in time, for it must be given a reasonable time after "delivery or tender," whereas the 2–607 notice must be given within a reasonable time after buyer discovers or should have discovered the breach. For reasons discussed in Chapter 9, it is fair and proper that the buyer who seeks to reject should be required to give notice and to act more quickly than one who seeks only to recover damages.

15. 329 F.2d 585, 2 UCC 110 (8th Cir.1964).

Chapter 13

DISCLAIMERS OF WARRANTY LIABILITY AND MODIFICATION OF BUYER'S REMEDIES

Analysis

---

§ 13–1 Introduction

Having surveyed the buyer's rights and remedies in regard to warranty, we turn to the seller's protection against warranty liability.[1] Seller's contract, bolstered by Code principles of freedom of contract, affords some protection for the seller who wishes to avoid liability that would otherwise arise from implied warranties or from express statements made in the heat of a sales pitch or otherwise. Section 1–102(3) provided that "[t]he effect of provisions of this Act may be varied by agreement, except as otherwise provided * * *."[2] Building on this general principle, as now set forth in 1–302 of Article 1, sections 2–316 and 2–719 delineate specific measures that the seller may take to disclaim warranty liability and to limit the buyer's remedies for breach. Also, 2–202, the Code's parol evidence rule, enables the seller sometimes to disavow statements made by salespersons that could be construed as express warranties, a topic we treated in Chapter 10.

But the seller does not have unlimited power to avoid liability. In fact, the freedom of contract shibboleth offers far more than it gives. Courts do not favor disclaimers—particularly when the plaintiff is an injured consumer. The Magnuson–Moss Warranty—Federal Trade Commission Improvement Act[3] imposes certain federal limitations on disclaimers to consumers. (In section 10–18 we have briefly treated this Act. Our discussion here ignores it.) The very Code provisions that purport to enable the seller to escape liability include significant restrictions on the form and content of disclaimers. These restrictions can be used as weapons to strike down disclaimers that appear to be insignificantly deviant to the objective eye. Moreover, the specter of unconscionability, specifically embodied in 2–719(3) and applicable to all contract terms under 2–302, constantly lurks above all consumer transactions.

Despite the specificity of 2–316 and 2–719, the effects of these provisions have been among the most unpredictable in the Code. This uncertainty is attributable to the availability of 2–302 as a policing device and to the use in 2–316, 2–317 (on cumulation and conflict of warranties), and in 2–719 of terms like "unreasonable,"[4] "consistent,"[5] and "circumstances."[6] This unpredictability is also

---

1. Disclaimer of the warranty of title is dealt with in § 10–16 *supra*.

2. Comment 2 to § 1–302 declares: "Subsection (a) states affirmatively at the outset that freedom of contract is a principle of the Code * * *." See generally, Friedman, Text and Circumstance: Warranty Disclaimers in a World of Rolling Contracts, 46 Arizona L. Rev. 677 (2004).

3. Act of 1975, Pub.L.No. 93–637, 88 Stat. 2183, 15 U.S.C.A. §§ 2301 et seq. (1982).

4. "Reasonable" or "unreasonable" appears twice in 2–316 and once in 2–317.

5. "Consistent" or "inconsistent" appears once in 2–316 and four times in 2–317.

6. Reference to "circumstances" is made twice in 2–316 and once in 2–719.

attributable to activist courts' sympathy toward consumers.[7] Partly because of these sources of uncertainty, the official reporters are filled with cases arising in this area.

Some of the responsibility for the uncertainties in the law lies at the feet of sellers. Apart from the magic words indorsed in 2–316, there are words that would tell a buyer—even an unsophisticated buyer—that the seller makes no warranty. Partly because section 2–316 blesses other less informative articulations ("not merchantable") but also because sellers sometimes want their cake and to eat it too, sellers mostly avoid more powerful articulations. In an exception to this rule, one of us recently saw a disclaimer on a computer program that read as follows: "If this program does not work, tough. If you use it and lose one million dollars, tough. That is your problem, not ours." Part of the reason that sellers' disclaimers are struck down is that sellers consciously reject the most informative statements.

Note too the difference between attempts to disclaim warranty liability and attempts to disclaim strict tort liability. Section 402A of the Restatement, Comment _m_ makes clear that the consumer's rights are "not affected by any disclaimer or other agreement."[8] Thus, at least in theory, Code law on procedures for disclaiming warranty liability has no bearing on the seller's liability in tort. Indeed some courts (including the California Supreme Court)[9] have explicitly held that a seller cannot disclaim strict tort liability. Other courts disagree,[10] but the wise lawyer appreciates that strict tort liability arises independently of any contractual relationship and may not be disclaimable.[11]

---

7. This sympathy may have reached its apogee in Henningsen v. Bloomfield Motors, Inc., 32 N.J. 358, 161 A.2d 69 (1960).

8. Restatement, Second, Torts § 402A, Comment _m_ at 356. On the successor to 402A, see 10–12, _supra_.

9. Vandermark v. Ford Motor Co., 61 Cal.2d 256, 37 Cal.Rptr. 896, 391 P.2d 168 (1964) (action against automobile manufacturer and dealer for personal injuries resulting from brake failure).

10. Where strict tort liability extends to property damage sustained by business entities, some courts have rejected the Restatement's nondisclaimability doctrine. See Delta Air Lines, Inc.

v. McDonnell Douglas Corp., 503 F.2d 239 (5th Cir.1974) (strict tort liability disclaimable under California law as to property damage to airplane), cert. denied, 421 U.S. 965, 95 S.Ct. 1953, 44 L.Ed.2d 451 (1975); Other courts have indicated that sellers may disclaim strict tort liability even as to personal injury. Turner v. International Harvester Co., 133 N.J.Super. 277, 336 A.2d 62, 16 UCC 1264 (1975) (where buyer is not ordinary consumer and language is unequivocal). See also McNichols, Who Says that Strict Tort Disclaimers Can Never Be Effective?—The Courts Cannot Agree, 28 Okl.L.Rev. 494 (1975).

11. On the successor to 402A, see 10–12 _supra_.

§ 13–2   Disclaimers of Express Warranties, Section 2–316(1)

A "disclaimer" of an express warranty may seem an oxymoron. How can a seller disavow an express representation that by hypothesis and definition is "part of the basis of the bargain"?[1] The draft of the 1952 Code explicitly prohibited a seller from doing this, for 2–316 then provided: "If the agreement creates an express warranty, words disclaiming it are inoperative."

Section 2–316(1) provides:

> Words or conduct relevant to the creation of an express warranty and words or conduct tending to negate or limit warranty shall be construed wherever reasonable as consistent with each other; but subject to the provisions of this Article on parol or extrinsic evidence (Section 2–202) negation or limitation is inoperative to the extent that such construction is unreasonable.

The above wording in 2–316(1) of the 1952 Official Text did not make a major change. If the factfinder determines that a seller's statement created an express warranty, words purportedly disclaiming that warranty will still be "inoperative", for the disclaiming language is inherently inconsistent.[2] Thus a seller who explicitly "warrants" or "guarantees" that a car is without defects may not set up a disclaimer of express warranties when sued for the cost of repairing the clutch.

Sometimes courts have used section 2–316(1) also to invalidate short time limits on express warranties. For example, in Wilson Trading Corp. v. David Ferguson, Ltd.[3] the seller expressly warranted yarn of "good merchantable" quality. The New York Court of Appeals held that a clause excluding liability for defects discovered more than ten days after delivery did not protect the seller from liability arising from breach of the express warranty. We question this case. Although we appreciate that a time limit can be struck down as manifestly unreasonable, we do not believe that time limits on express warranties should be read to violate section 2–316(1). After all, the Code does not oblige the seller to make any express warranty and if the time limit is an integral part of the express

§ 13–2

1. See § 2–313

2. See, e.g., Harris v. Ford Motor Co., 845 F.Supp. 1511, 25 UCC2d 53 (M.D.Ala. 1994) (allowing limitation in scope of express warranty); Hayes v. Bering Sea Reindeer Products, 983 P.2d 1280, 39 UCC2d 372 (Alaska 1999) (nongeneralized, conspicuous and clear disclaimer of express warranty valid); Tulger Contracting Corp. v. Star Building Systems, Inc., 2002 WL 986994, 52 UCC2d 917 (S.D.N.Y. 2002) (disclaimer barring all warranties was enforceable where conspicuous and where buyer was already familiar from prior jobs).

3. 23 N.Y.2d 398, 297 N.Y.S.2d 108, 244 N.E.2d 685, 5 UCC 1213 (1968).

warranty, as actually made, we do not believe that it violates the policy of section 2–316(1).[4]

Below we deal with 2–316(1) in two contexts: (1) when both warranty and disclaimer language are contained in a written agreement; and (2) when a parol warranty is made before the disclaimer is incorporated into a written contract.

§ 13–3   Disclaimers of Express Warranties, Section 2–316(1)—Conflict Within Written Agreement

Comment 1 to 2–316 indicates that subsection (1) "seeks to protect a buyer from unexpected and unbargained language of disclaimer by denying effect to such language when inconsistent with language of express warranty * * *." Express warranties arise under 2–313 via affirmations of fact or promise, descriptions, and samples or models. Most 2–316(1) questions arise when a seller sets up a disclaimer against an express affirmation or description appearing outside the specific warranty clause of the contract. If the affirmation or description creates a warranty, subsection (1) resolves the conflict in the buyer's favor. Yet 2–316(1) allows the factfinder to decide that the language of disclaimer itself prevents an affirmation or description which would otherwise create warranty from doing so.[1] Comment 1 to 2–316 states that subsection (1) "seeks to protect a buyer from *unexpected* and *unbargained* language of disclaimer by denying effect to such language when inconsistent with language of express warranty * * *." (Emphasis added.)

In U.S. Fibres, Inc. v. Proctor & Schwartz, Inc.,[2] the Sixth Circuit read language of warranty and disclaimer together to deny warranty protection. The parties jointly designed equipment for the production of resinated cotton pads, and the contract language reflected the experimental nature of the goods. The warranty clause itself read: "[Seller] warrants the machine against defects in materials or workmanship, but makes no other warranties, express or implied * * * unless the word 'guarantee' is used."[3] In a subse-

---

4. A number of courts have ignored 2–316(1) when assessing the validity of "time warranties." For example, Majors v. Kalo Labs., Inc., 407 F.Supp. 20, 18 UCC 592 (M.D.Ala.1975) (clause requiring buyer to notify seller of defects in soybean inoculant within 120 days of delivery unconscionable). For a case upholding time limits on express warranties, see Womco, Inc. v. Navistar International Corp., 84 S.W.3d 272, 48 UCC2d 130 (Tex.App. 2002) (requirement that disclaimer be reasonable applies only to express warranties).

§ 13–3

1. Professor Honnold suggested that the 1952 draft would have required courts to isolate language of express warranty and determine its effect prior to considering the effect of language of disclaimer. 1 N.Y. State Law Revision Comm'n, 1955 Report 409 (1955).

2. 509 F.2d 1043, 16 UCC 1 (6th Cir.1975).

3. *Id.* at 1045, 16 UCC at 3.

quent clause labeled "PERFORMANCE," the contract provided "that in view of the variables affecting the capacity of the machine, no guarantee can be extended."[4] When the machinery produced pads of non-uniform thickness, the buyer based his breach of warranty claim on the equipment description: "designed with a deflection tolerance of ± 1/32."[5] The court denied recovery, noting that the word "guarantee" was absent from the claimed warranty and holding that the only warranty was the general guarantee against defects in materials or workmanship:

> The language of description referred only to the expectations of the designers and in no way guaranteed that these expectations would be met. Furthermore, there is substantial evidence that executives of Fibres who participated in the purchase of the equipment never expected it to produce finished pads having a thickness tolerance of ± 1/32 inch across their width. Thus, the descriptive language was not "part of the basis of the bargain." * * * The district court correctly determined that the language which excluded an express warranty was not inconsistent with the language of description, UCC § 2–316(1), and gave it effect.[6]

The decision in *U.S. Fibres* probably conforms to the parties' legitimate expectations. The contract affirmatively evidenced the buyer's nonreliance on the seller's statement. Moreover, the buyer had participated in development of the product via a continuous bargaining process. In Wenner v. Gulf Oil Corp.,[7] the label on the seller's product proclaimed that "OUTFOX is a low carryover herbicide, and when applied at the recommended rate, normal crop rotation is possible the season following OUTFOX application."[8] The buyer applied the herbicide to his corn crop with successful results, but chemicals remained in the field and damaged the subsequent crop. Despite a disclaimer of any warranty that the product would not damage crops, the Minnesota Supreme Court affirmed buyer's recovery. The affirmation on the label created an express warranty that rendered any disclaiming language inoperative.[9]

The decisions in *U.S. Fibres* and in *Wenner* are sensible interpretations of 2–316. By directing the court to "construe" the alleged warranty and disclaimer as consistent with each other, the

4. *Id.* at 1045, 16 UCC at 2.

5. *Id.* at 1045, 16 UCC at 3.

6. *Id.* at 1046, 16 UCC at 3–4. Accord Terrell v. R & A Manufacturing Partners, Ltd., 835 So.2d 216, 50 UCC2d 151 (Ala.App. 2002) (inconspicuous remedy limitations and warranty disclaimers ineffective because not part of the basis

of bargain); Perry v. Gulf Stream Coach, Inc. 814 N.E.2d 634, 54 UCC2d 769 (Ind.App. 2004) (no warranties created).

7. 264 N.W.2d 374, 23 UCC 603 (Minn.1978).

8. *Id.* at 383, 23 UCC at 609.

9. *Id.* at 383–84, 23 UCC at 609.

legislature is directing more than a rote comparison. Particularly in a negotiated deal, where, as in *U.S. Fibres*, the parties have consciously chosen certain terms as express warranties and have specifically limited those warranties, it is sensible to interpret the terms as a whole and to recognize what otherwise might be described as an invalid disclaimer as an enforceable qualification of the express warranty.[10]

On the other hand, non-negotiated forms attached to products that appear at one place to warrant X and to say at another that X is not warranted, should receive the treatment given in *Wenner*. Drafters of those forms must understand that product descriptions and other affirmations that lay persons may not regard as "express warranties" are express warranties under section 2–313. They will therefore form the basis of liability notwithstanding a clause that purports to disclaim all "express warranties." Sellers' batting average would increase if they use language that is more forthcoming and more likely to be understood by a buyer as a warning: "If you use OUTFOX wrong it will kill not only your weeds but also your corn, soybeans, and alfalfa for the next 30 years. If it does, don't call us."

§ 13–4   Disclaimers of Express Warranties, Section 2–316(1)—Oral Warranties Made Prior to the Written Agreement

Section 2–316(1) makes clear that it is "subject to the provisions of this Article on parol or extrinsic evidence (Section 2–202) * * *."[1] Section 2–202 provides:

> Terms with respect to which the confirmatory memoranda of the parties agree or which are otherwise set forth in a writing intended by the parties as a final expression of their agreement with respect to such terms as are included therein may not be contradicted by evidence of any prior agreement or of a contemporaneous oral agreement but may be explained or supplemented
>
> (a) by course of dealing or usage of trade (Section 1–303) or by course of performance (Section 2–208); and

---

10. See Corey v. Furgat Tractor & Equip., Inc., 147 Vt. 477, 520 A.2d 600, 3 UCC2d 505 (1986) (tractor warranty did not cover logging purposes and so disclaimer was valid).

also Broude, The Consumer and the Parol Evidence Rule: Section 2–202 of the Uniform Commercial Code, 1970 Duke L.J. 881.

§ 13–4

1. For an extensive discussion of the parol evidence rule, see Chapter 3. See

(b) by evidence of consistent additional terms unless the court finds the writing to have been intended also as a complete and exclusive statement of the terms of the agreement.

According to Comment 2 to 2–316, the reference to the parol evidence rule is intended to protect the seller "against false allegations of oral warranties." However, the seller's protection is subject to two important restrictions. First, the written agreement may be contradicted by parol evidence if it was not intended by the parties as a *final* expression of their agreement. Thus a disclaimer in a nonfinal memorandum does not negate an oral warranty previously made by the seller.[2] Second, even if the writing was intended as the final expression of part of the parties' agreement, it may be supplemented with evidence of consistent additional terms if the writing was not intended as a complete and exclusive statement of the terms of the agreement. Thus the courts[3] have had, and continue to have, considerable discretion in deciding whether to admit evidence of oral warranties.[4]

An effectively worded merger or integration clause can have the same effect as a disclaimer.[5] That is, if a party includes a clause in a contract which states that the written contract is the "complete and exclusive statement of the terms of the agreement," the most likely legal consequence will be to exclude from evidence the proof of any oral warranty. The careful disclaimer drafter will not rely exclusively on 2–316 and 2–719 but will also consider 2–202 and the parol evidence rule.

Under pre-Code law, a clause providing that the contract "contains the entire agreement of the parties, and that there are no antecedent or extrinsic representations, warranties, or collateral provisions that are not intended to be discharged and nullified" was often effective to exclude evidence of alleged oral warranties.[6] Most courts have given similar language the same effect under the Code.[7]

2. See, e.g., Drier v. Perfection, Inc., 259 N.W.2d 496, 23 UCC 323 (S.D.1977) (parol evidence that seller of press would "make it print" admitted upon finding that security agreement containing disclaimer was not final agreement).

If, however, the writing that includes a disclaimer is intended to be final, most courts hold that parol warranties are "contradictory" within 2–202 and hence inadmissible. See Bakal v. Burroughs Corp., 74 Misc.2d 202, 343 N.Y.S.2d 541, 13 UCC 60 (1972) (representations in sales literature contradict disclaimer).

3. As § 2–202(b) indicates, rulings on parol evidence are for the court.

4. Of course parol evidence is admissible to show the invalidity of the docu-

ment itself. 3 A. Corbin, Contracts § 578 at 405 (1960).

5. See 1 W. Hawkland, A Transactional Guide to the Uniform Commercial Code 85 (1964); Moye, Exclusion and Modification of Warranty Under the U.C.C.—How to Succeed in Business Without Being Liable for Not Really Trying, 46 Denver L.J. 579 (1969).

6. 3 A. Corbin, Contracts § 578 at 402–403 (1960). But Comment 1 to 2–202 makes clear that the Code rejects several pre-Code propositions.

7. See, e.g., Quality Acceptance Corp. v. Million & Albers, Inc., 367 F.Supp. 771, 14 UCC 78 (D.Wyo.1973) (buyer has heavy burden to establish parol war-

Thus, in Betaco, Inc. v. Cessna Aircraft Co.,[8] the buyer was precluded from raising breach of warranty claims based on seller's prior oral representations where the parties signed an integrated agreement as their "only agreement." In Green Chevrolet v. Kemp,[9] which involved the sale of a used car, the conditional sales contract provided that it covered all conditions and agreements between the parties. The Arkansas Supreme Court held that 2–202 and the contract provision prevented the introduction of evidence that the salesperson made an oral guarantee concerning the mechanical parts.

Note, however, that the inclusion of a merger clause will not necessarily stop a court from deciding that the writing is incomplete.[10] In a particularly appealing case, a court may take the position that the merger clause is only *evidence* of the parties' intent. Moreover, if other language in the contract conflicts with the merger clause, the court may hold that the writing is incomplete and look to parol evidence for explanation or clarification.[11] In Leveridge v. Notaras,[12] a printed form contract contained both a printed disclaimer clause and the following handwritten notation:

> 30 day warranty
>
> Repair clutch as needed
>
> not too [sic] exceed $100.00
>
> date no later then [sic] Sat. Feb. 24, 1963

The court held that because this notation rendered the document ambiguous, evidence of an oral warranty against latent mechanical defects could be introduced.[13]

Since any attempt to disclaim an express warranty will encounter considerable judicial scrutiny, the only certain way to avoid liability for express warranties is to avoid making them in the first place. However, the seller can attain some protection against carelessly uttered (or falsely alleged) affirmations of fact by incorporat-

---

ranties where lease of business machines contains merger clause); Allmand Associates, Inc. v. Hercules Inc., 960 F.Supp. 1216, 34 UCC2d 353 (E.D.Mich. 1997) (conspicuous merger clause sufficient to exclude evidence of oral express warranties); Rawson v. Conover, 20 P.3d 876, 44 UCC2d 420 (Utah 2001).

8. 103 F.3d 1281, 31 UCC2d 1 (7th Cir. 1996).

9. 241 Ark. 62, 406 S.W.2d 142, 3 UCC 805 (1966).

10. For a lengthy discussion on merger clauses in other contexts, see Chapter 3.

11. See 3 A. Corbin, Contracts § 578 at 411 (1960); 4 S. Williston, Contracts § 643 at 1082 (3d ed. 1961).

12. 433 P.2d 935, 4 UCC 691 (Okl. 1967).

13. Note that the oral evidence was admitted despite the fact that the written contract contained the following merger clause: "It is agreed that no change, alteration, interlineation, or verbal agreement of any kind shall be effective to change, alter, or amend the printed terms of this agreement." *Id.* at 937, 4 UCC at 692.

ing a carefully drafted merger clause into the contract for sale. We offer the following as an example:

> MERGER CLAUSE, ORAL STATEMENTS NOT BINDING: The seller's sales people may have made oral statements about the merchandise described in this contract. Those statements are not warranties, should not be relied on by the buyer, and are not part of the contract for sale. The entire contract is embodied in this writing. This writing constitutes the final expression of the parties' agreement, and it is a complete and exclusive statement of the terms of that agreement.

If this clause conspicuously appears in the agreement, a court will have difficulty in giving effect to oral warranties that the buyer says the seller gave before the written agreement was signed. Moreover, this clause may provide the seller with a powerful bargaining tool during settlement negotiations.

§ 13–5 Disclaimers of Implied Warranties—Explicit Disclaimers of Implied Warranties, Section 2–316(2)

Disclaimers most often attempt to negate the implied warranties of merchantability and fitness for a particular purpose. Subsection 2–316(2) sets out specific requirements in this regard, and subsection (3) describes other circumstances that exclude implied warranties. Subsection (2) provides:

> Subject to subsection (3), to exclude or modify the implied warranty of merchantability or any part of it the language must mention merchantability and in case of a writing must be conspicuous, and to exclude or modify any implied warranty of fitness the exclusion must be by a writing and conspicuous. Language to exclude all implied warranties of fitness is sufficient if it states, for example, that "There are no warranties which extend beyond the description on the face hereof."

Consider several preliminary points. First, this provision applies to attempts to modify (for example by setting a time limit) as well as to attempts fully to exclude implied warranties. Any written disclaimer must be conspicuous, and the warranty of fitness can be disclaimed only in writing. While the implied warranty of merchantability can be orally excluded or modified, any attempt, written or oral, to disclaim that warranty must specifically mention the word "merchantability." On the other hand, general written language is sufficient to exclude the implied warranty of fitness for a particular purpose and, in fact, other words will do just as well as merchantability because of 2–316(3)(a). There are three questions involving subsection (2) that we will attempt to answer:

(1) What language satisfies the requirements of 2–316(2)?

(2) What does "conspicuous" mean?

(3) Is a disclaimer made after the time of contracting valid?

a. Required Language

Because section 2–316(2) states that "the language must mention merchantability" most disclaimers mention merchantability, and courts sometimes require that that word appear for a disclaimer to be effective. That requirement is contrary to the rule in 2–316. Because the rule in subsection (2) is "subject to subsection (3)", and because subsection (3) authorizes disclaimer "by expressions like 'as is', 'with all faults', or other language which in common understanding calls the buyer's attention to the exclusion of warranties and makes plain there is no implied warranty * * * *", it is not necessary to mention merchantability to have a valid disclaimer under 2–316. The word merchantability is blessed by subsection (2), but subsection (3) contemplates an unlimited array of words that could have the same effect. Moreover, most of us can think of many words that more clearly disclaim warranties than "Not Merchantable" does.[1] Because subsection (2) specifically blesses "merchantability" most drafters wisely include that word. But a careful drafter will do more and will recognize that other words can considerably strengthen a disclaimer.

Comment 4 states that the implied warranty of fitness for a particular purpose may be excluded by general language. For example, one court held that the following language is sufficient to negate this warranty: "The warranties and guaranties herein set forth are made by us and accepted by you in lieu of all statutory or implied warranties or guaranties, other than title."[2] The Code itself approves language that states " 'There are no warranties which extend beyond the description on the face hereof.' "[3] The seller's lawyer should remember, however, that under 2–316(1) that lan-

---

§ 13–5

1. See, e.g., Star–Shadow Productions, Inc. v. Super 8 Sync Sound System, 730 A.2d 1081, 38 UCC2d 1128 (R.I. 1999) (general disclaimer alerting buyer that no warranties exist beyond those on the face of the document is sufficient to disclaim warranties under 2–316(3)(a), without mention of merchantability). Sterner Aero AB v. Page Airmotive, Inc., 499 F.2d 709, 14 UCC 1080 (10th Cir.1974) (without discussion, court upheld disclaimer of implied warranty failing to mention merchantability); cf. Potler v. MCP Facilities Corp.,

471 F.Supp. 1344, 26 UCC 651 (E.D.N.Y. 1979) (court explicitly rejects decision in *Roto–Lith* and requires the word "merchantability").

2. Thorman v. Polytemp, Inc., 1965 WL 8338, 2 UCC 772, 774 (N.Y.Co.Ct. 1965) (sale of steam heater to dry cleaning establishment).

3. § 2–316(2). But bad faith can vitiate a disclaimer. See e.g., Potomac Plaza Terraces, Inc. v. QSC Products, Inc., 868 F.Supp. 346 26 UCC2d 1069 (D.D.C. 1994).

guage will not negate an express warranty that the goods being sold are fit for the buyer's special purpose. Moreover, language that is too general will fail. For example, the mere statement in a written express warranty that "no claim for labor or damages will be allowed" has been held insufficient to exclude the implied warranty of fitness for a particular purpose.[4]

It is comparatively easy to draft a disclaimer that complies with 2–316(2); to draft a disclaimer that a court will enforce is something else. Disclaimers with the right words are always subject to attack because the words are inconspicuous or the disclaimer is unconscionable. Whether a disclaimer is likely to be found unconscionable depends partly on how effectively it communicates its message to a typical buyer.

Consider common sellers' errors. Frequently disclaimers are mislabeled; the clause that contains the disclaimer may itself be labelled "WARRANTIES." Frequently disclaimers fail the test of conspicuousness discussed below. Sometimes they are on the back of the form and sometimes in print so small or poorly contrasting that it cannot be read. (We know of one plaintiff who won a case by asking the defendant's president to read its disclaimer on the witness stand. The contrast in the print was so faint that the president could not read the disclaimer.) Finally, a seller who is serious about disclaiming implied warranty liability may wish to use the vernacular of the street, vernacular that jars the buyer and truly alerts buyer to the risks.

Consider a plain vanilla disclaimer.

EXCLUSIONS OF WARRANTIES, NO WARRANTIES. The implied warranties of MERCHANTABILITY and fitness for a particular purpose and all other warranties, express or implied, are EXCLUDED from this transaction and shall not apply to the goods sold.

If the seller wants to provide the buyer with some limited protection—for example, the seller may be willing to repair or replace defective parts—the seller should spell out the nature of the express warranty and limited remedy in specific terms. The seller might then insert language to the effect:

The warranty described in this paragraph is IN LIEU OF any other warranty, express or implied, including but not limited to, any implied warranty of MERCHANTABILITY or fitness for a particular purpose.

---

4. See Murray v. Kleen Leen, Inc., 41 Ill.App.3d 436, 445, 354 N.E.2d 415, 423, 20 UCC 298, 306 (1976) (court held the following language ineffective to disclaim fitness warranty in lease of hogs for breeding: "Corporation makes no representation of profitability or warranty of results, and producer specifically acknowledges any livestock operation is affected by changes in costs, markets and unforeseeable factors which directly affect profits or loss.")

It is always desirable to use the magic words but it may be even better to add some spice to the disclaimer. For example, we can imagine a disclaimer as to used cars that might follow the plain vanilla merchantability disclaimer by saying "If this car stops working when you drive out of our lot, that is your problem, not ours." Or with respect to a TV—if the seller really means it—"We hope this TV will work when you get it home, but if it does not, that is your problem, not ours. We won't fix it." Since most sellers of new goods make broad express warranties and fear disparaging their goods, disclaimers of the sort we describe will rarely be included in the retail sale of new goods. That means the seller must use a plain vanilla merchantability disclaimer. The purpose of the disclaimer is not to escape responsibility for standard operation of the commodity, but is usually to avoid consequential liability or unforeseen claims under 2–314 about performance.

b. Conspicuousness in Contracting Generally

Subject to 2–316(3) section 2–316(2) requires that disclaimers of implied warranties be conspicuous. Section 1–201(10) defines "conspicuous" as follows:

> "Conspicuous", with reference to a term, means so written, displayed, or presented that a reasonable person against which it is to operate ought to have noticed it. Whether a term is "conspicuous" or not is a decision for the court. Conspicuous terms include the following:
>
> > (A) a heading in capitals equal to or greater in size than the surrounding text, or in contrasting type, font, or color to the surrounding text of the same or lesser size; and
>
> > (B) language in the body of a record or display in larger type than the surrounding text, or in contrasting type, font, or color to the surrounding text of the same size, or set off from surrounding text of the same size by symbols or other marks that call attention to the language.

Comment 10 emphasizes that subsection (10) merely indicates some of the methods of making a term conspicuous and that "the test is whether attention can reasonably be expected to be called to it." Indeed, some courts have indicated that methods may vary according to the bargaining strength and commercial sophistication of the buyer. In American Electric Power Co, Inc. v. Westinghouse Electric Corp.,[5] the parties arrived at a contract for the sale of a generator after more than two years of negotiations. Without any reference to the print or location of the clause disclaiming implied warranties, the court held the provision conspicuous, stating merely

---

5. 418 F.Supp. 435, 19 UCC 1009 (S.D.N.Y.1976).

that, "[i]t strains credulity to suggest that plaintiffs had not noticed or were unaware of the exclusion of implied warranties."[6] We agree with this approach since 1–201(10) phrases the test for conspicuousness of a clause in terms of a reasonable person "against whom it is to operate."

Many courts have assumed that the capitalization, typeface, and color methods described in 1–201(10) are absolute requirements; this reflects a judgment that terms embedded in a lengthy printed form contract are, in reality, not conspicuous unless there is something unusual about the way they are printed.[7] Absent something else to bring the disclaimer to a buyer's attention (e.g., Chanel No. 5) "[a] provision is not conspicuous when there is only a slight contrast with the balance of the instrument."[8] But in some courts it may be enough to alert the buyer to read the full agreement.[9]

A disclaimer's location on a document can be important. For example, in Massey–Ferguson v. Utley,[10] a contract for the sale of a combine attachment contained an express warranty clause, with a heading in capital letters that excluded all implied warranties. The Kentucky Court of Appeals held that because this provision was on the back of the contract form and was referred to by words in only ordinary type on the front, it was not conspicuous. Several other courts have adopted a similar rationale,[11] but the Kentucky court was quick to emphasize that disclaimers on the reverse side of contract forms are not invalid *per se*. In Childers & Venters, Inc. v.

---

6. *Id.* at 451 n.22, 19 UCC 1021 n.22. Courts often cite buyer sophistication as one of several factors supporting a finding of conspicuousness.

7. Courts have approved other attention-drawing methods as well. See, e.g., Architectural Aluminum Corp. v. Macarr, Inc., 70 Misc.2d 495, 333 N.Y.S.2d 818, 10 UCC 1159 (1972) (framed in black); Wilson v. Royal Motor Sales, Inc., 812 N.E.2d 133, 54 UCC2d 473 (Ind. App. 2004) (contrasting type and size from rest of the language is conspicuous).

8. Greenspun v. American Adhesives, Inc., 320 F.Supp. 442, 444, 8 UCC 439, 441 (E.D.Pa.1970). See also Sarnecki v. Al Johns Pontiac, 1966 WL 8826, 3 UCC 1121 (Pa.C.P.1966) (slight variation in contrasting type was perfunctory attempt to comply with Code); DeLamar Motor Co. v. White, 249 Ark. 708, 460 S.W.2d 802, 8 UCC 437 (1970) (disclaimer in italic type which was smaller and lighter than much of the rest of the form); Bailey v. Tucker

Equipment Sales, Inc., 236 Ga.App. 289, 510 S.E.2d 904, 38 UCC2d 292 (1999) ("as is" language in same size and color as the rest of terms is not conspicuous).

9. Perry v. Gulf Stream Coach, Inc., 814 N.E.2d 634, 54 UCC2d 769 (Ind. App. 2004).

10. 439 S.W.2d 57, 6 UCC 51 (Ky. 1969). Cf. Clements Farms, Inc. v. Ben Fish and Son, 120 Idaho 185, 814 P.2d 917, 15 UCC2d 799 (1991) (court's rationale for holding disclaimer inconspicuous included disclaimer's location in the middle of the front page).

11. Hunt v. Perkins Mach. Co., 352 Mass. 535, 226 N.E.2d 228, 4 UCC 281 (1967) (disclaimer on reverse side of form was concealed from buyer because form was on pad when he signed it); Parsley v. Monaco Coach Corp., 327 F.Supp.2d 797, 54 UCC2d 301 (W.D.Mich. 2004) (all-capitalized disclaimer conspicuous even on reverse because of multiple references to disclaimer on front in all capital letters, bold print, and contrasting color).

Sowards,[12] the court said that if the drafters intended a per se rule, they would have said so since they knew it was customary to print terms on the back of form contracts. The court therefore validated a disclaimer appearing on the back side of a contract for the sale of a used truck, since the clause was printed in larger and heavier print than was used on the rest of the form.[13] A case that may win the prize for valid reverse side disclaimers is Parsely v. Monaco Coach Corp.[14]

Several sellers have attempted to satisfy the conspicuousness requirement by printing only the heading of the combined express warranty and disclaimer clause in capital letters. In part because these headings have failed to disclose the true nature of the clause, some courts have denied effect to the disclaimer. For example, in the *Utley* case,[15] the disclaimer was contained in a paragraph headed in capital letters as "WARRANTY and AGREEMENT"; the disclaimer language itself was printed in the same type size and face as the rest of the contract. Said the court:

> It is true the *heading* was in large, bold-face type, but there was nothing to suggest that an exclusion was being made; on the contrary, the words of the heading indicated a *making* of warranties rather than a *disclaimer*.[16]

Similarly, the seller who emphasizes only the words "MERCHANT-ABILITY" or "FITNESS FOR A PARTICULAR PURPOSE" in the body of his disclaimer may find the disclaimer inoperative.[17] Perhaps the *safest* course for a seller to follow is to print all disclaimer language in bold-face capitals of a contrasting color.

The comment says a term is conspicuous if "attention can reasonably be expected to be called to it." It does not say that a consumer's attention must *actually* be called to a disclaimer. A court in New Jersey—where disclaimers have enjoyed little favor[18]

12. 460 S.W.2d 343, 8 UCC 433 (Ky. 1970).

13. Accord Houck v. DeBonis, 38 Md.App. 85, 379 A.2d 765, 23 UCC 60 (1977), cert. denied sub nom., Conklin v. Maryland, 434 U.S. 967, 98 S.Ct. 511, 54 L.Ed.2d 454 (1977) (front of form referenced reverse-side disclaimer that contrasted with rest of contract); See, however, Young v. Continental Crane and Rigging Co., 183 Or.App. 563, 53 P.3d 465, 48 UCC2d 846 (2002) (not conspicuous where on back in very light ink although party had initialed front saying agreed to terms on back). With this case, compare Wilson v. Royal Motor Sales, Inc., 812 N.E.2d 133, 54 UCC2d 473 (Ind. App. 2004) (valid, though on back where buyer's signature acknowledged disclaimer).

14. 327 F.Supp.2d 797, 54 UCC2d 301 (W.D.Mich. 2004) (all-capitalized disclaimer conspicuous even on reverse because of multiple references to disclaimer on front in all capital letters, bold print, and contrasting color).

15. Massey–Ferguson v. Utley, 439 S.W.2d 57, 6 UCC 51 (Ky.1969).

16. *Id.* at 59, 6 UCC at 53.

17. See International Harvester Co. v. Pike, 249 Ark. 1026, 466 S.W.2d 901, 10 UCC 1164 (1971) (sale of transport truck).

18. See Henningsen v. Bloomfield Motors, Inc., 32 N.J. 358, 161 A.2d 69 (1960).

—refused to give effect to a disclaimer of warranties concerning a new car. It did so partly because there was no evidence that the disclaimer had actually been brought to the buyer's attention or explained to the buyer in detail.[19] The Kentucky Court of Appeals has held that it is not necessary that the buyer's attention be specifically called to a disclaimer.[20] We believe that the Kentucky court reads the Code correctly since it accords with 1–201(10)'s "reasonable-person" standard, the language of the comment, and conventional contract doctrine that binds a party even to unread terms.

Can a seller achieve conspicuousness by orally drawing attention to an otherwise inconspicuous written disclaimer? Comment 1 to 2–316 indicates that the purpose of the conspicuousness requirement is to "protect the buyer from surprise" and from "unexpected and unbargained language of disclaimer." This purpose is accomplished when the buyer learns of the seller's disclaimer—conspicuous or inconspicuous. On the other hand, section 1–201(10) says, "A term or clause is conspicuous when *so written* * * *." (Emphasis added).

This situation is analogous to that described in the preceding paragraph, where the buyer attacks a disclaimer by testifying that the disclaimer was not actually pointed out to him. Giving legal effect to knowledge or lack of knowledge might reward the convincing liar who claims that the buyer was—or was not—made aware of the disclaimer. But we think the cases are different. Persons who sign contracts are bound by all of the terms—those read and those not read. Although effective disclaimers may need to be conspicuous, nothing in the Code conditions a disclaimer's effect on the buyer's knowledge—much less understanding—of the disclaimer and the cases that suggest otherwise are wrong. On the other hand, we believe that where the buyer—particularly a commercial buyer—admits to reading and understanding inconspicuous clauses or admits that the seller drew those clauses to his attention, the clauses should be valid and binding notwithstanding their inconspicuousness.[21]

c. *Conspicuousness in Electronic Contracting*

The definition of conspicuous in section 1–201(10), discussed immediately above applies to electronic contracting as well. Under that definition, a contract in electronic form can be relevantly

19. Zabriskie Chevrolet, Inc. v. Smith, 99 N.J.Super. 441, 240 A.2d 195, 5 UCC 30 (1968).

20. Childers & Venters, Inc. v. Sowards, 460 S.W.2d 343, 8 UCC 433 (Ky. 1970).

21. See Woodruff v. Clark County Farm Bureau Co-op. Ass'n, 153 Ind.App. 31, 286 N.E.2d 188, 11 UCC 498 (1972) ("as is" disclaimer inconspicuous in absence of evidence of buyer awareness).

conspicuous, as with a disclaimer of warranty under section 2–316(2). Because 1–201(10) provides that conspicuous means so written, displayed, or presented that a reasonable person against which it is to operate ought to have noticed it, the section recognizes that an electronic statement can be conspicuous.

d. Disclaimer Subsequent to Contracting

Sometimes the seller does not make a disclaimer until *after* the contract for sale has been made. For example, a buyer might sign a purchase agreement for a new car and the next week sign an installment sales contract that contains a printed disclaimer. That case is now covered not by former 9–206(2) but by Article 2 which governs all secured sales with respect to disclaimers of warranty. A disclaimer in a security agreement that is signed subsequent to the signing of the sales agreement should not affect either express or implied warranties created on the earlier date,[22] unless there is an effective modification under 2–209.

In a more common situation the buyer might be given a disclaimer at the time of the delivery of the goods. That disclaimer may be printed on a label, in an operator's manual, or on an invoice. According to most pre-Code law, "[I]f a bargain with even an implied warranty has once arisen, a subsequent disclaimer of warranty when the goods are delivered will not avail the seller."[23] The same rule has generally prevailed under the Code.[24] For example, in Koellmer v. Chrysler Motors Corp.[25] a properly worded disclaimer clause was contained in the operator's manual for a new truck. A Connecticut court held this clause ineffective because the manual was delivered after the sale had been consummated.[26]

The reader will recall that Comment 7 to 2–313 indicates that an express warranty made after the closing of the deal can be made a binding part of the contract so long as the parties comply with the provisions of 2–209 on contract modification. This analysis should be equally applicable to disclaimers made pursuant to 2–316. Compliance with 2–209 is not easy, for subsection (1) requires that the parties agree to any modifications. Thus, a warranty booklet stuffed in a glove compartment of a new car would not be binding on a

---

22. See Tennessee Carolina Transportation, Inc. v. Strick Corp., 283 N.C. 423, 196 S.E.2d 711, 12 UCC 1055 (1973) (disclaimers in security agreements executed after contract for sale of 150 trailers did not negate implied warranty of fitness).

23. 8 S. Williston, Contracts § 993A at 610 (3d ed.1961).

24. See, e.g., Zabriskie Chevrolet, Inc. v. Smith, 99 N.J.Super. 441, 240 A.2d 195, 5 UCC 30 (1968) (disclaimer for new car contained in warranty delivered after contract signed).

25. 6 Conn.Cir. 478, 276 A.2d 807, 8 UCC 668 (1970). A properly worded disclaimer "embedded" in the sales contract was inoperative because it was not conspicuous. *Id.* at 484, 8 UCC at 672.

26. *Id.* at 484, 8 UCC at 673.

buyer who receives the car three days after signing the sales agreement—unless the buyer "agreed" to the modification. In any event, section 2–209 does provide a forgetful seller who is willing to negotiate with a means of disclaiming warranties that arose when the seller closed the deal.

One case invokes the obligation of good faith in concluding that a disclaimer may not be binding.[27]

§ 13–6 Disclaimers of Implied Warranties—Other Methods, Section 2–316(3)

After setting out the specific requirements of subsection 2–316 (2), the Code continues to provide in subsection (3) several alternative and less formal means of disclaiming warranty liability "[n]otwithstanding subsection (2)."

Comment 6 to 2–316 explains:

The exceptions to the general rule * * * are common factual situations in which the circumstances surrounding the transaction are in themselves sufficient to call the buyer's attention to the fact that no implied warranties are made or that a certain implied warranty is being excluded.

One must keep in mind that each of the alternative routes depends to some extent on the circumstances surrounding the particular sale in question; these are not absolute rules.

a. "As Is" Clauses, Section 2–316(3)(a)

Perhaps the easiest way for a seller to avoid potential warranty liability is to provide in the sales agreement that the buyer takes the goods sold "as is." Section 2–316(3)(a) reads:

Notwithstanding subsection (2)

(a) unless the circumstances indicate otherwise, all implied warranties are excluded by expressions like "as is", "with all faults" or other language which in common understanding calls the buyer's attention to the exclusion of warranties and makes plain that there is no implied warranty * * *.

Comment 7 tells us that "[s]uch terms in ordinary commercial usage are understood to mean that the buyer takes the entire risk as to the quality of the goods involved." Thus, if one bottler agrees to sell used bottling equipment to another bottler "as is, where is," an experienced businessperson-buyer cannot hold the seller responsible for any defects in the equipment on an implied warranty

---

27. Potomac Plaza Terraces, Inc. v. QSC Products, Inc., 868 F.Supp. 346, 26 UCC2d 1069 (D.D.C. 1994).

theory.[1] The seller has other magic words available also: paragraph (a) mentions "with all faults" and Comment 7 adds "as they stand." It is unclear what other shibboleths would work. One court held that a statement in a sales contract to the effect that the buyer accepts the car "in its present condition" had the same effect as an "as is" clause;[2] yet another court, in a case involving an almost identical transaction, said the terms were not synonymous.[3]

Subsection 2–316(3)(a) does give the buyer an opportunity to nullify an "as is" clause by showing that "the circumstances indicate otherwise."[4] One such circumstance might be the fact that the buyer is an ordinary consumer without knowledge of the consequences of "as is," "with all faults," or "as they stand." A Florida appellate court reversed summary judgment for a seller who sold a used motorcycle "as is."[5]

Section (3)(a) and Comment 7 bear on these questions. The subsection refers to language which in "common understanding" conveys the message of disclaimer. Comment 7 refers to "ordinary commercial usage." If the Florida court is suggesting that a particular buyer must understand a particular articulation, we think the court is wrong. Even consumer buyers should be bound by language that would have a particular meaning in "common understanding", i.e., an understanding widely shared even though not understood by this particular buyer. While it is proper for courts to insist that language of disclaimer be widely understood to be effective, they should be skeptical of any buyer's claim that that buyer did not understand words to mean what a lay person would normally understand. Remember that consumer buyers lie too; they are not different from any other contracting parties who find it convenient to deny appreciation of what they have signed. Presumably the rule

§ 13–6

1. Crown Cork & Seal Co. v. Hires Bottling Co., 254 F.Supp. 424, 3 UCC 609 (N.D.Ill.1966), rev'd, 371 F.2d 256 (7th Cir.1967); Ladner v. Jordon, 848 So.2d 870, 49 UCC2d 138 (Miss. App. 2002).

2. First Nat. Bank of Elgin v. Husted, 57 Ill.App.2d 227, 205 N.E.2d 780, 2 UCC 777 (1965).

3. Hull–Dobbs, Inc. v. Mallicoat, 57 Tenn.App. 100, 415 S.W.2d 344, 3 UCC 1032 (1966).But see Quaker Alloy Casting Co. v. Gulfco Indus., Inc., 686 F.Supp. 1319, 7 UCC2d 429 (N.D.Ill. 1988) (where buyer's contract negotiator testified that it was its understanding that buyer bought work-in-progress parts without reserving further rights against seller, effect was same as "as is").

4. "Circumstances indicat[ing] otherwise" applies only to narrowly drawn situations. Pelc v. Simmons, 249 Ill. App.3d 852, 189 Ill.Dec. 353, 620 N.E.2d 12, 23 UCC2d 1113 (1993) ("as is" sign on car effectively disclaimed implied warranties, and statement by seller that he rebuilt engine did not create express warranty).

5. Knipp v. Weinbaum, 351 So.2d 1081, 22 UCC 1141 (Fla.App.1977). Relying in part on the phrase "unless circumstances indicate otherwise," the court remanded for a determination of the intended effect of the "as is" clause.

that binds one to what he has signed is to avoid this unreliable testimony. Assuming that the language carries the common meaning of disclaimer, it is no defense that a particular buyer did not understand the meaning of that language.[6]

A New Jersey court has indicated that the use of an "as is" clause in a contract for the sale of new goods may be inoperative. Gindy Manufacturing Corp. v. Cardinale Trucking Corp.[7] involved the sale of twenty-five new semi-trailers. The contract form, which the seller used for the sale of both new and used vehicles, contained an "as is" disclaimer. The court found that under the custom of the trade,[8] "as is" clauses are expected in contracts for the sale of used vehicles but not when new vehicles are involved.[9] It therefore held that under these circumstances the "as is" clause was not a disclaimer.[10]

A buyer's attempt to avoid an "as is" clause will almost surely be defeated by evidence that the parties bargained over the term. Chamberlain v. Bob Matick Chevrolet, Inc.[11] involved the sale of a used car, which turned out to have a defective master cylinder. The dealer finally agreed to sell the car for $325 "as is," but earlier the dealer had offered to sell it with a guarantee for $350. The court held that in light of these circumstances and the fact that the seller told the buyer that a sale at the lower price would be at the buyer's risk, the seller had made an effective disclaimer.[12]

A few pre-Code cases held that an "as is" clause did not operate to negate the seller's obligation to deliver goods as described. For example, in a misrepresentation case one court held the buyer of a 1933 truck "in its present condition" was entitled to rescission upon its discovery that the truck was actually a 1932 model.[13] Would the same result be reached under the Code? Under

---

6. Professor Honnold took the position that an "as is" clause should exclude all warranties, even in a contract with a consumer who is unaware of the trade meaning of the term. 1 N.Y. State Law Revision Comm'n, 1955 Report 409 (1955). See also § 2–316, Comment 1.

7. 111 N.J.Super. 383, 268 A.2d 345, 7 UCC 1257 (1970).

8. Comment 7 to 2–316 states, "The terms covered by paragraph (a) are in fact merely a particularization of paragraph (c) which provides for exclusion or modification of implied warranties by usage of trade."

9. 111 N.J.Super. at 397, 268 A.2d at 353, 7 UCC at 1268.

10. *Id.* at 399, 268 A.2d at 354, 7 UCC at 1269. The court suggested that

an "as is" clause in a contract for the sale of new goods, if accompanied by a statement that the goods are delivered in good condition means that the goods are in new and good mechanical condition.

11. 4 Conn.Cir.Ct. 685, 239 A.2d 42, 4 UCC 936 (1967).

12. *Id.* at 696, 239 A.2d at 46, 4 UCC at 942. See also Crown Cork & Seal Co. v. Hires Bottling Co., 254 F.Supp. 424, 3 UCC 609 (N.D.Ill.1966), rev'd, 371 F.2d 256 (7th Cir.1967) ("as is" clause insisted on by seller was effective because it had been the subject of bargaining).

13. Denenberg v. Jurad, 300 Mass. 488, 15 N.E.2d 660 (1938).

2–313(1)(b), any description of the goods that is made part of the basis of the bargain creates an express warranty that the goods conform to that description. Since 2–316(3)(a) provides a means of disclaiming *implied* warranties only, an express warranty based on a description of the truck as a 1933 model would not be disclaimed by an "as is" clause.[14] This clause would fail under 2–316(1) because of its inconsistency with the description warranty.[15] Comment 4 to section 2–313 states that a court cannot give literal effect to a clause that purports to disclaim *all* warranties, express or implied; at the very minimum, the seller cannot disclaim the obligation to deliver goods that conform to their description.

One final question remains under 2–316(3)(a). Must disclaimer language under this provision be conspicuous? The Code does not explicitly impose that requirement. Moreover, Comment 6 suggests that the very fact that an "as is" clause is included should be sufficient to call the buyer's attention to the seller's exclusion of implied warranties.[16] However, many courts have held that the conspicuousness requirement applies to "as is" clauses on the ground that otherwise that requirement's presence in subsection (2) would be useless.[17]

14. See, e.g., City Dodge, Inc. v. Gardner, 232 Ga. 766, 208 S.E.2d 794, 15 UCC 598 (1974) ("as is" clause did not negate express warranty that used car had never been wrecked); Bill Spreen Toyota, Inc. v. Jenquin, 163 Ga. App. 855, 294 S.E.2d 533, 35 UCC 419 (1982) (car purchased was not a Toyota as expressly warranted, but was one-half of such a car welded to one-half of another unidentified vehicle).

15. See 13–3 *supra*. See also Morningstar v. Hallett, 858 A.2d 125, 54 UCC2d 716 (Pa. Super. 2004). An "as is" clause in a writing intended to be final might, however, be effective against parol warranties. Section 2–316(1) is made subject to 2–202 which excludes terms contradicting a final writing. See Avery v. Aladdin Products Div., 128 Ga.App. 266, 196 S.E.2d 357, 12 UCC 628 (1973) (clause stating that machinery was sold "in its present condition" excluded evidence of seller's oral statement that machinery was in "good condition"); TIBCO Software, Inc. v. Gordon Food Service, Inc., 2003 WL 21683850, 51 UCC2d 102 (W.D.Mich. 2003) (excluded parol evidence where "as is" clause was part of a fully integrated agreement).

16. For an argument based on the comments that 2–316(3)(a) does not in-

corporate a conspicuousness requirement, see Hogan, The Highways and Some of the Byways in the Sales and Bulk Sales Articles of the Uniform Commercial Code, 48 Cornell L.Q. 1, 7–8, 8 n.29 (1962). See also Lord, Some Thoughts About Warranty Law: Express and Implied Warranties, 56 N.D.L.Rev. 509, 680–684 (1980). Further on conspicuousness, see Tulger Contracting Corp. v. Star Building Systems, 52 UCC2d 917 (S.D.N.Y. 2002); Parsley v. Monaco Coach Corp., 327 F. Supp.2d 797, 54 UCC2d 301 (W.D. Mich. 2004) (conspicuous though on back). Accord, Pitts v. Monaco Coach Corp., 330 F. Supp.2d 918, 54 UCC2d 316 (W.D. Mich. 2004) (were references on front to notice on back). See also Alcan Aluminum Corp. v. BASF Corp., 133 F.Supp.2d 482, 44 UCC2d 432 (N.D. Tex. 2001) (conspicuous though on back).

17. See, e.g., Woodruff v. Clark County Farm Bureau Co-op. Ass'n, 153 Ind.App. 31, 286 N.E.2d 188, 11 UCC 498 (1972) (sale of chickens); Dallas Aerospace, Inc. v. CIS Air Corp., 2002 WL 31453789, 49 UCC2d 142 (S.D.N.Y. 2002) ("as is" term in delivery form plus disclaimer in bold face validly disclaimed warranties as to airplane engine).

b. Disclaimer Because of Examination or Opportunity to Examine

Paragraph (b) of 2–316(3) provides an alternative method by which a seller may shift the risk of the quality of the goods to the buyer:

> (3) Notwithstanding subsection (2)
>
>   * * *
>
>   (b) when the buyer before entering into the contract has examined the goods or the sample or model as fully as he desired or has refused to examine the goods there is no implied warranty with regard to defects which an examination ought in the circumstances to have revealed to him.
>   * * *

The drafters have provided an unusually long and helpful Comment 8. The gist of (3)(b), according to the comment, is that by demanding that the buyer examine the goods sold, "[t]he seller * * * puts the buyer on notice that he is assuming the risk of defects which the examination ought to reveal." Thus it is not sufficient that the seller merely make the goods available for inspection.[18] Once the seller makes the demand, however, the seller is free of any implied warranty for defects that an examination should have revealed, even if the buyer does not examine the goods.[19] On the other hand, even if the seller does not make a demand, the seller receives the same protection if the buyer voluntarily examines the goods, or a sample or a model[20] as fully as the buyer wishes.[21] The seller should be aware, however, that a buyer's examinations or refusals to examine that occur *after* contract formation will not affect the existence of implied warranties.[22]

18. See, e.g., Holm v. Hansen, 248 N.W.2d 503, 20 UCC 879 (Iowa 1976) (seller failed to demand that buyer test cows for brucellosis).

19. See, e.g., Calloway v. Manion, 572 F.2d 1033, 23 UCC 1143 (5th Cir. 1978) (buyer refused to examine horse); Tarulli v. Birds in Paradiso, 99 Misc.2d 1054, 417 N.Y.S.2d 854, 26 UCC 872 (City Civ.Ct.1979) (buyer never had cockatoo examined by a veterinarian); Ladner v. Jordan, 848 So.2d 870, 49 UCC2d 138 (Miss.App. 2002) (failure to inspect horse at point of sale "as is" negated implied warranty of fitness).

20. While the words "sample or model" are used in connection with an actual examination by the buyer, they are not used in connection with his refusal to examine. This wording would indicate that a disclaimer does not arise by virtue of paragraph (b) when the buyer refuses to examine a sample or model. But cf. Austin Lee Corp. v. Cascades Motel, Inc., 123 Ga.App. 642, 182 S.E.2d 173, 9 UCC 462 (1971) (buyer's failure to examine sample bedspreads did not disclaim implied warranty because seller made no demand).

21. Cf. Sparks v. Stich, 522 N.Y.S.2d 707, 135 A.D.2d 989, 5 UCC2d 922 (1987) (suggesting that even a brief inspection by buyer may protect seller).

22. See, e.g., Murray v. Kleen Leen, Inc., 41 Ill.App.3d 436, 354 N.E.2d 415, 20 UCC 298 (1976) (examination of pigs at delivery did not negate implied warranties). But see Davis v. Pumpco, Inc., 519 P.2d 557, 14 UCC 89 (Okl.App.1974) (implied warranty negated because buy-

Comment 8 to 2–316 emphasizes the importance of "[t]he particular buyer's skill and the normal method of examining goods in the circumstances * * *." The comment then suggests a distinction between professional and nonprofessional buyers. For example, a governmental agency buying magnetic tape[23] or a farmer purchasing feeder pigs[24] will be held to have assumed the risk for any defects that professionals in their respective fields should have discovered upon examination.[25] On the other hand, a lay person purchasing an automobile cannot be expected to be able to discover subtle mechanical and design defects. Absent unusual circumstances, we expect that most courts would be reluctant to find that an examination by a consumer has excluded all implied warranties.[26] But unusual circumstances might exist where the buyer of a used car is a teen-age car freak or the buyer of a computer is himself a dedicated hacker.

Although paragraph (b), like paragraphs (a) and (c), deals only with the exclusion of implied warranties, a pre-contract examination may affect whether an express warranty arises as well. Alan Wood Steel Co. v. Capital Equipment Enterprises, Inc.[27] involved the 1966 sale of a "75 ton" crane which had been manufactured in 1942. The crane proved incapable of lifting more than 50 tons, and the buyer claimed breach of an express warranty by description. But the buyer was aware that the seller had not seen the used crane prior to the sale. Moreover, at the seller's urging, the buyer had examined the crane twice before his purchase. The court found that this examination was one factor preventing an *express* warranty from arising.[28] The language of "description" did not become part of the basis of the bargain.[29] Even when the examination does uncover an inconsistency with an express warranty, under all the

---

er discovered defect in pipe cement after sale but prior to use).

23. See Reeves Soundcraft Corp., 1964 WL 518, 2 UCC 210 (Armed Serv. Bd. of Contract Apps.1964).

24. See, e.g., Willis v. West Ky. Feeder Pig Co., 132 Ill.App.2d 266, 265 N.E.2d 899, 8 UCC 1010 (1971).

25. The buyer is only held to such defects as can be discovered under the circumstances. Thus, the buyer will not be held to latent defects or defects ascertainable only by testing procedures not reasonable under the circumstances. See § 2–316, Comment 8. See, e.g., Ambassador Steel Co. v. Ewald Steel Co., 33 Mich.App. 495, 190 N.W.2d 275, 9 UCC 1019 (1971) (buyer of steel not expected to make tests for carbon content).

26. See Overland Bond & Inv. Corp. v. Howard, 9 Ill.App.3d 348, 292 N.E.2d 168, 11 UCC 945 (1972) (even if buyer test drove car, one would not be expected to discover latent defects in transmission, gas line, and brakes); Doug Connor, Inc. v. Proto–Grind, Inc., 761 So.2d 426, 41 UCC2d 1153 (Fla.App. 2000) (implied, but not express, warranties waived by buyer's inspection).

27. 39 Ill.App.3d 48, 349 N.E.2d 627, 19 UCC 1310 (1976).

28. The court also cited contract language that "descriptions are approximate and intended to serve as a guide." *Id.* at 57, 349 N.E.2d at 635, 19 UCC at 1320.

29. See Chapter 10 *supra*.

circumstances, the buyer might still reasonably expect conformity by the time of sale.[30]

The buyer's examination can also lead to the *creation* of express warranties under 2–313.[31] For example, if the buyer examines a sample or model considered part of the basis of the bargain, an express warranty arises that the goods shall conform to the sample or model.[32] In a pre-Code case, the seller urged the buyer to examine surplus rope being sold on an "as is—where is" basis. The court held that when the seller accepted the buyer's offer based on his examination, the seller warranted that the rope would conform to its condition at the time of inspection.[33] Such a result might not be possible under the Code, since nothing in 2–313 provides that examination of goods prior to sale, without more, creates an express warranty that the goods should conform to the condition they were in at the time of the examination.[34] But a few words carelessly tossed out by the seller could be construed, in combination with the examination, to be an express warranty. Comment 8 to 2–316 tells us:

> [I]f the offer of examination is accompanied by words as to their merchantability or specific attributes and the buyer indicates clearly that he is relying on those words rather than on his examination, they give rise to an "express" warranty.

One should understand that examination of the goods or a sample or model, may modify, add to, or eliminate the seller's warranty responsibility.

c. Disclaimer by Other Circumstances, Section 2–316(3)(c)

Paragraph (c) of 2–316(3) is a "catch-all" provision for miscellaneous methods of excluding or modifying warranties. It provides:

> (3) Notwithstanding subsection (2) * * *
>
>   (c) an implied warranty can also be excluded or modified by course of dealing or course of performance or usage of trade.

This provision has little meaning without reference to section 1–303, which defines "course of dealing" and "usage of trade":

> (b) A "course of dealing" is a sequence of conduct concerning previous transactions between the parties to a particular

---

30. See also, Doug Connor, Inc. v. Proto–Grind, Inc., 761 So.2d 426, 41 UCC2d 1153 (Fla.App. 2000).

31. See § 10–2 et seq., *supra.*

32. § 2–313(1)(c).

33. United States v. Blake, 161 F.Supp. 76 (D.N.C.1958).

34. § 2–313 provides for the creation of express warranties only by affirmation of fact, description of the goods, or exhibitions of samples or models.

transaction that is fairly to be regarded as establishing a common basis of understanding for interpreting their expressions and other conduct.

(c) A "usage of trade" is any practice or method of dealing having such regularity of observance in a place, vocation or trade as to justify an expectation that it will be observed with respect to the transaction in question. The existence and scope of such a usage must be proved as facts. If it is established that such a usage is embodied in a trade code or similar record interpretation of the record is for the court.

In addition, 1–303(a) defines "course of performance":

(a) A "course of performance" is a sequence of conduct between the parties to a particular transaction that exists if:

(1) the agreement of the parties with respect to the transaction involves repeated occasions for performance by a party; and

(2) the other party, with knowledge of the nature of the performance and opportunity for objection to it, accepts the performance or acquiesces in it without objection.

"Course of performance" and "course of dealing" are closely related to each other since both arise solely from relationships between the parties. A "usage of trade," on the other hand, develops out of a history of transactions within a particular business community. To borrow a phrase from labor law,[35] course of performance and course of dealing represent the "common law" of the parties, while usage of trade embodies the "common law" of the trade of one or more of the parties.

How can a course of dealing or course of performance disclaim a warranty? In Country Clubs, Inc. v. Allis–Chalmers Manufacturing Co.,[36] a contract for the sale of electric golf carts contained an express warranty that was limited to repair and replacement of parts, and also purported to exclude all other warranties without using the word "merchantability." The carts developed problems, and the buyer returned them for repairs. The seller made the repairs at a total cost of $12,000 but billed the buyer for $4,663 to cover parts not within the warranty terms but which—in the seller's opinion—needed replacing because of ordinary wear and tear.[37] The buyer refused to pay and sued for breach of warranty to

---

35. See, e.g., United Steelworkers v. Warrior & Gulf Navigation Co., 363 U.S. 574, 579–80, 80 S.Ct. 1347, 1351, 4 L.Ed.2d 1409 (1960), which refers to the "common law of the shop."

36. 430 F.2d 1394, 7 UCC 1253 (6th Cir.1970).

37. When the buyer has paid for past repairs, a court may hold that the buyer's course of performance disclaimed implied warranties. See Gulash v. Stylarama, Inc., 33 Conn.Sup. 108, 364 A.2d 1221, 20 UCC 603 (1975) (assuming ar-

recover damages for the cost of the carts and lost profits. The court held that regardless of the language used in the disclaimer, the course of dealing and the course of performance were sufficient to exclude implied warranties because the parties had discussed and negotiated the warranty provisions and the buyer had asserted several claims under those provisions.[38] The buyer had ordered carts from the seller on two different occasions, so "a sequence of previous conduct between the parties" existed between them.[39]

When business persons have repeatedly used particular disclaimers in prior dealings, courts are likely to uphold otherwise invalid disclaimers. In Velez v. Craine & Clarke Lumber Corp.,[40] the buyer's employee sought recovery for personal injury sustained when scaffold planking collapsed. The seller's invoice contained a small print disclaimer—as had invoices in prior transactions between the parties for over fifteen years. Since the buyer had knowledge of past disclaimers on invoices, the court held the clause conspicuous "despite the smallness of the type."[41] The course of dealing did not by itself void implied warranties. Rather, the sequence of previous dealings over the years validated the written disclaimer.[42]

Establishing a disclaimer may be easier by trade usage than by course of performance or course of dealing. A court may refer to other members of the trade or to trade manuals or trade codes to learn trade usage. For example, the Nebraska Supreme Court upheld a trial court's determination that when a cattle buyer inspects cattle and cuts out those that do not suit the buyer, there is a usage of trade that his acceptance of others "is irrevocable and without recourse," and thus excludes all implied warranties.[43] Pre-

---

guendo that Code applies to sale and installation of swimming pool).

38. 430 F.2d at 1397, 7 UCC at 1256. The court also noted that the buyer's agent was a business person and attorney and that the buyer had referred to the warranty provisions in the contract when it defended against the seller's counterclaim.

39. Standard Structural Steel Co. v. Bethlehem Steel Corp., 597 F.Supp. 164, 40 UCC 1245 (D.Conn.1984) (course of dealing established between merchants after 62 years of business).

40. 41 A.D.2d 747, 341 N.Y.S.2d 248, 12 UCC 69 (1973), rev'd on other grounds, 33 N.Y.2d 117, 350 N.Y.S.2d 617, 305 N.E.2d 750, 13 UCC 793 (1973).

41. Id. at 749, 341 N.Y.S.2d at 252, 12 UCC at 73. The Velez court also cited the buyer's awareness that trade in-

voices commonly contain disclaimers to support its finding that the disclaimer was conspicuous.

42. Courts have employed similar reasoning to uphold written liability limitations received by the buyer on or after delivery. See, e.g., D.O.V. Graphics, Inc. v. Eastman Kodak Co., 46 Ohio Misc. 37, 75 O.O.2d 349, 347 N.E.2d 561, 19 UCC 842 (1976) (remedy limitation on packages of photographic paper became part of contract where similar clause was present in past party dealings). But prior dealings cannot validate a post-sale disclaimer. Bowdoin v. Showell Growers, Inc., 817 F.2d 1543, 3 UCC2d 1366 (11th Cir.1987).

43. R.D. Lowrance, Inc. v. Peterson, 185 Neb. 679, 682, 178 N.W.2d 277, 279, 7 UCC 1179, 1181 (1970). Compare Ruskamp v. Hog Builders, Inc., 192 Neb. 168, 219 N.W.2d 750, 14 UCC 1093

Code law frequently recognized a trade usage of seed sellers that excluded implied warranties and bound the purchaser, even if he did not know about the usage.[44] In Zicari v. Joseph Harris Co.,[45] a New York case, a seed seller tried to assert this usage of trade when the exclusionary language printed on its order forms failed to comply with 2–316(2). The seller contended that the alleged usage of trade should be binding on the buyer since other seed sellers in the area used similar exclusionary language and since only one out of 400 customers with damaged crops had complained to the seller. The court, however, concluded that these facts failed to establish "a usage of trade understood by all persons in the seed business and farming."[46]

Surely the court misspoke or erred when it suggested that "all" must understand. Members of the trade are bound despite their individual ignorance. Under pre-Code law, a trade usage was not operative against a party who was not a member of the trade unless the nonmember actually knew of it or the other party could reasonably believe the nonmember knew of it.[47] This view has been carried forward in 1–303(d), which provides that usages of trade "in the vocation or trade in which they are engaged or of which they are or should be aware * * * may give particular meaning to specific terms of the agreement and may supplement or qualify the terms of the agreement." In other words, a disclaimer by usage of trade is only binding on members of the trade involved or other persons who know or should know about it. Persons who should be aware of a trade usage doubtless include those who regularly deal with members of the relevant trade, and also members of a second trade who commonly deal with members of the relevant trade (for example, farmers should know something of farm equipment selling).[48]

d. Lessons From Amended Section 2–316

Even though Amended 2–316 will never become law, the amendment process and the final version have important lessons for the interpretation of existing law.

(1974) (seller failed to prove trade usage disclaiming implied warranty that gilt fit for breeding) with Torstenson v. Melcher, 195 Neb. 764, 241 N.W.2d 103, 19 UCC 484 (1976) (evidence supported jury finding that trade usage disclaims implied warranty that bull fit for breeding).

44. 8 S. Williston, Contracts § 993A at 610 (3d ed.1961).

45. 33 A.D.2d 17, 304 N.Y.S.2d 918, 6 UCC 1246 (1969).

46. *Id*. at 22, 304 N.Y.S.2d at 923–24, 6 UCC at 1250. Compare *Zicari* with

Bickett v. W.R. Grace & Co., 1972 WL 20845, 12 UCC 629 (W.D.Ky.1972) (farmers universally recognize trade usage excluding implied warranty as to seed corn).

47. 3 A. Corbin, Contracts § 557 at 248 (1960). See also Restatement of Contracts § 247, Comment *b* (1932); 5 S. Williston, Contracts § 661 at 113–18 (3d ed. 1961).

48. Spurgeon v. Jamieson Motors, 164 Mont. 296, 521 P.2d 924, 14 UCC 651 (1974).

Amended 2–316 would have made small but important changes. Most of these dealt with consumers. For example, the consumer safe harbor would have required a more elaborate statement than before. Some of the early drafts called for language that, according to the sellers, required them to denigrate their own products in order to make an effective disclaimer.[49] By 2003 most of that was gone.

§ 2–316. Exclusion or Modification of Warranties.

(2) Subject to subsection (3), to exclude or modify the implied warranty of merchantability or any part of it <u>in a consumer contract the language must be in a record, be conspicuous, and state "The seller undertakes no responsibility for the quality of the goods except as otherwise provided in this contract," and in any other contract</u> the language must mention merchantability and in case of a ~~writing~~ <u>record</u> must be conspicuous<u>,</u> ~~and to~~<u>.</u> <u>Subject to subsection (3), to</u> exclude or modify the implied warranty of fitness, the exclusion must be ~~by a writing~~ <u>in a record</u> and <u>be</u> conspicuous. Language to exclude all implied warranties of fitness <u>in a consumer contract must state "The seller assumes no responsibility that the goods will be fit for any particular purpose for which you may be buying these goods, except as otherwise provided in the contract," and in any other contract the language</u> is sufficient if it states, for example, that "There are no warranties ~~which~~ <u>that</u> extend beyond the description on the face hereof." <u>Language that satisfies the requirements of this subsection for the exclusion or modification of a warranty in a consumer contract also satisfies the requirements for any other contract.</u>

(3) Notwithstanding subsection (2)<u>:</u>

(a) unless the circumstances indicate otherwise, all implied warranties are excluded by expressions like "as is", "with all faults" or other language ~~which~~ <u>that</u> in common understanding calls the buyer's attention to the exclusion of warranties ~~and~~<u>,</u> makes plain that there is no implied warranty<u>, and, in a consumer contract evidenced by a record, is set forth conspicuously in the record</u>; ~~and~~

(b) ~~when~~ <u>if</u> the buyer before entering into the contract has examined the goods or the sample or model as fully as ~~he~~

---

49. An early draft suggested the following language would be sufficient: "These goods may not be merchantable; that is, not suitable for ordinary use" (for exclusion or modification of implied warranty of merchantability); "There are no warranties that these goods will conform to the purposes for which they are purchased made known to the seller" (for exclusion or modification of implied warranty of fitness). § 2–316(b)(2) (Revised Working Draft, Jan. 1996), available at http://www.law.upenn.edu/bll/ulc/ucc2/text3w.htm.

desired or has refused to examine the goods after a demand by the seller there is no implied warranty with regard to defects ~~which~~ that an examination ~~ought~~ in the circumstances ~~to~~ should have revealed to ~~him~~ the buyer; and

(c) an implied warranty ~~can~~ may also be excluded or modified by course of dealing or course of performance or usage of trade.

Consider the only amendment relating directly to non-consumers. This was the provision in 2–316(3)(b) which stated that a refusal to inspect goods frees the seller from liability for defects the buyer should have seen on inspection only if the refusal to inspect occurred "after a demand by the seller" that buyer inspect.

Comment 8 said the same thing:

In order to bring the transaction within the scope of "refused to examine" in paragraph (b), it is not sufficient that the goods are available for inspection. There must in addition be a demand by the seller that the buyer examine the goods fully. The seller by the demand puts the buyer on notice that he is assuming the risk of defects which the examination ought to reveal. The language "refused to examine" in this paragraph is intended to make clear the necessity for such demand.[50]

The existing requirement in Article 2 that the buyer "refuse to examine" might carry the implication that the seller had to make a demand for the section to work. The requirement of a demand would have been explicit in Amended Comment 6:

To bring the transaction within the scope of "refused to examine" in subsection (3)(b), it is not sufficient that the goods are available for inspection. There must in addition be an actual examination by the buyer or a demand by the seller that the buyer examine the goods fully. The seller's demand must place the buyer on notice that the buyer is assuming the risk of defects which the examination ought to reveal.[51]

There is a common misconception about disclaimers to consumers, and the drafters of Amended Article 2 did nothing to alleviate it. Subsection (2) of Unamended 2–316 and of the amendments says that to exclude the warranty of merchantability in a consumer contract the language "must" comply with (2), i.e., the disclaimer must be conspicuous, must use these magic words, etc. The presence of the verb "must" in that sentence misleads many first-time readers. That reader often overlooks the initial phrase in (2), "Subject to subsection (3)." Since all of the onerous requirements in (2) are "subject to" the more limited requirements of (3),

---

50. § 2–316, Comment 8 (1994).   **51.** § 2–316, Comment 6 (2003).

one can also disclaim—even against a consumer—by complying with these limited requirements in (3). Of course, any sensible drafter will use the safe harbor terms in (2) but, in a pinch, words like "as is" and "with all faults" or other language may do even if it is not conspicuous. The drafters could have made it clear that subsection (2) was a consumer safe harbor and not more, but they didn't.

A second ambiguity that was consciously carried forward in Amended Article 2 at the consumers' insistence is the initial clause in 2–316(3)(a), "unless the circumstances indicate otherwise." This was left despite the fact that no one is sure about what the "circumstances" are or should be that would make the terms in (3) not override (2). This retention of old and unclear language was consciously negotiated by the clever consumer representatives who hope someday to breathe life into these words to the consumer's benefit. The revisers (one of us included) should have been embarrassed at carrying forward such intentional ambiguities.

There were long and bloody battles during the revision process about the terminology that should be blessed as adequate to disclaim the warranty of merchantability in a consumer contract. Existing Article 2 requires only that the disclaimer be conspicuous and mention "merchantability." The amendments, quoted in full above, required a stronger statement: "seller undertakes no responsibility for the quality of the goods except as otherwise provided in the contract." Consumer advocates argued persuasively that mention of "merchantability" did not adequately convey the true state of affairs to a consumer.

In the early going, the consumer advocates were able to get even stronger language into proposed 2–316. Consider for example language that appeared in the May 16, 1997 Draft. Two alternative statements were suggested in consumer contracts: Alternative A— "Except as expressly provided in this contract, the seller makes no promise as to the merchantability, suitability, or fitness for purpose of the goods. This means that there is no promise that the goods will be fit for use for any particular purpose or even that they will be fit for the normal purpose for which such goods are used." Alternative B—"Unless we say otherwise in this contract, we make no promises about these goods. They may not work. They may not do what you want them to. If they don't, it's your problem."[52] Consumer advocates eventually retreated to the language that appeared in the final draft of Amended Article 2: "The seller undertakes no responsibility for the quality of the goods except as otherwise provided in the contract." This final articulation seemed

---

52. § 2–407(e)(3) (Draft, May 16, 1997), available at http://www.law. upenn.edu/bll/ulc/ucc2/597art2.htm.

a sensible compromise; it better conveyed the legal consequence to a buyer, but it did not require sellers to denigrate their products. There was a similar reformulation of the safe harbor words for disclaiming the warranty of fitness in a consumer contract.

The last sentence of Amended 2–316(2) made clear what everyone would have believed anyway, namely that what works against a consumer works against others. "Language that satisfies the requirements of this subsection for the exclusion or modification of a warranty in a consumer contract also satisfies the requirements for any other contract."

With consumers, the disclaimer had to be in a record; so it would not have been good enough to state the disclaimer orally. Under the existing law, theoretically a seller can make a written contract and give an effective disclaimer orally, even with a consumer. One can also make an oral contract with an effective oral disclaimer. Those possibilities would be gone if one wished to fit within Amended subsection (2); with consumers, only disclaimers that are in records would have fit in (2)'s safe harbor, but if the contract were oral, an oral disclaimer would have been potentially effective even in a consumer contract under subsection (3).

Disclaimers of the warranty of fitness for a particular purpose deserve a word. The proposed safe harbor language for consumers was: "The seller assumes no responsibility that the goods will be fit for any particular purpose for which you may be buying these goods, except as otherwise provided in the contract."[53] Assume that the buyer tells the salesperson that he is interested in driving his SUV in a particular kind of off-road use in rugged terrain that he describes to the salesman. Assume the salesman assures buyer that the SUV he is considering will do it with flying colors. The consumer signs a contract that has the disclaiming language quoted above. Is there a warranty of fitness for this particular off road use?

The buyer would argue that the use described is part of the contract because the salesman's assurance was a promise of just that performance. If this oral term made it into the contract, then the disclaimer, by its terms would have been ineffective. Better yet for the consumer, the salesman's statement might be an express warranty and the buyer may not need to march through the fitness thicket from 2–315. Of course the solution to this problem for the car dealer is to have a prominent merger clause in the sales agreement so that the salesman's statement, even if a promise, does not make it into the contract of the parties.

To qualify for the safe harbor in (2), disclaimers in records would have to have been conspicuous. With one exception, all disclaimers that are not conspicuous would have been invalid

---

53. § 2–316(2) (2003).

against consumer buyers. So the meaning of conspicuous is still important and that meaning now has a new dimension with the recognition and use of contracts in electronic form. For a discussion of the meaning of "conspicuous" in an electronic record, return to section 13–5(c). What was simple with a writing is complicated where a seller sends the contract electronically, and the buyer reads it on a computer screen or prints it out. As we warn above, what was sent as a conspicuous disclaimer on the seller's screen may arrive as an inconspicuous one on the buyer's screen.

We reiterate, Amended Article 2 will fade into the mists without a single adoption. The purpose of the foregoing exercise is to alert you to some of the issues that linger in the existing statute. (Or perhaps the purpose is to show off some knowledge, hard earned by one of us who is unwilling to concede that it is now useless.)

§ 13–7 Cumulation and Conflict of Warranties, Section 2–317

Sometimes warranties conflict with each other. In Section 13–3 we dealt with the common situation where disclaimer language in a printed warranty clause conflicts with an express warranty. Section 2–316(1) instructs us to construe these provisions as consistent unless this would be unreasonable.

Section 2–317 embodies a similar policy with regard to conflicts between any warranties, express or implied:

Warranties whether express or implied shall be construed as consistent with each other and as cumulative, but if such construction is unreasonable the intention of the parties shall determine which warranty is dominant. In ascertaining that intention the following rules apply:

(a) Exact or technical specifications displace an inconsistent sample or model or general language of description.

(b) A sample from an existing bulk displaces inconsistent general language of description.

(c) Express warranties displace inconsistent implied warranties other than an implied warranty of fitness for a particular purpose.

Comment 2 tells us that the purpose of this section is to assist in determining the intent of the parties as to which of two conflicting warranties shall prevail. But this determination is made only when the court has first decided (1) that it would be unreasonable to construe the warranties as consistent with each other and (2) that the seller is not estopped from denying such consistency. According to Comment 2, equitable estoppel operates against the seller when the seller has not acted in "perfect good faith" in making inconsistent warranties or when the seller has led the buyer to believe that all warranties could be performed.

In practice 2–317 is most often applied when the seller has made an express warranty and failed to exclude or limit the implied warranties. If the express warranty cannot reasonably be read as consistent with the implied warranties, the court must try to ascertain which warranty the parties intended to be dominant. Subsections (a), (b), and (c) list rules to aid this inquiry. While Comment 3 points out that these rules are not intended as absolute, other evidence of the parties' intent will usually be lacking. As a result, courts that have concluded that multiple warranties are inconsistent will usually be forced to apply one or more of the three rules presented in subsections (a), (b), and (c).

Subsection (c) requires that an express warranty displace inconsistent implied warranties other than the implied warranty of fitness for a particular purpose.[1] A common example of inconsistent express and implied warranties arises in sales of automobiles. Assume, for example, that a new car is sold with the following warranty clause: "This vehicle is warranted to be free of defects for 24,000 miles or twenty-four months, whichever occurs first; this warranty is given in lieu of all other warranties, express or implied." The clause is not conspicuously printed and it does not mention the word "merchantability." On the 26,000th mile the transmission fails as a result of a manufacturing defect. The buyer sues the dealer and manufacturer for breach of the implied warranty of merchantability, but the defendants move for summary judgment on the grounds that under 2–317(c) the express warranty displaced the implied warranty of merchantability. What result should a court reach?

If the court views the language of the express warranty clause as a whole, it might conclude that this clause was inconsistent with the implied warranty of merchantability. However, this would permit the seller to disclaim the warranty of merchantability in certain respects even though he had not complied with the formal requirements of 2–316(2)—conspicuousness, and use of the word "merchantability". Since the warranty clause really contained both an express warranty and a disclaimer, it would be appropriate to treat the two terms separately.[2] The "24,000 miles or 24 months"

---

§ 13–7

1. Where it is the specifications of the buyer that render a product defective, there is no breach of the implied warranty of merchantability. See, e.g., Murphy v. Eaton, Yale & Towne, Inc., 444 F.2d 317, 9 UCC 805 (6th Cir.1971)

(buyer ordered forklift truck without overhead guard); See also § 2–316, Comment 9.

2. Section 2–313 enumerates the types of express warranties that may be created under the Code. Nothing in 2–313 or in the accompanying comments

express warranty, viewed in isolation from the disclaimer language, and the implied warranty of merchantability may conceivably be construed as cumulative. We find this interpretation unpalatable and would argue that the 24,000 mile express warranty displaced any implied warranty on the same item at least as to damage covered by the express warranty. However, in Koellmer v. Chrysler Motors Corp.,[3] the court held that an automobile guarantee against defective parts for five years or 50,000 miles is not inconsistent with the implied warranty of merchantability. In that case the court separately evaluated the disclaimer language, which was similar to that used in our hypothetical case, in light of 2–316's requirement and held that it was ineffective because it was not conspicuous. Of course, even though our seller is obligated under the implied warranty, our seller may be able to avoid liability by persuading the court that a transmission that lasts for 26,000 miles is merchantable. It should be added that most courts since *Koellmer* permit recovery under an implied warranty of merchantability after the expiration of an express warranty, usually without reference to 2–317.[4]

Section 2–317(c) includes an important exception to its general rule: an express warranty does not displace an inconsistent implied warranty of fitness for a particular purpose. Suppose a contract for the purchase of a cold-storage room includes an express warranty that the motor is three horsepower and will deliver ten tons of refrigeration. If the buyer also has an implied warranty of fitness for a particular purpose based on the seller's knowledge of the buyer's needs and on the buyer's reliance on the seller's skill and judgment, that warranty would not be negated by the express warranty.[5]

suggests that the term "express warranty" encompasses language that excludes warranties; rather, express warranties are portrayed as affirmative obligations of the seller. Thus, the use of the term "express warranties" in 2–317(c) should not be construed as incorporating disclaimer language that happens to appear in the same printed paragraph.

3. 6 Conn.Cir.Ct. 478, 276 A.2d 807, 8 UCC 668 (1970).

4. See, e.g., Dennin v. General Motors Corp., 78 Misc.2d 451, 357 N.Y.S.2d 668, 15 UCC 102 (1974) (automobile). Cf. Gable v. Silver, 258 So.2d 11, 10 UCC 316 (Fla.App.1972), aff'd, 264 So.2d 418 (1972) (common law implied warranties attaching to air conditioning system survived express warranty). Where the express warranty is still in force, buyers have been allowed to sue

simultaneously upon ineffectively disclaimed implied warranties. See, e.g., Stream v. Sportscar Salon, Ltd., 91 Misc.2d 99, 397 N.Y.S.2d 677, 22 UCC 631 (City Civ.Ct. 1977).

5. 1 N.Y.State Law Revision Comm'n, 1955 Report 412 (1955).

Such conflicts should be rare. The implied warranty of fitness for a particular purpose requires buyer reliance which probably precludes reliance on conflicting language of express warranty. Thus, the express warranty language may not reach the basis of the bargain. On the other hand, where the buyer relies on express warranty language, the reliance requirement necessary for a conflicting fitness warranty would not be met. See Special Project, Article Two Warranties in Commercial Transactions, 64 Cornell L.Rev. 30, 211 n. 765 (1978). Comment 9

Subsections (a) and (b) of 2–317 contain two other rules of construction that help resolve conflicts between express warranties. In essence, these rules establish a hierarchy based on the specificity of the express warranties. Thus exact or technical specifications are given priority over inconsistent samples, models, or general descriptions, and a sample drawn from an existing bulk prevails over inconsistent general language of description. The scheme of 2–317, as reflected in all three rules, is to give effect to the more specific of conflicting warranties. Presumably, a specific express warranty would have "claimed the attention of the parties in the first instance," and hence, in the absence of contrary evidence, it was probably intended by the parties to be dominant.[6] The guidelines in subsections (a) and (b) for construing inconsistent express warranties should be considered in light of 2–313(1)(b) and (c) (creation of express warranty by description, sample, or model) and 2–316(1) (exclusion or modification of express warranties).

§ 13–8 Modification or Limitation of Remedies, Section 2–719

While 2–316 is primarily concerned with the exclusion or modification of warranties, it also tells the seller that the seller may limit by agreement the buyer's remedies for breach of warranty. Section 2–316(4) provides:

Remedies for breach of warranty can be limited in accordance with the provisions of this Article on liquidation or limitation of damages and on contractual modification of remedy (Sections 2–718 and 2–719).

Section 2–719 plays the dominant role in limiting the buyer's remedies, and that role may easily be confused with 2–316's exclusion of warranties role. For example, a tractor dealer may achieve similar immunity from a buyer's claims by disclaiming all warran-

---

to 2–316 sets forth one situation where an express warranty precludes the implied warranty of fitness for a particular purpose:

The situation in which the buyer gives precise and complete specifications to the seller is not explicitly covered in this section, but this is a frequent circumstance in which the implied warranties may be excluded. The warranty of fitness for a particular purpose would not normally arise since in such a situation there is usually no reliance on the seller by the buyer.

6. See § 2–313, Comment 3. Stewart–Decatur Security Sys., Inc. v. Von Weise Gear Co., 517 F.2d 1136, 17 UCC 24 (8th Cir.1975) illustrates when party

intent should supersede 2–317. The buyer tested and approved a model gear motor for opening jail doors. On the purchase order, however, the buyer specified an input speed different from that of the model. The court held that the buyer had improperly rejected motors conforming to the model because the parties intended the model rather than the specifications to govern the seller's obligation. Although the court held the Code's warranty sections inapplicable since the buyer did not accept the goods, it noted that strict application of 2–317's priority rules would have been inappropriate. *Id.* at 1140 n.12, 17 UCC at 30–31 n.12.

ties under 2–316 or by limiting the buyer's remedy to the repair or replacement of defective parts under 2–719(1). In either case, if the seller has complied with all statutory requirements the buyer will be barred from recovering consequential damages such as for lost crops or injury to property. Indeed, there is explicit authority that, to be valid, an exclusion of consequential damages need not necessarily be conspicuous.[1] However, one route may offer greater chance of court acceptance than another in certain circumstances. Before we compare 2–719 and 2–316, we examine 2–719.

§ 13–9 Modification or Limitation of Remedies— How to Limit the Buyer's Remedies, Section 2–719(1)

Section 2–719(1) provides:

Subject to the provisions of subsections (2) and (3) of this section and of the preceding section on liquidation and limitation of damages,

> (a) the agreement may provide for remedies in addition to or in substitution for those provided in this Article and may limit or alter the measure of damages recoverable under this Article, as by limiting the buyer's remedies to return of the goods and repayment of the price or to repair and replacement of non-conforming goods or parts; and

> (b) resort to a remedy as provided is optional unless the remedy is expressly agreed to be exclusive, in which case it is the sole remedy.

Comment 1 tells us: "Under this section parties are left free to shape their remedies to their particular requirements and reasonable agreements limiting or modifying remedies are to be given effect." Consistent with this policy of freedom of contract, 2–719 enables the parties to provide for remedies "in addition to or in substitution for" those normally available under the Code. In practice, however, the section is most often invoked to limit the buyer's remedies for breach. For example, in Dow Corning Corp. v. Capitol Aviation, Inc.[1] a contract for the sale of an executive passenger aircraft included a clause that limited the buyer's remedy for non-delivery to cancellation and refund of deposit. In an unsuccessful action by the buyer for consequential damages,[2] the court

---

§ 13–8

1. Lara v. Hyundai Motor America, 331 Ill.App.3d 53, 264 Ill.Dec. 416, 770 N.E.2d 721, 47 UCC2d 1379 (2002).

§ 13–9

1. 411 F.2d 622, 6 UCC 589 (7th Cir.1969).

2. The alleged consequential damages consisted of a judgment suffered by the buyer in favor of the buyer's customer. The customer recovered lost profits

held that 2–719(1)(a) authorized the clause. Section 2–719(3), which explicitly provides that the parties may opt to limit or exclude consequential damages, also supports the *Dow* decision. Comment 3 explains that 2–719(3) enables the parties to allocate "unknown or undeterminable risks." Although any contract term purporting to limit or exclude consequential damages is subject to judicial scrutiny under the unconscionability standard, courts usually uphold these clauses between business persons.[3]

One way for a buyer to get around a limitation-of-remedy clause is to show that the remedy stipulated was not expressly agreed to be exclusive. In that case, 2–719(1)(b) requires that the stipulated remedy be regarded as optional. Comment 2 says that "[s]ubsection (1)(b) creates a presumption that clauses prescribing remedies are cumulative rather than exclusive," but the seller can rebut this presumption through good drafting in the original agreement.[4] For example, Wyatt Industries, Inc. v. Publicker Industries, Inc.,[5] which involved the sale of a pressure vessel for a chemical plant, held that the following clause was sufficiently explicit to limit the buyer to the stipulated remedy:

> Guarantee: Fabricator warrants the completed work against defective material and workmanship, exclusive of corrosion, for the period of one year from completion thereof. Its liability under this warranty shall be limited to the replacement within the aforesaid time of any defective work or material f.o.b. Fabricator's shop, and Fabricator shall be liable for no other damages or losses * * *.[6]

among other things. *Id.* at 623–24, 6 UCC at 591. See also Bernath v. Potato Services of Michigan, 300 F.Supp.2d 175, 52 UCC2d 434 (D.Me. 2004) (limitation to return of price upheld).

3. In *Dow*, for example, the court held that the stipulated remedy was not unconscionable in light of the commercial setting, which involved a transaction between a manufacturer and distributor. *Id.* at 627, 6 UCC at 595. Proto Construction & Development Corp. v. Superior Precast, Inc., 2002 WL 1159593, 52 UCC2d 921 (E.D.N.Y. 2002) (effective remedy limitation between two sophisticated companies); Bernath v. Potato Services of Michigan, 300 F.Supp.2d 175, 52 UCC2d 434 (D.Me. 2004) (limitation enforceable under 2–719 because buyer and seller were sophisticated). Discussion in § 13–11 *infra*.

4. See, e.g., High Plains Natural Gas Co. v. Warren Petroleum Co., 875 F.2d 284, 8 UCC2d 1015 (10th Cir.1989) (clauses in natural gas sales contract demonstrated intent to limit seller's liability); Global Octanes Texas, L.P. v. BP Exploration & Oil Inc., 154 F.3d 518, 36 UCC2d 633 (5th Cir. 1998) (may effectively limit total recoverable in damages, but other remedies such as injunctive relief are not affected); Rheem Mfg. Co. v. Phelps Heating & Air Conditioning, Inc., 746 N.E.2d 941, 44 UCC2d 751 (Ind. 2001) (failed limited remedy clause has no effect on exclusion of consequential damages).

5. 420 F.2d 454, 7 UCC 105 (5th Cir.1969).

6. 420 F.2d at 456, 7 UCC at 106–107. The court upheld the exclusive remedy "regardless of the existence or nonexistence of any implied warranties of merchantability and/or fitness." *Id.* at 457, 7 UCC at 108.

The courts are divided over the interpretation of one common clause—that an exclusive remedy of repair or replacement is "expressly in lieu of any and all other warranties, express or implied, and of all other obligation on the part of the seller." An early Pennsylvania case[7] involving the sale of vegetable and dairy refrigerators held this language sufficiently specific to constitute an express agreement that the stipulated remedy be exclusive. However, a later Arkansas case, Ford Motor Co. v. Reid,[8] held almost identical language insufficient for the purposes of 2–719(1)(b). The court emphasized that the contract language dealt only with warranties and obligations and not with remedies.[9] It distinguished remedies from obligations as "the rights arising from failure to perform obligations"[10] and concluded that the printed clause did not expressly state that the *remedy* of repair or replacement was exclusive.

There are two lessons in these cases. First, the identity of the plaintiff and the nature of the injury may make a major difference. The plaintiffs in the first two cases were business persons who incurred commercial losses. Mr. and Mrs. Reid, on the other hand, were consumers whose house burned down as a result of defective wiring in their new car. Courts show more sympathy to consumers than to business persons.[11] A second lesson is that a seller should limit remedies in the most specific terms possible. For example, in the *Reid* case, the remedy clause could have provided, in addition to the disclaimer language:

> The buyer's exclusive remedy against the seller shall be for the repair or replacement of defective parts. No other remedy (including, but not limited to, incidental or consequential damages[12] for lost profits, lost sales, injury to person or property, or

7. Evans Mfg. Corp. v. Wolosin, 1957 WL 8308, 1 UCC 193 (Pa.C.P.1957). See also BOC Group, Inc. v. Chevron Chemical Co., 359 N.J.Super. 135, 819 A.2d 431, 50 UCC2d 489 (2003).

8. 250 Ark. 176, 465 S.W.2d 80, 8 UCC 985 (1971).

9. *Id.* at 184, 465 S.W.2d at 85, 8 UCC at 990.

10. *Id.* at 184, 465 S.W.2d at 85, 8 UCC at 991. See also In re Crysen–Montenay Energy Co., 156 B.R. 922, 23 UCC2d 748 (S.D.N.Y. 1993), and First Security Mortg. Co. v. Goldmark Plastics Compounds, Inc., 862 F.Supp. 918, 25 UCC2d 66 (E.D.N.Y. 1994).

11. Compare Fredonia Broadcasting Corp. v. RCA Corp., 481 F.2d 781, 12 UCC 1088 (5th Cir.1973) (provision that repair or replacement fulfills all seller "obligations" in commercial sale of broadcasting equipment created exclusive remedy), with Stream v. Sportscar Salon, Ltd., 91 Misc.2d 99, 397 N.Y.S.2d 677, 22 UCC 631 (City Civ.Ct.1977) (used car buyer recovered purchase price because contract limited "liability" rather than remedy to dealer's "famous one-year mechanical guarantee on parts and labor"); Proto Construction & Development Corp. v. Superior Precast, Inc., 2002 WL 1159593, 52 UCC2d 921 (E.D.N.Y. 2002) (effective limitation between two sophisticated companies); General Electric Co. v. Varig—S.A, 2004 WL 253320, 52 UCC2d 936 (S.D.N.Y. 2004) (effective limitation in contract painstakingly negotiated between two highly competent parties).

12. § 2–719(3) makes limitation of consequential damages for personal injuries in the case of consumer goods prima

any other incidental or consequential loss) shall be available to buyer.

Of course, a determined court can find any clause too vague or ambiguous, and a court always has the option of refusing to enforce a clause as unconscionable. Nevertheless, the more explicit the limitation-of-remedy clause is, the more likely it will be enforced. Moreover, even if an explicit clause would be a loser before an appellate court, it might win the case in negotiations or at the trial level. In sum, a well-drafted remedy limitation clause will in most situations protect the seller against enormous damage judgments.

A seller may limit remedy to repair or replacement and thereby exclude liability for personal injuries, subject to 2–719(3).[13] There may be no remedy for latent defects not manifested until after the warranty has expired.[14] Of course, a remedy limitation must be part of the basis of the bargain.[15]

The code distinguishes between "damages" and "remedies". Thus, a limited cap on damages still stands despite the presumption in 2–719 that remedies are cumulative.[16]

§ 13–10 Modification or Limitation of Remedies— Failure of Stipulated Remedy to Achieve Its Essential Purpose, Section 2–719(2)

The basic mechanism provided by 2–719 is not very difficult to understand or apply. However, even if a contract contains a perfectly drafted clause that explicitly states the exclusive remedy, the buyer can still resort to subsection (2) to avoid the effect of that clause. If the buyer can establish that the exclusive remedy provided in the contract "fails of its essential purpose" the buyer may disregard that term of the contract and pursue remedies to which the buyer otherwise might not have recourse. According to two commentators "it is hard to find any provision in Article 2 that has been more successfully used by aggrieved buyers in the last [25] years than Section 2–719(2)."[1]

---

facie unconscionable. Theoretically, the seller may overcome this presumption. The seller's chances of accomplishing that feat should be weighed against the possibility that a court would improperly strike the entire limitation-of-remedy clause because of the single unconscionable term. The chances of either occurrence are slight, and on balance it is probably wisest to make the clause as comprehensive as possible.

13. Reibold v. Simon Aerials, Inc., 859 F.Supp. 193, 24 UCC2d 496 (E.D. Va. 1994). See further, 13–11 *infra*.

14. Duquesne Light Co. v. Westinghouse Electric Corp., 66 F.3d 604, 27 UCC2d 823 (3d Cir. 1995).

15. Olathe Mfg., Inc. v. Browning Mfg., 259 Kan. 735, 915 P.2d 86, 30 UCC2d 495 (1996).

16. Global Octanes Texas, L.P. v. BP Exploration and Oil Inc., 154 F.3d 518, 36 UCC2d 633 (5th Cir. 1998).

§ 13–10

1. Clark & C. Smith, The Law of Product Warranties, 8–54 (1984) ("The failure of essential purpose doctrine is of

Comment 1 to 2–719 explains the policy behind subsection (2):

> [I]t is of the very essence of a sales contract that at least minimum adequate remedies be available. If the parties intend to conclude a contract for sale within this Article they must accept the legal consequence that there be at least a fair quantum of remedy for breach of the obligations or duties outlined in the contract.

The standards provided in this excerpt—"minimum adequate remedies" and "fair quantum of remedy"—are of limited assistance to the drafter or interpreter.

Section 2–719(2) raises two main questions, which can be attributed to the two clauses that make up the provision. When does an exclusive or limited remedy fail of its essential purpose? When a remedy fails, what remedies are available to the buyer?

a.   Application of Section 2–719(2)

Section 2–719(2) provides:

> Where circumstances cause an exclusive or limited remedy to fail of its essential purpose, remedy may be had as provided in this Act.[2]

Comment 1 explains that this subsection applies to "an apparently fair and reasonable clause," which "because of circumstances fails in its purpose or operates to deprive either party of the substantial value of the bargain * * *." Note that both the statutory language and the comment refer to "*its* [i.e., the limited or exclusive remedy's] essential purpose * * *" (emphasis added). That is, 2–719(2) should be triggered when the remedy fails of *its* essential purpose, not the essential purpose of the Code, contract law, or equity. And to use the words of Professor Honnold, this provision "is not concerned with arrangements which were oppressive at their inception, but rather with the application of an agreement to novel circumstances not contemplated by the parties."[3]

---

extreme importance because so many warranty forms provide a limited repair-or-replace remedy. If the product turns out to be a lemon and the seller cannot cure the defects within a reasonable period of time, the courts are not shy about invoking § 2–719(2) and freeing the other Article 2 remedies available to an aggrieved buyer.").

2. Commentaries on 2–719(2) include Anderson, "Failure of Essential Purpose and Essential Failure on Purpose: A Look at Section 2–719 of the Uniform Commercial Code," 31 Sw.L.J. 759 (1977); Eddy, "On the 'Essential' Purposes of Limited Remedies: The Me-

taphysics of UCC 2–719(2)," 65 Calif.L.Rev. 28 (1977). A limited remedy does not fail of its essential purpose simply because it limits recovery of particular relief sought. Gooch v. E.I. Du Pont de Nemours and Co., 40 F.Supp.2d 863, 38 UCC2d 796 (W.D. Ky. 1999). Nor does a remedy fail of its essential purpose merely where buyer thinks going back for repairs is "too much trouble". Trinity Industries, Inc. v. McKinnon Bridge Co., Inc., 77 S.W.3d 159, 46 UCC2d 119 (Tenn. App. 2001).

3. 1 N.Y. State Law Revision Comm'n, 1955 Report 584 (1955). "[W]hen unexpected circumstances pres-

When are "novel circumstances" present? The most frequent application of 2–719(2) occurs when under a limited "repair and replacement" remedy, the seller is unwilling or unable to repair the defective goods within a reasonable period of time.[4] Thus the limited remedy fails of its essential purpose, i.e., fails to cure the defect.[5] A remedy also fails when the seller is willing and able to repair, but the repairs cannot be done. This might happen because the goods have been destroyed.

Ordinarily, the buyer must provide the seller a reasonable opportunity to carry out the exclusive or limited remedy before the buyer can successfully argue failure of essential purpose.[6] Even then, the buyer may not succeed in establishing failure of essential purpose.[7] The reasonableness of the opportunity to repair varies with the type of goods involved, and some may require a lengthy repair period.

The wise buyer will give a seller a reasonable opportunity to repair or replace, and will also carefully document those efforts.[8] In Riley v. Ford Motor Co.,[9] the plaintiff purchased a new car under an exclusive remedy of repair or replacement of defective parts. The contract explicitly provided that the seller would not be responsible for consequential loss. During the first few weeks of ownership the buyer discovered at least fourteen major and minor defects in the car, which the dealer and the manufacturer's representatives were unable satisfactorily to repair.[10] The jury returned a verdict for the

ently prevent the agreed remedy from yielding its purported and expected relief then the remedy has failed of its essential purpose." Ritchie Enters. v. Honeywell Bull, Inc., 730 F.Supp. 1041, 11 UCC2d 1170 (D.Kan.1990) (citing J. White and R. Summers). Limitations that are "oppressive" at the outset face trouble under 2–302 and 2–719(3).

4. See Clark v. International Harvester Co., 99 Idaho 326, 581 P.2d 784, 25 UCC 91 (1978) (seller's inability to repair tractor within reasonable time caused the limited remedy to fail of its essential purpose); Arabian Agriculture Services Co. v. Chief Industries, Inc., 309 F.3d 479, 48 UCC2d 1394 (8th Cir. 2002) (failed of essential purpose where silo collapsed and seller refused to repair).

5. § 2–719(2) can apply either when the seller refuses to make repairs pursuant to the warranty or when the seller fails to make repairs within a reasonable time. Liberty Truck Sales, Inc. v. Kimbrel, 548 So.2d 1379, 9 UCC2d 908 (Ala. 1989).

6. See Corey v. Furgat Tractor &

Equip., Inc., 147 Vt. 477, 520 A.2d 600, 3 UCC2d 505 (1986) (involving logging tractor). Delmarva Power & Light Co. v. ABB Power T & D Co., 2002 WL 840564, 47 UCC2d 1033 (Del.Super. 2002) (remedy does not fail of essential purpose because numerous attempts at repair were required).

7. See Cline v. Allis–Chalmers Corp., 690 S.W.2d 764, 41 UCC 430 (Ky.App. 1985) (involving combine); BOC Group, Inc. v. Chevron Chemical Company, LLC, 359 N.J.Super. 135, 819 A.2d 431, 50 UCC 2d 489 (2003) (limitation remained effective where buyer had agreed to it and did not prove failure of essential purpose).

8. Sometimes the buyer, disgusted with the goods, simply returns them to the seller without affording any opportunity to repair. By this time, too, the buyer may have lost or misplaced his copy of the agreement.

9. 442 F.2d 670, 8 UCC 1175 (5th Cir.1971).

10. The plaintiff alleged both breach of warranty and negligent repair. *Id.* at 671, 8 UCC at 1176.

plaintiff in an amount far exceeding the cost of repairs. The Fifth Circuit held that the jury was justified "in its implicit finding that the warranty operated to deprive the purchaser 'of the substantial value of the bargain.' "[11] In other words, the exclusive remedy of repair and replacement of defective parts failed of its essential purpose because even after numerous attempts to repair, the car did not operate as should a new car free of defects.[12]

The buyer complained in essence that there was no remedy at all under the contract and that the new car was worth nothing since it could not be repaired. *Riley* fits the literal scheme of 2–719(2) because unusual circumstances caused the exclusive remedy to fail of its essential purpose. In usual circumstances, a few repairs and replacements can be expected to put a new car in good working condition.[13]

Although Comment 1 to 2–719 suggests there should be at least "minimum adequate remedies", the cases that conclude that failed repair and replacement agreements leave buyer with no minimum adequate remedy are questionable. At least business people could agree to a term under which the seller agreed to use its "best efforts" to repair, and if the seller could not repair, the loss would fall on the buyer. That would be a permissible and "minimum adequate" remedy even if it left the buyer with the loss. In a related setting, one court has held that an alternative of a purchase price refund was a minimum adequate remedy.

We believe that business people should be permitted to agree on any remedy they want and, having done so, that their allocation of loss should not be upset by a court. On the other hand, it would be both unfair and contrary to the parties' expectation to leave a consumer buyer with nothing where the seller is unable to repair or

---

11. *Id*. at 673, 8 UCC at 1178–79. Nonetheless, the court reversed because the jury verdict far exceeded the recovery permitted by the Code.

12. Accord, Beal v. General Motors Corp., 354 F.Supp. 423, 426, 12 UCC 105, 109 (D.Del.1973) (sale of diesel tractor):

The purpose of an exclusive remedy of replacement or repair of defective parts, the presence of which constitute a breach of express warranty, is to give the seller an opportunity to make the goods conforming [sic] while limiting the risks to which he is subject by excluding direct or consequential damages that might otherwise arise. From the point of view of the buyer the purpose of the exclusive remedy is to give him goods that conform to the contract within a reasonable time after a defective part is

discovered. * * * The limited, exclusive remedy fails of its purpose and is thus avoided under § 2–719(2), whenever the warrantor fails to correct the defect within a reasonable period.

See also Rose v. Colorado Factory Homes, 10 P.3d 680, 43 UCC2d 1160 (Colo.App. 2000) (buyer had right to revoke when seller failed to repair); Caudill Seed & Warehouse Co. v. Prophet 21, Inc., 126 F.Supp.2d 937, 43 UCC2d 849 (E.D.Pa. 2001) (claim for failure of essential purpose could be inferred from the complaint).

13. § 2–719, Comment 1. See, e.g., Canal Electric Co. v. Westinghouse Electric Corp., 756 F.Supp. 620, 14 UCC2d 765 (D.Mass.1990) (purchase price refund constituted a minimum adequate remedy).

replace. In that setting it is unlikely that either the buyer or seller intended that the buyer get nothing more than seller's best efforts to repair. Consumer cases such as *Riley* that rely on the "at least minimum adequate remedies" language doubtless come to the correct conclusion—even if the conclusion is justified on questionable grounds. We argue only that those grounds ought not be used to justify additional remedies in business deals where buyer has assumed the risk of seller's inability to repair.

Section 2–719(2) has been put to work in a second major class of cases in which the exclusive remedy fails because it requires the buyer to perform an act that cannot be performed because of the seller's breach. For example, suppose an automobile manufacturer limits remedy to repair and replacement of defective parts and provides that the defective parts must be delivered to its plant. If the entire car is destroyed as a result of defective wiring, the buyer would be unable to return the wiring to the manufacturer's plant. Even if the buyer could return the defective parts, repair and replacement of those parts would not restore the car to working condition. The exclusive remedy would fail of its essential purpose.[14]

Repair or replacement remedies can also fail because they take too long.[15] In Ehlers v. Chrysler Motor Corporation,[16] the South Dakota Supreme Court held that Chrysler's delay caused the repair and replacement remedy to fail of its essential purpose.

Buyer misbehavior—depriving the seller of a chance to repair or replace—is relevant to the question whether a remedy has failed of its essential purpose too. In Belcher v. Versatile Farm Equipment Co.,[17] a tractor dealer repaired a tractor, replaced defective parts, and returned it in good condition but the buyer made unauthorized alterations on it and refused to return it to the dealership until it broke down. In light of the buyer's alterations, which were made without the knowledge or consent of the seller,

14. Russo v. Hilltop Lincoln–Mercury, Inc., 479 S.W.2d 211, 10 UCC 768 (Mo.App.1972) (court allowed recovery of purchase price of car rendered irreparable by fire despite exclusive remedy of repair or replacement); Giarratano v. Midas Muffler, 166 Misc.2d 390, 630 N.Y.S.2d 656, 27 UCC2d 87 (1995) (remedy clause for new parts failed of essential purpose because conditioned on allowing seller to inspect entire system and make any repairs deemed necessary, at buyer's expense).

15. Krupp PM Engineering, Inc. v. Honeywell, Inc., 209 Mich.App. 104, 530 N.W.2d 146, 26 UCC2d 742 (1995). For cases where the courts recognized that unreasonable delay in repair or replacement may cause the remedy to fail of its

essential purpose but found no such delay, see Middletown Eng'g Co. v. Climate Conditioning Co., 810 S.W.2d 57, 15 UCC2d 746 (Ky.App.1991). Others not so finding include Proto Construction and Development Corp. v. Superior Precast, Inc., 2002 WL 1159593, 52 UCC2d 921 (E.D.N.Y. 2002) and Pearson v. DaimlerChrysler Corp., 349 Ill.App.3d 688, 286 Ill.Dec. 173, 813 N.E.2d 230, 53 UCC2d 18 (Ill.App. 2004) (question of fact whether manufacturer completed warranty repairs within a reasonable number of attempts).

16. 226 N.W.2d 157, 88 S.D. 612, 16 UCC 737 (1975).

17. 443 So.2d 912, 37 UCC 706 (Ala. 1983).

the court found that the repair-or-replace remedy did not fail of its essential purpose.

Should a court consider the seller's good faith or due care in determining whether a limited remedy has failed of its essential purpose? Several courts have answered in the affirmative but the majority have concluded that these factors are irrelevant.[18] This is consistent with the language of 2–719(2).

Wilson Trading Corp. v. David Ferguson, Ltd.[19] illustrates how a court may misapply 2–719(2). In that case, a contract for the sale of yarn provided: "No claims * * * shall be allowed if made after weaving, knitting, or processing, or more than 10 days after receipt of shipment."[20] It was possible that latent defects would render the yarn unmerchantable without the defect's being discoverable within the given time period. If so, said the New York Court of Appeals, the limited remedy would fail of its essential purpose since the buyer would be left with no remedy for those defects.[21]

In *Wilson Trading*, the exclusive remedy might have been unreasonable but it did not fail of its essential purpose. The exclusive remedy should have been invalidated, if at all, under Code provisions that deal with terms oppressive at inception.

A similar misapplication of 2–719(2) occurred in Neville Chem. Co. v. Union Carbide Corp.,[22] where the court held that the remedy of return of the purchase price failed of its essential purpose when consequential damages far exceeded that amount. The court rea-

---

18. Although the opinions are not always clear, most courts seem to agree that seller's good faith or due care is not relevant to whether a buyer is deprived of the substantial value of the bargain. See, e.g., County Asphalt, Inc. v. Lewis Welding & Eng'g Corp., 323 F.Supp. 1300, 8 UCC 445 (S.D.N.Y.1970), aff'd, 444 F.2d 372, 9 UCC 206 (2d Cir.1971), cert. denied, 404 U.S. 939, 92 S.Ct. 272, 30 L.Ed.2d 252 (1971) (repair or replacement remedy could fail under 2–719(2) even if seller acted in good faith); Pierce v. Catalina Yachts, Inc., 2 P.3d 618, 41 UCC2d 737 (Alaska 2000) (limitation against consequential damages unenforceable where manufacturer acted in bad faith in failing to honor warranty). But see Jones & McKnight Corp. v. Birdsboro Corp., 320 F.Supp. 39, 8 UCC 307 (N.D.Ill.1970) (if seller was unreasonable or willfully dilatory in making good on exclusive remedy to repair automated machinery, the buyer would not be limited to that remedy).

19. 23 N.Y.2d 398, 297 N.Y.S.2d 108, 244 N.E.2d 685, 5 UCC 1213 (1968).

20. *Id.* at 401, 297 N.Y.S.2d at 110, 244 N.E.2d at 686, 5 UCC at 1214.

21. *Id.* at 404, 297 N.Y.S.2d at 112–12, 244 N.E.2d at 688, 5 UCC at 1217. In reaching this conclusion, the court cited old 1–204(1), which provided:

Whenever this Act requires any action to be taken within a reasonable time, any time which is not manifestly unreasonable may be fixed by agreement.

The purpose of this provision, according to Comment 1, is to enable a court to disregard "a clause which whether by inadvertence or overreaching fixes a time so unreasonable that it amounts to eliminating all remedy under the contract." See also Ritchie Enterprises v. Honeywell Bull, Inc., 730 F.Supp. 1041, 11 UCC2d 1170 (D.Kan.1990) (limited remedy fails of its essential purpose where defects are latent and undiscoverable after a reasonable inspection).

22. 294 F.Supp. 649, 5 UCC 1219 (W.D.Pa.1968), aff'd in part, vac'd in part, 422 F.2d 1205 (3d Cir.1970).

soned that when a defect is latent and not discoverable within a reasonable period of time, return of the purchase price is a remedy "far below a fair minimum in quantum." Here, too, the remedy should have been invalidated, if at all, under Code provisions that deal with terms oppressive at inception.

A third possibility for misapplication of 2–719(2) arises when the goods are experimental.[23] Where the goods are experimental, the remedy is less likely to fail of its essential purpose because that purpose will not be a guarantee that the goods will work as hoped. Similarly, sometimes buyers buy for special purposes and even provide detailed specifications. In these cases, the limited or exclusive remedy may be only a promise that the seller will attempt to provide a remedy so that the goods will serve the special purposes.

b. *Protection Against Section 2–719(2)*

Where a seller limits its obligation to repair or replacement to a consumer, there is little seller can do to avoid the cases described above where the limited remedy is found to have failed of its essential purpose on seller's inability to repair or replace. In most cases the consumer buyer surely expects a new product to be repaired or replaced so that it is equivalent to what he expected originally from the new product. Even if a seller interprets the promise to be merely a promise to use "its best efforts" to make the product like new, that is not a reasonable interpretation of the promise to a consumer. Therefore most of the cases finding failure of essential purpose when the seller is unable to repair or replace are probably a correct interpretation of the expectations of the parties.

In the unusual case—one involving used goods, experimental goods, or the business context—other opportunities are open to the seller. If, in fact, the seller is promising merely to use his best efforts to repair or replace, he can so promise, if he does so in explicit language, the courts should find no failure of essential purpose. In those cases, the risk has been allocated to the buyer and if seller's best efforts do not make the goods work, that is buyer's tough luck.

In the case of experimental or specially built goods, it should be easy for the seller to make clear that it does not guarantee any particular level of performance and that its promise to "repair and replace" should not be interpreted otherwise.

Another way for a seller to protect against 2–719(2) is to provide an alternate, or "backup," remedy for cases where the primary repair-or-replace remedy fails of its essential purpose.

23. See, e.g., Myrtle Beach Pipeline Corp. v. Emerson Elec. Co., 843 F.Supp. 1027, 23 UCC2d 683 (D.S.C.1993).

These might be a purchase price refund, replacement with alternative and different goods, reasonable liquidated damages, or any combination of the three (perhaps with options for the seller or the buyer). A case illustrating the virtue of alternative remedies is Computerized Radiological Services v. Syntex Corp.,[24] where the seller of an X-ray scanner provided a price refund as a backup. The court found that this remedy prevented failure of essential purpose.

c.   *Consequential Damage Exclusions*

Inevitably, exclusive remedies—such as repair or replacement, or promise of refund of the purchase price—are accompanied by clauses that deny liability for consequential damages. Buyers are rarely satisfied merely to avoid the repair or replace limitation; usually they want consequential damages too. Successful in their arguments that the basic remedy fails of its essential purpose, buyers turn to two statements—one in 2–719(2) and one in Comment 1 to 2–719—to make the further argument that failure of essential purpose of the original remedy also blows away the restriction on recovery of consequential damages.[25] Subsection 2–719(2) states that "remedy may be had as provided in this Act" when the remedy fails of its essential purpose. Comment 1 says that a remedy that fails "must give way to the general remedy provisions of this Article." Buyers occasionally ride these statements to victory over separate or integrated clauses that purport to deny consequential damages.

In our opinion, courts that accept the buyer's argument are mistaken. Some courts favor buyers by narrow interpretations of the consequential damage disclaimer. For example, in Waters v. Massey–Ferguson, Inc.[26] the plaintiff was unable to plant his soybean crop because of a defect in a tractor. The plaintiff argued for lost profits notwithstanding a term in the contract that excluded consequential damages. The court interpreted the consequential damage exclusion to apply only to losses incurred by the buyer before the promise to repair was accomplished. In a similar case the Colorado Supreme Court[27] found the restriction on consequential damage was too vague to bar buyer's claims. Other courts simply rely on the language quoted above to find a term denying consequential damages to be invalid.[28] Nothing in the language of the

---

24.   595 F.Supp. 1495, 40 UCC 49 (E.D.N.Y.1984), aff'd in part, rev'd in part, 786 F.2d 72 (2d Cir.1986).

25.   For an analysis of this issue, see H. Foss, When to Apply the Doctrine of Failure of Essential Purpose to an Exclusion of Consequential Damages: An Objective Approach, 25 Duquesne L.Rev. 551 (1987).

26.   775 F.2d 587, 41 UCC 1553 (4th Cir.1985).

27.   Cooley v. Big Horn Harvestore Sys., Inc., 813 P.2d 736, 14 UCC2d 977 (Colo.1991).

28.   See Adams v. J.I. Case Co., 125 Ill.App.2d 388, 261 N.E.2d 1, 7 UCC 1270 (1970); Koehring v. A.P.I., Inc., 369 F.Supp. 882, 14 UCC 368 (E.D.Mich.

statute or the comments specifically addresses any additional clause on consequential damages.

The leading case favoring sellers is American Electric Power Co., Inc. v. Westinghouse Electric Corp.[29] That case represents the majority view. The court found "no reason to disturb the consensual allocation of business risk." The court concluded that this was not a case where the failure to repair left the plaintiff without a "minimum adequate remedy" because the contract provided for a damage recovery that was distinct from the repair remedy. Given this, the two provisions (i.e., the repair promise and the exclusion of consequential damages) were considered independent and the failure of the limited remedy under section 2–719(2) did not affect the consequential damage exclusion.[30]

In general, we favor the *American Electric Power* line of cases. Those cases are most true to the Code's general notion that the parties should be free to contract as they please. The text of the Code disfavors judges' and juries' rewriting contracts that allocate risks between the parties. UCC sections 1–302, 2–316, 2–719, and many others accord primacy to the terms of the contract over the general law of the Code. Indeed, as to remedies, 2–719(1)(a) and (b) provide that the parties may provide for remedies "in substitution for those provided in the article" and that the parties may make such remedies "exclusive."[31] General Electric Co. v. Varig—S.A.[32] is aptly illustrative. There, highly competent parties painstakingly negotiated the terms.

In our view the parties, better than the state, can allocate the loss to the one who can avoid it at the least cost. The state's agents should respect that allocation. This is particularly true when a knowledgeable buyer is using an expensive machine or consuming a

1974) (buyer did not anticipate that sole remedy would become a nullity, thus causing additional damages); Forest River, Inc. v. Posten, 847 So.2d 957, 51 UCC2d 711 (Ala.Civ.App. 2002) (buyers of RV with irreparable leaking and were not bound by limitation to repair costs, and could get damages for "mental anguish" under 2–714); Razor v. Hyundai Motor America, 349 Ill.App.3d 651, 286 Ill.Dec. 190, 813 N.E.2d 247, 54 UCC2d 737 (2004) (remedy failed of its essential purpose, thus provision excluding incidental and consequential damages had no effect).

29. 418 F.Supp. 435, 19 UCC 1009 (S.D.N.Y.1976).

30. To similar effect, see Chatlos Sys., Inc. v. National Cash Register Corp., 635 F.2d 1081, 30 UCC 416 (3d Cir.1980).

31. For this reason, nearly all the cases between sophisticated parties in which remedies were fully and carefully negotiated impose a heavy burden of proof and persuasion on the parties seeking to invalidate the agreement. A general survey of the cases shows that the party seeking to invalidate the agreement in such circumstances typically loses. See, e.g., American Electric Power Co. v. Westinghouse Electric Corp., 418 F.Supp. 435, 19 UCC 1009 (S.D.N.Y.1976); Proto Construction & Development Corp. v. Superior Precast, Inc., 2002 WL 1159593, 52 UCC2d 921 (E.D.N.Y. 2002) (not unconscionable where both parties were aware of risk and had explicitly allocated risk to buyer).

32. 2004 WL 253320, 52 UCC2d 936 (S.D.N.Y. 2004).

commodity in a business setting. It is the buyer who operates the machine, adjusts it, and understands the consequences of its failure. Sometimes flaws are inherent and attributable to the seller's faulty design or manufacture. But the fault may also lie in buyer neglect, inadequate training and supervision of the operators, failure to report difficulties, or even in intentional use in ways forbidden by the seller. Believing the parties to know their own interests best, we favor their allocations.

Although the consumer purchaser makes a more sympathetic case for court intervention, we would apply *General Electric* in those cases as well. When the consequential damages consist of personal injury or property damage, the buyer can recover in tort without regard to the 2–719 limitation. When it consists of other loss, the consumer may be the lowest cost risk avoider. Even consumers can read instructions; even they can appreciate the danger of lighting a match in the presence of gas fumes.

§ 13–11   Modification or Limitation of Remedies— Unconscionable Limitation of Remedy, Sections 2–719(3) and 2–302

We have already discussed the policies behind, and operation of, the court's power under section 2–302 to refuse to enforce unconscionable contracts and clauses generally.[1] Section 2–719(3) provides that a court should strike a clause that limits or excludes consequential damages if "the limitation or exclusion is unconscionable."

A failure to distinguish between warranty disclaimers and remedy limitations or exclusions has caused trouble here. A disclaimer[2] controls the seller's liability by reducing situations where the seller can be in breach. It adjusts the standard of conformity. A remedy limitation or exclusion, on the other hand, restricts the remedies once a breach is established. Assume, for example, that a new-car buyer sues for breach of warranty, and the seller raises defenses based on disclaimer and limitation or exclusionary clauses. The disclaimer defense denies the existence of any cause of action. An exclusionary-clause defense, on the other hand, denies that the buyer is entitled to the remedy he demands—for example, conse-

---

§ 13–11

1. See Chapter 5 *supra*. Johnson, Unconscionability and the Federal Chancellors: A Survey of UCC Section 2–302 Interpretations in the Federal Circuits During the 1980's, 16 Lincoln L.Rev. 21 (1985).

2. While the Code itself does not use the term "disclaimer," the comments refer to it. See § 2–316, Comments 1, 3, 5, 8; 2–719, Comment 3.

quential damages.[3] These clauses are easily confused.[4] We first consider unconscionability as applied to each in isolation. Then we look at the relationship among sections 2–316, 2–719, and 2–302.

a.   Unconscionable Consequential–Loss Exclusion

Section 2–719(3) states a rule and corollary:

Consequential damages may be limited or excluded unless the limitation or exclusion is unconscionable. Limitation of consequential damages for injury to the person in the case of consumer goods is prima facie unconscionable but limitation of damages where the loss is commercial is not.

Note first that subsection (3) is not the buyer's best friend: as the courts have recognized, the subsection explicitly authorizes the contractual exclusion of consequential damages.[5] Moreover, except in cases where consumer goods cause personal injuries, the buyer carries the burden of proving the unconscionability of the limitation-of-remedy clause.[6] Comment 1 further suggests that a remedy limitation clause should be deleted on the grounds of unconscionability only when it fails to provide "minimum adequate remedies."

Suppose Acme Motors sells a pick-up truck to a consumer, who plans to use it for fishing trips.[7] The printed form sales contract states that the buyer is not entitled to consequential damages. The buyer suffers serious injuries when the truck explodes on the way home from the showroom. Unless Acme comes forward with evidence rebutting the presumption of unconscionability of the exclusion clause,[8] the buyer may recover damages for personal injuries.

3. Since an exclusionary clause may reduce the period of limitation for a cause of action (see § 2–725), a defense based on such a clause may, in effect, deny the existence of a cause of action. Note also that an exclusionary clause may apply to all seller breaches, not just to breaches of warranty.

4. One manifestation of the confusion is a series of cases construing remedy limitations as modifications of the implied warranty of merchantability and hence requiring that the provisions mention "merchantability" to limit recovery under that warranty.

5. Southland Farms v. Ciba–Geigy Corp., 575 So.2d 1077, 14 UCC2d 404 (Ala.1991) (sale of agricultural chemical products).

Comment 3 indicates that the Uniform Commercial Code permits clauses excluding consequential damages because they are an allocation of unknown or undeterminable risks.

6. The statement "but limitation of damages where the loss is commercial is not" could mean that such a limitation is not prima facie unconscionable or that it is prima facie not unconscionable. The first alternative seems more probable.

7. Under § 9–102(23) of Amended Article 9, the truck would be a consumer good since it was bought "primarily for personal, family or household purposes." § 2–103(3) states that this definition applies to Article 2, and the courts have applied it to 2–719(3). See, e.g., Ford Motor Co. v. Tritt, 244 Ark. 883, 430 S.W.2d 778, 5 UCC 312 (1968).

8. The comments to 2–719 contain a cross-reference to § 2–302. Comment 1 to that section suggests that the purpose of the section is to prevent "oppression and unfair surprise." Therefore, it is possible that Acme could rebut the presumption if it could show that the exclusion clause was conspicuously printed, that it was explained to the buyer, that the parties bargained over it, and that the buyer knew that Acme's trucks had a tendency to explode. It is possible, but not likely. See, e.g., Matthews v. Ford Motor Co., 479 F.2d 399, 12 UCC 593

On the other hand, if the buyer had purchased the truck for delivering groceries from the buyer's store and the only injuries caused by the explosion were to the truck and to the groceries on board, the buyer would have to prove that the exclusionary clause was unconscionable.[9]

Can the buyer ever win in a commercial setting? The New York Court of Appeals said yes in a case where a contract for the sale of yarn required that all claims against the seller be made within ten days after the sale. The court indicated that the clause might be unconscionable if latent defects could not reasonably be discovered by the buyer, a sweater manufacturer, during the designated time period.[10] Similarly, a federal district court struck down a consequential damage exclusion that would have prevented a farmer from recovering for crop damage caused by a latent defect in the seller's soybean inoculant.[11] Moreover, other courts have held that when an automobile dealer suffers a judgment in favor of a consumer buyer who sustained personal injuries caused by a purchased automobile, a contractual arrangement limiting the manufacturer's liability to the dealer is unconscionable.[12] Absent a showing of procedural unconscionability, we are doubtful.

Findings of unconscionability should be and are rare in commercial settings.[13] For the kind of hardheaded analysis we favor,

(4th Cir.1973) (personal injuries from defect in car); Martin v. American Med. Sys., Inc., 116 F.3d 102, 32 UCC2d 1101 (4th Cir. 1997) (personal injuries). See, however, Reibold v. Simon Aerials, Inc., 859 F.Supp. 193, 24 UCC2d 496 (E.D. Va. 1994) (seller could negate contractual liability for personal injuries though not liability in tort); Pig Improvement Co., Inc. v. Middle States Holding Co., 943 F.Supp. 392, 31 UCC2d 422 (D. Del. 1996) (buyer had reason to know defect might be present and had means to discover). See also Pierce v. Catalina Yachts, Inc. 2 P.3d 618, 41 UCC2d 737 (Alaska 2000) (disclaimer of consequential damages unconscionable where buyers were consumers, and manufacturer acted in bad faith by failing to honor warranty).

9. § 2–302(1), which presumably applies to 2–719(3) requires that the court itself determine unconscionability. A clause excluding consequential damages for injury to the person in the case of goods that are not consumer goods apparently is not prima facie unconscionable. However, the fact of personal injuries should enhance the buyer's case.

10. Wilson Trading Corp. v. David Ferguson, Ltd., 23 N.Y.2d 398, 297

N.Y.S.2d 108, 244 N.E.2d 685, 5 UCC 1213 (1968).

11. Majors v. Kalo Labs., Inc., 407 F.Supp. 20, 18 UCC 592 (M.D.Ala.1975). Compare County Asphalt v. Lewis Welding & Eng'g Corp., 323 F.Supp. 1300, 8 UCC 445, 447 (S.D.N.Y.1970), aff'd, 444 F.2d 372, 9 UCC 206 (2d Cir.1971), cert. den., 404 U.S. 939, 92 S.Ct. 272, 30 L.Ed.2d 252 (1971) (unconscionability rare in commercial setting "absent undiscoverable 'latent defects' ") with Cyclops Corp. v. Home Ins. Co., 389 F.Supp. 476, 16 UCC 415 (W.D.Pa. 1975), aff'd, 523 F.2d 1050 (3d Cir.1975) (irrelevant whether defect in motor was latent).

Since Comment 3 to 2–719 refers to clauses excluding consequential damages as "merely an allocation of unknown or undeterminable risks" we question whether the mere latency of defects should render such clauses unconscionable in commercial sales.

12. See, e.g., Ford Motor Co. v. Tritt, 244 Ark. 883, 430 S.W.2d 778, 5 UCC 312 (1968).

13. County Asphalt, Inc. v. Lewis Welding & Eng'g Corp., 323 F.Supp. 1300, 8 UCC 445 (S.D.N.Y.1970), aff'd,

consider K & C, Inc. v. Westinghouse Electric Corp.[14] An experienced business person and an attorney formed the plaintiff corporation, which contracted to purchase coin operated dry cleaners from the defendant. The machines developed difficulties, and the plaintiff sued for consequential damages, even though the sales contracts purported to bar that remedy. The court concluded that "it is clear that the exclusion was not unconscionable here, where the buyer was hardly the sheep keeping company with wolves that it would have us believe."[15] To support this conclusion, the court cited the experience of the plaintiff's owners and the fact that they had carefully studied their investment for six months before making the purchase.

b. Unconscionable Disclaimer of Warranty

By specific reference in 2–719, certain remedy limitations must be tested against unconscionability. But there is no similar reference to unconscionability in 2–316. That omission from an otherwise elaborate and detailed set of conditions could not have been an oversight. Because unconscionability is nowhere mentioned in 2–316, some commentators—most notably Professor Leff in his classic article on unconscionability[16]—have argued that no disclaimer that meets the requirements of section 2–316 can be unconscionable. In the first place, the formal requirements of 2–316 are intended "to protect a buyer from unexpected and unbargained language of disclaimer,"[17] an intent that coincides with 2–302's purpose of preventing "oppression and unfair surprise."[18] Once a disclaimer has been expressed so conspicuously that a buyer's "attention can reasonably be expected to be called to it,"[19] the buyer can hardly complain that he or she was unfairly surprised or that the disclaimer was unexpected. Moreover, 2–316 makes no reference to 2–302, not even in the cross references listed in the official comment. Since several other sections in Article 2—including 2–719(3)—make such reference, it would seem that the drafters would have done so in 2–

444 F.2d 372, 9 UCC 206 (2d Cir.1971), cert. denied, 404 U.S. 939, 92 S.Ct. 272, 30 L.Ed.2d 252 (1971) (sale of equipment for use in asphalt plants). In some commercial contexts, an exclusionary clause is so widely accepted that is considered a "usage of trade" and therefore prima facie reasonable. See, e.g., Southland Farms, Inc. v. Ciba–Geigy Corp., 575 So.2d 1077, 14 UCC2d 404 (Ala. 1991) (consequential damages in context of sale of agricultural chemicals is accepted method of risk-shifting in the industry).

14.   437 Pa. 303, 263 A.2d 390, 7 UCC 679 (1970).

15.   Id. at 308, 263 A.2d at 393, 7 UCC at 682. See also Cryogenic Equip., Inc. v. Southern Nitrogen, Inc., 490 F.2d 696, 14 UCC 420 (8th Cir.1974) (sale of equipment for nitrogen liquification plant).

16.   Leff, Unconscionability and the Code—The Emperor's New Clause, 115 U.Pa. L. Rev. 485, 516–28 (1967).

17.   § 2–316, Comment 1.

18.   § 2–302, Comment 1.

19.   § 1–201(10), Comment 10 (definition of "conspicuous").

316 if they intended for it to be governed by 2–302. As Professor Leff sums up:

> Here is 2–316 which sets forth clear, specific and anything but easy-to-meet standards for disclaiming warranties. It is a highly detailed section, the comments to which disclose full awareness of the problem at hand. It contains no reference of any kind to section 2–302, although nine other sections of Article 2 contain such references. In such circumstances the usually bland assumptions that a disclaimer which meets the requirements of 2–316 might still be strikeable as "unconscionable" under 2–302 seems explainable, if at all, as oversight, wishful thinking or (in a rare case) attempted sneakiness.[20]

But there are some arguments in favor of the application of 2–302 to disclaimers. First of all, 2–302 applies to "any clause of the contract." There is nothing in that section barring it from any other Code sections, no matter how detailed. Similarly, section 2–316 does not state expressly that disclaimers meeting its requirements are immune from general policing provisions like 2–302 or 1–203 (obligations of good faith).

Further support for the argument that 2–302 applies to disclaimers can be found in the comments to 2–302. Comment 1 lists and describes ten cases which are presumably intended to illustrate the underlying basis of the section; in seven of those cases disclaimers of warranty were denied full effect. If the drafters intended 2–302 to have no effect on disclaimers, why did they use so many cases on disclaimers in the comments to section 2–302?[21]

While it may be hard to see how a disclaimer that meets the conditions of 2–316 could be procedurally unconscionable, it is easy to imagine a substantively unconscionable disclaimer. A powerful seller could certainly impose a "one-sided" or "oppressive" disclaimer on a buyer where the seller had power over the buyer. These words from the comment appear to have influenced the court in Henningsen v. Bloomfield Motors.[22] Although that court never mentions 2–302, it invalidates Chrysler's disclaimer for contraven-

---

20. Leff, *supra*, note 16 at 523. The author also argues that if the drafters had meant to outlaw all disclaimers they would have said so. *Id*. at 524. But just because the drafters did not manifest an intent to prohibit all disclaimers does not mean they intended to insulate particular disclaimers from the policing of 2–302. For further support of Leff's view, see 1 N.Y. State Law Revision Comm'n, 1955 Report 586 (1955).

21. According to Professor Leff, these cases are intended merely to illustrate "the skewing of legal doctrine that

may be caused by an emotional pressure to get a more heartwarming particular result." Leff, Unconscionability and the Code—The Emperor's New Clause, 115 U.Pa. L. Rev. 485, 527 (1967). While the cases doubtless do illustrate "manipulative techniques," one would think the comment writer would not have selected the majority of the cases from a substantive area that 2–302 was not supposed to touch.

22. 32 N.J. 358, 161 A.2d 69 (1960).

ing public policy. The *Henningsen* case is perhaps best viewed as a tort case; nevertheless it is among the most crude and dramatic in its discussion of the Code and Code policy.

On the other side, the Supreme Court of Appeals of Virginia[23] sides with those favoring the preemption view. In a pre-Code case involving a disclaimer clause like the one in *Henningsen*[24] in connection with the sale of a new car to a consumer, the court refused to follow the New Jersey court. In upholding the disclaimer, the court stated:

> [I]f there exist the "overriding reasons of public policy," as claimed by the complainant and as relied upon by the New Jersey court in the Henningsen case, those reasons surely would have been known to our legislature when, in 1964, it adopted the Uniform Commercial Code, effective January 1, 1966. And yet, while providing in Code, § 8.2–315 that there shall be an implied warranty of fitness attached to the sale of goods, the legislature specifically provided in Code, § 8.2–316 how such an implied warranty may be excluded.[25]

A number of cases have held "disclaimers" that were really remedy limitations, to be unconscionable. But we have found no cases that find a disclaimer conforming to 2–316 to be unconscionable. Five different courts, however, have indicated that a warranty disclaimer may be unconscionable. A Pennsylvania trial court asserted in a footnote that even if the new-car dealer in the case before it had used the proper forms for the disclaimer, the disclaimer might still be unconscionable under 2–302.[26] The Third Circuit Court of Appeals suggested in dicta that when a disclaimer is manifestly unreasonable, section 1–102(3)[27] "prevents the enforcement of unconscionable sales where, as in this instance, the goods exchanged are found to be totally worthless."[28] While the court did

---

23. Marshall v. Murray Oldsmobile Co., 207 Va. 972, 154 S.E.2d 140, 4 UCC 172 (1967).

24. See notes 29–31 *infra* and accompanying text.

25. 207 Va. at 978, 154 S.E.2d at 144–45, 4 UCC at 177.

26. Willman v. American Motor Sales Co., 1961 WL 8744, 1 UCC 100, 103–104, 104 n.3 (Pa.C.P.1961) (new car destroyed by fire while operating). It was unnecessary for the court to decide the unconscionability issue because it held that the disclaimer failed to use the clear and definite language required by the 1952 version of 2–316.

27. § 1–102(3) provided:

The effect of provisions of this Act may be varied by agreement, except as otherwise provided in this Act and except that the obligations of good faith, diligence, reasonableness and care prescribed by this Act may not be disclaimed by agreement but the parties may by agreement determine the standards by which the performance of such obligations is to be measured if such standards are not manifestly unreasonable.

Section 1–302 includes similar language.

28. Vlases v. Montgomery Ward & Co., 377 F.2d 846, 850, 4 UCC 164, 169 (3d Cir.1967) (sale of one-day-old chicks with avion bukosis, a form of bird cancer). The seller apparently had not used sufficiently specific disclaimer language to satisfy the requirements of 2–316.

not cite 2–302, the quoted language demonstrates the court's belief that disclaimers are subject to the general policing provisions of the Code and particularly to the unconscionability standard. A New Jersey appellate court was more explicit when it declared in dicta that the policy enunciated in *Henningsen* that disclaimers of the implied warranty of merchantability are "against public policy now finds statutory support not only in N.J.Stat.Ann. 12A:2–316(2) but also in N.J.Stat.Ann. 12A:2–302, N.J.S.A. (unconscionable contract or clause)."[29] The Sixth Circuit Court of Appeals explicitly recognized that warranty disclaimers which comply with 2–316 are limited by 2–302.[30]

Finally, a New York court suggested that a disclaimer provision that explicitly excludes the implied warranties of merchantability and fitness for a particular purpose may under some circumstances be unconscionable even though it is conspicuously printed. In Jefferson Credit Corp. v. Marcano,[31] the court excused the buyers from making further payments for a used car that was constantly in need of major repairs. The sales contract included a thirty-day warranty and an apparently flawless disclaimer which the Spanish-speaking couple could not fully understand since it was printed in English.[32] On three different occasions, the dealer led the buyers to believe that the car would be put in good condition, but at the end of the thirty days, the dealer denied all responsibility. The case was filled with juicy unconscionability equities: the dealer's deception in avoiding responsibility under the express warranty, the inability of the buyers to understand English, that the buyers paid out a total of $621.63 for the partial use of a defective used car for six months while both the dealer and the plaintiff-assignee apparently realized reasonable returns, that the assignee sold the repossessed car to the original dealer seven months after the sale for less than one-fifth of the total charges to the buyer under the installment contract, that the dealer had to spend $402 to put the car in salable condition.[33]

29. Zabriskie Chevrolet v. Smith, 99 N.J.Super. 441, 448, 240 A.2d 195, 199, 5 UCC 30, 35 (1968). The attempted disclaimer was not conspicuous, and it was delivered after the contract for sale was signed.

30. Martin v. Joseph Harris Co., 767 F.2d 296, 41 UCC 315 (6th Cir.1985).

31. 60 Misc.2d 138, 302 N.Y.S.2d 390, 6 UCC 602 (City Civ.Ct.1969).

32. It could be argued that a disclaimer written in English is not conspicuous to a buyer who cannot read English, since such a buyer's attention cannot reasonably be expected to be called to it. See the discussion of conspicuousness in § 13–5 *supra*.

33. 60 Misc.2d at 139–40, 302 N.Y.S.2d at 392–93, 6 UCC at 604–05. The original purchase price for the car was $1395, and the total price, which included tax and credit charges, was $1766.23. The plaintiff-finance company sued for the unpaid balance of $796.60 plus attorney's fees of $119.49. The dealer received a total of $1169.75 (including the down payment by the buyers and the amounts received from the assignee and resale purchaser), and the assignee received $749.88 (including amounts received from the buyers and from the dealer on resale) to cover the $650 it paid the dealer for the contract.

Although the court's judgment for defendant rested upon plaintiff's violation of the resale provisions in former section 9–504, it relied principally upon the disclaimer and the facts immediately surrounding it in declaring the contract unconscionable:

> It is my opinion that the lack of equality between the bargaining parties, the contract clauses under which the defendants unwittingly and unknowingly waived both the warranty of merchantability and the warranty of fitness for the particular purpose for which the motor vehicle was purchased and the defective condition of the motor vehicle are sufficient to render the contract unenforceable under the provisions of the Uniform Commercial Code, section 2–302 as between [defendants and the dealer-assignor].[34]

Dismal as the prospect is to at least one of your authors, we suspect that the courts have the bit in their teeth and that most are determined to apply 2–302 to warranty disclaimers whether or not those disclaimers comply with 2–316. One of us believes that these courts misread the intention of the drafters and that the drafters never intended 2–302 to be an overlay on the disclaimer provisions of 2–316. Nevertheless, the lawyer must recognize the judicial hostility to warranty disclaimers, particularly in contracts made with consumers. Aside from personal injury or property damage cases and despite the cases discussed above, we believe that a lawyer has a good chance with an argument that 2–316 has preempted the unconscionability doctrine with respect to warranty disclaimers.[35] Where the buyer is not a consumer, Leff's rigorous analysis should carry the day.

§ 13–12 Modification or Limitation of Remedies— Use of Section 2–719(3) to Invalidate an Otherwise Valid Disclaimer

Most buyers who have invoked the aid of the courts to nullify properly drafted disclaimers on grounds of unconscionability have not even bothered with 2–302. Rather, they have succeeded in convincing courts that 2–719(3)'s prohibition of unconscionable consequential loss exclusion clauses prevents a court from upholding a disclaimer that denies the plaintiff consequential damages. This trip around 2–316 violates the apparent intention of the

---

34. *Id.* at 142, 302 N.Y.S.2d at 394–95, 6 UCC at 606. It should be noted that the buyers in *Marcano* lacked one key "equity"—personal injuries.

The court in *Marcano* also had to overcome a clause in the sales contract in which the buyers waived all defenses against the assignee, a feat which was accomplished by a rather novel interpretation of former 9–504.

35. See, e.g., Arkwright–Boston Manufacturers Mutual Insurance Co. v. Westinghouse Electric Corp., 844 F.2d 1174, 6 UCC2d 73 (5th Cir.1988) (the court declined to read a requirement of "basic equity and fairness" into 2–316).

drafters.[1] Two cases from the Arkansas Supreme Court illustrate the point.

In Ford Motor Co. v. Tritt,[2] the plaintiff's husband purchased a new truck which was covered by the manufacturer's express warranty and exclusive remedy of repair and replacement. The warranty contained the following clause:

> This warranty is expressly in lieu of any other express or implied warranty, including any implied warranty of merchantability or fitness, and of any other obligation on the part of the Dealer.[3]

The buyer was killed when a defective axle caused the truck to turn over.[4] The court had little difficulty holding that it would be unconscionable to allow the printed disclaimer to preclude damages under implied warranty for wrongful death:

> The waiver of the implied warranty of merchantability or fitness certainly does not protect [the dealer] from liability, for to do so would be unconscionable under the Uniform Commercial Code within the meaning of Ark.Stat.Ann. § 85–2–719(3) (Add.1961) * * *.[5]

A couple of years later, Ford got involved in another Arkansas warranty suit in Ford Motor Co. v. Reid.[6] This time no one was hurt, but a new automobile purchased by the plaintiff caught fire in his garage and burned down his house. The car was sold with a warranty and disclaimer clause almost identical to the one involved in *Tritt*. But since there were no personal injuries, the contractual exclusion of consequential damages was not automatically unconscionable under 2–719(3). So the court took a different tack. It accepted at face value the manufacturer's express warranty regarding defective parts,[7] but it held that the language in the disclaimer

---

§ 13–12

1. Comment 3 to 2–719 states: "The seller in all cases is free to disclaim warranties in the manner provided in § 2–316."

2. 244 Ark. 883, 430 S.W.2d 778, 5 UCC 312 (1968).

3. *Id.* at 889, 430 S.W.2d at 781, 5 UCC at 315.

4. In the initial opinion, the court held there was no evidence establishing proximate cause. On rehearing, the court held that a proffer of evidence by an expert witness was sufficient to support the verdict in plaintiff's favor. *Id.* at 890, 430 S.W.2d at 783, 5 UCC at 312.

5. *Id.* at 889, 430 S.W.2d at 781, 5 UCC at 315. The court also held that the trial court could properly conclude that the disclaimer was unconscionable as between the dealer and the manufacturer. *Id.* at 890, 430 S.W.2d at 782, 5 UCC at 316.

6. 250 Ark. 176, 465 S.W.2d 80, 8 UCC 985 (1971).

7. The court relied on then 2–316(1), which directs that disclaimer language be construed whenever reasonable as consistent with express-warranty language, in order to construe a statement in the warranty that "[a]ll the warranties shall be fulfilled by the Selling Dealer" as explaining the seller's obligation rather than as limiting the buyer's rights to other remedies. 250 Ark. at 184, 465 S.W.2d at 84, 8 UCC at 990.

did not constitute an express agreement within the meaning of 2–719(1)(b) that repair and replacement would be the exclusive remedy. The court reached this conclusion by emphasizing that the disclaimer clause dealt with "obligations" and "warranties," not "remedies."[8] Thus, in the court's opinion, there was no language in the contract that prevented the buyer from recovering consequential damages for the seller's breach of its express warranty.

In *Tritt*, the court held that the language "This warranty is expressly in lieu of * * * any other obligations" was unconscionable because it excluded consequential damages. Then in *Reid* the court held that virtually identical language does *not* exclude consequential damages.[9] How can these two cases be reconciled? In the later case, the buyer's action was based on breach of express warranty. To permit recovery of consequential damages, the court merely had to construe language of remedy as nonexclusive. In *Tritt*, however, the buyer alleged breach of an implied warranty that had been disclaimed under 2–316(2). Thus, the only avenue to any recovery was foreclosed unless the court held the clause unconscionable.[10]

The holding of *Reid* appears to be reasonable. But the proposition enunciated by *Tritt*—that a *disclaimer of warranties* that has the effect of modifying or excluding consequential damages may be unconscionable under 2–719(3)—is out of line with the scheme of the Code. Comment 3 to 2–719(3) provides (emphasis added):

> Subsection (3) recognizes the validity of clauses limiting or excluding consequential damages but makes it clear that they may not operate in an unconscionable manner. Actually such

---

8. 250 Ark. at 184, 465 S.W.2d at 85, 8 UCC at 990. Support for this distinction was found in 2–301's definition of "obligation": "The obligation of the seller is to transfer and deliver * * * in accordance with the contract." The court might also have quoted from then Comment 34 to 1–201(34), which stated that remedial rights are "those to which an aggrieved party can resort on his own motion." Together, these two definitions suggest that obligations and remedies are counterparts; when the seller fails to do what is required by the contract, i.e., fails to perform the obligation, the buyer may invoke an appropriate remedy.

The distinction between remedy and obligation is well established in constitutional law. A state may significantly modify or alter contractual remedies without impairing the obligation of contract within the meaning of Article I, Section 10 of the Constitution. See e.g., Home Bldg. & Loan Ass'n v. Blaisdell,

290 U.S. 398, 54 S.Ct. 231, 78 L.Ed. 413 (1934).

9. The appellate court was apparently precluded from finding the disclaimer to be an unconscionable exclusion of consequential damages by the failure of the buyer to provide a factual basis for such a holding at the trial. 250 Ark. at 184, 465 S.W.2d at 84, 8 UCC at 989 (quoting from the manufacturer's brief).

10. Apparently the plaintiff in *Tritt* did not allege breach of an express warranty, although the 24 month or 24,000 mile warranty was still in effect. If an express warranty breach had been established, the court could have taken one of two routes. Either the repair or replacement remedy was not exclusive, or, even if it were, it was unconscionable under 2–719(3) because it excluded consequential damages for personal injury.

terms are merely an allocation of unknown or undeterminable risks. *The seller in all cases is free to disclaim warranties in the manner provided in Section 2–316.*

The last sentence seems to be telling the seller, "If you really want to limit your liability, why don't you disclaim all warranties? Then you won't have to worry about limiting damages." Note that the sentence appears after the discussion of remedy limitations and after the discussion of the extent to which such clauses are governed by the unconscionability doctrine and that it announces that the seller may disclaim warranties in all cases. These facts strongly indicate the drafters intended that disclaimers valid under 2–316 would be valid under 2–719.[11]

This implication is buttressed by Comment 2 to 2–316 (emphasis added):

> * * * This Article treats the limitation or avoidance of consequential damages as a matter of limiting remedies for breach, separate from the matter of creation of liability under a warranty. *If no warranty exists, there is of course no problem of limiting remedies for breach of warranty.*[12]

The comment's reasoning is elementary: there can be no consequential damages if there is no breach; there can be no breach of warranty if there is no warranty; there can be no warranty if the seller has disclaimed them pursuant to 2–316. Although a particular disclaimer may be unconscionable under 2–302, it seems clear that the scheme of the Code does not permit a court to disregard that disclaimer on the basis that it operates to exclude consequential damages that could not be excluded under 2–719(3).[13]

Nevertheless, some courts have struck down disclaimers on the ground that they are unconscionable under 2–719(3).[14] The *Tritt* case demonstrates how these courts have ignored the clear bound-

---

11. See also Leff, Unconscionability and the Code—The Emperor's New Clause, 115 U.Pa. L. Rev. 485, 520 (1967).

12. Prior to 1957, Comment 2 read:

It is the view of this Article that the desire to limit or avoid consequential damages by excluding all warranties has nothing to do with the creation of liability under a warranty but goes rather to the problem of limiting remedies for its breach. Subsection (3) [now (4)] indicates that this question is in no way affected by the present section but is fully covered in the sections of this Article on limitation of damages and remedy.

13. See Ford Motor Co. v. Moulton, 511 S.W.2d 690, 14 UCC 312 (Tenn. 1974), cert. den., 419 U.S. 870, 95 S.Ct. 129, 42 L.Ed.2d 109 (1974) (disclaimer of implied warranty coupled with expiration of express warranty in contract for sale of car precluded personal injury action based upon warranty).

14. See, e.g., Orlett v. Suburban Propane, 54 Ohio App.3d 127, 561 N.E.2d 1066, 13 UCC2d 70 (1989) (exculpatory clause relieving seller of negligence liability to gas consumers is prima facie unconscionable under 2–719(3)).

aries between 2–316 and 2–719. In Walsh v. Ford Motor Co.,[15] a personal-injury case involving the same disclaimer drafted by the same manufacturer who was sued in *Tritt*, a New York trial court treated the unconscionability issue. The defendants (manufacturer and dealer) had argued that their disclaimer of warranties was permitted by 2–316. The court conceded that point but ruled against them because they "tendered no factual proof to rebut the plaintiff's showing that under the statute (UCC § 2–719(3)) the exclusion of a cause of action for recovery of damages for personal injuries is *prima facie* unconscionable."[16] This holding, of course, misses the base because 2–719 deals with limitations of remedies, not causes of action.

Undoubtedly, the main reason why courts refuse to follow the literal scheme of the Code is its harshness.[17] If neither 2–302 nor 2–719(3) operates as a restriction on disclaimers complying with 2–316, then the seller may have the power to thrust on the consumer all risks of personal injury resulting from defects in its products. Even adherents of strict construction concede that such power is not needed in order to keep the wheels of commerce turning.[18] It is not surprising then that courts faced with a consumer plaintiff who has been seriously injured by a corporate defendant's product are often willing to disregard the literal meaning of the Code. One may nevertheless question the wisdom of twisting a carefully devised statutory scheme, especially when alternative theories of relief, like negligence or strict tort, may be available.

The effects of disclaimers on third parties are treated in some cases.[19] It is difficult to sum up all the law on disclaimers, exclusion clauses, and unconscionability. We can say with confidence that a clause purporting to limit the buyer's damages or remedies is subject to attack as unconscionable under 2–719(3). Successful

---

15. 59 Misc.2d 241, 298 N.Y.S.2d 538, 6 UCC 56 (1969).

16. *Id.* at 242, 298 N.Y.S.2d at 540, 6 UCC at 57.

17. It has also been argued that it does not make sense to prohibit a seller of consumer goods from excluding consequential damages for personal injuries but to permit him to exclude *all* warranty liability by complying with the formal requirements of 2–316. See R. Dusenberg & C. King, Sales and Bulk Transfers Under the Uniform Commercial Code § 7.03 at 7–47 n. 30 (1969); Peters, Remedies for Breach of Contracts Relating to the Sale of Goods Under the Uniform Commercial Code: A Roadmap to Article Two, 73 Yale L.J. 199, 282–83 (1963); Speidel, The Virginia "Anti–Privity" Statute: Strict Products Liabili-

ty Under the Uniform Commercial Code, 51 Va.L.Rev. 804, 838 (1965).

As we have observed, however, it may be extremely difficult under 2–316(1) for a seller to refrain from making express warranties. See Section 13–2 and 13–3 *supra.*

18. See Leff, Unconscionability and the Code—The Emperor's New Clause, 115 U.Pa. L. Rev. 485, 516 (1967).

19. Theos & Sons, Inc. v. Mack Trucks, Inc., 431 Mass. 736, 729 N.E.2d 1113, 41 UCC2d 1082 (2000) (conspicuous disclaimer effective, not only against original purchaser, but also against subsequent purchasers, although the disclaimer may not have been brought to their attention).

attacks will mostly be limited to consumer settings involving personal injuries. If the seller has made a disclaimer that complies with 2–316, it is not clear whether the buyer can attack it with 2–302. As a matter of statutory construction, one of us thinks disclaimers should be policed solely by 2–316, the other thinks 2–302 should be available at least for consumer buyers. It is clear that some courts will continue to invoke unconscionability as embodied in 2–302 and 2–719(3). In light of the cases decided thus far, we suspect that whenever a consumer's blood is spilled, even wild horses could not stop a sympathetic court from plowing through the most artfully drafted and conspicuously printed disclaimer clause in order to grant relief. On the other hand, when the buyer is a merchant, no court should apply unconscionability of any variety to a disclaimer that complies with 2–316.

Table of Cases

A

Aboudaram v. De Groote, 2004 WL 1242426 (D.D.C.2004)—§ **4–3, n. 8.**

A. C. Carpenter, Inc. v. Boyer Potato Chips, 1969 WL 10993 (U.S.Dept. Agric.1969)—§ **12–10, n. 4.**

Ace, Inc. v. Maynard, 108 N.C.App. 241, 423 S.E.2d 504 (N.C.App.1992)—§ **3–10, n. 7; § 3–11, n. 32.**

Acme Mfg. Co. v. Arminius Chemical Co., 264 F. 27 (4th Cir.1919)—§ **4–10, n. 64.**

Acme Pump Co., Inc. v. National Cash Register Co., 32 Conn.Supp. 69, 337 A.2d 672 (Conn.Com.Pl.1974)—§ **11–2, n. 1.**

Adams v. J. I. Case Co., 125 Ill.App.2d 388, 261 N.E.2d 1 (Ill.App. 4 Dist. 1970)—§ **13–10, n. 28.**

Adams v. Petrade Intern., Inc., 754 S.W.2d 696 (Tex.App.-Hous. (1 Dist.) 1988)—§ **3–6, n. 6.**

Addis v. Bernardin, Inc., 226 Kan. 241, 597 P.2d 250 (Kan.1979)—§ **10–14, n. 17.**

Addressograph–Multigraph Corp. v. Zink, 273 Md. 277, 329 A.2d 28 (Md. 1974)—§ **11–4, n. 29.**

Advanced Computer Sales, Inc. v. Sizemore, 186 Ga.App. 10, 366 S.E.2d 303 (Ga.App.1988)—§ **9–4, n. 5.**

Advent Systems Ltd. v. Unisys Corp., 925 F.2d 670 (3rd Cir.1991)—§ **2–1, n. 10.**

Aero Consulting Corp. v. Cessna Aircraft Co., 867 F.Supp. 1480 (D.Kan. 1994)—§ **2–7, n. 4.**

AES Technology Systems, Inc. v. Coherent Radiation, 583 F.2d 933 (7th Cir. 1978)—§ **7–5, n. 18.**

AFA Corp. v. Phoenix Closures, Inc., 501 F.Supp. 224 (N.D.Ill.1980)—§ **7–5, n. 2; § 10–7, n. 9.**

Afram Export Corp. v. Metallurgiki Halyps, S.A., 772 F.2d 1358 (7th Cir. 1985)—§ **8–6, n. 8; § 8–16, n. 18.**

A & G Const. Co., Inc. v. Reid Bros. Logging Co., Inc., 547 P.2d 1207 (Alaska 1976)—§ **2–7, n. 7, 24; § 3–4, n. 7.**

AGF, Inc. v. Great Lakes Heat Treating Co., 51 Ohio St.3d 177, 555 N.E.2d 634 (Ohio 1990)—§ **8–11, n. 3; § 12–10, n. 1.**

Agoos Kid Co. v. Blumenthal Import Corp., 282 Mass. 1, 184 N.E. 279 (Mass.1932)—§ **10–12, n. 17.**

Agrarian Grain Co., Inc. v. Meeker, 526 N.E.2d 1189 (Ind.App. 2 Dist.1988)— § **9–4, n. 37, 38; § 12–10, n. 1.**

Agriliance, L.L.C. v. Farmpro Services, Inc., 328 F.Supp.2d 958 (S.D.Iowa 2003)—§ **1–4, n. 15.**

Agway, Inc. v. Ernst, 394 A.2d 774 (Me. 1978)—§ **4–6, n. 26.**

Aircraft Trading and Services Inc. v. Braniff, Inc., 819 F.2d 1227 (2nd Cir. 1987)—§ **4–12, n. 7, 46.**

Airstream, Inc. v. CIT Financial Services, Inc., 111 Idaho 307, 723 P.2d 851 (Idaho 1986)—§ **3–11, n. 5.**

Akron Brick & Block Co. v. Moniz Engineering Co., Inc., 365 Mass. 92, 310 N.E.2d 128 (Mass.1974)—§ **8–3, n. 15.**

Alabama Great Southern R. Co. v. McVay, 381 So.2d 607 (Miss.1980)— § **3–4, n. 13; § 4–12, n. 21.**

Alamance County Bd. of Educ. v. Bobby Murray Chevrolet, Inc., 121 N.C.App. 222, 465 S.E.2d 306 (N.C.App. 1996)—§ **4–10, n. 37.**

Alamo Clay Products, Inc. v. Gunn Tile Co. of San Antonio, Inc., 597 S.W.2d 388 (Tex.Civ.App.-San Antonio 1980)—§ **4–8, n. 10; § 4–10, n. 26.**

Alamo Rent–A–Car, Inc. v. Mendenhall, 113 Nev. 445, 937 P.2d 69 (Nev. 1997)—§ **4–12, n. 38.**

Alan Wood Steel Co. v. Capital Equipment Enterprises, Inc., 39 Ill.App.3d 48, 349 N.E.2d 627 (Ill.App. 1 Dist. 1976)—§ **2–3, n. 27; § 13–6, n. 27.**

Alarm Device Mfg. Co. v. Arnold Industries, Inc., 65 Ohio App.2d 256, 417 N.E.2d 1284 (Ohio App. 6 Dist. 1979)—§ **3–5, n. 25.**

B

N

Q

S

*

Index

References are to Sections

---

†